Kont
6/93

C3
95

P9-DTA-428
A1

The Family, Law and Society
Cases and Materials

The Family, Law and Society
Cases and Materials

Third edition

Brenda M Hoggett QC, MA (Cantab)
Law Commissioner
Visiting Professor, King's College, London

David S Pearl MA, LLM, PhD (Cantab)
Professor of Law, Dean of the School of Law,
University of East Anglia, Norwich
Life Fellow, Fitzwilliam College, Cambridge

Butterworths
London, Dublin, Edinburgh
1991

United Kingdom   Butterworth & Co (Publishers) Ltd,
88 Kingsway, LONDON WC2B 6AB and 4 Hill Street,
EDINBURGH EH2 3JZ

Australia   Butterworths Pty Ltd, SYDNEY, MELBOURNE,
BRISBANE, ADELAIDE, PERTH, CANBERRA and
HOBART

Canada   Butterworths Canada Ltd, TORONTO and VANCOUVER

Ireland   Butterworth (Ireland) Ltd, DUBLIN

Malaysia   Malayan Law Journal Sdn Bhd, KUALA LUMPUR

New Zealand   Butterworths of New Zealand Ltd, WELLINGTON and
AUCKLAND

Puerto Rico   Equity de Puerto Rico, Inc, HATO REY

Singapore   Malayan Law Journal Pte Ltd, SINGAPORE

USA   Butterworth Legal Publishers, AUSTIN, Texas; BOSTON,
Massachusetts; CLEARWATER, Florida (D & S Publishers);
ORFORD, New Hampshire (Equity Publishing); ST PAUL,
Minnesota; and SEATTLE, Washington

All rights reserved. No part of this publication may be reproduced in any material form (including photocopying or storing it in any medium by electronic means and whether or not transiently or incidentally to some other use of this publication) without the written permission of the copyright owner except in accordance with the provisions of the Copyright, Designs and Patents Act 1988 or under the terms of a licence issued by the Copyright Licensing Agency Ltd, 90 Tottenham Court Road, London, England W1P 9HE. Applications for the copyright owner's written permission to reproduce any part of this publication should be addressed to the publisher.

Warning: The doing of an unauthorised act in relation to a copyright work may result in both a civil claim for damages and criminal prosecution.

© Butterworth & Co (Publishers) Ltd 1991

A CIP Catalogue record for this book is available from the British Library.

First edition 1983
Second edition 1987

ISBN 0 406 60870 9

Typeset by Colset Pte Ltd., Singapore
Printed and bound in Great Britain by
Mackays of Chatham PLC, Chatham, Kent

Preface

As we have always said, the aim of this book is to introduce the student of family law to a wider range of sources than can be found in the statutes and law reports of the conventional law library. The concept of the student's own portable library is becoming more important as numbers grow and resources shrink.

We have made as few changes as possible in this new edition, but obviously a major recasting of the chapters dealing with children has been necessary in the light of the Children Act 1989 which comes into force on 14 October this year. The Act was meant to simplify the law, but only time will tell whether it has succeeded in doing so. The Act has, however, enabled us to simplify the structure of the book, in both the private and the public law. Other notable developments have included the Law Commission's Report on the Ground for Divorce, the Child Support Act 1991 which is to be brought in force in January 1993, and the Human Fertilisation and Embryology Act 1990. All this activity testifies to the continuing vitality and fascination of the subject, long after it ceased to be principally concerned with the intimate details of marital behaviour.

As always, we are grateful to those who have allowed us to reproduce their work for the benefit of a wider audience. We must thank also the many people with whom we have worked in family law, especially colleagues at the Law Commission (in the case of BH) and at the Centre for Family Law and Family Policy at the University of East Anglia (in the case of DP), who have contributed so much to our own knowledge and understanding. The staff at Butterworths remain as efficient and friendly as ever. Finally, we continue to be grateful to our ever patient families who must think that work on this book is rather like the painting of the Forth Bridge. The errors and omissions, of course, are all our own.

8 August 1991

Brenda Hoggett
David Pearl

Contents

Table of statutes

References in this Table to *Statutes* are to Halsbury's Statutes of England (Fourth Edition) showing the volume and page at which the annotated text of the Act may be found. Page references printed in **bold** type indicate where an Act is set out in part or in full.

List of cases

Pages on which cases are principally treated are indicated by the use of **bold** figures.

Bibliography

[Asterisks indicate works from which extracts have been quoted.]

Chapter 1

* M. Anderson, *Approaches to the History of the Western Family (1500–1914)* (1980) London and Basingstoke, Macmillan, pp. 40, 51, 69.
* M. Anderson (ed.), *Sociology of the Family* (1980) Harmondsworth, Penguin Books, p. 81.
  R. Bailey, 'Decree of Nullity of Marriage of True Hermaphrodite who has Undergone Sex-change Surgery' (1979) 53 Australian Law Journal 659.
  R. Ballard, 'South Asian Families' in R.N. Rapoport, M. Fogarty and R. Rapoport (eds) *Families in Britain* (1982) London, Routledge.
  J. Barrow, 'West Indian Families: An Insider's Perspective' in R.N. Rapoport, M. Fogarty, and R. Rapoport (eds) *Families in Britain* (1982) London, Routledge.
  L.K. Berkner, 'Peasant Household Organization and Demographic Change in Lower Saxony (1689–1766)' in R.D. Lee (ed.), *Population Patterns in the Past* (1977) New York and London, Academic Press.
  A. Bradney, 'The Family in Family Law' (1979) 9 Family Law 244.
  A. Bradney, 'How Not to Marry People' (1989) 19 Family Law 408.
  A. Dickey, 'The Nature of Family in Law' (1982) 14 West Aust L Rev 417.
  G. Driver 'West Indian Families: An Anthropological Pespective' in R.N. Rapoport, M. Fogarty and R. Rapoport (eds) *Families in Britain* (1982) London, Routledge.
* *Efficiency Scrutiny of the Registration Service* (1985) London, HMSO, para. 46.2.
* F. Engels, *Origins of the Family, Private Property and the State* (1st edn., 1884) New York, Lawrence and Wishart, p. 244.
* R. Fletcher, *The Family and Marriage in Britain* (1966) Harmondsworth, Pelican Books, pp. 26–27, 128 (3rd edn., 1973).
* R. Fletcher, *The Shaking of the Foundations* (1988) London and New York, Routledge, p. 43.
  R. Fletcher, *The Abolitionists: The Family and Marriage under Attack* (1988) London and New York, Routledge.
  M.A. Glendon, *State, Law and Family* (1977) Amsterdam, North Holland.
  J. Goody, *The Development of the Family and Marriage in Europe* (1983) Cambridge, Cambridge University Press.
* E.K. Gough, 'The Nayars and the Definition of Marriage' (1959) 89 Journal of the Royal Anthropological Institute pp. 23, 32.
* W.J. Goode, *World Revolution and Family Patterns* (1963) The Free Press, a Division of Macmillan Publishing Company, p. 41.
* C.C. Harris, *The Family: an Introduction* (1979) London, Allen and Unwin, p. 49.
  J. Jackson, *The Formation and Annulment of Marriage* (2nd edn., 1969) London, Butterworths.
* T.E. James, 'The English Law of Marriage' in R.H. Graveson and F.R. Crane

(eds.), *A Century of Family Law* (1957) London, Sweet and Maxwell, pp. 32–33.

* P. Laslett and R. Wall, *Household and Family in Past Time* (1972) Cambridge, Cambridge University Press, pp. 28–30, 63, 64.

* E.R. Leach, 'Polyandry, Inheritance, and the Definition of Marriage' (1955) Man, no. 199, p. 183.

* Law Commission, *Report on Nullity of Marriage*, Law Com. No. 33 (1970) London, HMSO, paras. 24, 25, 52.

* Law Commission, *Report on Solemnisation of Marriage*, Law Com. No. 53 (1973) London, HMSO, paras. 14–16.

A. MacFarlane, *Origins of English Individualism: the Family, Property and Social Transition* (1978) Oxford, Blackwell.

* A. MacFarlane, *Marriage and Love in England 1300–1840* (1986) Oxford, Basil Blackwell, pp. 246–247.

K. Meselman, *Incest* (1979) New York, Jessey Bross.

* L. Mair, *Marriage* (1971) Harmondsworth, Pelican Books; (1977) London, Scolar Press, p. 19.

* K. O'Donovan, *Sexual Divisions in Law* (1985) London, Weidenfeld and Nicholson, pp. 45ff.

* A. Oakley, *Housewife* (1974) London, Allen Lane; (1976) Harmondsworth, Pelican Books, pp. 236–237.

R. Oakley, 'Cypriot Families' in R.N. Rapoport, M. Fogarty and R. Rapoport (eds) *Families in Britain* (1982) London, Routledge.

* Population Trends 'A Review of the 1980s', (1990) 62 Population Trends 1 at p. 11 (Table H) London, HMSO.

S. Parker, 'Informal Marriage, Cohabitation and the Law, 1750–1989' (1990) Basingstoke, Macmillan.

J. Priest, 'Child of the Family' (1984) 14 Family Law 134.

Registration: A Modern Service (Cm 531) (1989) London, HMSO.

* E. Shorter, *The Making of the Modern Family* (1975) New York, Basic Books; (1977) London, Fontana, p. 38.

* L. Stone, *The Family, Sex, and Marriage in England 1500–1800* (1977) London, Weidenfeld and Nicholson, pp. 26–27, 102–104.

L. Stone, *Road to Divorce; England 1530–1987* (1990) Oxford, Oxford University Press.

L.A. Tilly, 'Individual Lives and Family Strategies in the French Proletariat' (1979) Journal of Family History (IV).

* A. Wilson, *Family* (1985) London and New York, Tavistock Publications, pp. 78–81.

C. Winberg, 'Population Growth and Proletarianization' in S. Akerman et al. (eds.), *Chance and Change* (Odense University Studies in History and Social Sciences, Vol. 52). (1978) Odense, Odense University Press.

R. Wall (ed.), *Family Forms in Historic Europe* (1983) London, Edward Arnold.

* K. Wrightson, English Society 1580–1680 (1982) London, Hutchinson, pp. 71, 103, 104.

Chapter 2

W. Blackstone, *Commentaries on the Laws of England* (1765) 17th edition by Edward Christian and others (1830) London, Tegg.

S. Brownmiller, *Against our Will*, (1975) London, Secker and Warburg.

* Criminal Law Revision Committee, *11th Report* (Cmnd. 4991) (1972) London, HMSO, para. 147.

Criminal Law Revision Committee, *Working Paper on Sexual Offences* (1980) London, HMSO.

Criminal Law Revision Committee, *15th Report on Sexual Offences* (Cmnd. 9213) (1984) London, HMSO.

R. Cross and C. Tapper, *Cross on Evidence* (6th edn., 1985) London, Butterworths.

J. de Montmorency, 'The Changing Status of a Married Woman' (1897) 13 Law Quarterly Review 187.

* Equal Opportunities Commission, *The Taxation of Husband and Wife: Response of the Equal Opportunities Commission to the Government Green Paper* (1981) Manchester, Equal Opportunities Commission, paras. 10 et seq.

M.D.A. Freeman, *Violence in the Home* (1979) Farnborough, Gower.

* M.D.A. Freeman, 'Doing his Best to Sustain the Sanctity of Marriage' in N. Johnson (ed.) *Marital Violence* (1985) London, Routledge and Kegan Paul, p. 124 at 136–139.

* R. Graveson, 'The Background of the Century' in R.H. Graveson and F.R. Crane (eds.), *A Century of Family Law* (1957) London, Sweet & Maxwell, pp. 2–3.

Sir Matthew Hale, *History of the Pleas of the Crown* (1736) vol. 1, p. 629 ed. by George Wilson (1778) London, Sollom Emlyn.

* Inland Revenue, *The Taxation of Husband and Wife* (Cmnd. 8093) (1980) London, HMSO, paras. 14 et seq., 31–41, 83–85.

* Inland Revenue, *The Reform of Personal Taxation* (Cmnd. 9756) (1986) London, HMSO, paras. 3.10–3.21.

* H.D. Krause, *Family Law* (3rd ed) (1990) St Paul, Minnesota, West Publishing Company, p. 248.

* Law Commission, Working Paper no. 116, *Rape within Marriage* (1990) London, HMSO, paras. 4.20–4.24.

A. MacFarlane, *Marriage and Love in England* 1300–1840 (1986) Oxford, Basil Blackwell.

J. McFadyen, 'Interspousal Rape: the Need for Reform' in J.M. Eekelaar and S.N. Katz (eds.), *Family Violence: An International and Interdisciplinary Study* (1978) Toronto, Butterworths, p. 193.

S. Maidment, 'The Law's Response to Marital Violence: a Comparison Between England and the USA' in J.H. Eekelaar and S.N. Katz (eds.), *Family Violence: An International and Interdisciplinary Study* (1978) Toronto, Butterworths, p. 110.

A. Medea and K. Thompson, *Against Rape* (1975) London, Owen.

* C.A. Morrison, 'Tort' in R.H. Graveson and F.R. Crane (eds.), *A Century of Family Law* (1957) London, Sweet and Maxwell, pp. 91–93.

R.I. Parnas, 'Judicial Response to Intra-Familial Violence' (1970) 54 Minnesota Law Review 584.

R.I. Parnas, 'The Relevance of Criminal Law to Inter-Spousal Violence' in J.M. Eekelaar and S.N. Katz (eds.), *Family Violence: An International and Interdisciplinary Study* (1978) Toronto, Butterworths, p. 188.

* *Report of the Committee on One-Parent Families* (Chairman: The Hon. Sir Morris Finer) (Cmnd. 5629) (1974) London, HMSO, paras. 6.88–6.90.

O. Stone, *Family Law* (1977) London, Macmillan.

J. Temkin, 'Towards a Modern Law of Rape' (1982) 45 Modern Law Review 405.

* L.A. Tilly and J.W. Scott, *Women, Work and Family* (1987) New York and London, Methuen, pp. 4, 220, 253.

* *The Oregonian* (Rideout v Rideout), 20, 27 December 1978; 11 January 1979.

G.L. Williams, 'The Legal Unity of Husband and Wife' (1947) 10 Modern Law Review 16.

* O.P. Wylie, *Taxation of Husband and Wife* (1990) London, Butterworths, pp 4, 253.

A.A. Zuckerman, *The Principles of Criminal Evidence* (1989) Oxford, Oxford University Press.

Chapter 3

M. Anderson, 'Family, Household and the Industrial Revolution' in M. Anderson (ed.), *Sociology of the Family* (1980) Harmondsworth, Penguin Books.

Association of Market Survey Organisations, *Men and Domestic Work* (1987).

L. Baillyn, 'Career and Family Orientation of Husband and Wife' (1971) Human Relations 23, pp. 97 et seq.

M. Barrett and M. McIntosh, *The Anti-Social Family* (1982) London, Verso Editions.

J. Bernard, *The Future of the Family*, (1972) New York, World.

J. Burgoyne, R. Ormrod, M. Richards, *Divorce Matters* (1987) Harmondsworth, Penguin Books.

* Central Statistical Office, *Social Trends 21* (1991) London, HMSO, Table 4.2.

* Central Statistical Office, *Social Trends 17* (1987) London, HMSO, Table A.2, Chart 4.4.

E. Clive, 'Marriage: An Unnecessary Legal Concept' in J.M. Eekelaar and S.N. Katz (eds.), *Marriage and Cohabitation in Contemporary Societies: Areas of Legal, Social and Ethical Change* (1980) Toronto, Butterworths.

L. Comer, *Wedlocked Women* (1974) Leeds, Feminist Books.

W.B. Creighton, *Working Women and the Law* (1979) London, Mansell.

* R. Deech, 'The Work of the Law Commission in Family Law: The First Twenty Years' in M.D.A. Freeman (ed.) *Essays in Family Law 1985* (1986) London, Stevens, p. 57 at p. 74.

* Sir M. Finer and O.R. McGregor, 'The History of the Obligation to Maintain'. App. 5, *Report of the Committee on One-Parent Families* (Cmnd. 5629-I) (1974) London, HMSO, para. 36.

* D. Gittins, *The Family in Question* (1985) Basingstoke, Macmillan, pp. 27, 28, 131.

H. Gavron, *The Captive Wife* (1966) London, Routledge and Kegan Paul; Harmondsworth, Penguin Books.

* M.A. Glendon, *State, Law and Family* (1977) Amsterdam, North Holland, p. 75.

C. Glendinning and J. Millar, *Women and Poverty in Britain* (1987) Brighton, Wheatsheaf Books.

G. Gorer, *Sex and Marriage in England Today* (1971) London, Nelson.

D. Gowler and K. Legge, 'Dual Worker Families' in R.N. Rapoport, M.P. Fogarty, and R. Rapoport (eds.), *Families in Britain* (1982) London, Routledge and Kegan Paul.

E. Granseth, 'Work Sharing: a Norwegian Experience' in R.N. Rapoport and R. Rapoport (eds.), *Working Couples* (1978) London, Routledge and Kegan Paul.

* K. Gray, *Reallocation of Property on Divorce* (1977) Abingdon, Professional Books, p. 176.

M.W. Gray, 'Prescriptions for Productive Female Domesticity in a Transitional Era: Germany's Hausmutterliteratur 1780–1840', (1987) 8 History of European Ideas, p. 413.

E. Hobsbaum and G. Ridé, *Captain Swing* (1973) Harmondsworth, Penguin.

L. Hoffman and F. Nye, *Working Mothers* (2nd edn., 1978) New York, Jossey-Bass.

* *Home Office Statistical Bulletin* 21/1990 (1990) Map 1.

* P. Hudson and W.R. Lee 'Women's Work and the Family Economy in Historical Perspective' in P. Hudson and W.R. Lee (eds), *Women's Work and the Family Economy in Historical Perspective* (1990) Manchester and New York, Manchester University Press, pp. 26, 27, 28, 31, 32.

* Inland Revenue, *The Taxation of Husband and Wife* (Cmnd. 8093) (1980) London, HMSO, tables 1–3.

* Inland Revenue, *The Reform of Personal Taxation* (Cmnd 9756) (1986) London, HMSO, Charts 2.2, 2.3.

J. Jephcott, N. Seear, and J. Smith, *Married Women Working* (1962) London, Allen and Unwin.

* A. Honoré, *The Quest for Security: Employees, Tenants, Wives* (1982) London, Stevens, p. 62.

H. Land, 'Women: Supporters or Supported?' in D.L. Baker and S. Allen (eds.) *Sexual Divisions and Society: Process and Change* (1976), London, Tavistock.

H. Land, *Large Families in London* (1969) London, G. Bell & Sons.

P. Laslett, *The World We Have Lost* (2nd edn., 1971) London, Methuen.

* Law Commission, Working Paper No. 53, *Matrimonial Proceedings in Magistrates' Courts* (1973) London, HMSO, paras. 7–11, 24, 35, 42, 43.

* Law Commission, *Report on Matrimonial Proceedings in Magistrates' Courts*, Law Com No. 77 (1976) London, HMSO, paras. 2.8–2.11, 2.15, 2.60–2.61.

Law Commission, Working Paper No. 90, *Transfer of Money Between Spouses* (1985).

* Law Commission, *Report on Family Law: Matrimonial Property*, Law Com. No. 175 (1988) London, HMSO, paras. 5.1–5.4.

* Law Commission Report on *Family Law: The Ground for Divorce*, Law Com. No. 192 (1990) London, HMSO, paras. 4.22–4.28.

J. Lewis and D. Piachaud, 'Women and Poverty in the Twentieth Century' in C. Glendinning and J. Millar (eds) *Women and Poverty in Britain* (1987) Brighton, Wheatsheaf Books.

O.R. McGregor, *Social History and Law Reform* (1981) London, Stevens.

J. Martin and C. Roberts, *Women and Employment: A Lifetime Perspective* (1984) London, HMSO.

* J.G. Miller, *Family Property and Financial Provision* (2nd edn., 1983) London, Sweet and Maxwell, p. 313.

J. Mortimore, 'Dual-career Families – A Sociological Perspective' (1977) Conference Papers, Minnesota.

P. Morton, *Women's Work is Never Done* (1970) London, Leviathan.

P. Moss and I.P. Lewis, *Young Children in the Inner City* (1979) London, HMSO. (T. Coram Research Unit – Pre-school project).

K. O'Donovan, 'Should All Maintenance of Spouses be Abolished?' (1982) 45 Modern Law Review 431.

* A. Oakley, *The Sociology of Housework* (1974) London, Martin Robertson & Co., pp.122, 124.

A. Oakley, *Subject Women* (1981) London, Martin Robertson & Co., (1982) Harmondsworth, Penguin Books.

A. Oakley, 'Conventional Families' in R.N. Rapoport, M. Fogarty and R. Rapoport (eds.), *Families in Britain* (1982) London, Routledge and Kegan Paul.

* Office of Population Censuses and Surveys, *Family Formation Survey* (1979) London, HMSO.

S. Orden and M. Bradburn, 'Dimensions of Marriage Happiness' (1968) 74 Journal of Sociology 715.

J. Pahl, 'Patterns of Money Management Within Marriage' (1980) 9 Journal of Social Policy 313.

* J. Pahl, 'The Allocation of Money Within the Household' in M.D.A. Freeman (ed.) *State, Law and the Family* (1984) London and New York, Tavistock Publications, p. 36 at pp. 40–42, 44, 45.

* J. Pahl, *Money and Marriage* (1989) Basingstoke and London, Macmillan, pp. 94, 108, 178.

R.N. Rapoport, R. Rapoport and Z. Strelitz, *Fathers, Mothers and Others* (1977) London, Routledge and Kegan Paul.

R.N. Rapoport and R. Rapoport (eds.), *Working Couples* (1978) London Routledge and Kegan Paul.

* R.N. Rapoport and R. Rapoport, 'The Impact of Work on the Family' in P. Moss and N. Fonda (eds.), *Work and the Family* (1980) London, Temple Smith, pp. 172 et seq., 177.

R.N. Rapoport and R. Rapoport, 'Dual Career Families: Progress and Prospect' (1978) Marriage and Family Review.

* *Report of the Committee on One-Parent Families* (Chairman: The Hon Sir Morris Finer) (Cmnd. 5629) (1974) London, HMSO, paras. 4.386, 4.67–68.

* *Report of the Royal Commission on Marriage and Divorce* (Chairman: Lord Morton of Henryton) (Cmd. 9678) (1956) London, HMSO, paras. 1042–1046.

L. Rimmer, *Employment Trends and the Family* (1981) London, Study Commission on the Family.

H. Ross and I. Sawhill, *Time of Transition: the Growth of Families headed by Women* (1975) Washington, Urban Institute.

M. Rutter, *Maternal Deprivation Reassessed* (1972) Harmondsworth, Penguin Books.

S. Rowbotham, *Women's Consciousness, Man's World* (1973) Harmondsworth, Penguin Books.

H. Scott, *Working Your Way to the Bottom: the Feminisation of Poverty* (1984) London, Pandora Press.

* J. Todd and L. Jones, *Matrimonial Property* (1972) London, HMSO, paras. 4.0–4.2.

* L. Tilly and J. Scott, *Woman, Work and Family* (1987) New York and London, Methuen, pp. 21 et seq. 105, 123, 124, 176.

M. Weissman and E. Paykel, *The Depressed Woman* (1974) Chicago, University of Chicago Press.

* L. Weitzman, 'Legal Regulation of Marriage: Tradition and Change.' (1974) 62 California Law Review 1169.

A. Wilensky, 'Women's Work, Economic Growth, Ideology and Structure' (1968) 7 Industrial Relations 235.

* E. Wilson, *Women and the Welfare State* (1977) London, Tavistock, p. 176.

M. Young, 'Distribution of Income Within the Family' (1952) 3 British Journal of Sociology 303.

* M. Young and P. Willmott *The Symmetrical Family* (1973) London, Routledge and Kegan Paul (1980) Harmondsworth, Penguin Books, pp. 28 et seq.

F. Zweig, *The Workers in the Affluent Society* (1961) London, Heineman.

Chapter 4

* Sir William Beveridge, *Social Insurance and Allied Services* (Cmd. 6404) (1942) London, HMSO, para. 347.

J. Bradshaw and J. Millar *Lone Parent Families in the UK* (1991) Social Security Research Report, no. 6, London, HMSO.

* Central Statistical Office, *Social Trends 17* (1987) London, HMSO, table 2.6.

* Central Statistical Office, *Social Trends 20* (1990) London, HMSO, tables 1.2; 1.20.

* Central Statistical Office, *Social Trends 21* (1991) London, HMSO, table 5.18.

* *Children Come First*: (Cm 1264) (1990) London, HMSO, The Government's proposals on the maintenance of children vol. 1:1/16; Appendix C; vol; 2. 1.3.2.; 1.4.; 1.5.

DHSS/SBC, *Low Incomes* (1979) London, HMSO.

G. Douglas, 'Individual Economic Security for the Elderly and the Divorced: A Consideration of the Position in England and Wales' in M.T. Meulders-Klein and J. Eekelaar (eds) *Family, State and Individual Economic Security* (1988) Brussels, Story-Scientia, p. 491.

* J.M. Eekelaar, 'Public Law and Private Rights: the Finer Proposals' [1976] Public Law 64, pp. 70–77.

J. Eekelaar and D. Pearl (eds.) *An Aging World* (1989) Oxford, Oxford University Press.

Equal Opportunities Commission, *The Taxation of Husband and Wife: Response*

of the Equal Opportunities Commission to the Government Green Paper
(1981) Manchester, Equal Opportunities Commission.

F. Field, *Fair Shares for Families — the Need for a Family Impact Statement*
(1981) London, Study Commission on the Family.

V. George, *Social Security and Society* (1973) London, Routledge and Kegan
Paul.

* H. Green, *Informal Carers* (1988) OPCS (Social Survey Division) Series GH 5
no. 15 supp A, London HMSO, figs 2A, 4A.

* *Hansard*, House of Commons, vol. 192 (4 June 1991) cols 178–249.

* *Hansard*, House of Lords, vol. 526 (25 February 1991) cols 779, 781–782, 830.

* J. Haskey, 'One-Parent Families and Their Children in Great Britain: Numbers
and Characteristics' (1989) 55 Population Trends 27, table 4 at p. 30.

Home Office Statistical Bulletin 21/90 (1990).

House of Commons Social Security Committee, *Second Report*, (Session 1990–91)
(HC 277-I) paras. 7–8; 11.

* J. Leigh, 'Child Maintenance: A View from the Law Society' [1991] Journal of
Child Law, pp. 41 et seq.

P. Lewis, 'Cutting Poverty in Half' One-Parent Times, Spring 1979.

R. Lister, *Patching Up the Safety Net* (1977) London, Child Poverty Action
Group.

R. Lister, *The No-Cost, No-Benefit Review* (1979) London, Child Poverty Action
Group.

* R. Lister, 'Income Maintenance for Families with Children' in R.N. Rapoport,
M.P. Fogarty and R. Rapoport (eds.), *Families in Britain* (1982) London,
Routledge and Kegan Paul, p. 432.

* M. Maclean and J. Eekelaar, *Children and Divorce: Economic Factors* (1983)
Oxford, SSRC, p. 10.

A.J. Manners and I. Rauta, *Family Property in Scotland* (1981), Edinburgh,
HMSO.

J.E. Meade, *The Structure and Reform of Direct Taxation* (1978) London, George
Allen and Unwin.

M.T. Meulders-Klein and J. Eekelaar (eds) *Family, State and Individual
Economic Security* (1988) Brussels, Story-Scientia.

* S. Monk, 'Child Support: the View from the National Council for One-Parent
Families' [1991] Journal of Child Law, p. 47.

S. Parker, 'Child Support in Australia: Children's Rights or Public Interest' (1991)
vol. 5 Int Journal of Law and the Family, p. 24.

D. Piachaud, *The Cost of a Child* (1979) London, Child Poverty Action Group.

C. Pond, *The Poverty Trap* (1978) Milton Keynes, Open University Press.

* P. Paillat, 'Recent and Predictable Population Trends in Developed Countries
in J. Eekelaar and D. Pearl (eds.), *An Aging World* (1989) Oxford, Oxford
University Press, p. 25 at p. 35.

Reform of Social Security vol. I (1985) (Cmnd. 9517) London, HMSO.

* *Reform of Social Security* (Programme for Change) vol. II (1985) (Cmnd. 9518)
London, HMSO paras. 4.44–4.51.

Reform of Social Security (Programme for Action) (1985) (Cmnd. 9691) London,
HMSO.

* *Report of the Committee on One-Parent Families* (Chairman: The Hon. Sir
Morris Finer) (Cmnd. 5629) (1974) London, HMSO, paras. 4.179–4.183,
4.193, 4.207, 4.188–4.189, 5.104, 5.81–5.86.

Royal Commission on the Taxation of Profits and Income, *Second Report*
(Cmd. 9105) (1954) London, HMSO.

* Social Security Statistics (1990) London, HMSO, table H2.01.

Supplementary Benefits Commission, *Cohabitation* (1971) London, HMSO.

J.E. Todd and C.M. Jones, *Matrimonial Property* (1972) London, HMSO.

P. Townsend, *Poverty in the United Kingdom* (1981) Harmondsworth, Penguin
Books.

Supplementary Benefits Commission, *Response of the Supplementary Benefits Commission to Social Assistance* (1979) London, HMSO.
* The Independent Newspaper, November 2nd 1990 (comment by J. Eekelaar).
* The Independent Newspaper, April 25th 1991 (letter).
  J. Walley, *Social Security: Another British Failure?* (1972) London, Charles Knight.
  M. Wynn, *Family Policy* (1972) Harmondsworth, Penguin Books.

Chapter 5

* Central Statistical Office, *Social Trends 17* (1987) London, HMSO, table 8.1.
  General Household Survey (1984) London, HMSO.
  K. Gray *Reallocation of Property on Divorce* (1977) Abingdon, Professional Books.
* K. Gray, *Elements of Land Law* (1987) London, Butterworths, pp. 870, 871.
* *Insolvency Law and Practice* (Report of the Review Committee chaired by Sir Kenneth Cork) (Cmnd 8558) (1982) London, HMSO, para. 1118.
* O. Kahn-Freund, *Matrimonial Property: where do we go from here?* Joseph Unger Memorial Lecture, University of Birmingham, (1974) pp. 11, 20–21, 22, 23, 25, 46–47.
* Law Reform Commission of Canada, *Family Property*, Working Paper No. 8 (1975) Ottowa, Information Canada, pp. 9–10, 18, 19–22, 27.
* Law Commission, Working Paper No. 42, *Family Property Law* (1971) London, HMSO paras. 0.12, 0.13, 0.15, 0.16, 0.25–0.29, 0.37–0.41, 4.65, 4.71.
* Law Commission, *First Report on Family Property: A New Approach*, Law Com. No. 52 (1973) London, HMSO, paras. 21–24, 38, 39, 41, 44, 47–59.
  Law Commission, *Second Report on Family Property: Family Provision on Death*, Law Com. No. 61 (1974) London, HMSO.
* Law Commission, *Third Report on Family Property: The Matrimonial Home (Co-ownership and Occupation Rights) and Household Goods*, Law Com. No. 86 (1978) London, HMSO, paras. 1.113–1.119.
  Law Commission, *Property Law: The implications of Williams and Glyn's Bank Ltd v Boland*, Law Com. No. 115 (1982) London, HMSO.
* Law Commission, Working Paper No. 90, *Transfer of Money Between Spouses – the Married Women's Property Act 1964* (1985) London, HMSO, paras. 5.5–5.6.
* Law Commission, *Matrimonial Property: Second Consultation Paper* (1986) London, HMSO, paras. 1.1–1.6; 2.1, 2.2.
* Law Commission, *Property Law: 3rd Report on Land Registration*, Law Com. No. 158 (1987) London, HMSO paras. 2.6; 2.12.
* Law Commission, *Family Law, Matrimonial Property*, Law Com. No. 175 (1988) London, HMSO, para 1.4, footnote 21.
  Law Commission, *Distribution on Intestacy*, Law Com. No. 187 (1989) London, HMSO.
  A.J. Manners and I. Rauta, *Family Property in Scotland* (1981) Edinburgh, HMSO.
  J. Masson, 'A New Approach to Matrimonial Property' (1988) 18 Family Law 327.
  J.G. Miller, *Family Property and Financial Provision* (1974) (3rd edn. 1983) London, Sweet and Maxwell.
  J. Montgomery, 'A Question of Intention' (1987), Conveyancer 86 p. 16.
  M. Rheinstein and M. Glendon, 'Interspousal Relations' (1980) International Encyclopedia of Comparative Law, vol. IV.
* The Scottish Law Commission, *Family Law: Report on Matrimonial Property* (1984) Scot. Law Com. No. 86 HC 467. Edinburgh, HMSO, para. 3.
* Sir Jocelyn Simon, *With All My Wordly Goods*. Holdsworth Club, Presidential

Address, University of Birmingham (1964), pp. 1–4, 8–9, 10–13, 14–17, 100, 101, 102, 103.
* J. Todd and L. Jones, *Matrimonial Property* (1972) London, HMSO, p. 120.

Chapter 6

S. Anderson, 'Legislative Divorce — Law for the Aristocracy' in G.R. Rubin and N. Sugarman (eds.) *Law, Society and Economy: Essays in Legal History* (1984), Abingdon, Professional Books.
* G. Alpern, *Rights of Passage* (1982) Aspen, Colorado, Psychological Development Publications, p. 19.
A. Alvarez, *Life after Marriage: Love in an Age of Divorce* (1981) New York, Simon and Schuster.
J. Burgoyne, R. Ormrod, M. Richards, *Divorce Matters* (1987) Harmondsworth, Penguin Books.
* Central Statistical Office, *Social Trends 21* (1991) London, HMSO, chart 2.13, 2.15.
A.J. Cherlin, *Marriage, Divorce and Remarriage* (1981) Cambridge, Massachusets, Harvard University Press.
R. Chester (ed.), *Divorce in Europe* (1978) Leiden, Martin Nijhoff.
R. Chester and J. Streather, 'Cruelty in English Divorce: Some Empirical Findings' (1972) 34 Journal of Marriage and the Family, 706.
* J. Cleese and R. Skynner, *Families and How to Survive Them* (1983) London, Methuen.
E. Clive, *The Divorce (Scotland) Act 1976* (1976) Edinburgh, Green.
* G. Davis, A. Macleod and M. Murch, 'Special Procedure in Divorce and the Solicitor's Role' (1982) 12 Family Law 39, pp. 39, 43–44.
* G. Davis and M. Murch, *Grounds for Divorce* (1988) Oxford, Clarendon Press, pp. 78–85.
* R. Deech, 'Marriage as a Short-term Option' (1990) The Independent Newspaper, 2nd November 1990.
J. Dominian, 'Families in Divorce' in R.N. Rapoport, M.P. Fogarty and R. Rapoport (eds.), *Families in Britain* (1982) London, Routledge and Kegan Paul.
J. Eekelaar, *Family Law and Social Policy*, (2nd edn.) (1984) London, Weidenfeld and Nicolson.
J. Eekelaar, *Regulating Divorce* (1991) Oxford, Clarendon.
E. Elston, J. Fuller and M. Murch, 'Judicial Hearings of Undefended Divorce Petitions' (1975) 38 Modern Law Review 609.
* Sir Morris Finer and O.R. McGregor, 'The History of the Obligation to Maintain' App. 5, *Report of the Committee on One-Parent Families* (Cmnd. 5629-1) (1974) London, HMSO, paras. 1, 2, 4, 5, 6, 13, 14, 17, 18, 30, 31, 34, 42, 43.
M.D.A. Freeman, 'Divorce without Legal Aid' (1976) 6 Family Law 255.
C. Gibson, 'The Effect of Legal Aid on Divorce in England and Wales, Part I: Before 1950' (1971) 1 Family Law 90.
C. Gibson and A. Beer, 'The Effect of Legal Aid on Divorce in England and Wales, Part II: Since 1950' (1971) 1 Family Law 122.
C. Gibson, 'The Association between Divorce and Social Class in England and Wales' (1974) 25 British Journal of Sociology 79.
C. Gibson, 'Divorce and the Recourse to Legal Aid' (1980) 43 Modern Law Review 609.
* M.A. Glendon, *Abortion and Divorce in Western Law* (1987) Cambridge (Mass) and London, Harvard University Press, pp. 63–64, 66–68.
J. Haskey, 'The Proportion of Marriages ending in Divorce' (1982) 27 Population Trends 4.
* J. Haskey, 'Social Class and Socio-economic Differentials in Divorce in England and Wales' (1984) Population Studies, p. 38.

J. Haskey, 'Grounds for Divorce in England and Wales — a Social and Demographic Analysis' (1986) 18 J. Biosoc. Sci., p. 127, Fig. 2, Table 3.

J. Haskey, 'Recent Trends in Divorce in England and Wales: the Effects of Legislative Changes' (1986) 44 Population Trends, p. 9.

* J. Haskey, 'Trends in Marriage and Divorce 1837–1987' (1987) 48 Population Trends, p. 11, figure 6 (at p. 17).

* J. Haskey, 'Regional Patterns of Divorce in England and Wales' (1988) 52 Population Trends, p. 5, table 6 (at p. 13).

* J. Haskey, 'Children in Families Broken by Divorce' (1990) 61 Population Trends, p. 34, figure 1 (p. 35), table 1 (p. 35).

* Law Commission, *Reform of the Grounds of Divorce — The Field of Choice* (Cmnd. 3123) (1966) London, HMSO, paras. 11, 15, 19, 52, 120.

Law Commission, Working Paper No. 76, *Time Restrictions on Presentation of Divorce and Nullity Petitions* (1980) London, HMSO.

* Law Commission, *Report on Time Restrictions of Presentation of Divorce and Nullity Petitions*, Law Com. No. 116 (1982) London, HMSO, paras. 2.14, 2.15, 2.27, 2.30, 2.31, 2.33.

Law Commission, *Facing the Future — A Discussion Paper on the Ground for Divorce*, Law Com. No. 170 (1988) London, HMSO.

* Law Commission, *The Ground for Divorce*, Law Com. No. 192 (1990) London, HMSO, paras. 1.5–1.8; 2.8–2.21; 3.29–3.48; 5.75–5.77.

* Law Commission, *Court Record Study* Appendix C to *The Ground for Divorce*, Law Com. No. 192 (1990) London, HMSO, paras. 26, 31, 32, 36, 37, 44, 51, table 5.

* Law Reform Commission of Canada, Working Paper No. 13, *Divorce* (1975) Ottawa, Information Canada, pp. 31, 34, 35.

Law Society, Family Law Sub-Committee, *A Better Way Out: Suggestions for the Reform of the Law of Divorce and Other Forms of Matrimonial Relief; for the Setting Up of a Family Court; and for its Procedure* (1979) London, The Law Society, paras. 33, 35–38, 40, 42, 44, 46–52, 58, 69, 70.

Law Society, Standing Committee on Family Law, *A Better Way Out Reviewed* (1982) London, The Law Society, paras. 27, 28.

B.H. Lee, *Divorce Law Reform in England* (1974) London, Peter Owen.

* R. Leete, *Changing Patterns of Family Formation and Dissolution in England and Wales 1964–1976* OPCS Studies on Medical and Population Subjects No. 39 (1979) London, HMSO, tables 36, 38, figures 19, 20.

* Lord Chancellor's Department, *Judicial Statistics — Annual Reports 1989* (Cmnd. 1154) (1990) Table 5.3 (p. 57) and previous years.

O.R. McGregor, *Divorce in England — A Centenary Study* (1957) London, Heinemann.

M. Maclean and R.E.J. Wadsworth, 'The Interests of Children after Parental Divorce: A Long-term Perspective' (1988) 2 Int. J. of Law and the Family 155.

S. Maidment, *Judicial Separation — A Research Study* (1982) Oxford, Centre for Socio-Legal Studies.

M. Mears, 'Getting it Wrong Again? Divorce and the Law Commission' (1991) Family Law 231.

B. Mortlock, *The Inside of Divorce* (1972) London, Constable.

F. Pollock and F.W. Maitland, *The History of English Law Before the Time of Edward I* (2nd edn., 1898) Cambridge, Cambridge University Press.

* Report of a Group appointed by the Archbishop of Canterbury (Chairman: The Rt Rev. R.C. Mortimer, Lord Bishop of Exeter), *Putting Asunder — A Divorce Law for Contemporary Society* (1966) London, Society for Promoting Christian Knowledge, paras. 17, 18, 45(f), 55, 69.

* *Report of the Committee on One-Parent Families* (Chairman: The Hon. Sir Morris Finer) (Cmnd. 5629) (1974) London, HMSO, paras. 4.29–4.32.

* *Report of the Matrimonial Causes Procedure Committee* (Chairman: The Hon. Mrs. Justice Booth, D.B.E.) (1985) London, HMSO, paras. 2.9, 2.10.

Report of the Royal Commission on Divorce (Chairman: Lord Gorell), (Cd. 6478) (1912) London, HMSO.

Report of the Royal Commission on Marriage and Divorce (Chairman: Lord Morton of Henryton) (Cmd. 9678) (1956) London, HMSO.

M. Rheinstein, *Marriage Stability, Divorce and the Law* (1972) Chicago, University of Chicago Press.

* M.P.M. Richards, 'Divorce Research Today' [1991] Family Law, pp. 70–72.

M.P.M. Richards and M. Dyson, *Separation, Divorce and the Development of Children: a Review* (1982) London, DHSS.

L. Rimmer, *Families in Focus* (1981) London, Study Commission on the Family.

* St. Mark, 'Gospel according to St. Mark' *Holy Bible* Authorised King James version, ch. 10.

Sir Jocelyn Simon, 'Recent Developments in the Matrimonial Law' Riddell lecture, 1970. Printed in *Rayden on Divorce* (11th edn., 1971) London, Butterworths.

Society of Conservative Lawyers, *The Future of Marriage — A Report by a Research Sub-Committee* (1981) London, Conservative Political Centre.

* L. Stone, *Road to Divorce: England 1530–1987* (1990) Oxford, Oxford University Press, p. 27, 310.

S.D. Sugarman and H.H. Kay, *Divorce Reform at the Crossroads* (1990) New Haven and London, Yale University Press.

B. Thornes and J. Collard, *Who Divorces?* (1979) London, Routledge and Kegan Paul.

The Scottish Law Commission, *Report on Reform of the Ground for Divorce* (1989) Scot. Law Com. No. 116, Edinburgh, HMSO.

L. Tottie, 'The Elimination of Fault in Swedish Divorce Law' in J.M. Eekelaar and S.N. Katz (eds.), *Marriage and Cohabitation in Contemporary Societies: Areas of Legal, Social and Ethical Change* (1980) Toronto, Butterworths.

United States' National Conference of Commissioners on Uniform State Laws, *Uniform Marriage and Divorce Act* (1970), s. 305.

W. Wadlington, 'Divorce Without Fault Without Perjury' (1966) 52 Virginia Law Review 32.

J.S. Wallerstein and J.B. Kelly, *Surviving the Breakup* (1980) New York, Basic Books Inc.

J.S. Wallerstein and S. Blakeslee, *Second Chances* (1989) London, Bantam.

J. Walker, 'Divorce — Whose Fault?' [1991] Family Law 234.

L. Weitzman and R.B. Dixon, 'The Transformation of Marriage through No-Fault Divorce — The Case of the United States' in J.M. Eekelaar and S.N. Katz (eds.), *Marriage and Cohabitation in Contemporary Societies: Areas of Legal, Social and Ethical Change* (1980) Toronto, Butterworths.

S. Wolfram, 'Divorce in England 1700–1857' (1984) 5 Oxford Journal of Legal Studies 156.

Chapter 7

F.A.R. Bennion, 'First Consideration: A Cautionary Tale' (1976) 126 New Law Journal 2237.

J. Black and J. Bridge, *A Practical Approach to Family Law* (2nd edn.) (1989) London, Blackstone.

P. Bohannan (ed.), *Divorce and After* (1970) Garden City, New York, Doubleday.

* J. Burgoyne, R. Ormrod, M. Richards, *Divorce Matters* (1987) Harmondsworth, Penguin Books, pp. 73–74.

* E. Clive, 'The Financial Consequences of Divorce: Reform from the Scottish Perspective' in M.D.A. Freeman (ed.), *State, Law, and the Family*, (1984) London, Tavistock, p. 196 at pp. 206, 207.

* S. Cretney, 'Money After Divorce — The Mistakes We Have Made?' in M.D.A. Freeman (ed.), *Essays in Family Law 1985* (1986) London, Stevens, p. 34 at p. 54.

* R. Deech, 'The Principles of Maintenance' (1977) 7 Family Law 229, pp. 230–232.

R. Deech, 'Financial Relief: the Retreat from Precedent and Principle' (1982) 98 Law Quarterly Review 621.

* R. Deech, 'Divorce Studies and Empirical Studies' (1990) 106 Law Quarterly Review 229 at p. 237.

J. Dewar, 'Reforming Financial Provision: The Alternatives' [1984] Journal of Social Welfare Law 1.

A.R. Dewar, 'The Family Law (Scotland) Act 1985 in practice' (1989) Journal of the Law Society of Scotland (February 42).

* G. Douglas, 'The Clean Break on Divorce' (1981) 11 Family Law, pp. 42–53, 45, 48.

* J.M. Eekelaar, 'Commission Reports on the Financial Consequences of Divorce' (1982) 45 Modern Law Review 420 at p. 423.

J.M. Eekelaar, *Family Law and Social Policy* (2nd edn., 1984) London, Weidenfeld and Nicholson.

* J.M. Eekelaar and M. Maclean, *Maintenance After Divorce* (1986) Clarendon Press, p. 62, table 10 (p. 25), table 11 (p. 27).

J.M. Eekelaar and M. MacLean, 'Divorce Law and Empirical Studies — A Reply' (1990) 106 Law Quarterly Review 621.

* Sir Morris Finer and O.R. McGregor, 'The History of the Obligation to Maintain'. App. 5, *Report of the Committee on One-Parent Families* (Cmnd. 5629–I) (1974) London, HMSO, paras. 26–27, 32–33, 35–38.

D. Freed and H. Foster 'Divorce in the Fifty States: an Overview as of August 1st 1979' (1979) 5 Family Law Reporter.

J. Freedman, *Property and Marriage: An Integrated Approach* (IFS Report Series No. 29) (1988) London, Institute of Fiscal Studies.

M.A. Glendon, *The New Family and the New Property* (1981) Toronto, Butterworths, pp. 52 et seq., 57–58.

K. Gray, *Reallocation of Property on Divorce* (1977) Abingdon, Professional Books.

W.M. Harper, *Divorce and Your Money* (1979) London, Allen and Unwin.

S. Hoffman and G. Duncan, 'What Are The Economic Consequences of Divorce?' (1988) 25 Demography 641.

H. Joshi and H. Davies, *The Pension Consequences of Divorce* (1991) (Discussion Paper No. 550) London, Joseph Rowntree Foundation.

H. Land, 'Poverty and Gender, The Distribution of Resources within the Family' in M. Brown (ed.), *The Structure of Disadvantage* (1983) London, Heinemann.

* Law Commission, *The Financial Consequences of Divorce: the Basic Policy: a Discussion Paper* (Cmnd. 8041) (1980) London, HMSO, paras. 24–27, 59, 66, 70, 73, 75, 77, 80, 84, 86.

* Law Commission, *The Financial Consequences of Divorce* (Law Com. No. 112) (1982) London, HMSO, para. 17.

* The Law Society, *Maintenance and Capital Provision on Divorce* (1991), the Law Society, London, 2.17–2.25; 3.3.

P. McDonald (ed.), *Setting Up; Property and Income Distribution on Divorce in Australia* (1986) Institute of Family Studies' Family Reformation Project, Sydney, Prentice-Hall of Australia.

P. McDonald, *The Economic Consequences of Marriage Breakdown in Australia (A Summary)* (1985) Melbourne, Institute of Family Studies, pp. 33–36.

* M. Maclean and J.M. Eekelaar, *Children and Divorce: Economic Factors* (1983) Oxford, S.S.R.C., p. 34.

M.M. Marvin, *Divorced Man's Guide through Pain and Misery* (1981, 4th ed. 1984) Stilwell, Kansas, Deej Publishing Company.

A.C. Martin, 'Actuaries, Pensions and Divorce' [1991] Family Law 258.

J.G. Miller, 'Trusts and Financial Provision on Divorce' (1990) Trusts Law and Practice (May 42).

R. Mnookin, et al., 'Private Ordering Revisited: What Custodial Arrangements are Parents Negotiating?' in S. Sugarman and H.H. Kaye (eds) *Divorce Reform at the Cross Roads* (1990) New Haven and London, Yale University Press, p. 37.

* K. O'Donovan, 'The Principle of Maintenance: an Alternative View.' (1978) 8 Family Law 180–184.

* *Report of the Committee on One-Parent Families*, (Chairman: The Hon. Sir Morris Finer) (Cmnd. 5629) (1974) London, HMSO, table 5.1.

* *Report (Final) of the Royal Commission on Legal Services* (Cmnd. 7648) (1979) London, HMSO, vol. 1, para. 13.64.

* The Scottish Law Commission, *Report on Aliment and Financial Provision*, Scot. Law Com. No. 67 (1981) Edinburgh, HMSO, paras. 3.18–3.22, 3.62, 3.65–3.68, 3.92–3.94, 3.107–3.110.

* C. Smart, *The Ties that Bind* (1984) London, Routledge and Kegan Paul, pp. 223, 224, 227, 228.

* S. Sugarman, 'Dividing Financial Interests on Divorce', in S. Sugarman and H.H. Kaye (eds) *Divorce Reform at the Cross Roads* (1990) New Haven and London, Yale University Press, p. 149.

* P. Symes, 'Indissolubility and the Clean Break' (1985) 48 Modern Law Review 44 at pp. 46, 47, 51, 52, 53, 57, 59, 60.

R. Thornton, 'Homelessness Through Relationship Breakdown: The Local Authorities' Response' [1989] Journal of Social Welfare Law 67.

E. Wasoff, R.E. Dobash, and Harcus, *The Impact of the Family Law Scotland Act 1985 on Solicitors' Divorce Practice* (1990) Scottish Office, Central Research Unit Papers.

* L. Weitzman, *The Divorce Revolution* (1985) New York, The Free Press, table 12 (p. 152), figure 3 (p. 338), p. 362.

* L. Weitzman and R. Dixon, 'The Alimony Myth: Does No Fault Divorce Make a Difference?' (1980) 14 Family Law Quarterly 142, p. 151.

Chapter 8

H. Astor and J. Nothdurft, 'Report of the New South Wales Law Reform Commission on De Facto Relationships' (1985) 48 Modern Law Review at 61.

C. Barton, *Cohabitation Contracts, Extra Marital Partnerships and Law Reform* (1985) Aldershot, Gower, Coventry.

J. Bradshaw and J. Millar, 'Lone Parent Families in the UK', Department of Social Security Research Report No. 6, p. 98 (HMSO, 1991).

J. Bowlber, J. Jackson and E. Longbridge, *Living Together* (1991) London, Century.

C. Bruch, 'Non-marital Cohabitation in the Common Law Countries: A Study in Judicial-Legislative Interaction' (1981) 29 American Journal of Comparative Law p. 217.

E.H. Butler, *Traditional Marriage and Emerging Alternatives* (1979) Harper and Row, London.

* Central Statistical Office, *Social Trends 21* (1991) London, HMSO, table 2.16.

* E.M. Clive, 'Marriage: An Unnecessary Legal Concept' in J.M. Eekelaar and S.M. Katz (eds.), *Marriage and Cohabitation in Contemporary Societies: Areas of Legal, Social and Ethical Change* (1980) Toronto, Butterworths, p. 72.

S. Danielson, 'Unmarried Partners and their Children: Scandinavian Law in the Making' (1983) 3 Oxford Journal of Legal Studies 59.

* R. Deech, 'The Case Against Legal Recognition of Cohabitation' in J.M. Eekelaar and S.M. Katz (eds.), *Marriage and Cohabitation in Contemporary Societies: Areas of Legal, Social and Ethical Change* (1980) Toronto, Butterworths, pp. 309–310.

C. Fernandez, 'Beyond Marvin: A Proposal for Quasi-spousal Support' (1978) 30 Stanford Law Review 359.

H.A. Finley, A.J. Bradbrook and R.J. Bailey-Harris, *Family Law: Cases and Commentary* (1985) Sydney, Butterworths.

M.D.A. Freeman and C.M. Lyon, *Cohabitation Without Marriage* (1983) Aldershot, Gower.

* M.A. Glendon, 'Withering Away of Marriage' (1976) 62 Virginia Law Review 663, p. 686.

Hansard, House of Lords, vol. 429 (4 May 1982) col. 1104.

* C. Harpum, 'Adjusting Property Rights Between Unmarried Cohabitees' (1982) 2 Oxford Journal of Legal Studies 287.

* J. Haskey and K. Kiernan, 'Cohabitation in Great Britain — Characteristics and Estimated Number of Cohabiting Partners' (1989) 58 Population Trends, p. 23, tables 5.6, figs 1, 2, 4, 5, 9, 10.

Institute of Law Research and Reform, Alberta, *Towards Reform of the Law Relating to Cohabitation Outside Marriage* (1987) Issues Paper No. 2; (1989) Report No. 53.

* International Association of Young Lawyers, Conference in Philadelphia (1980), an *Example of a Cohabitation Contract*.

R. Johnson, 'Cohabitation Without Formal Marriage in England and Wales' (1986) 16 Family Law 47.

H.D. Krause, *Family Law* (3rd edn.) (1990) St. Paul, Minnesota, West Publishing Company.

* D. Meade, 'Consortium Rights of the Unmarried — Time for a Reappraisal' (1981) 12 Family Law Quarterly 213.

J.G. Miller, 'Provision for a Surviving Spouse' (1986) 102 Law Quarterly Review 445.

New South Wales Law Reform Commission (1983), *Report on De Facto Relationships* (LRC 36).

D. Oliver, 'The Mistress in Law' [1978] Current Legal Problems 81.

D. Oliver, 'Why Do People Live Together?' [1982] Journal of Social Welfare Law, p. 209.

* H. Oppenheimer, *Marriage* (1990) London, Mowbray, pp. 32–34.

S. Parker, *Cohabitees* (1987) London, Kluwer Law Publishes.

M.L. Parry, *The Law Relating to Cohabitation* (1988) London, Sweet & Maxwell.

J. Priest, *Families Outside Marriage* (1990) Bristol, Family Law.

Report of the Committee on One-Parent Families (Chairman: The Hon Sir Morris Finer) (Cmnd. 5629) (1974) London, HMSO.

* The Scottish Law Commission, *The Effects of Cohabitation in Private Law* (1990) Scot. Law Com. Discussion Paper No. 86, Edinburgh, HMSO, paras. 5.2, 5.5.

E.L. Van Deuson, *Contract Cohabitation: An Alternative to Marriage* (1975) New York, Avon Books.

* L. Weitzman, *The Marriage Contract: Spouses, Lovers, and the Law* (1981) London, Collier MacMillan, p. 361.

* L. Weitzman et al, 'Contracts for Intimate Relationships' (1978) Alternative Life-styles, vol. 1 no. 3, August, figure 1 (p. 303).

M. Welstead, 'Truly a Charter for Mistresses' (1990) Denning Law Journal, p. 117.

* W. Weyrauch, 'Metamorphoses of Marriage' (1980) 13 Family Law Quarterly 436.

W. Weyrauch and S. Katz, *American Family Law in Transition* (1983) Washington DC, The Bureau of National Affairs Inc.

A. Zuckerman, 'Formality and the Family — Reform and Status Quo' (1980) 96 Law Quarterly Review 248.

Chapter 9

L.J. Allen, 'Child Abuse: A Critical Review of the Research and the Theory' in J.P. Martin (ed.), *Violence and the Family* (1978) Chichester, Wiley.

Jasmine Beckford, see Brent Council.

V. Binney, G. Harkell and J. Nixon (WAFE/DOE research team), *Leaving Violent Men: A Study of Refuges for Battered Women* (1981) London, Women's Aid Federation, England.

B. Birns, S. Barsden and W.H. Bridges, *Individual Differences in Temperamental Characteristics of Infants* (1969) Transactions of New York Academy of Sciences.

M. Borkowski, M. Murch and V. Walker, *Marital Violence — the community response* (1983) London, Tavistock.

A. Bourlet, *Police Involvement in Marital Violence* (1990) Milton Keynes, Open University Press.

Brent Council, *A Child in Trust — The Report of the Panel of Inquiry into the Circumstances Surrounding the Death of Jasmine Beckford* (Chairman: L. Blom-Cooper Q.C.) (1985) London, London Borough of Brent.

Wayne Brewer, see Somerset Area Review Committee.

P.M. Bromley, *Family Law* (5th edn., 1976; now 7th edn., 1987) London, Butterworths.

B. Cade, 'Family Violence: An Interactional View' (1978) 9 Social Work Today, no. 26, p. 15.

Kimberley Carlile, see Greenwich London Borough Council.

J. Carter, 'Is Child Abuse a Crime?' in A.W. Franklin (ed.), *The Challenge of Child Abuse. Proceedings of a Conference Sponsored by the Royal Society of Medicine, 2–4 June 1976* (1977) London, Academic Press.

J. Carter (ed.), *The Maltreated Child* (1974) London, Priory Press.

J.R. Chapman and M. Gates (eds.) *The Victimisation of Women* (1978) Beverley Hills, California, Sage.

Ciba Foundation (R. Porter, ed.), *Child Sexual Abuse within the Family* (1984) London, Tavistock.

J. Clifton, *It's Lonely but We're Coping: A Follow-up Study of Women Who Used a Refuge* (1980).

* J. Clifton, 'Factors Predisposing Family Members to Violence', in Social Work Services Group, Scottish Education Department, *Violence in the Family — Theory and Practice in Social Work* (1982) Edinburgh, HMSO, pp. 25–32.

Maria Colwell, see under Reports.

J. Court, 'Characteristics of Parents and Children' in J. Carter (ed.), *The Maltreated Child* (1974) London, Priory Press.

B. Dawson and T. Faragher, *Battered Women's Project: Interim Report* (1977) Keele, University of Keele, Department of Sociology.

Department of Health, *Child Abuse: A Study of Inquiry Reports 1980–1989* (1991) London, HMSO.

DHSS, *Child Abuse: A Study of Inquiry Reports, 1973–81*, (1982) London, HMSO.

R. Dobash and R. Dobash, 'Wives: the Appropriate Victims of Marital Violence' and (with C. Cavanagh and M. Wilson) 'Wife Beating: the Victims Speak' (1978) 2 Victimology.

* R. Dobash and R. Dobash, *Violence Against Wives: A Case Against the Patriarchy* (1980) London, Open Books, p. 156.

R.E. Dobash and R.P. Dobash, 'Community response to violence against wives: charivari, abstract justice and patriarchy' (1981) 28 Social Problems 563.

R.E. Dobash and R.P. Dobash, 'The Nature and Antecedents of Violent Events' (1984) 24 British Journal of Criminology 269.

* M. Dow, 'Police Involvement' in M. Borland (ed.), *Violence in the Family* (1976) Manchester, Manchester University Press, pp. 132–133.

S.M. Edwards, 'A sociolegal evaluation of gender ideologies in domestic violence, assault and spousal homicides' (1985) 10 Victimology 186.

S.M. Edwards and A. Halpern, 'Conflicting interests: protecting children or protecting title to property' [1988] Journal of Social Welfare Law 110.

S.M. Edwards and A. Halpern, 'Protection for the victim of domestic violence: time for radical revision?' [1991] Journal of Social Welfare and Family Law 94.

J.M. Eekelaar, 'The Emergence of Children's Rights' (1986) 6 Oxford Journal of Legal Studies 161.

J.M. Eekelaar and S.N. Katz (eds.). *Family Violence: An International and Interdisciplinary Study* (1978) Toronto, Butterworths.

E. Evason, *Hidden Violence* (1982) Belfast, Farset Press.

* Family and Civil Committees of the Council of Her Majesty's Circuit Judges, 'Domestic Violence and Occupation of the Family Home' [1990] Family Law 225, pp. 225–227.

* T. Faragher, 'The Police Response to Violence Against Women in the Home', in J. Pahl (1985) op. cit., p. 117.

E. Farmer and R. Parker, *A Study of Interim Care Orders* (1985) Bristol, University of Bristol, Department of Social Administration.

M. Faulk, 'Men Who Assault Their Wives' (1974) 14 Medicine, Science and the Law 180.

* M.D.A. Freeman, *Violence in the Home* (1979) Farnborough, Saxon House (now Aldershot, Gower), p. 45.

M.D.A. Freeman, 'Violence Against Women: Does the Legal System Provide Solutions or Itself Constitute the Problem?' (1980) 7 British Journal of Law and Society 215.

M.D.A. Freeman, 'Legal ideologies, patriarchical precedents and domestic violence' in M.D.A. Freeman (ed.), *The State, the Law and the Family: Critical Perspectives* (1984) London, Stevens.

J.J. Gayford, 'Wife Battering: A Preliminary Survey of 100 Cases' (1975) British Medical Journal, no. 1, p. 194.

R. Gelles, *The Violent Home* (1972) Beverley Hills, Sage Publications.

D. Gil, 'Violence Against Children' in C. Lee (ed.), *Child Abuse: A Reader and Sourcebook* (1973) Milton Keynes, Open University Press.

Greenwich London Borough Council and Greenwich Health Authority, *A Child in Mind — The Report of the Commission of Inquiry into the Circumstances Surrounding the Death of Kimberley Carlile* (Chairman: L. Blom-Cooper Q.C.) (1987) London, London Borough of Greenwich.

M. Hayes, 'The Law Commission and the Family Home' (1990) 53 Modern Law Review 222.

Tyra Henry, see Lambeth London Borough Council.

Hillingdon Council, Area Review Committee on Child Abuse, *Report of the Review Panel into the Death of Heidi Koseda* (1986) London, London Borough of Hillingdon.

* Home Office Circular (60/90), *Domestic Violence*, London, Home Office, paras. 2, 4, 11–18, 21, 24.

M. Homer et al, 'The burden of dependency' in N. Johnson (ed.), *Marital Violence* (1985) London, Routledge and Kegan Paul.

* House of Commons Select Committee on Violence in Marriage, *Report, Minutes of Evidence and Appendices* HC 553-II (1974–75) London, HMSO, paras. 10, 20, 21 and pp. 366, 375–376.

House of Commons Select Committee on Violence in the Family, *Violence to Children. Vol. 1: Report (together with the Proceedings of the Committee)* HC 329-i (1976–77) (1977) London, HMSO.

M. Jobling, 'Battered Wives: A Survey' (1974) 47 Social Service Quarterly 142.

D.S. Kalmuss and M.A. Straus, 'A wife's marital dependency and wife abuse' [1981] Journal of Marriage and the Family 277.

G. Kaufman Kantor and M.A. Straus, *Stopping the Violence: Battered Women, Police Utilisation and Police Response* (1987) Paper presented to the American Society of Criminology Meeting, Montreal.

R.S. Kempe and C.H. Kempe, *Child Abuse* (1978) London, Fontana/Open Books.

D. Klein, 'Battered wives and the domination of women' in N.H. Rafter and E. Stanko (eds.), *Judge, Lawyer, Victim, Thief: Women, Gender Roles and Criminal Justice* (1982) Boston, Mass., Northeastern University Press.

Heidi Koseda, see Hillingdon Council.

Lambeth London Borough Council, *Whose Child? The Report of the Public Inquiry into the Death of Tyra Henry* (1987) London, London Borough of Lambeth.

Law Commission, *Report on Matrimonial Proceedings in Magistrates' Courts*, Law Com. No. 77, (1976) London, HMSO.

* Law Commission, Working Paper No. 113, *Domestic Violence and Occupation of the Family Home* (1989) London, HMSO, paras. 2.2–2.15, 3.19–3.25, 3.37.

M. Lynch, 'Ill health and Child Abuse' *Lancet*, 16 August 1975, p. 317.

M. Lystad, 'Violence at Home: A Review of the Literature' (1975) 45 American Journal of Orthopsychiatry 328.

S. Maidment, 'The Law's Response to Marital Violence in England and the U.S.A.' (1977) 26 International and Comparative Law Quarterly 403.

* S. Maidment, 'The Relevance of the Criminal Law to Domestic Violence' [1980] Journal of Social Welfare Law 26, pp. 29–31.

D. Marsden, 'Sociological Perspectives on Family Violence' in J.P. Martin (ed.), *Violence and the Family* (1978) Chichester, Wiley.

D. Marsden and D. Owens, 'The Jekyll and Hyde Marriages' *New Society*, 8 May 1975.

D. Martin, *Battered Wives* (1976) San Francisco, Glide Publications.

D. Martin, 'Battered women: society's problem' in J.R. Chapman and M. Gates, *The Victimisation of Women* (1978) Beverley Hills, California, Sage.

J.P. Martin (ed.), *Violence and the Family* (1978) Chichester, Wiley.

J.S. Mill, *The Subjection of Women* (1869); reprinted in Everyman's Library (1929) London, Dent.

M. Morash, 'Wife Battering' [1986] Criminal Justice Abstracts 252.

National Society for the Prevention of Cruelty to Children, *At Risk: An Account of the Work of the Battered Child Research Department* (1975) London, Routledge and Kegan Paul.

* New York Task Force Report, 'Domestic Violence' (1987) 15 Fordham Urban Law Journal 28, pp. 38–40.

J.E. O'Brien, 'Violence in Divorce Prone Families' (1971) 33 Journal of Marriage and the Family 692.

C. Ounsted and M.A. Lynch, 'Family Pathology as Seen in England' in R.E. Helfer and C.H. Kempe (eds.), *Child Abuse and Neglect: The Family and the Community* (1976) Cambridge, Mass., Ballinger.

M. Pagelow, *Battered Women — A New Perspective* (1977) Dublin, International Sociological Association.

J. Pahl, *A Refuge for Battered Women: A Study of the Role of a Women's Centre* (1978) London, HMSO.

J. Pahl, 'Police Response to Battered Women' [1982] Journal of Social Welfare Law 337.

J. Pahl (ed.), *Private Violence and Public Policy. The needs of battered women and the response of the public services* (1985) London, Routledge and Kegan Paul.

S. Parker, 'The Legal Background' in J. Pahl (1985) *op cit*.

R.I. Parnas, 'Judicial Response to Intra-family Violence' (1970) 54 Minnesota Law Review 585.

R.I. Parnas, 'The Relevance of the Criminal Law to Inter-spousal Violence' in J.M. Eekelaar and S.N. Katz (eds.) *Family Violence: An International and Interdisciplinary Study* (1978) Toronto, Butterworths.

E. Pence, *Criminal Justice Response to Domestic Assault Cases* (1985) Duluth, Minnesota, Domestic Abuse Intervention Project, Minnesota Program Development Inc.

* E. Pizzey, *Scream Quietly or the Neighbours Will Hear* (1974) Harmondsworth, Penguin Books, pp. 98, 119–121.

* J. Renvoize, *Children in Danger* (1974) London, Routledge and Kegan Paul; (1975) Hardmondsworth, Penguin Books, p. 20.

Report of the Committee of Inquiry into the Care and Supervision provided in relation to Maria Colwell (Chairman: T.G. Field-Fisher Q.C.) (1974) London, HMSO.

* *Report of the Committee of Inquiry into the Provision and Co-ordination of Services to the Family of John George Auckland* (Chairman: P.J.M. Kennedy Q.C.) (1975) London, HMSO, paras. 45–47, 49, 54, 57, 58, 164, 181–183, 185, 194, 195, 206, 214, 215, 217, 224, 238, 241–243.

* *Report of the Inquiry into Child Abuse in Cleveland 1987* (Chairman: The Hon. Mrs. Justice Butler-Sloss D.B.E.) Cm. 412 (1988) London, HMSO, pp. 4–9.

M. Roy (ed.), *Battered Women* (1977) New York, Van Nostrand Reinhold.

H.R. Schaffer and P.E. Emerson, 'Patterns of Response to Physical Contact in Early Human Development' (1964) 5 Journal of Child Psychology and Psychiatry 1.

P. Scott, 'Battered Wives' (1974) 125 British Journal of Psychiatry 433.

A.E. Skinner and R.L. Castle, *78 Battered Children: a Retrospective Study* (1969) London, NSPCC.

* L. Smith, *Domestic Violence: an overview of the literature*, Home Office Research Study 107 (1989) London, HMSO, pp. 27–29.

S.M. Smith, *The Battered Child Syndrome* (1975) London, Butterworths.

Somerset Area Review Committee of Non-Accidental Injury to Children, *Wayne Brewer — Report of the Review Panel* (1977).

B. Steele and C. Pollock, 'A Psychiatric Study of Parents who abuse Infants and Small Children' in R. Helfer and C.H. Kempe (eds.), *The Battered Child* (1968) Chicago, Chicago University Press.

S. Steinmetz and S. Straus (eds.), *Violence in the Family* (1974) New York, Dodd, Mead.

A. Storr, *Human Aggression* (1974) Harmondsworth, Penguin Books.

M.A. Straus, 'A sociological perspective on the prevention and treatment of wife-beating' in M. Roy (ed.), *Battered Women* (1977) New York, Van Nostrand Reinhold.

H.I. Subin, *Criminal Justice in a Metropolitan Court: the Processing of Serious Criminal Cases in the District of Columbia Court of General Sessions* (1966) Washington, Office of Criminal Justice, US Department of Justice.

R. Thornton, 'Homelessness through relationship breakdown: the local authorities' response' [1989] Journal of Social Welfare Law 67.

L.E. Walker, *The Battered Woman Syndrome* (1984) New York, Springer.

F. Wasoff, 'Legal Protection from Wife Beating: The Processing of Domestic Assaults by Scottish Prosecutors and Criminal Courts' (1982) 10 International Journal of the Sociology of Law 187.

A. Weir, 'Battered Women: Some Perspectives and Problems' in M. Mayo (ed.), *Women in the Community* (1977) London, Routledge and Kegan Paul.

W.A. Westley, *Violence and the Police: a Sociological Study of Law, Custom and Morality* (1970) Cambridge, Mass., M.I.T. Press.

R. Whitehurst, 'Violence in Husband-Wife Interaction' in S. Steinmetz and M. Straus (eds.), *Violence in the Family* (1974) New York, Dodd, Mead.

* E. Wilson, *The Existing Research into Battered Women* (1976) London, National Women's Aid Federation (now Women's Aid Federation, England), pp. 5–6.

E. Wilson, *What is to be done about Violence against Women?* (1983) Harmondsworth, Penguin.

M.E. Wolfgang and F. Ferracuti, *The Subculture of Violence: Towards an Integrated Theory in Criminology* (1967) London, Tavistock.
* Women's National Commission, *Violence Against Women*, Report of an ad hoc Working Group (1985) London, Cabinet Office, paras. 108, 111, 113, 115.

Chapter 10

R. Adler and A. Dearling, 'Children's Rights: A Scottish Perspective' in B. Franklin (ed.), *The Rights of Children* (1986) Oxford, Basil Blackwell.
* Anon., 'Mental Hospitalisation of Children and the Limits of Parental Authority' (1978) 88 Yale Law Journal 186, pp. 194–208.
A. Bainham, 'The Balance of Power in Family Decisions' [1986] Cambridge Law Journal 262.
Jasmine Beckford, see Brent Council.
* Sir William Blackstone, *Commentaries on the Laws of England* (1st edn., 1765) Oxford, Clarendon Press, book 1, pp. 434–435, 440–441.
J. Bowlby, *Attachment and Loss. Vol. 1: Attachment* (1965) London, Hogarth Press and Institute of Psycho-Analysis; (1971) Harmondsworth, Penguin Books.
J. Bowlby, *Attachment and Loss. Vol. 2: Separation — Anxiety and Anger* (1973) London, Hogarth Press and Institute of Psycho-Analysis; (1975) Harmondsworth, Penguin Books.
Brent Council, *A Child in Trust — The Report of the Panel of Inquiry into the Circumstances Surrounding the Death of Jasmine Beckford* (Chairman: L. Blom-Cooper Q.C.) (1985) London, London Borough of Brent.
* Central Statistical Office, *Social Trends 21* (1991) London, HMSO, Table 3.11.
A.M. Clarke and A.C.B. Clarke, *Early Experience: Myth and Evidence* (1976) London, Open Books.
J.E. Coons and R.H. Mnookin, 'Toward a Theory of Children's Rights' in I.F.G. Baxter and M.A. Eberts (eds.), *The Child and the Courts* (1978) London, Sweet and Maxwell.
* Council of Europe, *European Convention for the Protection of Human Rights and Fundamental Freedoms* (1950), articles 8 and 9, protocol no. 1, article 2.
* Department of Health, *An Introduction to the Children Act 1989* (1989) London, HMSO, paras. 1.4–1.5.
DHSS, Health Circular HC (86), 1 *Family Planning Services for Young People* (1986) London, DHSS.
* DHSS, *Review of Child Care Law — Report to Ministers of an Interdepartmental Working Party* (1985) London, HMSO, paras. 2.12–2.13, 15.11.
B.M. Dickens, 'The Modern Function and Limits of Parental Rights' (1981) 97 LQR 462.
* J. Eekelaar, 'Parental Responsibility: State of Nature or Nature of the State?' [1991] Journal of Social Welfare and Family Law 37, pp. 38–39.
J.M. Eekelaar, *Family Law and Social Policy* (2nd edn., 1984) London, Weidenfeld and Nicholson.
* J. M. Eekelaar, 'The Emergence of Children's Rights' (1986) 6 Oxford Journal of Legal Studies 161, pp. 169–174, 176, 180–182.
R. Farson, *Birthrights* (1978) Harmondsworth, Penguin Books.
R. Frank, 'Family Law and the Federal Republic of Germany's Basic Law' (1990) 4 International Journal of Law and the Family 214.
B. Franklin (ed.), *The Rights of Children* (1986) Oxford, Basil Blackwell.
M.D.A. Freeman, 'The Rights of Children in the International Year of the Child' [1980] Current Legal Problems 1.
M.D.A. Freeman, *The Rights and Wrongs of Children* (1983) London, Frances Pinter.

A. Freud and D. Burlingham, *Young Children in War Time: A Year's Work in a Residential Nursery* (1944) London, Allen and Unwin.

A. Freud and D. Burlingham, *Infants Without Families: The Case For and Against Residential Nurseries* (1944) London, Allen and Unwin.

J. Goldstein, A. Freud and A.J. Solnit, *Beyond the Best Interests of the Child* (1973) London, Collier Macmillan.

* J. Goldstein, A. Freud and A.J. Solnit, *Before the Best Interests of the Child* (1980) London, Burnett Books, pp. 8–10, 11–12, 16–17, 92, 93–94.

A. Grubb and D. Pearl, 'Medicine, Health, the Family and the Law' (1986) 16 Family Law 227.

Tyra Henry (1987) — see Lambeth London Borough Council.

J. Holt, *Escape from Childhood* (1974) New York, Dutton.

House of Commons Social Services Committee, Second Report Session 1983–84, *Children in Care* HC 360 (1984) London, HMSO.

J. Kagan, R.B. Kearsley and P.R. Zelazo, *Infancy: Its Place in Human Development* (1978) Cambridge, Mass., Harvard University Press.

R.B. Kearsley, P.R. Zelazo, J. Kagan and R. Hartman, 'Separation Protest in Day-Care and Home-Reared Infants' (1975) 55 Paediatrics 171.

I. Kennedy, 'The Karen Quinlan Case: Problems and Proposals' (1976) 2 Journal of Medical Ethics 3, p. 6.

Lambeth London Borough Council, *Whose Child? The Report of the Inquiry into the Death of Tyra Henry* (1987) London, London Borough of Lambeth.

Law Commission, *Report on Illegitimacy*, Law Com. No. 118 (1982) London, HMSO.

Law Commission, Working Paper No. 91, *Review of Child Law: Guardianship* (1985) London, HMSO.

* Law Commission, Working Paper No. 91, *Review of Child Law: Custody* (1986) London, HMSO, paras. 6.20–6.22.

* Law Commission, *Report on Guardianship and Custody*, Law Com. No. 172 (1988) London, HMSO, paras. 2.4–2.16.

N. MacCormick, 'Children's Rights: A Test Case for Theories of Right' (1976) 62 Archiv für Rechts und Sozialphilosophie 305.

J.S. Mill, *On Liberty* (first published 1859) (1985) Harmondsworth, Penguin Classics.

J. Montgomery, 'Confidentiality and the Immature Minor' (1987) 17 Family Law 101.

P.H. Pettitt, 'Parental Control and Guardianship' in R.H. Graveson and F.R. Crane (eds.), *A Century of Family Law* (1957) London, Sweet and Maxwell.

J. Piaget, *The Construction of Reality in the Child* (1937); translated by M. Cook (1955) London, Routledge and Kegan Paul.

Report of the Committee on the Age of Majority (Chairman: Mr. Justice Latey) Cmnd. 3342 (1967) London, HMSO.

Review of Child Care Law, see DHSS.

M. Richards, 'Developmental Psychology and Family Law: A Discussion Paper' (1986) British Journal of Developmental Psychology.

C.M. Rogers and L.S. Wrightsman, 'Attitudes towards Children's Rights: Nurturance or Self-Determination' (1978) 34 Journal of Social Issues, no. 2, p. 59.

R.M. Rolfe and A.D. MacClintock, 'The Due Process Rights of Minors "Voluntarily Admitted" to Mental Institutions' (1976) 4 Journal of Psychiatry and Law 333.

M. Rutter, *Maternal Deprivation Reassessed* (1972; 2nd edn. 1981; rep. 1986) Harmondsworth, Penguin Books.

B. Tizard, *Adoption: A Second Chance* (1977) London, Open Books.

* United Nations, *Convention on the Rights of the Child* (1989), Arts. 3, 9, 12, 13, 18, 30.

C.A. Wringe, *Children's rights – A philosophical study* (1981) London, Routledge and Kegan Paul.

Chapter 11

D. Barber, *Unmarried Fathers* (1975) London, Hutchinson.
* Sir William Blackstone, *Commentaries on the Laws of England* (1st edn., 1765) Oxford, Clarendon Press, book 1, p. 447.
* E. Blyth, 'Assisted reproduction: what's in it for the children?' (1990) 4 Children and Society 167, pp. 174–177.
P. Braidwood, 'Artificial choices' (1989) The Observer, 23 July.
J. Brandon and J. Warner, 'A.I.D. and Adoption: Some Comparisons' (1977) 7 British Journal of Social Work 235.
C. Brinton, *French Revolutionary Legislation on Illegitimacy 1789–1804* (1936) Cambridge, Mass., Harvard University Press.
British Agencies for Adoption and Fostering, *AID and after* papers from BAAF, BASW and a Scottish working party (1984) London, British Agencies for Adoption and Fostering.
P.M. Bromley, 'Aided Conception: the alternative to adoption' in P. Bean, (ed.), *Adoption: Essays in Social Policy, Law and Sociology* (1984) London, Tavistock.
* N. Bruce, 'On the Importance of Genetic Knowledge' (1990) 4 Children and Society 183, pp. 191–192.
* Cellmark Diagnostics, *DNA Fingerprinting Information and Procedures Guide.*
* Central Statistical Office, *Social Trends 21* (1991) London, HMSO, Graphs 2.21, 2.22, Table 2.26.
Children Come First, Cm. 1263 (1990) London, HMSO.
* Ciba Foundation Symposium, No. 17 (new series), G.E.W. Wolstenholme and D.W. Fitzsimmons (eds.), *Law and Ethics of A.I.D. and Embryo Transfer* (1973) Amsterdam, Associated Scientific Publishers, pp. 63, 66.
R. Collins and A. Macleod, 'Denials of paternity: the impact of DNA tests on court proceedings' [1991] Journal of Social Welfare and Family Law 209.
R. Collins and A Macleod, *The End of Illegitimacy*, Research Report (1990) British, University of Bristol.
Council for Science and Society, *Human Procreation: Ethical Aspects of the New Techniques* (1984) Oxford, Oxford University Press.
* Council of Europe, *European Convention for the Protection of Human Rights and Fundamental Freedoms* (1950).
* Council of Europe, *European Convention on the Legal Status of Children born out of Wedlock* (1981).
E. Crellin, M.L. Kellmer Pringle and P. West, *Born Illegitimate: Social and Educational Implications* (1971) Windsor, National Foundation for Educational Research.
K.R. Daniels, 'Semen donors in New Zealand: their characteristics and attitudes' (1987) 5 Clinical Reproduction and Fertility 177.
K.R. Daniels, 'Semen donors: their motivations and attitudes to their offspring' (1989) 7 Journal of Reproductive and Infant Psychology 121.
* K. Davis, 'Illegitimacy and the Social Structure' (1939) 45 American Journal of Sociology 215, pp. 215, 216, 219, 221, 223.
R. Deech, 'The Reform of Illegitimacy Law' (1980) 10 Family Law 101.
D. Derrick (ed.), *Illegitimate – the Experience of People Born Outside Marriage* (1986) London, National Council for One-Parent Families.
* DHSS, *Legislation on Human Infertility Services and Embryo Research, A Consultation Paper*, Cm 46 (1986) London, HMSO, paras. 8–13.
R.J. Edelmann and K.J. Connelly, 'Psychological aspects of infertility' (1986) 59 British Journal of Medical Psychology 209.

* H. Elisofon, 'A Historical and Comparative Study of Bastardy' (1973) 2 Anglo-American Law Review 306, p. 318.

F. Engels, *The Origin of the Family, Private Property and the State* (1st edn., 1884) New York, Lawrence and Wishart.

* Sir Morris Finer and O.R. McGregor, 'The History of the Obligation to Maintain' App. 5, *Report of the Committee on One-Parent Families* (Cmnd. 5629-I) (1974) London, HMSO, paras. 56, 57, 59–62, 64, 74, 75.

R. Fox, *Kinship and Marriage* (1967) Harmondsworth, Penguin Books.

J. Fratter, 'How adoptive parents feel about contact with birth parents after adoption' (1989) 13(4) Adoption and Fostering 18.

C. Gibson, 'The Association between Divorce and Social Class in England and Wales' (1974) 25 British Journal of Sociology 79.

D. Gill, *Illegitimacy, Sexuality and the Status of Women* (1977) Oxford, Basil Blackwell.

J. Glover, *Fertility and the Family: The Glover Report on Reproductive Technologies to the European Commission* (1989) London, Fourth Estate.

S. Golombek, A. Spencer, and M. Rutter, 'Children in single parent and lesbian households: psychosexual and psychiatric appraisal' (1983) 24(4) Journal of Psychiatry and Psychology 551.

* Hansard (House of Lords), Vol. 516, cols. 1097–1098.

J. Harris, *The Value of Life: An Introduction to Medical Ethics* (1985) London, Routledge.

J. Haskey, 'Marital Status before Marriage and Age at Marriage: their Influence on the Chance of Divorce' (1983) 32 Population Trends 4.

* M. Hayes, 'Law Commission Working Paper No. 74: Illegitimacy' (1980) 43 Modern Law Review 299, p. 299.

U.R.Q. Henriques, 'Bastardy and the New Poor Law' (1967) 37 Past and Present.

D. Howell and M. Ryburn, 'New Zealand: new ways to choose adopters' (1987) 11(4) Adoption and Fostering 38.

Human Fertilisation and Embryology Authority, *Code of Practice* (1991) London, Human Fertilisation and Embryology Authority.

H.D. Krause, *Illegitimacy, Law and Social Policy* (1971) Indianapolis, Bobbs, Merrill.

* L. Lambert and J. Streather, *Children in Changing Families: A Study of Adoption and Illegitimacy* (1980) London and Basingstoke, Macmillan, pp. 55–57, 136, 140–142.

* P. Laslett, *The World We Have Lost* (2nd edn., 1971) London, Methuen, pp. 137, 140–141.

P. Laslett, *Family Life and Illicit Love in Earlier Generations* (1977) Cambridge, Cambridge University Press.

P. Laslett, K. Oosterven, and R.M. Smith (eds.), *Bastardy and Its Comparative History* (1980) London, Arnold.

Law Commission, Working Paper No. 91, *Review of Child Law: Guardianship* (1985) London, HMSO.

* Law Commission, Working Paper No. 74, *Illegitimacy* (1979) London, HMSO, paras. 2.10–2.12, 3.2–3.6, 3.8–3.9, 3.14–3.16, 9.12, 9.18, 9.23, 9.24, 9.27, 9.28, 9.33, 9.40, 9.47, 10.5, 10.6, 10.8, 10.9, 10.11, 10.17, 10.25, 10.26.

* Law Commission, *Report on Guardianship and Custody*, Law Com. No. 172 (1988) London, HMSO, paras. 2.18–2.20.

* Law Commission, *Report on Illegitimacy*, Law Com No. 118, (1982) London, HMSO, paras. 4.26, 4.39, 4.44, 4.45, 4.49, 4.50, 4.51, 10.6, 10.7, 10.8, 10.10, 10.11, 10.12.

Law Commission, *Report on Declarations in Family Matters*, Law Com. No. 132 (1984) London, HMSO.

* Law Commission, *Illegitimacy (Second Report)*, Law Com. No. 157 (1986) London, HMSO, paras. 3.1–3.3, 3.4, 3.14, 3.18–3.19.

* R. Leete, 'Adoption Trends and Illegitimate Births' (1978) 14 Population Trends 9, pp. 11, 13, 14, 15.

* L. Mair, *Marriage* (1971) Harmondsworth, Pelican Books, pp. 11–14, 16.
  A. McWhinnie, 'The case for greater openness concerning AID' in *AID and After* (1984) London, British Agencies for Adoption and Fostering.
  J. Montgomery, 'Artificial reproduction and the Family Law Reform Act 1987' (1988) 18 Family Law 23.
* National Council for One-Parent Families, *An Accident of Birth – A Response to the Law Commission's Working Paper on Illegitimacy* (1980) London, One-Parent Families, pp. 2–4, 9, 11–12.
  S. Pollock and J. Sutton, 'Father's Rights, Women's Losses' (1985) 8 Women's Studies International Forum 593.
  G.R. Quaife, *Wanton Wenches and Wayward Wives* (1979) London, Croom Helm.
  S. Reid, *Labour of Love: Story of the World's first Surrogate Grandmother* (1988) Oxford, Bodley Head.
  Report of the Advisory Group on the Law of Rape (Chairman: The Hon. Mrs Justice Heilbron D.B.E.) (Cmnd. 6352) (1975) London, HMSO.
* *Report of the Committee of Inquiry into Human Fertilisation and Embryology* (Chairman: Dame Mary Warnock) (Cmnd. 9314) (1984) London, HMSO, paras. 6.8, 8.10–8.16.
* *Report of the Committee on the Law of Succession in relation to Illegitimate Persons* (Chairman: The Rt. Hon. Lord Justice Russell) (Cmnd. 3051) (1966) London, HMSO, para. 19.
  Report of the Departmental Committee on Human Artificial Insemination (Chairman: The Earl of Feversham) (Cmnd. 1105) (1960) London, HMSO.
  G. Rowntree, 'Some Aspects of Marriage Breakdown in the Last Thirty Years' (1964) 18 Population Studies 147.
  D. Saunders, 'Assessment of the infertile couple for AID' in C. Wood, J. Leeton, and G. Kovacs (eds.), *Artificial Insemination by Donor* (1980) Melbourne, Brown, Prior Anderson Property Ltd.
  H.R. Schaffer, 'Family structure or interpersonal relationships' (1988) 2(2) Children and Society 91.
* Scottish Law Commission, *Family Law – Illegitimacy*, Consultative Memorandum No. 53 (1982) Edinburgh, Scottish Law Commission, paras. 1.15, 1.16.
* Scottish Law Commission, *Report on Illegitimacy*, Scot. Law Com. No. 82 (1984) Edinburgh, HMSO, paras. 9.2, 9.3.
  J. Seglow, M.L. Kellmer Pringle and P. Wedge, *Growing Up Adopted* (1972) London, National Foundation for Educational Research.
  C. Smith, *Adoption and Fostering* (1984) London, Macmillan.
  R. Snowden and G.D. Mitchell, *The Artificial Family – A Consideration of Artificial Intermination by Donor* (1981) London, George Allen and Unwin.
  R. Snowden and E.M. Snowden, *The Gift of a Child* (1984) London, George Allen and Unwin.
  M.T. Sverne, 'The Swedish view of artificial insemination by donor' in *Artificial procreation, genetics and the law* (1986) Proceedings of the Lausanne Colloquium.
  P. Tapp, 'The Social and Legal Position of Children of Unmarried Cohabiting Parents' in J.M. Eekelaar and S.N. Katz (eds.), *Marriage and Cohabitation in Contemporary Societies: Areas of Legal, Social and Ethical Change* (1980) Toronto, Butterworths.
  J. Triseliotis, 'Foster care outcomes: a review of key research findings' (1989) 13(3) Adoption and Fostering 5.
  United Nations, *Convention on the Rights of the Child* (1989).
  United Nations, *Declaration on the Rights of the Child* (1959).
  D. Webb, 'The Use of Blood Grouping and DNA "Finger printing" Tests in Immigration Proceedings' (1986) 1 Immigration and Nationality – Law and Practice 53.

V. Wimperis, *The Unmarried Mother and Her Child* (1960) London, Allen and Unwin.

Chapter 12

C. Ahrons, 'The Continuing Co-Parental Relationship between Divorced Spouses' (1981) 51 American Journal of Orthopsychiatry 415.

F.R. Bennion, 'First consideration: a cautionary tale' (1976) 126 New Law Journal 1237.

B. Bettelheim, 'Fathers Shouldn't Try to Be Mothers' *Parents' Magazine*, October 1956, cited in J.A. Levine, *Who Will Raise the Children? New Options for Fathers (and Mothers)* (1976) Philadelphia, Lippincott.

Booth Committee, see Report of the Matrimonial Causes Procedure Committee.

* J. Bowlby, *Child Care and the Growth of Love* (2nd edn., 1965) Hardmondsworth, Pelican Books, pp. 13–15.

J. Brophy, 'Child Care and the Growth of Power: the status of mothers in custody disputes' in J. Brophy and C. Smart (eds.) *Women in Law* (1985) London, Routledge and Kegan Paul.

J. Burgoyne, *Breaking Even: Divorce, Your Children and You* (1984) Harmondsworth, Penguin.

* J. Burgoyne and D. Clark, 'Reconstituted Families' in R.N. Rapoport, M.P. Fogarty and R. Rapoport (eds.), *Families in Britain* (1982) London, Routledge and Kegan Paul, pp. 299–301.

* J. Burgoyne and D. Clark, *Making a go of it — A study of stepfamilies in Sheffield* (1984) London, Routledge and Kegan Paul, Table 6.1.

J. Burgoyne, R. Ormrod, and M. Richards, *Divorce Matters* (1987) Harmondsworth, Penguin.

* Central Statistical Office, *Social Trends 19* (1989) London, HMSO, Graph 2.18.

* Central Statistical Office, *Social Trends 21* (1991) London, HMSO, Graph 2.8, 2.9.

L. Clarke, *Children's changing circumstances: recent trends and future prospects*, Centre for Population Studies Research Paper 89-4 (1989).

L. Clarke and S. Eldridge, *The structure and characteristics of families: a review of the circumstances of children in the 1980s*, Centre for Population Studies Research Paper 89-3 (1989).

C. Clulow and C. Vincent, *In the Child's Best Interests? Divorce court welfare and the search for a settlement* (1987) London, Tavistock.

G. Davis, A. Macleod and M. Murch, 'Undefended Divorce: Should Section 41 of the Matrimonial Causes Act 1973 be Repealed?' (1983) 46 Modern Law Review 121.

* Departmental Committee on the Adoption of Children (Chairman: Sir William Houghton), *Working Paper* (1970) London, HMSO, paras. 92–94.

R. Dingwall and J. Eekelaar, 'Judgements of Soloman: psychology and family law' in M. Richards and P. Light, *Children of Social Worlds* (1986) Cambridge, Polity Press.

M. Dodds, *A Study of the Practice of the Divorce Courts in relation to Children* (1981) University of Manchester, LL.M. Thesis.

M. Dodds, 'Children and Divorce' [1983] Journal of Social Welfare Law 228.

J.W.B. Douglas, 'Broken Families and Child Behaviour' (1970) 4 Journal of the Royal College of Physicians 203.

J.M. Eekelaar, 'What Are Parental Rights?' (1973) 89 Law Quarterly Review 210.

J.M. Eekelaar, 'Children in Divorce: Some Further Data' (1982) 2 Oxford Journal of Legal Studies 62.

* J.M. Eekelaar, 'Custody appeals' (1985) 48 Modern Law Review 704, p. 705.

J.M. Eekelaar, 'Gillick in the Divorce Court' (1986) 136 New Law Journal 184.

* J.M. Eekelaar and E. Clive with K. Clarke and S. Raikes, *Custody After Divorce: The Disposition of Custody in Divorce Cases in Great Britain* (1977) Oxford, Centre for Socio-legal Studies, paras. 3.6, 6.1, 6.3, 6.4, 6.5, 13.7, 13.23, 13.25–27, 13.29, tables 8, 15 and 34.

E. Ferri, *Growing Up in a One-Parent Family* (1976) Windsor, N.F.E.R. Publishing.

H. Foster and D. Freed, 'Life with Father' (1978) 11 Family Law Quarterly 321.

A. Freud, 'Child Observation and Prediction of Development' (1958) 13 The Psychoanalytic Study of the Child 92.

L. Fuller, *Interaction Between Law and Its Social Context* (1971) Class material for Sociology of Law, University of California, Berkeley.

F.F. Furstenberg, *Renegotiating Parenthood After Divorce and Remarriage* (1981) Paper presented at Biennial Meeting of the Society for Research in Child Development, Boston, USA.

V. George and P. Wilding, *Motherless Families* (1972) London, Routledge and Kegan Paul.

* J. Goldstein, A. Freud and A.J. Solnit, *Beyond the Best Interests of the Child* (1973) London, Collier Macmillan, pp. 31–34, 37, 40–41, 49–50, 51, 53, 62–63.

M. Goldzband, *Consulting in Child Custody* (1982) Lexington, Lexington Books.

W.J. Goode, *After Divorce* (1956) New York, Free Press.

N. Hart, *When Marriage Ends: A Study in Status Passage* (1976) London, Tavistock.

J. Haskey, 'Widowhood, Widowerhood and Remarriage' (1982) 30 Population Trends 15.

J. Haskey, 'Social class differentials in remarriage after divorce: results from a forward linkage study (1987) 47 Population Trends 34.

J. Haskey and K. Kiernan, 'Cohabitation in Great Britain — characteristics and estimated numbers of cohabiting partners' (1989) 58 Population Trends 23.

J. Haskey, 'One-parent families and their children in Great Britain: numbers and characteristics' (1989) 58 Population Trends 23.

* J. Haskey, 'Children of Families broken by Divorce' (1990) 61 Population Trends 34, pp. 41–42.

* A. Heath-Jones, 'Divorce and the Reluctant Father' (1980) 10 Family Law 75, p. 75.

M.E. Hetherington, 'Effects of Father's Absence on Personality Development in Adolescent Daughters' (1972) 1 Developmental Psychology 313.

Houghton, Working Paper — see Departmental Committee on the Adoption of Children.

Houghton, Report — see Report of the Departmental Committee on the Adoption of Children.

* Inter-departmental Review of Adoption Law, *The Nature and Effects of Adoption*, Discussion Paper No. 1 (1990) London, Department of Health, paras. 131–134.

* C. Itzin, *Splitting Up: Single Parent Liberation* (1980) London, Virago, pp. 130, 138.

* Justice, *Report on Parental Rights and Duties and Custody Suits* (1975) London, Stevens, paras. 89(h), 91.

H.F. Keshet and K.M. Rosenthal, *Father Presence: Four Types of Post-marital Separation Fathering Arrangements* (1978) Paper presented at N.I.M.H. Symposium on Mental Health Consequences of Divorce on Children, Washington D.C.

* M. King, *Childhood, Welfare and Justice* (1981) London, Batsford Academic and Educational, p. 124.

M. King, 'Playing the Symbols — Custody and the Law Commission' (1987) 17 Family Law 186.

* Law Commission, *Report on Guardianship and Custody*, Law Com. No. 172 (1988) London, HMSO, paras 3.2–3.9, 3.13–3.14, 3.18–3.19, 3.22–3.25, 4.2–4.21, 4.55–4.57.

Law Commission, Working Paper No. 91, *Review of Child Law: Guardianship* (1985) London, HMSO.

* Law Commission, Working Paper No. 96, *Review of Child Law: Custody* (1986) London, HMSO, paras. 4.8–4.10, 4.35–4.38, 4.40–4.45, 6.40–6.43.

Law Commission, Working Paper No. 100, *Care, Supervision and Interim Orders in Custody Proceedings* (1987) London, HMSO.

J.A. Levine, *Who Will Raise the Children? New Options for Fathers (and Mothers)* (1976) Philadelphia, Lippincott.

C. Lewis, (1986) *Becoming a Father* (1986) Milton Keynes, Open University Press.

N. Lowe, 'The Legal Status of Fathers − Past and Present' in L. McKee and M. O'Brien (eds.), *The Father Figure* (1982) London, Tavistock.

D.A. Luepnitz, *Child Custody: A Study of Families After Divorce* (1982) Lexington, Mass., Lexington Books.

M. Lund, 'The non-custodial father', in C. Lewis and M. O'Brien (eds.), *Reassessing Fatherhood* (1987) London, Sage.

A. Macleod with M. Borkowski (1985) *Access after Divorce: The Follow-Up to the Special Procedure in Divorce Project* (1985) Bristol, University of Bristol.

* B. Maddox, *Step-parenting* (1980) London, Unwin Paperbacks, pp. 37–39.

* S. Maidment, 'Access Conditions in Custody Orders' (1975) 2 British Journal of Law and Society 182, pp. 185–187.

S. Maidment, 'A Study in Child Custody' (1976) 6 Family Law 195 and 236.

S. Maidment, *Child Custody: What Chance for Fathers?* Forward from Finer No. 7 (1981) London, One-Parent Families.

S. Maidment, *Child Custody and Divorce* (1984) London, Croom Helm.

S. Maidment, 'Step-parent and Step-children: Legal Relationships in Serial Unions' in J.M. Eekelaar and S.N. Katz (eds.), *Marriage and Cohabitation in Contemporary Societies: Areas of Legal, Social and Ethical Change* (1980) Toronto, Butterworths.

D. Marsden, *Mothers Alone: Poverty and the Fatherless Family*, (1969) Harmondsworth, Penguin Books.

* J. Masson, D. Norbury and S. Chatterton, *Mine, Yours or Ours? A study of step-parent adoption* (1984) London, HMSO, pp. 84, 103–105.

* A. Mitchell, *Children in the Middle: Living through Divorce* (1985) London, Tavistock, pp. 125, 140–141.

* R.H. Mnookin, 'Child Custody Adjudication: Judicial Functions in the Face of Indeterminacy' (1975) 39 Law and Contemporary Problems 226, pp. 249–255, 256–261, 286–287. © 1975 Duke University School of Law.

P. Morgan, *Child Care: Sense and Fable* (1975) London, Temple Smith.

* M. Murch, *Justice and Welfare in Divorce* (1980) London, Sweet and Maxwell, pp. 129–131, 160, 161–162, 194.

* *New English Bible* (1972) The Bible Societies, 1 Kings 3, vs. 22–27.

E. Newson and J. Newson, *Patterns of Infant Care in an Urban Community* (reprinted 1972) Harmondsworth, Penguin Books.

A. Oakley, *Becoming a Mother* (1979) Oxford, Martin Robertson.

M. Patrician, 'Child Custody Terms: Potential Contributors to Custody Dissatisfaction and Conflict' (1984) 3 Mediation Quarterly 41.

* J.A. Priest and J.C. Whybrow, *Custody Law in Practice in the Divorce and Domestic Courts*. Supplement to Law Commission W.P. No. 96, *Review of Child Law: Custody* (1986) London, HMSO, para. 5.6, Tables 6, 7, Figure F.4, Map M.2.

Probation and Aftercare Service, *Specimen Welfare Officer's Report* (1981).

R.N. Rapoport, R. Rapoport and Z. Strelitz, *Fathers, Mothers and Others* (1977) London, Routledge and Kegan Paul.

Report of the Committee on Human Fertilization and Embryology (Chairman: Dame Mary Warnock) (Cmnd. 9314) (1984) London, HMSO.

Report of the Committee on One-Parent Families (Chairman: The Hon. Sir Morris Finer) (Cmnd. 5629) (1974) London, HMSO.

* *Report of the Departmental Committee on the Adoption of Children* (Chairman:

Sir William Houghton, later Judge F.A. Stockdale) (Cmnd. 5107) (1972) London, HMSO, para. 108.

Report of the Matrimonial Causes Procedure Committee (Chairman: The Hon. Mrs. Justice Booth D.B.E.) (1985) London, HMSO.

Report of the Royal Commission on Marriage and Divorce (Chairman: Lord Morton of Henryton) (Cmd. 9678) (1956) London, HMSO.

* M. Richards, 'Post Divorce Arrangements for Children: A Psychological Perspective' [1982] Journal of Social Welfare Law 133, pp. 135–136, 142–149.

M. Richards, 'Parents and Kids: the New Thinking' *New Society*, 27 March 1987.

M. Richards and M. Dyson, *Separation, Divorce and the Development of Children: A Review* (1982) Child Care and Development Group, University of Cambridge.

N. Richards and P. Light (eds.), *Children of Social Worlds* (1986) Cambridge, Polity Press.

Rights of Women, *Lesbian Mothers on Trial. A report on Lesbian mothers and child custody* (1985) London, Rights of Women.

M. Richards, 'Behind the Best Interests of the Child: An Examination of the Arguments of Goldstein, Freud and Solnit Concerning Custody and Access at Divorce' [1986] Journal of Social Welfare Law 77.

M. Roman and W. Haddad, *The Disposable Parent: The Case for Joint Custody* (1978) New York, Penguin Books.

* M. Rutter, *Maternal Deprivation Reassessed* (1972; 2nd edn. 1981; rep. 1986) Harmondsworth, Penguin Books, pp. 126–127.

G. Sanctuary and C, Whitehead, *Divorce – and After* (1970) Harmondsworth, Penguin Books.

H.R. Shaffer and P.E. Emerson, 'The Development of Social Attachments in Infancy' (1964) 29 Monograph Soc. Res. Child Development, no. 3, p. 1.

J. Shulman and V. Pitt, 'Second Thoughts on Joint Custody: Analysis of Legislation and Its Impact for Women and Children' (1982) 12 Golden Gate University Law Review 539.

S. Steinman, 'The Experience of Children in a Joint Custody Arrangement' (1981) 51 American Journal of Orthopsychiatry 403.

M. Wadsworth, 'Parenting Skills and their Transmission through Generations' (1985) 9 (1) *Adoption and Fostering* 28.

M. Wadsworth, 'Evidence from Three Birth Cohort Studies for Long Term and Cross Generational Effects on the Development of Children' in M. Richards and P. Light (1986) *op. cit.*

Y. Walczak with S. Burns, *Divorce: The Child's Point of View* (1984) London, Harper and Row.

* J.S. Wallerstein and J.B. Kelly, *Surviving the Breakup: How Children and Parents Cope with Divorce* (1980) London, Grant McIntyre, pp. 292–293.

A. Watson, 'Children of Armageddon: Problems of Custody Without Care' (1969) 21 Syracuse Law Review 55.

R.S. Weiss, *Marital Separation* (1975) New York, Basic Books.

R.S. Weiss, *Going It Alone: The Family Life and Social Situation of the Single Parent* (1979) New York, Basic Books.

L. Weitzman, *The Divorce Revolution – The Unexpected Social and Economic Consequences for Women and Children in America* (1985) London, Free Press.

L.J. Weitzman and R.B. Dixon, 'Child Custody Awards: Legal Standards and Empirical Patterns for Child Custody, Support and Visitation after Divorce' (1979) 12 UC Davis Law Review 473.

Chapter 13

M. Adcock and R. White (eds.), *Terminating Parental Contact: An Exploration of the Issues relating to Children in Care* (1980) London, Association of

British Adoption and Fostering Agencies (now British Agencies for Adoption and Fostering).

M. Adcock, R. White and O. Rowlands, *The Administrative Parent: A Study of the Assumption of Parental Rights and Duties* (1983) London, British Agencies for Adoption and Fostering.

* Lady Allen of Hurtwood, 'Whose Children? Wards of State or Charity' *The Times*, 15 July 1944.

P. Bean and J. Melville, *Lost Children of the Empire* (1988) London, Unwin.

D. Berridge, *Children's Homes* (1985) Oxford, Basil Blackwell.

J. Bowlby, *Child Care and the Growth of Love* (1953; 2nd edn., 1965) Harmondsworth, Penguin Books.

Brent Council, *A Child in Trust — The Report of the Panel of Inquiry into the Circumstances surrounding the Death of Jasmine Beckford* (Chairman: L. Blom-Cooper Q.C.) (1985) London, London Borough of Brent.

Children's Legal Centre, *'It's my life not theirs' — A Children's Legal Centre survey of current reviewing practice for children and young people in care* (1985) London, Children's Legal Centre.

Childright, News feature, 'Running Away — Under Pressure' (1987) 33 Childright 16.

Cleveland Report, see Report of the Inquiry into Child Abuse in Cleveland 1987.

Dartington, see S. Millham *et al, op. cit.*

* Department of Health. *The Care of Children — Principles and Practice in Regulations and Guidance* (1990) London, HMSO, pp. 18–19.

* Department of Health, *Working Together — A guide to arrangements for inter-agency co-operation for the protection of children from abuse* (draft) (1991) London, Department of Health, paras. 5.4, 5.9, 5.15, 5.25, 6.1–6.17.

* Department of Health, Guidance and Regulations on the Children Act 1989, vol. 1, *Court Orders* (1991) London, HMSO, paras. 3.77, 4.6, 4.9, 4.12, 4.15, 4.28, 4.29, 4.31, 4.44.

Department of Health, *Child Abuse — A Study of Inquiry Reports 1980–1989* (1991) London, HMSO.

DHSS, *Child Abuse — A Study of Inquiry Reports, 1973–1981* (1982) London, HMSO.

* DHSS, *Review of Child Care Law — Report to Ministers of an Interdepartmental Working Party* (1985) London, HMSO, paras. 2.20–2.25, 15.12–15.24, 18.5–18.15.

* DHSS, *Social Work Decisions in Child Care — Recent Research Findings and their Implications* (1985) London, HMSO, pp. 9–12, 36–37, 38.

* DHSS and others, *The Law on Child Care and Family Services*, Cm. 62 (1987) London, HMSO, paras. 16–18, 20–22, 42–43.

* R. Dingwall, J.M. Eekelaar and T. Murray, *Care or Control? Decision-Making in the Care of Children Thought to have been Abused or Neglected. A Summary of the Final Report* (1981) Oxford, Centre for Socio-legal Studies, pp. 40–42.

R. Dingwall, J.M. Eekelaar and T. Murray, *The Protection of Children: State Intervention and Family Life* (1983) Oxford, Basil Blackwell.

* R. Dingwall, 'The Jasmine Beckford Affair' (1986) 49 Modern Law Review 489, pp. 493–495, 497–501.

* J.M. Eekelaar, R. Dingwall and T. Murray, 'Victims or Threats? Children in Care Proceedings' [1982] Journal of Social Welfare Law 67, pp. 71–78.

Family Rights Group, *Promoting links: keeping families and children in touch* (1986) London, Family Rights Group.

E. Farmer and R. Parker, *A Study of the Discharge of Care Orders* (1985) Bristol, Department of Social Administration, University of Bristol.

E. Farmer and R. Parker, *A Study of Interim Care Orders* (1985) Bristol, Department of Social Administration, University of Bristol.

M. Fisher, P. Marsh, and D. Phillips, with E. Sainsbury, *In and Out of Care —
The Experiences of Children, Parents and Social Workers* (1986) London,
Batsford/BAAF.

Greenwich London Borough Council and Greenwich Health Authority, *A Child
in Mind — the Report of the Commission of Inquiry into the Circumstances
Surrounding the Death of Kimberley Carlile* (Chairman: L. Blom-Cooper
Q.C.) London, London Borough of Greenwich.

* Hansard, House of Commons, Vol. 190, Written Answers, col. 364.

* J.S. Heywood, *Children in Care: The Development of the Service for the Deprived
Child* (3rd edn., 1978) London, Routledge and Kegan Paul, pp. 7–10, 63–65,
92–93.

L. Hilgendorf, *Social Workers and Solicitors in Child Care Cases* (1981) London,
HMSO.

Hillingdon Council, Area Review Committee on Child Abuse, *Report of the
Review Panel into the Death of Heidi Koseda* (1986) London, London
Borough of Hillingdon.

A.S. Holden, *Children in Care* (1980) London, Comyn.

Home Office, *The Child, the Family and the Young Offender* (Cmnd. 2742) (1965)
London, HMSO.

Home Office, *Children in Trouble* (Cmnd. 3061) (1968) London, HMSO.

House of Commons Social Services Committee, *Children in Care, Minutes of
Evidence*, HC 26–i and ii (1982–83) (1982) London, HMSO.

House of Commons Social Services Committee, Second Report Session 1983–84,
Children in Care, HC 360 (1984) London, HMSO.

B. Kahan, *Growing Up in Care: Ten People Talking* (1979) Oxford, Basil
Blackwell.

Kimberley Carlile — see Greenwich London Borough Council.

Law Commission, Working Paper No. 113, *Domestic Violence and Occupation
of the Family Home* (1989) London, HMSO.

* Law Commission, Working Paper No. 101, *Wards of Court* (1987) London,
HMSO, para. 3.30.

P. Marsh, 'Natural families and children in care: an agenda for practice
development' (1986) 10 (4) Adoption and Fostering 20.

Marsh and Fisher, see M. Fisher *et al.*, *op. cit.*

S. Millham, R. Bullock, K. Hosie and M. Haak (Dartington Social Research
Unit), *Lost in Care — The problems of maintaining links between children
in care and their families* (1986) Aldershot, Gower.

National Children's Bureau, see J. Vernon and D. Fruin, *op cit.*

T.L. Norris and N. Parton, 'The Administration of Place of Safety Orders' [1987]
Journal of Social Welfare Law 1.

* J. Packman, *The Child's Generation: Child Care Policy in Britain* (2nd edn., 1981)
Oxford, Basil Blackwell, pp. 57–59, 64–65, 156, 161.

* J. Packman, with J. Randall and N. Jacques, *Who Needs Care? Social-Work
Decisions about Children* (1986) Oxford, Basil Blackwell, pp. 194–197 and
Table 4.2.

* *The Pindown Experience and the Protection of Children: The Report of the
Staffordshire Child Care Inquiry* (Allan Levy Q.C. and Barbara Kahan)
(1991) London, HMSO, paras. 11.17–11.35.

* J. Renvoize, *Children in Danger* (1974) London, Routledge and Kegan Paul;
(1975) Harmondsworth, Penguine Books, p. 24.

* *Report by Sir Walter Monckton, KCMG, KCVO, MC, KC, on the circumstances
which led to the boarding-out of Denis and Terence O'Neill at Bank Farm,
Minsterley, and the steps taken to supervise their welfare* (Cmd. 6636) (1945)
London, HMSO, paras. 2,3 and 54.

* *Report of the Care of Children Committee* (Chairman: Miss M. Curtis) (Cmd.
6922) (1946) London, HMSO, paras. 10, 138, 140, 144, 154, 171, 193, 370,
425 (ii), 427, 440, 441, 443.

Report of the Committee on Children and Young Persons (Chairman: Viscount Ingleby) (Cmnd. 1191) (1960) London, HMSO.

Report of the Committee of Inquiry into the Provision and Co-ordination of Services to the Family of John George Auckland (Chairman: P.J.M. Kennedy Q.C.) (1975) London, HMSO.

Report of the Committee on Local Authority and Allied Personal Social Services (Chairman: F. Seebohm) (Cmnd. 3703) (1968) London, HMSO.

* *Report of the Inquiry into Child Abuse in Cleveland 1987* (Chairman: The Hon. Mrs. Justice Butler-Sloss D.B.E.) (Cm. 412) (1988), London, HMSO, paras. 10.6–10.13, 12.1–12.60, (1984).

Review of Child care Law – see DHSS (1985).

J. Rowe, H. Cain, M. Hundleby and A. Keane, (1984) *Long-Term Foster Care* (1984) London, Batsford.

* J. Rowe and L. Lambert, *Children Who Wait* (1973) London, Association of British Adoption Agencies (now British Agencies for Adoption and Fostering), pp. 36–37.

M. Rutter, *Maternal Deprivation Reassessed* (1972; 2nd edn. 1981; rep. 1986) Harmondsworth, Penguin Books.

M. Rutter and N. Madge, *Cycles of Disadvantage* (1976) London, Heinemann.

R. Sinclair (1984) *Decision making in Statutory Reviews on Children in Care* (1984) Aldershot, Gower.

* J. Stroud, *The Shorn Lamb* (1960) London, Longman, pp. 242–243.

J. Thoburn, A. Murdoch, and A. O'Brien, *Permanence in Child Care* (1986) Oxford, Basil Blackwell.

J. Tunnard, 'The Case for Family Involvement' in *Accountability in Child Care – Which Way Forward?* (1982) London, Family Rights Group.

J. Vernon, and D. Fruin, *In Care – A Study of Social Work Decision-Making* (1986) London, National Children's Bureau.

G. Wagner, *Children of the Empire* (1981) London, Weidenfeld and Nicholson.

Chapter 14

G. Adamson, *The Caretakers* (1973) Bristol, Bookstall Publications.

M. Adcock, 'Alternatives to Adoption' (1984) 8 (1) Adoption and Fostering 12.

J. Aldgate, 'Identification of Factors Influencing Children's Length of Stay in Care' in J. Triseliotis (ed.), *New Developments in Foster Care and Adoption* (1980) London, Routledge and Kegan Paul.

C. Bagley, 'Adjustment, Achievement and Social Circumstances of Adopted Children in a National Survey' (1980) 102 Adoption and Fostering 47.

P. Bean (ed.), *Adoption: Essays in Social Policy, Law and Sociology* (1984) London, Tavistock.

Jasmine Beckford, see Brent Council.

D. Berridge and H. Cleaver, *Foster Home Breakdown* (1987) Oxford, Blackwell.

Brent Council, *A Child in Trust – The Report of the Panel of Inquiry into the Circumstances Surrounding the Death of Jasmine Beckford* (Chairman: L. Blom-Cooper Q.C.) London, London Borough of Brent.

* E. Bullard and E. Malos, with R.A. Parker, *Custodianship – A Report to the Department of Health on the Implementation of Part II of the Children Act 1975 in England and Wales from December 1985 to December 1988* (1990) Bristol, Department of Social Policy and Social Planning, University of Bristol, paras. 9.31–9.40.

* Central Statistical Office, *Social Trends 21* (1991) London, HMSO, Chart 2.29.

M. Colton, *Dimensions of substitute child care* (1988) Avebury, Gower.

C. Day, 'Access to Birth Records: General Register Office Study' (1979) 3 (4) Adoption and Fostering 17.

J.de Hartog, *The Children* (1969) London, Hamish Hamilton.

* Department of Health, Circular CI(90)17, *Adoption of Children from Overseas*, London, Department of Health, paras. 1, 2, 6–8.

DHSS, *Review of Child Care Law — Report to Ministers of an Interdepartmental Working Party* (1985) London, HMSO.

J.M. Eekelaar, *Family Law and Social Policy* (1st edn. 1978) London, Weidenfeld and Nicholson.

D. Fanshel and E.B. Shinn, *Children in Foster Care: A Longitudinal Study* (1978) New York, Columbia University Press.

M.D.A. Freeman, 'Subsidised adoption' in P. Bean (ed.), *op. cit.*

V. George, *Foster Care: Theory and Practice* (1970) London, Routledge and Kegan Paul.

E. Goffman, *Stigma: notes on the management of spoiled identity* (1963) Harmondsworth, Penguin Books.

E. Grey with R.M. Blunden, *A Survey of Adoption in Great Britain*, Home Office Research Studies No. 10 (1971) London, HMSO.

* E. Haimes and N. Timms, *Adoption, Identity and Social Policy — The search for distant relatives* (1985) Aldershot, Gower, p. 92.

* J. Heywood, *Children in Care: The Development of the Service for the Deprived Child* (3rd edn., 1978) London, Routledge and Kegan Paul, pp. 150–151, 173–174.

M. Hill, L. Lambert and J. Triseliotis, *Achieving Adoption with Love and Money* (1989) London, National Children's Bureau.

R. Holman, *Trading in Children: A Study of Private Fostering* (1973) London, Routledge and Kegan Paul.

* R. Holman, 'The Place of Fostering in Social Work' (1975) 5 British Journal of Social Work 3, pp. 8–14.

* Inter-departmental Review of Adoption Law, Discussion Paper No. 1, *The Nature and Effects of Adoption* (1990) London, Department of Health, paras. 97–114.

R. Jenkins, 'Long term Fostering' (1969) 15 Case Conference, no. 9, p. 349.

S. Jenkins and E. Norman, *Filial Deprivation in Foster Care* (1973) Columbia University Press.

H. Kirk, *Shared Fate* (1964) Free Press.

M. Kornitzer, 'The adopted adolescent and the sense of identity' (1971) 65 Child Adoption.

L. Lambert, M. Buist, J. Triseliotis and M. Hill, *Freeing Children for Adoption: Final Report to the Social Work Services Group* (1989) Edinburgh, Scottish Office; see also *Freeing for Adoption*, Research Series No. 7 (1990) London, British Agencies for Adoption and Fostering.

L. Lambert and J. Streather, *Children in Changing Familes* (1980) London, Macmillan.

* Law Commission, Working Paper No. 96, *Review of Child Law: Custody* (1986) London, HMSO, paras. 5.15, 5.17, 5.19, 5.23, 5.37, 5.39, 5.41, 5.42, 5.46.

* N. Lowe, 'Freeing for Adoption — the Experience of the 1980s' [1990] Journal of Social Welfare Law 220, pp. 232–233.

A. McWhinnie, *Adopted Children, how they grow up* (1966) London, Routledge and Kegan Paul.

A. McWhinnie, 'Who am I?' (1970) 62 Child Adoption.

S. Millham, R. Bullock, K. Hosie and M. Haak, *Lost in Care — The problems of maintaining links between children in care and their families* (1986) Aldershot, Gower.

H. Napier, 'Success and failure in foster care' (1972) 2 British Journal of Social Work 187.

News of the World, 10 October 1976.

D. Owen, J. Tunstill, T. White, J. Triseliotis and J. Rowe, *A review of the Children Act 10 years on — its effects on foster care, policy and practice* (1986) London, National Foster Care Association.

* M.L. Kellmer Pringle, 'In Place of One's Own — A Look into the Future' in J. Seglow, M.L. Kellmer Pringle and P. Wedge, *Growing Up Adopted* (1972) Windsor, National Foundation for Educational Research, pp. 170, 176.

L. Raynor, *The Adopted Child Comes of Age* (1980) London, George Allen and Unwin.

* *Report (first) of the Child Adoption Committee* (Chairman: Mr Justice Tomlin) (Cmd. 2401) (1925) London, HMSO, paras. 4, 9, 11, 15, 18, 19, 28.

* *Report of the Adoption Practices Review Committee* (1990) New Zealand, Ministry of Social Welfare, pp. 39–43.

Report of the Committee on Child Adoption (Chairman: Sir Alfred Hopkinson K.C.) (Cmd. 1254) (1921) London, HMSO.

Report of the Departmental Committee on Adoption Societies and Agencies (Chairman: Miss Florence Horsbrugh M.P.) (Cmd. 5499) (1937) London, HMSO.

Report of the Departmental Committee on the Adoption of Children (Chairman: His Honour Sir Gerald Hurst Q.C.) (Cmd. 9248) (1954) London, HMSO.

* *Report of the Departmental Committee on the Adoption of Children* (Chairman: Sir William Houghton, later Judge F.A. Stockdale) (Cmnd. 5107) (1972) London, HMSO, paras. 33–36, 38, 83–88, 93–94, 116, 120–122, 125–127, 144, 146, 168.170, 221, 223–224, 237, 244, 252, 253, 301–303, 326, 327.

Review of Child Care Law, see DHSS.

L. Ripple, 'A Follow-up Study of Adopted Children' (1968) 42 Social Service Review, no. 4, p. 479.

G. Rosner, *Crisis of Self Doubt* (1961) New York, Child Welfare League of America.

* J. Rowe, 'Fostering in the 1970s' (1977) Adoption and Fostering, no. 4, 15, pp. 15–17.

J. Rowe, 'The realities of adoptive parenthood' (1970) 59 Child Adoption.

J. Rowe and L. Lambert, *Children Who Wait* (1973) London, Association of British Adoption Agencies (now British Agencies for Adoption and Fostering).

* J. Rowe, H. Cain, M. Hundleby and A. Keane, *Long-Term Foster Care* (1984) London Batsford and BAAF, pp. 223–226.

J. Rowe, H. Cain, M. Hundleby and A. Keane, *Long-term fostering and the Children Act — a study of foster parents who went on to adopt* (1984) London, British Agencies for Adoption and Fostering.

J. Rowe et al, *Child Care Placements — Patterns and Outcomes* (1989) London, British Agencies for Adoption and Fostering.

H.J. Sants, 'Genealogical bewilderment in children with substitute parents' (1967) 37 British Journal of Medical Psychology.

* J. Seglow, M.L. Kellmer Pringle and P. Wedge, *Growing Up Adopted* (1972) Windsor, National Foundation for Educational Research, pp. 9–10, 157, 170, 176.

J. Thoburn, *Review of Research Relating to Adoption*, Interdepartment Review of Adoption Law, Background Paper No. 2 (1990) London, Department of Health.

J. Thoburn, A. Murdoch and A. O'Brien, *Permanence in Child Care* (1986) Oxford, Basil Blackwell.

R. Thorpe, 'Mum and Mrs So and So' (1974) 4 Social Work Today, no. 22, p. 691.

* R. Thorpe, 'The Experience of Children and Parents Living Apart' in J. Triseliotis (ed.), *New Developments in Foster Care and Adoption* (1980) London, Routledge and Kegan Paul, pp. 90–95.

* B. Tizard, *Adoption: A Second Chance* (1977) London, Open Books, pp. 1, 3–8, 206–209.

G. Trasler, *In Place of Parents* (1960) London, Routledge and Kegan Paul.

J. Triseliotis, 'Identity and Adoption' (1974) 78 Child Adoption.
* J. Triseliotis, *In Search of Origins: The Experiences of Adopted People* (1973) London, Routledge and Kegan Paul, pp. 84, 85, 101.
* J. Triseliotis, 'Growing Up in Foster Care and After' in J. Triseliotis (ed.), *New Developments in Foster Care and Adoption* (1980) London, Routledge and Kegan Paul, pp. 138 and 148.
J. Triseliotis, 'Identity and Security in Adoption and Long-Term Fostering (1983) 7 (1) Adoption and Fostering 22.
* J. Triseliotis, 'Obtaining birth certificates' in P. Bean (ed.), *Adoption: Essays in social policy, law and sociology* (1984) London, Tavistock, pp. 51–52.
J. Triseliotis and J. Russell, *Hard to Place: The Outcome of Late Adoption and Residential Care* (1984) London, Heinemann.
* J. Triseliotis, 'Foster care outcomes: a review of key research findings' (1989) 13(3) Adoption and Fostering 5, pp. 12–15.
* C. Walby and B. Symons, *Who am I? Identity, adoption and human fertilisation*, Discussion Series No. 12 (1990), London, British Agencies for Adoption and Fostering, pp. 39–41, 68.
E.A. Weinstein, *The Self Image of the Foster Child* (1960) New York, Russell Sage Foundation.
C. Wilkinson, *Prospect, Process and Outcome in Foster Care*, University of Edinburgh, M. Phil. Thesis (1988).

Chapter 15

ACAS, The Advisory, Conciliation and Arbitration Service, *The ACAS Role in Conciliation, Arbitration and Mediation* (1979) London, HMSO.
Association of County Councils, *Juvenile Justice* (1984) London, Association of County Councils.
Association of Directors of Social Services, *Children Still in Trouble* (1985) London, ADSS.
Booth Committee, see Report of the Matrimonial Causes Procedure Committee.
* A. Bottomley, 'Resolving family disputes – a critical view' in M.D.A. Freeman (ed.), *The State, the Law and the Family: Critical Perspectives* (1984) London, Stevens, pp. 294–298.
* British Agencies for Adoption and Fostering and Association of Directors of Social Services, *Family justice – a structure for the family court* The Report of the BAAF/ADSS Family Courts Working Party (Denis Allen, ed.) (1986) London, BAAF, paras. 29–31, 70–73.
British Association of Social Workers, *Family Courts – A Discussion Document* (1984) Birmingham, BASW.
* L. Neville Brown, 'The Legal Background to the Family Court' [1966] British Journal of Criminology 139, p. 149.
G. Davis, 'Conciliation or Litigation?' [1982] L.A.G. Bulletin, April, p. 11.
G. Davis, 'Conciliation and the Professions' (1983) 13 Family Law 6.
G. Davis, 'Mediation in Divorce: A Theoretical Perspective' [1983] Journal of Social Welfare Law 131.
G. Davis, *Partisans and Mediators* (1988) Oxford, Oxford University Press.
G. Davis and K. Bader, *In Court Mediation on Custody and Access Issues – The Files Study* (1983a) Bristol, Department of Social Administration, University of Bristol.
G. Dvais and K. Bader, *In Court Mediation on Custody and Access Issues at Bristol County Court – The Observation Study* (1983b) Bristol, Department of Social Administration, University of Bristol.
G. Davis with K. Bader, *Research Report on the Pre-trial Review Scheme at the Principal Registry* (1982) Bristol, University of Bristol.
* G. Davis and K. Bader, 'In-court Mediation: the Consumer View' (1985) 15 Family Law 42, and 82, pp. 48, 85.

G. Davis, A. Macleod and M. Murch, 'Divorce and the Resolution of Conflict' The Law Society's Gazette, 13 January 1982.

* G. Davis and M. Murch, *Grounds for Divorce* (1988) Oxford, Clarendon Press, pp. 53–56.

* Department of Health, *An Introduction to the Children Act 1989* (1989) London, HMSO, para. 3.4.

* Department of Health, Guidance and Regulations on the Children Act 1989, vol. 1, *Court Orders* (1991) London, HMSO, paras. 1.13–1.15.

R. Dingwall and J.M. Eekelaar (eds.), *Divorce Mediation and the Legal Process* (1988) Oxford, Clarendon Press.

J. Donzelot, *The Policing of Families* (1980) London, Hutchinson.

J.M. Eekelaar and R. Dingwall, 'The development of conciliation in England' in R. Dingwall and J.M. Eekalaar (eds.), *Divorce Mediation and the Legal Process* (1988) Oxford, Clarendon Press.

Eisenberg, 'The Bargain Principle and its Limits' (1982) 95 Harvard Law Review 741.

Family Courts Campaign, *A Court Fit For Families* (1986) London, Family Courts Campaign.

M.D.A. Freeman, 'Towards a More Humane System of Divorce: Murch and Participant Justice' (1981) 145 Justice of the Peace 173.

T. Fisher (ed.), *Family Conciliation within the UK* (1990) Bristol, Family Law.

D. Fraser, 'Divorce Avon Style: the Work of a Specialist Welfare Team' (1980) 11(30) Social Work Today 12.

C. Fried, *Contract as Promise* (1981).

M.A. Glendon, *State, Law and Family* (1977) London, North Holland.

Judge J. Graham Hall, 'Outline of a Proposal for a Family Court' (1977) 1 Family Law 6.

P.H. Gulliver, *Neighbours and Networks* (1971) Berkeley, University of California Press.

* B.M. Hoggett, 'Family courts or family law reform — which should come first?' (1986) 6 Legal Studies 1, pp. 3–5.

* Home Office, *Marriage Matters. A Consultative Document by the Working Party on Marriage Guidance set up by the Home Office in consultation with the DHSS* (1979) London, HMSO, paras. 1.12, 1.15–1.16, 7.10–7.11.

Interdepartmental Review of Family and Domestic Jurisdiction, *A Consultation Paper* (1986) London, Lord Chancellor's Department.

Justice, *Report on Parental Rights and Duties and Custody Suits* (1975) London, Stevens.

Justices' Clerks' Society, *Towards a Workable Family Court* (1976) London, Justices' Clerks' Society.

* Law Commission, *Court Record Study*, Appendix C to the Report on the Ground for Divorce, Law Com. No. 192 (1990) London, HMSO, paras. 13–15, 21–22.

Law Commission, *Reform of the Grounds of Divorce — The Field of Choice* Cmnd. 3123 (1966) London, HMSO.

* Law Commission, *Report on the Ground for Divorce*, Law Com. No. 192 (1990) London, HMSO, paras. 5.29–5.30, 5.33–5.39.

* Law Reform Commission of Canada, *The Family Court*, Working Paper 1 (1974) Ottowa, Information Canada, pp. 7–8.

Law Society, Family Law Sub-Committee, *A Better Way Out: suggestions for the reform of the Law of Divorce and Other Forms of Matrimonial Relief; for the Setting-up of a Family Court; and for its Procedure* (1979) London, The Law Society.

Law Society, Standing Committee on Family Law, *A Better Way Out Reviewed* (1982) London, The Law Society.

Law Society, Standing Committee on Family Law, *A Family Court —
Consultation Paper* (1985) London, The Law Society.

Law Society, Standing Committee on Family Law, *A Suggested Model for the
Family Court* (1986) London, The Law Society.

Lord Chancellor's Department, *Family Jurisdiction of the High Court and County
Courts* Consultation Paper (1983) London, Lord Chancellor's Department.

A.H. Manchester and J.M. Whetton, 'Marital Conciliation in England and Wales'
(1974) 23 International and Comparative Law Quarterly 339.

J.S. Mill, *On Liberty* (1859), London.

R.H. Mnookin, 'Bargaining in the Shadow of the Law: The Case of Divorce'
[1979] Current Legal Problems 65, p. 65.

* R.H. Mnookin, 'Divorce Bargaining: the Limits on Private Ordering' in
J.M. Eekelaar and S.N. Katz (eds.), *The Resolution of Family Conflict:
Comparative Legal Perspectives* (1984), Toronto, Butterworths, pp. 366–372,
376–379.

* M. Murch, *Justice and Welfare in Divorce* (1980) London, Sweet and Maxwell,
p. 223.

Newcastle Report, see University of Newcastle.

L. Parkinson, 'Bristol Courts Family Conciliation Service' (1982) 12 Family Law
13.

L. Parkinson, 'Conciliation: Pros and Cons' (1983) 13 Family Law 22.

L. Parkinson, 'Conciliation: A New Approach to Family Conflict Resolution'
(1983) 13 British Journal of Social Work 19.

* L. Parkinson, *Conciliation in Separation and Divorce: Finding common ground*
(1986) London, Croom Helm, pp. 52, 65.

G.M. Parmiter, 'Bristol In-Court Conciliation Procedure' Law Society's Gazette,
25 February 1981.

J. Pugsley et al, 'Conciliation and Report Writing: Tasks for One Officer' (1986)
16 Family Law 169.

* *Report of the Committee on One-Parent Families* (Chairman: The Hon. Sir
Morris Finer) (Cmnd. 5629) (1974) London, HMSO, paras. 4.282–3,
4.285–6, 4.288–9, 4.290, 4.298–4.300, 4.404–5.

Report of the Committee on Procedure in Matrimonial Causes (Chairman: The
Hon. Mr. Justice Denning) (Cmd. 7024) (1947) London, HMSO.

Report of the Inter-departmental Committee on Conciliation (1983) London,
HMSO.

* *Report of the Matrimonial Causes Procedure Committee* (Chairman: The Hon.
Mrs. Justice Booth D.B.E.) (1985) London, HMSO, paras. 3.11–3.12.

Report of the Royal Commission on Marriage and Divorce (Chairman: Lord
Morton of Henryton) (Cmd. 9678) (1956) London, HMSO.

I. Ricci, *Mom's House/Dad's House* (1980).

S. Roberts, 'Mediation in Family Law Disputes' (1983) 46 Modern Law Review
537.

S. Roberts, *Order and Dispute* (1979) Harmondsworth, Penguin Books.

S. Roberts, 'The Location and Occasion of Mediation' in *The Role of Mediation
in Divorce Proceedings: A Comparative Perspective* (1987) University of
Vermont.

Society of Conservative Lawyers, *The Case for Family Courts* (1978) London,
Conservative Political Centre.

* E. Szwed, 'The Family Court' in M.D.A. Freeman (ed.), *The State, the Law and
the Family: Critical Perspectives* (1984) London, Stevens, p. 272.

* University of Newcastle Conciliation Project Unit, *Report to the Lord Chancellor
on the Costs and Effectiveness of Conciliation in England and Wales*
(1989) Newcastle, University of Newcastle upon Tyne, paras. 2.20–2.38, 20.1,
20.5–20.10, 20.18–20.19.

J.A. Walker, 'Divorce Mediation — Is it a Better Way?' in J. McCrory (ed.), *The Role of Mediation in Divorce Proceedings: A Comparative Perspective* (1987) University of Vermont.

* J.A. Walker, 'Conciliation Research' in T. Fisher (ed.), *Family Conciliation within the UK* (1990) Bristol, Family Law, p. 156.

M. Wilkinson, *Children and Divorce* (1981) Oxford, Basil Blackwell.

E. Wilson, *Women and the Welfare State* (1977) London, Tavistock.

CHAPTER 1

The family and marriage

1 Definitions of 'household' and 'family'

Most people understand that the word *family* refers to a group of persons related to each other by blood and/or marriage. The introduction of an additional word, such as 'immediate', suggests that the members of the family probably live together within a single household, and (although to a variable extent) pool their resources for the common well-being of the unit. However, many important questions are immediately raised by this series of assumptions. Is it necessary for the members of the family to be related in the manner described? Is it a prerequisite that there be a single household? Why should members pool resources?

The family's structure will vary from culture to culture. Most are based on monogamous marriages although there are still some cultures which tolerate polygamous marriages. It is also still the case that most cultures are strongly patriarchal rather than matriarchal; although there are exceptions.

Question

Bradney, in an article entitled 'The Family in Family Law' (1979) states: 'It seems clear that there is at least room for debate about the type of family, or types of family, which should be found in family law.' Do you agree with this view, and if so, which types would you have in mind?

In the England of the 1990s, we must not assume that the answer to the question 'What is a family?' is necessarily going to produce a simple and straightforward response. In the context of a traditional Indian family, or a Chinese family, the familial group may be much larger than a simple household; there may be a pooling of certain resources only, financial obligations may be extended to a wider kinship group than the familial nexus.

A *household* according to Stone, writing about the family in England from 1500–1800, consists of persons 'living under one roof'. In *The Family, Sex and Marriage* (1977), he says:

The core of any household is clearly the family, namely members related by blood or marriage, usually the conjugal pair and their unmarried children, but sometimes including grandparents, the married children, or occasionally kin relatives. But most households also included non-kin inmates, sojourners, boarders or lodgers, occupying rooms vacated by children or kin, as well as indentured apprentices and resident servants, employed either for domestic work about the house or as an additional resident labour force for the fields or the shop.

Laslett and Wall, in their seminal work published in 1972 entitled *Household and Family in Past Time*, define the two words 'household' and 'family' in the context of the historical demographic data which they collect and analyse:

It must be strongly stressed that in this vocabulary the word *family* does not denote a complete coresident domestic group, though it may appear as an abbreviated title. The word *household* particularly indicates the fact of shared location, kinship and activity. Hence all solitaries have to be taken to be households, for they are living with themselves, and this is the case when they have servants with them, since servants are taken as household members. . . .

The expression *simple family* is used to cover what is variously described as the *nuclear family*, the *elementary family* or (not very logically, since spouses are not physiologically connected), the *biological family*. It consists of a married couple, or a married couple with offspring, or of a widowed person with offspring. The concept is of the conjugal link as the structural principle, and conjugal linkage is nearly always patent in the lists of persons which we are using. For a simple family to appear then, it is necessary for at least two individuals connected by that link or arising from that link to be coresident: *conjugal family unit* (CFU) is a preciser term employed to describe all possible groups so structured.

No solitary can form a conjugal family unit and for such a group to subsist it is necessary for at least two immediate partners (spouses and/or offspring) to be present. More remotely connected persons, whose existence implies more than one conjugal link, do not constitute a conjugal family unit if they reside together with no one else except servants. Nor do brothers and sisters. Hence a widow with a child forms a conjugal family unit, but a widow with a grandchild does not, nor does an aunt with a nephew. Whenever a conjugal family unit is found on its own, it is always taken to be a household, just as solitaries are, and such a coresident domestic group is called a *simple family household*. The first mentioned person in the household of this and all other types is always taken to be head. . . .

An *extended family household* [or stem family] consists in a conjugal family unit with the addition of one or more relatives other than offspring, the whole group living together on its own or with servants. It is thus identical with the simple family household except for the additional item or items. If the resident relative is of a generation earlier than that of the head, say a married head's father, or a spouse's mother, or a widowed head's aunt, then the extension is said to be upwards.

Similarly the presence of a grandchild (without either parent) or a nephew or niece creates downward extension, and that of a brother, sister or cousin of the head or of his spouse, implies sideways or lateral extension. Some groups are extended vertically and laterally, and it should be noted that the presence of any kin or affine of the conjugal family unit creates extension however distant the relationship, though the relatives of a servant do not do so. It is particularly important that the whole phrase 'extended family household' be used for this category of domestic group, because the words 'extended family' by themselves have a highly significant but quite separate further meaning, which covers all relatives in habitual contact with a person, irrespective of whether they live with him.

Multiple family households comprise all forms of domestic group which include two or more conjugal family units connected by kinship or by marriage. Such units can be simple or extended, and can be disposed vertically and laterally. The disposition of a secondary unit, that is of a constituent unit which does not contain the head of the whole household, is said to be UP if its conjugal link involves a generation earlier than that of the head, as for example when his father and mother live with him. Such a secondary unit can include offspring of the head's parents other than the head himself, that is his resident unmarried brothers or sisters, and the presence of such persons keeps this secondary unit in being if one or other of the head's parents dies. A secondary unit is disposed DOWN if, for example, a head's married son lives with him along with his wife and perhaps offspring, with similar implications about siblings and widowhood. . . .

If conjugal family units within households of the multiple kind are all disposed laterally, as when married brothers and/or sisters live together, the overall arrangement is the one often referred to as the 'fraternal joint family' by social anthropologists. The expression 'joint family' is also widely used, however, to refer to all the forms of multiple family household.

It is necessary to consider another introductory matter, namely the difference between *familial experience* and *familial ideology*. There may be a correspondence between experience and ideology; however, it has been argued by Laslett and Wall that although the nuclear monogamous family has a claim to universality, it has never possessed a normative and ideological force:

There must be few behavioural institutions of which it can be said that ideology and experience are entirely congruent. No one would question that the English society of our day is correctly described as monogamous, because monogamous behaviour is nearly universal amongst a people whose belief in monogamy as a value is very widespread, and whose conduct is consistent with monogamy as the norm. It could be called the marital institution under which the English live, for no other distinct practice-with-belief exists alongside it as an alternative. Yet divorce is now quite frequent, scepticism about single spouse unions often encountered, and sexual intercourse outside marriage a commonplace. Indeed we know that children have been begotten illegitimately in appreciable numbers in England during the whole period for which figures can be recovered. . . .

Departure from the monogamous ideal of behaviour, amongst English people nowadays, and perhaps amongst their ancestors, has been particularly conspicuous within the élite, and rejection of the beliefs associated with monogamy especially common with the intellectuals, the makers of opinions and of norms. Monogamy as an institution, then, has been underwritten by a general correspondence of ideology and experience, but is consistent with an appreciable degree of disharmony between the two. We do not find ourselves enquiring how much they could diverge before a practice ceased to be *the* institution, and became one amongst others, *an* institution. We do not easily contemplate a situation where plural institutions, or highly variable behaviour, exist in one society at one time in such matters as sexual behaviour and marriage.

Yet if we turn to the question of how far any of the forms of the coresident domestic group, . . . could be called *the* institution, or *an* institution, of the societies where examples of them are found, this issue becomes inescapable. Glancing again at England as it is today, it seems safe enough to claim that the nuclear family, the simple family household, is *the* familial institution, and that again because experience of it, belief in it, willingness to obey its norms, are in fact all congruent with each other. The nuclear family, of course, complements the English institution of monogamy in a particular way. But it has, and has had for hundreds of years as far as we can yet see, a markedly better claim to universality in behaviour and experience than monogamous marriage with exclusively marital sexual intercourse. Yet the nuclear family never seems to have possessed the normative force, certainly not the ideological potential of monogamy, in England or indeed in Western culture.

The hiatus, therefore, between familial experience and familial ideology is of a somewhat different character than that which divides the two in the matter of monogamy. The intellectuals and opinion makers who deal in the ideology of our world, have a tendency to deplore the circumstance that the complex family household is not sufficiently established as a norm in our society. Extended and even multiple households exist amongst us, but not in anything like enough numbers to ensure that the widowed and the elderly unmarried have a family to live in, or our children the emotional advantage of the presence of the extended kin in the households where they grow up.

Laslett and Wall's definition of monogamy may be contrasted with the following extract from Engels, *Origins of the Family, Private Property and the State* (1884):

Sex love in the relation of husband and wife is and can become the rule only among the oppressed classes, that is, at the present day, among the proletariat, no matter whether this relationship is officially sanctioned or not. But all the foundations of classical monogamy are removed. Here there is a complete absence of all property, for the safeguarding and inheritance of which monogamy and male domination were established. Therefore, there is no stimulus whatever here to assert male domination. . . .

Moreover, since large-scale industry has transferred the woman from the house to the labour market and the factory, and makes her, often enough, the bread winner of the family, the last remnants of male domination in the proletarian home have lost all foundation — except, perhaps, for some of that brutality towards women which became firmly rooted with the establishment of monogamy. Thus, the proletarian family is no longer monogamian in the strict sense, even in cases of the most passionate love and strictest faithfulness of the two parties, and despite all spiritual and worldly benedictions which may have been received. . . .

In short, proletarian marriage is monogamian in the etymological sense of the word, but by no means in the historical sense.

Questions

(i) Polygamy is permitted in some cultures; for example, according to the classical Islamic law a man is permitted four wives; the husband inherits a large slice of his wife's property, but she does have rights of ownership while she is alive and can inherit a share of the estate of her deceased father. Do you think that polygamy has anything to do with: (*a*) control of property and (*b*) male domination?

(ii) Do you think that a male worker has a vested interest in the domination of his wife and children?

(iii) Section 8(3) of the Immigration Act 1971 states that the provisions introduced under the Act for immigration control shall not apply to any person so long as he is a member of a mission, or 'a person who is a member of the family and forms part of the household of such a member'. Are the following exempt from control:

  (*a*) the distant cousin of a Burmese diplomat who has been looked after by this diplomat and his wife after the death of the parents;

  (*b*) the fourth wife of a Yemeni diplomat who has been provided with separate accommodation by her husband in Yemen in accordance with Islamic law; and

  (*c*) the young brother of an Indian diplomat who has equal rights with the diplomat in the joint property they have both inherited from their father?

See *Re Wirdestedt*, reported as a note [1990] Imm AR 20 where the Court of Appeal held that a 'firm, stable and lasting homosexual relationship' was not a relationship which was capable of recognition within the Immigration Rules. A homosexual partner was not a 'close relative' and thus was not qualified for admission for settlement on the application of the sponsor.

(iv) Private sector tenancies: the Housing Act 1988, s. 17(4) defines a tenant's spouse, who can succeed to a periodic assured tenancy, as including 'a person who was living with the tenant as his or her wife or husband'. Does this rule apply to the following: (*a*) a close friend of the original tenant, where both had for many years lived together in a platonic association; (*b*) the survivor of two old cronies who had shared a house; (*c*) a lady of 'independence' who had lived with the deceased for many years as his cohabitant but who had deliberatedly remained unmarried?

(v) In *Carega Properties SA v Sharratt* [1979] 2 All ER 1084, [1979] 1 WLR 928, the House of Lords emphasised that the relevant question under the Rent Act 1977 (then in force) is whether the 'ordinary man' would regard the relationship in question as establishing 'a broadly recognisable familial nexus'. Historically, is this phrase restricted to a biological or marital connection? (See p. 362, below, for further discussion of this provision).

(vi) Public sector tenancies: Section 113(1) of the Housing Act 1985 states:

'A person is a member of another's family . . . if—
  (a) he is the spouse of that person, or he and that person live together as husband or wife, or
  (b) he is that person's parent, grandparent, child, grandchild, brother, sister, uncle, aunt, nephew or niece.'

In *Harrogate Borough Council v Simpson* [1986] 2 FLR 91, [1986] Fam Law 359, the Court of Appeal held that a woman who lived in council accommodation with another woman, a secured tenant, and who shared a 'committed, monogamous, homosexual relationship' with her, was not a 'member of the tenant's family' within the meaning of s. 113(1), (2) of the Housing Act 1985, and accordingly was not entitled to succeed to the tenancy on the death of the tenant. (Section 87 of the 1985 Act).

Would you be prepared to make a case in favour of extending the section so as to include monogamous yet homosexual relationships? And what of cousins or other collaterals who live together in an extended family which operates a system of joint property?

(vii) In *M v M* (1981) 2 FLR 39, the Court of Appeal refused an application of a wife for a maintenance order against her husband in favour of a child of hers. The court decided that the husband had not treated the child as a child of the family (s. 52(1) of the Matrimonial Causes Act 1973; see now s. 105(1) of the Children Act 1989). The parties were married in September 1970. They separated in April 1971. After the separation the wife became pregnant by another man. The wife did not want her family to know that the husband was not the father. The husband acquiesced in this state of affairs and allowed the wife's family to think the child was his.

Ormrod LJ: In my judgment the first question the learned judge had to ask himself was, 'Could there possibly be said to have been at any time during this child's life a family of which he could be treated as part?' In my judgment, the answer to that must be 'No'. These two parties, husband and wife, had been living apart in the full sense of the phrase ever since April 1971. There had been nothing whatsoever in their relationship which bore any relation to that of husband and wife. The learned judge himself put it that they were, if anything, friends, still on friendly terms. . . .

Here the husband has filed his petition (he has not got his decree yet) on the ground that the parties had been living apart in that sense for five years, and the one thing that emerges perfectly clearly from the facts of this case is that neither of them regarded the marriage as subsisting. Once you get to that stage, it seems to me wholly artificial to say that the family as a social unit continued to exist. It must, as a family, using the language in ordinary sense, come to an end when the parties regard their marriage as at an end. These two parties plainly regarded their marriage as at an end from April 1971 onwards. It is not necessary to go any further than that except to say that these two parties would not be treated as living together for any other purpose of the Matrimonial Causes Act. They would be separate individuals for the purposes of income tax, for example, and for affiliation proceedings.

They were living apart, held together only by the empty shell of this marriage which could have been dissolved at any time. . . .

My conclusions on the facts of this case are, firstly, that there was in fact at no time during this child's life a family. Therefore, it was not possible to treat the child as a child of this (non-existent) family; secondly on the question of 'treatment', it is a matter of fact to be judged by looking at and carefully considering what the husband in this case did and how he behaved towards the child. The difficulty in this case is that the husband, if he did anything, behaved towards this child not as if the child were a child of the family but as if, for certain purposes, the child was his own natural child. That is, he took part in the pretence without protesting. I do not think the evidence goes any further than that. The fact that he put the word 'Dad' on some Christmas cards and presents does not, in my judgment, amount to anything more than following the line he had taken up at the request of the wife, which was to cover up for her to all intents and purposes. He, as he said himself, was quite fond of the child as a child. He was kind to the boy and was quite pleased to see him on the rare occasions when he visited the mother. It goes no further than that.

(viii) Does a 'household' include a man who has been committed to prison for nine months? (See *Taylor v Supplementary Benefit Officer* [1986] 1 FLR 16, [1986] Fam Law 16, CA.)

(ix) Is 'child of the family' the same thing as 'child of the household'? (See the article by Jacqueline Priest 'Child of the Family' in (1984) 14 Fam Law p. 134 where other cases are discussed; in particular *W v W* [1984] FLR 796; and *Teeling v Teeling* [1984] FLR 808.)

Read what Lord Langdale MR said in 1836 in relation to wills in *Blackwell v Bull* (1836) 1 Keen 176, 5 LJ Ch 251:

It is evident that the word 'family' is capable of so many applications that if any one partic-ular construction were attributed to it in wills, the intention of testators would be more fre-quently defeated than carried into effect. Under different circumstances it means a man's household, consisting of himself, his wife, children and servants; it may mean his wife and children, or his children excluding his wife; in the absence of wife and children, it may mean his brother and sisters or his next of kin, or it may mean the genealogical stork from which he may have sprung. All these applications of the word and some others are found in common parlance.

In the case of a will we must endeavour to ascertain the meaning in which the testator employed the word, by considering the circumstances and situations in which he was placed, the object he had in view, and the context of the will.

(See also *Re Barlow's Will Trusts* [1979] 1 All ER 296, [1979] 1 WLR 278. For an interesting article see A. Dickey, 'The Notion of Family in Law' (1982) 14 U West Aust L Rev 417.)

The United States Supreme Court has had to consider the definition of 'family' and 'household' on a number of occasions. In *Department of Agri-culture v Moreno* 413 US 528 (1973) the court declared unconstitutional a provision of the Food Stamp Act which failed to provide assistance to house-holds containing any unrelated individuals.

The second case is *Belle Terre v Boras* 416 US 1 (1973). This concerned a so-called 'zoning' Ordinance which restricted occupancy to one-family units with 'family' as 'one or more persons related by blood, adoption, or marriage, living or cooking together as a single housekeeping unit, exclusive of household servants'. There was a proviso to this definition which per-mitted two unrelated persons to constitute a family, but no more than two such persons in any housekeeping unit. Belle Terre enforced the Ordinance against a property owner who had rented his home to six students. The Supreme Court held the Ordinance to be constitutional.

The third US case is *Moore v City of Cleveland* 431 US 494 (1977) which also concerned a Housing Ordinance. East Cleveland's Ordinance limits occupancy of dwelling units to single families, and by s. 1341.08 defines 'family' in this way:

'Family' means a number of individuals related to the nominal head of the household or to the spouse of the nominal head of the household living as a single housekeeping unit in a single dwelling unit, but limited to the following:

(a) Husband or wife of the nominal head of the household.
(b) Unmarried children of the nominal head of the household or of the spouse of the nominal

head of the household, *provided*, however, that *such unmarried children have no children residing with them*.

(c) Father or mother of the nominal head of the household or of the spouse of the nominal head of the household.

(d) *Nothwithstanding* the provisions of subsection (b) hereof, a family may include not more than one dependent married or unmarried child of the nominal head of the household or of the spouse of the nominal head of the household and the spouse and dependent children of such dependent child. For the purpose of this subsection, a dependent person is one who has more than fifty percent of his total support furnished for him by the nominal head of the household and the spouse of the nominal head of the household.

(e) A family may consist of one individual. [Italics added]

The Supreme Court declared this provision unconstitutional in the following circumstances. The appellant, Mrs Moore, lived in her home with her son and two grandsons, one of whom was the child of the son living with her, and the other who was the child of her deceased daughter. Mrs Moore was charged with a criminal offence in violation of the Ordinance. The Supreme Court distinguished *Belle Terre*.

Powell J: But one overriding factor sets this case apart from *Belle Terre*. The ordinance there *affected only unrelated individuals*. It expressly allowed all who were related by 'blood, adoption, or marriage' to live together, and in sustaining the ordinance we were careful to note that it promoted 'family needs' and 'family values'. 416 US at 9. *East Cleveland, in contrast*, has chosen to regulate the occupancy of its housing by *slicing deeply into the family itself*. This is no mere incidental result of the ordinance. On its face *it selects certain categories of relatives who may live together and declares that others may not*. In particular, it makes a crime of a grandmother's choice to live with her grandson in circumstances like those presented here.

When thus examined, this ordinance cannot survive. The city seeks to justify it as a means of preventing overcrowding, minimizing traffic and parking congestion, and avoiding an undue financial burden on East Cleveland's school system. Although these are legitimate goals, the ordinance before us serves them marginally, at best. For example, the ordinance permits any family consisting only of husband, wife and unmarried children to live together, even if the family contains a half dozen licensed drivers, each with his or her own car. At the same time it *forbids an adult brother and sister to share a household*, even if both faithfully use public transportation. The ordinance would permit a grandmother to live with a single dependent son and children, even if his school-age children number a dozen, yet it forces Mrs. Moore to find another dwelling for her grandson John, simply because of the presence of his uncle and cousin in the same household. We need not labor the point. Section 1341.08 *has but a tenuous relation to alleviation of the conditions mentioned by the city*. [Italics added]

Questions

(i) Do you find attractive the distinction suggested in *Moore* between that case and *Belle Terre*?

(ii) Is the legal meaning of family different according to the functional context in which it is used? If so, should it be?

2 Approaches to the history of the family

In *Approaches to the History of the Western Family* (1980) Anderson distinguishes three approaches to family history: the demographic approach, the sentiments approach, and the household economic approach. These three schools of thought emphasise different aspects of the available source material. The extracts in this section have been selected to provide illustrations of the debate upon which family historians are currently engaged.

(a) THE DEMOGRAPHIC APPROACH

Peter Laslett and his co-workers at the Cambridge ESRC group for the History of Population and Social Structure are the major writers who adhere to this approach.

A particular matter which must be of considerable interest for the policy-makers of the present time is the historical evidence relating to the size of households, and whether this information has a bearing on the size, type and function of the family. It is to this question that the Laslett team has directed its gaze. Laslett suggests that the 'mean household size' (including servants in England) 'has remained more or less constant at about 4.75 from the sixteenth century right through the industrialisation period until the end of the nineteenth century when a steady decline set in to a figure of about three in contemporary censuses.' The work of the Group is based on 100 English communities at dates between 1574 and 1821. 70% of households are classed as two-generational and 24% as one generational. Only 6% contain relatives of three different generations and less than 1% of four generations. The major conclusion is that a nuclear familial form 'may have been one of the enduring and fundamental characteristics of the Western family system.' Indeed, Alan MacFarlane in *Origins of English Individualism* (1978) has argued that the nuclear family as a behavioural fact has existed in England since 1200.

However, recent research has tended to suggest that this view is a gross exaggeration and overgeneralisation. In Southern and Eastern Europe, households were of a more complex type (see Berkner, 1977). Indeed even in relation to England, Laslett's conclusions have been doubted, as Anderson (1980) explains:

If we imagine a household where land is transferred to a son on his marriage and the son subsequently has children of his own, then, if this occurs before his father's death, a three-generation family will appear in a census listing. A few years later, when the father has died, only a widow, married child and grandchildren will be left and the evidence for a stem household becomes ambiguous. On the widow's death, a nuclear household will result and the census listing will reveal no evidence of any extension at all. Nevertheless — and this is the crucial point — while no stem-family[1] *household* is present, a stem-family *organisation* remains since, in due course, the same process will be repeated by the next generation. Indeed, even where no stem-family system is in operation the availability of data on ages frequently shows a marked life-cycle effect in household data which is not apparent in aggregate data.

What is at issue is the life cycle of the family: first, newly-married couple; second, nuclear family with children; third, extended family; and fourth, back again to nuclear family. Static listings of households conceal this pattern.

The conclusions of Laslett and other members of the group are also criticised by Edward Shorter, in *The Making of the Modern Family* (1975):

---

1. Extended.

In earlier writings on the history of the family, sociologists acquired the bad habit of assuming that families before the Industrial Revolution were organized in clans or were at least highly 'extended'. Because any historian with even a passing familiarity with Europe's social history would realize at once the inaccuracy of that assumption, a revisionist reaction developed in the 1960s: the nuclear family was 'unearthed' time and again in history, to the accompaniment of loud shouts of discovery. As often happens to revisionists, these writers fell over backwards attempting to overturn the conventional wisdom; instead of merely correcting the sociologists' fantasies about clans and sprawling patriarchies, they tended to proclaim that at most times and places it was the conjugal family — mother, father, children, and servants — that had prevailed. The revisionists thus proceeded to create a little fantasy of their own; the nuclear family as a historical constant.

Now, many kinless families did exist; indeed, they often represented a majority of all households. But to get a sense of the typical experience of the average person, we must ask what kind of household a child would most likely have been socialized in: extended (stem), or nuclear? And there is a good chance that in better-off households as opposed to poorer ones, and in east Europe as opposed to west Europe, the average child was raised in a dwelling that contained many relatives besides his mother and father. . . .

Conjugal groups *minus* kin also turned up frequently enough in rural Europe. There were, for example, the pastoral regions of the Netherlands, where the grandparents seldom lived with the farmer and his wife. In Norwegian villages relatives co-resided with propertied peasants only about a fifth of the time, and the percentage was even lower among the cottagers. Across much of Lower Austria and in at least two well-documented villages in Salzburg province, three-generation households were unusual. . . .

Yet we must still consider the possibility that in such communities many households might, at some point in time, have contained several generations, but that death snatched away the grandparents before the census-taker arrived. Thus in the census they appeared as single-family units, whereas they might actually have been, for a period of years, stem families.

However, in many other areas of western and central Europe, the stem family was common-place and the kinless family an anomaly. Frédéric Le Play, the nineteenth-century French sociologist, coined the term *famille souche* to denote families that passed on a given farm undivided from one generation to the next over long periods of time.

(b) THE ECONOMIC APPROACH

A question often asked is why a detailed knowledge of household composition should necessarily tell us much about familial behaviour? Indeed, there are many who see household composition as a by-product of more fundamental economic processes. There is a group of writers who seek to interpret the historical data relating both to households and to families in the context of the economic realities of the period and of the region. The major question is based around the value of the household as a means of production. Anderson summarises these writings for us, in the context of the family economy of the Western peasant, in *Approaches to the History of the Western Family* (1980):

This approach has taken as its central concept the often unconscious 'strategies' employed by family members to maintain a customary standard of living, both for themselves in the present and, under certain circumstances, for themselves and their descendants in the future. The types of strategies available are constrained in a number of ways: by the family's resource-generating potential (particularly its age/sex composition); by the mode of production in which the family is involved; by the income-generating relationships which are implied by that mode; by law, and custom regarding property acquisition (including inheritance); by the possibilities of access to alternative resource-generating activities (including wage-labour or domestic manufacturing) or resource-providing rights (including, for example, both customary rights to pasture animals on common land and social welfare provision); by the intervention of powerful groups external to the family (landlords, employers and others with power in the local community); by customs limiting the range of resource-generating options which individuals see as practically available at a point in time (for example, ideas over what is appropriate work for women). (Tilly, 1979).

For the Western peasant or yeoman farmer, the principal scarce resource was land, so family strategies were constrained by the conditions under which land could be obtained and by the labour inputs required to work it. The literature on continental Europe, on Ireland, and on some areas of England even in the early nineteenth century, portrays the dominant peasant/ yeoman pattern as one where the family's subsistence needs could be met only through the continual application of the labour of all its members to productive tasks in agriculture or, to a greater or lesser extent, in certain craft or other domestically organised productive activities. Almost all production was intended either for family use or for local and known markets.

One of the central problems of the peasant family, from this perspective, was the need to ensure that enough labour was available to meet current and future needs while yet not having too many mouths to feed for the resource-generating capacity of the means of production (Winberg, 1978). On the one hand it was necessary to avoid childless marriages, which gave no security for old age (hence perhaps norms encouraging premarital intercourse to ensure marriage only to fertile girls). On the other hand too many children threatened current subsistence. This problem could, however, in some places be solved by one or more strategic responses. For example: one could acquire more productive resources as children grew . . . , one could expand non-agricultural activities and devote more effort to domestic craft production (but this was not always available) . . . , one could restrict family size by marriage to older women . . . , by some form of contraception (found in seventeenth-century England, eighteenth- and early-nineteenth-century Sweden and many other places) . . . or by some other strategy such as prolonging breast feeding. Finally, as in England, Scandinavia and elsewhere, poor households could regulate their numbers by sending 'surplus' children into service at an early age.

(c) THE SENTIMENTS APPROACH

There is another group of writers which is not prepared either to see household composition as a by-product of fundamental economic processes, or to deduce the historical development of the Western family from demographic sources. Shorter (1975) and Stone (1977, 1990) in particular have emphasised what has been termed 'the tale of sentiments.' Anderson illustrates the difference in the approach between Laslett, and the work of Shorter and Stone: 'The demographic approach started from a particular set of documents, by which their questions and conclusions have been constrained. The sentiments writers began with a set of questions about the ideas associated with family behaviour and were then faced with the problem of finding suitable source material to throw light on such ideas.'

The following extract is taken from Stone's chapter on family characteristics, in *The Family, Sex and Marriage* (1977):

In the sixteenth century, relations between spouses in rich families were often fairly remote. Living in big houses, each with his or her own bedroom and servants, husband and wife were primarily members of a functioning social universe of a large household and were rarely in private together. . . . Their marriage was usually arranged rather than consensual, in essence the outcome of an economic deal or a political alliance between two families. The transaction was sealed by the wedding and by the physical union of two individuals, while the emotional ties were left to develop at a later date. If they did not take place, and if the husband could find sexual alternatives through casual liaisons, the emotional outlet through marriage was largely non-existent for either husband or wife.

In any case, the expectations of felicity from marriage were pragmatically low, and there were many reasons why disappointment was minimal. The first is that the pair did not need to see very much of one another, either in elite circles, where they could go their own way, or among the plebs, where leisure activities were segregated, with the men resorting to the ale-house, and the women to each other's houses. . . .

The second reason why such a system was so readily accepted was the high adult mortality rates, which severely reduced the companionship element in marriage and increased its purely reproductive and nurturance functions. There was a less than fifty-fifty chance that the husband and wife would both remain alive more than a year or two after the departure from the home of the last child, so that friendship was hardly necessary. William Stout's comment on a marriage in 1699 could stand as an epitaph for many sixteenth- and seventeenth-century couples: 'they lived very disagreeably but had many children.'

Nor was the position very different amongst the lower classes in pre-nineteenth century France:

Eighteenth-century middle-class observers of social relations among the labouring classes, peasants and urban *petite bourgeoisie* in France could find no trace of affection in the marital relationship. Their observations may be biased by class and background, but if they are at all accurate, they must reflect a permanent feature of the traditional European society. All over France, 'If the horse and the wife fall sick at the same time, the . . . peasant rushes to the blacksmith to care for the animal, and leaves the task of healing his wife to nature.' If necessary, the wife could be replaced very cheaply, while the family economy depended on the health of the animal. This peasant pragmatism was confirmed by traditional proverbs, such as 'rich is the man whose wife is dead and horse alive.' The same lack of marital sentiment was evident in the towns. '*L'amitié*, that delicious sentiment, is scarcely known. There are in these little towns only marriages of convenience; nobody appreciates that true happiness consists in making others happy, who always reward us in kind.'

This bleak portrait is modified in a number of ways by Stone himself:

This rather pessimistic view of a society with little love and generally low and widely diffused affect needs to be modified if it is accurately to reflect the truth. Romantic love and sexual intrigue was certainly the subject of much poetry of the sixteenth and early seventeenth centuries, and of many of Shakespeare's plays. It was also a reality which existed in one very restricted social group: the one in which it had always existed since the twelfth century, that is the households of the prince and the great nobles. Here, and here alone, well-born young persons of both sexes were thrown together away from parental supervision and in a situation of considerable freedom as they performed their duties as courtiers, ladies and gentlemen in waiting, tutors and governesses to the children. They also had a great deal of leisure, and in the enclosed hot-house atmosphere of these great houses, love intrigues flourished as nowhere else.

The second modification of the pessimistic general description of affective relations concerns a far wider group, including many who were subjected to the loveless arranged marriage, which was normal among the propertied classes. It is clear from correspondence and wills that in a considerable number of cases, some degree of affection, or at least a good working partnership, developed after the marriage. In practice, as anthropologists have everywhere discovered, the arranged marriage works far less badly than those educated in a romantic culture would suppose, partly because the expectations of happiness from it are not set unrealistically high, and partly because it is a fact that sentiment can fairly easily adapt to social command. In any case, love is rarely blind, in the sense that it tends to be channelled along socially acceptable lines, towards persons of the other sex of similar background. This greatly increases the probability that an arranged marriage, provided it is not undertaken purely for mercenary considerations and that there is not too great a discrepancy in age, physical attractiveness or temperament, may well work out not too badly. This is especially the case where leisure is segregated, so that the pair are not thrown together too much, and where both have a multitude of outside interests and companions to divert them. In a 'low affect' society, a 'low affect' marriage is often perfectly satisfactory.

The final modification to be made to the bleak affective picture is that, owing to the high adult death rate and the late age of marriage, by no means all marriages among persons of property in the sixteenth century were arranged by the parents, since many of them were dead: marriages by choice certainly occurred, although freedom of choice was far more difficult to achieve for women other than widows.

Similar considerations are the basis of Shorter's work. Here he describes the change to 'domesticity', in *The Making of the Modern Family* (1975):

The 'companionate' marriage is customarily seen as the hallmark of contemporary family life, the husband and wife being friends rather than superordinate and subordinate, sharing tasks and affection. Perhaps that is correct. But the emotional cement of the modern family binds more than the husband and wife; it fixes the children, as well, into this sentimental unit. The notion of companionship doesn't necessarily say anything about the relationship between the couple and their children. Also, 'companionship' implies incorrectly that some form of intense romantic attachment continues to unite the couple. Both ideas are incomplete, and for that reason I prefer the expression 'domesticity' in demarcating the modern family from the traditional.

Domesticity, or the family's awareness of itself as a precious emotional unit that must be protected with privacy and isolation from outside intrusion, was the third spearhead of the great onrush of sentiment in modern times. Romantic love detached the couple from communal sexual supervision and turned them towards affection. Maternal love created a sentimental nest within which the modern family would ensconce itself, and it removed many women from involvement with community life. Domesticity, beyond that, sealed off the family as a whole from its traditional interaction with the surrounding world. The members of the family came to feel far more solidarity with one another than they did with their various age and sex peer groups.

Stone's thesis has been commented on critically by other historians. For example, Keith Wrightson in *English Society 1580–1680* (1982) writes:

Stone's powerful arguments and adventurous hypotheses constitute the most ambitious attempt yet undertaken to interpret the development of the English family over time. Nevertheless they are seriously open to question in both their characterization of family life in later sixteenth and seventeenth century England and in their account of change within this period. Although he is undoubtedly aware of the major distinctions which may have existed between social groups in England, Stone has devoted insufficient care to the exploration of the experience of the mass of the population. As a result his interpretation has been elaborated on the basis of the historical experience of the aristocracy, upper gentry and urban plutocracy with which he is primarily concerned and retains at its heart the tacit assumption that analytical categories derived from their experience can somehow be extended to encapsulate phases in the history of the English family. This is a mistaken assumption. For whatever their historical prominence, the familial behaviour of the English elite was very far from representative of that of their countrymen. Nor can shifts in their behaviour be asserted to have been significant advances in familial development when set in the full context of the already established and persisting characteristics of the family life of their social inferiors.

In a later extract, Wrightson continues:

Of marital relations in late sixteenth- and seventeenth-century England, much remains obscure. The weight of the evidence reviewed here, however, suggests that, despite the inevitable counter-examples and the individual and social variation which is to be expected, there is little reason to follow Professor Stone in regarding the rise of the companionate marriage as a new phenomenon for the later seventeenth and eighteenth centuries. It seems to have been already well established. It is true that the best of our evidence is derived from the diaries of deeply religious people, puritans who had especial cause to follow the advice of moral teachers on the subject of mutuality. Yet such supplementary evidence as can be gathered does not suggest that they were unusual in their marital relations, while the teachings of the moralists themselves were neither new, nor distinctively Puritan. They represented for the most part the mainstream of opinion on the best practice in marriage. In the present state of our knowledge it would seem unwise to make too sharp a dichotomy between the 'patriarchal' and the 'companionate' marriage, and to erect these qualities into a typology of successive stages of family development. It may well be that these are less evolutionary stages of familial progress, than the poles of an enduring continuum in marital relations in a society which accepted both the primacy of male authority and the ideal of marriage as a practical and emotional partnership. Most people established their roles within marriage somewhere between the two, with the emphasis, for the most part, on the latter.

Given these wide differences of perspective, it is appropriate to pause and to ask what relevance is there for a twentieth century lawyer to have answers to the questions raised by the historians. It is to this matter that we now turn.

(d) THE RELEVANCE OF THE HISTORY OF THE FAMILY?

Anderson asks the question whether family history can 'justify itself', in *Sociology of the Family* (now 1980):

. . . It can do so above all by drawing out the implications of these changes for the kind of family life which is possible today and, above all, by demonstrating that old moralities and old behaviours cannot meet new situations and that, accordingly, present problems require new and not obsolete solutions.

Perhaps the most significant, and certainly analytically the most difficult of these changes have been in the family's relation to production. The peasant household was the locus of production with head and spouse organizing production using the household's own labour and exploiting and co-ordinating the contribution of all household members. Each class of individual had a clearly prescribed role and each member was dependent on the activities of all the others. In this situation there is a high degree of role interdependence both between spouses and between generations. . . . Not merely was production a joint activity but almost all consumption was either shared or was undertaken in some way or other on behalf of the household.

By contrast, under our kind of capitalist system of production, work for the mass of the population becomes directed by others who select and reward labour on an individualistic basis. One or more household members leaves the domestic arena and each is remunerated by outsiders on a basis which normally takes no account of his or her family situation. The wage received is the personal property of the individual, is dependent on the individual's own level of activity and achievement, and is paid to the individual in private leaving him or her to negotiate with the rest of the family over how and to what extent the money is to be distributed in order to satisfy their wants.

The contrast between the jointness of income generation in the peasant family and its individualistic basis under capitalism was, to a considerable extent, concealed under early capitalist production by the continued participation of all except the youngest family members in income-generating activities. Even after legislation had removed children from full time factory employment there remained within local communities significant opportunities for children to add to family resources through cash or goods in kind obtained in return for odd jobs done outside school hours. In addition, the substantial levels of labour input required to process food and other materials for domestic consumption, together with the significant amount of domestic productive activity for both home production and for the market, allowed those who remained in the domestic arena to contribute significantly to family resource generation processes. Thus, in as far as the husband earned income outside the home on behalf of the family, the children (and particularly the male children) sought odd jobs on behalf of the family, and the wife (aided by the female children) produced domestically on behalf of the family, all resources being pooled together, the role interdependence remained and there was little analytical difference between this situation and the peasant system where the husband and male children worked in the outfield producing in part marketable products to pay the rent, while wife and female children worked in the infield and the home on the production and reproduction of labour power. Of course, because wages were the private property of the individual there was no guarantee that wages were in fact pooled — as the harrowing descriptions of the wives of nineteenth-century factory workers trying to extract their husbands from public houses on pay day testify. . . .

Models which assume that family-based decision making took place over how necessary income should be generated and over who should work in which sectors of production, have a clear empirical fit with data from most nineteenth- and early twentieth-century working-class communities.

However, developments of the last fifty years have moved most families significantly away from this position. Children have become almost totally dependent. They leave the home daily for education which is oriented far more to their individual futures than to their current family roles and subsequently enter the labour force to receive pay much of which is again retained for their own use even in the very few years that now typically remain between starting work and marriage. In this way children have almost totally ceased to be part of an interdependent resource-generating system. Similarly, in as far as both spouses enter the labour force and each receives a private reward for labour (and particularly as in many dual career families where outside workers come in to perform most of the domestic work, which anyway can now if desired require a much smaller labour input), the work of the spouses can no longer so easily be seen as a co-operative productive activity or even as involving a complementary division of labour where each performs different but interrelated tasks on behalf of the family unit. . . . The ties between family members thus become based not on an interdependence rooted in co-operative productive activity essential for survival, but on personal interdependence oriented towards the joint attainment of essentially intrinsic 'projects' of highly diverse kinds.

However, these aspirations are much more susceptible to change over time than are the basic survival objectives of pre-industrial European societies, and their interpersonal basis is much more fragile. . . . Thus it is not surprising that wherever we see communities moving from family groups based on property and co-operative production, so we also see a decline in parental involvement in mate selection and, usually, a fall in the age of marriage and a rise in marital instability.

These changes are further facilitated by the parallel changes in the roles of children in the family, which involve both a drastic reduction in the power of parents over their children and in their 'interests' in their children's future welfare. . . .

Viewed in a historical perspective, therefore, there is in the contemporary capitalist world a marked lack of structural support for familial bonds. In addition, demographic changes have increased the emphasis on intrinsic functions of marriage through the reduction in the period of the family life cycle which is devoted to the bearing and rearing of small children. Marriage at a younger age and an increase in life expectancy among adults have combined roughly to double the average duration of marriages unbroken by social dissolution; the median duration of such marriages is rapidly appoaching fifty years. At the same time, the fall in family size and the concentration of childbirth into the earlier years of marriage has led for the first time to a situation where the majority of the life span of marriages does not involve the bearing of and caring for, small children; far from being a brief interval in old age, the 'empty nest' situation, with all its attendant problems of role reallocation, is fast coming to comprise a majority of the marital cycle. Increased leisure has only come to extend still further the time and the energy available for interpersonal relationships between spouses and thus, by inference at least, to make more problematical a lack of success in them. . . .

Equally importantly, the other main prop to traditional family morality — close community supervision — has also been undermined and, indeed, in a comparative perspective, family behaviour has become the most private and personal of all areas of behaviour, almost totally free from external supervision and control.

Anderson concludes his review:

The study of the history of the Western family shows quite clearly that we cannot go back to a strict conformity to the family morality that we have inherited from the past without also — which is clearly impossible — reverting to the economic and social relations of the past. We are not peasants any more and thus cannot sustain a peasant morality. We have to develop new institutions and new behaviours to cope with new situations.

One aspect of family forms which is often overlooked when discussing the history of the family is the fact that the UK has a history of population migration, and immigration has necessarily brought with it a number of family forms different from traditional patterns. Adrian Wilson summarises this trend for us in *Family Forms* (1985).

Such families put a much greater emphasis on the demands and duties of kinship. Asian families are a clear example of this. Family members feel that they have obligations both to their kin in Britain and also to the rest of their family, who are still resident in the home village. Many Indian families in Britain continue to provide financial support for their relatives in India.

The family structure of many ethnic groups tends to be both hierarchical and patriarchal. Ballard (1982) argues that the basic pattern of the south Asian family consists of a man, his sons and grandsons, together with their wives and unmarried daughters. This family has been transferred into a British setting. The man is clearly the head of the household, controlling the family finances, and negotiating the major family decisions. R. Oakley (1982) suggests that a similar pattern is true for Greek Cypriot families living in London. The Cypriot husband is an authoritarian figures, the source of family discipline. It is the husband who handles all the external dealings of the family with the wider society. Conjugal roles are essentially segregated, although complementary to each other.

The male-dominated nature of family life creates a very different experience for women within the ethnic minorities. In the early years of immigration, many women found themselves cut off from outside society. Social and language barriers kept them trapped in the domestic setting. Some Asian families created a state of purdah for their womenfolk, setting them apart from society at large. Oakley contrasts the social isolation of Cypriot women in England with the physical openness and outdoor character of life in Cyprus.

The reason for the attempt by ethnic minorities to control the lives of women lies in the need to maintain family honour. It is important that family members do not bring shame on the family name. Every member should be seen to behave properly. Inevitably, life in a British environment has thrown up major challenges to this traditional view of family life.

Serious problems have been created with the second generation, the immigrants' children, who were born and have been brought up in the United Kingdom. School teaches these children to want more independence. The socializing influence of the family stresses loyalty and obedience. It must also be remembered that many of the first-generation immigrants grew up in societies where there was no such thing as adolescence or youth culture, so conflict is inevitable when their children act like British teenagers. However, ethnic minority families have proved to be more flexible than was at first expected. An example of this flexibility can be seen in the way that the traditional arranged marriage is being modified to allow young people some say in the process.

West Indian families in Britain present a further distinct family pattern that reflects their culture of origin. The colonial system that was based on slavery weakened the bonds between men and women. The lack of a stable employment system left the man unable to support a family by his own efforts. The mother-child relationship became the central structure of the family.

Driver (1982) and Barrow (1982) use studies of family structures in the West Indies to suggest three models of family life. The first type is the conventional nuclear family household. Such a family form was most typical of the respectable and more affluent section of the community. The second type was a common-law household, where a man and a woman lived together with their children, but without a formal marriage. Third, there was the female-dominated household, where women had to care for their children and provide an income, without the presence of a man. Studies conducted in the West Indies suggested that each type accounted for about a third of all households in the West Indies.

Driver suggests that these family forms have been transplanted into the British West Indian community. He suggests that there are two types of black family structure in Britain. There is the nuclear family, where both partners share the full range of domestic roles. But there is also the mother-centred family. Driver says this is again associated with the lack of stable employment for men. The black mother is left to bring up the children, run the home, and provide an income. She must do this in England without the range of support that she could have obtained from female relatives in the West Indies. This kind of family might even be growing in Britain, providing a clear contrast to both Asian and traditional English family patterns.

It is hard to predict how ethnic minority families will develop with the third and subsequent generations. The size of minority families is dropping rapidly. Young couples seem to be more sceptical about the need to maintain such a wide family network. But the young Asians, Chinese, and Cypriots are well aware of their different cultural heritages. For many of these young people, their family life will be a compromise between the two cultures they inhabit.

Indian News (November 1990) reported that a Crown Court judge in Nottingham sentenced a 57 year old Muslim father to two years' imprisonment for kidnapping his own step-daughter to prevent her from marrying a Christian. In sentencing the defendant, the judge said: 'In a Muslim country, Christians are rightly expected to obey Muslim laws, and so it should be the other way round in this country.' The step-daughter pleaded with the judge not to send her step-father to prison as the marriage had in fact gone ahead and the family now accepted the marriage.

Questions

(i) Does a possibly false view of family history in this country prevent us from accepting that families fall today and have always fallen into different types?
(ii) Do you believe that the judge in this case was entitled to say that Christians in Muslim countries should be expected to obey Muslim laws?
(iii) What was the justification for a two year custodial sentence in this case?

3 The family as a social group

The historical strands — the nuclear unit, the rise of domesticity, the economic inter-relationship — are viewed, as we have seen, in different ways by the scholars who have looked at the evidence. Similarly, the modern family has been described by sociologists in many variations. Two extremes are Fletcher (1966) and Oakley (1974). The following extract is from Ronald Fletcher's *The Family and Marriage in Britain* (1966) and emphasises the sense of 'belonging' which is, for him, so important:

The family is, in fact, a community in itself: a small, relatively permanent group of people, related to each other in the most intimate way, bound together by the most personal aspects of life; who experience amongst themselves the whole range of human emotions; who have to strive continually to resolve those claims and counter-claims which stem from mutual but often conflicting needs; who experience continual responsibilities and obligations towards each other; who experience the sense of 'belonging' to each other in the most intimately felt sense of that word. The members of a family share the same name, the same collective reputation, the same home, the same intricate, peculiar tradition of their own making, the same neighbourhood. They share the same sources of pleasure, the same joys, the same sources of profound conflict. The same vagaries of fortune are encountered and overcome together. Degrees of agreement and degrees of violent disagreement are worked out amongst them. The same losses and the same griefs are shared. Hence the family is that group within which the most fundamental appreciation of human qualities and values takes place — 'for better for worse': the qualities of truth and honesty, of falsehood and deceit; of kindliness and sympathy, of indifference and cruelty; of cooperation and forbearance, of egotism and antagonism; of tolerance, justice, and impartiality, of bias, dogmatism, and obstinacy; of generous concern for the freedom and fulfilment of others, of the mean desire to dominate — whether in overt bullying or in psychologically more subtle ways. All those values, and all those discriminations and assessments of value, which are of the most fundamental importance for the formation of adult character are first experienced and exercised by children in the context of the family. Furthermore, these qualities are not 'taught' or 'learned' in any straightforward or altogether rational way; they are actually embodied in people and their behaviour.

Later, Fletcher offers a definition of the contemporary British family summarising the points developed in the book. He asserts that the modern British family is:

1. contracted or founded at an early age, and therefore of long duration,
2. consciously planned,
3. small in size,
4. to a great extent separately housed, and in an improved material environment,
5. economically self-responsible, self-providing, and therefore (*a*) relatively independent of wider kindred, and (*b*) living at a 'distance' from wider kindred, sometimes geographically, but also in terms of a diminished degree of close and intimate social life shared with them,
6. entered into and maintained on a completely voluntary basis by partners of equal status, and therefore entailing a marital relationship based upon mutuality of consideration,

7. democratically managed, in that husband and wife (and frequently children) discuss family affairs together when decisions have to be taken, and

8. centrally concerned with the care and upbringing of children — to such an extent that it is frequently called 'child-centred'.

Finally, we might add:

9. that the importance of the modern family is widely recognized by government and by the whole range of social services, and is therefore aided in achieving health and stability by a wide range of public provisions.

When these points are considered, there can surely be little doubt that the characteristics of the family in contemporary Britain manifest considerable moral improvements upon the family types of the past. How, then, does it come about that the modern family is said to be in a condition of 'instability'? Why is it said that the family is 'declining in importance as a social institution'? On what grounds can it be argued that there is evidence of 'moral decline'?

Questions

(i) Do you agree with each of these nine points?

(ii) Is Fletcher correct in saying that the contemporary British family manifests a considerable 'moral improvement'?

(iii) What answers can you give to Fletcher's final three questions? (Remember that the book was published in 1966.)

Fletcher writes with passion in defence of the family in *The Shaking of the Foundations* (1988)

I can only confess that the more I reconsider these relatively recent condemnations of the family, the more absurd, the more lacking in any serious sense of perspective, they seem to be. If a grave and restless disorder, a profound disorientation, a decline of conviction in beliefs, principles and morality, assailed — and continues to assail — our society, it does not seem to me at all surprising. During a time in which every secure foundation of every society in the world has been thrown into a vast vortex of war and social change, when the entire order of civilized thought in the world is undergoing a process of rapid transformation the outcome of which we cannot yet foresee, how can it be even remotely sensible to make *the family* the butt of our criticisms? The very highest levels of supposed authority — in international affairs, in other societies, and in our own society — rock with uncertainty, indecision, and unprincipled manipulation. The doctrines of all religions, including those of our own national church, are riddled with doubts, cleavages, illogicalities, and even downright simple-mindedness. The realities of public corruption are only occasionally and partially glimpsed (though now with increasing frequency), but none the less very revealingly so, in the pages of the press and the procedures of the courts. And yet, for some curious reason, it is *the family* which is the scapegoat. It is *'the breakdown of the family'* within the supposed *'laxities of the Welfare State'* — or it is *'the reactionary strength of the family'* and the pernicious influences of *'the intensity of its too-private world'* — which is blamed for our bad behaviour! But surely, if anything seems true in all this, it is that the family in society, and all its members, have been the *victims* of society's disasters, not their *causes*?

Ann Oakley in her book *Housewife* (1974) presents a very different picture:

A greater equality may characterize the relationships between husband and wife in some areas — legal rights for instance — but mother and father roles, husband and wife roles, remain distinct, and — conspicuous of all — the allocation to women of the housewife role endures. Apparent changes, such as the increasing likelihood of a wife's employment, may not be changes at all, and we should not be taken in by surface appearances, nor by that pseudo-egalitarian phrase the 'dual-career' marriage. . . .

The capacity of the housewife's employment to affect fundamentally and permanently the structure of marital roles is undermined by the ideology of non-interchangeability, of role-segregation, subscribed to by the married couple — the ideology of gender differentiation which is basic to marriage as an institution.

Question

Ann Oakley is talking about marriage as an institution; and what is more, it is the nuclear arrangement which is the object of her scorn. But would an extended family household make the structure of personal relationships and sex differentiation any different?

4   The definition of marriage

We turn our attention to the definition of the conjugal unit or marriage. This is not as easy to describe as may at first appear. Harris (1979) expressed the problem in the following way: 'The inhabitants of Europe and America have an idea which they call marriage. People in other cultures have other ideas which are similar to, but not the same as, our ideas. Traditionally the argument has been about how dissimilar the ideas have to get to force us to stop describing their ideas as "marriage".' Leach (1955) argues that no definition can be found which applies to all institutions which ethnographers and anthropologists commonly refer to as marriage. Therefore he submits for consideration a definition based on a 'bundle of rights'. At least one part of the bundle must be present before the term 'marriage' can be used. The list, which according to Leach is not closed, is as follows:

A. To establish the legal father of a woman's children.
B. To establish a legal mother of a man's children.
C. To give the husband a monopoly in the wife's sexuality.
D. To give the wife a monopoly in the husband's sexuality.
E. To give the husband partial or monopolistic rights to the wife's domestic and other labor services.
F. To give the wife partial or monopolistic rights to the husband's labor services.
G. To give the husband partial or total rights over property belonging or potentially accruing to the wife.
H. To give the wife partial or total rights over property belonging or potentially accruing to the husband.
I. To establish a joint fund of property – a partnership – for the benefit of the children of the marriage.
J. To establish a socially significant 'relationship of affinity' between the husband and his wife's brothers.

In contrast with Leach, there are other scholars, of whom E. Kathleen Gough, in *The Nayars and the Definition of Marriage* (1959), is representative, who argue that 'the status of children born to various types of union (is) critical for decisions as to which of these unions constitute marriage.' As a tentative definition that would have cross-cultural validity, and will fit the unusual cases such as that of the Nayar,[2] Gough suggests: 'Marriage is a relationship established between a woman and one or more other persons which provides that a child born to the woman under circumstances not

---

2. In a period before the British took control of India. Nayar women customarily had a small but not a fixed number of husbands. When a woman became pregnant, it was essential for one of those men to acknowledge probable paternity. The genitor, however, had no economic, social, legal or ritual rights in nor obligations to his children once he had paid the fees of their births. Their guardianship, care and discipline were entirely the concern of their matrilineal kinsfolk.

prohibited by the rules of the relationship, is accorded full birth-status rights common to normal members of his society or social stratum.'

A slightly different way of looking at the problem is suggested by Harris (1979). He says that the major question is to consider *tasks*. The only significant question is the following: 'How do societies arrange for the orderly procreation and rearing of future generations and the transmission of material and cultural possessions?' Harris emphasises child rearing. We shall see later in Chapter 11, below, how judges in English courts have been preoccupied by similar considerations.

If nothing else, then, marriage is about the licence to beget children. There are therefore three questions which assume importance in legal terms. First, who is entitled to marry so as to produce these children? Second, when if at all, should society step in to prevent a marriage from being solemnised or pronounce a decree of nullity? Third, how is such a relationship formalised? We deal with these matters in turn.

5 Who can marry?

In *Corbett v Corbett (otherwise Ashley)* [1971] P 83, [1970] 2 All ER 33, Ormrod J said: 'on the other hand, sex is clearly an essential determinant of the relationship called marriage, because it is and always has been recognised as the union of man and woman. It is the institution on which the family is built, and of which the capacity for natural heterosexual intercourse is an essential element'. Ormrod J defined a person's sex according to his birth, regardless of any sex change operation.

In *Rees v UK* [1987] Fam Law 157, the applicant, who was born with all the physical and biological characteristics of the female sex, applied to the European Court of Human Rights contending that the UK Government was in breach of his right to respect for his private life under article 8 (see p. 407, below) and article 12 of the European Convention for the Protection of Human Rights and Fundamental Freedoms, in that the Registrar General refused to amend the birth certificate notwithstanding surgical sexual conversion under the National Health Service. Article 12 provides that 'Men and women of marriageable age have the right to marry and to found a family, according to the national laws governing the exercise of this right'. The Court held that there was no violation of article 12 because that provision referred to the traditional marriage between persons of opposite biological sex.

Rees v UK was endorsed by the European Court of Human Rights in *Cossey v UK* (1990) which was a male to female transsexual case. Having determined that there was no violation of article 8, the majority turned to article 12:

44. Miss Cossey placed considerable reliance, as did the Delegate of the Commission, on the fact that she could not marry at all: as a woman, she could not realistically marry another woman and English law prevented her from marrying a man.

In the latter connection, Miss Cossey accepted that Article 12 referred to marriage between a man and a woman and she did not dispute that she had not acquired all the biological characteristics of a woman. She challenged, however, the adoption in English law of exclusively biological criteria for determining a person's sex for the purposes of marriage and the Court's endorsement of that situation in the *Rees* judgment, despite the absence from Article 12 of any indication of the criteria to be applied for this purpose. In her submission, there was no good reason for not allowing her to marry a man.

45. As to the applicant's inability to marry a woman, this does not stem from any legal impediment and in this respect it cannot be said that the right to marry has been impaired as a consequence of the provisions of domestic law.

As to her inability to marry a man, the criteria adopted by English law are in this respect in conformity with the concept of marriage to which the right guaranteed by Article 12 refers.

46. Although some Contracting States would now regard as valid a marriage between a person in Miss Cossey's situation and a man, the developments which have occurred to date cannot be said to evidence any general abandonment of the traditional concept of marriage. In these circumstances, the Court does not consider that it is open to it to take a new approach to the interpretation of Article 12 on the point at issue. It finds, furthermore, that attachment to the traditional concept of marriage provides sufficient reason for the continued adoption of biological criteria for determining a person's sex for the purposes of marriage, this being a matter encompassed within the power of the Contracting States to regulate by national law the exercise of the right to marry.

There were however strong dissenting opinions, in particular the joint dissent of Judges Palm, Foignel and Pekkanen:

5. When drafting Article 12 of the Convention the draftsmen probably had in mind the traditional marriage between persons of opposite biological sex as the Court stated in *Rees*. However, transsexualism was not at that time a legal problem, so that it cannot be assumed that the intention was to deny transsexuals the right to marry. Moreover, as we have tried to show above, there have been significant changes in public opinion as regards the full legal recognition of transsexualism. In view of the dynamic interpretation of the Convention followed by the Court, these social and moral developments should also be taken into account in the interpretation of Article 12.

Gender reassignment surgery does not change a person's biological sex. It is impossible for Miss Cossey to bear a child. Yet, in all other respects, both psychological and physical, she is a woman and has lived as such for years.

The fact that a transsexual is unable to procreate cannot, however, be decisive. There are many men and women who cannot have children but, in spite of this, they unquestionably have the right to marry. Ability to procreate is not and cannot be a prerequisite for marriage.

The only argument left against allowing Miss Cossey to marry a man is the fact that biologically she is considered not to be a woman. But neither is she a man, after the medical treatment and surgery. She falls somewhere between the sexes. In this situation a choice must be made and the only humane solution is to respect the objective fact that, after the surgical and medical treatment which Miss Cossey has undergone and which was based on her firm conviction that she is a woman, Miss Cossey is psychologically and physically a member of the female sex and socially accepted as such.

It should also be borne in mind that Miss Cossey has no possibility of marrying unless she is allowed to marry a man as she wishes. It would be impossible, both psychologically and physically, for her to marry a woman. There would certainly also be doubts as to the legality of a marriage of this kind.

6. For these reasons we are of the opinion that in the present case there is a violation of Articles 8 and 12 of the Convention.

Questions

(i) Is it only a matter of time before the European Court of Human Rights changes its mind about transsexuals?

(ii) And what do you think the Court would say about homosexuals having the right to marry?

We turn our attention now to prohibitions based on affinity and consanguinity. The Marriage Acts 1949–86 state that marriages between certain relatives are void.

Schedule 1 to the Marriage Act 1949 (as amended) lists the following prohibitions based on consanguinity:

Male	*Female*
Mother	Father
Adoptive mother or former adoptive mother	Adoptive father or former adoptive father
Daughter	Son
Adoptive daughter or former adoptive daughter	Adoptive son or former adoptive son
Father's mother	Father's father
Mother's mother	Mother's father
Son's daughter	Son's son
Daughter's daughter	Daughter's son
Sister	Brother
Father's sister	Father's brother
Mother's sister	Mother's brother
Brother's daughter	Brother's son
Sister's daughter	Sister's son

The surviving prohibitions based on affinity are laid down in the Marriage (Prohibited Degree of Relationship) Act 1986. Section 1 and Sch. 1 are as follows:

1.—(1) A marriage solemnized after the commencement of this Act between a man and a woman who is the daughter or granddaughter of a former spouse of his (whether the former spouse is living or not) or who is the former spouse of his father or grandfather (whether his father or grandfather is living or not) shall not be void by reason only of that relationship if both the parties have attained the age of twenty-one at the time of the marriage and the younger party has not at any time before attaining the age of eighteen been a child of the family in relation to the other party.

(2) A marriage solemnized after the commencement of this Act between a man and a woman who is the grandmother of a former spouse of his (whether the former spouse is living or not) or is a former spouse of his grandson (whether his grandson is living or not) shall not be void by reason only of that relationship.

(3) A marriage solemnized after the commencement of this Act between a man and a woman who is the mother of a former spouse of his shall not be void by reason only of that relationship if the marriage is solemnized after the death of both that spouse and the father of that spouse and after both the parties to the marriage have attained the age of twenty-one.

(4) A marriage solemnized after the commencement of this Act between a man and a woman who is a former spouse of his son shall not be void by reason only of that relationship if the marriage is solemnized after the death of both his son and the mother of his son and after both the parties to the marriage have attained the age of twenty-one.

(5) In this section 'child of the family' in relation to any person, means a child who has lived in the same household as that person and been treated by that person as a child of his family.

Part II
Degrees of affinity referred to in section 1(2) *and* (3) *of this Act*

Daughter of former wife	Son of former husband
Former wife of father	Former husband of mother
Former wife of father's father	Former husband of father's mother
Former wife of mother's father	Former husband of mother's mother
Daughter of son of former wife	Son of son of former husband
Daughter of daughter of former wife	Son of daughter of former husband

Part III
Degrees of affinity referred to in section 1(4) *and* (5) *of this Act*

Mother of former wife	Father of former husband
Former wife of son	Former husband of daughter

But most people do not marry their kin.

MacFarlane in *Marriage and Love in England 1300–1840* (1986) provides historical background to the move from kinship marriages to what he refers to as 'free-floating' marriages:

. . . We may wonder when and how it originated. Is there any evidence in the period from the fifteenth to the nineteenth century of a transformation from the marriage system based on kinship rules, to the free-floating marriages based on psychology and economics which exist today? In answering the questions concerning the curious link between economics and demography raised by Malthus and Wrigley, we need to pursue this further. A marriage system embedded in kinship is close to biological restraints: marriage for women will very often be at or near puberty. Marriages will not adjust sensitively to economic changes, since they are mainly determined by kinship. Nor will there be space for personal psychological pressures. Likes and dislikes, love and passion, have no formal place where the decision about whom to marry is encoded in the kinship structure. . . .

. . . Essentially one may marry all except members of the nuclear family and all those, including uncles and aunts, nephews and nieces, in the ascending and descending generations. First cousin marriage is now, as it was from 1540, legal, if often disapproved of. At marriage the couple became 'one blood'. Thus a man was forbidden from marrying the same range of wife's kin as of his own blood relatives. For instance, he could not marry his wife's aunt even though she was not a blood relative. The prohibitions continued after the spouse's death. Hence marriage with a deceased wife's sister was forbidden.

In the three centuries before 1540 the prohibitions were wider. By the decision of the Fourth Lateran Council of 1215, impediments of consanguinity and affinity were set at the fourth degree, according to the canonical computation. Thus a person could not marry his own or his wife's third cousin, or any nearer relative. Furthermore, wide rules of spiritual affinity prevented those related by godparenthood from marrying. On the other hand, dispensations were easily available, for a price, from the Church. There was a very limited prohibition in early Anglo-Saxon England, then a widening of the ring of prohibited persons, and then a narrowing again, so that England in 1540 returned to the situation that had prevailed in the seventh century. The change at the Reformation was important, but it was neither unprecedented nor indicative of a shift from 'elementary' to 'complex' structures. Indeed, by allowing all to marry first and second cousins without dispensation, the Reformers, if anything, encouraged a move towards the possibility of an elementary system. It is difficult to see how preferential kin marriages can have been enormously attractive and common when the whole weight of the Church forbade them.

More important in assessing the presence of kinship pressures are the positive rules. To prevent estates going out of the family, or to consolidate social, political and other ties, most societies are organized so that strong pressures are put on the individual stating which kin he should marry. To find a person standing in the right kinship relationship is one of the central tasks of an elaborate kinship vocabulary, as well as of the 'marriage brokers' who exist in many societies.

Questions

(i) What do you see as the advantages of a preferential kin system?

(ii) The criminal law prohibits only sexual intercourse between direct ascendants and descendants and brothers and sisters (Sexual Offences Act 1956, ss. 10 and 11): how would you account for the difference?

(iii) Why should both parties to a marriage involving a step relationship have to be over 21 at the time of the marriage?

(iv) 'Child of the family' is defined as a child who has lived in the same household as that person and been treated by that person as a child of his family. Do you think that this restriction serves any useful purpose, and, if so, what purpose? Would it be possible for the child in *M v M* (see p. 5, above) to marry a former wife of his father?

(v) Do you agree that a marriage should only be possible between a man and his mother-in-law after the death of both the former wife and the father of the former wife? The father of the former wife may not necessarily have been married to the mother. Should this make a difference?

(vi) Do you believe that the changes which have been made to the bars based on affinity undermine the integrity of family life?

(vii) What justification is there for retaining any bars based on consanguinity or affinity?

The Law Commission, in their Report on *Nullity of Marriage* (1970), saw no need to change the law relating to consanguinity:

52 (a) In so far as the question is biological, the answer depends on an evaluation of scientific evidence. The marriage of uncle and niece, or nephew and aunt is permitted in some countries and by some religions and it may well be that there is no such biological objection to these marriages as to justify legal prohibition. They may well be no more objectionable biologically than the marriage of a man with his grandparent's sister or of a woman with her grandparent's brother, which is not within the prohibited degrees.

(b) Nevertheless, the question raises social and moral problems, the answer to which must depend on public opinion. Would public opinion tolerate or object to marriages between uncle and niece or nephew and aunt and, if it objects to such unions, does it wish to extend the prohibition to great-uncle and great-niece and great-nephew and great-aunt? Many people would no doubt instinctively hold the view that such marriages are unnatural and wrong, just as they would view with revulsion a marriage between brother and sister, even if there were no biological reasons against such a union. There are some matters of conviction on which men hold strong feelings of right and wrong though they cannot place their fingers on any particular reason for this conviction. It may be that such unions would be generally regarded as just as wrong as a marriage between adopter and adopted child — a union which is clearly considered objectionable although there cannot be any biological ground for this.

Marriages which would be void under the present English law do take place elsewhere:

Cheni v Cheni
[1965] P 85, [1962] 3 All ER 873, [1963] 2 WLR 17, High Court, Family Division

The parties, who were uncle and niece, were married in Cairo in 1924 in accordance with Jewish rites. The intention of both was to enter into a monogamous union. According to expert evidence the marriage was valid by Jewish and Egyptian law and although potentially polygamous at its inception became irrevocably monogamous on the birth of a child of the marriage in 1926. The parties continued to live in Egypt until 1957 when they settled in England where they became domiciled. In 1961 the wife filed a petition praying that the marriage be declared null and void on the ground of consanguinity or, in the alternative, that the marriage be dissolved on the ground of the husband's cruelty. On the issue of nullity:

Sir Jocelyn Simon P: . . . Dr Gaon[3] told me that a marriage between uncle and niece is in accordance with general Jewish law. This was spelt out further by Professor James, Professor of the History of Religions at London University, and formerly a member of the Archbishop's Commission on Kindred and Affinity, 1937. In the Levitical Code marriage between aunt and nephew was prohibited, but not marriage between uncle and niece (see The Book of Leviticus,

---

3. Dr Gaon, who gave evidence to the Court, was at that time the Chief Rabbi of the Sephardi Jewish Community in the United Kingdom.

Ch. 18, verses 12–14). The distinction reflected the Jewish emphasis on the family as a primary unit of society, the aunt-nephew relationship reversing the natural order of authority, whereas in the uncle-niece relationship there is no confusion of authority. In Christianity up to the schism between the Eastern and Western Catholic Churches marriage was prohibited up to the relationship of first cousins, so that the relationship of uncle and niece, which was closer, invalidated a marriage. After 1064 the Western Church maintained its prohibition of marriages between uncle and niece and first cousins, but the impediment was capable under special circumstances of dispensation by the Pope. The uncle-niece impediment would be dispensed with only to avoid some greater evil, generally of a political nature. This is still much the situation in the Roman Catholic Church: the Revised Codex of 1918 shows that close consanguinous relationship in marriage is discouraged, though dispensable up to the first degree collaterally, i.e., the brother-sister relationship. The Reformation involved a general reaction against the papal system of dispensation. Luther dismissed the whole process and returned to the Levitical Code as the expression of God's will. The uncle-niece relationship is therefore permitted in many Lutheran churches, and the aunt-nephew relationship prohibited; though some Lutheran churches, such as those in this country and the United States, follow, as they are bound to, the law of the land. Calvin, on the other hand, did not accept the Levitical Code literally, but applied it by parity of reasoning. Uncle-niece and aunt-nephew stand in the same degree of blood relationship; the Levitical prohibition of aunt-nephew marriages was therefore applied to uncle-niece marriages. The Anglican communion in this respect followed the Calvinist line.

Mr Stirling accepts that this marriage was valid by the law of the parties' domicile, which is the proper law by which capacity to marry is to be tested. But, he says, there is an exception to this general rule, in that the courts of this country will not recognise the validity of a marriage which, even though valid by its proper law, is incestuous by the general consent of all Christendom, or, as he prefers to put it, by the general consent of civilised nations or by English public policy.

The President rejected Counsel's argument:

. . . The marriage in this case was in my judgment a valid one. I do not consider that a marriage which may be the subject of papal dispensation and will then be acknowledged as valid by all Roman Catholics, which without any such qualification is acceptable to all Lutherans, can reasonably be said to be contrary to the general consent of Christendom; . . . If the general consent of civilised nations were to be the test, I do not think that the matter can be resolved by, so to speak, taking a card-vote of the United Nations and disregarding the views of the many civilised countries by whose laws these marriages are permissible. As Mr Argyle observed, Egypt, where these people lived and where the marriage took place, is itself a civilised country. If domestic public policy were the test, it seems to me that the arguments on behalf of the husband, founded on such inferences as one can draw from the scope of the English criminal law, prevail. Moreover, they weigh with me when I come to apply what I believe to be the true test, namely, whether the marriage is so offensive to the conscience of the English court that it should refuse to recognise and give effect to the proper foreign law. In deciding that question the court will seek to exercise common sense, good manners and a reasonable tolerance. In my view it would be altogether too queasy a judicial conscience which would recoil from a marriage acceptable to many peoples of deep religious convictions,. lofty ethical standards and high civilisation. Nor do I think that I am bound to consider such marriages merely as a generality. On the contrary, I must have regard to this particular marriage, which, valid by the religious law of the parties' common faith and by the municipal law of their common domicile, has stood unquestioned for 35 years. I must bear in mind that I am asked to declare unmarried the parents of a child who is unquestionably legitimate in the eyes of the law: *Re Bischoffsheim, Cassel v Grant* [1948] Ch 79, [1947] 2 All ER 830. In my judgment, injustice would be perpetrated and conscience would be affronted if the English court were not to recognise and give effect to the law of the domicile in this case.

Question

Are there any objections to amending the law still further so as to permit marriages between uncle and niece or aunt and nephew?

6 Age at marriage

W.J. Goode in *World Revolution and Family Patterns* (1963) describes the history of attitudes to the proper age to marry thus:

It seems likely that toward the end of the nineteenth century Western attitudes did alter toward a belief that very young girls should not marry. Prior to the twentieth century, marriages of girls aged 15–17 were not disapproved of providing that the man was sufficiently well-to-do. In the absence of sufficient data my hypothesis is that chronological maturity as a prerequisite for marriage was not an important focus of social attention in the West until about the turn of the century.

Let us consider this point. Prior to the French Revolution, the legal minimum age for marriage in France was 14 years for boys and 12 years for girls. These were also the legal minimum marriage ages accepted under both the older English law and Roman law. In most cases these minimum ages — the assumed ages of puberty for each sex — probably permitted parents to arrange the marriages of their children whenever it seemed suitable. Children of so young an age could not marry independently, and marriage in many Western nations without the consent of parents is even now forbidden to young people under 21 years of age. In the West, there has generally been a substantial difference between the legal minimum age for marriage and the minimum age at which young people might marry *without* parental consent. Since one youngster may be forbidden to marry because of parental refusal, and another of the same age may marry *with* parental consent, it is clear that Western laws concerning minimum ages at marriage were aimed at maintaining the power of the parent, *not* at enforcing a 'right' age at marriage. Over the past generation, a typical legal change has been to narrow the gap between the two age minimums by raising the age at marriage *with* parental consent, or establishing a lower age at marriage without consent.

Since marriage was not thought in the West to be properly based on free courtship until late in the nineteenth century, 'maturity' as measured by years was given no great weight. If a good match could be made for a girl of 15 or 16 years, her age was no barrier, and there were indeed many youthful marriages. Within noble or well-to-do rural families, a young couple could be married precisely because they did *not* have to support themselves or assume the responsibility of a profession.

In contrast to upper-class families, farming families in regions without free land did not ordinarily permit their children to marry until much later, when the parents were ready to relinquish control of the property, or had accumulated sufficient money to afford the marriage. Without land, marriage was not possible. And, of course, servants and apprentices might not marry at all, since their status was viewed as a semi-familial one, and they had no right to introduce a spouse into the family circle. However, a 'proper' age was not the question. Instead, it was whether there was adequate land or income available. Until the end of the nineteenth century the couple had either to wait for land or, if the productive unit was large enough, to become part of a larger kin group, taking part in its economic activities and sharing from the common store. Thus, age in itself was of little importance.

We must therefore conclude that in most parts of the West, until some time in the nineteenth century, marriage came relatively late for the bulk of the population, and the myth that marriages occurred extremely early as we go back in time comes from the fact that the many marriages at very young ages occurred among the most conspicuous classes. . . .

In the contemporary West, however, a 'proper' age (varying from country to country and from class to class — higher in the upper strata) has now come to be accepted, since, under the conjugal family system, a couple must be self-sufficient. The young couple cannot be extremely young, since they have to take care of themselves; on the other hand, they do not have to be very old, because they can be independent.

Here, we encounter an empirical puzzle. It seems likely that in the early period of England's industrialization, the age of marriage would not have changed greatly because, although they did work in the factories, for the most part children were given their jobs through relatives and often were supervised by their own male parents. They were not independent workers, and the traditions of the times dictated that they should give their pay to their parents. It was only when they obtained jobs on their own, without the intervention of parents or relatives, that they could make their own decision about choice of spouse or age at which to marry. However, the age at marriage did not change substantially until still later, i.e., in this century, and now seems to be tied at least in part to the independent participation of *females* in the labor force. The job becomes the young girl's 'dowry' in the unskilled and semiskilled white- and blue-collar strata, where, in fact, the highest proportion of women are to be found in the labor force.

The author continues by giving the figures of the median age at marriage for men and women (i.e. the age below which 50% of persons married in any one year):

Marriage age for spinsters and bachelors and number of minors married per thousand marriages in England and Wales, 1876–1956

Year	Median age of marrying		Number of minors (under 21 years of age) per thousand marriages	
	M	F	M	F
1881–1885	25.9	24.4	73.0	215.0
1891–1895	26.6	25.0	56.2	182.6
1901–1905	26.9	25.4	48.3	153.1
1911–1915	27.5	25.8	39.2	136.6
1921–1925	27.5	25.6	48.2	149.2
1931–1935	27.4	25.5		
1941–1945	26.8	24.6	33.8	163.8
1951–1955	26.6	24.2	65.0	271.1
1956	26.2	23.7		

The median age at marriage increased during the 1970s and 1980s following a drop in the 1960s. We give below a table taken from *Population Trends* (Winter 1990).

Questions

(i) (*a*) Why do you think the median age dropped in the 1950s and 1960s? (*b*) Why do you think it increased in the 1970s and 1980s? (*c*) What do you think will happen in the 1990s?

(ii) Bearing in mind the association between the age at marriage and divorce (page 229, below), should there be any changes in the law?

(iii) Should the minimum age of marriage be the same as the age of consent to sexual intercourse?

Table H   Marriages by previous marital status and median age of marriage (England and Wales)

	Total number of marriages	Percentage of marriages which were:			Median age at marriage (years)					
		First for both partners	First for one partner	Second or later for both partners	Bachelors	Divorced men	Widowers	Spinsters	Divorced women	Widows
1971	405	79	12	8	23.3	37.0	60.1	21.4	33.0	54.2
1977	357	67	18	15	23.8	35.7	60.7	21.5	32.6	55.0
1980	370	65	19	16	24.0	35.8	60.1	21.8	33.1	55.3
1981	352	65	19	16	24.1	35.9	60.6	22.0	33.4	55.3
1982	342	64	19	16	24.3	36.3	61.0	22.1	33.8	55.7
1983	344	64	19	17	24.5	36.6	61.3	22.3	34.0	56.0
1984	349	64	19	16	24.7	37.0	61.5	22.6	34.3	55.6
1985	346	64	19	16	24.9	37.3	61.2	22.8	34.4	55.2
1986	348	63	20	17	25.1	37.7	61.7	23.1	34.6	55.5
1987	352	64	20	16	25.3	37.8	61.7	23.3	34.7	55.0
1988	348	63	20	17	25.6	38.4	61.9	23.6	35.1	55.3
1989	347	63	20	17	26.3	39.2	62.5	24.4	35.9	56.1

7 Void and voidable marriages

Grounds on which a marriage is voidable are as follows:

12. A marriage celebrated after 31st July 1971 shall be voidable on the following grounds only, that is to say —

   (*a*) that the marriage has not been consummated owing to the incapacity of either party to consummate it;

   (*b*) that the marriage has not been consummated owing to the wilful refusal of the respondent to consummate it;

   (*c*) that either party to the marriage did not validly consent to it, whether in consequence of duress, mistake, unsoundness of mind or otherwise;

   (*d*) that at the time of the marriage either party, though capable of giving a valid consent, was suffering (whether continuously or intermittently) from mental disorder within the meaning of the [Mental Health Act 1983] of such a kind or to such an extent as to be unfitted for marriage;

   (*e*) that at the time of the marriage the respondent was suffering from venereal disease in a communicable form;

   (*f*) that at the time of the marriage the respondent was pregnant by some person other than the petitioner.

Singh v Singh
[1971] P 226, [1971] 2 All ER 828, [1971] 2 WLR 963, 115 Sol Jo 205, CA.

The wife was a 17 year-old girl from an orthodox Sikh family. She went through a ceremony of marriage in a Register Office with a 21 year-old Sikh boy. The marriage was arranged by her parents, and the bride had never seen the bridegroom before the actual ceremony of marriage. The plan was that there would be a religious ceremony of marriage and then the parties would commence living together. When the wife saw the husband at the Register Office, she did not like what she saw, and although she participated in the civil ceremony, she refused to go through with the religious ceremony or to live with the husband. She petitioned for a decree of nullity on two grounds, namely, duress and incapacity to consummate due to her invincible repugnance. Her petition was dismissed. Karminski LJ dealt with the issue of duress and continued:

There is the alternative matter of repugnance. It is true that the wife never submitted herself to the physical embraces of the husband, because after the ceremony of marriage before the registrar it does not appear that she saw him again or went near him. Having taken the view which she did, that she did not want to be married to him, it is understandable that she did not want to have sexual intercourse with him; but that again seems to be a very long way from an invincible repugnance. True, as counsel for the wife argued, invincible repugnance can have a number of forms; and he reminded us of a decided case where the wife refused to undress when she went to bed so that the husband could not have intercourse with her. But here the wife abandoned the idea of her marriage altogether, and there is nothing of a psychiatric or sexual aversion on her part which is in any way established. In my view that ground of nullity fails completely.
Appeal dismissed.

Hirani v Hirani
(1982) 4 FLR 232, CA.

The wife was 19 and she was living with her parents. The family is Hindu. The girl became friendly with a young Indian Muslim, a Mr Husain. When the parents discovered this relationship, they immediately made arrangements for her to marry a Mr Hirani, who like them was a Hindu of the same caste and linguistic background. She had never seen this man nor had her parents. The Judge recalled the pressure which was put on her by her parents to marry in this way: 'You want to marry somebody who is strictly against our religion; he is a Muslim, you are a Hindu. You had better marry somebody we want you to — otherwise pick up your belongings and go.' She married him, lived with him for six weeks and then left her husband and went to Mr Husain's house. Her petition for a decree of nullity on the ground of duress was dismissed. On appeal:

Ormrod LJ: The crucial question in these cases . . . is whether the threats, pressure or whatever it is is such as to destroy the reality of consent and overbears the will of the individual. It seems to me that this case . . . is a classic case of a young girl, wholly dependent on her parents being forced into a marriage with a man she has never seen in order to prevent her (reasonably from her parents point of view) continuing in an association with a Muslim which they would regard with abhorrence. But it is as clear a case as one could want of the overbearing of the will of the petitioner and thus invalidating or vitiating her consent.
Appeal allowed.

In *MK (otherwise M McC) v F McC* [1982] ILR 277, an Irish case, the petitioner became pregnant. Her parents threatened her with expulsion from the family home unless she married the respondent. For his part, he was told by his mother than he could no longer remain at home. His father stopped speaking to him. The young couple, aged 19 and 21, went through a ceremony of marriage, but after three years' cohabitation they separated. The judge granted the wife a decree of nullity based on duress:

I am satisfied that the will, not merely of one partner but of both husband and wife, was overborne by the compulsion of their respective parents and that they were driven unwillingly into a union which neither of them desired, or gave real consent to, in the true sense of the word, and which was doomed to failure from the outset . . . An unwilling bride and resentful husband were dragged to the altar and went through a ceremony of marriage which neither of them wanted, and without any genuine feelings of attraction or affection which might have led on to a happy union in the course of time.

Questions

(i) Is it necessary to have genuine feelings of attraction or affection for a marriage to be valid in English law? What about arranged marriages?
(ii) Do you think the absence of divorce in Ireland makes a difference in the way judges in that jurisdiction consider nullity petitions? Should it?
(iii) Is there a difference between saying 'I can't' and 'I won't'?
(iv) Does the decision in *Hirani v Hirani* open the floodgates to large numbers of nullity petitions on this ground?
(v) Can you really see the difference between the wife who refuses to undress because of a repugnance to her husband and the wife who refuses to comply with the requirements of contracting a marriage according to her religious beliefs because of a repugnance to the man she married in a civil form? (See *A v J (Nullity Proceedings)* [1989] 1 FLR 110 where it was held that a wife's insistence on the postponement of a religious ceremony because she was 'disappointed by the husband's cool and inconsiderate behaviour to her' amounted to wilful refusal on her part to consummate the marriage.)

(vi) What is the point of keeping alive, even for a short time longer, a marriage such as the one contracted in the *Singh v Singh* litigation?

(vii) It is clear that inability to consummate does not render the marriage void. Should it?

(viii) Why should 'mistake' render a marriage merely voidable rather than void?

(ix) Should English law retain the concept of a voidable marriage in relation to ss. 12(*a*) and 12(*b*) of the Matrimonial Causes Act 1973?

The Law Commission Report on *Nullity of Marriage* (1970) provides the following four reasons for retaining nullity of a voidable marriage:

24 (*a*) It is not true to say that the difference between a nullity decree of a voidable marriage and a decree of divorce is a mere matter of form. It may be that the consequences of the two decrees are substantially similar, but the concepts giving rise to the two decrees are quite different: the decree of nullity recognises the existence of an impediment which prevents the marriage from initially becoming effective, while the decree of divorce records that some cause for terminating the marriage has arisen since the marriage. This distinction may be of little weight to the lawyer, but is a matter of essence in the jurisprudence of the Christian Church.

(*b*) The Church attaches considerable importance to consent as a pre-requisite to marriage. Consent to marriage includes consent to sexual relations and, hence, impotence can be regarded as having the effect of vitiating consent. Likewise, the grounds under section 9(1)(*b*), (*c*) and (*d*) of the Act of 1965 (mental disorder, epilepsy, pregnancy by another or venereal disease) can be considered to fall under the head of conditional consent [see now s. 12(*d*)(*e*)(*f*) Matrimonial Causes Act 1973] and are acceptable to the Church. Except with regard to wilful refusal to consummate, which the Church of England considers should cease to be a ground for nullity and be a ground for divorce, the Church is satisfied with the existing law of nullity. Therefore, so radical a change as is involved in the substitution of a decree of divorce for a decree of nullity in respect of matters which the Church regards as relevant to the formation of marriage and irrelevant to divorce, is likely to be unwelcome to the Church. It is also likely to be resented by people not necessarily belonging to the Church who associate a stigma with divorce and who would therefore prefer to see such matters as impotence and mental disorder, which are illnesses, remain grounds for annulling the marriage rather than causes for dissolving it.

(*c*) It may be that many people do not appreciate the distinction between divorce and nullity. They, presumably, would not oppose turning a nullity of a voidable marriage into a divorce. If, however, such a change is likely to cause offence to a substantial minority, then the proposal cannot be recommended unless some worthwhile advantage is to be gained from the change. The only advantage to be gained would be that one of the present voidable marriages (*i.e.,* one voidable for wilful refusal to consummate), might be thought by some to fit in more 'neatly' among divorces than among nullities.

(*d*) The assimilation of voidable marriages and dissolvable marriages could not be complete so long as we retained the bar on divorce within three years of the marriage. [This has now been changed: see later p. 222.] Such a bar would be wholly inappropriate to nullity cases.

25. We are therefore, opposed to the abolition of the class of voidable marriages and think that it should be retained. But the effect of the decrees of nullity of a voidable marriage should be modified so as to make it clear that the marriage is to be treated in every respect as a valid marriage until it is annulled and as a nullity only from the date when it is annulled.

On wilful refusal, in particular, they said:

(*a*) Wilful refusal to consummate is in most cases the alternative allegation to impotence as it is often uncertain whether the respondent's failure to consummate is due to one cause or the other; the petitioner may not know whether the respondent refuses to consummate the marriage because he is unable to have sexual intercourse or because, though able to have sexual intercourse, he does not want to have it; in such cases the court must draw an inference from the evidence before it and it seems unreal that the relief granted to the petitioner — nullity or divorce — should depend in any given case on the court's view as to which of the two reasons prevented the consummation of the marriage.

(b) Failure to consummate, whether it be because the respondent is unable or because he is unwilling to have sexual intercourse, deprives the marriage of what is normally regarded as one of its essential purposes. Parties would think it strange that the nature of the relief should depend on the court's decision whether non-consummation was due to the respondent's inability or whether it was due to his unwillingness. From the parties' point of view the relevant fact would be that the marriage had never become a complete one. To tell them that, in the eyes of the law, failure to complete it due to one cause results in their marriage being annulled, whereas such failure due to another cause results in their marriage being dissolved, would seem to them to be a strange result.

Questions

(i) What advantages, other than those mentioned by the Law Commission, can you see for retaining the concept of nullity in this context?

(ii) Do you agree with the four arguments referred to in the Law Commission Report generally?

(*Note*: The three year discretionary bar to a divorce petition has now been replaced by a one year absolute bar. See later p. 222.)

(iii) Are the two arguments in relation to wilful refusal sufficient reasons by themselves to justify the retention of the present state of the law?

8 The formalities of marriage

As Lucy Mair explains in *Marriage* (1971):

There are some societies in which it is possible to get married almost without any formalities at all, and some in which a marriage without formality is a permitted alternative for people who cannot afford the formalities or do not attach importance to them. . . .

There is a correlation between the amount of formality and display and the importance of the alliance that is being created. There are also in some societies — but these are different ones — ways of circumventing parental choice and forcing the consent of elders to a marriage agreed on by a young couple.

Informal Marriages
It is possible for a marriage to be created and announced in one breath by the simple fact that a couple are seen to be eating together. This is what happens in the Trobriand Islands in the Pacific, as they were described by Malinowski (in the *Sexual Life of Savages* (1929)) in the first ethnographic account to clothe formal statements of rules with the reality of actual behaviour. Since a marriage is concluded in such a simple way, a couple can marry in defiance of parental opposition. . . .

England is not the Trobriand Islands, although prior to the Council of Trent (1545–1563) all that was necessary to constitute a valid marriage according to the canon law was the free consent of the parties expressed in any way so as to provide evidence that they contemplated a permanent and lawful union. Even after the Council, 'informal' marriages were recognised by the ecclesiastical courts. Lord Hardwicke's Marriage Act of 1753 was designed primarily to prevent these informal and often clandestine marriages from being performed although the reasons for this may not have been entirely altruistic. As K. O'Donovan (1985) states:

The proponents of the new Act were not concerned about popular common law marriage but about the threat to the propertied classes and to patriarchy of clandestine marriage:

> 'How often have we known the heir of a good family seduced, and engaged in a clandestine marriage, perhaps with a common strumpet? How often have we known a rich heiress carried off by a man of low birth, or perhaps by an infamous sharper? What distress some of our best families have been brought into what ruin some of their sons or daughters have been involved in, by such means, every gentleman may from his own knowledge recollect.'

(Parliamentary History of England, vol. 13 (1813) col. 3)

Not all the Members of Parliament were convinced that the legislature had the power to declare null and void a conjugal promise. Robert Nugent pointed out:

> '. . . the most pernicious consequence of this Bill will be, its preventing marriage among the most useful, I will not scruple to say, the best sort of our people. The healthy, the strong, the laborious and the brave, I may justly call so. . . . Shall we for the sake of preventing a few misfortunes to the rich and great amongst us, make any law which will be a bar to the lawful procreation of such sort of men in this country?'

(Ibid. col. 17)

Several speakers suggested that the cost of a licence deterred many of the poor from marrying in church and that those labourers mobile by trade would be prevented from marrying at all. Parental failure to control marriage among the rich might result in 'a great disappointment to the avarice or ambition of the parents'; but now the poor would be prevented from marriage.

The arguments of patriarchy carried the day: 'It is not only the interest but the duty of every parent to take care that his child shall not contract a scandalous or infamous marriage, and if he cannot do this by paternal authority the laws ought to assist him,' said Lord Barrington. 'I cannot suppose that any gentleman who has ever known what it is to be a father, will be against it,' was the view of the Solicitor-General.

A short description of the present English law is given by T.E. James, 'The English Law of Marriage' in *A Century of Family Law* (1957):

From 1753 until 1836 the formalities required for a valid marriage had all to be in accordance with the rites of the Church of England.[4] After 1836 civil marriages were permitted. . . . There have been a large number of statutes modifying and extending the formal requirements; but now the matter is governed by the Marriage Act, 1949, which consolidated existing legislation and modified it to some extent.

Marriage according to the rites of the Church of England can be solemnised in four ways, that is, after due publication of banns,[5] by special licence,[6] by common licence[7] or by the certificate issued by a Superintendent Registrar without a licence. The resulting ceremonies, according to the rites of the Church of England, require the presence of at least two witnesses and of a clergyman in holy orders. . . .

The distinction between the superintendent registrar's certificate with and without a licence lies in the procedure to be followed which affects the time of residence and the display of the notice of marriage prior to the granting of the certificate.

Marriages by virtue of the superintendent registrar's certificate may be solemnised in the appropriate parish church or authorised chapel, if according to the rites of the Church of England; if they are in accordance with other rites, then in a registered building[8] or the office

---

4. Except for Quakers and Jews.
5. The banns must be published on three Sundays preceding the marriage. If the parties reside in the same parish, the banns must be published in the parish church. If they reside in separate parishes, then the banns must be published in both parishes. A clergyman is not obliged to publish banns unless the parties deliver or cause to be delivered seven days' notice in writing with their full names, place of residence and the period during which each has resided there.
6. These are special dispensations granted by the Archbishop of Canterbury enabling marriages to be solemnised according to the rites of the Church of England at any convenient time or place.
7. The common licence is issued under the authority of the bishop of the diocese. It can be granted only for the marriage in a church or chapel of an ecclesiastical district in which one of the parties has had his usual place of residence for 15 days immediately before the grant of the licence, or a parish church or chapel which is the usual place of worship of one or both of the parties.
8. This is defined as a 'separate building of public religious worship.'

of the Superintendent Registrar, or according to the usages of the Society of Friends or of the Jews.

As a result of the Marriage (Registrar General's Licence) Act 1970, there is power for the civil authorities to authorise a marriage to be solemnised at any convenient time or place. The Registrar General has to be satisfied, inter alia, that one of the persons to be married is seriously ill and is not expected to recover. In addition, the Marriage Act 1983 enables a marriage to be solemnised on the authority of a Superintendent Registrar's Certificate of a person who is housebound or is a detained person at a place where that person usually resides.

The Law Commission's Report on *Solemnisation of Marriage* (1973) presents a powerful case for uniform civil preliminaries:

The need for compulsory civil preliminaries
14. We have said that the primary objectives of preliminaries are to ensure that 'there should be proper opportunity for the investigation of capacity (and, in the case of minors, parental consent) before the marriage, and that the investigation should be carried out, uniformly for parties to all marriages, by persons trained to perform this function,' and that 'there should be proper opportunity for those who may know of a lawful impediment to a marriage to declare it'. In fact it is difficult to imagine a system less calculated to achieve these objectives. It is not uniform. It does not ensure that there is always a proper opportunity for investigation or that the investigation is carried out by those who have been trained for that role. Nor does it ensure that those whose consents are required or who may know of impediments have an adequate opportunity of stopping the marriage. These strictures are least justified in the case of marriages after a superintendent registrar's certificate. There, at any rate, there is a three-week waiting period, an opportunity of investigation by trained personnel, and some information on which to base an investigation and a right to demand some further evidence. But, even there, there is no method whereby those who wish to object can be sure of doing so effectively. Potential objectors may in practice have no idea where the couple propose to marry. It is impracticable to search every marriage notice book in the country; and a search will be ineffective if the couple choose to marry in Church after ecclesiastical preliminaries. Nor will there be time to make searches if the couple have paid a little extra in order to cut down the waiting period from 21 days to one day. The outstanding absurdity of the present position is, perhaps, that the payment of an extra fee enables the major safeguard of a waiting period to be by-passed.
15. Although in the case of banns there is generally an equally long waiting period it is a less effective safeguard. . . . there is no legal requirement that the parties shall make any declaration about capacity, nor is there any legal duty upon the person to whom application is made for the publication of banns (who is not necessarily the incumbent himself) to satisfy himself on these matters although many clergymen do so. The historical justification for banns is, of course, that their publication will give adequate advance public notice of the couple's intention to marry which will enable anyone knowing of an impediment to come forward. In social conditions which prevailed in this country before the present century this may have been sound. To-day, with the growth and increased mobility of the population and the increase in urban living, it clearly is not. Unless the banns happen to be published in a church regularly attended by the parties and their friends and relations the chances of any impropriety coming to light are remote.
16. In our view, it is impossible adequately to reform the present system unless uniform civil preliminaries are made compulsory in the case of all marriages and unless the civil preliminaries are themselves reformed. Only then will it be possible to ensure that there is adequate investigation and to provide an effective system of raising objections. This is far from being a novel or revolutionary suggestion. When the Marriage Bill was introduced in 1836 it in fact provided for civil preliminaries to all marriages. The clauses which required this in the case of Church of England marriages were removed during the course of the Bill's passage in order to hasten the enactment of the Bill's major reforms. But the Government of the day then expressed the view that it would be necessary on a future occasion to carry the whole of the original plan into effect. Such preliminary enquiries as we have made suggest that the Church of England would not now oppose this rationalisation. It will not, of course, prevent the Church requiring publication of banns as an ecclesiastical preliminary to a Church wedding. All that we are proposing is that

the publication of banns should cease to be a requirement of the civil law. This could, if desired by the Church, be coupled with the removal of the present obligation on incumbents to marry any of their parishioners (even though they have never set foot in the Church before), affording them the same freedom as ministers of the Roman Catholic and Free Churches to decide whether or not they will perform a particular marriage. Marriage by common licence would necessarily disappear. We would see no objection to the retention of the Archbishop's special licence but this would not be essential if the legislation were amended so that the Registrar General's licence could be used as a preliminary to a marriage according to the rites of the Church of England.

Questions

(i) Why do you think that these recommendations have not been the subject of any legislation? Were the Law Commission correct in their view that the Church authorities would not oppose universal preliminaries? (There is certainly some opinion in the Church, referred to in the Report, which feels that there would be a reduction of 'pastoral opportunities' and that 'universal civil preliminaries might lead to the eventual introduction of a compulsory civil ceremony'.)
(ii) The *Efficiency Scrutiny of the Registration Service* (1985) considered that universal civil preliminaries would assist the efficiency of the Registration Service. It made a number of detailed comments on the present non-Church of England procedures primarily designed to cut costs and increase choice, for example that 'authorised persons' (who solemnise and register marriages) be registered without reference to a building, that there be no limitation on the register office a couple can choose to be married in, that the marriage notice book be discontinued and that marriage notices no longer be displayed on public notice boards. In keeping with the rationale for the scrutiny, the Report recommends improvements in the Register Office 'ambiance'.

'46.2. The normal wedding room could be provided at the standard fee, but a local historic house owned by the Council might be available for an extra fee . . .'

Are you in favour of this last proposal? (The Government Green Paper *Registration: A Modern Service* (1989) also makes a large number of recommendations; none of them, however, providing a major structural change.)
(iii) There are two other models different from the one which exists at present — whether it be modified or not by the Law Commission recommendations. One model would be to have universal civil procedures followed by a ceremony of marriage anywhere. Marriages would not be confined to Churches, places of public religious worship, or register offices. Another model, moving the other way, would be to impose compulsory civil ceremonies of marriage, which could be followed by religious blessings if the parties so desired. Do you favour either of these reforms? Why shouldn't people be able to marry wherever they like? (See A. Bradney, *How Not to Marry People* [1989] Fam Law 408 for a critique of the Green Paper *Registration: A Modern Service*.)

Mary Ann Glendon (1977) distinguishes compulsory pre-marital procedures from compulsory ceremonies necessary for the actual creation of a contract of marriage. As to the first, she states: 'the preliminaries required by modern States before a marriage can take place are revealing as indications of the degree to which the State is actively involved in regulation of marriage formation, as opposed to contenting itself with the promulgation of rules which describe ideal behaviour in the area but which have no real sanction.'

In commenting on the English law of marriage preliminaries, Glendon states that: 'the apparent complexity of the system. . . . masks the fact that the system as a whole exercises little control over the formation of marriage and that the English State takes little advantage of the occasion of marriage to promote any particular social policies.'

Question

What social policies do you think that the State should promote? In particular do you think that the State should impose longer waiting periods, greater publicity, compulsory counselling, compulsory medical tests (for instance for HIV antibodies), or evidence of financial or residential security? Or are all these impositions contrary to the basic freedom to marry?

CHAPTER 2

The legal structure of marriage

Blackstone's *Commentaries on the Laws of England* (1765):

. . . . By marriage, the husband and wife are one person in law: that is, the very being or legal existence of the woman is suspended during the marriage, or at least is incorporated and consolidated into that of the husband: under whose wing, protection, and *cover*, she performs every thing; and is therefore called in our law-french a *feme-covert, foemina viro co-operta*; is said to be *covert-baron*, or under the protection and influence of her husband, her *baron*, or lord; and her condition during her marriage is called her *coverture*. Upon this principle, of a union of person in husband and wife, depend almost all the legal rights, duties and disabilities, that either of them acquire by the marriage. . . .

William Cobbett, *Advice to Young Men and (incidentally) to Young Women* (1837) [quoted in A. MacFarlane, *Marriage and Love in England 1300*–1840 (1986)]

[She] makes a surrender, an absolute surrender, of her liberty, for the joint lives of the parties: she gives the husband the absolute right of causing her to live in what place, and in what manner and what society, he pleases; she gives him the power to take from her, and to use, for his own purposes, all her goods, unless reserved by some legal instrument; and, above all, she surrenders to him her *person*.

1 The common law

In this chapter, we discuss the legal rights and duties which accrue on marriage. As we can see from the quotations above, the common law 'incorporated and consolidated' the wife's legal existence into that of her husband. In *A Century of Family Law* (1957), Ronald Graveson sketched the legal position at common law in his introductory essay, 'The Background of the Century':

The English family in the years following Waterloo differed in many ways from the family of today. The husband was in a real sense the authoritarian head of the family, with very extensive powers over both person and property of his wife and children. But his right to inflict personal chastisement on his wife had greatly declined in importance since Blackstone had described it half a century before as one which the lower orders took seriously and cherished dearly. On marriage husband and wife became for many purposes one person in law, a doctrine of common law of great antiquity. In the words of a late nineteenth-century lawyer, 'The Creator took from Adam a rib and made it Eve; the common law of England endeavoured to reverse the process, to replace the rib and to remerge the personalities.' [de Montmorency (1897)] On marriage all the wife's personal chattels became the absolute property of the husband, while the husband could dispose of the wife's leasehold property during his life and enjoyed for his own benefit her freehold estate during her life. Subject to the institution by the Court of Chancery of what was known as the wife's separate estate in equity, the married woman, both physically and economically, was very much in the position of a chattel of her husband. But her position was not completely black. The doctrine of the legal identity of husband and wife was never applied to its extreme limit. In the words of de Montmorency, 'The English judges were too reasonable to be logical, if they could possibly help it.'

In criminal law a presumption existed that a wife who committed a felony (other than the most serious ones) had been coerced by her husband. Civilly the husband was liable for torts, such as slander, committed by his wife, while rules of evidence prevented husband and wife bearing witness against one another in all but the most exceptional circumstances. Each of these aspects of the nineteenth-century relationship of husband and wife . . . reflect the general position in the early nineteenth century when the relations of society were largely relations of status, that is, a legal position imposed by rules of general law by virtue of persons being in certain relationship with one another, such as husband and wife, parent and child, master and servant. The dominant character of these relationships was one of an often profitable guardianship to the person to whom the law gave control. But the idea of guardianship carried with it one of responsibility for the acts and defaults of what we may call the junior member of the relationship. Thus, while the husband obtained great economic advantages from marriage, he was liable to a great extent, both criminally and civilly, to suffer for the misdeeds of his wife, in a somewhat similar manner to that in which a master was and still is liable for the wrongful acts of his servant committed in the course of his employment.

2 Making decisions — sexual relations

It is clear that so far as the law is concerned, one spouse no longer automatically predominates. However, the movement towards equality and joint responsibility has by no means been a simple process:

R v Clarence
(1888) 22 QBD 23, 58 LJMC 10, 59 LT 780, 53 JP 149, 37 WR 166, 5 TLR 61, 16 Cox CC 511, High Court

Mr Clarence had been convicted of an assault upon his wife occasioning 'actual bodily harm' and of unlawfully and maliciously inflicting upon her 'grievous bodily harm.' It appears that Mr Clarence, to his knowledge, was suffering from a form of gonorrhoea yet he nevertheless had marital intercourse with his wife without informing her of this fact. He infected her, and from this infection, it was claimed that his wife suffered grievous bodily harm. He was convicted, but he appealed successfully to the Queen's Bench Division against conviction. The case was considered by all of the thirteen judges: nine quashed the conviction and four dissented.

Hawkins J: . . . The wife *submits* to her husband's embraces because at the time of marriage she gave him an irrevocable right to her person. The intercourse which takes place between husband and wife after marriage is not by virtue of any special consent on her part, but is mere submission to an obligation imposed upon her by law. Consent is immaterial.

A. L. Smith J: . . . At marriage the wife consents to the husband exercising the marital right. The consent then given is not confined to a husband when sound in body, for I suppose no one would assert that a husband was guilty of an offence because he exercised such right when afflicted with some complaint of which he was then ignorant. Until the consent given at marriage be revoked, how can it be said that the husband in exercising his marital right has assaulted his wife? In the present case at the time the incriminated act was committed, the consent given at marriage stood unrevoked. Then how is it an assault?

The utmost the Crown can say is that the wife would have withdrawn her consent if she had known what her husband knew, or, in other words, that the husband is guilty of a crime, viz., an assault because he did not inform the wife of what he then knew. In my judgment in this case, the consent given at marriage still existing and unrevoked, the prisoner has not assaulted his wife.

This case is not solely of historic interest for it was reported in the Independent, (1 November 1989) that the plaintiff, a Mr Sheppard, sought compensation for personal injury, loss and damage against a Miss Davies. The plaintiff alleged that between October 1986 and January 1987 his then partner 'recklessly and knowingly exposed him to a "poisonous or noxious substance" namely herpes simplex virus'. A number of cases in the US have been brought between sexual partners in similar situations, for example *Kathleen K v Robert B* 150 Cal App 3d 992 (1984, Ca Ct App) and *Long v Adams* 333 SE 2d 852 (1985, Georgia App).

Questions

(i) Would Mrs Clarence have been guilty of the offence charged against Mr Clarence if she had been suffering from venereal disease, or the AIDS virus, undisclosed to her husband?
(ii) Is Mr Sheppard in a stronger or a weaker position in his action against Miss Davies because he is not married to her?

But it is the so-called 'marital immunity' to rape which has caused the greatest controversy. This immunity is allegedly based on the pronouncement of Sir Matthew Hale in *History of the Pleas of the Crown* (vol 1 1736, p. 629) where he said:

But the husband cannot be guilty of a rape committed by himself upon his lawful wife, for by their mutual matrimonial consent and contract the wife hath given up herself in this kind unto her husband, which she cannot retract.

Many American states such as California, New Jersey, Nebraska, Florida and Oregon, have totally abolished the marital exemption. Oregon was the scene of a case which provided newspaper copy for many weeks: *Rideout v Rideout* (Or. Cir Ct. 5 Fam 2164). The following account is taken from issues of the *Oregonian* in December 1978 and January 1979:

Rideout was indicted . . . on a charge of first-degree rape, stemming from an . . . incident in which police say he raped and beat his . . . wife, Greta.
    At the time of the alleged incident, the Rideouts shared their . . . apartment. Since then, they have separated, and Mrs Rideout has filed for divorce.
    In her testimony, . . . Mrs Rideout said she and her husband had been arguing about sex and money the night before the . . . incident.
    During that argument, she said, they discussed the fact that women in Oregon can charge their husbands with rape. Mrs Rideout said she learned of the 1977 statute about three weeks before the incident in her home.
    Mrs Rideout testified that . . . she refused her husband's request to have sexual relations. She said her husband became very angry and told her ' "You are my wife and you should do what I want." '
    Mrs Rideout said she attempted twice to run out of their apartment to escape her husband, but both times he followed her. On the second occasion, when Rideout caught up with her in a park near the apartment, Mrs Rideout said he took her by the arm and escorted her to the apartment, where he again demanded they have sex.
    'He asked me, "Are you going to cooperate with me?" and I said no,'. . . . She testified that

he repeated that question twice, and when she answered negatively, he hit her on the left side of the face.

'I said to John, "Why are you picking on me?" and he said, "It's because I can't stand you, I can't stand you," ' she said. 'So I said, "Why don't you let me go?" And he said, "Because I love you, Greta." '

Mrs Rideout said she attempted to struggle and scream while her husband was forcing her to have intercourse with him. Finally, she testified, she decided to submit to his demands because she feared if he continued to hit her on the face, he would break her jaw.

. . .

Mrs Rideout said that, when the assault was over, she hid in a neighbor's home, where she called the . . . Women's Crisis Center and the . . . police.

. . . Rideout said he hit his wife only after she had hit him a number of times during their . . . altercation. He said he struck her once, using more force than he had intended.

'She hit me first. She slapped me. I grabbed ahold of her arms and she slapped me again,' Rideout testified.

'Then I felt a pain . . . she had kneed me in the groin. I stepped back and then stepped forward and slapped her,' he continued. 'I stopped myself because I realized I was really angry. I had never hit my wife before intentionally. I said, "Greta, I'm sorry, I didn't mean to do it." '

Rideout said he and his wife went into their bathroom to look at the injury to her face. He said she appeared to have some redness around one of her eyes. Rideout said he apologized to his wife, and then they had sex.

. . . John . . . Rideout was acquitted . . . of a charge that he raped his wife.

In the Supreme Court of New Jersey in 1981, *State v Smith* (85 N J 193, 426 A 2d 38). Pashman J commented on the issue of 'implied consent' in the following way:

. . . this implied consent rationale, besides being offensive to our valued ideals of personal liberty, is not sound where the marriage itself is not irrevocable. If a wife can exercise a legal right to separate from her husband and eventually terminate the marriage 'contract', may she not also revoke a 'term' of that contract, namely, consent to intercourse? Just as a husband has no right to imprison his wife because of her marriage vow to him, he has no right to force sexual relations upon her against her will. If her repeated refusals are a 'breach' of the marriage 'contract', his remedy is in a matrimonial court, not in violent or forceful self-help.

However, the Criminal Law Revision Committee, which produced its Report on *Sexual Offences* (15th Report) in 1984, recommended by a majority to retain the immunity in all cases except where the parties are living apart:

11. Marital rape

2.55 There is wide divergence of opinion on this Committee and elsewhere on the question whether the offence of rape should apply generally between spouses. A number of women's groups formed to assist victims of rape were strongly of opinion that the offence should be so extended, even where the spouses were living together as husband and wife at the time. The remainder of our commentators were divided, with strong opinions expressed on both sides. The Policy Advisory Committee have advised us specifically upon this subject and a majority of their Members are of opinion that the offence should apply in all cases between spouses.

2.56 . . . We all agree that at least the present law should be retained, by which in a limited set of circumstances a husband may be convicted of raping his wife. We would also all like to see the present law extended so that a husband could be prosecuted for rape where he and his wife had ceased cohabiting with each other. There are, however, difficulties in defining cohabitation for these purposes and any definition would be likely to involve an investigation into the parties' domestic arrangements, which some of us think would be unsuitable for a criminal trial. In the absence of an acceptable definition of cohabitation, the choice lies between extending the offence of rape to cover all marriages or leaving the law as it is. Given that choice, a number of us would extend the offence to all marriages but a narrow majority of us would leave the law as it is. . . .

Arguments for retaining the present law in relation to married couples cohabiting at the time of the act of sexual intercourse

2.64 The majority of us, who would not extend the offence of rape to married couples cohabiting at the time of the act of sexual intercourse, believe that rape cannot be considered in the abstract as merely 'sexual intercourse without consent'. The circumstances of rape may be peculiarly grave. This feature is not present in the case of a husband and wife cohabiting with each other when an act of sexual intercourse occurs without the wife's consent. They may well have had sexual intercourse regularly before the act in question and, because a sexual relationship may involve a degree of compromise, she may sometimes have agreed only with some reluctance to such intercourse. Should he go further and force her to have sexual intercourse without her consent, this may evidence a failure of the marital relationship. . . .

2.65 . . . At present a person convicted of rape is usually sentenced to immediate imprisonment, often for a substantial period. . . . For rape between cohabiting spouses, however, immediate imprisonment might not be appropriate; where no physical injury was caused to the wife, imprisonment would be most unlikely. A category of rape that was dealt with leniently might lead to all rape cases being regarded less seriously. . . .

2.66 There are also several grave practical consequences which would flow from an extension of the offence to all marriages and which might be detrimental to marriage as an institution. It is the common experience of practitioners in domestic violence cases that allegations of violence made by a wife against her husband are often withdrawn some days later or not pursued. Violence occurs in some marriages but the wives do not always wish the marital tie to be severed, whatever their initial reaction to the violence. Once, however, a wife placed the facts of an alleged rape by her husband before the police she might not be able to stop the investigation process if she wanted to. . . . All of this, more likely than not, would be detrimental to the interests of any children of the family.

2.67 This would be unfortunate enough if it was the wife on her own who made the decision to go to the police in full knowledge of the consequences. This degree of foresight is likely to be rare; moreover she may not always be left to make up her own mind. She might be persuaded by others to embark upon a course of action which she might later regret and from which she might find difficulty in withdrawing.

2.68 Nor would the actual investigation of the offence be easy. The fact of sexual intercourse having occurred would prove little unless it was allied to other evidence. . . .

2.69 There are also other considerations . . . Some of us consider that the criminal law should keep out of marital relationships between cohabiting partners — especially the marriage bed — except where injury arises, when there are other offences which can be charged.

Married couples not cohabiting at the time of the act of sexual intercourse

2.81 We have said that we are divided on marital rape. There is, however, one proposition that unites us all, namely that, if a satisfactory definition could be achieved, the offence of rape should be extended to all cases where husband and wife are no longer cohabiting. This would be a logical, and modest, extension of the offence to cover bad cases not amounting at present to the offence, for example, where a husband forces his way into his wife's residence after they have ceased to cohabit but where she has not yet had recourse to a court. . . .

The Law Commission, Working Paper 116, *Rape Within Marriage* (1990) find the view of the CLRC hard to accept.

4.20 First, and most fundamentally, if the rights of the married and the non-married woman are in this respect the same, those rights should be protected in the same way, unless there are cogent reasons of policy for taking a different course.

4.21 Second, it is by no means necessarily the case that non-consensual intercourse between spouses has less serious consequences for the woman, or is physically less damaging or disturbing for her, than in the case of non-consensual intercourse with a stranger. Depending on the circumstances the wife whose husband thrusts intercourse upon her may suffer pain from the act of intercourse itself; or the fear or the actuality of venereal or other disease; or the fear or the actuality of an unwanted pregnancy if because of the suddenness of the attack she has taken no contraceptive precautions or such precautions are unacceptable or impossible for medical reasons; and in the event of actual pregnancy a termination may be unavailable or morally offensive to her. All of these hazards may apply equally in the case of marital as of non-marital rape.

4.22 Third, we think that there is a danger that the CLRC underestimated the emotional and psychological harm that a wife may suffer by being subjected by her husband to intercourse against her will, even though on previous occasions she has willingly participated in the same act with the same partner. In *Kowalski*[1] the Court of Appeal approved the trial judge's ruling, in respect of an act of fellatio that the husband compelled the wife to perform on him, that she was entitled to say —

'I agree I have done that with you before. I agree I did not find it indecent when we did it as an act of love, but I now find it indecent; I find it repell[e]nt; I find it abhorrent.'

It is well recognised that unwanted sexual intercourse can be a particularly repellent and abhorrent experience for a woman: that is one main justification for the existence of the offence of rape. We see no reason why a wife cannot say that she feels that abhorrence for such intercourse with her husband, whether or not she has willingly participated on previous occasions.

4.23 Fourth, for a man to oblige his wife to have intercourse without her consent may be equally, or even more, 'grave' or serious as when that conduct takes place between non-spouses. In the case of the husband, he abuses not merely an act to which, as a matter of abstract principle, society attaches values, but the act that has been or should have been his means of expressing his love for his wife. There seems every reason to think that that abuse can be quite as serious on the part of the husband, and quite as traumatic for the wife, as is rape by a stranger or casual acquaintance.

4.24 Fifth, in many cases where the husband forces intercourse on his wife they will be living in the same household, or at least she will be in some sort of dependent relationship with him. It is likely to be harder, rather than easier, for such a woman to avoid her husband's insistence on intercourse, since to do so she may for instance have to leave the matrimonial home. That is a further respect in which non-consensual intercourse by a husband may be a particular abuse.

The Court of Appeal eventually came to the rescue in *R v R (a husband)* [1991] 2 All ER 257, [1991] 2 WLR 1065:

Lord Lane CJ: The appellant, married his wife on 11 August 1984. They had one son who was born in 1985. On 11 November 1987 the parties had separated for a period of about two weeks before becoming reconciled. On 21 October 1989, as a result of futher matrimonial difficulties, the wife left the matrimonial home with their son, who was then aged four, and returned to live with her parents. She had by this time already consulted solicitors regarding her matrimonial affairs and indeed had left a letter for the appellant in which she informed him that she intended to petition for divorce. However no legal proceedings had been taken by her before the incident took place which gave rise to these criminal proceedings. It seems that the appellant had on 23 October spoken to his wife by telephone indicating that it was his intention also to 'see about a divorce'.

Shortly before 9 o'clock on the evening of 12 November 1989, that is to say some 22 days after the wife had returned to live with her parents, and while the parents were out, the appellant forced his way into the parents' house and attempted to have sexual intercourse with the wife against her will. In the course of that attempt he assaulted her, in particular by squeezing her neck with both hands. That assault was the subject of count 2. The appellant was interviewed by the police after his arrest and admitted his responsibility for these events as his eventual plea of guilty indicates. The only other matter which need be noted is that on 3 May 1990 a decree nisi of divorce was made absolute.

The question which the judge had to decide was whether in those circumstances, despite her refusal in fact to consent to sexual intercourse, the wife must be deemed by the fact of marriage to have consented. The argument before us has ranged over a wider field and has raised the question whether there is any basis for the principle, long supposed to be part of the common law, that a wife does by the fact of marriage give any implied consent in advance for the husband to have sexual intercourse with her; and secondly, the question whether, assuming that the principle at one time existed, it still represents the law in either a qualified or unqualified form.

. . .

It seems clear from the passage we have cited [from Hale. See p. 37, above] that he founded the proposition that a husband could not be guilty of rape upon his lawful wife on the grounds (a) that on marriage a wife 'gave' up her body to her husband; and (b) that on marriage she gave her irrevocable consent to sexual intercourse. These two grounds are similar, though not identical.

The theory that on marriage a wife gave her body to her husband was accepted in matrimonial cases decided in the Ecclesiastical Courts. Thus in *Popkin v Popkin* (1794) 1 Hag Ecc 765n Lord

---

1. [1988] 1 FLR 447, [1988] Fam Law 259.

Stowell, in a suit by a wife for divorce a mensa et thoro, stated, at p. 767: 'The husband has a right to the person of his wife', though he added the important qualification, 'but not if her health is endangered'.

These concepts of the relationship between husband and wife appear to have persisted for a long time and may help to explain why Hale's statement that a husband could not be guilty of rape on his wife was accepted as an enduring principle of the common law.

. . . [I]n *R v Miller* [1954] 2 QB 282, Lynskey J., having examined the authorities, ruled that Hale's proposition was correct and that the husband had no case to answer on a charge of rape although the wife had before the act of intercourse presented a petition for divorce, which had not reached the stage of a decree nisi.

Having considered the other authorities, Lord Lane CJ continued by quoting from the ruling of the judge at the trial:

In the course of his ruling upon the submission, Owen J., having set out the authorities, reached a conclusion in the following terms [1991] 1 All ER 747, 754:

'What, in law, will suffice to revoke that consent which the wife gives to sexual intercourse upon marriage and which the law implies from the facts of marriage? . . . It must be sufficient for there to be an agreement of the parties. Of course, an agreement of the parties means what it says. It does not mean something which is done unilaterally . . . As it seems to me, from his action in telephoning her and saying that he intended to see about a divorce and thereby to accede to what she was doing, there is sufficient here to indicate that there was an implied agreement to a separation and to a withdrawal of that consent to sexual intercourse, which the law, I will assume and accept, implies. The next question is whether a third set of circumstances may be sufficient to revoke that implicit consent. Mr. Milmo argues that the withdrawal of either party from cohabitation is sufficient for that consent to be revoked . . . I accept that it is not for me to make the law. However, it is for me to state the common law as I believe it to be. If that requires me to indicate a set of circumstances which have not so far been considered as sufficient to negative consent as in fact so doing, then I must do so. I cannot believe that it is a part of the common law of this country that where there has been withdrawal of either party from cohabitation, accompanied by a clear indication that consent to sexual intercourse has been terminated, that that does not amount to a revocation of that implicit consent. In those circumstances, it seems to me that there is ample here, both on the second exception and the third exception, which would enable the prosecution to prove a charge of rape or attempted rape against this husband.'

The judge then reviewed possible solutions, and concluded:

What should be the answer?

Ever since the decision of Byrne J. in *R v Clarke* [1949] 2 All ER 448, courts have been paying lip service to the Hale proposition, whilst at the same time increasing the number of exceptions, the number of situations to which it does not apply. This is a legitimate use of the flexibility of the common law which can and should adapt itself to changing social attitudes.

There comes a time when the changes are so great that it is no longer enough to create further exceptions restricting the effect of the proposition, a time when the proposition itself requires examination to see whether its terms are in accord with what is generally regarded today as acceptable behaviour.

For the reasons already adumbrated, and in particular those advanced by the Lord Justice-General in *S v HM Advocate* 1989 SLT 469, with which we respectfully agree, the idea that a wife by marriage consents in advance to her husband having sexual intercourse with her whatever her state of health or however proper her objections (if that is what Hale meant), is no longer acceptable. It can never have been other than a fiction, and fiction is a poor basis for the criminal law. The extent to which events have overtaken Hale's proposition is well illustrated by his last four words, 'which she cannot retract.'

It seems to us that where the common law rule no longer even remotely represents what is the true position of a wife in present day society, the duty of the court is to take steps to alter the rule if it can legitimately do so in the light of any relevant Parliamentary enactment. That in the end comes down to a consideration of the word 'unlawful' in the Act of 1976. It is at the best, perhaps a strange word to have used if the draftsman meant by it 'outside marriage'. However sexual intercourse outside marriage may be described, it is not 'unlawful' if one gives to the word its ordinary meaning of 'contrary to law'. We have not overlooked the decision in

R v Chapman [1959] 1 QB 100 . . ., but if the word is to be construed as 'illicit' or 'outside marriage', then it seemingly admits of no exception. The husband who is the subject of an injunction or undertaking to the court or in respect of whose marriage a decree nisi has been pronounced or is a party to a formal separation agreement would be nevertheless immune from prosecution for raping his wife. This would apply equally to a husband who is the subject of a family protection order, a situation which was the subject of a judgment by Swinton Thomas J. in the Crown Court at Stafford in *R v S* (15 January 1991, unreported).

The alternative to that unwelcome conclusion would be to interpret the word as including the various exceptions to the husband's immunity which we have examined earlier in this judgment. If so, one asks whether the situation crystallises at the date the Act came into force. If that is the case, then all the decisions since the time when the Act of 1976 came into force which have narrowed the husband's immunity would have been wrongly decided.

It may be on the other hand that the draftsman intended to leave it open to the common law to develop as it has done since 1976.

The only realistic explanations seem to us to be that the draftsman either intended to leave the matter open for the common law to develop in that way or, perhaps more likely, that no satisfactory meaning at all can be ascribed to the word and that it is indeed surplusage. In either event, we do not consider that we are inhibited by the Act of 1976 from declaring that the husband's immunity as expounded by Hale no longer exists. We take the view that the time has now arrived when the law should declare that a rapist remains a rapist subject to the criminal law, irrespective of his relationship with his victim.

The remaining and no less difficult question is whether, despite that view, this is an area where the court should step aside to leave the matter to the Parliamentary process. This is not the creation of a new offence, it is the removal of a common law fiction which has become anachronistic and offensive and we consider that it is our duty having reached that conclusion to act upon it.

Had our decision been otherwise and had we been of the opinion that Hale's proposition was still effective, we would nevertheless have ruled that where, as in the instant case, a wife withdraws from cohabitation in such a way as to make it clear to the husband that so far as she is concerned the marriage is at an end, the husband's immunity is lost.
The appeal fails and is dismissed.

Questions

(i) Now that the Court of Appeal (although — at the time of publication — not yet the House of Lords) has finally spoken, do you think that legislation is no longer required?

(ii) Is the *Rideout* case from Oregon a typical example of what may happen now that the immunity is no longer recognised?

(iii) Do you believe there is any strength in the argument advanced by some that if a category of rape ends up being dealt with leniently this might lead to all rape cases being regarded less seriously?

3 Making decisions — life and death

There is one particular matter on which the law does grant the casting vote to the wife, and this is the decision whether to abort a foetus or to give birth to the child already in the womb. This is of course a different question from the one relating to whether or not to have sexual relations, or indeed whether to have those relations with or without contraceptives. The law does not in these matters provide either party with a casting vote or a veto. So far as a possible abortion is concerned, however, the law clearly excludes the husband from any right to demand or to refuse such an operation for his wife:

Paton v British Pregnancy Advisory Service Trustees
[1979] QB 276, [1978] 2 All ER 987, [1978] 3 WLR 687, 122 Sol Jo 744,
High Court, Queen's Bench Division

The plaintiff, William Paton, was the husband of the second defendant, Joan Mary Paton. On 8 May 1978, the wife's general practitioner confirmed that she was pregnant. The wife thereafter applied for and obtained the necessary medical certificate entitling her to an abortion within the terms of the Abortion Act 1967. On 16 May 1978, the wife left the matrimonial home.

On 17 May 1978, the husband applied for an injunction to restrain the first defendants, the trustees of the British Pregnancy Advisory Service, and the wife from causing or permitting an abortion to be carried out on the wife. Sir George Baker P adjourned the case for one week to 24 May 1978, to enable all the parties to be represented. Also on 17 May the wife filed her petition for divorce.

The husband originally put his case on the basis that the wife had no proper legal grounds for seeking the termination of her pregnancy and that she was being spiteful, vindictive and utterly unreasonable in so doing. At the resumed hearing on 24 May it was accepted by all the parties that the provisions of the Abortion Act 1967 had been correctly complied with. The husband contended that he had the right to have a say in the destiny of the child he had conceived.

Sir George Baker P: By a specially endorsed writ the plaintiff, who is the husband of the second defendant, seeks an injunction in effect to restrain the first defendants, a charitable organisation, and particularly his wife, the second defendant, from causing or permitting an abortion to be carried out upon his wife without his consent.

Such action, of course, arouses great emotions, and vigorous opposing views as was recently pointed out in 1972 in the Supreme Court of the United States by Blackmun J in *Roe v Wade* 93 S Ct 705 (1973), 708–709. In the discussion of human affairs and especially of abortion, controversy can rage over the moral rights, duties, interests, standards and religious views of the parties. Moral values are in issue. I am, in fact, concerned with none of these matters. I am concerned, and concerned only, with the law of England as it applies to this claim. My task is to apply the law free of emotion or predilection.

Nobody suggests that there has ever been such a claim litigated before the courts in this country. Indeed, the only case of which I have ever heard was in Ontario. It was unreported because the husband's claim for an injunction was never tried.

In considering the law the first and basic principle is that there must be a legal right enforceable in law or in equity before the applicant can obtain an injunction from the court to restrain an infringement of that right. That has long been the law.

The law is that the court cannot and would not seek to enforce or restrain by injunction matrimonial obligations, if they be obligations, such as sexual intercourse or contraception (a non-molestation injunction given during the pendency of divorce proceedings could, of course, cover attempted intercourse). No court would ever grant an injunction to stop sterilisation or vasectomy. Personal family relationships in marriage cannot be enforced by the order of a court. An injunction in such circumstances was described by Judge Mager in *Jones v Smith* 278 So Rep 339 (1973) in the District Court of Appeal of Florida as 'ludicrous.'

I ask the question, 'If an injunction were ordered, what could be the remedy?' and I do not think I need say any more than that no judge could even consider sending a husband or wife to prison for breaking such an order. That, of itself, seems to me to cover the application here; this husband cannot by law stop his wife by injunction from having what is now accepted to be a lawful abortion within the terms of the Abortion Act 1967. . . .

The Abortion Act 1967 gives no right to a father to be consulted in respect of a termination of a pregnancy. True, it gives no right to the mother either, but obviously the mother is going to be right at the heart of the matter consulting with the doctors if they are to arrive at a decision in good faith, unless, of course, she is mentally incapacitated or physically incapacitated (unable to make any decision or give any help) as, for example, in consequence of an accident. The husband, therefore, in my view, has no legal right enforceable in law or in equity to stop his wife having this abortion or to stop the doctors from carrying out the abortion.

In *C v S* [1988] QB 135, [1987] 1 All ER 1230 a similar case was heard in connection with the application by the father to prevent his former girlfriend from having an abortion. The argument primarily was centred around the meaning of 'capable of being born alive' as defined in the Infant Life Preservation Act 1929, and whether the termination of the girl's pregnancy was a potential criminal abortion.[2]

Heilbron J agreed with Sir George Baker P in *Paton v BPAST* that the Abortion Act 1967 had not given the father the right to be consulted in respect of a termination of pregnancy. The point was not considered by the Court of Appeal.

Missouri in the United States once had a spousal consent provision:

Section 3. No abortion shall be performed prior to the end of the first twelve weeks of pregnancy except:

(1) By a duly licensed, consenting physician in the exercise of his best clinical medical judgment;

(2) After the woman, prior to submitting to the abortion, certifies in writing her consent to the abortion and that her consent is informed and freely given and is not the result of coercion;

(3) With the written consent of the woman's spouse, unless the abortion is certified by a licensed physician to be necessary in order to preserve the life of the mother;

(4) With the written consent of one parent or person in loco parentis of the woman if the woman is unmarried and under the age of eighteen years, unless the abortion is certified by a licensed physician as necessary in order to preserve the life of the mother.

Planned Parenthood of Missouri v Danforth
428 US 52, 49 L Ed 2d 788, 96 S Ct 2831, (1976) Supreme Court

The plaintiffs, a non-profit-making organisation which maintains a facility in Missouri for the performance of abortions, brought proceedings to obtain declaratory relief on the grounds, amongst others, that certain provisions of the Act deprived the organisation and its doctors and their patients of various constitutional rights; the right to privacy in the physician-patient relationship, the female patients' right to determine whether to bear children and other constitutional rights.

The Supreme Court concluded that both s. 3(3) and 3(4) were unconstitutional: we report here their *opinion* relating to s. 3(3) (for a discussion of parental control over their children, see Chapter 10):

The appellees defend § 3(3) on the ground that it was enacted in the light of the General Assembly's 'perception of marriage as an institution,' Brief for Appellee Danforth 34, and that any major change in family status is a decision to be made jointly by the marriage partners. Reference is made to an abortion's possible effect on the woman's childbearing potential. It is said that marriage always has entailed some legislatively imposed limitations: reference is made to adultery and bigamy as criminal offenses; to Missouri's general requirement, Mo Rev Stat § 453.030.3 (1969), that for an adoption of a child born in wedlock the consent of both parents is necessary; to similar joint-consent requirements imposed by a number of States with respect to artificial insemination and the legitimacy of children so conceived; to the laws of two States requiring spousal consent for voluntary sterilization; and to the long-established requirement of spousal consent for the effective disposition of an interest in real property. It is argued that

---

2. See now *Rance v Mid-Downs Health Authority* [1991] 1 All ER 801, [1991] 2 WLR 159.

'[r]ecognizing that the consent of both parties is generally necessary . . . to begin a family, the legislature has determined that a change in the family structure set in motion by mutual consent should be terminated only by mutual consent,' Brief for Appellee Danforth 38, and that what the legislature did was to exercise its inherent policymaking power 'for what was believed to be in the best interests of all the people of Missouri.' Id., at 40.

The appellants, on the other hand, contend that § 3(3) obviously is designed to afford the husband the right unilaterally to prevent or veto an abortion, whether or not he is the father of the fetus, and that this not only violates *Roe* [*v Wade*] 410 US, 93 S Ct 705 but is also in conflict with other decided cases. See, e.g., *Poe v Gerstein* 517 F2d 787, 794–796 (CA5 1975), appeal docketed, No. 75-713; *Wolfe v Schroering*. 388 F Supp, at 636–637; *Doe v Rampton*, 366 F Supp 189, 193 (Utah 1973). They also refer to the situation where the husband's consent cannot be obtained because he cannot be located. And they assert that § 3(3) is vague and overbroad.

In *Roe* [*v Wade*] we specifically reserved decision on the question whether a requirement for consent by the father of the fetus, by the spouse, or by the parents, or a parent, of an unmarried minor, may be constitutionally imposed. 410 US, at 165 n 67, 35 L Ed 2d 147, 93 S Ct 705. We now hold that the State may not constitutionally require the consent of the spouse, as is specified under § 3(3) of the Missouri Act, as a condition for abortion during the first 12 weeks of pregnancy. We thus agree with the dissenting judge in the present case, and with the courts whose decisions are cited above, that the State cannot 'delegate to a spouse a veto power which the state itself is absolutely and totally prohibited from exercising during the first trimester of pregnancy.' 392 F Supp, at 1375. Clearly, since the State cannot regulate or proscribe abortion during the first stage, when the physician and his patient make that decision, the State cannot delegate authority to any particular person, even the spouse, to prevent abortion during that same period.

We are not unaware of the deep and proper concern and interest that a devoted and protective husband has in his wife's pregnancy and in the growth and development of the fetus she is carry-ing. Neither has this Court failed to appreciate the importance of the marital relationship in our society. See, e.g., *Griswold v Connecticut*, 381 US 479, 486, 14 L Ed 2d 510, 85 S Ct 1678 (1965); *Maynard v Hill*, 125 US 190, 211, 31 L Ed 654, 8 S Ct 723 (1888). Moreover, we recognize that the decision whether to undergo or to forgo an abortion may have profound effects on the future of any marriage, effects that are both physical and mental, and possibly deleterious. Notwithstanding these factors, we cannot hold that the State has the constitutional authority to give the spouse unilaterally the ability to prohibit the wife from terminating her pregnancy, when the State itself lacks that right. See *Eisenstadt v Baird*, 405 US 438, 453, 31 L Ed 2d 349, 92 S Ct 1029 (1972).

It seems manifest that, ideally, the decision to terminate a pregnancy should be one concurred in by both the wife and her husband. No marriage may be viewed as harmonious or successful if the marriage partners are fundamentally divided on so important and vital an issue. But it is difficult to believe that the goal of fostering mutuality and trust in a marriage, and of strengthening the marital relationship and the marriage institution, will be achieved by giving the husband a veto power exercisable for any reason whatsoever or for no reason at all. Even if the State had the ability to delegate to the husband a power it itself could not exercise, it is not at all likely that such action would further, as the District Court majority phrased it, the 'interest of the state in protecting the mutuality of decisions vital to the marriage relationship.' 392 F Supp, at 1370.

We recognize, of course, that when a woman, with the approval of her physician but without the approval of her husband, decides to terminate her pregnancy, it could be said that she is acting unilaterally. The obvious fact is that when the wife and the husband disagree on this deci-sion, the view of only one of the two marriage partners can prevail. Inasmuch as it is the woman who physically bears the child and who is the more directly and immediately affected by the pregnancy, as between the two, the balance weighs in her favor. Cf. *Roe v Wade*, 410 US, at 153, 35 L Ed 2d 147, 93 S Ct 705.

We conclude that § 3(3) of the Missouri Act is . . . unconstitutional.

Questions

(i) Are these cases examples of the judiciary: (*a*) being reluctant to interfere in domestic relations; (*b*) championing the rights of women; or (*c*) suppress-ing the rights of men?

(ii) If you think these cases suppress the rights of men, do you consider that a man should be able to compel his wife to have an abortion, or be relieved from maintenance if she does not have the abortion and goes ahead with the birth?

(iii) If a father cannot obtain an injunction what else can he do?

(iv) Can you think of any decisions taken by husband and wife in their marriage which the courts would actually force the parties to make jointly, by way of injunction if need be?

Jones v Smith
59 Fl App 278, So 2d 339 (1973) District Court of Appeal of Florida

The case turned upon the constitutional provision relating to the right of privacy. The court decided that the decision to terminate a pregnancy is one that is purely personal to the mother and a matter between her and the attending physician. The court held further that 'any unreasonable governmental interference must yield to the mother's right of privacy.' The facts of the case are set out in the judgment.

Mager J: . . . This is an appeal from an order denying a claim for injunctive relief seeking to restrain the 'obtaining or aiding in the obtaining of an abortion'. Although pseudonyms are used the parties are real persons.

The primary question presented is whether a potential putative father has the right to restrain the natural mother from terminating a pregnancy resulting from their cohabitation. The appellant, who acknowledges that he is the father of the unborn child, is twenty-seven years old, was formerly married and is the father of a six-year-old daughter by such previous marriage. The appellee-mother is nineteen years old and unmarried and had been dating the appellant for approximately six months during which time the parties were frequently intimate. The appellant in seeking injunctive relief has indicated his desire to marry the appellee and to assume all the obligations financial and otherwise for the care and support of the unborn child; that, notwithstanding such affirmations, the appellee-mother, who has expressed her desire not to marry the appellant, has sought to terminate the pregnancy.

Although the appellant alleged in his complaint below 'that the mother's mental and physical health will not be endangered by bringing the child to term in allowing its natural birth' there is no allegation and proof that the proposed termination of pregnancy does not comply with Florida's newly enacted 'Termination of Pregnancy' law (Chapter 72-196, Laws of Florida, numbered as Section 458.22, Florida Statutes, F.S.A.). It is interesting to note a suggestion by the appellant that his own health would be affected if the pregnancy is terminated; testimony from a psychiatrist examining the appellant suggested 'the possibility of him suffering depressive symptoms and depressive reactions in the future'.

The main thrust of the appellant's position is that as a potential putative father he has the 'right' to participate in the decision to terminate the pregnancy.

Because of the time factors involved and in particular the fact that the mother is reaching the end of the first trimester of pregnancy this court has granted an emergency hearing and has expedited its review.

The appellant contends that whatever right of privacy that the mother might have enjoyed, such right was 'waived' by virtue of her consent to and participation in the sex act. This argument is somewhat tenuous. The right of privacy of the mother with respect to a termination of pregnancy as delineated by the decisions of the United States Supreme Court is a right separate and apart from any act of conception. The determination of whether to carry the child the full term is not 'controlled' or 'waived' by virtue of the act of conception no more so than the fact that were the child conceived in the State of Florida would give the State the right to interfere with the termination of pregnancy during the first trimester. Moreover, whatever purported 'waiver' might have occurred as a result of the conception, the interest or 'right' of the natural father must remain subservient to 'the life or health of the female' (See F.S. Section 458.22(2)(*a*), F.S.A.).

Questions

(i) In the course of his judgment, Judge Mager asked the following question: 'Could a potential putative father (or for that matter a husband) seek an injunction to restrain the woman from using contraceptives or compel the woman to bear children?' What would be your answer to this question? Do you think there should be a different answer depending on whether the father is or is not married to the mother? (Judge Mager's answer is referred to in the judgment of Baker P in *Paton v British Pregnancy Advisory Service Trustees* [1979] QB 276, [1978] 2 All ER 987.)

(ii) If English law introduced a paternal veto, would it be contrary to article 8 of the European Convention of Human Rights (set out on p. 407, below)?

Krause (1990) reports the following story:

New York Times, Nov. 14, 1968, p. 36, col. 1. Hempstead, L.I., Nov. 13 (AP) — A 24-year-old mother of three children, who was injured in an automobile crash, died today after her husband had refused on religious grounds to allow doctors to give her a blood transfusion.

The police said the victim, Betty Jackson, was pinned in her car when it struck a utility pole at Wellsley Street and Rumsem Avenue near her home. She was admitted to Hempstead General Hospital at about 11:30 A.M.

Doctors said examination showed Mrs. Jackson was suffering from multiple injuries and bleeding internally. They sought permission from her husband, Clemons Jackson, to administer a transfusion.

Mr. Jackson, a follower of Jehovah's Witnesses, refused. He remained adamant, despite the pleading of several doctors, and at 4:30 P.M. the hospital administrator appealed to State Supreme Court Judge William Sullivan.

'If I allow blood to be given into her and if she lived, she wouldn't be considered my wife,' the Nassau County police said Mr. Jackson had told the doctors.

Judge Sullivan refused to order the transfusion. Mrs. Jackson died at 6:30 P.M. Her three children, who were with her when the car struck the utility pole, were also in the hospital and reported in fair condition.

Questions

(i) What do you think an English judge would do in this situation?

(ii) If the doctor failed to obtain the consent of a judge, would he be guilty of any crime?

4 Making decisions — the choice of a home

The law governing the choice of the matrimonial home has developed since the second world war, not only in response to women's participation in the labour market (on which see Tilly and Scott (1987)), but also in response to a growing respect for their right to a voice in where they shall live. It is relevant, first, in divorce or other matrimonial cases in which it is alleged that one spouse has deserted the other; and secondly, in connection with the modern protection of rights of occupation in the matrimonial home. An example of the first is the following case:

Dunn v Dunn
[1949] P 98, [1948] 2 All ER 822, [1949] LJR 87, 65 TLR 570, 112 JP 436,
92 Sol Jo 633, 46 LGR 521, Court of Appeal

Denning LJ: In his able argument counsel for the husband put forward the proposition that the husband has the right to decide where the parties shall live, and that, if the wife refuses to join him, she is guilty of desertion unless she can prove that she had a just cause for her refusal.

If that were a proposition of law it would put a legal burden on the wife to justify her refusal, but it is not a proposition of law. . . . It is simply a proposition of ordinary good sense arising from the fact that the husband is usually the wage-earner and has to live near his work. It is not a proposition which applies in all cases. The decision where the home should be is a decision which affects both the parties and their children. It is their duty to decide it by agreement, by give and take, and not by the imposition of the will of one over the other. Each is entitled to an equal voice in the ordering of the affairs which are their common concern. Neither has a casting vote, though, to be sure, they should try so to arrange their affairs that they spend their time together as a family and not apart. If such an arrangement is frustrated by the unreasonableness of one or the other, and this leads to a separation between them, then the party who has produced the separation by reason of his or her unreasonable behaviour is guilty of desertion. The situations which may arise are so various that I think it unwise to attempt any more precise test than that of unreasonableness. Views as to unreasonableness may vary, and the decision is essentially one for the trial judge with which this court should not interfere unless the conclusion is one which could not reasonably be drawn. If a wife refuses to join her husband at a place when he is ready to receive her, that is, of course, a factor of great weight, but it is not necessarily decisive. Take this case. The judge has held that the wife's refusal was not unreasonable. She was living with the two children, aged 14 and 7, in the matrimonial home at Morpeth. She had never been away from Morpeth except for a few days in 1934. The husband wanted to uproot them for a stay in wartime at Immingham or Barrow. The stay was to be of uncertain duration and it might be for a few weeks or a few months. It was to be in rooms. The wife was deaf and had difficulty in making herself understood by strangers. A considerate husband would have recognised her difficulty and not have insisted on her coming. A considerate wife would have put up with the difficulties and gone. Neither was considerate. Neither was unreasonable. From his point of view he was not acting unreasonably; from her point of view she was not acting unreasonably. Each insisted on their own point of view, and hence the marriage came to an end. The decisive matter, to my mind, is that throughout the matrimonial home was at Morpeth and the wife was ready and willing to have him there on his leave whenever he could get there, and that is where the family were. Her refusal to go for a short stay elsewhere in the circumstances which I have mentioned, it seems to me, was not unreasonable. At all events, there was ample ground on which the learned judge could come to the conclusion which he reached, that it was not unreasonable on her part to fail to go and stay with him. Unless I could say that finding was unreasonable I do not think this court should interfere. I cannot say that, and, therefore, I think the appeal should be dismissed.

Question

In this case, Denning LJ held that neither spouse was being unreasonable, although equally neither party was considerate. Would another finding have been that *both* parties were unreasonable?

The second aspect of this question is the right to occupy the matrimonial home. At common law, each spouse had a personal right, as against the other spouse, to occupy a matrimonial home to which that other was entitled. But this gave no rights against third parties to whom the owning spouse might seek to dispose of his interest. The Matrimonial Homes Act 1967 (see now 1983) was passed to remedy this problem, but in the process it had also to provide a statutory definition of the rights of the parties inter se:

Protection against eviction, etc., from matrimonial home of spouse not entitled by virtue of estate, etc., to occupy it

1. − (1) Where one spouse is entitled to occupy a dwelling house by virtue of a beneficial estate or interest or contract or by virtue of any enactment giving him or her the right to remain in occupation, and the other spouse is not so entitled, then, subject to the provisions of this Act, the spouse not so entitled shall have the following rights (in this Act referred to as 'rights of occupation') −

    (a) if in occupation, a right not to be evicted or excluded from the dwelling house or any part thereof by the other spouse except with the leave of the court given by an order under this section;

    (b) if not in occupation, a right with the leave of the court so given to enter into and occupy the dwelling house.

(2) So long as one spouse has rights of occupation, either of the spouses may apply to the court for an order −

    (a) declaring, enforcing, restricting or terminating those rights, or

    (b) prohibiting, suspending or restricting the exercise by either spouse of the right to occupy the dwelling house, or

    (c) requiring either spouse to permit the exercise by the other of that right.

(3) On an application for an order under this section, the court may make such order as it thinks just and reasonable having regard to the conduct of the spouses in relation to each other and otherwise, to their respective needs and financial resources, to the needs of any children and to all the circumstances of the case, and, without prejudice to the generality of the foregoing provision −

    (a) may except part of the dwelling house from a spouse's rights of occupation (and in particular a part used wholly or mainly for or in connection with the trade, business or profession of the other spouse),

    (b) may order a spouse occupying the dwelling house or any part thereof by virtue of this section to make periodical payments to the other in respect of the occupation,

    (c) may impose on either spouse obligations as to the repair and maintenance of the dwelling house or the discharge of any liabilities in respect of the dwelling house.

(4) Orders under this section may, in so far as they have a continuing effect, be limited so as to have effect for a period specified in the order or until further order.

(5) Where a spouse is entitled under this section to occupy a dwelling house or any part thereof, any payment or tender made or other thing done by that spouse in or towards satisfaction of any liability of the other spouse in respect of rent, rates, mortgage payments or other outgoings affecting the dwelling house shall, whether or not it is made or done in pursuance of an order under this section, be as good as if made or done by the other spouse.

(6) A spouse's occupation by virtue of this section shall, for the purposes of the Rent (Agriculture) Act 1976, and of the Rent Act 1977 (other than Part V and sections 103 to 106), be treated as possession by the other spouse and for purposes of Part IV of the Housing Act 1985 and Part I of the Housing Act 1988 be treated as occupation by the other spouse.

(7) Where a spouse is entitled under this section to occupy a dwelling house or any part thereof and makes any payment in or towards satisfaction of any liability of the other spouse in respect of mortgage payments affecting the dwelling house, the person to whom the payment is made may treat it as having been made by that other spouse, but the fact that that person has treated any such payment as having been so made shall not affect any claim of the first-mentioned spouse against the other to an interest in the dwelling house by virtue of the payment.

. . .

(10) This Act shall not apply to a dwelling house which has at no time been a matrimonial home of the spouses in question; and a spouse's rights of occupation shall continue only so long as the marriage subsists and the other spouse is entitled as mentioned in subsection (1) above to occupy the dwelling house, except where provision is made by section 2 of this Act for those rights to be a charge on an estate or interest in the dwelling house.

(11) It is hereby declared that a spouse who has an equitable interest in a dwelling house or in the proceeds of sale thereof, not being a spouse in whom is vested (whether solely or as a joint tenant) a legal estate in fee simple or a legal term of years absolute in the dwelling house, is to be treated for the purpose only of determining whether he or she has rights of occupation under this section as not being entitled to occupy the dwelling house by virtue of that interest.

Section 1 of the 1967 Act provided a remedy which was not clearly available as between spouses who were jointly entitled to the matrimonial home.

Accordingly, s. 4 of the Domestic Violence and Matrimonial Proceedings Act 1976 was passed and is now incorporated into the Matrimonial Homes Act 1983 by s. 9 of that Act which provides;

9. – (1) Where each of two spouses is entitled, by virtue of a legal estate vested in them jointly, to occupy a dwelling house in which they have or at any time have had a matrimonial home, either of them may apply to the court, with respect to the exercise during the subsistence of the marriage of the right to occupy the dwelling house, for an order prohibiting, suspending or restricting its exercise by the other or requiring the other to permit its exercise by the applicant.

(2) In relation to orders under this section, section 1(3), (4) and (9) above shall apply as they apply in relation to orders under that section.

(3) Where each of two spouses is entitled to occupy a dwelling house by virtue of a contract, or by virtue of any enactment giving them the right to remain in occupation, this section shall apply as it applies where they are entitled by virtue of a legal estate vested in them jointly.

(4) In determining for the purposes of this section whether two spouses are entitled to occupy a dwelling house, there shall be disregarded any right to possession of the dwelling house conferred on a mortgagee of the dwelling house under or by virtue of his mortgage, whether the mortgage is in possession or not.

Section 1 of the Matrimonial Homes Act 1983 raises the question of how great a voice the non-owning spouse should have in the choice of a matrimonial home.

Wroth v Tyler
[1974] Ch 30, [1973] 1 All ER 897, [1973] 2 WLR 405, 117 Sol Jo 90, 25 P & CR 138, High Court, Chancery Division

The wife registered a charge under the Matrimonial Homes Act 1967 after her husband, who was the sole legal and beneficial owner of the house, had signed a contract for the sale of the house. The registration of the charge meant that the sale with vacant possession could not be completed, and the husband was thus held liable in damages. It is not immediately apparent from the facts of the case why the husband did not seek an order under s. 1(3) of the Matrimonial Homes Act 1967, as it then was, for the wife's right of occupation to be terminated so as to allow the completion to go ahead. It certainly appears on the face of it that the wife had led both the husband and the prospective purchasers, a newly married couple, reasonably to believe that she was not actively dissenting from the wish of the husband to move from Kent, where they had previously lived, so as to set up home in a cottage in Norfolk. Megarry J commented on the facts in the following manner:

Let me add that I would certainly not regard proceedings under the Act by the defendant against his wife as being without prospect of success. As the evidence stands (and of course I have not heard the defendant's wife) there is at least a real prospect of success for the defendant. He does not in any way seek to deprive his wife of a home; the difference between them is a difference as to where the matrimonial home is to be. In that, the conduct of the wife towards the plaintiffs and the defendant must play a substantial part.

Megarry J was not prepared to order specific performance of the contract, for to do so would be to indirectly force the husband to take proceedings under the Matrimonial Homes Act against his wife. This was a decision which only he could take. Perhaps therefore, one should not feel too concerned about the fate of the husband — who had to pay damages amounting to £5,500 — for after all the remedy was in his own hands. Certainly, on the result of *Wroth v Tyler*, the wife had the 'casting vote'.

Questions

(i) A husband sells the matrimonial home of which he is the sole legal and beneficial owner and, with the proceeds of sale, purchases a house in which he instals his mistress. The entire transaction takes place whilst the wife is away looking after her aged mother.
(a) Would a court assume jurisdiction and hear a wife's claim 'to enter into and occupy the dwelling house?'
(b) If the court does assume jurisdiction, what are her chances of success?
(c) Could the wife obtain an order to exclude the mistress?
(d) Could any order which the wife obtains include provisions restraining the husband from taking away the furniture?

The question which we are concerned with in the present chapter — making decisions about where to live — will of course be resolved from time to time by the decision of the courts. This is particularly true in the rented sector. Section 1(5), (6) of the Matrimonial Homes Act 1983 is an important provision regarding rented property. If the tenancy is a protected or a statutory tenancy under the Rent Act 1977 or a periodic assured tenancy under the Housing Act 1988 (private tenancies) or a secure tenancy under the Housing Act 1985 (council tenancies) an occupying spouse may keep the tenancy of the other spouse 'alive', even though the latter spouse is not living in the accommodation. (In addition, Sch. 1 of the Matrimonial Homes Act 1983 gives a spouse a right to seek transfer of a protected, statutory or secure tenancy or assured tenancy on the granting of a decree of divorce etc., or at any time thereafter.)

Questions

(i) Does this mean that the tenant spouse cannot defeat the occupation rights of the wife by purporting to surrender the tenancy to the landlord? (See *Middleton v Baldock* [1950] 1 KB 657, [1950] 1 All ER 708, CA.)
(ii) Do you think that the local authority should be under an obligation to provide alternative accommodation for the ex-tenant?
(iii) In the case of a periodic joint tenancy, when one of the tenants gives notice to quit, it seems that the tenancy terminates (see *Greenwich London Borough Council v McGrady* (1982) 81 LGR 288, 6 HLR 36, CA; *Hammersmith and Fulham London Borough Council v Monk* (1990) Times, 5 November, CA. See p. 168 below). Is this a sufficient protection for a wife who has the support of a housing authority?

Such 'secure' tenancies were originally confined to private tenancies. The *Report of the Committee on One-Parent Families* (The Finer Report) discussed this in 1974:

6.88 The reasons for the exclusion of council tenancies from the statutory protection appear to be that the landlord in these cases is a democratically elected public body which can be trusted to behave reasonably in dealing with its tenants, and which also may find itself in a position where its duty to the tenant conflicts with some other public duty, to resolve which it has to retain a free hand. . . .

6.90 . . . we can see no continuing good reason for depriving local authority or New Town tenants of the basic protection in security of tenure which the Rent Acts give to the tenants of private landlords. . . .

Our recommendation in principle is that security of tenure similar to the Rent Acts protection be extended to tenancies in the public sector. It should be noted that one effect would be always to interpose the court between an authority wanting possession and a tenant unwilling to go — a safeguard that we think would be of special value when the dispute with the authority was connected with or happened to coincide with some breakdown of marital relations within the home.

This recommendation was accepted, and council house tenancies are in most cases secure tenancies within the meaning given to that phrase under the Housing Act 1985 (see further Chapter 5, below). In particular the s. 1(5) protection applies to secure council tenancies. Further, if proceedings are brought against the tenant and as a result of those proceedings the tenancy is ended as against the tenant then in certain cases at least, the spouse in occupation has the right to ask the court to adjourn the proceedings, postpone the date of possession, and stay or suspend execution of the order.

Questions

(i) The Finer Report (1974) stated that 'the protection which the wife and children may require when the family live in rented accommodation is protection in occupancy, which may be achieved irrespective of rights of ownership.' In the context of council housing, (*a*) do you think that it is appropriate that this protection should be exercised by the courts rather than by the local authorities, and if so, (*b*) why do you have this view? (For the courts' powers to transfer a tenancy, both private and council, after the termination of the marriage under the Matrimonial Causes Act 1973 see Chapter 7, below.)

(ii) A number of authorities have introduced clauses into their tenancy agreements which state that violence or threats of violence constitute a breach of the tenancy agreement and can thus be grounds for possession giving the local authority the power to determine the tenancy. Do you feel that such clauses are appropriate, or would you deal with the problem of domestic violence in some other way (see further, pp. 393ff).

Under s. 2 of the Act, the non-legal owner is entitled to register a Class F land charge (or a caution in the case of registered land) so as to protect the right of occupation provided by s. 1 of the Act. The impact of such a registration was the issue in the following case:

Barnett v Hassett
[1982] 1 All ER 80, [1981] 1 WLR 1385, 125 Sol Jo 376, High Court, Family Division

The parties, both married previously, married one another in February 1980. The wife owned a large and expensive house, 2 Spaniard's Close, as a result of the orders made in her favour at the end of her first marriage. The husband's previous house was sold in March 1980, and no doubt in anticipation of setting up the new combined families, he exchanged contracts for the purchase of a house and paid a deposit of £41,000. The exchange of contracts took place in November 1979. He moved into 2 Spaniard's Close in March 1980 and left it in July 1980. Clearly, the new marriage had not worked, and, in May 1980, the husband informed the vendors of the house he intended to purchase that he could not complete. He forfeited the deposit. In December 1980, the husband applied to register a Class F land charge on 2 Spaniard's Close.

Wood J: . . . Before turning to the law I analyse the husband's case as follows: (i) he has rights under section 1(1)(*b*) of the Matrimonial Homes Act 1967 [now 1983] as a spouse not in occupation of the matrimonial home; (ii) he does not wish to occupy that home or any part of it; (iii) he does not now wish to prevent its sale (although I doubt whether that was his attitude until very recently); (iv) he wants to freeze part of the proceeds of sale — £60,000; (v) he therefore registered a Class F charge to force his wife to apply to this court to set it aside.

I turn to the Act of 1967 itself. It is unnecessary for me to review the history of the rights between husband and wife prior to the passing of this Act; suffice it to say that the provisions of the Act introduce new rights.

. . . The whole emphasis of the Act is to create and protect the right to occupation of a spouse not in occupation or a spouse already in occupation. This is made clear throughout the Act. The right to occupation must relate to a matrimonial home, and only continues during the existence of the marriage. A Class F charge is intended to protect that right.

One thing is abundantly clear, namely that this husband does not seek 'to enter into and occupy' the whole or any part of the matrimonial home. Is he entitled to ask the court to freeze any part of the proceeds of sale? I do not think so. . . . Section 3 of the Act seems to me to emphasise that any interest other than a right to occupy is to be excluded or disregarded. By that section a charge can only be registered on one matrimonial home at a time. If the intention of the Act had been to allow a spouse to place his or her hands upon proceeds of sale or to allow the prevention of such a sale then I would have thought that a charge on a matrimonial home not in occupation and when a sale was likely would be an obvious source for funds.

. . . in my judgment, the registration of this Class F charge in the circumstances of the present case was not a proper use of the process set up by the Act of 1967 and the charge will be set aside.

Question

What is the difference between *Wroth v Tyler* (see p. 50, above), and the behaviour of the wife in that case, and *Barnett v Hassett*, and the behaviour of the husband?

Megarry J in *Wroth v Tyler* called the statutory right of occupation 'a weapon of great power and flexibility:'

I can now say something about the nature of the charge and the mode of operation of the Act. First, for a spouse in occupation, the right seems to be a mere statutory right for the spouse not to be evicted. There appears to be nothing to stay the eviction of others. For example, if a wife is living in her husband's house with their children and her parents, her charge, even if registered, appears to give no protection against eviction to the children or parents. . . . Nor if the wife takes in lodgers does there seem to be anything to prevent the husband from evicting them. If, for example, the husband is himself living in the house, it would be remarkable if the Act gives the wife the right to insist upon having other occupants in the home against his will. The statutory right appears in essence to be a purely personal right for the wife not to be evicted; and it seems wholly inconsistent with the Act that this right should be assignable or otherwise disposable. I may add that there is nothing to require the wife to make any payment to the husband for her occupation, unless ordered by the court under section 1(3), though if she is in occupation against his will and by virtue of her statutory rights, it may be that she will be in rateable occupation.

Second, although the right given to an occupying wife by section 1(1) is merely a right not to be evicted or excluded 'by the other spouse,' and so at first sight does not appear to be effective against anyone except that other spouse, section 2(1) makes the right 'a charge' on the husband's estate or interest; and it is this, rather than the provisions for registration, which makes the right binding on successors in title. The operation of the provision for registration seems to be essentially negative; the right is a charge which, if not duly protected by registration, will become void against subsequent purchasers, or fail to bind them. In this, the right seems not to differ from other registrable charges, such as general equitable charges or puisne mortgages. Yet there is this difference. For other charges, the expectation of the statute is plainly that they will all be protected by registration, whereas under the Act of 1967 there does not seem to be the same expectation.

Questions

(i) If statutory co-ownership is introduced (see p. 162, below), will the protection afforded under the Matrimonial Homes Act 1983 be of any value?

(ii) Does the wife's right of occupation give her the right to invite visitors to the home? (See *R v Thornley* (1980) 72 Cr App Rep 302.)

The Matrimonial Homes Act 1983 is confined to matrimonial homes, and only spouses obtain protection under its terms. Cohabitants are excluded. In Scotland the position is different. Section 18 of the Matrimonial Homes (Family Protection) (Scotland) Act 1981 states:

If a man and a woman are living with each other as if they were man and wife (a cohabiting couple) in a home which, apart from the provisions of this section—
   (a) one of them is entitled, or permitted by a third party to occupy; and
   (b) the other . . . is not so entitled to occupy.
the court may, on the application of the non-entitled partner, if it appears that the man and the woman are a cohabiting couple in the house, grant occupancy rights therein to the applicant for such period, not exceeding three months, as the court may specify.
   Provided that the court may extend the said period for a further period or periods, no such period exceeding six months.

If occupancy rights under this Act are granted, the 'non-entitled' partner has the right (a) if in occupation, not to be evicted and (b) if not in occupation, a right to enter into and occupy.

Questions

(i) Do you favour similar amendments to the English law?
(ii) What problems would arise?

(See Chapter 8, below for a general discussion of the question of cohabitation.)

5 The unity doctrine remaining today?

(a) TORT

Under the common law, as the husband and wife became 'one person in law' neither could sue the other and the wife could not be sued directly by a third party; all proceedings were brought against her husband. The common law position together with the amendments made to it by the legislation of the nineteenth century is summarised in the following extracts from C.A. Morrison's essay on Tort, in *A Century of Family Law* (1957):

At common law
(1) The wife still retained sufficient separate identity to be able to commit a tort or to have torts inflicted upon her. She might sue or be sued for these, but she had no procedural existence alone and her husband had to be joined with her in the action, and might thereupon become liable.
(2) The husband thus found himself under a liability for torts committed by his wife whether before or during marriage, but it was a joint liability with her. His liability might be justified on the legal ground that she had no procedural personality without him and he had to be joined as co-defendant; on the moral ground that he had her property, and that if his wife brought an action, he would acquire any damages she obtained.
(3) Husband and wife could not sue each other in tort.

As a result of statutory changes in the nineteenth century
In the second half of the nineteenth century there came a period of twelve years of reform by a series of Married Women's Property Acts which greatly altered the picture. The effects of the French and the Industrial Revolutions and perhaps the example of the Queen herself all aided in this feverish period of reform, which in little more than a decade changed the law of centuries. The 1870 [Married Women's Property] Act, designed primarily to protect the earnings of the married woman, did not affect the position in tort. The 1874 Act affected the position only of torts committed by the wife before marriage and reduced the husband's liability for these so that he was liable only to the extent of certain specified assets which he had acquired from or through his wife on marriage.
Judgment was to be a joint one to the extent to which the husband was liable and a separate one against the wife for the residue, if any. The main reform however came with the Act of 1882, which affected torts committed before or during marriage. This Act deprived the husband of all the interest he acquired by marriage in his wife's property and earnings, then, having recognised the married woman's capacity to acquire and dispose of property, it went on to regularise and protect that new position by altering the law in tort and contract. It was necessary that the separate property now recognised by statute should be protected against her husband and against outsiders. This meant, first, that against outsiders she needed the right to sue in her own name, for it would appear that she could not have compelled her husband to join with her to protect her property. This was achieved by dispensing with the need to join her husband in actions by or against her. It meant, secondly, that her property might need protection against even her husband. The Act recognised this by permitting an exception to the rule that husband and wife could not sue each other in tort. By section 12 the wife was given civil and criminal rights of action against her husband for the protection and security of her property. To these two main reforms was added a further which made the married woman herself liable to the extent of her separate property for her torts, whether committed before or during marriage, and liable to be sued alone for these torts. But she could be made bankrupt to the extent of her separate property only if she were carrying on a trade separately from her husband.

The doctrine of unity still prevailed in to the twentieth century. There were criticisms of this state of the law as early as 1930. In *Gottliffe v Edelston* [1930] 2 KB 378 McCardie J said: '. . . wives however wealthy of purse or independent of character, possess powers and privileges which are wholly denied to husbands. Husbands are placed under burdens from which wives are free. . . . Upon the husband there has fallen one injustice after another.'

Question

Would you criticise the common law in this way?

In 1935, five years after this judgment was delivered, the Law Reform (Married Women and Tortfeasors) Act abolished the rule which prevented wives from being sued by third parties. By s. 1, a married woman may sue or be sued in all respects as if she were a feme sole and is made subject to the law relating to bankruptcy and to the enforcement of judgments and orders. Section 3 provides that a husband shall not, by reason only of his being her husband, be liable in respect of any tort committed by his wife whether before or during the marriage. Finally, the Law Reform (Husband and Wife) Act 1962 abolished the common law prohibition preventing one party to the marriage from suing the other.

The common law fiction that husband and wife are in law one person was described by Oliver J in *Midland Bank v Green (No 3)* [1979] Ch 496, [1979] 2 All ER 193; in the following way: 'It is a useful instrument for the furtherance of the policy of the law to protect the institution of marriage, but as an exposition in itself of the living law it is as real as the skeleton of the brontosaurus in a museum of natural history.' Oliver J was concerned in that case with the question of whether a husband and wife who agree with one another to injure a third person, and by their concerted action do injure him, are liable in damages for the tort of conspiracy. Oliver J's affirmative response to that question was the subject of an appeal.

Midland Bank Trust Co Ltd v Green (No 3)
[1982] Ch 529, [1981] 3 All ER 744, [1982] 2 WLR 1, 125 Sol Jo 554, Court of Appeal

Lord Denning MR: The point of principle raised by Mr Munby for the appellant is this. He says that the doctrine of unity between husband and wife is an established doctrine in English law. So well established that the doctrine and its ramifications are still part of our law today: and must still be applied by the courts except in so far as it has been altered by statute. One of the ramifications of the doctrine (that husband and wife are one) is that they cannot be guilty as conspirators together. So they cannot be made liable in damages for a conspiracy.

The authorities cited by Mr Munby show clearly enough that mediaeval lawyers held that husband and wife were one person in law: and that the husband was that one. It was a fiction then. It is a fiction now. It has been eroded by the judges who have created exception after exception to it. It has been cut down by statute after statute until little of it remains. It has been so much eroded and cut down in law, it has so long ceased to be true in fact, that I would reject Mr Munby's principle.

I would put it in this way. Nowadays, both in law and in fact, husband and wife are two persons, not one. They are partners — equal partners — in a joint enterprise, the enterprise of maintaining a home and bringing up children. Outside that joint enterprise they live their own lives and go their own ways — always, we hope, in consultation one with the other, in complete loyalty one with the other, each maintaining and deserving the trust and confidence of the other. They can and do own property jointly or severally or jointly and severally, with all the consequences that ownership entails. They can and do enter into contracts with others jointly or severally or jointly and severally, and can be made liable for breaches just as any other contractors can be. They can and do commit crimes jointly or severally and can be punished severally for them. They can and do commit wrongs jointly or severally and can be made liable jointly or severally just as any other wrong-doers. The severance in all respects is so complete that I would say that the doctrine of unity and its ramifications should be discarded altogether, except in so far as it is retained by judicial decision or by Act of Parliament.

I turn now to our particular case — conspiracy. So far as criminal conspiracy is concerned, a husband and wife cannot be found guilty of conspiring with one another. That is now statutory in section 2(2)(*a*) of the Criminal Law Act 1977. But they can be found guilty if the two of them jointly conspire with a third person.

Mr Munby says that the tort of conspiracy should be treated in the same way as the crime of conspiracy. He says that husband and wife cannot be made liable in tort for conspiracy with one another. But they can, he admits, be made liable if the two of them jointly conspire with a third person. For instance, he agrees that if the conspiracy charged in this case was between Walter (the husband) and Evelyne (the wife) and their other son Derek, and it was found that all three conspired together, all could be made liable in damages. But as the only conspiracy charged is against Walter and Evelyne alone, they cannot be made liable at all. That seems to me a most illogical and unreasonable state of the law, not to be accepted unless covered by authority, and there is none to cover it, no decision and really no statement of authority as far as I can discover. . . .

I see no good reason for applying the doctrine of unity to the modern tort of conspiracy. It is clear that in a like case father and son could be made liable in conspiracy; so mother and daughter; so man and mistress. Why then should not husband and wife be made liable? If the allegations against Walter and Evelyne are correct, they did a grievous wrong to Geoffrey. Together with their son Derek they deprived Geoffrey of his birth right, just as Jacob deprived Esau. Both are now dead, but their estates can be made liable in conspiracy, or at any rate Walter's estate which is the only one now before the court. It seems to me that Mrs Kemp [Walter's executrix] would be liable in full if the conspiracy were established which is alleged. And if she were held liable for the conspiracy and the damages which flow from it after giving any credit from the solicitors' action she would be liable for it, and then her only recourse would be against the lawyers who failed on her behalf to plead plene administravit, if she could prove that they were in any way at fault.

For these reasons I agree with the decision of Oliver J and would dismiss the appeals.

(b) EVIDENCE

At common law, as a general rule, a party's spouse was incompetent as a witness both for or against him. It is also suggested that there was a prohibition on disclosure of marital communications by any witness.

The Evidence Amendment Act 1853 allowed a husband or a wife of a party in a civil case to be a permissible witness for that party and also to give evidence on the other side. A competent witness is normally obliged to give evidence at the instance of either party; thus in this sense the husband or the wife are compellable witnesses in civil actions. Section 3 of that Act gave a privilege in civil proceedings to the spouse to whom a statement was made not to be compelled to disclose this statement. The privilege was abolished by the Civil Evidence Act 1968, s. 16(3) although s. 14(1)(b) confers on the witness in a civil trial 'a right to refuse to answer any question or produce any document or thing if to do so would tend to expose the husband or the wife of that person to proceedings for any . . . criminal offence or for the recovery of . . . a penalty'.

So far as criminal trials are concerned, s. 80 of the Police and Criminal Evidence Act 1984 has now swept away the previous unsatisfactory position.

(1) In any proceedings the wife or husband of the accused shall be competent to give evidence—
  (a) subject to subsection (4) below, for the prosecution; and
  (b) on behalf of the accused or any person jointly charged with the accused.
(2) In any proceedings the wife or husband of the accused shall, subject to subsection (4) below, be compellable to give evidence on behalf of the accused.
(3) In any proceedings the wife or husband of the accused shall, subject to subsection (4) below, be compellable to give evidence for the prosecution or on behalf of any person jointly charged with the accused if and only if—
  (a) the offence charged involves an assault on, or injury or a threat of injury to, the wife or husband of the accused or a person who was at the material time under the age of sixteen; or
  (b) the offence charged is a sexual offence alleged to have been committed in respect of a person who was at the material time under that age; or
  (c) the offence charged consists of attempting or conspiring to commit, or of aiding, abetting, counselling, procuring or inciting the commission of, an offence falling within paragraph (a) or (b) above.
(4) Where an information or indictment charges a husband and his wife jointly with an offence neither spouse shall at the trial of the information or indictment be competent or

compellable by virtue of subsection (1)(*a*), (2) or (3) above to give evidence in respect of that offence unless that spouse is not, or is no longer, liable to be convicted of that offence at the trial as a result of pleading guilty or for any other reason.

The policy which lay behind the Act is identified in the following extract from the Criminal Law Revision Committee's 11th Report (1972):

147. How far the wife of the accused should be competent and compellable for the prosecution, for the accused and for a co-accused is in these days essentially a question of balancing the desirability that all available evidence which might conduce to the right verdict should be before the court against (i) the objection on social grounds to disturbing marital harmony more than is absolutely necessary and (ii) what many regard as the harshness of compelling a wife to give evidence against her husband. Older objections, even to competence, based on the theoretical unity of the spouses or on the interest of the accused's wife in the outcome of the proceedings, and in particular on the likelihood that his wife will be biased in favour of the accused, can have no place in the decisions as to the extent of competence and compellability nowadays. But the question of the right balance between the considerations of policy mentioned is one on which different opinions are inevitably — and sometimes strongly — held. The arguments relate mostly to compellability for the prosecution but, as will be seen, not entirely so. The argument for more compellability for the prosecution is the straightforward one that, if it is left to the wife to choose whether to give evidence against her husband, the result may be that a dangerous criminal will go free. The argument to the contrary is that, if the wife is not willing to give the evidence, the state should not expose her to the pitiful clash between the duty to aid the prosecution by giving evidence, however unwillingly, and the natural duty to protect her husband whatever the circumstances. It has been argued strongly in support of this view that the law ought to recognize that, as between spouses, conviction and punishment may have consequences of the most serious economic and social kind for their future and that neither of them should in any circumstances be compelled, against his or her will, to contribute to bringing this about. It is also pointed out that there is at least a considerable likelihood that the result of more compellability will be either perjury or contempt by silence. The particular provisions which we recommend are intended (in addition to simplifying the law) as a compromise between these views.

Questions

(i) Note that the Act does not make the spouse compellable for the prosecution in all cases. Should it have done so?

(ii) Is the accused's wife compellable against him if he kisses a fifteen-year-old? Is the accused's wife compellable against him if he rapes and murders a sixteen-year-old? [See Zuckerman (1990) p. 294.]

Can you justify the different answers you give to these questions?

(iii) Section 14(1)(*b*) of the Civil Evidence Act 1968 (see p. 57) has no corresponding provision in criminal law. When a witness testifies in a criminal trial, he or she has no right to refuse to answer a question on the ground that to answer would incriminate his or her spouse. However, the privilege of communication between spouses still exists in criminal law although it has now been abolished in a civil action. Are these rules consistent?

(c) PUBLIC LAW

(i) Rates/community charge

Cardiff Corpn v Robinson
[1957] 1 QB 39, [1956] 3 All ER 56, [1956] 3 WLR 522, 120 JP 500, 100 Sol Jo 588, 49 R & IT 571, 1 RRC 83, 54 LGR 506, Divisional Court, Queen's Bench Division

A husband lived with his wife and children in a house owned by his father. In November 1954, after differences had arisen between the husband and the wife, the husband left his wife and went to live elsewhere. The father raised no objection to the wife and children remaining in the house. The husband and wife agreed that the wife should remain in the house rent free and he should pay her £6 per week by way of maintenance. He paid the rates to the end of the financial year 31 March 1955, and then informed the Cardiff Corporation that as he was no longer the occupier of the house his liability to pay rates ceased. The Cardiff Corporation preferred a complaint against the husband that being a person duly rated and assessed in their area by a general rate in the sum of £19.1s.4d (the first instalment of the 1955-6) rates, he had not paid that sum. The Stipendiary Magistrate stated a case to the Divisional Court.

Lord Goddard CJ: . . . The position is that, the respondent having left his wife and children, he is under an obligation to maintain them and, among other things, to provide a roof over their heads. He has done that by telling the wife that she may continue to occupy this house. Of course, that would only be so long as his father allowed the wife and children to live there. It seems to me obvious, therefore, that the husband has made this provision for his wife as part of the obligation he is under to maintain her. Therefore, he is using this house, which his father has allowed him to occupy, in the most beneficial way he can by housing his wife and children in respect of whom he is liable to provide a home. It is agreed, and no one can deny, that if the respondent goes out of the house and leaves his furniture in it, he is liable, so long as his furniture is there, to pay the rates because there is a beneficial occupation. If he chooses to leave the house and leave his wife and family there, why is it any different from leaving his furniture there? He may come to an arrangement between himself and his wife under which his wife agrees to pay the rates. That may be, but the local authority are not bound by any arrangement of that sort. The only question here is: has the husband got a beneficial occupation? I think that he has, because it enables him to provide for his wife and family who, if they had to provide a home for themselves, would naturally require more money from him.

But the situation has now changed. Under the Local Government Finance Act 1988 (which will remain in force until 1993), s. 16(9) there is joint and several liability in respect of community charge for people: (*a*) who are married to each other and are members of the same household, or (*b*) who are not married to each other but are living together as husband and wife.

Question

If an earning husband fails to pay the community charge for either himself or his wife, why should his non-earning wife have to pay for both of them?

(ii) Taxation

Income tax law once aggregated the resources of husband and wife and treated them as those of the husband. A married man received an allowance higher than that given to a single person. In addition, the husband whose wife went out to work, received an additional earned income allowance.

These allowances were not transferable.

Some married men tried to get the best of both worlds.

Holmes v Mitchell (Inspector of Taxes)
[1991] FLR 512, [1991] Fam Law 217, [1991] STC 25, High Court, Chancery Division

The taxpayer married his wife, a teacher, in 1959. By 1962 they had begun to live separate lives while remaining in the same house. The taxpayer paid all the outgoings on the house but otherwise he and his wife maintained themselves out of their own incomes.

From 1972 onwards they lived, the commissioners held, 'as separate households under the same roof . . . and more or less ignored each other'. In 1987, the taxpayer was granted a decree of divorce absolute based on two years separation by consent.

Section 8(1) of the Income and Corporation Taxes Act 1970 provided for the relief if a husband proved: '(i) that for the year of assessment he had his wife living with him, or (ii) that his wife is wholly maintained by him . . .'

Section 42 provided: '(i) A married woman shall be treated for income tax purposes as living with her husband unless — (a) they are separated under an order of a court of competent jurisdiction, or by deed of separation, or (b) they are in fact separated in such circumstances that the separation is likely to be permanent.'

The issue was whether the taxpayer was entitled to deduct for income tax purposes personal allowances at the higher rate appropriate to a married man living with his wife for the years under appeal.

Vinelott J: [T]he commissioners decision that the taxpayer had not satisfied the requirement laid down in section 8(1)(a)(ii) of having 'wholly maintained' his wife during the relevant years was plainly correct.

Turning then to section 8(1)(a)(i), did the taxpayer have his wife living with him during the relevant years? Or to put it in the terms set out in section 42(1) of the Act, were they 'separate in such circumstances that the separation is likely to be permanent.'

It was well established that a husband and wife might be separated and that one might be said to have deserted the other even though they were living under the same roof. In *Hopes v Hopes* ([1949] P 227, 236), a case concerning divorce based on desertion, Denning LJ said that the 'line was to be drawn at the point where the parties are living separately and apart. In cases where they are living under the same roof, that point is reached when they cease to be one household and become two households, or, in other words, when they are no longer residing with one another or cohabiting with one another'.

That case, not being concerned with the provisions of section 42 of the 1970 Act, was not direct authority. But the principle there laid down that spouses may be 'apart' when living in the same house, in the sense of not being in the same household, was appropriate.

The commissioners in reaching their decision had not misunderstood the principles to be applied. They were entitled to hold that the taxpayer lived separately, although under the same roof, from his wife during the relevant years. Further, they were right to conclude that the taxpayer's action in seeking a divorce confirmed that that *de facto* separation was one that was likely to be permanent.

In recent years, the Government has produced two Green Papers, one in 1980 and the other in 1986.

The 1986 Green paper, entitled *The Reform of Personal Taxation*, moved towards a fully transferable allowance:

Husband and wife

3.10 If transferable allowances were introduced, married women would be treated as independent taxpayers; they would be responsible for their own tax affairs, be able to fill in their own tax returns, and to pay their own tax. It follows that the legislation which deems a married woman's income to be her husband's for tax purposes would be abolished.

3.11 Transferable allowances would give married women an opportunity for complete privacy in tax matters. Couples where the husband and wife both had income above the tax threshold would be treated, in effect, wholly independently. For other couples, any transfer of allowances would be wholly voluntary: people would not have to make any transfer, or they could transfer an amount less than the whole of their unused allowances if they so chose (accepting that their partner would be entitled to less tax relief in consequence of their choice).

3.12 A system of transferable allowances would thus reflect the Government's belief that a married woman should have the same right to deal with her own tax affairs as any other taxpayer. . . .

The family

3.14 Transferable allowances would provide a means for recognising through the tax system that, at different times and for different reasons, one partner in a marriage may be financially dependent on the other. The Government reject the view that the tax system should pay no regard to the special relationship and responsibilities that exist within marriage. The aim is to recognise these in a way that is straightforward, flexible, and does not seek to make invidious distinctions between couples in different circumstances.

3.15 With transferable allowances there would no longer be discrimination against couples where, for whatever reason, the wife was not in paid employment. And since transferability could operate both ways between a husband and wife, the system would give equal recognition to circumstances where the husband did not have income but his wife did.

3.16 Transferable allowances would ensure that a couple's total allowances remained the same, and did not fall when one partner left paid work. This is often at a time when the couple may be under financial pressure, for example when they start a family. . . .

3.18 The Government believe that the tax system should not discriminate against families where the wife wishes to remain at home to care for young children. Transferable allowances would direct more tax relief to such families.

3.19 The effect of transferable allowances on the willingness of married women to go out to work would need to be carefully considered. Since it would give everybody the same tax allowance, the system would treat married men and married women in exactly the same way. What it would remove is the present special incentive for two-earner couples, introduced in the war-time conditions of 1942. Such positive discrimination is neither necessary nor economically desirable at a time of high unemployment, particularly among the young (of both sexes). In principle, transferable allowances are neither an incentive nor a deterrent for married women seeking work.

3.20 It is sometimes argued that transferable allowances would deter married women from seeking work because they would suffer tax on every pound that they earned. That would not be the position: a married woman would be entitled to a single allowance against her earnings or other income, in precisely the same way as any man or single woman. A variant of this argument is that, in practice, the husband would regard both allowances as a married man's allowance, and would not want his wife to go back to work because he would lose the benefit of her tax allowance. There can be no direct evidence for or against this view. But it is interesting to note that Denmark, which has operated a form of transferable tax allowance for some time, has the highest proportion of married women working of any country in the European Community.

3.21 By taxing a husband and wife separately and giving a married woman her own allowance and tax rate bands in the same way as any other taxpayer, transferable allowances could remove the tax penalty which arises for married-couples where the wife has more than a modest amount of savings income. . . .

This proposal became law under the Finance Act 1988 as from April 1990.

Income tax law no longer aggregates all resources and treats them as that of the husband. However, tax law still contains within it certain vestiges of the former system, as the following extract from Wylie, *The Taxation of Husband and Wife* (1990), makes clear:

. . . apart from choosing the individual as the unit of taxation, the Government had opted for two basic principles. First, independent taxation should operate with non-transferable personal allowances; and, second, there should be no losers as a result of the change from aggregate taxation to independent taxation. One consequence of this latter decision is that the married man's allowance has been retained in another guise, the married couple's allowance, equal to the difference between the married and single person allowance.[3] Further, the married couple's allowance can only be deducted from the husband's income and may not be deducted from the wife's income unless the husband has insufficient income to exhaust it, in which case the unused balance is transferable. Again, for a limited period a husband's but not a wife's, unused personal allowance may be transferred to the other spouse, and the special arrangements for elderly taxpayers continue to exist. The change to independent taxation has therefore not resulted in a married couple being equated for all tax purposes with two single people, and has produced its own anomalies.

. . . However the balance of taxation has swung against cohabitation and, if anything, is now in favour of marriage. Virtually all the tax disadvantages of marriage have been removed. Spouses now have their incomes and gains taxed as if they were unmarried rather than have them aggregated, and cohabitees no longer have the ability to claim double mortgage interest relief, or double additional personal allowance if they have two or more children. Indeed a married couple without children are now significantly better off than their unmarried counterpart. The husband is entitled to claim married couple's allowance, and assets can be freely transferred from one spouse to the other with no capital gains tax or inheritance tax penalty.

Of these concessions in favour of marriage perhaps the most anomalous is the married couple's allowance. This was retained mainly to ensure that married men did not suffer a significant drop in their take home pay following the introduction of independent taxation, but in an era of legislation against discrimination on the grounds of sex, it is difficult to see why it can only be deducted from a wife's income if her husband has insufficient taxable income against which to offset it, and even then only on a claim to transfer the unused allowance being made by the husband. It is also difficult to see why marriage, as such, should qualify a couple for higher tax allowances than if they remained unmarried.

Questions

(i) Married couples' allowances still continue. Why?

(ii) Would some people object that the abolition of the married couple's allowance and the use of the revenue to increase child benefit: (*a*) discriminates in favour of families with children; (*b*) discriminates in favour of high-income two worker families; and (*c*) does nothing to help the low paid — especially if only one works and there is only one child, or no child?

(iii) If a system of wholly independent taxation is introduced, do you think that more people would decide that there is no point in getting married?

(iv) Do you think that the present system 'is a compromise which seems to be broadly acceptable to many people'?

(v) Do you agree with the view expressed in the Green Paper (1986) that transferable allowances do not deter married women from seeking work?

---

3. But frozen in the 1991 Budget on previous year's figures.

CHAPTER 3

Family economics — income

The economic arrangements of a husband and a wife do not exist in isolation. There is a need for a body of flexible rules within which the husband and wife are free to regulate their affairs. These rules exist in all marriages; whether they be created by the parties themselves, by the society and the culture within which they live, or imposed upon them by judicial or other external intervention. The concern of the lawyer in this area tends to be expressed most often in terms of finding sensible solutions to the re-allocation of the economic assets of the parties after the marriage has broken down and the parties are divorced or separated. However, no legal solution to this particular problem can reflect a logical and realistic re-adjustment of the tangled affairs unless there is a clear understanding of the economic expectations of the husband and the wife during the marriage. Thus, the question 'what happens to property after divorce?' is closely inter-linked with the question 'what were the economic arrangements of the husband and the wife when they were married?' There are also two important ideological questions to be raised relating to support obligations of spouses for one another and the state involvement in the support of the family.

These chapters, therefore, are concerned both with marriage and with divorce; for a sensitive law on matrimonial property and support obligations must be aware of the possibility of divorce, and likewise a law on divorce re-allocation must be soundly based on the economic structure of the marriage as a going concern.

Professor Tony Honoré is fully aware of the link which we have just made between the dynamic and subsisting marriage and what has been described as the 'pathology of family law', when he categorises marriage ideologically into three distinct groups — as a partnership, as a contract, and thirdly as an arrangement by which a husband assumes the role of provider. The following extract is taken from *The Quest for Security: Employees, Tenants, Wives* (1982).

There are three main ways of viewing marriage. Some see it as a *partnership*. On a traditional view, it is a partnership, come what may, for life. In that case, after divorce the partnership notionally continues, and the wife is entitled to the support she would have received had the marriage not broken up, or at any rate to a standard of living which continues to be the equal of her husband's. . . . More often, marriage is now seen as an equal partnership which lasts, like other partnerships, until it is dissolved. On that view there must on divorce be a fair division of the profits of the partnership, including property acquired during the marriage. . . .

Another conception of marriage is that of an *arrangement* (a collateral contract?) *by which a husband induces his wife to change her career*. Had it not been for the marriage she might, for example, have had good earning prospects. She gives these up to marry. On divorce she must now retrain, sometimes late in life, with diminished prospects. If so, her husband must compensate her by keeping her, during a transitional period, while she brings up the children, if she wants to, and redeploys. If, after a long time together, she has become emotionally attached to her status as a wife, her husband may also be required to compensate her for the wrench.

Yet another conception views marriage not as a contract but *as an arrangement by which a husband assumes the role of providing for his wife's needs and those of their children*. This idea, more ancient and deeply rooted in genetics than the contractual ones, makes the husband to some extent the wife's insurer. If she is in need, it is to him, rather than the state, that she turns in the first instance. It is he who must see to her subsistence, and perhaps more, in ill-health, old age or disablement. It is only in this framework of anticipated security that childbearing and childrearing can flourish. But how far does the husband's responsibility extend? How far, in modern conditions does that of the state or community? [italics added]

These three categories must be borne in mind when we consider the historical evidence from both an economic and a sociological perspective.

1 The economic evidence

It is argued that the economic process of change in the family has proceeded through three stages, as explained by M. Young and P. Wilmot in *The Symmetrical Family* (1973):

Even though there is so much in common between family life at each stage, and even though the boundaries between one stage and another are somewhat arbitrary, the rough-and-ready division seems to us useful, as does the generalization, even though it cannot any more than most generalizations do justice to all the evidence. In the first stage, the pre-industrial, the family was usually the unit of production. For the most part, men, women and children worked together in home and field. This type of economic partnership was, for working-class people, supplanted after a bitter struggle by the Stage 2 family, whose members were caught up in the new economy as individual wage-earners. The collective was undermined. Stage 2 was the stage of disruption. One historian has pointed the contrast in this way (E.P. Thompson 1963).

'Women became more dependent upon the employer or the labour market, and they looked back to a "golden" period in which home earnings from spinning, poultry and the like, could be gained around their own door. In good times the domestic economy, like the peasant economy, supported a way of life centred upon the home, in which inner whims and compulsions were more obvious than external discipline. Each stage in industrial differentiation and specialisation struck also at the family economy, disturbing customary relations between man and wife, parents and children, and differentiating more sharply between "work" and "life". It was to be a full hundred years before this differentiation was to bring returns, in the form of labour-saving devices, back into the working woman's home. Meanwhile, the family was roughly torn apart each morning by the factory bell.'

The process affected most the families of manual workers (and not all of these by any means). The trends were different in the middle class family, where the contrasts for both husbands and wives were somewhat less sharp than they had been in the past. But as working-class people were preponderant most families were probably 'torn apart' by the new economic system. In the third stage the unity of the family has been restored around its functions as the unit not of production but of consumption.

It is clearly not possible, since social history is unlike political or military history, to do more by way of dating than to indicate a rough manner when the successive waves of change started going through the social structure. The Stage 1 family lasted until the new industry overran it in a rolling advance which went on from the eighteenth well into the nineteenth century. The development of the new industry was uneven as between different parts of the country, coming much later to London than to the industrial north. It also outmoded the old techniques of production more slowly in some occupations than in others. But come it did, eventually, along with many other forms of employment which shared one vital feature, that the employees worked for wages. This led to the Stage 2 family. The third stage started early in the twentieth century and is still working its way downwards. At any one period there were, and still are, families representing all three stages. But as first one wave and then another has been set in motion, the proportions in Stage 2 increased in the nineteenth century and in Stage 3 in the twentieth.

The new kind of family has three main characteristics which differentiate it from the sort which prevailed in Stage 2. The first is that the couple, and their children, are very much centred on the home, especially when the children are young. They can be so much together, and share so much together, because they spend so much of their time together in the same space. Life has, to use another term, become more 'privatized'. . . . This trend has been supported by the form taken by technological change.

The second characteristic is that the extended family (consisting of relatives of several different degrees to some extent sharing a common life) counts for less and the immediate, or nuclear, family for more. . . .

The third and most vital characteristic is that inside the family of marriage the roles of the sexes have become less segregated.

Social historians, Louise Tilly and Joan Scott, describe each of these three stages in *Women, Work and Family* (1987). They speak first of the family as the labour and consumption unit:

In both England and France, in city and country, people worked in small settings, which often overlapped with households. Productivity was low, the differentiation of tasks was limited. And many workers were needed. The demand for labor extended to women as well as men, to everyone but the youngest children and the infirm. Jobs were differentiated by age and by sex, as well as by training and skill. But, among the popular classes, some kind of work was expected of all able-bodied family members. . . . But whether or not they actually worked together, family members worked in the economic interest of the family. In peasant and artisan households, and in proletarian families, the household allocated the labor of family members. In all cases, decisions were made in the interest of the group, not the individual. This is reflected in wills and marriage contracts which spelled out the obligation of siblings or elderly parents who were housed and fed on the family property, now owned by the oldest son. They must work 'to the best of their ability' for 'the prosperity of the family' and 'for the interest of the designated heir.' Among property-owning families the land or the shop defined the tasks of family members and whether or not their labor was needed. People who controlled their means of production adjusted household composition to production needs. For the propertyless, the need for wages — the subsistence of the family itself — sent men, women, and children out to work. These people adjusted household composition to consumption needs. The bonds holding the proletarian family together, bonds of expediency and necessity, were often less permanent than the property interest (or the inheritable skill) which united peasants and craftsmen. The composition of propertied and propertyless households also differed. Nevertheless, the line between the propertied and propertyless was blurred on the question of commitment to work in the family interest.

One of the goals of work was to provide for the needs of family members. Both property owning and proletarian households were consumption units, though all rural households were far more self-sufficient than urban households. Rural families usually produced their own food, clothing, and tools, while urban families bought them at the market. These differences affected the work roles of family members. Women in urban families, for example, spent more time marketing and less time in home manufacture. And there were fewer domestic chores for children to assist with in the city. In the urban family, work was oriented more to the production of specific goods for sale, or it involved the sale of one's labor. For the peasant family, there were a multiplicity of tasks involved in working the land and running the household. The manner of satisfying consumption needs thus varied and so affected the kinds of work family members did.

When the number of household members exceeded the resources available to feed them, and when those resources could not be obtained, the family often adjusted its size. Non-kin left to work elsewhere when children were old enough to work. Then children migrated. Inheritance systems led non-heirs to move away in search of jobs, limited positions as artisans forced children out of the family craftshop, while the need for wages led the children of the propertyless many miles from home. People migrated from farm to farm, farm to village, village to town, and country to city in this period. Although much migration was local and rural in this period, some migrants moved to cities, and most of these tended to be young and single when they migrated. Indeed, in this period cities grew primarily by migration; for urban death rates were high and deaths often outnumbered births, a result largely of the crowded and unsanitary conditions that prevailed. Migrants came to the city from nearby regions.

In the second stage, the family wage economy, we enter a distributive period. As Kevin Gray (1977) says: 'In the distributive stage, production occurs outside the family, and the family merely distributes among the family members the economic product of the labour performed by the provider husband, the house-maker wife of course playing a vital role in this secondary process of distribution.'

Tilly and Scott emphasise that this distributive period (the 'family wage economy', as they call it) developed gradually during the mid-nineteenth century:

Under the family wage economy married women performed several roles for their families. They often contributed wages to the family fund, they managed the household, and they bore and cared for children. With industrialization, however, the demands of wage labor increasingly conflicted with women's domestic activities. The terms of labor and the price paid for it were a function of employers' interest, which took little account of household needs under most circumstances. Industrial jobs required specialization and a full-time commitment to work, usually in a specific location away from home. While under the domestic mode of production women combined market-oriented activities and domestic work, the industrial mode of production precluded an easy reconciliation of married women's activities. The resolution of the conflict was for married women not to work unless family finances urgently required it, and then to try to find that work which conflicted least with their domestic responsibilities. . . .

In general, married women tended to be found in largest numbers in the least industrialized sectors of the labor force, in those areas where the least separation existed between home and workplace and where women could control the rhythm of their work.

Question

The authors concentrate on working class families. Do you have the feeling that their comments might need modifying for the middle classes in the nineteenth century?

The authors then describe how the third stage, the consumer economy, developed:

By the early twentieth century the higher wages of men particularly and the availability of cheap consumer goods raised the target income of working-class families. Necessities now included not only food and clothing, but also other items that once had been considered luxuries. What we have termed the family consumer economy then was a wage earning unit which increasingly emphasized family consumption needs.

The organization of the family consumer economy was not dramatically different from that of the family wage economy. The management of money and of family affairs in an increasingly complex urban environment did, however, require additional time and a certain expertise. As a result, the household division of labor tended to distinguish even more sharply than in the past between the roles of husband and wife and of daughters and wives. Husbands and unmarried children were family wage earners, while wives devoted most of their time to child care and household management. Wives continued, however, to work sporadically in order to earn wages to help raise the family's level of consumption.

Tilly and Scott inform us that women who worked chose to do so not simply from individualistic motives and certainly hardly ever for financial independence. Rather the prime motive was to improve the financial position of the family and to raise its standard of living. The mother's work was a supplement to her domestic responsibilities.

Question

Would it surprise you to be told that this view of a woman's reasons for working is now controversial?

The three models of family organisation described by Tilly and Scott and by Young and Wilmot have been criticised by Hudson and Lee in their introductory essay to *Women's Work and the Family Economy* (1990):

The temporal sequence of organisational change from the traditional family economy to the family wage economy, and finally to the family consumer economy based on a 'symmetrical' marriage structure is of only limited usefulness. It is also problematic to view work at home for pay as constituting a 'transitional model', given both its traditional and contemporary prevalence. Even within the middle class, adherence to the Victorian cult of domesticity was not always translated into the reality of separate spheres of activity and maintaining the 'paraphernalia of gentility' was often financially impossible. With changing economic conditions participation by middle-class women in the public sphere became 'both respectable and necessary', and there is increasing evidence of their role in decision-making in relation to their husbands' careers and family businesses. To this extent nineteenth-century middle-class practice was not too dissimilar from the joint responsibility for financial matters enshrined in the earlier German tradition of *Hausmutterliteratur*.[1] Furthermore, despite the apparent pervasiveness of patriarchy in the later nineteenth century, there were certain industries, such as pottery, where the male breadwinner ethos failed to take root, and where women retained a strong presence, even in trade-union organisations. A joint contribution to the family economy could also encourage mutuality in dealing with domestic responsibilities.

Pottery was an exception.

Diana Gittins in *The Family in Question* (1985) describes how the ideology of a single male breadwinner per family developed during the nineteenth century:

Although never an entirely secure institution, marriage in pre-industrial society had provided women with a reasonable means of economic survival involving both production and domestic work in and around the home, with a good chance of some minimal security in the event of widowhood. The growth of wage labour and the increasing separation of home from work put women more than ever before at the mercy of two increasingly unstable markets: the marriage market and the labour market. In both their position was weak, and economic survival was precarious whether a woman entered one or both.

In other areas the response to mechanisation, de-skilling and proletarianisation was different. Sometimes machine breaking was an immediate response, as in the Luddite and Captain Swing riots (Hobsbaum and Rudé, 1973). More often, men in skilled crafts or industries formed themselves into associations or unions. Their general purpose was to defend their members against further capitalist exploitation, mechanisation and wage cuts, and to protect themselves from cheap labour. Since most cheap labour was made up of women and children, the unions tended to contribute further to the already disadvantaged position of women. Until the second half of the nineteenth century, however, the majority of unions were made up of men from only the most skilled trades and crafts, and one of their main aims was to procure a 'family wage' — a single wage that was adequate to support a man and dependent wife and children on his work alone. This new emphasis on the father/husband as sole earner was a powerful factor in the development of modern notions of 'masculinity'. While the concept of a single male breadwinner had started with the rise of the middle classes in the late eighteenth century, this was the first time a sector of the working class — and a very small sector at that — did so.

As Hilary Land (1976) points out, it is hard to know whether their argument for wanting to keep their wives and children out of the workforce was more a matter of conviction or a rationale for higher wages that they knew would appeal to middle-class ears. Whatever the

---

1. M.W. Gray 'Prescriptions for Productive Female Domesticity in a Transitional Era: Germany's *Hausmutterliteratur* 1780–1840', History of European Ideas 8 (1987) pp. 413–26.

rationale, the ideal of a family wage became increasingly important as an ideal of the organised trade union movement, and it was an ideal which coincided with the new middle-class ideology of women and children as dependants of the husband/father.

During the nineteenth century, however, the proportion of working-class families who could survive on the basis of the man's wage alone was very small. Nevertheless, the objective of a single male breadwinner per family was one of the most radical changes in family ideology of the modern era, and one that had dramatic effects on notions of fatherhood, masculinity, motherhood, femininity, family life and family policy, and still has. The ideal, then as now, was often very far removed from the reality, and the majority of working-class families in the nineteenth century still relied heavily on a household economy based on several wages. Working-class men and women, but women in particular, were therefore dependent on both wage labour in the labour market and a partner through the marriage market in order to survive economically. Both markets were insecure and in fact many individuals had to find extra economic support through children's or other kin's labour.

Question

Do you feel that this campaign was one worth winning?

2 The sociological evidence

In *Legal Regulation of Marriage: Tradition and Change* (1974), Lenore Weitzman writes:

The sociological data . . . are closely related to the economic data . . ., for in large part it is the changing position of women with respect to men in the larger society which has influenced and altered the position of the two sexes within the family. Thus the increased labor force participation of married women has probably been instrumental in causing a decline in the absolute authority of the husband, with a consequent growth in the wife's role in the family decision-making. With an expansion in women's roles, especially economic roles, outside the family, roles within the family have also become less strongly differentiated. Wives are assuming more responsibility for financial and domicile decisions, and husbands are assuming a greater share of the responsibility for housework and child care. In general, there is a strong trend toward egalitarian family patterns, those in which authority is shared and decisions are made jointly by the husband and the wife.

The spread in egalitarian family patterns may be briefly noted in several areas. First, there is an increase in the sharing of financial decisions within the family. As the wife's contribution to the total family budget assumes greater relative importance, financial responsibilities within the family are more equally shared. Decisions on family expenditures, savings, and the general 'struggle for financial security' are now made jointly or apportioned on a less sex-stereotyped basis. Second, the determination of the family domicile and the decision of when and where to move has become more of a family decision, with the needs and interests of the wife and children assuming a much greater importance than in the past. Although both of these trends represent a decline in the traditional authority of the husband, there is also a significant decline in the traditional authority of the wife as the husband assumes a more important role in household decisions and in household tasks. . . .

A third area in which there is a significant trend toward more egalitarian patterns is that of sexuality. The current sexual revolution has focused increased attention and emphasis on the wife's participation and satisfaction in sexual relations, and consequently on more mutual and egalitarian sexual relationships. . . .

A fourth and closely related trend is in the increased sharing of responsibility for birth control. Knowledge and use of some form of contraception has become nearly universal in the United States today. By 1965, 97% of white and black couples in a national sample had used or expected to use contraception at some point in their married lives. The most recently introduced and most highly effective methods of contraception, the pill and the I.U.D., are the first to give women independent control over their reproductive decisions, and the first to allow couples a real choice about the number and timing of children. With technological advances in effective methods of female contraception, the decision of when to have children, as well as the decision of when to have sexual relations, may be increasingly decided by the husband and wife together.

Fifth, and most important, is an extended range of family roles which are now being shared or alternated between husbands and wives.

Question

Is Weitzman saying that industrialisation and changes in women's labour force participation are responsible for changes in family patterns?

Although between the end of the Second World War and the 1990s, the proportion of economically active women has risen dramatically (see p. 81, below), the evidence all points to the fact that women still bear the primary burden of domestic labour in the household. The table on p. 70 is taken from *Social Trends 17* (1987).

Questions

(i) Is it not true that 'most women still regard family and domestic roles and responsibilities as their chief source of personal worth and fulfilment'? (Burgoyne, Ormrod and Richards, 1987).
(ii) Would it surprise you to be told that a larger percentage of working-class couples shared the housework between them than that of middle-class couples?

Todd and Jones' survey of *Matrimonial Property* (1972) provides additional evidence of the general financial management of household affairs. It was carried out in early 1971 on behalf of the Law Commission:

4.1 Household duties involving regular expenditure
We wanted to have some picture of how the couple organised their roles with regard to handling their money, and we also wanted to lead up to asking the wife how interested she was in financial matters. In the first series of questions we asked the couple who usually bought the food, paid the gas or electricity bills, paid the rates, rent or mortgage and who, if there was any money left, dealt with the surplus. In these questions we were asking who carried out the tasks, not who provided the money for them.

Who usually dealt with: —	Buying food	Paying for gas or electricity	Paying rates, rent, mortgage	Dealing with any surplus
	%	%	%	%
Husband	3	38	45	20
Wife	89	49	45	36
Either or both	7	10	8	43
Other answer	1	3	2	1
	100	100	100	100
Base	(1877)	(1877)	(1877)	(1877)

In some cases someone other than one of the spouses carried out the duties, or there was some special method of payment, for example, payment by standing order. The wife was predominantly the person responsible for buying the food but in the other matters there was a fairly even split of responsibility between the couple. We examined in more detail whether the housing and earnings situation of the couple were associated with the sharing of responsibilities for paying bills for heating and lighting, and rates, rent or mortgage.

Table A.2: Household division of labour: by marital status, 1984
Great Britain

Percentages

Household tasks (percentage[3] allocation)	Married people[1]						Never-married people[2]		
	Actual allocation of tasks			Tasks should be allocated to			Tasks should be allocated to		
	Mainly man	Mainly woman	Shared equally	Mainly man	Mainly woman	Shared equally	Mainly man	Mainly woman	Shared equally
Washing and ironing	1	88	9	–	77	21	–	68	30
Preparation of evening meal	5	77	16	1	61	35	1	49	49
Household cleaning	3	72	23	–	51	45	1	42	56
Household shopping	6	54	39	–	35	62	–	31	68
Evening dishes	18	37	41	12	21	64	13	15	71
Organisation of household money and bills	32	38	28	23	15	58	19	16	63
Repairs of household equipment	83	6	8	79	2	17	74	–	24
Child-rearing (percentage[3] allocation)									
Looks after the children when they are sick	1	63	35	–	49	47	–	48	50
Teaches the children discipline	10	12	77	12	5	80	16	4	80

1 1,120 married respondents, except for the questions on actual allocation of child-rearing tasks which were answered by 479 respondents with children under 16.

2 283 never-married respondents. The table excludes results of the formerly married (widowed, divorced, or separated) respondents.

3 'Don't knows' and non-response to the question mean that some categories do not sum to 100 per cent.

Source: British Social Attitudes Survey, 1984,
Social and Community Planning Research

Who usually deals with: —	Paying for gas or electricity		Paying rates, rent, mortgage	
	Method of payment from husband's employment			
	cash	not cash	cash	not cash
	%	%	%	%
Husband	26	58	30	65
Wife	61	31	60	23
Either or both	9	10	7	10
Other answers	4	1	3	2
	100	100	100	100
Base	(1099)	(534)	(1099)	(534)

The method by which the husband is paid is closely associated with which spouse pays both types of bills, fuel and rates, rent or mortgage. Where the husband is paid in cash there is a much greater likelihood that the wife carries out these duties. Where the husband is not paid in cash it is most likely that he has responsibility for these bills.

We next examine whether these duties are associated at all with whether the matrimonial home is owned by the couple or not.

Who usually deals with: —	Paying for gas or electricity		Paying rates, rent, mortgage	
	Ownership of the matrimonial home			
	Couple do not own the home	Couple own the home	Couple do not own the home	Couple own the home
	%	%	%	%
Husband	27	49	29	59
Wife	58	40	61	30
Either or both	10	10	6	11
Other answers	5	1	4	—
	100	100	100	100
Base	(896)	(978)	(896)	(978)

The variation here is similar to that in the previous table. Where the couple own their own home the husband is more likely to take the responsibility for paying the bills for fuel and housing. Where the couple do not own their home these duties are more frequently carried out by the wife.

Thus the duties that the spouses carry out in relation to these particular household responsibilities are associated with other factors in their domestic situation.

4.2 Wife's interest in money matters

After the series of questions about household management we asked wives whether they liked to know about money matters or whether they preferred to leave such things to their husbands. We first classified separately those wives who said they received the whole pay packet and were obviously responsible themselves for domestic financial management.

Wife's interest in money matters

	%
Is given the whole pay packet	5
Likes to know about money matters	76
Prefers to leave such things to husband	19
	100
Base	(1877)

Giving the whole pay packet to the wife is often talked of as a regional phenomenon so we examined to what extent the 5% of wives in this position varied in the different economic planning regions.

Region	Proportion of wives who receive pay packet	
		Base
North	15%	(122)
East Midlands	8%	(142)
South West	8%	(152)
Wales	8%	(99)
Yorkshire and Humberside	5%	(199)
West Midlands	4%	(201)
East Anglia	3%	(62)
North West	3%	(275)
South East	2%	(391)
Greater London	2%	(234)
England and Wales	5%	(1877)

It is thus a way of life occurring most frequently in the North but also occurring more than average in the East Midlands, the South West and Wales.

Distribution of family income between its members is a difficult research field. Notwithstanding the difficulties, Jan Pahl in *Money and Marriage*, (1984, 1990) attempts a structure for the research she and others have conducted in this field:

Patterns of allocation of money
There is an infinite variety of different allocative systems within the great variety of types of households. . . . In reality, the proposed typology represents points on a continuum of allocative systems, but previous research suggests that the typology has considerable validity both within Britain and in other parts of the world. Two criteria are central in distinguishing one system from another: these are, first, each individual's responsibility for expenditure between and within expenditure categories, and second, each individual's access to household funds, other than those for which he or she is responsible.

The whole wage system
In this system one partner, usually the wife, is responsible for managing all the finances of the household and is also responsible for all expenditure, except for the personal spending money of the other partner. The personal spending money of the other partner is either taken out by him before the pay packet is handed over, or is returned to him from collective funds. If both partners earn, both pay packets are administered by the partner who manages the money. Where a whole wage system is managed by a husband, his wife may have no personal spending money of her own and no access to household funds.

The allowance system
In the most common form of this system the husband gives his wife a set amount, which she adds to her own earnings if she has any; she is responsible for paying for specific items of household expenditure. The rest of the money remains in the control of the husband and he pays for other specific items. Thus each partner has a sphere of responsibility in terms of household expenditure. If a wife does not earn she only has access to the 'housekeeping' allowance and, since this is allocated for household expenditure, she may feel that she has no personal spending money of her own: the same phenomenon can also be seen in the case of the whole wage system where the wife is responsible for all family expenditure but has no personal spending money. The allowance system has many variations, mainly because of the varying patterns of responsibility. At one extreme a wife may only be responsible for expenditure on food; at the other extreme she may be responsible for everything except the running of the car and the system may come close to resembling the whole wage system. The allowance system is also known as the 'wife's wage' and the 'spheres of responsibility' system, while the whole wage system is sometimes called the 'tipping up' system (Barrett and McIntosh 1982).

The shared management or pooling system
The essential characteristic of this system is that both partners have access to all or almost all the household money and both have responsibility for management of the common pool and for expenditure out of that pool. The partners may take their personal spending money out of the pool. On the other hand one or both of them may retain a sum for personal spending; when this sum becomes substantial the system begins to acquire some characteristics of the independent management system. . . .

The independent management system
The essential characteristic of this system is that both partners have an income and that neither has access to all the household funds. Each partner is responsible for specific items of expenditure, and though these responsibilities may change over time, the principle of keeping flows of money separate within the household is retained.

The political economy of the household
Distinguishing different types of allocative system is, however, only a beginning. What are the variables which determine the allocative system adopted by any one couple at any one time? What are the implications for the couple as a whole, and for individuals, of adopting one system rather than another?

Pahl (1990) provides interesting information regarding the reasons given by her sample of wives and husbands for their system of money management.

Table 6.1 Reasons given by wives and husbands for their system of money management

		Number mentioning each reason	
		Wives	*Husbands*
	'Ideological' reasons		
1	System seemed natural/right/fair	41	53
	'Practical' reasons		
2	Seemed more efficient/'it just works for us'	27	22
3	Response to way in which wages/salaries paid	22	19
4	More convenient/one partner able to get to bank	19	15
	'Psychological' reasons		
5	Wife 'better manager' so she manages money	23	15
6	Husband 'better manager' so he manages money	10	9
	'Generational' reasons		
7	Tried to avoid parents' mistakes	5	2
8	Money management similar to parents' system	4	1

Note: Numbers add up to more than sample because some individuals gave more than one reason.

Questions

(i) Are you impressed by the 'ideological' reasons given, or do you think that people simply drift into particular arrangements?
(ii) Is it more or less likely that parties to a marriage where one or both of them have been married before will opt for an independent management system?
(iii) Is it more or less likely that cohabitants will opt for an independent management system?

Pahl (1990) moves the debate along by writing:

... It has become clear that, far from protecting them, women's assumed and actual dependence on men constitutes a major cause of their poverty (Glendinning and Millar, 1987). Women carry the burden of scarcity, not just because they are more likely than men to be poor, but also because when a household is poor it is women who are usually responsible for seeing that the money goes round; when money is short it is typically women who go without. The recent idea of the 'feminisation of poverty' implies that women are now at greater risk of poverty than men (Scott, 1984). However, evidence from Britain suggests that throughout the twentieth century women have been more likely to fall into poverty than men (Lewis and Piachaud, 1987).

Question

What should politicians do with this information?

3 An ideological basis?

Mary Ann Glendon, in *State, Law and Family: Family Law in Transition in the United States and Western Europe* (1977), emphasises the difficulties which appear when this question is explored.

The prevailing ideologies of marriage have never been alike for all groups of any large population. In Western society, however, one ideology has been dominant and until modern times has found universal expression in the law. The family law of Western legal systems has traditionally embodied ideas of separate spheres of activity appropriate for women and men. It has carried the image of the woman as principal caretaker of the home and children, the man as principal provider, and of a family authority structure dominated by the husband and father. This should not be understood as meaning that the woman's *exclusive* task has been to care for home and children. In pre-industrial society, the wife was often a co-worker with the husband on the farm, in the craft and in the shop. The exclusively housewife-marriage seems to be a phenomenon of the 20th century. Already this period is beginning to appear to have been a brief interlude in history. Today, as more and more women engage in economic activity outside the home, housewife-marriage is only one of many current marriage patterns. Where housewife-marriage exists, it is now more apt to be a phase of a marriage than a description of the marriage from beginning to end.

Organized around a hierarchical model, with a clear division of roles between the sexes, traditional family law placed primary responsibility for support of the family on the male partner and vested authority in him to determine the place and mode of family life and to deal with all the family property, including that of the wife. Among the wealthy, property matters could to some extent be arranged so that the interests of the wife (and her family of origin) could be protected. The law paid little attention to the needs of the poor, even when large numbers of women began to be employed outside the home in the early 19th century in England, and later in France and Germany. The set of legal rules organized along these traditional lines persisted in England, France, the United States and Germany well into the 20th century, long after behavior of many married people had ceased to correspond to the image enshrined in the laws.

This model was constantly adjusted, beginning in the late 19th century and in the first half of the 20th century, but at last the center could not hold. Laws which might have been appropriate for the family production community, or for the housewife marriage when divorce was rare, no longer worked when many women's economic activity had been transferred to the marketplace and when divorce had become pandemic.

Although Glendon's point is a necessary reminder of the shift in emphasis of the women's economic activity, it is appropriate to recall the material contained at p. 70 that housework and child care continue to a great extent to be the responsibility of women. Elizabeth Wilson, in *Women and the Welfare State* (1977), asks the question why:

Because more and more married women are going out to work, and because, although there has been a rise in the number of women who bear a child or children at some point in their lives maternity has become quantitatively less and less absorbing, the importance, drudgery, and significance of domestic work in the home has become more and more clear (Gardiner 1975). Why then is it retained? Why has it not been socialized when in the industrial sphere capitalism constantly seeks to transform and revolutionize its technology? The economic significance of domestic labour has been discussed for some years in the Women's Movement (e.g. Benston 1969; Morton 1970; Rowbotham 1973) and more recently the subject has been taken up by a number of socialist and Marxist economists (Harrison 1974; Secombe 1974). Whatever the precise nature of its relationship to surplus value it is clear that the domestic unpaid work of the housewife helps to keep costs down for the employer by making it possible for the worker to be cared for much more cheaply than would otherwise be possible. The socialized care of the worker — canteens, living accommodation, laundry — alone would be likely in this country to cost the capitalist more than the efforts of the housewife who takes pride in making do. Where it is cheaper for the workman to be separated from his family — as is the case in South Africa where black workers can be compelled to live in barracks — that is what happens. The strength of the working class has also much to do with the achievement of more tolerable living conditions.

There is a second reason for the retention of domestic work: the supportive emotional functions of the family. The intensity of the parental–child relationships within the family make for the vulnerability of the child and therefore the family is a highly functional ideological institution for the upbringing of children in such a manner that they conform, as adults, to authoritarian/submissive social relationships. Then there is the marriage relationship. It is pleasanter for workers to be married. The marriage relationship may have its problems, men may feel henpecked or hamstrung; the sexual relationship may have its inhibitions and disappointments, especially for the woman; yet State brothels could hardly provide an adequate substitute. . . .

A third reason for the retention of the unwaged housewife and her children as the dependants of the individual worker is that this arrangement reinforces the incentive of the father to work regularly and hard. The ability to support a family is early equated in the male child's mind as an essential part of his manhood. Much value is attached to virility and loss of his job can lead to the man losing also his sense of identity in his own and his wife's eyes. . . . The male role thus reinforces the work ethic quite directly.

Elizabeth Wilson's thesis is that even though women are now increasingly available to seek employment, there is an ideology which continues to define them narrowly as wives and mothers, responsible for the domestic work within the nuclear family.

Ann Oakley, in *The Sociology of Housework* (1974), provides an interesting table of self-assessment. She states that asking women to describe themselves is likely to yield the following:

I am a housewife	I am a good housewife
I am a mother	I am good to my children
I am ordinary	I am good at housework
I am a wife	I am good to my husband
I am happy	I am good at washing
I am reasonably attractive	I am fed up at times
I am a sister	I am bad tempered at times
I am a neighbour	I am very happy with my work
I am a friend	I am happy with my children
I am sociable	I am seldom unhappy

Question

Would you add to the list, or delete anything from it?

Diana Gittins, in *The Family in Question* (1985), places the debate in a feminist framework:

Understanding why 'a woman's work is never done' means first of all accepting the dual nature of the 'work' for women. For a very long time the idea of womanhood — and increasingly wifehood — has been synonymous with a woman's 'natural' responsibility for child-care and domestic work. However a society or household is organised, there has always been the assumption that a certain core of domestic work is by definition woman's work. This regardless of whether she engages in paid work, whether she is totally or partly dependent on a husband or father, regardless of whether she is single, married, widowed or divorced, young or old. There is no equivalent assumption for men. A man *may* empty the rubbish, bath the baby, wash the dishes or sweep the floor, but if he elects not to do so — as many have and do — he is in no way socially or economically ostracised or penalised. His domestic participation is totally and always voluntary.

If a woman chooses not to keep the house clean, not to supervise the children adequately, she is in danger of being labelled as a 'bad' mother or a bad wife — she can be divorced, she can have her children taken away from her by the State. Housework and child-care are not voluntary for married women in contemporary society, unless their class position is such that they have the financial resources to pay others to carry out their responsibilities. But they remain their responsibilities.

Domestic labour does have more than just a use value. It can be bought, exchanged and sold, and frequently is. Although domestic labour is an integral and implicit part of the marriage contract, it is not specific to married women only — single mothers are equally held responsible for carrying out domestic work for their children.

Questions

(i) Do you believe that society in the 1990s in the UK is ordered on a gender role basis, legitimising patriarchal power?

(ii) If you do believe this, should the law leave people free to arrange their lives thus, or should it encourage some different pattern?

(iii) If the latter, what and how?

4 Women and employment

Hudson and Lee, in *Women's Work and the Family Economy in Historical Perspective* (1990), describe the scale of married women's involvement in the formal labour market, which has altered dramatically in the twentieth century:

. . . The post-1945 period in particular witnessed a rapid development in women's employment in advanced industrial economies despite the resurgence of a 'back to the kitchen ideology' in the 1970s fuelled by official concern about male unemployment. The abolition of the marriage bar in public-sector employment in Britain aided this trend. There were significant changes in a variety of areas, with women increasingly dominating such occupations as clerical work, retail sales, elementary teaching and nursing. The increasing importance of 'new industries' in the 1920s and 1930s, including rayon manufacture, light engineering, food processing, and white goods provided a boost for female employment in the formal sector, although on a regionally selective basis and with an emphasis on 'semi-skilled' and 'unskilled' work. Furthermore, the inter-war period generally was characterised by official restrictions on married women's employment as a reaction to male unemployment.

'New' female occupations in the service sector continued to expand after 1945, particularly in retailing, banking, public administration and other forms of clerical work. This trend was assisted by a variety of factors, including improved levels of female pay in certain sectors, shorter working hours, lower fertility, and the gradual provision of suitable, if still inadequate welfare support. . . . Technological innovations in the production and conception of household consumer durables such as vacuum cleaners, cookers and electric irons were potentially a source of reduction of domestic burdens as they slowly percolated down the social scale, especially from the 1960s, but new higher standards of domestic cleanliness and decor put pressure on women to spend as much time as in the past on homemaking.

Despite growth in the employment of married women in the formal economy in the twentieth century, many of the factors which determined female labour force participation in the early stages of capitalist development continue to affect occupation choice, gender segregation and women's overall subordination in work. Married women frequently choose jobs which do not directly challenge the prevailing concept of a 'woman's proper place', and many people still 'view it unseemly and inappropriate for wives to work'. Women's occupational choices are clearly influenced by a variety of factors, both work and non-work related. The nature of the labour-market is important but persistently negative facets of women's employment, such as sex-typed jobs, low-ranking position and low comparative earnings, reflect the continued operation of more long-term and deep-seated factors. Married women are still not expected to express any dissatisfaction with their domestic status, so that a return to formal employment frequently has to be legitimised in a socially accepted fashion, with hours tailored to suit child care (for example, mothers' evening shifts in factories) and with earnings treated as 'pin money', or with work portrayed as an emergency measure. As important is the assertion that women have a different relationship to money and wages from men, a notion which has helped to cement the social construction of gender dependency.

Just as women's wage labour in the early phases of capitalist development was frequently an extension of home-based skills, so the general expansion of the service sector, particularly in the twentieth century, has tended to replicate a similar bond between the domestic and work environments. There has been an unprecedented expansion in nursing services since the nineteenth century, accompanied by the formation of professional nursing associations, but these have been based on women's 'traditional' role as carer. Moreover, gender segregation in the health sector as a whole has been associated with persistent low pay for nurses in comparison with other sections of the medical profession. Librarianship has also provided a fast-growing demand for low-paid, but educated, female recruits. Women librarians have frequently been employed because of their submissive attitudes or, as in Tsarist Russia, because of their function as 'guardians of traditional culture'. Even in the retail trades women have been employed not just because they were cheaper than men but because they had such positive virtues as 'politeness' and 'sobriety'. They could also function effectively in a 'world of women', linking women as workers with women as consumers.

In the long term, therefore, despite an unprecedented expansion in the employment of married women in the formal economy, many of the earlier facets of women's work have been retained, particularly in relation to economic marginalisation, pay discrimination, occupational segregation and trade-union participation.

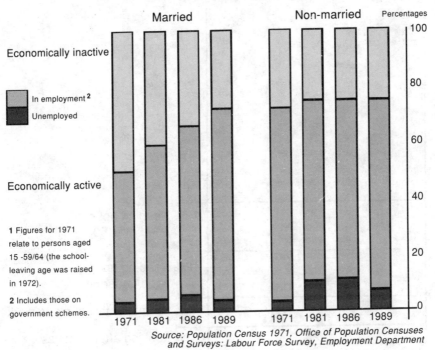

Females aged 16-59[1]

Source: Population Census 1971, Office of Population Censuses and Surveys: Labour Force Survey, Employment Department

1 Figures for 1971 relate to persons aged 15 -59/64 (the school-leaving age was raised in 1972).

2 Includes those on government schemes.

Social Trends 21, ©Crown copyright 1991

Question

Is there gender segregation in the legal profession?

Social Trends 21 (1991) (above, p. 77) provides a useful chart illustrating the economic activity of married and unmarried women. Whereas the position of unmarried women has been constant, the position of married women has changed a great deal from 1971–1989.

Evidence of why women seek employment is available from the OPCS *Family Formation Survey* (1979):

Reason for working between first and second live births in four different time periods

Worked because:	1956–60	1961–65	1966–70	1971–5
Really needed the money	52	51	48	47
Wanted extra things	27	25	27	27
Liked it	16	19	20	22
Other reason	5	5	5	4

Source: Dunnell (1979) Table 6.5. Crown copyright.

From the other perspective, *The Reform of Personal Taxation* (1986) gives reasons why women are economically inactive:

Reasons given by married women for being economically inactive

	63% Looking after children
	12% Keeping house: aged over 50
	12% Keeping house: aged under 50
	5% Permanently unable to work
	3% Looking after relatives
	4% Other reasons

Tilly and Scott, in *Women, Work and Family* (1987), remind us that the timing of women's workforce participation is very different today from what it has been in previous periods. We reproduce below a schematic diagram taken from their book:

Schematic Diagram showing percent women employed by Life/Family cycle stage, England

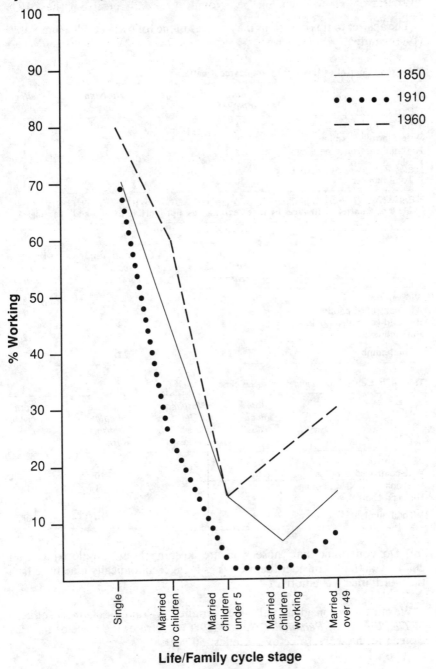

Questions

(i) Ann Oakley, in *Subject Women* (1981), suggests that these surveys show that the 'public acceptability of selfish and work-centred reasons for employment may be growing.' Do you agree?

(ii) Do you think there is any correlation between the control and allocation of money described by Jan Pahl (see p. 73) and whether the wife has employment?

The answer to this questions may appear in the following table from Pahl's (1990) study:

Table 6.5: Control of finances by employment pattern

	Both employed	Wife only	Husband only	Neither employed
Wife control	5	—	5	4
Wife-controlled pooling	19	—	7	1
Husband-controlled pooling	17	—	19	3
Husband control	9	1	9	3
Total number	50	1	40	11

Table 6.6: Control of finances by wife's earnings as a proportion of husband's earnings

	Wife's earnings		
	Over 30% of husband's earnings	Under 30% of husband's earnings	Wife had no earnings
Wife control	6	—	8
Wife-controlled pooling	12	8	7
Husband-controlled pooling	5	14	20
Husband control	5	5	12
Total number	28	27	47

Table 6.7: Control of finances by social class

	Both middle class	Husband middle class wife working class	Wife middle class husband working class	Both working class
Wife control	3	2	2	7
Wife-controlled pooling	10	0	10	7
Husband-controlled pooling	18	6	1	14
Husband control	7	2	3	10
Total number	38	10	16	38

(iii) Do you think that those who are 'keeping house' or 'looking after children' actually consider themselves as being 'economically inactive'? Isn't the word 'inactive' emotive?

We must now consider 'dual career' families. A dramatic chart reproduced in *The Reform of Personal Taxation* (1986) illustrates the place of married women in the work force over the last 50 years.

The proportion of married women working or looking for work

Percentage

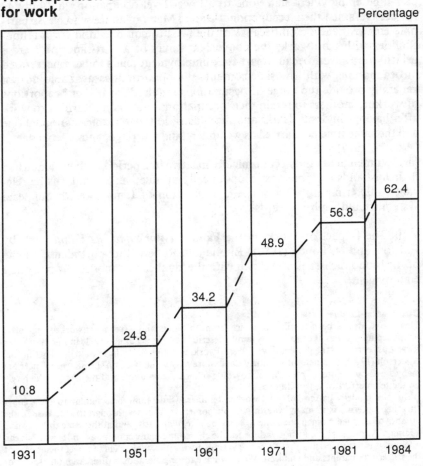

Source: Censuses of Population and Labour Force Survey 1984

Questions

(i) What type of allocative system exists, do you think, in families from South Asia and from the West Indies?

(ii) In *Women and Employment: A Lifetime Perspective* (1984) it was found: 'amongst the mothers who were interviewed, there were marked differences in the types of occupational changes made by them before and after having their first child. Before childbirth, only 18 per cent of mothers who worked had experienced downward occupational mobility when they changed jobs, while 62 per cent had maintained a level occupational status (as defined by the classification used). On returning to work after childbirth the first job found by 37 per cent of mothers was lower down the occupational scale than their previous job, while only about half (49 per cent) of them found a job which was of the same occupational status. Much of this downward movement was associated with mothers entering part-time employment on return to the labour market; 45 per cent of those who took part-time employment had gone to a lower level occupation, and only 42 per cent retained their occupational status. Many of those who chose part-time employment did so because of the need to combine domestic responsibilities with paid work; the convenient hours of a part-time job were a priority. However, because part-time employment tends to be concentrated in occupations with low skill content, the opportunities available do not generally provide the range of occupations required for higher proportions of working mothers to retain their occupational status on returning to work after having children'. Is this another illustration that 'women cannot at one and the same time be married as we understand marriage, and independent?' (Wilson, 1977)

(iii) Women are mainly economically inactive in a period in their lives when their husbands may be most economically productive. Should this be relevant in determining what sort of distribution of family wealth our legal system should aspire towards?

In 'The Impact of Work on the Family' (*Work and the Family*, ed. by P. Moss and N. Fonda (1980)) Rhona and Robert Rapoport identify some of the economic issues associated with the 'dual career' model of family and employment:

Dual-worker families

There have always been families in which both husbands and wives have worked regularly. Shopkeeping families like the baker's family described by Peter Laslett (1971) in *The World We Have Lost* persist to the present day; and shiftworking couples like those described by Michael Anderson (1973) for nineteenth-century Lancashire may actually be on the increase. There are many small businesses — pubs, inns, boarding schools, restaurants and the like — which rely on the team effort of a working couple.

But the modern pattern of dual-worker families, while somewhat similar to these long-standing patterns, is in many ways a new phenomenon. It arises through the increase in the number of married women choosing to work on a regular basis, and at the same time to have a family. As there are many motivations for the choice and many conditions under which it can operate, it is not surprising that there are various forms it can take. These affect the impact of the pattern on parents and children. We now have three generations of research on aspects of this pattern (Rapoport and Rapoport, 1978); with all the variations there are some generic issues that occur, and some characteristic ways of resolving them (Gowler and Legge, 1981).

Peter Moss has indicated some of the *economic* issues associated with the pattern. The consequences, if not the intentions, of operating the pattern are very different for those at the lower end of the social-class scale than for those higher up. At the lower end, it has the effect of keeping families above the poverty line. Higher up the scale, it enables families to increase their standard of living, taking holidays abroad, making home extensions or buying second homes and so on. It also has the effect of providing security against rapid downward mobility in the event of unemployment or career reversals of a breadwinner.

Another general feature of the pattern, also mentioned above, is that though there is a substantial basis in social values, particularly middle-class values, to support the pattern as an expression of an egalitarian orientation, the observed behaviour of husbands leads to the conclusion that this is often lip-service. Generally speaking, husbands do not replace the time by which their wives reduce household work. Sometimes, as Ann Oakley (1974) has shown, part of the husband's replacement takes the form of skimming off more enjoyable elements like playing with the children, leaving his wife with a more unremitting portion of drudgery. One writer on 'dual-career' families (Mortimer, 1977) noted that husbands in such families are often not aware of the discrepancy between what they say and what they do.

Nor is work outside the home a panacea, even when freely chosen. Weissman and Paykel (1974) noted that employed wives who are mismatched with their jobs are prone to depression in a way not dissimilar to 'captive housewives'. If a married woman, for example, takes a job for which she is over-qualified in order to escape the loneliness and boredom of being a housewife, she may come to feel that she has jumped from the frying pan into the fire, as regards the degree of personal stress she has to endure. This highlights the importance of 'fit' between person and role as an important intervening variable.

Just as there is a sub-group of conventional housewives who are reluctant in their role and would prefer to be at work, there is a sub-group of reluctant working wives. A recent study (Moss and Lewis, 1979) suggests that these women are more prevalent in the lower income groups, and that most of them would not like to stop work altogether but would rather work a little less in order to achieve a better balance between what a recent Russian study with similar findings called their functions as 'toilers, mothers, child-rearers and home-makers' (reported in *New Society*, 30 August 1979). Though this is a statistical tendency, reflecting the strains on women who have low income, ungratifying jobs and unsupportive husbands, it probably has wider validity.

However, for various reasons and in various ways, increasing proportions of families are adopting a dual-worker pattern. It is not, as some early commentators on research on dual-career families held, a freakish pattern tenable in peacetime only by a privileged minority. It is being chosen by increasing numbers of families because of its appeal to ordinary people — and its demonstrated feasibility. But, as with other patterns of work/family interrelationship, it has both gains and strains.

We are now able to define the issues with a fair degree of precision. Research on dual-worker families has now reached a state where it is possible to say that many of the early 'doomwatcher' hypotheses are 'unproven', and many of the 'advocacy' hypotheses can now be placed in perspective for further investigation. To illustrate this, there are two 'doomwatcher' hypotheses which can be examined:

(a) that dual-worker marriages will produce marital conflict;
(b) that dual-worker marriages will produce a poor environment for parenthood, leading to neglected 'latchkey' children who will swell the ranks of the delinquent, retarded and mentally disordered.

Impact on parents. Most of the reviews of literature that could help us to assess the hypothesis are inconclusive. Either they relate to overlapping but not identical populations (e.g. Hoffman and Nye's (1974) review of literature on working mothers; and Michael Rutter's (1972) review of literature on maternal deprivation); or they show no statistically significant relationship (which does not, of course, mean that there are never any negative consequences of the pattern). There are, however, some useful studies which contribute insight into the issues involved.

One American study by Orden and Bradburn (1968) of the National Opinion Research Center in Chicago suggests that marital happiness depends less on whether or not both partners work than on whether their choice was freely entered into. This work highlights the importance of the *meaning of work* (as well as the fact of working) as part of assessing work's impact on family life.

A study of British graduate couples by Lotte Bailyn (1971) indicates that while conventional families show a slightly higher proportion stating that their marriage is 'very happy', the proportions are not significantly less for working couples. Moreover, the latter are less likely to give stereotyped 'happiness' responses. But the subgroup which are markedly *low* on marital satisfaction are those in which the husband is extremely 'career-oriented' — i.e. seeks his major life satisfactions from his work and not at all from his family life (as distinct from men who place career first but also rate family as an important source of satisfaction). This circumstance occurs in conventional families, as well as dual-worker families.

Heather Ross and Isabel Sawhill (1975) of the Urban Research Institute in Washington note an association between the rising divorce rate and the rising rate of wives at work. They observe that the economic benefits of marriage are less decisive for wives who are independent earners, and that divorce has a different sub-cultural meaning among secular urban couples than in more conventional settings. The whole issue of the significance of divorce, and its occurrence at different points in the family and career cycles is involved here, but research to date provides more questions than answers.

On the other side of the coin is the body of literature from case studies of dual-worker families in which wives who hold satisfying jobs by choice express the view that they are more fulfilled; while husbands view them as more interesting marital partners. They emphasise the idea that both as spouses and parents, it is 'quality' rather than 'quantity' that counts, and that though the pattern is stressful they prefer it to the alternatives that they see for themselves, e.g. operating the conventional pattern and feeling bored and resentful.

Question

What do you think of the *second* hypothesis as a statement? Do *you* think it is unproven?

5 Domestic arrangements and the law

Balfour v Balfour
[1919] 2 KB 571, [1918–19] All ER Rep 860, 88 LJKB 1054, 121 LT 346, 35 TLR 609, 63 Sol Jo 661, Court of Appeal

A husband agreed to give to his wife £30 per month whilst she was in England recuperating from an illness. He returned to Ceylon where he was employed. The Court of Appeal refused to enforce this agreement.

Atkin LJ: The defence to this action on the alleged contract is that the defendant, the husband, entered into no contract with his wife, and for the determination of that it is necessary to remember that there are agreements between parties which do not result in contracts within the meaning of that term in our law. The ordinary example is where two parties agree to take a walk together, or where there is an offer and an acceptance of hospitality. Nobody would suggest in ordinary circumstances that those agreements result in what we know as a contract, and one of the most usual forms of agreement which does not constitute a contract appears to me to be the arrangements which are made between husband and wife. It is quite common, and it is the natural and inevitable result of the relationship of husband and wife, that the two spouses should make arrangements between themselves — agreements such as are in dispute in this action — agreements for allowances, by which the husband agrees that he will pay to his wife a certain sum of money, per week, or per month, or per year, to cover either her own expenses or the necessary expenses of the household and of the children of the marriage, and in which the wife promises either expressly or impliedly to apply the allowance for the purpose for which it is given. To my mind those agreements, or many of them, do not result in contracts at all, and they do not result in contracts even though there may be what as between other parties would constitute consideration for the agreement. The consideration, as we know, may consist either in some right, interest, profit or benefit accruing to one party, or some forbearance, detriment, loss or responsibility given, suffered or undertaken by the other. That is a well-known definition, and it constantly happens, I think, that such arrangements made between husband and wife are arrangements in which there are mutual promises, or in which there is consideration in form within the definition that I have mentioned. Nevertheless they are not contracts, and they are not contracts because the parties did not intend that they should be attended by legal consequences. To my mind it would be of the worst possible example to hold that agreements such as this resulted in legal obligations which could be enforced in the Courts. It would mean this, that when the husband makes his wife a promise to give her an allowance of 30s. or £2 a week, whatever he can afford to give her, for the maintenance of the household and children, and she promises so to apply it, not only could she sue him for his failure in any week to supply the allowance, but he could sue her for non-performance of the obligation, express or implied, which she had undertaken upon her part. . . . They are not sued upon, not because the parties are reluctant to enforce their legal rights when the agreement is broken, but because the parties, in the inception of the arrangement, never intended that they should be sued upon. Agreements such as these are outside the realm of contracts altogether. The common law does not regulate the form of agreements between spouses. Their promises are not sealed with seals and sealing wax. The consideration that really obtains for them is that natural love and affection which counts for so little in these cold Courts. The terms may be repudiated, varied or renewed as performance proceeds or as disagreements develop, and the principles of the common law as to exoneration and discharge and accord and satisfaction are such as find no place in the domestic code. The parties themselves are advocates, judges, Courts, sheriff's officer and reporter. In respect of these promises each house is a domain into which the King's writ does not seek to run, and to which his officers do not seek to be admitted.

Questions

(i) The Crown's officers may not seek on their own initiative to be admitted into the house, but why make it difficult for the parties themselves to invite the judges, advocates and courts into the house?
(ii) Is the natural inequality in bargaining power of the spouses in house-wife marriages an argument for or against making agreements for domestic financing enforceable?
(iii) Should spouses be free to make such agreements as they wish or should the law impose a preferred pattern?
(iv) If the latter, what pattern do you have in mind?

In *Jones v Padavatton* [1969] 2 All ER 616, [1969] 1 WLR 328, CA, Dankwerts LJ stated that there was 'no doubt that the principles [in *Balfour v Balfour*] apply to dealings between other relations, such as father and son and daughter and mother'. Salmon LJ in the same case said that the pre-sumption against intention to create legal relations 'derives from experience of life and human nature which shows that in such circumstances men and women usually do not intend to create legal rights and obligations, but intend to rely solely on family ties of mutual trust and affection'.

Questions

(i) Is a promise by a parent to pay a son or daughter an allowance during a course of study at college enforceable (*a*) by the son or daughter, (*b*) by the college authorities?
(ii) If not, should it be?
(iii) Is a promise by a husband to pay his wife an allowance whilst she com-pletes Law School enforceable?
(iv) If not, should it be?

6 The duty to support

(a) AT COMMON LAW

Manby v Scott
(1663) 1 Keb 482, 1 Lev 4, 1 Mod Rep 124, 0 Bridg 229, 1 Sid 109, King's Bench Division

Hyde J: . . . In the beginning, when God created woman an helpmate for man, he said, 'They twain shall be one flesh'; and thereupon our law says, that husband and wife are but one person in law: presently after the Fall, the judgment of God upon woman was, 'Thy desire shall be to thy husband, for thy will shall be subject to thy husband, and he shall rule over thee' (Gen iii, 16). Hereupon our law put the wife *sub potestate viri*. . . .
[His wife] was bone of his bone, flesh of his flesh, and no man did ever hate his own flesh so far as not to preserve it.

Question

Has the duty of support at common law anything to do with the law relating to unity of property?

The details of the common law are described by Gareth Miller, in *Family Property and Financial Provision* (1983):

At common law a husband is under the duty to maintain his wife in accordance with his means, but there is no corresponding duty on a wife to maintain her husband. A husband will normally perform his duty by providing first, a suitable home where he and his wife will live together, and, secondly, necessaries such as food and clothing. It is unlikely that he will wish to undertake the management of the household himself, and instead he will generally provide his wife with an appropriate allowance. However, at common law a wife has never had the right to a separate allowance, but if she is living with her husband she is presumed to have his implied authority to pledge his credit for necessary household expenses.

This authority does not arise from the fact of marriage, but from the wife's usual position as housekeeper from which it can be inferred that the husband has held her out as his agent. It is open to a husband expressly to forbid his wife to pledge his credit and there need be no communication of this to any tradesman. However, if he has in the past held out his wife to a particular tradesman as having apparent authority, then it will be necessary to give an express warning to that tradesman. A husband may also rebut the presumption of implied authority by showing that she already had a sufficient allowance with which to purchase necessaries, or that she was already supplied with sufficient of the goods in respect of which a claim is made against him.

Generally a wife is not entitled to separate maintenance in a separate home unless she has a good reason for living apart from her husband. A husband's duty to maintain his wife is suspended while she is in desertion, but it revives on termination of the desertion. If she commits adultery which has not been connived at or condoned then her right to be maintained ceases altogether. Indeed, if the wife's conduct is such as to induce in the husband a reasonable (though of course mistaken) belief in her adultery, then he is not obliged to maintain her as long as he continues to have reasonable grounds for that belief.

A wife may, however, be living apart from her husband because he is in desertion or because she has been forced to do so by his misconduct. In such circumstances, in the absence of misconduct on her part, she is still entitled to be maintained. If a husband then failed to provide for his wife she was formerly entitled to pledge his credit for necessaries suitable to their joint style of living before the separation. The basis of this right was the so-called 'agency of necessity.' This could not be terminated by the husband forbidding his wife to pledge his credit or even by expressly forbidding tradesmen to give her credit. However, its value was limited because tradesmen were naturally reluctant to give credit if they were likely to become involved in a matrimonial dispute.

The wife's agency of necessity was abolished by section 41 of the Matrimonial Proceedings and Property Act 1970, but this leaves untouched the authority which she is presumed to have while running the husband's household, or any authority which she may have been held out by the husband as having.

The practical utility to a wife of the husband's common law obligation to maintain her has been limited owing to the difficulty of enforcement, but its influence has been, and continues to be, considerable. Although a wife will, wherever possible rely on one of the statutory remedies [see p. 97, below] . . . the courts have constantly referred to the principles surrounding the common law obligation in interpreting the scope of these remedies. It has also played an important part in protecting the wife's occupation of the matrimonial home after a marriage has broken down but before it has been terminated by divorce. Once a marriage has been terminated by divorce then of course the husband's obligation is also terminated and financial provision thereafter is dependent entirely on statute.

Question

Mrs Splash buys a new dress from Newstyle, instructing the assistant to send the account to her husband. In fact her husband told her the day before that if she wanted a new dress she would have to pay for it herself. Advise Newstyle as to their rights.

(b) MAINTENANCE AND 'HOUSEKEEPING'

Even after the Married Women's Property Act 1882 allowed the wife to keep anything she acquired by gift or purchase, money received for housekeeping remained the property of the husband. She simply had custody of it and any savings belonged to him. (See *Hoddinot v Hoddinot* [1949] 2 KB 406 at p. 89, below.) Further, the statutes under which she could apply for a maintenance order only permitted her to enforce any order after the parties had separated. This restriction was discussed in the Report of the Royal Commission on *Marriage and Divorce* (1956):

The husband's liability where the wife is cohabiting with her husband
1042. Some witnesses suggested that if a wife's only complaint against her husband is that of wilful neglect to provide reasonable maintenance for her or her children, she should be able to obtain an order which should be fully effective notwithstanding that she and her husband continue to live together as man and wife. They pointed out that a husband's neglect to provide for his wife may not be deliberate or malicious but may be due rather to thoughtlessness or improvidence and that the existence of an effective court order may then be sufficient to keep him up to the mark. . . .
1043. Against this proposal it was argued that the existence of an effective order could only further exacerbate relations which were already strained, to the point where the final breakdown of the marriage would be inevitable. Moreover, it was said that the proposal would be impracticable. The amount of the order is based on what the wife requires to keep herself when living apart from her husband. If husband and wife were in fact living together then the husband could argue that he was being asked to pay too much since he was providing her with a home; on the other hand, she might say that she was not getting enough under the order since she was expected to make all the housekeeping expenses out of a sum intended for her own needs.
1044. Other witnesses were concerned more with the status of the wife in the home. It was said that a wife should not be dependent on the whim of her husband for the amount which he allows her for housekeeping; every wife should have a right to a housekeeping allowance. Some of these witnesses proposed that the amount should be fixed by law as a certain proportion of the family income; others considered that the wife should be able to apply to the court for an order fixing the amount. These proposals we are unable to accept. The first would be clearly impracticable. The second would require the court in effect to determine the standard of living of the family.
1045. We are impressed, however, by the argument that the present law fails to make any provision for the case where the wife has constant difficulty in getting money from her husband but at the same time does not want to break up the home. We have been told that in fact quite often a wife who has obtained a maintenance order does not leave her husband and that the situation improves because he, not realising that her order is unenforceable, makes her regular payments. We therefore think that it would be desirable to allow a wife who has obtained a maintenance order solely on the ground of her husband's wilful neglect to provide reasonable maintenance for her (or for the children) to be able to enforce that order without leaving her husband.
1046. We have carefully considered the arguments advanced against the proposal but in our opinion their force has been exaggerated. If relations between husband and wife are already seriously strained, we think it unlikely that the fact that the wife has obtained a court order which is enforceable will make matters any worse. But where the situation has not gone so far we believe that in some cases at least there is reasonable hope that the making of an order may bring the husband to his senses. Moreover, the very fact that the court has power to make such an order may in itself have a salutary effect on those husbands who are apt to be careless of their financial responsibility for their families. . . .
1047. As to the practical difficulty referred to in paragraph 1043, we feel confident that it is not insuperable. If the wife wishes to go on living with her husband we see no reason why the court, when assessing the amount of the order, should not take into account the fact that the husband is paying the rent. At the same time the court could point out to the husband that if

he expects his wife to run his household he must pay her a sum over and above that specified in the order. If the wife subsequently left her husband she could apply for an increase in the amount of the order to meet the cost of providing accommodation for herself.

The Law Commission in their Working Paper on *Matrimonial Proceedings in Magistrates' Courts* (1973) agreed with the Royal Commission. The Law Commission felt that there might be advantages if an order which is made on the ground of failure to provide reasonable maintenance (see p. 97, below) could be enforceable for the period of six months whilst the parties continued to live together. If the parties continued to live together for more than six months the order would become unenforceable. In their subsequent Report (1976), the Law Commission commented on the evidence submitted on this topic:

2.60 This tentative proposal by the Working Party, not unnaturally, aroused strong feelings amongst those commenting on the working paper. The feeling of the majority was that such a provision would be useful, but it was pointed out that there would be practical difficulties. How, for example, would payments be made under such an order? Would a husband who had failed to maintain his wife be required to send payments to the court each week for collection by his wife? Or would he be expected to make payments direct to her? Neither course would be free of difficulty. Another significant criticism of this proposal was that it might lead to a number of wives asking the court to 'fix the housekeeping'.
2.61 We have no doubt that cases occur in which the sole cause, or the real cause, of matrimonial difficulties is the husband's carelessness of his financial responsibilities. Where the parties are still living together in such cases, it seems to us to be wrong that the court should be unable to make an immediately enforceable financial order in favour of the wife. The result is that a wife who stays with her husband is worse off financially than she would be by leaving him. While the law is in such a state it may be argued that it is providing an inducement for the wife to leave her husband and is thus favouring the break down of the marriage instead of its repair. We, therefore, think that a maintenance order made in favour of a spouse while the parties are cohabiting should be enforceable notwithstanding the cohabitation.

The recommendation of the Law Commission is contained in s. 25(1) of the Domestic Proceedings and Magistrates' Courts Act 1978 (as amended by the Children Act 1989):

25. — (1) Where —
   (*a*) periodical payments are required to be made to one of the parties to a marriage (whether for his own benefit or for the benefit of a child of the family) by an order made under section 2 or 6 of this Act or by an interim maintenance order made under section 19 of this Act (otherwise than on an application under section 7 of this Act), . . .
the order shall be enforceable notwithstanding that the parties to the marriage are living with each other at the date of the making of the order or that, although they are not living with each other at that date, they subsequently resume living with each other; but the order shall cease to have effect if after that date the parties continue to live with each other, or resume living with each other, for a continuous period exceeding six months.

Questions

(i) Is an order for maintenance of the wife and/or the children the same thing as an order for a housekeeping allowance?
(ii) When the wife obtains a maintenance order, whom should she spend it on?
(iii) At the end of six months, the wife will have to decide either to leave with an order, or stay without one. Does this rule make matters worse?

At common law, any savings which the wife was able to accumulate from housekeeping allowances from the husband, and any property which she purchased out of such savings, belonged to the husband:

Hoddinot v Hoddinot
[1949] 2 KB 406, 65 TLR 266, 93 Sol Jo 286, Court of Appeal

A husband and wife regularly invested in football pools, in the husband's name, the savings on housekeeping moneys. Forecasting was the result of their joint effort. Their forecast won a prize of £138. 7s which was paid into the husband's bank account. Part of the money was used to purchase furniture in the home. The parties quarrelled and separated and the wife claimed the furniture or at least part of it.

Bucknill LJ: . . . I am not at all satisfied that she had got any legal interest in the housekeeping money as such. The money belonged to the husband, and I should have thought she held it in trust for him for keeping them both, and if the husband decides to take some of it away from the purchase of food and such things to invest it in football pools, it seems to me that the money still remained his, and that in the absence of any contract between them the proceeds or winnings on that housekeeping money also belong to him.

Questions

(i) If the wife holds the housekeeping money in trust for the husband, for keeping them both, might she not at least be entitled to retain sufficient of the money to maintain herself at their standard of living?
(ii) The husband decides the standard of living. What can a wife do about this if the standard of living is not appropriate to his means?
(iii) Husband and wife are both earning similar amounts. The wife does the household shopping one week and the husband does it the next week. In one week, when it is the wife's turn, she gives the husband her purse and asks him to do the shopping. There is more than enough in the purse. Will she be entitled to the change?

The Married Women's Property Act 1964 provides:

1. If any question arises as to the right of a husband or wife to money derived from any allowance made by the husband for the expenses of the matrimonial home or for similar purposes, or to any property acquired out of such money, the money or property shall, in the absence of any agreement between them to the contrary, be treated as belonging to the husband and the wife in equal shares.

Question

Has this provision made any difference to your answer to question (iii) above?

The Law Commission's Working Paper, *Transfer of Money Between Spouses* (1985) recommended reform in part so that the sexually discriminatory aspect of the 1964 Act be removed. The responses to the Working

Paper persuaded the Law Commission to look at the whole issue in a much broader context. The recommendations in *Family Law: Matrimonial Property* are as follows:

5.1 We *recommend* that in future the purchase of property (with some exclusions) by one or both spouses for their joint use or benefit should give rise to joint ownership of that property subject to a contrary intention on the part of the purchasing spouse, known to the other spouse.

5.2 We further *recommend* that transfer of property by one spouse to the other for their joint use or benefit should give rise to joint ownership of that property subject to a contrary intention on the part of the transferring spouse, known to the other spouse. If the transferred property is not for joint use or benefit it should become the sole beneficial property of the spouse to whom it is transferred, subject to a contrary intention on the part of the transferring spouse, known to the other spouse.

5.3 These recommendations do *not* extend to property purchased or transferred for business purposes.

5.[4] We *recommend* that the Married Women's Property Act 1964 be repealed.

(We discuss these recommendations in detail in Chapter 5.)

7 The enforcement of the duty of support

The history of the magistrates' matrimonial jurisdiction is not free from controversy. The Law Commission Working Paper (1973) describes the development in the following way:

7. The Matrimonial Causes Act 1857 established a secular court to hear and determine matrimonial causes. Named 'the Court for Divorce and Matrimonial Causes', it was empowered to dissolve marriages (a power previously exercisable only by Act of Parliament) and to grant judicial separation (a remedy previously available only in the ecclesiastical courts). The remedies provided in the 1857 Act (divorce, judicial separation, nullity and restitution of conjugal rights) dealt with breakdown of marriage but had little or no relevance save in the context of breakdown induced by grievous matrimonial offence, and the Act made no provision, except in one respect, for the exercise of any matrimonial jurisdiction by magistrates. The provision it did make was really directed towards a situation of irretrievable breakdown — the 'protection order' which magistrates were empowered to make to protect 'any money or property [a deserted wife] may acquire by her lawful industry' or otherwise against the claims of her husband and his creditors.

8. The 1857 Act was of very little value to anyone outside the propertied classes. The great majority of wives whom their husbands abandoned or maltreated had to make do with such relief as they could find in the poor law or the criminal law. The first help to the ill-treated woman was given by section 4 of the Matrimonial Causes Act 1878, which brought together the strands of the criminal and the poor law for her benefit. It provided that, if a husband was convicted summarily or otherwise of an aggravated assault upon his wife, the court or magistrate before whom he was convicted, if satisfied that the wife's future safety was in peril, should have power to order that she should no longer be bound to cohabit with her husband (such order to have the force and effect in all respects of [sic] a decree of judicial separation on the grounds of cruelty). The order might further provide for:
(i) the husband to pay the wife weekly maintenance, and
(ii) the legal custody of any children under 10 to be given to the wife.

9. The 1878 Act was followed by a wider ranging reform in 1886, when the Married Women (Maintenance in Case of Desertion) Act gave a more direct and economically useful remedy to wives. Under this Act if a married woman could establish that her husband was able to support her and his children but had refused or neglected to do so and had deserted her, a magistrates' court could award her maintenance of up to £2 a week. Powers under the 1878 Act were unaffected. The Summary Jurisdiction (Married Women) Act 1895 gave magistrates' courts their general matrimonial jurisdiction. It repealed section 4 of the 1878 Act and the whole

of the 1886 Act, replacing their limited provisions by a general code of matrimonial relief available to married women (but not men) in courts of summary jurisdiction. In brief, the grounds upon which a wife could apply to a magistrates' court were that her husband had been convicted of violence to her, that her husband had deserted her, that her husband had been persistently cruel to her, or that her husband had wilfully neglected to provide reasonable maintenance for her and her infant children. The magistrates could make a non-cohabitation order, order payment of maintenance of up to £2 a week, and grant the wife custody of a child under the age of 16. The wife's adultery, unless condoned, connived at or conduced to, was a bar to an order in her favour.

10. The 1895 Act was a major advance. While following the 1886 Act in allowing maintenance orders to be made without the court also having to make a non-cohabitation order, it empowered magistrates to order the payment of a weekly sum of money where the husband's only offence was 'wilful neglect to provide reasonable maintenance'. Thus, it constituted a code of matrimonial relief designed to deal with the situation where matrimonial breakdown had occurred but was not irretrievable, and to provide relief before it became irretrievable. This code remained the basis of the magistrates' law until 1960. The Licensing Act 1902 added habitual drunkenness by either spouse as a ground for an order. The Married Women (Maintenance) Act 1920 corrected the anomaly that no money could be ordered for the support of a child in the wife's custody by making possible an order for 10s a week. The Summary Jurisdiction (Separation and Maintenance) Act 1925 added to the grounds for an order, that the husband was guilty of persistent cruelty to the children, that he insisted on having sexual intercourse while knowingly suffering from a venereal disease, that he was forcing his wife to engage in prostitution, or that he was a drug addict. The Matrimonial Causes Act 1937 not only added to the grounds for an order that of adultery, but introduced the significant provision that a husband (as well as being able to apply for an order on the grounds of his wife's habitual drunkenness) could apply for an order if his wife committed adultery. The Matrimonial Proceedings (Magistrates' Courts) Act 1960 attempted to rationalise and modernise the law in the light of the recommendations of the Morton Commission on Marriage and Divorce (1956) and of the Arthian Davies Committee (1959). The major advance was that the Act made relief generally available to husbands as well as wives (though the husband had to prove impairment of earning capacity to obtain a money order) and gave power to make orders providing for the custody and support of children, even when the wife (or husband) failed to prove her (or his) ground of complaint.

11. Over the years Parliament has raised the limits of financial relief that the magistrates can order (there has never been a limit on the powers of the divorce court in this respect). . . . Finally, the Maintenance Orders Act 1968, on the recommendation of the Departmental Committee on Statutory Maintenance Limits, abolished the upper limit for the maintenance of both spouse and child.

The *Finer Committee on One-Parent Families* (1974) suggested that the Law Commission was guilty of a 'seriously mistaken interpretation of history' in asserting that the magistrates' jurisdiction was designed to deal with situations where matrimonial breakdown had occurred but was not irretrievable. The view of the Finer Report is as follows:

36. The creation, . . . of a matrimonial jurisdiction to be exercised in the magistrates' courts was to have a profound and lasting effect on the arrangements, both substantive and procedural, which English law makes for regulating the consequences of matrimonial breakdown. All of the following characteristics were implanted into this part of our legal system. First, two separate jurisdictions, High Court and summary, existing side by side, but administering different and overlapping rules and remedies, came into being for the purpose of dealing with the same human predicament. Secondly, while the reforms of 1857 were designed to remove matrimonial disputes to the arbitrament of a superior and civil court of record, the jurisdiction created in 1878 was vested in inferior tribunals, given over to the criminal process, and universally known, because of their close association with the police, as 'police courts.' Thirdly, whereas the 1857 reformers regarded legal intervention into matrimony, maintenance and the custody of children as so delicate and important that the jurisdiction had to be entrusted to professional judges of the highest rank, the 1878 jurisdiction was to be exercised by a magistracy overwhelmingly lay in its composition. Finally, the concern for extending to a larger population the benefits which the 1857 reforms had afforded to the wealthy bore fruit in the creation of a secondary system designed for what were considered to be the special and cruder requirements of the poor.

The different treatment of the history led the two bodies to formulate different principles upon which the law and procedure should be based. The Law Commission's Working Paper suggested:

24. There is a clear contrast between the magistrates' jurisdiction and that exercised by the divorce court under the 1969 and 1970 Acts. The magistrates' jurisdiction is normally exercised at a stage earlier than irretrievable breakdown and is not concerned with change of status. Indeed, the marriage may only temporarily have run into difficulties. There is evidence that many orders made by the magistrates come to an end because the parties are reconciled. The role of the magistrates' court in dealing with those involved in matrimonial breakdown may perhaps be illustrated by comparing it with a casualty clearing station. All the casualties of marriage can be brought to the magistrates' court. Some are clearly mortal; they should go on to be laid to rest by proceedings in the divorce court; some are serious, being more likely than not to end in final breakdown; some however will respond to local treatment and may well recover completely; others are trivial, requiring no more than sympathetic handling and encouragement. It is the duty of those who work in a casualty clearing station to give attention and interim or substantive treatment to all, to do nothing which might turn a minor case into a major one, and to refrain from attempting to treat those whom they have not the competence or equipment to treat. So too the magistrates in their matrimonial jurisdictions. They must look to the possibility that no more may be needed than sympathy and the opportunity for reconciliation. But they must also have the means of treating the more serious casualties of marriage. Turning away from the language of metaphor, we suggest therefore that the role of the magistrates — the principle and objectives of their matrimonial jurisdiction — should be to enable them to intervene on the application of either party to a marriage:
(i) to deal with family relations during a period of breakdown which is not necessarily permanent or irretrievable
   (*a*) by relieving the financial need which breakdown can bring to the parties,
   (*b*) by giving such protection to one or other of the parties as may be necessary, and
   (*c*) by providing for the welfare and support of the children; and
(ii) to preserve the marriage in existence, where possible.

The Finer Report refuted the 'casualty clearing station' approach:

4.383 We think the working party has allowed itself to be misled concerning the actual role of magistrates' courts in matrimonial breakdown by the attractions of a medico-military analogy. We have assembled compelling evidence to demonstrate that the very existence and persistence of the dual jurisdiction, and of the attitudes and institutions stemming from it, account for the presence in magistrates' courts of many very poor folk who possess neither knowledge nor expectation of any other legal cure for their marital ills. Nor is the analogy compelling when we find that two thirds of the casualties on the books in January 1966 were to be found there in July 1971, that nearly half of the discharges during this period had been patients for ten years or more at the time of their discharge, and that on 1 July 1971 there were some 58,000 magistrates' orders in force which were ten years old, or older. We doubt whether many clearing stations would find this a satisfactory work record.

The Finer Report argued strongly that the matrimonial jurisdiction of the magistrates' court used, as it is, by only one section of the community, serves to highlight the social divisions within the community. We discuss the argument advanced in favour of a family court in Chapter 15, below. The Finer Report is quite clear that 'a more general use of the magistrates' courts by all classes of the community' would be unrealistic. The thrust of the Report is contained in the following passage:

4.67 However, the most important feature of the contrast between the two systems is that they expose and give encouragement and effect to inconsistent public policies. The public policy of the latter part of the twentieth century is to promote the welfare of individuals and enhance respect for the law by disposing of dead marriages with decency and dignity, and a minimum of bitterness, distress and humiliation, and to do so in a manner that will encourage harmonious relations between the parties and their children in the future. This policy has been accepted by

Church and State, has been legislated into the divorce law, and is implemented in the superior system of courts of law. The public policy of the latter part of the nineteenth century was to provide police court protection for the lower orders in their matrimonial troubles, and this, . . ., remains at the heart and sets the tone of the summary jurisdiction. There is evidence to suggest that one half of the complainants who obtain matrimonial orders in the summary courts never proceed to a divorce, but remain in a matrimonial limbo in which they are single in reality but married in law. In the five years 1968–1972 the number of matrimonial orders made by the magistrates averaged some 22,000 a year. On this footing, the summary jurisdiction embalms 11,000 dead marriages every year. But it could reasonably be held that the number of applications to the magistrates provides a more realistic measure of the number of collapsed marriages in this category than does the number of orders. Many women are refused orders because they have committed a matrimonial offence, even though their husbands have deserted them and no longer give them financial support (and, besides, may well themselves be guilty of a matrimonial offence at least as serious). On this view, the 11,000 cases above mentioned will be nearer 16,000 a year. It is notorious that a high proportion of the husbands and a lower proportion of the wives in this situation set up illicit unions and have illegitimate children.

4.68 We conclude that not merely do the two matrimonial jurisdictions co-exist as formerly, but one of them is founded on principles which have been rejected by the other. Even in the act of reforming itself, English matrimonial law has so far failed to escape from its habit of dispensing two brands of matrimonial justice, whose antinomy is now stronger than ever before.

Ruth Deech in 'The Work of the Law Commission in Family Law: The First Twenty Years' in M.D.A. Freeman (ed.) *Essays in Family Law 1985* (1986) states:

The relationship between the Law Commission and the Finer Committee, incidentally, was curious: the Commission's project on limited reform of the magistrates' jurisdiction was started exactly one year after the Finer Committee had commenced work, as if to imply that Finer could never produce anything practicable; and some have deplored the fact that the Commission seemingly collaborated with the government of the day in perpetuating the domestic jurisdiction of magistrates in its unsatisfactory form and thereby reducing the pressure to implement Finer. (McGregor, 1981)

Questions

(i) Surely the achievement of the possible is more useful than the elucidation of the desirable yet unattainable, or is it? (See p. 97.)

(ii) Now that the law applied by the magistrates' courts has been reformed along the lines advanced by the Law Commission in their Report and Working Paper (see p. 97, below), is there much force left in the Finer Report's criticism?

(iii) One of the most important aspects of the magisterial jurisdiction in the present dual system is as a registration and enforcement agency of county court orders. Many of the applications to the magistrates' courts seek variation of these orders and/or remission of arrears which have accrued. Is the effect of a refusal to remit arrears as serious to a paying party as a decision on a successful application by the payee to vary an order?

(iv) If a family court system is introduced, is there a case for enforcement of arrears to be dealt with by a body other than the new court? (See later Chapter 15.)

(v) Are applications to remit linked to enforcement or to variation?

Under the 1960 Act, in order to obtain a matrimonial order in the magistrates' court, the applicant had to prove that the respondent had committed a matrimonial offence. The Working Paper fully accepted that the time had come for the obligation of each spouse to maintain the other to be recognised as the cornerstone to the new grounds. The obligation of support should be seen to be fully reciprocal. Given this general principle the Working Paper went on to consider the possible new grounds:

35. If the obligation to maintain were to be recognised in the general matrimonial law as fully reciprocal, in what circumstances should magistrates have power to order maintenance and what facts should they take into account in doing so? For the purpose of discussion we tentatively put forward the proposition that the principal ground upon which a court should have power to order maintenance should be failure by one of the parties to the marriage to provide such maintenance for the other party or for any children as is reasonable in all the circumstances. We recognise that such a formulation, which relies upon the concept of 'reasonable in all the circumstances', leaves a very wide discretion to the court. But we think this is a good starting point, particularly for the lay magistracy.

Questions

(i) Do you think it a good idea for the lay magistracy to have such a wide discretion?
(ii) Do you think it a good idea for anyone to have such a wide discretion?

The Working Party considered additional grounds. They put forward the proposition that it should be open to either party to a marriage to apply for a maintenance order on the ground that the respondent has behaved in such a way that the applicant cannot reasonably be expected to live with the respondent, mainly because they thought that a wife should be able to 'escape from her husband and obtain financial relief if she needs it'. So far as desertion was concerned, they said:

42. . . . If the parties have ceased to cohabit, it will often happen that a deserting husband will continue to maintain his wife. If he does not, then the failure to maintain ground is available to the wife; but if he does, on what ground could intervention by the courts be justified? Should the courts be able to intervene solely on the ground that the respondent refuses to live with the applicant, or, put in terms of the existing law, should desertion continue to be a ground for an order? One ground for intervention, we suggest, might be as a protection against the future. The wife in these circumstances might be thought to be justified in wanting an order as security against her husband's future failure to maintain her. We wonder, however, whether the effect of enabling the courts to intervene in this situation might not be simply to encourage unnecessary litigation. If there is genuine need for relief, for example because maintenance (though substantial) is irregularly paid, the court should be able to intervene on the ground that the husband is not maintaining, i.e. not providing reasonable maintenance. The same arguments apply a fortiori where there are any children of the marriage. Another possible justification for the court's intervention is that desertion can be difficult to prove and, as it remains a ground for establishing irretrievable breakdown and thus obtaining a divorce, it should be possible for the applicant to prove desertion as soon as it begins. But this alone may not be an adequate ground for an exercise of the magistrates' matrimonial law. . . .
43. Nevertheless, our own inclination would be to preserve the existing position. We therefore provisionally propose that there should be a third ground on which it should be possible to apply to the court for an order: namely, that the respondent is in desertion.

Questions

(i) What arguments can you present against the retention of desertion as a ground?
(ii) Why is adultery not included?
(iii) Section 7(1) of the Domestic Proceedings and Magistrates' Courts Act 1978 states: 'Where the parties to a marriage have been living apart for a

continuous period exceeding three months, neither party having deserted the other, and one of the parties has been making periodical payments for the benefit of the other party or of a child of the family, that other party may apply to a magistrates' court for an order under this section, and any application made under this subsection shall specify the aggregate amount of the payments so made during the period of three months immediately preceding the date of the making of the application.' In view of this, is there any reason to retain desertion as a ground?

The Working Paper stimulated a large number of comments. Some are reported by the Law Commission in their Report (1976):

2.8 The Working Party's analysis of the principles and objectives underlying the summary matrimonial jurisdiction was generally approved in the consultation. . . . Opinions were, however, divided when it came to the three grounds of application for a matrimonial order proposed in substitution for the existing provisions in section 1 of the 1960 Act. . . . The Bar Council . . . thought that it would be sufficient to provide for an 'application for reasonable maintenance' without specifying the grounds on which the application might be made, and that if a ground of application was to be specified it should be limited to a failure to provide reasonable maintenance. Our own view is that it is right to give some guidance to the court by specifying the grounds on which an application may be made. We agree with the majority of those who commented on the working paper that both failure to provide reasonable maintenance and unreasonable behaviour should be grounds so specified.
2.9 On whether desertion should be retained as a separate ground opinion was more or less evenly divided. . . . Some argued that desertion was simply a specific form of unreasonable behaviour, which, like adultery, would already be covered by the general ground. Others contended that desertion was a highly technical offence, difficult to prove and thus not appropriate to the magistrates' matrimonial jurisdiction.
2.10 Other commentators argued that the effect of including desertion as a ground would be to encourage applicants to institute proceedings to safeguard them against possible future failures to maintain. As for the argument that, since desertion remains a ground for establishing irretrievable breakdown and thus obtaining a divorce, it should be possible for the applicant to prove desertion as soon as it begins, it was asserted that magistrates' courts should not be used as a stepping stone to the divorce court since this would not be conducive to a conciliatory atmosphere.
2.11 We can see the force in all these arguments. We think, however, that the balance of advantage lies in retaining in the magistrates' matrimonial jurisdiction some means by which a wife who has been deserted can obtain a maintenance order soon after the desertion, whether or not her husband has ceased to maintain her. We do not think that a deserted wife for whom her husband is providing reasonable maintenance should be required to wait until that maintenance has ceased before making her application.

Questions

(i) What *is* the difference between wilful neglect to maintain and failure to provide reasonable maintenance?
(ii) Does the Law Commission answer the views of those such as the Bar Council who were unhappy about the retention of the 'conduct' grounds?
(iii) If so, is it a satisfactory answer?
(iv) Is desertion 'unreasonable behaviour'? (See further in Chapter 6, below)?
(v) Do you think that the acceptance of the general principle that *each* spouse has a duty to support the other advances the status of women?

On the relevance of a wife's adultery to her claim to support, the Law Commission reported that:

2.15 The Working Party considered at length the question whether, and if so to what extent, the courts, when considering the making of a maintenance order on one of the three grounds proposed in the working paper, should have regard to the conduct of the respective parties to the marriage. They concluded that, as regards adultery, it was not desirable and no longer acceptable to public opinion that the commission by the wife of a single act of adultery should be regarded as sufficient to disqualify her automatically from all financial relief. They could see no justification nowadays for a court's being bound to refuse to make a maintenance order in favour of an otherwise deserving wife because she has committed adultery; the more so since adultery is not a bar to an award of maintenance in divorce proceedings. . . .

These proposals were welcomed by all who commented on the working paper and we concur in them.

Question

Write a brief on behalf of an invented society — the Society for the Preservation of Standards in Marriage — designed to oppose the views of the Law Commission and the subsequent law.

On the role of conduct generally, the Law Commission invited comments in the Working Paper on four possible approaches:

(*a*) the obligation to maintain should be regarded as absolute and reciprocal and, thus, matrimonial conduct should not be taken into account in determining liability or quantum; or

(*b*) the conduct should be relevant in every case as regards liability, but should not be taken into account in determining the amount of an order; or

(*c*) conduct should be relevant, both as regards liability and quantum; or

(*d*) conduct should be relevant in every case, both as regards liability and quantum, but if the court decides to make an order, it should not reduce the amount it would have ordered below a sum sufficient to provide the applicant with the basic necessities of life.

The Law Commission accepted approach (*c*). Thus,

[In] determining whether and if so how to exercise its powers to order financial provision the court should, to the extent to which it is just to do so, have regard to the conduct of the parties. Conduct may therefore, in a proper case, be relevant both to liability and to quantum. It seems to us that that principle, established as it has been by Parliament, must be accepted as equally applicable to cases where a magistrates' court is considering whether one party to a marriage should be ordered to make financial provision for the other while the marriage is still subsisting, and if so what provision should be ordered. We therefore think that in deciding whether to order such financial provision, and if so what provision to order, a magistrates' court should be required by statute to have regard to the conduct of the parties to the marriage to the extent to which it is just to do so.

Questions

(i) Do you think the Law Commission was right to propose principles based on the divorce jurisdiction?

(ii) Does the acceptance of proposal (*c*) mean that conduct is or is not relevant to the question of whether the husband has failed to provide reasonable maintenance for the wife?

When considering factors other than conduct which courts should take into account in determining whether or not to make an order, and if so for what amount, the Working Party had recommended that the court should have regard to

(a) the income, earning capacity, property and other financial resources of each of the parties; and
(b) the financial needs, obligations and responsibilities of each of the parties.

The Law Commission's Report took the view that these two sets of factors were not adequate. They felt that the right course was to reproduce as far as possible the guidelines contained in s. 25 of the Matrimonial Causes Act 1973.

Amendments have now been made to s. 25 by the Matrimonial and Family Proceedings Act 1984 see below p. 256; and the guidelines contained in the amended s. 25 are reproduced in the amended s. 3 of the Domestic Proceedings and Magistrates' Courts Act. The Act now reads:

1. Either party to a marriage may apply to a magistrates' court for an order under section 2 of this Act on the ground that the other party to the marriage (in this Part of this Act referred to as 'the respondent') —
    (a) has failed to provide reasonable maintenance for the applicant; or
    (b) has failed to provide, or to make a proper contribution towards, reasonable maintenance for any child of the family; or
    (c) has behaved in such a way that the applicant cannot reasonably be expected to live with the respondent; or
    (d) has deserted the applicant.

2. — (1) Where on an application for an order under this section the applicant satisfies the court of any ground mentioned in section 1 of this Act, the court may, subject to the provisions of this Part of this Act, make any one or more of the following orders, that is to say —
    (a) an order that the respondent shall make to the applicant such periodical payments, and for such term, as may be specified in the order;
    (b) an order that the respondent shall pay to the applicant such lump sum as may be so specified;
    (c) an order that the respondent shall make to the applicant for the benefit of a child of the family to whom the application relates, or to such a child, such periodical payments, and for such term, as may be so specified;
    (d) an order that the respondent shall pay to the applicant for the benefit of a child of the family to whom the application relates, or to such a child, such lump sum as may be so specified.

(2) Without prejudice to the generality of subsection (1)(b) or (d) above, an order under this section for the payment of a lump sum may be made for the purpose of enabling any liability or expenses reasonably incurred in maintaining the applicant, or any child of the family to whom the application relates, before the making of the order to be met.

(3) The amount of any lump sum required to be paid by an order under this section shall not exceed £500 or such larger amount as the Secretary of State may from time to time by order fix for the purposes of this subsection. . . .

3. — (1) Where an application is made for an order under section 2 of this Act, it shall be the duty of the court, in deciding whether to exercise its powers under that section and, if so, in what manner, to have regard to all the circumstances of the case, first consideration being given to the welfare while a minor of any child of the family who has not attained the age of eighteen.

(2) As regards the exercise of its powers under subsection (1)(a) or (b) of section 2, the court shall in particular have regard to the following matters —
    (a) the income, earning capacity, property and other financial resources which each of the parties to the marriage has or is likely to have in the foreseeable future, including in the case of earning capacity any increase in that capacity which it would in the opinion of the court be reasonable to expect a party to the marriage to take steps to acquire;
    (b) the financial needs, obligations and responsibilities which each of the parties to the marriage has or is likely to have in the foreseeable future;
    (c) the standard of living enjoyed by the parties to the marriage before the occurrence of the conduct which is alleged as the ground of the application;
    (d) the age of each party to the marriage and the duration of the marriage;

(e) any physical or mental disability of either of the parties to the marriage;

(f) the contributions which each of the parties has made or is likely in the foreseeable future to make to the welfare of the family, including any contribution by looking after the home or caring for the family;

(g) the conduct of each of the parties, if that conduct is such that it would in the opinion of the court be inequitable to disregard it.

The Law Commission in their Report, *Family Law: The Ground for Divorce* (1990) recommended repeal of s. 1(c) and 1(d). The major restructuring of divorce law as recommended by them (see Chapter 6) undermines the previous views of the Law Commission (see pp. 95ff):

4.22 One of the broad objectives of the Law Commission's recommendations, which resulted in the Domestic Proceedings and Magistrates' Courts Act 1978, was indeed 'to bring the family law administered by the magistrates' courts, so far as can appropriately be done, into line with the law administered by the divorce court'. This was not, however, the primary reason for the inclusion of the behaviour and desertion grounds. Behaviour was included to cover the case of a wife who is anxious to leave her husband because of his conduct, but knows that if she does so he would cease to maintain her. The Commission wished to avoid a situation whereby a woman was compelled to continue to live with a husband who was treating her badly for fear that she would be left destitute. Similarly, desertion was included so as to enable a deserted wife whose husband was providing her with reasonable maintenance to obtain an order immediately, without having to wait for him to stop doing so. It was thought that this would enable her to obtain some security against his future failure to maintain her. An additional advantage of including behaviour and desertion was stated to be the preservation of evidence which could later be used in divorce proceedings. This would, of course, no longer be relevant in the context of our recommendations.

4.23 In practice, it is unlikely that either of these grounds is able to provide the degree of security which the Commission envisaged. A woman who is in fear of her husband is unlikely to take the risk of applying for maintenance before she leaves him. Once they are separated, he will either continue to maintain her voluntarily, in which case she should be able to obtain either an agreed order under section 6 of the Act, or eventually a confirmation of voluntary payments order under section 7; or he will cease to do so, in which case she can allege failure to maintain under section 1(a). If there is indeed a need to obtain an order to gain security in advance of such a failure, it is illogical to distinguish between desertion and other reasons for separating. In any event, the availability of income support cannot be ignored in the context of a woman who fears that she may be left destitute. Whatever arrangements may eventually be negotiated or ordered, this is a far more reliable immediate safety net than any court-based procedure could ever be.

4.24 It is not known how many marriages in respect of which financial orders are made by magistrates later proceed to divorce. Undoubtedly quite a number do so. It seems undesirable that cases which might later proceed to the divorce court should have started off by one of the parties alleging fault. This could undermine the objectives of the proposed reforms for divorce. When the divorce court comes to deal with children and financial matters during the period for consideration and reflection, it is unlikely that a husband will forget that his wife has already made a number of allegations in court about his behaviour. This could also serve to undermine the effectiveness of any attempts at conciliation or mediation.

4.25 A further factor which should not be ignored is that an application to a magistrates' court leaves the door open to reconciliation. However unlikely this may be in many cases, it is even more desirable than it is in divorce to seek so far as possible to minimise the bitterness and conflict between them, so as to preserve the possibility of an amicable and peaceful resumption of cohabitation.

4.26 Finally, it is worth bearing in mind the findings of earlier research that the magistrates' jurisdiction is predominantly the resort of the poor. This may now have changed, particularly since the introduction of agreed orders under section 6 of the 1978 Act, but the law should seek to avoid giving the impression of 'one law for the rich and another for the poor' which has for so long been a criticism of our matrimonial procedures.

Conclusion

4.27 In our view, the power to make an order on the ground of failure to provide reasonable maintenance, together with the power to make an agreed order, and the power to make an order where the parties have been living apart for three months and one party has been voluntarily paying maintenance to the other or for a child of the family, would cover all the practical requirements of those who are likely to use this jurisdiction. Any short intervening period where maintenance is either not being paid, or is below subsistence level, will be covered by income support or family credit. There is separate legal machinery available to the Department of Social Security to recover income support from a liable relative. It is therefore unlikely that any person would be left destitute as a result of a reform in the grounds for obtaining a financial provision order in the magistrates' court.

4.28 We there *recommend* the abolition of the separate grounds of behaviour and desertion, and accordingly that section 1(*c*) and section 1(*d*) of the Domestic Proceedings and Magistrates' Courts Act 1978 should be repealed. Further, the power in section 7, to make an order where the parties have been living apart for three months and one has been voluntarily maintaining the other or any child of the family, should no longer be limited to cases where neither has deserted the other but cover all types of separation. The deletion of desertion from sections 1 and 7 would incidentally result in an enormous simplification of family law, for desertion is one of the most complex and technical concepts which it contains.

Questions

(i) Is there an argument for abolishing the magistrates' courts jurisdiction in these matters outright? (See Chapter 15.)

(ii) Since the 1978 Act was passed, is there anything left of the husband's common law duty to maintain?

(iii) Is an earning wife under any duty to provide housekeeping money (*a*) to a non-earning husband or (*b*) to an earning husband?

(iv) Section 6 of the 1978 Act as amended states:

6.—(1) Either party to a marriage may apply to a magistrates' court for an order under this section on the ground that *either the party making the application* or the other party to the marriage has agreed to make such financial provision as may be specified in the application and, subject to subsection (3) below, the court on such an application may, if—

(*a*) it is satisfied that the applicant or the respondent, as the case may be, has agreed to make that provision, and

(*b*) it has no reason to think that it would be contrary to the interests of justice to exercise its powers hereunder,

order that the *applicant* or the respondent, as the case may be, shall make the financial provision specified in the application.

What advantages are there, for a payee and a payer in obtaining an order under s. 6?

(v) In *Simister v Simister* [1987] 1 All ER 233, [1986] 1 WLR 1463, Waite J said that 'maintenance is normally very much a dunning process, with one side pressing for as much, and the other side holding out for as little, as each can fairly get or give.' (*a*) Is such a process desirable? (*b*) If you think that it is not desirable, how would *you* change the law to lessen this effect?

Three cases on the Act are the following. In the first case there were no children.

Robinson v Robinson
[1983] Fam 42, [1983] 1 All ER 391, [1983] 2 WLR 146, 4 FLR 243, 13 Fam Law 48, Court of Appeal

The parties were married in 1976. The husband was a soldier and the wife ceased her employment after she married him. They lived in married quarters. In late 1980, the husband was posted to Belize, and the wife returned to her parents. When the husband returned from overseas duty in March 1981, the wife decided that she was not going back to him, although she did not tell him of her decision until August 1981. The wife applied for maintenance under s. 2 of the Domestic Proceedings and Magistrates' Courts Act 1978. The magistrates' found that the wife had deserted her husband and that this behaviour was 'gross and obvious'. The magistrates' court said 'the wife's desertion of her husband, he not having committed any misconduct, was a matter of the gravest importance in relation to this marriage and was a matter to be taken into account together with all the other matters set out in section 3 of the 1978 Act when deciding what financial provision order, if any, should be made in favour of the applicant.' The magistrates' court awarded her periodical payments of £15 per week, one-tenth of the joint income, for a period of five years from the date of the order. The wife appealed unsuccessfully to the Divisional Court and on further appeal to the Court of Appeal.

Waller LJ: The magistrates held that (the conduct of the wife) was 'gross and obvious misconduct' and in so doing were referring to the test applied by Lord Denning MR and Ormrod J (in *Wachtel v Wachtel* [1973] Fam 72, [1973] 1 All ER 827). The words 'gross and obvious misconduct' can be somewhat misleading, but as I understand it they were referring to the fact that this was an unusual case far removed from those where much blame could be put on both sides and it was a case where it would have been unjust to give the financial support which would normally be given. In answer to the question would it offend a reasonable man's sense of justice that this wife's conduct should be left out of account in deciding the financial provision which the husband should make, the magistrates were answering 'Yes it would' when they said: 'The wife's desertion of her husband, he not having committed any misconduct was a matter of the gravest importance in relation to the marriage . . .'. On the facts found the behaviour of the wife was quite capable of being within the terms I have outlined above. In my opinion it is quite impossible to interfere with the decision of the magistrates.
Appeal dismissed.

In the second case, there was a child.

Vasey v Vasey
[1985] FLR 596, [1985] Fam Law 158, Court of Appeal.

The magistrates' court granted the custody of the child of the family to the wife with access to the husband. They ordered that the husband pay £15 a week for the child but refused to make an order for the maintenance of the wife because she had deserted her husband. The wife appealed unsuccessfully to the Divisional Court and then to the Court of Appeal.

Dunn LJ: In *Robinson v Robinson* the magistrates had found, as in this case, that conduct was a relevant consideration and, accordingly, they made a substantial reduction in the maintenance order as compared with the order they would have made in the absence of such a finding. . . .
    In this case there is no appeal against the finding of the magistrates that conduct was relevant. Indeed, there could have been no such appeal since the wife left the husband after less than 9 months of marriage and did not attempt to justify her leaving. But what is said in this court by Mr Lightwing (counsel for the wife) is that the magistrates failed to take into account matters which they were required to take into account by reason of the provisions of s. 3 of the Act; that, accordingly, they failed to carry out the balancing exercise required by that section and consequently, by reason of the decision of this court in *Dicocco v Milne* (1982) 4 FLR 247, an appellate court was free to carry out the balancing exercise since there was sufficient evidence to enable it to do so. . . . The proper approach for magistrates in considering any application

under s. 2 of the Act is therefore to make findings seriatim upon each of the matters set out in [s. 3(2)] and then to balance the factors against one another so as to arrive at an order which is just and reasonable. The weight to be attached to any particular matter is for the magistrates, but they must take account of all of them. The most important function of magistrates is usually to balance needs and responsibilities against financial resources; and if, in an exceptional case, the magistrates decide that conduct is relevant, that must be put into the balance. I say 'an exceptional case' because experience has shown that it is dangerous to make judgements about the cause of the breakdown of a marriage without full inquiry, since the conduct of the one spouse can only be measured against the conduct of the other, and marriages seldom break down without faults on both sides.

In this case the magistrates do not appear to have considered either para. (*a*) or (*b*) of [s. 3(2),] the most important paragraphs dealing with financial resources and needs, and they carried out apparently no balancing exercise at all. With respect to the Divisional Court, the fact that they may have considered the alternative of a reduction of maintenance for the wife is, in my judgment, no indication that they took into account any factor save conduct.

[Dunn LJ then dealt with the various matters relating to the needs and resources of the parties, and continued . . .]

Mr Lightwing submitted that were it not for the relevant conduct, the wife in this case could have expected to receive an order in excess of £5,000 a year less tax, if the conventional one-third approach was applied as a starting figure. But because of the finding as to conduct he conceded that there should be a substantial reduction. He submitted that the wife should at least be put into the position in which she now is on social security, which I should emphasize is, by definition, to put her at subsistence level. That would involve, said Mr Lightwing, an order of between £30 and £40 a week for her, in addition to £15 a week for the child. That would still leave her below the tax belt.

In my view this proposal by Mr Lightwing is by no means an excessive one, and Mr Briggs (counsel for the husband) accepted that if we were to come to the conclusion that it was open to us to review the magistrates' order his proposal was a reasonable one — indeed, I would say that it is a modest one. It would give the wife about £55 a week for herself and the child under the terms of the order and, in addition, she would be entitled to £10.55 a week child allowance and single parent allowance. Of course the wife, out of those moneys, would have to pay her own rent of £20 of £25 a week. . . .

I would only add that I would make these orders on the basis that the wife is not working. If and when she is able to work, it would be open to the husband to apply for an appropriate reduction having regard to the means of the parties at that time.

Appeal allowed: £33 p.w. for wife, £20 p.w. expenses to be paid direct to the child.

Question

Are you relieved by the approach taken by the Court of Appeal in *Vasey v Vasey*?

In the third case, there were step-children.

Day v Day
[1988] FCR 470, [1988] 1 FLR 278, High Court, Family Division

The marriage had lasted only six weeks. Nevertheless, the husband married the wife after a long relationship and both treated and accepted the children as children of the family. He had in effect 'taken on a commitment'. The magistrates' court made an order for the husband to pay £15 per week to the wife and £5 per week to each of the children on the basis of his admitted desertion. On appeal, the husband contended that the court should have made a nominal order for five reasons: (i) the wife, now on social security benefits, was in fact better off financially without her husband than with him; (ii) she was of an age to go out to work; (iii) the husband had no means to pay such amounts to his wife because of his outgoings; (iv) the marriage had been a short one; and (v) although the husband's desertion could be criticised it did not entitle any payment to be increased.

Wood J: This is an appeal from a decision of the justices sitting at Tottenham on 23 September 1985. . . .

The justices found that this husband knew what he was doing in accepting these two children as children of the family; that he did so, and that he provided subsistence and maintenance for them during the short duration of the cohabitation.

Having found those general facts, the justices looked at the means of the wife, namely, the receipts that she had from the DHSS and her outgoings.

Prior to the marriage, the wife and children had been on social security and after the departure of the husband they returned to remain on social security and, to a substantial extent, they are still reliant upon social security. It is right to point out that any money paid by this husband towards the maintenance of his wife and the children of the family will reduce the liability of the taxpayer, but that is conceded not to be a relevant factor.

Mr Marks [for the husband] submits that, based upon those factors which I have mentioned [the five factors above], the justices really did not take into consideration the various factors set out in s. 3 of the 1978 Act, the financial resources, the need and obligations, the standard of living, the ages and duration. They ignored the amendment [in 1984] and ignored the fact that somebody else, namely the natural father, should have been maintaining these children. Looking at the reasons it is quite clear that the justices, in their reasons, expressly referred to s. 3 and the amendment. It is quite apparent that the many factors which are mentioned by Mr Marks are taken into account in their findings of fact and their reasoning if one looks at the document as a whole, and, in my judgment, it would not be right to seek to look upon the reasons given by justices as one would a carefully reserved judgment and to search with too fine a toothcomb for the phraseology and the criticisms which are possible. I have no doubt here that these justices took the very greatest care, as one can see from their reasons in this case. They saw and heard the witnesses, they have indicated whose evidence they preferred and they have referred to the correct statutory provisions which they must have had before them. They also had the assistance of Mr Marks who, I am sure, presented the case before them with the skill and determination with which he has presented this appeal.

I am satisfied here that there are no reasons for this appeal to succeed and it is dismissed.

Question

Can you find any common thread which runs through the judgments?

The judicial statistics for domestic proceedings in magistrates' courts suggest a dramatic drop in applications for 'married women maintenance orders' — from 28,004 in 1968 to 6,851 in 1978. Applications increased during the early 1980s to 13,900 in 1984, but then dropped again to 11,070 in 1985. There has been a continuing fall, and there were only 8,590 applications in 1989. Applications under s. 6 (agreed payments orders) show a similar drop from 8,340 in 1986 to 5,190 in 1989. Applications under s. 7 have always been low; in 1989 there were just 30. The magistrates' courts are often used to register orders made elsewhere, and in 1989, some 7,930 orders made by other courts were registered. There were also 44,450 applications for variation, revival or revocation of financial provision orders. Both these figures, however, represent significant falls from the figures some four years ago when there were 58,410 applications for variation, revival or revocation, and 10,960 registrations from other courts. (Home Office Statistical Bulletin 21/1990.)

Domestic proceedings per 100,000 population in magistrates' courts — England and Wales 1989

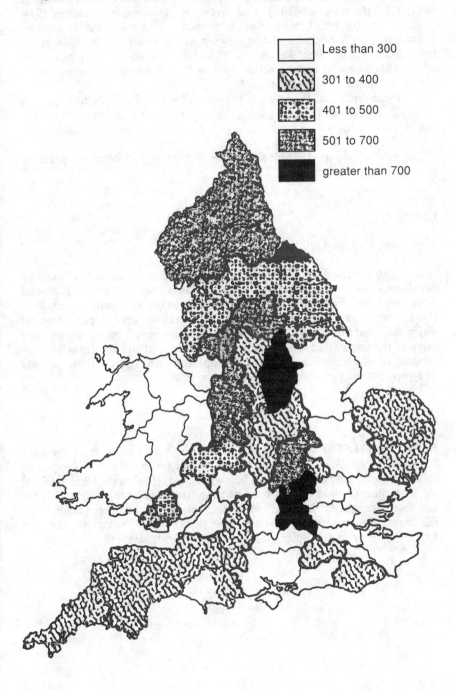

Source: Home Office Statistic Bulletin, 21/1990

Questions

(i) Which of the following do you consider the most likely explanation for the fall: (*a*) the reform of the law of divorce which came into force in 1971; (*b*) a fall in the number of married women needing support from their husbands; (*c*) the decision of the supplementary benefit authorities at the time, following the Finer Report (1974) no longer to advise married women who claimed benefit to take action against their husbands; (*d*) some other reason or combination of reasons?
(ii) Do you think that the reforms brought about by the Child Support Act (1991) (see Chapter 4, below) will result in an increase in 'married women maintenance orders'?

The map above (p. 103) illustrates the distribution of domestic proceedings in magistrates' courts in 1989.

Question

What does this map tell us?

It is also possible for a spouse to apply to a divorce court for financial provision under s. 27 of the Matrimonial Causes Act 1973, on the ground of failure to provide reasonable maintenance for the applicant or a child of the family. The court may then award secured or unsecured periodical payments, and/or a lump sum of unlimited amount. Divorce courts have none of the unpleasant 'police court' connotations of the magistrates' jurisdiction, to which the Finer Committee took such strong exception, yet only 151 applications under s. 27 were made in 1989.

Questions

(i) Which of the following do you consider the most likely explanation for the rarity of applications: (*a*) that most would prefer to seek a divorce or judicial separation (see Chapter 6, below) instead; (*b*) that the legal aid fund would require a good reason for resorting to this remedy while a cheaper equivalent existed in the magistrates' court; or (*c*) some other reason?
(ii) Do the figures on maintenance applications support the views of the Law Commission or of the Finer Committee (see p. 92, above)?

CHAPTER 4

State support and private support

This chapter considers the complex questions which surround the question of state involvement in family income support. Of necessity, the chapter is concerned with priorities and with parity of treatment. It looks at lone parent families, some of whom may well have forms of support other than the state; it looks at poor two-parent families, who may well have no other means of support; and it looks at those families where there is a dependent elderly adult living in the household.

We consider first the issue of claims to income support by women and their children from their husbands and their fathers. This question necessarily links up with the section in the previous chapter on maintenance claims in the domestic court. An examination of this area is also important in an appreciation of parity with other families when it comes to considering competing claims to state funds.

1 Poverty and the lone parent family

The growth in the number of lone parent families in Great Britain is apparent from the following table from *Population Trends 55* (1989).

Growth in lone parent families

Thousands and percentages

Type of family with dependent children*	Numbers (thousands)				Percentage increase 1976–86	Percentage (from GHS 1985–87)	
	1971	1976	1985	1986			
One parent families							
Single mothers	90	130	210	230	+77	23	3.2
Separated mothers	170	185	180	190	+3	18	2.6
Divorced mothers	120	230	400	410	+78	41	5.6
Widowed mothers	120	115	90	80	−30	8	1.1
ALL mothers	500	660	880	910	+38	90	12.5
ALL fathers	70	90	90	100	+11	10	1.4
ALL parents	570	750	970	1,010	+35	100	13.9
*Married couple families***							86.1
ALL families							100.0

* Dependent children are defined as aged under 16 or 16 to 18 and in full time education.
** Includes some cohabitating couples.

Sources: Population Trends 55 Spring 1989

Lone parents now comprise almost 14% of all households in Great Britain with dependent children, a percentage increase of 35% from 1976–1986. It is not surprising to find that there has been a similar marked increase in the number of lone parents dependent on State support; from 330,000 in 1980 to 770,000 in 1989.

To place the numbers in perspective, we print below the following two tables from *Social Trends 17* (1987) and *21* (1991).

People in households: by type of household and family in which they live[1]

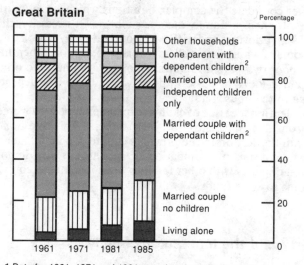

Great Britain

1 Data for 1961, 1971 and 1981 are taken from the Population Censuses for those years: the 1985 data are from the General Household Survey

2 These family types may also include independent children

Source: Office of Population Censuses and Surveys

Thus a substantial proportion of lone-parent families are living at the officially defined subsistence level, but Maclean and Eekelaar in *Children and Divorce: Economic Factors*, (1983) speaking of children of divorced parents, emphasise the importance of relating the problems of the poverty level for dependent children of lone parent families to other children in comparable situations:

. . . but these children have potential sources of support not available to children of sick or unemployed fathers, or children in large families. On divorce there are essentially four sources from which support might be found to arrest the decline in the economic circumstances of the former family. The first comprises *the resources of the former family* as they stood at the moment of the dissolution. However, as most studies have shown, these are generally meagre (Todd and Jones, 1972; Manners and Rauta, 1981). But where an independent household existed, a dwelling, either owner-occupied or rented, is likely to be the most significant item. The second is *the earning capacity of the custodial parent* (which we assume for simplicity to be the mother). The third is *the earning capacity of the non-custodial parent* (the father). And the last resource is to be found in *State provisions*.

Composition of the lowest quintile group of household income:[1] by economic status of family head[2], 1981 and 1987

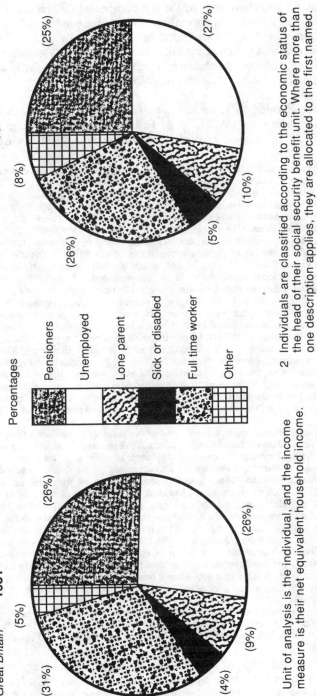

Great Britain

1981

(5%)
(26%)
(31%)
(4%)
(9%)
(26%)

1987

(25%)
(8%)
(26%)
(5%)
(10%)
(27%)

Percentages

Pensioners
Unemployed
Lone parent
Sick or disabled
Full time worker
Other

1 Unit of analysis is the individual, and the income measure is their net equivalent household income.

2 Individuals are classified according to the economic status of the head of their social security benefit unit. Where more than one description applies, they are allocated to the first named.

Source: Department of Social Security, Households below average income, from Family Expenditure Survey

Social Trends 21, © Crown copyright 1991

Questions

(i) Why do you think that whilst the number of divorced lone parents has increased by 78% and the number of single lone mothers has increased by 77%, the number of widowed mothers has actually declined?

(ii) Maclean and Eekelaar actually identify in their examination of potential sources of support for children of divorced parent a 'fifth and powerful economic resource'. What do you think they are referring to?

In her chapter on Income Maintenance for Families with Children, in *Families in Britain* (1982), Ruth Lister described the framework of the system of state support up until the reforms in the Social Security Act 1986.

The basic framework for today's income maintenance provisions was laid down in the Beveridge Report of 1942. The Beveridge Plan envisaged a comprehensive 'scheme of social insurance against interruption and destruction of earning power' combined with a 'general system of children's allowances, sufficient to meet the subsistence needs' of children. Family allowances (for all children but the first) and contributory national insurance benefits (such as unemployment and widows' benefits) were introduced after the war. The Beveridge Plan also included the safety-net of a means-tested national assistance scheme designed to protect the minority who fell through the meshes of the insurance scheme. It was intended that this safety-net would wither away until it was catering for only a tiny minority. Instead, because of the failure to pay adequate national insurance benefits, as recommended by Beveridge, the numbers claiming means-tested assistance (renamed supplementary benefit in 1966) trebled from one to three million between 1948 and 1978. Further, governments have attempted to bolster up inadequate income maintenance provisions for both those in and out of work through the introduction of a range of means-tested benefits, which have been much criticised. A classic example was the introduction, in 1971, of Family Income Supplement for poor working families, as an alternative to fulfilling an election pledge to increase family allowances. The failure to pay high enough national insurance benefits and family allowances was one reason for the growing dependence on means-tested benefits. The other was the exclusion from the Beveridge Plan of people such as the congenitally disabled who could not meet the contribution conditions attached to the insurance benefits. During the 1970s a number of non-contributory benefits were, therefore, introduced to help the disabled and those at home to care for disabled relatives.

The overall picture today is, thus, one of a confusing patchwork of contributory, non-contributory and means-tested benefits. Much of this patchwork has grown up in isolation from the other main element in our income maintenance provisions: the tax system. . . . The system of personal tax allowances was supposed to ensure that 'there should be no income tax levied upon any income which is insufficient to provide the owner with what he requires for subsistence' (Royal Commission on the Taxation of Profits and Income, 1954). [However] the personal tax allowances patently no longer perform this function. The value of the tax allowances has been so eroded since the war that people can now start to pay tax at incomes which are below the poverty line. . . . When you take the growing dependence on means-tested benefits and add to it the growing numbers of low income working families drawn into the tax net, the result is one of the more ludicrous aspects of the income maintenance scheme: 'the poverty trap'. The 'poverty trap' is a term 'used to describe the situation in which a family loses more in terms of extra tax paid and reduced benefits received than it gains from a pay increase which brought them about' (Pond, 1978). It is families with children who are most vulnerable to the poverty trap.

The most recent development in income maintenance provision for families has been the introduction of the child benefit scheme. This represented the fusion of two hitherto separate strands of financial support for children: family allowances and child tax allowances.

The Social Security Act 1986 replaced the supplementary benefit with a system known as income support. A claimant is entitled to Income Support if he or she is aged 18 or over and available for employment although not engaged in 'remunerative work'. There are certain categories of claimant exempt from the requirement of having to show evidence of availability for employment. Lone parents may qualify for Income Support at 16. The income of the claimant must not exceed an 'applicable amount'. Likewise, the capital must not exceed a 'prescribed level'. The amount which is paid by way of Income Support is based on a complicated formula of allowances and premiums, described in this way in Appendix C to *Children Come First* (1990):

The personal allowance is the basic element of the Income Support payment and is intended to cover all normal living expenses. Premiums are additions to Income Support allowances for groups of people with extra needs. Normally, a person who qualifies for more than one premium will only get the one that gives them the most money. However, a person entitled to the family, disabled child, severe disability or carer premium can get them as well as any other premiums they qualify for.

Weekly Personal Allowances
[as from April 1991]

Single People
18-24 years old £31.15
18 years and over and bringing up a child £39.65
25 years old and over £39.65

Couples
both under 18 .... £47.30
with at least one of the couple 18 or over £62.25

And for each child
under 11 .... £13.35
11 to 15 years old £19.75
16 to 17 years old, doing a full-time course not above A
  level, Scottish Certificate of Education (Higher Grade) or
  equivalent £23.65
18 years old, doing a full-time course not above A level, Scottish Certificate of Education (Higher Grade) or equivalent   £31.15

Weekly Premiums
Premiums for people with children

Family Premium
for people with at least one child £7.95

Disabled Child Premium
for people with a child who is getting Attendance Allowance
  or Mobility Allowance or who is registered blind £16.65

Lone Parent Premium
for people bringing up one or more children on their own .. £4.45

Premiums for long term sick or disabled people

	Single Person	Couple
Disability Premium for people getting Invalidity Benefit, Severe Disablement Allowance, Mobility Allowance, Attendance Allowance, registered blind or who are sick and cannot work and have been sending doctor's statements for at least 28 weeks	£16.65	£23.90
Severe Disability Premium for people getting Attendance Allowance and living alone and no-one gets Invalid Care Allowance for looking after them.		
Single person	£31.25	
Couple both partners get Attendance Allowance but someone gets Invalid Care Allowance for looking after them		£31.25
Couple, both partners get Attendance Allowance, no-one gets Invalid Care Allowance for looking after either of them		£62.50

Premiums for Carers
Carer Premium

	Single Person	Couple
for people getting Invalid Care Allowance	£10.80	£10.80 (for each person on ICA)

There are also premiums for people aged 60 or over.

Help with Housing and Community Charge Costs
Income Support can include money to help people to meet interest charges on a mortgage or home loan.

The Social Security Act 1986 also made two other changes in terminology. First, Single Payments were replaced by a scheme known as the Social Fund which provides Social Fund Officers with a wide discretion to meet needs, albeit often by loans. Secondly, Family Credit (see p. 130, below) is introduced to replace FIS so as to provide some limited assistance for low income families where the claimant or partner is responsible for a child member of the household.

The two reports which are still of profound importance are Sir William Beveridge's Report on *Social Insurance and Allied Services* (1942) and Sir Maurice Finer's *Report of the Committee on One-Parent Families* (1974).

Sir William Beveridge's Report on *Social Insurance and Allied Services* (1942) had this to say of the divorced and separated:

347. **End of marriage otherwise than by widowhood**
Divorce, legal separation, desertion and voluntary separation may cause needs similar to those caused by widowhood. They differ from widowhood in two respects: that they may occur through the fault or with the consent of the wife, and that except where they occur through the fault of the wife they leave the husband's liability for maintenance unchanged. If they are regarded from the point of view of the husband, they may not appear to be insurable risks; a man cannot insure against events which occur only through his fault or with his consent, and if they occur through the fault or with the consent of the wife she should not have a claim to benefit. But from the point of view of the woman, loss of her maintenance as housewife without her consent and not through her fault is one of the risks of marriage against which she should be insured; she should not depend on assistance. Recognition of housewives as a distinct insurance class, performing necessary service not for pay, implies that, if the marriage ends otherwise than by widowhood, she is entitled to the same provision as for widowhood, unless the marriage maintenance has ended through her fault or voluntary action without just cause. That is to say, subject to the practical considerations mentioned in the note below she should get temporary separation benefit (on the same lines as widow's benefit), and guardian or training benefit where appropriate.

NOTE. — The principle that a married woman who without fault of her own loses the maintenance to which she is entitled from her husband should get benefit is clear. It is obvious, however, that except where the maintenance has ended through divorce or other form of legal separation establishing that the default is not that of the wife, considerable practical difficulties may arise in determining whether a claim to benefit, as distinct from assistance, has arisen. There will often be difficulty in determining responsibility for the break-up of the marriage. There will in cases of desertion be difficulty in establishing the fact or the permanence of desertion. There will in all cases be the problem of alternative remedies open to the wife. The point to which the principle of compensating a housewife for the loss of her maintenance otherwise than by widowhood can be carried in practice calls for further examination. It may for practical reasons be found necessary to limit the widow's insurance benefit to cases of formal separation, while making it clear that she can in all cases of need get assistance and that the Ministry of Social Security will then proceed against the husband for recoupment of its expenditure.

The proposal was not adopted. A major reason why the idea did not meet with approval may lie in the need to reconcile the collective security involved in an insurance scheme with the concept of individual responsibility. In a welfare state, the moral virtue of contributing to a scheme which will provide relief against, for example, sickness and unemployment — both your own and your neighbours — is, one hopes, self-evident. Contributing to a scheme which provides relief for the wives in other people's broken marriages, however, is not so easy to justify. Another problem, even assuming that the philosophical difficulty could be overcome, would be the difficulties inherent in asking civil servants to allocate blame for a marriage breakdown.

Question

Do you consider that the state has a responsibility to ensure that children do not spend most of their childhood living at the officially-defined subsistence level? If you do think this way should state resources be directed at (*a*) enforcing the 'liable relative' obligation (see p. 121, below) or (*b*) helping to alleviate the poverty of children and others in comparable situations?

The Finer Committee looked for an alternative state benefit to resolve the lone parent's problems, and opted for a 'guaranteed maintenance allowance' (GMA). There were, for the committee, six 'ideal' requirements or principles upon which such a benefit should be based. These are summarised and discussed by John Eekelaar in *Public Law and Private Rights: The Finer Proposals* (1976):

The six principles
(i) GMA should be 'a replacement, so far as the recipient is concerned, for maintenance payments, so that lone mothers should be freed from the worry and distress which the inadequacy and uncertainty of these payments now produce.'

It follows from this principle that the benefit becomes payable without regard as to whether the mother seeks or obtains a maintenance order on her own account. Her support becomes entirely a matter of public law. The administering authority is, in its turn, free to recoup what it may from the liable relative, but that, too, is a matter of public law. The rights between the adults are irrelevant because the benefit is for the child, for whom the liable relative retains liability irrespective of the equities between the parents. Hence the Report recommends that the authority administering GMA should be able to make an 'administrative order,' immediately binding on the liable relative, based on disclosed principles of assessment. . . .

Yet although the Committee sought to achieve 'a rational relationship between State support for one-parent families and the private obligation to maintain' it is precisely concerning this relationship where the Report is at its weakest. If the right of the administering authority against the liable relative is a right of the public deriving from its support for the parties' children, the authority must surely be entitled to ascertain the relevant information about the liable relative from the recipient. Yet all the Report says is that the mother would be 'asked' to give information initially to enable the authority to identify and communicate with the liable relative. There is certainly no reason to suppose the information will be readily forthcoming, especially in the case of unmarried mothers. Yet the Report says nothing about what should happen if the mother refuses to disclose the father's identity. It may even be that the Committee contemplated that the whole recoupment process should depend on the voluntary co-operation of the recipient, for they say, in connection with a similar proposal for recoupment by the SBC of supplementary benefit, that the SBC should be enabled to make its 'administrative order' against the liable relative 'if the lone mother wishes it.' . . .

But this is not all. Impressed by the prospective efficiency of the 'administrative order' system, the Committee recommends that the authority administering GMA should be free to assess the liable relative to pay an amount exceeding the sums which it is paying the recipient by way of GMA. No longer would the authority be acting as a public agency recouping payments from public funds, but it would be an agent of the recipient, enforcing her private rights against the liable relative. It is not clear whether the recipient must expressly authorise this. The Committee recognises that, to the extent by which the assessment is in excess of the GMA payments, the liable relative should be entitled to raise any defences (*e.g.* conduct) he may have against the other party. But as the administering authority's assessment would become immediately binding (like a tax assessment), the onus would clearly lie with the liable relative to contest the matter in court. The harnessing of bureaucratic power on the side of one party in a dispute over private rights could be severely oppressive to the liable relative.

(ii) GMA should be 'large enough to offer the lone parent a genuine choice about whether or not to work'; and

(iii) 'designed to provide effective help for those with part-time or low full-time earnings.'

The case for a special benefit for one-parent families rests on two propositions. One is that these families suffer special deprivation. The other is that they have special needs. Both propositions are amply supported by the Report. The main source of income for 40% of all fatherless families is supplementary benefit. Nearly one-half receive it for periods exceeding two years. Those not in receipt of supplementary benefit are characterised by an exceedingly low level of general earnings due, largely, to the low earnings of lone mothers. Yet 'the expenses of running a home do not change greatly because there is one adult less'. Household costs (fuel, rates, rent) remain the same. If the parent works, there is less time to economise and greater dependence on prepared foods. Child-minding may add to the expense. It is therefore concluded that GMA should be above supplementary benefit level. But the Report goes further in accepting the principle that it should be sufficient to provide a genuine choice whether or not to work. '. . . a woman should not be obliged by financial pressures to go out to work when she feels it is in the best interests of her children for her to be at home.' At the same time, lone mothers who wish to work should not be discouraged from doing so. One of the Committee's major criticisms of the supplementary benefits scheme is that the earnings disregards are so low that this discourages part-time working. As for full-time employment (when supplementary benefit ceases to be available), the earnings of women are so low that they will often be better off on supplementary benefit.

To meet these points, GMA, though structured like supplementary benefit, is pitched higher. . . .

The benefit departs radically from supplementary benefit, however, by being payable whether or not the recipient is in full-time work. So as not to discourage employment, the 'adult' portion of GMA would only cease to be payable when the recipient earnings reached about the level of average *male* earnings. After an initial disregard, GMA would taper off until the earnings reached that level. But the 'child' additions would remain payable. The principle upon which these recommendations is based is surely sound. That the community should regard the mother's basic needs while caring for her child as the child's needs is surely right . . .

(iv) GMA should be 'of universal application; that is, it should be available to all kinds of one-parent families, without discrimination, since all are at a disadvantage.'

This principle is a logical corollary of seeing the benefit as a benefit for the child. It would be available equally to widows as to unmarried mothers, though in the case of the former their national insurance benefits would be taken into account in assessing their income . . .

(v) GMA should be 'simple to claim, avoiding face to face interviews, searching inquiries and constant reporting of changes.'

This principle seeks to meet the constant stream of criticism levelled against the supplementary benefits administration where, it is alleged, claims are often made in humiliating conditions, there is constant prying into claimants' affairs . . .

(vi) GMA should be 'equitable, in the sense that it should not tip the scales too far in favour of one-parent families as compared with low income two-parent families.' . . .

The Committee's sixth principle holds good, not as an inducement for parties to remain married, but because the justification for the benefit is (i) that the recipient unit is a one-parent family and (ii) such units suffer special deprivation. If the unit suffers no such deprivation, justification for payment ceases. For this reason the benefit is means-tested. For the same reason the cohabitation rule must apply. The reason for the rule is not the enforcement of 'conventional' morality, nor the expectation that the cohabiting man must support his mistress's children. It is that, insofar as the fact of cohabitation has made more funds available for the mother, she must look to those funds and no longer to the public for support during child-care.

The ten main features of the proposed benefit are summarised in the Finer Report:

(1) The allowance would normally, in the hands of the lone parent, be a substitute for maintenance payments; maintenance payments would be assessed and collected by the authority administering the allowance; they would be offset against the allowance paid and any excess paid to the mother; the need for lone mothers to go to court to sue for maintenance awards would be largely eliminated;

(2) the level of the benefit would be fixed in relation to supplementary benefit payments, and, like them, would be reviewed regularly, so that, taken in conjunction with whatever family support was generally available (family allowances or tax credits) it would normally be sufficient to bring one-parent families off supplementary benefit even if they had no earnings;

(3) all one-parent families would be eligible for the benefit, including motherless families;

(4) the benefit would be non-contributory;

(5) the benefit would consist of a child-care allowance for the adult and a separate allowance for each child;

(6) the benefit would not be adjusted to the particular needs of individual families, except in so far as it would reflect the size of the family;

(7) for lone parents who are working or have other income the benefit would be tapered, after an initial disregard, so that it fell by considerably less than the amount by which income increased;

(8) the adult benefit would be extinguished by the time income reached about the level of average male earnings, but the child benefit would continue to be payable to all lone parents, whatever their income;

(9) once awarded, benefit would be fixed at that level for three months at a time, without in the normal way being affected by changes in circumstances. There would thus normally be no need for changes, including the beginning of a cohabitation, to be reported, until a fresh claim to benefit was made. Taken in conjunction with subparagraph (6) above this should much reduce the need for detailed enquiries;

(10) the benefit would be administered by post, on the lines of the family income supplements scheme.

Questions

(i) The Finer proposals have not been adopted: besides the obvious economic reasons, why do you think the Conservative and the Labour parties, for their differing reasons, have both been slow to support the scheme?
(ii) Do you think that public opinion in the 1990s would object to a *contributory* scheme for lone parent families?

It is noteworthy that only a very small proportion of lone parent families headed by widows are obliged to rely upon income support. This is because widowed mothers are entitled to a widowed mother's allowance if the deceased husband has paid the necessary contributions (and the contribution conditions are not very severe). The parent is entitled to a flat-rate benefit and an addition for each child. There is no reduction for earnings, or indeed for any other income, such as a pension from her deceased husband's occupational pension scheme, or from life insurance.

Question

Are there any arguments against extending this benefit to include unmarried, divorced and separated mothers? Or separated fathers?

2 The private law obligation and the state — maintenance and income support

Section 26(3) of the Social Security Act 1986 as amended by s. 5 of the Social Security Act 1989 states:

(*a*) a man shall be liable to maintain his wife and any children of whom he is the father, and

(*b*) a woman shall be liable to maintain her husband and any children of whom she is the mother.

Yet the State, as we have seen, has an obligation to provide income support in the case of need.

Can a departing partner morally argue that his new responsibility is with a new liaison, leaving the State to provide support for his former partner and the children by that relationship? It is this question which lies at the heart of the *Report of the Committee on One-Parent Families*, the Finer Report (1974):

The dilemma of liable relatives
4.179 At this stage, it will be helpful to create the characters in an everyday drama. John, let it be supposed, contracted a marriage by which there are children of school age, or younger. He earns an average wage in a semi-skilled occupation. His marriage has broken down, and he has left home. He may or may not be divorced. Mary is John's former or deserted wife. Her lack of training, or the demands of the children, or both, prevent her from taking employment, or, at any rate, from earning more than a small amount in part-time work, insufficient for the needs of herself and the children. John is living with his second wife, or with his mistress. She and John have children of their own, or, it may be, she has children by a former marriage or association whom John looks after as his own. This woman also earns little or nothing.
4.180 In the postulated circumstances, there are two families in being for the purposes of supplementary benefits [now called income support]: Mary's family, consisting of herself and her children; and John's family, consisting of himself, his second wife or his mistress, and the children of their household. Mary, being unemployed or in part-time work only, is eligible for supplementary benefit, the amount of which will depend upon the calculation of the requirements and resources of her family. If John falls out of work, he will be entitled to benefit, the amount of which will depend upon the calculation of the requirements and resources of his family; but if he is in full-time work, then no member of his family is eligible for benefit. . . .
4.181 If John is still married to Mary he has a statutory obligation to support Mary's family, . . . that is to say, he is a 'liable relative'. Further, whether still married to Mary or not, John may be under an obligation to maintain Mary's family under a maintenance order made by the magistrates or in the divorce jurisdiction. Given John's earning capacity, however, it is clear that he cannot, when in work, earn enough money to maintain both the families. If he elects to do his duty by Mary's family, he will to that extent relieve the Supplementary Benefits Commission [now the DSS] from paying money to Mary, but the inevitable effect will be to deprive the family of which he is a current member of the means of subsistence in circumstances where, since he is in work, they will not themselves be eligible for benefit. If, on the other hand, he elects to maintain the latter family, then, with equal inevitability, he has to break his obligations towards Mary's family. But she, in that case, can claim supplementary benefit; in such circumstances neither family starves.
4.182 When a man is put in such a dilemma the solution he will lean towards is tolerably clear. He will feed, clothe and house those with whom he is living, knowing that the State will provide for the others.

This view of the dilemma and its solution is illustrated by the following cases.

Delaney v Delaney
[1991] FCR 161, [1990] 2 FLR 457, [1991] Fam Law 22, Court of Appeal

The parties married in January 1978. They separated in February 1987 and were divorced in March 1989. There were three children of the marriage — a boy aged eleven, a girl aged ten and another boy aged five. In February 1989 the wife applied for periodical payments for herself and the three children. On September 8, 1989 the deputy district judge ordered that the husband should pay £10 a week in respect of each child. He further made a nominal order for the wife of 5p a year. The husband appealed to the judge. The husband and his girl friend had acquired a three bedroomed semi-detached house in conjunction with a housing association. They were paying a mixture of mortgage repayments and rent, amounting to £40.28 per week each. The judge found that this exceeded their needs and the husband had deliberately taken on unnecessary and excessive obligations after he had an obligation to the children. He dismissed the appeal.

The husband appealed.

Ward J: . . . The wife's income was found to be £98.75 a week made up as follows: (1) From her . . . employment as a sales assistant she earned £50 a week basic with some possibilities for overtime which the Judge quite rightly ignored. After payment of her national insurance contribution she was left with £48 a week net. (2) She continued the part-time employment where she earned £29.32. (3) She was in receipt of child benefit of £21.75 for the three children. She is, therefore, a hard working lady to whom all credit must be given. . . .

It does not appear to have been drawn to the Judge's attention that she was entitled as of right to a further benefit, being the single parent benefit currently of £5.60 a week. She was not making claims for nor in receipt of any other state benefit and gave evidence that she had not inquired into those matters. Nor was it explored before the Judge . . ., that having regard to the wife's earned income she is entitled to family credits of £45.35 a week. She will receive that amount on a basis that there is no order for periodical payments either in her favour or in favour of the children. If an order is made in respect of either her or the children, . . . that benefit will be reduced by £0.70 for every pound which she receives up to that limit of £45.35.

Considering, therefore, what this lady is entitled to, if one has regard to those state benefits, the arithmetic then is to this effect: from her income some £79.32, from her child benefit £21.75, from her single parent benefit £5.60, and there is family credit of £45.35, which adds up to a total of some few pence short of £152 a week.

As against that, she expressed in her affidavit her weekly expenditure which totalled £112.70 per week. . . . Her rent was £33 a week and £3 was paid off the arrears that had accumulated making £36 a week in all. Her food bills were modestly pitched at £30 a week for herself and her three children. Her mail order catalogue, . . . was £12 a week. Because she has struggled, . . . she has not always been able to meet all her expenditure. The result is she has incurred certain penalties for non-payment of rates, water rates and the television licence, and the poor lady has certain fines to pay as a result of that misfortune, and those fines are included in those outgoings.

The Judge said this of her income and her need: 'After paying her rent and rates, she has left £50, with which to feed and clothe herself and her three children. This patently is not enough', and quite clearly it is not. Her express need was for £71.70 in addition to that commitment for rent and rates, and that was modest, as was conceded, and rightly conceded, by counsel for the husband both in the court below and before us.

The real issue, therefore, is the extent to which the husband can meet that need for this wife and this family. His position is that following the separation from his wife he has established a relationship with another lady whom he hopes soon to marry and with whom he hopes then to start a new family. For a while after the separation he lived with his father, but then he took a tenancy in the private sector of a one-bedroomed flat which was costing him £26 a week. The Judge appears, . . . to accept that the flat with its one bedroom was not convenient for access to the children on rainy days, nor, I would add, is it convenient for the children for the purpose of staying access, and ordinarily one would hope and expect that a father would enjoy staying access, . . .

Faced with life in that one-bedroomed flat and his hopes for the future, this husband and his girl friend embarked on the purchase of alternative accommodation. . . . They have availed themselves of those opportunities, which may be rare opportunities and are certainly beneficial opportunities, to buy a property in conjunction with a housing association. The basis of the arrangement is that the young couple acquire a one-half interest in the property and the other half is acquired by the association, who then let it to the couple. Consequently, they pay a mixture of mortgage repayments and rent.

That opportunity presented itself in respect of a three-bedroomed semi-detached house, three and a half years old, . . . The cost was £60,000 and the couple borrowed £30,000 for their half share, for which their mortgage commitment, . . . was £67.84 per week, and their rent in respect of the half they did not own £12.72 per week, making a total outgoing of £80.56 per week. If that is shared between them, the cost of providing the roof over his head is £40.28 per week.

The husband gave evidence that this was regarded by them to be a very reasonable price to be paid on a market which was then still rising, that a two-bedroomed property would have been inadequate for their needs once they had started a family, and that it would have been a waste of money having regard to the duplication of the costs of sale in the not too distant future as they saw it. The Judge found that that property far exceeded the husband's needs, that he did not need a house of that size for access purposes, and that he had 'deliberately taken on unnecessary and excessive obligations after he had an obligation to the children'.

The Judge also observed that the couple ran a motor car. This was a Metro motor car, the lowest in the range, acquired by the girl friend in August of 1988 . . . It is now used to convey both of them to work and his is a 12 mile journey. . . . [I]t was accepted [by Miss Wall for the wife] that the car, being most modest of its kind, was essential to this couple for their working lives as well as for collecting the children on access.

Miss Wall mounted some attack against the husband's expenditure of some £12.92 per week on the hire purchase commitment he and the girl friend took, and I assume took after these proceedings were well under way, to buy for themselves a refrigerator and some furniture. . . . Bearing in mind that the husband left the matrimonial home with the contents intact for the wife and children, he cannot be criticized in my judgment for wishing to equip himself with some modest furniture, . . .

That apart, the major issue which counsel for the wife raises is whether or not the mortgage commitment could be justified.

To that Mr. Smith, for the husband, has two answers. Firstly, he says that of the total expenditure of £80.56 only one half of it should be regarded as the husband's liability — that is to say, some £40 per week, and he says that that cannot be regarded as an unreasonable amount to pay towards the cost of his home. Secondly, Mr. Smith submits that the Judge was not justified in his finding that the husband deliberately took on unnecessary and excessive obligations without regard to all the circumstances of the case. . . . There was no evidence, he submitted, of the availability of housing association accommodation which justified the Judge's finding that the respondent could rent a house from a housing association at a rent similar to that paid by the petitioner of £33 a week.

In my judgment the approach of this court in this case must be, firstly, to have regard to the need of the wife and the children for proper support. Having assessed that need, the court should then consider the ability of the husband to meet it. Whilst this court deprecates any notion that a former husband and extant father may slough off the tight skin of familial responsibility and may slither into and lose himself in the greener grass on the other side, nonetheless this court has proclaimed and will proclaim that it looks to the realities of the real world in which we live, and that among the realities of life is that there is a life after divorce. The respondent husband is entitled to order his life in such a way as will hold in reasonable balance the responsibilities to his existing family which he carries into his new life, as well as his proper aspirations for that new future. In all life, for those who are divorced as well as for those who are not divorced, indulging one's whims or even one's reasonable desires must be held in check by the constraints imposed by limited resources and compelling obligations. But this husband's resources, even when one adds to them the contribution made by his girl friend, are very limited indeed. He brings in £115 a week net and she brings in £97 a week net. Their joint income is £212 per week. Their expressed outgoings, as found by the Judge, . . . were £179.39, and that took no account of food, clothing, entertainment, holidays, house repairs, car repairs, servicing, the television licence or the road fund tax. . . . After meeting those expenses their joint income is then reduced to something in the region of £25 a week on which this man and his girl friend have to feed and clothe themselves and maintain the first family.

In my judgment this father was reasonably entitled to say that for the welfare of his children, . . . he should have accommodation sufficient for proper access and so suitable to be able to offer them staying access. Two bedrooms may have been sufficient, but three bedrooms does not far exceed his need having regard to the fact that the wife herself lives in a three-bedroomed house. . . . I find it difficult to say that this husband, in incurring these liabilities, was behaving in an extravagant fashion. That was the test applied in the case of *Furniss v Furniss* (1981) 3 FLR 46. The approach in *Barnes v Barnes* [1972] 1 WLR 1381 was to permit expenditure to a proper standard. The approach in *Preston v Preston* [1982] Fam 17 was to look at need within the context of s. 25 of the Matrimonial Causes Act in terms of what was reasonably required. So whether one judges this man by a standard of extravagant expenditure or of living to an improper standard or of behaving unreasonably, I do not find it possible to judge him to have gone beyond the limit of what is permissible. His share of £40.28 per week is not out of proportion to the wife's rental of £33 per week. Consequently, I find that this expenditure as set out is reasonably incurred by him and I find, as a result, that the £25 a week or thereabouts left for himself and the girl friend to feed and clothe themselves is barely adequate to sustain any reasonable way of life.

In my judgment, therefore, this father would find it extremely difficult, if not impossible, to meet the obligation he has and which ordinarily he should honour to maintain his children. In paying him due credit, I observe that he has paid £10 a week to the children, being the most that he felt he could afford.

This court is entitled, as the authority of *Stockford v Stockford* (1981) 3 FLR 58 makes clear, to approach the case upon a basis that if, having regard to the reasonable financial commitments undertaken by the husband with due regard to the contribution properly made by the lady with whom he lives, there is insufficient left properly and fully to maintain the former wife and children, then the court may have regard to the fact that in proper cases social security benefits are available to the wife and children of the marriage; that having such regard, the court is enabled to avoid making orders which would be financially crippling to the husband. Benefits are available to this family of which the Judge was not made aware, and I have come to the conclusion that the husband cannot reasonably be expected to contribute at all to the maintenance of his previous family without financially crippling himself. In my judgment, it is far better that the spirit of effecting a clean break and starting with a fresh slate be implemented in this case, not by dismissing the claims of the wife and the children, but by acknowledging that now and, it is likely, in the foreseeable future he will not be able to honour the obligations he has recognised towards his children, and in my judgment the appeal should be allowed and I would substitute a nominal order to each of the children for the order of £10 which each of them is currently ordered to receive.

Appeal allowed; an order of £0.50 per annum per child substituted for the order made by the judge in the court below.

The judge in *Delaney v Delaney* referred to the case of *Barnes v Barnes*:

Barnes v Barnes
[1972] 3 All ER 872, [1972] 1 WLR 1381, 116 Sol Jo 801, Court of Appeal

The parties were married in 1960. They had four children — aged eleven, ten, eight and seven. In March 1971, the wife obtained a decree nisi of divorce, the decree being made absolute in June 1971. In July 1971, the husband remarried. The second child, Peter, remained with his father until May 1971, then went to his mother, returned for a short time to his father, and at the time of the appeal in this case was in a residential home.

The other children remained with their mother. In March 1971, the county court judge made an order in favour of each of the three children who were with their mother in the sum of £2.50 per week. He made no order for the wife. By the order of 30 June 1971, the judge reduced the weekly payments to the three children to £2.00 each and made an order with respect to Peter for £2.00. He made a nominal order of 5p per annum in respect of the wife. On 13 March 1972, the judge ordered that the husband should pay only £1.50 for each of the children and the payment of 5p for the wife should continue. The wife appealed against the orders of 30 June 1971 and 13 March 1972 on the ground that the judge erred in making only nominal orders for periodical payments for herself.

Edmund Davies LJ: [referred to the order made on 30 June 1971 and continued]: . . ., the conclusion to which I have come is that in the first place when the court is seeking to arrive at what would be a proper order, it is desirable that regard should not be had to social security benefits but that one should, looking at all the features of the case, . . . seek to arrive at a fair figure. But if the case is one in which the income of the parties is of modest proportions, and if the total available resources of both parties are so modest that an adjustment of that totality would result in the husband's being left with a sum quite inadequate to enable him to meet his own financial commitments, then the court may have regard to the fact that in proper cases social security benefits will be available to the wife and the children of the marriage. Having such regard, the court is enabled to avoid making such an order as would be financially crippling to the husband if it considered only the combined income, earning capacity and property of the parties. It would be, I am persuaded, unrealistic to take any other course, . . .

I think the time has come when the wife should have an order made in her favour. How much better off she is going to be is extremely open to doubt; nevertheless, I would be for allowing the appeal against this second order to this extent and to this extent only: while leaving the four children to have the sum of £1.50 a week each, I would be in favour of ordering that the wife receive the sum of £2, making a totality of £8. That would mean that the husband would have something in the region of £12 weekly for himself and his wife. I hope and believe that that would meet the justice of the case; beyond that I would not be prepared to go. To that extent I would allow the appeal against the second order.

Russell LJ: I wish to add only a few words with regard to the impact on these matters of social security benefits.

What should be the proper approach? Prima facie a husband, or former husband, ought to support his wife and children — subject, of course, to any independent income or earnings of the wife — and he ought to support them to a proper standard. But in the lower income groups, this is frequently not possible out of the earnings of the husband, consistently with the husband being able to maintain himself to a proper standard and having regard also to any new responsibility he undertakes, as by law he is entitled to undertake, in the shape of a second wife and perhaps a second family. It is at this stage that the social security benefits to the first wife come into the picture.

The existence of such benefits enables the court in effect to deal with a larger purse than would otherwise be available; but it would be quite wrong to say (and indeed it is not said) that the existence of those social security benefits either enables, or entitles, a husband to throw on to social security the burden which he ought himself to bear, consistently with being left himself with a proper standard. In my view the approach should in general be that the husband may be left with a proper standard, though his contribution to the wife and children is as a result inadequate to provide by itself a proper standard for the first wife and children, bearing in mind that social security benefits will provide sufficient addition to his contribution to the wife and children, producing a proper standard for them.

Tovey v Tovey
(1978) 8 Fam Law 80, Court of Appeal

Ormrod LJ: The question then was should he be able literally to off-load the whole of his obligation to his wife and his three children on to the State, simply by taking over another woman with two children? It seemed . . ., even in these days, a startling proposition that a man who was in regular work should be required to make no contribution at all to the maintenance of his own children. It was true that it could be argued that he had taken two children off social security by going to live with this lady, and that from the tax-payers' point of view was a benefit. But at the same time, as a pure matter of public policy it was very undesirable indeed that a man should not, even in a purely formal sense, continue to contribute to the children who were his primary liability. It was very unfortunate that the liability was blurred by considerations such as the supplementary benefits regulations; they blurred that responsibility, which was very unfortunate.

In *Tovey v Tovey* the husband was ordered to pay £1.00 per week for each child. Only a nominal order was made for the wife. This award nonetheless reduced the husband to an income level below the supplementary benefit rates then applicable to himself and his new dependants.

Berry v Berry

[1987] Fam 1, [1986] 2 All ER 948, [1986] 3 WLR 257, [1987] 1 FLR 105,
[1986] Fam Law 304, Court of Appeal

Both husband and former wife were in receipt of supplementary benefit.
The wife had a periodical payments order in her favour of £5 per week which
was registered in the magistrates' court. The husband remarried and was
unemployed and was in receipt of £4.66 per week benefit. On an application
by the husband, the justices varied the order to £2 a week. The husband
appealed, and we report that part of Arnold P's judgment which refers to
quantum, with which both Bush and Booth JJ agreed. Further appeals in this
case relate to issues of jurisdiction with which we are not concerned.

The grounds which are taken by the husband are that the justices failed to take any proper
account of his means and ability to pay the maintenance and that they failed to distinguish adequately or at all between his means and ability to pay the maintenance and those of his present
wife; and that they failed to take any or any proper account of the fact that the respondent —
that is the ex-wife — would gain no benefit from the order for maintenance or for the enforcement of arrears as she was and is in receipt of supplementary benefit.

As regards that last ground, it seems to me to be wholly unjustified. It is perfectly true that
the respondent to this appeal is in receipt of supplementary benefit, and will continue to be in
receipt of supplementary benefit irrespective of the order which the court makes on this appeal,
or indeed irrespective of any order which the justices could have made. But that is not a ground
for allowing the appeal. Supplementary benefit is available under the relevant statutes for those
whose means are insufficient to enable them to live without the payment of social security
benefits: and the proper level of those benefits has to be determined after the means of the
claimant have been assessed, and if the claimant is able to obtain a larger sum by means of a
maintenance order, then plainly the amount of the supplementary benefit would be reduced.
So that the mere circumstance that the claimant is in receipt of supplementary benefit does not
by itself reduce the proper level of maintenance which should be ordered.

But the other grounds of appeal seem to me to be well sustained. It was held by this court
in *Fletcher v Fletcher* [1985] Fam 92:

> 'that where a husband and wife and their dependants were living on supplementary benefit,
> the proper conclusion, in the absence of special circumstances, was that there would be no
> margin between the husband's level of subsistence and the amount of his benefit to justify
> the making of a substantial maintenance order against him; . . .'

Now in the present case, this husband was at the date of the hearing before the justices in
receipt of a supplementary benefit payment of £4.66 a week, after taking account of the earnings of his present wife; and the wife was, as I have already mentioned, in receipt of supplementary benefit payments as well. There were no circumstances whatsoever which suggested that
the husband could in those circumstances have afforded any substantial payment to his former
wife, and consequently that part of the husband's averment on the appeal is well justified.

There is also the circumstance that the justices in their reasons said:

> 'We were told by Mr. Berry that his wife now works as a secretary, earning £65 a week'
> — and then there is a reference to a car — 'and in view of the fact that his supplementary
> benefit each week amounted to £4.66, we took the accumulated figures as one when calcu-
> lating the moneys coming into the household.'

Exactly for what purpose they were calculating the moneys coming into the household is not
stated in the reasons. In so far as it was right for them to consider (as of course they must consider) how far the husband's ability to pay was reduced by any maintenance for his present wife
which he was compelled to find, it would be relevant for them to consider her earnings and their
combined funds. But in so far as they were assessing what he could afford to pay to his former
wife, it would be quite wrong to take the present wife's earnings into account; and it does appear
to me in the circumstances of this case that it was in relation to the latter matter that the justices
must have taken the present wife's earnings into account.

For all those reasons, I would accordingly allow this appeal in so far as it is an appeal against
the level of maintenance, and substitute a payment of 5p per annum for the payment of £2 per
week which was ordered by the justices.

Appeal allowed.

Questions

(i) Do you agree with the proposition that a court should strive to avoid making orders that are financially crippling to the husband? Does not this approach encourage irresponsibility on the part of the husband? Or do you think that an order is justified so as to impress upon fathers that their primary obligation is to their own children and their first wives?

(ii) Is there any principle at *all* which comes over to you from an examination of these cases?

(iii) Do you think that ss. 2, 3 of the 1978 Act (see p. 97, above) helps or hinders solving the problems which arise?

(iv) Can you think of *any* advantages from the point of view of the wife for obtaining a court order in her favour in a case such as *Barnes v Barnes* [1972] 3 All ER 872, [1972] 1 WLR 1381?

(v) As a tax payer, can you see any justification for the legal aid fund being used in this case on behalf of the wife's applications?

(vi) Home Office statistics reveal that in 1989, some 480 men were committed to prison forthwith for non-payment of maintenance. There were a further 3,120 suspended committals. (Home Office Statistical Bulletin 21/1990). Do you see any value at all in sending a man to prison for non-payment of maintenance payments?

(vii) In England and Wales in 1989, there were 7,000 'attachment of earnings' orders. Can you see any disadvantages in the use of these orders?

(viii) *Is* there a difference between failure to pay 'wife support' and failure to pay 'child support'?

(ix) Bradshaw/Millar (1990) found that only 30% of lone mothers received regular payments of maintenance. They also found that maintenance formed less than 10% of lone parent's total net income compared with 45% for income support and 22% for net earnings. *Children Come First* (1990), complains: 'The contribution made by maintenance to the income of lone parent families therefore remains too low.' Do you agree with this statement?

The Finer Report discusses the practice of the supplementary benefit authority, as it then was, in relation to private support claims:

The allegations of pressure

4.193 Several of the organisations which gave evidence showed concern that women who are reluctant to institute legal proceedings for maintenance against liable relatives are, or at least feel themselves to be, subjected to pressure from officials to do so. We quote from some of the representations we have received:

'. . . health visitors have noted with concern the distress of some deserted or unmarried mothers when social security officers insist that legal proceedings be instituted . . . undue pressure is sometimes brought to bear at a time when the mother is already under considerable stress (Health Visitors' Association).'

'While the Department of Health and Social Security deny that pressure is ever brought on women to apply for court orders against liable relatives, we have knowledge of many cases in which the woman had been given the definite impression that her supplementary benefits would cease if she omitted to take such action. Women in this situation frequently sue their husbands for a matrimonial offence when in fact they have no case and as a result have a very humiliating and embarrassing experience in court. We have known cases of women who have left their husbands by mutual agreement but have, as a result of this misunderstanding, sued them for desertion . . .' (Women's National Commission).

'Pressure by the Department of Health and Social Security is often the cause of such (maintenance) proceedings where it might not otherwise be taken' (NSPCC).

If a woman eligible for income support applies for and obtains a maintenance order in her favour which is less than the full rate of her benefit entitlement, she may authorise the magistrates' clerk to divert any payments which are received to the DSS:

4.207 . . . When such a transfer is effected, the wife receives an order book entitling her to supplementary benefit (calculated on the basis that there is no maintenance order) which she can cash at the post office: and the clerk of the court transmits to the Department whatever is paid in to the collecting office under the maintenance order. (The procedure is also available in the much rarer case where the amount of the maintenance order exceeds the supplementary benefit entitlement; but here no invitation to transfer the maintenance order is made until the circumstances, such as repeated failure to pay on the order, show this to be desirable.) The effect is that the wife receives her full entitlement regularly, whether the maintenance order is paid in full, intermittently or not at all. She is relieved of the anxiety of irregular payments and the harassment and indignity of commuting between different officials and different procedures.

(This 'diversion' procedure was, of course, only available where the order was either made or registered in the magistrates' court, so that payment was not made direct to the recipient but through the magistrates' clerk).

Section 24B of the Social Security Act 1986 (inserted by the Social Security Act 1990) permits the DSS to enforce a lone parent's private maintenance order where the parent is on income support. In addition, the DSS will accept an offer of payment from a liable relative if it forms the view that the offer is reasonable.

But this was clearly not enough.

It is put in this way in *Children Come First* (1990) 'The Government's Proposals on the Maintenance of Children: The Background':

1.3.2 When a lone parent claims Income Support the DSS tries to ensure that the absent parent pays enough maintenance to remove his dependants' need for Income Support, or as much towards that amount as he can reasonably afford. A separated parent is asked to pay enough to support the claimant and the children fully so that payment of Income Support can stop. Divorced parents and parents who were never married who are not liable to maintain each other are currently asked to pay an amount equal to the personal benefit rates for the children they are liable to maintain plus the family and lone parent premiums payable under Income Support because there are children in the household. The Social Security Act 1990 has provided for courts to be able to include the amount to be recovered from the absent parent in recognition that it is responsibility for the care of the children which prevents the claimant working.

Children Come First proposed a major change in approach both by the courts and the DSS:

2.1 The Government proposes to establish a system of child maintenance which will be equally available to any person seeking maintenance for the benefit of a child and which will:
  • ensure that parents honour their legal and moral responsibility to maintain their own children whenever they can afford to do so. It is right that other taxpayers should help to maintain children when the children's own parents, despite their own best efforts, do not have enough resources to do so themselves. That will continue to be the case. But it is not right that taxpayers, who include other families, should shoulder that responsibility instead of parents who are able to do it themselves;
  • recognise that where a liable parent has formed a second family and has further natural children, he is liable to maintain all his own children. A fair and reasonable balance has to be struck between the interests of the children of a first family and the children of a second;
  • produce consistent and predictable results so that people in similar financial circumstances will pay similar amounts of maintenance, and so that people will know in advance what their maintenance obligations are going to be;

- enable maintenance to be decided in a fair and reasonable way which reduces the scope for its becoming a contest between the parents to the detriment of the interests of the children;
- produce maintenance payments which are realistically related to the costs of caring for a child;
- allow for maintenance payments to be reviewed regularly so that changes in circumstances can be taken into account automatically;
- recognise that both parents have a legal responsibility to maintain their children;
- ensure that parents meet the cost of their children's maintenance whenever they can without removing the parents' own incentives to work, and to go on working;
- enable caring parents who wish to work to do so as soon as they feel ready and able;
- provide an efficient and effective service to the public which ensures that:
  - (*a*) maintenance is paid regularly and on time so that it provides a reliable income for the caring parent and the children and
  - (*b*) produces maintenance quickly so that the habit of payment is established early and is not compromised by early arrears;
- avoid the children and their caring parent becoming dependent on Income Support whenever this is possible and, where it is not possible, to minimise the period of dependence.

The proposal, contained in the Child Support Act 1991 (and coming into force in January 1993) was for an 'integrated package' involving a formula for the assessment of how much maintenance should be paid, a child support agency which will have responsibility for tracing absent parents and for the assessment, collection and enforcement of maintenance payments, and changes in the rules of Social Security to encourage caring parents to go to work if they wish to do so.

A summary of the scheme is provided by Jane Leigh in 'Child Maintenance: a view from the Law Society' (1991):

All children whose parents have separated will be entitled to a minimum of maintenance from their natural or adoptive parents. The government suggests that a stepfather should only be liable to pay maintenance to his stepchildren in exceptional circumstances, such as where a natural parent is dead or completely untraceable. This represents a change from the current position where a stepfather is potentially liable to maintain any 'child of the family' following a divorce.

The amount of the 'maintenance bill' which a father should, if possible, pay will be calculated according to income support rates and will be made up of the following elements [1991/92 figures]:

Child Allowances	Variable depending upon age
Family Premium	£7.95
Lone Parent Premium	£4.45
Parent as Carer	£39.65
Less Child Benefit	£8.35 (from October 1991)

A question mark remains as to whether disabled children will be entitled to claim an enhanced level of maintenance by including the disabled child premium payable under the income support scheme in their maintenance bill. In a more wealthy family the children will be entitled to claim an increasing amount of maintenance to reflect their parents' standard of living. The government has suggested that this should be deducted at a rate of 15 per cent from the paying parent's 'assessable' income after the basic maintenance bill for the child(ren) has been met. The 'assessable' income is net income less the exempt slice of income.

All fathers who are potentially liable to pay maintenance will be entitled to an exempt slice of income designed to provide for their essential needs and those of any of their natural children living with them. The exempt slice of income will not be increased by the presence of a second wife. Step-children will only lead to an increase in the exempt slice in exceptional circumstances. It is envisaged that the exempt income will be deducted from income, net of tax and national insurance, and will be made up of the personal allowance which a father would be entitled to if he were on income support and his reasonable housing costs. The exempt slice of income may be increased to include 50 per cent of any superannuation contributions. Above this exempt slice 50 per cent of a father's income will be deducted to provide maintenance for his children subject to three safeguards:

(i) Maintenance, in whole or in part, will not be provided if it would lead to a father and his dependents (if any) being reduced to below subsistence level (the family's notional entitlement to income support plus £5 per week);

(ii) A cap on the level of earnings which can be susceptible to claims for child maintenance will be imposed to ensure that excessive and unrealistic claims for maintenance are avoided, although the government has not suggested at what level this should be set;

(iii) The income (if any) of the mother will be taken into account in calculating the amount of child maintenance that should be paid. This will be subject to the deduction of an exempt slice of income.

It is planned that fathers on income support should pay a nominal five per cent of their benefit to their children as maintenance. Where the maintenance which is paid is £3 or less per week the government suggests that a system of standard minimum payments should be introduced to prevent the need to spend vast amounts of money in calculating minimal variations to the maintenance awarded.

It may be possible in exceptional circumstances to depart from the formula or substitute some other provision instead of continued payments of maintenance, for example a lump sum, although at the moment the government appears keen to limit the scope for departure or substitution.

The amount of maintenance payable under the formula will be reviewed each year to take account of any changes in circumstances. The government proposes that if a 'big change' should take place in between the annual reviews this should trigger an additional review. The government thinks that a 'big change' should be defined as a rise or fall in maintenance of more than £5 per week.

. . .

The Government intends to set up the Agency as a 'Next Steps Agency'. The concept of a Next Steps Agency grew from a review of methods of improving management in government entitled 'Improving Management in Government: The Next Steps' which was carried out in 1988. This review was prompted by the size and diversity of the Civil Service and the consequent problems that were experienced.

The review recommended that a number of semi-independent agencies should be set up to carry out executive functions within departments. These agencies would have a well defined framework consisting of clear policies, a budget and specific targets for results to be achieved, combined with as much management freedom and accountability to Parliament and Ministers as possible. It is envisaged that the Child Support Agency will be set up as a Next Steps Agency within the Department of Social Security to build on the expertise in liable relative sections that already exists within these offices across the country.

The second volume of the White Paper consists of the results of research into the current system of child maintenance and it may well be that this will form the basis for setting performance targets for the Agency.

The government has identified ten functions that it expects the Agency to carry out as follows:

- to provide information and advice to the public on, for example, how to make a claim for child maintenance, how the formula works, the services provided by the Agency;
- to identify and trace liable persons if their whereabouts are unknown;
- to obtain information on the incomes and circumstances of the parents of the child for whom maintenance is claimed;
- on the basis of that information, to assess the maintenance to be paid by applying the rules laid down;
- to make an estimated assessment in the absence of all the required information;
- to notify both parents of the assessment made and make arrangements for a suitable method of payment;
- to record and monitor the payments made where appropriate;
- to take appropriate enforcement action at an early date when payments are not made;
- to review the assessment at regular intervals;
- to present the facts when an appeal against an assessment is made.

. . .

The introduction of the Child Support Agency and the formulaic calculation of maintenance is to be combined with changes to the rules relating to family credit, housing benefit and community charge benefit (but not income support), designed to increase work incentives for lone parents. Namely:

   (i) A maintenance disregard of £15 per week;

   (ii) A reduction in the number of hours worked per week which are necessary for a claim for family credit to be possible from 24 hours to 16 hours.

   (iii) The upper hours limit for receiving income support will also change from 24 hours to 16 hours — protection will be provided for those people currently receiving income support and working between 16 and 24 hours per week.

These measures will be combined with increased help for lone parents seeking work through Training and Enterprise Councils and Job Centres.

Perhaps the most controversial of the government's proposals is that relating to mothers who refuse to name the fathers of their children. Unless the child concerned is the product of rape or incest the government has said that it will deduct 20 per cent from a mother's income support if she fails to name the father.

An illustration of how the formula may work for low income families appears as example 6: *Children Come First*:

Sarah and Mark are 16 and 14, living with Marie. Sarah is still at school.

David [Sarah's former partner] has married Sue who has a daughter Katy aged 5 from her own previous marriage. David and Sue have a baby, James. Sue is not working.

David, Sue, Katy and James are living in a house where the mortgage payments are £75 per week.

. . .

The maintenance bill is [1990/91 figures]:

	£ per week
children's allowance	21.90 for Sarah
	18.25 for Mark
family premium	7.35
lone parent premium	4.10
parent as carer	31.20
subtotal	82.80
less child benefit	14.50
Total maintenance bill	**£68.30 per week (rounded £69)**

David's exempt income is calculated. He is liable to maintain James as well as Sarah and Mark. So his exempt income is:

	£ per week
personal allowance	36.70
child allowance	12.35 for James
family premium	7.35
housing	45.00 for David and James
total exempt income	**£101.40 per week (rounded £102)**

David's assessable income is:

	£ per week
net income	200
less exempt income	102
Total assessable income	**£ 98 per week**

David pays 50% of his assessable income in maintenance for Sarah and Mark. This is £49 or 24.5% of his total net income. He keeps £151 or 75.5% of his total net income.

. . .

The **total amount of maintenance** is £59 a week of which David contributes £49 . . . This is less than the maintenance bill which is £69.

Lord Mackay, in moving that the Child Support Bill be read a second time in the House of Lords stated that the Bill provided a firm foundation for assessing what people can afford to pay in a coherent and equitable way. He said this:

> . . . There are four basic elements.
> First, there is the maintenance requirement. This is an amount, which will be calculated with reference to the income support rates, which represents the basic costs of maintaining the children who qualify for a formula award. Secondly, there is the assessable income. This is derived by deducting an exempt income from the parents' net income, that is, income after tax and national insurance. This exempt income represents the weekly amount which it is considered parents need for their own essential day-to-day expenses. It will be based on income support allowances, and will include reasonable housing costs and the costs of any children for whom they are liable. The remaining income is the assessable income, such income of both parents will be taken into account.
> Thirdly, there is the deduction rate. A percentage of the assessable income of each parent will be taken into account in order to meet the maintenance requirement, where possible. We intend that, until the maintenance requirement is met, assessable income should be shared equally between the absent parent and his children who qualify under the Bill. A smaller percentage will apply in individual cases after the maintenance requirement has been met. Beyond that, there will be an upper limit to the operation of the formula and, as I indicated earlier, in high income cases above that limit the parties will be able to seek additional maintenance for the child from the courts.
> Fourthly and lastly, there is the protected income. This is the income level below which no family of a person liable to maintain a child will be allowed to fall as a result of his meeting his maintenance obligations and his essential living expenses. It will protect those who are working, or who have other sources of income, from being left with an income less than a level set on the basis of income support levels.

John Eekelaar is clearly suspicious that the main reason for the Child Support Act 1991 is to reduce this level of expenditure if at all possible (the Independent, Friday 2 November 1990):

> Readers of the Government's White Paper, *Children Come First*, may believe it would have been better entitled *Taxpayers Come First*.
> It points out that lone parents cost the taxpayer £3.6bn, compared with £1.75bn in 1981/82. It then sets out a formula that the proposed child support agency would apply to recover this cost.
> The formula is based unashamedly on a 'maintenance bill' that reflects the state benefits many lone parents and their children receive. The absent father will be required to pay the Exchequer 50 per cent of his disposable income after allowances — the highest rate the Government believes it can collect without driving him to give up work — until this 'bill' is met.
> Courts may be stopped from making property settlements that favour children if the taxpayer suffers because of any resulting reliance on benefits.
> There is a suspicion that the Government's claims about benefiting children are a cover for cutting public spending.
> For some, this is confirmed by plans for the agency's first customers to be those solely dependent on income support. In fact, it is these people who will least need the agency's enforcement services because many absent parents are unlikely to pay more than a lone parent receives in benefits.
> Where they do pay more, however, the Department of Social Security will be able to reduce income support pound for pound.
> That it is the state, not the single-parent family, that has most to gain from maintenance payments is implicitly recognised in the proposal that lone parents who failed, without good reason, to take action through the agency to make the absent parent pay risk a cut in their benefits of up to 20 per cent.

See s 6
CSA 1991

Question

See the table on p. 126, below, taken from *Social Security Statistics 1990* revealing expenditure on non-contributory benefits. Do you think Eekelaar has reason to be suspicious?

Finance: Table H2.01
Expenditure on non-contributory benefits (£ million)

	Year ended 31 March						
	1975	1980	1985	1986	1987	1988	1989
Consolidated fund payment in respect of:							
Attendance allowance and invalid care allowance	62	207	587	699	883	1081	1177
Non-contributory retirement pensions	31	35	39	41	45	37	36
Non-contributory invalidity pensions/Severe Disablement Allowance	–	85	232	247	285	295	316
Mobility allowance	–	79	356	422	514	596	675
Lump sum payments for pensions	–	5	6	7	8	9	9
Family allowances (child benefit)	344	2830	4276	4468	4513	4598	4514
One-parent benefit (child benefit)	–	–	120	134	148	163	179
Family income supplement	12	27	126	130	161	180	7
Family Credit	–	–	–	–	–	0.4	387
Non-contributory maternity grant	–	–	19	17	14	–	–
Supplementary pensions and allowances	992	2502	6452	7509	8099	8068	209
Income Support	–	–	–	–	–	–	7507
Social Fund[1]	–	–	–	–	–	29	149
Housing Benefit:							
Rate rebates	–	–	1291	1442	1562	1677	1336
Rent rebates	–	–	2065	2225	2356	2461	2531
Rent allowances	–	–	645	792	951	1012	1035
Administration costs of rating housing and local authorities	–	–	87	101	109	122	128
Development costs of rating, housing and local authorities	–	–	5	1	–	–	–
War pensions[2]	204	375	544	581	589	599	610
Administration	335	402	919	1006	1121	1312	1595

Notes: 1. Net expenditure after payment of loans.
2. Includes Northern Ireland.

Others are concerned that the Act pushes back the debate in favour of a family court, as Lord Mishcon states in the Parliamentary debate on 25 February 1991:

The first aspect of the Bill which one considers is the setting up of the agency. I should like to share with the House a deep anxiety that I feel when I see that a fundamental view taken by this House — supported also by the noble and learned Lord the Lord Chancellor — has been slightly eroded. I refer to the view that we all held that the most desirable way of dealing with family problems concerning the husband, wife and children was to ensure that they were dealt with in one court. That was the reason why, many of us pleaded for a family court; that is the reason when the noble and learned Lord dealt with the enactment of the Children Bill in 1989, we supported him to the full when he spoke of the problems of children and families being dealt with in one court.

Maintenance is a fundamental part of the matters with which one must deal in regard to children and families. Therefore I doubt whether the setting up of an agency is preferable to the fulfilment of the dream of a family court with similar powers.

and is contrary to the principle of the clean break developed by the divorce court (see p. 297, below).

At the moment the family home is usually the only asset that a family in the middle and lower income groups possesses — possibly the upper end of the lower income group, but nevertheless, in spite of the difficulties occasioned by mortgages and high interest rates in these latter days, it is more and more the pride of the family to have a family home. What happens now — in fulfilment of an aim of our recent divorce legislation, of which the noble and learned Lord is a great supporter — is that it is the rule and the desirability in many cases to achieve a clean break. That means that the husband or father, as a rule, does not have round his neck a millstone of unceasing maintenance for the years ahead. It means providing the ability to create new lives; to write new chapters when the old ones are unhappy. The way that the courts achieve the clean break is often by suggesting — and certainly agreeing to any consent order — that the father transfers the family home over to the mother. Often the mother will thereupon get income support, the idea being that spouse maintenance ceases when the father or husband does that, and the child maintenance order is a pretty low one.

. . . Faced with a maintenance order under the statutory provisions that we are now looking at, the court will be unable to make an order transferring the house to the wife for the benefit of the children and their security.

The husband will say, 'Goodness gracious me, I face a continuing liability'. There is no question now of the ability to carry out the provisions of the divorce legislation which has pertained until now, and which cut off the liability and allowed such a settlement to be made.

Question

In his evidence to the House of Commons Social Security Committee (Session 1990/91), Eekelaar outlined a further concern:
'when circumstances allow it, the main objective of courts, and also of most caregiving parents, is to retain the house for the children [see Chapter 7, below]. The rest of the package is fashioned to achieve that purpose. Under the [Child Support Act 1991] the child support element is fixed; it may not then be possible to fashion the package so as to prevent the homelessness of the children'.
Is this (*a*) a real or (*b*) an acceptable risk?

The House of Commons Social Security Committee was so concerned by these aspects that they issued an interim report:

7. The Government's Child Support Bill, after completing Committee stage in the House of Lords, includes a clause, which is designed to allow people to continue to make private agreements about maintenance. Clause 8[1] (Agreements about maintenance) specifies that the existence of any such agreement will not prevent either party from seeking a new assessment by the Child Support Agency for a maintenance award. Courts will not be permitted to alter existing agreements between parents to take account of an award made by child support officers. In the case of agreements that include a provision that neither party will apply for an assessment of maintenance, clause 8 subsection 4[2] provides that the provision shall be void.
8. There is provision under the present clause 33[3], special cases, for the Secretary of State to define and take account of 'special cases'. The clause gives examples including cases in which both parents are 'absent' in respect of the child or where more than one person has care of the child, but the example of an existing capital settlement is not included.
. . .

Effect of the new system on divorce settlements
11. There is a danger that two parallel systems of child maintenance will develop. New cases will be handled by Child Support officers. Cases considered by both parties and the courts to have been settled by agreement or negotiation will in effect be reactivated because a maintenance bill is calculated. The Law Society expressed particular anxieties about the effect that legislation is already having on divorce settlements involving children in the courts, as well as doubts about the new system for child support. They told us that, as a result of the provisions in the Social Security Act 1990, it was possible that a fresh claim for maintenance could be made in cases where 'the matrimonial home was conveyed to the wife as part of the clean break'. Mr David Salter, of the Law Society, explained how this might occur in the future:

> 'The husband will refer back to the court saying that there has been a fundamental change in the underlying circumstances which govern that order and invite the court to effectively appeal out of time to set the order aside because he will have given up far more capital in the expectation that he was not going to face a future claim for maintenance'.

Mr Henry Hodge, also of the Law Society, told us that solicitors were already drafting clauses in clean break divorce agreements to the effect that a clean break would be overturned if the husband was approached by the DSS or the Agency with a claim for maintenance. As we note above in paragraph 7 a clause in the Child Support Bill will render such arrangements void, but we believe that, in cases where a substantial amount of capital has been foregone in the expectation of a clean break, it is not reasonable to return to the case to pursue a further claim for the financial security of the child. . . .

Questions

(i) Do you prefer the approach of this arithmetical formula or the judicial discretion for (*a*) those families on or close to income support and (*b*) those families a long way away from income support?

(ii) Liable relatives on low incomes pay a much larger proportion of their income as maintenance than those with above average incomes (Monk, 1991). Is it harmful for children (*a*) in the former case to operate a deduction rate of 50% (above the exempt slice of income), (*b*) in the latter case to operate an additional deduction rate of 15% from the paying parent's 'assessable' income?

(iii) Do you think that there should be a residual discretion to allow courts to vary the formula (*a*) upwards and/or (*b*) downwards?

(iv) When assessing the father's exempt income, the presence of step-children is overlooked except in exceptional cases. Is this approach reconcilable with the philosophy underlying the Children Act 1989?

(v) Is it an exceptional case that a step-father has assumed responsibility for looking after the children of his new partner and treated them as children of the family?

(vi) Eight academic observers wrote to the Independent on 25 April 1991:

---

1. Section 9, Child Support Act 1991.
2. Section 9(4), Child Support Act 1991.
3. Section 42, Child Support Act 1991.

Shortcomings of the Child Support Bill

From Mrs R. Deech and others
Sir: As university law teachers, we wish to express our concern over the Government's opposition to amendments to the Child Support Bill designed to give a parent the option to seek child support through the proposed agency or in the courts.

The Bill, which will be at report stage this week, contains the power to order child support to the agency, using a formula, with the following consequences:

1. Parties in disagreement over their divorce settlement will need to have child support liability and other aspects of the settlement (property, capital, school fees, children's residence) determined by separate institutions using different procedures and at different times, adding to costs and delay; if a court makes a property settlement after child support is ordered, they may need to return to the agency for adjustment to the child support order.
2. Child support will become non-negotiable. A financial settlement, even if approved by a court, in which child support liability as dictated by the formula is modified in favour of other benefits will not prevent the agency later making a full child support order. This could inhibit people from reaching sensible agreements.

Views differ over the merits of the agency and the formula. But it makes no sense to introduce them in such a way as to undermine the policies of reducing legal costs and delay and encouraging negotiated settlement and consumer choice.
Your sincerely,

R. DEECH (Principal, St Anne's College, Oxford), G. DOUGLAS (Lecturer, Cardiff), J. EEKELAAR (Reader, Oxford), M. FREEMAN (Professor, London), M. HAYES (Reader, Sheffield), N. LOWE (Professor, Cardiff), J. MASSON (Professor, Warwick), D. PEARL (Professor, East Anglia)

Do you believe that child support should be non-negotiable?
(vii) Do you think that the money spent on establishing and running the Child Support Agency would have been better spent on placing resources at the courts' disposal?
(viii) Do you think that a mother should have a reduction in her income support or family credit if she fails to provide information which will allow maintenance to be recovered from an absent parent where there is a risk of her or of any child living with her suffering harm or undue distress as a result (s. 6(2)(*a*); s. 46, Child Support Act 1991)?
(ix) The Spastics Society had this to say as quoted by Lord Prys-Davies in the Debate in the House of Lords on 25 February 1991:

The possibility that there should be sanctions to ensure the naming of an absent parent so that maintenance can be collected by the Agency is a cause of grave concern to the Spastics Society. Where a relationship has foundered on the birth of a disabled child, such measures might put unnecessary and regrettable pressure on the caring parent who might prefer to severe connections with as little pain as possible.

What do you think 'undue distress' means, and would it cover this example?

3 Support for other families with children and families with elderly and/or disabled dependents

There has been some attempt to allocate resources towards families with children. From 1945, there was in existence a system of family allowances. The philosophy behind this scheme was that the State should not meet the whole cost of the needs of children. The amount of the allowance therefore was based on the estimates of the cost of meeting physical needs only, for example, for food, clothing and housing. There was no notional account taken of items such as toys or books.

In particular, allowances were not payable for the first child of the family. Family allowances were subject to a tax 'claw-back'. But, under a child tax allowance scheme, tax payers could obtain exemption from a certain amount of their income from taxation for each dependent child. Tax allowances of course only benefited those subject to tax, and would hardly be of any value to those categories of persons who fall within or close to the poverty trap. Child benefit was phased in as from 1977, and provides a merger of child tax allowances and family allowances. Child benefit is a universal, non-means tested and tax-free cash benefit for all children. There is an additional payment, known as the one-parent benefit, for a lone-parent. The benefit was seen by politicians from all parties as a way 'to put cash into the hands of mothers and to give a measure of independence to mothers' (Patrick Jenkin MP on 9 February 1977, in a debate on the Child Benefit Scheme in the House of Commons). In the same debate the then Minister, Mr Stan Orme MP said:

Child Benefit is non-means tested and non-taxable. The scheme has two big advantages over the present method of family support which relies on child tax allowances and family allowances. The child benefit will be paid to the mother, as it is typically the mother who is responsible for the house keeping in raising the children. This contrasts with the child tax allowances, which typically go to the father. Thus, income is transferred within the family from father to mother. Wage earners who earn under the tax threshold do not get the benefit of the child tax allowances, but they will get the child benefit.

However, another MP present during this debate, Mr John Ovenden MP said:

Successive Governments have a pretty shameful record of support for families. They have an even worse record if we attempt to make international comparisons. There are few European and non-European countries with which we stand any comparison in this league. That is why it is important to talk about the whole level of family support and why we should commit ourselves to policies aimed at relieving the problem of family poverty.

The Government has responded to these criticisms by introducing the system of family credit. The argument in favour of these changes is contained in Volume II of *Reform of Social Security (Programme for Change)* (1985):

Child benefit and one-parent benefit
4.44 As we have made clear the Government accept the case for continuing the system of child benefit. It is right that families with children at all income levels should receive some recognition for the additional costs of bringing up children and that the tax/benefit system should allow for some general redistribution of resources from those without children to those who have responsibility for caring for them. Child benefit is simple, well understood and popular. The system of payment usually to the mother is also well established and appreciated and, although the result is that the value of the benefit as part of general household income is often over-looked, the Government do not wish to change it. Accordingly, child benefit will continue on its present basis as a universal benefit, generally payable to the mother and paid at a flat rate for each child. Similarly one parent benefit will continue to be paid on a universal basis as at present as a contribution to the additional costs faced by lone parents in bringing up children alone. The fact that one-parent families can also obtain extra help through the tax system does not undermine the case for one parent benefit but the Government will consider further whether there would be value in rationalising the assistance available through the tax and benefit sytems.

A new family credit system
4.45 Although the general principle of providing support to families through child benefit is important, the greatest priority for additional resources in the area of family support is to provide better targetted help for those on low incomes. The proposals for the new income support scheme have been designed to give greater relative priority to families with children. But it is

clear that the present arrangements for assisting low-income working families with children must be improved. The existing family income supplement is not effective in meeting this need. It will, therefore, be abolished and a new family credit system will be introduced.

4.46 The objectives of the new family credit will be:

first, to provide an effective bridge between the higher level of support for children available to those in the income support scheme (which is intended to cover the full costs of caring for children) and the general recognition of family costs implied by child benefit;

second, to ensure that families do not find themselves worse off in work than they would be if they were not working;

third, to provide such extra help as is required as part of income from work rather than as a separate payment through the benefit system;

fourth, to avoid the position, which can occur now where net family income can be reduced as earnings rise over significant ranges of earnings;

fifth, to give greater freedom of choice to the families concerned by providing assistance in cash rather than in kind;

4.47 The new family credit scheme will use the same basic structure as the income support scheme. Maximum entitlement to benefit at the lowest income levels will comprise a substantial premium payable to all families (including one-parent families) augmented by allowances for each child which, when taken together with child benefit, will exceed the allowances within the income support scheme. The aim will be to ensure that at earnings above the income support level for a couple, a family with children should not be worse off in work. Entitlement will be assessed by the Department of Health and Social Security but the benefit will be paid by employers as an offset to tax and national insurance or, where appropriate, as an addition to gross pay. Above the lowest income levels, the benefit entitlement will be reduced proportionately as income rises. But the assessment will be based on net income so that the reduction in benefit resulting cannot exceed any increase in earnings. The benefit will also be treated as income for the assessment of housing benefit so that the combined effect of the two benefits cannot lead to a marginal tax rate above 100 per cent.

4.48 A key feature of the scheme will be its impact on the poverty and unemployment traps. By adopting a similar structure to income support, and a similar net income test to both income support and housing benefit, it should be possible both to ensure that those in work are better off than if they were not working and that the worst effects of the poverty trap are eliminated. The scope of the family credit scheme will cover a wide range of incomes and have wider eligibility than family income supplement. Anybody working more than 24 hours a week will also be entitled to claim, whereas under family income supplement only lone parents have entitlement to benefit if working less than 30 hours a week.

4.49 The value of the allowances to be paid through family credit can only be set in relation to the levels of income support which are finally determined. But the structure which has been laid down for the scheme ensures that it will provide an effective bridge between incomes in and out of work. Nonetheless it will inevitably require a greater volume of resources than family income supplement does now. The Government believe that it will be right to give greater priority to assistance for families in the income range covered by family credit than to the assistance given to families as a whole through child benefit. We will therefore have regard to the need to concentrate resources in this area both in setting the differentials between income support and family credit and in determining the overall level of child benefit.

4.50 It will be essential to the successful introduction of family credit that it should be simple to administer and to pay. The use of a common income test for income support, housing benefit and family credit will assist in this. We also intend to adopt a simple approach to the assessment of family credit. But, to avoid the potential for manipulation involved in the current FIS system, entitlement will be assessed in relation to normal weekly earnings over a thirteen week period. Awards will be made for a period of six months (irrespective of changes in circumstances) rather than one year as under family income supplement. The new scheme should offer significant advantages for employers in ensuring that employees perceive more clearly the total net remuneration they receive rather than earnings net of tax and national insurance alone. The Government expect that, because of the extended period of awards and because assessment will be the responsibility of the Department of Health and Social Security, the credit should prove even simpler to operate than the successful statutory sick pay scheme.

4.51 Since one of the objectives of family credit is to leave working families with sufficient income from the pay packet to meet their needs, the Government have concluded that, so far as possible, assistance should be provided by means of cash rather than benefits in kind. We have, therefore, decided not to extend the availability of free school meals and welfare foods to families receiving family credit although they will be exempt from NHS charges. The school meals service has an important role to play but the extension of free school meals to a wider range of children is undesirable in principle. A substantial proportion of those entitled to benefits in kind do not take advantage of them and the Government believe it is better to give the families concerned adequate resources and the freedom to choose how to use them. Accordingly, the rates of assistance for children within the family credit scheme will be set at a higher level than those in the income support scheme. The low-income scheme for welfare foods and the discretionary power of local authorities to provide free and reduced cost school meals will therefore be ended. Families receiving income support will continue to get free welfare foods and free school meals. To ensure that mothers of infants who are not breast fed can afford proprietary brands of modified baby milks, they will be available at reduced cost to those on family credit.

But very little has really changed. It has been estimated that in 1989 approximately 20% of households in Great Britain had a gross income below £100 per week, and approximately two-thirds of these were lone person households (Parliamentary Answer, 30 January 1991). The number of families with children who were receiving FIS fell from about 89,000 in December 1977 to an average of about 77,000 in 1979. From 1979, there was a marked increase, and in December 1981, the number of families on FIS had increased to 132,000. By September 1986, this figure had further increased to 210,000. Family credit then replaced FIS, and at the end of November 1990 the family credit case load was 324,000.

Questions

(i) Might family credit be a palliative? Why do we not (*a*) introduce a national minimum wage, and/or (*b*) allow employer and employee to negotiate a true national wage?

(ii) Is there any merit in abolishing child benefit and using the money to target more help to more people through the mechanism of family credit?

(Before you answer this question you may care to ponder that 74% of total Government expenditure on child benefit goes to families below the 'mean' income level. Thus 26% of total Government expenditure goes to families above this level. Parliamentary Answer, 28 January 1991.)

We must now return to the question of priorities. The age structure of the population has changed in recent years. There is a lower proportion of children aged under 16 in 1988 than in 1971, and a higher proportion aged 65 to 79. Both the 65 to 79 and the 80 and over groups are projected to increase further as the table from *Social Trends 20* (1990) (opposite) illustrates.

Another table from *Social Trends 20* (1990) (see below, p. 134) shows that all EC countries project a similar growth.

These figures suggest that many more people than at present are likely to be involved in caring for dependent relatives. The information obtained by Hazel Green on informal carers for the *General Household Survey* (1985) suggest that about 1.7 million adults in Great Britain are caring for someone living with them, 1.4 million are spending at least 20 hours per week on providing help or supervision and about 3.7 million are bearing the main responsibility for the care of someone. This information is broken down in the following way (see below pp. 134, 135) by Hazel Green's study:

1.2 Age and sex structure of the population
United Kingdom (Millions)

	Under 16	16-39	40-64	65-79	80 and over	All ages
Mid-year estimates						
1951	—	—	15.9	4.8	0.7	50.3
1961	13.1	16.6	16.9	5.2	1.0	52.8
1971	14.3	17.5	16.7	6.1	1.3	55.9
1981	12.5	19.7	15.7	6.9	1.6	56.4
1986	11.7	20.6	15.8	6.8	1.8	56.8
1988	11.5	20.4	16.2	6.9	2.0	57.1
Males	5.9	10.3	8.0	2.9	0.6	27.8
Females	5.6	10.1	8.2	3.9	1.4	29.3
Mid-year projections[1]						
1991	11.7	20.2	16.5	6.9	2.2	57.5
1996	12.5	19.8	17.0	6.8	2.4	58.5
2001	12.8	19.2	18.0	6.7	2.5	59.2
2006	12.6	18.4	19.4	6.6	2.6	59.6
2011	12.1	18.1	20.2	7.0	2.7	60.0
2025	12.1	18.6	19.0	8.5	2.9	61.1

1 1988-based projections.

Source: Office of Population Censuses and Surveys;
Government Actuary's Department

Population aged 70 and over : EC comparison

United Kingdom

Belgium

Denmark

France

Germany
(Fed. Rep.)

Greece

Irish Republic

Italy

Luxembourg

Netherlands

Portugal

Spain

Legend:
- 1985
- 2000
- 2020

Thousands: 0   2   4   6   8   10

Social Trends 20, © Crown copyright 1990

Source: EUROSTAT Demographic Statistics

Number of hours caring per week (for all dependents) by whether the dependent lived inside or outside the carer's household; Great Britain, 1985

Hours caring per week*	Carers with dependents in the same household**	Carers with dependents in another private household only	All carers
50 or more	45%	8% / 20% / 25%	14% / 10% / 19%
20 to 49	17%	47%	20%
10 to19	15%		37%
5 to 9	8%		
Under 5	14%		
Base	(723)	(1737)	(2460)

* Includes time when carer was available in case help needed

** Includes people caring for someone in the same household and someone in another private household

Percentages of carers who were the main carers of a dependent and percentages who were caring for someone for at least 20 hours per week, by whether the dependent lived inside or outside the carer's household; Great Britain, 1985

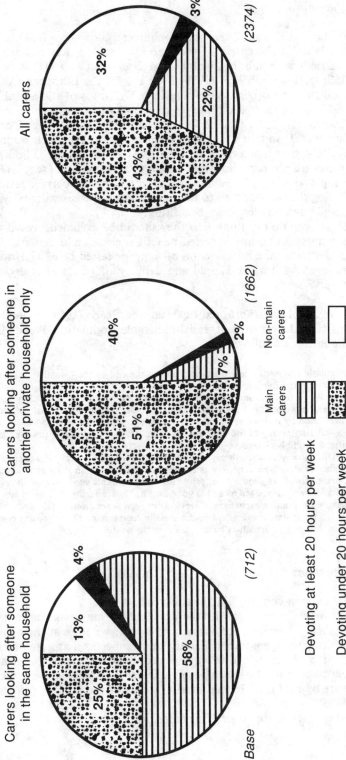

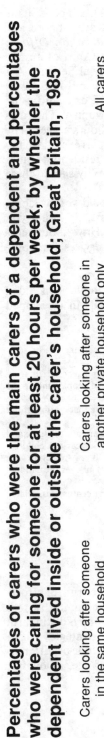

Carers looking after someone in the same household

(712)

Base

Carers looking after someone in another private household only

(1662)

All carers

(2374)

Main carers

Non-main carers

Devoting at least 20 hours per week

Devoting under 20 hours per week

Questions

(i) Before 23 June 1986, the invalid care allowance (ICA), which is made available to the carers of the severely disabled, was not available to any married or cohabiting woman. In *Drake v Chief Adjudication Officer*: 150/85 [1987] QB 166, [1986] 3 All ER 65, the European Court of Justice held that the original provision in s. 37(3)(*a*)(i) of the Social Security Act 1975 contravened the principle of equality of treatment set out in Council Directive 79/7 EEC. The Government changed the law (a day before the judgment!) so that the benefit is made available to such women. The rules for ICA state that a carer must provide care for at least 35 hours a week. The 'disregard' for part-time work is now £30 per week. These rules exclude many people, especially those who look after relatives who live in residential homes during the week and go to the carer's home at weekends. Why should these people be excluded from benefiting?

(ii) If you do not think that they should be excluded, would you welcome a universal non-means tested benefit such as child benefit, or would you prefer to see the introduction of a means-tested benefit? How about zero-rating VAT for the supply and delivery of goods and services for home carers?

In *An Aging World* (ed Eekelaar and Pearl) (1989) P. Paillat concluded his remarks on 'Recent and Predictable Population Trends in Developed Countries' as follows:

Population trends in developed countries at the end of the [twentieth] century can be summarized in the following way:
    — A low fertility, much lower than the replacement level and including a generalized aging process, expressed on the one hand by an increase of the proportion of old people, and on the other hand by internal aging of the working age population;
    — A lengthening of life after age 50, without anyone being able to state that quality of life after 80 will also improve.
    This latter issue is worth paying attention to. Problems in very old age are not the same and cannot be solved the same way in a young population or in an aging one. 60-year-old 'children' cannot provide as good a care for old dependent parents aged 85, as a 40-year-old child with a father or mother, aged 65 and in good health. The scattering of families all over the national territory is limiting exchanges of services between generations.
    . . . [P]opulation aging will be the socially central issue of the coming century, associated with disrupting population balance all over the world.

Questions

(i) Do you consider Paillat alarmist?

(ii) Would you agree with the view that we 'may make more fruitful efforts in tackling poverty [of various groups] if we look at the common factors which unite them rather than the more superficial aspects which distinguish their problems. In this way, we could perhaps develop strategies which encompass all who live in poverty, rather than seeking to exclude or differentiate by means of formal marital status or the accident of age.' (Douglas, 1985)?

Maybe there are no priorities after all!

CHAPTER 5

Matrimonial property

In the last two chapters we have concentrated on income. In this chapter, we turn our attention to a discussion of matrimonial property. For many families, until comparatively recently, only the former question had much relevance. However, there has always been a substantial group who have enjoyed the fortune of land, chattels, and stocks and shares. Rules have developed to regulate and administer this property during the marriage, and after the termination of the marriage by death. In contrast to the modern concern for what has been termed by the Finer Report as the 'pathology of the family', traditional property law has been concerned with a law 'which fortifies and regulates an institution central to society'. In Chapter 3, we looked at the development of the consumer society, where families spend the money which is earned on food, shelter, clothes and luxuries. This economic shift has resulted in a need to apply matrimonial property law as traditionally conceived to new types of wealth. The 'new property' of the last quarter of the twentieth century is the property which can be earned and which is paid by employers in return for an individual's work, both as wages and as a deferred sum by way of a pension expectancy. Simultaneously with this change in the subject matter of property, there has been an expansion in the number of those who enjoy the new wealth. Major sections of the community now own luxury items and belong to pension schemes. Thus although matrimonial property law was developed in a different age by the land owners and the bourgeoisie who in effect made their own laws by contracts, trusts, and wills, there has been a 'proletarisation' during the present century. The only restraint on this expansion is the ever present shadow of state involvement (interference?) through taxation, social security law, and death duties. Traditional property law was mainly concerned about devolution rules within the kinship group. Modern commercial activity now involves third parties; banks, building societies and other creditors. Courts are increasingly asked to adjudicate between competing claims.

1 Historical background

The law which at present governs family property is based on the principle of separate property: 'each spouse may acquire and deal with his or her property as if he or she were single.' (Law Commission Working Paper on *Family Property Law* 1971.) But this was not always the case, as Sir Jocelyn Simon explains in *With all my Worldly Goods* (1964):

I invite you to accompany me to a village church where a wedding is in progress. The mellifluous cadences of the vicar's voice fall hypnotically on the ear —'. . . honourable estate . . . mutual society, help and comfort . . . comfort her, honour and keep her. . . .' Now he has reached the ceremony of the ring. The bridegroom bends a gaze of ineffable tenderness on his bride —. . . with this ring . . . with my body . . . and with all my worldly goods I thee endow.' I hold my breath, aghast. Will the vicar rend his cassock? Will he sprinkle on his head ashes from the ancient coke stove? Will he hurl the bridegroom from the chancel steps with imprecation and anathema? For the man has committed the most horrible blasphemy. In that holy place, at this most solemn moment, actually invoking the names of the Deity, he has made a declaration which is utterly false. He is not endowing the bride with a penny, a stick, a clod. Nor does he intend ever to do so. And yet the service proceeds as if nothing untoward has happened. How does this come about?

The phrase originates in the ancient Use of Sarum, where it is almost unique in liturgy. It reflects a mediaeval custom, the endowment of the bride at the church door, dower *ad ostium ecclesiae* itself a relic, I surmise, of a still more archaic usage, the payment of the brideprice negotiated between the families of bride and bridegroom.

Dower *ad ostium ecclesiae*, however, gave way to common law dower, where the law itself determined what interest the wife should have in her husband's property. That was a life estate after the death of her husband in one third of any land of which the husband had ever been solely seised at any time during the marriage for an estate of inheritance to which issue of the wife by the husband might possibly succeed.

But this was small compensation for the proprietary and personal rights that the wife lost at Common Law on her marriage.

In this country the feudal theory was, under the Norman kings, applied in all its rigour. The proper purpose of a tenement — and wealth at that time was largely to be measured in land — was the maintenance of a vassal in such a state that he could suitably perform his feudal services to his lord — not least military service. A married woman was considered to be generally incapable of performing the feudal services. Any freehold estate of which the wife was seised was therefore vested in the husband as well as the wife during coverture, and it was under his sole management and care. If there was any issue of the marriage born alive, the husband immediately gained an estate in the wife's freeholds corresponding to her dower in his lands, but extending to the whole estate, not merely to one third: this was significantly called the husband's estate by the courtesy of England. As soon as issue was born alive, he had therefore a life estate in his wife's land which he could charge to the full. Chattels being more evanescent than land, the Common Law took the simple course of letting the husband have them as his. Any goods, including money, in the wife's actual possession, came under his absolute ownership forthwith. Any property to which the wife might be entitled by bringing an action at law — her 'chose in action'; for example, any debt due to her — became the husband's if during coverture he recovered it or otherwise reduced it into possession. When leasehold interests began to be created, for the investment of money rather than for the enjoyment of land, the Common Law treated them largely as chattels: though they did not in theory become the husband's property, he might nevertheless sell them and take the proceeds as his own. During coverture the husband was entitled to the whole of the wife's income from any source, including her own earnings or the rent from her leasehold or freehold property. She could only bequeath her personal property with the consent of her husband; and such consent might be revoked by him at any time. On the wife dying intestate by virtue of this rule, all her personal property, including her leaseholds and her choses in action, passed to her husband. In such circumstances, it was a real triumph for 18th century self-satisfaction that Blackstone could write: 'Even the disabilities which the wife lies under are for the most part intended for her protection and benefit: so great a favourite is the female sex of the laws of England.' It could have been little less inconvenient to have been a favourite of Haroun-al-Raschid.

However, in mediaeval England, the wife did enjoy some limited rights. As Sir Jocelyn Simon says:

It is almost certain that in the 12th and 13th centuries our own law recognised, . . . a reserved portion of a man's chattels of which he might not dispose by will if he left wife or child. After payment of debts the estate was divided into 'wife's part', 'bairns' part', and 'dead's part' (the two former were also called 'the reasonable parts'). Only over the 'dead's part' was there freedom of disposition.

Why did they not lead the lawyers to adopt a system of Community of Goods similar to that of our continental neighbours? Why, indeed, did it not survive in England, as it has in Scotland to this day? I think there were two reasons. First, with the invention of the English system of heirship in land, the heir took the whole of the freehold estate, the widow only a life interest and only in a third. Furthermore, she did not automatically enter the land as of right at the death of her husband: she had to wait to be assigned her portion by the heir. In the field of devolution which remained firmly within the view of the common lawyers, the widow, therefore, looked like a pensioner of the heir rather than a partner of the ancestor.

Secondly, in the eyes of the mediaeval Church intestacy was almost a sin: the 'dead's part' must be suitably devoted to such pious uses (especially ecclesiastic benefaction) as would mitigate the transcendental pains and penalties which would otherwise be the reward for the deceased's terrestrial shortcomings. In order to make sure that nothing went wrong about this, the Church — in this country alone — secured jurisdiction over probate of wills. The common lawyers became intensely jealous. Moreover, the interference of the Church courts with morals made them highly unpopular with laymen too. Thus neither common lawyers nor laymen were in the least disposed to follow the Church courts or their law. So it came about that in Edward III's reign the Lords in Parliament expressly disapproved the custom of the 'reasonable part' of the personal estate reserved from disposition by will — it was an intolerable interference with freedom. Under such disapprobation the custom had died out in the province of Canterbury by the end of the 15th century. In the northern province it lasted until 1692, but was then abolished by Act of Parliament. The excuse was that a system of jointuring widows had been invented, and if they enjoyed both jointure and 'wife's part' there would be too little left for the younger children; so it was helpfully arranged that a testator could thenceforward leave his children with nothing at all.

It is well known that equity intervened. Simon puts it in the following way:

During the Middle Ages the influence of the Church and the cults of chivalry and courtly love had brought about a steady rise in the status of women. . . . But others besides the wife were interested in what happened to her property, not least her kinsfolk. They will wish to make suitable provision for her on her marriage, to ensure in particular that the children of the marriage, who will be their own blood relations, are properly advanced. But if there is no issue of the marriage the primary interest of the wife's kinsfolk is that the property which they have put into the marriage should return to them, rather than pass to the husband's family. This consideration was until quite modern times particularly potent among the ruling classes, where marriages were to be considered, at least partly, as political and economic alliances. But by the end of the Middle Ages a number of things had occurred which increased the relative value of personal as against real property, and thus eroded the interest of the kinsfolk as against that of the husband. First, the great contraction in population, which probably fell by one third during the 14th century, involved a considerable fall in the value of land to the upper classes: and 'in the long run the peasantry alone profited by the change from services in kind to services in money.' Secondly, as a result of the decline in the labour force, large portions of demesne land of manors which had previously been farmed directly by landowners were leased. . . . Leaseholds became classified as a species of chattel, so that the husband could sell them and pocket the proceeds, and would in any event take them on the death of the wife: only if the husband predeceased the wife without having sold them or given them away did she take them by survivorship so that they were capable of passing to her heirs. Thirdly, the rise of mercantilism to replace the largely agricultural society of the Middle Ages and the discovery of the wealth of the New World meant a further augmentation in the property which lay within the husband's field of claim as against that of the wife's kinsfolk. . . .

By this time, however, the Common Law was too far committed to the interest of the husband to be able to recognise the claims of the wife and her kinship group. It had lost the flexibility to provide new remedies for new needs as they arose. . . .

[But] a woman about to enter matrimony, or her kinsfolk, could transfer property to a trustee: at Common Law it was in his ownership; but in Chancery he was bound to deal with it according to the terms of the trust — which could, simply, be according to the married woman's wishes. Or the trust could provide that, in the absence of any issue of the marriage to take a vested interest in the property, it should after the wife's death or that of her husband revert to her kinsfolk. Moreover, if the husband had recourse to the Court of Chancery, with its superior remedies, for the purpose of asserting his common law rights over the wife's property, that Court would as a condition of its aid compel the husband to settle on his wife and children part of any such property; and ultimately the wife herself or the children could initiate the claim. Over the wife's interest acquired in these two ways Equity at last gave her nearly all the rights of a single woman: she could give it away or sell it, or leave it by will to whoever she wished, or charge it with her contracts. A married woman could thus possess separate property over which her husband had no control whatever, and against which neither he nor his creditors had any claim. But in safeguarding in this peculiar way the interests of the married woman and of her kinship group, Equity took a further and decisive step away from any system of Community of Goods between married people.

Equity created a regime of separate property for married women. This regime was limited, however, to the investment property of the wealthy. Simon explains how the doctrines of equity were used in the late nineteenth century to deal with the needs of 'middle and lower middle classes':

First, the proponents of reform, led by John Stuart Mill, were principally interested in abrogating the subjection of women and in giving them equal political and civil rights with men. Men owned their own property, virtually untrammelled by any claims by their spouses. So women must be given similar rights. To entrench, say, the married woman's right to occupation of her husband's house would be to treat her as an unequal. Even Fitzjames Stephen, who controverted in this very field Mill's theory of equality, supported Mill's property proposals without pausing to consider whether there might not be some fairer régime for what he saw as the inevitable, the proper, role of the married woman. Secondly, Mill was at this time in the full tide of his individualism. Indeed, there was as yet no significant movement of thought orientated towards the foundation of society on small voluntary groupings, such as the family, of which the law of property should take specific cognizance. Thirdly, together with Mill there was a vociferous group of emancipated women writers, who were acutely conscious that the Common Law delivered over to their husbands the fruits of their professional activities, but who were understandably less concerned with the claims of all the housewives and mothers whose real needs were security in the matrimonial home and the right to participate in the proprietary benefits which their husbands enjoyed through their own economic self-abnegation. Fourthly, comparative jurisprudence was virtually unstudied at this time; and there was in any event a tendency to regard French political and social institutions with a well-bred distaste. Lastly, and most important, legal reform proceeds largely on the principle of inertia, not least in countries where the rule of precedent colours legal thinking. A movement once started continues of its own momentum. We have already seen the Common Law operate in that way in this very field. And now Parliament. Equity had permitted married women of the wealthier classes to own their separate property: how could it be denied to the generality of married women? So the Married Women's Property Acts did not attempt to remove married women's incapacities in any general way; still less in their interests to put restriction on the freedom of disposition of married men. Statute merely followed Equity in permitting married women to hold and handle and bind themselves with regard to any property which might come to them.

Questions

(i) Do you see similarities between the individualism of the nineteenth century and trends in the present generation which have led to the introduction of a system of independent taxation?

(ii) Modern feminists would regard chivalry and courtly love as the reverse of equalising the status of women. Why?

(iii) Do you think that a major reason why the Married Women's Property Acts were enacted could have been the tradesmen's difficulties in enforcing their debts?

2 Criticisms and survival of separation of property

Sir Jocelyn Simon made the following observation in his 1964 lecture:

But men can only earn their incomes and accumulate capital by virtue of the division of labour between themselves and their wives. The wife spends her youth and early middle age in bearing and rearing children and in tending the home; the husband is thus freed for his economic activities. Unless the wife plays her part the husband cannot play his. The cock bird can feather his nest precisely because he is not required to spend most of his time sitting on it.

In such a state of affairs a system of Separation of Goods between married people is singularly ill adapted to do justice. Community of Goods, or at the least community in acquisitions and accumulations, is far more appropriate. And as one leaves the sphere of those who enjoy investment property for that of those whose property largely consists of the home and its contents a régime of Separation is utterly remote from social needs.

The difficulties are taken up by the English Law Commission in 1971 in a Working Paper on *Family Property Law*:

0.12 It is said that equality of power, which separation of property achieves, does not of itself lead to equal opportunity to exercise that power; it ignores the fact that a married woman, especially if she has young children, does not in practice have the same opportunity as her husband or as an unmarried woman to acquire property; it takes no account of the fact that marriage is a form of partnership to which both spouses contribute, each in a different way, and that the contribution of each is equally important to the family welfare and to society.

The Law Commission give an example of how the principle works unfairly. This is what strict separation of property used to mean:

0.13 Mr Brown earns the family income. The home is in his name and he is responsible for the mortgage repayments and outgoings. Mrs Brown has given up her employment and earnings to attend to domestic affairs and to look after the family. She has no savings or private income, and cannot contribute in cash to the acquisition of property. If the marriage breaks down, the law regards the home, its contents, and any other property or savings acquired by Mr Brown in his name, as his sole property. Mrs Brown has a right to occupy the home and to be maintained, but she does not own the home or any other property acquired out of Mr Brown's earnings. On a decree of divorce, nullity or judicial separation she may apply to the court for property to be transferred to or settled on her [see Chapter 7, below]. If Mr Brown dies leaving a will which disinherits her (though this is relatively uncommon) she has a limited right of support, available only on application to a court and at its discretion: she has no right other than to ask for what is normally needed for her support. In short, she has no right of property in her dead husband's estate if he has made a will which disinherits her.

There are three reasons given for dissatisfaction with the principle of separation: (i) unfairness, (ii) uncertainty, particularly in relation to the matrimonial home, and (iii) that even when adjustments can be made, these adjustments depend on the discretion of the court after the termination of the marriage. As Sir Otto Kahn-Freund explains in *Matrimonial Property: Where do we go from here?* (1971):

0.15 Mr and Mrs Jones have been married for ten years and have three children. When they married they bought a house on mortgage. The deposit was paid partly from Mrs Jones' savings and partly from a loan from Mr Jones' employer. The mortgage instalments have usually been paid by Mr Jones. At the beginning Mrs Jones had a job; she went back to part-time work when the children were older. From her wages she paid a large part of the household expenses and bought some of the furniture. Occasionally she paid the mortgage instalments. A car and a washing machine were bought on hire-purchase in Mr Jones' name, but the instalments were sometimes paid by him and sometimes by her. Mr Jones has now left his wife and children and is living with another woman.

0.16 If, in the above situation, Mrs Jones asks what her property rights are so that she can make arrangements, she will receive no clear answer. In effect, the law will ask her what intentions she and her husband had about the allocation of their property, and to this she would only be able to reply that they had no clear intention.

Question

Which of the three reasons for dissatisfaction do you consider the most powerful reason for reform?

It is necessary to discuss the alleged uncertainty of the law in detail. Lord Denning had attempted to introduce an element of discretion, both through his interpretation of the courts' powers under s. 17 of the Married Women's Property Act 1882 (see below) and through his approach to the ownership of 'family assets'. This may have made the law even more uncertain, but in his view it certainly made it more fair. In the event, the House of Lords, in *Pettitt v Pettitt* [1970] AC 777, [1969] 2 All ER 385 and *Gissing v Gissing* [1971] AC 886, [1970] 2 All ER 780 overruled his interpretation of s. 17 and emphasised that the interests of husband and wife in property must be determined in accordance with the ordinary rules of property law. A spouse who contributes to the cost of acquiring or improving a home which is legally owned by the other will be entitled to a beneficial interest, but the circumstances in which a trust (resulting, implied or constructive) will arise are notoriously difficult to predict.

Pettitt v Pettitt

[1970] AC 777, [1969] 2 All ER 385, [1969] 2 WLR 966, 113 Sol Jo 344, House of Lords

The case was concerned with work carried out by a husband upon a matrimonial home which was owned by his wife. The facts appear in the speech of Lord Reid.

Lord Reid: My Lords, the appellant was married in 1952. For about nine years she and her husband lived in a house which she had inherited. During that time her husband carried out a number of improvements, largely redecorating, on which he says he spent some £80. In 1961 this house was sold and she acquired another. After this had been paid for there was a surplus of a few hundred pounds and he used this money, apparently with the consent of the appellant, in paying for his car. The spouses lived for about four years in the new house. Then the appellant left her husband, alleging cruelty, and she obtained a divorce in 1967. The husband then left the house and raised the present proceedings. He said that during those four years he carried out a considerable number of improvements to the house and garden and estimated that in doing so he performed work and supplied material to a value of £723. He sought a declaration that he was beneficially interested in the proceeds of sale of the house in the sum of £1,000 and an order on the appellant to pay. Then an order was made that she should pay him £300. The Court of Appeal reluctantly dismissed her appeal, holding that they were bound by the decision in *Appleton v Appleton* [1965] 1 All ER 44, [1965] 1 WLR 25. They gave leave to appeal.

For the last twenty years the law regarding what are sometimes called family assets has been in an unsatisfactory state. There have been many cases showing acute differences of opinion in the Court of Appeal. Various questions have arisen, generally after the break-up of a marriage. Sometimes both spouses have contributed in money to the purchase of a house; sometimes the contribution of one spouse has been otherwise than money: sometimes one spouse owned the house and the other spent money or did work in improving it: and there have been a variety of other circumstances. . . .

Many of the cases have been brought by virtue of the provisions of section 17 of the Married Women's Property Act 1882. That is a long and complicated section: the relevant part is as follows:

'In any question between husband and wife as to the title to or possession of property, either party . . . may apply by summons or otherwise in a summary way to any judge of the High Court of Justice . . . and the judge . . . may make such order with respect to the property in dispute . . . as he thinks fit.'

The main dispute has been as to the meaning of the latter words authorising the judge . . . to make such order with respect to the property in dispute as he thinks fit. They are words normally used to confer a discretion on the court: where discretion is limited, the limitations are generally expressed: but here no limitation is expressed. So it has been said that here these words confer on the court an unfettered discretion to override existing rights in the property and to dispose of it in whatever manner the judge may think to be just and equitable in the whole circumstances of the case. On the other hand it has been said that these words do not entitle the court to disregard any existing property right, but merely confer a power to regulate possession or the exercise of property rights, or, more narrowly, merely confer a power to exercise in proceedings under section 17 any discretion with regard to the property in dispute which has already been conferred by some other enactment. And other intermediate views have also been expressed.

I would approach the question in this way. The meaning of the section cannot have altered since it was passed in 1882. At that time the certainty and security of rights of property were still generally regarded as of paramount importance and I find it incredible that any Parliament of that era could have intended to put a husband's property at the hazard of the unfettered discretion of a judge (including a county court judge) if the wife raised a dispute about it. Moreover, this discretion, if it exists, can only be exercised in proceedings under section 17: the same dispute could arise in other forms of action; and I find it even more incredible that it could have been intended that such a discretion should be given to a judge in summary proceedings but denied to the judge if the proceedings were of the ordinary character. So are the words so unequivocal that we are forced to give them a meaning which cannot have been intended? I do not think so. It is perfectly possible to construe the words as having a much more restricted meaning and in my judgment they should be so construed. I do not think that a judge has any more right to disregard property rights in section 17 proceedings than he has in any other form of proceedings. . . .

I would therefore refuse to consider whether property belonging to either spouse ought to be regarded as family property for that would be introducing a new conception into English law and not merely developing existing principles. There are systems of law which recognise joint family property or communio bonorum. I am not sure that those principles are very highly regarded in countries where they are in force, but in any case it would be going far beyond the functions of the court to attempt to give effect to them here.

Similar observations about matrimonial property were made by Lord Morris:

I cannot agree that section 17 empowers a court to take property from one spouse and allocate it to the other. But something may depend upon what is meant by 'family assets.' If what is referred to is an asset separately owned by someone who is a member of a family, then once the ownership is ascertained it cannot, under section 17, be changed. If what is referred to is property which, on the evidence, has been decided to be property which belongs beneficially to husband and wife jointly, I do not consider that section 17 enables a court to vary whatever the beneficial interests were ascertained to be. There would be room for the exercise of discretion in deciding a question as to whether a sale should be ordered at one time or another but there would be no discretion enabling a court to withdraw an ascertained property right from one spouse and to grant it to the other. Any power to do that must either be found in some existing provision in relation to matrimonial causes or must be given by some future legislation.

And by Lord Hodson:

The notion of family assets itself opens a new field involving change in the law of property whereby community of ownership between husband and wife would be assumed unless otherwise excluded. This is a matter of policy for Parliament, and I agree is outside the field of judicial interpretation of property law.

And by Lord Upjohn:

My Lords, we have in this country no doctrine of community of goods between spouses and yet by judicial decision were this doctrine of family assets to be accepted some such doctrine would become part of the law of the land.

As a result of this case, Parliament enacted s. 37 of the Matrimonial Proceedings and Property Act 1970:

It is hereby declared that where a husband or wife contributes in money or money's worth to the improvement of real or personal property in which or in the proceeds of sale of which either or both of them has or have a beneficial interest, the husband or wife so contributing shall, if the contribution is of a substantial nature and subject to any agreement between them to the contrary express or implied, be treated as having then acquired by virtue of his or her contribution a share or an enlarged share, as the case may be, in that beneficial interest of such an extent as may have been then agreed or, in default of such agreement, as may seem in all the circumstances just to any court before which the question of the existence or extent of the beneficial interest of the husband or wife arises (whether in proceedings between them or in other proceedings).

Questions

(i) Mr Pettitt lost his case: would s. 37 have made any difference?
(ii) What interest would Mr Pettitt have acquired if he had spent his money on a new roof or on rewiring?

Gissing v Gissing

[1971] AC 886, [1970] 2 All ER 780, [1970] 3 WLR 255, 114 Sol Jo 350, House of Lords

The facts are set out in the speech of Lord Diplock:

In the instant appeal the matrimonial home was purchased in 1951 for £2,695 and conveyed into the sole name of the husband. The parties had by then been married for some 16 years and both were in employment with the same firm, the husband earning £1,000 and the wife £500, per annum. The purchase price was raised as to £2,150 on mortgage repayable by instalments, as to £500 by a loan to the husband from his employers, and as to the balance of £45 and the legal charges was paid by the husband out of his own moneys. The wife made no direct contribution to the initial deposit or legal charges, nor to the repayment of the loan of £500 nor to the mortgage instalments. She continued earning at the rate of £500 per annum until the marriage broke down in 1961. During this period the husband's salary increased to £3,000 per annum. The husband repaid the loan of £500 and paid the mortgage instalments. He also paid the outgoings on the house, gave to his wife a housekeeping allowance of £8 to £10 a week out of which she paid the running expenses of the household and he paid for holidays. The only contribution which the wife made out of her earnings to the household expenses was that she paid for her own clothes and those of the son of the marriage and for some extras. No change in this arrangement was made when the house was acquired. Each spouse had a separate banking account, the wife's in the Post Office Savings Bank, and each made savings out of their respective earnings. There was no joint bank account and there were no joint savings. There was no express agreement at the time of the purchase or thereafter as to how the beneficial interest in the house should be held. The learned judge was prepared to accept that after the marriage had broken down the husband said to the wife: 'Don't worry about the house — it's yours'; but this has not been relied upon, at any rate in your Lordships' House, as an acknowledgment of a pre-existing agreement on which the wife had acted to her detriment so as to give rise to a resulting, implied or constructive trust, nor can it be relied upon as an express declaration of trust as it was oral only.

On what then is the wife's claim based? In 1951 when the house was purchased she spent about £190 on buying furniture and a cooker and refrigerator for it. She also paid about £30 for improving the lawn. As furniture and household durables are depreciating assets whereas houses have turned out to be appreciating assets it may be that she would have been wise to have devoted her savings to acquiring an interest in the freehold; but this may not have been so apparent in 1951 as it has now become. The court is not entitled to infer a common intention to this effect from the mere fact that she provided chattels for joint use in the new matrimonial home; and there is nothing else in the conduct of the parties at the time of the purchase or thereafter which supports such an inference. There is no suggestion that the wife's efforts or her earnings made it possible for the husband to raise the initial loan or the mortgage or that her relieving her husband from the expense of buying clothing for herself and for their son was undertaken in order to enable him the better to meet the mortgage instalments or to repay the loan. The picture presented by the evidence is one of husband and wife retaining their separate proprietary interests in property whether real or personal purchased with their separate savings and is inconsistent with any common intention at the time of the purchase of the matrimonial home that the wife, who neither then nor thereafter contributed anything to its purchase price or assumed any liability for it, should nevertheless be entitled to a beneficial interest in it.

Earlier in his speech, Lord Diplock looked at the role of the agreement in the creation of an equitable interest in real property.

Any claim to a beneficial interest in land by a person, whether spouse or stranger, in whom the legal estate in the land is not vested must be based upon the proposition that the person in whom the legal estate is vested holds it as trustee upon trust to give effect to the beneficial interest of the claimant as cestui que trust. The legal principles applicable to the claim are those of the English law of trusts and in particular, in the kind of dispute between spouses that comes before the courts, the law relating to the creation and operation of 'resulting, implied or constructive trusts.' Where the trust is expressly declared in the instrument by which the legal estate is transferred to the trustee or by a written declaration of trust by the trustee, the court must give effect to it. But to constitute a valid declaration of trust by way of gift of a beneficial interest in land to a cestui que trust the declaration is required by section 53(1) of the Law of Property Act 1925, to be in writing. If it is not in writing it can only take effect as a resulting, implied or constructive trust to which that section has no application.

A resulting, implied or constructive trust — and it is unnecessary for present purposes to distinguish between these three classes of trust — is created by a transaction between the trustee and the cestui que trust in connection with the acquisition by the trustee of a legal estate in land, whenever the trustee has so conducted himself that it would be inequitable to allow him to deny to the cestui que trust a beneficial interest in the land acquired. And he will be held so to have conducted himself if by his words or conduct he has induced the cestui que trust to act to his own detriment in the reasonable belief that by so acting he was acquiring a beneficial interest in the land.

This is why it has been repeatedly said in the context of disputes between spouses as to their respective beneficial interests in the matrimonial home, that if at the time of its acquisition and transfer of the legal estate into the name of one or other of them an express agreement has been made between them as to the way in which the beneficial interest shall be held, the court will give effect to it — notwithstanding the absence of any written declaration of trust. Strictly speaking this states the principle too widely, for if the agreement did not provide for anything to be done by the spouse in whom the legal estate was not to be vested, it would be a merely voluntary declaration of trust and unenforceable for want of writing. But in the express oral agreements contemplated by these dicta it has been assumed sub silentio that they provide for the spouse in whom the legal estate in the matrimonial home is not vested to do something to facilitate its acquisition, by contributing to the purchase price or to the deposit or the mortgage instalments when it is purchased upon mortgage or to make some other material sacrifice by way of contribution to or economy in the general family expenditure. What the court gives effect to is the trust resulting or implied from the common intention expressed in the oral agreement between the spouses that if each acts in the manner provided for in the agreement the beneficial interests in the matrimonial home shall be held as they have agreed.

An express agreement between spouses as to their respective beneficial interests in land conveyed into the name of one of them obviates the need for showing that the conduct of the spouse into whose name the land was conveyed was intended to induce the other spouse to act to his or her detriment upon the faith of the promise of a specified beneficial interest in the land and that the other spouse so acted with the intention of acquiring that beneficial interest. The agreement itself discloses the common intention required to create a resulting, implied or constructive trust.

But parties to a transaction in connection with the acquisition of land may well have formed a common intention that the beneficial interest in the land shall be vested in them jointly without having used express words to communicate this intention to one another; or their recollections of the words used may be imperfect or conflicting by the time any dispute arises. In such a case — a common one where the parties are spouses whose marriage has broken down — it may be possible to infer their common intention from their conduct.

As in so many branches of English law in which legal rights and obligations depend upon the intentions of the parties to a transaction, the relevant intention of each party is the intention which was reasonably understood by the other party to be manifested by that party's words or conduct notwithstanding that he did not consciously formulate that intention in his own mind or even acted with some different intention which he did not communicate to the other party. On the other hand, he is not bound by any inference which the other party draws as to his intention unless that inference is one which can reasonably be drawn from his words or conduct. It is in this sense that in the branch of English law relating to constructive, implied or resulting trusts effect is given to the inferences as to the intentions of parties to a transaction which a reasonable man would draw from their words or conduct and not to any subjective intention or absence of intention which was not made manifest at the time of the transaction itself. It is for the court to determine what those inferences are.

In drawing such an inference, what spouses said and did which led up to the acquisition of a matrimonial home and what they said and did while the acquisition was being carried through is on a different footing from what they said and did after the acquisition was completed. Unless it is alleged that there was some subsequent fresh agreement, acted upon by the parties, to vary the original beneficial interests created when the matrimonial home was acquired, what they said and did after the acquisition was completed is relevant if it is explicable only upon the basis of their having manifested to one another at the time of the acquisition some particular common intention as to how the beneficial interests should be held. But it would in my view be unreasonably legalistic to treat the relevant transaction involved in the acquisition of a matrimonial home as restricted to the actual conveyance of the fee simple into the name of one or other spouse. Their common intention is more likely to have been concerned with the economic realities of the transaction than with the unfamiliar technicalities of the English law of legal and equitable interests in land. The economic reality which lies behind the conveyance of the fee simple to a purchaser in return for a purchase price the greater part of which is advanced to the purchaser upon a mortgage repayable by instalments over a number of years, is that the new freeholder is purchasing the matrimonial home upon credit and that the purchase price is represented by the instalments by which the mortgage is repaid in addition to the initial payment in cash. The conduct of the spouses in relation to the payment of the mortgage instalments may be no less relevant to their common intention as to the beneficial interests in a matrimonial home acquired in this way than their conduct in relation to the payment of the cash deposit.

It is this feature of the transaction by means of which most matrimonial homes have been acquired in recent years that makes difficult the task of the court in inferring from the conduct of the spouses a common intention as to how the beneficial interest in it should be held. Each case must depend upon its own facts but there are a number of factual situations which often recur in the cases.

Where a matrimonial home has been purchased outright without the aid of an advance on mortgage it is not difficult to ascertain what part, if any, of the purchase price has been provided by each spouse. If the land is conveyed into the name of a spouse who has not provided the whole of the purchase price, the sum contributed by the other spouse may be explicable as having been intended by both of them either as a gift or as a loan of money to the spouse to whom the land is conveyed or as consideration for a share in the beneficial interest in the land. In a dispute between living spouses the evidence will probably point to one of these explanations as being more probable than the others, but if the rest of the evidence is neutral the prima facie inference is that their common intention was that the contributing spouse should acquire a share in the beneficial interest in the land in the same proportion as the sum contributed bore to the total purchase price. This prima facie inference is more easily rebutted in favour of a gift where the land is conveyed into the name of the wife: but as I understand the speeches in *Pettitt v Pettitt* [1970] AC 777, [1969] 2 All ER 385 four of the members of your Lordships' House who were parties to that decision took the view that even if the 'presumption of advancement' as between husband and wife still survived today, it could seldom have any decisive part to play in disputes between living spouses in which some evidence would be available in addition to the mere fact that the husband had provided part of the purchase price of property conveyed into the name of the wife.

Similarly when a matrimonial home is not purchased outright but partly out of moneys advanced on mortgage repayable by instalments, and the land is conveyed into the name of the husband alone, the fact that the wife made a cash contribution to the deposit and legal charges not borrowed on mortgage gives rise, in the absence of evidence which makes some other explanation more probable, to the inference that their common intention was that she should share in the beneficial interest in the land conveyed. But it would not be reasonable to infer a common intention as to what her share should be without taking account also of the sources from which the mortgage instalments were provided. If the wife also makes a substantial direct contribution to the mortgage instalments out of her own earnings or unearned income this would be prima facie inconsistent with a common intention that her share in the beneficial interest should be determined by the proportion which her original cash contribution bore either to the total amount of the deposit and legal charges or to the full purchase price. The more likely inference is that her contributions to the mortgage instalments were intended by the spouses to have some effect upon her share.

Where there has been an initial contribution by the wife to the cash deposit and legal charges which points to a common intention at the time of the conveyance that she should have a beneficial interest in the land conveyed to her husband, it would be unrealistic to regard the wife's subsequent contributions to the mortgage instalments as without significance unless she pays them directly herself. It may be no more than a matter of convenience which spouse pays particular household accounts particularly when both are earning, and if the wife goes out to work and devotes part of her earnings or uses her private income to meet joint expenses of the household which would otherwise be met by the husband, so as to enable him to pay the mortgage instalments out of his moneys this would be consistent with and might be corroborative of an original common intention that she should share in the beneficial interest in the matrimonial home and that her payments of other household expenses were intended by both spouses to be treated as including a contribution by the wife to the purchase price of the matrimonial home.

Even where there has been no initial contribution by the wife to the cash deposit and legal charges but she makes a regular and substantial direct contribution to the mortgage instalments it may be reasonable to infer a common intention of the spouses from the outset that she should share in the beneficial interest or to infer a fresh agreement reached after the original conveyance that she should acquire a share. But it is unlikely that the mere fact that the wife made direct contributions to the mortgage instalments would be the only evidence available to assist the court in ascertaining the common intention of the spouses.

Where in any of the circumstances described the above contributions, direct or indirect, have been made to the mortgage instalments by the spouse into whose name the matrimonial home has not been conveyed, and the court can infer from their conduct a common intention that the contributing spouse should be entitled to *some* beneficial interest in the matrimonial home, what effect is to be given to that intention if there is no evidence that they in fact reached any express agreement as to what the respective share of each spouse should be?

I take it to be clear that if the court is satisfied that it was the common intention of both spouses that the contributing wife should have a share in the beneficial interest and that her contributions were made upon this understanding, the court in the exercise of its equitable jurisdiction would not permit the husband in whom the legal estate was vested and who had accepted the benefit of the contributions to take the whole beneficial interest merely because at the time the wife made her contributions there had been no express agreement as to how her share in it was to be quantified.

In such a case the court must first do its best to discover from the conduct of the spouses whether any inference can reasonably be drawn as to the probable common understanding about the amount of the share of the contributing spouse upon which each must have acted in doing what each did, even though that understanding was never expressly stated by one spouse to the other or even consciously formulated in words by either of them independently. It is only if no such inference can be drawn that the court is driven to apply as a rule of law, and not as an inference of fact, the maxim 'equality is equity,' and to hold that the beneficial interest belongs to the spouses in equal shares.

The same result however may often be reached as an inference of fact. The instalments of a mortgage to a building society are generally repayable over a period of many years. During that period, as both must be aware, the ability of each spouse to contribute to the instalments out of their separate earnings is likely to alter, particularly in the case of the wife if any children are born of the marriage. If the contribution of the wife in the early part of the period of repayment is substantial but is not an identifiable and uniform proportion of each instalment, because her contributions are indirect or, if direct, are made irregularly, it may well be a reasonable inference that their common intention at the time of acquisition of the matrimonial home was that the beneficial interest should be held by them in equal shares and that each should contribute to the cost of its acquisition whatever amounts each could afford in the varying exigencies of family life to be expected during the period of repayment. In the social conditions of today this would be a natural enough common intention of a young couple who were both earning when the house was acquired but who contemplated having children whose birth and rearing in their infancy would necessarily affect the future earning capacity of the wife.

The relative size of their respective contributions to the instalments in the early part of the period of repayment, or later if a subsequent reduction in the wife's contribution is not to be accounted for by a reduction in her earnings due to motherhood or some other cause from which the husband benefits as well, may make it a more probable inference that the wife's share in the beneficial interest was intended to be in some proportion other than one-half. And there is nothing inherently improbable in their acting on the understanding that the wife should be entitled to a share which was not to be quantified immediately upon the acquisition of the home but should be left to be determined when the mortgage was repaid or the property disposed of, on the basis of what would be fair having regard to the total contributions, direct or indirect, which each spouse had made by that date. Where this was the most likely inference from their conduct it would be for the court to give effect to that common intention of the parties by determining what in all the circumstances was a fair share.

Difficult as they are to solve, however, these problems as to the amount of the share of a spouse in the beneficial interest in a matrimonial home where the legal estate is vested solely in the other spouse, only arise in cases where the court is satisfied by the words or conduct of the parties that it was their common intention that the beneficial interest was not to belong solely to the spouse in whom the legal estate was vested but was to be shared between them in some proportion or other.

Where the wife has made no initial contribution to the cash deposit and legal charges and no direct contribution to the mortgage instalments nor any adjustment to her contribution to other expenses of the household which it can be inferred was referable to the acquisition of the house, there is in the absence of evidence of an express agreement between the parties no material to justify the court in inferring that it was the common intention of the parties that she should have any beneficial interest in a matrimonial home conveyed into the sole name of the husband, merely because she continued to contribute out of her own earnings or private income to other expenses of the household. For such conduct is no less consistent with a common intention to share the day-to-day expenses of the household, while each spouse retains a separate interest in capital assets acquired with their own moneys or obtained by inheritance or gift. There is nothing here to rebut the prima facie inference that a purchaser of land who pays the purchase price and takes a conveyance and grants a mortgage in his own name intends to acquire the sole beneficial interest as well as the legal estate: and the difficult question of the quantum of the wife's share does not arise.

Lord Diplock concluded that he was unable to draw an inference that there was any common intention that the wife should have any beneficial interest in the matrimonial home.

Lord Dilhorne and Lord Morris were against indirect contributions entitling a spouse to some beneficial interest in the matrimonial home. Lord Reid and Lord Pearson would appear to permit a beneficial interest to be acquired through indirect contributions but do not elaborate this concept.

Thus, the separation of property principle survived the attempt by Lord Denning and others to sweep it away. However, Parliament stepped in to grant discretionary powers to courts to re-allocate property after the termination of marriage. Such discretionary powers can take into account non-financial contributions. These provisions, now contained in the Matrimonial Causes Act 1973, are looked at in detail in Chapter 7, below.

Question

If Lord Diplock had drawn an inference that there was a common intention that the wife should have a beneficial interest in the matrimonial property, would this have been sufficient *without more* to have decided the case in her favour?

Strict property law is still important as we can see from:

Lloyds Bank plc v Rosset
[1991] 1 AC 107, [1990] 1 All ER 1111, House of Lords

The husband and wife bought a semi-derelict property as a family home. The acquisition was in the husband's sole name, apparently because of the insistence by the Swiss trustees of the husband's family trust. However, the wife carried out a considerable amount of the decorating work and generally supervised the builders. A lot of this work was done prior to exchange of contracts. The cost of the renovation was met by an overdraft on the husband's account. The husband signed the bank's form of legal charge. The husband left the house in 1984, and the loan was not repaid. In a claim by the bank for possession and an order for sale, the wife resisted the claim on the basis that she had a beneficial interest in the property under a constructive trust that qualified as an overriding interest under s. 70(1) (g) of the Land Registration Act 1925 (See p. 164, below) because she had been in actual occupation at the relevant date. The House of Lords, in following *Abbey National Building Society v Cann* [1991] 1 AC 56, [1990] 1 All ER 1085, held that the relevant date for ascertaining whether an interest in registered land was protected by actual occupation so as to prevail against the holder of a legal estate as a overriding interest under s. 70(1)(g) was that of the transfer or creation of the estate rather than its registration. However, it was not necessary to determine whether she was in actual occupation at the relevant date, because the House was of the unanimous view that she did not possess a beneficial interest.

Lord Bridge of Harwich: The first and fundamental question which must always be resolved is whether, independently of any inference to be drawn from the conduct of the parties in the course of sharing the house as their home and managing their joint affairs, there has at any time prior to acquisition, or exceptionally at some later date, been any agreement, arrangement or understanding reached between them that the property is to be shared beneficially. The finding of an agreement or arrangement to share in this sense can only, I think, be based on evidence of express discussions between the partners, however imperfectly remembered and however imprecise their terms may have been. Once a finding to this effect is made it will only be necessary for the partner asserting a claim to a beneficial interest against the partner entitled to the legal estate to show that he or she has acted to his or her detriment or significantly altered his or her position in reliance on the agreement in order to give rise to a constructive trust or a proprietary estoppel.

In sharp contrast with this situation is the very different one where there is no evidence to support a finding of an agreement or arrangement to share, however reasonable it might have been for the parties to reach such an arrangement if they had applied their minds to the question, and where the court must rely entirely on the conduct of the parties both as the basis from which to infer a common intention to share the property beneficially and as the conduct relied on to give rise to a constructive trust. In this situation direct contributions to the purchase price by the partner who is not the legal owner, whether initially or by payment of mortgage instalments, will readily justify the inference necessary to the creation of a constructive trust. But, as I read the authorities, it is at least extremely doubtful whether anything less will do.

The leading cases in your Lordships' House are *Pettitt v Pettitt* [1970] AC 777 and *Gissing v Gissing* [1971] AC 886 [see pp. 142, 144, above]. Both demonstrate situations in the second category to which I have referred and their Lordships discuss at great length the difficulties to which these situations give rise.

. . .

Outstanding examples on the other hand of cases giving rise to situations in the first category are *Eves v Eves* [1975] 1 WLR 1338 and *Grant v Edwards* [1986] Ch 638 [see Chapter 8, below]. In both these cases, where the parties who had cohabited were unmarried, the female partner had been clearly led by the male partner to believe, when they set up home together, that the property would belong to them jointly. In *Eves v Eves* the male partner had told the female partner that the only reason why the property was to be acquired in his name alone was because she was under 21 and that, but for her age, he would have had the house put into their joint names. He admitted in evidence that this was simply an 'excuse'. Similarly in *Grant v Edwards* the female partner was told by the male partner that the only reason for not acquiring the property in joint names was because she was involved in divorce proceedings and that, if the property were acquired jointly, this might operate to her prejudice in those proceedings. As Nourse L.J. put it, at p. 649:

'Just as in *Eves v Eves* [1975] 1 WLR 1338, these facts appear to me to raise a clear inference that there was an understanding between the plaintiff and the defendant, or a common intention, that the plaintiff was to have some sort of proprietary interest in the house; otherwise no excuse for not putting her name on to the title would have been needed.'

The subsequent conduct of the female partner in each of these cases, which the court rightly held sufficient to give rise to a constructive trust or proprietary estoppel supporting her claim to an interest in the property, fell far short of such conduct as would by itself have supported the claim in the absence of an express representation by the male partner that she was to have such an interest. It is significant to note that the share to which the female partners in *Eves v Eves* and *Grant v Edwards* were held entitled were one quarter and one half respectively. In no sense could these shares have been regarded as proportionate to what the judge in the instant case described as a 'qualifying contribution' in terms of the indirect contributions to the acquisition or enhancement of the value of the houses made by the female partners.

I cannot help thinking that the judge in the instant case would not have fallen into error if he had kept clearly in mind the distinction between the effect of evidence on the one hand which was capable of establishing an express agreement or an express representation that Mrs. Rosset was to have an interest in the property and evidence on the other hand of conduct alone as a basis for an inference of the necessary common intention.

Appeal allowed.

Question

Is Lord Bridge saying the same as Lord Diplock in *Gissing v Gissing*? (See p. 148, above.)

Midland Bank plc v Dobson
[1986] 1 FLR 171, [1986] Fam Law 55, 75, Court of Appeal.

Mr and Mrs Dobson were married in 1951. They lived initially in the house of Mr Dobson's mother. This house was sold two years later and the proceeds were put into the cost of a house which was bought in the joint names of Mr Dobson and his mother. The balance of the purchase of this house was secured by way of a legal charge in favour of a building society. The mortgage was discharged in 1970, the mother died in 1971 and Mr Dobson became the absolute owner. Mr Dobson became a director of a company in 1978 which required a bank loan to finance a transaction. Midland Bank plc provided this loan but required Mr Dobson to give security in the form of a legal charge on the matrimonial home. It also required a letter of consent to be signed by Mrs Dobson. The company then got into difficulties and the bank sought to enforce the legal charge. The husband had no answer to the claim for possession, but Mrs Dobson resisted it on two grounds. First, she said that she was entitled to a substantial beneficial interest, and secondly, she submitted that the circumstances in which she signed the letter of consent made it not binding on her. The county court judge decided in favour of the wife on both points and the bank appealed. Fox LJ, in giving the judgment of the court, decided that although there was a common intention that the parties should have a beneficial interest, it was necessary to inquire whether Mrs Dobson had acted to her detriment by reason of that common intention as to joint ownership of the matrimonial home:

She made no direct contribution to the purchase price and there was never any agreement or understanding that she would do so. The purchase price was provided as to nearly two-thirds by Mr Dobson's mother from the proceeds of sale of the . . . house which belonged to her. The remainder was raised on mortgage. It was, I would suppose, a 20-year instalment mortgage, but, be that as it may, all the actual payments towards its discharge were made by Mr Dobson. For 10 years after the house was purchased Mrs Dobson was not working and had no income. It was not until 12 years, or thereabouts, after the purchase that she earned any income of consequence (about £200 in 1965). By 1965 the amount outstanding on the mortgage was small (and the whole was redeemed by 1970). It is not suggested that Mrs Dobson made any direct contribution to that or was ever asked to do so. She did use part of her earnings for household expenses, including the purchase of domestic equipment. But it is not suggested that she did that in reliance upon any understanding as to joint ownership of the house. She did it, presumably, simply because she thought the expenditure appropriate and she had the money. She also did some ordinary periodic decorating, but I see no reason to suppose that was because of any arrangement that she would do so on account of a common intention as to joint ownership. It was the sort of work that members of a family do in a house.

But it is said, as I understand the argument, that Mrs Dobson suffered a detriment in that there was a common understanding that all their property was to be held jointly. The proposition that Mrs Dobson was in some way inhibited in dealing with her earnings or other personal property by reason of a common intention of joint ownership seems to me quite unreal. I do not think that the judge investigated that aspect of the matter in any detail or reached conclusions upon it. Mrs Dobson's evidence in the affidavit which she swore on 14 January 1983 is clear. In para. 4 she deposes as follows:

'I have not worked during the marriage except for a small amount of market research work occasionally undertaken. The defendant [i.e. Mr Dobson] discharged the mortgage with which the property was purchased and paid the rates bill and gave me housekeeping money with which I paid all food, gas and electricity bills. The money I earned from the small amount of market research work I used for my own purposes. Throughout the marriage I have performed all wifely duties and have cared for and brought up the two children of the marriage and therefore I am advised that I have thereby acquired an interest in the matrimonial home.'

In her oral evidence Mrs Dobson said that by 'own purposes' she meant 'householdwise as well, not just for clothes'. She added that she did not seek to say that para. 4 was wrong and did not seek to resile from it. As I have said, she always had bank accounts in her own name.

The result, in my view, is that Mrs Dobson does not demonstrate that she was induced to act to her detriment upon the basis of a common intention of ownership of the house or that there was otherwise any nexus between the acquisition of the property and something provided or foregone by Mrs Dobson.

I should add that I see no basis for any claim by Mrs Dobson simply by way of resulting trust unaccompanied by a specific agreement. Thus she made no direct contribution to the purchase price. There was no arrangement that she should go out to work and provide money which directly or indirectly would be used to pay off the mortgage. Mrs Dobson, of course, performed various household duties and purchased various household items, but those facts are quite consistent with Mr Dobson's absolute ownership of the house itself.

The result, in my opinion, is that Mrs Dobson does not establish that she is entitled to any beneficial interest in Tower Road. The result is that the case is one of a mortgage by the absolute beneficial owner of the fee simple (Mr Dobson). The bank is, under the legal charge, entitled to possession accordingly.

Appeal allowed. [The question of the effect of the letter of consent did not arise.]

Question

Would you consider that the local authority should have a duty under s. 59 of the Housing Act 1985 to rehouse Mrs Rosset and Mrs Dobson after the sale of the property as persons in priority need?

Bankruptcy is another example where there can be conflict between the rights of the spouse to occupy the matrimonial home and the rights of third parties to realise their interest. This is now regulated by ss. 336 and 337 of the Insolvency Act 1986.

336.(2) — Where a spouse's rights of occupation under the [Matrimonial Homes Act 1983] are a charge on the estate or interest of the other spouse or of trustees for the other spouse and the other spouse is adjudged bankrupt —

(*a*) the charge continues to subsist notwithstanding the bankruptcy and . . . binds the trustee of the bankrupt's estate and persons deriving title under that trustee; and

(*b*) any application for an order under section 1 of that Act shall be made to the court having jurisdiction in relation to the bankruptcy.

(3) Where a person and his spouse or former spouse are trustees for sale of a dwelling house and that person is adjudged bankrupt, any application by the trustee of the bankrupt's estate for an order under section 30 of the Law of Property Act . . . shall be made to the court having jurisdiction in relation to the bankruptcy.

(4) On such an application as is mentioned under subsection (2) or (3) the court shall make such order under section 1 of the Act of 1983 or section 30 of the Act of 1925 as it thinks just and reasonable having regard to —

(*a*) the interests of the bankrupt's creditors,

(*b*) the conduct of the spouse or former spouse, so far as contributing to the bankruptcy,

(*c*) the needs and financial resources of the spouse or former spouse,

(*d*) the needs of any children, and

(*e*) all the circumstances of the case other than the needs of the bankrupt.

(5) Where such an application is made after the end of the period of one year beginning with the first vesting . . . of the bankrupt's estate in a trustee, the court shall assume, unless the circumstances of the case are exceptional, that the interests of the bankrupt's creditors outweigh all other considerations.

(Section 337 applies the principles of s. 336 to the situation where the bankrupt has no spouse with occupational rights, and children under 18 'had their home' with him. The needs of the children are to be taken into account but not the needs of the bankrupt himself. Section 337(6) is to the same effect as s. 336(5).)

These provisions have their origin in *Insolvency Law and Practice* (The Cork Committee) (1982) which states:

1118: It would be consistent with present social attitudes to alleviate the personal hardships of those who are dependent on the debtor but not responsible for his insolvency, if this can be achieved by delaying for an acceptable time the sale of the family home.

Question

Would Mrs Dobson and Mrs Rossett have fared better if their respective husbands been declared bankrupt?

In *Re Holliday (a bankrupt), ex p Trustee of the Bankrupt v Bankrupt* [1981] Ch 405, [1980] 3 All ER 385, the Court of Appeal decided that the interests of the wife and her children should prevail over the interests of the creditors to the extent that the sale of the house should be deferred for a substantial period.

Sir David Cairns: I reach that view because I am satisfied that it would at present be very difficult, if not impossible, for the wife to secure another suitable home for the family in or near Thorpe Bay; because it would be upsetting for the children's education if they had to move far away from their present schools, even if it were practicable, having regard to the wife's means, to find an alternative home at some more distant place; because it is highly unlikely that postponement of the payment of the debts would cause any great hardship to any of the creditors;

However, in *Re Citro (a bankrupt)* [1990] 3 All ER 952, [1990] 3 WLR 880, involving two bankrupts and their wives, the majority of the Court of

Appeal distinguished the earlier case. At first instance, Hoffmann J imposed a provision for postponement of sale on the application of the trustee in bankruptcy until the youngest child in each case reached 16 years of age. He was of the opinion that if immediate orders for sale were made, the half shares to which each of the wives were entitled would be insufficient for them to acquire other accommodation in the area which would inevitably disturb the education of the children. In reversing the decision of Hoffmann J at first instance, Nourse LJ said:

Did Hoffmann J. correctly apply [the law] to the facts which were before him? I respectfully think that he did not. First, for the reasons already stated, the personal circumstances of the two wives and their children, although distressing, are not by themselves exceptional. Secondly, I think that the judge erred in fashioning his orders by reference to those which might have been made in the Family Division in a case where bankruptcy had not supervened. . . . Thirdly, and perhaps most significantly, he did not ask himself the critical question whether a further postponement of payment of their debts would cause hardship to the creditors. . . .

Finally, I refer to section 336 of the Insolvency act 1986 which, although it does not apply to either of these cases, will apply to such cases in the future. In subsection (5) of that section the court is required, in the circumstances there mentioned, to 'assume, unless the circumstances of the case are exceptional, that the interests of the bankrupt's creditors outweigh all other considerations'. I have no doubt that that section was intended to apply the same test as that which has been evolved in the previous bankruptcy decisions, and it is satisfactory to find that it has. I say that not least because section 336 only applies to the rights of occupation of those who are or have been married. The case law will continue to apply to unmarried couples, who nowadays set up house together in steadily increasing numbers. A difference in the basic tests applicable to the two classes of case would have been most undesirable.

Question

Both of these cases were decided under the old law. Suppose that Harry is declared bankrupt, and he lives with his wife, Wendy, and their three children in a house which they jointly own. The eldest child is physically handicapped and the house has been adapted for her purposes. The other two children are gifted twins and attend a local school for gifted children. Harry is a self-employed builder and many of his creditors are local traders with families. Do you think that the court would (*a*) make an immediate order for sale? (*b*) if the application for sale is made after the end of one year beginning with the first vesting of the estate in Harry's trustee, postpone the sale for a further period? (*c*) in either (*a*) or (*b*) would it make any difference if Harry has the sole legal and beneficial interest? (*d*) in either (*a*) or (*b*) would it make any difference if Harry and Wendy were not married? (*e*) in either (*a*) or (*b*) would it make any difference if Harry and Wendy were not married and if Harry has the sole legal and beneficial interest?

The Insolvency Act 1986 does not deal with charging orders which are described by Gray *Elements of Land Law* (1987) as follows:

If the creditor's application is granted by the court, the charging order has the effect of imposing on specified property of the debtor a 'charge for securing the payment of any money due . . . under the judgment or order'. The charging order thus converts what was at most a contractual debt into an enforceable security with proprietary attributes. The judgment creditor may protect his charge against third parties by the expedient of a registration against the debtor's name under the Land Charges Act 1972 (in the case of unregistered land) or by the entry of a notice in the register of the debtor's title (in the case of registered land).

. . .

The principal advantage of a charging order is that the charge imposed by the court becomes enforceable 'in the same manner as an equitable charge created by the debtor by writing under his hand'. Accordingly the judgment creditor has a right to invoke legal process in the realisation of his security, and is entitled to apply to the court either for an order for sale of the property charged or for the appointment of a receiver.

Gray continues:

. . . Armed with his charging order, the judgment creditor has locus standi to apply to the court for an order directing the sale of the entire co-owned land, his own charge being satisfied out of the proceeds attributable to the debtor's aliquot share. Given the traditional preference in favour of creditors under s. 30, it becomes acutely apparent that the charging order carries a realistic and highly potent threat to residential security in the family home.

An example of an attempt to use a charging order is the following case:

Harman v Glencross
[1986] Fam 81, [1986] 1 All ER 545, [1986] 2 WLR 637, [1986] 2 FLR 241, [1986] Fam Law 215, Court of Appeal.

This case concerned the application by a wife to vary a charging order absolute which was made against the husband's interest in a property which was in the joint names of both parties. The wife was in exclusive occupation with the two children. Both the district judge and the circuit judge postponed the charging order to await any order made on the wife's application in the divorce proceedings. The Court of Appeal refused to interfere with the exercise of the discretion of the judge, but Balcombe LJ dealt with wider issues. He considered the competing advantages of a *Mesher v Mesher* order against a 'clean break' (see pp. 298ff, below) and continued:

Of greater importance, when considering the balance between the wife's rights and claims and those of the judgment creditor, an order which merely postpones the sale of the matrimonial home can leave her 'locked in' to the particular house which was the matrimonial home at the date of the break-up of the marriage, and although family circumstances may render it desirable for her to be able to sell the house and move to a smaller house, or to a different district, she will be unable to do so if the result of a sale of the existing house, and the consequent division of the proceeds of sale, will leave her with insufficient funds to buy a new house.

It is for reasons such as these that an outright transfer of the husband's interest in the matrimonial home may be the appropriate way to protect fully the wife's right to have a roof over the heads of herself and the children, and it was, of course, such an order that the registrar made (and the judge affirmed) in the present case. Indeed, one of the points made in support of the wife's case, and accepted by the judge, was that if the charging order absolute stood, and was followed by a sale, she would not have enough money left to rehouse herself and the children. However, unless the transfer of the husband's share in the house to the wife is necessary to give her adequate protection so that she may have a home for herself and the children, it is difficult to see why the judgment creditor's undoubted rights should not take preference to the wife's claim to a transfer of property order.
Appeal dismissed.

Question

If Mrs Glencross had had no proprietary right in the home, what would have happened?

3 The field of choice

(a) THE ISSUES

There are three possibilities: a complete freedom of choice for the parties with little or no judicial discretion available to the judges; a system of fixed property rights; and a freedom of choice but with a power for the courts to readjust the parties rights either during the marriage or at the end of the marriage.

The distinction between the fixed and discretionary system is highlighted in the First Report on *Family Property — A New Approach* (1973) where the Law Commission acknowledge that there is a body of opinion that would oppose the introduction of any form of fixed property rights between husband and wife on the ground that this is unnecessary and in itself objectionable:

10 . . . They believed that in so far as the existing law led to any injustice, the proper remedy was to allow the court to exercise its discretionary powers in matrimonial or family provision proceedings. It was claimed that all necessary reforms could be achieved by developing the traditional discretionary systems, which ensured great flexibility. The principal reasons for considering any form of fixed property rights undesirable were as follows:

  (*a*) fixed property rights would cause more dissension and injustice than they would alleviate;
  (*b*) the state should not interfere in the relations between spouses by imposing automatic rules regulating their property rights;
  (*c*) fixed property rights would deter marriage and compel people to take advice before marrying.

Questions

Is advice before marriage a good thing which should be encouraged?

By contrast, the Canadian Law Reform Commission (1975) put the alternative point of view:

Another drawback to a discretionary system lies in its lack of fixed legal rights. Even were equality to be stated as a general legislative policy, the essential nature of judicial discretion would leave the court free to make whatever sort of property disposition seemed to be appropriate in any given case. A married person would not have a *right* to equality, but only a *hope* to obtain it. If no concept of equality were contained in the law establishing a discretionary system, then it would be accurate to say that a married person would have no property rights at all at the time of divorce. Our concern here is not limited to the way things would work out in practice, since the courts would do their best to ensure that arbitrary dispossession did not occur. Rather, it includes the psychological advantage that accrues to a person who knows he or she has a positive right that is guaranteed and protected by law.

But if there is to be a fixed system, what would it mean?

The following extract is taken from the Canadian Law Reform Commission (1975):

The community property concept of marital property rights is based upon the assumption that marriage, among other things, is an economic partnership. As such, the partnership, or community, owns the respective talents and efforts of each of the spouses. Whatever is acquired as a result of their talents and efforts is shared by and belongs to both of them equally, as *community property*.

Community property regimes exist in Quebec, in many European countries and in eight of the United States. Quebec's community property regime, like the separate property regime in that province, is an option available to married persons who choose not to be governed by the basic regime providing for separate ownership of property during a marriage, with fixed sharing upon divorce.

The essential idea of community property is very simple: the earnings, and property purchased with the earnings, of either spouse become community property in which each spouse has a present equal legal interest. Where the community is terminated — for example by divorce — the community property, after payment of community debts, is divided equally between the spouses. The community is also terminated by the death of a spouse, and in some jurisdictions, including Quebec, by an agreement between the spouses to switch to some other regime or to regulate their property relations by a contract. This simple formula conceals some rather complex rules. We can do no more in this paper than touch upon the general principles and a few of the major problem areas involved in community property systems without dealing with finer points in any great detail.

Under community regimes, there are three kinds of property: the separate property of the husband, the separate property of the wife, and community property. Typically, the property owned by either spouse before marriage is the separate property of that spouse, along with property acquired after marriage by a spouse by way of gift or inheritance. Separate property is not shared at the time of divorce, but rather is retained by the owner-spouse. All other property, however acquired, becomes community property, in which each spouse has a present interest as soon as it is purchased or obtained, and an equal share in its division upon divorce. In some jurisdictions, someone giving property to a married person must specify that the property is to be the separate property of the recipient. Otherwise it will be treated as a gift to both spouses, even though it is only given to one, and will become community property. In the Province of Quebec, some types of property owned before marriage become community property, but it is possible for persons giving such types of property to a single person to make the gift on the condition that it remain the separate property of the recipient should he or she thereafter marry under the regime of community property.

Under a community property regime, all property owned by either spouse at the time of a divorce is generally presumed in law to be community property unless it can be proved to be separate. In many marriages the spouses will not have adequate records of ownership or the source of funds used to acquire property. This produces the legal phenomenon of 'commingling' — that is, the separate property of each spouse eventually becomes mixed with that of the other spouse and with the community property, resulting in all the property being treated as sharable community property at the time of divorce. Commingling makes it impossible for the spouses to establish that certain items of property were owned before marriage, or otherwise fall into the classification of separate property.

Community property regimes, however, are enacted into law on the assumption that commingling is not what most people desire, and they therefore contain rather elaborate rules and formulae designed to deal with the fact that married persons will be using and enjoying the three different types of property created by the law of this regime—that is, the husband's separate property, the wife's separate property and the community property. These rules and formulae tend to make the essentially simple concept of community of property a rather complicated system in practice. For example, one typical rule is that property acquired after marriage in replacement of separate property does not become community property. This means that a spouse who wishes to replace or keep replacing property that was owned before marriage must keep an account and record of every transaction, so that at the time of divorce items purchased after marriage for which separate property status is claimed can be traced back to the original property owned before marriage, and can be shown to be replacements for such original property. If a person does not have adequate records, the replacement property will be presumed to belong to the community and shared between the spouses when the marriage is dissolved.

Even assuming that the separate property of a spouse can in fact be kept identifiable, it is necessary to have rules governing the situation where community funds are expended with respect to such property. If, for example, a husband owns a house as separate property and has it repaired, using community funds, the community property is entitled to reimbursement at the time of divorce to the extent of the value of the repairs. Or if he sells the house and buys another, using for the purchase some community funds plus proceeds of the sale, the rule might be that if more than fifty per cent of the price of the second house came from the first house, it remains separate property subject to an appropriate compensation to the community upon divorce. If more than fifty per cent of the price of the second house came from community funds, then it loses its character as separate property and becomes community property. In the latter case there would be a compensation paid from the community at the time of divorce to the husband's separate property equal to the amount realized on the sale of the first house. When it is recognized that most families only have available the earnings of one spouse, which belong to the community, and that many items of separate property over the course of a marriage would be maintained and repaired out of these earnings, or sold and 'traded up' for newer property using the proceeds of the sale of the separate property plus community funds, then some of the practical difficulties in accounting during the marriage and sorting out community and separate property at its termination become readily apparent.

In some community property jurisdictions, the income produced by a spouse's separate property (such as the profits from renting an apartment house owned separately by one spouse) becomes community property. In other jurisdictions, the rule is the other way, so that a spouse is entitled to keep such income separate so long, of course, as he is able to establish at the time of divorce that the source of the income was his separate property.

With respect to liability for indebtedness, some community property jurisdictions distinguish between debts contracted as community obligations, such as necessaries for any member of the family or the debts connected with the prosecution of a community business, and debts contracted with respect to the acquisition or disposition of separate property or the management of a separately owned business of one spouse. In other jurisdictions, the community property is liable for the debts of the husband but not the debts of his wife.

Deferred Community is described in detail in the Canadian Law Reform Commission's Working Paper (1975).

Deferred sharing, or deferred community of property as it is sometimes called, is based on the idea that there should be separate ownership of property during marriage, and an equal distribution of property on divorce. Deferred sharing, therefore, lies somewhere between the extremes of separate property on the one hand and full community of property on the other. Deferred sharing regimes exist in Denmark, Sweden, Norway, Findland, West Germany and Holland. In Canada, Quebec adopted a deferred sharing regime in 1970 — the 'partnership of acquests' — as its basic family property law, applicable to all married persons who did not make a positive choice of community property or separate property. In addition, the Ontario Law Reform Commission, in the spring of 1974, made a formal and detailed proposal to the government of that province that legislation be enacted to create a deferred sharing system, known as the 'matrimonial property regime', to replace many fundamental aspects of the law of separate property in Ontario. Although there are some conceptual differences, its results are essentially similar to Quebec's partnership of acquests.

The basic theory of the deferred sharing system is simple. In general terms, all property acquired by either spouse during marriage is to be shared equally when the marriage partnership is dissolved.

The possibility of a deferred community regime was raised in the English Law Commission Working Paper (1971), and the Law Commission commented on the results of the consultation in the First Report (1973):

47. The proposals relating to such a system of 'deferred community' attracted far more interest and comment than did those relating to legal rights of inheritance. No clear view, however, emerged from the consultation. Some supported the principle of community with enthusiasm. Others opposed it forcefully. In between were those who were neutral or mildly interested and those who thought community would be unnecessary if co-ownership of the matrimonial home were introduced. On balance, the majority did not support deferred community. Some thought that community would give effect to the partnership element in marriage and create definite property rights without the need to depend upon the exercise of the court's discretion; it was seen as a natural extension of the principle of co-ownership of the home into a wider field. Others thought that community could be unfair if applied arbitrarily without regard to the circumstances and to conduct, that it would be a cause of dissension and that it would be inconsistent with the independence of the spouses. . . .
49. Very few took the extreme view that fixed principles of deferred community should replace the present discretionary powers exercisable on divorce or in family provision proceedings. The vast majority thought that existing discretionary powers should be retained.
50. The Social Survey asked married couples what they thought would be a fair settlement in the following circumstances:

'A married couple with no children acquire during their marriage a house on mortgage, the furniture, a car and some savings — altogether worth about £3,000. Then by mutual agreement they decide to separate and some financial arrangement has to be made.'

The situation was considered on the basis that both spouses had been earning and on the basis that the husband had been working and the wife had been looking after the home. A range of solutions was offered for each situation.

51. Excluding those who said they 'did not know', the proportion of people who chose some form of sharing in each of the situations was over 90%. Predominantly (in at least 75% of cases) half-and-half sharing was preferred, and there was little difference in the views of husbands and wives:

'Changing the situation from one where both spouses were earning to only one spouse earning did not result in a large shift of opinion as to what would be a fair settlement in the event of a breakdown of marriage. Nine out of ten thought the possessions should be shared and three quarters thought the method of sharing should be half and half.'

52. The Survey stressed that they had expressly excluded from the situation factors which might have led to qualification, for example, whether there were any children or whether the separation was wanted by both spouses. Nevertheless, the results indicate that many people would consider that in principle some form of sharing at the end of marriage would be fair.

53. The principle of deferred community should be considered in the light of the conclusions we have already reached in this Report, namely that the principle of co-ownership of the home is a necessary measure which would be widely accepted as better achieving justice than the present law, and that a system of fixed legal rights of inheritance is neither necessary nor desirable. Assuming, for the moment, that the principle of co-ownership of the home will be implemented, is the further step of introducing a system of community needed in order to attain the proper balance of justice?

54. The Working Paper pointed out that anomalies could arise if a fixed principle of sharing were limited to just one asset. It would apply only where there was a matrimonial home. Further, the spouse who acquired an interest in the matrimonial home under the co-ownership principle might own other assets of similar or greater value which did not have to be shared. It was suggested that a wider principle of sharing might appear fairer. The results of the Social Survey throw some light on both these points. The Survey confirms that spouses who do not own their home seldom have assets of any substantial value. It also indicates that where a home is owned, it represents a substantial proportion of the total value of the spouses' assets. For the majority of home-owners, sharing the home would, in effect, be sharing the most substantial asset of the family. How far is deferred community necessary as a means of eliminating the anomalies in other cases? . . .

59. *Our conclusion* is that if the principle of co-ownership of the matrimonial home were introduced into English law much of what is now regarded as unsatisfactory or unfair would be eliminated, and the marriage partnership would be recognised by family property law in this very important context. Having regard to our conclusions regarding co-ownership of the matrimonial home, to the broad interpretation by the court of its powers to order financial provision on divorce, and to our conclusion that the court should have similar powers in family provision proceedings, we do not consider that there is at present any need to introduce a system of deferred community.

A system similar to deferred community has been introduced in Scotland by s. 10 of the Family Law (Scotland) Act 1985. (See Chapter 7, below.)

Sharing of value of matrimonial property

10.—(1) In applying the principle set out in section 9(1)(a) of this Act, the net value of the matrimonial property shall be taken to be shared fairly between the parties to the marriage when it is shared equally or in such other proportions as are justified by special circumstances.

(2) The net value of the matrimonial property shall be the value of the property at the relevant date after deduction of any debts incurred by the parties or either of them—

(a) before the marriage so far as they relate to the matrimonial property, and

(b) during the marriage.

which are outstanding at that date.

(3) In this section 'the relevant date' means whichever is the earlier of—

(a) subject to subsection (7) below, the date on which the parties ceased to cohabit;

(b) the date of service of the summons in the action for divorce.

and to be honest with ourselves, in England as a result of case law developments (see Chapter 7, below).

Question

Is the introduction of deferred community good enough (*a*) for women in the higher paid sectors of the employment market (*b*) for women who do not work, or who work only part time? (See Chapter 7, below.)

(b) THE MATRIMONIAL HOME

The two areas which feature predominantly in Law Commission reports in England are the matrimonial home and household goods. We discuss each in turn. It is natural that discussions should centre around the home.

As we have seen (p. 149, above), problems invariably involve third party creditors.

The English Law Commission Working Paper, *Family Property Law* (1971) discussed the topic in detail, and formed the conclusion that a system of co-ownership should be introduced to meet many of the objections to the present law:

0.25 The matrimonial home is often the principal, if not the only, family asset. Where this is the case, if satisfactory provision could be made for sharing the home, the problem of matrimonial property would be largely solved. Under present rules, apart from any question of gift or agreement, ownership is decided on the basis of: (1) the documents of title, and (2) the financial contribution of each spouse. Part 1 of the Paper considers whether there should be alternative ways or additional considerations for determining ownership.

0.26 One possibility would be to allow the court to decide ownership of the home on discretionary grounds whenever a dispute arose between the spouses, taking into account various factors, including the contribution of each spouse to the family. The provisional conclusion is reached that, on balance, this would not be a worthwhile reform in view of the existing discretionary powers to award financial provision (which include powers to order a transfer or settlement of the property of either spouse) on a decree of divorce, nullity or judicial separation. Further, it would leave ownership uncertain in the absence of litigation.

0.27 Another possibility would be to introduce a presumption that the matrimonial home is owned by both spouses equally. Unless one of the spouses contested the matter, the presumption would apply. In the event of a contest equality would prevail unless the presumption was rebutted. The chief problem under such a system would be to determine the circumstances in which the presumption should be rebutted. The choice may lie between narrow, and perhaps arbitrary, grounds and broad discretionary grounds which might result in considerable uncertainty.

0.28 A third possibility would be to go further than a presumption, which could be rebutted, and to provide that, subject to any agreement to the contrary, the beneficial interest in the matrimonial home should be shared equally by the spouses. We refer to this as the principle of co-ownership. The interests of the spouses would arise not from any financial contribution, nor from any contribution to the welfare of the family, nor from any other factors to be assessed by the court, but from the marriage relationship itself. There are advantages in this solution: it would in the absence of agreement to the contrary apply universally; it would acknowledge the partnership element in marriage by providing that the ownership of the principal family asset should be shared by the spouses; it would provide a large measure of security and certainty for a spouse in case of breakdown of marriage or on the death of the other spouse; and it would help to avoid protracted disputes and litigation.

0.29 The chief argument against the principle of co-ownership is that it could operate unfairly in individual cases. For example, a husband who paid for the house might find that, while he had to share ownership of it with his wife, he had no right to share *any* of her property. Since the sharing would operate only where spouses owned their home, the principle would not help [a wife] if [a husband] chose to invest his money and live in rented accommodation. An automatic rule might even induce him not to buy a home. Besides these objections there are certain practical problems to be overcome. One is to decide to what extent a spouse who is given an interest should be responsible for the liabilities in respect of the home which she may have no means of discharging unless she shares in assets other than the home. A second is to determine whether a spouse should be called upon to share a home which he or she may have owned absolutely before marriage. A third and serious problem is how to protect the interest of a spouse whose name is not on the legal title, while at the same time safe-guarding the interests of a purchaser or mortgagee. This, however, is essentially a matter of conveyancing machinery which should not be impossible to solve if it were decided to introduce the principle of co-ownership. The conclusion is reached that it would be practicable to introduce co-ownership, and that it would, on balance, have advantages over the present law. The Paper proposes that a new form of matrimonial home trust should apply whenever the beneficial interest in the home is shared between the spouses, in order that they should have a direct interest in the property.

In their First Report on *Family Property — A New Approach* (1973) the Law Commission stated that the principle of co-ownership was widely supported.

21. It emerged clearly from the consultation that the principle of co-ownership of the matrimonial home is widely supported both as the best means of reforming the law relating to the home, and as the main principle of family property law. The great majority who supported co-ownership included legal practitioners, academic lawyers, women's organisations and members of the public. Those who opposed co-ownership were those who were opposed to any form of fixed property rights, and they were relatively few in number.
22. Widespread approval of the principle of co-ownership of the matrimonial home was also revealed by the Social Survey [Todd and Jones, 1972]. Married couples were asked the following question:
    'Some people say that the home and its contents should legally be jointly owned by the hus-
    band and wife irrespective of who paid for it. Do you agree or disagree with that?'
91% of husbands and 94% of wives who took part in the survey agreed with the proposition: the remainder disagreed. In the case of owner occupiers who had their home in the name of one spouse 87% of both husbands and wives said that they regarded the home as belonging to both of them.
23. The opinions expressed favouring the co-ownership principle are supported by a change in the pattern of ownership of the matrimonial home in recent years. The Social Survey analysed the pattern and found that 52% of couples owned their home; among the home owners 52% had their home in joint names. However, when the figures were broken down by the year of purchase of the home it was clear that a marked increase in the rate of joint ownership began in the middle 1960's and is continuing. . . . In cases where the wife had made some financial contribution to the home the proportion of homes put into joint names was higher than in cases where there had been no such contribution. The rate of joint ownership was also very high in cases where the couple had owned more than one home.
24. The Survey considered the reasons for the trend towards joint ownership and concluded that
    'the factors associated with joint ownership of the matrimonial home were not those related
    to the couple themselves, such as the length of marriage and social class. Instead there were
    factors relating to the circumstances of purchase of the home; the year the present home
    was acquired; the number of times the couples had been through the process of buying a
    house and whether the wife had made any financial contribution to it'.

Having examined this evidence, the Law Commission arrived at the conclusion that, subject to the proviso that a husband and wife remain free to make any arrangements they choose, the principle of automatic co-ownership of the matrimonial home should be introduced.

The Scottish Law Commission in their Report on *Matrimonial Property* (1984) disagreed with the English proposals:

(i) Statutory co-ownership of the matrimonial home would not be a good way of giving expression to the idea of marriage as an equal partnership. In some cases it would go too far, particularly if it applied to a home owned before marriage, or acquired by gift or inheritance during the marriage. These are not the results of the spouses' joint efforts. In other cases it would not go far enough and could produce results which were unfair as between one spouse and another. If the wife, say, owned the home and the husband owned other property, he could acquire a half share in the home without having to share any of his property. A spouse with investments worth thousands of pounds could allow the other to buy a home and then claim half of it without contributing a penny. The scheme would also work very unevenly as between different couples. If Mr A had invested all his money in the matrimonial home while his next-door neighbour Mr B had mortgaged his home to its full value in order to finance his business, the law would operate very unevenly for the benefit of Mrs A and Mrs B. It would, in short, be a hit or miss way of giving effect to the partnership ideal. .

(ii) Statutory co-ownership of the matrimonial home would not be a good way of recognising contributions in unpaid work by a non-earning spouse. It would benefit the undeserving as well as the deserving. Extreme cases can be imagined. A man might marry a wealthy widow, encourage her to buy an expensive house, claim half of her house and leave her. Even in less extreme cases statutory co-ownership would be a poor way of rewarding unpaid work. Most housewives would get nothing from the new law because its effects would be confined to owner-occupiers. Only about 37% of married couples in Scotland live in owner-occupied accommodation.[1] Even where the new law did apply, its effects would be totally arbitrary. Not only would the net value of the home vary enormously from case to case, and from time to time, but so too would the respective values of the spouses' contributions.

(iii) Statutory co-ownership of the matrimonial home would not necessarily bring the law into line with the views of most married people. We know that most married owner-occupiers in Scotland favour voluntary co-ownership of the matrimonial home.[2] We do not know that most married people in Scotland would favour forcing co-ownership on an unwilling owner regardless of the circumstances of the particular case.

(iv) It is not self-evident that property which is used in common should be owned in common. Even if this proposition were accepted, it would lead further than co-ownership between spouses. It would lead to co-ownership between the members of a household, including for example, children and parents.

(v) A scheme for statutory co-ownership of the matrimonial home would be very complex. The scheme we outlined in our consultative memorandum was as simple as we could make it, but even so it raised many difficult questions. Should, for example, co-ownership come about automatically by operation of law (in which case how would third parties, such as people who have bought the house in good faith, be protected) or should it come about only, say, on registration of a notice by the non-owner spouse (in which case would non-owner spouses bother to register before it was too late)? Should co-ownership apply to a house owned by one spouse before the marriage? Should it apply to a home which is part of commercial or agricultural property? Should it apply to a home bought by one spouse after the couple have separated? If not, should it make any difference if the spouses resume cohabitation for a short period? Should the spouses become jointly liable for any debts secured on the home? When should it be possible for one spouse, or both, to opt out of co-ownership and how should this be done? Should a spouse be able to claim half of the sale proceeds of one home, refuse to contribute to the purchase price of a new home, and then claim half of that one too? If not, how can this be remedied without forcing one spouse to invest in a home he or she does not want to invest in? These are just some of the less technical questions which would have to be answered.

(vi) Statutory co-ownership of the matrimonial home would not benefit many people. . . . The majority of . . . owner-occupier couples already have their home in joint names. Of those owner-occupiers who have their home in the sole name of one spouse, a number will have a good reason for this and would presumably opt out of a statutory scheme. In many cases a co-ownership scheme would confer no long-term benefit on the non-owner spouse because he or she would succeed to the house on the death of the other in any event, or would receive as much by way of financial provision on divorce as he or she would have received if the scheme had applied.

(vii) A scheme for statutory co-ownership of the matrimonial home would have to co-exist with the law on financial provision on divorce. It would make little sense, it might be said, to introduce a complicated scheme for fixed co-ownership rights in the home during the marriage if the whole financial circumstances of the spouses were to be thrown into the melting-pot on divorce. The supposed benefit of fixed rights would be illusory. It would be most useless when most needed.

(viii) Finally, a scheme for forced co-ownership could exacerbate matrimonial disputes. If

---

1. In Great Britain as a whole, 69% of married men are owner-occupiers (GHS, 1984).
2. A.J. Manners and I. Rauta *Family Property in Scotland* (1981).

co-ownership came about only when the non-owner spouse registered a notice, the act of registration might well be seen as a deliberate raising of the level of a domestic dispute. An intimation by one spouse that he or she was opting out of co-ownership would also be unlikely to promote good domestic relations.

Questions

(i) Which if any of these criticisms do you agree with, and why?
(ii) The Law Commission proposal was that the legal estate would remain in the sole name of the spouse whose name was on the title. The spouses would therefore become equitable joint tenants. Why did the Law Commission not recommend joint legal ownership?

One of the problems of co-ownership by operation of law is that there are bound to be exceptions. In their Third Report on *Family Property* (1978), the Law Commission returned to a consideration of the major exceptions which would be necessary if the principle were to be introduced. The first is in relation to an interest in property acquired on or before marriage. The Law Commission recommended that a home of this kind should be subject to statutory co-ownership unless the owner spouse takes positive action to exclude it. Such action can only be taken before the marriage:

1.113 We also recommend that it should affect only the particular home in question: it should not operate to exclude any subsequent home even if that home is purchased with the proceeds of sale of the first one. Finally, we emphasise that the owner spouse is to have this power of exclusion only when he holds a separate interest — an interest, that is, which is held by him otherwise than as a joint tenant or tenant in common *with the other spouse* (or, more accurately, with the person who is to become the other spouse).

There is disagreement about whether an owning spouse should be allowed to make a 'secret reservation'. The majority of the Law Commissioners recommend that a reservation need not be communicated to a future spouse, but that there should be a written declaration, signed and attested by a witness to the effect that statutory co-ownership is not to apply. One Law Commissioner, Mr Marsh, considers, however:

that it would be potentially harmful to good matrimonial relations to allow one spouse by his own secret reservation to spring a surprise, perhaps after years of marriage, on the other spouse as to the ownership of the matrimonial home. He thinks therefore that a declaration should not have effect unless it has been communicated to the other spouse before marriage (which he emphasises does not necessarily mean that the other spouse consents).

Questions

(i) What arguments can you advance against the view that property acquired before marriage can be treated as community property?
(ii) Do you agree with Mr Marsh or with the other Commissioners about 'secret reservations'?
(iii) Or would you not permit any reservations at all?

Another exception canvassed in the Working Paper (1971) which had been the subject of considerable discussion related to homes acquired by one spouse from a third party by gift or inheritance during, or by gift in contemplation of, the marriage. The original view of the Law Commission was:

1.116 'If co-ownership were to apply automatically, the donor could not make an absolute gift to one spouse without asking the other spouse to agree to exclude co-ownership. It seems undesirable that a donor should have to ask for such an agreement. The result would probably be that the donor would either refrain from making the gift or resort to some other device (such as granting a life interest) to achieve his purpose.'
. . . We reached the provisional conclusion that homes of this kind should not be subject to co-ownership at all (though it was recognised that the donee spouse could always agree to share with the other spouse if he wished to do so).

However, in their Third Report on *Family Property* (1978), the Law Commission state:

1.117. The weight of opinion expressed in consultation was against this conclusion. We see the force of the views expressed by those who disagreed. It can certainly be argued, for instance, that a spouse who acquires a home by gift is already fortunate enough, and that there is no reason to multiply his good fortune, and at the same time to prevent his spouse from participating in it, by excluding her from co-ownership. On the other hand we think the arguments advanced in the working paper are also sound.
1.118. We have therefore arrived once more at a compromise solution — namely, that co-ownership *should* apply to a home of this kind *unless* the donor (a term which we use to include a testator or settlor) directs, in the instrument making the gift, that it shall not.
1.119. Our reasons for recommending this solution are much the same as our reasons for recommending a similar solution to the problem of homes owned by one spouse before the marriage. In this case, however, the solution was considered in the working paper and provisionally rejected on the ground that a declaration by the donor 'could appear invidious, and may be even more undesirable than an agreement to exclude.' Although the first part of this statement is obviously true — . . . we are no longer inclined to support the second part. We feel, moreover, that this solution, imperfect though it may be, is really the only one open to us. In view of our consultation and the further thought which we ourselves have given to the matter, we no longer feel able to recommend the automatic exclusion proposed in the working paper. But we do not feel it right to deny the donor any means whatever of bringing about an exclusion.

The third case where automatic co-ownership might be excluded is when there is an agreement between the spouses. The Law Commission recommend however that statutory co-ownership should only be excluded 'when the spouses have spelt out the beneficial holding which is to replace it.'

Turning to the question of third parties, the Law Commission (1978) recommended that statutory co-ownership should only give protection against third parties if the interest is registered, and that it would not be an overriding interest. However, the House of Lords decided that beneficial interests in registered land were overriding in certain circumstances:

Williams and Glyn's Bank Ltd v Boland
[1981] AC 487, [1980] 2 All ER 408, [1980] 3 WLR 138, 124 Sol Jo 443, [1980] RVR 204, 40 P & CR 451, House of Lords

In 1969 Michael Boland bought a house in his sole name (the land was registered land) and went to live there with his wife and son. The wife made a substantial contribution to the purchase price. A loan was subsequently guaranteed to the husband by the bank to whom he charged the house as security. The bank made no enquiries about the wife's interest. Subsequently, the bank brought proceedings for possession, with a view to its sale with vacant possession and the recovery, from the proceeds, of so much of the loan as remained due. Mrs Boland maintained that she had rights which prevailed against those of the bank. She claimed that she was entitled to a property interest in the house by reason of her contribution to the purchase; that she occupied the house and was entitled to continue to occupy it; and that her rights constituted an 'overriding interest' under s. 70(1)(g) of the Law Registration Act 1925 which prevailed against the bank. The bank succeeded at first instance, but the judgment was reversed by the Court of Appeal whose decision was unanimously upheld by the House of Lords. (The case was heard together with a similar appeal in *Williams and Glyn's Bank Ltd v Brown*.)

Lord Wilberforce: There was physical presence, with all the rights that occupiers have, including the right to exclude all others except those having similar rights. The house was a matrimonial home, intended to be occupied, and in fact occupied by both spouses, both of whom have an interest in it: it would require some special doctrine of law to avoid the result that each is in occupation. Three arguments were used for a contrary conclusion. First, it was said that if the vendor (I use this word to include a mortgagor) is in occupation, that is enough to prevent the application of the paragraph. This seems to be a proposition of general application, not limited to the case of husbands, and no doubt, if correct, would be very convenient for purchasers and intending mortgagees. But the presence of the vendor, with occupation, does not exclude the possibility of occupation of others. . . . Then it was suggested that the wife's occupation was nothing but the shadow of the husband's — a version I suppose of the doctrine of unity of husband and wife. This expression and the argument flowing from it was used by Templeman J in *Bird v Syme-Thomson* [1978] 3 All ER 1027, [1979] 1 WLR 440, a decision preceding and which he followed in the present case. The argument was also inherent in the judgment in *Caunce v Caunce* [1969] 1 All ER 722, [1969] 1 WLR 286 which influenced the decisions of Templeman J. It somewhat faded from the arguments in the present case and appears to me to be heavily obsolete. The appellant's main and final position became in the end this: that, to come within the paragraph, the occupation in question must be apparently inconsistent with the title of the vendor. This, it was suggested, would exclude the wife of a husband-vendor because her apparent occupation would be satisfactorily accounted for by his. But, apart from the rewriting of the paragraph which this would involve, the suggestion is unacceptable. Consistency, or inconsistency, involves the absence, or presence, of an independent right to occupy, though I must observe that 'inconsistency' in this context is an inappropriate word. But how can either quality be predicated of a wife, simply qua wife? A wife may, and everyone knows this, have rights of her own; particularly, many wives have a share in a matrimonial home. How can it be said that the presence of a wife in the house, as occupier, is consistent or inconsistent with the husband's rights until one knows what rights she has? And if she has rights, why, just because she is a wife (or in the converse case, just because an occupier is the husband), should these rights be denied protection under the paragraph? If one looks beyond the case of husband and wife, the difficulty of all these arguments stands out if one considers the case of a man living with a mistress, or of a man and a woman — or for that matter two persons of the same sex — living in a house in separate or partially shared rooms. Are these cases of apparently consistent occupation, so that the rights of the other person (other than the vendor) can be disregarded? The only solution which is consistent with the Act (section 70(1)(g)) and with common sense is to read the paragraph for what it says. Occupation, existing as a fact, may protect rights if the person in occupation has rights. On this part of the case I have no difficulty in concluding that a spouse, living in a house, has an actual occupation capable of conferring protection, as an overriding interest, upon rights of that spouse.

Lord Wilberforce goes on to consider whether such rights as a spouse has under a trust for sale are capable of recognition as overriding interests. He examines the structure of the Land Registration Act 1925, and reaches the conclusion that such rights are indeed capable of recognition.

Lord Scarman: . . . But the importance of the House's decision is not to be judged solely by its impact on conveyancing or banking, practice. The Court of Appeal recognised the relevance, and stressed the importance, of the social implications of the case. While the technical task faced by the courts, and now facing the House, is the construction to be put upon a sub-clause in a subsection of a conveyancing statute, it is our duty, when tackling it, to give the provision, if we properly can, a meaning which will work for, rather than against, rights conferred by Parliament, or recognised by judicial decision as being necessary for the achievement of social justice. The courts may not, therefore, put aside, as irrelevant, the undoubted fact that if the two wives succeed, the protection of the beneficial interest which English law now recognises that a married woman has in the matrimonial home will be strengthened whereas, if they lose, this interest can be weakened, and even destroyed, by an unscrupulous husband. Nor must the courts flinch when assailed by arguments to the effect that the protection of her interest will create difficulties in banking or conveyancing practice. The difficulties are, I believe, exaggerated; but bankers, and solicitors, exist to provide the service which the public needs. They can — as they have successfully done in the past — adjust their practice, if it be socially required. Nevertheless, the judicial responsibility remains — to interpret the statute truly according to its tenor. The social background is, therefore, to be kept in mind but can be decisive only if the particular statutory provision under review is reasonably capable of the meaning conducive to the special purpose to which I have referred. If it is not, the remedy is to be found not by judicial distortion of the language used by Parliament but in amending legislation.

Fortunately, these appeals call for no judicial ingenuity — let alone distortion. The ordinary meaning of the words used by Parliament meets the needs of social justice.

In *Boland* the land was registered. In *Kingsnorth Trust Ltd v Tizard* [1986] 2 All ER 54, [1986] 1 WLR 783, the court was faced with a case where the disputed property was unregistered title. The question was whether the plaintiff's legal mortgage was subject to the wife's agreed equitable rights in the house. In the course of his judgment the judge said: 'if the purchaser or mortgagee carries out such inspections "as ought reasonably to be made" and does not either find the claimant in occupation or find evidence of that occupation reasonably sufficient to give notice of the occupation, then I am not persuaded that the purchaser or mortgagee is in such circumstances fixed with notice of the claimant's rights'. On the facts, the plaintiffs should have been alerted to make further inquiries, they did not do so, and accordingly they were fixed with notice of her interest.

Questions

(i) In the light of these cases, do you think that there is any substantial difference between the situation of registered land compared with unregistered land?

(ii) Surely not all married women have beneficial interests in the matrimonial home? (See p. 144, above.)

(iii) As a result of the *Boland* decision, it was said that the cost of conveyancing has increased, and new sources of delay and complication have been created (See for instance *Winkworth v Edward Baron Development Co Ltd* [1987] 1 All ER 114, [1986] 1 WLR 1512, HL). Is this a reasonable price to pay for the additional protection accorded to those, especially married women, who have equitable interests in the family home?

(iv) If Mrs Boland had been asked to agree to the charge, in order to secure her husband's business and source of income, do you think that she would have done so? (See *Bristol and West Building Society v Henning* [1985] 2 All ER 606, [1985] 1 WLR 778.)

(v) What would have been the position if the bank had advanced capital moneys to two trustees? (See *City of London Building Society v Flegg* [1988] AC 54, [1987] 3 All ER 435, HL.)

The Law Commission, in their paper, *The Implications of Williams and Glyn's Bank Ltd v Boland* (1982) still considered that registration was the solution, provided that this was accompanied by a requirement for spouses to consent to dispositions *and* the implementation of their earlier co-ownership scheme. This proposal was not widely welcomed. Instead, the Land Registration and Law of Property Bill was introduced in 1985. This Bill would have retained the entitlement to automatic protection enjoyed by spouses who occupied dwelling houses, whilst at the same time removing from others the 'overriding interest' status who would be protected only by notice or caution. Similar provisions were proposed for unregistered land. The Bill was withdrawn owing to lack of parliamentary time when aspects of the Bill proved controversial.

In looking afresh at the whole question, the Law Commission in the *Third Report on Land Registration* (1987) state:

2.6 . . . The ideal of a complete register of title is certainly compatible with the policy of the law for over one hundred and fifty years of both simplifying conveyancing and maintaining the security of property interests on the one hand and the marketability of land on the other. But the longevity of a policy hardly guarantees its acceptability to-day in the light of modern developments affecting land ownership. Plainly no policy should be followed blindly which works against rather than for 'rights conferred by Parliament or recognised by judicial decision, as being necessary for the achievement of social justice'. Put simply, it may be unjust to require that a particular interest be protected by registration on pain of deprivation. Apart from this basic aspect, also militating against the ideal of a complete register are the various matters the nature of which is such that recording them on the register would be 'unnecessary, impractible or undesirable'. Thus there are self-evident difficulties in reproducing in verbal form on the register rights which are acquired or arise without any express grant or other provision in writing. Again some rights may seem so transient as to be not worth the trouble of recording. Beyond this, other rights may be so readily discoverable by any purchaser without recourse to the register that no greater protection would be conferred by recording them. Similarly, perhaps, there is clearly common-sense behind the general rule relieving the registrar from the necessity of entering on the register notice of any liability, right, or interest appearing to him to be 'of a trivial or obvious character, or the entry of which on the register is likely to cause confusion or inconvenience'. In addition, requiring an entry on the register to protect a right or interest otherwise accepted and exercised may be to provoke litigation unnecessarily soon: neighbours as well as spouses may see a notice or caution as a hostile act. Finally to be borne fully in mind is the point that, as the law now stands, any reduction in the list of overriding interests inevitably involves a corresponding increase in the number of potential claims for indemnity (these provisions are not at present available where losses are in respect of overriding interests). These considerations persuade us to adopt two principles, with the first being subject to the second: (1) 'in the interests of certainty and of simplifying conveyancing, the class of right which may bind a purchaser otherwise than as the result of an entry in the register should be as narrow as possible' *but* (2) interests should be overriding where protection against purchasers is needed, yet it is either not reasonable to expect or not sensible to require any entry on the register. Thus far the welfare of the conveyancer, or rather his client, is our first but not our paramount consideration. However, particularly perturbed by thoughts of honest and careful purchasers suffering losses because of principle (2), we will proceed to propose that the ordinary indemnity provisions should become available for claims occasioned by overriding interests. . . .

Principle (2) deals with the implication of *Williams and Glyn's Bank v Boland*. The Law Commission (1987) then go on to propose that in order to protect the 'honest and careful purchaser' who could suffer loss as a result of principle (2), the ordinary indemnity provisions should become available for claims occasioned by overriding interests.

2.12 However various further arguments for an extension of the indemnity provisions to cover losses suffered by reason of overriding interests themselves may be urged. To begin with, as a matter of long-standing policy, registration of title is rapidly being made compulsory for the whole of England and Wales in the public interest. But the public interest being pursued here is undoubtedly that of providing quicker and cheaper conveyancing with particular reference to house transfer. Achievement of this interest would certainly be facilitated by the abolition of overriding interests, but as a matter of conflicting policy it has been decided that the system should remain subject to these. In other words, the ideal of a complete register could have been imposed in the interests of purchasers, but instead certain third party interests are, many think rightly, to be protected as paramount. This being so, as second best to the complete protection of purchasers, the machinery of registered conveyancing ought to be oiled by means of a 'state guarantee' of title. A precedent for the provision of compensation out of public funds as a just solution for a defective system established by Act of Parliament may be seen in relation to land charges registered against pre-root estate owners. In our opinion there is no good reason why indemnity should be completely precluded, all other matters being equal, when an overriding interest is asserted against a registered proprietor. The availability of indemnity, will, we believe, go some way to enabling an acceptable balance to be achieved between competing innocent interests.

Questions

(i) Do you consider that this proposal will solve the problems?
(ii) If practitioners have now come to terms with the implications of the *Boland* decision, why worry?
(iii) The Law Commission take the ascertainment of beneficial interests a stage further in *Matrimonial Property* (1988) (see p. 171, below). The Law Commission exclude land and hence the matrimonial home. Should they have done?

The Law Commission propose that the co-ownership principle should be extended to the rented sector. Local authorities increasingly use joint tenancy agreements in the case of husband and wife. If the tenancy is a joint one, the Housing Act 1985 provides that in general the tenancy is 'secure' so long as at least one of them occupies the dwelling house as his or her only or principal home (s. 81). The two major components of secure tenancies are the right of succession on the death of the first tenant and the security from eviction. Whether the tenancy is sole or joint, there is provision for only *one* succession on the death of the first tenant. Succession will be in favour, first of the tenant's spouse provided that that person 'occupied the dwelling house as his only or principal home at the time of the tenant's death,' or secondly, failing this, of any other member of the tenant's family who has resided with the tenant throughout the period of 12 months ending with the tenant's death. The other major element of the security of tenure conferred by the Housing Act 1985 relates to the circumstances in which possession of a dwelling house let on a secure tenancy may be recovered. A landlord cannot get possession from a secure tenant without a court order and the court cannot make such an order except on the grounds specified in detail in Sch. 2 to the Housing Act 1985. These include non payment of rent, deterioration in the condition of the dwelling house, nuisance or annoyance and so on.

Questions

(i) It is often argued that joint tenancies have a psychological effect. However, where there is a joint tenancy, each partner is jointly and severally liable for the rent even if the arrears were due purely to the 'fault' of one of them. Is this too high a price to pay for the alleged psychological advantage of joint tenancies?

(ii) Why restrict rights of succession to one?

(iii) If the husband dies in 1991 and the wife dies in 1992, what then happens to the children?

(iv) Is the position of the children in (iii) the same under the scheme for succession to a Rent Act 1977 tenancy? (See p. 362, below.)

(v) The power of the local authority to transfer a tenancy agreement on its own initiative is no longer available in the case of secure tenancies. Do you think that this is an unfortunate restriction of the local authority's powers? [In Scotland, the Tenants' Rights, Etc. (Scotland) Act 1980 allowed authorities to apply for termination of tenancies on marital breakdown. The Matrimonial Homes (Family Protection) (Scotland) Act 1981 repealed this provision.]

(vi) How, if at all, can a local authority remove a person's tenancy rights after serious domestic violence? (See further Chapter 9, below. Read *Greenwich London Borough Council v McGrady* (1982) 81 LGR 288, 6 HLR 36, CA and *Hammersmith and Fulham London Borough Council v Monk* (1990) Times, 5 November, CA; see p. 51, above.)

(c) THE FAMILY ASSETS OTHER THAN THE MATRIMONIAL HOME

Professor Sir Otto Kahn-Freund was a strong advocate of an introduction of 'community' in the family assets, and we quote the following extracts from his Unger Memorial Lecture (1971):

What I suggest is a general rule that such assets as form the matrimonial aggregate, — 'family assets', — should, in the absence of special circumstances, be shared by the spouses half and half. The special circumstances would have to be found by the court in the light of the facts of the case. It is here that the court should have a wide discretion, especially in assessing the significance in each case of various conflicting considerations. Some of the considerations enumerated in section 5 of the Matrimonial Proceedings and Property Act 1970 [now s. 25(1) of the Matrimonial Causes Act 1973 as amended; see Chapter 7, below] would be relevant, including above all, the value of pensions expectations which either spouse, — in most cases the wife, — stands to lose as a result of the termination of a marriage. Occasionally the court may also have to assess the value of the contributions made by either spouse to the welfare of the family, 'including any contribution made by looking after the home and caring for the family'. But this should only be done in exceptional cases, — and normally the value of the contributions should be deemed to be equal. . . .

But, of course, this leaves us with two fundamental problems: how should the assets which make up the aggregate be identified? And, equally important, is all this to affect the spouses themselves only, or also third parties?

Kahn-Freund answers his first question in the following manner;

I should identify the assets which are to constitute the aggregate not by reason of how, when, by whom and with whose resources they were acquired. My criterion of selection would not be their origin, but their purpose. My question would not be whether they have been acquired before or during the marriage, or acquired through work or thrift or through inheritance or gift. I should ask: what object are they intended to serve? Are they assets for investment, acquired and held for the income they produce or the profit they may yield on resale? Or are they household assets, family assets, which form the basis of the life of husband, wife and children?

Kahn-Freund rejects historical examples of 'family assets' which in his view 'belong to the dustheap of history'. There were three motivations in former times for introducing community schemes into continental Europe:

The first was to protect the wife who was assumed to be incapable of defending her property and of managing her affairs. The second was to protect the widow or the widower against the next of kin of the predeceasing spouse. The third was to provide capital for the husband's enterprise.

Kahn-Freund says of the first reason, 'to us the assumption that women are incapable of defending their property and are in need of tutelage looks absurd'. Kahn-Freund continues:

An asset is a family asset if, at any given time it is by consent of the spouses, dedicated to the common use of the household family, irrespective of whether it was acquired before or after the marriage, or through the spouses' work or thrift or through inheritance or gift. It comprises the family home and its contents (furniture and equipment), but also a family car and other implements intended to be enjoyed by the family. It also includes such funds, however invested, as are, by the spouses' consent, at any given moment dedicated to future family expenditure, including expenditure for the benefit of a child of the family, or as have been saved by either spouse without the knowledge of the other and been dedicated by him for future family expenditure. In the absence of proof to the contrary any house or flat used as a matrimonial home is presumed to be a family asset, and so are all chattels in common use. No other asset belonging to either spouse is presumed to be a family asset.

The major problem relating to family assets is whether any principle of co-ownership should affect third parties. The Law Commission, possibly aware of this difficulty, state that in their view the primary consideration should be to devise a scheme which protects the 'occupation rights' of the spouses (see p. 48, above). In the First Report (1973), they say:

. . . It is more important at this stage to protect the use and enjoyment of those goods than to change the ownership rules. The reason for this is that such goods usually have a rapidly diminishing realisable value; in most cases a spouse's share in the proceeds of sale of second-hand furniture would not go far towards the cost of its replacement (save in the case of antiques). Because of this a spouse's main concern is to retain the use and enjoyment of the goods and we propose that the spouse in occupation of the home should have this right. This would be essentially a support right supplementing the rights of occupation which are protected under the Matrimonial Homes Act 1967 [now 1983].

However, the Law Commission's Working Paper, *Transfer of Money Between Spouses* (1985) recommends more extensive reform:

5.5 *Money or property acquired with it* Property acquired with the money should be co-owned in the same way as the money iself is co-owned. Property acquired with the money in effect represents the money and it would be illogical not to extend co-ownership so far. The effect would therefore be to impose co-ownership on some household goods of married couples, and in some cases on the matrimonial home, . . . Where chattels are concerned we provisionally recommend that, if acquired with money made available for a purpose within the provision and that, of course, would include money made available to buy the chattel itself if it is a joint one, they should be jointly owned at law, and not merely in equity. There are no special formalities required to create legal interests in chattels and we do not think there is any difficulty in creating legal co-ownership by statute. If a spouse were to acquire an interest in equity only, this would introduce a trust, and this seems to us an unnecessary complication. However, where land is concerned legal title can only be conferred by deed (and where title is registered, by registration) and it would be difficult to confer legal title by statute. Where land is concerned we therefore suggest that any title acquired as a result of this proposal should be equitable only. . . .

5.6 *The transfer*　We have been using the word 'transfer'. This may be unduly restrictive and we would suggest the phrase 'made available' which would cover a wide range of circumstances, as for example where a spouse is permitted to draw on the other spouse's bank account. It would also enable the proposal to cover the arrangements some couples adopt whereby they create a notional pool of their resources. In other words they do not pay money into a joint bank account but each pays for separate items, for example one may pay the mortgage and fuel bills while the other buys food and saves for their holiday. Where both spouses use their income for joint purposes in this way we would suggest that all the money so used should be considered to be made available for joint purposes.

Their original proposal, the reaction to it by those who responded to the Working Paper, and their further thoughts are summarised in the Second Consultation Paper (1986):

1.1 The major reform suggested by the working paper was that, rather than co-ownership applying to savings from a housekeeping allowance as at present, all money transferred by one spouse to another for common purposes should be jointly owned. There was substantial support for this suggestion. However, the underlying objective of the reform was to produce co-ownership in all cases where there is good reason to suppose that this was what was in fact intended, or would have been if the parties had addressed their minds to it at the time, and to do so irrespective of whether the correct formalities for achieving this under the present law had been adopted. In the light of that objective, we now incline to the view that in one respect our provisional proposals may have been too wide, whereas in another they may have been too narrow. . . .

1.2 Our provisional proposals may have been too wide in that we considered that joint ownership should apply unless the spouses had both agreed otherwise. It was not our idea, nor would it command significant support, to impose joint ownership on the reluctant. To insist on a contrary agreement would do this, as the providing spouse would have to ask for an agreement and might be hesitant to ask or unaware of the need to do so. We therefore now envisage that joint ownership will not apply where either spouse can prove that he or she did not intend it. Usually, of course, it will be the providing spouse who will want to prove this but occasionally the other spouse may be unwilling to become a joint owner of the property or money concerned.

1.3 We believe that this modification of our original proposals is essential if any significant widening of the scope of the Married Women's Property Act 1964 is to be acceptable. However, in respect of the savings from a house-keeping allowance which are now covered by that Act, the scope would be somewhat narrowed, as the act at present requires a contrary agreement if co-ownership is not to arise. . . .

1.4 Our original proposals may, however, have been too narrow in that they were confined to the transfer of money from one spouse to the other and to the purchase of property with that money. As we have said, there was substantial support for the proposition that money transferred for common purposes should (in the absence, as we now propose, of a contrary intention by the transferor) be jointly owned. However, we were anxious not to exclude couples who organise their finances for common purposes but do so without any transfer, e.g. where one pays for their accommodation while the other shops for food and cleaning materials. The concept of the 'notional pool' had been developed by the courts as one means of identifying contributions to the purchase of a matrimonial home and seemed capable of application in this context too. Once again, there was considerable support for our suggestion that such circumstances should be covered.

1.5 One means of doing so would be to provide that where both parties spend money for common purposes, the whole shall be treated as jointly owned. On further consideration, however, this seems somewhat arbitrary in its operation. It would give rise to full joint ownership, where one spouse had spent only a tiny amount on common purposes, while the other had spent a great deal, but not where one spouse had spent nothing at all. It would be difficult to identify a time-scale within which the expenditure of one spouse could or could not be treated as a contribution to the notional pool with the expenditure of the other. It would also be difficult to distinguish those who had operated their finances separately by choice, and with the intention of retaining individual ownership, and those who had operated separately by chance or for convenience but with the intention of pooling their resources.

1.6 The crux of the matter remains, in our view, not the way in which the parties have organised their finances, but the purposes to which that finance has been put. Consultation confirmed our impression that, in the united households with which we are concerned, a prima facie rule that money spent or set aside for common purposes results in joint ownership will in most cases produce the effect which the parties in fact intended, or would have intended if they had thought about it at the time (it is, of course, common for married couples to give no thought to legal ownership when acquiring property for their joint use or benefit). In combination with our present suggestion that the provider of the money should be able to show a contrary intention, therefore, such a rule would be just.

Similar observations were made by Todd and Jones (1972):

We asked the wives whether they had contributed to the major items of matrimonial property and if so by what means. Among the couples who owned the home 79% of wives said they had contributed to it; among the couples who owned cars 57% said they have contributed to it; 85% of wives said they had contributed to the furniture and 76% said they had contributed to big items such as the cooker, refrigerator, washing machine etc. We suggested five possible means of contributing and asked each wife who had contributed which methods she had used. In terms of the home and contents over two thirds of those who had contributed said they did so from earnings during marriage, about a half said that their effort in the home had been a contribution, and a quarter to a third said that savings from before marriage had been used for the house or furniture.

Thus a large proportion of wives felt that they have contributed to the matrimonial property, and a considerable number considered that their effort in the home had been a contribution.

Questions

(i) Does this constitute evidence in support of co-ownership for major household goods?

(ii) What do you do with those spouses who think that they have made no contribution? Would they be entitled to automatic co-ownership rights as well?

And then comes the Law Commission Report on *Matrimonial Property* (1988) (see Chapter 3, above). They reviewed their earlier work:

1.4 There were two consistent themes running through all the Commission's earlier work. The first was the persistent observation that the present rules for determining the ownership of property during marriage were arbitrary, uncertain and unfair. The second was that the ownership of property while a marriage continues is important and that it is not right to consider marital property only in relation to what happens when a marriage ends. There are those who have said, and no doubt will continue to say, that since English law now provides for the discretionary re-allocation of property between spouses on various events, for example death or divorce, the precise detail of the ownership of property during marriage does not matter. It has also been said that in their attitudes to, and arrangements for, ownership of their property, married couples vary so greatly that it is impossible to generalise about the way in which such property would or should be regarded. If the parties did give thought to the ownership of property which they acquired for their joint use and benefit, they would not do so on any consistent or common basis. We cannot, however, accept these arguments, for the following main reasons:

    (i) To a partner who is the sole or main wage earner in the family, the present rules for determining ownership may seem as unimportant during the marriage as they are important when the marriage has broken down; to the partner who has no separate income, on the other hand, they may appear as unfair during the marriage as they do when it ends. Respondents to our Working Paper who represented the latter were unanimously of this view. . . .

(ii) It is a false dichotomy to split marriages into the happy and the unhappy, and to say that while the couple are happy, property ownership does not matter and that, if they are not, they will get divorced and that the court will reallocate the property. Most marriages do not end in divorce. There may be occasions during a marriage when knowledge of who owns what property is important to either or both spouses. We believe that a law which aims to reduce uncertainty and to reflect the intentions of both parties is more likely to further stability in the relationship of marriage than one which does not.

(iii) Although it is undoubtedly true that the attitude of the spouses to family property will vary enormously and will depend upon individual expectations, nevertheless the law already provides an extensive body of rules affecting the property rights of the spouses. Changes in the principles upon which these rules are based will not alter the fact that the law finds it necessary to make provision for such rules, which are just as much an intrusion into the private lives of the parties whether they are made by Parliament or by judges.

(iv) It is clear that in some cases property rights during marriage are important when either spouse becomes bankrupt or dies. Even when the court has to reallocate property on divorce, rules which have become common knowledge and which clarify the ownership of property acquired for joint use and benefit during the marriage could provide a more satisfactory basis for reallocation and could reduce the arguments, acrimony and delay in reaching a settlement of property rights.

With one amendment, the proposal of the Second Consultation Paper (1986) is followed (see p. 170, above). The amendment is contained in square brackets.

39 . . . where money is paid by either spouse to the other or to buy property and the payment or purchase is for common purposes, the money or property will be jointly owned, subject to a contrary intention on the part of [the purchasing spouse known to the other spouse].
. . . To expand a little, the purchase of property for common purposes would give rise to joint ownership, even though there had been no transfer of money to the other spouse and no expenditure on common purposes by the other spouse. This avoids the likely difficulties of the 'notional pool'. It might be thought that it would go too far and produce more joint ownership than is warranted. However, it would give way to a contrary intention which need not be communicated to the other spouse, so a spouse who wishes to retain sole ownership can do so. The main effect would be to produce co-ownership in household assets even though there was no thought given to it at the time and/or the formalities technically required for a transfer to the other spouse (such as delivery of goods or a declaration of trust) had not been complied with. It might be thought that this proposal alone is sufficient. However, it makes no provision for ownership of money that is not spent, ... Hence we would retain the idea of making money paid by one spouse to the other for common purposes into jointly owned money.

However, the Law Commission does not speak with one voice on the question.

B. Davenport QC: I do not share the view of my colleagues that to give effect to the policy expressed in this report by enactment of the draft Bill in Appendix A would bring about an improvement in English Law. Some of my principal reasons are, in summary, as follows:-
   (a) Apart from making technical changes to the Married Women's Property Act 1964 [see p. 89, above], I am not persuaded that there is any real need for reform in that area of the law. The reform suggested is as likely to lead to matrimonial quarrelling as to matrimonial concord.
   (b) Having regard to the almost infinite variety in relations between husbands and wives, the law should be very cautious before imposing any statutory regime of property rights upon them. The policy recommended in this report . . . is to provide a series of rules which are intended positively to lay down when property is to be jointly owned. These rules are, I consider, too inflexible to be applied satisfactorily to every marriage. Indeed, it is not difficult to think of situations where an application of the rules can lead to consequences which many might regard as unjust.
   (c) Assumptions made about household goods, generally of limited value, cannot safely be extrapolated to motor vehicles or to securities (both of which are excluded from the

Scottish Act [see below]). The title to both vehicles and securities is likely to pass from person to person and claims for damages for wrongful interference or conversion by a spouse who had not consented to the sale would seem an almost inevitable consequence of giving effect to the draft Bill. Indeed, the sale of "family" motor vehicles might become significantly more difficult, as might the sale of securities, unless special protection is given to *bona fide* purchasers.

Questions

(i) What situations can you think of which might lead to unjust consequences?

(ii) Who do you agree with — Mr Davenport or his colleagues?

(iii) The Law Commission decided to exclude life insurance policies and to include motor cars. Why?

(iv) The Family Law (Scotland) Act 1985, s. 25 states:

Presumption of equal shares in household goods

25. — (1) If any question arises (whether during or after a marriage) as to the respective rights of ownership of the parties to a marriage in any household goods obtained in prospect of or during the marriage other than by gift or succession from a third party, it shall be presumed, unless the contrary is proved, that each has a right to an equal share in the goods in question.

(2) For the purposes of subsection (1) above, the contrary shall not be treated as proved by reason only that while the parties were married and living together the goods in question were purchased from a third party by either party alone or by both in unequal shares.

(3) In this section 'household goods' means any goods (including decorative or ornamental goods) kept or used at any time during the marriage in any matrimonial home for the joint domestic purposes of the parties to the marriage, other than —

(*a*) money or securities;

(*b*) any motor car, caravan or other road vehicle;

(*c*) any domestic animal.

What about the pet Labrador? The Scottish Law Commission suspect that animals would often be regarded by the spouses as belonging fairly definitely to one of them. Are they right?

4 Rights of inheritance

(a) FIXED SHARE FOR THE SURVIVING SPOUSE?

In their Working Paper (1971) the Law Commission discuss a system of inheritance under which a surviving spouse would be entitled as of right to a fixed proportion of the estate of the deceased spouse whether he died intestate or testate and regardless of the terms of the will:

0.37 Such a system is to be distinguished from community of property and from the right to apply for family provision. Although theoretically it could co-exist with 'community', it would be a needless complication in a law which recognised and enforced a genuine community of property; accordingly we discuss it as an alternative or substitute for 'community'. It differs from the law of family provision in that an order for family provision is discretionary [see p. 175, below], and the amount of the order is assessed having regard to the means, needs and conduct of the applicant. A legal right of inheritance would be a property right in no way dependent upon the means, needs and conduct of the surviving spouse, all of which factors would be irrelevant. The system put forward for consideration is comparable with systems in certain other countries, including Scotland.

0.38. If any system of legal rights of inheritance were introduced, various questions would have to be answered. Chief of these is whether the system should replace the present law of family provision for a surviving spouse, or whether it should be in addition to that law. Provisionally we favour the latter view.

0.39. Other questions which arise are: —

    (a) what minimum amount or proportion of the estate should go, *as of right*, to the survivor,

    (b) whether a spouse should be able to waive a right of inheritance,

    (c) whether, and if so, how benefits received from the deceased during his life should be taken into account,

    (d) how to deal with dispositions made by the deceased with the intention of defeating rights of inheritance,

    (e) the relationship between rights of inheritance and the intestacy rules,

    (f) whether children should enjoy rights of inheritance.

0.40 We make a number of tentative suggestions as to the way in which these questions might be answered. For instance, we reach the provisional view that children should not have a legal right of inheritance; we suggest £2,000 or one-third of the estate (whichever is the greater) for the surviving spouse; and we indicate that it may be better not to complicate the law by seeking a solution within a system of rights of inheritance of the problems of benefits received or dispositions made during the lifetime of the deceased. The appropriate context in which to consider these problems may well be that of family provision, where the courts will continue to have a discretion to set aside dispositions and to make such financial orders as are considered necessary for the support of the survivor.

0.41. A legal right of inheritance would accrue to a spouse only on the death of the other: thus it could not touch their property rights while both were alive, and would not be available to a spouse on divorce, separation, or nullity (though its loss as a result of divorce, nullity or judicial separation would, like the loss of a pension right, be considered by the court awarding maintenance). These limitations are in contrast with a system of community of property, . . . which would operate during joint lives and would be available to the spouses, however their marriage ended. While 'community' has the advantage that its rights do not depend upon death, a system of rights of inheritance is less complicated and involves less interference with existing property law. In the great majority of cases — i.e. those in which a spouse makes adequate provision for his widow, or is content to leave the distribution of his estate to the rules governing an intestacy — there would be no need to invoke the law: a genuine disadvantage of 'community' is that it presents all spouses with a complicated legal situation that more often than not requires legal advice to handle successfully.

Question

Would this raise problems similar to those of common law dower?

The Working Paper itself drew attention to a major disadvantage of fixed rights of inheritance:

4.71 A system of legal rights would be an imprecise way of protecting the survivor's interest in the family assets. It would take no account of the fact that the bulk of the family assets might already be vested in the survivor: the survivor's assets would be irrelevant unless derived from the deceased. It would not be limited to that part of the deceased's estate which could properly be regarded as family assets, and since it would operate only on death it would create a distinction between property rights on divorce and those on death.

Legal rights of inheritance are seldom of significance when a spouse dies intestate. Under the present law, the surviving spouse inherits personal chattels, a statutory legacy of £75,000 of the estate and a life interest in half of any residue where there are children; or the personal chattels, a statutory legacy of £125,000 plus half the balance where there are no children but other close relatives. In other cases, the surviving spouse inherits the whole estate.[3]

Thus fixed shares are significant only when a testator fails to make adequate provision for a surviving spouse. In those circumstance, is it better for a fixed share or should there be legislation which enables a court to order provision to be taken out of the estate?

The Working Paper dealt with the issue as follows:

4.65 Both legal rights of inheritance and family provision law are designed to take care of the case where a deceased has accidentally or deliberately failed to make adequate provision for the surviving spouse. What is adequate would be decided in the case of legal rights by a fixed rule, and in the case of family provision by a court exercising its discretion in the light of all the circumstances. Legal rights would have the advantage of establishing a fixed standard capable of application without resort to the court: family provision enables the court to do justice in the light of the actual circumstances of the estate and the survivor.

Questions

(i) Are you not concerned that money could go to the unmeritorious survivor?

(ii) It is really fair that children of former marriages could end up inheriting none of what was originally their parent's property?

(iii) How far is the Inheritance (Provision for Family and Dependants) Act 1975 a solution (see p. 176, below)?

The First Report (1973) noted the lack of support for the principle of legal rights of inheritance for a surviving spouse:

38. In the light of all the comments and views received we have considered again the principle of fixed legal rights of inheritance for a surviving spouse and its relation to family provision law. If one were starting from the position as it was in England before the introduction of family provision law [in 1939], it would be necessary to consider the best means of protecting the interests of the family of a deceased person and to weigh up the relative advantages and disadvantages of an automatic system of legal rights and a discretionary system of family provision operating through an application to the court. However, as the Working Paper suggested, and as the results of our consultation confirm, the issue now is whether it is necessary to supplement or reinforce family provision law by a system of legal rights.

39. Under family provision law the court can, in the exercise of its discretion, take into account the means and needs of all the parties concerned.

The Law Commission recommend substantial improvements to the family provision legislation. They rejected the introduction of a principle under which the surviving spouse would have a *legal* right to inherit part of the estate of the deceased spouse.

(b) FAMILY PROVISION

Writing in 1974, Miller said that 'the aim of the present law of family provision is to ensure that reasonable provision is made for the *maintenance* of certain dependants of the deceased. It is not designed to enable members of

---

3. In the Law Commission's Report *Distribution on Intestacy* (1989), the recommendation is that on intestacy, a surviving spouse should always receive the whole estate.

the deceased's family to acquire a share in his estate without reference to their need for support, or in other words, dependency.'

The Law Commission at first advanced the belief that maintenance should remain as the governing factor. However, they subsequently had second thoughts and, so far as the wife is concerned, in their First Report (1973) recommended a change in objective:

41. At present, the aim, as expressed in the legislation, is to secure reasonable provision for the *maintenance* of the deceased's dependants, and this is clearly narrower in concept than the provision of a fair share (although in any particular case it may amount to much the same thing). 'Maintenance' is no longer the principal consideration in fixing the amount of financial provision for a spouse on divorce, and we have come to the conclusion that it would be anomalous to retain it as the main objective in determining family provision for a surviving spouse.

The recommendations of the Law Commission were enacted in the Inheritance (Provision for Family and Dependants) Act 1975:

1. Application for financial provision from deceased's estate
(1) Where after the commencement of this Act a person dies domiciled in England and Wales and is survived by any of the following persons: —
    (*a*) the wife or husband of the deceased;
    (*b*) a former wife or former husband of the deceased who has not remarried;
    (*c*) a child of the deceased;
    (*d*) any person (not being a child of the deceased) who, in the case of any marriage to which the deceased was at any time a party, was treated by the deceased as a child of the family in relation to that marriage;
    (*e*) any person (not being a person included in the foregoing paragraphs of this subsection) who immediately before the death of the deceased was being maintained, either wholly or partly, by the deceased;
that person may apply to the court for an order under section 2 of this Act on the ground that the disposition of the deceased's estate effected by his will or the law relating to intestacy, or the combination of his will and that law, is not such as to make reasonable financial provision for the applicant.
(2) In this Act 'reasonable financial provision'—
    (*a*) in the case of an application made by virtue of subsection (1)(*a*) above by the husband or wife of the deceased (except where the marriage with the deceased was the subject of a decree of judicial separation and at the date of death the decree was in force and the separation was continuing), means such financial provision as it would be reasonable in all the circumstances of the case for a husband or wife to receive, whether or not that provision is required for his or her maintenance;
    (*b*) in the case of any other application made by virtue of subsection (1) above, means such financial provision as it would be reasonable in all the circumstances of the case for the applicant to receive for his maintenance.
(3) For the purposes of subsection (1)(*e*) above, a person shall be treated as being maintained by the deceased, either wholly or partly, as the case may be, if the deceased, otherwise than for full valuable consideration, was making a substantial contribution in money or money's worth towards the reasonable needs of that person.

2. Powers of court to make orders
(1) Subject to the provisions of this Act, where an application is made for an order under this section, the court may, if it is satisfied that the disposition of the deceased's estate effected by his will or the law relating to intestacy, or the combination of his will and that law, is not such as to make reasonable financial provision for the applicant, make any one or more of the following orders: —
    (*a*) an order for the making to the applicant out of the net estate of the deceased of such periodical payments and for such term as may be specified in the order;
    (*b*) an order for the payment to the applicant out of that estate of a lump sum of such amount as may be so specified;
    (*c*) an order for the transfer to the applicant of such property comprised in that estate as may be so specified;

(*d*) an order for the settlement for the benefit of the applicant of such property comprised in that estate as may be so specified;

(*e*) an order for the acquisition out of property comprised in that estate of such property as may be so specified and for the transfer of the property so acquired to the applicant or for the settlement thereof for his benefit;

(*f*) an order varying any ante-nuptial or post-nuptial settlement (including such a settlement made by will) made on the parties to a marriage to which the deceased was one of the parties, the variation being for the benefit of the surviving party to that marriage, or any child of that marriage, or any person who was treated by the deceased as a child of the family in relation to that marriage.

(2) An order under subsection (1)(*a*) above providing for the making out of the net estate of the deceased of periodical payments may provide for—

(*a*) payments of such amount as may be specified in the order,

(*b*) payments equal to the whole of the income of the net estate or of such portion thereof as may be so specified,

(*c*) payments equal to the whole of the income of such part of the net estate as the court may direct to be set aside or appropriated for the making out of the income thereof of payments under this section,

or may provide for the amount of the payments or any of them to be determined in any other way the court thinks fit.

(3) Where an order under subsection (1)(*a*) above provides for the making of payments of an amount specified in the order, the order may direct that such part of the net estate as may be so specified shall be set aside or appropriated for the making out of the income thereof those payments; but no larger part of the net estate shall be so set aside or appropriated than is sufficient, at the date of the order, to produce by the income thereof the amount required for the making of those payments.

(4) An order under this section may contain such consequential and supplemental provisions as the court thinks necessary or expedient for the purpose of giving effect to the order or for the purpose of securing that the order operates fairly as between one beneficiary of the estate of the deceased and another and may, in particular, but without prejudice to the generality of this subsection—

(*a*) order any person who holds any property which forms part of the net estate of the deceased to make such payment or transfer such property as may be specified in the order;

(*b*) vary the disposition of the deceased's estate effected by the will or the law relating to intestacy, or by both the will and the law relating to intestacy, in such manner as the court thinks fair and reasonable having regard to the provision of the order and all the circumstances of the case;

(*c*) confer on the trustees of any property which is the subject of an order under this section such powers as appear to the court to be necessary or expedient.

3. Matters to which court is to have regard in exercising powers under s. 2

(1) Where an application is made for an order under section 2 of this Act, the court shall, in determining whether the disposition of the deceased's estate effected by his will or the law relating to intestacy, or the combination of his will and that law, is such as to make reasonable financial provision for the applicant and, if the court considers that reasonable financial provision has not been made, in determining whether and in what manner it shall exercise its powers under that section, have regard to the following matters, that is to say—

(*a*) the financial resources and financial needs which the applicant has or is likely to have in the foreseeable future;

(*b*) the financial resources and financial needs which any other applicant for an order under section 2 of this Act has or is likely to have in the foreseeable future;

(*c*) the financial resources and financial needs which any beneficiary of the estate of the deceased has or is likely to have in the foreseeable future;

(*d*) any obligations and responsibilities which the deceased had towards any applicant for an order under the said section 2 or towards any beneficiary of the estate of the deceased;

(*e*) the size and nature of the net estate of the deceased;

(*f*) any physical or mental disability of any applicant for an order under the said section 2 or any beneficiary of the estate of the deceased;

(*g*) any other matter, including the conduct of the applicant or any other person, which in the circumstances of the case the court may consider relevant.

(2) Without prejudice to the generality of paragraph (*g*) of subsection (1) above, where an application for an order under section 2 of this Act is made by virtue of section 1(1)(*a*) or 1(1)(*b*) of this Act, the court shall, in addition to the matters specifically mentioned in paragraphs (*a*) to (*f*) of that subsection, have regard to —

(*a*) the age of the applicant and the duration of the marriage;

(*b*) the contribution made by the applicant to the welfare of the family of the deceased, including any contribution made by looking after the home or caring for the family;

and, in the case of an application by the wife or husband of the deceased, the court shall also, unless at the date of death a decree of judicial separation was in force and the separation was continuing, have regard to the provision which the applicant might reasonably have expected to receive if on the day on which the deceased died the marriage, instead of being terminated by the death, had been terminated by a decree of divorce.

(3) Without prejudice to the generality of paragraph (*g*) of subsection (1) above, where an application for an order under section 2 of this Act is made by virtue of section 1(1)(*c*) or 1(1)(*d*) of this Act, the court shall, in addition to the matters specifically mentioned in paragraphs (*a*) to (*f*) of that subsection, have regard to the manner in which the applicant was being or in which he might be expected to be educated or trained, and where the application is made by virtue of section 1(1)(*d*) the court shall also have regard —

(*a*) to whether the deceased had assumed any responsibility for the applicant's mainte- nance and, if so, to the extent to which and the basis upon which the deceased assumed that responsibility and to the length of time for which the deceased discharged that responsibility;

(*b*) to whether in assuming and discharging that responsibility the deceased did so knowing that the applicant was not his own child;

(*c*) to the liability of any other person to maintain the applicant.

(4) Without prejudice to the generality of paragraph (*g*) of subsection (1) above, where an application for an order under section 2 of this Act is made by virtue of section 1(1)(*e*) of this Act, the court shall, in addition to the matters specifically mentioned in paragraphs (*a*) to (*f*) of that subsection, have regard to the extent to which and the basis upon which the deceased assumed responsibility for the maintenance of the applicant and to the length of time for which the deceased discharged that responsibility.

(5) In considering the matters to which the court is required to have regard under this section, the court shall take into account the facts as known to the court at the date of the hearing.

(6) In considering the financial resources of any person for the purposes of this section the court shall take into account his earning capacity and in considering the financial needs of any person for the purposes of this section the court shall take into account his financial obligations and responsibilities.

4. Time-limit for application

An application for an order under section 2 of this Act shall not, except with the permission of the court, be made after the end of the period of six months from the date on which represen- tation with respect to the estate of the deceased is first taken out.

Questions

(i) Do you think that orders for periodical payments should cease on the remarriage of a *surviving* spouse?

(ii) Do you think that such orders should cease on the remarriage of a *former* spouse?

Two of the few reported decisions on widows' applications are the following:

Re Besterman, Besterman v Gursin

[1984] Ch 458, [1984] 2 All ER 656, [1984] 3 WLR 280, [1984] FLR 503, [1984] Fam Law 203, Court of Appeal.

Dr Theodore Besterman died in 1976 aged 71. Apparently, he believed he was the reincarnation of Voltaire, and he left most of his £1.3 million fortune to the Taylor Institute at Oxford University so that his life's work, the publishing of Voltaire manuscripts, could continue. He bequeathed to his wife chattels worth £790 and a life interest in war loan stock producing a gross income of £3,500. The widow applied under the 1975 Act for provision out of the estate of the deceased.

The trial judge made an order that the wife receive £259,250 out of the estate. The wife appealed.

The Court of Appeal was more generous to the widow, and the lump sum was increased to £378,000. In giving the judgment of the Court of Appeal, Oliver LJ referred to the fundamental flaw in the trial judge's calculation.

Oliver LJ: He should I think have looked at the position as a whole for the purpose of assessing what a reasonable provision would be in all the circumstances for the widow of a millionaire with no obligations to anyone else, and, indeed, a millionaire who had expressed himself as desirous of making very ample provision for her. What he did in fact, was to start from the position that particularly in the case of a large estate (and I am not quite clear why the size of the estate should be of particular relevance for this purpose) the court should start from the position that the provisions of the will must be upheld except to the extent that they are displaced by the obligation to maintain the widow during her lifetime. It was that which led him to adopt as the basis for his calculation the price of what he considered an adequate annuity and which led him to provide a figure which, for my part, I think was, in all the circumstances of this case, a good deal too low. . . .

In my judgment, therefore, the learned judge misdirected himself and this is, therefore, a case in which it is open to this court to review the exercise of his discretion and to form its own conclusion.

What then is to be done? In the first place, I think that we must give much greater weight than did the learned judge to the provision which the plaintiff might have expected to get if the marriage had ended in divorce. What that is is a matter of speculation, but I would not seriously quarrel with Mr Johnson's suggestion that an overall sum of £350,000 could not be considered excessive. At the same time I do not think that I can accept that because the marriage did not terminate by divorce in fact, therefore and a fortiori, she must be entitled to more – Mr Johnson puts it (perhaps rather arbitrarily) at £100,000 more. As I have pointed out, however odd the result may be, the two Acts are not necessarily directed to achieving the same result and under this Act the overall criterion is what is reasonable.

I also think that the absence, which is inherent in a lump sum order, of an opportunity to return to the court does mean that, in assessing the lump sum, the court must take rather greater account than might otherwise be the case of contingencies and inflation. I accept Mr Johnson's submission that reasonable provision, in the case of a very large estate such as this and a wholly blameless widow who is incapable of supporting herself, should be such as to relieve her of anxiety for the future. I say 'in the case of a very large estate' not because there is any difference in principle but simply because the existence of a large estate makes that which is desirable also practically possible.

. . . Now bearing in mind that the plaintiff is the only person to whom it could be said that the deceased owed any duty to make provision and that he left an estate of about £1.5 million, that is by no means a generous figure. It amounts to a little over one-sixth of the estate and so far as one can judge from those reported cases in the Family Division where very wealthy spouses have been involved it appears to bear very little relation to the provision which she would have been likely to have achieved if the marriage had ended in divorce.

Re Bunning, Bunning v Salmon
[1984] Ch 480, [1984] 3 All ER High Court, Chancery Division

The defendants, amongst others, were the University of Cambridge and the Royal Society for the Protection of Birds, who were the primary beneficiaries of the estate. Mr. Bunning's major interest in his lifetime was animals, and he wished to establish a Fellowship with the object of facilitating investigation into cats and dogs. The applicant was his widow. He had married her in 1963 when she was 34 and he was 56. She left him in 1978 and she never returned. She had helped him considerably in his business activities during the time that the marriage was a going concern. He died in 1982 leaving some £220,000 net in the estate. Vinelot J made an order in favour of the widow of £60,000 (about one quarter of the net estate).
     The judge justified the finding in the following way:

Bearing in mind the considerable contribution made by the wife during the marriage and the disparity in the spouses' ages, I think that the court might well have regarded £36,000 as the appropriate as well as the maximum figure.
     With that in mind, I turn to the question what, in the terms of the Act of 1975, is 'such financial provision as it would be reasonable in all the circumstances of the case' for the wife to receive, whether or not required, for her maintenance. The figure of £36,000 cannot be taken as limiting the provision which it is reasonable for the wife to receive out of the estate. 'Pine Croft' has now been sold. Not only is there now no longer need to provide for the husband, but he has no other dependants for whom to provide. In assessing what is reasonable provision I must bear in mind, on the one hand, the matters specifically mentioned in section 3(2) of the Act of 1975 and, in particular, the fact that the wife is comparatively young and, having regard to the history which I have outlined, entitled to a reasonable degree of financial security during what is likely to be a lengthy widowhood. I must bear in mind, on the other hand, that the husband's assets were built up by his own efforts in large measure before he married. The court should not interfere with his right to dispose of those assets by his will except to the extent necessary to make reasonable provision for the wife.
     Bearing these matters in mind, I have come to the conclusion that the right figure is £60,000. It is impossible to demonstrate by any deductive process that that is the appropriate figure. However, that it is the right figure is, I think, confirmed by the following. First, while I have not calculated the figure of £60,000 as a proportion of the spouses' aggregate resources, the figure of £60,000 will in fact achieve rough equality. If the costs of this application, which I understand are estimated to amount to £26,000, are deducted from the husband's estate but accrued interest is included, the value of the estate is £211,000. Taking the wife's assets at the conservative figure of £95,000 − and it must be borne in mind that some of her assets, such as the contents of the house, are not in fact realisable − the aggregate is £306,000 and one half is £153,000. Secondly, a lump sum of £60,000 is comparable with the life interest in residue which in 1979 the husband himself thought a reasonable provision to make for his wife. Thirdly, a sum of £60,000 will, I think, enable the wife to buy the cottage which she hopes to be able to buy at Hunstanton and provide the income she needs and provide a reserve adequate to provide for exceptional demands and unforeseen contingencies. If she spends another £30,000 in replacing her present house with a more expensive one, and furnishing and decorating it, she will be left with assets, apart from her car and the contents of her house, worth some £60,000, and £60,000 will bring this figure up to £120,000. Assuming a net yield of 4 per cent. after standard rate tax and a reasonably balanced portfolio of investment income, her income, including the state and deferred pensions, will be some £2,000 short of her needs. On the other hand, I would expect her to be able to prefer to earn some money by part-time work. If so, then, while she will have to draw on capital over the next few years, she will only have to do so to a limited extent. In five or ten years time she may wish to purchase an annuity. She would be unwise to do so at her present age. Quotations have been obtained showing that an annuity of £6,165 per annum with a capital content of £1,931, giving a total net income of £4,895 after standard rate tax on the income content would cost £50,000. An annuity increasing at a compound rate of 5 per cent. per annum to take account of inflation at that level, bought at a cost of £50,000, would provide only £2,934 per annum after standard rate tax on the income content. However, in five or ten years time, if the wife feels she no longer wishes to work, the cost of an annuity will be very much less and future rates of inflation may be more easy to predict. A lump sum

of £60,000 will, therefore, put the wife into a position where she can confidently expect to have available the moneys she will then require to maintain a by no means extravagant style of life and be left with a reasonable but not excessive reserve.

Questions

(i) Do you think that the sums awarded in these cases were reasonable?
(ii) Can't a man have a duty to organisations and charities that have been able to illustrate their worth to the testator to such a degree that he wishes to leave the bulk of his estate to them?
(iii) Both these cases concerned wealthy men. Do you think that the yardstick of about one quarter of the estate would be suitable in cases of people with more modest means?
(iv) Only 183 writs were issued under the 1975 Act in 1989. (This is in relation to all claimants.) Why do you think so few actions were brought under this Act?

The policy of the law, so far it applies to former spouses, is well explained by Ormrod LJ in the following case.

Re Fullard, Fullard v King
[1982] Fam 42, [1981] 2 All ER 796, [1981] 3 WLR 743, 125 Sol Jo 747, 11 Fam Law 116, Court of Appeal

The plaintiff was married to the deceased in 1938. They had two children. In 1976 the plaintiff petitioned for divorce and the decree was made absolute on 31 December 1976. At the time of the divorce, the plaintiff had £3,000 in savings plus an old age pension. The deceased had a similar amount. The matrimonial home, valued at £9,000 was in joint names. As part of the divorce settlement, the plaintiff paid the deceased £4,500 in cash and the house was transferred to the wife. The deceased went to share a house with the beneficiary. He died in January 1978. The plaintiff applied for reasonable provision from his estate. The judge dismissed her application and she appealed.

Ormrod LJ: . . . The question is – and it is a simple question to my mind – is it unreasonable, or was it unreasonable, that this man made no financial provision by his will for his former wife? He thought he and the plaintiff had sorted out their financial claims as between each other when they reached the agreement about the house. It is right to say that if the plaintiff had been dissatisfied with that arrangement, she had her remedy. She could have applied to the court for an order and she might have succeeded in getting the whole of the house transferred to her without having to pay anything – or perhaps on payment of very much less. . . .
. . . It seems to me that the number of cases which, since the court acquired its wide powers under the Matrimonial Proceedings and Property Act 1970 to make property adjustments, can now get in within the umbrella of the Inheritance (Provision for Family and Dependants) Act 1975 post divorce must be comparatively few. In the course of argument I suggested one case where a periodical payments order has been going on for a long time and the husband is found to have a reasonable amount of capital in his estate. . . . Mr Reid [for the plaintiff] suggested that there was another possible situation – where a substantial capital fund was unlocked by the death of the deceased, such as insurance or pension policies. Those are cases which could come within the Act of 1975. Apart from those, it seems to me there cannot be many cases which qualify.
Appeal dismissed.

Question

Ormrod LJ referred to two situations where he felt that a successful application could be brought by a former spouse against the estate. Can you think of any others?

In *Re Fullard* [1982] Fam 42, [1981] 2 All ER 796 emphasis was placed on the importance of the post-divorce settlement. Ormrod LJ said, at the end of the judgment, '. . . the responsibility and obligations of a former husband for the maintenance of a former wife are to comply with such orders as the court has made or that the parties may have agreed between themselves. There are certainly no other legal obligations. In these days it might be quite difficult to say that he had a moral obligation — though there may be cases where it could be argued that he had'.

In addition, s. 15(1) of the 1975 has been amended and now states:

(1) On the grant of a decree of divorce, a decree of nullity of marriage or a decree of judicial separation or at any time thereafter the court, if it considers it just to do so, may, on the application of either party to the marriage, order that the other party to the marriage shall not on the death of the applicant be entitled to apply for an order under section 2 of this Act.

Ormrod LJ regards an application under s. 15 as a form of insurance against applications being made under the 1975 Act.

These issues lead us into the discussion of the financial re-allocation and rearrangement after a divorce. We have tried so far as possible to follow the rule that the property rights of the husband and the wife are rights which are capable of being ascertained without awaiting a divorce adjustment. Leaving divorce on one side has, however, to some extent been artificial, if only because many of the circumstances which create the difficulties only arise on marital breakdown. It is therefore to divorce itself that we now turn.

CHAPTER 6

Divorce

'Divorce is an institution only a few weeks later in origin than marriage.'
[Voltaire, quoted in A. Alvarez, (1981).]

An American psychologist, Gerald Alpern in *Rights of Passage* (1982) has
tried to provide a guide to the emotional realities of divorce:

Some divorces are simple happenings, a graceful parting in which two people go off in different
directions to new lives. Other divorces occur so gradually, over so many years, that the divorce
process is not a deeply felt experience. For others, the marriage involved a connection so casual
that a legal divorce is but a formality.

However, the majority of divorces are very powerful experiences which, for many, are
devastating. For most people, divorce necessitates major revisions in life goals, expectations,
and personal identities. People involved in divorce find themselves acting in unfamiliar ways.
They may behave irrationally, become vicious or promiscuous, or suddenly plan to desert loved
children. These unfamiliar actions and feelings are very frightening and cause grave self-doubts
which exacerbate the depression so common to divorcing men and women. The most disorient-
ing experience is the wide mood swings which accompany the vacillating positive and negative
feelings about the divorce. At one moment the person is high on thoughts of being independent,
of being free of a spouse no longer loved. The next moment or day the same person may be
crying, longing for the missing spouse and planning an attempt at reconciliation.

John Cleese and Robin Skynner in *Families and How to Survive Them* (1983)
remind us that we are perhaps asking for trouble by entering into the types
of marriage expected of us in this period of our history:

John Let's start with an easy one . . . Why do people decide to marry each other?
Robin Because they're in love.
John Oh, come on.
Robin No, I'm being serious.
John Well, perhaps, but this falling in love routine is very bizarre. You find perfectly
ordinary, rational people like computer programmers and chartered accountants, and there
they are, happily computing and chartering away, and suddenly they see someone across a
crowded room and think, 'Ah, that person is made for me, so I suppose I'd better spend the
rest of my life with them.' It borders on the occult.
Robin Perhaps you'd have preferred it three hundred years ago when parents arranged all
the marriages for sensible reasons like land and money and social climbing. They all regarded
'falling in love' as the worst possible basis for marriage — a recipe for disaster.
John Yes, Samuel Johnson said that all marriages should be arranged by the Lord Chancellor
without reference to the wishes of the parties involved.
Robin So the point I'm making is that nowadays we are free to marry the person we love, the
one who can really make us happy.
John And of course we have the highest divorce rate in history.
Robin Since you and I have both made a contribution to those statistics, we'd better not sound
too critical.
John I'm sorry if I did. Actually, I think divorce is underrated. It gives you insights into some
of the trickier aspects of marriage, the more delicate nuances as it were, that couples who've

been happy together for thirty years wouldn't begin to grasp. But nevertheless, divorced or not, here we are, millions upon millions of us, all blithely pairing off, thinking, 'This is the one for me.' So what's going on, Doctor?
Robin   What do you think falling in love is about?

We turn our attention first of all to the history of our divorce law up until the major changes of the Divorce Reform Act 1969.

1 The history of English divorce law

We should first ponder on the important words of Lawrence Stone in *Road to Divorce* (1990). It is his view that there does not exist any single model of change which can explain the history of marital breakdown and divorce in a single country for all periods of time and for all classes of society. He writes:

Any historian who claims that either the law has always shaped marital practices or that marital practices have always shaped the law, or that the causes of change were at bottom either legal, or economic and social, or cultural and moral, or intellectual, is offering a simplistic solution which is unsupported by the evidence. History is messier than that.

The Gospel according to St Mark, in Chapter 10, lays the foundation for the Christian view of marriage and divorce which has influenced our law for so long.

2. And the Pharisees came to him, and asked him, Is it lawful for a man to put away his wife? tempting him.
3. And he answered and said unto them, What did Moses command you?
4. And they said, Moses suffered to write a bill of divorcement, and to put her away.
5. And Jesus answered and said unto them, For the hardness of your heart he wrote you this precept.
6. But from the beginning of the creation God made them male and female.
7. For this cause shall a man leave his father and mother, and cleave to his wife.
8. And they twain shall be one flesh: so then they are no more twain, but one flesh.
9. What therefore God hath joined together, let not man put asunder.
10. And in the house his disciples asked him again of the same matter.
11. And he saith unto them, Whosoever shall put away his wife, and marry another, committeth adultery against her.
12. And if a woman shall put away her husband, and be married to another, she committeth adultery.

An almost identical account appears in St Matthew's Gospel (Chapter 19, verses 3 to 9), but with the significant addition of the words 'except it be for fornication' in his version of Mark's verse 11.

A helpful summary of developments up until the second Royal Commission on Divorce (1912) appears in *The History of the Obligation to Maintain*, by Sir Morris Finer and Professor O.R. McGregor, which is Appendix 5 to the Report of the (Finer) Committee on *One-Parent Families* (1974):

The canon law of marriage
1. In medieval times most men, whether of high or low degree, married with the primary object of advancing their interests. For women, marriage was a protective institution. Monogamy did not require, or imply, that people should contract only one marriage in a lifetime, and remarriage was a frequent occurrence in all social groups thereby helping to fill the gaps among the married population which resulted from early deaths. Remarriage protected widows from the dangers of living alone in a violent society as well as feudal superiors from the risk that

unmarried dependants would fail in the full performance of services due from them. Moreover, the medieval laity were motivated by a desire 'to place the satisfaction of the flesh under the shelter of the sacrament'.

2. From the middle of the twelfth century until the Reformation, the law regulating marriage in England was the canon law of the church of Rome administered in courts christian. The canon law was framed in the belief that marriage is a permanent union of the natural order established by God in the creation, and consequently it affirmed that marriage made man and woman one flesh and partook of the nature of a sacrament signifying the unity betwixt Christ and his Church. Medieval christendom regarded marriage as an eternal triangle within which spouses established unbreakable bonds not only with each other but also with God. For this reason, the church maintained that marriage was indissoluble and that no earthly power, not even the Pope himself, could break the bond of a christian marriage. . . .

The canon law of nullity

14. In early English law, church and state recognised divorce *a vinculo matrimonii*. This was a divorce in the full sense. It dissolved the bond of marriage and left the parties free to marry again. The church of Rome, treating marriage as indissoluble, abolished divorce in this sense. Thereafter, the ecclesiastical courts granted in the case of a validly contracted marriage only a more limited form of relief. As against a spouse guilty of adultery, cruelty, heresy or apostasy, they might pass sentence of divorce *a mensa et thoro*. This had the effect of a modern judicial separation. It relieved the spouses of the obligation to live together — to share board and bed — but preserved intact the marriage tie.

5. Yet the practical realities of life in the middle ages demanded a method of legitimate avoidance of the rigours of the doctrine of indissolubility. The church provided such a method by developing an elaborate theory of nullity. It was argued that only a valid, consummated, christian marriage was indissoluble. If an impediment to the validity of a marriage had existed when it was contracted, then that marriage would be held by the ecclesiastical courts never to have taken place at all. Many impediments were soon established; the most important were the degrees of consanguinity and affinity within which marriage was prohibited. Before the Lateran Council of 1215, marriage was forbidden between persons to the seventh degree of blood relationship; afterwards, the prohibition was narrowed to the fourth degree, that is, to third cousins. To the impediments of blood were added those of affinity. Since sexual union made man and woman one flesh, it followed that all the blood kinswomen of a man's wife or even of his mistress, were themselves connected to him by affinity. To the impediments of sexual affinity the church then added yet another series created by the spiritual relationships of god-children. . . . [See further in Chapter 1, above.]

The effect of the Reformation

6. By the time of the Reformation, many reformers were rejecting the canon law of marriage developed by the medieval church. They no longer regarded virginity as superior to marriage; they abandoned sacerdotal celibacy; they urged that marriage should be treated as a civil contract regulated by the state; and they favoured the dissolubility of marriage, although differing as to the grounds on which a divorce *a vinculo* ought to be granted. Nevertheless, the protestant doctrines of divorce, though much discussed in the second half of the sixteenth century, did not become part of the law of the land. On the contrary, by the beginning of the seventeenth century, the new church of England had affirmed its belief in the indissolubility of marriage mitigated only by divorce *a mensa et thoro*. . . . At the same time, it rejected the extravagances of the canon law of nullity. Thus, ironically enough, the principal effect of the Reformation on marriage in England was the sealing up of the loopholes and the rejection of the evasions and absurdities by which the medieval system had been made tolerable in practice. Yet whatever formal respect the rich and powerful accorded to christian theology, they were no more prepared than were their ancestors to tolerate the inconveniences inseparable from a system of rigidly indissoluble marriage. In seventeenth and eighteenth century England, these classes both sustained monogamous marriage and encouraged the accumulation of private property. It was natural, therefore, for them to be more sensitive to the immediate damage which hasty and easily contracted marriages could inflict upon the orderly disposition of family property than to the remoter danger that sexual immorality might imperil their immortal souls. For these reasons, the state broke the exclusive familial jurisdiction of the ecclesiastical courts in two ways. First, it stepped in to regulate and formalise the procedure by which a valid marriage could be contracted. Secondly, it provided a machinery for the dissolution of valid marriages by Act of Parliament. . . .

Parliamentary divorce[1]

13. As the ecclesiastical courts had no power to dissolve a valid marriage *a vinculo* and as the secular courts refused to invade the spiritual jurisdiction, only Parliament could break the indissoluble bond of marriage by intervening in particular cases through the procedure of sovereign legislation. The following Table shows the extent of its interference for this purpose by the passing of private Acts of divorce:

Period							Number	Percentage
Before 1714	...	...	...	...	...	...	10[2]	3
1715–1759	...	...	...	...	...	...	24	8
1760–1779	...	...	...	...	...	...	46	14
1780–1799	...	...	...	...	...	...	53	17
1800–1819	...	...	...	...	...	...	49	15
1820–1839	...	...	...	...	...	...	59	19
1840–1856	...	...	...	...	...	...	76	24
Total	...	...	...	...	...	...	317	100

Source: Adapted from PP 1857, Session 2 (106–I), Volume XLII, page 117.

[The table] shows how rare parliamentary divorces were before the accession of George I and how their use increased steadily thereafter, so that one quarter of all the private Acts were passed in the twenty years before the system was abolished in 1857. Before the eighteenth century the main reason for Parliament's willingness to grant the privilege of marrying again was to continue the succession to peerages in the male line. When the Duke of Norfolk successfully petitioned the House of Lords for his divorce bill of 1700, he stated that his wife had 'made full proof of her adultery' and that he 'hath no issue, nor can have any probable expectation of posterity to succeed him in his honours, dignities, and estate, unless the said marriage be declared void by authority of Parliament. . . .'[3] This soon ceased to be the only circumstance in which Parliament would intervene. Later Acts were passed in favour of professional men (including seventeen clergymen) and people engaged in business; indeed, such folk accounted for half the Acts passed between the middle of the eighteenth century and 1857. Nevertheless, all the promoters had one characteristic in common: they were very wealthy. They had to be, for the cost of a private Act and the related proceedings was formidable.

14. After the adoption of a series of Resolutions framed by Lord Chancellor Loughborough in 1798, the House of Lords imposed a standard procedure upon all applications. Before coming to Parliament a petitioner had first to obtain both a decree of divorce *a mensa et thoro* from the spiritual court, and an award of damages for criminal conversation against the wife's seducer in the secular court. The Resolutions further required that the petitioner should attend the House so that he might if necessary be examined as a witness, with reference both to collusion or connivance and also to another point which was always deemed of primary importance in judging divorce bills: whether at the time of the adultery he was living apart from his wife and had thereby contributed to her offence. . . .

17. This procedure, cumbersome, expensive and intricate as it was, could in practice be utilised only by aggrieved husbands. Only four wives were ever granted Acts and these were all passed in the nineteenth century. The first occurred in 1801. We quote Frederick Clifford's account of Mrs Addison's Act in full, both for its intrinsic interest and to show how, even at the close of the Age of Reason, the House of Lords could still be moved and bemused by arguments based upon the canonists' doctrine of the carnal affinities.

---

1. See also Sybil Wolfram, 'Divorce in England 1700–1857', Oxford Journal of Legal Studies vol. 5 (1984) pp. 155–186, and S. Anderson, 'Legislative Divorce — Law for the Aristocracy' in G. Rubin and D. Sugarman (eds) *Law, Society and Economy. Essays in Legal History* (1984).

2. The case of Lord Roos in 1670 is discussed in detail by Stone (1990). The case, described by Charles II as 'better than a play', apparently gave birth to the famous nursery rhyme 'Mary Mary quite contrary, how does your garden grow . . . pretty maids all in a row' after the alleged succession of extramarital liaisons of his wife Anne. Unlike 'Mary', 'Anne' does not rhyme with 'contrary'!

3. Stone (1990) informs us that Norfolk died in 1701 before he had had time to remarry so that the whole purpose of the Act was frustrated.

'Mr Addison had maintained a criminal intercourse with his wife's sister, a married woman. Her husband, Dr Campbell, obtained a verdict against him with £5,000 damages. Mrs Addison, after obtaining in the Ecclesiastical Court a divorce *a mensa et thoro*, applied to Parliament for a divorce *a vinculo*. Her husband did not appear. Lord Thurlow . . . made a powerful speech for the Bill. Every principle of justice, he said, would be violated by its rejection. But Lord Thurlow did not assert a woman's general right to the same legislative relief as was given to an injured husband. He found his chief defence of the Bill upon the old doctrine of the canonists, that commerce between the sexes creates affinity. In this case, he argued, if Mr Addison had previously had illicit intercourse with her sister, he could not have married his present wife, because such marriage would have been tainted by incest, and might have been pronounced void by an Ecclesiastical Court. A like result occurred by reason of this incestuous adultery. It made reconciliation legally impossible, for, by the affinity it had created, renewed cohabitation between Mr and Mrs Addison would become incestuous.'

Lord Thurlow's subtleties prevailed upon the Lord Chancellor, Lord Eldon, to withdraw his intended opposition to the establishment of this precedent. There is no record of any opposition in the House of Commons, and Mrs Addison obtained her Act. But Parliament held thereafter to the principle that adultery without more by the husband was not a sufficient ground for a wife to obtain an Act. Of the three other instances, in Mrs Turton's case in 1830 the adultery was incestuous; in Mrs Battersby's case in 1840 there was adultery aggravated by cruelty and followed by bigamy for which her husband was transported; and in Mrs Hall's case in 1850 there was also bigamy.

18. Two of the characteristics of the procedure of divorce by private Act of Parliament are now plain. It was so expensive that only the wealthy could avail themselves of it; and within the exclusive social sphere for which the procedure catered, it made a further discrimination between men and women. The discrimination which Parliament maintained between husbands and wives, in respect of the grounds on which it was prepared to dissolve a marriage, was justified in terms of the different effect of their adultery. As Lord Chancellor Cranworth explained to the House of Lords:

'A wife might, without any loss of caste, and possibly with reference to the interests of her children, or even of her husband, condone an act of adultery on the part of the husband but a husband could not condone a similar act on the part of a wife. No one would venture to suggest that a husband could possibly do so, and for this, among other reasons . . . that the adultery of the wife might be the means of palming spurious offspring upon the husband, while the adultery of the husband could have no such effect with regard to the wife.'

R v Hall 1845
(cited by Stone (1990))

Maule J: Prisoner at the bar, you have been convicted before me of what the law regards as a very grave and serious offence: that of going through the marriage ceremony a second time while your wife was still alive. You plead in mitigation of your conduct that she was given to dissipation and drunkenness, that she proved herself a curse to your household while she remained mistress of it, and that she had latterly deserted you; but I am not permitted to recognise any such plea . . . Another of your irrational excuses is that your wife had committed adultery, and so you thought you were relieved from treating her with any further consideration — but you were mistaken. The law in its wisdom points out a means by which you might rid yourself from further association with a woman who had dishonoured you; but you did not think proper to adopt it. I will tell you what that process is. You ought first to have brought an action against your wife's seducer, if you could have discovered him; that might have cost you money, and you say you are a poor working man, but that is not the fault of the law. You would then be obliged to prove by evidence your wife's criminality in a Court of Justice, and thus obtain a verdict with damages against the defendant, who was not unlikely to turn out pauper. But so jealous is the law (which you ought to be aware is the perfection of reason) of the sanctity of the marriage tie, that in accomplishing all this you would only have fulfilled the lighter portion of your duty. You must then have gone, with your verdict in your hand, and petitioned the House of Lords for a divorce. It would cost you perhaps five or six hundred pounds, and you do not seem to be worth as many pence. But it is the boast of the law that it is impartial, and makes no difference between the rich and the poor. The wealthiest man in the kingdom would have had to pay no less than that sum for the same luxury; so that you would have no reason to complain. You would, of course, have to prove your case over again, and at the end of a year, or possibly two, you might obtain a divorce which would enable you legally to do what you have thought proper to do without it. You have thus wilfully rejected the boon the legislature offered you, and it is my duty to pass upon you such a sentence as I think your offence deserves, and that sentence is, that you be imprisoned for one day; and in as much as the present assizes are three days old, the result is that you will be immediately discharged.

Question

As we can see from this sentence on the unfortunate Mr Hall, there was one law for the rich and another law for the poor. Could it be that only the rich needed to divorce? What social changes in the years leading up to 1857 might have made it necessary for others to seek this remedy?

The story is taken up by Sir Morris Finer and Professor O. R. McGregor:

The first Royal (Campbell) Commission on divorce

30. In 1850 a Royal Commission, under the chairmanship of Lord Campbell, was appointed 'to enquire into the present state of the law of divorce'. The commission was an explicit response to the dissatisfaction with the existing law we have been describing: 'the grave objection,' as Lord Chancellor Cranworth explained, 'that such complicated proceedings were too expensive for the pockets of any but the richest sufferers, and that relief was put beyond the reach of all but the wealthiest classes.' It followed, as Lord Campbell himself said, that the object of the commission was not in any way to alter the law, but only the procedure by which the law was carried into effect. The same points were made repeatedly in the debates on the Matrimonial Causes Act 1857, whereby the recommendations of the Campbell Report were given effect. Thus, the Act of 1857 did not, as is sometimes mistakenly thought, introduce divorce into England or discard a hitherto sacred principle of indissolubility of marriage. The Act (apart from some minor innovations) did no more than consolidate and transfer to a civil and more accessible court of law the jurisdictions that were already being respectively exercised by Parliament and the ecclesiastical courts. The only substantial change which it effected was to make more widely available matrimonial remedies which only the very few had until then enjoyed.

The Matrimonial Causes Act 1857

31. The principal provisions of the Act of 1857 were, accordingly, as follows. The matrimonial jurisdiction of the ecclesiastical courts was abolished, but re-created in a new court called 'the Court for Divorce and Matrimonial Causes'. In exercising the transferred jurisdiction, the divorce court was to proceed on the same principles as had guided the ecclesiastical courts. The remedy which those courts had formerly granted under the name of a decree of divorce *a mensa et thoro* was henceforth to be called a decree of judicial separation. The divorce court would also deal with petitions for the dissolution of marriage. A husband could present a petition for divorce on the ground of his wife's adultery; a wife, on the ground of adultery aggravated by some other conduct (such as incestuous adultery, adultery coupled with cruelty or with desertion for two years or upwards) or on the ground of sodomy or bestiality. It is notable that Gladstone, while vigorously opposing the passage of the Act, was equally strong in contending that if it were passed at all it should not discriminate between the sexes:

'It is impossible to do a greater mischief than to begin now, in the middle of the nineteenth century, to undo with regard to womankind that which has already been done on their behalf, by slow degrees, in the preceding eighteen centuries, and to say that the husband shall be authorised to dismiss his wife on grounds for which the wife shall not be authorised to dismiss her husband. If there is one broad and palpable result of Christianity which we ought to regard as precious, it is that it has placed the seal of God Almighty upon the equality of man and woman with respect to everything that relates to these rights.' [See the extract from St Mark's Gospel at the beginning of this chapter.]. . . .

The number of divorces

34. The Act of 1857 opened the door to matrimonial relief for many whom the expense of the earlier procedures had excluded. In the four years following the passing of the Act 781 petitions for divorce and 248 petitions for judicial separation were filed in the new court. On the other hand, the Act, as these figures demonstrate, opened no floodgate. The highest number of

decrees granted in any one year up to 1900 was 583 divorces (in the year 1897) and 57 decrees for judicial separation (in the year 1880). The new jurisdiction was wholly centralised in London, which acted as a deterrent to its employment by those who resided at a distance. Further, although the costs were not so wildly exorbitant as previously, they were still very considerable, and beyond the reach of people of ordinary means. It was not long before the criticisms which had preceded the Act regained currency. . . .

The Second Royal (Gorell) Commission on Divorce
42. In 1909, a Royal Commission was appointed, under the chairmanship of Lord Gorell 'to enquire into the present state of the law of England and the administration thereof in divorce and matrimonial causes and applications for separation orders, especially with regard to the position of the poorer classes in relation thereto.' By this time, while the High Court was dealing every year with some 800 petitions for divorce and judicial separation, the magistrates were dealing with some 15,000 applications for matrimonial orders. [This jurisdiction is discussed in Chapter 3, above.] In the ten years 1897–1906 the magistrates made more than 87,000 separation orders. Almost all of the magistrates' clientele were the poor, whose problems the terms of reference expressly recognised. Indeed, the themes and anxieties which had dominated the discussion in the preceding century, and which the intervening reforms had not laid to rest, continued to be strongly reflected in the evidence given to the commission: discrimination between the sexes; discrimination against the poor. . . . It continues . . . to impress by a quality of vision and humanity which may be illustrated by a passage which refers to the obligation:

> 'to recognise human needs, that divorce is not a disease but a remedy for a disease, that homes are not broken up by a court but by causes to which we have already sufficiently referred, and that the law should be such as would give relief where serious causes intervene, which are generally and properly recognised as leading to the break-up of married life. If a reasonable law, based upon human needs, be adopted, we think that the standard of morality will be raised and regard for the sanctity of marriage increased.'

43. As regards the law of divorce and its administration, the Gorell Report proposed, first, 'that the law should be amended so as to place the two sexes on an equal footing as regards the grounds on which divorce may be obtained'. . . . This recommendation was not followed until 1923. Next, the report proposed the broadening of the grounds on which either spouse might petition for divorce, by adding to adultery the offences of desertion for three years and upwards, cruelty, incurable insanity, habitual drunkenness and imprisonment under commuted death sentence. Extensions on these lines had to wait upon the Matrimonial Causes Act 1937. Thirdly, the Gorell Report recommended a decentralisation of procedure so that the High Court could sit and exercise divorce jurisdiction locally, for the benefit, in particular, of people of small means. It took another committee, in 1946, to produce any effective change in this respect.

The story since then is taken up in the main body of the Finer Report:

Lord Buckmaster's Act in 1923 had put husbands and wives on a footing of formal equality in respect of the grounds of divorce, by making it possible for each to petition against the other on the grounds of simple adultery. But it was not until the legal aid scheme of 1949 compensated wives for their lack of income or low earnings that they won practical equality of access to the court.[4]

The Third Royal (Morton) Commission on Marriage and Divorce
4.30 In 1951, Mrs Eirene White proposed, in a private member's bill, to permit divorce to spouses who had lived apart for seven years: that is to say, divorce which depended on the fact of separation over this period, and did not involve the proof, by one spouse against the other, of the commission of a matrimonial offence. Coming as it did, at the time when legal aid regarded as a social service was replacing help for the poor as a form of professional charity dispensed by lawyers, and the financial bar to the divorce courts was being lifted, Mrs White's bill was seen by its opponents as a measure to open the floodgates. Nevertheless, to the alarm of its opponents, and to the surprise of many of the supporters of the bill, it appeared as though the House might respond favourably. At this juncture, the government offered Mrs White a Greek gift in the shape of a Royal Commission. Mrs White accepted.

---

4. This observation is based upon the respective proportions of husbands and wives who were subsequently legally aided (Gibson and Beer, 1971), but it should be recalled that part of the husband's common law duty to maintain his wife was to give security for her costs in litigation.

4.31 The Report of the Morton Commission in 1956, though divided, was decidedly against change. Reformers had urged that the doctrine of the matrimonial offence was out of step with people's actual behaviour and expectations in marriage, that the law was brought into contempt by the perjury thereby encouraged, and that the result was illicit unions and the birth of illegitimate children. The Church of England was the most influential opponent of change in the matrimonial law. It explained to the Royal Commission that the doctrine of the matrimonial offence was 'entirely in accord with the New Testament', asserted that divorce was 'a very dangerous threat to the family and to the conception of marriage as a lifelong obligation', and upheld its traditional view that, although much individual suffering and hardship might be relieved by making divorce easier to obtain, the damage to the social order must outweigh such benefits. . . .

The pressure for reform
4.32 In 1956, it must have seemed that the Morton Commission and the Church of England had between them put the quietus on divorce law reform for many years to come. But the appearances were deceptive. The report proved to be little more than a ripple on the surface of a tide that was moving strongly in the other direction.

Nevertheless, it was a group set up in the 1960s by the Archbishop of Canterbury (under the chairmanship of the Rt. Rev. R.C. Mortimer, Lord Bishop of Exeter) that cleared the way for major reform. Its report was published in 1966, under the title *Putting Asunder — A Divorce Law for Contemporary Society*. It drew three main conclusions.

First, as Jesus himself had accepted the Mosaic law for those whose 'hardness of heart' made them unable to understand the truth of Jesus' own teaching about life-long fidelity, and today's secular society was full of such people:

17. There is therefore nothing to forbid the Church's recognizing fully the validity of a secular divorce law within the secular sphere. It follows that it is right and proper for the Church to co-operate with the State, and for Christians to co-operate with secular humanists and others who are not Christians, in trying to make the divorce law as equitable and as little harmful to society as it can be made. Since ex hypothesi the State's matrimonial law is not meant to be a translation of the teaching of Jesus into legal terms, but [to] allow properly for that 'hardness of heart' of which Jesus himself took account, the standard by which it is to be judged is certainly not the Church's own canon law and pastoral discipline. . . .
18. The only Christian interests that need to be declared are the protection of the weak and the preservation and strengthening of those elements in the law which favour lasting marriage and stable family life; and these are ends which Christians are by no means alone in thinking socially important. . . .

Secondly, having considered the interpretation of the fault-based grounds; the stratagems to which these put couples who were determined on divorce; and the inconsistency of having some fault and some (like incurable insanity and cases of cruelty for which the respondent could not morally be blamed) no-fault grounds:

45(*f*) . . . We are far from being convinced that the present provisions of the law witness to the sanctity of marriage, or uphold its public repute, in any observable way, or that they are irreplaceable as buttresses of morality, either in the narrower field of matrimonial and sexual relationships, or in the wider field which includes considerations of truth, the sacredness of oaths, and the integrity of professional practice. As a piece of social mechanism the present system has not only cut loose from its moral and juridical foundations: it is, quite simply, inept.

Thirdly, the courts should be empowered, after an enquiry into every case, to recognise in law the fact that a marriage had irretrievably broken down:

55. . . . As we see it, the primary and fundamental question would be: Does the evidence before the court reveal such failure in the matrimonial relationship, or such circumstances adverse to that relationship, that no reasonable probability remains of the spouses again living together as husband and wife for mutual comfort and support? That is in line with Lord Walker's definition of a broken marriage as 'one where the facts and circumstances affecting the lives of the parties adversely to one another are such as to make it improbable that an ordinary husband and wife would ever resume cohabitation' (Morton Report, 1956). The evidence falling to be considered by the court would be all the relevant facts in the history of the marriage, including those acts and circumstances which the existing law treats as grounds for divorce in themselves. The court would then dissolve the marriage if, and only if, having regard to the interests of society as well as of those immediately affected by its decision, it judged it wrong to maintain the legal existence of a relationship that was beyond all probability of existing again in fact.

In the light of what eventually happened, however, one further conclusion reached by the group should be stressed:

69. We may enumerate three principal objections to reducing the principle of breakdown to a verbally formulated 'ground' and introducing it into the existing law cheek by jowl with the 'grounds' defining matrimonial offences.

(a) The mutual incompatibility of the two principles would be glaringly obvious
The existing law is almost entirely based on the assumption that divorce ought to be seen as just relief for an innocent spouse against whom an offence has been committed by the other spouse. If then there were inserted into this law an additional clause enabling a guilty spouse to petition successfully against the will of an innocent, the whole context would proclaim the addition unjust. Conversely, if the legislature came to the conclusion that it was right and proper to grant divorce, on the petition of either party and without proof of any specific offence, when — and only when — a marriage was shown to have broken down irreparably, how could it justify retaining grounds which depended on the commission of specific offences, on which only injured parties might petition, and which required no evidence of breakdown at all? . . .

(b) The superficiality inseparable from verbally formulated 'grounds' would tend to render the principle of breakdown inoperative
One of our reasons for recommending the principle of breakdown is that it would enable the courts to get to grips with the realities of the matrimonial relationship instead of having to concentrate on superficialities. But if the principle were introduced into the law in the shape of yet another verbally formulated 'ground' . . ., the advantage hoped for would be lost. . . .

(c) The addition of a new 'ground' embodying the principle of breakdown would make divorce easier to get without really improving the law
As we have said, we have no reason to believe that the entire substitution of breakdown for the matrimonial offence would, in the long run, make divorce easier or increase the number of decrees granted to a significant extent; but quite obviously the mere addition of a 'ground of separation' would do both, since it would make divorce available where now it is not, while leaving undisturbed the opportunities now existing. . . .

Immediately following the publication of *Putting Asunder*, the Lord Chancellor referred the matter to the Law Commission. Their report, entitled *Reform of the Grounds of Divorce — The Field of Choice*, was published only five months later. Their conclusions were summarised thus:

120. (1) The objectives of a good divorce law should include (*a*) the support of marriages which have a chance of survival, and (*b*) the decent burial with the minimum of embarrassment, humiliation and bitterness of those that are indubitably dead. . . .
(2) The provision of the present law whereby a divorce cannot normally be obtained within three years of the celebration of the marriage may help to achieve the first objective. . . . But the principle of matrimonial offence on which the present law is based does not wholly achieve either objective. . . .

(3) Four of the major problems requiring solution are:

 (*a*) The need to encourage reconciliation. Something more might be achieved here; though little is to be expected from conciliation procedures after divorce proceedings have been instituted. . . .

 (*b*) The prevalence of stable illicit unions. As the law stands, many of these cannot be regularised nor the children legitimated. . . .

 (*c*) Injustice to the economically weaker partner — normally the wife. . . .

 (*d*) The need adequately to protect the children of failed marriages. . . .

(4) The field of choice for reform is circumscribed by a number of practical considerations and public attitudes, which cannot be ignored if acceptable and practicable reforms are to be undertaken. . . .

(5) The proposals of the Archbishop's Group on Divorce made in *Putting Asunder*, though they are to be welcomed for their rejection of exclusive reliance on matrimonial offence, are procedurally impracticable. They propose that there should be but one comprehensive ground for divorce — breakdown of the marriage — the court being required to satisfy itself by means of a thorough inquest into the marriage that it has failed irretrievably. It would not be feasible, even if it were desirable, to undertake such an inquest in every divorce case because of the time this would take and the costs involved. . . .

(6) However, the following alternative proposals, if any of them were thought desirable, would be practicable in the sense that they could be implemented without insuperable legal difficulty and without necessarily conflicting with the critical factors referred to in (4):

 (*a*) *Breakdown without Inquest* — a modification of the breakdown principal [sic] advocated in *Putting Asunder*, but dispensing in most cases with the elaborate inquest there suggested. The court would, on proof of a period of separation and in the absence of evidence to the contrary, assume that the marriage had broken down. If, however, this were to be the sole comprehensive ground of divorce, it would not be feasible to make the period of separation much more than six months. If, as seems likely, so short a period is not acceptable, breakdown cannot become the sole ground, but might still be introduced as an additional ground on the lines of proposal (*c*) below. . . .

 (*b*) *Divorce by Consent* — This would be practicable only as an additional, and not a sole comprehensive, ground. It would not be more than a palliative and would probably be unacceptable except in the case of marriages in which there are no dependent children. Even in the case of childless marriages, if consent were the sole criterion, it might lead to the dissolution of marriages that had not broken down irretrievably. . . .

 (*c*) *The Separation Ground* — This would involve introducing as a ground for divorce a period of separation irrespective of which party was at fault, thereby affording a place in the law for the application of the breakdown principle. But since the period would be substantially longer than six months, it would be practicable only as an addition to the existing grounds based on matrimonial offence. The most comprehensive form of this proposal would provide for two different periods of separation. After the expiration of the shorter period (two years is suggested) either party, subject to safeguards, could obtain a divorce if the other consented, or, perhaps, did not object. After the expiration of the longer period (five or seven years) either party, subject to further safeguards, could obtain a divorce even if the other party objected. . . .

(7) If any of these proposals were adopted, the following safeguards would appear to be necessary: —

 (*a*) The three year waiting period should be retained. . . .

 (*b*) The court should have power to adjourn for a limited period to enable the possibilities of reconciliation to be explored. . . .

 (*c*) The court should have a discretion to refuse a decree if attempts had been made by the petitioner wilfully to deceive it; but the present absolute and discretionary bars would be inapplicable to petitions on these new grounds. . . .

 (*d*) Additional safeguards would be needed to protect the respondent spouse and the children. These should include: —

  (i) A procedure to ensure that the respondent's decision to consent to or not oppose a divorce, had been taken freely and with a full appreciation of the consequences. . . .

  (ii) Retention, and possible improvement, of the provisions of the present law designed to ensure that satisfactory arrangements are made for the future of the children. . . .

  (iii) Provisions protecting an innocent party from being divorced against his or her will unless equitable financial arrangements are made for him or her. . . .

 (*e*) It is for consideration whether there should be a further discretionary bar based on protection of interests wider than those of the parties alone. If such a bar were introduced, it should be defined as precisely as possible so as to promote consistency in its exercise and to enable legal advisers to give firm advice to their clients. . . .

Question

In the light of this summary, do you think that to title the Report *The Field of Choice* was 'inaccurate'?

The 'practical considerations and public attitudes' referred to in paragraph 120 (4) above are of particular interest:

52. . . .
   (*a*) Public opinion would not accept any substantial increase in the difficulty of obtaining a divorce or of the time it takes, unless it could be shown that an appreciable number of marriages would be mended as a result.
   (*b*) Experience shows that the chances of reconciliation between the parties have become almost negligible by the time that a petition for a divorce is filed.
   (*c*) Whether a divorce is obtainable or not, husbands and wives in modern conditions will part if life becomes intolerable. The ease with which names can be changed under English law simplifies the establishment of a new and apparently regular 'marriage'; where the deception is not complete, the resulting children are the main sufferers because of the stigma that still attaches to the status of illegitimacy.
   (*d*) Children are at least as vitally affected by their parents' divorce as are the parents themselves.
   (*e*) Breakdown of a marriage usually precedes the matrimonial offence on which the divorce petition is based. Thus, an isolated act of adultery or isolated acts with different partners may be the grounds for divorce, but are likely to be the result of the breakdown of the marriage rather than its cause.
   (*f*) Public opinion would be unlikely to support a proposal which had the effect of, say, doubling the amount spent on divorce proceedings; in so far as more Judges, more courts and more Legal Aid would impose a burden on public funds, it would be felt that the money could be better spent on other subjects, including, for example, marriage guidance and conciliation.
   (*g*) Public opinion would be equally unlikely to support a great expansion of the Queen's Proctor's Office or the employment of additional public servants with the function of investigating the truth of the evidence given by parties to divorce proceedings. At the present time there is a shortage of trained welfare officers attached to the courts and no sudden addition to their numbers can be hoped for in the near future.
   (*h*) Even where a marriage is childless, divorce granted automatically if the parties consent ('Post Office divorces') would not be acceptable; there must be an independent check if only to ensure that the economically weaker party really and freely consents to the divorce and to approve the financial arrangements worked out by the parties and their solicitors. The need for outside intervention is, of course, far greater where there are children.

Question

The Law Commission did not base these statements on any scientific opinion poll (although they were described as 'hard facts' in the Report) — how many of them, would hold good today?

2 The law

The Divorce Reform Act 1969, by and large, translated the Law Commission's clear preferences into law. It came into force on 1 January 1971 and has since been consolidated with other relevant legislation in the Matrimonial Causes Act 1973. [For a fascinating account of the passage of the Act on to the statute book, see B. H. Lee's study, *Divorce Law Reform in England* (1974)]:

1. Divorce or breakdown of marriage   (1) Subject to section 3 below, a petition for divorce may be presented to the court by either party to a marriage on the ground that the marriage has broken down irretrievably.

(2) The court hearing a petition for divorce shall not hold the marriage to have broken down irretrievably unless the petitioner satisfies the court of one or more of the following facts, that is to say —

(*a*) that the respondent has committed adultery and the petitioner finds it intolerable to live with the respondent;

(*b*) that the respondent has behaved in such a way that the petitioner cannot reasonably be expected to live with the respondent;

(*c*) that the respondent has deserted the petitioner for a continuous period of at least two years immediately preceding the presentation of the petition;

(*d*) that the parties to the marriage have lived apart for a continuous period of at least two years immediately preceding the presentation of the petition (hereafter in this Act referred to as 'two years' separation') and the respondent consents to a decree being granted;

(*e*) that the parties to the marriage have lived apart for a continuous period of at least five years immediately preceding the presentation of the petition (hereafter in this Act referred to as 'five years' separation').

(3) On a petition for divorce it shall be the duty of the court to inquire, so far as it reasonably can, into the facts alleged by the petitioner and into any facts alleged by the respondent.

(4) If the court is satisfied on the evidence of any such fact as is mentioned in subsection (2) above, then, unless it is satisfied on all the evidence that the marriage has not broken down irretrievably, it shall, subject to sections 3(3) and 5 below, grant a decree of divorce.

(5) Every decree of divorce shall in the first instance be a decree nisi and shall not be made absolute before the expiration of six months from its grant unless the High Court by general order from time to time fixes a shorter period,[5] or unless in any particular case the court in which the proceedings are for the time being pending from time to time by special order fixes a shorter period than the period otherwise applicable for the time being by virtue of this subsection.

2. Supplemental provision as to facts raising presumption of breakdown   (1) One party to a marriage shall not be entitled to rely for the purposes of section 1(2)(*a*) above on adultery committed by the other if, after it became known to him that the other had committed that adultery, the parties have lived with each other for a period exceeding, or periods together exceeding, six months.

(2) Where the parties to a marriage have lived with each other after it became known to one party that the other had committed adultery, but subsection (1) above does not apply, in any proceedings for divorce in which the petitioner relies on that adultery the fact that the parties have lived with each other after that time shall be disregarded in determining for the purposes of section 1(2)(*a*) above whether the petitioner finds it intolerable to live with the respondent.

(3) Where in any proceedings for divorce the petitioner alleges that the respondent has behaved in such a way that the petitioner cannot reasonably be expected to live with him, but the parties to the marriage have lived with each other for a period or periods after the date of the occurrence of the final incident relied on by the petitioner and held by the court to support his allegation, that fact shall be disregarded in determining for the purposes of section 1(2)(*b*) above whether the petitioner cannot reasonably be expected to live with the respondent if the length of that period or of those periods together was six months or less.

(4) For the purposes of section 1(2)(*c*) above the court may treat a period of desertion as having continued at a time when the deserting party was incapable of continuing the necessary

---

5. The period is now fixed at six weeks.

intention if the evidence before the court is such that, had that party not been so incapable, the court would have inferred that his desertion continued at that time.

(5) In considering for the purposes of section 1(2) above whether the period for which the respondent has deserted the petitioner or the period for which the parties to a marriage have lived apart has been continuous, no account shall be taken of any one period (not exceeding six months) or of any two or more periods (not exceeding six months in all) during which the parties resumed living with each other, but no period during which the parties lived with each other shall count as part of the period of desertion or of the period for which the parties to the marriage lived apart, as the case may be.

(6) For the purposes of section 1(2)(*d*) and (*e*) above and this section a husband and wife shall be treated as living apart unless they are living with each other in the same household, and references in this section to the parties to a marriage living with each other shall be construed as references to their living with each other in the same household.

(7) Provision shall be made by rules of court for the purpose of ensuring that where in pursuance of section 1(2)(*d*) above the petitioner alleges that the respondent consents to a decree being granted the respondent has been given such information as will enable him to understand the consequences to him of his consenting to a decree being granted and the steps which he must take to indicate that he consents to the grant of a decree.

5. Refusal of decree in five year separation cases on ground of grave hardship to respondent
(1) The respondent to a petition for divorce in which the petitioner alleges five years' separation may oppose the grant of a decree on the ground that the dissolution of the marriage will result in grave financial or other hardship to him and that it would in all the circumstances be wrong to dissolve the marriage.

(2) Where the grant of a decree is opposed by virtue of this section, then—
    (*a*) if the court finds that the petitioner is entitled to rely in support of his petition on the fact of five years' separation and makes no such finding as to any other fact mentioned in section 1(2) above, and
    (*b*) if apart from this section the court would grant a decree on the petition,
the court shall consider all the circumstances, including the conduct of the parties to the marriage and the interests of those parties and of any children or other persons concerned, and if of opinion that the dissolution of the marriage will result in grave financial or other hardship to the respondent and that it would in all the circumstances be wrong to dissolve the marriage it shall dismiss the petition.

So that we can see the English law in context, we reproduce Table 2 (p. 196, below) from Mary Anne Glendon in *Abortion and Divorce in Western Law* (1987). As Mary Ann Glendon explains, England was not alone:

Between 1969 and 1985 divorce law in nearly every Western country was profoundly altered. Among the most dramatic changes was the introduction of civil divorce in the predominantly Catholic countries of Italy and Spain, and its extension to Catholic marriages in Portugal. Other countries replaced or amended old, strict divorce laws. Most of these laws had been virtually unchanged since the grounds for ecclesiastical separation from bed and board became the basis for the secular institution of divorce. The chief common characteristics of all these changes were the recognition or expansion of nonfault grounds for divorce, and the acceptance or simplification of divorce by mutual consent. When California in 1969 became the first Western jurisdiction completely to eliminate fault grounds for divorce, the move was thought by some to prefigure the direction of reforms in other places. But it soon became clear that the purist approach was not to find wide acceptance. That same year England, too, passed a new divorce law which purported to make divorce available only when a marriage had irretrievably broken down. But since the English statute permitted marriage breakdown to be proved by evidence of traditional marital offenses as well as by mutual consent or long separation, it did not really repudiate the old fault system. As it turned out, compromise statutes of the English type (resembling those already in place in Australia, Canada, and New Zealand) became the prevailing new approach to the grounds of divorce.

Glendon writes:

The changes in divorce law were themselves part of a more general process in which the legal posture of the state with respect to the family was undergoing its most fundamental shift since family law had begun to be secularized at the time of the Protestant Reformation. Beginning

Table 2: Grounds for divorce in nineteen countries[a]

Mixed Fault and Nonfault Grounds			Nonfault Grounds Only	
Required waiting period of more than 1 year for contested unilateral nonfault divorce	Required waiting period of 1 year or less for contested unilateral nonfault divorce	Mutual consent required for nonfault divorce	Judicial discretion to deny contested unilateral divorce	No judicial discretion to deny divorce
Austria (1978)	Canada (1968–86)	U.S. (2 states)	Netherlands (1971)	Sweden (1973)
Belgium[b] (1974–82)	Switzerland[b] (1907)		West Germany (1976)	U.S. (18 states and D.C.)
Denmark (1969)	U.S. (22 states)			
England[b] (1969)				
Finland[c] (1929–48)				
France[b] (1975)				
Greece (1983)				
Iceland[b] (1921)				
Italy (1970–75)				
Luxembourg[b] (1975–78)				
Norway (1918)				
Portugal (1975–77)				
Spain (1981)				
U.S. (8 states)				

[a] This table classifies countries according to two criteria: the extent to which their divorce statutes have (1) abandoned the fault principle and (2) accepted the possibility of divorce by one spouse of a partner who opposes the divorce and has committed no marital "fault." The dates of the most recent major changes relating to the grounds of divorce are in parentheses. Countries vary, of course, in the extent to which these ideas are put into practice by the courts, the cost of implementing statutory rights, the opportunities offered for tactical delay, and so on. Ireland, which allows no divorce, is not included in table.

[b] In these systems of mixed grounds, the court has discretion to deny a divorce sought by one spouse against a nonconsenting partner who has committed no "fault" in the technical sense of the divorce laws.

[c] In 1986, the Finnish government introduced a bill to make marriage dissolution available on nonfault grounds only, with no discretion to deny divorce.

in the 1960s, movement in Western family law had been characterized, broadly speaking, and in varying degrees, by a withdrawal of much official regulation of marriage: its formation, its legal effects, and its termination. The removal of many legal obstacles to marriage; the effect of new attitudes of tolerance for diversity combined with older policies of nonintervention in the ongoing marriage; and the transformation of marriage itself from a legal relationship terminable only for serious cause to one increasingly terminable at will, amounted to a dejuridification of marriage. This process of deregulation of the formation and dissolution of marriage, and of the relations of the spouses during marriage, was typically accompanied, however — again in varying degrees — by a continued, and sometimes intensified, state interest in the economic and child-related consequences of marriage dissolution.

Question

Do you agree with Glendon's analysis of the fundamental shift, and if you do, do you welcome this process of 'deregulation' and 'dejuridification'?

(a) THE 'FAULT-BASED' FACTS

At first sight, these provisions combine fault and no-fault 'grounds' for divorce in just the way so deplored by the Archbishop's group in *Putting Asunder*. In fact, as the following cases illustrate, the apparently fault-based 'grounds' are not always what they seem.

Cleary v Cleary
[1974] 1 All ER 498, [1974] 1 WLR 73, 117 Sol Jo 834, Court of Appeal

The wife left her husband and committed adultery. She then returned to her husband and they lived together for five or six weeks. She left again but did not repeat the adultery. She took proceedings unsuccessfully in a magistrates' court complaining of her husband's persistent cruelty and wilful neglect to maintain her. A few months later she petitioned for divorce on the basis of her husband's behaviour. The husband denied this and cross-prayed for divorce on the basis of her adultery. She withdrew her petition and the case proceeded undefended upon the husband's cross-prayer. The county court judge dismissed the suit and the husband appealed.

Lord Denning MR: . . . [On the words of section 1(2)(*a*)] a point of law arises on which there is a difference of opinion between the judges. The question is whether the two facts required by section [1(2)(*a*)] are severable and independent, or whether they are interconnected. In other words, is it sufficient for the husband to prove (*a*) that the wife has committed adultery and (*b*) that he finds it intolerable to live with her? Or has he to prove that (*a*) the wife has committed adultery and (*b*) that *in consequence thereof* he finds it intolerable to live with her? Are the words 'in consequence thereof' to be read into section [1(2)(*a*)]?

On the one hand, in *Goodrich v Goodrich* [1971] 2 All ER 1340, [1971] 1 WLR 1142, Lloyd-Jones J quoted from *Rayden on Divorce*, 11th ed. (1971), p. 175, where it was submitted that the two phrases are in the context independent of one another. The judge said: 'In my judgment that view is acceptable.' On the other hand, more recently in *Roper v Roper and Porter* [1972] 3 All ER 668, [1972] 1 WLR 1314, Faulks J took a different view. He said:

'I think that common sense tells you that where the finding that has got to be made is that the respondent has committed adultery, and the petitioner finds it intolerable to live with the respondent, it means, "*and in consequence* of the adultery the petitioner finds it intolerable to live with the respondent." '

So Faulks J would introduce the words 'in consequence thereof,' whereas Lloyd-Jones J would not. Which is the right view?

As a matter of interpretation, I think the two facts in section [1(2)(*a*)] are independent and should be so treated. Take this very case. The husband proves that the wife committed adultery and that he forgave her and took her back. That is one fact. He then proves that, after she comes back, she behaves in a way that makes it quite intolerable to live with her. She corresponds with the other man and goes out at night and finally leaves her husband, taking the children with her. That is another fact. It is in consequence of that second fact that he finds it intolerable — not in consequence of the previous adultery. On that evidence, it is quite plain that the marriage has broken down irretrievably. He complies with section [1(2)(*a*)] by proving (*a*) her adultery which was forgiven; and (*b*) her subsequent conduct (not adultery), which makes it intolerable to live with her.

I would say one word more. In *Rayden on Divorce*, 11th ed., p. 175, it is suggested (referring to an extra-judicial lecture by Sir Jocelyn Simon [Riddell Lecture 1970, see *Rayden*, pp. 3227, 3234]): 'It may even be his own adultery which leads him to find it intolerable to live with the respondent.' I cannot accept that suggestion. Suppose a wife committed adultery five years ago. The husband forgives her and takes her back. He then falls in love with another woman and commits adultery with her. He may say that he finds it intolerable to live with his wife, but that is palpably untrue. It was quite tolerable for five years: and it is not rendered intolerable by his love for another woman. That illustration shows that a judge in such cases as these should not accept the man's bare assertion that he finds it intolerable. He should inquire what conduct on the part of the wife has made it intolerable. It may be her previous adultery. It may be something else. But whatever it is, the judge must be satisfied that the husband finds it intolerable to live with her.

On the facts of this case I think the judge could and should have found on the evidence the two elements required, (1) the adultery of the wife and (2) the husband found it intolerable to live with her.

Appeal allowed.

Questions

(i) Husband and wife agree that they will live on the wife's earnings from prostitution; after some months of this the husband falls in love with a young virgin; he finds it intolerable to live with his wife; is he entitled to an immediate divorce?

(ii) The same husband leaves his wife to wait until he is free to marry his young virgin; is his wife entitled to an immediate divorce?

(iii) Do you find your answers to questions (i) and (ii) either (*a*) just, or (*b*) sensible?

(iv) If you are not happy with the answers to questions (i) and (ii), ought the result to be (*a*) that neither is entitled to an immediate divorce, or (*b*) that both are entitled to an immediate divorce?

(v) What difference, if any, would it have made to any of your answers if the husband's distaste for his wife had developed because she contracted the AIDS virus in the course of her prostitution?

(vi) Does not the answer to Lord Denning's last example lie in s. 2(1)?

(vii) But if 'adultery' and 'intolerability' need have nothing to do with one another, why is s. 2(2) expressed as it is?[6]

(viii) In the magistrates' matrimonial jurisdiction (Chapter 3, above), adultery is only a ground for financial relief insofar as it falls within 'behaviour': what difference, if any, does this make?

---

6. A differently constituted Court of Appeal was troubled by this point in *Carr v Carr* [1974] 1 All ER 1193, [1974] 1 WLR 1534, but reluctantly accepted the *Cleary* interpretation of s. 1(2)(*a*).

Livingstone-Stallard v Livingstone-Stallard
[1974] Fam 47, [1974] 2 All ER 766, [1974] 3 WLR 302, 118 Sol Jo 462, 4
Fam Law 150, High Court, Family Division

The husband and wife married in December 1969; they were then aged 56
and 24 respectively. Two months later, 'as the result of one of the few scenes
of violence which took place during the marriage', the wife left. But in
September 1970 they were reunited. The marriage ended for practical purposes in September 1972, when the wife left after the husband became
enraged in the course of an argument. The wife petitioned on the basis
of her husband's behaviour. Most of the incidents were 'trivial in themselves', and we quote only one of those described because of the significance
attached to it by the judge. It took place shortly after the wedding and before
the first parting.

Dunn J: . . . The wife also complained about another incident which was, perhaps, the most
illuminating incident so far as the husband's character was concerned. They had, naturally, had
some photographs taken at their wedding, and not very long afterwards the photographer came
round with the wedding album. The husband was out and the wife, exercising what one would
imagine was normal courtesy and hospitality, offered the photographer a glass of sherry which
he accepted and she had a glass of sherry too to keep him company. When the husband came
home he went to his cocktail cabinet, took out the sherry bottle and said, 'You have drunk half
a bottle of sherry. Don't you ever go to my cocktail cabinet again.' He asked her who she had
been drinking with and she told him what had happened. He forbade her to 'give refreshment
to trades people again.' He was naturally cross-examined about his attitude and it appeared to
be that if his wife took a glass of sherry with a tradesman — and he apparently classed the
photographer as a tradesman — then the glass of sherry might, as he put it, impair her faculties,
so that the tradesman might make some kind of indecent approach to her; and that was the
justification of his conduct on that occasion. To my mind, it is typical of the man. . . .
   I am quite satisfied that this marriage has broken down. The wife told me that in no circumstances would she continue to live with her husband, partly because he is so irresponsible with
Jason [their son] and takes so little interest in him. I cannot, of course, dissolve this marriage
unless I am satisfied that the husband has behaved in such a way that the wife cannot reasonably
be expected to live with him. That question is, to my mind, a question of fact, and one approach
to it is to suppose that the case is being tried by a judge and jury and to consider what the proper
direction to the jury would be, and then to put oneself in the position of a properly directed
jury in deciding the question of fact.
   Mr Reece, for the husband, has referred me to the cases — all of which have been so far
decided at first instance — *Ash v Ash* [1972] Fam 135, [1972] 1 All ER 582; *Pheasant v
Pheasant* [1972] Fam 202, [1972] 1 All ER 587; and *Katz v Katz* [1972] 3 All ER 219, [1972]
1 WLR 955 and has submitted that incompatibility of temperament is not enough to entitle a
petitioner to relief, that the behaviour must be of sufficient gravity so that the court can say
that it would, under the old law, have granted a decree of divorce on the ground of constructive
desertion. Mr Reece has submitted that the best approach is to apply the test which was applied
in the constructive desertion cases, bearing in mind that the parties are married and that the
conduct must be sufficiently grave to justify a dissolution of the marriage; weighing the gravity
of the conduct against the marriage bond or, as Mr Reece put it, against the desirability of
maintaining the sanctity of marriage. I have in the past followed the reasoning of Ormrod J
in *Pheasant v Pheasant* [1972] Fam 202, [1972] 1 All ER 587 but, on reflection and with respect,
I am not sure how helpful it is to import notions of constructive desertion into the construction
of the Matrimonial Causes Act 1973. Nor, speaking for myself, do I think it helpful to analyse
the degree of gravity of conduct which is required to entitle a petitioner to relief under section
1(2)(*b*) of the Act. As Lord Denning MR has emphasised in another context (*Wachtel v Wachtel*
[1973] Fam 72, [1973] 1 All ER 829), the Act of 1973 is a reforming statute and section 1(2)
is in very simple language which is quite easy for a layman to understand. Coming back to my
analogy of a direction to a jury, I ask myself the question: Would any right-thinking person
come to the conclusion that this husband has behaved in such a way that this wife cannot
reasonably be expected to live with him, taking into account the whole of the circumstances and
the characters and personalities of the parties? It is on that basis that I approach the evidence
in this case.

The wife was young enough to be the husband's daughter and plainly considerable adjustment was required on both sides. Mr Reece submitted that she had known him a long time and that she knew exactly the kind of man that she was marrying; that the complaints which she made are trivial; and that she cannot bring herself within section 1(2)(*b*) simply because the character of her husband does not suit her. He further submitted that the reality of this case was that this young woman had simply got fed up and walked out, and walked out pretty soon too. I accept that the wife was a strong-minded young woman, but I am satisfied that she was anxious for the marriage to last and wished it to continue, that she wished to have children and bring them up and to have her own home, and that she did her best so far as she was able to adjust to her husband's character.

The husband was said, by Mr Reece, to be meticulous. I agree with Mr Beckman [for the wife] that more suitable adjectives would be self-opinionated, didactic and critical and I accept that the husband's approach was to educate the wife to conform entirely to his standards. He, in my judgment, patronised her continually and submitted her, as I have found, to continual petty criticisms and his general attitude is well exemplified by the incident of the sherry and the photographer whom he called 'the tradesman.' I accept that many of the incidents were, or might appear to be, trivial in themselves and that there is a paucity of specific incidents between September 1970 and November 1972. But taking the facts as I have found them in the round in relation to the husband's character, in my judgment, they amount to a situation in which this young wife was subjected to a constant atmosphere of criticism, disapproval and boorish behaviour on the part of her husband. Applying the test which I have formulated, I think that any right-thinking person would come to the conclusion that this husband had behaved in such a way that this wife could not reasonably be expected to live with him. There will accordingly be a decree nisi under section 1(2)(*b*) of the Matrimonial Causes Act 1973.

Buffery v Buffery
[1988] FCR 465, [1988] 2 FLR 365, Court of Appeal

The parties were married in 1964. In December 1985 the wife petitioned for divorce under s. 1(2)(*b*) of the Matrimonial Causes Act 1973. The recorder considered that the conduct alleged against the husband had to be 'grave and weighty' and such that the wife could not reasonably be expected to continue to live with him. He concluded from the evidence that the cause of the breakdown of the marriage could not be blamed on the husband in the sense that he had been guilty of misbehaviour of a grave and weighty nature and that the breakdown could not be directed at either party since they had merely drifted apart. Accordingly, he held that the wife had failed to prove her case under s. 1(2)(*b*) and dismissed the petition. The wife appealed.

May LJ: . . . This was a suit based upon the provisions of s. 1(2)(*b*) of the Matrimonial Causes Act 1973. The judge found, and there is no dispute, that the marriage had irretrievably broken down. The wife, however, contends that in considering whether the court was satisfied of the requirement in subs. (2)(*b*) the judge below applied the wrong test. It was submitted that had he applied the right test he ought to have granted a decree, or alternatively that the matter should go back to be reheard.

The parties were married in July 1964. They are now respectively 51 and 62 years of age. There are three children, all of them girls. They are now grown up and employed; two live at home. Although, when the matter came before the recorder, the husband and wife were still living under the same roof, we understand that recently the situation has altered to the extent that, at any rate temporarily, the wife has moved out of the matrimonial home and is living elsewhere. The two girls apparently still remain at home.

The petition was filed on 6 December 1985. The particulars of behaviour relied upon, even with later additions, could not be said to raise the strongest of cases under the statutory provisions.

Before turning to the findings of the recorder, it is convenient to deal with a preliminary question which arose in the course of argument. In his judgment the recorder referred to the cause of the irretrievable breakdown and held that this could not be blamed on the husband. It was submitted on behalf of the wife, and not contended otherwise on behalf of the husband, that the requirements in s. 1(1) and (2) of the 1973 Act are to be read disjunctively; that is to say that there is no requirement, on a proper construction of the relevant statutory provision, that the behaviour of the husband complained of must be a cause of the irretrievable breakdown before the statutory requirements are satisfied. I agree that they are separate requirements. First, that the marriage has irretrievably broken down and, secondly, that the court is satisfied of one or more of the facts set out in the paragraphs in subs. (2). . . .

We were referred to a number of cases. The latest one, *O'Neill v O'Neill* [1975] 1 WLR 1118, refers to the earlier case of *Livingstone-Stallard v Livingstone-Stallard* [1974] Fam 47. There is a brief passage in that earlier case which I wish to quote. The question in issue was the husband's behaviour, the extent of it and the test which had to be applied to decide whether or not it satisfied the statutory requirements. At p. 54 Dunn J referred to the earlier decision of Ormrod J in *Pheasant v Pheasant* [1972] Fam 202, and went on to say:

'. . . I am not sure how helpful it is to import notions of constructive desertion into the construction of the Matrimonial Causes Act 1973. Nor, speaking for myself, do I think it helpful to analyze the degree of gravity of conduct which is required to entitle a petitioner to relief under s. 1(2)(*b*) of the Act.'

It may be that particular conduct can be stigmatized as so grave that it is behaviour after which the petitioner cannot reasonably be expected to live with the respondent. But for my part, with Dunn J in that case, on a proper reading of the statute and an assessment of the facts of a given case, the gravity or otherwise of the conduct complained of is of itself immaterial. What has to be asked, as will appear from the judgment in *O'Neill*, is whether the behaviour is such that the petitioner cannot reasonably be expected to live with the respondent. If it is grave, the answer is probably no.

The case of *O'Neill* was again a conduct case within s. 1(2)(*b*) of the Matrimonial Causes Act 1973 in which the question of the proper approach arose. At p. 1121, after disagreeing with the test which had been applied by the judge below, Cairns LJ put the matter in this way:

'The right test is, in my opinion, accurately stated in *Rayden on Divorce* . . .:

"The words 'reasonably be expected' prima facie suggest an objective test. Nevertheless, in considering what is reasonable, the court (in accordance with its duty to inquire, so far as it reasonably can, into the facts alleged) will have regard to the history of the marriage and to the individual spouses before it, and from this point of view will have regard to *this* petitioner and *this* respondent in assessing what is reasonable." '

Thus one looks to this husband and this wife, or vice versa, but one also looks at what is reasonable. That is the point referred to by Roskill LJ in his judgment in the same case, at p. 1125, where he adopted as correct the test which Dunn J had applied in the *Livingstone-Stallard* case in a part of his judgment which I have not quoted. Roskill LJ said:

'I would respectfully adopt as correct what Dunn J said in *Livingstone-Stallard*, at p. 54:

"Coming back to my analogy of a direction to a jury, I ask myself the question: Would any right-thinking person come to the conclusion that this husband has behaved in such a way that this wife cannot reasonably be expected to live with him, taking into account the whole of the circumstances and the characters and personalities of the parties." '

That, in effect, is posing precisely the same test as referred to by Cairns LJ quoting from *Rayden*. One considers a right-thinking person looking at the particular husband and wife and asks whether the one could reasonably be expected to live with the other taking into account all the circumstances of the case and the respective characters and personalities of the two parties concerned. . . .

That, however, is not an end of the matter, because the recorder did make certain findings of fact in the context of the petition and answer before him. . . .

The matters of which complaint is made in the original and supplemental particulars went, first, to the questions of finances between husband and wife and the way in which the husband had dealt with them and, secondly, to whether the husband ever took his wife out on social occasions, she contending that he did not. That failure on his part was at least part of the behaviour of which she complained, which led to the reasonable conclusion that she could not be expected to live with him.

In so far as going out together socially was concerned, the recorder made a more precise finding:

'I think the situation was this — the wife was not keen to go out when the children were growing up and they simply got to a stage when they did not go out socially except on rare occasions. By the time the children had grown up and they could have gone out socially, they were quite unable to communicate. In that respect, I do not think the blame is attached to one more than the other. As the wife put it on more than one occasion — we just do not communicate. We have nothing in common.'

Then, towards the end of his judgment, the recorder said:

'Although the [wife] has established that the marriage has irretrievably broken down, the cause of the breakdown cannot really be levelled at the [husband] in the sense that he has been guilty of misbehaviour of a grave and weighty nature. The [wife] has been quite candid about this; when asked she said the marriage has broken down; we cannot communicate; we have nothing in common — and there lies, in my view, the crux of the matter. The situation is that neither is really at fault.'

Reading the judgment of the recorder in full, I conclude that in so far as any dissension over money matters was concerned, although the husband had been somewhat insensitive, nevertheless this did not constitute sufficient behaviour within the relevant statutory provision. In truth, what has happened in this marriage is the fault of neither party; they have just grown apart. They cannot communicate. They have nothing in common and there lies, as the recorder said, the crux of the matter.

It was submitted that if the matter went back to the recorder he could make various findings on the evidence about the sensitivity, for instance, of the wife in relation to these matters and various further findings of fact about the nature and extent of the husband's behaviour complained of. I, for my part, do not think he could. He heard all the evidence and the conclusion to which he came was that nobody was really at fault here, except they both had grown apart. In those circumstances, in my judgment, clearly the wife failed to make out her case under s. 1(2)(*b*), although she satisfied the recorder that the marriage had broken down irretrievably. I do not think any advantage would be gained by sending this matter back for a retrial. The matter was fully investigated and the recorder made the findings to which I have referred. In those circumstances, I would reach the same conclusion as did the recorder, namely that the petition should be dismissed.

Appeal dismissed.

Questions

(i) If Mr Livingstone-Stallard and Mr Buffery had petitioned for divorce based on s. 1(2)(*b*), what would have been the result?

(ii) The facts in *Pheasant v Pheasant* [1972] Fam 202, [1972] 1 All ER 587, to which Dunn J refers, were that a husband complained that the wife was unable to provide him with the 'spontaneous, demonstrative affection' which his character and personality demanded. This lack of affection made it impossible for him to live with his wife. The husband's petition was rejected by Ormrod J. If Mrs Pheasant had petitioned for divorce based on s. 1(2)(*b*) would she have obtained the same result as Mrs Livingstone-Stallard?

In *Balraj v Balraj* (1980) 11 Fam Law 110, CA, p. 214, below, Cumming-Bruce LJ said:

In behaviour cases, where the ground relied upon to prove the breakdown or a condition precedent to breakdown is the effect of behaviour, the court has to decide the single question whether the husband (for example) has so behaved that it is unreasonable to expect the wife to live with him. In order to decide that, it is necessary to make findings of fact of what the husband actually did and then findings of fact upon the impact of his conduct on that particular lady. As has been said again and again between a particular husband and a particular lady whose conduct and suffering are under scrutiny, there is of course a subjective element in the totality of the facts that are relevant to the solution but, when that subjective element has been evaluated, at the end of the day the question falls to be determined on an objective test.

Questions

(i) Are you attracted by this test?

(ii) Is it different from the test in *Buffery v Buffery*?

(iii) H became an alcoholic and his condition so disgusted W that she left him in January. By August, he was cured and at his request W returned. After five months she decides that, although the cure seems to be permanent, she no longer enjoys being married to him and she left again. Can W obtain an immediate divorce? Should she be able to?

Stringfellow v Stringfellow
[1976] 2 All ER 539, [1976] 1 WLR 645, 120 Sol Jo 183, 6 Fam Law 213, Court of Appeal

Ormrod LJ: . . . The allegations which are said to constitute behaviour within the limits of s. 1(2)(b) of the 1973 Act are simply these, that having been married since 1969, having had two children, and having been, I assume, reasonably happy together, the situation between them changed in January 1975 when the husband, to quote the words of the petition —
'ceased to show any interest in keeping the said marriage alive and has failed and refused to show any affection towards the [wife]. (b) . . . has refused to have sexual intercourse with the [wife] and has rejected all approaches made by the [wife] saying that he was not in the mood or that he was feeling depressed. (c) [He] has regularly gone out in the evenings but has failed to take the [wife] out saying that he had no feelings for her. (d) [He] has told the [wife] that he could not stand her being near to him. (e) [He] is interested in sport and puts his sporting activities before the [wife] and the said children as a result whereof the said children have had no family life (f) [He] told the [wife] to go to her parents for a week so that he could sort out his feelings saying that he no longer loved the [wife] and that he wanted his freedom which he had lost by marrying her at the age of 19.'
The wife went to her parents, and returned after a week, but the husband insisted that he wished to part from her; and it is said, naturally enough, that his rejection of her upset her. And finally, on 23 March 1975, he left and has lived apart from her ever since.
. . . What is the relationship between the two grounds (b) and (c) set out in s. 1(2) of the 1973 Act? (c) of course is desertion; and, if one reads (b) literally, it would be easy to conclude that no spouse could reasonably be expected to live with a spouse who had deserted him or her. In other words, ground (b) has to be given some meaning which is not quite its literal grammatical one if it is to co-exist with (c) because it is clear to me that if (b) is to be read literally there will not in fact be any case coming before the court on the ground of desertion because every deserted spouse could maintain that the deserter had behaved in such a way that he or she could not be expected to live with him. So it cannot mean that; it must mean something more than that; and, in my judgment, it means some conduct other than the desertion or the behaviour leading up to the desertion. It means something which justifies the court in finding that the marriage had irretrievably broken down before the period of two years had elapsed after the separation. So there must be some conduct on the part of the respondent spouse which goes beyond mere desertion or the steps leading up to mere desertion.
This case on the evidence seems to me to be a classic case of desertion simpliciter, if I may put it that way. The whole married life came quickly to an end following a change in the husband which took place in January 1975. No complaint is made about his behaviour prior to that at all. In that month either he was ill or something happened to him which altered his attitude completely towards his wife. He did no more as far as I can see than indicate to her that his attitude had changed. His attitude having changed, he could not display affection to her, he could not have sexual intercourse with her, or would be very reluctant to do so, and inevitably during those weeks between January and his departure in March this relationship was breaking down. But I do not see any allegation in the petition which goes beyond describing the basic facts of a relationship between husband and wife which has for one reason or another broken down, and I cannot see any behaviour on his part outside the limits of that situation. So for my part I would certainly hold that the wife here failed to show that the husband had behaved in such a way that she could not reasonably be expected to live with him within ground (b). She certainly has a case on desertion, but under the Act in its present form she has to wait two years.

Questions

(i) Would a jury think it reasonable to expect a wife to go on living with a husband who was no longer there to be lived with?
(ii) But what if the reason that the husband was not there was that he was suffering from an incurable disease with which the wife was no longer able to cope?

Thurlow v Thurlow
[1976] Fam 32, [1975] 2 All ER 979, [1975] 3 WLR 161, 119 Sol Jo 406, 5 Fam Law 188, High Court, Family Division

The wife suffered from epilepsy and a severe physical neurological disorder. From June 1969, her mental and physical condition gradually deteriorated. Her husband made a 'genuine, sustained and considerable effort' to cope with her at home, but was forced to give up, and since July 1972 she had required full-time institutional care and would continue to do so for the rest of her life. In 1974, the husband petitioned on the basis of her behaviour.

Rees J: . . . The husband's case therefore consists of allegations of both negative and of positive behaviour on the part of the wife. The negative behaviour alleged and proved is that between the middle of 1969 and 1 July 1972, she gradually became a bedridden invalid unable to perform the role of a wife in any respect whatsoever until she reached a state in which she became unfitted even to reside in an ordinary household at all and required to be removed to a hospital and there reside for the rest of her life. The positive behaviour alleged and proved is that during the same period she displayed bad temper and threw objects at her mother-in-law and caused damage by burning various household items such as towels, cushions and blankets. From time to time she escaped from the home and wandered about the streets causing alarm and stress to those trying to care for her.

I am satisfied that by July 1972 the marriage had irretrievably broken down and since the wife, tragically, is to spend the rest of her life as a patient in a hospital the husband cannot be expected to live with her. But the question remains as to whether the wife's behaviour has been such as to justify a finding by the court that it is unreasonable to expect him to do so. . . .

Questions of interpretation of the words in section 1(2)(b) of the Act of 1973 which arise from the facts in the instant case include the following: Does behaviour which is wholly or mainly negative in character fall within the ambit of the statute? Is behaviour which stems from mental illness and which may be involuntary, capable of constituting relevant behaviour?

I consider these questions separately. As to the distinction which has been made between 'positive' and 'negative' behaviour I can find nothing in the statute to suggest that either form is excluded. The sole test prescribed as to the nature of the behaviour is that it must be such as to justify a finding that the petitioner cannot reasonably be expected to live with the respondent. It may well be that in practice such a finding will more readily be made in cases where the behaviour relied upon is positive than those wherein it is negative. Spouses may often, but not always, be expected to tolerate more in the way of prolonged silences and total inactivity than of violent language or violent activity. I find myself in respectful agreement with the views expressed by Davies LJ in the Court of Appeal in *Gollins v Gollins* [1964] P 32 at 58:

'. . . I do not find the contrast between "positive" conduct and "negative" conduct either readily comprehensible or helpful, although these expressions are undoubtedly to be found in the decided cases. Almost any sort of conduct can at one and the same time be described both as positive and as negative. An omission in most cases is at the same time a commission.' . . .

I now turn to the question as to whether behaviour which stems from mental illness and which may be involuntary is capable of falling within the statute. . . .

. . . I propose to follow the principle stated by Lord Reid in *Williams v Williams* [1964] AC 698 at 723 and cited by Sir George Baker P in *Katz v Katz* [1972] 3 All ER 219 at 224:

'In my judgment, decree should be pronounced against such an abnormal person . . . simply because the facts are such that, after making all allowances for his disabilities and for the temperaments of both parties, it must be held that the character and gravity of his acts were such as to amount to cruelty.'

Sir George Baker P usefully suggested that this statement of principle may be adapted to meet the present law by substituting for the final words: '. . . the character and gravity of his behaviour was such that the petitioner cannot reasonably be expected to live with him.'

Accordingly the facts of each case must be considered and a decision made, having regard to all the circumstances, as to whether the particular petitioner can or cannot reasonably be expected to live with the particular respondent. If the behaviour stems from misfortune such as the onset of mental illness or from disease of the body, or from accidental physical injury, the court will take full account of all the obligations of the married state. These will include the normal duty to accept and to share the burdens imposed upon the family as a result of the mental or physical ill-health of one member. It will also consider the capacity of the petitioner to withstand the stresses imposed by the behaviour, the steps taken to cope with it, the length of time during which the petitioner has been called upon to bear it and the actual or potential effect upon his or her health. The court will then be required to make a judgment as to whether the petitioner can fairly be required to live with the respondent. The granting of the decree to the petitioner does not necessarily involve any blameworthiness on the part of the respondent, and, no doubt, in cases of misfortune the judge will make this clear in his judgment.

In the course of his most helpful submissions on behalf of the wife Mr Holroyd Pearce drew attention to some difficulties which he urged would arise if the law were such as to enable a decree to be granted in the instant case. It would mean, he said, that any spouse who was afflicted by a mental or physical illness or an accident so as to become a 'human vegetable' could be divorced under section 1(2)(*b*) of the Matrimonial Causes Act 1973. This was repugnant to the sense of justice of most people because it involved an implication of blameworthiness where none in truth existed and it was not what Parliament intended. The remedy was open to the petitioner in such cases to seek a decree of divorce on the ground of five years' separation under section 1(2)(*e*) of the Act of 1973 and if this were done no blame would be imputed to the respondent and also the special protection for the interests of the respondents provided by sections 5 and 10 of the Act of 1973 would be available whereas it would not if a decree were granted under section 1(2)(*b*). He cited two extreme examples to illustrate the point. One was the case of a spouse who was suddenly reduced to the state of a human vegetable as a result of a road traffic accident and was immediately removed to a hospital and there remained for life. The other was one in which supervening permanent impotency brought marital relations to an end.

There is no completely satisfactory answer to these submissions but what may properly be said is that the law as laid down in *Williams v Williams* [1964] AC 698, [1963] 2 All ER 994 does provide a remedy by divorce for a spouse who is the victim of the violence of an insane respondent spouse not responsible in law or fact for his or her actions and in no respect blameworthy. The basis for that decision is the need to afford protection to the petitioner against injury. So also in the insanity cases where the behaviour alleged is wholly negative and no violence in deed or word is involved but where continuing cohabitation has caused, or is likely to cause injury to health, it should be open to the court to provide a remedy by divorce. Before deciding to grant a divorce in such cases the court would require to be satisfied that the petitioner could not reasonably be expected to live with the respondent and would not be likely to do so in the case referred to by Mr Holroyd Pearce unless driven to it by grave considerations which would include actual or apprehended injury to the health of the petitioner or of the family as a whole. It is now common knowledge that health may be gravely affected by certain kinds of negative behaviour whether voluntary or not and if the granting of a decree under section 1(2)(*b*) is justified in order to protect the health of petitioners injured by violence so it should be in cases where the petitioner's health is adversely affected by negative behaviour. The safeguard provided for the interests of respondents is that it is the judge and not the petitioner who must decide whether the petitioner can reasonably be expected to live with the respondent; and that decision is subject to review upon appeal.

I do not propose to state any concluded view upon the case postulated in which a spouse is reduced to a human vegetable as the result of a road traffic accident and is removed at once to hospital to remain there for life . . .

In reaching the decision the judge will have regard to all the circumstances including the disabilities and temperaments of both parties, the causes of the behaviour and whether the causes were or were not known to the petitioner, the presence or absence of intention, the impact of it upon the petitioner and the family unit, its duration, and the prospects of cure or improvement in the future. If the judge decided that it would be unreasonable to expect the petitioner to live with the respondent then he must grant a decree of divorce unless he is satisfied that the marriage has not irretrievably broken down.

Approaching the facts in the instant case upon the basis of these conclusions I feel bound to decide that a decree nisi of divorce should be granted. This husband has conscientiously and courageously suffered the behaviour of the wife for substantial periods of time between 1969 and July 1972 until his powers of endurance were exhausted and his health was endangered. This behaviour stemmed from mental illness and disease and no blame of any kind can be nor is attributed to the wife.

Questions

(i) Is it possible for anyone nowadays to define the 'obligations of the married state'? How can a judge guess what a jury of 'right-thinking' people would think they were?

(ii) The Family Law Sub-Committee of the Law Society, in *A Better Way Out* (1979), stated that, in undefended cases, 'the evidence presents little difficulty — after several years of marriage, virtually any spouse can assemble a list of events which, taken out of context, can be presented as unreasonable behaviour [sic] sufficient on which to found a divorce petition.' Does this surprise you?

(iii) If you were drafting a petition based upon the other's behaviour would you be inclined to make it look as bad as possible (lest the court be tempted to probe more deeply) or as little as you think you can get away with (lest the respondent be goaded into defending either the petition itself or ancillary issues)?

(iv) How little do you think you can get away with?

A selection of newspaper cuttings on defended divorce petitions during the period 1984–1991 reveals successful petitions brought against the following:

(i) a handyman husband who started many jobs in the house and garden, but seldom finished them. He was moody, aggressive and difficult (2/11/84);

(ii) a husband who deliberately annoyed his wife by hiding her underwear; if she did or said something he did not like he would become moody and not speak to her for days (17/4/86);

(iii) a husband who sat in the matrimonial home all day in his pyjamas shouting his opinions at anyone prepared to listen and even those not prepared to (1/3/85);

(iv) a wife who often forced her husband to sleep in the car and did not allow him to use the downstairs bathroom (14/2/86);

(v) a husband who was something of 'a martinet' and put his children on parade before him from time to time (17/6/85);

(vi) a wife who went to Athens where her husband was a diplomat, and attacked his mistress in a public cinema. Earlier, when they were stationed in Istanbul where she was unhappy with the sewerage system, she had threatened to pour a pail of sewage over the Consul General's dining-room table if something was not done (25/3/87);

And unsuccessful petitions against the following:

(vii) an undemonstrative husband (16/4/86);

(viii) a man of 'outstanding forbearance' who had shown 'patience and sympathy' for a wife who was 'cold, utterly self-centred and somewhat neurotic' (24/1/85);

(ix) a man who was alleged to be 'of dominant mind and character', especially in financial matters (18/1/90).

Questions

(i) Was there really any point defending the petitions in the first six cases?

(ii) Would you have advised the respondents in the last three cases to defend?

(iii) What would have happened if the last three cases had been undefended?

(iv) Is 'adultery' or 'unreasonable behaviour' the more acceptable basis for a marriage to be terminated against (a) a male respondent, and (b) a female respondent?

(b) THE 'NO-FAULT' FACTS

Santos v Santos
[1972] Fam 247, [1972] 2 All ER 246, [1972] 2 WLR 889, 116 Sol Jo 196, Court of Appeal

This was a wife's undefended petition on the basis of two years' separation and her husband's consent. The judge dismissed the petition because on three occasions since the separation the wife had stayed with her husband for a short while. These did not amount to more than six months and they had been apart for the requisite total of two years in all, but the judge's attention was not drawn to what is now s. 2(5) of the Matrimonial Causes Act 1973. The wife appealed and the Court of Appeal took the opportunity to consider a totally new point as to the meaning of 'living apart.' The judgment was that of the whole court.

Sachs LJ: . . . The appeal first came before the court, differently constituted, on November 11, 1971. Then, after having heard the submissions of Mr Picard for the wife, it became apparent that it raised a very important issue as to the meaning of the words 'living apart' in section [1(2)(d)]. Does this relate simply and solely to physically not living under the same roof, or does it import an additional element which has been referred to in various terms — 'absence of consortium,' 'termination of consortium,' or an 'attitude of mind' — phrases intended to convey either the fact or realisation of the fact that there is absent something which is fundamental to the state of marriage. It was, accordingly, decided to refer the case to the Queen's Proctor for inquiry and such assistance as he considered that he could offer to the court. The appeal came on again for hearing on 16 December, when the Queen's Proctor was represented by Mr Ewbank, who presented to the court the result of a great amount of research in a most learned and interesting set of submissions for which we are much indebted. . . .

In the course of the argument before us reference was frequently made to the position of diplomats en poste in insalubrious foreign capitals, to those serving sentences in prison, to those in mental and other hospitals, and to prisoners of war — in the main, involuntary separations. None the less there are larger and no less important categories of separations which start voluntarily, such as business postings, voyages of exploration or recuperation trips when one party has been ill — all of which must also be looked at when endeavouring to determine what the legislature intended by the words 'living apart.'

As part of the fruits of that research already mentioned there was fully and fairly put before us material enabling us in relation to those words to examine a considerable range of parallel Commonwealth statutes and also decisions upon them reached in Australia, Canada and New Zealand. In addition, Mr Ewbank referred us to the comprehensive and helpful review by Professor Wadlington in the *Virginia Law Review*, vol. 52 (1966), p. 32, of the effect of comparable provisions in the legislation of a large number of individual states of the U.S.A. . . .

Their lordships then reviewed the Commonwealth authorities on comparable divorce legislation and the English authorities on similar expressions in English tax and criminal legislation.

The cogent volume of authority, to which we have been referred, makes it abundantly clear that the phrase 'living apart' when used in a statute concerned with matrimonial affairs normally imports something more than mere physical separation. This is something which obviously must be assumed to have been known to the legislature in 1969. It follows that its normal meaning must be attributed to it in the Act of 1969, unless one is led to a different conclusion either by the general scheme of the statute coupled with difficulties which would result from such an interpretation, or alternatively by some specific provision in that statute. . . .

Obviously this element is not one which necessarily involves mutual consent, for otherwise the new Act would not afford relief under head (*e*) in that area where it was most plainly intended to be available — where the 'innocent' party adheres to the marriage, refusing to recognise that in truth it has ended, often despite the fact that the 'guilty' one has been living with someone else for very many years. So it must be an element capable of being unilateral: and it must, in our judgment, involve at least a recognition that the marriage is in truth at an end — and has become a shell, to adopt a much-used metaphor.

If the element can be unilateral in the sense of depending on the attitude of mind of one spouse, must it be communicated to the other spouse before it becomes in law operative? That is a question that gave particular concern in the course of the argument. There is something unattractive in the idea that in effect time under head (*e*) can begin to run against a spouse without his or her knowledge. Examples discussed included men in prison, in hospital, or away on service whose wives, so far as they knew, were standing by them: they might, perhaps, thus be led to fail to take some step which they would later feel could just have saved the marriage. On the other hand, communication might well be impossible in cases where the physical separation was due to a breakdown in mental health on the part of the other spouse, or a prolonged coma such as can occasionally occur. Moreover, need for communication would tend to equate heads (*d*) and (*e*) with desertion — which comes under head (*c*) — something unlikely to be intended by the legislature. Moreover, bowing to the inevitable is not the same thing as intending it to happen.

In the end we have firmly concluded that communication by word or conduct is not a necessary ingredient of the additional element.

On the basis that an uncommunicated unilateral ending of recognition that a marriage is subsisting can mark the moment when 'living apart' commences, 'the principal problem becomes one of proof of the time when the breakdown occurred'. . . . Sometimes there will be evidence such as a letter, reduction or cessation of visits, or starting to live with another man. But cases may well arise where there is only the oral evidence of the wife on this point. One can only say that cases under heads (*d*) and (*e*) may often need careful examination by the first instance judge and that special caution may need to be taken. . . .

The difficulties arising from some of these problems at one stage led to hesitation as to whether after all 'living apart' in this particular Act might not refer merely to physical separation. But there are at any rate two cogent reasons against holding that the standard meaning does not apply. First, in any statute in which those words are used the same problems are normally inherent to a considerable degree — and it cannot be said that they have such a special impact in the Act of 1969 as to lead to the inference that the standard meaning is negatived. Secondly — perhaps more importantly — there are the injustices and absurdities that could result from holding that 'living apart' refers merely to physical separation; these, in our judgment, outweigh any hard cases or difficulties that can arise from the standard interpretations.

One category under head (*e*) is exemplified by the case of a long sentence prisoner whose wife has, with his encouragement, stood by him for five years — only for her to find that when he comes out he files a petition for divorce relying on ground (*e*). But the more usual categories relate to men who could unjustly find time running against them through absences on public service or on business in areas where, out of regard for the welfare of the wife or the children of the family, the former remains in this country: particularly hardly could this bear on men whose home leave did not for some years total the six months referred to in section [2(5)].

Turning from hardships under head (*e*) to absurdities under head (*d*), read in conjunction with section [2(5)] of the Act, it is plain that in cases arising under the latter head the spouses can spend up to 20% of their time together without interrupting the continuity of the separation (i.e. six months in two years and six months). Thus, if living apart means mere physical separation, a man who came home on leave for less than 20% of the two to two-and-a-half years immediately preceding the filing of the petition would be in a position to satisfy the court under head (*d*), even though he and his wife had been on excellent terms until they had a row on the last day of his last leave. As petitions under head (*d*) are normally undefended, there would be no evidence to rebut this presumption that the breakdown of the marriage was irretrievable and the decree would be granted. Unless — contrary to our view — the Act intended to permit divorce by consent simpliciter such a result would be absurd. On the contrary, the tenor of section [1(2)] is to ensure that under heads (c), (d) and (e) a breakdown is not to be held irretrievable unless and until a sufficiently long passage of time has shown this to be the case. . . .

The only specific provision of the Act upon which Mr Picard felt able to rely, if his general submissions failed, was section [2(6)] . . . [p. 195, above] . . . Those terms, he contended, should be interpreted as making it clear that no other element than physical separation could be taken into account under grounds (d) and (e).

It is unfortunately by no means plain what exactly the legislature had in mind when enacting this subsection — nor even what is its general objective. Three points on its phraseology are however to be noted. First, it does not use the word 'house,' which relates to something physical, but 'household,' which has an abstract meaning. Secondly, that the words 'living with each other in the same household' should be construed as a single phrase. Thirdly, it specifically refrains from using some simple language referring to physical separation which would achieve the result for which Mr Picard contended. On the contrary, use is again made of words with a well settled matrimonial meaning — 'living together,' a phrase which is simply the antithesis of living apart, and 'household,' a word which essentially refers to people held together by a particular kind of tie, even if temporarily separated and which has been the subject of numerous decisions in matrimonial as well as in other cases. Whatever the object of this subsection, the combination of the first and third points makes it plain that it does not produce the result which has been urged on behalf of the wife.

We are, however, inclined to think that its object is simply to ensure that the long drawn out conflict — so fully and comprehensively discussed in *Naylor v Naylor* [1962] P 253, [1961] 2 All ER 129 between on the one hand the series of cases exemplified by *Smith v Smith* [1940] P 49, [1939] 4 All ER 533 and the views expressed by Denning LJ in *Hopes v Hopes* [1949] P 227 at 236, and, on the other hand, the series started by *Evans v Evans* [1948] 1 KB 175, [1947] 2 All ER 656 should for the purposes of the Act of 1969 be conclusively resolved in favour of the former. Thus, the subsection makes it clear beyond further debate that when two spouses are living in the same house, then, as regards living apart, a line is to be drawn, in accordance with the views of Denning LJ, and they are to be held to be living apart if not living in the same household. If the subsection has some other meaning it will, incidentally, give rise to many problems, as for instance where husband and wife are in different arms of the services and there is for some time no matrimonial home. . . .

. . . Therefore 'living apart' referred to in grounds (d) and (e) is a state of affairs to establish which it is in the vast generality of cases arising under those heads necessary to prove something more than that the husband and wife are physically separated. For the purposes of that vast generality, it is sufficient to say that the relevant state of affairs does not exist whilst both parties recognise the marriage as subsisting. . . .

The case was therefore sent back for trial before a High Court judge.

Questions

(i) From the point of view of the innocent and loyal wife of the long sentence prisoner, why is it 'absurd and unjust' if he makes up his mind to divorce her just before he is released, but apparently not if he makes up his mind five years earlier and tells her nothing about it?

(ii) Is the real reason not that this is absurd and unjust to her, but that such a recent decision is not conclusive evidence that the breakdown is irretrievable?

(iii) Suppose a couple whose marriage is going through a bad patch have a trial separation but keep returning to one another for brief periods until they finally decide that it is all over: is that decision any less likely to be 'irretrievable' than that of a couple whose initial separation was 'for good' but who kept changing their minds? (The logic of *Santos* coupled with s. 2(5) would appear to be that the second couple get their divorce whereas the first couple do not.)

However, the notion that 'living with each other in the same household' is as much an abstraction as a physical reality can be very helpful to those couples who are still under the same roof:

Fuller (otherwise Penfold) v Fuller
[1973] 2 All ER 650, [1973] 1 WLR 730, 117 Sol Jo 224, Court of Appeal

Husband and wife separated in 1964, when the wife left the matrimonial home, taking their two daughters, and went to live with a Mr Penfold in the latter's home. She took the name of Mrs Penfold and they lived together as husband and wife. Four years later, Mr Fuller had a coronary thrombosis and was no longer able to live alone. He therefore 'went and became a lodger in the house' where his wife lived with Mr Penfold. The wife gave him food and he ate with others in the house. The wife also did the washing. He paid a weekly sum for board and lodging. After four years of this, the wife petitioned for divorce on the basis of five years' separation and the husband did not defend. The judge refused the decree and the wife appealed.

Lord Denning MR: . . . At the hearing the judge held that he had no jurisdiction to grant a divorce because he thought that when the husband came back to the house, he and his wife were not living apart. The judge referred to the cases under the old law, such as *Hopes v Hopes* [1949] P 227, [1948] 2 All ER 920; and also the cases under the new Act: *Mouncer v Mouncer* [1972] 1 All ER 289, [1972] 1 WLR 321 and *Santos v Santos* [1972] 2 All ER 246.

In *Santos v Santos* this court stressed the need, under the new Act, to consider the state of mind of the parties and, in particular, whether they treated the marriage as subsisting or not. Clearly they treated it in this case as at an end.

In this case we have to consider the physical relationship of the parties. From 1964 to 1968 the parties were undoubtedly living apart. The wife was living with the other man as the other man's wife in that household, and the husband was separate in his household. From 1968 to 1972 the husband came back to live in the same house but not as a husband. He was to all intents and purposes a lodger in the house. Section 2(5) says they are to be treated as living apart 'unless they are living with each other in the same household'. I think the words 'with each other' mean 'living with each other as husband and wife'. In this case the parties were not living with each other in that sense. The wife was living with Mr Penfold as his wife. The husband was living in the house as a lodger. It is impossible to say that husband and wife were or are living with each other in the same household. It is very different from *Mouncer v Mouncer* where the husband and wife were living with the children in the same household — as husband and wife normally do — but were not having sexual intercourse together. That is not sufficient to constitute 'living apart'. I do not doubt the correctness of that decision. But the present case is very different. I think the judge put too narrow and limited a construction on the Act. I would allow the appeal and pronounce the decree nisi of divorce.

Stamp LJ: I agree. I can only say that to my mind the words 'living with each other in the same household' in the context of the Act relating to matrimonial proceedings are not apt to describe the situation where the wife is indisputably living with another man in the same household and her husband is there as a paying guest in the circumstances Lord Denning MR has described. 'Living with each other' connotes to my mind something more than living in the same household: indeed the words 'with each other' would otherwise be redundant.

Appeal allowed.

Questions

(i) Until this case, we had all thought that the operative concept was that of a common 'household' — were they sharing such things as meals and television, and was the wife still doing some things for her husband, even if they were not sharing a bed? — but does it now seem that the operative words are 'with each other'? Does that make the words 'in the same household' redundant?

(ii) If that be so, why should not withdrawal to a separate bedroom, together with the state of mind envisaged in *Santos v Santos* [1972] Fam 247, [1972] 2 All ER 246, be sufficient?

(iii) Why do the judges apparently think that it is more important when a wife stops cooking and washing for her husband than when she refuses to share a bed with him?

(iv) Suppose a woman comes to you and explains that she and her husband have had little to do with one another for some time and would now like a divorce, although for convenience they are still living under the same roof: will you explain the law carefully to her before you seek further and better particulars of their circumstances?

(v) What questions would you then ask?

(vi) How do you think all this accords with the concern felt by the Archbishop of Canterbury's group for 'considerations of truth, the sacredness of oaths and the integrity of professional practice'?

We turn now to the s. 5 defence:

Mathias v Mathias
[1972] Fam 287, [1972] 3 All ER 1, [1972] 3 WLR 201, 116 Sol Jo 394, Court of Appeal

The parties married in 1962 and had one daughter, now aged nine and a half. They separated in 1964. The wife had done very little work of any kind since then, believing it her duty to devote herself to the child. She lived on maintenance topped up with supplementary benefit. In 1971, the husband petitioned for divorce on the basis of five years' separation. The wife alleged that a decree would cause her grave financial hardship, through the possible reduction in her maintenance payments and eventual loss of widow's pension. The judge granted a decree and the wife appealed.

Davies LJ: . . . when a wife, as in this case, is 'put away' under [s. 1(2)(*e*) of the 1973] Act, if I may use the expression, in the overwhelming number of cases there must be, I should have thought, some financial hardship. But on what we have before us in this case I am very far indeed from being satisfied that the hardship that this lady has suffered and will suffer could properly be called 'grave' financial hardship. And, of course, if there is not shown by her — and speaking for myself I have no doubt at all that the onus is on her to show — the probability of 'grave' financial hardship, then no question of refusing a decree can arise.

On the second part of the section, I would say, in the light of the history and of the factors that Karminski LJ has set out, that, so far from it being wrong to dissolve this marriage, I am absolutely satisfied that it would be wrong not to do so. The ages of the parties are about 35 and 32 respectively. We do not know the age of the husband's lady friend, but no doubt she is a young woman. All three of the parties, the husband, the wife and the lady, would, in the ordinary course of events, have many years to keep alive in this shell of a marriage and prevent perhaps all three of the parties settling down to a happier life in happier circumstances. The cohabitation lasted for some [1¾] years. They have been living apart now for some 7¾ years. I should have thought that the sooner that latter situation is put to an end the better. I agree, therefore, that the appeal should be dismissed.

Question

At first instance, Park J had said that in any subsequent proceedings for financial provision, he would want to know why the wife was not working: to what extent is it relevant that the financial hardship is 'self-inflicted'?

Le Marchant v Le Marchant
[1977] 3 All ER 610, [1977] 1 WLR 559, 121 Sol Jo 334, Court of Appeal

The husband was a post office employee and about to retire. He petitioned for divorce on the basis of five years' separation. The wife alleged that the possible loss of an index-linked widow's pension would cause her grave financial hardship. The judge granted a decree and the wife appealed.

Ormrod LJ: . . . It would be quite wrong to approach this kind of case on the footing that the wife is entitled to be compensated pound for pound for what she will lose in consequence of the divorce. She has to show, not that she will lose something by being divorced, but that she will suffer grave financial hardship, which is quite another matter altogether. It is quite plain that, prima facie, the loss of the pension, which is an index-linked pension, in the order of £1,300 a year at the moment, is quite obviously grave financial hardship in the circumstances of a case like this unless it can be in some way mitigated. The learned judge, however, did not approach the case in this way. He said that s. 5 had to be read with s. 10 of the 1973 Act. Section 10 is the section which provides, in sub-s (3), that before a decree nisi is made absolute in cases such as the present, the court is required at the request of the wife to investigate the financial position and not to make the decree absolute until it is satisfied either that the petitioning husband should not be required to make any financial provision for the wife or that the financial provision made by him is reasonable and fair or (and these are the words which cause the trouble) is 'the best that can be made in the circumstances'. So, as counsel for the wife says, s. 10 offers an elusive or, perhaps better, an unreliable protection to a wife placed in the position in which this wife is placed. The marriage would have been dissolved by the decree nisi, there would have been therefore a finding of fact that she has not suffered grave financial hardship in consequence of the decree and she would then have to do the best she could under s. 10.

It is also right to point out that there are many cases, and this is one, in which the powers of the court, extensive as they are under ss. 23 and 24 as well as s. 10, are not wide enough to enable the court to carry out by order various things which a petitioner husband can do voluntarily, even if compelled to do it voluntarily, so s. 10 is not an adequate substitute. The learned judge, in a sentence, took the view that if he could see from the husband's financial position that he would be able one way or the other to alleviate sufficiently the financial hardship falling on the wife as a result of the loss of her pension, that was good enough. In the view of this court, that is not right. The right way to approach this problem is Cumming-Bruce J's approach in *Parker v Parker* [1972] Fam 116, [1972] 1 All ER 410, that is that the answer should set up a prima facie case of financial hardship, that the petition should be dismissed unless the petitioner can meet that answer in his reply by putting forward a proposal which is acceptable to the court as reasonable in all the circumstances and which is sufficient to remove the element of grave financial hardship which otherwise would lead to the dismissal of the petition. . . .

Now, at the last minute, and this is really one minute to midnight, counsel for the husband has at least made an offer. The offer is this. His client offers to transfer the matrimonial home or his interest in the matrimonial home to the wife forthwith. Secondly, he offers to pay her £5,000 when he receives the capital sum under his pension scheme (his position has clearly improved since the figures in the document P1 were worked out) and in addition to that he proposes to take out a life insurance policy on his own life to provide on his death the sum of £5,000 which will be payable to the wife if she survives him and which she can then use as she thinks fit. That offer is without prejudice to any order for periodical payment which may be made hereafter by a registrar when the respective income positions have been investigated. . . .

The view which I have formed is that the present offer is a reasonable one in the sense that it will, if implemented, remove the element of grave financial hardship so far as the wife is concerned, and remove therefore the defence which she has to the present petition. . . .

I need only say that the decree absolute will not be made in this case until the matrimonial home has been transferred and the insurance policy has been taken out, and the lump sum paid over, to the satisfaction of the wife's advisers. In those circumstances, and in those circumstances only, would I be in favour of allowing a decree nisi to stand.

Rukat v Rukat
[1975] Fam 63, [1975] 1 All ER 343, [1975] 2 WLR 201, 119 Sol Jo 30, 4 Fam Law 81, Court of Appeal

The husband, a Pole, and the wife, a Sicilian, married in 1946. Both were Roman Catholics. They had not lived together since 1947, when the wife had visited Sicily with their daughter and the husband had written telling her not to return as he had fallen in love with another woman. Since then the wife had kept up the pretence that the marriage was still subsisting. In 1972, the husband petitioned for divorce on the basis of five years' separation. The wife alleged that this would cause her hardship on the grounds that: (i) the prospect of divorce was an anathema to her on religious and moral grounds because she was a Roman Catholic; (ii) because of the social structure of the area where she lived, divorce would cause serious repercussions for her and her child; and (iii) if a decree were pronounced she would not be accepted in her community in Sicily and would not be able to return to her home. The judge granted a decree and the wife appealed.

Lawton LJ: . . . One has to start, I think, by looking at the context in which the phrase 'grave financial or other hardship' occurs. The word 'hardship' is not a word of art. It follows that it must be construed by the courts in a common sense way, and the meaning which is put on the word 'hardship' should be such as would meet with the approval of ordinary sensible people. In my judgment, the ordinary sensible man would take the view that there are two aspects of 'hardship' — that which the sufferer from the hardship thinks he is suffering and that which a reasonable bystander with knowledge of all the facts would think he was suffering. That can be illustrated by a homely example. The rich gourmet who because of financial stringency has to drink vin ordinaire with his grouse may well think that he is suffering a hardship; but sensible people would say he was not.

If that approach is applied to this case, one gets this situation. The wife undoubtedly feels that she has suffered a hardship; and the learned judge, in the passages to which Megaw LJ has referred, found that she was feeling at the time of the judgment that she could not go back to Sicily. That, if it was genuine and deeply felt, would undoubtedly be a 'hardship' in one sense of that word. But one has to ask oneself the question whether sensible people, knowing all the facts, would think it was a hardship. On the evidence, I have come to the conclusion that they would not, and for this reason. The wife has been separated from her husband now since 1947. She returned in that year to Sicily. She has been living in Palermo with her mother and father. Her relatives have been around her; they must have appreciated that something had gone wrong with the marriage. I make all allowances for the undoubted fact that many male Sicilians leave their country to work elsewhere, and wives may be left alone for months and years on end. Nevertheless, 26 years is a very long time; and such evidence as there was before the learned judge was to the effect that it was almost inevitable that her family and those who knew her would have appreciated that there was something wrong. There would be some social stigma attached to that; she might be thought to have failed as a wife. But she has lived that down; and the fact that there had been a divorce in some foreign country would add very little to the stigma. . . .

Ormrod LJ: . . . The court has first to decide whether there was evidence on which it could properly come to the conclusion that the wife was suffering from grave financial or other hardship; and 'other hardship' in this context, in my judgment, agreeing with Megaw and Lawton LJ, must mean other *grave* hardship. If hardship is found, the court then has to look at the second limb and decide whether, in all the circumstances, looking at everybody's interests,

balancing the respondent's hardship against the petitioner's interests in getting his or her freedom, it would be wrong to dissolve the marriage. . . .
Appeal dismissed.

In *Reiterbund v Reiterbund* [1974] 2 All ER 455, [1974] 1 WLR 788, Finer J held that the possible loss of a state widow's pension to a woman of 52 who would have to rely, as she was then relying, on supplementary benefit was *not* a grave financial hardship. He added this:

> Finally, I would add a word on the second limb of the defence. It seems to me that the word 'wrong' must there be construed to mean 'unjust'. However, in determining whether in all the circumstances it would be wrong, or unjust, to dissolve the marriage, it seems to me that the court must be careful to avoid subverting the policy which led to the inclusion of s. 1(2)(e) as one of the facts establishing irretrievable breakdown by, so to speak, treating the para. (e) 'fact' as of a lower order than the other four. Irretrievable breakdown is now the sole ground for divorce, and it may be established through any one of the matters set out in s. 1(2), all of which carry equal weight in expressing the object of the legislation. It seems to me, therefore, that in considering the s. 5 defence, the court has to exclude from its consideration that a petition based on five years separation is brought by a 'guilty' husband (in the phraseology of the old law) against a non-consenting wife, for this would be tantamount to striking s. 1(2)(e) out of the Act altogether. (I might parenthetically point out that the Civil Judicial Statistics for 1972 [Table 10] show that of the 19,270 petitions for dissolution filed that year based on five years separation, 10,003 were by husbands and 9,267 by wives; so that the fear, to which s. 5 was largely a response, that the five years separation rule constituted, as it was said, a Casanova's charter, might with roughly equal ineptitude have been expressed by a reference to Messalina.) In the course of the argument I was referred to the bulk of the authorities so far decided on the construction and application of the s. 5 defence; I do not find any of them inconsistent with the view I have just expressed. The parties in this case are not young, but even if there were no prospect at all of the husband marrying again (and, as I said previously, there is at least a hint that he may) I do not consider that it would be wrong to dissolve this marriage. On the contrary, I think it is a case which is well within the policy embodied in the new law which aims, in all other than exceptional circumstances, to crush the empty shells of dead marriages.

Balraj v Balraj
(1980) 11 Fam Law 110, Court of Appeal

The parties, both Indians, married there in 1952 as child bride and child groom. They started living together in 1962 when the husband was 23 and the wife was 18. The husband left the wife a year later when the wife was pregnant. He came to the UK in 1968. In 1979, the husband petitioned for divorce based on five years' separation. She filed an answer under s. 5. At first instance, the following facts were found:

> (1) That the petitioner and the respondent belonged to a community which is truly a Kshatriyas community or is an aspirate to Kshatriyas status and could be expected to adopt the norms and prejudices appropriate to Kshatriyas.
> (2) That Kshatriyas would not be accustomed to the conception of customary divorce.
> (3) That a divorced woman who is Kshatriyas would be in an anomalous position and have no ascertainable status.
> (4) That a divorced woman who is a Kshatriyas would be disadvantaged by her loss of status.
> (5) That the effect of divorce on the marriage prospects of the daughter of the parties would constitute a hardship for the respondent and for the daughter of the parties.
> [He then said:] I cannot conclude on that material that, objectively considered, those hardships must be regarded as grave.

The judge dismissed the defence. The wife appealed on the ground that the trial judge had failed to apply the correct test as to what constitutes grave hardship within the meaning of s. 5 of the Matrimonial Causes Act

1973. Counsel for the wife submitted that the judge should have applied a subjective rather than an objective test. The Court of Appeal rejected this submission:

Cumming-Bruce LJ: . . . in my view the President was right in taking the view that, having made that appraisal of the respondent's own expectation about her suffering, he must stand back and then look at all the circumstances and form an objective view as to whether the prospective situation for the lady would constitute gravé hardship or not.
Appeal dismissed.

Questions

(i) Can you describe a case, other than one such as *Le Marchant v Le Marchant* [1977] 3 All ER 610, [1977] 1 WLR 559, see p. 212, in which a divorce would cause grave hardship to the respondent *and* it would be wrong to dissolve the marriage? (See *Johnson v Johnson* (1981) 12 Fam Law 116).
(ii) Is it necessary for the 'grave hardship' to be caused by the divorce rather than by the breakdown of the marital relationship?
(iii) If it is necessary, why should this be?
(iv) What advice would you give to Mrs Balraj and Mrs Rukat? [Read s. 10(2)(3), MCA 1973.]

(c) DOES FAULT MATTER?

Grenfell v Grenfell
[1978] Fam 128, [1978] 1 All ER 561, [1977] 3 WLR 738, 121 Sol Jo 814, 7 Fam Law 242, Court of Appeal

Husband and wife married in 1951 and separated in 1969. In 1974, shortly before they had been separated for five years, the wife petitioned for divorce on the basis of her husband's behaviour. The husband waited until the five years had elapsed and then filed an answer denying her allegations of behaviour and cross-praying on the basis of five years' separation. The wife filed a reply admitting separation but alleging that a divorce would cause her grave hardship, for the following reasons:

(1) She is of the Greek Orthodox faith. (2) As a practising Christian her conscience would be affronted if the marriage were to be dissolved otherwise than for grounds of substance whereby the true cause of the breakdown of the marriage will be determined by the court and a decree pronounced accordingly. (3) Further and alternatively the petitioner contends that the financial provisions set forth in the reply are inadequate in any event and that if implemented after a decree had been granted to the respondent the petitioner would suffer grave financial hardship.

The third reason was later abandoned. The registrar ordered, in effect, that the wife's reply should be struck out and that the case should proceed first on the prayer in the husband's answer. The wife appealed, first to the judge without success, and then to the Court of Appeal.

Ormrod LJ: . . . It is quite clear that the purpose of section 5 is to permit a party to a marriage to object to a decree being granted on the ground of five years' separation where dissolution of the marriage would result in grave financial or other hardship to that party. The only thing to be looked at is the dissolution of the marriage. The question is simply and solely: Will the dissolution of this marriage cause grave financial or other hardship? It has got nothing to do, in my judgment, with which of the parties initiates the proceedings, nor with the ground for the proceedings. The wife in this case, having herself asked for a decree of dissolution, cannot be heard to say that if her marriage is dissolved she will suffer grave financial or other hardship. It would be a plain case of blowing hot and cold, which, of course, is not a form of pleading which can be tolerated. Consequently, in my judgment, the registrar and the judge were entirely right to strike out the reply.

There is in fact no defence to the husband's prayer for a dissolution of marriage on the ground of five years' separation, in the light of the admissions made by the wife partly in the reply and partly in the petition.

I turn now to the second matter. The second point in this appeal is whether the wife should be permitted to go on with the allegations of behaviour in her petition in view of what has happened. It might be more accurate perhaps to put the question the other way round, in view of Mr Ewbank's submission [for the wife], and ask whether the court has power to grant a decree on the husband's answer on the ground of five years' separation, all the necessary facts being admitted, and to refuse to hear the allegations of behaviour set out in the petition. I agree that it was a perfectly proper petition when it was filed, and I agree with the registrar that it would not be appropriate to strike it out under Order 18 on the ground that it was frivolous and vexatious. But it is necessary, I think, to draw attention to the wide powers the court has in its inherent jurisdiction to stay proceedings whenever it seems that it is appropriate to do so and the interests of justice as such require that course to be taken. . . .

To deal with this question which has arisen several times in the past, though I think this is the first time it has arisen in this court, it is necessary to remind ourselves what the Divorce Reform Act 1969 in fact did. There is one ground, and one ground only now, upon which the court has power to dissolve a marriage, and that is now set out in section 1 of the Act of 1973. The ground is that the marriage has broken down irretrievably. Parliament then went on in section 1(2) to prescribe five separate facts, one of which has to be established in order to prove that the marriage has broken down irretrievably. They are, of course, the well-known five. On proof of any one of the five — and Parliament plainly chose each of those five facts as being facts which would raise in any reasonable mind a presumption that the marriage had broken down — Parliament provided that the court should grant a decree of divorce unless it is satisfied on all the evidence that the marriage has not broken down irretrievably. In other words, on proof of any one of the five facts, there is a presumption, rebuttable, it is true, of irretrievable breakdown, and the onus is quite plainly on the party who is asserting that the marriage has not irretrievably broken down to satisfy the court by evidence that the presumption should be treated as rebutted. It is not, therefore, an adversary proceeding in any way comparable to the proceedings in other divisions of this court. Whichever side proves a fact under section 1(2), proves prima facie that the marriage has irretrievably broken down, and the court is not, in my judgment, concerned with anything else. . . .

On the pleadings in this case, as I have already said, once the reply was struck out, there was an admission by the wife that the marriage had irretrievably broken down and that the parties had been separated for five years. So that the court would be bound to grant a decree of divorce as soon as those matters were brought to the attention of the court. The wife would not be in a position to rebut the presumption of irretrievable breakdown and that would be that.

Mr Ewbank has sought to rely on section 1(3) of the Act of 1973, which provides:

'On a petition for divorce it shall be the duty of the court to inquire, so far as it reasonably can, into the facts alleged by the petitioner and into any facts alleged by the respondent.'

He says that that requires the court, imposes a statutory duty on the court, to conduct an inquiry into the facts alleged by the petitioner and by the respondent. The first comment to make on that is this: When the court is proceeding on the husband's prayer for a dissolution of marriage on the ground of five years' separation, he to all intents and purposes is the petitioner and the court's duty is to inquire into any relevant fact relating to his allegations. The wife, in her turn, is the effective respondent for the purposes of subsection (3), and it is the duty of the court to inquire into any relevant facts alleged by her. But, in the nature of things, on the facts in this case, there are no other relevant facts, other than the fact that the parties have been apart for five years and that the wife herself has asked for a decree and has herself admitted that the marriage has irretrievably broken down. There is nothing else to be inquired into.

There is no point, as I see it, in a case like this of conducting an inquiry into behaviour merely to satisfy feelings, however genuinely and sincerely held by one or other of the parties. To do so would be a waste of time of the court and, in any event, would be running, as I think, counter to the general policy or philosophy of the divorce legislation as it stands today. The purpose of Parliament was to ensure that where a marriage has irretrievably broken down, it should be dissolved as quickly and as painlessly as possible under the Act, and attempts to recriminate in the manner in which the wife in this case appears to wish to do should be, in my judgment, firmly discouraged. . . .

In those circumstances, I am quite satisfied that it would be entirely wrong to permit the wife to go on with her petition in this case, for the simple reason that facts sufficient to enable the court to grant a decree of dissolution are plain on the face of the pleadings.

Appeal dismissed.

Questions

(i) Do you think, from what you can gather from all these cases, that 'the general policy or philosophy of the divorce legislation as it stands today' is the same as it was in 1971?

(ii) What advice would you give to a couple who came to you wanting an immediate divorce?

(iii) What advice would you give to a wife who wanted to divorce as soon as possible from a husband who did not?

(iv) What advice would you give to the husband in question (iii)?

(v) Do you think that the answers you have given to questions (ii), (iii) and (iv): (*a*) reflect any credit upon the law; or (*b*) represent the reformers' original intentions?

3 The procedure

One feature which has militated against attempts to restrict divorce is the impossibility of forcing respondents to defend. By 1966, 93% of divorces were undefended, and the position now is that less than 1,000 cases a year are likely to result in a defended divorce hearing. (In 1989, only 285 defended divorces proceeded to a hearing.) A so-called 'special procedure' was invented for the very simplest of cases and extended to all undefended divorces in 1977. The 'special procedure' is described in appendix C to the Law Commission's Report *The Ground for Divorce* (1990):

26. . . . This requires the [district judge] to scrutinise the petition, supporting affidavit and any other evidence, in order to satisfy himself that the contents of the petition have been proved and that the petitioner is entitled to a decree. Thus the documents are checked both for their procedural regularity and for their sufficiency in substance to prove the petitioner's case. If they are found to be lacking in some way, the [district judge] may request further information or evidence. If the [district judge] is satisfied, he will issue a certificate that the petitioner is entitled to a decree and the judge will pronounce it formally in open court. If the [district judge] is not satisfied, he will remove the case from the special procedure list and require that it be heard before the judge.

Appendix C to the Report is a summary of a Court Record Study carried out by the Law Commission. One of the major aims of the study was to discover more about the circumstances in which district judges refused their certificates. This is what they report:

31. Procedural or administrative problems fell into the following broad categories: inaccuracies on the face of the documents, . . . documents, for example the marriage certificate, not filed or the wrong document, for example an acknowledgement of service relating to the wrong fact, filed; disagreement or problems over costs; problems with service; and respondents under a disability for whom a guardian ad litem might have to be appointed . . .

32. Substantive problems arose where the [district judge] had questioned the method or sufficiency of proof of the fact asserted in the petition and whether the petitioner was entitled to a decree. These fell into the following broad categories: insufficient evidence of adultery . . .; failure to name the person with whom the adultery was alleged to have been committed . . . and parties still living at the same address. . . .

36. Unsurprisingly, the effect of stop notices was to increase the overall length of the proceedings. As against a median length of 182 days for all proceedings, where there had been stops the median was 200 days, and where there had been no stops the median was 150 days. This suggests that as a distinct factor in affecting the overall length of proceedings, stop notices have a slightly greater effect (50 days) than the presence of children of the family (43 days).

Table 5 to the appendix illustrates the point in tabular form:

Table 5: Length of proceedings by fact relied on

Adultery	190 days (6 months)
Behaviour	193 days (6 months)
Desertion	*
Two years	148 days (5 months)
Five years	210 days (7 months)
Overall Median	182 days (6 months)

The Court Record Study then gives detailed examples of some of the problems noted on the files. In adultery cases:

37. A substantial proportion of problems noted on the files related to proof of adultery . . . A good example of the problems was a case in which neither party was represented, where the petition read:

'The parties separated by mutual consent due to incompatibility. The respondent subsequently committed adultery with an unknown woman who he now wishes to marry. I now feel that my marriage is seriously prejudicing my chances of forming another lasting relationship.'

The [district judge] objected that 'there is not even a hint of a shred of evidence' and required the petitioner to name the other woman if possible and join her as a party. [This practice is based on *Bradley v Bradley and Queen's Proctor (intervening)* [1986] 1 FLR 128]. A letter was received from the respondent who asserted that he did want to marry his new partner but was not prepared to admit to adultery. The petition was re-presented and the [district judge's] certificate refused a second time because 'there is still no evidence of adultery'. The case did eventually reach decree absolute.

And in behaviour cases:

44. It might have been thought that assessing behaviour cases would also cause some problems. [district judges] might have been unpersuaded, either that the behaviour complained of had in fact taken place or had the effect alleged, or that however accurately described it was such that it was unreasonable to expect the petitioner to live with the respondent. The files examined did not reveal evidence of this, apart from the problems arising where the couple were still living at the same address. The behaviour itself was generally proved by the assertions made in the petition and subsequently confirmed in the petitioner's affidavit.

The study concludes:

51. It is certainly difficult to conclude from the files which we studied that the intervention of the courts, considerable though this may be, has a noticeable impact upon the outcome of cases. Of the cases which failed to proceed, far more did so because of the decisions of the parties themselves than because of the problems of proving the ground. Of the cases where there had been such problems, the great majority eventually reached a decree.

At the same time as the so-called special procedure was introduced, legal aid was withdrawn from undefended divorce proceedings, although it remains available for 'ancillary relief'. The impact of this has been studied by Gwynn Davis, Alison Macleod and Mervyn Murch in *Special Procedure in Divorce and the Solicitor's Role* (1982):

Background to the procedural changes
The measures in question were introduced primarily to save money. The proportion of people qualifying for legal aid declined after 1950 as the eligibility limits did not keep pace with inflation, but civil legal aid expenditure escalated rapidly during the 1970s. By 1976, divorce accounted for the bulk of the civil legal aid budget. This was due to a number of factors, including the rising divorce rate, the increasing proportion of women petitioners who were more likely to be legally aided, and the growing practice of financially assisted petitioners not applying for costs against the respondent. Research had shown that judicial hearings of undefended divorce petitions served little practical purpose (Elston, Fuller and Murch, 1975). It was thought that their abolition, by removing the need for representation, would bring savings to the legal aid fund. It was also hoped that the changes would encourage more petitioners to prepare their own petitions, although this could still be done with a solicitor's help under the legal advice and assistance ('Green Form') scheme. This is limited to specified sums for petitioner and respondent, although solicitors can apply to the Area Legal Aid Committee for extensions. The services covered are also limited and do not normally include representation in court.
    Although the primary legislation remained the same, when the changes were introduced they were thought to be significant for the following reasons:
   (i) formal responsibility for the conduct of the divorce in Green Form cases passed from the solicitor to the petitioner;
  (ii) it was thought that the changes might contribute to a greater use of alternative sources of legal help, such as citizens' advice bureaux and law centres; they might also bring more people into direct contact with county court staff and increase reliance on their informal advice;
 (iii) there was no longer to be a judicial hearing of the petition in open court;
 (iv) for the first time since the legal aid scheme was introduced it was being withdrawn from one area; and
  (v) since almost all divorces are now undefended, the above changes were likely to affect the majority of the divorcing population.
The Lord Chancellor's withdrawal of legal aid was challenged by The Law Society. They argued that:
   (i) the Green Form limits (then £45 for petitioners, £25 for respondents) would be inadequate to allow the necessary work to be done and would dilute the quality of service to clients;
  (ii) people would need representation at the new judicial appointments;
 (iii) the use of legal advice and assistance 'in tandem' with legal aid, with an unclear division of responsibility between solicitor and client, would be confusing and inefficient;
 (iv) the restrictions would mean a two-tier system, with one level of service for those who could afford to pay and another for those who could not.

The authors then describe their research and its results, which they summarise as follows:

1. The great majority of petitioner and respondent [parties] still consult solicitors. While technically they may be 'petitioners in person', this phrase is misleading, as practically all are advised by solicitors at some stage.
2. Although a quarter of our sample had sought information from CABs or legal advice centres, most had done so as a preliminary to seeking solicitors' advice.
3. Solicitors continue to deal with most of the paperwork associated with special procedure divorce. The complexity of the documentation and procedure encourages dependence on solicitors.
4. Some solicitors find it necessary to do work not covered by the Green Form.
5. Some of those interviewed told us that, at least in retrospect, they thought that their solicitor had not adequately explored the possibility of reconciliation. [See Chapter 15, below.]
6. The research identified a number of problems concerning the legal aid and advice schemes. These include:

(a) people's uncertainty concerning whether or not they are eligible for help;
(b) the distinction between the role of adviser under the Green Form scheme and representation under legal aid is not understood;
(c) some people are deterred by worries about cost from seeking a lawyer's help as early as they might do otherwise;
(d) some disturbing cases were encountered where it appeared that solicitors had not adequately informed their clients about their entitlement to legal aid;
(e) some respondents are being advised not to defend the divorce because of cost and many feel aggrieved about this.

Conclusion

What impact has the extension of the special procedure and the withdrawal of legal aid had upon the provision of legal services for those who divorce? The changes relate primarily to people's entry into the legal system. They affect the mechanics of obtaining an undefended divorce but do not touch custody battles, disputes about finance or property, or contested divorces, all of which may be pursued under a full legal aid certificate as before.

Much of the policy debate between the Lord Chancellor's Legal Aid Advisory Committee and The Law Society about the withdrawal of legal aid from undefended divorce hinged on the question of what legal services were necessary in these cases. Many solicitors were unhappy with the limits. As we have seen, some provide their clients with extra services for which they do not get paid. This raises the question of whether the State should provide anything other than the minimum service necessary to meet the strictly legal requirements of the case.

We would argue that the divorce lawyer also has a responsibility to consider the social and emotional aspects, if only because these have a bearing on the legal issues. For example, clients may well use their lawyers as sounding-boards while working out problems such as access arrangements. . . . Some solicitors refuse to see their role as consisting entirely in the performance of a series of straightforward administrative tasks, although the Green Form scheme is designed to support little more than this:

'The special procedure has simplified the process but divorce is an emotional experience and people want support. Currently there is no system designed to do this. I'd say that three-quarters of my time is spent counselling.'

We may at present have the worst of both words: a system of legal advice and representation which does not allow solicitors to give adequate time to their divorcing clients and yet, through comparatively generous support for representation in ancillary matters, encourages a litigious approach.

Meanwhile, the hope that divorce under the Green Form would substantially reduce the cost to the legal aid fund of ancillary matters has not been realized. The number of legal aid certificates in matrimonial cases rose by 18% in 1980/81. The Law Society comment that the number of certificates in matrimonial proceedings has increased 'at a rate far in excess of the increase in the number of divorce petitions'. There has been no fall in the use of solicitors because there has been no fundamental change in divorce law or procedure. Overall the measures have made little impact on a system which is still largely adversarial in character and which, therefore, does not encourage genuine litigants in person.

Gwynn Davis and Mervyn Murch bring together the research on the Special Procedure and the research on Conciliation (see, p. 233 below in *Grounds for Divorce* (1988):

It is worth noting, incidentally, that one party's need to obtain a quick divorce can leave them open to pressure to grant what they consider to be unreasonable concessions in respect of 'ancillary' matters, usually finance or property. This, for example, was the experience of one man who petitioned for divorce on the basis of his wife's adultery: 'They held out the adultery confession as the prize for being a good boy and splitting up the house. If I'd refused, I probably wouldn't have got the divorce — or I *may* not; it would have been more difficult. I'd have had to get a private detective or whatever people do.' The fact of there being a judicial test of breakdown — which in practice is allowed to rest entirely on the respondent's acceptance of behaviour or adultery allegations — is bound to invite manipulation of this kind. Anyone anxious to obtain a quick divorce is vulnerable in this respect.

Many of the couples whom we interviewed had come to recognize the truth of Chester and Streather's dictum that 'whatever the client's reason for wanting divorce, the lawyer's function is to discover grounds' (Chester and Streather, 1972). In the words of one husband, 'As it stands now you choose a reason, whatever is the easiest, and you don't ever really involve the courts in the real reason for the breakdown of the marriage. It's just something that they recognize, so you choose one of them.' This element of contrivance (and of acceptance on the respondent's part) was most marked in respect of petitions based on adultery, a point also noted by Eekelaar (1984). Use of the 'behaviour' basis was, however, far more problematic. This emerged in the course of our Special Procedure survey when we asked the parties how 'amicable' their divorce had been. The 'behaviour' basis stood out, containing proportionately far fewer 'amicable' (or even remotely reasonable) partings than did the other four 'facts'. Divorces based on 'adultery', on the other hand, were said to have been 'amicable' (or 'fairly amicable') as often as those based on two years separation. 'Adultery', in other words, appears to be employed with a degree of emotional neutrality, whereas 'behaviour' seldom is.

Since divorce can no longer be refused because the suit is collusive, there is little doubt that 'adultery' is employed by many couples who simply find it inconvenient to wait two years to obtain a decree. . . .

Questions

(i) Do you think the introduction and the extension of the 'special procedure' and the withdrawal of legal aid more radical departures than the introduction of irretrievable breakdown as the sole ground of divorce?

(ii) Is it necessary or desirable that the termination of the marriage be obtained in a formal or judicial manner?

(iii) In some circumstances, we recognise divorces obtained abroad by judicial or other proceedings and even, on occasions, in cases where the divorce is not accompanied by 'other proceedings' (Family Law Act 1986, s. 46(2)(*b*)). If we recognise such divorces obtained abroad, why not allow administrative divorces here?

(iv) Or do we already have that given that almost all divorces are granted each year under the 'special procedure'?

(v) Although we no longer have many defended divorces, the number of cases where the respondent at some stage indicates an intention to defend is by no means insignificant. (See the Law Commission's Court Record Study (1990).) Why is it that so few of these initially contested cases reach the point of a full hearing before a judge?

4 Time restrictions on petitioning

One stratagem, introduced in 1937, to stem the tide of divorce was the so-called 'three-year' rule. This rule prevented divorce petitions being presented to court before the expiration of the period of three years from the date of the marriage unless special leave was granted on the ground either of exceptional hardship suffered by the petitioner or of exceptional depravity on the part of the respondent. This restriction was recommended to be retained both by *Putting Asunder* (1966) and the *Field of Choice* (1966). However, the Law Commission reconsidered it in a Working Paper (1980) and Report, *Time Restrictions on Presentation of Divorce and Nullity Petitions* (1982) which recommended replacing the previous discretion with an absolute bar on petitioning within a year of the marriage.

2.14 . . . It is perhaps a little simplistic to think of measuring the effectiveness of the restriction solely, for example, in terms of the number of marriages saved, as the underlying objective is more subtle: it is to shape an attitude of mind. . . .

2.30 In the Working Paper we said that the arguments in favour of the proposal that there should be an absolute bar on the presentation of divorce petitions within a stipulated period from the date of the marriage could be put in this way:

'The justification for a time restriction is one of public policy; it would devalue the institution of marriage to make divorce readily obtainable within days of the marriage. The present law is on this view based on a sound principle, but is objectionable because of the unsatisfactory nature of the exceptions whereby the court may allow a petition to be presented on proof of exceptional hardship or depravity. Although it would be possible to construct other exceptions, none of them is entirely satisfactory. The law would on this view be simpler and more comprehensible if it asserted the general policy by means of an absolute bar on divorce early in marriage.'

2.31 There was widespread support in the response to the Working Paper for the view that such a bar would have the obvious advantage of certainty and consistency, and would provide an adequate expression of public concern that the institution of marriage should not be devalued by precipitate divorce. It is, of course, true that such a bar may involve hardship. However, the response to the Working Paper reinforces us in our view that such hardship may, in many cases, be more apparent than real (provided that the period during which petitions may not be presented is comparatively short) particularly in view of the fact that, even where a marriage breaks down in the very early stages, the parties are eligible to apply for a wide range of legal remedies, by way of financial provision, protection and arrangements for custody of and access to children. Indeed the only relief which will not be available is the liberty to re-marry. Thus the number of cases involving actual hardship is likely to be minimal. . . .

2.33 We are, however, conscious that a considerable number of those who wrote to us favoured the total abolition of the restriction. We have sympathy with the logic of their arguments; yet we firmly believe in the public policy arguments recited above and the need to avoid the apparent scandal of divorce petitions being presented immediately after the marriage. We think that a one-year absolute bar is the least intrusive and most straightforward of restrictions which accords with many of the views which have been expressed to us and is, accordingly, likely to be the most generally acceptable.

The reform proposed by the Law Commission was implemented by s. 1 of the Matrimonial and Family Proceedings Act 1984.

Questions

(i) After the three year bar was reduced to one year in 1984, the number of petitions for judicial separation fell sharply. The number of petitions in 1989 was 2,741 and there were 1,678 decrees. The figures in 1983 were 7,430 petitions and 4,852 decrees. Do you agree with the Law Commission (1990) that judicial separation should remain available as an alternative to divorce, and if so, why?

(ii) The effect of the Law Commission's proposals (1990) (see, p. 244, below) is that no divorce could be granted until at least two years after the marriage. The Law Commission recommend that there be no abridgement of this period. Do you anticipate hardship in some cases if the proposals are introduced without the removal of the one year ban?

5 The factual context

We now turn to the facts behind the law. One question which arises immediately is the relationship between the divorce rate and changes in the law. The possible impact upon numbers is demonstrated by the following graph from Richard Leete's study of *Changing Patterns of Family Formation and Dissolution 1964–76* (1979):

Divorces, 1966-76 England and Wales

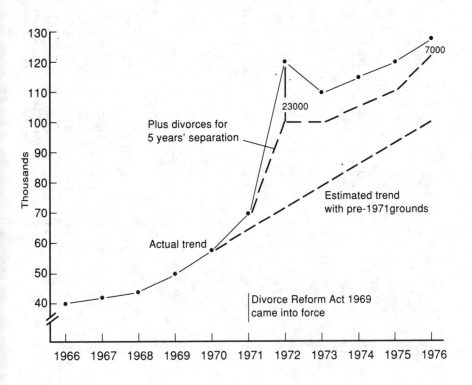

Questions

(i) If in 1976 there were 7,000 more divorces than might have been expected from an extrapolation of the pre-1971 trend together with the five year cases, how would you account for the increase? Is it (*a*) that the law was allowing more already broken marriages to be dissolved; or (*b*) that more marriages were breaking down than even the pre-1971 trend would have suggested; or (*c*) a bit of both?

(ii) If you are inclined to favour explanation (*b*), does the increase of 7,000 (in a total of 126,000 in 1976) strike you as being large or small?

(iii) Look at the table on p. 224 giving the numbers of decrees absolute (including nullity), and the rates per thousand married people, from 1961 to 1989: does this cause you to revise your view?

(iv) If you think that the law contributes to an attitude of mind (see the views of the Law Commission on p. 193, above), do you think that this is most potent when the law is changed? Does the trend in the 1980s support this?

(v) How many *other* reasons can you think of for the rise in the divorce rate?

Changes in the numbers and rates of divorce are important, but so also are changes in the numbers of petitions and decrees nisi, and in the proportions of petitions brought by husbands and wives, as the graph from Haskey *Trends in Marriage and Divorce 1837–1987* (1987) (p. 225) and Table 2.13 from *Social Trends 21* (1991) (p. 224) make clear.

Table 2.13: Divorce[1]

	1961	1971	1976	1981	1984	1985	1986	1987	1988	1989
Petition filed[2] (thousands)										
England & Wales										
By husband	14	44	43	47	49	52	50	50	49	50
By wife	18	67	101	123	131	139	131	133	134	135
Total	32	111	145	170	180	191	180	183	183	185
Decrees nisi granted (thousands)										
England & Wales	27	89	132	148	148	162	153	150	155	152
Decrees absolute granted (thousands)										
England & Wales	25	74	127	146	145	160	154	151	153	151
Scotland	2	5	9	10	12	13	13	12	11	12
North Ireland	–	–	1	1	2	2	2	2	2	2
United Kingdom	27	80	136	157	158	175	168	165	166	164
Persons divorcing per thousand married people										
England & Wales	2.1	6.0	10.1	11.9	12.0	13.4	12.9	12.7	12.8	12.7
Percentage of divorces where one or both partners had been divorced in an immediately previous marriage										
England & Wales	9.3	8.8	11.6	17.1	21.0	23.0	23.2	23.5	24.0	24.7
Estimated numbers of divorced people who had not remarried (thousands)										
Great Britain										
Men	101	200	405	653	847	918	990	1,047	..	..
Women	184	317	564	890	1,105	1,178	1,258	1,327	..	..
Total	285	517	969	1,543	1,952	2,096	2,248	2,374	..	..

Source: Office of Population Censuses and Surveys;
Lord Chancellor's Department;
General Register Office (Scotland)

1 This table includes annulment throughout.
2 Estimates based on 100 per cent of petitions at the Principal Registry together with a 2 month sample of county court petitions (March and September).

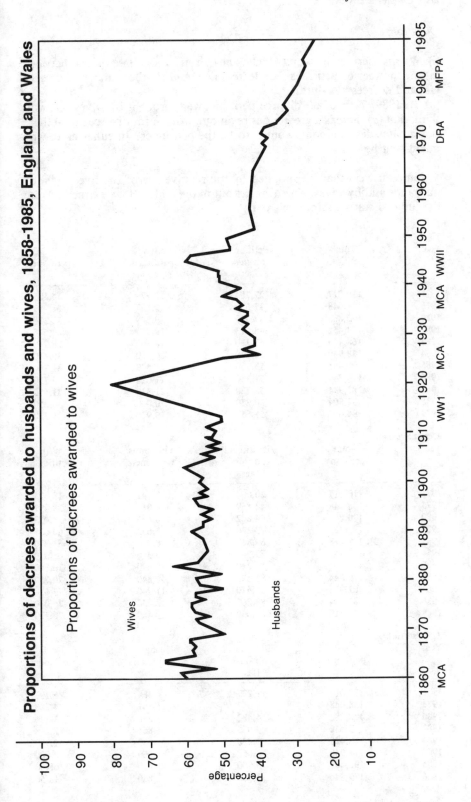

Proportions of decrees awarded to husbands and wives, 1858-1985, England and Wales

Proportions of decrees awarded to wives

Wives

Husbands

Questions

(i) Why is there such a gap (which is never retrieved in later years) between (*a*) the number of petitions and decrees nisi, and (*b*) the number of decrees nisi and decrees absolute?

(ii) In 1989, 72% of all divorce petitions were brought by wives. Do you think that (*a*) there is a greater desire among women for divorce or (*b*) there is a greater desire among women to be the petitioner? In either case, why might that be?

Some answers may be supplied by the relative use of the five 'facts' by husbands and by wives. These are set out in the table below, extracted from the judicial statistics for each year:

1. Adultery

Year	Total petitions	Petitions on this fact	Husbands petitioners	Wife petitioners
1971	110,017	27,284	12,779	14,505
1975	138,048	37,650	15,867	21,783
1980	170,882	47,919	19,549	28,370
1982	173,452	48,013	19,335	28,678
1983	168,428	47,130	18,360	28,770
1984	178,940	50,720	20,310	30,410
1985	190,481	53,330	21,570	31,760
1986	179,844	51,730	21,020	30,710
1987	182,934	52,780	21,330	31,450
1988	182,804	50,250	20,000	30,250
1989	184,610	51,650	19,920	31,370

2. Behaviour

Year	Total petitions	Petitions on this fact	Husbands petitioners	Wife petitioners
1971	110,017	20,004	2,281	18,323
1975	138,048	42,869	4,012	38,857
1980	170,882	64,882	6,870	58,012
1982	173,452	72,320	7,633	64,687
1983	168,428	69,850	8,040	61,810
1984	178,940	73,340	8,330	65,010
1985	190,481	81,220	10,690	70,520
1986	179,844	81,590	10,840	70,750
1987	182,934	85,410	11,740	73,670
1988	182,804	88,260	12,230	76,030
1989	184,610	89,050	12,460	76,590

3. Desertion

Year	Total petitions	Petitions on this fact	Husbands petitioners	Wife petitioners
1971	110,017	11,277	4,484	6,793
1975	138,048	5,847	1,561	4,286
1980	170,882	4,482	1,286	3,196
1982	173,452	3,079	861	2,218
1983	168,428	2,450	730	1,720
1984	178,940	3,060	1,060	2,000
1985	190,481	8,000	1,590	6,400
1986	179,844	2,580	830	1,750

3. Desertion (continued)

Year	Total petitions	Petitions on this fact	Husbands petitioners	Wife petitioners
1987	182,934	2,153	720	1,440
1988	182,804	2,180	730	1,450
1989	184,610	2,050	650	1,390

4. Two year separation and consent

Year	Total petitions	Petitions on this fact	Husbands petitioners	Wife petitioners
1971	110,017	16,057	6,436	9,621
1975	138,048	33,085	12,626	20,449
1980	170,882	39,760	16,042	24,719
1982	173,452	37,704	13,139	24,565
1983	168,428	36,930	12,700	24,240
1984	178,940	38,950	13,670	25,290
1985	190,481	36,460	12,940	23,520
1986	179,844	32,760	11,660	21,110
1987	182,934	31,150	10,960	20,190
1988	182,804	30,860	11,450	19,410
1989	184,610	30,610	11,460	19,150

5. Five year separation

Year	Total petitions	Petitions on this fact	Husbands petitioners	Wife petitioners
1971	110,017	29,911	16,466	13,445
1975	138,048	13,987	6,646	7,341
1980	170,882	12,510	5,775	6,735
1982	173,452	11,389	5,284	6,104
1983	168,428	11,330	5,130	6,190
1984	178,940	10,780	4,970	5,810
1985	190,481	10,210	4,980	5,230
1986	179,844	10,200	4,850	5,350
1987	182,934	10,420	4,770	5,650
1988	182,804	9,830	4,220	5,610
1989	184,610	10,100	4,670	5,430

Source: figures taken from Judicial Statistics, Annual Reports 1989 (and previous years)

The information, in percentage form, appears in *Social Trends 21* (1991), below, p. 228.

Before we leap to conclusions, we should take a slightly closer look. John Haskey, in *Grounds for Divorce in England and Wales – A Social and Demographic Analysis* (1986), analysed the decrees obtained in 1981, firstly by age groups, below p. 229.

Then by social class of husband (1979) and of wife (1981) and by whether they had children (1981), below p. 230.

Haskey returns to the question of children of divorcing couples in a further study *Children in Families Broken by Divorce* (1990) as shown in the chart and table on pp. 231 and 232 respectively.

Divorce — party granted decree: by grounds[1]

England and Wales

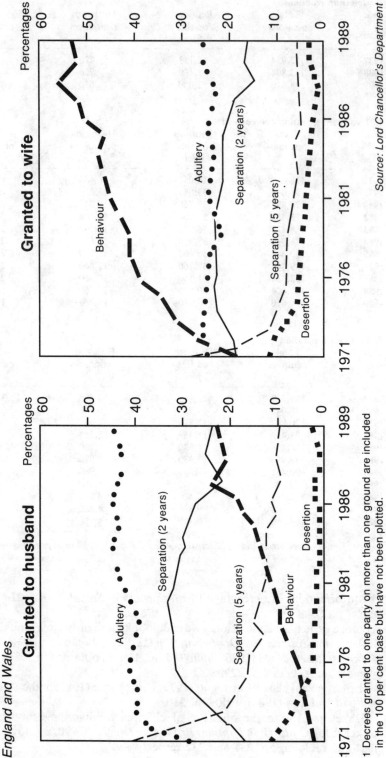

Source: Lord Chancellor's Department

1 Decrees granted to one party on more than one ground are included in the 100 per cent base but have not been plotted.

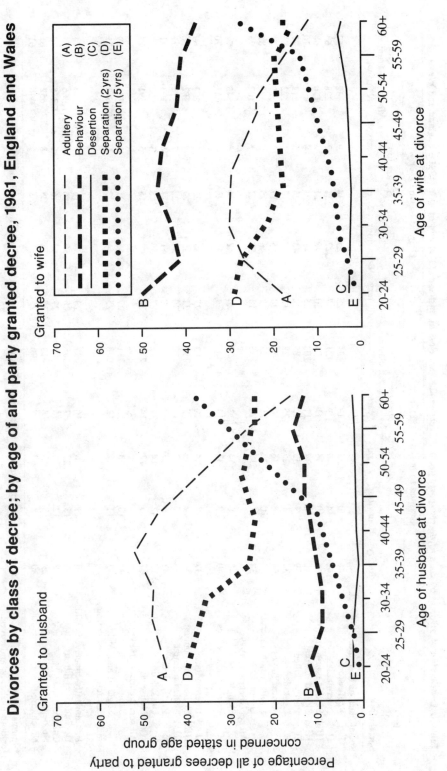

Divorces by class of decree; by age of and party granted decree, 1981, England and Wales

Table 3: Distribution of divorces by class of decree, party granted decree and social class of husband (1979) and of wife (1981), England and Wales

Social class	Granted to husband (%)					Granted to wife (%)				% of decrees
	Adultery	Behaviour	Separation 2 years	Separation 5 years	All classes N^*	Adultery	Behaviour	Separation 2 years	Separation 5 years	All classes granted N^* to wife
Social class of husband, 1979										
I Professional	46	0	33	13	24	25	25	38	9	32	57
II Intermediate	40	4	45	9	121	37	27	31	2	228	65
IIIN Skilled non-manual	45	10	34	11	71	30	40	21	6	150	68
IIIM Skilled manual	46	6	34	11	202	25	41	23	8	482	70
IV Partly skilled	39	7	33	12	85	22	43	25	5	212	71
V Unskilled	32	11	25	25	28	15	67	13	4	123	81
Armed forces	64	0	36	0	11	24	55	17	3	29	73
Economically inactive	37	10	23	21	52	12	46	25	10	223	81
Unemployed	34	11	17	26	35	13	57	21	2	107	75
All social classes, 1979†										
Sample	42	6	34	13	628	24	42	24	6	1,540	71
England and Wales	40	9	33	14	42,407	24	41	24	7	96,661	70
Social class of wife†										
II Intermediate	37	8	44	10	93	27	39	26	6	203	69
IIIN Skilled non-manual	44	7	39	9	198	31	35	27	4	382	66
IIIM Skilled manual	33	17	37	10	30	30	38	22	7	73	71
IV Partly skilled	47	6	37	9	79	19	51	21	6	193	71
V Unskilled	18	32	14	32	22	27	56	8	3	62	74
Housewives	47	15	22	14	219	28	49	15	5	591	73
All social classes, 1981										
Sample	41	10	33	13	781	27	45	21	5	1,723	69
England and Wales	43	11	31	12	43,088	25	44	23	6	103,643	71
Family characteristics of couple, 1981										
Pre-maritally conceived child	60	11	16	10	97	23	54	16	4	274	74
Dependent children	55	13	22	7	368	28	50	16	3	1,066	75
Children	48	12	22	15	491	27	49	16	5	1,275	72
No dependent children	29	8	43	8	413	25	35	28	8	652	61
No children	30	8	50	8	290	25	31	35	5	448	61

* Forms base of 100%; includes decrees of nullity and of divorce for desertion. Multiple facts counted under each fact and joint decrees counted in figures for both husbands and wives.

† Includes those whose occupation was inadequately described and those not normally assigned a social class.

‡ By own occupation

Divorcing couples and children* in their families, 1970-89, England and Wales

*Aged under 16 at date of petition

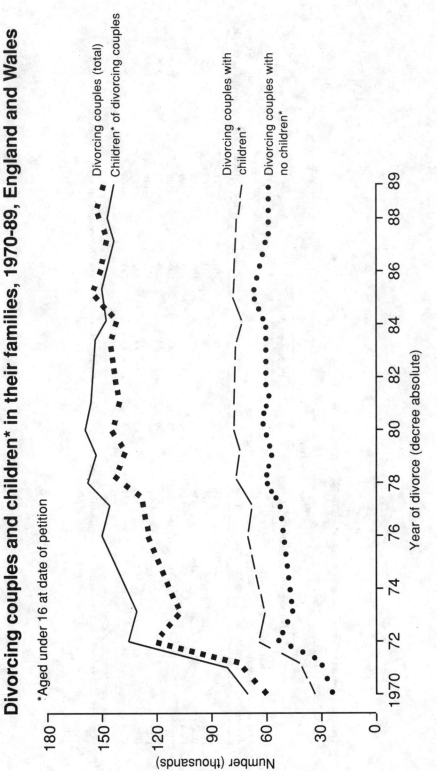

Divorcing couples (total)

Children* of divorcing couples

Divorcing couples with children*

Divorcing couples with no children*

Number (thousands)

180
150
120
90
60
30
0

1970 72 74 76 78 80 82 84 86 88 89

Year of divorce (decree absolute)

Table 1: Divorcing couples and their children*, 1970–89, England and Wales

numbers and percentages

Year of divorce	Divorcing couples						Children* of divorcing couples	Average number of children* per divorcing couple
	Numbers (thousands)			Percentage			No. (thousands)	
	With at least one child*	With no children*†	Total	With at least one child*	With no children*†	Total		
1970	36	22	58	62	38	100	71	1.22
1975	74	47	121	61	39	100	145	1.20
1980	88	60	148	59	41	100	163	1.10
1984	84	61	145	58	42	100	149	1.03
1985	89	71	160	55	45	100	156	0.97
1986	86	68	154	56	44	100	152	0.99
1987	84	67	151	56	44	100	149	0.99
1988	84	68	153	55	45	100	150	0.98
1989	83	68	151	55	45	100	148	0.98

* Aged under 16 at date divorce petition filed.
† Couples with no children aged under 16 comprise those with no children of any age, plus those whose children are all aged 16 or over.

The point about social class is emphasised in an earlier article on *Social Class and Socio-economic Differentials in Divorce in England and Wales* (1984), in which Haskey calculated the 'expected' number of divorces in each social class and compared it with the actual number, giving a standardised rate showing the extent of deviation from the expected 100:

Social class of husband		Standardised divorce rate
I	Professional	47
II	Intermediate	83
IIIN	Skilled, non-manual	108
IIIM	Skilled, manual	97
IV	Partly skilled	111
V	Unskilled	220
	Armed Forces	270
	Unemployed	225

Some observations from these and other statistics, as well as more general arguments relating to questions of 'fault' are provided for us by the work of Davis and Murch (See p. 220, above) and Martin Richards. Davis and Murch in *Grounds for Divorce* (1988) write:

It is clear that choice of 'fact' is class-based. Social Classes I and II opt for 'adultery' in about 45 per cent of cases and have as many petitions based on two years separation as they have on 'behaviour'. The lower the social class, the more popular 'behaviour' petitions become until, in Social Class V, they comprise 57 per cent. Correspondingly, the proportion of 'adultery' petitions declines to the point where in Social Class V it is less than half that in Social Class I.

These patterns are confirmed by the larger (and more assuredly representative) study conducted by Haskey (1986). He also points out the parallels with the social class distribution under the old law, particularly in relation to the ground of 'cruelty' as analysed by Chester and Streather (1972). Those researchers found that amongst petitions based on the ground of cruelty, there was an over-representation of couples where the husband worked in a partly skilled or unskilled occupation, and a corresponding under-representation of Social Classes I and II.

Whilst it is possible to derive a degree of harmless amusement from speculating as to why adultery should be so popular amongst the upper classes, it is certain that we need to look for more broadly social (or extra-marital) explanations for these patterns, rather than regard them as reflecting (albeit with many distortions) the actual marital circumstances of couples within these social groups. They may reflect, for example, different social groups' tolerance of the stigma of fault, or commitment to an interactionist view of marital breakdown.

The class breakdown may also reflect legal practitioners' views as to what is an appropriate (or acceptable) basis for divorce for couples from a given social background. These days, 'adultery' provides an almost totally non-stigmatic route to divorce. This is especially true of those cases in which the third party is not even cited, it being alleged simply that the respondent has committed adultery with a person unknown to the petitioner. 'Behaviour' . . . has not been sanitized in this way. Middle class people, perhaps more aware of the various options, or more anxious to preserve their dignity, tend to avoid it; or else their solicitors, alive to the social cost which a 'behaviour' petition entails, avoid it on their behalf.

As with the evidence relating to the parties' age or to the sex of the petitioner, one possible conclusion to be drawn from this breakdown of 'fact' by social class is that it undermines any case for the continued existence of the present legal categories. This is on the assumption, difficult to establish empirically, that social class variation in the choice of 'fact' does not reflect an objective reality in terms of marital circumstances.

The variation in use of the five 'facts' across the social classes probably accounts for the different patterns which we observed *within each court*. In Table 13 we give this breakdown for each of the courts in which we conducted the Special Procedure survey, focusing on the three most commonly used 'facts' of adultery, behaviour, and two years separation. It can be seen that choice of 'fact' does vary quite significantly by court. . . . The underlying influence of social class is suggested by the fact that Newport and Cardiff, which had the highest incidence of 'behaviour' petitions, also had considerably more men who were unemployed or working in unskilled occupations. It is doubtful, therefore, whether Yeovil is the hotbed of adultery that the figures might suggest, or whether one should regard intolerable behaviour within marriage as another manifestation of Welsh culture, along with fine singing voices and a genius for rugby football.

Table 13: 'Fact' cited by court (Special Procedure survey)

Court	No.	Adultery %	Behaviour %	2 years sep. %
Bristol	615	32	42	20
Cardiff	255	24	55	15
Gloucester	447	34	45	14
Newport ·	273	30	51	13
Swindon	268	37	37	20
Taunton	222	37	32	23
Yeovil	163	44	34	19

. . .

Despite the elements of collusion and contrivance which are readily apparent in present-day decree proceedings, we would not wish to suggest that the parties' marital history plays *no* part in the choice of 'fact', even if the relationship between the two is not clear-cut. For example, when in the course of the Special Procedure project we asked petitioners what had led them to start divorce proceedings, 31 per cent of those petitioning on adultery cited their former spouse's relationship with someone else; only 4 per cent of 'behaviour' petitioners give this as the main reason. We also asked petitioners whether there had been any incidents of physical violence in their marriage. Of those petitioning on 'behaviour', 55 per cent said that there had been violence, as compared with 35 per cent of those petitioning on 'adultery' and 32 per cent of those petitioning on two years separation. It is also possible that the more severe or repeated violence may have been experienced by 'behaviour' petitioners, although this cannot be determined on the basis of our quantifiable information.

But rather than trying to ascertain whether there is any objective relationship between behaviour in marriage and 'fact' cited in the divorce petition, it might be more fruitful to ask whether the parties regard it as appropriate that the law should allow scope for public recrimination in divorce: if the answer to that question is 'yes', it might be argued that the 'fault' element should be retained. In the Special Procedure survey we asked everyone whether the idea of 'the guilty party' had any relevance as far as they were concerned. Thirty-one per cent said that it did, with a further 16 per cent giving equivocal responses. Since the Special Procedure research focused on uncontested cases, amongst which questions of 'fault' might be thought to have less relevance, it is evident that questions of guilt or innocence are still important for many people. But it was also apparent that the listing of one spouse's marital failings, whilst giving expression to the resentment felt by the petitioner, often provoked a sense of profound injustice on the part of the respondent. This, indeed, was the reason given by some men for wanting divorce to remain a public matter: they wished to see these false allegations openly challenged.

Not surprisingly, petitioners and respondents who had experienced the fault-based 'facts' were more likely to regard the question of which party was responsible for the marriage breakdown as being an appropriate element in divorce law, although the variation across the five 'facts' was not very dramatic. In general, respondents were *more* likely than petitioners to say that the issue of guilt or blame mattered to them. This was particularly true of those who had experienced the 'behaviour' fact, with 60 per cent of respondents saying that they were concerned about questions of 'fault', as against only 33 per cent of petitioners. This might suggest that the experience of being on the receiving end of a 'behaviour' petition actually promotes this way of thinking, so that the respondent is prompted to defend the allegations, or perhaps to recriminate in turn. The 'adultery' group was the only one in which petitioners were more likely than respondents to say that questions of guilt or innocence still mattered to them (52 per cent as against 37 per cent).

Our informants advanced a number of arguments in favour of retaining the 'fault' element. The first was that the drift away from fault has undermined the significance of marriage, making it more akin to other types of relationship. As one male respondent put it, 'It [the question of responsibility for the breakdown] matters a hell of a lot to me. By getting away from that, they've taken a lot of the importance out of marriage.'

Secondly, there was the argument that the 'innocent' spouse should be protected against divorce; in other words, if you lead a blameless marital life, you should be able to feel secure in your marital status. As it was put by another man whom we interviewed, 'To my mind, if you've done something wrong – OK, let someone divorce you. But if you've done nothing at all wrong, how can the other person divorce you?' Whilst some 'innocent' petitioners regarded it as appropriate that their spouse should be identified as the person whose conduct ended the marriage, they might nevertheless feel very aggrieved that all the trauma and responsibility of obtaining the divorce fell to them, so that in that sense the 'guilty' party escaped scot-free.

And Martin Richards in *Divorce Research Today* (1991):

The incidence of divorce
After a lull in the 1950s, divorce rates in Britain and, indeed, through most of the industrialised world, began to rise steeply in the early 1960s. This increase persisted until the late 1970s when the curve flattened out and it has remained more or less stable ever since. The fact that this pattern of change is so widespread, geographically, means that we should not look for its causes in local factors. Clearly, attitudes to marriage have undergone a very widespread change in the post-war years.

While it is widely believed that increasing rates of divorce are the consequence of reducing the legal hurdles involved in ending a marriage, the evidence suggests the opposite process is the more important: that as divorce has become more common, jurisdictions have found it necessary to reform their divorce law and to simplify the process in order to accommodate the growing numbers.

There have been many suggestions about how we might account for the rising rates. Rising expectations for marriage and a growing feeling that, if you do not succeed at first, you should try again, seem part of the pattern. Rising divorce rates, at least until very recently, have been associated with parallel increases in rates of remarriage, so the increasing divorce rates seem more to reflect a disenchantment with a particular partner, rather than any more general flight from marriage. But in recent years there may have been a change in this pattern and in many countries there has been an increase in cohabitation, especially for those who have been previously married. As the great majority of divorces are initiated by women, it is reasonable to assume that they most often make the decision to leave the marriage, so it is not surprising to find evidence that divorce rates are associated with the ease, or difficulty, with which women with children can support themselves financially on their own. Housing is probably of great importance and it has been suggested that the housing shortage and, especially the lack of council housing, may currently be acting to depress divorce rates especially in South-East England.

Regional differences in rates remain significant, so that, within the UK, we have very low rates in Northern Ireland, among the lowest in Europe, while those in England are towards the upper end of the European distribution.

It is often suggested that divorce is contagious. There may well have been an effect of this kind while rates were rising rapidly. As people saw those around them divorce and were increasingly likely to have friends or relatives who had been through the process, they may have been encouraged to use this means of trying to alleviate their own domestic problems. In the 1960s the literature on divorce tended to emphasise its potential positive results for adults and had little to say about the difficulties. But in recent years there have been indications of an opposite kind of influence. As the negative effects of divorce, in both personal and economic terms, become much more widely appreciated, people may be much more reluctant to leave a marriage and instead may try to make greater efforts to keep it going.

Taking a wider historical perspective, it is clear that there has been an accelerating increase in divorce since it first became a matter for the civil courts in the middle of the 19th century. It is tempting to relate this growth to the changing nature of marriage, which has been seen increasingly as an exclusive companionate relationship which should, ideally, at least, satisfy most or all adult needs for friendship and emotional, and sexual companionship. There has been a growing expectation that a couple should spend most of their non-working time together and share not only interests, but all their thoughts and feelings with each other. Some, at least, experience the social and emotional exclusiveness of modern marriage as isolation and it is plausible to suggest that these changing expectations are a significant contributor to marital instability and rising divorce rates. Further support for ideas of this kind is provided by societies where the notion of companionate marriage is less strong. In the Middle East, for example, where many marriages are still arranged by families and the roles for men and women are very distinct, divorce remains very much lower than in Northern Europe.

At a more individual level, research has not been particularly successful in predicting which marriages are likely to last and which may end in divorce. It is well established that those who marry young, especially under 20 (or over 35 for a first time), are particularly prone to divorce, as are those who have children before or soon after marriage. These effects may well be associated with the economic difficulties that those who marry young may often experience. Attempts to find particular kinds of personality or styles of relationship which are associated with increased divorce rates have met with little success.

Maybe where you live has something to do with it as the researchers show. Haskey provides the following table in *Regional Patterns of Divorce* (1988):

Table 6: **Estimated divorce rates by standard region of England and Wales, 1981 and 1985**

Standard region or area	1981		1985	
	Divorce rate (per 1,000)	— as a percentage of that for England and Wales	Divorce rate (per 1,000)	— as a percentage of that for England and Wales
South West	12.8	106	13.6	101
Yorkshire and Humberside	12.7	106	14.3	107
East Anglia	12.6	105	13.0	97
South East	12.5	104	13.0	97
North West	12.4	103	13.5	101
England and Wales	*12.0*	*100*	*13.4*	*100*
North	11.9	99	13.0	97
West Midlands	11.2	93	11.8	88
Wales	10.2	85	12.2	91
East Midlands	9.6	80	10.3	77
(Greater London)	(14.8)	(124)	(14.9)	(111)

Questions

(i) Notice that the percentage of decrees granted to wives is higher (*a*) in the lower socio-economic classes, and (*b*) when there are dependent children: why is that?

(ii) What conclusions do you draw from the fact that the most numerous single category is behaviour petitions by wives?

(iii) Why are so few petitions based on desertion?

(iv) Do the figures on the five year fact confirm or dispel fears that it would become a 'Casanova's Charter'?

(v) How would you account for Haskey's finding that 'husbands who divorce their wives who are housewives tend to establish irretrievable marriage breakdown on their wives' adultery relatively more often than the average husband'?

(vi) Why are couples without children more than twice as likely to divorce by consent after two years' separation as couples with children?

(vii) Can you hazard a guess at which groups of petitioners would be most affected by moves to make divorce (*a*) easier, or (*b*) more difficult?

6 A brighter future?

In 1988, the Law Commission published *Facing the Future A Discussion Paper on the Ground for Divorce*. In *Family Law: A Ground for Divorce* (1990) the Law Commission report on their inquiries and the responses to the discussion paper:

1.5 Our inquiries have made three things absolutely plain. First, of the existence of the problem there can be no doubt. The response to Facing the Future [1988] overwhelmingly endorsed the criticisms of the current law and practice which it contained. The present law is confusing and unjust. It now fulfils neither of its original objectives. These were, first, the support of marriages which have a chance of survival, and secondly, the decent burial with the minimum of embarrassment, humiliation and bitterness of those that are indubitably dead.

1.6 Secondly, it is clear that those basic objectives of a 'good' divorce law, as set out by our predecessors in 1966, still command widespread support, difficult though it may be to achieve them in practice. In 1990, however, any summary would include two further objectives: to encourage so far as possible the amicable resolution of practical issues relating to the couple's home, finances and children and the proper discharge of their responsibilities to one another and their children; and, for many people the paramount objective, to minimise the harm that the children may suffer, both at the time and in the future, and to promote so far as possible the continued sharing of parental responsibility for them.

1.7 Thirdly, there was overwhelming support for the view expressed in Facing the Future that irretrievable breakdown of the marriage should remain the fundamental basis of the ground for divorce. This means, first, that divorce should continue to be restricted to those marriages which have clearly broken down and should not be available for those which are capable of being saved; and secondly, that any marriage which has broken down irretrievably should be capable of being dissolved. The criticism is not of the principle itself, but of the legal rules and processes by which the irretrievable breakdown of a marriage is at present established in the courts.

1.8 Our consultations have led us to the firm conclusion that there is one particular model for reform which is to be preferred. It has not only received the support of the great majority of those who responded to Facing the Future, but has also been shown by our public opinion survey to be acceptable to a considerable majority of the general population. This was the model described in Facing the Future as divorce as a 'process over time' but here described as divorce after a period of consideration and reflection, colloquially a 'cooling-off' period or breathing space. [Our recommendations] constitute in many ways a radical departure from the present law: one designed to retain what are seen as the strengths of the present system while meeting the most serious criticisms.

They identify six criticisms of the present law and practice:

(i) *It is confusing and misleading*

2.8 There is a considerable gap between theory and practice, which can only lead to confusion and lack of respect for the law. Indeed, some would call it *downright dishonest*. There are several aspects to this. First, the law tells couples that the only ground for divorce is irretrievable breakdown, which apparently does not involve fault. But next it provides that this can only be shown by one of five 'facts', three of which apparently do involve fault. There are several recent examples of divorces being refused despite the fact that it was clear to all concerned that the marriage had indeed irretrievably broken down.[7] The hardship and pain involved for both parties can be very great.

2.9 Secondly, the fact which is alleged in order to prove the breakdown need not have any connection with the *real reason* why the marriage broke down.[8] The parties may, for example, have separated because they have both formed different associations, but agree to present a petition based on the behaviour of one of them, because neither wishes their new partner to be publicly named. The sex, class and other differences in the use of the facts make it quite clear that these are chosen for a variety of reasons which need have nothing to do with the reality of the case. This is a major source of confusion, especially for respondents who do not agree with the fact alleged. As has long been said, 'whatever the client's reason for wanting divorce, the lawyer's function is to discover grounds'. [See p. 220, above.]

2.10 The behaviour fact is particularly confusing. It is often referred to as 'unreasonable behaviour', which suggests blameworthiness or outright cruelty on the part of the respondent; but this has been called a 'linguistic trap',[9] because the behaviour itself need be neither unreasonable nor blameworthy: rather, its *effect* on the petitioner must be such that it is unreasonable to expect him or her to go on living with the respondent, a significantly different and more flexible concept which is obviously capable of varying from case to case and court to court.

---

7. *Buffery v Buffery* [1988] FCR 465, [1988] 2 FLR 365 (see p. 200, above).
8. *Stevens v Stevens* [1979] 1 WLR 885.
9. *Bannister v Bannister* (1980) 10 Fam Law 240 per Ormrod LJ.

Although the test is to be applied by an objective reasonable outsider, the character and personality of the petitioner are particularly relevant in deciding what conduct he or she should be expected to bear.[10]

2.11 Finally, and above all, the present law pretends that the court is conducting an inquiry into the facts of the matter, when in the vast majority of cases it can do no such thing. This is not the fault of the court, nor is it probably any more of a problem under the present law and procedure than it was under the old. It may be more difficult to evaluate the effect of the respondent's behaviour from the papers than from the petitioner's account in the witness box, but it has always been difficult to get at the truth in an undefended case. Moreover, the system still allows, even encourages, the parties to lie, or at least to exaggerate, in order to get what they want. The bogus adultery cases of the past may have all but disappeared, but their modern equivalents are the 'flimsy' behaviour petition or the pretence that the parties have been living apart for a full two years. In that 'wider field which includes considerations of truth, the sacredness of oaths, and the integrity of professional practice',[11] the present law is just as objectionable as the old.

(ii) *It is discriminatory and unjust*

2.12 83% of respondents to our public opinion survey thought it a good feature of the present law that couples who do not want to put the blame on either of them do not have to do so, but these couples have to have lived apart for a least two years. This can be extremely difficult to achieve without either substantial resources of one's own, or the co-operation of the other spouse at the outset, or an ouster order from the court. A secure council house tenancy, for example, cannot be re-allocated between them without a court order which is only obtainable on divorce or judicial separation.[12] The law does recognise that it is possible to live apart by conducting two separate households under the same roof. In practice, this is impossible in most ordinary houses or flats, especially where there are children: it inevitably requires the couple to co-operate in a most unnatural and artificial lifestyle. It is unjust and discriminatory of the law to provide for a civilised 'no-fault' ground for divorce which, in practice, is denied to a large section of the population. A young mother with children living in a council house is obliged to rely upon fault whether or not she wants to do so and irrespective of the damage it may do.

2.13 The fault-based facts can also be intrinsically unjust. 'Justice' in this context has traditionally been taken to mean the accurate allocation of blameworthiness for the breakdown of the marriage. Desertion is the only fact which still attempts to do this: it requires that one party has brought about their separation without just cause or consent. Desertion, however, is hardly ever used, because its place has been taken by the two year separation fact. A finding of adultery or behaviour certainly need not mean that the respondent is any more to blame than the petitioner for the breakdown of the marriage. If one has committed adultery or behaved intolerably there is usually nothing to stop the other obtaining a divorce based upon it, even though that other may have committed far more adulteries or behaved much more intolerably himself or herself. Nor does the behaviour fact always involve blame: it may well be unreasonable to expect a petitioner to live with a spouse who is mentally ill or disabled[13] or has totally incompatible values or lifestyle.[14] Even when the catalogue of complaints contained in the petition includes violence of other obviously blameworthy behaviour, this might look different if weighed against the behaviour of the other. In a defended case, the petitioner's own character and conduct may be relevant in determining the effect of the respondent's conduct upon her, but if his conduct is sufficient, it is irrelevant that she may have behaved equally badly in some other way. In an undefended case, of course, the matter will appear even more one-sided.

2.14 This inherent potential for injustice is compounded by the practical problems of defending or bringing a cross-petition of one's own. It is extremely difficult to resist or counter allegations of behaviour. Defending them requires time, money and emotional energy far beyond the resources of most respondents. Even if the parties are prepared to go through this, what would be the point? If the marriage is capable of being saved, a long-fought defended divorce, in which every incident or characteristic that might amount to behaviour is dragged up and examined in detail, is not going to do this. It can only serve to make matters worse and to consume resources

---

10. *Astwood v Astwood* (1981) 131 NLJ 990.
11. *Putting Asunder* (1966) (see, p, 190, above).
12. Unless it is a joint tenancy and one of them voluntarily surrenders it, but this brings the whole tenancy to an end. See *Greenwich London Borough Council v McGrady* (1982) 81 LGR 288 (see pp. 51, 168, above).
13. *Thurlow v Thurlow* [1976] Fam 32 (see p. 204, above).
14. *Livingstone-Stallard v Livingstone-Stallard* [1974] Fam 47 (see p. 199, above).

which are often desperately needed elsewhere, particularly if there are children. Legal aid will only be granted if the case cannot be disposed of as an undefended suit without detriment to the interests of either party. As the basis on which the divorce is granted is usually irrelevant to ancillary issues, the parties' *legal* positions are unlikely to be affected whatever their personal views. Small wonder, then, that lawyers advise their client not to defend and that their clients feel unjustly treated.[15]

(iii) *It distorts the parties' bargaining positions*

2.15 Not only can the law be unjust in itself, it can also lead to unfair distortions in the relative bargaining positions of the parties. When a marriage breaks down there are a great many practical questions to be decided: with whom are the children to live, how much are they going to see of the other parent, who is to have the house, and what are they all going to live on? Respondents to Facing the Future told us that the battles which used to be fought through the ground for divorce are now more likely to be fought through the so-called ancillary issues which in practice matter so much more to many people. The policy of the law is to encourage the parties to try and resolve these by agreement if they can, whether through negotiation between solicitors or with the help of a mediation or conciliation service. Questions of the future care of children, distribution of family assets, and financial provision are all governed by their own legal criteria. It is not unjust for negotiations to be affected by the relative merits of the parties' cases on these matters. Yet negotiations may also be distorted by whichever of the parties is in a stronger position in relation to the divorce itself. The strength of that position will depend upon a combination of how anxious or reluctant that party is to be divorced and how easy or difficult he or she will find it to prove or disprove one of the five facts. That might not matter if these represented a coherent set of principles, reflecting the real reasons why the marriage broke down; but as we have already seen, they do not. The potentially arbitrary results can put one party at an unfair disadvantage.

(iv) *It provokes unnecessary hostility and bitterness*

2.16 A law which is arbitrary or unjust can exacerbate the feelings of bitterness, distress and humiliation so often experienced at the time of separation and divorce. Even if the couple have agreed that their marriage cannot be saved, it must make matters between them worse if the system encourages one to make allegations against the other. The incidents relied on have to be set out in the petition. Sometimes they are exaggerated, one-sided or even untrue. Allegations of behaviour or adultery can provoke resentment and hostility in a respondent who is unable to put his own side of the story on the record. We are not so naive as to believe that bitterness and hostility could ever be banished from the divorce process. It is not concerned with cold commercial bargains but with the most intimate of human relations. The more we expect of marriage the greater the anger and grief when marriage ends. But there is every reason to believe that the present law adds needlessly to the human misery involved. Our respondents confirmed this.

(v) *It does nothing to save the marriage*

2.17 None of this is any help with the law's other objective, of supporting those marriages which have a chance of survival. The law cannot prevent people from separating or forming new relationships, although it may make it difficult for people to get a divorce. The law can also make it difficult for estranged couples to become reconciled. The present law does make it difficult for some couples—in practice a very small proportion—to be divorced, but does so in an arbitrary way depending upon which facts may be proved. It also makes it extremely difficult for couples to become reconciled. A spouse who wishes to be divorced is obliged either to make allegations against the other or to live apart for a lengthy period. If the petitioner brings proceedings based on behaviour, possibly without prior warning, and sometimes while they are still living together, the antagonism caused may destroy any lingering chance of saving the marriage. The alternative of two or five years' separation may encourage them to part in order to be able to obtain a divorce, when their difficulties might have been resolved if they had stayed together. From the very beginning, attention has to be focussed on how to prove the ground for divorce. The reality of what it will be like to live apart, to break up the common home, to finance two households where before there was only one, and to have or to lose that day-to-day responsibility for the children which was previously shared, at least to some extent: none of this has to be contemplated in any detail until the decree nisi is obtained. If it had, there might be some petitioners who would think again.

---

15. See particularly the work of Davis and Murch (see p. 234, above).

2.18 It is a mistake to think that, because so few divorces are defended, the rest are largely consensual. There are many, especially behaviour cases, in which the respondent indicates an intention to defend, but does not file a formal answer, or files an answer which is later withdrawn. Some of these are a reaction to the unfairness of the allegations made against them, but some reveal a genuine desire to preserve the marriage. A defended suit is not going to do this, and if a case is, or becomes, undefended, there is little opportunity to explore the possibility of saving the marriage. An undefended decree can be obtained in a matter of weeks. If both parties are contemplating divorce, the system gives them every incentive to obtain a 'quickie' decree based on behaviour or separation, and to think out the practical consequences later.

(vi) *It can make things worse for the children*

2.19 The present system can also make things worse for the children. The children themselves would usually prefer their parents to stay together. But the law cannot force parents to live amicably or prevent them from separating. It is not known whether children suffer more from their parents' separation or from living in a household in conflict where they may be blamed for the couple's inability to part.[16] It is probably impossible to generalise, as there are so many variables which may affect the outcome, including the age and personality of the particular child. But it is known that the children who suffer least from their parents' break-up are usually those who are able to retain a good relationship with them both. Children who suffer most are those whose parents remain in conflict.[17]

2.20 These issues have to be faced by the parents themselves, as they agonise over what to do for the best. However regrettably, there is nothing the law can do to ensure that they stay together, even supposing that this would indeed be better for their children. On the other hand, the present law can, for all the reasons given earlier, make the conflict worse. It encourages couples to find fault with one another and disputes about children seem to be more common in divorces based on intolerable behaviour than in others. The alternative is a long period of separation during which children can suffer from the uncertainty before things can be finally sorted out or from the artificiality of their parents living in separate households under the same roof. This is scarcely an effective way of encouraging the parents to work out different ways of continuing to discharge their shared parental responsibilities. It is often said that couples undergoing martial breakdown are too wrapped up in their own problems to understand their children's needs. There are also couples who, while recognising that their own relationship is at an end, are anxious to do their best for their children. The present system does little to help them to do so.

Conclusion

2.21 These defects alone would amount to a formidable case for reform. The response to Facing the Future very largely endorsed its conclusion that 'Above all, the present law fails to recognise that divorce is not a final product but part of a massive transition for the parties and their children'. It is all too easy to think of divorcing couples in simple stereotypes. In fact they come in many different shapes and sizes. But for most, if not all, the breakdown of their relationship is a painful process, and for some it can be devastating. It affects each party in different ways: one may be far ahead of the other in withdrawing from the relationship before the other even realises that there is a problem. The anger, guilt, bitterness and regret so often felt have little to do with the law, which can seem an irrelevant game to be played by the lawyers. But the law does nothing to give the parties an opportunity to come to terms with what is happening in their lives, to reflect in as calm and sensible a way as possible upon the future, and to re-negotiate their relationship. Both emotionally and financially it is better for them and their children if they can do this by agreement rather than by fighting in the courts. There are always going to be some fights and the courts are there to resolve them. But the courts should be kept to their proper sphere of adjudicating upon practical disputes, ensuring that appropriate steps are properly taken, and enforcing the orders made. They should not be pretending to adjudicate upon matters they cannot decide or in disputes which need never arise.

---

16. That there are adverse effects upon some children from some divorces cannot be doubted; see, e.g. J.S. Wallerstein and J.B. Kelly, *Surviving the Breakup* (1980); however the claims of J.S. Wallerstein and S. Blakeslee in *Second Chances* (1989) as to the high risks of such effects, have to be treated with some caution. One difficulty is distinguishing the effects of divorce itself from the poverty and consequent disadvantages which so often result; see M. Maclean and R.E.J. Wadsworth 'The Interests of Children after Parental Divorce: A Long-Term Perspective' (1988) 2 Int. J of Law and the Family 155.
17. M.P.M. Richards and M. Dyson, *Separation, Divorce and the Development of Children: a Review* (1982).

Questions

(i) Do you accept these criticisms?
(ii) Can you think of other criticisms which can be levelled at the present law and practice of divorce?
(iii) Those are the criticisms. What are the strengths of the present law?

The Law Commission rejected the retention of 'fault'; the introduction of a full judicial inquest into the marriage and the possibility of saving it; immediate divorce either unilaterally or by mutual consent; and a divorce after a fixed minimum period of separation. They recommend a divorce after a fixed minimum period for reflection and consideration of the arrangements: the process over time.

3.29 Several features particularly commended themselves to respondents. One was the recognition that divorce is not a single event but a social, psychological and only incidentally a legal process, which takes place over a period of time. Relate Marriage Guidance considered that acknowledging the time people need to adapt emotionally, socially and psychologically to their new circumstances could have far reaching — and beneficial — effects, not only for the parties and their children, but also for any new families formed through re-marriage. It is thought that one reason why so many re-marriages fail is the unresolved legal and emotional legacy of the first.

3.30 Another advantage emphasised was the encouragement given to focus upon the practical consequences of separation and divorce and to work these out *before* rather than after the divorce itself. Several respondents, including Relate, the Law Society, and the Association of Chief Officers of Probation, believed that the encouragement to look to the future instead of attacking the past would foster constructive rather than destructive attitudes towards the practical issues. The removal of the need to allege fault should reduce the temptation to adopt hostile and adversarial positions in the parties' discussions. This was seen as an incentive for the parties to recognise and meet their responsibilities towards the family, and therefore as a protection for the children and the financially weaker party. The financial position of the weaker spouse would also be improved by the power to make orders during this period. The period itself would assist in negotiations by providing a clear beginning and end to the process.

3.31 The potential for the increased use of conciliation and mediation, in order to resolve practical issues in a more constructive atmosphere, was also favoured, not only by professionals who are currently engaged in conciliation or mediation, including the Association of Chief Officers of Probation, the National Family Conciliation Council, and the Family Mediators' Association, but also by the legal profession and many others. One advantage seen was that the parties could set their own pace for the proceedings, giving time for a person who was less ready to cope emotionally, rather than progress at a pace dictated by one of them. The more constructive environment which this proposal would bring to the provision of counselling services was also welcomed by many respondents, including Relate Marriage Guidance.

3.32 Several features were thought likely to increase rather than decrease the chances of reconciliation. First was the removal of the need to separate or allege fault, with all the accompanying stigma and bitterness. Second was the encouragement to work out the practical consequences of a divorce before committing themselves to it. Third was the period of time itself, which would prevent hasty divorces and discourage people from rushing into remarriage. One respondent thought that it might even be sufficiently onerous to act as a deterrent to divorce itself.

3.33 Finally, it was though that all these features would foster more constructive and co-operative attitudes towards the children's future and reduce the damage which they can suffer from prolonged uncertainty and hostility.

3.34 This model therefore received very substantial support from a wide variety of quarters. There is also good reason to believe from our public opinion survey that it would be acceptable to the general public. 87% of respondents to our public opinion survey thought a model along these lines might be 'acceptable', but that was alongside other models. More importantly, it was approved as the sole ground for divorce by 67% and disapproved by 15%, an 'acceptability' rate well above that for separation as the sole ground for divorce. If the law is to be reformed, as respondents to Facing the Future clearly thought that it should, then this is evidently the model to be preferred.

3.35 However, there was understandable concern among some of our respondents about the details of how it would work in practice. We . . . should point out here the central features which were implicit, or in some cases explicit, in the support which it received. First, a substantial period of time should be required to elapse, in order to demonstrate quite clearly that the marriage has irretrievably broken down. There can be no better proof of this than that one or both parties to the marriage have stated their belief that their marital relationship has broken down and that either or both of them persist in that belief after the lapse of a considerable period. This must be longer than the present interval between petition and decree, which is six months or less in a substantial proportion of cases. It must also give the parties a realistic time-scale within which, in the great majority of cases, the practical questions about the children, the home and the finances can be properly resolved. It must avoid rushing them towards a resolution of those issues, so that they can go at their own pace and draw back if they wish. It must discourage hasty and ill-thought-out applications. In our views, an overall period of one year would be required to achieve all these objectives. . . .

3.36 Secondly, there should be an orderly but unhurried procedural timetable during the period, for the exchange of information and proposals, the negotiation of those matters which can be resolved by agreement, and the adjudication of those which cannot, together with the possibility of making orders to have effect during the period, and of extending it where matters have not been properly resolved.

3.37 Many respondents also attached particular importance to the provision of adequate counselling and conciliation services during this time. The National Campaign for the Family, for example, argued that there should be professionally monitored counselling and conciliation services available in all localities, with trained staff and a firm funding base. . . . counselling and conciliation are two very different things: counselling may either help a couple who wish to try to save their marriage or give support to one or both of them, or to a child, who is suffering particular trauma or distress from the breakdown of a marriage which cannot be saved. Conciliation or mediation provide a neutral figure who helps both parties to negotiate an agreed solution to the issues concerning their children, and sometimes their property and finances, which will have to be resolved if the divorce proceeds. It was considered important that both such services should be available for all couples (and their children) who want them and that opportunities to make use of them should be built into the procedure itself.

3.38 We share our respondents' views of the importance of both counselling and conciliation services. Indeed, we think this just as great whether or not the law of divorce is to be changed. Similarly, we would consider our proposals a great improvement upon the present law, whether or not more resources were to be made available for these services; but there is no doubt that, just as our proposals would provide a much more constructive and less damaging context for both counselling and conciliation to be successful, so would our proposals greatly benefit from increased provision for them. We say this because we believe that it is by the provision of these services, to the people who want and need them, that the most harmful emotional, social and psychological effects of marital breakdown and divorce can best be avoided or mitigated. The law and legal processes cannot do this, although they can, and at present do, make matters worse. The law's processes are principally designed to adjudicate disputes and to oblige people to meet their financial and legal liabilities. This is an important element in the model which we propose.

3.39 There were of course some respondents who specifically rejected this model. It is necessary, therefore, both to explain their objections and if possible to attempt to meet them.

3.40 Some objections centred round the removal of fault from the ground for divorce. Two different types of advantage are claimed for retaining fault. The first is that it provides a moral base for conduct within marriage. The main difficulty with this is that, logically, it can only be done by returning to a system based wholly on fault. The present mixed system of fault and no-fault 'grounds' is, as the authors of *Putting Asunder* recognised in 1966, incapable of supplying a coherent and consistent moral base. . . . Furthermore, granting or withholding the divorce itself is an inappropriate and ineffective sanction against marital misbehaviour; the real and effective sanction is the unwanted breakdown of the marriage. Conduct still has a part to play in determining the practical consequences of that breakdown.

3.41 Secondly, it is argued that the retention of fault provides a public affirmation of 'guilt' and 'innocence' within the marriage which enables the innocent party to feel vindicated in his or her decision to end it. This is an important psychological point. However, one of the difficulties with the whole concept of divorce for fault is that it assumes that fault is the only possible justification for divorce. People who hold this belief, whether for religious or other reasons, may well need to feel that they are morally justified in what they have done. Unfortunately for them, experience has shown the law cannot accurately allocate moral blameworthiness, for there are always two sides to every marital history and different people assess these in different ways; nor do the great majority of divorcing couples want it to do so. They may wish that something could have been done to stop the other spouse behaving as he or she did, or even for the other to be publicly branded in some way, but they shrink from the detailed examination of their marital lives which would necessarily be involved in making a proper assessment in every case. The human as well as the financial costs in making the attempt would be enormous. If that is so, then the sometimes (although obviously not invariably) inaccurate allocation which takes place at present is itself morally wrong, quite apart from the other problems it can cause.

3.42 Another objection was that this model amounts to divorce by unilateral demand, albeit not immediately. This is the inevitable consequence of any system based on irretrievable breakdown of the marriage, including the present one. The present law expressly provides for unilateral divorce after five years' separation, and 71% of respondents to our public opinion survey thought this period too long. In practice, it also provides for divorce by unilateral demand a great deal more quickly, because of the practical and legal problems of defending a petition based on behaviour or, sometimes, adultery.

3.43 It is also the case that this model does not supply an opportunity for one spouse to contest the other's allegation that the marriage has broken down. There are many divorces where one party believes that the marriage can be saved. Sometimes both may do so. Contests in court, however, cannot be the way to do this. As the Booth Committee observed, 'The court itself discourages defended divorce not only because of the futility of trying a contention by one party that the marriage has not broken down despite the other party's conviction that it has, but also because of the emotional and financial demands that it makes upon the parties themselves and the possible harmful consequences for the children of the family'. A reasonably long period of delay, where each party has every opportunity to reflect upon the position and explore the alternatives, coupled with the availability of counselling services if need be, and the removal of the necessity to make damaging allegations against one another, stand a better chance of helping those marriages which can and should be preserved.

3.44 However, it is one thing to accept that the marriage has irretrievably broken down once one party has become convinced, after a considerable period of delay, that it has done so. It is another thing to conclude that that person should 'be able to switch resources to a new family' irrespective of the hardship caused to the first. Under the present law, it is possible to resist a divorce, although only if based on five years' separation, on the ground that the divorce will cause the respondent grave financial or other hardship. In the vast majority of marriages, of course, it is the break-up and separation which cause the hardship, rather than the divorce as such. However, it would be both possible and logical to combine this model with such a hardship bar, if this were considered appropriate. [See p. 245, below.] . . .

3.45 On the other hand, there were some respondents who objected that this model would in fact make divorce more difficult, particularly for couples who are agreed upon divorce and for petitioners who need a speedy decree for other reasons. Both groups would, however, be catered for by the availability of ancillary remedies at the outset, so that all they have to wait for is the decree itself, with its consequent permission to remarry. While we appreciate that there are young and childless couples who realise early in their marriage that they have made a mistake, it does not seem unduly intrusive to require a period of delay before granting what is, in effect, a licence to remarry.

Easier or harder?

3.46 This debate indicates quite clearly how impossible it is to characterise any particular divorce system as 'too easy' or 'too difficult'. 'Easy' may mean short or painless, whereas 'hard' may mean long or painful. For some, the model we are recommending might provide 'easier' divorce, in that they would not have to separate for years before proceeding; for others, for example most of those who now rely on adultery or behaviour, it would be 'harder' because they would have to wait for longer than they do at present. For some, it might be 'easier', because they would no longer, justly or unjustly, be branded the wrongdoer; for others, it might be 'harder', because they would have to disclose their financial circumstances and confront their responsibilities towards their families before they could obtain a decree.

3.47 The emotional pain which many people feel at the breakdown of their marriages is not necessarily linked in any way to the ease or difficulty of the legal process. Divorce is almost always painful for their children, but if there is to be a divorce at all, the system should certainly try to make it as easy for them as it can. This was the unanimous view of all those organisations whose principal concern is the welfare of children.

Conclusion

3.48 For all these reasons, we therefore *recommend*:

(i) that irretrievable breakdown of the marriage should remain the sole ground for divorce; and

(ii) that such breakdown should be established by the expiry of a minimum period of one year for consideration of the practical consequences which would result from a divorce and reflection upon whether the breakdown in the marital relationship is irreparable.

Ruth Deech is no supporter of the Law Commission's work in this area. She puts her point in the following article in the Independent (1990):

Marriage as a short-term option

The last time divorce law was reformed, we all still believed that human behaviour was rational and could be shaped by legal rules.

The Law Commission said its 1969 Act, which introduced simpler divorce by separation, would promote marriage stability and reconciliation. It would encourage spouses to omit recriminations from their petitions.

Twenty-one years later, the inaccuracy of the reformers' predictions about the new law's effect on people's lives is striking.

Cohabiting couples would regularise their unions, they said, the illegitimacy rate would drop as a result of the freedom to remarry, and the divorce rate would not rise. Instead, we find a marked increase in cohabitation and a divorce rate that has trebled to some 190,000 petitions each year.

So why are we about to embark on another reform, and why is the Law Commission . . . implicitly repeating naïve claims that a new law will improve the lot of children?

Liberalised divorce law has not, so far, resulted in a greater sum of human happiness. It has given us over one million unremarried divorcees, many of whom are largely dependent on social security.

Feminists have remained largely silent on the question of easier divorce, presumably because women have diametrically opposed personal interests: one woman's bitter divorce and abandonment is another woman's freedom to claim the man or liberty she wants. Yet it could be argued that, if women as a sex ought to be protesting about anything, it is about this issue.

The public at large does not seem to want any change in the law, including the latest proposal to rid it of fault-based grounds and allow a couple to divorce after working out arrangements over children and finances. Neither is there any pressing need to liberalise the law, because all those whose marriages have broken down can readily obtain their divorces under the existing arrangements.

The reason for reform is one given several times before: that the law should reflect social reality and the fact that many divorces are undefended and uninvestigated.

On each occasion the law has been brought into line with practice, however, it has simply made divorce easier. Once the rate rises it never drops back to its previous level. The resulting increased faith in divorce as a solution to marital problems leads to increased willingness to use it, which in turn leads to a relaxation of divorce procedure and then a fresh call for further changes to bring the law into line with reality.

That happened in 1937, 1949 and 1969 and is about to happen again. It is a spiralling process that Parliament should not encourage, for the sake of children, if no one else.

Common sense, as well as academic research, has shown us that the children of divorce (unlike widows' children) suffer from the divorce itself. It results in lower educational achievement and worse employment and emotional prospects for the children.

From the research, it seems that the most hurtful episode for children in the divorce process is the time of separation. The proposals for a more effective maintenance system and for civilised agreements between parents about access can have no remedial effect: most children want their parents to stay together. Any change in divorce law is irrelevant to children's post-divorce suffering and we should not delude ourselves otherwise.

Rational lawyers, such as the Lord Chancellor, are reported to believe that something can be built into a new divorce process to encourage parents to concentrate on their children's welfare, and maybe to change their minds for the sake of their offspring.

That is much wishful thinking because, by the time a couple has initiated the divorce process, it is too late. In the great majority of cases, the children will remain with their mother and there are no real alternatives on offer. Many fathers soon stop visiting, and recent research by Newcastle University shows that conciliation services have little lasting impact.

The law reformers' argument is that divorce law should bury a dead relationship; it is never conceded that the law itself might have played a part in infecting the couple with a fatal virus.

Everything except the law, has been blamed for the breakdown of marriage – housing short-ages, shotgun marriages, youthful marriages, unions, unemployment, living longer and legal aid.

My own hypothesis is that the most important element in divorce law is the *message* it conveys to the public. We all absorb the prevailing divorce ethos long before we ourselves ever seriously consider ending a marriage, and it is that earlier influence which counts in determining our response. . . .

Everything points to the desirability of leaving the law of divorce unchanged. It would be better for the reformers to focus their efforts on informing teenagers and married couples of the harm done by divorce. It is far too late in a relationship to rely on the divorce law to do so.

Question

Ruth Deech is concerned about the message the proposed law conveys to the public. Can you write a short paragraph describing that message? Now write another short paragraph describing the message the present law conveys to the public.

The Law Commission wish to retain, and indeed extend, the s. 5 bar (see p. 211, above):

5.75 . . . those respondents to Facing the Future who discussed this issue were all in favour of retaining the bar. It provides an important protection for a small group of people who may still face serious hardship which the law is unable at present to redress in other ways. If it retains substantially the same form as the present bar, it is unlikely to be invoked, and even less likely to succeed, in any but a tiny minority of cases. On balance, therefore, we *recommend* that it should be possible to resist the grant of a divorce, on the ground that the dissolution of the marriage would result in grave financial or other grave hardship to the person concerned, and that it would be wrong, in all the circumstances, for the marriage to be dissolved.

5.76 Given that the hardship bar can only apply to divorce rather than separation, it follows that an application to invoke such a bar can only be made once an application for a divorce order has been made. The court will then normally have only the one month period of transition to consider the merits of such an application before the divorce order is issued. However, this should not usually cause insuperable difficulties, as it is almost inconceivable that the financial position of the parties as it is likely to be after divorce would not already have become clear to the court. The person wishing to invoke the bar should have made his or her position apparent in all the exchanges taking place during the period of consideration and reflection. . . . [I]n appropriate cases, the court should give consideration at the preliminary assessment to whether or not the bar is likely to be raised. It should at that stage be possible to require a spouse to state whether he or she intends to invoke it should an application for divorce be made, and if so on what grounds. Occasionally, however, it may be impossible to resolve matters within the month between application and divorce. The court must therefore have power to delay the divorce for this purpose. It is vital, however, that this be strictly limited, so that it cannot be used as a tactical weapon in every case. Accordingly, we *recommend* that the court should have power to postpone the divorce but only where it is probable that the hardship part of the grounds can be established, there are exceptional circumstances making it impracticable to decide the application within the month, and postponement is desirable in order to enable it to be properly determined. Any delay in notifying the other party of an intention to invoke the bar, or any matters relevant to it, should be taken into account in deciding this. Thus, for example, it may only just have become apparent that the applicant will suffer hardship, because the other spouse has only just disclosed details of his pension scheme. On the other hand, the applicant may now be seeking to rely on matters which she could easily have raised much earlier. In the one case delay might well be desirable, in the other not. Only if it is probable that the applicant will succeed in establishing hardship should it be possible to delay in order for the full circumstances to be properly explored.

5.77 It would also be unjust were a bar imposed by the court on the ground of hardship to remain in force indefinitely, despite any change in the financial position of the parties. We therefore *recommend* that the court have power to revoke an order imposing a bar, upon application by either or both parties, where it is satisfied that the grounds for continuing the bar no longer exist. Revocation might be appropriate, for example, where the party who applied for the bar wished to re-marry or where the other party found the financial resources to compensate for any loss of pension rights. We further *recommend* that, provided all the other conditions have been met, the court should then have power to make an order for divorce either after the usual one month period of transition or earlier if appropriate. It would not at that stage make sense to require a further period of consideration.

Question

(i) Given that the Law Commission has rejected the philosophy of the fault-based divorce, why retain the bar?

(ii) Do you think the retention of the bar will be (*a*) the last recourse of the bloody-minded or (*b*) provide much needed protection for dependents and spouses who would otherwise be discarded at will?

(iii) Is pension splitting an answer? (See p. 309, below).

Finally, we return to Martin Richards (1991):

The process of divorce

In the earlier research, marital breakup tended to be seen as a single event. We now appreciate that it is a long drawn-out process that may span several years, from the time when difficulties in the marriage first became apparent to a point when both partners may have settled into new living arrangements after a separation; and it is a process with many alternative pathways. For some, there is a long period of marital difficulty, perhaps with intervals of trial separation, before the final break comes, while for others the process of uncoupling is much more sudden and, indeed, can come as a complete surprise for one spouse. New partners may be involved before the separation, or not until some time after the break. Some move straight from one relationship into another while others may have a long period living on their own. The legal divorce has a variable position in the process. Some begin legal action before they separate, while for others it comes long after the effective end of the marriage, perhaps as the first step towards a new marriage. The timing of the various moves, the advent of new partners and the degree of overt conflict between parents are all of great consequence to children.

Social scientists often contrast male and female experiences of marriage, but it is only recently that there has been much discussion of 'his' and 'her' divorce. There has been a growing tendency for women to be petitioners and to be the ones who decide to end a marriage. Indeed, it has been suggested that men rarely end a marriage unless they have a new partner in prospect, while women are more likely to leave simply to end the relationship and move out of the situation. Thus, the general pattern may be for men deciding to divorce in order to marry (or cohabit with) someone else, while women divorce to get out of a marriage. Financially, the consequences are likely to be very different for men and women. For women, at least for those with children, a period on state benefits will be the experience of the majority, while men usually experience a much smaller drop in living standards and may even become better off.

Illness, both mental and physical, is strongly associated with divorce. Some studies suggest that the effects are more marked on men. This is possibly because many men become dependent on what has been called the 'emotional and social housekeeping' of their wives and may become very lost and disorientated when they suddenly find themselves on their own. Effectively, they may lose all social and emotional support and, indeed, have little idea how to organise their social life, but much will depend on the situation. A mother with children, struggling on her own in poverty, is very likely to suffer from depression, while a husband who has moved in with his lover in comfortable circumstances may feel a good deal better than he did in his conflictual marriage.

Remarriage (or cohabitation) has attracted a good deal of research attention. While many adults may search very actively for a new partner after divorce, the advent of a new adult in the household may produce a much more complex situation for children. In terms of both educational achievement and behavioural measures, there is evidence that some children may be worse off with a step-parent than with a parent who is living alone. On the other hand, household incomes tend to rise with remarriage but, on average, do not quite return to pre-divorce levels.

Perhaps, surprisingly, expectations of a second marriage may be higher than they were the first time round, but second marriages tend to be of shorter duration, especially if there are children from the first marriage. For a minority, a divorce may herald a whole series of relatively short-term relationships which will bring a disrupted life for children with repeated moves and changes of school.

With changes in the law and in the services and support available to divorcing parents and their children, the process of divorce may be changing. Prominent in recent years has been the growth of conciliation.

Questions

(i) Do you think that it is possible for the parties to negotiate sensible arrangements for their home, children and finances if there is doubt about the outcome of the divorce petition?

(ii) But what about those cases where sensible negotiations can never take place?

(iii) Does it surprise you to learn that the Divorce Act 1985 in Canada provides for divorce after one year's separation, or for physical or mental cruelty, or for adultery?

(iv) Does it surprise you to learn that the Scottish Law Commission conclude that adultery and behaviour should be retained as alternatives to the two separation 'facts'; these should be reduced to one year in the case of consent and two years where there is no consent (Report on *Reform of the Ground for Divorce* (1989))?

CHAPTER 7

Maintenance and capital provision on divorce

1 The historical background

At common law the wife acquired the right to be supported by her husband throughout the marriage, albeit how and when the husband chose. (See Chapter 3 above.) When divorce was introduced into English law in 1857, it was thought to be only correct that the wife would have the right to apply to a court to obtain an order for support to substitute the voluntary payments to which she would have been entitled had the marriage continued.

Until recently, English law was dominated by a system of divorce based on the doctrine of the matrimonial offence (see Chapter 6, above). It necessarily followed that the court would attempt to make awards which kept an 'innocent' wife in the position in which she would have been had her husband properly discharged his marital obligations towards her. The Law Commission discussion paper entitled *The Financial Consequences of Divorce: the Basic Policy* (1980) reminds us of the following never to be forgotten words of Sir James Wilde (later Lord Penzance) in the Victorian case *Sidney v Sidney* (1865) 4 Sw & Tr 178, 34 LJPM & A 122:

. . . If, it was said, a man can part with his wife at the door of the Divorce Court without any obligation to support her, and with full liberty to form a new connection, his triumph over the sacred permanence of marriage will have been complete. To him marriage will have been a mere temporary arrangement, conterminous with his inclinations, and void of all lasting tie or burden. To such a man the Court may truly say with propriety, 'According to your ability you must still support the woman you have first chosen and then discarded. If you are relieved from your matrimonial vows it is for the protection of the woman you have injured, and not for your own sake. And so much of the duty of a husband as consists in the maintenance of his wife may be justly kept alive and enforced upon you in favour of her whom you have driven to relinquish your name and home.'

Further,

It is the foremost duty of this Court in dispensing the remedy of divorce to uphold the institution of marriage. The possibility of freedom begets the desire to be set free, and the great evil of a marriage dissolved is, that it loosens the bonds of so many others. The powers of this Court will be turned to good account if, while meting out justice to the parties, such order should be taken in the matter as to stay and quench this desire and repress this evil. Those for whom shame has no dread, honourable vows no tie, and violence to the weak no sense of degradation, may still be held in check by an appeal to their love of money; and I wish it to be understood that, so far as the powers conferred by the section go, no man should, in my judgment, be permitted to rid himself of his wife by ill-treatment, and at the same time escape the obligation of supporting her.

Question

Do you think that the knowledge that there is no escape from the financial ties and obligations of a marriage would operate today as a deterrent against divorce and a buttress to the institution of marriage?

What of a 'guilty' wife? Historically, a wife who had deserted her husband or committed adultery lost her common law right of maintenance. Although the position was ameliorated to a certain extent, the function of divorce was seen to be that of giving relief where a wrong had been done. This inevitably deprived many women of support after a divorce.

Finer and McGregor describe the position in the following way in their *History of the Obligation to Maintain* (Appendix 5 to the Finer Report (1974)):

Alimony in the ecclesiastical courts
26. A right to maintenance in the strict sense — meaning a claim for the payment of money directly enforceable against the husband — was available to the wife only in the ecclesiastical courts, and even there was only ancillary to the power of these courts to pronounce a decree of divorce *a mensa et thoro*. Such a decree, if granted on its own, might have left the wife without the means of survival. The court would therefore at the same time pronounce a decree of alimony, under which the husband would be required to pay his wife an annual sum, calculated as a proportion of his income, or, if the wife had separate estate, a proportion of their joint incomes. It was common to award one third, sometimes less, sometimes — especially where the husband's property had come substantially from the wife — more. A decree of alimony could not be made separately from a decree of divorce *a mensa et thoro*, for which it followed that a wife who could not establish one of the offences on which such a decree could be granted could not be granted alimony either. Moreover, the means of enforcing an award of alimony were of more theoretical than practical utility. Alimony could not be sued for as a debt in the civil courts. Just as the common law courts refused to award maintenance on the grounds that this would have interfered with the ecclesiastical jurisdiction, so on the same grounds they refused to enforce the awards made in that jurisdiction. Before 1813, the only sanction for non-payment of alimony was excommunication or other ecclesiastical censure. Thereafter, a machinery for the imprisonment of the defaulting husband on a writ of *de contumace capiendo* became available, but there is little evidence to suggest that the threat of punishment here and now proved to be any more effective than the threat of punishment in the hereafter.

Maintenance after parliamentary divorce
27. A second species of maintenance attached to divorce by private Act of Parliament. The women who benefited from these awards of maintenance were very few in number. But the parliamentary practice is of cardinal historical importance because it established the principles that were adopted by the legislature as governing the right to maintenance when it established for the first time, in 1857, a system of divorce in the civil courts. The earliest Divorce Acts contained express provisions to ensure that the divorced wife should not be left in a state of destitution. Subsequently, a different practice prevailed:
'In the House of Commons there was a functionary called "The Ladies' Friend", an office generally filled by some member interested in the private business of Parliament, who undertook to see that any husband petitioning for divorce made a suitable provision for his wife. No clause to this effect was inserted in the Bill, lest it should be rejected in the other House, but, as a condition of obtaining relief, a husband was made to understand that, before the Bill passed through Committee, he must enter into a bond securing some moderate income to his wife.'
Two features of this practice call for special note. First, unlike the practice in the ecclesiastical court, which granted alimony only to an innocent wife, Parliament deliberately saw to it that a man could not use its process to rid himself of his wife, whatever her matrimonial misconduct might have been, without making some financial provision for her. Secondly, also in contrast with alimony, the provision which had to be made was not for the periodic payment of a sum

of money. A husband seeking divorce by Act of Parliament had to make secured provision: that is to say, he had to make property available which, under the terms of an appropriate deed, was permanently set aside to secure whatever gross or annual amount he was to pay.

Finer and McGregor describe the beginning of the divorce court (as to which see Chapter 6, above) and then continue:

Maintenance for wives under the new procedure
32. . . . The new divorce court could grant alimony ancillary to a decree of judicial separation on the same principles as alimony could previously attach to a decree of divorce *a mensa et thoro*. It could also in granting a decree of divorce dissolving the marriage, insist on the husband making financial provision for the wife of the kind which the Ladies' Friend, under the parliamentary divorce procedure, had previously secured for her benefit. In this connection, the Act provided that on any decree of dissolution of marriage the court might order the husband to secure to the wife such gross sum of money, or such annual sum of money for any term not exceeding her own life, as having regard to her fortune (if any), to the ability of the husband, and to the conduct of the parties, the court should deem reasonable.
33. The use which the divorce court made of its powers of securing maintenance to the wife when dissolving her marriage took rather a curious course. Despite the fact that the distinctive feature of the parliamentary procedure which the court was supposed to have inherited was precisely that it guaranteed provision for the guilty (respondent) wife, the divorce court at first ruled that it would do this only in the rarest of cases. More than that, by 1861 (*Fisher v Fisher* (1861) 2 Sw & Tr 410, 31 LJPM & A 1) Sir Cresswell Cresswell, the first Judge Ordinary of the court, was saying that a wife petitioner should be awarded less by way of maintenance on being granted a decree of divorce than she would have been granted by way of alimony had she sought a judicial separation, for this would tend towards the preservation of the sanctity of marriage. Four years later, this view of the law was rejected by the court, (*Sidney v Sidney* (1865) 4 Sw & Tr 178, 34 LJPM & A 122) which indicated in the same case that it would welcome a power, in dissolving a marriage, to make financial provision for the wife by way of an order for periodical payments, as well as by way of a secured sum. This power was granted by the Matrimonial Causes Act 1866, which provided that if a decree for dissolution of marriage were obtained against a husband who had no property on which the payment of a gross or annual sum could be secured, he might be ordered to pay such monthly or weekly amounts to his former wife, during their joint lives, as the court should think reasonable. By about the 1880s, the maintenance jurisdiction in divorce had come to be exercised to the following broad effect: the guilty wife, as under the old parliamentary practice, would have some modicum awarded to her; the innocent wife, as under the old ecclesiastical practice, would be granted a proportion, almost always one third, of the joint income, and, in addition, an amount in respect of any children committed to her custody.
37. In 1873, as part of the general re-organisation of the superior courts which then took place, the jurisdiction of the Court for Divorce and Matrimonial Causes, set up in 1857, was transferred to the High Court of Justice to be exercised in the Probate, Divorce and Admiralty Division of the High Court.
38. . . . the court began to state that the rule, borrowed from the ecclesiastical jurisdiction, of awarding one third of the joint income to the innocent wife was not a rule of thumb, and that in awarding maintenance it had to take into account all the circumstances of the particular case. Secondly, signs emerged of a recognition that the moral blame, if there was any, for the breakdown of a marriage might not be coincident with the finding of guilt in the divorce suit. It followed that an adulterous wife might in justice be entitled to a larger award than the sustenance which, following the former Parliamentary practice, the divorce court had conceded to her. As ultimately established, the rule was stated to be:
> 'Nowhere . . . is there to be found any warrant for the view that a wife who had committed adultery thereby automatically loses her right to maintenance regardless of the other circumstances of the case. . . . In practice a wife's adultery may or may not disqualify her from succeeding in her application for maintenance and may or may not reduce the amount allotted. At one end of the scale her adultery may indeed disqualify her altogether. It may do so, for example, where it broke up the marriage, where it is continuing and where she is being supported by her paramour. At the other end of the scale, her adultery will not disqualify her and have little, if any, influence on the amount,' (*Iverson v Iverson* [1967] P 134, [1966] 1 All ER 258).

Nevertheless, the discretionary nature of the jurisdiction gave ample opportunity to judges so inclined to take an idiosyncratic view on these matters.

The Divorce Reform Act 1969 altered completely the conceptual basis of divorce (see Chapter 6, above). Necessarily, the preconceptions inherent in the legal status of the husband and the wife, especially in relation to the doctrine of unity and the concept of lifelong support obligation unless the wife committed a matrimonial offence — all this could no longer form the underlying philosophy of a marriage. At the same time, there was awareness that in reality, certainly in conventional marriages and perhaps also in dual career marriages (see p. 82, above) a wife's performing the 'domestic chores' *was* a significant contribution in its own right towards the resultant value of the family assets. There was also a view, although perhaps it did not play a major role in the reform, that marriage itself was a substantial impediment to a woman's self-sufficiency in many cases. All this resulted in the enactment of the Matrimonial Proceedings and Property Act 1970. That Act permitted all financial orders to be made in favour of either husband and wife, enabling the court to rearrange *all* the couple's assets through periodical payments (secured and unsecured), lump sum payments and property adjustment orders.

The Act also set out detailed guidelines designed to assist the court in the exercise of its powers. These guidelines were simply that; for the basic philosophy inherent in the Act was to permit a broad discretion within the framework of the legislative target. It is to that target that we must turn.

2 The law from 1970–1984; the principles and the criticisms

The 1970 Act was consolidated in the Matrimonial Causes Act 1973. Section 25, relevant to both maintenance and capital provision, provided that it was the duty of the court to:

> . . . exercise those powers as to place the parties, so far as it is practicable and, having regard to their conduct, just to do so, in the financial position in which they would have been if the marriage had not broken down and each had properly discharged his or her financial obligations and responsibilities towards the other.

The Law Commission, in their discussion paper *The Financial Consequences of Divorce: the Basic Policy* (1980), identified four specific complaints:

(a) Inconsistency with the modern law of divorce
24. A fundamental complaint is, we think, that the underlying principle of the law governing the financial consequences of divorce is inconsistent with the modern divorce law. The law (it is said) now permits either party to a marriage to insist on a divorce, possibly against the will of the other party, regardless of the fact that the other party may have honoured every conceivable marital commitment. Why (it is asked), if the status of marriage can be dissolved in this way, should the financial obligations of marriage nevertheless survive — particularly in cases where divorce has been forced on an unwilling partner, or where a wholly innocent partner is required to support one whose conduct has caused the breakdown? Instead (it is argued), divorce ought to provide a 'clean break' with the past in economic terms as well as in terms of status, and, so far as possible, encourage the parties to look to the future rather than to dwell in the past.

(b) Hardship for divorced husbands
25. We have been told that the continuing financial obligations imposed by divorce often cause severe economic hardship for those who are ordered to pay, normally of course the husband.

It is not uncommon for a man to be ordered to pay as much as one-third of his gross income to his ex-wife until she either remarries or dies, and to be deprived of the matrimonial home (which may well represent his only capital asset) at least during the minority of the children. Unless she remarries this obligation to maintain an ex-wife can put divorced husbands under financial strain not only over a very long period of years but even into retirement. The obligation to maintain an ex-wife is particularly resented if the husband feels that it is his wife who is really responsible for the breakdown of the marriage; and such feelings are further exacerbated where he believes that his ex-wife has either chosen not to contribute toward her maintenance by working, or has elected to co-habit with another man, who might be in a position to support her but whom she has decided not to marry so as not to be deprived of her right to maintenance from her first husband.

(c) Hardship for second families

26. . . . Particular resentment seems to be felt by men who have remarried after a divorce, and by their second wives. The burden of continuing to provide for a first wife can involve financial deprivation for a man who does not remarry, but the burden may well be acute if he remarries and has a second family. In such cases the impoverishment caused by the first wife's continuing claim upon her husband may well fall on all the members of his new family. . . . In particular the effect on a man's second wife is a frequent source of comment. It is claimed that she is invariably forced to accept a reduced standard of living by reason of the fact that part of her husband's income is being diverted to support his first wife; it is also claimed that a second wife may be forced, notwithstanding family commitments, to work, even although her husband's first wife, who possibly has no family commitments, chooses not to do so. Indeed some second wives have told us that they feel that they are being required personally to support their husband's first wife because the courts take a second wife's resources into account when assessing a husband's financial circumstances and his capacity to make periodical payments to a former spouse.

(d) Hardship suffered by divorced wives

27. . . . There is no doubt that many divorced wives feel that the law still fails to make adequate provision for them. Not only is the starting point for assessing the provision to be made for a divorced wife only one-third [See *Wachtel v Wachtel* [1973] Fam 72, [1973] 1 All ER 829, CA [see p. 265, below] (as opposed to one-half) of the parties' joint resources, but in practice divorced wives often face great difficulty in enforcing any order which the court has made. The law, it is true, requires that so far as practicable, the wife should be kept in the position she would have been in had the marriage not broken down, but, as the Finer Committee remarked in 1974, private law is not capable of providing the 'method of extracting more than a pint from a pint pot'. We have seen that economic realities often make it difficult for a husband to provide for his second family. The same economic factors also make it difficult for him to provide for his former wife. . . .

One particular aspect of the debate still relevant in the 1990s is the question of whether married women are justified in looking primarily to their husbands for support if their marriages break down. After all, so the argument goes, emphasis is now placed on equality of opportunity for men and women, and it is indeed a fact that most women are employed outside the home for at least some period during their married lives. The argument has been forcefully presented by Ruth Deech. We quote here from *The Principles of Maintenance* (1977):

For some time now there have been available to married women reliable contraception, education and full legal status. Legislation provides for equal opportunities and equal pay: 40% of the working force of employees are female, of whom two-thirds are married and 85% of married women have been in employment at some time during their marriage. But the concept of female dependency on the male continues to permeate the maintenance laws and in addition the comparatively recent state pensions and tax provisions are based on sexual stereotypes of the husband as provider and the wife as full-time housekeeper and child-rearer. This legal supposition of female dependency tends to deny freedom of choice to married and formerly married persons; it is widely considered degrading to women and it perpetuates the common law proprietary relationship of the husband and wife even after divorce. While they express the superiority of the male the maintenance laws are at the same time an irritant to the increasing number of divorced men who have always to be able to provide and who suffer the perpetual drain on their income represented by a former wife. Maintenance awards are emotionally charged with the desire on the part of the wife for retribution and by their nature are unlikely to be readily enforceable because of the hostility surrounding their creation and the fact that the ex-husband is paying money without getting anything in return.

Deech concludes by stating that maintenance should be rehabilitative and a temporary measure confined to spouses who are incapable of work because of infirmity or child care.

A different view, however, is presented by Katherine O'Donovan in *The Principles of Maintenance: An Alternative View* (1978):

Whilst it cannot be denied that laws based on sexual stereotypes are undesirable and ought to be eliminated what both Deech and Gray (1977) fail to see is that the current organisation of family life is premissed on the assumption that one partner will sacrifice a cash income in order to rear children and manage the home. The dependence of the non-earning spouse on the wage-earner is inevitable under present family arrangements. This leads in turn to inequality of earning power of spouses. Without a major change in social and family structures the Deech or Gray proposals merely serve to perpetuate an already unfair situation and will not ensure equality.

. . .

. . . The idea of a family wage adequate to support a wife and children with the addition of child benefit has been built into wage structure since the nineteenth century. So the expectation of society is that a wife's work is covered by her husband's wages. On divorce, without maintenance, the housewife will have little or no income from wage-earning and no National Insurance benefits to fall back on. If she does get a job, as already pointed out, her earning ability will be low.

Deech and Gray both propose that on divorce there should be a distribution of property acquired during marriage. Deech suggests that the Law Commission's proposals on co-ownership of the matrimonial home should be enacted (see Chapter 5, above). Gray proposes that an equal division of property take place. Both approaches involve recognition that the spouse who works at home is an equal partner in the marriage. But neither fully appreciate that without a regime of community of property true equality cannot be said to exist in matrimonial property law. . . .

For the majority of couples there will be a period in their marriage when their major asset, other than possible ownership of the matrimonial home, is the earning ability of the husband. This is why the law gives dependants a right of support after [divorce], and not the fact that they are parasites – as suggested by Deech. . . .

Ruth Deech's argument is ultimately against marriage itself. If the spouse who undertakes housekeeping and child care should not consider marriage as (in part) an alternative career to one which is economically productive, then the answer is either not to marry, or to engage in paid work during marriage. But society does not seem ready for marriages in which both spouses work full-time. The present provision for nursery and pre-school facilities is inadequate. Children are prone to illness and are naturally dependent. Schools are not open for a full working day. And at present there is high unemployment. Participation in the workforce is not necessarily the answer, where there are young children; at least not without major changes in society, with the provision of communal laundries, cheap family restaurants, full-time nurseries etc. And male work attitudes would have to change to enable fathers to share equally in child care functions. It seems unlikely that this will happen. Deech argues that mothers with children should receive maintenance on divorce, and that it is only those who could earn who should be deprived. But withdrawal from the labour market at any time, current or past, affects earning ability, and it is fair that this diminution in earning ability be shared by both spouses.

Carol Smart in *The Ties That Bind* (1984) points to the difficulty of both positions in the context of a feminist viewpoint:

The question that proponents on either side of this debate have posed is, 'Should individual husbands support their ex-wives after divorce?' This question does not allow for a 'feminist answer' as such because whichever side of the debate a woman supports she does a disservice to feminist arguments. Basically feminists have argued for the financial independence of women, hence dependency on men either during or after marriage is recognised as a major problem. But equally feminists have argued for a recognition of the value of domestic labour which benefits not only the state but also individual men. Hence it can be argued that if domestic labour has a value to both the state and individual men, *both* should recompense the woman who has lost material benefits whilst individual men and the state have been reaping them. If we consider these conflicting principles within the existing framework of family law there is no satisfactory solution. Abolishing maintenance for ex-wives does not give women their financial independence, it just means that even more women have to rely on inadequate supplementary benefit (assuming they cannot work outside the home or cannot earn a living wage). On the other hand arguing that individual men should pay for their privileges ignores the fact that many simply cannot afford to pay. But in addition this argument has the deleterious effect of containing the 'problem' within the private sphere, with the consequence that women's dependency remains a private issue and a personal conflict, and does not become a matter of public policy. It is an untenable situation for feminists *precisely* because the original question was framed outside feminist priorities.

Questions

(i) Notice that O'Donovan argues that Deech's argument is ultimately against marriage itself. We know Deech's views about the divorce law reforms (see p. 244, above). Can her argument on maintenance in her 1977 article be reconciled with her views in 1990 on divorce law reform, and if so, how?

(ii) Why is the idea that men should be able to avoid all financial responsibility for their own children through realistic child benefits attractive to an 'emergent feminist policy'?

(iii) Should an able-bodied house-husband be expected to support himself after divorce?

(iv) What do you suppose Carol Smart means by the phrase 'feminist priorities'?

(v) Do you think that the main question is really about how women can advance in the labour market?

Deech thinks that matters will only improve when the ideological basis of a support-dominated maintenance law is abolished; O'Donovan believes that a support-dominated maintenance law can only be abolished after the infrastructure of employment laws, support services for child care, pension and social security laws, and taxation provisions have all been reorganised to permit a woman to survive without the need for support from her former provider.

Questions

(i) Which of these two views do you believe to be *politically* realistic?

(ii) Are they asking the right questions?

In Part IV of their discussion paper, *The Financial Consequences of Divorce: the Basic Policy* (1980), the Law Commission describe seven models which might form the basis of a law to govern the financial consequences of divorce. These are discussed as separate options, and more briefly in combination. It should be recalled that the Commission were dealing mainly with the parties' finances and only incidentally with reallocation of their property. We summarise below the major characteristics of each model:

Model 1: Retention of section 25 of the Matrimonial Causes Act 1973
59 . . . Whilst it is true that the failure of the Act to give any indication of the weight to be attached to any particular circumstance, or indeed to 'the circumstances' as a whole, can make it difficult for practitioners to advise clients on how a case is likely to be decided, it is claimed that any such disadvantage is more than outweighed by the advantage to be gained from the court having a discretion which cannot only be adapted to the infinitely varied facts of each case (which can be foreseen neither by a judge nor by the legislature) but also to changing social circumstances. Moreover, in this view it is not only inevitable, but indeed desirable, that it should be left to case law to provide the coherent but evolving guidance on how to deal with such specific problems . . .

Model 2: Repeal of the direction to the court in section 25 to seek to put the parties in the financial position in which they would have been had the marriage not broken down
66 . . . We consider the most fundamental issue raised by the present controversy over section 25 to be whether or not it is desirable to retain the principle of life-long support which that section seems to embody. It might therefore be argued that the simplest solution to the criticisms of the present law would be for Parliament to repeal the specific direction at the end of section 25(1), but otherwise to leave the section intact; the court would simply be directed to make whatever order it considered appropriate in the light of all the circumstances, including the circumstances listed in sub-sections (*a*) to (*g*) of section 25(1). This would enable the courts to adopt a flexible approach, taking into account not only all the relevant individual circumstances of the parties, but also changing economic factors such as the availability of housing and changing attitudes to the proper purpose of financial provision. . . .

Model 3: The relief of need
70 Under this model, the economically weaker party would be eligible to receive financial assistance from the economically stronger party if, and so long as, he or she could show that, taking into account his or her particular social and economic conditions, there is actual need of such assistance. The principle adopted would thus be one of individual self-reliance: after a marriage had broken down neither of the parties would have any automatic right to support, but rather only a qualified right insofar as it could be justified by special circumstances. . . .

Model 4: Rehabilitation
73 . . . The concept of rehabilitative financial provision has been explained in a recent American case as:
> 'sums necessary to assist a divorced person in regaining a useful and constructive role in society through vocational or therapeutic training or retraining, and for the further purpose of preventing financial hardship on society or the individual during the rehabilitative process' *Mertz v Mertz* (1973, 287 So 2d 691 at 692).

The onus is therefore firmly placed on the spouse in receipt of a rehabilitative award to take steps to become self-sufficient, and in this respect we think that such an approach might often result in the wife having to accept a significantly lower standard of living after divorce than that which she enjoyed before. She would be given an opportunity to develop such skills as she possessed, but ultimately she would be expected to fend for herself. . . .
75 . . . The rehabilitative period might be limited by statute, to a maximum of two or three years or to the duration of some course of training, or it might lie in the discretion of the court. . . .

Model 5: The division of property — the 'clean break'
77 The essence of this model is the analogy of partnership. Where a partnership is dissolved, the partnership property is divided amongst the partners and that is the end of the matter. This, it is said, should also be the case where a marriage is dissolved (Gray, 1977). The principle might be adopted in one of a number of forms. At the one extreme it would involve no continuing financial relationship between ex-spouses: their rights and duties inter se would be resolved at the time of the divorce by dividing the matrimonial property between them. Such division might involve using a fractional approach (e.g. both parties would be entitled to half of the property available for distribution) or it might reflect some other principle such as the 'rehabilitative' or 'needs' models suggested above. Alternatively, the division might be effected solely on the basis of the court's discretion in each individual case. However, other variations on the basic theme

that the financial consequences of divorce ought to be resolved by means of a division of the matrimonial property might also be possible. Thus a law based on this model might provide, for instance, for a delay in the division where the matrimonial home is needed to accommodate a growing family, or for additional payments of maintenance on a rehabilitative or needs basis. . . .

Model 6: A mathematical approach

80 . . . On this approach the spouses' financial rights and duties inter se on divorce would be resolved by reference to fixed mathematical formulae which might then be adjusted to take into account particular factors such as the care of children or the length of the marriage. The result, it is said, would be two-fold. First, the parties and their legal advisers would in most cases be able to save time and money by negotiating a settlement in the knowledge that it accurately reflected current practice. Secondly, adjudicators would be able to decide cases in an entirely consistent fashion. . . .

Model 7: Restoration of the parties to the position in which they would have been had their marriage never taken place

84 On this view (e.g. Gray) the court should seek to achieve 'not the position which would have resulted if the marriage had continued, but the position which would have occurred if the marriage had never taken place at all'. The model is therefore a guiding principle, and might be carried into effect either by imposing an obligation to make periodical payments or by a once and for all division of the parties' capital (or a combination of both) which would be designed to compensate the financially weaker spouse for any loss incurred through marriage. . . .

A combination of models

86 . . . It might be argued however that many of the problems which could result if a particular model were to be adopted as the sole governing principle might be avoided if the law were to be based on a combination of these models. For instance, elements of the needs or rehabilitative approaches could be used to temper some of the difficulties that might arise if the division of property model were to be adopted by itself. Alternatively it would no doubt be possible, whilst maintaining the main structure of the existing law, to amend the guidelines at present contained in section 25, so as to direct the court's attention more specifically to certain matters, for example the possibility that a wife should be expected to rehabilitate herself after divorce.

In *The Financial Consequences of Divorce* (1981), the Law Commission make the following recommendation:

17. We have come to the conclusion that the duty now imposed by statute to seek to place the parties in the financial position in which they would have been if the marriage had not broken down is not a suitable criterion; and in our view it should be removed from the law.

The Report goes on to recommend that the guidelines in s. 25(1) should be revised to give greater emphasis: (*a*) to the provision of adequate financial support for children which should be an overriding priority, and (*b*) to the importance of each party doing everything possible to become self-sufficient. The latter should be formulated in terms of positive principle and weight should be given to the view that, in appropriate cases, periodical financial provision should be primarily concerned to secure a smooth transition from the status of marriage to the status of independence. Thus, of the models advanced in the discussion paper, the English report argues for the retention of a discretion-based framework.

The proposals were introduced into law by the Matrimonial and Family Proceedings Act 1984 replacing the old s. 25 and adding a new s. 25A of the Matrimonial Causes Act 1973:

25. — (1) It shall be the duty of the court in deciding whether to exercise its powers under section 23, 24 or 24A above and, if so, in what manner, to have regard to all the circumstances of the

case, first consideration being given to the welfare while a minor of any child of the family who has not attained the age of eighteen.

(2) As regards the exercise of the powers of the court under section 23(1)(*a*), (*b*) or (*c*), 24 or 24A above in relation to a party to the marriage, the court shall in particular have regard to the following matters—

(*a*) the income, earning capacity, property and other financial resources which each of the parties to the marriage has or is likely to have in the foreseeable future, including in the case of earning capacity any increase in that capacity which it would in the opinion of the court be reasonable to expect a party to the marriage to take steps to acquire;

(*b*) the financial needs, obligations and responsibilities which each of the parties to the marriage has or is likely to have in the foreseeable future;

(*c*) the standard of living enjoyed by the family before the breakdown of the marriage;

(*d*) the age of each party to the marriage and the duration of the marriage;

(*e*) any physical or mental disability of either of the parties to the marriage;

(*f*) the contributions which each of the parties has made or is likely in the foreseeable future to make to the welfare of the family, including any contribution by looking after the home or caring for the family;

(*g*) the conduct of each of the parties, if that conduct is such that it would in the opinion of the court be inequitable to disregard it;

(*h*) in the case of proceedings for divorce or nullity of marriage, the value to each of the parties to the marriage of any benefit (for example, a pension) which, by reason of the dissolution or annulment of the marriage, that party will lose the chance of acquiring.

(3) As regards the exercise of the powers of the court under section 23(1)(*d*), (*e*) or (*f*), (2) or (4), 24 or 24A above in relation to a child of the family, the court shall in particular have regard to the following matters—

(*a*) the financial needs of the child;

(*b*) the income, earning capacity (if any), property and other financial resources of the child;

(*c*) any physical or mental disability of the child;

(*d*) the manner in which he was being and in which the parties to the marriage expected him to be educated or trained;

(*e*) the considerations mentioned in relation to the parties to the marriage in paragraphs (*a*), (*b*), (*c*) and (*e*) of subsection (2) above.

(4) As regards the exercise of the powers of the court under section 23(1)(*d*), (*e*) or (*f*), (2) or (4), 24 or 24A above against a party to a marriage in favour of a child of the family who is not the child of that party, the court shall also have regard —

(*a*) to whether that party assumed any responsibility for the child's maintenance, and, if so, to the extent to which, and the basis upon which, that party assumed such responsibility and to the length of time for which that party discharged such responsibility;

(*b*) to whether in assuming and discharging such responsibility that party did so knowing that the child was not his or her own;

(*c*) to the ability of any other person to maintain the child.

25A.—(1) Where on or after the grant of a decree of divorce or nullity of marriage the court decides to exercise its powers under section 23(1)(*a*), (*b*) or (*c*), 24 or 24A above in favour of a party to the marriage, it shall be the duty of the court to consider whether it would be appropriate so to exercise those powers that the financial obligations of each party towards the other will be terminated as soon after the grant of the decree as the court considers just and reasonable.

(2) Where the court decides in such a case to make a periodical payments or secured periodical payments order in favour of a party to the marriage, the court shall in particular consider whether it would be appropriate to require those payments to be made or secured only for such term as would in the opinion of the court be sufficient to enable the party in whose favour the order is made to adjust without undue hardship to the termination of his or her financial dependence on the other party.

(3) Where on or after the grant of a decree of divorce or nullity of marriage an application is made by a party to the marriage for a periodical payments or secured periodical payments order in his or her favour, then, if the court considers that no continuing obligation should be imposed on either party to make or secure periodical payments in favour of the other, the court may dismiss the application with a direction that the applicant shall not be entitled to make any further application in relation to that marriage for an order under section 23(1)*a*) or (*b*) above.

Sections 23, 24 and 24A are as follows:

23. Financial provision orders in connection with divorce proceedings, etc.

(1) On granting a decree of divorce, a decree of nullity of marriage or a decree of judicial separation or at any time thereafter (whether, in the case of a decree of divorce or of nullity of marriage, before or after the decree is made absolute), the court may make any one or more of the following orders, that is to say—

    (a) an order that either party to the marriage shall make to the other such periodical payments, for such term, as may be so specified in the order;

    (b) an order that either party to the marriage shall secure to the order to the satisfaction of the court such periodical payments, for such term, as may be so specified;

    (c) an order that either party to the marriage shall pay to the other such lump sum or sums as may be specified;

    (d) an order that a party to the marriage shall make to such person as may be specified in the order for the benefit of a child of the family, or to such a child, such periodical payments, for such term, as may be so specified;

    (e) an order that a party to the marriage shall secure to such person as may be so specified for the benefit of such a child, or to such a child, to the satisfaction of the court such periodical payments, for such term, as may be so specified;

    (f) an order that a party to the marriage shall pay to such person as may be so specified for the benefit of such a child, or to such a child, such lump sum as may be so specified;

subject however, in the case of an order under paragraph (d), (e) or (f) above, to the restrictions imposed by section 29(1) and (3) below on the making of financial provision orders in favour of children who have attained the age of eighteen.

(2) The court may also, subject to those restrictions, make any one or more of the orders mentioned in subsection (1)(d), (e) and (f) above—

    (a) in any proceedings for divorce, nullity of marriage or judicial separation, before granting a decree; and

    (b) where any such proceedings are dismissed after the beginning of the trial, either forthwith or within a reasonable period after the dismissal.

(3) Without prejudice to the generality of subsection (1)(c) or (f) above—

    (a) an order under this section that a party to a marriage shall pay a lump sum to the other party may be made for the purpose of enabling that other party to meet any liabilities or expenses reasonably incurred by him or her in maintaining himself or herself or any child of the family before making an application for an order under this section in his or her favour;

    (b) an order under this section for the payment of a lump sum to or for the benefit of a child of the family may be made for the purpose of enabling any liabilities or application for an order under this section in his favour to be met; and

    (c) an order under this section for the payment of a lump sum may provide for the payment of that sum by instalments for such amount as may be specified in the order and may require the payment of the instalments to be secured to the satisfaction of the court.

(4) The power of the court under subsection (1) or (2)(a) above to make an order in favour of a child of the family shall be exercisable from time to time; and where the court makes an order in favour of a child under subsection (2)(b) above, it may from time to time, subject to the restrictions mentioned in subsection (1) above, make a further order in his favour of any of the kinds mentioned in subsection (1) (d), (e) or (f) above.

(5) Without prejudice to the power to give a direction under section 30 below for the subsection (1)(a), (b) or (c) above on or after granting a decree of divorce or nullity of marriage, neither the order nor any settlement made in pursuance of the order shall take effect unless the decree has been made absolute.

(6) Where the court—

    (a) makes an order under this section for the payment of a lump sum; and

    (b) directs—

        (i) that payment of that sum or any part of it shall be deferred; or

        (ii) that that sum or any part of it shall be paid by instalments,

the court may order that the amount deferred or the instalments shall carry interest at such rate as may be specified by the order from such date, not earlier than the date of the order, as may be so specified, until the date when payment of it is due.

24. Property adjustment orders in connection with divorce proceedings, etc.

(1) On granting a decree of divorce, a decree of nullity of marriage or a decree of judicial separation or at any time thereafter (whether, in the case of a decree of divorce, or of nullity of marriage, before or after the decree is made absolute), the court may make any one or more of the following orders, that is to say—

(*a*) an order that a party to the marriage shall transfer to the other party, to any child of the family or to such person as may be specified in the order for the benefit of such a child such property as may be so specified, being property to which the first-mentioned party is entitled, either in possession or reversion;

(*b*) an order that a settlement of such property as may be so specified, being property to which a party to the marriage is so entitled, be made to the satisfaction of the court for the benefit of the other party to the marriage and of the children of the family or either or any of them;

(*c*) an order varying for the benefit of the parties to the marriage and of the children of the family or either or any of them any ante-nuptial or post-nuptial settlement (including such a settlement made by will or codicil) made on the parties to the marriage;

(*d*) an order extinguishing or reducing the interest of either of the parties to the marriage under any such settlement;

subject, however, in the case of an order under paragraph (*a*) above, to the restrictions imposed by section 29(1) and (3) below on the making of orders for a transfer of property in favour of children who have attained the age of eighteen.

(2) The court may make an order under subsection (1)(*c*) above notwithstanding that there are no children of the family.

(3) Without prejudice to the power to give a direction under section 30 below for the settlement of an instrument by conveyancing counsel, where an order is made under this section on or after granting a decree of divorce or nullity of marriage, neither the order nor any settlement made in pursuance of the order shall take effect unless the decree has been made absolute.

24A. Orders for sale of property
(1) Where the court makes under section 23 or 24 of this Act a secured periodical payments order, an order for the payment of a lump sum or a property adjustment order, then, on making that order or at any time thereafter, the court may make a further order for the sale of such property as may be specified in the order, being property in which or in the proceeds of sale of which either or both of the parties to the marriage has or have a beneficial interest, either in possession or reversion.

(2) Any order made under subsection (1) above may contain such consequential or supplementary provisions as the court thinks fit and, without prejudice to the generality of the foregoing provision, may include—

(*a*) provision requiring the making of a payment out of the proceeds of sale of the property to which the order relates, and

(*b*) provision requiring any such property to be offered for sale to a person, or class of persons, specified in the order.

(3) Where an order is made under subsection (1) above on or after the grant of a decree of divorce or nullity of marriage, the order shall not take effect unless the decree has been made absolute.

(4) Where an order is made under subsection (1) above, the court may direct that the order, or such provision thereof as the court may specify, shall not take effect until the occurrence of an event specified by the court or the expiration of a period so specified.

(5) Where an order under subsection (1) above contains a provision requiring the proceeds of sale of the property to which the order relates to be used to secure periodical payments to a party to the marriage, the order shall cease to have effect on the death or re-marriage of that person.

(6) Where a party to a marriage has a beneficial interest in any property, or in the proceeds of sale thereof, and some other person who is not a party to the marriage also has a beneficial interest in that property or in the proceeds of sale thereof, then, before deciding whether to make an order under this section in relation to that property, it shall be the duty of the court to give that other person an opportunity to make representations with respect to the order; and any representations made by that other person shall be included among the circumstances to which the court is required to have regard under section 25(1) below.

3 A Scottish alternative

Proposals from the Scottish Law Commission in *Aliment and Financial Provision* (1981) and the resultant legislation in Scotland provides an interesting contrast:

Need for balance between principle and discretion
3.62 One of the main criticisms made of the present law on financial provision is that it leaves too much to the unfettered discretion of the court. We think that this criticism is justified. On the other hand we have no doubt that the courts must be left with considerable discretion to take account of the great variety of circumstances in cases which come before them. One of our main concerns in this Report has been to try to strike the right balance between principle and discretion. We take as our starting point the proposition that an order for financial provision should be made if, and only if, it is justified by an applicable principle. . . .

FAIR SHARING OF MATRIMONIAL PROPERTY

A principle of quantification
3.65 When we refer to the principle of fair sharing of matrimonial property we are not talking about the division of specific items of property. How the value of a spouse's share would be satisfied would depend on the resources available at the time of the divorce. The court's powers would not be limited to matrimonial property (as defined) but would extend to all of the spouses' resources at the time of the divorce. The concept of matrimonial property would be relevant only as a means of arriving at a figure. . . . The basic idea is that it covers property acquired by the spouses, otherwise than by gift or inheritance, in the period between the marriage and their final separation.

The norm of equal sharing
3.66 It would be too vague to empower the courts to award simply a 'fair share' of matrimonial property. One of the major criticisms of the present law is that it provides no guidance on the amount of a capital sum which can be expected on divorce. It would, on the other hand, be too rigid to lay down a fixed rule of apportionment for all cases. We think that the best solution is to provide that matrimonial property should normally be divided equally between the parties but that the court should be able to depart from this norm of equal sharing in special circumstances. . . . [We] can see no good reason for giving either spouse, whether legal owner or not, whether wife or husband, less than half of the matrimonial property. The underlying idea is that of partnership in marriage and the only fair solution seems to us to be an equal division of the 'partnership' assets as the norm. We are confirmed in this conclusion by the fact that no system of matrimonial property of which we are aware provides for a division of such property in any fixed proportions other than equal shares.
3.68 Where there are special circumstances justifying a departure from equal sharing . . . we think that the court should be directed to share the matrimonial property in such proportions as may be fair in those circumstances. It would be impossible to provide with precision for the infinite variety of special circumstances which may arise. We therefore recommend:
>   32. (*a*) The principle of fair sharing of matrimonial property is that the net value of the matrimonial property should be shared equally or, if there are special circumstances justifying a departure from equal sharing, in such other proportions as may be fair in those circumstances. . . .

Having defined matrimonial property essentially in terms of property acquired during marriage and discussed the special circumstances justifying the departure from equal sharing, they turn to a discussion of the recognition of contributions:

·3.92 The first is where the contributions of one spouse have contributed to an improvement in the other's economic position. A husband, for example, may have paid off a loan over a house owned by his wife before the marriage, or he may have worked for years extending and improving her house. Similarly a wife may have worked for years, unpaid, in a small business owned by her husband before the marriage and may have helped to build up its value. In all these cases one spouse has contributed to an increase in the capital of the other and we think it reasonable that the court should be able to award some financial provision on divorce in recognition of the contributions. The position is essentially the same where one of the spouses has contributed to an increase in the other's earning potential. A wife, for example, may have bought the husband into a partnership or franchise arrangement on such terms that there are minimal rights to capital but a valuable earning potential. A husband may have worked over-time to pay his wife's fees for some special course of further education or training. A wife may have helped her husband with his work on an unpaid basis (e.g. as a personal secretary or business manager) but because of the nature of his work (e.g. author, doctor, advocate, professional sportsman, entertainer) the result of her contributions may be an increase in his earning potential rather than in the capital value of a business. Again, there may be cases where one spouse's unpaid services as a housekeeper, hostess, domestic manager and child-minder could be shown to have contributed directly or indirectly to an improvement in the other spouse's economic position. It may be possible to prove, for example, that a wife's contributions of this nature have enabled her husband to work long hours furthering his career. In all these cases, where there is a demonstrable link between one spouse's contributions and an improvement in the other spouse's economic position, it seems to us that there is a strong case for enabling the contribution to be recognised where this is not already done by means of a share in matrimonial property.

3.93 The position becomes more difficult, however, if there is no link between the contributions and any improvement in the other spouse's economic position. Suppose, for example, that three men all started work in the same employment at the age of 20. The first married a wife who assumed the traditional housewife's role and did all the domestic work. The second married an idle woman and did most of the domestic work himself. The third remained unmarried and did all his own domestic work. All three lived in rented accommodation. None accumulated any savings. All advanced remorselessly up their salary scale. If the first man was divorced at the age of 40 it would certainly not be obvious that his wife's contributions over the years had contributed to any improvement in his economic position, although they may well have contributed to an increase in the time available to him for leisure activities. Should an industrious wife receive more than an idle wife in this case? Should the principle of fair recognition of contributions extend to contributions to the welfare of the family even if they have not improved the other spouse's economic position? One submission made to us was that such contributions were made voluntarily and should therefore be ignored. The same point could, however, be made about many contributions which have directly improved the other spouse's economic position. Another view put to us was that the law should take a hard line on the question of a housewife's contributions in order to encourage women to preserve their economic independence during marriage. In our view, however, it is not the function of financial provision on divorce to encourage people to adopt any particular life style during marriage. The law in our view ought to be neutral in this respect. We therefore reject these two arguments. We think, however, that there are other grounds for not recognising a claim based on contributions which have not resulted in any improvement in the other spouse's economic position. First, such contributions will often be evenly balanced. If, in the traditional type of marriage, a housewife could make a claim on the basis of contributions in work towards the welfare of the family, her husband could often do the same. One of the findings of the survey on family property in Scotland in 1979 was that 50% of married informants said that the contributions of the husband and the wife in unpaid work in the home were about the same. Moreover, if a wife could make a claim on the basis of her contributions in work, her husband could often make a claim on the basis of his contributions in money to the welfare of the family. In some cases (for example the lazy wife, the wife with domestic help) the husband would be able to make a claim on this basis for a payment out of the wife's separate property. We doubt whether this would be acceptable. Secondly, an attempt to work out which spouse had contributed more to the welfare of the family during the marriage would often involve an unproductive examination and investigation of conduct over many years. Thirdly, and more fundamentally, the purpose of financial provision on divorce is not, in our view, the punishment of bad conduct or the reward of good conduct. In our view its concern should be with the economic effects of marriage and divorce . . .

3.94 There is a further problem. One spouse may have sustained an economic disadvantage in the interests of the other party or of the family. The standard illustration is the well-qualified woman who married, say, 20 or 30 years ago and who gave up her own career prospects, perhaps with the encouragement or passive approval of her husband, in order to look after and bring up the family. There are other illustrations. A husband may have given up career prospects (for example the chance of a lucrative post abroad) in his wife's interests. An older woman may have given up a good position on marriage in order to look after her husband and may be unable to obtain employment again after divorce. One of the parties may have given up a tenancy in order to live with the other party on marriage. In all such cases there should in our view be the possibility of financial provision on divorce in recognition of the economic disadvantages sustained. . . .

FAIR PROVISION FOR ADJUSTMENT TO INDEPENDENCE

The principle
3.107 In many cases divorcing spouses will already be economically independent by the time of the divorce. In many cases an award of financial provision under one of the principles

discussed above would be sufficient to provide for any necessary adjustment to post-divorce independence. In other cases, however, we think that a reasonable objective of an award of financial provision on divorce is to enable a spouse to adjust, over a relatively short period, to the cessation on divorce of any financial dependence on the other spouse. Depending on the circumstances, the purpose of the award might be to enable the payee to undertake a course of training or retraining, or to give the payee time to find suitable employment, or to enable the payee to adjust gradually to a lower standard of living. It would be essential to specify a maximum time over which the adjustment would have to be made because otherwise there would, in many cases, be no way of ensuring that a transitional provision did not become permanent life-long support. We think that a period of three years from the date of divorce would be an adequate maximum period, given that in most cases the final separation between the parties would be some considerable time before that. We considered whether an adjustment provision ought to be available for, say, three years after the termination of a period of child-care after divorce. We have concluded, however, that this would not be justified. The main purpose of a provision under this principle is to provide time to adjust. . . .

Factors to be taken into account

3.108 In addition to the usual factors such as the needs and resources of the parties, we think that it would be desirable to refer specifically, in relation to this principle, to the earning capacity of the payee, to the duration and extent of the payee's past dependency on the payer and to any intentions of the payee to undertake a course of education or training. . . .
3.109 We therefore recommend as follows:
   35. (a) The principle of fair provision for adjustment to independence is that where one party to the marriage has been financially dependent on the other and the dependence has come to an end on divorce, the dependent party should receive such financial provision as is fair and reasonable to enable him to adjust, over a period of not more than three years from the date of divorce, to the cessation of that dependence.
   (b) In deciding what financial provision is fair and reasonable under this recommendation the court should have regard to the age, health and earning capacity of the applicant, to the duration and extent of the applicant's past dependency on the payer, to any intention of the applicant to undertake a course of education or training, to the needs and resources, actual or foreseeable, of the parties, and to the other circumstances of the case. . . .

RELIEF OF GRAVE FINANCIAL HARDSHIP

Purpose and scope

3.110 It could be argued that the . . . principles which we have discussed so far are adequate to cover all cases where financial provision on divorce is justified. This would mean that if there was no matrimonial property, if there was no claim based on contributions or disadvantages, and if there were no dependent children, then a divorced spouse could be awarded at most a provision designed to ease his or her adjustment to independence over a period of not more than three years. Thereafter he or she would have no claim against the former spouse. While there is much to be said for this approach, we have rejected it. The . . . principles discussed already would not always ensure that a spouse who suffered severe financial hardship as a result of the marriage and the divorce could recover some financial provision in appropriate cases. A wife might, for example, have gone with her husband to some tropical country and might have contracted a disabling disease. Or she might have been permanently disabled as a result of injury in childbirth. We think that in such cases financial provision on divorce would be justified if it were reasonable having regard to the parties' resources. We have more doubt about whether a former spouse should ever be expected to relieve the hardship of the other if the hardship does not arise in any way from the marriage. If we were approaching the matter as one of pure principle we would be inclined to reject such a proposition as contrary to the idea that divorce ends the marriage. Financial provision on divorce is not, however, simply a matter of abstract principle. It is essential that any system should be acceptable to public opinion and it is clear from the comments we have received that many people would find it hard to accept a system which cut off, say, an elderly or disabled spouse with no more than a three-year allowance after divorce, no matter how wealthy the other party might be. We have concluded therefore that the law ought to provide, as a 'long-stop', for the case where one spouse would suffer grave financial hardship as a result of the divorce. In such a case the court should be able to award such financial provision as is fair and reasonable in the circumstances to relieve the hardship over such period as the court may determine. We do not intend this principle to be a gateway to support after divorce in all cases just as if the marriage had not been dissolved. We do not think, for example, that a man who suffers hardship on being made redundant at the age of 52 should have a claim for financial provision against a former wife whom he divorced thirty years before. We think that the general principle should be that after the divorce each party bears the risk of *supervening* hardship without recourse against the other. It should therefore be made clear in the legislation that it is only where the likelihood of grave financial hardship is established at the time of the divorce that a claim will arise under this principle.

Questions

(i) Does the approach of the Scottish Law Commission differ substantially from that of the English Law Commission?
(ii) If so, whose approach do you prefer?

The Family Law (Scotland) Act 1985 states:

Principles to be applied
9. — (1) The principles which the court shall apply in deciding what order for financial provision, if any, to make are that —
  (a) the net value of the matrimonial property should be shared fairly between the parties to the marriage;
  (b) fair account should be taken of any economic advantage derived by either party from contributions by the other, and of any economic disadvantages suffered by either party in the interests of the other party or of the family;
  (c) any economic burden of caring, after divorce, for a child of the marriage under the age of 16 years should be shared fairly between the parties;
  (d) a party who has been dependent to a substantial degree on the financial support of the other party should be awarded such financial provision as is reasonable to enable him to adjust, over a period of not more than three years from the date of the decree of divorce, to the loss of that support on divorce;
  (e) a party who at the time of the divorce seems likely to suffer serious financial hardship as a result of the divorce should be awarded such financial provision as is reasonable to relieve him of hardship over a reasonable period.
  (2) In subsection (1)(b) above and section 11(2) of this Act —
  'economic advantage' means advantage gained whether before or during the marriage and includes gains in capital, in income and in earning capacity, and 'economic disadvantage' shall be construed accordingly;
  'contributions' means contributions made whether before or during the marriage; and includes indirect and non-financial contributions and, in particular, any such contribution made by looking after the family home or caring for the family.

Question

Note that 'grave' financial hardship recommended by the Scottish Law Commission has been replaced by 'serious' financial hardship. Is there a difference?

Criticisms of the Scottish legislation are summarised by the Family Law Committee of the Law Society in their memorandum on *Maintenance and Capital Provision on Divorce* (1991):

2.17 The principles in the Scottish legislation were subject to criticism at the time of the legislation's enactment and this criticism has been borne out in research into the effect the Act has had on advice given by solicitors to their clients (*see Wasoff, Dobash and Harcus 'The Impact of the Family Law Scotland Act 1985 on Solicitors' Divorce Practice'* 1990).

2.18 At the time the Act was passed [Stephen] Cretney argued in *'Money After Divorce — The Mistakes We Have Made'* (1986) that although the Scottish system does seem to reduce judicial discretion nevertheless three criticisms can be made of it. First, that although certainty has been achieved through the implementation of a framework of principles, scope for uncertainty still exists. If you take the judge's discretion under the existing English law as being as long as a piece of string, and replace it by five pieces of string each of indeterminate length, as under the Scottish legislation, it is far from clear that the position has been improved. Secondly, he argues that the Scottish legislation is unfavourable to women as the court cannot make an order for periodical payments unless it is satisfied that an order for the payment of a capital sum or transfer of property would not by itself be appropriate or sufficient to give effect to the five principles embodied in the legislation. Thirdly, if the court does order periodical payments they must not be for a longer period than three years from the date of divorce unless these payments are required in order to satisfy the two principles of fair sharing of the burden of child care or relief from serious financial hardship. In addition, another limitation on any settlement is the fact that spouses are entitled to receive 'fair recognition of contributions and disadvantages'. There is also a proviso that claims are only to be accepted under this heading if they have resulted in an improvement in the spouse's economic position.

2.19 Under the Scottish Code there is no reference to the welfare of the child(ren) because claims in respect of the child(ren) are dealt with independently of claims of parents in divorce proceedings. Thus, when considering the allocation of income and property, attention is not specifically directed to the interests of the children although the court must have regard to the economic burden of child care. It is the Family Law Committee's view that any set of principles dealing with maintenance and capital provision on divorce should include within it recognition that the interests of any children should be the first consideration.

2.20 The Committee believes that the principles in the Scottish legislation have the potential to produce arbitrary results. This concern is backed up . . . by A R Dewar *'The Family Law (Scotland) Act 1985 in Practice'* (1989) in which he stated that the courts were relying on the fifth principle of relief from serious financial hardship to an unexpected degree in order to avoid this. The results of the research carried out by Wasoff, Dobash and Harcus [1990] also lend support to this argument as well as revealing a number of other problems experienced by solicitors in their interpretation of the legislation.

2.22 . . . the research shows that the existence of the principles does not seem to be a universal panacea for a number of reasons. First, the principles have not led to identical advice being given by solicitors when presented with identical facts. This is partly because the solicitors participate in a process of negotiation and it is inherent in negotiation that a process of give and take occurs. Certainty is by definition therefore impossible; however, the field for negotiation did not seem to be greatly reduced by the existence of principles. Commonly, by the end of the first interview the solicitors were able to give their clients an indication of the boundaries of what would be an acceptable solution — this represents only a small improvement on what solicitors operating under the Matrimonial Causes Act 1973 are able to do at the end of a first interview.

2.23 Secondly, most if not all, of the solicitors interviewed stressed the need for negotiated settlements. Solicitors had both positive and negative reasons for not wishing to go to court and the negative reasons indicate a second problem with the use of principles. On the positive side the solicitors emphasised the emotional and financial benefits (in terms of costs) to the parties of a negotiated settlement. On the negative side, they expressed concern at their ignorance of how the five principles would be interpreted by the court — thus revealing the extent of discretion still present in the system despite the introduction of principles. They also suggested that a negotiated settlement would be more in their (female) client's interest than the strict application of the principles — this reflects the concerns highlighted by [Stephen] Cretney at the time of the Act's implementation.

2.24 Thirdly, linked with the solicitors' reluctance to go to court were calls for greater information on how the principles should be applied to particular facts, whether by case law or through a guide to the Act. Specific areas of concern for the solicitors were what to do when a conflict between two or more principles arose, the number of possible qualifications to the principles and the uncertain interpretation of specific principles. Taking each of these in turn, many solicitors thought that the inter-relationship between the principles of a clean break, equal sharing of matrimonial property and continuing maintenance for children might not always lead to consistent results. Moreover, the problem of the qualifications to principles was shown when solicitors tried to interpret when 'fair' sharing should not be 'equal'. Solicitors found the fourth and fifth principles were difficult to apply and often seemed not to have understood when the fifth principle could be used. The principles were also of no help in the quantification of child or spousal maintenance which remained vague, arbitrary and haphazard, as under the English legislation.

2.25 Difficulties encountered by English solicitors can be attributed to a lack of principles. However, it is clear from the analysis set out above that while a set of principles is a useful tool it does not represent the complete answer. Indeed, the use of principles seems to introduce a new problem of when and how to apply them. The Committee was particularly concerned about the problems experienced when a conflict between different principles arose and the possible adverse effect on the former wife's financial position. The Committee's view, therefore, is that their introduction would not greatly increase certainty — particularly if the effect is merely to shift an argument from the issue of which principles should be applied to when and how to apply them.

We let two of the major authors of the respective reports, Eric Clive and Stephen Cretney, have the final word — at least for the time being! In *The Financial Consequences of Divorce: Reform from a Scottish Perspective* (1984), Eric Clive, a Scottish Law Commissioner says:

What objectives should the courts be trying to achieve in making orders for financial provision and property distribution on divorce? This in my view is a nettle that has to be grasped. There is no point in telling the court to give first consideration to this and to have regard to that if there is absolutely no indication of the objectives to be achieved. We have tried in the Scottish Law Commission to provide a framework of principles that would be regarded as acceptable by reasonable spouses of both sexes and would provide a more satisfactory basis for amicable settlements than the present law . . .

Stephen Cretney, an English Law Commissioner at the time, in *Money after Divorce — The Mistakes We have Made*? (1986) states:

Where litigation is about money and sex, only the most optimistic would suppose that reason would ever predominate . . . But the underlying questions of principle remain and I suppose it is unrealistic that they can be quickly or easily solved.

4 Court decisions

(a) THE STARTING POINT

We start with the leading case on the pre-1984 law:

Wachtel v Wachtel
[1973] Fam 72, [1973] 1 All ER 829, [1973] 2 WLR 366, 117 Sol Jo 124, Court of Appeal

The parties were granted cross-decrees of divorce, and the dispute between the parties over the financial consequences of the divorce was dealt with in subsequent ancillary proceedings. The facts of the case are stated in the first few paragraphs.

Lord Denning MR: Mr and Mrs Wachtel were married on January 9, 1954. They were both then 28 years of age. They have two children, a son aged now 14, and a girl of 11. The husband is a dentist in good practice. On 31 March 1972, the wife left the home. On 21 July 1972, there was a divorce. . . . In consequence many things have to be settled. The parties have made arrangements for the children. The son is with the father. He is a boarder . . . where his fees are paid by his grandfather. The daughter is with the mother. She goes to day-school. There remain the financial consequences. . . .

On 3 October 1972, Ormrod J ordered the husband to pay to his wife (i) a lump sum of £10,000, or half the value of the former matrimonial home in Norbury, South London, whichever be the less: (ii) periodical payments of £1,500 per annum, less tax: and (iii) further payments of £500 per annum (£9.50 weekly), less tax, in respect of the eleven-year-old daughter.

The husband appeals to this court. The appeal raises issues of wide importance. This court is asked to determine, for the first time, after full argument, the principles which should be applied in the Family Division when granting ancillary relief pursuant to the powers conferred by the Matrimonial Proceedings and Property Act 1970 (in this judgment called the Act of 1970). . . .

The crucial finding of fact is that the responsibility for the breakdown of the marriage rested equally on both parties:. . . . The judge, having made that finding, determined that the only capital asset, namely, the matrimonial home, should be divided more or less equally between the parties. Since the evidence before the judge showed that the equity of the house in Norbury. (after discharging the outstanding mortgage amounting to some £2,000) was about £20,000, he ordered the husband to pay to his wife a lump sum of £10,000 or half the net value of the house if and when sold, whichever was the less. So far as the periodical payment of £1,500 per annum is concerned, the judge appears to have worked on an earning capacity on the part of the husband of £4,000 to £5,000 gross taxable income. He appears not to have allowed anything for the wife's earning capacity, at least in terms of monetary value. On this basis the £1,500 represents about one-third of the judge's assessment of the husband's earning capacity. But if one adds to that figure of £1,500 the further sum of £500 gross which the judge ordered to be paid by the husband to the wife in respect of the eleven-year-old daughter, the total is £2,000 gross, considerably more than one-third of the figure which the judge took as the husband's earning capacity.

The husband's appeal was founded on the ground that in effect he had been ordered to pay his wife one-half of his capital, and about one-half of his income. Particular criticism was levelled in this respect at an important passage in the judge's judgment . . ., stating that Parliament had intended in the Act of 1970 'to bring about a shift of emphasis from the concept of "maintenance" . . . to one of re-distribution of assets and . . . "purchasing power." ' Mr Ewbank, for the husband, contended that the judge had but lightly concealed his view that the Act of 1970 had brought about a new concept of community of property so that it was just to give every wife — or at least almost every wife — half the value of the matrimonial home on the break-up of the marriage, and about half her husband's income. If that were right in the case of a wife held equally to blame with her husband for the breakdown of the marriage, what, he asked rhetorically, was the position of a wife who was wholly innocent of responsibility for such a breakdown? He further asked this: If as in the past, one-third of the combined available income of the parties had been regarded as proper maintenance for a blameless wife, with a reduction (we avoid the use of the word 'discount') in the case of a wife who was not free from blame, how could periodical payments totalling nearly one-half of the husband's earning capacity be justified in a case where the wife was found equally to blame with the husband for the breakdown?

Mr Ewbank also complained that the judge had really started from a presumption that equal division was right and had worked back from the starting point and, allowing nothing — or almost nothing — for 'conduct' had arrived at the determination we have stated. He contested the judge's view that it was right to disregard conduct where blame had been found to exist, especially as Parliament in section 5(1) of the Act of 1970 [the unamended s. 25(1) of the Matrimonial Causes Act 1973] had enjoined the courts to have regard to the conduct of the parties. He also said that no, or no sufficient, account had been taken of the wife's earning capacity and that the £500 ordered to be paid for the child was in any event too high. He offered a lump sum of £4,000, together with a guarantee of any mortgage instalments which the wife might have to pay in connection with the acquisition of a new home for herself and the child. He urged this court in any event to reduce the £1,500 to £1,000; and the £500 to £300, or less.

Mr Gray, for the wife, supported the judgment on the broad ground that the long line of cases decided over the last century and more, which dealt with the issue of conduct, especially in relation to a guilty or blameworthy wife, were all decided when the foundation of the right to relief in matrimonial causes was the concept of a matrimonial offence. Now that concept had been swept away by the Act of 1969, the whole question of conduct in relation to ancillary relief required to be reconsidered, even though section 5(1) of the Act of 1970 preserved the obligation on the courts to have regard to 'conduct' in language not easily distinguishable from that of the earlier statutes from 1857 onwards. . . . Mr Gray particularly criticised the continued application of the so-called 'one third rule' under present day conditions. . . .

The conduct of the parties

It has been suggested that there should be a 'discount' or 'reduction' in what the wife is to receive because of her supposed misconduct, guilt or blame (whatever word is used). We cannot accept this argument. In the vast majority of cases it is repugnant to the principles underlying the new legislation, and in particular the Act of 1969. There will be many cases in which a wife (though once considered guilty or blameworthy) will have cared for the home and looked after the family for very many years. . . . There will no doubt be a residue of cases where the conduct of one of the parties is in the judge's words[1] 'both obvious and gross,' so much so that to order one party to support another whose conduct falls into this category is repugnant to anyone's sense of justice. In such a case the court remains free to decline to afford financial support or to reduce the support which it would otherwise have ordered. But, short of cases falling into this category, the court should not reduce its order for financial provision merely because of what was formerly regarded as guilt or blame. To do so would be to impose a fine for supposed misbehaviour in the course of an unhappy married life. Mr Ewbank disputed this and claimed that it was but justice that a wife should suffer for her supposed misbehaviour. We do not agree. Criminal justice often requires the imposition of financial and indeed custodial penalties. But in the financial adjustments consequent upon the dissolution of a marriage which has irretrievably broken down, the imposition of financial penalties ought seldom to find a place.

The family assets
The phrase 'family assets' is a convenient short way of expressing an important concept. It refers to those things which are acquired by one or other or both of the parties, with the intention that there should be continuing provision for them and their children during their joint lives, and used for the benefit of the family as a whole. . . .

The family assets can be divided into two parts: (i) those which are of a capital nature, such as the matrimonial home and the furniture in it: (ii) those which are of a revenue-producing nature, such as the earning power of husband and wife. When the marriage comes to an end, the capital assets have to be divided; the earning power of each has to be allocated.

Until recently the courts had limited powers in regard to the capital assets. They could determine the property rights of the parties. They could vary any ante-nuptial or post-nuptial settlements. But they could not order a transfer of property from one to the other. They could not even award a lump sum until 1963. The way in which the courts made financial provision was by way of maintenance to the wife. This they often did by way of the 'one-third' rule.

Now under the Act of 1970 the court has power, after a divorce, to effect a transfer of the assets of the one to the other. It set out in section 5 various criteria [now s. 25 of Matrimonial Causes Act 1973]. It was suggested that these were only codifying the existing law. Despite what has been said, we do not agree. The Act of 1970 is not in any sense a codifying statute. It is a reforming statute designed to facilitate the granting of ancillary relief in cases where marriages have been dissolved under the Act of 1969, an even greater measure of reform. . . .

The matrimonial home
The matrimonial home is usually the most important capital asset. Often the only one. This case is typical. When the parties married in 1954 they started in a flat. He was a dentist. She a receptionist. They both went out to work. They pooled such money as they had to get the flat and furniture and keep it going. Two years later, in 1956, they bought a house, no. 37 Pollards Hill North, Norbury, and moved in there. It has been their matrimonial home ever since. The purchase price in 1956 was £5,000. They did not put any money cash down, but bought it with a 100% mortgage. It was taken in the husband's name. The husband paid the mortgage instalment. The mortgage over the years has been reduced from £5,000 to £2,000. The house has increased in value from £5,000 to £22,000, or more.

After they moved into the house in 1956, the wife continued to go out to work until the son was born in 1958. She then stayed at home and looked after the children. But she helped her husband in various ways in his practice, such as by filling in the National Health forms, and helping as a receptionist from time to time. He put down a salary to her as part of his expenses against tax. This continued for all the years till 31 March 1972, when the wife left the house.

During the divorce proceedings the wife took out a summons under section 17 of the Act of 1882 claiming that, by reason of her financial contributions, she was entitled to one half of the equity in the house. Alternatively she claimed that, . . . there should be a transfer to her of half the house or its value by way of a lump sum.

Before the Act of 1970 there might have been much debate as to whether the wife had made financial contributions of sufficient substance to entitle her to a share in the house. The judge

1. Lord Denning MR here adopts the terminology of Ormrod J at first instance.

said . . ., that it 'might have been an important issue.' We agree. But he went on to say that since the Act of 1970 it was 'of little importance' because the powers of transfer under section 4 enabled the court to do what was just having regard to all the circumstances. We agree.

How is the court to exercise its discretion under the Act of 1970 in regard to the matrimonial home? We will lead up to the answer by tracing the way in which the law has developed. Twenty-five years ago, if the matrimonial home stood in the husband's name, it was taken to belong to him entirely, both in law and in equity. The wife did not get a proprietary interest in it simply because she helped him buy it or to pay the mortgage instalments. Any money that she gave him for these purposes would be regarded as gifts, or, at any rate, not recoverable by her: see *Balfour v Balfour* [1919] 2 KB 571, 88 LJKB 1054 [see p. 84, above]. But by a long line of cases, starting with *Re Rogers' Question* [1948] 1 All ER 328 and ending with *Hazell v Hazell* [1972] 1 All ER 923, [1972] 1 WLR 301, it has been held by this court that, if a wife contributes directly or indirectly, in money or money's worth, to the initial deposit or to the mortgage instalments, she gets an interest proportionate to her contribution. In some cases it is a half-share. In others less.

The court never succeeded, however, in getting a wife a share in the house by reason of her other contributions: other, that is, than her financial contributions. The injustice to her has often been pointed out.

In 1965 Sir Jocelyn Simon, when he was President, used a telling metaphor [see p. 141, above]: 'The cock can feather the nest because he does not have to spend most of his time sitting on it.'. . .

But the courts have never been able to do justice to her. In April 1969 in *Pettitt v Pettitt* [1970] AC 777 at 811 [see p. 142, above] Lord Hodson said: 'I do not myself see how one can correct the imbalance which may be found to exist in property rights as between husband and wife without legislation.'

Section 5(1)(*f*) [see now s. 25(2)(*f*) of the Matrimonial Causes Act 1973]

Now we have legislation. In order to remedy the injustice Parliament has intervened. The Act of 1970 expressly says that, in considering whether to make a transfer of property, the court is to have regard, among other things, to:

'(*f*) the contributions made by each of the parties to the welfare of the family, including any contributions made by looking after the home or caring for the family.'

Mr Ewbank suggested that there was nothing new in these criteria in section 5(1)(*f*). [See now s. 25(2)(*f*) of the Matrimonial Causes Act 1973.]

Lord Denning MR considered the Law Commission's Report on *Financial Provision in Matrimonial Proceedings* (1968) and continued:

. . . we may take it that Parliament recognised that the wife who looks after the home and family contributes as much to the family assets as the wife who goes out to work. The one contributes in kind. The other in money or money's worth. If the court comes to the conclusion that the home has been acquired and maintained by the joint efforts of both, then, when the marriage breaks down, it should be regarded as the joint property of both of them, no matter in whose name it stands. Just as the wife who makes substantial money contributions usually gets a share, so should the wife who looks after the home and cares for the family for 20 years or more.

The one-third rule

In awarding maintenance the Divorce courts followed the practice of the Ecclesiastical courts. They awarded an innocent wife a sum equal to one-third of their joint incomes. Out of it she had to provide for her own accommodation, her food and clothes, and other expenses. If she had any rights in the matrimonial home, or was allowed to be in occupation of it, that went in reduction of maintenance.

That one-third rule has been much criticised. In *Kershaw v Kershaw* [1966] P 13 at 17, Sir Jocelyn Simon P spoke of it as the 'discredited' 'one-third rule.' But it has retained its attraction for a very simple reason: those who have to assess maintenance must have some starting point. They cannot operate in a void. No better starting point has yet been suggested than the one-third rule. In *Ackerman v Ackerman* [1972] Fam 225 at 234, Phillimore LJ said: 'the proper course is to start again. I would begin with the "one-third rule" — bearing in mind that it is not a rule.'

There was, we think, much good sense in taking one third as a starting point. When a marriage breaks up, there will thenceforward be two households instead of one. The husband will have to go out to work all day and must get some woman to look after the house — either a wife, if he remarries, or a housekeeper, if he does not. He will also have to provide maintenance for the children. The wife will not usually have so much expense. She may go out to work herself, but she will not usually employ a housekeeper. She will do most of the housework herself, perhaps with some help. Or she may remarry, in which case her new husband will provide for her. In any case, when there are two households, the greater expense will, in most cases, fall on the husband than the wife. As a start has to be made somewhere, it seems to us that in the past it was quite fair to start with one third. Mr Gray criticised the application of the so-called 'one-third rule' on the ground that it no longer is applicable to present-day conditions, notwithstanding what was said in *Ackerman v Ackerman* [1972] Fam 225, [1972] 2 All ER 420. But this so-called rule is not a rule and must never be so regarded. In any calculation the court has to have a starting point. If it is not to be one third, should it be one half or one quarter? A starting point at one third of the combined resources of the parties is as good and rational a starting point as any other, remembering that the essence of the legislation is to secure flexibility to meet the justice of particular cases, and not rigidity, forcing particular cases to be fitted into some so-called principle within which they do not easily lie. There may be cases where more than one third is right. There are likely to be many others where less than one third is the only practicable solution. But one third as a flexible starting point is in general more likely to lead to the correct final result than a starting point of equality, or a quarter.

There is this, however, to be noted. Under the old dispensation, the wife, out of her one third, had to provide her own accommodation. If she was given the right to occupy the matrimonial home, that went to reduce the one third.

Under the new dispensation, she will get a share of the capital assets: and, with that share, she will be able to provide accommodation for herself, or, at any rate, the money to go some way towards it.

If we were only concerned with the capital assets of the family, and particularly with the matrimonial home, it would be tempting to divide them half and half, as the judge did. That would be fair enough if the wife afterwards went her own way, making no further demands on the husband. It would be simply a division of the assets of the partnership. That may come in the future. But at present few wives want their former husbands to make periodical payments as well to support them; because, after the divorce, he will be earning far more than she; and she can only keep up her standard of living with his help. He also has to make payments for the children out of his earnings, even if they are with her. In view of those calls on his future earnings, we do not think she can have both — half the capital assets, and half the earnings.

Under the new dispensation, she will usually get a share of each. In these days of rising house prices, she should certainly have a share in the capital assets which she has helped to create. The windfall should not all go to the husband. But we do not think it should be as much as one half, if she is also to get periodical payments for her maintenance and support. Giving it the best consideration we can, we think that the fairest way is to start with one third of each. If she has one third of the family assets as her own — and one third of the joint earnings — her past contributions are adequately recognised, and her future living standards assured so far as may be. She will certainly in this way be as well off as if the capital assets were divided equally — which is all that a partner is entitled to.

We would emphasise that this proposal is not a rule. It is only a starting point. It will serve in cases where the marriage has lasted for many years and the wife has been in the home bringing up the children. It may not be applicable when the marriage has lasted only a short time, or where there are no children and she can go out to work.

The lump sum provision

In every case the court should consider whether to order a lump sum to be paid by her husband to her. Before 1963 a wife, on a divorce, could not get a lump sum paid to her. All that she could get was weekly or monthly payments secured or unsecured. By section 5(1) of the Matrimonial Causes Act 1963, the court was empowered to make an order for the payment of a lump sum. [See now s. 23(1)(c) of the Matrimonial Causes Act 1973.] . . . The circumstances are so various that few general principles can be stated. One thing is, however, obvious. No order should be made for a lump sum unless the husband has capital assets out of which to pay it — without crippling his earning power.

Another thing is this: when the husband has available capital assets sufficient for the purpose, the court should not hesitate to order a lump sum. The wife will then be able to invest it and use the income to live on. This will reduce any periodical payments, or make them unnecessary. It will also help to remove the bitterness which is so often attendant on periodical payments. Once made, the parties can regard the book as closed. The third thing is that, if a lump sum is awarded, it should be made outright. It should not be made subject to conditions except when there are children. Then it may be desirable to let it be the subject of a settlement. In case she remarries, the children will be assured of some part of the family assets which were built up for them.

But the question of a lump sum needs special consideration in relation to the matrimonial home. The house is in most cases the principal capital asset. Sometimes the only asset. It will usually have increased greatly in value since it was acquired. It is to be regarded as belonging in equity to both of them jointly. What is to be done with it? This is the most important question of all.

Take a case like the present when the wife leaves the home and the husband stays in it. On the breakdown of the marriage arrangements should be made whereby it is vested in him absolutely, free of any share in the wife, and he alone is liable for the mortgage instalments. But the wife should be compensated for the loss of her share by being awarded a lump sum. It should be a sum sufficient to enable her to get settled in a place of her own, such as by putting down a deposit on a flat or a house. It should not, however, be an excessive sum. It should be such as the husband can raise by a further mortgage on the house without crippling him.

Conversely, suppose the husband leaves the house and the wife stays in it. If she is likely to be there indefinitely, arrangements should be made whereby it is vested in her absolutely, free of any share in the husband: or, if there are children, settled on her and the children. This may mean that he will have to transfer the legal title to her. If there is a mortgage, some provision should be made for the mortgage instalments to be paid by the husband, or guaranteed by him. If this is done, there may be no necessity for a lump sum as well. Furthermore, seeing that she has the house, the periodical payments will be much less than they otherwise would be.

Remarriage

In making financial provision, ought the prospects of remarriage to be taken into account? The statute says in terms that periodical payments shall cease on remarriage: see section 7(2)(*a*), (*b*). [See now s. 28(1) of the Matrimonial Causes Act 1973.] But it says nothing about the prospects of remarriage. The question then arises: ought the provision for the wife to be reduced if she is likely to remarry?

So far as the capital assets are concerned, we see no reason for reducing her share. After all, she has earned it by her contribution in looking after the home and caring for the family. It should not be taken away from her by the prospect of remarriage.

So far as periodical payments are concerned, they are, of course, to be assessed without regard to the prospects of remarriage. If the wife does in fact remarry, they cease. If she goes to live with another man — without marrying him — they may be reviewed.

The present case

Coming now to the facts of the present case. The matrimonial home belongs in law to the husband. On the figures before the judge, its gross value was about £22,000; and, as already stated, the equity is worth about £20,000 . . . we allowed Mr Gray . . . to argue that the judge, consistently with the principles which he sought to apply, should have ordered a lump-sum payment of £10,000, or half the net value of the house, whichever was the greater, and not, as the judge in fact ordered, whichever was the less.

So far as the husband's earning capacity is concerned, . . . We propose to proceed on the basis of the husband's earning capacity (i.e. his gross taxable income) being not less than £6,000 per annum. . . . We put the wife's potential earning capacity on part-time work as a dental nurse at £15 per week gross — say £750 per annum. The combined earning capacity is thus £6,750 per annum gross, of which one third (if that be the right starting point) is £2,250. If one deducts the £750 from that latter figure of £2,250, the result is £1,500 — the same figure as the judge arrived at though he reached that figure by a different route.

The husband is presently living at the former matrimonial home. The son of the marriage, aged 14, is now at a boarding school at the grandfather's expense. The boy lives with his father in the holidays. The father has to clothe and maintain him in the holidays. Clearly this requires the father to maintain a home for the son. Both parties gave their ages as 46. Remarriage is thus a possibility, though not it seems an imminent probability. The wife undoubtedly contributed to the home for some 18 years and, so far as the evidence goes, was in every respect an excellent mother. This is clearly a case in which the wife has made a substantial contribution to the home, as, of course, the husband has out of his earnings.

Any lump sum ordered to be paid will, we were told, be raised by the husband by increasing the sum for which the house is mortgaged. To require him to pay a lump sum of £10,000 raised in this way might cost him around £900 per annum in interest; and, of course, he will have to repay the principal as well. If £900 is added to the total of £1,500, plus the £500 (i.e., £2,000), the result is the equivalent of an order for a periodical payment of almost half of what we have taken to be the husband's gross taxable income. We think an order for a periodical payment on this scale (omitting any consideration of a lump sum payment) would be too high, having regard to the wife's needs and to the husband's needs. But, even if the matter be approached by a different route, we still think the £10,000 figure is too high. The wife should be able to make a substantial deposit in order to purchase suitable accommodation (assuming she wishes to buy, and not to rent) with the aid of a considerably smaller sum; and, if the order for £1,500 as a periodical payment is upheld, there seems to us to be a margin within that figure beyond the requirements of ordinary living expenses out of which repayments of mortgage, principal and interest could be made. On the other hand, we think the husband's offer of £4,000 is too low . . .

On the basis that the order for a periodical payment of £1,500 per annum is left untouched, we think the proper lump sum, taking everything into account that the Act of 1970 requires, is £6,000, and we would vary the judge's order for £10,000 accordingly. We think the wife should have that sum, £6,000, free of any trust, or other terms.

We, therefore, see no reason to interfere with the order for £1,500 in favour of the wife on the basis of the figures we have just mentioned. . . . We see no reason whatever on the facts of this case, as found by the judge, for making any reduction of any kind on the ground that the judge found the wife equally responsible with the husband for the breakdown of their marriage. To do so would be quite inconsistent with the principles which we think should be adopted in future in relation to conduct.

Looking at it broadly
In all these cases it is necessary at the end to view the situation broadly and see if the proposals meet the justice of the case. On our proposals here the wife gets £6,000 (nearly one third of the value of the matrimonial home). She gets it without any conditions at all. This seems to represent a fair assessment of her past contributions, when regard is had to the fact that she will get periodical payments as well. She also gets £1,500 a year by way of periodical payments, which is about one third of their joint incomes. She will also have the management of £300 a year for the daughter who is at a good school, and aged 11. These provisions are as much as the husband can reasonably be expected to make. It will mean that each will have to cut down their standard of living: but it is as much as can be done in the circumstances.
Appeal allowed by varying lump sum payment of £10,000 to £6,000 and reducing payments in respect of daughter from £500 per annum to £300 per annum (£6 a week gross of tax).

Questions

(i) Lord Denning MR gives two reasons for substituting one-third for the one-half approach used by the trial judge: does either of them convince you?

(ii) Would either reason have been valid if the wife had been working full time and: (*a*) earning as much as her husband, or (*b*) earning less than he did?

(iii) Do you think that a court would reach a similar result to Lord Denning MR, applying the principles in s. 25 of Matrimonial Causes Act 1973 as amended?

(b) ONE-THIRD RULE

An examination of the case law illustrates how the one-third rule has, to some extent at least, been marginalised.

(i) Substantial assets

Gojkovic v Gojkovic
[1990] 2 All ER 84, [1990] FCR 119, [1990] 1 FLR 140, Court of Appeal

The husband and wife, both Yugoslavs, arrived in England in 1966 with very little money. In 1969 they started to live together and they were married in 1978. Their life together consisted of hard work and sacrifice. Whilst in other employment, they turned a property into a hotel. The wife worked hard from dawn to midnight, did night-portering and made the hotel successful. The husband and his brothers were involved in other enterprises and expanded their business into other hotels and properties. During the later years of the marriage, the wife ran the hotel side of the business and the husband and his brothers concentrated on successful property speculation. The marriage broke down in 1986 and they were divorced in 1987. In ancillary proceedings, the husband's share of the family assets was approximately £4m. The wife's legal share amounted to very little. It was agreed between the parties that there should be a 'clean break' order and that the wife should have a maisonette worth £295,000. The husband's solicitor offered the wife a lump sum of £532,000 calculated to reflect the reasonable needs and requirements of a former wife of a wealthy husband. The wife wanted to continue with the hotel business and asked for a lump sum to enable her to acquire and run her own hotel.

The judge found that the wife's contributions had been exceptional by ordinary standards and were equal to the husband's, that there had been a quasi-partnership with the wife playing a unique role in establishing a supply of custom to the hotel and her efforts had helped develop and sustain the business. He concluded that her contributions had earned her a share in the family assets which had to be taken into account in the final award. Accordingly he awarded the wife a lump sum of £1m to enable her to buy and run a hotel. The husband appealed contending that the judge had erred in making the award to enable the wife to purchase and run her own hotel and that the amount had been excessive. He further contended that the effect of s. 25 of the Matrimonial Causes Act 1973 as amended by the Matrimonial and Family Proceedings Act 1984 had limited the discretion of the court to provide self-sufficiency for the wife, and that her self-sufficiency would be fully met by the husband's offer and the property but did not extend to the wife's requirement for the purchase of business assets.

Butler-Sloss LJ: Prior to the hearing before the judge, the husband, through his legal advisers, made an open offer based upon calculations provided by the accountants Cooper and Lybrand. That open offer was that the wife should receive a maisonette worth £295,000, about which there is no dispute, and that she should receive a lump sum of £532,000. That figure was carefully calculated in accordance with what has been called the '*Duxbury* principles' or '*Duxbury* calculations',[2] . . . The difference between the award of the judge and the offer of the husband

---

2. This principle is referred to by Ward J in *B v B (financial provision)* [1990] FCR 105, [1990] 1 FLR 20 in this way:

. . . accountants or investment consultants calculate from a computer programme the lump sum, which, if invested on assumptions as to life expectancy, inflation, return or investments, growth of capital and incidence of income tax, would produce enough to meet the recipient's needs for life. . .

is therefore approximately half a million pounds. It was agreed between the parties that this was a suitable case for a 'clean break' order.

This court has been urged to provide guidelines as to the correct approach to big money cases. Our attention has been drawn to the two cases of *Preston v Preston* (1981) 2 FLR 331 and *Duxbury v Duxbury* [1987] 1 FLR 7. In *Preston* the judge accepted that £500,000 was required to provide the wife with a net income after tax of £20,000 a year. In *Duxbury* the figure of £20,000 net income for the wife of a rich man in 1980 was accepted in principle by the legal advisers as an appropriate sum and was adjusted to the 1985 figure of £28,000. On that basis, and with the assistance of detailed figures, the judge in *Duxbury* arrived at the lump sum award of £540,000 to meet in full the wife's entitlement and reasonable requirements. The lack in *Preston* of detailed information as to the financial implications of a lump sum awarded to provide income, criticised by Ormrod LJ, was remedied in *Duxbury*, and the computerised formulation accepted by the judge in that case has provided, we are told, a very useful guide to the settlement of cases in this bracket in the last 2 years. Both in *Preston* and in *Duxbury*, this court upheld the lump sum orders without being asked to consider in any detail the level of income appropriate in such cases. Moreover, I do not read those decisions of this court as laying down an income bracket suitable for the needs of every former wife of a millionaire. In *Preston*, where the wife made a substantial financial contribution during the early part of the marriage which subsisted for 24 years, and in *Duxbury*, where the wife did not go out to work but brought up the family and did all that was required of her as a wife, the formulation arrived at by the accountants may provide a most helpful guide to the assessment of the needs or reasonable requirements of a wife where the husband is wealthy, taking into account the contribution which she has made to the family and the marriage. It can only, however, be a guide and should not be elevated to a rigid mathematical calculation. Each case must be decided on its own facts and in accordance with the principles set out in s. 25 of the Matrimonial Causes Act 1973 as amended by the Matrimonial and Family Proceedings Act 1984. The wide discretion of the court under s. 25 must not be fettered.

Mr Wall, on behalf of the husband, in his attractive argument urges us to treat the present appeal as a *Duxbury* type of case. He makes two main points:

(i) that the judge was wrong in principle to make an award to enable the wife to buy and run a hotel; and

(ii) if not wrong in principle, the amount was excessive, and he erred in the exercise of his discretion in making so large an award

In considering (i) he argued that the effect of the repeal and reenactment of s. 25 of the 1973 Act as amended by s. 3 of the Matrimonial and Family Proceedings Act 1984, had the effect of limiting the discretion of the court under the new s. 25 to providing for the wife to become self-sufficient. Considerations of the future standard of living of the former spouse were irrelevant, although he accepted that the contribution of the applicant spouse during the marriage would affect or enhance her subsequent standard of living after divorce.

For my part, I do not see the repeal and replacement of s. 25 as having that effect. By the original s. 25(1) it was the duty of the court, in deciding whether to exercise its powers under s. 23 or s. 24, to have regard to all the circumstances of the case, including seven specific matters:

'and so to exercise those powers as to place the parties, so far as it is practicable and, having regard to their conduct, just to do so, in the financial position in which they would have been if the marriage had not broken down and each had properly discharged his or her financial obligations and responsibilities towards the other'.

That section has not been repealed. It has been replaced by s. 25(1), (2), which sets out that the court must have regard to all the circumstances, and lists eight specific matters to which the court shall have regard. It no longer requires the court to attempt that which was impossible in the vast majority of cases. It does not, however, in my view circumscribe the descretion of the court, as is suggested by Mr Wall. The new s. 25A lays a responsibility upon the court to consider whether financial obligations should be terminated and to make orders designed to enable the spouse to adjust without due hardship to the termination of financial dependence on the other spouse. By s. 25(1)(*a*) an applicant's future earning capacity is relevant. So also, however, is the standard of living enjoyed by the family before the breakdown of the marriage. The proposed standards of living of both spouses must be a relevant consideration and where finances permit, they should not be wholly out of proportion to each other.

In my judgment, a *Duxbury* calculation cannot by itself provide the answer as to the sum to which the wife is entitled, though it produces a figure to which the judge is entitled to have regard in deciding what is the right answer. The judge found that the wife had made an exceptional contribution to the wealth generated during their relationship and marriage, a contribution greater than that often made by wives after long marriages. He found that in 1969, at the inception of their relationship, she 'was in at the beginning, committed — as he was — to contributing financially, physically and emotionally', and that she took with him the first steps towards the current financial empire of the wider family. As was said in *Page v Page* (1981) 2 FLR 198, 'this wife has earned her share'. That share is not to be calculated exclusively in relation to her needs. It is clear that her needs in one sense would be met by the offer of suitable accommodation and a lump sum producing an income of £30,000 a year net. Equally important as financial need is, however, the contribution made by each of the parties to the welfare of the family, a contribution found by the judge to be exceptional. This case has much in common with *S v S* (16 July 1980, unreported) with which we have been provided with a transcript. In *S v S* the spouses farmed together, starting from the minimum, working 'flat out', living frugally and building up a considerable farming business. According to Sir John Arnold P, 'all of it was therefore traceable to the first small beginnings to which up to 1943 Mrs S had made such an enormous contribution'. In that case, the offer of the husband of £200,000 would have met her reasonable requirements. But it did not sufficiently take into account the very substantial contributions made by the wife, and Balcombe J made a lump sum order of £375,000. He said:

'While this considerably exceeds what is necessary for the wife's needs it gives some measure of recognition of her contribution in building up the husband's present assets, while not being such an amount that to realise it would cripple the husband.'

The approach of Balcombe J was accepted by this court.

Mr Wall criticised the findings of the judge that they were engaged in a joint enterprise and a quasi-partnership. He argued that the wife was not considered by the husband to be a partner and was never so described. It was, indeed, a matter of dissent between the spouses, particularly when at a later stage other members of the family were made partners. This position may have owed much to the husband's view of the wife as his wife, rather than a recognition of her own contribution to the making of the business. Further, he saw himself as creating the wealth for the wider family of some sixteen people and being in a sense a trustee of it. It was available for use by all of them, according to him, but not individually. His view of the wealth of the family cannot displace an objective assessment of the wife's entitlement.

During the marriage, both spouses worked so hard that they did not have the time or opportunity to enjoy a comfortable standard of living. The wife does not now wish to sit back and be comfortable. The effect of the breakdown of the marriage was to deprive her of her way of life, the running of the hotel. She now desires to buy and run a small hotel. The judge found, and there was evidence upon which he could come to that finding, that she required £1.5m to buy such a hotel. She would be able to raise £500,000 and service the interest and therefore required £1m for her project. Mr Wall submitted that all her reasonable requirements were met by £532,000 and the property in which she was living, and the requirements of s. 25 did not include her needs at a higher level. She was self-sufficient at the figure of the husband's offer.

If his wife's contribution was adequately taken into account by the figure offered by the husband, her desire, however strong, to have a greatly increased lump sum to enable her to run a hotel would not be reasonable, but weight must be given to the fact that this is a working wife with a recognised expertise in the management of hotels. It is a viable proposition that she puts forward although one which will require her to continue a life of hard work. A wife who is entitled to a lump sum on the *Minton* 'clean break' principle is not obliged to deal with that money in any particular fashion. She is perfectly entitled to use it as working capital if this is the sum of money to which, taking into account her contribution and all other aspects of s. 25, she is entitled. In principle I cannot see how the judge can be criticised for making an order which enabled her to buy a hotel so long as all the relevant criteria were satisfied. This is not, in my view, an issue of principle.

Mr Wall's second question in my view is the only issue in this case: did the judge in exercising his discretion make an order which was so out of proportion that it was plainly wrong? However great the contribution of the wife to the family, the order to her must not be out of proportion to the total assets and must do justice between the parties. The judge considered this aspect very carefully. There was no suggestion that this order would be impossible for the husband to comply with or that it would cripple his business interests. On joint assets of £4m, subject to costs, he will retain £2.7m or so. The judge not only considered it from the point of view of the wife's desire to buy a hotel; he tested it in other ways: half the value of the hotel she had been running and approximately a third of the joint assets, though he was at pains to say he was not making his decision in reliance upon either of those bases.

This is an award which is not excessively generous and I cannot say it is outside the 'generous ambit of disagreement' that would entitle an appellate court to interfere with the discretion of the judge. I would dismiss this appeal.

Appeal dismissed.

Question

The husband in this case had argued that he was the trustee of the 'family wealth'. This argument was rejected by the judge and the Court of Appeal. Can you think of any situation where such an argument would be acceptable to the court?

(ii) Average resources

Scallon v Scallon
[1990] FCR 991, [1990] 1 FLR 194, Court of Appeal

The parties were married in 1943 and divorced in 1987. In ancillary proceedings, the district judge ordered that on the husband's transfer of his interest in the matrimonial home to the wife together with its contents and certain insurance policies, all her other financial claims should be dismissed. The former matriomonial home had an equity value of £68,400. The husband had debts of £11,000. He appealed contending that the order had left him with no capital assets. At the time of the appeal, both parties were employed, the husband was earning £12,000 p.a. and the wife £8,500 p.a. The recorder discharged the district judge's order. She concluded that each party should be in a position to have alternative homes and that having regard to the long marriage and the wife's contributions towards the family, she should have the protection of a nominal periodical payments order in case she should need maintenance in the future. She ordered that the house be sold and the net proceeds of sale be divided three fifths to the wife and two fifths to the husband. Both parties were legally aided with costs estimated at £3,500 each. The wife appealed contending, inter alia, that the recorder should have taken into account the impact of the legal aid charge when considering the order and should have deducted that sum from the wife's share and that as things stood she would have insufficient funds to purchase an alternative home.

Parker LJ: . . . The recorder proceeded on the basis that it would be just and equitable so to deal with the capital assets, if possible, as to provide that each party should be able to provide themselves with an alternative home. That approach is not challenged and, in my view, was clearly right. It is contended, however, that under the recorder's order neither party but principally the wife would be able to purchase an alternative property, and that that is wrong in principle. I accept that if the order made was an order which would result in the wife being unable to house herself, the husband's position being of less importance in this connection since it is the wife who is appealing, it would be proper for this court to interfere. The question, therefore, which is central to this appeal is whether the order . . . did achieve the objective of enabling the wife to purchase a suitable alternative property.

The net proceeds, as I have said, were £68,400. The distribution ordered by the recorder results in a figure of £41,040 for the wife and £27,360 for the husband. The proceeds of the policies, as I have said, were £4,560. The debts of the wife were substantially the same, £4,645, so that the £41,000 was available to be spent upon a new property. As to the legal aid costs, it was submitted by Mr Pointer that those costs would have to be deducted, leaving in the wife's hands available for a new property the sum not of £41,040 but, broadly speaking, £37,500. That was based upon an observation which was made in the case of *Simmons v Simmons* (1983) 4 FLR 803, in which this court considered, somewhat incidentally, the matter of the position of the legal aid charges. The judgment of the court in essence was given by Purchas LJ, who in the last paragraph of his judgment said as follows:

'I revert to the comment made by the President [Sir John Arnold] in *Jones v The Law Society*; amendments to s. 9(6) of the 1974 Act and the regs 88 and 91 to exclude the

proceeds of the sale of the matrimonial home or funds allocated for the purchase of a
primary home for either of the parties to the marriage or a child of the marriage to whom
s. 41 of the 1973 Act applies would avoid the hardship caused in this case. A person's home
and the tools of his trade are already excluded from assessment under the 1974 Act.
However, a mere discretion granted to the Law Society would not, in my judgment, be
sufficient to permit the court to assume that the monies would not be collected, nor a
charge enforced unless the position was secured by direct enactment.'

Since then the regulations have been amended and the regulations presently in force are the
Civil Legal Aid (General) Regulations 1989 (SI 1989 No. 339) which came into force on 1 April
1989. Regulation 96 reads as follows:

96 Postponement of enforcement of charges over money
>   (1) This regulation applies where in proceedings under — . . .
>> (*b*) The Matrimonial Causes Act 1973, . . .
>>> there is recovered or preserved for the assisted person a sum of money which
>>> by order of the court, or under the terms of any agreement reached, is to be
>>> used for purchasing a home for himself or his dependants.
>   (2) Where the assisted person —
>> (*a*) wishes to purchase a home in accordance with the order or agreement; and
>> (*b*) agrees in writing on a form approved by the Board to comply with the conditions
>> set out in sub-paragraph (3) the Board may, if the Area Director is satisfied that
>> the property to be purchased will provide adequate security for the sum referred
>> to in paragraph 3(*b*), agree to defer enforcing any charge over that sum.

It is thus apparent that there is still a discretion in the Law Society, even where the order of
the court is in the terms envisaged by para. (1). In the present case the wording of the order
which was made appears to me to satisfy the condition, for it is in these terms:

'That the former matrimonial home . . . be sold and that the net proceeds of sale be divided
into three-fifths to the petitioner and two-fifths to the respondent to be used by each party
for the purpose of purchasing a home.'

That condition is thus satisfied. But, it is true that a discretion still remains in the Legal Aid
Board and it is not for this court to direct how the Legal Aid Board should exercise its discretion.
However, in my view, the court is entitled to proceed on the basis that the Legal Aid Board
would so exercise its discretion as to further and not to defeat an order of this court. In a case
where the entire order of the court could be frustrated if the charge were enforced and the result
was that neither party could obtain a home, it appears to me to be unlikely in the extreme that
the Board would exercise the charge and thus frustrate the order of the court. Accordingly, it
does not appear to me to be justified, when considering the figures in this case, to deduct from
the wife's share of the proceeds of £41,040 any figure for legal aid costs. The amount available
to her initially is, therefore, £41,040.

It is submitted that that figure is not sufficient to enable her to house herself. The evidence
before the judge given by the wife was that she could support a mortgage of £25,000, albeit she
was then contemplating that that mortgage would be on the matrimonial home, which was a
three-bedroom house in which she could have taken lodgers and still provide for her son to have
a room of his own on occasion when he visited her.

It is abundantly apparent from the evidence which was given and from a further document,
which is not in the main court bundle but which was filed as a supplemental bundle which was
before the court, that £25,000 is a sum which she could raise from the building society. Those
two figures, taken together, amount to £66,000. The recorder concluded that the wife could
purchase a suitable property for a figure in the region of £65,000. On that basis there would
appear to be a margin of some £1,000 available to meet removal expenses. It is submitted by
Mr Pointer that the recorder's figure of £65,000 was too low and that the figure should be considerably higher, probably as high as £69,000. But the recorder had before her a large number
of particulars showing various house prices in and outside Oxford, some for one-bedroom
accommodation, which should be disregarded because it was common ground that the wife
should have a two-bedroom house, and some of which were, albeit it a short distance, outside
Oxford. The recorder was left, because no evidence was given as to the suitability or outgoings
or anything else relating to any of those houses, to do the best she could on the material before
her. For my part I am quite unable to see how it could possibly be said that she erred in any
way in reaching the figure of £65,000. The particulars, as one might expect, give the asking
prices that the agents suggest the sellers require. It would be flouting common sense if one were
to assume that those prices would be achieved in every case. Doing the best she could on the
material which she had, it appears to me the recorder's conclusion that the wife could purchase
a house for a sum in the region of £65,000 is unassailable. It indeed appears to me to be a figure
which is towards the top figure rather than the lower figure, and it may well be that the wife

can acquire a suitable property at less than £65,000. If that be right, then, on the face of it, the wife would only be short of a very small amount, if anything; and, bearing in mind that there is in existence a maintenance order, albeit a nominal one, should it turn out in the future that she is unable to meet her outgoings, it would be possible for her to apply to the court.

Next, it is said that the wife cannot really support a mortgage of £25,000. Although the matter was not developed in his opening, Mr Pointer in his reply put before us a number of figures to suggest that the wife was not able to support a mortgage of that amount. In my judgment, the position must be dealt with as it stood on the evidence, which was that the wife could afford a mortgage of £25,000. As against this, the only matter that is raised is that it appears on the evidence that she was then assuming that she would have an income from lodgers. But it must be borne in mind that the figures for outgoings, which were laid before the court in the form of the wife's affidavit, have to be reduced considerably because they include payments on the mortgage which would not be rightly included if one is doing the sort of calculation which Mr Pointer invited us to do. For my part I am not satisfied that she is unable to raise or should not prudently raise £25,000 on mortgage. Nor am I satisfied that the division of the proceeds in accordance with the recorder's order would not enable her to buy a suitable house elsewhere. It is, therefore, clear that although the recorder was dealing with figures which necessarily meant that she would be near the borderline in each case, I do not consider that it would be proper for this court to interfere on the ground that the figures demonstrate that the wife could not purchase a property. As to the husband, it is unnecessary to consider the matter. It is not suggested on his behalf that he would be unable to purchase another property and, indeed, it could not be so suggested because his percentage of the proceeds is £27,360 and his capacity in regard to raising a mortgage would be in the amount of some £36,000. It is thus abundantly apparent that, being a single man with no need for a two-bedroom residence, he could have purchased a property quite simply.

Appeal dismissed.

Question

Why has he no need for a two-bedroom residence?

The question of the Law Society charge has long exercised the courts, and Parker LJ's optimism is not necessarily borne out by practice:

Hanlon v Law Society
[1981] AC 124, [1980] 2 All ER 199, [1980] 2 WLR 756, 124 Sol Jo 360,
House of Lords

Mrs Hanlon wished to sell the house which had been transferred to her. (On these issues see p. 304, below.) It was worth £4,000 and was subject to a £4,000 mortgage. It was in need of repair and she wished to buy a smaller and no doubt more convenient house.

On the question whether the Law Society held a charge on the whole house pursuant to the legal aid regulations, the House of Lords held that this was indeed the case.

Lord Lowry: In the result I concur in dismissing the appeal and also join with your Lordships in expressing the hope that The Law Society will exercise the discretion which we all believe it has in relation to the charge on the appellant's home.

But the appeal has thrown into relief a problem which may be thought more difficult of solution than any of the questions which your Lordships have been called upon to answer. The object of legal aid is to provide the means of achieving justice through the courts which would otherwise be denied to persons of limited means. Yet the appellant, who has twice appealed successfully and who has ultimately been awarded the sole ownership of the matrimonial home, now emerges from litigation so costly, I might even say so ruinous, that if The Law Society decides, as it is quite entitled to do, to enforce its statutory charge, she will no longer have a house for herself and her children to live in.

Suggestions will, no doubt, be more appropriate on a legislative rather than a judicial occasion, but I might venture to put forward one idea. I do not, with respect, believe that the solution lies in making contributions on the instalment plan or in merely raising the threshold of liability to charge. Nor is it either reasonable or effective to try to frighten the parties into settling. Irresponsible advisers would not be deterred by a sanction directed only against their client and even highly responsible advisers (as in these proceedings) may advise an appeal (or more than one) in the hope (which may not be realised) of improving the lot of their client.

I am attracted by the Royal Commission's recommendation that the matrimonial home should once again be freed from any charge (Royal Commission on Legal Services, Final Report (1979) (Cmnd. 7648), vol. I, para. 13.64, p. 149). If this is done, I suggest that reform should be radical. For example, the registrar could be treated as an arbitrator whose decision on a section 23 and 24 application would be final subject to a case stated on a point of law. To give this method a chance of working the registrar would have to discuss his proposals with the parties before making up his order.

Questions

(i) Do you agree with Lord Lowry that the matrimonial home should be freed from the Law Society charge?

(ii) Do you think that the present system of the Law Society charge places a fetter on the discretion of the judges in legally aided cases?

(iii) What are the arguments for and against Lord Lowry's 'radical' solution of an arbitrator whose decision on ss. 23 and 24 applications should be final?

(iv) Are the arguments for his solution equally appropriate in the case of two non-legally aided litigants?

(iii) Limited resources

Cann v Cann
[1977] 3 All ER 957, [1977] 1 WLR 938, 121 Sol Jo 528, 7 Fam Law, High Court, Family Division

This was an application by the husband to vary an order made in the magistrates' courts in 1960, when the parties were still married. They were divorced in 1961. The couple were pensioners, the husband's total weekly income was £23.46p and the wife's total weekly income was £13.30p. The husband also had small savings amounting to £830 and he owned a motor car valued at £250. The current amount of the order was £7.00 per week. The husband's application to vary was unsuccessful and he appealed.

Hollings J: . . . Mr Jones [for the husband] submits that the one-third approach is right, and if one applies the calculation it leaves £12.25 as the wife's as it were, entitlement. She has more than that and therefore he submits that she should receive nothing and that any order should be entirely nominal. The result for the husband, he says, would be that he would have £23.46, expenses of £19.61, leaving £3.85 over for the husband. He submits that the gap suffered by his wife should be filled by social security payments. As Sir George Baker P pointed out in the course of Mr Jones' submission, that would only mean that the Department of Health and Social Security would be entitled to, and probably would, take advantage of her entitlement to claim against the husband in respect of social security payments because of the savings which he has, and make that claim against his savings.

Hollings J rejected this approach:

Now clearly the husband's situation has altered for the worse since November 1974. He no longer works, his income is reduced and is in the form of a pension. There was a discussion as to the way in which any savings which the husband has should be taken into account, if they are to be taken into account. So far as counsel are aware, and so far as I am aware, there is no authority dealing with the question as to whether justices can take into account for the purposes of making periodical payment orders, a description that stresses the income aspect, a capital sum owned by the husband. Of course, one can take into account the interest or notional interest, that is interest that could be earned in normal investment upon those savings; but there is no authority to indicate whether the capital element can or should be taken into account. It might in future be useful to explore the possibility of dealing with savings in the same way as damages are calculated in personal injury actions, that is take the lump sum for its capital value and its income producing value, take into account the respective ages of the parties — here I should say the husband is 67 and the wife 70 — and applying the actuarial table find out what annuity could be obtained from that sum, and apply a portion, if not the whole of that annuity, towards supplementing the order. I do not think in investigating this case, that exercise is necessary. One reason is that the sum of £830 has, sadly and regrettably, been seriously depleted by the contribution which the husband had to make in respect of his legal aid for the purpose of this appeal, a contribution of no less than £260 payable by 12 instalments of £21.70.

So far as the car is concerned, one knows the value of such an item is not always to be realised, so the sum that is left in the hands of the husband is not, in my judgment, a substantial amount of money for the exercise to which I have referred to be applied to it.

For myself I am satisfied that the one-third approach is quite inappropriate, in circumstances of this kind where neither party is earning; then one has to look at each party's needs and see what can best be done in all the circumstances. I have in mind particularly the words of the statute under which the justices have jurisdiction. What was a reasonable sum in all the circumstances of the case? Bearing that aspect in mind, I would hold that the justices were wrong in not effecting some reduction, but by no means a reduction of the size contended for on behalf of the husband. If one reduces the order made by the justices of £7 to the sum of £5, that is reducing it by £2, the wife will have £18 and the husband will be left with £18.46 to cover expenses of £19.61. That leaves him with £1.15 deficit. That deficit, I think, should properly be financed out of interest from his savings, such as are left, or if necessary the interest plus capital. In that way, the parties would, so far as it is possible in the circumstances of this case, be left with a fair division of the respective pensions to which they are entitled. . . .

Perhaps Sir George Baker P exposed the real reason for the court's apparent lack of concern for the husband's position, when he said in his judgment in this case: 'Thirdly, it passes my comprehension how a man can spend three-tenths of his capital sum in legal aid in trying to vary an order for his ex-wife.'

Question

Let us assume that in each of the above three cases there are minor children of the family. Do you think that the decisions would have been any different? (See p. 298, below.)

(iv) Short marriages

Foley v Foley
[1981] Fam 160, [1981] 2 All ER 857, [1981] 3 WLR 284, 125 Sol Jo 442, Court of Appeal

The parties began to cohabit in 1962 when each was married to someone else. They had three children. They married in 1969, separated in 1974, and were divorced in 1977. The wife applied for financial provision for herself and the one child who was living with her. She had good employment; she also had realisable capital assets. The husband was not working and his future prospects were not very good; he owned a property (not the matrimonial home). The wife agreed to her claim for periodical payments (for herself) being dismissed but she claimed a lump sum payment.

In assessing the amount of the lump sum payment the judge distinguished the period of the marriage and the period of cohabitation, indicating that in so far as s. 25(1)(*d*) of the Matrimonial Causes Act 1973 [now s. 25(2)(*d*)] referred to the duration of the marriage he was not prepared to treat this as a marriage which had subsisted prior to 1969 but that as part of 'all the circumstances of the case' he took into account the wife's contribution to the family during the whole of the period they were living together. The judge was of opinion that the one-third calculation was not an appropriate starting point for computing the lump sum in this case. The one-third calculation would have given the wife £14,000. The judge awarded her £10,000. The wife appealed. The appeal was dismissed.

Eveleigh LJ gives more information about the circumstances of the parties:

Eveleigh LJ: The husband had an unusual career with various occupations. He was described as a bullion dealer, a firearms dealer, a dealer in antiques. He and the wife lived well during the period of their cohabitation and the period of their marriage. At first they lived in a mews flat at 12 Pindock Mews, London, W 9. In 1972 they moved to a spacious flat in Ashworth Mansions, London, W 9. That was a rented flat and the wife now lives there. In 1959, before meeting his wife, Mr Foley bought a freehold property, 55 Upper Montague Street, London, W 1., for £5,250. He and his first wife converted the ground floor to a sandwich bar and they let it and it remains let. The top two floors were in a bad condition. They were let, however, on controlled tenancies. In the mid-1960s the second Mrs Foley [Mr Foley had been married before] who was, of course, not at that date married to Mr Foley, helped in this renovation of the upper floor of that property and Mr Foley spent some £4–5,000 on improvements. The wife (and I shall call her 'the wife' for the purposes of this judgment) helped in furnishing those flats and in the decoration and she collected the rents when they fell due.

Today, as the learned judge has found, the wife is an attractive woman, who dresses well. She is employed as a hairdresser in the Edgware Road at £75 a week and the learned judge estimated that she received tips of about £15 a week. She lives in the flat and she has the furniture. The learned judge made this finding, that the wife will be able to maintain the style of life that she has enjoyed over the last few years for some years to come. He assessed her capital at £10,000 and this was jewellery, paintings, a fur coat and some cash — her current realisable assets, as the learned judge called them. The two boys — because the daughter, it will be appreciated, was of responsible years — at first lived with the husband but in 1980 D went to live with the wife.

As to the husband, he was in arrears for maintenance to his first wife and the learned judge found that his free assets did not exceed his debts. . . .

As I have said, the learned judge [Balcombe J] came to the conclusion that the proper sum to award the wife was £10,000.

The wife now appeals and the first ground of her appeal is to the effect that the learned judge failed to take into account the period of cohabitation, that is to say, the period when the parties were living together before the marriage.

[However,] . . . in my view, the two periods, namely, cohabitation and marriage, are not the same. What weight will be given to matters that occurred during those periods will be for the learned judge to decide in the exercise of his discretion, but one cannot say that those two periods are the same. Ten years of cohabitation will not necessarily have the same effect as 10 years of marriage. During the period of cohabitation the parties were free to come and go as they pleased. This is not so where there is a marriage. In the great majority of cases public opinion would readily recognise a stronger claim founded upon years of marriage than upon years of cohabitation. On the other hand, in deciding these difficult financial problems there may be cases where the inability of the parties to sanctify and legitimize their relationship calls for a measure of sympathy which will enable the court to take what has happened during the period of cohabitation into account as a very weighty factor. *Kokosinski v Kokosinski* [1980]

Fam 72, [1980] 1 All ER 1106 is one such case. *Campbell v Campbell* [1976] Fam 347, [1977] 1 All ER 1 is certainly not.

I do not regard Balcombe J as saying that the years of cohabitation are irrelevant. He simply says that they are not years of marriage within section 25(1)(*d*). That section requires the court to have regard to all the circumstances. Circumstances may be relevant for consideration in one case which would not be relevant in another, and the two cases, *Campbell v Campbell* and *Kokosinski v Kokosinski*, provide examples of this. But the matters specifically listed in s. 25 will always be relevant, because Parliament has said so. . . .

I therefore see no error in the approach of the learned judge to the problem and I cannot say that he wrongly exercised his discretion in this case, in so far, for the moment, as he considered what weight should be given to the years of cohabitation.

On the relevance of the one-third formula to the case, on which the Court of Appeal again supported the trial judge, Eveleigh LJ said:

. . . the second ground of appeal is that the learned judge should have started on the basis that one-third was the proper proportion for the wife. Mr Jackson [for the wife] argued that, starting from one-third, the wife, on the facts of this case, should actually have received more than the £14,000 which a 'one-third' calculation would have produced, and he referred the court to the authorities relating to the 'one-third' proportion. As I see it, one-third in many cases is a very useful starting point for the court in deciding what should be the final figure. It is a useful proportion to take and then adjust one way or another as the case demands. But it is in no way a rule of law, as I see it. It is an aid to the mental process when arriving at the appropriate figure and there are many cases where the 'one-third' figure would not enter the mind of the court, because it would be obvious from the start that the proportion would be nothing like that. For example, the young marriage that lasts but a day or two. It is an extreme case but it is not unknown in this court. So that I do not find it possible to criticize the learned judge because he in fact said that he did not regard the one-third as the starting point in this case.
Appeal dismissed.

One of the cases cited by Eveleigh LJ was the following:

Campbell v Campbell
[1976] Fam 347, [1977] 1 All ER 1, [1976] 3 WLR 572, 120 Sol Jo 116, 6 Fam Law 214, High Court, Family Division

The question at issue was whether the three-and-a-half years of premarital cohabitation should be taken into account.

Sir George Baker P: . . . Mr Sleeman [for the wife] attempts to persuade me that the 3½ years of pre-marital cohabitation should be taken into account in assessing the length of the marriage. The way he puts it is: 'She was for 3½ years performing wifely duties before marriage.' Now I entirely reject that argument. Mrs Campbell was then a married woman with a large number of children, most of them in care, living with a youngster. There is an increasing tendency, I have found in cases in chambers, to regard and, indeed, to speak of the celebration of marriage as 'the paper work'. The phrase used is: 'We were living together but we never got round to the paper work'. Well that is, to my mind, an entirely misconceived outlook. It is the ceremony of marriage and the sanctity of marriage which count; rights, duties and obligations begin on the marriage and not before. It is a complete cheapening of the marriage relationship, which I believe, and I am sure many share this belief, is essential to the well-being of our society as we understand it, to suggest that pre-marital periods, particularly in the circumstances of this case, should, as it were, by a doctrine of relation back of matrimony, be taken as a part of marriage to count in favour of the wife performing, as it is put, 'wifely duties before marriage'. So I take this as a marriage of 2 years and a month or two; after which it ended.

Questions

(i) Judgments such as these are based, to some extent at least, on an ideological commitment to marriage. Do you think that such sentiments actually help to enhance the status of marriage?

(ii) On the facts of *Foley v Foley*, do you think that the one-third formula was rejected because, in the view of both the trial judge and the appellate court, a five-year marriage is a 'short' marriage?

(iii) Is the rationale for the one-third rule the need to balance present shares against future needs?

(iv) If it is, would legislating for automatic equal distribution of property deprive us: (*a*) of the one-third approach to income distribution, or (*b*) the rationale for *any* income distribution?

(v) Now that there is no longer an obligation as far as practicable to keep the parties in the position in which they would have been if the marriage had not broken down, is there *more* or *less* justification for adopting a one-third approach?

(vi) Do you think that the one-third formula is appropriate in cases where the husband is applying for provision from his wife?

(vii) If not, why not?

(v) Net effect

The approach that the courts have been adopting in the 1980s and early 1990s is the so-called 'net effect' method. Jill Black and Jane Bridge in *A Practical Approach to Family Law* (1990) describe the method in the following way:

It is very helpful to the court to work out how a proposed order (be it a one-third order or an order arrived at on a different basis) would work in practice.

To do this it is necessary to calculate each party's tax liability on the basis of the proposed order. From the payer's gross income is then deducted the tax he would have to pay, and his expenses of earning it. What is left is his spendable income — is it enough to enable him to meet his reasonable expenses? If not, the proposed order may well be too high. If he would have a significant sum over after meeting his expenses, the order may be too low. The position of the payee must also be considered. From her gross income, including the proposed maintenance, child benefit and one-parent benefit, must be deducted tax and her earning expenses. Is her spendable income sufficient for her reasonable expenses?

The net effect approach can be a very valuable way of showing up inequalities between the parties that might not otherwise be apparent; for instance, if the proposed order leaves the husband with £200 a month to spend and the wife with minus £10, the proposed order will obviously have to be adjusted so that the husband pays more. It may well be, however, that *both* parties are left with too little to cover their expenses — an all too common situation following the breakdown of a marriage. In such a case there is no possibility of carrying out a fine balancing exercise to distribute surplus income — the court must do the best it can and may have to work on the basis that one or the other party (or both) will require state benefits.

An illustration of this approach is:

Allen v Allen
[1986] 2 FLR 265, Court of Appeal

The parties were married in 1976 and divorced in 1984. There were two children of the family. The wife, who was in receipt of supplementary benefit, applied for a financial provision order. The husband earned £134 a week gross. After the parties separated, the husband purchased a house for £13,950 with a mortgage of £13,250. The mortgage repayments and rates amounted to £36 a week. The district judge ordered the husband to pay £5 a week for the wife and £5 a week for each child, a total of £15 a week. The wife appealed. The recorder found that the husband's net income after tax and national insurance and the mortgage and rates were deducted was £53.71 a week. He ordered the husband to pay £5 a week for the wife and £15 a week for each of the two children, a total of £35 a week. The recorder found that although the husband was justified in buying the house, he should be prepared to make some sacrifices for it or to use it to enhance his means. He further found that although the house was sparsely furnished it would not be difficult for the husband to be accepted for credit agreements.

The husband appealed.

Purchas LJ: . . . The wife, and the children who are with her, depend entirely upon payments from the Department of Health and Social Security. It is common ground that whatever order is made within reason in this case, as matters stand at the moment its effect will not touch upon her. . . .

The husband is in good employment. There was before the recorder some debate as to his precise earnings. Those figures are now agreed, as a result of his findings, at a gross annual income of £7,000 (i.e. £134.61 per week).

The debate has turned upon the approach which the court ought to make where one party (in this case the wife) is in receipt of social security payments and, apart from some undetermined event in the future which might bring her into a substantial earning category, the effect of the order, as I have already said, does not touch upon her.

The appeal is brought before this court on the basis that the recorder erred in principle in more than one respect. Mr Wall, who has presented the appeal, accepts that in his judgment the recorder correctly applied the approach of taking the net income available to the husband and did not approach the matter on the gross effective income of the parties. But Mr Wall submits that the recorder erred in principle in the exercise of discretion in relation to a house at 21 Mindale Road, Wavertree, Liverpool, which the husband was buying on mortgage. I hope I summarize the point accurately. Having found that the husband was 'justified at his age' in wanting a place of his own and that he would have great difficulty in obtaining rented accommodation, and that the property was modest, he said that acquiring the house constituted gaining an asset in respect of which the husband should 'be prepared to make some sacrifices for it, or to use it as best he may to enhance his means'. He continued:

'He will need to have some money to furnish it, but with his job it should not be difficult for him to be accepted for credit agreements. It will cost him money to live, but this will be largely offset by what he at present pays his mother.'

I should add some background to this point. At the time of the hearing before the [district judge] and also before the recorder the evidence was that the husband stayed during the week with his mother, to whom he paid £20 per week, but that at the week-end he went to the house which he was buying, with the assistance of an extremely substantial mortgage, because 'he got peace and was on his own'.

With respect [to] the recorder, it was not justified, in my judgment, for him to regard that property as anything more than necessary accommodation to which, as the recorder himself found, the husband was entitled. We are told, although it is not relevant to this appeal and does not form any part of my judgment, that in fact the husband is now living permanently at the house. The point is that, on the findings of the recorder, it is costing no more than the money he would pay to his mother, and certainly no more than he would have to pay if he became a tenant, whether in private or council accommodation; so that to impose a penalty upon the husband because of his acquiring the house was, in my judgment, a wrong approach in this case. It is an important feature of the case because the expenditure involved in connection with the acquisition of that house amounts of £36 per week. That goes to the mortgage payment. The mortgage is £13,250 out of a total purchase price of £13,950. And it also covers an endowment policy premiums, rates and water rates.

The suggestion by the recorder that the husband could without difficulty raise money to furnish the house is again a matter of some significance where, with respect to the recorder, I have to dissent from his conclusion. First there is a suggestion that the husband should use the property 'to enhance his means', which, as I read it, could only mean that one of the two bedrooms at this terraced house might be used to take in lodgers. That certainly could not be done in the state of the property at the moment. It is common ground that it is sparsely furnished; and the recorder found that further furnishing would be necessary. . . .

In the context of this case the exercise is to look at the net amount of money available to the husband. In view of the position which the wife enjoys in relation to social security provisions, one is able to ignore the effect of the order upon her. In my judgment the recorder should have considered the relationship between the net effect of his order and those figures published for supplementary benefit under the social security scheme. If he had done this, in my judgment he would have paused and considered again the effect of the order which he was about to make.

On those two grounds, in my judgment, Mr Wall has succeeded in demonstrating that the recorder erred in a matter of principle which brings the case within the classical dictum of Asquith LJ in *Bellenden v Satterthwaite* [1948] 1 All ER 343, as referred to in the speech of Lord Fraser of Tullybelton in *G v G* [1985] FLR 894 at p. 899 as lying outside the so-called 'generous ambit' of discretion and demonstrating, in my judgment, an error of principle and approach at that final stage so far as the calculation of the figures was concerned, and at the earlier stage in the recorder's approach to the impact of the cost incurred in acquiring his house by the husband.

That being so, the next question which falls to be decided is what course this court ought to take in dealing with the matter.

Mr Wall has submitted that there are but two courses. One is to remit the matter for further review by the [district judge], or to exercise our own discretion upon the admitted facts in this case and to make an order.

In my judgment it is appropriate in this court to bear in mind that these cases, important as they are to the parties concerned, are a burden upon the public purse and if, consistent with doing justice between the parties, that burden can be alleviated, then this court should take such a course. We have here first of all a starting point in the order made by the [district judge]. Those figures are not up-to-date, but there are balancing features. Reviewing the position both as to the new amount of money available to the wife under the State scheme and the position of the husband, I am prepared to accept the very frank and helpful approach of Mr Wall that, although at the time those advising him thought that the [district judge] made an order slightly higher than they would have expected, he does not feel able to challenge those figures for the purpose of an exercise of the discretion of this court today. I do not consider that this court ought to make an order in excess of that made by the [district judge]. The figures in the [district judge's] order, as adjusted, would leave the husband with a net income at the end of the day of £43.21 (£53.71 less £10.50). When this figure is compared with the long-term figure for supplementary benefit of £37.50, which comes into effect after 12 months, the excess income available to the husband is a modest £5.71 per week. I do not think that this is in any way an excessive amount to leave available to the husband from the point of view of the public responsibility to pay to the wife the amount that she will receive of £60 per week.

The last point to which I would advert was the point made by Miss de Haas that it is of some importance to the wife that this order should be as high as it ought to be — and indeed that must be right — because if at some time in the future she does obtain gainful employment, then she may move above the supplementary benefit limits and have to rely upon the order. But, in that event, that would be a substantial change of circumstances and, as Mr Wall has said, the matter would be subject to review in the ordinary way under s. 31 of the Matrimonial Causes Act 1973.

For those reasons I would allow this appeal and restore the [district judge's] orders.

Appeal allowed.

(c) CONDUCT

You will recall that s. 25(2)(*g*) of the *Matrimonial Causes Act 1973* states that the court shall have regard to the conduct of each of the parties if that conduct is such that it would in the opinion of the court be inequitable to disregard it. Lord Denning MR, in *Wachtel v Wachtel* [1973] Fam 72, [1973] 1 All ER 829, p. 265, above, used the phrase 'obvious and gross' when describing that conduct which would justify the court in departing from the then statutory objective. Sir George Baker P, in *W v W* [1976] Fam 107, [1975] 3 All ER 970, said that he would be entitled to take account of conduct in a case which would cause an ordinary mortal to throw up his hands and say 'surely that woman is not going to be given any money!' The problem with a definition such as that is that 'ordinary mortals' *are* ordinary mortals, and might be tempted to throw up their hands in cases where the judges would consider that some financial provision was appropriate:

Harnett v Harnett
[1973] Fam 156, [1973] 2 All ER 593, [1973] 3 WLR 1, 117 Sol Jo 447, High Court, Family Division

Bagnall J deduced the following proposition from *Wachtel v Wachtel* [1973] Fam 72, [1973] 1 All ER 829:

It will not be just to have regard to conduct unless there is a very substantial disparity between the parties on that score. . . .

His Lordship then described the final parting thus:

The final separation was sudden and tempestuous. For some eight months before June 1969, the wife (as she later admitted) had been having a ridiculous affair with a youth half her age to whom the parties had given occasional hospitality when he was a schoolboy and his parents were abroad, and who was then staying with them because his work was near. In the late evening of 27 June 1969, they were caught virtually in the act by the husband returning home unexpectedly early. He reacted understandably. He threw the boy out of the house and, after some violence, the wife also. She managed to return and stayed uneasily until 30 June 1969, when she left with the children and went to her parents. She never returned, and apart from the last five months of 1969, the children have been with her. Her association with the boy did not survive.
  [However by] her answer in the suit the wife alleged cruelty including a number of incidents of physical violence as well as the incident (admitted by the husband) of 27 June 1969. . . .
  In deciding the question of conduct I do not think it necessary to make findings on the specific allegations made by the wife. I think that before 1969 the marriage was foundering, and, if any serious crisis occurred, liable to break. This was due partly to misfortune in the husband's illness, mainly to the temperaments of the parties, partly even to the passage of time [the parties had been married for fifteen years]. The husband conceded that he was in part responsible for the breakdown. The wife clearly behaved foolishly and reprehensibly; I think that the need she sought to satisfy was solely physical, with no intention of destroying the marriage; she simply thought — if she thought at all — that she would not be found out. This behaviour was, in my view, susceptible of forgiveness by a reasonable and loving husband, who thought his marriage worth preserving and who wanted to maintain the unity of his family. . . . I am satisfied that the conduct of the wife fell far short of being gross and obvious, certainly in comparison with that of the husband, and probably also absolutely.

Question

(i) What do you think that an 'ordinary mortal' would have thought of the wife's conduct in this case? Do you think that the answer would be different depending on whether the 'ordinary mortal' viewed events in 1973 as opposed to the 1990s?

As Ormrod J also observed in *Wachtel v Wachtel* [1973] Fam 72, [1973] 1 All ER 113, there is no reason to suppose that conduct must be directly related to the breakdown of the marriage. For example, in *Jones v Jones* [1976] Fam 8, [1975] 2 All ER 12, the husband had made a violent attack upon his wife after the breakdown of their marriage, and this had reduced her capacity to earn her own living. As Orr LJ remarked:

It was argued that conduct is to be considered as relevant only for the purpose of cutting down a claim by a wife to a share of matrimonial property and cannot be applied so as to increase it. I for myself cannot accept the validity of this contention. As was pointed out in argument, the question in cases of this kind involves conflicting claims to matrimonial property, and an increase of one involves inevitably a decrease of the other. Moreover, in my judgment, this was a case in which the conduct of the husband had been of such a gross kind that it would be offensive to a sense of justice that it would not be taken into account.

Burgoyne, Ormrod and Richards (1987) discuss whether the 1984 amendment (see p. 256, above) will make any difference. They point to the fact that the removal of the 'gross and obvious' hurdle, if indeed it is removed by the courts, will mean that it will be somewhat easier to get a hearing on questions of conduct. It will of course not be possible to conclude that it would be inequitable to disregard conduct without investigating the conduct of both parties in some depth. If conduct is raised, argument is likely to last for some considerable period of time. This is indeed what happened in the following case:

Leadbeater v Leadbeater
[1985] FLR 789, [1985] Fam Law 280, High Court, Family Division

The judge heard evidence lasting some two weeks. Both parties had been married before and both had children from earlier relationships. Balcombe J summarised the problems of the new marriage in this way:

Balcombe J: There was, first, the husband's obsessive feelings about the custody of his children. There were some 16 hearings in the divorce suit between the husband and the former wife about custody of their children, which eventually the husband largely lost, although in the event the eldest child, a girl who is some 18 years of age, has now come to live with him in Tenerife; the middle child tragically died; the youngest child, a boy, is with his mother and the husband does not see him. But that sort of litigation imposes an immense strain on the parties to it and that must have been, and clearly was, a great strain on the parties' marriage, and indeed everybody else concerned.

Another problem allied to the first was the wife's inability to establish any satisfactory relationship with the husband's children. She accepts that on one or two occasions when she was drunk she did make the remark that she wished they were dead, a remark which she regretted bitterly when later the middle child died. But that failure to establish a relationship with her husband's children by his first marriage was clearly another major problem.

Then a great problem throughout was the relationship of the wife's son, both with his sister and with the adults. He had had some psychiatric outpatient treatment during the first year or so of this marriage, but at the time, at any rate, that did not appear to be effective and, the suggestion of in-patient treatment was not followed up. The son's problems manifested themselves in outbreaks of violence.

Then there was the wife's alcoholism. That was only really under control during the first 9 months of the marriage. Again I quote but two passages from the evidence which I noted. In her own evidence under cross-examination she said: 'It was under control for the first 6 to 9 months of the marriage'; the husband, in his evidence, said: 'From early 1980 onwards she was regularly drunk'. Although I accept, as I indicated during the course of the hearing, that alcoholism is a disease, nevertheless one cannot ignore the effects that that disease may have on the other persons concerned, and that was a major problem.

Then there was the wife's adultery in Cyprus. The husband, naturally, was upset by it, but he treated it, as he himself said, in a civilized manner. He attributed it to her drink, and by itself it could probably have been overcome. But it was not.

Finally, at the end of the marriage, there was this introduction of the 16-year-old girl, Miss D, into the household. Even had there been no form of sexual attraction between the husband and Miss D, in my judgment the husband was wholly unreasonable in insjsting that this 16-year-old girl should be a part of the family, against his wife's wishes. Even if there had been no other relationship, it seems to me quite unreasonable for a husband to insist that a complete stranger be adopted as part of a family against his wife's objections. But, in any event, I find that from an early stage there was some form of sexual attraction between the husband and Miss D. I do not say that there were actual sexual relations until much later. It is now accepted that there were sexual relations in November 1983 and Miss D had the husband's child born in July 1984. I do not accept that the husband's relationship with Miss D was wholly innocent from the beginning. It very soon must have become a question of sexual attraction and I accept the wife's evidence that the husband (as she put it) was besotted by Miss D. But the introduction of Miss D into the household was certainly not the sole, nor even the main cause, of the breakdown of this marriage. It was the last in a whole series of failures of relationships. . . .

In my judgment it would not be inequitable to disregard conduct in this case. To put it another way, if I have to take the husband's conduct into account in bringing Miss D into the house, then equally I have to take the wife's conduct into account in her attitude over her son, her alcoholism, and indeed also the question of the adultery in Cyprus. In my judgment it is proper in this case not to give any effect to conduct, even in the way that Mr Feder (for the wife) invited me to do, namely, by saying that if it had not been for the husband's conduct in bringing Miss D into the house this would not have been merely a 4-year marriage. I leave conduct out of account and there is here a 4-year marriage.

Question

Would you have left conduct out of account?

Conduct was deemed more relevant in the following case:

Kyte v Kyte
[1988] Fam 145, [1987] 3 All ER 1041, [1987] 3 WLR 1114, [1988] FCR 325, Court of Appeal.

Purchas LJ: . . . This is an appeal by Graham Rodger Kyte ('the husband') against an order made by Ewbank J. on 16 January 1987 at Manchester when the judge allowed an appeal from an order made by the [district judge] on 7 October 1986 to the extent that, in addition to the orders made by the [district judge], the husband was ordered to pay to Diana Kathleen Kyte ('the wife') a lump sum of £14,000. . . .

The short background to the application was as follows. The parties were married on 25 July 1975. There are four children of the family, two of whom were the wife's children by a former marriage, namely Paul, born on 21 September 1965, and Andrea, born on 29 January 1969; and two who were the issue of the parties to the marriage, Victoria, born on 7 October 1977, and Rachel, born on 17 January 1980. The marriage appears to have come under stress at or soon after the birth of Rachel. The husband suffered from depression and spent numerous periods in hospital under treatment for this condition. In the particulars of behaviour upon which the wife relied in support of her petition for dissolution of marriage based upon section

1(2)(*b*) of the Matrimonial Causes Act 1973, which generally were accepted by the husband, it appears that, as a result of his depression, he was unpredictable and suicidal. Particularly severe incidents are recorded in April 1981. In the summer of 1982 he attempted suicide at his office and was rescued only by the wife and his office driver who, missing him, had called the wife for assistance. Other suicidal incidents occurred in the summer of 1983.

On the findings of fact reached by the [district judge], which were generally accepted by the judge on appeal, the wife started associating with a Mr. Gregory as early as June 1983, although she did not start living with him permanently until 1984. The husband's case, which was accepted by the [district judge], was that, although one of the serious suicidal attempts in the summer of 1983 was caused by the wife withdrawing her support from him, he was not at that time aware of the wife's association with Mr. Gregory. Subsequently, he realised that she was only using his conduct as a means to dissolve the marriage and set up home with Mr. Gregory.

Having initiated the suit, the wife obtained an injunction ousting the husband from the matrimonial home in February 1984. It is his assertion that this application was contrived to enable her to set up home with Mr. Gregory in the matrimonial home. The [district judge] found that, in presenting her version of these events to him, the wife had lied on oath. . . .

The district judge found that the wife had connived at his suicide attempts with a view to gaining as much of his assets as possible.

I accept the submission made by Mr. Burns [for the husband] that it is abundantly clear from the long and careful judgment of the [district judge] that he took into account the conduct of the wife in the context of the conduct of the husband and all the circumstances arising during the marriage and that the judge, with great respect to him, was not entitled to criticise his judgment in this respect in the way in which he did. . . .

I have, reluctantly, come to the conclusion that the judge was wrong to have reversed the [district judge] on the findings of conduct. The test as to conduct which the [district judge] set for himself is as apt an interpretation of the phrase 'inequitable to ignore it' that I can readily envisage. The conduct of the wife not only in actively assisting or, alternatively, taking no steps to prevent the husband's attempts at suicide in the presence of the motive of gain which the [district judge] found on ample evidence to be established, together with her wholly deceitful conduct in relation to her association with Mr. Gregory, would amount to conduct of a gross and obvious kind which would have fallen within the concept under the old law and, in my judgment, could certainly render it inequitable to ignore it even against the conduct of the husband which contributed to the unhappy conditions which existed during the marriage and afterwards as a result of the husband's manic depression.

I have, therefore, come to the conclusion that his appeal must be allowed on one of the two aspects upon which the judge in turn reversed the order of the [district judge]. This leaves the question of what this court ought to do in those circumstances. I am unable to accept Mr. Burns' submission that the court should adopt the view that the order of the [district judge] provided the financial provision that was required to comply with the interests of the minors within section 25(1) of the Act of 1973 and that, therefore, no further payment should be made to the wife in any event. This would place too much weight on the conduct of the wife and would be inconsistent with the approach of the [district judge] ('I do not think that her conduct is such as to disentitle her altogether . . .'). On the other hand, I cannot accept Mr. Allweis' submission that conduct should not affect the distribution of the extra £40,000 of capital assets and that the judge's decision to give the wife £14,000 of it as a matter of discretion ought not to be disturbed. This ignores the fact that the judge was working on the basis that conduct was irrelevant, and we have found that he was in error in doing this. The judge also had the matter of costs in mind. Although the husband appeared in person in order to reduce costs, the wife has at all stages been an assisted person under the Legal Aid Act 1974. Before the [district judge] the wife's costs of the ancillary relief proceedings were expected to be in the region of £5,000. Before the judge her costs were said to be £15,000 in respect of which there would be a charge in the favour of The Law Society. On inquiring about this extraordinary difference, the court was told that the figure for the wife's costs included costs incurred in numerous applications involving the children. Although the information given to the court was not very clear, I understand that certainly not all the additional £10,000 costs related to the costs of this appeal. Again on the basis that the [district judge] was wrong over conduct, the judge awarded costs to the wife both before the [district judge] and on appeal.

In view of the decision we have reached in this court, it would be quite wrong to allow the judge's orders on costs to stand. The order of the [district judge], i.e. no order as to costs, should be restored and . . . it would appear that the husband should be awarded the costs of the appeal against the wife, such order not to be enforced without leave of the court. In these circumstances, it appears probable that, apart from the protected part of any lump sum award, The Law Society charge will absorb the balance. This is, of course, no reason for not making an award.

The approach which I propose to adopt is to vary the judge's apportionment of the £40,000 additional capital to take into account the question of conduct which he wrongly ignored. Bearing in mind that the interests of the minors have already been catered for and that the wife enjoys the support of Mr. Gregory, and her conduct, which I considered was extremely grave, even taking into account the difficulties of the marriage, I would reduce the lump sum to £5,000. *Appeal allowed with costs.*

Questions

(i) Suppose that a divorced wife who is in receipt of periodical payments from her ex-husband has an affair with another man: is this conduct which the court should refuse to regard as relevant?

(ii) If the answer to question (i) is 'yes,' suppose further that she becomes pregnant as a result of the affair and is obliged to give up her part-time job: how would you put her ex-husband's case in reply to her application for an increase in her periodical payments?

(iii) Suppose that the behaviour of the ex-wife in *Kyte v Kyte* had been entirely due to her own psychiatric disorder: would this have made the situation any different?

K v K (conduct)
[1990] FCR 372, [1990] 2 FLR 225, High Court, Family Division

The parties married in 1977 having previously lived together for about 3 years and there were no children. In 1982, they purchased their matrimonial home for about £17,261, which involved a substantial discount to the true market price of about £70,000. (The discount was available because they had previously been involved in a co-ownership scheme.) They obtained a 100% mortgage from a bank. The husband had been made redundant in 1980 and had remained unemployed since that time and it was therefore the wife's earnings which enable the parties to obtain the mortgage. The husband received redundancy money of about £12,500, most of which was spent on general living expenses. The marriage ran into difficulties, the most serious of which concerned the husband's excessive drinking. In 1984 the wife left the matrimonial home and commenced divorce proceedings. The divorce was made absolute in 1987. However, in May 1985 the bank mortgagee obtained an order for sale and in 1987 sold the property for £125,000 leaving net proceeds of £97,379 which was paid into court. At the time of the hearing that sum had increased to £101,000 with the accretion of interest. The wife merely sought payment of the half share of the net proceeds of sale, to which (it was conceded) she was beneficially entitled. The husband sought not only his half share of the net proceeds of sale but also ancillary relief from the wife by way of a lump sum and/or periodical payments. The wife had a present gross income of £24,600 p.a. having made efforts to improve her financial position since the marriage broke down. She lived in a flat, now worth about £85,000, which was purchased with the assistance of a mortgage and further loans from relatives, friends and other sources. She had other assets by way of shares, building society accounts, jewellery and some family silver, all of which had been valued at less than £20,000. Further, there was the possibility of an inheritance at some future date from either or both parents.

The husband had not worked since 1980. He had no capital except his half share of the former matrimonial home. He moved from one bed-sit to another as required by the local authority who treated him as a homeless person. He suffered from a personality disorder but was capable of taking sedentary employment. He received benefits of various kinds amounting to about £50 per week. He owed the wife some £3,230 by way of costs of the divorce proceedings. His own costs were estimated at about £6,000, as opposed to the wife's costs estimated to be about £12,000. He contended for £70,000 by way of capital out of the monies held in court in order to enable him to buy a house in London, and capitalised periodical payments of £5,000 a year for 3 years amounting to £15,000, i.e. some £85,000 in total.

Scott Baker J: . . . I have come to the conclusion that in this case the conduct of the parties is a factor to be taken into account and that the conduct of the parties is one of the matters that has to be weighed in the scales in deciding whether any order ought to be made in favour of the husband and, if it ought to be made, what order ought to be made.

What are the relevant features in this case? I find that the wife has made great efforts to improve her own financial position, in contra-distinction to the husband who, on his own admission in evidence, could and should have obtained employment. It may be that he could not, even with reasonable efforts, and I do not think he really did make reasonable efforts, have got employment at quite the same level as he had before but I am satisfied that he could have obtained some employment from which he could have obtained a respectable income. That is the first point.

The second point is that the husband has had quite a serious drink problem. His general practitioner says that there is no evidence that he has seen that the problem still remains today. In my judgment, there is really no firm evidence one way or the other although I am bound to say I still have some doubt as to the extent of the husband's current drinking.

In these circumstances, I think it would be inequitable to disregard the conduct of the parties, which is, as I have said, one of the factors to be weighed in the scales. What conduct ought to be taken into account? In my judgment there should be taken into account first of all the fact that the husband did not get other employment, and secondly the fact that he has had a drink problem and the disagreeable behaviour relating to it including, for example, neglecting the house and ultimately the forced sale of the property. These are both matters of some significance. It is also significant in my judgment that the husband has a personality disorder and that his present situation, although partly due to extraneous causes beyond his control, is largely self-inflicted.

The next step is to go through s. 25 as amended and to draw attention to what to me seem the salient features as regards this case. Before I do so I should say that I accept the evidence of the wife whom I regard as an honest, reliable and by and large accurate witness. Insofar as there is any conflict between the evidence of the husband and the evidence of the wife and witnesses who were called by the wife, I unhesitatingly accept the evidence of the wife and her witnesses.

Turning then to s. 25 and the matters to be taken into account:

'(*a*) the income, earning capacity, property and other financial resources which each of the parties has or is likely to have in the foreseeable future, including in the case of earning capacity any increase in that capacity which it would be in the opinion of the court reasonable to expect the party to the marriage to take steps to acquire'.

The wife has a significant income and is going to go on having a significant income. In my judgment the husband has an earning capacity to obtain sedentary employment, albeit it may take him some time to find it.

'(*b*) the financial needs, obligations and responsibilities which each of the parties to the marriage had or is likely to have in the forseeable future'.

The crucial factor in my judgment is the husband's need for accommodation. He has urgent need for housing and that, in my judgment, is one of the most important factors in this case.

'(*c*) the standard of living enjoyed by the family before the breakdown of the marriage'.

It is plain that they lived to a reasonable standard and that they were both earning a good income. I also take into account the age of the parties insofar as it is relevant and the fact that although this was not a short marriage, neither was it a very long one.

'(*e*) any physical or mental disability of either of the parties'.

There is some physical and mental disability on the part of the husband. The physical disability is not in my judgment going to have a significant effect on his earning capacity. The mental disability, on the other hand, may do, but I bear in mind that the mental disability has been brought about to an extent by his own conduct.

Then I turn to the contributions at para. (*f*) and here it is plain that each in their own way contributed to the value of the matrimonial home and it is owned in equal shares and in my judgment it is justly owned in equal shares. Each since the breakdown of the marriage has had his or her opportunity of making his own contribution to his own welfare thereafter.

The conduct of the parties I have already referred to and the extent to which I think it ought to be brought into the scales. As far as pensions and other benefits are concerned, in my judgment those matters have little bearing on this case. The wife has pensionable employment. The husband has the benefit at some time in the future of pension provision resulting from his former employment; it is not very large and it is not effective for some years.

Taking all these matters into account, I have come to the conclusion that it would not be just to make an order against the wife that she should pay periodical payments to the husband. On the other hand I think that the husband has a very great need for accommodation. It is a need which he might have satisfied before if he had taken a more prudent course than pursuing these proceedings to the hearing that has now taken place. I have got to look at the position as it is today.

I do not think it is realistic to expect that he can obtain accommodation in London without using up, bearing in mind the costs that have to be paid, a disproportionately large amount of the proceeds of sale of the former matrimonial home. I do think it ought to be possible for him to obtain suitable accommodation elsewhere in the country. I think in all the circumstances that it is right to make an order under s. 24 by way of a lump sum because I think the husband's needs are such that it is appropriate that he should have more than simply his half share of the former matrimonial home, but I do not think that he should have very much more.

In the circumstances, the order that I propose to make is that he should have a lump sum of £60,000 to be paid out of the proceeds standing in court currently at £101,000. I bear in mind that necessarily some £3,000 of that will go to meet the wife's existing order for costs. . . . I dismiss the husband's other claims for financial relief.

Questions

(i) Is it really relevant that the husband's 'conduct' (i.e. his drink problem) is largely self inflicted?

(ii) If it had been the wife who had the drink problem and the husband who had made the great efforts to improve his financial position, do you think that the judge would have made the same order?

(iii) Do you think that wives should have to provide for their husbands?

(iv) Was *K v K (conduct)* really about conduct at all?

(v) Can the results of the cases in this section be explained by gender bias on the part of the judges?

Conduct was treated as an aspect of the contribution made by the parties to the welfare of the family in:

E v E (financial provision)
[1989] FCR 591, [1990] 2 FLR 233, High Court, Family Division

The parties were married in Israel in 1972. The husband, who was the only son of a rich man living in Israel, worked for his father for a modest salary. The father kept a tight control over his assets. He did not make over any capital to his son, but he bought the parties a matrimonial home and supplemented the husband's salary to the extent that they were able to live at the rate of some £350,000 p.a. net. In 1983 the last matrimonial home of the parties was settled on discretionary trusts, the beneficiaries being the husband, the wife and the three children of the marriage and any future children and future wife of the husband. By a protector clause the father was chosen to be protector. From about 1980 the wife started disengaging herself from the family. She was said to have had affairs with two men in 1982 and 1983 which she denied. In 1986 she had an affair with a third man and in 1988 she left home to live with him. The children were left with their father. A decree nisi was pronounced in June 1988. The wife applied for financial relief and property adjustment including variation of the post-nuptial settlement relating to the matrimonial home. She agreed that her husband should have an order for care and control of the children. The husband alleged that his father had refused to countenance a capital settlement on the wife and that that had led to a violent dispute and a rupture of their relationship, so that he had had to give up his posts in his father's companies and his salary had been discontinued. He could no longer afford to live in the last matrimonial home and had moved back to an earlier one which he still owned. His only assets were that matrimonial home and the post-nuptial settlement worth £1.25m. The wife contended that the rupture was a facade with a view to avoiding her claims. At the time of the hearing she was receiving interim periodical payments of £50,000 p.a. In February 1989 the husband made an open offer of £500,000 to the wife. She rejected it on the basis that the post-nuptial settlement was worth £3m. She did not formulate a counter-offer. The total costs of the case prior to the hearing amounted to over £300,000.

Ewbank J: . . . From about 1980 the wife started disengaging herself from the family. The home was staffed so there was little for her to do there, I suppose, and she became involved in her own concerns. She is said to have been neglecting the children from about 1980, and is said to have had affairs with various men in the ensuing years. In 1982 it is said that she had an adulterous affair with a Mr R. He denies the allegation, as does the wife. He has taken no part in the proceedings. In 1983 she is alleged to have had an affair with Mr B. He says (through his solicitors) that he makes no admissions of that adultery, and he too has played no part in the case. The wife denies that adultery too. In 1986 she became friendly with Mr N, and in April 1986 she first committed adultery with him. Mr N has a wife and two children. The husband became friendly with Mrs N and he committed adultery with her from October 1987 for a period of about 4 months.

It is said by the husband that the wife's disengagement from the family, neglect of the children, and adulterous affairs with other men indicate that her contribution to the welfare of the family has been negative rather than positive. It is also said that her conduct is such that it ought to be taken into account in these proceedings.

. . .

Under s. 25 of the Matrimonial Causes Act 1973 I have to consider the contribution of the parties to the welfare of the family in the past and in the foreseeable future, the contribution made by looking after the home or caring for the family. The husband says that the wife's contribution in this case has been minimal for the last 9 years and that that is a factor which ought to be taken into account. The section was originally introduced in order to do justice to wives and mothers who stayed at home to look after the home and the family. Her husband says that on three counts the wife's contribution is negligible: (1) her extravagance; (2) her neglect or abandonment of the children; and (3) her adultery during the marriage.

I deal firstly with the assertion of extravagance. The wife says this. Immediately prior to the breakdown of the marriage her rate of expenditure was:

clothes	£60,000 p.a.
beauty treatments	£8,000 p.a.
hair dressing	£5,000 p.a.
housekeeping	£30,000 p.a.
discharge of credit card liabilities	£5,000 p.a.

These figures probably speak for themselves, although it has to be said that the husband provided the means whereby the wife was able to spend this amount of money. The husband was away a great deal; the house had servants; the wife was moving away, as she said, from the children, and she seems to have had little else to do but spend money. But, however understandable her spending of money may be, I do not think it can be said to be a positive contribution to the welfare of the family.

In relation to the children, the welfare officer puts it this way, and I do not believe the wife dissents from this:

'The wife was a loving and involved mother until about 1980. When the family moved into [the last matrimonial home], the wife changed in a way that was destructive to the family life. The husband, though heir to a huge fortune, was not master of his own destiny. He spent a very substantial time away on business. When he was at home he spent time with his children. He is not a social party person, more serious. He grew up in a home without love except from the nanny. With the wife it became a lonely marriage devoid of love. She compensated by spending money and retreating from her children, since there was a staff to take care of everything. This happened gradually without any conscious decision.'

So the husband says that her contribution to the welfare of the family from 1980 was very small. Initially she contested that this was the case. She said in an affidavit, 'I strenuously deny that I ceased to be a full member of the household', but in her evidence she has conceded that that was the case.

It is rare nowadays to have charges of adultery in this type of case, but the husband has asserted that the wife committed adultery during this period of unhappiness, after 1980, and he has produced evidence of this adultery from various servants in the house. They have sworn affidavits and they have given evidence. Their affidavits constitute a strong *prima facie* case of adultery. I doubt if it is of value to go through their evidence; it is available there to be read. They were cross-examined. Discrepancies were shown in parts of their evidence but these were respectable women and I believe the basic facts of their evidence were true. The wife asserts that she not only has not committed adultery with the two men I have mentioned but that they had no other form of relationship other than as friends of the family. I am unable to accept her evidence. I accept and trust the evidence of the servants, and I find adultery with both men. The adultery is not of particular significance in itself: it is part of the pattern of disengagement from the family from 1980.

The wife started her affair with Mr N in 1987, and she has been asked questions about her spending during the period of her affair. It appears that she spent £17,000 on clothes in July 1987, and £8,000 in August. The wife says that these were items that she had actually bought before the affair started, but I do not accept that. The husband says that such spending on his account when she is having an affair with another man is distasteful. It is also pointed out that she bought a watch for Mr N in February or March 1987 which cost some £700. The husband in an affidavit says that the wife insisted on her spending, and he remembers an occasion in June 1987 (which was during the course of this affair) when three taxi loads of clothes arrived at the house, the contents of, as he puts it, 'a buying spree' at two shops. He asked her to explain and she said the Mr N liked to see her dressed well. The wife went on a number of journeys with Mr N; she went to America, to France, to Italy and to Israel, and she says that she paid her fare and Mr N paid the rest. She left home and set up with Mr N in April 1988. According to the husband, whom I have no reason to doubt on this aspect, she left behind seventy pairs of shoes, some of them in their unopened boxes, and clothes which filled twenty packing cases with which he had to deal. Between August 1987 and January 1989 she apparently sold a number of clothes to raise money and obtained £10,000 on those sales.

I have to say that from early 1987 the wife's contribution to the welfare of the family was negative, and from 1980 it has been minimal. In assessing her needs I bear in mind that she now has no financial obligation to the children. She is living with Mr N and he is sharing the expenses of her home. She is comparatively young, being 36, and proposes to start a business, and there is no reason why she should not be successful in such a business. In dealing with the application for a lump sum and for variation of the post-nuptial settlement, I have to consider the various matters set out in s. 25 of the 1973 Act. I have to give first consideration to the welfare of the children of the family, and that is particularly important when I come to deal with the post-nuptial settlement. I have to consider the financial resources and the financial needs of the parties. I do not find it necessary to consider conduct as a separate item. Such conduct as has been shown can properly be dealt with by considering the contribution the wife has made to the welfare of the family.

The judge made the following findings:

[1] The wife's contribution to the welfare of the family had been minimal from 1980 and negative from 1987. She had committed adultery as alleged but such conduct as had been shown could be dealt with in the context of that contribution. She was living with a man who shared her expenses and was likely to be successful in the business she proposed to set up. On the other hand, consideration must be given to the fact that her children, being the grandchildren of a very rich man, should not see their mother in straitened circumstances.

[2] Having regard to the above and to all the other relevant matters set out in s. 25 of the Matrimonial Causes Act 1973, the proper lump sum for the husband to pay from the first matrimonial home was £200,000. From the post-nuptial settlement, bearing in mind that the first consideration was to the welfare of the children and the second consideration was that the court should not interfere with it more than necessary for the purpose of s. 25 of the 1973 Act, £250,000 would be taken out and made into a separate fund for the wife, £50,000 to go to her absolutely and the balance to be settled on her for life with the remainder to the children. The remainder of the fund would be left on trust for the husband and children. There would be a change of trustees and the father would be removed as protector. Maintenance would be terminated.

[3] As regards costs, the court had unfettered discretion. . . . Furthermore, in view of the wife's negative contribution to the welfare of the family and the fact that the husband was having the continuing care of the children, the offer of £500,000 had been a fair offer, even if the husband's assets had been more than he asserted. In those circumstances, the wife should have her costs up to the date of her refusal of the offer and there should be no order for costs thereafter.

A particular aspect of the problems facing judges which has attracted considerable public controversy is the question of balancing the obligations of a husband who has remarried against his obligations to his former wife. In some cases, this question is also seen as an aspect of conduct.

Blezard v Blezard and Mul
(1978) 1 FLR 253, 9 Fam Law 249, Court of Appeal

Lawton LJ: This is a case, all too familiar, in which a man in his late 40s, who had been married for 25 years to a wife aged 51, left her with two children to look after for a younger woman in her mid-30s. It was his decision to leave and to set up home with and marry the younger woman. Through his counsel he submitted that, when a balance sheet was drawn up of the assets and liabilities of himself and his first wife and she was found to have more assets and less liabilities than he had, an adjustment should be made to enable him and his new wife to have a more comfortable and secure future. . . .

The idea has . . . got around amongst some lawyers, but not perhaps amongst right-thinking members of the public, that nowadays leaving one's spouse to set up home with another was a mere accident of life, which should be borne by the wife without fuss and which should not be taken into account when the court exercised its jurisdiction to rearrange the finances of the broken family . . . that was not the law. Such conduct may be of the greatest importance when the court came to make a property disposition order under s. 24 of the Matrimonial Causes Act 1973. When, as in this case, the husband's conduct had brought about his first wife's present situation and he had not alleged that she was responsible in any way for the breakdown of the marriage, [I] could see no reason why her living standards should be reduced to the same level as his. He decided to take another wife and the woman he married must have known that he had been married before and had left his first wife to marry her. The husband made the new conjugal bed and he should not be allowed now to say that it was uncomfortable to lie in. When this kind of situation arose in cases where the husband could not support two women, both may have to suffer, because any other result would be impracticable within the meaning of the 1973 Act. That was not this case. The first wife and the two children could be supported in something approaching the old standard of living. For these reasons, it seemed . . . that conduct was a material factor.

The other judge in *Blezard v Blezard*, Orr LJ, did not express himself in these terms. The question for him was whether the former matrimonial home, where the former wife was living with the daughter, should be sold in order to enable the husband to realise his only real asset. The younger girl was still 14 and the judge thought that her interests should be considered. He therefore ordered that the house should not be sold until the younger child had attained the age of 18.

Questions

(i) Do you approve of the views expressed by Lawton LJ in this case?
(ii) In *B v B (financial provision)* [1990] FCR 105, [1991] 1 FLR 20, Ward J said:

This wife has made the fullest contribution that could be expected of her. She did everything the husband required of her to be a good wife and help around the farm, and a good mother to his four children. She has earned the award I must make.

(*a*) Would, or (*b*) should, it have made any difference to the order if she had not been a good wife and mother?

(d) SHARES VERSUS NEEDS

H v H (family provision: remarriage)
[1975] Fam 9, [1975] 1 All ER 367, [1975] 2 WLR 124, 118 Sol Jo 579, 5 Fam Law 17, High Court, Family Division

In this case both parties had remarried. The main question for decision was the effect of the wife's remarriage to a man of means, with a new home in their joint names, upon her claim for the former matrimonial home to be settled on her ex-husband and herself in equal shares, but in trust until the youngest child reached 18 or alternatively for a lump sum of £17,000. The children of the marriage, two girls and two boys, lived with the father in the former home.

Sir George Baker P: The wife does not suggest that she has any property rights in the sense of a legal interest, or a beneficial interest arising from a joint tenancy, under section 17 of the Married Women's Property Act 1882 or by virtue of improvements under section 37 of the Matrimonial Proceedings and Property Act 1970. Her case is that she has contributed to the welfare of the family, including looking after the home and caring for the family: [see now section 25(2)(*f*) of the Matrimonial Causes Act 1973;] that in the 15 years of marriage she bore the four children, was a wife and mother, and in the early days washed, ironed, cooked for and looked after a paying guest; that with the husband she decorated a flat they had early in the marriage and part of a house they had in 1963; that she cleaned the stairs and bathroom of a tenanted house the husband owns; and that she gardened and supervised decoration and workmen. Under the new law such contributions can and must be adequately recognised on the division of the family assets, either as a moral claim, or as an accrued right, a beneficial interest, already in existence at the end of the marriage earned by her contribution: see per Lord Denning MR in *Wachtel v Wachtel* [1973] Fam 72 at 94.

Mr Jackson, for the wife, rightly points out that continuing financial provision orders [see now section 28(1) of the Matrimonial Causes Act 1973] end on remarriage, but that a property adjustment order can be made after remarriage. The sole prohibition, contained in section 28(3) of the Matrimonial Causes Act 1973, is that a party to a remarriage shall not be entitled to apply for a financial provision order, and the courts have consistently held that that means 'make a new application.' An application which has already been made can be pursued. . . . This must, he submits, be because a proprietary right has already accrued as a result of the wife's contribution under section 25(2)(*f*) of the Act of 1973. She has earned that right and remarriage only affects that right by making it unenforceable if a claim, that is an application for its recognition, has not already been made. If such a claim has been made it would be imposing a penalty on the wife to hold, in the absence of a statutory provision, that her right ends with remarriage.

Mr Holroyd Pearce, for the husband, submits that this is a misconceived claim and that the wife has no entitlement in law or justice to such a claim because of, first, her remarriage to the second respondent and, secondly, an agreement made on 4 January 1973. I can dispose briefly of the agreement. . . .

The wife was concerned primarily about the children and I accept that she did not intend to give up any claim she might have in the house. The husband may have thought he was securing the house for the children but there is clearly no estoppel. In any event the agreement was reached before judgment was delivered in *Wachtel v Wachtel* [1973] Fam 72, [1973] 1 All ER 829 on 8 February 1973, and I doubt if legal advice at that time would have been able to accurately forecast the possibilities, I therefore disregard the agreement.

After referring to a few old decisions, and quoting from the judgment of Lord Denning MR in *Wachtel v Wachtel* (see p. 265, above), the judge said:

Lord Denning MR was careful to deal with the prospects, the likelihood, of remarriage. He said nothing of the fact of remarriage in relation to capital assets. It is said that the passage is obiter and its guidance is not binding upon me, but in a reserved judgment given in chambers on 27 March 1972, allowing an appeal by a wife against a lump sum award of £350,000 I had myself said:

'It would be strange, indeed repugnant, if, in the face of section 4 of the Law Reform (Miscellaneous Provisions) Act 1971, which prohibits the court from taking into account a widow's remarriage or prospects of remarriage in assessing damages in respect of the death of her husband, this court had to embark on an inquiry into this lady's prospects of remarriage before deciding upon the lump sum.'

In *Trippas v Trippas* [1973] Fam 134, [1973] 2 All ER 1 the wife was living with another man whom she might marry, but that did not affect her entitlement. The prospect, chance or hope of remarriage is, I think, irrelevant, but the fact of remarriage, which does not admit of speculation, is in my judgment, something which the court must consider. This accords with Bagnall J's view in *Jackson v Jackson* [1973] Fam 99 at 104, that the wife's intervening marriage is a factor to be weighed with all the others in a particular case, and with at least part of Latey J's conclusion in *S v S* (1973) Times, 11 December, reached after reviewing *Mesher v Mesher (1973)* [1980] 1 All ER 126. . . . *Hector v Hector* [1973] 3 All ER 1070, [1973] 1 WLR 1122 and *Chamberlain v Chamberlain* [1974] 1 All ER 33, [1973] 1 WLR 1557 that

'. . . the following emerges as guidance . . . If the wife had remarried or was going to remarry her financial position on remarriage had to be considered. If it was guesswork whether she would or would not remarry, prospective remarriage should be ignored.'

To ignore remarriage entirely would be to ignore the financial needs of the parties in the foreseeable future: [see now section 25(2)(b) of the Matrimonial Causes Act 1973.]

It seems to me that the real problem in any particular case is to decide how to translate a new marriage into money. How it is to be regarded and what part is it to play in the financial provision? Mr Jackson argues that a wife who remarries a poor man should get no more, and therefore a wife who remarries a rich man gets no less. I do not accept that submission. Remarriage to a poor man would reflect in her financial resources and financial needs, and would probably result in her receiving the full share of what she had earned. Equally, marriage to a wealthy man has a bearing on her financial needs and resources just as her own capital would be taken into account, for as Bagnall J said in *Harnett v Harnett* [1973] Fam 156, 164: 'Where the wife has some capital, that must be taken into account in determining what she should be given by the husband.' . . .

The husband has a salary of £20,000 per annum and about £500 per annum from rents and dividends. The matrimonial home was bought by him in 1968 for £25,000 as the perfect home for the children. . . . The value has been taken for the purposes of this case as £65,000. The husband has two accounts with his bank one of which is designated 'House Purchase Account'. It is overdrawn to the limit of £20,000. Of this, £9,718 arose from house improvements and £6,516 from accumulated overdraft interest, of which, it is submitted for the wife, only a half should be charged against the house. His other account was overdrawn £20,358 in August 1973 (limit £20,000). Both accounts are secured by the title deeds of the matrimonial home. Only a part of the overdraft interest will in future be allowable against tax. The household effects are valued at £4,505 but half of this sum has already been paid to the wife.

The judge then considered various other aspects of the husband's resources, and continued:

To summarise the husband's capital position, he can be treated broadly as having £35,000–£40,000.

Turning next to the second respondent [the second husband] he has an income of about £14,000 per annum gross which, after tax, will not be very greatly less than that of the husband. I do not think that it is necessary or desirable for me to go into his capital position in detail. Suffice it to say that I have studied his lengthy affidavit in his own matrimonial proceedings and have regard to his oral evidence before me which I accept. I find that, as he said, he has capital, after allowing for capital gains tax, of approximately £50,000. There are some uncertainties. Mr Jackson and the wife were prepared to accept that the second respondent's capital position is roughly the same as the husband's. I find he is the better off; on any view his capital position is no worse.

Now the wife: the house where she lives with the second respondent was bought in January 1973 for a total of £65,000, of which £35,000 was for adjoining plots which, the second respondent hopes, are to be sold at a profit. The house and garden, which was put into their joint names, is therefore worth £30,000 plus £4,000 spent on it by the second respondent. The equity is probably about £14,000 although there is no very clear evidence. The wife is also a beneficiary under her grandfather's will subject to life interests. Her interest is valued at the present day at £2,250.

. . . She can fairly, I think, be treated as having notional capital of £7,000–£9,000.

In these circumstances, and with due regard to them all, I think, first, that it is unjust and impracticable to make the husband pay a lump sum. He cannot raise more money on the house, he has to pay for the four children and he has little other capital.

The wife needs no flat or house and I think most people would find it distasteful and unjust that a lump sum should be given to a wife for the probable benefit of the new family.

The judge then made the following comment about the wife's claim:

But, the wife says, she has earned a share in the house and will accommodate her first family by allowing it to remain with them till the youngest is 18. She says that that share should be one-third of the house. If the concept of earning is to be applied to a domestic situation, then it should be applied with all its normal consequences. One is that if the job is left unfinished you do not earn as much. A builder agrees to build four houses. He goes off to a job which he prefers to do, leaving them in varying stages of completion. Leaving aside any question of special contractual terms, the best he could hope to receive is the value of work actually done, remembering also that the owner has to have the work completed. Is there any difference between four houses and four children? I think not. Any payment will in fact put her in a better financial position than if the marriage had continued and I would give her one-twelfth of the unencumbered value of the house (at present £65,000), her entitlement thereto to rank after the present charges for the bank overdrafts and not to be payable until the youngest child is 18.

Questions

(i) Is the comment about an 'unfinished' job a disguised way of making 'conduct' relevant?

(ii) In this case, the husband needed the house for the children, whereas the wife did not need the house for that purpose. Do you think that this fact affected the decision?

(iii) Do you think that the wife would have received less if the 1984 amendments had been in force at the time this case was decided?

(e) THE CLEAN BREAK

The doctrine of the clean break has emerged from the haze of the judicial involvement as one major target which, within the framework of s. 25 of the Act, must be in the forefront of the judge's mind.

Minton v Minton
[1979] AC 593, [1979] 1 All ER 79, [1979] 2 WLR 31, 122 Sol Jo 843, House of Lords

In this case, the House of Lords collectively, and Lord Scarman in particular, stressed the requirement that the parties put the past behind them and begin a new life which is in no way overshadowed by a former relationship:

. . . There are two principles which inform the modern legislation. One is the public interest that spouses, to the extent that their means permit, should provide for themselves and their children. But the other − of equal importance − is the principle of 'the clean break.' The law now encourages spouses to avoid bitterness after family break-down and to settle their money and property problems. An object of the modern law is to encourage each to put the past behind them and to begin a new life which is not overshadowed by the relationship which has broken down. It would be inconsistent with this principle if the court could not make, as between the spouses, a genuinely final order unless it was prepared to dismiss the application. The present case is a good illustration. The court having made an order giving effect to a comprehensive settlement of all financial and property issues as between spouses, it would be a strange application of the principle of the clean break if, notwithstanding the order, the court could make a future order on a subsequent application made by the wife after the husband had complied with all his obligations.

Questions

(i) Is Lord Scarman being cruel to be kind?
(ii) Is the clean break approach consistent with the interests of the children?

Suter v Suter and Jones
[1987] Fam 111, [1987] 2 All ER 336, [1987] 3 WLR 9, 131 Sol Jo 471, Court of Appeal

The husband and wife, who had married in 1971, were divorced in 1985, on the husband's petition, on the ground of the wife's adultery with the co-respondent. Care and control of the two children of the marriage, born in 1972 and 1978, was awarded to the wife who continued to live with them in the former matrimonial home. The co-respondent, who earned £7,000 per annum, paid rent to his mother for a room in her house and had his meals there, but spent most nights with the wife, who neither sought nor received any contribution from him towards the expenses of running the home. The husband remarried. On the wife's application for financial provision, the district judge in the county court ordered, inter alia, the husband to transfer to the wife all his interest in the former matrimonial home, subject to the mortgage, together with the surrender value of two insurance policies, and to make periodical payments of £100 per month to her until she remarry or both children attain the age of 18 and periodical payments of £110 and £90 per month respectively to the children during their respective minorities. Without the periodical payments to her, the wife's outgoings would have exceeded her income by £570 per annum. The circuit judge dismissed the husband's appeal against the periodical payments order in favour of the wife, on the basis that a 'clean break' could not be ordered, under section 25A(2), where there were children under 18, that section 25(1) of the Act of 1973 made the welfare of the children the paramount consideration in deciding whether to make a periodical payments order and its amount, and that the children's welfare required the order to be made so as to ensure that they continued to have a roof over their heads.

On the husband's appeal:

Sir Roualeyn Cumming-Bruce: This appeal raises questions about the meaning and application of section 25(1) of the Matrimonial Causes Act 1973, as amended by section 3 of the Matrimonial and Family Proceedings Act 1984, and the correct exercise of the powers and duties conferred on the court by section 25A of the Act of 1973.

. . .

Counsel for the appellant husband's first submission was that the judge misdirected himself in that he never carried out the exercise prescribed as a mandatory duty upon the court by section 25A. By section 25A(1) it is the duty of the court to consider whether it would be appropriate to exercise the powers so that financial obligations of each party towards the other will be terminated as soon after the grant of the decree as the court thinks just and reasonable. By subsection (2), where the court decides to make a periodical payments order in favour of a party to a marriage, the court shall in particular consider whether it would be appropriate to require those payments to be made for such term as would in the opinion of the court be sufficient to enable the party in whose favour the order is made to adjust without undue hardship to the termination of his or her financial dependence on the other party.

Those provisions, introduced by the Act of 1984, enshrine in statute law the principle that after dissolution of marriage a time may have come, or can be foreseen in the future, when the party in whose favour financial provision has been made can so adjust his or her life as to attain sufficient financial independence to enable that party to live without undue hardship without any further dependence on the other party. This has been described as the principle of a 'clean break,' the phrase used by Lord Scarman in his speech in *Minton v Minton* [1979] AC 593, 608. In a number of cases which were decided before the new legislation came into force the court observed that where there were children for whom the parties shared a continuing obligation there is likely to be little or no room for the father and mother to have a clean break from each other: see, for example, *Pearce v Pearce* (1979) 1 FLR 261 and *Moore v Moore* (1980) 11 Fam Law 109, in which Ormrod L.J. observed at p. 109:

> 'It is one thing to talk about a 'clean break' when there are sufficient financial resources to make a comprehensive settlement. Where there are no capital resources, as here, it is unrealistic to talk about a 'clean break' if there are children. It is not possible for the father and mother of dependent children to have a clean break from one another. . . . So, in my judgment, the so-called principle of the 'clean break' has no application where there are young children.'

I agree with the submission of counsel that the new section 25A imposes a mandatory duty in every case to apply itself to questions set out in section 25A(2) whenever a court decides to make a periodical payments order in favour of a party to the marriage. The judgments in the cases before 1984 have to be read with that in mind. Though the parties may have to co-operate wth each other over children still dependent upon them, it may be possible on the facts to recognise a date when the party in whose favour the order is made will have been able to adjust without undue hardship to the termination of financial dependence on the other party. I also agree that the judge appears to have been influenced by the earlier cases to approach the question of termination of financial dependence without specifically addressing himself to the question whether this wife could and should find a way of adjusting her way of life so as to attain financial independence of her husband. So this court is entitled to consider the facts for itself and to carry out the statutory duty prescribed by section 25A. Having said that, I am clear that on the facts it is not possible at this date to predict with any more confidence than the [district judge] when the wife will have been able to make the adjustment which leads to the inference that it will then be just and reasonable to terminate her right to claim periodical payments from her husband. The children are growing up. It is likely that it will become progressively easier for the wife to organise and increase her earning capacity. But there are too many uncertainties to predict the development of events over the next 10 years. Likewise in connection with the financial advantages which on the judge's finding she can expect to derive, if she wishes, from her association with the co-respondent. It is their declared intention at present not to marry. There has already been one interruption in the continuity of their cohabitation, if that is the right description of their present arrangements, as I think it is. She may become increasingly and permanently financially dependent on the co-respondent. She may not. Consideration of the facts in evidence before the [district judge] does not at this date enable the court to predict with any confidence whether she will in the next 10 years have had the opportunity so to adjust herself that her claim for periodical payments can be terminated without undue hardship. The [district judge] warned her that such would be the position once the younger child reached the age of 18. It may be that that situation will be attained earlier. It is not impossible that even after the younger child is 18, consideration of the wife's needs and earning capacity will still make it just and reasonable for her to claim some support from her husband, though I would expect it to be unlikely. For those reasons I reject the submission that the judge was wrong in refusing to make an order terminating the husband's financial obligations towards his wife.

I do not however found that conclusion upon the judge's reasoning and approach. I am satisfied for the reasons that I have stated, that he misdirected himself by failing to apply the test prescribed in section 25A(2). This court is therefore entitled to consider the facts in the way that section 25A(2) has enjoined, and then to exercise the discretionary power itself. So directing myself I come to the conclusion that it would be premature to make an order terminating the wife's claim for periodical payments for her support from her husband.

The second submission made on behalf of the husband is that the judge, following the approach of the [district judge], misdirected himself upon the proper construction and effect of section 25 of the Act of 1973, as amended by section 3 of the Act of 1984.

By section 25(1):

'It shall be the duty of the court in deciding whether to exercise its powers under section 23, 24 or 24A above and, if so, in what manner, to have regard to all the circumstances of the case, first consideration being given to the welfare while a minor of any child of the family who has not attained the age of 18.'

This subsection is new, and in effect replaces the words formerly enacted in section 25 at the end of the list of matters in paragraphs (*a*) to (*g*) of section 25(1) and paragraphs (*a*) to (*e*) of section 25(2) to which the court had to have regard amongst all the circumstances of the case.

The husband submits that both the judge and the [district judge] treated the welfare of the children as first and paramount, in the sense in which that phrase was interpreted by Lord MacDermott in the context of section 1 of the Guardianship of Infants Act 1925: see *J v C* [1970] AC 668, 711. There Lord MacDermott considered the two adjectives in the phrase, and said:

'That is the first consideration because it is of first importance and the paramount consideration because it rules upon or determines the course to be followed.'

I agree with the submission that counsel culled from a commentary by a distinguished commentator [F.A.R. Bennion (1976)] that the phrase 'first and paramount' means simply 'overriding,' and that if the draftsman had omitted the adjective 'first' the meaning and effect of the single adjective 'paramount' would have been the same. We are faced with the problem of discovering the intention of Parliament when it used the phrase 'the first consideration' without the conjunction of the adjective 'and paramount' which gave the phrase in section 1 of the Guardianship of Infants Act 1925 its dominant force and effect.

The duty of the court under section 25(1), as amended, is to have regard to all the circumstances, first consideration being given to the welfare while a minor of any child of the family under the age of 18. As regards the exercise of the powers in relation to a party to the marriage, the court shall in particular have regard to the matters set out in section 25(2) in the subparagraphs lettered (*a*) to (*h*). Sub-paragraph (*g*) introduces a matter not previously included: 'the conduct of each of the parties, if that conduct is such that it would in the opinion of the court be inequitable to disregard it; . . .'

Having regard to the prominence which the consideration of the welfare of children is given in section 25(1), being selected as the first consideration among all the circumstances of the case, I collect an intention that this consideration is to be regarded as of first importance, to be borne in mind throughout consideration of all the circumstances including the particular circumstances specified in section 25(2). But if it had been intended to be paramount, overriding all other considerations pointing to a just result, Parliament would have said so. It has not. So I construe the section as requiring the court to consider all the circumstances, including those set out in subsection (2), always bearing in mind the important consideration of the welfare of the children, and then try to attain a financial result which is just as between husband and wife.

Consideration of the judge's judgment, taken in conjunction with paragraphs 15 and 16 of the judgment of the [district judge] which he clearly approved, shows that the judge treated the consideration of the children's welfare as paramount; and controlling the effect of the interplay of all other matters. Though the [district judge] and the judge gave some effect by way of reduction of the periodical payments to the financial contribution of the co-respondent to the wife's finances, which the judge held would be substantial, the order was calculated in such a way as to provide the wife with a periodical payments order which would enable her to make all the mortgage payments. And the reasoning thus proceeded because it was considered that the children's welfare required that solution, although the [district judge] for the reasons that he gave thought that ordinary people would regard the result as unjust. In my view the judge fell into error in treating section 25(1) as requiring him to give effect to a consideration of the children's welfare as the overriding or paramount consideration. This was a misdirection, and this court is entitled to review the facts, apply the statute on its proper construction, and decide how to determine the wife's financial claim for periodical payments.

The judge then considered the position of the co-respondent.

. . . the wife has invited her lover to live for the foreseeable future in the former matrimonial home with herself and the children, without seeking or receiving any contribution to the expenses of maintaining that house. He is a bachelor aged 21 with a gross income of not less than £7,000, subject to tax. The figures demonstrate that the payment of the mortgage amounts to £2,148 per annum, and that after payment thereof she has a deficit of £570 per annum. It is reasonable to infer that the co-respondent is in a position to contribute at least £12 per week for the privileges which he enjoys in the furnished residence which, as a consequence of the husband's transfer of property, now belongs wholly to the wife, subject to the mortgage. It is material to bear in mind that since he moved to reside in the wife's house the co-respondent has continued to pay £16 per week to his mother for the room in which he no longer sleeps. As the wife is now for practical purposes living with the co-respondent in the former matrimonial home, it is just and reasonable to make an order on the basis that she require him to contribute not less than £600 per annum for the expenses of the house which she has invited him to enjoy. On that basis I would not think it just that the husband should do more than he has done by making the capital transfers already completed and by continuing to make payments to the children amounting to £200 per month. In that situation the wife's and children's needs are met, she can afford to run the home and pay the mortgage, and the husband and wife can expect to enjoy a comparable standard of living in the accommodation in which they respectively live.

I would move that the appeal be allowed and that the husband's obligation to contribute to her support be reduced to a nominal order of £1 per year.

Appeal allowed.

Questions

(i) Purchas LJ described a 'clean break' in *Scallon v Scallon* [1990] FCR 911, [1990] 1 FLR 194 (see p. 275, above) as follows:

Finally, I wish to say a word about "clean break" which is a phrase which arises since the amendments to the 1973 Act were introduced to ensure that, where there were short-term marriages, one party should not get what is described as "a meal ticket for life" upon the dissolution of such a marriage. Furthermore, it was to encourage spouses who hitherto had not earned their living to face up to the fact that after the dissolution they should earn their living.

But if the husband insisted that the wife remained at home during the marriage, is it really fair on her that she should now be encouraged to 'face up to the fact . . . that she should earn her living?' Perhaps it is too late?

(ii) When making a 'clean break' should the emphasis be on 'need' or 'earned share'? (See *B v B (financial provision)* [1990] FCR 105, [1990] 1 FLR 20, p. 295, above).

(iii) Do you think that the policy of the 'clean break' is consistent with the principles behind the Child Support Act 1991? (See Chapter 4, above.)

(iv) Will a 'clean break' be harder to achieve once the Child Support Act 1991 has been brought into force?

The ideology of the clean break is discussed in *Indissolubility and the Clean Break* (1985) by Pamela Symes:

The Logic of the Clean Break Principle

The limitations of the old section 25 directive were soon apparent and therefore a realistic and workable alternative needed to be found. The clean break principle is arguably a logical step forward in the long march towards liberal divorce and sexual equality but it is possible that in principle, it carries almost as much potential conflict and inconsistency as the old directive — equally capable of producing unjust and inequitable results, but for different reasons. The former section 25 directive embodied an *inherent* contradiction ('to place the parties . . . in the financial position in which they would have been if the marriage had not broken down'). By contrast, the clean break principle has an inherent logic about it based, as it is, on the assumption that the marital relationship is ending rather than being continued. The potential contradictions are not inherent — rather they are *internal* to the legislation (for example, trying to reconcile the clean break with the other policy objective of giving priority to children's needs) and *external*, such as when the clean break is not recognised by the D.H.S.S., for instance, who may still require contributions from an ex-husband after a clean break settlement. (*Hulley v Thompson* [1981] 1 All ER 1128.) [See now the Child Support Act (p. 122, above).]

After looking at the English and the Scottish proposals, Symes raises the basic issue of 'who pays'?

One very fundamental question was never satisfactorily answered before the Divorce Reform Act 1969 was enacted — namely, how is it going to be paid for? Divorce and remarriage it was realised would involve the creation of many new households; where were the extra resources to come from to finance this exercise? The wider fiscal implications of such a change in the divorce law seem to have been largely ignored . . .

The husband's obligation to maintain his wife, is the very nub of the problem. It is debatable whether such an obligation should arise during marriage, but if it does not end on divorce then what does divorce mean? This leads to the second basic question which has still not been satisfactorily answered: does divorce constitute the termination of the marital relationship, or merely a readjustment of it? These two questions have chased one another in a kind of conundrum for the last 15 years. Unable to accept the full logic of the position that divorce should constitute a complete and final termination of the parties' legal and financial relationship with the parties reverting to being 'legal strangers,' we have been forced to accept that it must therefore be a readjustment of their former marital relationship. Our present law is still ambiguous; while apparently signalling the end of the marital relationship, the financial provisions point to its readjustive function. But in one respect the law is quite clear and unambiguous: it incorporates a licence to remarry.

She argues that marriage 'as it has been traditionally practiced, is not intended to be ended by divorce':

Indeed, traditional housewife marriage has a most potent feature of indissolubility built right into it — dependency. When that dependency is reinforced in the social infrastructure (both explicitly through social security and taxation laws and implicitly in the underlying assumptions about marriage) then the marriage bond becomes practically indissoluble. The accumulation of responsibilities and obligations, the consequences of an unequal partnership based on dependency — all mean that an absolute severance of the bond without massive adjustment would be manifestly unjust, more likely impossible.

She ends her article in this way:

Conclusion

Present divorce is so often merely a readjustment of the former marital relationship. It results in the parties being released from the obligation to share bed and board but they are still saddled with the ongoing financial obligations of the marriage, not unlike judicial separation. Thus the licence to remarry is something of an illusion. In so many ways the parties are *not* free to remarry, as the evidence from numerous pressure groups will testify. Thus divorce, as granted in most cases, is only *a mensa et thoro* simply because most marriages are still indissoluble. True divorce *a vinculo matrimonii* can only be granted when, because the marriage is short, childless or the parties are sufficiently rich, the bond can be truly severed and a clean break imposed

— the marriage is, by practical definition, dissoluble. This is because, at the time the reformed divorce law came into operation, we failed to introduce simultaneously the effective means whereby the *vinculum*, the marriage bond could be broken (*i.e.* the necessary changes in the infrastructure). The ongoing marriage tie is reflected in the continuing support obligation which is imposed — admittedly imposed but often not met . . . If the support obligation is met, there is financial strain where remarriage follows as limited resources are spread between two families; if it is ignored or only partly met, then usually the resort is to subsistence on State benefit for the first family.

This was the inevitable result of attempting the impossible, of trying to introduce divorce for indissoluble marriage. With the passing of the Matrimonial and Family Proceedings Act 1984 the clean break principle now has embryonic statutory form. While it remains unsupported by a reformed social policy it will at best be a non-event, at worst, it will simply open the way to more injustice and suffering. For only when a radical change in the marital relationship takes place, when it becomes a partnership of two economically independent individuals through the abolition of marital dependency and when the corresponding changes in the social infrastructure are brought about, will there be any chance of formulating a coherent, clean break divorce law.

Questions

(i) After reading this, are you inclined to give up searching for a coherent policy?

(ii) How does one stop well meaning judges using phrases such as 'This wife has made the fullest contribution that could be expected of her?' (see p. 295, above) Why shouldn't they use such phrases?

(f) HOUSING

It will have been apparent from the cases already discussed that one of the most significant problems concerns what is to be done with the matrimonial home. There are a number of options available to the court. First, the court may decide to allow the husband to retain an interest in the matrimonial home even though the former wife remains in the home with the children. It may be considered appropriate for the sale of the home to be postponed until the youngest child has completed his or her education:

Mesher v Mesher and Hall
(1973) [1980] 1 All ER 126, Court of Appeal

The marriage took place in 1956 and the one child of the marriage (aged 9) lived with the mother. The house was in joint names. The judge ordered that the house be transferred to the wife, and the husband appealed.

Davies LJ: . . . Counsel for the husband submits that it would be quite wrong to deprive the husband of the substantial asset which his half-interest in the house represents . . ., one has to take a broad approach to the whole case. What is wanted here is to see that the wife and daughter, together no doubt in the near future with Mr Jones, [whom the wife intended to marry] should have a home in which to live rather than that she should have a large sum of available capital. With that end in view, I have come to the conclusion that counsel's submission for the husband is right. It would, in my judgment, be wrong to strip the husband entirely of any interest in the house. I would set aside the judge's order so far as concerns the house and substitute instead an order that the house is held by the parties in equal shares on trust for sale but that it is not to be sold until the child of the marriage reaches a specified age or with the leave of the court.

Harvey v Harvey
[1982] Fam 83, [1982] 1 All ER 693, [1982] 2 WLR 283, 126 Sol Jo 15, Court of Appeal

The parties were married in 1960. They had six children. The marriage broke down in 1979 and it was dissolved in May 1981. The judge made an order in the form used in *Mesher v Mesher*, namely that the home should be held in joint names of husband and wife on trust for sale in equal shares and that the sale of the property should be postponed until the youngest child attained 16 or completed her full-time education, whichever was later, when the wife should be at liberty to purchase the husband's share in the property at a valuation then made. The wife appealed.

Purchas J: . . . I am of the opinion that the wife is entitled to live in this house as long as she chooses so to do, . . . I do that on the basis that was adopted in *Martin v Martin* [1978] Fam 12, [1977] 3 All ER 762, that, had the marriage not broken down, that is precisely what she would have been entitled to do.

I would vary the judge's order, first of all to say that the asset (the matrimonial home) be transferred into the joint names of the wife and the husband on trust for sale in the shares two-thirds to the wife and one-third to the husband; and further that such sale shall be postponed during the lifetime of the wife, or her remarriage, or voluntary removal from the premises, or her becoming dependent on another man. I have in mind that if she begins to cohabit with another man in the premises, then obviously that man ought to take over the responsibility of providing accommodation for her. Until one or other of those events occur, she should be entitled to continue to reside at these premises, but after the mortgage has been paid off, or the youngest child has reached the aged of 18, whichever is the later, she should pay an occupation rent to be assessed by the [district judge].

Ormrod LJ: I agree. This is another case which illustrates very aptly the proposition which has been stated many times in this court, that the effect of making a *Mesher v Mesher* order is simply to postpone the evil day to avoid facing the facts now.

Questions

(i) Are you attracted by this solution? In *Carson v Carson* [1983] 1 All ER 478, [1983] 1 WLR 285, Ormrod LJ said that the facts of that case, where the judge had made the type of order in *Mesher v Mesher*, were 'a very good example of the chickens coming home to roost.' What exactly does he mean?
(ii) Why should a new man take over responsibility of providing accommodation for an ex-wife remaining in the former matrimonial home?
(iii) Assume the ex-wife is disabled and unable to contemplate moving out of a purpose built bungalow which is the former matrimonial home. There are no children. Is her disability a sufficient reason by itself to transfer the matrimonial home into her name alone? (Read *Chadwick v Chadwick* [1985] FLR 606, [1985] Fam Law 96, CA.)

In contrast, the court may decide not to postpone sale but rather to transfer title to the wife absolutely (*Hanlon v Law Society* [1981] AC 124, see p. 277, above). The husband may be ordered to continue to pay the mortgage. Or the wife may be ordered to pay a lump sum to the husband; in effect to buy him out. The deciding factor in determining whether to postpone sale or to transfer ownership is often whether the court considers that the husband cannot or will not pay periodical payments. However, the court is bound to think hard before it deprives the husband of the only real capital asset he has.

Comparative merits of *Mesher* orders, *Harvey* orders (or *Martin* orders as they are generally known) and orders transferring the home absolutely are discussed in the following case:

Clutton v Clutton
[1991] 1 All ER 340, [1991] 1 WLR 359, Court of Appeal

The parties, who were married in 1964, had two children, now aged 23 and 16. In 1970 the husband bought the matrimonial home in his sole name for about £4,500, subject to a small mortgage. The parties separated in 1984 and a decree absolute dissolving the marriage was granted in 1985. The husband remarried in that year. In 1984 the wife had applied for ancillary relief, seeking transfer of the matrimonial home into her sole name or at least an order that she be allowed to remain there with the children and be not required to sell the house until death or remarriage 'or such order as the court shall think fit.' The district judge made an order transferring the house to the wife, subject to a charge in the husband's favour for £7,000, not to be enforced until 1 January 1991. In addition he awarded the wife maintenance of £10 per week, arrears of maintenance and maintenance of £25 per week for the younger child. On appeal by the husband the judge was told that the matrimonial home was the sole capital asset of the parties, the equity being worth £50,000; that the husband, whose debts amounted to £17,000, had a net disposable income, taking account of debt repayments, of £127 per week, while his second wife ran a small business which brought in £2,000 per annum; and that the wife, who had a stable sexual relationship with another man but had declared her intention of not remarrying or cohabiting, earned £66 per week from part-time work. The judge held that it was a clear case for a 'clean break' and ordered that the charge over the matrimonial home in the husband's favour should be set aside and that the husband should pay maintenance of £25 per week for the younger child until the end of the July following her sixteenth birthday so long as she remained in full-time education. He made no order for payments of maintenance to the wife. The judge refused the husband's application for leave to appeal against the order transferring the matrimonial home to the wife absolutely.

Lloyd LJ: An order whereby the sale of the matrimonial home is postponed until the youngest child of the family is 18, or some other age, is usually known as a *Mesher* order: see *Mesher v Mesher and Hall (Note)* [1980] 1 All ER 126. An order whereby the sale is postponed until the wife dies, remarries or cohabits with another man, is usually known as a *Martin* order: see *Martin (BH) v Martin (D)* [1978] Fam 12. It will be seen that while, in 1984, the wife was asking for an out-and-out transfer of the matrimonial home, she would have been content, in the alternative, with a *Martin* order.

The principle of the clean break was, of course, well established long before the Matrimonial and Family Proceedings Act 1984: see for example *Minton v Minton* [1979] AC 593, *per* Viscount Dilhorne, at p. 601, and *per* Lord Scarman, at p. 608. It is now enshrined in section 25A(1) of the Matrimonial Causes Act 1973 by virtue of section 3 of the Act of 1984. But there is perhaps a danger in referring to it as a 'principle', since it might lead courts to strive for a clean break, regardless of all other considerations. This is not what section 25A requires. It requires the court to consider the appropriateness of a clean break, neither more nor less. It is salutary to remind oneself from time to time of the language of section 25A(1):

'it shall be the duty of the court to consider whether it would be appropriate so to exercise those powers that the financial obligations of each party towards the other will be terminated as soon after the grant of the decree as the court considers just and reasonable.'

Another danger is that 'clean break' may mean different things to different people. In origin it referred to an agreement whereby the wife abandoned her right to claim maintenance in return for a transfer by the husband of a capital asset, usually, though not always, the matrimonial home, thus encouraging the parties to put the past behind them, and, in the words of Lord Scarman in *Minton v Minton*, at p. 608, 'to begin a new life which is not overshadowed by the relationship which was broken down.'

. . .

Where the judge went wrong, and plainly wrong in my opinion, was in refusing to make a *Martin* order. As I have pointed out, this is what the wife was originally content to accept. It is also what the husband was asking for. Why then did the judge not make a *Martin* order? We cannot tell, because we do not know his reasons. It cannot surely have been because a *Martin* order would offend against the principle of the clean break. A charge which does not take effect until death or remarriage could only be said to offend against the principle of the clean break in the most extended sense of that term. The only clue we have is the argument on behalf of the wife that she did not want to be spied on.

I see some force in that argument, although it was scarcely pressed before us. Indeed it was not mentioned at all until it was raised by the court. Whatever the force of the argument, it is far outweighed by the resentment which the husband will naturally feel if the wife remarries within a year or two and continues thereafter to occupy the matrimonial home. She says she has no intention of marrying Mr. Davidson. But it remains a distinct possibility. In *Leate v Leate* (1982) 12 Fam Law 121 Ormrod L.J. recognised that it is 'very galling' for a husband if the family assets are handed over to the wife, who then remarries. He said:

'Some provision as to the wife's remarriage was reasonable and there ought to be a charge enforceable by the husband in the event of her death or remarriage.'

In *Simpson v Simpson* (16 March 1984, unreported); Court of Appeal (Civil Division) Transcript No. 119 of 1984, Lincoln J., giving the first judgment of the Court of Appeal, said:

'Such then was her intention. On that evidence the judge was entitled to conclude that on the balance of probability she did not then intend to and might never marry Mr. Cook, and that he was no more than a man friend employing her at £25 a week as his secretary and helping with petrol for the car and its insurance. But the matter does not stop there. Such a finding, if it had been expressly made, would not be inconsistent with a further finding that there was still a real possibility that she might marry him. She accepts that her feelings for him have deepened recently, she had been considering marriage with him and his relationship with her was clearly a close one. In the circumstances her intention, though truly and genuinely described today as negative, could change with the passage of time. If it did and if the present order for an out-and-out transfer remained, then the wife would be joined in her occupation at the matrimonial home by her second husband or cohabitee, the latter having contributed nothing to its original acquisition, and meanwhile the husband would have lost his half interest. I agree with the husband's contention that this would scarcely appear to be a just and fair solution. A trust for sale in which the power of sale becomes exerciseable on remarriage or permanent cohabitation would remedy that unfairness. An out-and-out order by definition cannot do so.'

In *Hendrix v Hendrix* (27 January 1981 unreported); Court of Appeal (Civil Division) Transcript No. 57 of 1981, where the facts were very similar to the present, a court consisting of Ormrod L.J. and Purchas J. ordered that the matrimonial home be transferred into the name of the wife, on her paying the husband a capital sum of £3,000, and further ordered that the house stand charged in favour of the husband as to 25 per cent. of the proceeds of sale, payable on the wife's death or remarriage, or on her cohabiting. In other words, the court made a *Martin* order.

It is true that, in the present case, the husband's earning capacity is very much greater than that of the wife. In due course, when he has paid off his debts, he will be able to get back on to the property ladder without insuperable difficulty. But the same was also true in *Hendrix v Hendrix*. The question is whether the difference in earning capacity, and the severance of the maintenance tie, justified an out-and-out transfer of the sole capital asset to the wife. In my judgment it did not. The very least which the judge should have done was to order a charge in favour of the husband in the event of the wife's death or remarriage.

Cohabitation raises a separate problem. But if, as Lord Scarman said in *Minton v Minton* [1979] AC 593, the reason underlying the principle of the clean break is the avoidance of bitterness, then the bitterness felt by the husband when he sees the former matrimonial home occupied by the wife's cohabitee must surely be greater than the bitterness felt by the wife being subject, as she fears, to perpetual supervision.

Not to have made a *Martin* order in this case was therefore in my opinion manifestly unfair to the husband. It deprived him forever of any share in the sole capital asset of the marriage, without any sufficient corresponding benefit to the wife.

. . .

I would be happy to leave the matter there. But Mr. Mostyn is not now content with a *Martin* order, as was his instructing solicitor, who appeared in this case in the court below. He asks us to consider making a *Mesher* order so that the charge would become effective on Amanda attaining the age of 18 or some other age.

The rise and fall of the *Mesher* order has been charted in many previous decisions of this court. Though decided in 1973, the case was not reported until 1980: *Mesher v Mesher and Hall (Note)* [1980] 1 All ER 126. It caught on very quickly, so much so that by the time of *Martin (BH) v Martin (D)* [1978] Fam 12 Ormrod L.J. felt it necessary to say that the *Mesher* order was never intended to be a general practice.

> 'There is no magic in the fact that there are children to be considered. All it means is that the interests of the children take priority in these cases, so that often there can be no question of sale while the children are young. But the situation that will arise when the children reach the age of 18 requires to be carefully considered. Otherwise a great deal of hardship may be stored up in these cases by treating it as a rule of thumb that the matrimonial home should then be sold. It is not a rule of thumb.'

Omrod L.J. went on to say, however, that in some cases a *Mesher* order might be the only way of dealing with the situation.

The dangers of the *Mesher* order were emphasised in a number of cases in the early 1980s. In *Mortimer v Mortimer-Griffin* [1986] 2 FLR 315 Sir John Donaldson M.R. said, at pp. 318–319:

> 'It does seem to me that both orders suffer from the defects to which Ormrod L.J. drew attention, that "chickens come home to roost" at an unpredictable time and in unpredictable circumstances; and that while an adjustment based on percentages seems attractive at the time, experience shows that it is subject to all kinds of difficulties and objections when it is worked out in the event.'

Parker L.J. said at p. 319:

> 'I would also add that I wholly endorse what my Lord, the Master of the Rolls, has said with regard to what is known as a *Mesher* order. It has been criticised since its birth; it is an order which is likely to produce harsh and unsatisfactory results. For my part, I hope that that criticism, if it has not got rid of it, will at least ensure that it is no longer regarded as the "bible".'

It seems to me, with respect to Parker L.J., that there are still cases where, if only by way of exception, the *Mesher* order provides the best solution. Such a case might be where the family assets are amply sufficient to provide both parties with a roof over their heads if the matrimonial home were sold, but nevertheless the interests of the children require that they remain in the matrimonial home. In such a case it may be just and sensible to postpone the sale until the children have left home, since, ex hypothesi, the proceeds of sale will then be sufficient to enable the wife to rehouse herself. In such a case the wife is 'relatively secure': see the judgment of Ormrod L.J. in *McDonnell v McDonnell* (1976) 6 Fam Law 220.

But where there is doubt as to the wife's ability to rehouse herself on the charge taking effect, then a *Mesher* order should not be made. That is, as I see it, the position here. The split suggested by the husband would give the wife two thirds of £50,000. It must be very uncertain whether this would be sufficient to enable the wife to rehouse herself in a few years' time when Amanda leaves home. That is no doubt the reason why the [district judge] declined to make a *Mesher* order. I would agree with him. But the *Martin* order does not suffer from the same disadvantages.

In conclusion I would reject Mr. Mostyn's submission that we should make a *Mesher* order, but accept his submission that we should make a *Martin* order. The split which he suggests seems about right. Accordingly, I would grant leave and allow the appeal to that extent.

Ewbank J: I agree. It is of course important to retain flexibility to meet the circumstances of individual cases and changes in social conditions. On the other hand, justice and the provisions of the statute usually indicate that an asset which has been acquired by the joint efforts of the spouses should eventually be shared. Where the only asset is a jointly acquired home of modest value it is often necessary to give its occupation to the parent with custody of children or to the spouse with the greater need. The clean break principle does not, however, mean that the other spouse is to be deprived for all time of any share. Experience has shown that postponing such an interest until the children are grown up often merely postpones and exacerbates the problems in re-housing that the occupying spouse will have. This is why the *Mesher* type of order is regarded as unsuitable unless there is going to be sufficient capital available to provide a suitable alternative home. But postponement until death, remarriage or cohabitation does not produce the same problem and is not generally disadvantageous to the occupying spouse. It does ensure that the other spouse receives eventually an appropriate share in the jointly acquired asset.

This is such a case. The judge was wrong, in my view, in depriving the husband of all interest in the house. The proper order would be for proceeds of sale of the house to be divided in the proportions of one third [to the husband] to two thirds [to the wife] on the death, remarriage or cohabitation of the wife.

Questions

(i) As a woman living in the former matrimonial home with your children, which would you prefer: (*a*) the knowledge that the house has to be sold when the youngest of your children goes to university and you receive one half of the equity; (*b*) the knowledge that the house has to be sold when you commence a 'permanent cohabitation' with your boy friend so as to provide your husband with one third of the equity. Would your answer differ in either case according to whether you were in receipt of maintenance payments?

(ii) Should property adjustment orders be capable of variation? (Read section 31 of the Matrimonial Causes Act 1973 and *Thompson v Thompson* [1986] Fam 38, [1985] 2 All ER 243.)

We now consider the question of tenancies. Whereas orders of the court regulating the occupation of the home can be made under the Matrimonial Homes Act 1983 only during the marriage, there is jurisdiction to order the transfer of a private or council tenancy if there is security of tenure from one spouse to the other in a case where the marriage is terminated by divorce or a decree of nullity (Matrimonial Homes Act 1983, Schedule 1). The court has the power to order the transfer, on granting a decree of divorce, nullity or judicial separation, or with leave of the court, at any time thereafter. The landlord's consent is not required, but he does have a right to be heard before an order is made.

Questions

(i) Do you think that this provision is an unnecessary interference in the powers and responsibilities of local authorities to determine housing priorities in their area?

(ii) Under s. 24(1)(*a*) of the Matrimonial Causes Act 1973, the court has a general power to order that one spouse shall transfer to the other, or to or for the benefit of a child of the family, 'such property as may be so specified.' Transfer of property orders may be made with respect to council tenancies. Can you think of any reason why an applicant should seek a transfer of property order under s. 24(1)(*a*) of the Matrimonial Causes Act 1973 rather than an order under Schedule 1 of the Matrimonial Homes Act 1983 with respect to a council tenancy?

(iii) Could *one* answer to question (ii) be that under s. 24(1)(*a*), the landlord has no express right to be heard?

(iv) Do you think that to allow a housing authority to reallocate the home before the judicial decision was made would prejudge the matter and hamper the ousted party's chances of custody?

(v) There is some evidence that women are sometimes unable to obtain custody without housing and unable to obtain housing without custody. (Watson and Austerberry, 1986.) If this is correct, who should break this vicious circle, the court or the housing authority?

What of women who leave home because they find the relationship intolerable although there is no question of violence? Indeed one reason why courts are asked to make orders may be because housing authorities often treat childless women or women who have left their children behind as intentionally homeless under the Housing Act 1985 and therefore not under a duty to rehouse. Rosy Thornton (1987) discovered that 54% of housing authorities in her survey (more than 100) would find such women intentionally homeless.

(g) PENSIONS

The Law Society Memorandum (1991) identifies six benefits which require consideration:

3.3 (a) the payment of a lump sum on retirement;
    (b) the pension the husband will become entitled to on retirement;
    (c) a widow's pension which may be payable following the husband's death after retirement;
    (d) a lump sum which could be payable to the husband's estate should he die in service;
    (e) a widow's pension payable should the husband die in service; and
    (f) the possibility of substantial life cover which would be payable to the husband's estate in the event of his death.

However, there have been difficulties:

(a) Under Section 25(1)(a) of the Matrimonial Causes Act 1973 the court must look at what will occur in the foreseeable future. The courts seem to limit the foreseeable future to about four or five years following the divorce, or at most ten — thus, if a couple divorce more than ten years before a pension is due, the wife is unlikely to benefit.
(b) The court does not have the power to order a husband to take out life or term insurance, assign pension benefits, or continue pension or insurance premiums. It is also not possible to order that a service gratuity be split (see section 203 of the Army Act 1955). As a result most arrangements for pensions for divorcees are made by consent.
(c) It is very difficult to value a pension accurately before it has accrued as the value will either depend on the final salary of the contributor or the amount of contributions made to a personal scheme and the performance of the investment. Traditional reliance has been placed on transfer values, however, it appears that these tend to underestimate the benefits accrued.
(d) It has been suggested in relation to family trusts (see J.G. Miller *'Trusts and Financial Provision on Divorce'* (1990)) . . . that orders contingent on an event occurring i.e. a pension accruing should be made. Although this approach has been used in the past (see *Milne v Milne* (1981) 2 FLR 286) it leaves a former wife dependent on a series of events occurring over which she has no control. It may be that her former husband becomes unemployed or dis-entitled to his pension or that he manages to avoid liability to his former wife by some other means.
(e) Often the terms of the pension schemes do not allow the assignment or commutation of benefits.
(f) Under the present system the only solution is often for a former husband to consent to taking out a policy for his former wife's benefit. This will often not be possible because of a lack of resources.
(g) Again, a sheer lack of resources often means that it is virtually impossible for a husband to compensate his wife adequately in some other way for the loss of pension rights, particularly when this is combined with the fact that women, whether married or

divorced, tend to earn less (and therefore have lower pension entitlements) than their male counterparts.

Little attempt has been made in English law to take account of these matters:

3.6 . . . the possibility of a widow's pension is ignored as by definition a divorcee cannot be the widow of her former husband. The possibility of death in service benefits is also not dealt with. The proportion of the lump sum is calculated according to the length of the marriage and the anticipated date of retirement of the husband. An attempt is also made to compensate the wife for the fact that she will be unable to benefit from any periodical payments received from a pension fund during her husband's retirement.

The Memorandum then summarises the proposals of the Institute of Fiscal Studies (1988), the proposals of the Labour Party, as well as Scottish[3] and German law: the Memorandum concludes by recommending:

3.22 The Committee, therefore, *recommends* that
  (i)   the courts should be given power to make pension adjustment orders in proceedings for ancillary relief brought under the Matrimonial Causes Act 1973;
  (ii) the courts should be provided with powers similar to those available under the Scottish legislation. In addition there should be a power to allow payments by a former husband into a personal pension scheme for a wife.
  (iii) Guidance should be issued on how and when a pension should be valued and in what shares it should be split.

5 Empirical evidence

It has been suggested on many occasions that a proper appreciation of the problems discussed in this chapter cannot be obtained because of a lack of hard evidence of what actually happens. Some idea is now beginning to emerge. Eekelaar and MacLean *Maintenance after Divorce* (1986) undertook to describe the present financial circumstances of a nationally representative sample of those who have divorced in England and Wales since the introduction of no-fault divorce in 1971. They chose an 'omnibus survey' which approached a quota sample of 8,000 individuals in England and Wales in May 1981; from this they were given permission to approach 92 of the men and 184 of the women. As the researchers admit, 'our final sample of 276 individuals is, of course, relatively small. It was, however, central to our strategy that it should be as closely representative of the divorcing population at large as we could make it. We therefore chose not to distort our original sample by interviewing additional cases with particular characteristics'.

In an earlier publication, *Children and Divorce* (1983) the authors publish the following two tables:

---

3. 3.17 The Family Law (Scotland) Act 1985 also makes some provision for pension splitting on divorce. Under the terms of section 10 of the Act [see p. 158, above], pensions and life assurance benefits are included in the definition of matrimonial property which should be split on divorce.

Table 10. Single mothers receiving and not receiving maintenance by source of income (n = 47)

Source of income	Mothers receiving maintenance	Mothers not receiving maintenance	Total
Full-time earnings	6	5	11
Part-time earnings	5	3	8
Part-time earnings plus Supplementary Benefit	5	3	8
Supplementary Benefit (incl. I ICA)	12	5	17
Other	2	1	3
Total	30	17	47

Table 11 Maintenance received as a percentage of household income

Percentage of household income	One parent families (n = 30) No.	%	Reconstituted families (n = 30) No.	%
up to 5	4 ⎫		10 ⎫	
6–10	2 ⎭	20	9 ⎭	63
11–20	9 ⎫		6 ⎫	
20–30	2 ⎭	50	1 ⎭	24
31–50	5 ⎫		1 ⎫	
over 50	2 ⎭	24	2 ⎭	10
not known	2		1	

Questions

Does this information suggest in any way at all that divorced women 'live off' the resources of their former husbands?

Eekelaar and Maclean (1986) comment in detail on the housing position:

A distinction needs to be drawn between occupants of local authority housing at the time of separation and those enjoying other types of housing provision. In the former case, the childless invariably left the accommodation. But where there were children, 79 per cent of the women interview respondents (n = 52) and 30 per cent of the men (n = 21) stayed; all but one of the men having custody of the children. . . . Of the few women who left, three returned (with their children) to their own families, four moved into a house with their new partners; and in one case both parents left and were re-housed by the local authority. For these people, then, housing circumstances in themselves played no significant role in altering their living standards on divorce. The effects of divorce would primarily be felt in respect to income. A similar pattern was found among the long-term mothers interviewed in 1984. Eight out of the ten in local authority housing at separation stayed there, the other two moving into owner-occupation (one with married children and one buying her council house).

But when we look at the housing outcome with respect to the owner-occupiers, a more complex picture emerges. . . . childless and children divorces share one feature regarding the home. In almost half of each category, the owner-occupied home was sold on divorce. In the case of the childless, the reason for the sale seems to have been to allow the wife to realize her half-share in the house, for half the homes of such couples which were in their joint names were sold. If the house was not sold, it was much more likely that the husband would stay on in the home than the wife, but in the event the wife would invariably leave with a lump sum payment; the husband had bought her out. In the three cases (13 per cent) where the wife left without a share, she went straight into a home provided by another man. If the house was in the husband's name alone, he was overwhelmingly likely to remain in it and the wife to leave without any lump sum payment. It is possible that in some of those cases the wife went uncompensated for any beneficial interest she may have acquired in the home by reason of direct or indirect monetary contributions to its acquisition. The advantage, from a wife's point of view, of joint legal ownership is clear, and the message of these findings seems to be that for childless marriages, a lump sum payment made to the wife is likely to be in the form of strict compensation for the transfer to the husband of a property interest.

It is striking that owner-occupied homes are just as likely to be sold in the case of divorces involving dependent children as where the marriage was childless, despite the well-established policy of the courts that one of the primary goals of divorce settlement is to secure accommodation for the children, usually by keeping them in the matrimonial home. [See p. 295, above, *H v H (family provision remarriage)* [1975] Fam 9, [1975] 1 All ER 367.] Are the children of divorcees who live in the owner-occupier sector subject to greater disruption than those of divorcees who live in public-sector housing?

In a number of cases it might be unnecessary to keep the home for the children because they and the wife will be moving into accommodation provided by another man. In four (28 per cent) of the cases where the house was sold the woman moved in with a new partner. So in over a quarter of the cases where the home was sold, no accommodation problem for the children arose. What of the other cases? It seems that the sales in these cases might either have been desired by the caregiving parent wanting to move from the area, or forced on her by the financial situation. This can be deduced from the fact that the wife stayed on in the house only once (3 per cent) in the childless cases, but did so in *one-quarter* of the children cases, irrespective of whether the house was in joint names or in the husband's name alone. Put another way, the wife stayed in half of the cases where the home was not sold. The reason for this is undoubtedly to provide accommodation for the children, and there is no reason to believe that this would not have happened in those cases where the house was sold were it not for the fact that the wife desired the sale or had it forced on her. Indeed, a small number of the sales (10 per cent) were in fact the result of foreclosure by the mortgagee. Others may well have taken place to prevent this eventuality.

It is at this point, of course, that the difficulties which the families with children experience over income have direct impact on their housing conditions. Yet, about three-quarters of the divorced mothers, still single and with dependent children, who had been in owner-occupation at the time of their separation were still living in *the private sector* at the time of interview. The lump sum acquired by the sale, or support from the former husband, or payments of mortgage interest by the supplementary benefit authorities, cushioned the *extent* of the deterioration in their housing circumstances; or, at least, the degree to which they needed to go to the public housing authorities for assistance. It is plausible to suppose that a move from the private sector will frequently cause greater social disruption, especially as regards the children's school environment, than moves within a sector. Our data showed that, of the women who moved, half (seven) were able to buy in the private sector (three of them later remarried). Only three (21 per cent) moved into public housing.

Our findings regarding the housing circumstances of divorcing men fail to show any disturbing degrees of hardship. In the childless cases, the man either kept the house or sold it, taking his share. Even where there were children, he stayed on in the house in one-quarter of the cases. Where the wife stayed, we found no evidence that she was joined by a cohabitee or new husband. The pattern seems clearly to be that, where a new partner enters the scene, he will provide a home for the wife and children. Where, in the divorces involving dependent children, the home was sold, the husband invariably took his share. There were, however, a few cases (thirteen (22 per cent) of those where either the house was sold or the wife remained in it) where the husband left without any apparent immediate compensation for his capital loss. However, four involved a 'Mesher' arrangement whereby the house is settled on trust for sale for both parents but sale is postponed until the youngest child reaches a certain age (usually eighteen or on completion of full-time education), or until a court order is made. Thus the husband is not deprived of his capital; his enjoyment of it is simply postponed. Of the seven cases where the husband left without taking any share of the asset, three forewent their share in discharge of their support obligation, one went to a new partner with a house and we had no information on the others. It should be remembered, of course, that when it is the man who leaves, it will usually be very difficult for the wife to raise sufficient capital to pay him a lump sum. Her inferior earning power and commitments to the children effectively preclude such a course.

The long-term mothers in owner-occupation at the time of separation were perhaps more firmly established in this sector. Even so, in half of the cases the home was sold and the proceeds shared enabled the women to buy a smaller property. Of the cases where the house was not sold, in half the house was occupied in lieu of maintenance (in one case with a 'Mesher' agreement), and in the two remaining cases the wife purchased her husband's interest, one with her own resources and the other with parental help.

We should conclude this review of the economic conditions of families after divorce by remarking on the significance of housing provision. Were it not for the relative security provided by public-sector housing, the position of many divorced single mothers would be far worse than it is. As we have seen, there is no potential in income transfers to substitute for its absence. We might make the same observation with respect to health care. It is fortunately not essential for these mothers to rely on income provision, from the state or from the absent parent, to meet the medical expenses of their children. These fall on the community through the national health service. But even outside the ambit of community-financed services, we note that, as far as accommodation is concerned, the position of mothers living in the private sector is not totally bleak. Most managed to stay in that sector, even if precariously. The attention given to the accommodation of children by judicial policy seems, according to our data, to have borne some fruit and, in so far as it has done so, has reduced the extent to which the receipt of income maintenance is critical to the most fundamental needs of these families [see Chapter 4, above]. The Social Security Review of 1985 revealed that the government was concerned about the burden which housing-related benefit (whether by way of rate rebates, payment of rent and mortgage interest, and of water and heating charges) was placing on the social security budget (*Reform of Social Security* (1985)). The implications of any erosion of these benefits for families broken by divorce do not seem to have been considered. The result might be to throw them into greater dependence on maintenance from the absent parent, to undermine the already precarious degree to which stability in housing those in owner-occupation has been achieved and to put new pressure on the public sector.

Questions

(i) What conclusions do you draw from Eekelaar and Maclean's work?
(ii) Is dependance on maintenance from the absent parent a good thing or a bad thing? (See Chapter 4, above).
(iii) Ruth Deech in *Divorce Studies and Empirical Studies* (1990) has hard words to say:

Likewise, Eekelaar and Maclean's figures in *Maintenance After Divorce* do not assess, and overlook the value of lump sums and property transferred after divorce. In emphasising weekly payments, they are, by definition, but without sufficient clarification of the bias, concentrating on and counting the awards to the wives of poorer husbands. Of those that responded to the Eekelaar and Maclean request for a sample, more than half were in local authority housing. Where childless owner-occupiers were surveyed, conclusions were drawn from a total of only 27 houses, a number too small, it is suggested, for broad conclusions to be drawn. There are widely accepted scientific criteria for the taking of samples and their sizes, and many small exercises in family law would not be accepted as valid for national purposes by professional statisticians.

The preconceptions relating to policy held by researchers are in general spelled out by them but, it is submitted, detract from the wider significance of the figures gathered in support. A clear example of this is provided by Eekelaar and Maclean's study. There is a presumption throughout that a family unit, impliedly the first family, remains bonded despite divorce and therefore perpetually liable to each other after divorce. Moreover, the authors apparently disapprove of working mothers. It used to be argued that divorced mothers could not be expected to seek self-support because of the unemployment rates. Now that that argument is less tenable, child welfare is cited instead.

Has she a point?

(The debate continues. See the reply to Deech by Eekelaar (1991)).

A dramatic table illustrating the position in California in Lenore Weitzman, *The Divorce Revolution* (1985) shows the change in standards of living of divorced men and divorced women in her sample, one year after the divorce. (See below, p. 314.)

In her book, the American researcher states:

Divorce laws that treat women equally and assume that all women are equally equipped to survive the break-up of their families without support from their ex-husbands or society only serve to enlarge the gap between men and women and create even greater inequalities.

Change in standards of living* of divorced men and women (approximately one year after divorce)

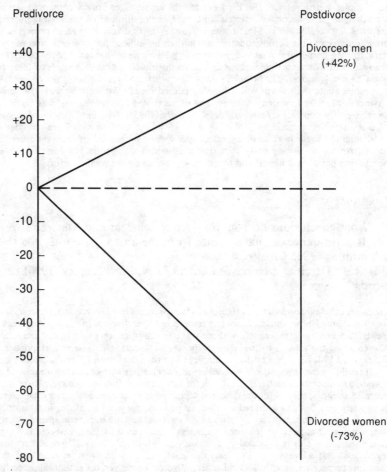

*Income in relation to needs with needs based on U.S. Department of Agriculture's low standard budget.

Based on weighted sample of interviews with divorced persons, Los Angeles County, California, 1978

California has a community of property system, and we must of course be wary of translating the debate of what happens there into the English scene.

Weitzman's work has been subjected to criticism by Stephen Sugarman in *Divorce Reform at the Crossroads* (edited by Sugarman and Kay, 1990). Sugarman objects also to a declared policy that states that the courts should aim for an 'equal standard of living':

Perhaps Weitzman's most frequently quoted finding is this: 'The research shows that, on the average, divorced women and the minor children in their households experience a 73 percent decline in their standard of living in the first year after divorce. Their former husbands, in contrast, experience a 42 percent rise in their standard of living.' I contend that not only is this conclusion both exaggerated and misleadingly precise, but also that, in any event, such disparities by themselves say nothing about the fairness of the way no-fault divorce is functioning. Following that discussion I search for what arguments might be made on behalf of the principle that no fault divorce should assure former spouses equal living standards and find nothing persuasive.

Without explaining precisely where her calculations went astray, Saul Hoffman and Greg Duncan have already shown that Weitzman's much-repeated finding about the decline in divorced women's living standards is inconsistent with previous research, implausibly large, and incompatible with other data she reports. They suggest that a 30 percent decline in living standards for women in the first year of divorce, rather than the 73 percent Weitzman claims, is far more likely to be typically the case. Although 30 percent is by no means a trifling amount, the difference between the two estimates is dramatic.

It is also clear that the most sensible time period for comparing the financial circumstances of the former spouses is the first year after divorce. When I think about the point one year after divorce, I imagine that relatively few men or women have remarried, and that, whereas he is probably both settled back into his job and settled into new quarters, her life, especially if she has their children, may be still very much in transition. Admitting that this is a loose generalization and that its accuracy in individual cases may depend, for example, upon the time between when the marriage broke up and when the divorce occurred, it will serve to make my point. Let us now consider instead the situation that might pertain if we compared the living standards of former couples three or five or ten years after divorce. By then, many more women may have entered the paid labor force or may have increased their earnings. Also, many women and even more men would be remarried and both burdened with new responsibilities and aided by a new spouse. As a result, it is certainly possible that the differences between the earlier divorced men's and women's living standards would be considerably less than they appear to be one year after divorce.

If this surmise is right, then the wisdom of measuring men/women differences for the first year after divorce depends on what the purpose of the measurement is. If, for example, we are interested in how financially well positioned the former spouses are to carry on with their lives as singles, the Weitzman's approach seems to make sense. If instead (or in addition) we are interested in long-run financial consequences of divorce as reflected in terms of the former spouses' standards of living, then it would have been better if Weitzman had provided similar data for periods of time longer removed from the initial divorce.

I also have some concerns about how one goes about making comparison between men's and women's living standards after divorce. I will assume initially that the goal is to concentrate on comparing incomes, rather than trying to measure utility levels. Even so, one must contend with the matter of 'imputed' income. For example, economists point out that the rental value of the family home to whoever is still living in it creates imputed income. So do do-it-yourself activities. Consider, for example, as Weitzman recognizes, that wives traditionally do most of the housework and that after divorce former husbands are deprived of this benefit, and thus have a lowered standard of living to that extent. I could not find any indication that these imputed income items were included by Weitzman in the measurements reported in her book. Another question is whether the comparison should be in terms of gross income or, say, income after taxes and reasonably necessary work expenses (including child-care expenses). I would think that the latter, although perhaps more difficult to ascertain, would be a more appropriate basis of comparison. It would appear that Weitzman used gross income figures in her study.

Next, if there are children and one spouse has primary physical custody, then a comparison of the spouses' living standards somehow has to take into account the expenses of the children. One solution would be to assume that child support awards (or payments) take care of that need. On this approach, one would exclude the child support from both the payor's and payee's income and would ignore the existence of the children. But if, realistically, the custodial spouse spends more than the child support payments for the needs of the children, this is an inadequate solution that would overestimate the financial condition of the custodial parent. Understandably, then, Weitzman sought to compare the living standard of the noncustodial parent with how well the custodial parent (usually the woman) and the children can together live on all of their income.

Yet, an approach that considers only the financial burden of the children and gives no weight to the nonfinancial benefits that children produce takes us back to wondering about the wisdom of the initial choice to compare incomes rather than utility. To be sure, sometimes the children are a drag that neither party wants. Parents without physical custody may clearly value the leisure they have obtained more than whatever benefits they would derive from custody of their children. In these situations, men-women differences (where women have custody) are reduced, rather than exaggerated, by looking at income differences. But where women have physical custody of the children and men feel that they have, as a result, lost something terribly important to them, it is deeply troubling to compare the former spouses' living standards in terms that treat the children solely as a liability. And as Robert Mnookin points out in chapter 2 [of *Divorce Reform at the Crossroads*], substantial numbers of divorcing husbands claim they want more physical custody of their children than they are able to obtain. Since it is unclear how one would go about dealing with this consideration, this just reinforces the ambiguity that surrounds the measuring of former spouses' comparative states.

Nonetheless, let me assume that, even after taking into account all the points just made, recently divorced men were still shown to enjoy a significantly higher standard of living than recently divorced women. Indeed, I am willing to assume for these purposes that men's living standards typically go up and women's down. Is that unfair? I do not think we can possibly say so without having a theory of what would be fair? Such disparities would certainly show that divorce, at least initially, is financially bad for women (and children) and good for men, and might, for example, be the basis for predicting that men would be more likely to initiate divorce than women. But until it is shown that fairness requires equal living standards, these difference would only be facts.

Although Weitzman does not, as I see it, really try to *argue* for the equal living standards norm, at several places she seems to endorse it. Just what is the case for it? I am still trying to figure that out.

While it is in some sense true that in the typical marriage vow the couple agrees to support each other forever, they also in the same sense promise to love each other and stay married forever. Since they are free to change their minds about the latter, something more needs to be added to the equation to explain why the former obligation would nonetheless continue. There are, after all, many marriages that end in less than one year, and a majority end in less than ten years, often without children. And if the equal standard of living principle is not meant to apply to all marriage and forever, on what basis is it meant to be limited? Once we go down that road — for example, for a period of five years, or for as long as the marriage lasted, or only for marriages lasting more than fifteen years — then it is really some other principle that is being applied.

Although women typically begin their divorces with lower standards of living than their former husbands, it is also the case that they typically enter marriage with lower personal economic prospects in the paid labor force. Even though it may be that men as a class have partly caused women's condition in the job market, I do not see why the particular man, who now happens to be a former husband, should be responsible for redressing this much larger social problem. In short, I think that a case for society-based income transfers from men to women, or strong affirmative action plans favoring women over men in employment settings, would be easier to make than the case that a former husband should remain a lifetime provider for his former wife.

Another puzzle is whether, under the equal living standards idea, the lower earning spouse would be assured only some specified standard of living that is once and for all determined at the time of the divorce. That, however, would not seem to capture the point as I see it. Rather, is it not the idea that their future financial condition is to be bound up with both of their financial futures just in the way that it would have been had they remained married (even though they did not)? But implications of that, it seems to me, are disquieting in other ways. What, for example, are we to do about all the changed circumstances that occur when they go their separate ways — such as a second marriage (and the assumption of new family obligations) and then, possibly, a second divorce?

In the end, the case for equal standards of living seems to me to rest on a tautology: the spouses were equal partners in marriage, and everything they have, including their future income potential, is theirs and is to be divided equally on divorce. But this begs the question of whether the moment of marriage should be seen to merge their human capital together, and a convincing case for that has yet to be made.

Research on the reasons acceptable as justification for alimony payments (periodical payments) was carried out in 1978 in Los Angeles County, California by Lenore Weitzman and Ruth Dixon, *The Alimony Myth: Does no*

Fault Divorce Make a Difference (1980). Weitzman summarises the findings in the following manner in *The Divorce Revolution* (1985):

Table 1
Attitudes toward alimony
From interviews with divorced men and women,
Los Angeles County, California, 1978

	PERCENTAGE WHO AGREE (Weighted Sample*)	
	Women (n = 111)†	Men (n = 112)
	(Percentage)	
A. A woman deserves alimony if she has helped her husband get ahead because they are really *partners* in his work	68	54
B. A woman does not deserve alimony if she had an *affair* and was unfaithful to her husband	23	40
C. A woman deserves alimony for at least a year or two so she can *adjust* to the divorce	31	21
D. A woman deserves alimony if she wants to go back to school or to be *retrained* so that she can get a good job to support herself	73	52
E. A woman deserves alimony if she's been married a long time and is *too old* to get a good job	87	66
F. A woman deserves alimony if she has young *children* and wants to stay home to care for them	67	63
G. A woman does not deserve alimony if she can go to work and support herself	65	85
H. A woman deserves alimony if her husband left her for another woman	29	39
I. A woman deserves alimony if she is *disabled* and can't support herself	94	87
J. A woman deserves alimony because when she got married her *husband promised to* support her for the rest of her life	9	3
K. A woman deserves alimony because her husband should *pay her back* for her years of work as a homemaker and/or mother	25	19
L. A woman deserves alimony because she can never recapture the years she has given to her marriage and the *opportunities* she *missed* to have a career of her own	20	4

  * The interview sample was weighted to reflect the characteristics of the total divorcing population in Los Angeles County.
  †n refers to the number of cases (i.e., interviews) on which the percentages are based.

Questions

(i) How many of these 12 statements do you agree with, and how many do you disagree with?
(ii) Carry out a similar exercise amongst your colleagues.
(iii) The results may well be different. If they are, do you think that the differences result from the fact that the California research was confined to *divorced* men and women?
(iv) How many of these 12 statements do you think most English judges would agree with?
(v) Do you think any of these responses are contradictory?
(vi) Having read through this chapter: (*a*) what underlying principle would

you adhere to in income and property redistribution on divorce? (b) what guidelines would you provide for the courts to reach solutions based on these principles? (c) would everyone be happy?

(vii) Do you think that a convincing case has been made for the moment of marriage as the date to merge 'human capital' between the husband and wife which should be equally split on the event of a subsequent divorce?

A major study by Jonathan Bradshaw and Jane Millar, *Lone Parent Families in the UK* (1991) provides further detailed information relating both to maintenance and housing enjoyed by the parties after divorce. They summarise their findings as follows:

Maintenance

This is the first survey that has provided evidence on the proportion of all lone parents who received payments from the absent parents and the level of payments they receive. It has shown that 29 per cent of all lone parents at any one time receive regular payments from the absent parent and that the proportion varies with the marital status of the lone parent and whether or not they receive income support or are employed. Only 13 per cent of single lone parents on income support receive maintenance. One in five lone parents not receiving maintenance say they do not want it and a further 29 per cent think that the absent parent is unemployed or cannot afford to pay. Two thirds of lone parents receiving maintenance were receiving it in respect of their children only. The level of maintenance is variable but is low. The modal payment is £10 per week and the mean payment per child about £16 per week. (This was at a time when DSS expected the absent parents to pay the family premium, the lone parent premium and the children rates: this totals £22.15 per child per week for children under 11 in a one child family.) Multivariate analysis was not particularly successful in producing a reliable model which predicted whether lone parents received maintenance. Only about a third of lone parents receiving no maintenance thought that the absent parent could pay anything. Among those lone parents who knew the circumstances of the absent parent it was estimated that 41 per cent of those paying nothing could pay something. Sixty five per cent of the lone parents who had received income support had been asked for the name and address of the absent parent. Forty six per cent had given DSS the details and a further 21 per cent said they would now give details if asked. Eleven per cent who had been asked had refused and a further 13 per cent said they would refuse if asked. The main reasons for not giving the details was that they did not know where the absent parents were or did not want to have anything more to do with them. Only 17 per cent of those receiving less than £10 per week gave our interviewer the name and address of the absent parent. . . .

Housing

The housing consequences of lone parenthood are profound. Fifty-eight per cent had to move following the breakdown of their relationship. Over half of those who moved thought that their accommodation was better than it had been before and only 25 per cent thought it was worse. Only 17 per cent of the sample were dissatisfied with their present housing.

Lone parents are very dependent on public sector housing. More lone parents come from local authority accommodation and the majority of those who move either pass through or eventually are housed by local authorities. It is a credit to public sector housing that satisfaction is as high as it is. The survey confirms previous research evidence that there is a shift downmarket following relationship breakdown. However it appears that absent parents experience this as much as lone parents. Absent parents are less likely to remain in owner occupied or local authority accommodation and they are also more likely to drift into households shared with others. In particular they are likely to go back to their parents.

Lone parents who moved tended to have had to move more than once in order to find a satisfactory housing solution and many of them had passed through episodes of living with relatives, or in temporary local authority or voluntary accommodation. Some lone parents had moved a number of times in a short while and 41 per cent of tenants had experienced rent arrears at some time since separation.

Question

Are you surprised by their conclusions?

CHAPTER 8

Cohabitation

1 The factual background

Perhaps the major change which has occurred in the organisation of the family, both in the United States and in Western Europe, over the last few decades has been the fact that, whereas once cohabitation may have existed but was concealed, today various forms of relationships outside marriage are accepted by the wider community as perfectly appropriate behaviour.

'Cohabitation' is defined in *Social Trends 21* (1991) as 'living together as husband and wife without having legally married'. A similar definition is adopted by the Scottish Law Commission in their discussion paper *The Effects of Cohabitation in Private Law* (1990) but they add that it matters not whether the couple pretend to others that they are married to each other.

There is also a difficulty over terminology. Previous editions of this book refer to 'cohabitees'. This, as Stephen Parker in *Cohabitees* (1987) points out, is an ugly irregular form of 'cohabitant'. We have abandoned the irregular form in this edition.

One thing is sure. The numbers are large. We look at some details later, but the information shown in Table 9 (opposite) from Haskey and Kiernan (1989) will suffice for the present. Until recently, 'informal' arrangements have been confined to a large extent to intellectual elites and the sub-cultures of the poor and racial and ethnic minorities for whom the structures of traditional marriage and divorce law have been to a large extent irrelevant. This is no longer the case.

Mary Ann Glendon, in *Withering Away of Marriage* (1976), reflects on some of the reasons for the acceptance by society of informal arrangements:

Today, however, informal marriage is increasingly common among other social groups and, perhaps more significant, increasingly accepted. These two facts interact. The more persons in a particular group 'live together,' the more such behaviour becomes accepted. The more acceptance this alternative to formal marriage gains, the more people employ it. Thus, informal marriage has become a recurring subject in popular songs and cartoons and was discussed in the 1972 federal government report on population. Cohabitation is favored among young people, among pensioners and others receiving benefits terminable or reducible upon formal marriage, and increasingly among other diverse social groups. It has been estimated that six to eight million people are involved in such arrangements and the writer of a legal handbook on cohabitation asserts that Bureau of the Census figures show that the number of couples living together without formal marriage increased by over 700% from 1960 to 1970. (King, 1975) . . .

Motivations to enter informal rather than legal marriage include economic advantages as in the case of many elderly people, inability to enter a legal marriage, unwillingness to be subject to the legal effects of marriage, desire for a 'trial marriage,' and lack of concern with the legal thousands

Table 9: Estimated numbers of men and women cohabiting, 1986–87, Great Britain

Age	Men					Women				
	Single	Separated	Divorced	Widowed	Total	Single	Separated	Divorced	Widowed	Total
Under 25	224	2	8	–	234	335	3	12	–	350
25–29	226	5	40	–	271	161	7	34	–	202
30–34	83	9	58	–	150	50	4	57	–	111
35–39	28	6	68	–	102	16	4	52	3	75
40–49	28	17	75	–	120	8	11	74	7	100
50–59	8	13	41	6	68	4	3	17	6	30
Total 16–59	597	52	290	6	945	574	32	246	16	868

institution. This lack of concern is nothing new among grc.ns accustomed to forming and dissolving informal unions without coming into contact with legal institutions. Among these groups legal marriage is but an aspect of the irrelevance of traditional American family law, law that is viewed as being property-oriented and organized around the ideals of a dominant social group. Lack of concern with marriage law has been growing, however, among many who definitely are not outside the mainstream of American life. Until recently these converts accepted unquestioningly the traditional structures of the enacted law, but they now find that on balance the enacted law offers no advantages over informal arrangements.

Helen Oppenheimer in *Marriage* (1990) presents a thoughtful message from the liberal Christian viewpoint.

The harder moral argument is about relationships which are physical, emotional, social and even high-minded, but decline to be irrevocable. Once it is granted that sexuality is not as such unclean, why must it be confined so rigidly to matrimony? Why talk about 'fornication' at all, except perhaps for relationships which are irresponsibly ephemeral? Of course faithfulness is a good and life-enhancing thing, but must it be the only consideration? To answer these questions satisfactorily in a still traditional way one must keep one's head and consider the real good and the real harm in the partial commitments.

Sometimes what is missing is fairly clear: the relationship is simply one-sided and means more to one partner than to the other. Then we do well to wonder, though not triumphantly, whether somebody is being exploited or is presently going to be hurt. It is not moralistic to be convinced that such liberty to be unshackled does not constitute a moral breakthrough.

Nor is it moralistic still to look rather suspiciously for lopsidedness when the claim is made that options are being kept open: 'It would be nice if it lasted but if we get tired of one another it is nobody's else's business. So long as we are not irresponsible or inefficient enough to have a child, there is no question of blame or "immorality" if we live together for a while and then split up. Much better that than all the miserable struggle of divorce. We can try it out without getting too involved and see how we get on.' There is not much safeguard here for the emotionally weaker party against misery and bitterness not easily distinguishable from the misery and bitterness of divorce. To ask them how sure they really can be that they are totally at one in the degree of commitment is like asking a polygamist whether he can be quite sure of loving his wives equally. Practical experience is not altogether on their side.

Lovers sometimes part 'good friends'. They sometimes do after a broken marriage. But an advance promise of mature detachment is no more likely to be easy to keep in the end than an advance promise of faithfulness. How many people truly like it when their partners take care to keep their options open? This is the sort of freedom that is not so happy in the claiming as in the propounding. How many middle-aged women would want to allow the lovers of their youth to feel quite free to leave them, with no ill-feelings? Indeed how many fairly young women will go on being content with the condition they thought they could accept: no child?

Traditionalists who have taken the old morality for granted and lived contentedly by it all their lives torment themselves nowadays with the idea that this generation, maybe their own sons and daughters, are badly brought up and indeed immoral. They would be justified in forgetting the word 'fornication' but remembering these real questions about human happiness.

It is only fair to add, and even insist, that sometimes when people live together unmarried the commitment really is there, or is beginning to be there, and all that is lacking is the wedding ceremony. Instead of bandying about the idea of 'living in sin' a Christian would do well to consider honestly whether what we have here truly is a kind of marriage.

The standard way to make a marriage is a wedding. The couple take each other as husband and wife before witnesses. It is their consent that makes the marriage, not the ministrations of registrar or even priest. The wedding ceremony is a solemn way of making that consent public, and to ask for the blessing of family and friends and especially, for religious people, the blessing of God. But if what makes the marriage is consent, to dispense with the ceremony may not invalidate the consent.

There are a good many couples today who have seen the previous generation's notions about marriage and their ensuing ups and downs as hindrance rather than help. When people try to work out a different and more humanly satisfying way for themselves, it must be recognized that what they are engaged upon is a moral enterprise. At least in all seriousness let it not be nipped in the bud for the sake of respectability.

If we think, as well we may, that people who avoid formal commitment are living dangerously, we ought not to wash our hands of them but stand by to help pick up the pieces if necessary, which does not mean being ready to say 'I told you so'.

Question

Is this an argument in favour of providing cohabitation with the legal consequences of marriage?

Some cohabitants remain so simply because they do *not* want to become trapped with the legal implications of a marriage. But this is not the case for all.

Meade, in *Consortium Rights of the Unmarried — Time for a Reappraisal* (1981), tends towards the view that there are a large number of inter-related reasons why couples opt out of traditional marriage. They include the following:

(1) a desire to avoid the sex-stereotyped allocation of roles associated with marriage
(2) a belief that marriage is unnecessary or irrelevant if no children are involved
(3) a reluctance to enter a supposedly permanent marriage
(4) bohemian philosophy
(5) a conscientious objection to state regulation of marriage
(6) a desire to avoid the expense and trauma of a possible divorce
(7) an insouciant outlook on legally sanctioned relationships
(8) the desire for various forms of companionship
(9) a trial period to test suitability for marriage
(10) the need to share expenses in the face of long-lasting inflation.

One reason left out of Meade's list which will be relevant in some cases is simply that the parties are *unable* to marry because previous legal ties have not yet been broken.

Question

Do you think any of the reasons given by Meade to be more important than any other?

Table 2.16: Percentage of women cohabiting: by age

Great Britain — Percentages and numbers

	1979	1981	1986	1988[1]
Age group (percentages)				
18–24 years	4.5	5.6	9.0	12.4
25–49 years	2.2	2.6	4.6	6.3
18–49 years	2.7	3.3	5.5	7.7
Women in sample (= 100%) (numbers)				
18–24 years	1,353	1,517	1,194	1,215
25–49 years	4,651	5,007	4,320	4,250
18–49 years	6,004	6,524	5,514	5,465

1 1988–89 data. The General Household Survey changed from calendar years to financial years in 1988.

Source: General Household Survey

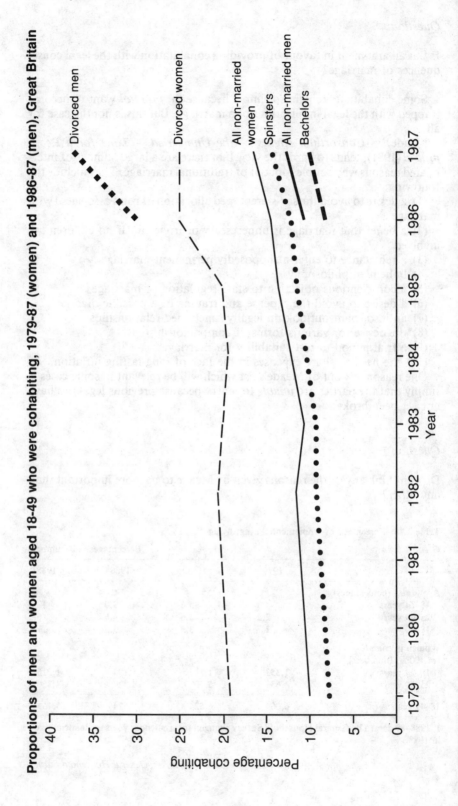

Proportions of men and women aged 18-49 who were cohabiting, 1979-87 (women) and 1986-87 (men), Great Britain

Statistical information obtained from the General Household Survey in Great Britain since 1979 traces the recent trends and gives an indication of the level of extramarital cohabitation. Our first table (see above, p. 323) comes from *Social Trends 21* (1991) from which it can be seen that the percentage of women cohabiting is most common amongst the 18–24 year old age group.

John Haskey and Kathleen Kiernan in *Cohabitation in Great Britain — Characteristics and Estimated Numbers of Cohabiting Partners* (1989) illustrate the substantial increases these figures represent.

Table 10: Estimated numbers of women cohabiting, 1979 and 1987, Great Britain

thousands

| | Women aged 18–49 | | | |
| Marital status | Estimated numbers | | | Percentage increase* |
	1979	1987	Increase	
Single	185	617	+ 432	+ 230
Separated/divorced	142	270	+ 128	+ 90
Total	327	887	+ 560	+ 170

* Rounded.

They also provide a breakdown of men and women who were cohabiting, according to age and to whether they were divorced or bachelors or spinsters (see p. 324).

They look also at other indicators. First, the proportions of married men and married women who pre-maritally cohabited with their future spouse, by year of marriage and whether the marriage was their first (see pp. 326 and 327). The distribution of length of time the couple have been cohabiting for both single and divorced men and women is then considered (see p. 328). Haskey and Kiernan have also done work on the socio-economic divisions, educational levels, and regional variations of cohabitation (see pp. 329, 330 and 331).

Questions

(i) Is it important for the lawyer to ask whether cohabitation is becoming: (*a*) institutionalised as an alternative to marriage; or (*b*) a new phase in a courtship process in which couples set up home before, rather than after, the 'paperwork'?
(ii) If you think it important, why do you think so?
(iii) Do you find any surprises in the tables relating to socio-economic divisions, educational levels and regional variations. If so, what are they?

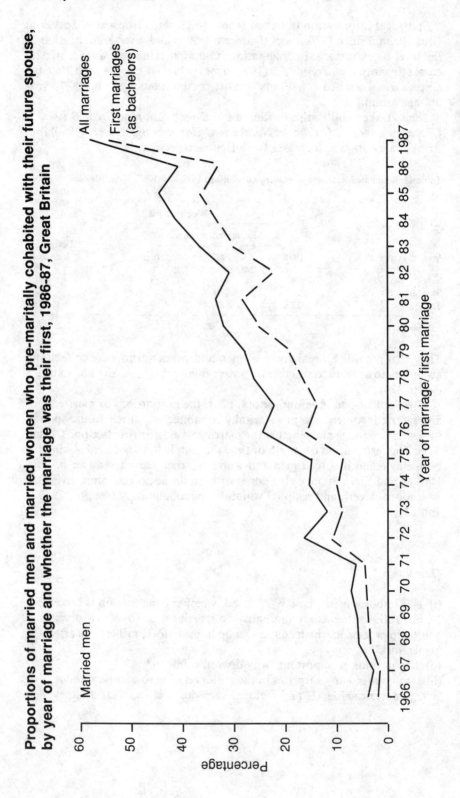

Proportions of married men and married women who pre-maritally cohabited with their future spouse, by year of marriage and whether the marriage was their first, 1986-87, Great Britain

Proportions of married men and married women who pre-maritally cohabited with their future spouse, by year of marriage and whether the marriage was their first, 1986-87, Great Britain

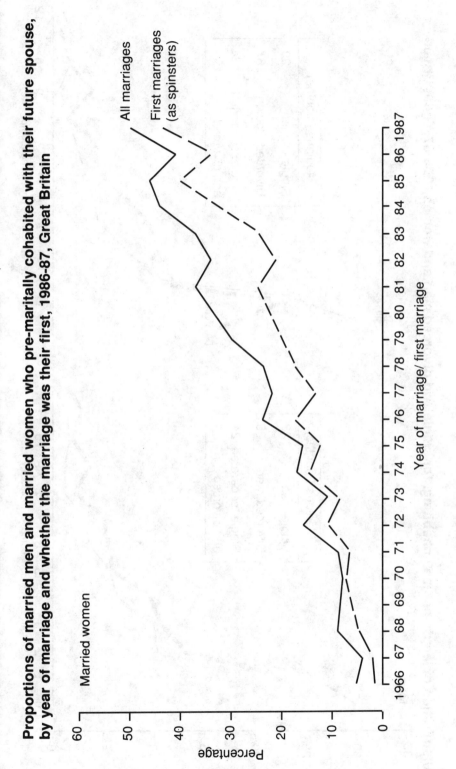

Married women

All marriages

First marriages
(as spinsters)

Year of marriage/ first marriage

Distribution of length of time cohabiting, for single and divorced men and women,1986-87, Great Britain

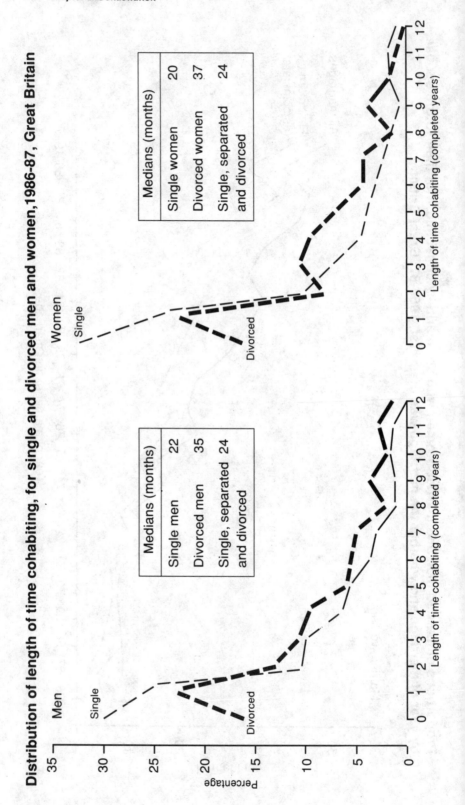

Table 5: Proportions of men and women, aged 20–39, who were cohabiting, by educational level, 1986–87, Great Britain

Educational level (highest qualification*)	Single				Divorced and separated			
	Men		Women		Men		Women	
	Percentage	Sample number	Percentage	Sample number	Percentage	Sample number	Percentage	Sample number
Degree (first or higher)	17	342	26	200	29	17	40	25
Higher education below degree level	18	261	22	185	16	37	20	49
GCE 'A' level†	13	476	13	326	30	47	33	43
GCE 'O' level†	14	526	20	529	50	64	21	145
CSE** and commercial	14	274	22	245	40	10	23	105
No qualifications	18	532	20	349	37	107	22	284
All educational levels‡	15	2,480	20	1,932	36	302	24	672

† Or equivalent(s).
* CSE grade 1 is equivalent to GCE 'O' level, and is *not* included under CSE and commercial qualifications.
‡ Includes other qualifications: foreign and other qualifications, and apprenticeships.

Table 6: **Proportions of men and women, aged 20–39, who were cohabiting, by socio-economic group, 1986–87, Great Britain**

Socio-economic group	Single				Divorced and separated			
	Men		Women		Men		Women	
	Percentage	Sample number	Percentage	Sample number	Percentage	Sample number	Percentage	Sample number
Professional	18	154	25	55	30	10	56	9
Employers and managers	20	271	28	154	47	47	32	56
Intermediate non-manual	17	313	22	411	17	29	24	105
Junior non-manual	9	266	18	669	37	27	21	192
Skilled manual	17	768	19	119	35	130	25	68
Semi-skilled manual and personal service	15	466	19	411	44	45	20	189
Unskilled manual	12	146	31	26	25	12	28	39
All socio-economic groups	16	2,395	20	1,845	36	302	23	658

Regional variations in the proportions of single, separated and divorced persons* who were cohabiting 1986-87, Great Britain

*aged 16-59

Percentage cohabiting in
Great Britain, p =13.5%

p greater than16%
p between 13.5% and16.0%
p between 11.5% and 13.5%
p less than 11.5%

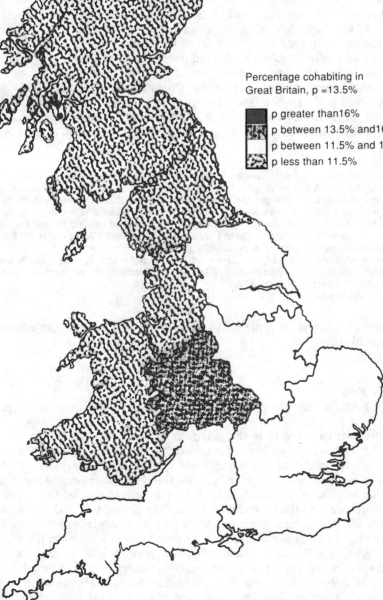

2 Property claims

Cooke v Head
[1972] 2 All ER 38, [1972] 1 WLR 518, 116 Sol Jo 298, Court of Appeal

The plaintiff formed a relationship with the defendant, a married man, in 1962. In 1964, they decided to acquire land in order to build a bungalow for their use. It was their hope that the defendant would obtain a divorce from his wife. The conveyance was taken in the defendant's name, and he paid a deposit and raised a mortgage from a building society. The plaintiff helped in the construction of the bungalow. To adopt the words used by Lord Denning MR in his judgment: 'She used a sledge hammer to demolish some old buildings. She filled the wheelbarrow with rubble and hard core and wheeled it up the bank. She worked the cement mixer, which was out of order and difficult to work. She did painting and so forth. The plaintiff did much more than most women would do.' The bungalow was nearing completion when, in 1966, the couple separated. The defendant sold the bungalow, and the plaintiff issued a writ to determine the way in which the proceeds of sale were to be divided. The trial judge held that she should have one-twelfth of the proceeds. She appealed against that decision to the Court of Appeal:

Lord Denning MR: . . . I do not think it is right to approach this case by looking at the money contributions of each and dividing up the beneficial interest according to those contributions. The matter should be looked at more broadly, just as we do in husband and wife cases. We look to see what the equity is worth at the time when the parties separate. We assess the shares as at that time. If the property has been sold, we look at the amount which it has realised, and say how it is to be divided between them. Lord Diplock in *Gissing v Gissing* [1971] AC 886 at 909 intimated that it is quite legitimate to infer that:

'the wife should be entitled to a share which was not to be quantified immediately upon the acquisition of the home but should be left to be determined when the mortgage was repaid or the property disposed of.'

Likewise with a mistress.

The court decided that the plaintiff's share of the net proceeds of sale should be one-third.

Eves v Eves
[1975] 3 All ER 768, [1975] 1 WLR 1338, 119 Sol Jo 394, Court of Appeal

The plaintiff (referred to in the judgment of Lord Denning MR as 'Janet' because 'she has had four surnames already') met the defendant in 1968. The relationship lasted four and a half years and during this time she took his surname and had two children by him. He was a married man and they lived together initially in his house. In 1969, they moved to another house which was conveyed into the defendant's name. The house was paid for in part by the sale of the former house and in part by a mortgage raised by the defendant. As in *Cooke v Head*, the plaintiff put in a lot of initial work. Lord Denning MR said 'she stripped the wallpaper in the hall. She painted woodwork in the lounge and kitchen. She painted the kitchen cabinets. She painted the brickwork in the front of the house. She broke up the concrete in the front garden. She carried the pieces to a skip. She, with him, demolished a shed and put up a new shed. She prepared the front garden for turfing.' The couple separated in 1972, and she applied to the county court for a declaration of an interest in the house. On appeal to the Court of Appeal:

Lord Denning MR: . . . Although Janet did not make any financial contribution, it seems to me that this property was acquired and maintained both by their joint efforts with the intention that it should be used for their joint benefit until they were married and thereafter as long as the marriage continued. At any rate, Stuart Eves cannot be heard to say to the contrary. He told her that it was to be their home for them and their children. He gained her confidence by telling her that he intended to put it in their joint names (just as married couples often do) but that it was not possible until she was 21. The judge described this as a 'trick,' and said that it 'did not do him much credit as a man of honour.' The man never intended to put it in joint names but always determined to have it in his own name. It seems to me that he should be judged by what he told her — by what he led her to believe — and not by his own intent which he kept to himself. Lord Diplock made this clear in *Gissing v Gissing* [1971] AC 886 at 906. It seems to me that this conduct by Mr Eves amounted to a recognition by him that, in all fairness, she was entitled to a share in the house, equivalent in some way to a declaration of trust; not for a particular share, but for such share as was fair in view of all she had done and was doing for him and the children and would thereafter do. By so doing he gained her confidence. She trusted him. She did not make any financial contribution but she contributed in many other ways. She did much work in the house and garden. She looked after him and cared for the children. It is clear that her contribution was such that if she had been a wife she could have had a good claim to have a share in it on a divorce: see *Wachtel v Wachtel* [1973] Fam 72 at 92–94.

Brightman J: The defendant clearly led the plaintiff to believe that she was to have some undefined interest in the property, and that her name was only omitted from the conveyance because of her age. This, of course, is not enough by itself to create a beneficial interest in her favour; there would at best be a mere 'voluntary declaration of trust' which would be 'unenforceable for want of writing': *per* Lord Diplock in *Gissing v Gissing* [1971] AC 886 at 905. If, however, it was part of the bargain between the parties, expressed or to be implied, that the plaintiff should contribute her labour towards the reparation of a house in which she was to have some beneficial interest, then I think that the arrangement becomes one to which the law can give effect. This seems to be consistent with the reasoning of the speeches in *Gissing v Gissing*.

The Court of Appeal decided that the defendant held the legal estate on trust for sale in the proportion one-quarter to the plaintiff and three-quarters to the defendant.

Bernard v Josephs
[1982] Ch 391, [1982] 3 All ER 162, [1982] 2 WLR 1052, 126 Sol Jo 361, Court of Appeal

The facts are given in the first paragraph of the judgment:

Lord Denning MR: This is all about a young lady, Maria Teresa Bernard, the plaintiff. In August 1973 it was her 21st birthday. On that very day she became engaged to be married. It was to Dion Emmanuel Josephs, the defendant. He was 30. Unknown to her he was already a married man, not yet divorced. They arranged to get a house and set up home together. It was 177, Dunstan's Road, SE 22. It was conveyed to them on 21 October 1974, in their joint names. It was a simple transfer by the vendor as beneficial owner 'to Dion Emmanuel Josephs and Maria Teresa Bernard,' without more, no declaration of trust, or anything. ·

The purchase price was £11,750. The whole of it was raised on mortgage from the Southwark Borough Council. They both signed the legal charge to secure it. They each paid some of the incidental expenses. She paid £200 of her own money. He paid £250 and £400 which he borrowed. They went into occupation and lived together as man and wife. The house was quite large. So they let off much of it to tenants. This helped greatly towards the mortgage instalments. Both went out to work. Their earnings enabled them to pay the rest of the outgoings and food, and so forth. Then after a year or two they quarrelled. She says that he was violent to her. So in July 1976 she left. He stayed on in the house. She applied for the house to be sold and for one-half of the proceeds. Meanwhile, in June 1975, he had got a divorce from his lawful wife. In April 1978 he married another woman. He took her to live with him in the house. They are childless.

The law
In our time the concept of marriage — I am sorry to say — is being eroded. Nowadays many couples live together as if they were husband and wife, but they are not married. They hope and expect that their relationship will be permanent. They acquire a house in their joint names. Most of the purchase price is obtained on mortgage in both their names. They are both responsible for payment of the instalments. Both go out to work. They pay the outgoings out of their joint resources. One paying for the food and housekeeping. The other paying the mortgage instalments. And so forth. Just as husband and wife do. But later on, for some reason or other, they fall out. They go their own separate ways. One or other leaves the house. The other stays behind in it. There is no need to divorce. They just separate. What is to happen to the house? Is it to be sold? If so, are the proceeds to be divided? And, if so, in what proportion? Or is one of them to be allowed to stay in it? If so, on what terms? If they had been husband and wife, our matrimonial property legislation would give the Family Division a very wide discretion to deal with all these problems. It is contained in sections 23 to 25 of the Matrimonial Causes Act 1973. But there is no such legislation for couples like these. . . .

In my opinion in ascertaining the respective shares, the courts should normally apply the same considerations to couples living together (as if married) as they do to couples who are truly married. The shares may be half-and-half, or any such other proportion as in the circumstances of the case appears to be fair and just.

Applied to this case
The judge assessed the shares in the house as half-and-half. He took it at the date of acquisition. But I think on the facts it would be the same — half-and-half — at the date of separation. Mr Josephs and his present wife have been in the house for over three years now. Miss Bernard has not been in it for five years. It would be unduly harsh to turn Mr Josephs and his wife out of this house — simply in order to provide funds for Miss Bernard. But, seeing that he has the use of her share, it would only be fair that he should pay an occupation rent in respect of it: see *Dennis v McDonald* [1982] Fam 63, [1982] 1 All ER 590. No doubt, however, he has been paying the whole of the mortgage instalments and this should be taken into account as well. It may relieve him of paying any occupation rent for her half-share.

The problem is to calculate the sum which Mr Josephs should pay to Miss Bernard to buy her out. This is to be done by taking the price obtainable for the house if it were sold now with vacant possession. Then deduct the sum payable to redeem the mortgage. Then deduct one-half of the amount paid by Mr Josephs since the separation for mortgage instalments (deducting, of course, the amount received from the tenants). He should only get credit for one-half, because he has had the benefit of her half-share. Then make any other special adjustments.

One of the problems in Lord Denning's approach is that some couples remain unmarried because they do not wish to make the commitment of marriage. As Griffiths LJ said, in his judgment in *Bernard v Josephs*, the task of the judge in cases under s. 17 of the Married Women's Property Act 1882 or, in the case of unmarried couples, under s. 30 of the Law of Property Act 1925:

. . . is to look at all the evidence placed before it and decide whether it indicates an intention by the parties that the beneficial ownership of the house should be held (in a case where the house is in joint names in law as here) in other than equal shares . . ., but the nature of the relationship between the parties is a very important factor when considering what inferences should be drawn from the way they have conducted their affairs. There are many reasons why a man and a woman may decide to live together without marrying, and one of them is that each values his independence and does not wish to make the commitment of marriage; in such a case it will be misleading to make the same assumptions and to draw the same inferences from their behaviour as in the case of a married couple. The judge must look most carefully at the nature of the relationship, and only if satisfied that it was intended to involve the same degree of commitment as marriage will it be legitimate to regard them as no different from a married couple.

Questions

(i) Reread *Gissing v Gissing* [1971] AC 886, [1970] 2 All ER 780, HL and *Pettitt v Pettitt* [1970] AC 777, [1969] 2 All ER 385, HL. (See pp. 142, 144, above). Is there any justification for Lord Denning MR's views given the speeches of Lord Diplock in those two cases?

(ii) Applying the principles you know from *Gissing v Gissing* [1971] AC 886, [1970] 2 All ER 780 (p. 144, above), if the litigants in each of these cases had been married, and the issues arose in the context, for instance, of the bankruptcy of the men, do you think that the women would have been entitled to the shares they were given?

(iii) If you do not think that this would have been the case, is it your view that Lord Denning MR was applying a disguised *Wachtel v Wachtel* [1973] Fam 72, [1973] 1 All ER 829 (p. 265, above), approach?

Perhaps it comes as no surprise that the opportunity was taken to limit the extent of the 'Lord Denning approach' at the first available opportunity.

Burns v Burns

[1984] Ch 317, [1984] 1 All ER 244, [1984] 2 WLR 582, [1984] FLR 216, [1984] Fam Law 244, Court of Appeal

The plaintiff and the defendant set up house together in 1961. In 1963, when the plaintiff was expecting their second child, the defendant decided to buy a house. This was purchased, and conveyed in the sole name of the defendant. He financed the purchase price out of his own money and paid the mortgage. The plaintiff remained at home in order to look after the two children and maintain the home. She did not go out to work until 1975. Subsequent to that date she used some of her earnings to pay for the rates and telephone bills and buy certain items for the house. She also redecorated the interior of the house. The relationship deteriorated, and the plaintiff left the home in 1980. She claimed that she was entitled to a beneficial interest in the house by reason of her contributions to the household over the 17 years she had lived in the house with him. The judge dismissed her claim and she appealed.

Fox LJ rejected the proposition that there was any evidence of a payment or payments by the plaintiff which it can be inferred was referable to the acquisition of the house. He also felt that the redecoration gave no indication of a common intention that she had a beneficial interest. (*Pettitt v Pettitt* [1970] AC 777, [1969] 2 All ER 385, HL. See p. 142, above.) He then turned to the question of housekeeping and domestic duties.

There remains the question of housekeeping and domestic duties. So far as housekeeping expenses are concerned, I do not doubt that (the house being in the man's name) if the woman goes out to work in order to provide money for the family expenses, as a result of which she spends her earnings on the housekeeping and the man is thus able to pay the mortgage instalments and other expenses out of his earnings, it can be inferred that there was a common intention that the woman should have an interest in the house − since she will have made an indirect financial contribution to the mortgage instalments. But that is not this case.

During the greater part of the period when the plaintiff and the defendant were living together she was not in employment or, if she was, she was not earning amounts of any consequence and provided no money towards the family expenses. Nor is it suggested that the defendant ever asked her to. He provided, and was always ready to provide, all the money that she wanted for housekeeping. The house was not bought in the contemplation that the plaintiff would, at some time, contribute to the cost of its acquisition. She worked to suit herself. And if towards the very end of the relationship she had money to spare she spent it entirely as she chose. It was in no sense 'joint' money. It was her own; she was not expected and was not asked to spend it on the household.

I think it would be quite unreal to say that, overall, she made a substantial financial contribution towards the family expenses. That is not in any way a criticism of her; it is simply the factual position.

But, one asks, can the fact that the plaintiff performed domestic duties in the house and looked after the children be taken into account? I think it is necessary to keep in mind the nature of the right which is being asserted. The court has no jurisdiction to make such order as it might think fair; the powers conferred by the Matrimonial Causes Act 1973 in relation to the property of married persons do not apply to unmarried couples. The house was bought by the defendant in his own name and, prima facie, he is the absolute beneficial owner. If the plaintiff, or anybody else, claims to take it from him, it must be proved the claimant has, by some process of law, acquired an interest in the house. What is asserted here is the creation of a trust arising by common intention of the parties. That common intention may be inferred where there has been a financial contribution, direct or indirect, to the acquisition of the house. But the mere fact that parties live together and do the ordinary domestic tasks is, in my view, no indication at all that they thereby intended to alter the existing property rights of either of them. As to that I refer to the passage from the speech of Lord Diplock in *Pettitt v Pettitt* [1970] AC 777, 826 which I have already mentioned; and also to the observations of Lord Hodson in *Pettitt v Pettitt* at p. 811 and of Lord Reid at p. 796. The undertaking of such work is, I think, what Lord Denning MR in *Button v Button* [1968] 1 WLR 457, 462 called the sort of things which are done for the benefit of the family without altering the title to property. The assertion that they do alter property rights seems to me to be, in substance, reverting to the idea of the 'family asset' which was rejected by the House of Lords in *Pettitt v Pettitt* [1970] AC 777. The decision in *Gissing v Gissing* [1971] AC 886 itself is really inconsistent with the contrary view since the parties lived together for ten years after the house was bought. In *Hall v Hall* (1981) 3 FLR 379, 381, Lord Denning MR did say:

'It depends on the circumstances and how much she has contributed − not merely in money − but also in keeping up the house; and if there are children in looking after them.' With respect I do not find support for that in the other authorities and I do not think that it is consistent with principle. I am not clear to what extent the matter was material in *Hall v Hall*. So far as looking after children is concerned, it appears that there were no children: see *per* Dunn LJ, at p. 382. The case seems to have proceeded on the concession made by the man that the woman was entitled by way of resulting trust to a share in the house. The parties lived together for seven years and it was accepted by the man that they could not have bought the house but for the fact that both were earning: see *per* Lord Denning MR, at p. 381. The parties, in fact, pooled their resources: see the findings of the judge at p. 383. Accordingly, it seems to me that the case may well have been one where the woman, through the pooling of their income, made a contribution, direct or indirect, to the mortgage payments.

The result, in my opinion, is that the plaintiff fails to demonstrate the existence of any trust in her favour.

May LJ agreeing with Waller LJ and Fox LJ referred to the unfortunate position that the plaintiff found herself:

When one compares this ultimate result with what it would have been had she been married to the defendant, and taken appropriate steps under the Matrimonial Causes Act 1973, I think that she can justifiably say that fate has not been kind to her. In my opinion, however, the remedy for any inequity she may have sustained is a matter for Parliament and not for this court. *Appeal dismissed.*

The principles were considered by Scott J in the following case:

Layton v Martin
[1986] 2 FLR 227, High Court, Chancery Division

The plaintiff met the deceased in 1967 and they became cohabitants. She was 29 and unmarried. He was a married man of 50, whose wife was in poor health. In a letter dated 25 May the deceased, whose wife was by then having medical treatment abroad, asked the plaintiff to live with him, offering 'what emotional security I can give, plus financial security during my life and financial security after my death'. He implied that he would marry her after his wife died. Thereafter, the plaintiff lived with him as his wife in all but name. He paid her a salary of £100 per month, later raised to £120, plus £30 per week for housekeeping. The deceased wife's died in 1977 but he did not in the event marry the plaintiff. It seemed that the plaintiff brought no pressure upon him to do so. She gave him love and affection during their time together and was wholly unmercenary in her dealings with him. He made some provision for her in a number of wills.

However, the relationship between them ran into difficulties culminating in the deceased cutting the plaintiff out of his will and giving to her, in June 1980, a 'written notice of dismissal'. They parted without rancour and kept in touch from time to time up to the deceased's death in April 1982. In 1983 the plaintiff made a claim to financial provision out of the estate of the deceased, the defendants being the deceased's executors. Her claim was based on the contents of the letter of 25 May 1975 under three heads: (i) that the deceased had represented to her that if she came to live with him he would make financial provision for her in his will, that relying on that representation she had done so, and that in the circumstances the estate was subject to a constructive trust to give effect to their common intention; (ii) that under the doctrine of proprietary estoppel, equity would subject the estate to such beneficial interests in her favour as would give effect to the representation on which she relied; (iii) that the representation constituted an offer which she by her subsequent conduct had accepted and that she was entitled to enforce the contract thereby concluded.

The claim was dismissed under all three heads. We consider here the first head, (see p. 350, below for head ii).

Scott J: I will assume, that the plaintiff when she went to live with the deceased did so in reliance on the deceased's representation that if she did he would make financial provision for her.

Counsel for the plaintiff contends that one partner in a quasi-matrimonial relationship can claim a beneficial interest in assets owned by the other partner provided that the claimant should have a beneficial interest therein, and provided that it can be regarded in all the circumstances of the case as unconscionable that the beneficial interest should be withheld from the claimant.

Counsel for the plaintiff supports this contention, first, by reliance on dicta from such well-known cases as *Pettit v Pettit* [1970] AC 777 at 818; *Gissing v Gissing* [1971] AC 886 and a more recent authority in the Court of Appeal, *Burns v Burns* [1984] FLR 216. These authorities and the dicta in them are, in my view, no use whatever to counsel for the plaintiff. They are all dealing with the circumstances in which a person can claim a beneficial interest in specific assets, standing in the name of another person, but which have been acquired or preserved, at least in part, by contributions made by the claimant. They establish a principle that if there is a common intention on the part of the parties that the contributing claimant should have a beneficial interest in the assets, then equity will impose on the assets and the legal owner thereof, a constructive trust to give effect to that beneficial interest. In *Pettit v Pettit* and *Gissing v Gissing*, as in most cases of this type, the critical question was whether the nature of the claimant's contribution to the acquisition or preservation of the assets justified attributing to the parties the common intention that on account of that contribution the claimant should have a beneficial interest in the assets. In both *Pettit v Pettit* and *Gissing v Gissing*, and also *Burns v Burns*, the conclusion was that it did not. In some cases there is evidence of an actual (as opposed to inferred) intention of the parties that the claimant should have a beneficial interest. In those cases the only question is the size of the beneficial interest justified by the actual contribution made by the claimant. *Eves v Eves* [1975] 1 WLR 1338 was a case of this type. It is to be noted, however, that it was made clear by the Court of Appeal in *Eves v Eves* that an express common intention that the claimant should have a beneficial interest, unsupported by any *quid pro quo* moving from the claimant, would not suffice to entitle the claimant to a beneficial interest in accordance with the common intention (see the judgement of Brightman J (as he then was)).

But all these cases, of whichever type, involve an inferred or actual common intention directed to specific property. They involve contributions to the acquisition or preservation of specific property. This feature is not just an incidental circumstance. It lies at the heart of the circumstances which create the claimant's equitable interest in the specific assets in question.

. . . An agreement by one party to pay the other, say £5,000 a year, or a lump sum of £15,000, is enforceable, if it complies with the requirements of contracts, as a contract. It does not create any equitable interest in any assets of the promissor. An agreement to pay an unspecified amount can obviously not be in any better state to create an equity in the promissor's assets. Nor can an agreement in such general terms as 'to make provision', or 'to provide financial security' create any equity in the promissor's assets.
Judgment for the defendant.

Grant v Edwards
[1986] Ch 638, [1986] 2 All ER 426, [1986] 3 WLR 114, [1987] 1 FLR 87, [1986] Fam Law 300, Court of Appeal

The plaintiff, a married woman who was separated from her husband, set up a home with the defendant. In 1969, the defendant purchased a house and moved into it with the plaintiff, their child and the two children of the plaintiff's first marriage. The house was conveyed into joint names of the defendant and his brother. It was alleged that the defendant told the plaintiff that her name was not included in the title simply because of possible difficulties in relation to her divorce. He paid the deposit and the mortgage instalments, although the plaintiff made substantial contributions to general household expenses. The parties separated in 1980 and the plaintiff claimed a beneficial interest in the house. The judge dismissed the claim, and the plaintiff appealed.

Nourse LJ: In order to decide whether the plaintiff has a beneficial interest in 96, Hewitt Road we must climb again the familiar ground which slopes down from the twin peaks of *Pettitt v Pettitt* [1970] AC 777 and *Gissing v Gissing* [1971] AC 886. In a case such as the present, where there has been no written declaration or agreement, nor any direct provision by the plaintiff of part of the purchase price so as to give rise to a resulting trust in her favour, she must establish a common intention between her and the defendant, acted upon by her, that she should have a beneficial interest in the property. If she can do that, equity will not allow the defendant to deny that interest and will construct a trust to give effect to it.

In most of these cases the fundamental, and invariably the most difficult, question is to decide whether there was the necessary common intention, being something which can only be inferred from the conduct of the parties, almost always from the expenditure incurred by them respectively. In this regard the court has to look for expenditure which is referable to the acquisition of the house: see *per* Fox LJ in *Burns v Burns* [1984] Ch 317, 328H–329C. If it is found to have been incurred, such expenditure will perform the twofold function of establishing the common intention and showing that the claimant has acted upon it.

There is another and rarer class of case, of which the present may be one, where, although there has been no writing, the parties have orally declared themselves in such a way as to make their common intention plain. Here the court does not have to look for conduct from which the intention can be inferred, but only for conduct which amounts to an acting upon it by the claimant. And although that conduct can undoubtedly be the incurring of expenditure which is referable to the acquisition of the house, it need not necessarily be so.

The clearest example of this rarer class of case is *Eves v Eves* [1975] 1 WLR 1338. That was a case of an unmarried couple where the conveyance of the house was taken in the name of the man alone. At the time of the purchase he told the woman that if she had been 21 years of age, he would have put the house into their joint names, because it was to be their joint home. He admitted in evidence that that was an excuse for not putting the house into their joint names, and this court inferred that there was an understanding between them, or a common intention, that the woman was to have some sort of proprietary interest in it; otherwise no excuse would have been needed. After they had moved in, the woman did extensive decorative work to the downstairs rooms and generally cleaned the whole house. She painted the brickwork of the front of the house. She also broke up with a 14-lb. sledge hammer the concrete surface which covered the whole of the front garden and disposed of the rubble into a skip, worked in the back garden and, together with the man, demolished a shed there and put up a new shed. She also prepared the front garden for turfing. Pennycuick V-C at first instance, being unable to find any link between the common intention and the woman's activities after the purchase, held that she had not acquired a beneficial interest in the house. On an appeal to this court the decision was unanimously reversed, by Lord Denning MR on a ground which I respectfully think was at variance with the principles stated in *Gissing v Gissing* [1971] AC 886 and by Browne LJ and Brightman J [in a different way, see before, p. 333]

About that case the following observations may be made. First, as Brightman J himself observed, if the work had not been done the common intention would not have been enough. Secondly, if the common intention had not been orally made plain, the work would not have been conduct from which it could be inferred. That, I think, is the effect of the actual decision in *Pettitt v Pettitt* [1970] AC 777. Thirdly, and on the other hand, the work was conduct which amounted to an acting upon the common intention by the woman.

It seems therefore, on the authorities as they stand, that a distinction is to be made between conduct from which the common intention can be inferred on the one hand and conduct which amounts to an acting upon it on the other. There remains this difficult question: what is the quality of conduct required for the latter purpose? The difficulty is caused, I think because although the common intention has been made plain, everything else remains a matter of inference. Let me illustrate it in this way. It would be possible to take the view that the mere moving into the house by the woman amounted to an acting upon the common intention. But that was evidently not the view of the majority in *Eves v Eves* [1975] 1 WLR 1338. And the reason for that may be that, in the absence of evidence, the law is not so cynical as to infer that a woman will only go to live with a man to whom she is not married if she understands that she is to have an interest in their home. So what sort of conduct is required? In my judgment it must be conduct on which the woman could not reasonably have been expected to embark unless she was to have an interest in the house. If she was not to have such an interest, she could reasonably be expected to go and live with her lover, but not, for example, to wield a 14-lb. sledge hammer in the front garden. In adopting the latter kind of conduct she is seen to act to her detriment on the faith of the common intention.

. . . .

Was the conduct of the plaintiff in making substantial indirect contributions to the instalments payable under both mortgages conduct upon which she could not reasonably have been expected to embark unless she was to have an interest in the house? I answer that question in the affirmative. I cannot see upon what other basis she could reasonably have been expected to give the defendant such substantial assistance in paying off mortgages on his house. I therefore conclude that the plaintiff did act to her detriment on the faith of the common intention between her and the defendant that she was to have some sort of proprietary interest in the house.

I should add that, although *Eves v Eves* [1975] 1 WLR 1338 was cited to the judge, I think it doubtful whether the significance of it was fully brought to his attention. He appears to have assumed that the plaintiff could only establish the necessary common intention if she could point to expenditure from which it could be inferred. I do not find it necessary to decide whether, if the common intention had not been orally made plain, the expenditure in the present case would have been sufficient for that purpose. That raises a difficult and still unresolved question of general importance which depends primarily on a close consideration of the speeches of their Lordships in *Gissing v Gissing* [1971] AC 886 and the judgments of Fox and May LJJ in *Burns v Burns* [1984] Ch 317. If it be objected that the views which I have expressed will expose the possibility of further fine distinctions on these intellectual steeps, I must answer that that is something which is inherent in the decision of the majority of this court in *Eves v Eves* [1975] 1 WLR 1338. Be that as it may, I am in no doubt that that authority is a sure foundation for a just decision of the present case, a justness which was fully demonstrated in the concise and commonsensical argument of Mr St Ville on behalf of the plaintiff in this court. . . . I would therefore hold that the plaintiff is entitled to a half interest in the house.

For these reasons, I would allow this appeal.

Questions

(i) What if in *Burns v Burns*, the man had left and he had then tried to evict the woman?

(ii) Is *Burns v Burns* a different case, or do you think the decision simply reflects the consensus amongst the judiciary that Lord Denning had gone too far?

(iii) How would you answer the difficult and still unresolved question of general importance mentioned by Nourse LJ in *Grant v Edwards*?

Most cases concern a woman's claim to establish a beneficial interest in the house. It need not always be so.

Thomas v Fuller-Brown
[1988] 1 FLR 237, Court of Appeal

The plaintiff Pamela Thomas and defendant Harry Fuller-Brown started to live together in 1983 when the plaintiff was 42 and the defendant 39. The defendant lived in the plaintiff's house, first in her former matrimonial home and then in a house purchased in her sole name and paid for solely by her. The defendant was unemployed and was kept by the plaintiff. In April 1984 the plaintiff obtained a grant for improvements to the house and reached an agreement with the defendant whereby he was to carry out the work in return for his keep. After the work, which was substantial, had been completed the relationship between the parties deteriorated and the plaintiff left. She served a notice on the defendant terminating what was stated to be his licence to occupy the property and when he did not vacate it she issued proceedings for possession. The defendant counterclaimed for a declaration that the plaintiff held the property on trust for herself and him in the proportions of one-third to two-thirds respectively, or alternatively that he was entitled to some other interest in it or an equitable lien on it. The judge dismissed the defendant's counterclaim and ordered that he should give up possession of the house to the plaintiff. The defendant appealed, contending, which the plaintiff denied, they they had agreed to marry and she had offered him a 50% interest in the house, and, further, that the only reasonable inference from the parties' conduct was that they both intended that he should have an interest in the house in exchange for the work he had carried out in it.

Slade LJ: . . . It is perhaps understandable that the defendant, having devoted a substantial amount of labour to the house, though no money, and having seen it correspondingly increase in value, should consider that he should be entitled in law to claim some interest in it. However, it must be said that under English law the mere fact that A expends money or labour on B's property does not by itself entitle A to an interest in the property. In the absence of express agreement or a common intention to be inferred from all the circumstances or any question of estoppel, A will normally have no claim whatever on the property in such circumstances. The decision of the House of Lords in *Pettitt v Pettitt* [1970] AC 777 makes this clear . . .

. . . I think that an implicit, as well as an explicit, promise by the owner might suffice to confer on the other party an interest in the land in the circumstances which Lord Upjohn [in *Pettitt v Pettitt* (see p. 143, above)] was discussing.

That, I think, is the remaining point in the present case. Can such an inference of any common intention properly be made in the present case? I emphasize the word 'common' in that phrase 'common intention'. The judge thought not but the defendant has submitted to us that she was quite wrong in declining to make the inference. I think his strongest point was this. He submitted that it is not realistic to suppose that he would have designed and constructed what he described in his notice of appeal as a valuable two-storey extension, made major alterations and other improvements in return for meals, lodgings on site, pocket-money and cohabitation. He vigorously rejected the suggestion that he did all this work with any covert ulterior motive such as that suggested by the judge. Translated into legal terms, his submission is that the only reasonable inference from the parties' conduct is that they both intended that, in exchange for what he was doing for the plaintiff and for the house, he should have a beneficial interest in it.

I see the force of that submission but for my part I am not able to accept it. The defendant in the course of his argument strongly attacked the judge's finding that the plaintiff had no financial need to use the defendant to do the work. He pointed out that he did quite a bit of work beyond that provided for by the grant. By a careful analysis of her financial situation he sought to persuade us that the plaintiff could not possibly have had all that work done if she had had to employ and pay for outside labour for the purpose of doing it. That may be so. I see the force of his submissions on this point too.

Nevertheless, even if it be so, in my judgment the conduct of both parties was still perfectly capable of being rationally explained in the manner in which the judge thought it was to be explained. And this was the explanation which she preferred after seeing both parties and hearing all the evidence. She was sure that the defendant went to Bosham with the plaintiff on the same terms as those on which he had been living with her at Selsey, namely, as a licensee doing the odd job here and there and being, as she put it, a kept man provided by the plaintiff with board and lodging. As Miss Brann pointed out, the financial benefit of board and lodging in this day and age is very considerable in itself. The judge was sure that after the arrangement had been made that he would do the work covered by the council grant, the arrangement between them continued in exactly the same basis as before, save that he was to receive some additional money by way of what he called weekly pocket-money. I see nothing inherently incredible or irrational in such a continuing arrangement. I have no doubt that the defendant for his part hoped, and may well have expected, that the plaintiff would in due course marry him and that he would receive a beneficial interest in the house. But as I have already emphasized, it is the *common* intention of the parties that is relevant. It takes two parties to make an agreement or form a common intention, not merely one. On the basis of the judge's findings of primary fact, which I think we cannot disturb, the plaintiff never did agree to marry him and never did lead him to suppose that by doing these improvements he would ever acquire an interest in the house.

In the circumstance, I can see no room on the evidence, or on the judge's findings of primary fact, for differing from her conclusion that there was no common intention that the defendant would acquire an interest in the house. . . .

The defendant may perhaps feel himself harshly treated by the plaintiff or by the law of this country, or both, if the conclusion which I have reached is the correct one. However, I am afraid that this case illustrates, as many previous cases have done, that a man who does work by way of improvement to his cohabitee's property without a clear understanding as to the financial basis on which the work is to be done does so at his own risk.

For the reasons which I have sought to give I would dismiss this appeal.

Question

Do you think you have an answer to Nourse LJ's question in *Grant v Edwards* (see p. 339, above)?

Windeler v Whitehall
[1990] FCR 268, [1990] 2 FLR 505, High Court, Chancery Division

The plaintiff went to live with the defendant and they became cohabitants. The defendant was very much in love with her and wanted to marry her, but she consistently refused and occasionally had affairs with other men. The defendant was a successful theatrical agent, first as an employee of an agency and then on his own with a partner. The plaintiff looked after his house and entertained for him, but the work of the agency was essentially done by the defendant in his office. In 1979 the defendant sold his house and bought a larger one. The plaintiff made no contribution to the purchase. She had no money of her own, never worked or earned money and was supported by the defendant. She supervised some minor building works carried out on the new house. In June of that year the defendant made a will leaving the plaintiff his residuary estate. By 1980 the relationship was deteriorating and in 1984 it ended. The plaintiff accepted some money from the defendant and removed her belongings from the house, together with some items belonging to the defendant. In January 1987 the plaintiff brought a claim for a proprietary interest in the house and the business.

Millett J: If this were California, this would be a claim for palimony, but it is England and it is not. English law recognises neither the term nor the obligation to which it gives effect. In this country a husband has a legal obligation to support his wife even if they are living apart. A man has no legal obligation to support his mistress even if they are living together. Accordingly, the plaintiff does not claim to be supported by the defendant but brings a claim to a proprietary interest in his business and his home.

English courts exercise a statutory jurisdiction to adjust the property rights of married persons on the dissolution of their marriage, but there must be a marriage to dissolve. The courts possess neither a statutory nor an inherent jurisdiction to disturb existing rights of property on the termination of an extra-marital relationship, however long established the relationship and however deserving the claimant.

The plaintiff, Victoria Windeler, claims a share in the house in which she formerly lived with the defendant, Michael Whitehall, and a share in his business as a successful West End theatrical agent. They never married. To succeed, therefore, it is not enough for Miss Windeler to persuade me that she deserves to have such a share. She must satisfy me that she already owns it. In each case legal ownership is vested in Mr Whitehall. Miss Windeler, therefore, must satisfy me that in equity she is a part owner. This depends on the intention of the parties and such intention must be proved directly or inferred from their conduct. But it is important to bear in mind, that it is to that narrow issue alone that the parties' conduct is relevant.

. . .

Let me turn at once to the real issues in this case. Was there a common intention on the part of Mr Whitehall and Miss Windeler that she should have an interest in either house, 53 Lillian [Road] or 38 Sterndale Road, or in his business, either while he was employed or when he was a shareholder and director in the business which belonged to Leading Artists?

I will deal with the house first. As far as Mr Whitehall's intention is concerned, there is no direct evidence whatever that it was his intention that she should have any interest in the house. 53 Lillian Road was in his sole name and belonged entirely and beneficially to him at the outset of the parties' relationship. The question is whether he ever intended to make a gift to her of an interest in the house. In view of the instability of the relationship which they had, he would have been extremely foolish to have made any such gift. In fact he denied it and there is no evidence whatever that it was his intention to make a gift to her of either house. It is not suggested that he ever said or did anything which would lead Miss Windeler to believe that that was his intention in regard to either house

. . .

When asked about it, Mr Whitehall said: 'She never thought she was a part owner of either my business or my house. On the contrary, she did not want possessions; they would tie her down'. That accords entirely with my impression of Miss Windeler. One witness described her in 1974 or 1975, at the outset of the relationship, as being mature. I think that was entirely the wrong word. I think the witness must have meant sophisticated, because maturity is the last word that I would use to describe Miss Windeler. I think she was essentially immature. She never shook off an adolescent desire to be free and to avoid being tied down. Her counsel submitted to me that she saw her life and future with Mr Whitehall. I do not think she did. I do not think she ever saw the relationsip as a permanent arrangement. She saw it only lasting as long as she chose to make it last.

She told me in the witness box that she gave Mr Whitehall the stability necessary to pursue his career. I think that is the last thing she gave him. She had no stability herself. I think she gave him love and beauty and excitement. But, apart from her love, the greatest gift that a woman can bring to a man is security, tranquillity and peace of mind; something I think Miss Windeler was never able to give to Mr Whitehall.

Not only is there no direct evidence of any common intention but there is evidence which I accept that it was not Mr Whitehall's intention that Miss Windeler should have an interest in the house or, for that matter, in the business. That really is the end of the case.

But as to the business, Millett J went further:

This is not a case where a woman has worked full-time or for substantial periods in the business without wages and in a way which would lead anyone to believe that she must have been encouraged in the expectation that she had or would have an interest in the business. What Miss Windeler did was not work for which Mr Whitehall would have paid anyone to do in any circumstance whatever. In the present case Miss Windeler would not have been entitled even to a quantum meruit claim, and the idea that her conduct entitled her to a proprietary interest in the business is, in my judgment, ridiculous. I dismiss the action.

It it *were* California:

Marvin v Marvin
(1976) 134 Cal Reptr 815, 557 P.2d 106, Supreme Court, State of California

Michelle Marvin contended that in 1964, she and the defendant, the film actor Lee Marvin, entered into an oral agreement that: 'while the parties lived together they would combine their efforts and earnings and would share equally any and all property accumulated as a result of their efforts whether individual or combined.' Furthermore, she said that they had agreed to hold themselves out to the general public as husband and wife, and that she would 'further render her services as a companion, housekeeper and cook.' She gave up what she said was a lucrative career as an entertainer and a singer to devote herself full time to Lee Marvin. She alleged that she lived with the defendant for six years and fulfilled her obligations under the agreement. When the relationship broke up, the plaintiff sought a declaration of constructive trust upon one-half of the property acquired during the course of the relationship.

Tobriner J: We base our opinion on the principle that adults who voluntarily live together and engage in sexual relations are nonetheless as competent as any other persons to contract respecting their earnings and property rights. Of course, they cannot lawfully contract to pay for the performance of sexual services, for such a contract is, in essence, an agreement for prostitution and unlawful for that reason. But they may agree to pool their earnings and to hold all property acquired during the relationship in accord with the law governing community property; conversely they may agree that each partner's earnings and the property acquired from those earnings remains the separate property of the earning partner. So long as the agreement does not rest upon illicit meretricious consideration, the parties may order their economic affairs as they choose, and no policy precludes the courts from enforcing such agreements.

In the present instance, plaintiff alleges that the parties agreed to pool their earnings, that they contracted to share equally in all property acquired, and that defendant agreed to support plaintiff. The terms of the contract as alleged do not rest upon any unlawful consideration. We therefore conclude that the complaint furnishes a suitable basis upon which the trial court can render declaratory relief.

The court went on to add that, in the absence of an express agreement, the court may look to a variety of other remedies in order to protect the parties' legitimate expectations:

The courts may inquire into the conduct of the parties to determine whether that conduct demonstrates an implied contract or implied agreement of partnership or joint venture . . ., or some other tacit understanding between the parties. The courts may, when appropriate, employ principles of constructive trust . . . or resulting trust. . . . Finally, a nonmarital partner may recover in quantum meruit for the reasonable value of household services rendered. . . .

We conclude that the judicial barriers that may stand in the way of a policy based upon the fulfillment of the reasonable expectations of the parties to a nonmarital relationship should be removed.

The mores of the society have indeed changed so radically in regard to cohabitation that we cannot impose a standard based on alleged moral considerations that have apparently been so widely abandoned by so many. Lest we be misunderstood, however, we take this occasion to point out that the structure of society itself largely depends upon the institution of marriage, and nothing we have said in this opinion should be taken to derogate from that institution. The joining of the man and woman in marriage is at once the most socially productive and individually fulfilling relationship that one can enjoy in the course of a lifetime.

There was further litigation in this case culminating in the California Court of Appeal (1981) (122 Cal App 3rd 871) deleting the trial judge's rehabilitative award of $104,000 to the plaintiff. The Appellate Court held that there was no basis for a finding of damage or unjust enrichment, and there was no evidence of a wrongful act on the part of the defendant with respect to either the relationship or its termination.

Question

Perhaps the situation between England and California is not all that different?

3 Cohabitation contracts — express and implied

Weyrauch, *Metamorphoses of Marriage* (1980) writes:

The legal device of contract is particularly useful for women from the middle classes and of high educational attainment who are self-assertive and competitive in their relations with men. It is less adequate for parties of the lower classes and those who, because of continued differential treatment of the sexes, lack equal bargaining power. The courts may then fall back on traditional conceptions of marriage as status and emphasize the conjugal obligations of the husband. If there is no marriage, the courts may surreptitiously apply public policy by reading into a supposedly implied contract provisions that never occurred to the parties. A host of legal theories, equitable in nature, may also affect the obligations of parties to quasi-marital relationships. Thus, the courts may develop remedies akin to those in modern contract law when dealing with terms that are manifestly unfair and oppressive, and may borrow the reasoning from commercial litigation when deciding marital and quasi-marital disputes. They may refuse to enforce unconscionable terms that have been found to exist between the parties, married or not, and imply a duty of good faith and fair dealing.

This is a contract drawn up by a firm of Philadelphia lawyers:

1. The parties desire to maintain their relationship as independent persons and to have their relationship be a natural consequence of their mutual love and affection without material or

economic considerations. Each of the parties has, prior to the date hereof, achieved a measure of material independence and by the execution hereof, each party expresses his or her intention not to claim any interest whatsoever in the property accumulated by the other party prior or subsequent hereto, or in any of the income or appreciation derived therefrom except as expressly provided herein.

2. The parties intend and desire to hereby define and clarify their respective rights in the property of the other and in any jointly owned property they might accumulate after the date hereof and to avoid such interests, which, except for the operation of this agreement, they might otherwise acquire in the property of the other as a consequence of their relationship.

3. The parties desire that all property presently owned by either of them of whatsoever nature and wheresoever located and all income derived therefrom and all increases in the value thereof, shall be and remain their respective separate property. The parties agree that in no time during their relationship shall there be any transmutation of any of their separate property interests into jointly owned property, except by an express written agreement. The following events shall, under no circumstances, be evidence of any intention by either party of an agreement between the parties to transmute their separate property interests into jointly owned property or to transmute their separate income into joint income:

(a) The filing of joint tax returns;

(b) The designation of one party by the other as a beneficiary of his or her estate;

(c) The co-mingling by one party of his or her separate funds or property with jointly owned funds or property or with the separate funds or property of the other party;

(d) Any oral statement by either party;

(e) Any written statement by either party other than the express written agreement of transmutation;

(f) The payment from jointly held funds of any separate obligation, including but not limited to the payment of mortgage, interest or real property taxes on a separately owned residence or other separately owned real estate;

(g) The joint occupation of a separately owned or leased residence.

4. Both parties to this Agreement have made to each other a full and complete disclosure of the nature, extent and probable value of all their property and estate. Attached hereto as Exhibit 'A' is a statement of the separate property of the parties as of the date hereof. It is understood that as a result of income from or increases in the value of their presently existing separate property, each party may acquire other and different separate property in the future.

5. Except as otherwise provided herein with regard to the income and appreciation of the parties' separate property, and except as the parties may otherwise agree in writing, property heretofore acquired by the parties or hereafter acquired by the parties, and the earnings themselves, shall remain separate property.

Each of the parties covenants and agrees that all property now owned by either of the parties of whatsoever nature and wheresoever located and any property which he or she may hereafter acquire, whether real, personal or mixed, including but not limited to any earnings, salaries, commissions, or income resulting from his or her personal services, skills and efforts shall be and remain the sole and separate property of the party acquiring same and each party may dispose of said property as said party sees fit. . . .

8. In full settlement of any and all claims by either party to the property of the other of whatsoever nature and wheresoever located and any property which might be hereafter acquired, whether real, personal or mixed, including but not limited to any earnings, salaries, commissions, or income heretofore or hereafter earned, [A] agrees that upon separation or the acquiring of separate living quarters by the parties, [B] shall receive as follows:

(a) Ten Thousand ($10,000.00) Dollars;

(b) payment of the premiums for Blue Cross, Blue Shield for a period of one (1) year from the date of separation;

(c) all right, title and interest to the property as set forth in Schedule 'B' attached hereto and made a part hereof.

9. This Agreement shall continue in force until it is modified by a writing executed by both parties.

10. This Agreement shall be construed under the laws of the Commonwealth of Pennsylvania.

11. The terms, provisions and conditions of this Agreement shall be binding upon any and all of the heirs, executors, administrators, successors or assigns of either of the respective parties hereto.

Questions

(i) Lord Wright in *Fender v St John Mildmay* [1938] AC 1, [1937] 3 All ER 402 said: 'the law will not enforce an immoral promise, such as a promise between a man and a woman to live together without being married or to pay a sum of money or to give some other consideration in return for an immoral association.' Scarman LJ in *Horrocks v Forray* [1976] 1 All ER 737, [1976] 1 WLR 230 said: 'When an illegitimate child has been born, there is certainly nothing contrary to public policy in the parents coming to an agreement, which they intend to be binding in law, for the maintenance of the child and the mother.' Do you think that a contract similar to the Philadelphia contract would be enforceable in English law?

(ii) Would Mrs Burns, Miss Layton, Mrs Grant, Mr Fuller-Brown, and Miss Windeler have been in a better or a worse position if they had signed a document similar to this?

In *Contracts for Intimate Relationships* (1978), four researchers from the University of California (Weitzman et al) looked at a sample of contracts. Included in the group were contracts written by married couples, as those identified as pursuing a 'trial marriage', and those who seek an alternative to marriage (cohabitants). The table opposite is revealing.

But perhaps California is not really typical of the rest of the world. For instance there is in force in Berkeley a non-discrimination 'Domestic Partnership' policy.

CITY OF BERKELEY, CALIFORNIA, DOMESTIC PARTNERSHIP POLICY, STATEMENT OF GENERAL POLICY, December 4, 1984.

It shall be contrary to the policy of the City of Berkeley, within any program, procedure, or contract, to grant benefits or assign liabilities on the basis of a marital relationship unless a substantially equal application is created for 'domestic partnership' relationships as defined by the City Council. The creation of substantially equal application to a broader category of relationships or persons which includes within it the 'domestic partnership' relationships shall also be a proper compliance with this policy.

Domestic Partnership Defined. A 'domestic partnership' shall exist between two persons (regardless of their gender) and each of them shall be the 'domestic partner' of the other if they both complete, sign, and cause to be filed with the designated City Department an 'affidavit of Domestic Partnership' attesting to the following: (a) the two parties reside together and share the common necessities of life; (b) the two parties are: not married to anyone; eighteen (18) years or older, not related by blood closer than would bar marriage in the State of California, and mentally competent to consent to contract; (c) the two parties declare that they are each other's sole domestic partner and they are responsible for their common welfare; (d) the two parties agree to notify the City if there is a change of the circumstances attested in the affidavit; (e) the two parties affirm, under penalty of perjury, that the assertions in the affidavit are true to the best of their knowledge.

Termination. A member of a domestic partnership may end said relationship by filing a statement with the designated City Department. In the statement the individual filing must affirm, under penalty of perjury, that: (1) the partnership is terminated, and (2) a copy of the termination statement has been mailed to the other partner.

New Statements of Domestic Partnership. No individual who has filed an affidavit of domestic partnership may file another such affidavit until six (6) months after a statement of termination of the previous partnership has been filed with the designated City Department.

Civil Actions. Any person defrauded by a false statement contained in an Affidavit of Domestic Partnership may bring a civil action for fraud to recover his/her losses.

Range of Benefits to be Extended to Domestic Partners. (1) Medical Coverage; (2) Dental Coverage; (3) Cash payments in lieu of double health/dental benefits; (4) Bereavement leave; (5) Family sick leave; (6) Pensions; (7) Survivor's benefits; (8) Credit Union membership.

Items 1–5 are basically City-controlled benefits. Consequently, the City may unilaterally

Aims and expectations for the relationship

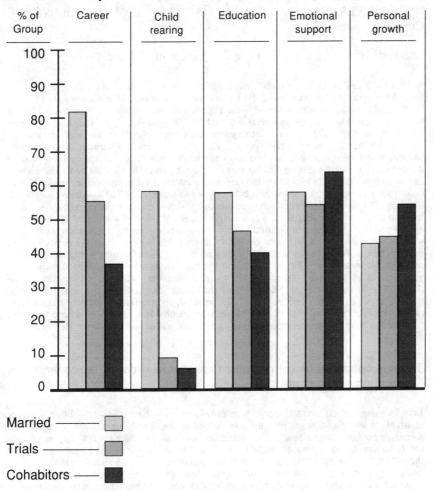

include domestic partners as recipients of these benefits. The other items will require agreement by other agencies before domestic partners can be extended these benefits.

Questions

(i) Does this policy discriminate *against* married partners?
(ii) If your local council decided to introduce a similar scheme, would you:
(*a*) welcome it? (*b*) fight against it? (*c*) do nothing at all on the ground that it will make little difference?

Claims in England have occasionally succeeded using doctrines of contractual licence or proprietary estoppel.

Tanner v Tanner
[1975] 3 All ER 776, [1975] 1 WLR 1346, 119 Sol Jo 391, 5 Fam Law 193, Court of Appeal

The facts of this case are given in the judgment of Lord Denning MR:

In 1968 Mr Eric Tanner, the plaintiff, was a milkman during the day and a croupier at night. He had been married for many years. He had a daughter then aged 19 and a son aged 12. They lived together at 26 Achilles Road in West Hampstead. But, to use his own words, he got 'disgusted' with his marriage and went out and had 'a good time.' He went out with three women, he said, 'simultaneously,' meaning separately but during the same weeks or months. One of these women was an attractive Irish girl, Miss Josephine MacDermott, the defendant. She was a cook in a nursing home. She had a flat in 33 Steels Road, Hampstead, on the third floor. He visited her frequently. She became pregnant by him. She took his name and became known as Mrs Tanner. In November 1969 she gave birth to twin daughters. They decided it was best to get a house for her and the twin babies. They found one at 4 Theobalds Avenue, North Finchley. The plaintiff borrowed a sum on mortgage with a local authority. In applying for it, he filled in a form. He said that he was 45. His wife was 41. He had a son aged 14, a daughter age 20 and twin daughters of 6 months. That was a very misleading application, because he was not getting it for his wife and his older children. He wanted it for the defendant and the twin babies. By means of that misrepresentation the plaintiff got the house on mortgage. It was in his own name. The defendant and the baby twins moved in there. She brought a good deal of her furniture and spent £150 on furnishings for it. She moved into the ground floor. They let the first floor. She managed the lettings and collected the rent. Previously, whilst she was in her flat in Steels Road, Hampstead, the plaintiff had paid her £5 a week maintenance for the twins. But after she moved into Theobalds Avenue he paid her nothing for them or for her. She got a supplementary allowance under social security from the local authority.

This was an appeal by the defendant against the order of the county court for vacation of the premises.

Lord Denning MR: It is said that they were only licensees — bare licensees — under a licence revocable at will: and that the plaintiff was entitled in law to turn her and the twins out on a moment's notice. I cannot believe that this is the law. This man had a moral duty to provide for the babies of whom he was the father. I would go further. I think he had a legal duty towards them. Not only towards the babies. But also towards their mother. She was looking after them and bringing them up. In order to fulfil his duty towards the babies, he was under a duty to provide for the mother too. She had given up her flat where she was protected by the Rent Acts — at least in regard to rent and it may be in regard also to security of tenure. She had given it up at his instance so as to be able the better to bring up the children. It is impossible to suppose that in that situation she and the babies were bare licensees whom he could turn out at a moment's notice. . . . In all the circumstances it is to be implied that she had a licence — a contractual licence — to have accommodation in the house for herself and the children so long as they were of school age and the accommodation was reasonably required for her and the children. There was, it is true, no express contract to that effect, but the circumstances are such that the court should imply a contract by the plaintiff — or, if need be, impose the equivalent of a contract by him — whereby they were entitled to have the use of the house as their home until the girls had finished school. It may be that if circumstances changed — so that the accommodation was not reasonably required — the licence might be determinable. But it was not determinable in the circumstances in which he sought to determine it, namely, to turn the defendant out with the children and to bring in his new wife with her family. It was a contractual licence of the kind which is specifically enforceable on her behalf: and which the plaintiff can be restrained from breaking; and he could not sell the house over her head so as to get her out in that way.

Browne LJ: . . . I agree that there was here a licence by the plaintiff to the defendant for good consideration: it could not be revoked at will. What has troubled me is what the duration of this licence was to be. With some hesitation I agree with Lord Denning MR's view of what it was to be; that is, in substance it was a licence to the defendant to occupy accommodation in the house so long as the children were of school age and such accommodation was reasonably required for her and the twins, subject to any relevant change of circumstances, such as her remarriage.

There was no express contract in *Tanner v Tanner*. However, the court decided that it could infer the existence of a contractual licence because of the presence of consideration, namely the giving up of the flat and looking after their children.

Pascoe v Turner
[1979] 2 All ER 945, [1979] 1 WLR 431, 123 Sol Jo 164, 9 Fam Law 82, Court of Appeal

In 1961, the plaintiff met the defendant, a widow. In 1963, the defendant moved into the plaintiff's home, at first as his housekeeper. In 1964, the plaintiff and defendant began to 'live in every sense as man and wife'. In 1965, they moved to another house. The plaintiff paid the purchase price and he also paid for the contents. In 1973, the plaintiff moved out. The defendant stayed on in the house and, in reliance upon the plaintiff's declarations that he had given her the house and the contents, she spent money and herself did work on redecorations, improvements and repairs. In 1976, the plaintiff tried to evict the defendant from the house. It was the man's determination to get her out of the house which persuaded the Court of Appeal to conclude that a fee simple rather than a life licence was the right answer.

Cumming Bruce LJ: . . . The principle to be applied is that the court should consider all the circumstances and, the (defendant) having no perfected gift or licence other than a licence revocable at will, the court must decide what is the minimum equity to do justice to her having regard to the way in which she changed her position for the worse by reason of the acquiescence and encouragement of the legal owner. The defendant submits that the only appropriate way in which equity can here be satisfied is by perfecting the imperfect gift as was done in *Dillwyn v Llewelyn* (1862) 4 De GF & J 517.

This court appreciates that the moneys laid out by the defendant were much less than in some of the cases in the books. But the court has to look at all the circumstances. When the plaintiff left her she was, we were told, a widow in her middle fifties. During the period that she lived with the plaintiff her capital was reduced from £4,500 to £1,000. Save for her invalidity pension that was all that she had in the world. In reliance upon the plaintiff's declaration of gift, encouragement and acquiescence she arranged her affairs on the basis that the house and contents belonged to her. So relying, she devoted a quarter of her remaining capital and her personal effort upon the house and its fixtures. In addition she bought carpets, curtains and furniture for it, with the result that by the date of the trial she had only £300 left. Compared to her, on the evidence the plaintiff is a rich man. He might not regard an expenditure of a few hundred pounds as a very grave loss. But the court has to regard her change of position over the years 1973 to 1976.

We take the view that the equity cannot here be satisfied without granting a remedy which assures to the defendant security of tenure, quiet enjoyment, and freedom of action in respect of repairs and improvements without interference from the plaintiff. The history of the conduct of the plaintiff since 9 April 1976, in relation to these proceedings leads to an irresistible inference that he is determined to pursue his purpose of evicting her from the house by any legal means at his disposal with a ruthless disregard of the obligations binding upon conscience. The court must grant a remedy effective to protect her against the future manifestations of his ruthlessness. It was conceded that if she is granted a licence, such a licence cannot be registered as a land charge, so that she may find herself ousted by a purchaser for value without notice.

If she has in the future to do further and more expensive repairs she may only be able to finance them by a loan, but as a licensee she cannot charge the house. The plaintiff as legal owner may well find excuses for entry in order to do what he may plausibly represent as necessary works and so contrive to derogate from her enjoyment of the licence in ways that make it difficult or impossible for the court to give her effective protection.

Weighing such considerations this court concludes that the equity to which the facts in this case give rise can only be satisfied by compelling the plaintiff to give effect to his promise and her expectations. He has so acted that he must now perfect the gift.

Coombes v Smith
[1986] 1 WLR 808, High Court, Chancery Division

The plaintiff, Mrs Coombes, sought relief against the defendant, Mr Smith in respect of property owned by the defendant but in which the plaintiff had been living since 1977. She sought an order that the defendant convey and transfer the property to her absolutely. As an alternative, she sought a declaration that the defendant was bound to allow her to occupy the property during her life and to discharge the mortgage. The plaintiff's action was based on proprietary estoppel and contractual licence. The trial judge distinguished *Pascoe v Turner* [1979] 2 All ER 945, [1979] 1 WLR 431, CA (See before, p. 349) on the ground that in this case the plaintiff had not held a belief that she would have a right to remain in the house indefinitely, and she had not acted to her detriment in any way on the facts of the case (this was despite becoming pregnant, leaving her husband, looking after the house and child, improving the house and not looking for a job!) On the contractual licence point, the judge said:

Nor in the instant case is there any evidence before me as to the plaintiff's circumstances when she was living with her husband, save that they were living in a council maisonette, and that the marriage was not a happy one. This is in contrast to *Tanner v Tanner* [1975] 1 WLR 1346, where the court found that the defendant was granted a licence in consideration for her giving up her rent-controlled flat and looking after the children in the new property. All I am left with in the instant case is the mere fact that the plaintiff decided to leave her husband and move to 67, Bulwark Road, with a view to the defendant joining her there subsequently. No doubt the plaintiff hoped that her relationship with the defendant would prove happier than her marriage had been, and that the defendant would look after her. But on the evidence before me I am wholly unable to infer an enforceable contract under which, as from the moment when the plaintiff moved to 67, Bulwark Road, the defendant became obliged to provide a roof over her head for the rest of her life. Nor was any lesser contractual right either pleaded or contended for. Accordingly, in my judgment, the plaintiff's claim based on contractual licence fails.

In the result, the action was dismissed on the defendant's undertaking to provide free accommodation at the house for the plaintiff and child until the child was 17.

Questions

(i) Given the undertaking by the defendant, is the result any different in this case to *Tanner v Tanner*?

(ii) Is it consideration to look after the child of the relationship?

(iii) In *Layton v Martin* [1986] 2 FLR 227 (see p. 337, above for the discussion on constructive trusts), the judge dismissed the claim based on proprietary estoppel. He said that the question whether an owner of property could by insisting on his strict legal rights defeat an expectation of an interest which he had raised by his conduct could not arise otherwise than in connection with some specific asset. A mere promise of 'financial security' did not suffice. Can you distinguish *Layton v Martin* from *Pascoe v Turner*, and, if so, how?

4 Legislative interventions

Charles Harpum, in *Adjusting Property Rights between Unmarried Cohabitees* (1982) states:

What is required is a broad statutory discretion (broader than that conferred by the Matrimonial Causes Act 1973 because the situations that exist are far more varied) to adjust the rights of cohabitees when they cease to live together. Already by statute, on the death of one cohabitee the other may have a claim against the estate of the deceased for reasonable financial provision, if the survivor was in some way economically dependent on the deceased: s. 1(1)(e) of the Inheritance (Provision for Family and Dependants) Act 1975. If on death, why not in life? The example of the 1975 Act could be followed and the trigger for the discretion could be a situation of total or partial economic dependence by one cohabitee on the other. The sooner such legislation is enacted the better.

(a) AUSTRALIA AND CANADA

One of the most significant legislative interventions comes from New South Wales where the De Facto Relationships Act 1984 was passed to put into effect the recommendations of the New South Wales Law Reform Commission (1983) relating both to property rights and to contractual claims.

14.(1)—Subject to this Part, a de facto partner may apply to a court for an order under this Part for the adjustment of interests with respect to the property of the de facto partners or either of them or for the granting of.maintenance, or both.
(2) An application referred to in subsection (1) may be made whether or not any other application for any remedy or relief is or may be made under this Act or any other law.
. . .
17.(1)—Except as provided by subsection (2), a court shall not make an order under this Part unless it is satisfied that the parties to the application have lived together in a de facto relationship for a period of not less than 2 years.
(2) A court may make an order under this Part where it is satisfied—
   (*a*) that there is a child of the parties to the application; or
   (*b*) that the applicant—
      (i) has made substantial contributions of the kind referred to in section 20(1)(*a*) or (*b*) for which the applicant would otherwise not be adequately compensated if the order were not made; or
      (ii) has the care and control of a child of the respondent,
and that the failure to make the order would result in serious injustice to the applicant.
18.(1)—Except as provided by subsections (2) and (3), where de facto partners have ceased to live together as husband and wife on a bona fide domestic basis, an application to a court for an order under this Part shall be made before the expiration of the period of 2 years after the day on which they ceased, or last ceased, as the case may require, to so live together.
(2) A court may, at any time after the expiration of the period referred to in subsection (1), grant leave to a de facto partner to apply to the court for an order under this Part (other than an order under section 27(1) made where the court is satisfied as to the matters specified in section 27(1)(*b*)) where the court is satisfied, having regard to such matters as it considers relevant, that greater hardship would be caused to the applicant if that leave were not granted than would be caused to the respondent if that leave were granted.

(3) Where, under subsection (2), a court grants a de facto partner leave to apply to the court for an order under this Part, the de facto partner may apply accordingly.

19. In proceedings for an order under this Part, a court shall, so far as is practicable, make such orders as will finally determine the financial relationships between the de facto partners and avoid further proceedings between them.

20.(1) – On an application by a de facto partner for an order under this Part to adjust interests with respect to the property of the de facto partners or either of them, a court may make such order adjusting the interests of the partners in the property as to it seems just and equitable having regard to –

    (a) the financial and non-financial contributions made directly or indirectly by or on behalf of the de facto partners to the acquisition, conservation or improvement of any of the property of the partners or either of them or to the financial resources of the partners or either of them; and

    (b) the contributions, including any contribution made in the capacity of homemaker or parent, made by either of the de facto partners to the welfare of the other de facto partner or to the welfare of the family constituted by the partners and one or more of the following namely:

        (i) a child of the partners;

        (ii) a child accepted by the partners or either of them into the household of the partners, whether or not the child is a child of either of the partners.

(2) A court may make an order under subsection (1) in respect of property whether or not it has declared the title or rights of a de facto partner in respect of the property. . . .

45.(1) – Notwithstanding any rule of public policy to the contrary, a man and a woman who are not married to each other may enter into a cohabitation agreement or separation agreement.

(2) Nothing in a cohabitation agreement or separation agreement affects the power of a court to make an order with respect to the right to custody of, maintenance of or access to or otherwise in relation to the children of the parties to the agreement.

46. Except as otherwise provided by this Part, a cohabitation agreement or separation agreement shall be subject to and enforceable in accordance with the law of contract, including, without limiting the generality of this section, the Contracts Review Act, 1980.

47.(1) – Where, on an application by a de facto partner for an order under Part III, a court is satisfied –

    (a) that there is a cohabitation agreement or separation agreement between the de facto partners;

    (b) that the agreement is in writing;

    (c) that the agreement is signed by the partner against whom it is sought to be enforced;

    (d) that each partner was, before the time at which the agreement was signed by him or her, as the case may be, furnished with a certificate in or to the effect of the prescribed form by a solicitor which states that, before that time, the solicitor advised that partner, independently of the other partner, as to the following matters:

        (i) the effect of the agreement on the rights of the partners to apply for an order under Part III;

        (ii) whether or not, at that time, it was to the advantage, financially or otherwise, of that partner to enter into the agreement;

        (iii) whether or not, at that time, it was prudent for that partner to enter into the agreement;

        (iv) whether or not, at that time and in the light of such circumstances as were, at that time, reasonably foreseeable, the provisions of the agreement were fair and reasonable; and

    (e) that the certificates referred to in paragraph (d) are endorsed on or annexed to or otherwise accompany the agreement.

the court shall not, except as provided by sections 49 and 50, make an order under Part III in so far as the order would be inconsistent with the terms of the agreement.

(2) Where, on an application by a de facto partner for an order under Part III, a court is satisfied that there is a cohabitation agreement or separation agreement between the de facto partners, but the court is not satisfied as to any one or more of the matters referred to in subsection (1)(b), (c), (d) or (e), the court may make such order as it could have made if there were no cohabitation agreement or separation agreement between the partners, but in making its orders, the court, in addition to the matters to which it is required to have regard under Part III, may have regard to the terms of the cohabitation agreement or separation agreement.

(3) A court may make an order referred to in subsection (2) notwithstanding that the cohabitation agreement or separation agreement purports to exclude the jurisdiction of the court to make that order.

48. Where a cohabitation agreement or separation agreement does not satisfy any one or more of the matters referred to in section 47(1)(*b*), (*c*), (*d*) or (*e*), the provisions of the agreement may, in proceedings other than an application for an order under Part III, be enforced notwithstanding that the cohabitation agreement purports to exclude the jurisdiction of a court under Part III to make such an order.

49.(1) – On an application by a de facto partner for an order under Part III, a court may vary or set aside the provisions, or any one or more of the provisions, of a cohabitation agreement (but not a separation agreement) made between the de facto partners, being a cohabitation agreement which satisfies the matters referred to in section 47(1)(*b*), (*c*), (*d*) and (*e*), where, in the opinion of the court, the circumstances of the partners have so changed since the time at which the agreement was entered into that it would lead to serious injustice if the provisions of the agreement, or any one or more of them, were, whether on the application for the order under Part III or on any other application for any remedy or relief under any other Act or any other law, to be enforced.

(2) A court may, pursuant to subsection (1), vary or set aside the provisions, or any one or more of the provisions, of a cohabitation agreement notwithstanding any provision of the agreement to the contrary.

50. Without limiting or derogating from the provisions of section 46, on an application by a de facto partner for an order under Part III, a court is not required to give effect to the terms of any cohabitation agreement or separation agreement entered into by that partner where the court is of the opinion –

    (*a*) that the de facto partners have, by their words or conduct, revoked or consented to the revocation of the agreement; or

    (*b*) that the agreement has otherwise ceased to have effect.

Question

(i) Is this what Harpum (see p. 351) is suggesting for England?

(b) SCOTLAND

The Scottish Law Commission's Discussion Paper on the *Effects of Cohabitation on Private Law* (1990) describes the New South Wales Act as well as other legislation from Australia and Canada.

5.2 Several Canadian provinces have enacted legislation which enables a cohabitant to apply to a court, during the cohabitation or within a specified period after its end, for an order for support against the other cohabitant. [Institute of Law Research and Reform, Alberta, *Towards Reform of the Law Relating to Cohabitation Outside Marriage* (Issues Paper No 2, 1987)] The details vary. In Ontario, for example, an application may be made by

'either a man or a woman who are not married to each other and have cohabited

    (*a*) continuously for a period of not less than 3 years, or

    (*b*) in a relationship of some permanence if they are the natural or adoptive parents of a child.' [Family Law Act 1986, s. 29. The New Brunswick Family Services Act 1980 s. 112(3) is broadly similar.]

In Manitoba the required period of cohabitation is 1 year if there is a child of the union and 5 years if there is not. [Family Maintenance Act 1978 (as amended) s. 2(3).] In British Columbia the required period of cohabitation is not less than 2 years, whether or not there is a child of the union. [Family Relations Act 1979, s. 1(*c*).] In Nova Scotia one year's cohabitation as husband and wife suffices, [Family Maintenance Act 1980 (as amended) s. 2(*m*).] while in the Yukon Territory all that is required is cohabitation in a relationship of some permanence. [Matrimonial Property and Family Support Ordinance 1979 (as amended) s. 30.6.] In a recent report the Alberta Law Reform Institute has, by a majority, recommended that an order for the maintenance of one cohabitant by the other should be possible where

    '(i) the applicant for maintenance has the care and control of a child of the cohabitational relationship and is unable to support himself or herself adequately by reason of the child care responsibilities; or

    (ii) the earning capacity of the applicant has been adversely affected by the cohabitational relationship and some transitional maintenance is required to help the applicant to re-adjust his or her life.' [*Towards Reform of the Law Relating to Cohabitation Outside Marriage* (Report No 53, 1989)]

5.3 There have also been interesting developments in Australia. One of them took place more than a hundred and fifty years ago. Tasmania has had since 1837 a provision [Now in s. 16 of the Maintenance Act 1967] enabling a woman who has cohabited with a man for at least a year to obtain a maintenance order if the man, without just cause or excuse, leaves her without adequate means of support, or deserts her, or is guilty of such misconduct as to make it unreasonable to expect her to continue to live with him. More recently, New South Wales, following on a report by the New South Wales Law Reform Commission [1983] passed the De Facto Relationships Act of 1984. This allows a cohabitant, who must normally have cohabited with his or her partner for at least two years, to claim maintenance if he or she is unable to support himself or herself adequately and if the inability is due either to having the care of a child of the union or to having suffered a reduction in earning capacity as a result of the cohabitation. An order based on the applicant's reduced earning capacity resulting from the cohabitation ceases 3 years from the date of the order or 4 years from the end of the cohabitation, whichever is earlier. The Act also gives the court power to make such order adjusting the interests of the cohabitants in their property as seems just and equitable, having regard to their contributions (financial or otherwise) to the property and to their financial resources. In Victoria, the Property Law (Amendment) Act 1988 enables a court in settling property disputes between cohabitants to take into account contributions of various kinds to the property of the cohabitants and the welfare of the family. The Northern Territory Law Reform Committee in its Report on *De Facto Relationships* [1988] recommended rules on maintenance and property adjustment similar, in their essential features, to those enacted in New South Wales.

Two of the options identified by the Scottish Discussion Paper (1990) are first,

do nothing:

5.5 Leave the law as it is. It would be quite possible to make no legislative provision for financial provision or property readjustment on the termination of cohabitation. This would leave matters to be regulated by the common law.

Secondly, apply all the principles applicable to financial provision on divorce in Scotland.

But they take the view in the Discussion Paper that:

5 There is no adequate justification for applying the principles of equal sharing of property and relief of long-term hardship in section 9(1)(a) and (e) of the Family Law (Scotland) Act 1985 to cohabitants.

It will be recalled that the principles applicable on divorce in Scotland are set out on p. 263, above.

Questions

(i) Do you agree with the Scottish Law Commission that (*a*) and (*e*) should not apply, and if so, why?

(ii) What about (*b*) (*c*) and (*d*)?

(iii) In England, different considerations apply. Will it be necessary to introduce a law similar to the Family Law (Scotland) Act 1985 for divorcing couples prior to providing relief for former cohabitants, or would the extension of the principles in the Matrimonial Causes Act 1973 to former cohabitants suffice?

5 English legislative initiatives

There has been a number of interventions in England. There is the Fatal Accidents Act 1976 under which a claim can be made by a dependant of the deceased against the tortfeasor. If the deceased's death was brought about by the fault of another giving rise to a cause of action, a cohabitant may claim under s. 1(3) of the Fatal Accidents Act 1976. This Act defines a dependant as including:

(b) any person who—
  (i)   was living with the deceased in the same household immediately before the date of the death; and
  (ii) had been living with the deceased in the same household for at least two years before that date; and
  (iii) was living during the whole of that period as the husband or wife of the deceased;

Section 3(4) states:

. . . there shall be taken into account (together with any other matter that appears to the court to be relevant to the action) the fact that the dependant had no enforceable right to financial support by the deceased as a result of their living together.

In the House of Lords' debate on the Bill (4 May 1982) Lord Elwyn Jones said this:

We feel that, as there are in this country today hundreds of thousands of men and women living together over the years in a settled, permanent relationship as reputed spouses, in the event of the man — or possibly in some cases the woman — being deprived of the person on whom there was dependency, it would be proper that he or she should be embraced in the provisions of the Bill to deal with dependency when the person dependent has suffered loss through the negligence of a third party causing even the death of one of the reputed spouses concerned. I recall recollecting how, in our constituency surgeries, we came across that sort of tragic situation — of a sudden catastrophe happening — of, say, the husband being killed by a negligent driver with nothing left for the so-called common law wife.

Lord Elwyn-Jones, in this speech, adopts the philosophy of pretending that cohabitation is, in certain cases, like marriage, and attributes to it the traditional incidents of marriage.

Question

Glendon (1976) states: 'What in effect were cohabitation cases were disguised as cases involving presumptively legal marriages, estoppels, and implied agreements to pay for services. . . .'
  Do you agree with this analysis of the cases?

  Under the Inheritance (Provision for Family and Dependants) Act 1975, s. 1(1)(e) a court may award reasonable maintenance to any person who 'immediately before the death of the deceased was being maintained, either wholly or partly, by the deceased.' It is important to remember, however, that the widow may apply under the same Act not only for maintenance, but for such 'financial provision as it would be reasonable in the circumstances of the case for a husband or wife to receive, whether or not that provision is required for his or her maintenance' (see Chapter 5, above). The unmarried partner is, therefore, in a much weaker position. She has no automatic rights on intestacy; and her rights under the 1975 Act are limited to the provision of maintenance. If the relationship was entirely *independent*, no rights at all under the 1975 Act will accrue. Likewise, it appears that no rights will accrue in a situation of 'mutual dependency'.

s. 1(3) For the purposes of subsection (1)(e) . . . a person shall be treated as being maintained by the deceased, either wholly or partly, as the case may be, if the deceased, otherwise than for full valuable consideration, was making a substantial contribution in money or money's worth towards the reasonable needs of that person.

She also has no claim if the relationship came to an end before the death of her cohabitant.

Jelley v Illiffe
[1981] Fam 128, [1981] 2 All ER 29, [1981] 2 WLR 801, 125 Sol Jo 355, Court of Appeal

The facts of the case are fully set out in Stephenson LJ's judgment:

On 19 August 1979, the plaintiff, Thomas William Jelley, an old age pensioner, applied under the Inheritance (Provision for Family and Dependants) Act 1975, for reasonable financial provision to be made for his maintenance out of the estate of Mrs Florence Lilian May Illiffe, deceased, a widow, with whom the plaintiff had lived for eight years before her death.

The deceased was the widow of the plaintiff's wife's brother, who died in 1970. The plaintiff's wife died in 1968. In 1971 the plaintiff went to live with the deceased. . . . Her husband had left the house to her for her life and after her death to their three children, but by a deed of arrangement in 1970 they conveyed the freehold to her. It was clearly understood by them — and they said by the plaintiff also, though he denied it — that the house should go to the children after her death. And so it did. By her will made on 22 May 1972, of which the first defendant[1] and the plaintiff were executors and trustees, she left all her property, real and personal, to them upon trust to divide her residuary estate between her three children in equal shares. At her death on 8 April 1979, the house, valued at £16,000, constituted by far the greatest part of her estate, which was valued when probate was granted to the first defendant at £17,303.86 net.

The case took the form of an application for the proceedings to be struck out on the ground that there was no reasonable cause of action.

[The object of the Act] is surely to remedy, wherever reasonably possible, the injustice of one, who has been put by a deceased person in a position of dependency upon him, being deprived of any financial support, either by accident or by design of the deceased, after his death. To leave a dependant, to whom no legal or moral obligation is owed, unprovided for after death may not entitle the dependant to much, or indeed any, financial provision in all the circumstances, but he is not disentitled from applying for such provision if he can prove that the deceased by his conduct made him dependent upon the deceased for maintenance, whether intentionally or not.

Accordingly, I am of opinion that the court has to consider whether the deceased, otherwise than for valuable consideration (and irrespective of the existence of any contract), was in fact

---

1. The deceased's son. The deceased had three children, one son and two daughters, who were the defendants to the action.

making a substantial contribution in money or money's worth towards the reasonable needs of the plaintiff, on a settled basis or arrangement which either was still in force immediately before the deceased's death or would have lasted until her death but for the approach of death and the consequent inability of either party to continue to carry out the arrangement. To discover whether the deceased was making such a contribution the court has to balance what she was contributing against what he was contributing, and if there is any doubt about the balance tipping in favour of hers being the greater contribution, the matter must, in my opinion, go to trial. If, however, the balance is bound to come down in favour of his being the greater contribution, or if the contributions are clearly equal, there is no dependency of him on her, either because she depended on him or there was mutual dependency between them, and his application should be struck out now as bound to fail. Where what B does gives full valuable consideration for the substantial contribution A makes there is no dependency and B's claim under the Act should be struck out.

The court declared that there was a reasonable cause of action, and allowed the trial to proceed. Stephenson LJ, however, did express his doubts about the ultimate success of the plaintiff's case:

Here there are several indications that the plaintiff's case is likely to fail. He did a lot for the deceased, perhaps enough to equal what she did for him, including the provision of rent-free accommodation, so he may not have been on balance dependent on her. Then the house was her children's until they conveyed it to her and she remained under a moral obligation to leave it back to them on her death. He had a home with a daughter to go to.

Bishop v Plumley
[1991] 1 All ER 236, [1991] 3 WLR 582, Court of Appeal

In 1974 the applicant, Evelyn Bishop, and the deceased, Douglas Plumley, who were both married to other people, began to live together and thereafter they cohabited until the death of the deceased in November 1984. Until January 1984 their circumstances were similar in that they lived together in rented accommodation on their pooled resources, consisting of social security benefits, his earnings as a farm labourer and later as a part-time grass cutter and her occasional earnings. In 1983 an uncle of the deceased died leaving the deceased a substantial portion of his estate which the deceased used to buy a house in which the deceased and the applicant lived from January 1984 until the deceased died. They both continued to claim social security benefit. From 1981 the deceased suffered from angina and received exceptionally devoted care and attention from the applicant. The deceased made a will in 1974, during a short period when he and the applicant were separated, in which he left his estate to his son and daughter and made no provision for the applicant. The applicant, who had no assets of her own and continued to live in the deceased's house on social security benefit after his death, applied for provision out of his estate under s. 1(1)(e) of the Inheritance (Provision for Family and Dependants) Act 1975, on the ground that immediately before his death she was 'being maintained' by the deceased within s. 1(3) of that Act since 'the deceased, otherwise than for full valuable consideration, was making a substantial contribution in money or money's worth towards [her] reasonable needs'. The district judge found that the applicant and the deceased had cohabited as husband and wife, that during the early period of their cohabitation he had largely supported her from his earnings but by the end of 1983 their circumstances were similar and they were pooling their modest resources and that the benefits the plaintiff gave to the deceased by way of looking after him as he became progressively more ill equalled the benefits the deceased gave to the plaintiff in the form of a secure rent-free home from January 1984, and that therefore the applicant had given full valuable consideration for the contribution made to her needs by the deceased. He accordingly dismissed the application and on appeal his decision was affirmed by the judge. The applicant appealed.

Butler-Sloss LJ: The object of the legislation is to remedy, wherever reasonably possible, the injustice of one who has been put by a deceased person in a position of dependency on him being deprived of any financial support, either by accident or by design of the deceased, after his death (see *Jelley v Iliffe* [1981] 2 All ER 29 at 36, [1981] Fam 128 at 137 per Stephenson LJ).

The issue in this case and the one on which both the [district judge] and the judge found against the applicant is whether she qualifies as one who was being maintained, wholly or partly, by the deceased.

. . . There is no argument on these facts that, if the applicant was maintained at all by the deceased, it was immediately before his death. Despite an argument to the contrary by counsel for the applicant, I am entirely satisfied that the applicant could not be said to be maintained even partly by the deceased prior to January 1984. Their circumstances were similar, living in rented accommodation and pooling their supplementary benefit and his grass-cutting earnings. The change of circumstances by the purchase of the house into which they both moved in January 1984 founds the basis of the present application.

As I understand the structure of the legislation, the question whether an applicant was being maintained is to be looked at in the light of the provisions of s. 1(3). I agree both with Megarry V-C in *Re Beaumont, Martin v Midland Bank Trust Co Ltd* [1980] Ch 444, [1980] 1 All ER 266 and Stephenson LJ in *Jelley v Iliffe* [1981] 2 All ER 29 at 34, [1981] Fam 128 at 136 that s. 1(3) exhaustively or exclusively defines what s. 1(1)(e) means by 'being maintained', and does not include in those words a state of affairs which is not within s. 1(1)(e) and would extend its ambit. This interpretation appears both to be settled law and common sense.

The test laid down in s. 1(3) is in two parts: (1) was the deceased making a substantial contribution in money or money's worth towards the reasonable needs of the applicant and, (2) if so, was the contribution made for full valuable consideration by the applicant?

If the answer to (1) is Yes and to (2) No, the applicant qualifies as being maintained either wholly or in part. The assessment of the contributions of the deceased and the applicant requires an analysis and assessment of the relevant facts and is an entirely different exercise from the exercise of the discretion of the court under s. 3, which requires the court to have regard to many factors and involves a careful balancing exercise, somewhat analogous to the exercise undertaken by the court under ss. 25 and 25A of the Matrimonial Causes Act 1973 (as amended).

The comparison of substantial contribution and full valuable consideration at the earlier stage is factual and involves no exercise of discretion. If the flow of benefits from the one to the other is broadly commensurate, full valuable consideration will be demonstrated; if there is an obvious imbalance in favour of the applicant, he or she will have surmounted the first hurdle. Griffiths LJ in *Jelley v Iliffe* [1981] 2 All ER 29 at 38, [1981] Fam 128 at 141 was dealing with the first limb, ie was the contribution made to the applicant by the deceased substantially greater when valued in money or money's worth?, when he said:

'Only if the balance comes down heavily in favour of the applicant will it be shown that the deceased was "making a substantial contribution in money or money's worth towards the reasonable needs" of the applicant.'

But he went on to qualify this statement:

'In striking this balance the court must use common sense and remember that the object of Parliament in creating this extra class of persons who may claim benefit from an estate was to provide relief for persons of whom it could truly be said that they were wholly or partially dependent on the deceased. It cannot be an exact exercise of evaluating services in pounds and pence. By way of example, if a man was living with a woman as his wife and providing the house and all the money for their living expenses she would clearly be dependent on him, and it would not be right to deprive her of her claim by arguing that she was in fact performing the services that a housekeeper would perform and it would cost more to employ a housekeeper than was spent on her and indeed perhaps more than the deceased had available to spend on her. Each case will have to be looked at carefully on its own facts to see whether common sense leads to the conclusion that the applicant can fairly be regarded as a dependant.'

I do not read the judgment as saying more than that, in determining whether or not the deceased was making a substantial contribution, one must look at the problem in the round;

apply a commonsense approach, avoiding fine balancing computations involving the value of normal exchanges of support in the domestic sense. Griffiths LJ's example of the provision of a house and connubial services in exchange would indicate that, in providing a secure home for the applicant, the deceased must be taken as having made a substantial contribution.

The provision of secure accommodation at the house purchased was a substantial contribution by the deceased. The case for this applicant is that her contribution to the deceased was that of a woman acting in all ways as a wife. Counsel for the applicant argues that her contribution by way of love and support in such a relationship ought to be disregarded in calculating the benefits flowing from her.

Counsel for the beneficiaries argues that on her own evidence the applicant gave services which were out of the ordinary, and by this exceptional care she was giving him full valuable consideration. I do not consider that her evidence that she did everything for him over a period of years can be assessed in isolation from the mutuality of the relationship. If a man or a woman living as man and wife with a partner gives the other extra devoted care and attention, particularly when the partner is in poor health, is he or she to be in a less advantageous position on an application under the Act than one who may be less loving and give less attention to the partner? I do not accept that this could have been the intention of Parliament in passing this legislation. In the case of this applicant, she is now 64, herself in poor health, with no assets, on supplementary benefit from which she is repaying overpayments to the Department of Social Security and, if unsuccessful in this claim, homeless. In that regard, the [district judge] found that, although the circumstances of the beneficiaries were modest, the applicant's needs were greater than theirs.

In my view, both the [district judge] and judge fell into error in their approach to the test to be applied under s. 1(3). Neither referred to or appeared to take into account the passage from the judgment of Griffiths LJ in *Jelley v Iliffe* to which I have just referred. If the [district judge] and the judge had approached the factual analysis of substantial contribution and full valuable consideration by including the mutual love and support of the couple, demonstrated as it was by the applicant in the devotion she gave him in the final years of their cohabitation, it is inconceivable that either would have excluded the applicant from advancing to the second stage to be resolved by ss. 2 and 3 of the Act.

I would allow this appeal, and find that the deceased had made a substantial contribution towards the applicant's reasonable needs other than for full valuable consideration, and remit the application to the [district judge] for consideration under ss. 2 and 3 whether an order and, if so, what order should be made.

Appeal allowed.

Questions

(i) Would Mrs Burns, Miss Layton, Mrs Grant, Mr Fuller-Brown and Miss Windeler have been successful in a claim under s. 1(1)(e) of the Inheritance (Provision for Family and Dependants) Act 1975 if Mr Burns, Mr Martin, Mr Edwards, Miss Thomas and Mr Whitehall died?

(ii) Would Mr Burns, Mr Martin, Mr Edwards, Miss Thomas and Mr Whitehall have succeeded if Mrs Burns, Miss Layton, Mrs Grant, Mr Fuller-Brown and Miss Windeler died?

(iii) Does 'status' or 'contract' determine the rights which accrue under the Fatal Accidents Act 1976 and the Inheritance (Provision for Family and Dependants) Act 1975?

(iv) Can you see any justification for the difference in qualification under the two Acts, and if you can, what is it?

(v) The Law Commission is their Report on *Distribution on Intestacy* (1989) have recommended an extension of the class of cohabitants who can claim under the 1975 Act. Would you extend the class to include (a) those who can benefit under the 1976 Act; (b) those who can benefit under the Ontario Family Law Act 1986 (see p. 353, above); (c) those who would benefit under the reforms of the Alberta Law Reform Institute (1989) (See p. 353, above); (d) or some other definition; or (e) leave well alone?

(vi) Would you recomend extending the law on intestacy to include cohabitants? If you do recommend such an extension would you extend the law to include all or some of the following (*a*) a long cohabitation which has resulted in children; (*b*) a short cohabitation which has resulted in children; (*c*) a long childless cohabitation, and (*d*) a short childless cohabitation?

Entitlement to or increases in social security contributory benefits for adult dependants are generally restricted to married partners. In contrast to entitlement, cohabitation with a man has the effect of depriving the woman of benefit, for benefits such as widow's payment, widowed mother's allowance and the widow's pension, and secondly, an individual entitlement to income support, family credit and housing benefit.

In the latter case, s. 20(5)(c) of the Social Security Act 1986 states: 'A person is entitled to income support if − (c) he is not engaged in remunerative work and, if he is a member of a married or unmarried couple, the other member is not so engaged . . .'

Crake v Supplementary Benefits Commission
Butterworth v Supplementary Benefits Commission
[1982] 1 All ER 498, 2 FLR 264, High Court, Queen's Bench Division

In *Butterworth*, the applicant, who was a divorcee, was seriously injured in a road accident. The daughter-in-law arranged for a man friend of the applicant to move in with her, which he did out of a sense of loyalty. He had his own bedroom, there was no sexual relationship between them, and he cooked and looked after her. In assessing the applicant's entitlement for supplementary benefit, the SBC treated her as cohabiting with the man and withdrew her benefit. The Tribunal affirmed this decision on the grounds that the couple were members of the same household. The applicant appealed.

In *Crake*, the applicant was a woman who had left her husband and was living in the house of another man. She said that she was simply acting as his housekeeper. The SBC withdrew her benefit, and the Tribunal affirmed this decision. The applicant appealed.

Dealing with the *Butterworth* appeal:

Woolf J: It is not sufficient, to establish that a man and woman are living together as husband and wife, to show that they are living in the same household. If there is the fact that they are living together in the same household, that may raise the question whether they are living together as man and wife, and, indeed, in many circumstances may be strong evidence to show that they are living together as man and wife; but in each case it is necessary to go on and ascertain, in so far as this is possible, the manner in which and why they are living together in the same household; and if there is an explanation which indicates that they are not there because they are living together as man and wife, then they would not fall within para 3(1); they are not two persons living together as husband and wife.

It is impossible to categorise all the explanations which would result in para 3(1) being inapplicable but it seems to me that if the reason for someone living in the same household as another person is to look after that person because they are ill or incapable for some other reason of managing their affairs, then that in ordinary parlance is not what one would describe as living together as husband and wife, as required by the paragraph.

Quite clearly if that were not the position, housekeepers performing no other functions, other than those of housekeepers, could be regarded as falling within this paragraph. A couple who live together because of some blood relationship could be treated as falling within this paragraph. In my view it was not the intention of Parliament that they should. What Parliament had in mind was . . . namely that where a couple live together as husband and wife, they shall not be in any different position whether they are married or not; and once one has established a relationship between the couple which is properly regarded as one between husband and wife in fact, then the paragraph applies, and of course thereafter it will continue to apply until that relationship ceases. Once one has established the relationship to exist then it is much easier to show that it continues, and it may well be that although many of the features of living together between husband and wife have ceased, perhaps because of advancing years or for other reasons, the paragraph will still continue to apply. This would be the position even though a court would have come to a different conclusion as to whether the paragraph applied, if at the outset all that existed was that state of affairs. . . . [The Tribunal] seemed to have attached too much importance to the fact that there were not two separate households. If there had been two separate households, then clearly they would not fall within para 3 of the schedule. But the fact that there were not two separate households does not mean that they do fall within that paragraph. Before they could fall within that paragraph the tribunal had to be satisfied that they were living together as husband and wife. If the only reason that Mr Jones went to that house temporarily was to look after Mrs Butterworth in her state of illness and, albeit, while doing so, acted in the same way as an attentive husband would behave towards his wife who suffered an illness, this does not amount to living together as husband and wife because it was not the intention of the parties that there should be such a relationship. Looked at without knowing the reason for Mr Jones going to live there, it would appear that they were living together as husband and wife, but when the reason was known that would explain those circumstances, and once the explanation was accepted by the tribunal, as clearly it was here, and it was a matter for them, they should have come to the conclusion that in his case para 3 did not apply.

Accordingly it seems to me that this is a case where Mrs Butterworth's appeal should be allowed, and in so far as on the facts found by the tribunal, a decision has to be made in relation to para 3, it seems to me not necessary for the matter to go back before the tribunal and I can here substitute my decision for that of the tribunal.
Appeal allowed.

[On the *Crake* appeal, Woolf J said that the Tribunal had properly directed their minds to the issues, and that the decision of the Tribunal was a proper one and he would not wish to interfere with it.]
Appeal dismissed.

Questions

(i) Why should contributory benefits not be paid for increased expenditure if there is evidence of actual dependence? (After all, dependant increases are paid for wives as an entitlement – and it does not follow that wives are necessarily dependent).
(ii) Is it odd that a widow's pension can be paid to a woman who has been separated from her husband for many years before his death, yet there is no pension entitlement for a cohabitant who may have been living with him for many years?
(iii) The Finer Report (1974) justifies the cohabitation rule in the law of non-contributory benefits as follows: 'It cannot be right to treat unmarried women who have the support of a partner both as if they had no such support and better than if they were married.' Do you agree with this?
(iv) Should there be a different approach to the 'cohabitation rule' in cases of widow's benefits as opposed to income support (After all, has not her husband paid for her widow's pension with his contributions?)
(v) If you think that there should be a difference, why do you think this?

Eric Clive, in *Marriage: An Unnecessary Legal Concept* (1980), stresses the growth of individualism and its implications for tax and social security:

Indeed if the object (of social security) is the relief of need it is not immediately obvious why the old widow or the old cohabitee should be preferred to the old spinster who has never cohabited with anyone, while if the object is the payment of benefits bought by contributions it is not immediately obvious why the contributor should not be allowed to nominate the beneficiary. On either view, marriage is irrelevant. It may be objected that while a man can have only one wife he may have several cohabitees and that the state could not afford to abandon the 'one man—one woman' system. Two answers may be ventured. First, a man may already have several wives successively in a contribution career. So nothing would change in that respect. The 'one man—one woman' system has already been abandoned. Secondly, if one man has several concurrent cohabitees then the chances are that some other man has none. Unless large numbers of cohabitees are drafted in from overseas it is unlikely that the pool of dependent women would be increased by abolishing marriage. There is, in any event, something fundamentally repulsive about this whole idea of dependent women. The long-term goal in this area should be the abolition of private dependency, by encouraging independence and treating poverty as an individual rather than a family phenomenon. Even before that goal is reached, however, it does not seem necessary to preserve the legal concept of marriage for the purposes of tax and social security laws.

Questions

(i) Do you agree with this statement?
(ii) Once again, how many of those referred to in question (i) on p. 359, above, would be deprived of income support because of the cohabitation rule?
(iii) If you were asked to draft a clause to make provision for cohabitants would you define 'cohabitation': (*a*) by the reason that it was established; or (*b*) by whether there is dependence; or would you (*c*) refuse to define cohabitation until you were told what the legislation was about, and then try to define it accordingly?

An unmarried partner may qualify as a member of the family of a tenant for the purpose of transmission of the tenancy on his death. In the case of local authority housing, the Housing Act 1985, s. 87 states that a secure tenancy can devolve upon any person who was 'another member of the tenant's family and has resided with the tenant throughout the period of twelve months ending with the tenant's death'. A person is a member of another's family, inter alia, if he is the spouse of that person or if he and that person live together as husband and wife. In the private sector, the Housing Act 1988, s. 17(4) defines a tenant's spouse, who can succeed to a periodic assured tenancy, as including 'a person who was living with the tenant as his or her wife or husband.' Only *one* 'statutory succession' is now permitted in both the public and private sector.

Watson v Lucas
[1980] 3 All ER 647, [1980] 1 WLR 1493, 124 Sol Jo 513, 40 P & CR 531, Court of Appeal

The defendant married in 1953 but his wife left him after a year. There was no divorce. In 1958, the defendant went to live with a widow, some 15 years his senior, in her flat, of which she was the protected tenant. The widow died in 1977. The plaintiff brought an action to recover possession of the flat.

Stephenson LJ: The ordinary man has to consider whether a man or a woman is a member of a family in the light of the facts, and whatever may have been held before *Dyson Holdings Ltd v Fox* [1976] QB 503, [1975] 3 All ER 1030, I do not think a judge, putting himself in the place of the ordinary man, can consider an association which has every outward appearance of marriage, except the false pretence of being married, as not constituting a family. If it looks like a marriage in the old and perhaps obsolete sense of a lifelong union, with nothing casual or temporary about it, it is a family until the House of Lords declares . . . that the case of *Dyson Holdings Ltd v Fox* was wrongly decided because the reasoning of the majority was wrong. The time has gone by when the courts can hold such a union not to be 'familial' simply because the parties to it do not pretend to be married in due form of law.

(In *Dyson Holdings Ltd v Fox* [1976] QB 503, [1975] 3 All ER 1030 the court drew a distinction between the case where the relationship was stable, and where it was 'casual or intermittent.')

Helby v Rafferty
[1978] 3 All ER 1016, [1979] 1 WLR 13, 122 Sol Jo 418, 8 Fam Law 207, 37 P & CR 376, Court of Appeal

Miss Taylor was the tenant of a flat. Mr Rafferty moved into this flat and they then lived together until her death in 1977. For the last three years of her life, Miss Taylor was ill (she was an alcoholic) and Mr Rafferty looked after her. After her death, he continued to live in the flat. The landlord brought an action against him for possession. This was successful, and Mr Rafferty appealed.

Stamp LJ: The question accordingly turns on whether Mr Rafferty was at the date of Miss Taylor's death a member of Miss Taylor's family within the meaning of Sch 1, para 3.

Had the case fallen to be decided prior to *Dyson Holdings Ltd v Fox* [1976] QB 503, [1975] 1 All ER 1030, we would have been constrained to dismiss the appeal on the authority of *Gammans v Ekins* [1950] 2 KB 328, [1950] 2 All ER 140, a decision of this court which was subsequently applied by this court in *Ross v Collins* [1964] 1 All ER 861, [1964] 1 WLR 425.

The ordinary or natural meaning of the expression 'member of a family' would not, in my judgment, apply to a person in the position of Mr Rafferty. The way the matter was put in *Gammans v Ekins* by Asquith LJ who gave the first judgment in that case (a very short judgment) was this:

'The judge has not found which, and says that it makes no difference; but if their relations were platonic, I can see no principle on which it could be said that these two were members of the same family, which would not require the court to predicate the same of two old cronies of the same sex innocently sharing a flat. If, on the other hand, the relationship involves sexual relations, it seems to me anomalous that a person can acquire a 'status of irremovability' by living or having lived in sin, even if the liaison has not been a mere casual encounter but protracted in time and conclusive in character. But I would decide the case on a simpler view. To say of two people masquerading, as these two were, as husband and wife (there being no children to complicate the picture) that they were members of the same family, seems to be an abuse of the English language, and I would accordingly allow the appeal.'

I interpolate at that point to make it perfectly clear that there was no masquerading on the part of Mr Rafferty and Miss Taylor. There is no evidence that Miss Taylor ever called herself Mrs Rafferty. Jenkins LJ in that same case remarked that it would be extending the relevant section, which was then slightly different in wording, beyond all reason to hold that it applied when it was no more than a liaison between two elderly people who chose to pose as a married couple when they were not in fact.

However, the majority of the court in *Dyson Holdings Ltd v Fox* (that is to say James and Bridge LJJ), following the view expressed in *Brock v Wollams* [1949] 2 KB 388, that the word 'family' should be given its popular meaning, felt able to distinguish *Gammans v Ekins* [1947] 1 All ER 715 on the ground that during the period intervening between that decision and the relevant time in *Dyson Holdings Ltd v Fox* the popular meaning of 'family' had changed and by then comprised a situation where the two parties, man and woman, had been living together permanently and for a very long time, in that case some 40 years.

I confess that, apart from authority, I would have taken the view that the language of a statute by whatever process you apply to its construction, whether you construe it in its natural and ordinary meaning or whether you construe it in a popular way or whether you construe it in what has sometimes been called 'a legal way' (and I am not sure I understand what the difference is) cannot alter its meaning from time to time and that, in order to find out what Parliament intended by the statute, you must ascertain what the words of the statute meant when Parliament used those words. There is the further difficulty, as I see it, that the language of the relevant statutory provision has been repeated in successive Rent Acts with only a very slightly different arrangement of the words. As I rather indicated, I think, it appears to me that the difficulty of determining whether a particular meaning of the words in an Act of Parliament would be given to those words by popular vote or not would be of a different kind. Do you listen to the vociferous minority or do you imagine what the silent majority might have said at a particular time?. . . . In *Dyson Holdings Ltd v Fox*, the facts (which I take from the headnote) are these:

'The defendant lived with the tenant of a house as if she were his wife for 21 years until his death in 1961. They never married and had no children. After his death the defendant continued to live in the house for which she paid rent as if she were his widow until the plaintiffs, who owned the house, learned in 1973 that she was not in fact his widow. The plaintiffs accepted no further rent and brought proceedings for possession of the house against her as a trespasser. The defendant pleaded that at all times after the commencement of the tenancy and before the tenant's death she had resided with him as a member of his family and that she continued to occupy the house as her residence.'

As I have indicated, the Court of Appeal held that her claim was well-founded.

In the instant case the association between Mr Rafferty and Miss Taylor endured for five years and it only came to an end as a result of Miss Taylor's comparatively early death. I will refer to the facts of this case hereafter. If, however, one were to follow the dicta of Lord Denning MR in *Dyson Holdings Ltd v Fox*, it would hardly be possible to distinguish the facts of the instant case from those in *Dyson Holdings Ltd v Fox*. The only guidance to be found in the judgments of James and Bridge LJJ in *Dyson Holdings Ltd v Fox* as to the approach to be adopted when you define this kind of situation is this. First James LJ, referring to the relationship, says:

'. . . it is not restricted to blood relationships and those created by the marriage ceremony. It can include de facto as well as de jure relationships. The popular meaning of "family" in 1975 would, according to the answer of the ordinary man, include the appellant as a member of Mr Wright's family. That is not to say [and this is the important passage, I think, in his judgment] that every mistress should be so regarded. Relationships of a casual or intermittent character and those bearing indications of impermanence would not come within the popular concept of a family unit.'

It seems to me, if I may say so, to follow that in every case a judge has, in the view of James LJ, to decide whether the relationship was of such a casual or intermittent character as not to constitute the relationship required in order to satisfy the provision of the section.

Bridge LJ put the matter in a somewhat similar way. He said this:

'. . . It is, I think, not putting it too high to say that between 1950 and 1975 there has been a complete revolution in society's attitude to unmarried partnerships of the kind under consideration. Such unions are far commoner than they used to be. The social stigma that once attached to them has almost, if not entirely, disappeared. The inaccurate but expressive phrases "common law wife" and "common law husband" have come into general use to describe them. The ordinary man in 1975 would, in my opinion, certainly say that the parties to such a union [and here come, I think, the important words] provided it had the appropriate degree of apparent permanence and stability, were members of a single family whether they had children or not.'

I make the same comment on that passage as I made on the passage just quoted from the judgment of James LJ.

I conclude that *Dyson Holdings Ltd v Fox* established two propositions: first, that, notwithstanding *Gammans v Ekins*, a relationship between an unmarried man and an unmarried woman living together over a very long period can constitute the family relationship which is necessary in order to satisfy the section, and second, that on the facts in *Dyson Holdings Ltd v Fox* such a relationship was established. One has to ask: has the union such a degree of apparent permanence and stability that the ordinary man would say that the parties were, in the words of Bridge LJ, 'members of a single family'?

In my judgment, the judge in the court below, deriving such assistance as he could from

Dyson Holdings Ltd v Fox, approached the question which he had to decide quite correctly. He summarised the facts which pointed in each direction and he concluded that there was not such a permanence and stability as to justify the view that each of the parties in the instant case was a member of the family of the other. . . .

The relevant facts in the instant case are these. Mr Rafferty, as I have said, took up residence about five years before Miss Taylor's death. They lived together, sharing a bed. They shared expenses, the life of each being bound up very closely with the life of the other. They went out together. They went about together. They went to shows together. They did shopping together. They went, I think, to the cinema together. As she got more ill, as unhappily she did, Mr Rafferty did all the things for her that a loving husband might be expected to do. He nursed her as a husband would have done. If it stopped there you might conclude that the situation was just such a one as the Court of Appeal in *Dyson Holdings Ltd v Fox* held satisfied the definition. But there was another side of the picture. In the first place, there was no charade. Miss Taylor did not call herself Mrs Rafferty. Nor was any attempt made, as I understand it, to throw dust in the eyes of friends as to the true nature of the relationship. Far from passing themselves off as husband and wife, when the time came for the mother to visit the flat, the parties did put up something in the nature of a charade in pretending that they were less intimate than was in fact the case.

The Court of Appeal took the view that Mr Rafferty had not been a member of Miss Taylor's family at the time of her death.

Questions

(i) Why should pretending to the woman's mother that there was less intimacy than in fact was the case be of any relevance to the *actual* situation?
(ii) Do you think that Miss Taylor would have succeeded had Mr Rafferty been the tenant and died?
(iii) Assuming the properties in question to have been secure tenancies in each of the circumstances in question (i) on p. 359, above, would those persons have been able to succeed to the tenancy had they lived there until the partners died?

Section 1(2) of the Domestic Violence and Matrimonial Proceedings Act 1976 (see Chapter 9, below) states that the rights under that Act to prevent molestation, enforce occupation of the common home, and exclude the other from the common home 'shall apply to a man and a woman who are living with each other in the same household as husband and wife as it applies to the parties to a marriage and any reference to the matrimonial home shall be construed accordingly.'

Davis v Johnson
[1979] AC 264, [1978] 1 All ER 1132, [1978] 2 WLR 553, 122, Sol Jo 178, House of Lords

The respondent, a young unmarried mother, who had the joint tenancy of the council flat with the appellant, the father of her child, left the home with the child because of his violent behaviour to her. She applied to the county court for injunctions to restrain him from molesting her or the child and to exclude him from the home. A deputy circuit judge granted the injunctions asked for. Subsequently, a division of the Court of Appeal in *B v B* [1978] Fam 26, [1979] 1 All ER 821 construed s. 1 of the Domestic Violence and Matrimonial Proceedings Act 1976 as procedural only. Following this decision and another case in the Court of Appeal, *Canliff v Jenkins* [1978] Fam 47, [1978] 1 All ER 836, the judge in the county court in this case rescinded that part of the order of the deputy judge which excluded the appellant from the home: he went back to the flat; and the respondent and the child returned to an overcrowded home for battered wives.

On the respondent's appeal, the Court of Appeal (of five judges) by a majority declined to follow the earlier decisions and allowed the appeal. On the appellant's appeal, four of the five judges dismissed the appeal and construed s. 1(1)(c) and 1(2) of the Act as enabling a woman with no property or tenancy rights in the home to apply to the court to obtain an injunction to exclude her partner from the property for a limited period.

Lord Scarman: The availability of paragraphs (c) and (d)) of subsection (1) to unmarried partners without any express restriction to those who have a property right in the house has an important bearing on the answer to the question which I consider to be crucial to a correct understanding of the scope of the section; i.e., what is the mischief for which Parliament has provided the remedies specified in subsection (1)? It suggests strongly that the remedies are intended to protect people, not property: for it is highly unlikely that Parliament could have intended by the sidewind of subsection (2) to have introduced radical changes into the law of property. Nor is it necessary so to construe the section. The personal rights of an unmarried woman living with a man in the same household are very real. She has his licence to be in the home, a right which in appropriate cases the courts can and will protect: She has also her fundamental right to the integrity and safety of her person. And the children living in the same household enjoy the same rights.

Bearing in mind the existence of these rights and the extent to which they are endangered in the event of family breakdown, I conclude that the mischief against which Parliament has legislated by section 1 of the Act may be described in these terms: — conduct by a family partner which puts at risk the security, or sense of security, of the other partner in the home. Physical violence, or the threat of it, is clearly within the mischief. But there is more to it than that. Homelessness can be as great a threat as physical violence to the security of a woman (or man) and her children. Eviction — actual, attempted or threatened — is, therefore, within the mischief: likewise, conduct which makes it impossible or intolerable, as in the present case, for the other partner, or the children, to remain at home. . . .

I find nothing illogical or surprising in Parliament legislating to over-ride a property right, if it be thought to be socially necessary. If in the result a partner with no property right who obtains an injunction under paragraph (c) or (d)) thereby obtains for the period of the injunction a right of occupation, so be it. It is no more than the continuance by court order of a right which previously she had by consent: and it will endure only for so long as the county court thinks necessary. . . .

Section 1 of the Act is concerned to protect not property but human life and limb. But, while the section is not intended to confer, and does not confer upon an unmarried woman property rights in the home, it does enable the county court to suspend or restrict her family partner's property right to possession and to preserve to her a right of occupancy (which owes its origin to her being in the home as his consort and with his consent) for as long as may be thought by the court to be necessary to secure the protection of herself and the children.

How, then does the section fit into the law? First, the purpose of the section is not to create rights but to strengthen remedies. Subsection (2) does, however, confer upon the unmarried woman with no property in the home a new right. Though enjoying no property right to possession of the family home, she can apply to the county court for an order restricting or suspending for a time her family partner's right to possession of the premises and conferring upon her a limited right of occupancy. In most cases the period of suspension or restriction of his right and of her occupancy will prove, I expect, to be brief. But in some cases this period may be a lengthy one. The continuance of the order will, however, be a matter for the discretion of the county court judge to be decided in the light of the circumstances of the particular case.

Secondly, the section is concerned to regulate relations between the two family partners. It does not, for instance, prevent the property owner from disposing of his property. . . .

Thirdly, and most importantly, the grant of the order is in the discretion of the county court judge. It is for him to decide whether, and for how long, it is necessary for the protection of the applicant or her child. The remedy is available to deal with an emergency; it is, . . . a species of first aid.

Appeal dismissed.

Davis v Johnson [1979] AC 264 was considered in the following case:

O'Neill v Williams
[1986] FLR 1, Court of Appeal

In 1979 the applicant and the respondent, who were not married, began to live together as husband and wife. At first they lived at the home of the applicant's parents. In March 1981 they moved into a flat as joint tenants. Their relationship deteriorated in 1982. In July of that year the applicant went away on holiday. On her return she was unable to get into the flat as the respondent had changed the locks. Soon after, the respondent went away on holiday and the applicant gained entry and returned to the flat. On his return at the end of August 1982 the respondent seriously assaulted the applicant causing a laceration to her lip and severe bruising. As a result she left and went to stay with her parents. In October 1982 she consulted solicitors but they were unable to act as an emergency legal aid certificate was refused. She obtained legal aid in February 1983 and on 1 March 1983 made her originating application under s. 1 of the Domestic Violence and Matrimonial Proceedings Act 1976 that the respondent be excluded and restrained from returning to the property, and that he be restrained from assaulting, molesting or otherwise interfering with her.

On appeal from the dismissal of the application by the county court judge for want of jurisdiction:

Cumming-Bruce LJ: The draftsman's words describe a man and woman who are living with each other in the same household and it is with the construction and effect of the present tense in the verb in that subsection that this appeal is concerned.

As the judge stated in his judgment, the court has to give a liberal construction to the words 'living with' as had been pointed out in previous authority. On the facts disclosed in the applicant's affidavit, the effective separation of the parties was on 27 or 28 August 1982 when she went back to live with her parents. The judge held that, having regard to the words of the section, he was not able to hold that a delay of 6 months between the date of the violence alleged, which is alleged to have brought about the determination of cohabitation, was such that after that delay the parties could possibly be said to be living together and the judge held that in such circumstances he had no jurisdiction.

. . . In *McLean v Nugent* (1980) 1 FLR 26, Ormrod LJ examined the draftsman's phrase in subs. (2), . . . and concluded that the Parliamentary intention was to grant jurisdiction to an applicant who was living with the respondent in the same household as husband and wife at the time when the violence complained of took place even though, as a result, the applicant had been forced temporarily to terminate cohabitation. In the course of that judgement, Ormrod LJ expressed himself at p. 31v as follows:

'The fact that she is also complaining of subsequent acts of violence after the relationship had come completely to an end is not particularly important except in this respect. The subsequent incidents throw a good deal of light on the nature of the earlier incidents before they separated and of course the subsequent incidents will indicate whether the court ought to interfere for her protection. It might have been a different story if there had been no violence whatever between them until after the parting and, of course, the longer the time that elapses between the cessation of their relationship and the summons, the more difficult it will be for an applicant to bring herself within the section.'

I have some doubt whether in that passage Ormrod LJ, when he referred to the effective passage of time, addressing his mind expressly to the question of jurisdiction as compared to the question as to whether, when there has been a long lapse of time since the determination of cohabitation, it was appropriate in the exercise of discretion for the court to grant the relief claimed.

In the case of *McLean v Burke* (1982) 3 FLR 70 in this court, the President presiding, it is quite clearly accepted that the test, for the purposes of jurisdiction, was whether, at the date of the violence complained of, the applicant and the respondent were at that time fulfilling the condition described in s. 1(2).

I derive from those judgments guidance that, though the precise situation considered in the instant appeal did not arise for decision, the approach of the courts hitherto has consistently been to regard the relevant test of the application of subs.(2) to inquire whether it was proved that at the date of the violence complained of the parties were then fulfilling the condition of living together in one household as husband and wife.

The judge took a different view. He had observed that in the authorities from 1978 onwards the courts had abandoned a literal construction of subs.(2) and had substituted a liberal construction for the purpose of enabling the remedy not to be frustrated and, considering the lapse of time in the history before him on the applicant's affidavit, he came to the conclusion that it was altogether too unreal to hold that in March 1983 the applicant and the respondent could, in any realistic sense, still be said to be within the contemplation of s. 1(2).

With respect to the judge, I readily appreciate the strong common sense of his approach; the more so when the speeches of their Lordships in the House of Lords in *Davis v Johnson* are considered. It emerges quite plainly from those speeches that the purpose of s. 1 was to provide not a long-term remedy for parties at odds about cohabitation but to afford, in appropriate circumstances, short-term relief so that the aggrieved party might continue to live at home while the two parties set about obtaining a solution in the long term of their practical difficulties arising from the attempt to share premises. In his speech Lord Salmon suggested that a period of a month might well be the appropriate period for an initial order in the county court followed, if necessary, by a further extension of another month or more but with a view to affording short-term relief within the kind of limit of 6 months, which ought to be enough to enable the parties, either by negotiation or recourse to the courts, to determine their rights at common law or under other statutes such as the Law of Property Act 1925. Having regard to that clear declaration in their Lordship's House, that this Act was concerned with providing short-term relief in an emergency where a party alleges that he or she is being excluded from the quasi-matrimonial home by virtue of the violence of the other party, it is easy to see that there were good grounds for reluctance on the part of the judge to be persuaded that he still had jurisdiction upon an originating application dated 1 March 1983 claiming an ouster or non-molestation injunction in respect of violence alleged to have brought about determination of cohabitation at the end of August 1982. At first sight such an application is inconsistent with the grant of a short-term remedy which this Act was designed to provide. But the submission on behalf of the appellant is that there are good reasons for holding that the judge was wrong, having regard to the clear indication in earlier authority that the test is: Did the violence take place at the date when the parties were then within the meaning of s. 1(2)?

. . .

It is submitted on behalf of the appellant that there were three periods accounting for the delay. The lady was always wanting to return home, meaning thereby the flat where she had lived as a joint tenant with a legal interest for a year, where she kept her clothes and belongings. In the first period she had desisted from legal action deliberately because she thought that negotiation would get her back into the flat. When that failed, as she could not afford to institute proceedings unaided, her solicitors applied for an emergency certificate. If that application had been successful the application might well have come before the court very soon after the end of October. But it did not succeed — not, it is submitted, by reason of any action or inaction on the applicant's part but because the legal aid authorities were not satisfied with the state of emergency although, it is submitted, at all times she was eager to return to the flat provided she could get the respondent out. And the third period of delay is likewise explained by the inevitable delay in processing the legal aid certificate. There was a fourth period of delay because, as I have observed, a month elapsed from the grant of a certificate to the filing of the originating application. That is explained, no doubt, as due to the time needed by the applicant's solicitor to proceed on the application with proper care. So, it is submitted, though the whole period appears to be quite inconsistent with an application under 1976 Act and with exclusion through violence at the end of August, there were good reasons, and it should not be a matter, as a test of jurisdiction, as to whether as a question of fact and degree the particular circumstances of any given applicant are to be regarded as justifying delay as compared to excusing it. One can think of hypothetical circumstances which would support that submission. The applicant might not have been as lucky as she was in only sustaining a cut on her lip and some bruises; she might have broken her leg, as at one time she thought she had. She might have been subjected to such injuries that she was in hospital for months, but on emerging she might have been eager to get home at once, turning the respondent out or, alternatively, getting a non-molestation injunction. How could it be right in such a situation to say that the mere fact that she lay in hospital for 3 or 4 months, deprived the court of jurisdiction?

Another hypothetical case which would support the appellant's submission is the case where the appellant is a woman with one or more dependent children of very tender age. It is not difficult to conceive of circumstances in which, having been excluded by violence from the home, such an applicant might be precluded by the sheer necessities of her situation — trying to find temporary accommodation for the children and to obtain means of support for herself and the children — such that, in any real sense, many weeks might pass before it was feasible for her to make an application to the court under the 1976 Act. If jurisdiction is to depend on an investigation of the individual facts and circumstances, hardships and difficulties, facing the victims of violence and individual cases, it would, in my view, be a very inconvenient, and probably impractical, method for testing the jurisdiction, and I would be reluctant to hold that it was the intention of Parliament that the jurisdiction to invoke this emergency relief should depend on an accurate assessment of questions of fact and degree in order to explain the circumstances excusing, if it could be excused, the interval between the ouster and the date of the originating summons.

. . .

For those reasons I would hold that the test hitherto propounded by the court is to be regarded as the correct test of jurisdiction. If at the date of the alleged exclusion by violence, alleged to have been committed by the respondent, the applicant and the respondent were then living with each other in the same household as husband and wife, I would hold that the condition precedent of jurisdiction is established and that there is no other condition which has to be satisfied before the court has jurisdiction. For that reason I would hold that the judge was wrong in dismissing the application on the grounds of want of jurisdiction.

. . .

In the ordinary way the case would be sent back to the judge to continue the hearing in order to decide whether or not to grant discretionary relief. I am satisfied that that course would be wrong because it would be unnecessary and pointless. On consideration of the facts alleged in the affidavits of the applicant and considering those facts as uncontested facts for this purpose, in spite of the fact that many of the relevant facts have been placed in issue by the affidavit of the respondent, on the facts alleged by the applicant was it a case in which it could have been right for the judge to grant either of the remedies sought in the application as a matter of discretion?

. . . I bear in mind the words of Ormrod LJ in *McLean v Nugent*, that the longer the time that elapses between cessation of the relationship and the summons, the more difficult it will be for the applicant to bring herself within the section.

I would apply that approach in this way, that the longer the time elapses the less and less likely it will become that any judge would, or could, find it right to grant the remedy or any of the remedies afforded by the 1976 Act, because that is an Act which deals with short-term relief, not with long-term solution of conflicts in matters of property.

Appeal dismissed.

Questions

(i) In *F v F (protection from violence: continuing cohabitation)* [1989] 2 FLR 451 in the York County Court, Judge Fricker refused to grant a non-molestation order to a woman (admittedly married) where the parties were still cohabiting and the woman required an injunction to inhibit her husband from using violence against her and molesting her when he was drunk, also to protect their child from seeing and hearing distressing attacks upon her.

You have a client who tells you that her cohabitant is so drunk that when he attempts to punch her he misses. She is living in a climate of considerable tension but it is better than going on the streets. Do you advise her (*a*) to make sure he hits her and then apply for an exclusion and non-molestation order (*b*) decide once and for all that the relationship is over, leave him and apply to the court for an exclusion order, or (*c*) neither of these suggestions. If so, what do you advise.

(ii) What can an unmarried woman do when the man, with whom she has been living and who has been ousted by an order under s. 1 of the Domestic Violence and Matrimonial Proceedings Act 1976, stops paying the rent and purports to surrender his sole protected or secure tenancy to the landlord?

(iii) Would the following women, whose circumstances are described in the cases quoted earlier in this chapter, have protection under the Domestic Violence and Matrimonial Proceedings Act 1976: (*a*) Janet Eves; (*b*) the defendant in *Pascoe v Turner*; (*c*) Maria Bernard *after* she had left; (*d*) Mrs Tanner; (*e*) Mrs Coombes?

CHAPTER 9

Dangerous families

Home is generally regarded as a place of safety but in this chapter we begin to examine some of the dangers which can face both adults and children within it. We shall look first at the different kinds of abuse, ill-treatment and neglect which can be suffered by adults (usually women) and children, and then at some of the research into explanations, before turning to the remedies in criminal and civil law. We shall deal only with the private law remedies available to protect adult and child victims in this chapter. The remedies available to local social services authorities, the NSPCC and others in public law for the protection of children will be dealt with in Chapter 13, after we have looked generally at the legal relationship between parents, children and the state.

1 What are the dangers?

'I burned him later with the iron; I did it deliberately. I'd look at him, and think, oh you little bastard, you know? I just got hold of him and burned him on the back of the hand. I was so fed up! He'd been grizzling; he was tired out in the daytime because he didn't sleep at night. And of course *I* was tired too, and he wouldn't stop grizzling. I was ironing on the floor in the lounge because it was just something quick I wanted — I was kneeling down and he was sitting over by the window. I just got hold of his hand and I said, *that'll* make you sleep! It was all done in such a quick second, you know, that I didn't . . . it wasn't sort of premeditated; I just looked at him, had the iron in my hand, and did it.'

'I have had ten stitches, three stitches, five stitches, seven stitches, where he has cut me. . . .' 'I have had a knife stuck through my stomach; I have had a poker put through my face; I have no teeth where he knocked them all out; I have been burnt with red hot pokers; I have had red hot coals slung all over me; I have been sprayed with petrol and stood there while he has flicked lighted matches at me. . . .' These assaults did not just take place when he was drunk, but 'at any time; early in the morning; late at night; in the middle of the night he would drag me out of bed and start hitting me, he would do it in front of the children. He never bothered if the children were there. . . .' 'I have been to the police. I nicked my husband. He gave me ten stitches, and they held him in the nick over the weekend and he came out on Monday. He was bound over to keep the peace, that was all. On the Tuesday he gave me the hiding of my life'.

Samantha's mother died when she was very young and her father brought up her younger brother and herself singlehanded. He began to abuse her when she was 4. When she was little he covered her head and top half with a blanket and interfered with her vagina. By the age of 10 it was regular sexual intercourse and thereafter it included buggery and oral intercourse. 'He made me say that I enjoyed it, that I wanted it. He wouldn't like any disagreement.' As she got older she began to realise that this did not happen to other girls. She said that: — 'it got to the stage that if I wanted a favour, to go out with a friend, or buy a new pair of shoes, I had to let him do it first.'

She had no-one to confide in, no-one to turn to: — 'I thought any adult would not believe me — they would think I was making up a story. . . . I didn't know what might happen. For my brother's sake I didn't want my family split up. . . . I loved my father so much. I respected him as a father. But I was confused, didn't understand. I wanted it to stop. I hated that part of it so much.'

So said, respectively, the mother who told her story to Jean Renvoize for her investigation into *Children in Danger* (1974) and Mrs X who gave evidence to the House of Commons Select Committee on *Violence in Marriage* (1975) and 'Samantha' whose history is told in the Report of the *Inquiry into Child Abuse in Cleveland 1987 (1988)*. An even more chilling illustration of the multifarious problems involved is provided in the dispassionate account in the *Report of the Committee of Inquiry into the Provision and Co-ordination of Services to the Family of John George Auckland* (1975):

45. On 13 November 1965 Mr John Auckland married Miss Barbara Marsden, a local girl then 18 years old, whom he had been courting for some four months. His parents, Mr and Mrs George Auckland, were opposed to the marriage, partly on the grounds that it was taking place in such a rush, and Miss Marsden herself sought and obtained an assurance from Mr John Auckland that the reason for his wanting to marry her did not stem from [an] argument that he had had with his parents. After the marriage, Mr John Auckland and his wife moved into a small terraced house of their own at 11 Churchfield Avenue, Cudworth.
46. It soon became apparent that Mrs Barbara Auckland had no previous training whatsoever in domestic duties, and was incompetent at managing household finance. As she told us herself, she could not even peel potatoes. By 17 January 1966 things had reached such a pitch that both Mr and Mrs John Auckland sought the advice of Mr Tindall, the probation officer to whom Mr John Auckland was reporting, both agreeing that Mrs Barbara Auckland, who was working full-time, needed help and guidance with household management and cooking. Mr Tindall found Mrs Barbara Auckland to be at that time immature and not very capable, but willing to learn. He felt that, given time, she would develop more confidence in her own abilities and, to help with this process, he asked Mrs Mary Auckland to give her daughter-in-law some assistance. There is some evidence that Mrs Barbara Auckland was already being subjected to violence by her husband.
47. By February 1966 the marital situation seemed to be improving but it soon relapsed. Mrs Barbara Auckland left her husband at the beginning of March, and Mr John Auckland had medical treatment, which he claims was for nervous upset occasioned by his wife's slovenly habits. The separation was not long-lasting but it set a pattern for the future. It is some evidence of Mrs Barbara Auckland's state of mind at this time that she was admitted to hospital in April 1966 having swallowed a quantity of a rubbing ointment in what appears to have been a suicidal gesture. . . .
. . .
49. Mrs Barbara Auckland became pregnant for the first time in 1967. Her husband welcomed this, as he had been anxious for some time to have a family. The baby girl, Marianne, was born on 9 April 1968. She was not premature but weighed only 4 1b 13 oz. . . .
. . .
54. The events of the night when Marianne died are recounted in a statement which Mr John Auckland made to the police seven hours after the event. In this statement he says that on the previous day he had ceased taking the 13 tablets prescribed for him by Dr Murray Park because he felt they were making him unwell. Instead he went out for some beer, and returned home at 9.30 p.m. with a headache, played cards for a while with his wife, ate some ham sandwiches, and drank some tea. The baby started crying upstairs, Mr John Auckland went up to quieten her, and then in his own words, 'this thing came over me like some evil, and I started banging her. Wife came upstairs and she tried to stop me, and I hit her as well'.

Before his trial for Marianne's murder, John Auckland was examined by several doctors:

57. . . . Dr Quinn's diagnosis is worth quoting for it reveals a pattern of behaviour on Mr John Auckland's part which we now know was to recur: '. . . I have formed the opinion that he (John Auckland) is an emotionally unstable individual, prone to alterations of mood. In the face of difficulties which he cannot readily reject or resolve, depression of mood reaches pathological intensity and renders him temporarily unable to evaluate and deal with his problems in a

controlled and rational manner. The combination of constitutional factors and environmental pressures led over a number of months to the development of a depressive illness.'

58. At his trial at Leeds Assizes on 14–17 October 1968 Mr John Auckland was found guilty of manslaughter, by reason of diminished responsibility, and was sentenced to 18 months' imprisonment. After the verdict had been given, and before sentence was passed, Dr Orr was recalled by the Judge, Mr Justice Bridge, to give his prognosis and he then said that Mr John Auckland had all but recovered from his depressive illness and remained a person of average intelligence but of weak character. On being asked if there was a danger that if he were released in the near future he would commit a further offence Dr Orr replied that in his view the possibility was very remote indeed.

When John Auckland was released from prison, he was reunited with his wife. They moved from Cudworth to Shafton and had two more children, John Roy (born on 6 January 1971) and Mandy (born 17 March 1972). Then:

164. On 25 March 1973 Susan Auckland was born prematurely at Barnsley District General Hospital. Mrs Barbara Auckland was discharged home after 24 hours but the baby, only weighing 4 lb 1 oz, had to remain in the Special Care Baby Unit until 20 April. . . .
. . .

181. On Wednesday 27 March 1974, following an argument between herself and her husband, Mrs Barbara Auckland packed a few possessions into a carrier bag, put the baby Susan into a pram, and pushed the pram several miles to the home of her aunt, Mrs Doreen Nunn, who lived at Kendray. She arrived at Kendray about 11.40 p.m., and slept that night on the sofa. The next morning at about 9.00 or 10.00 a.m. Mrs Nunn telephoned Mr Martin Nurcombe, a social worker employed by the County Borough of Barnsley, to ask if the social services could help to find accommodation for Mrs Barbara Auckland and the child as she did not have room for them. Mr Nurcombe went to Mrs Nunn's home where he saw Mrs Barbara Auckland who said that she had left home and pushed the pram to Kendray because of her husband's cruelty to her, and because of the constant insinuations by his family that she was incapable of running a home. Mrs Barbara Auckland also told Mr Nurcombe that her husband was drinking heavily and beating her. She also told him that the family had been receiving help from Mr Jones of the Barnsley Division of the West Riding County Council Social Services Department, so Mr Nurcombe promised to contact Mr Jones and ask him to call and see her.
182. Meanwhile Mr John Auckland had informed the police of his wife's departure with Susan, and they had notified Mr Jones, who went to visit Mr John Auckland at his parents' home. Mr John Auckland had with him the two other children and he seems to have set out to prove himself to be the innocent husband and father who had been wronged by the deserting wife. . . .
183. On the same day, 28 March 1974, Mr Nurcombe tried unsuccessfully to contact Mr Jones to tell him where to find Mrs Barbara Auckland and Susan, but he was able to make contact early the following morning, and Mr Jones went straight to Mrs Nunn's home, where he arrived at about 9.30 a.m. Unfortunately, Mr Nurcombe did not tell Mr Jones that Mrs Barbara Auckland had complained to him of being ill treated, but when he arrived at the house Mr Jones found her very distressed and complaining that her husband and his family 'picked on her'. She made some complaint of being maltreated and said at one point 'I have told you lies before, I have not told you what it is like', but Mr Jones did not invite her to explain further because he was mainly concerned with her intentions in relation to Susan. Mrs Barbara Auckland was proposing to go to her parents in London, whom she had not seen for seven years, and who lived in a school caretaker's flat where children were not allowed, so Mr Jones regarded her proposal to take Susan with her as misconceived. Furthermore, Susan was suffering from a bad 'nappy rash', of which Mrs Nunn rightly told Mr Jones, and which he later was able to observe for himself. Mr Jones persuaded Mrs Barbara Auckland to allow him to take Susan to her husband and other children who were at Mr and Mrs George Auckland's, and he summoned Mrs Angela Baines, a social work assistant, to act as escort for the journey. As they left Mrs Barbara Auckland, Mr Jones recalls her saying of the children, with an air of resignation, 'I suppose he will have them,' and she asked Mr Jones not to tell Mr John Auckland where she was, which, as Mr Jones appreciated, indicated that she was afraid of her husband. . . .
. . .
185. The two other children at Cudworth, John Roy and Mandy, were pleased to see their baby sister, and Mrs Mary Auckland was willing to accept responsibility for her so Mr Jones and Mrs Baines left her there. It does not seem to have occurred to either of them to go back to Mrs Barbara Auckland to tell her how Susan had been received, or to hear anything more she might want to say to them. . . .
. . .

194. On 5 April 1974 Mr Jones visited the Auckland children at their grandmother's and recorded that Mr John Auckland was 'still unsure of his future. He presumes that he will have a divorce but is presently looking for a "housekeeper". Prospects in this field seem poor. Mrs Auckland (senior) would like to go away for a fortnight. She asked if we could take Susan for a while'.

195. In response to Mrs Mary Auckland's request to be relieved of Susan for a time Mr Jones consulted Mr Carlson [the area officer] who agreed that she should be received temporarily into care, and placed in a foster home. The child was to go into care on 11 April 1974, and for that purpose certain forms had to be completed by Mr Jones which he signed on that day. The first form was a personal case record of the child (form CHN2) in which he entered as the reason for reception into care 'No suitable home — for a month'. Later in the form Mr Jones wrote:

'Mr Auckland is content to leave his children in the care of his mother. Indeed he has little choice at present. Mrs Auckland, Grandmother, is a capable woman, happy to look after the children, who are themselves happiest in their own company . . . Susan will be able to return to her Grandmother when the latter returns from her holiday. Her future then lies, at least in the near future, with her Grandmother, until Mr Auckland can sort out his home'. (our underlining)

The committee underlined those last words because they were typed on a different machine and the committee thought that they had been added later. The Report does not accept that the social workers had ever contemplated that when Susan was discharged from care she might go, not to her grandmother in Cudworth, but to her father, and her brother and sister, in Shafton. Another reason for the committee's view was the following:

206. On 30 April 1974 Mr Jones received a letter from Mrs Barbara Auckland the material part of which read:

'Would you please be good enough to let me know how my three children are going on?' The letter gave Mr Jones Mrs Barbara Auckland's London address, but he was asked to keep it to himself. . . . [And] on 1 May he replied to Mrs Barbara Auckland as follows:

'. . . your three children, staying with their Grandmother, are well. Susan has been staying for a month with a foster mother while Mrs Auckland has been on holiday.' . . .

. . .

214. [John Auckland] appeared at the social services department on Monday 6 May 1974, where he was seen by Mrs Baines. According to the note made by Mrs Baines, he claimed to have cleaned and decorated the home at Shafton, and to be having John Roy and Mandy back to live with him there on Wednesday or Thursday. He said that he would very much like Susan to join them. . . .

215. [Mrs Baines'] note reads:

'Advised him (John Auckland) Mr Jones was now on holiday but I would look into it sometime this week. Explained I would visit his mother to make sure adequate arrangements for care of children had been made. He was agreeable to this, he was also most anxious for me to visit his home in Shafton to see decorating he had done.'. . .

. . .

217. Then on Friday 10 May 1974 Mrs Baines visited Mrs Mary Auckland, and obtained confirmation that she and her daughters were prepared to give 'all the help and support that was required.' John Roy and Mandy had returned to Shafton on the preceding day, so Mrs Baines went on to Shafton, where she found the family just finishing lunch and Mr John Auckland showing justifiable pride in his housekeeping. All seemed well, so Mrs Baines decided to return Susan that day. . . .

. . .

224. Mr Jones very soon learnt of Susan's return to her father, because she was returned on Friday 10 May 1974 and he was told what had happened on his return to work on the following Monday. On Tuesday 14 May 1974 he visited the family at Shafton. . . . [His note] reads:

'Visited Mr Auckland, who is now looking after all three children. He is coping well and receiving considerable support from his mother. Children all healthy — no apparent serious problems.'

. . .

226. . . . It goes on —

'Mrs Auckland has contacted me once by 'phone to enquire after the children's health. She has told me that she is taking legal advice towards a divorce.'

The wording does not suggest that the note was made on the same day as the telephone call, but Mr Jones told us that he did receive the telephone call on 14 May 1974, and that he told

Mrs Barbara Auckland then of the return of the children to their father. Her attitude he said was one of resignation, reflecting her comment [in paragraph 183 earlier] when he had taken Susan from the house of Mrs Nunn. . . .

. . .

238. As to Mrs Barbara Auckland's activities during this period, on 25 June 1974, she telephoned Mr Jones to ask whether she could have her children to stay with her for a short period and he explained that this was impracticable but that arrangements could be made for her to see them if she came to Barnsley. Also on that day, she called to see Mr Douglas Drane, a social worker on duty in the Hounslow area of London. The following day, Mr Drane dictated a report of the visit which says that Mrs Barbara Auckland called for advice about housing so that she could have her three children in London with her. She recounted something of her history to Mr Drane, ...

. . .

241. On the night of 10 July 1974, Mr John Auckland left his three children in the care of Mr Michael Beaumont, his brother-in-law, and a neighbour, and went out for a drink, returning shortly after 10.00 p.m. Early the following morning he viciously assaulted his baby daughter so causing her death; the pathologist, Dr Alan Usher, on examining her body, found over a hundred marks of violence of different ages, the vast majority being soft tissue bruises which had been inflicted in the last ten to fourteen days of her life, many within the last thirty-six hours. To quote from his report —
> 'the injuries in this case though they fall short of the degree of violence required to break bones are far too numerous to be accounted for by a domestic accident or even a series of domestic accidents and I am in no doubt this child has been grossly physically abused by an adult.'

242. Mr John Auckland was subsequently charged with murder, tried at Sheffield Crown Court between 26–29 November 1974, and found guilty of manslaughter. He was sentenced to five years imprisonment which he is still serving. A charge that he had wilfully ill-treated his other daughter Mandy was not proceeded with, although there were three obvious marks of violence on her head and face at the time of Susan's death. Mr Jones failed to notice those marks when he went to the home after the killing, and he recorded that the surviving children were 'well'.

243. After the death of Susan, John Roy and Mandy were received into care and placed with foster-parents. Mrs Barbara Auckland subsequently took charge again of her two remaining children, and returned to live in Shafton; she was closely supervised by the social services and other agencies and to facilitate this, Barnsley Metropolitan Borough Council applied for a supervision order early in 1975, but were instead granted a care order which, even though the children remain with their mother, enables the local authority to remove them immediately should this prove necessary. Miss Ebo is currently supervising the family on behalf of the social services and we understand that the children are in good health and happy. Mrs Barbara Auckland is apparently coping well.

But violence and neglect are only part of the story, as the *Cleveland Report* (1988) makes plain:

1. Child abuse, the non-accidental injury of a child, received increasing attention in this country in the 1960s, and followed upon its recognition in the United States. . . . A parallel can be drawn between the reluctance to recognise physical abuse in the United Kingdom in the 1960s and the reluctance by many to accept the reality of certain aspects of child sexual abuse in the 1980s.

2. Child abuse has many forms; the concerns may centre upon physical abuse, sexual and emotional abuse, or upon neglect. Dr Cameron in discussing the 3 categories of active child abuse: — physical, emotional, and sexual abuse, pointed out that, while it was helpful to the diagnostician to have distinct forms of child abuse in mind, not infrequently, in practice, a child is subject to more than one form of abuse. It is obviously important to recognise that the categories of the abuse are not closed. Experts gave us figures indicating that as much as 30% of children referred because of other forms of abuse may also show medical evidence of sexual abuse.

Definitions of Child Sexual Abuse

4. The definition of child sexual abuse by Schechter and Roberge is widely quoted: —
> 'Sexual abuse is defined as the involvement of dependent, developmentally immature children and adolescents in sexual activities that they do not fully comprehend and to which they are unable to give informed concent or that violate the social taboos of family roles.'

In other words it is the use of children by adults for sexual gratification. Dr Cameron described it as inappropriate behaviour which involved: — 'the child being exploited by the adult either for direct physical gratification of sexual needs or for vicarious gratification'.

5. Child sexual abuse may take place within the family circle or outside, for example, by a neigbour or a complete stranger. According to Dr Paul (1986) abuse within the family is the most common form. The type of sexual abuse, its degree of seriousness, the age of the child and whether it is within the family all affect not only the presentation but also the response to it by the community and the action required of the professionals charged with the duty of protecting the abused child. It is essential in any consideration of child sexual abuse to be clear at all times as to the definition and description being used.

. . .

The Children
12. The Inquiry was provided with evidence about Cleveland children primarily in respect of allegations of the most serious offences of incest, unlawful sexual intercourse and buggery of girls and buggery of boys and indecent assault almost all within the family, including digital penetration, fondling, mutual masturbation, anal and oral/genital contact. From the evidence presented to the Inquiry a majority of children sexually abused in the U.K. are girls but there are significant numbers of boys. . . .
13. The abuse may be one incident, occasional, a gradual but escalating level of abuse; or it may be frequent and regular. For some children it may become a way of life and only in adolescence do they realise they have not enjoyed a 'normal' family life. At the time it may not necessarily be experienced as distasteful by the child and it is only later that the child realises it is what it is. On the other hand it may be coercive and frightening from the beginning.
14. Some children appear to be specially vulnerable, for example those with physical or mental handicaps, others treated as scapegoats, or those who are particularly immature. It may occur where the older child has a parenting role. Alcohol, drugs, absence of the other parent from home; a single parent with succession of male partners, violence, marital or sexual difficulties may be factors. Other factors suggested include chaotic or inadequate families, or the sub-normality of a parent.
15. The children caught up in the crisis in Cleveland ranged in age from under a year to adolescence. It would be impossible to say how many sexually abused children in Cleveland were boys. But there were some boys sexually abused during the period and significant proportions in respect of whom allegations were made.
16. There were some unusual complaints, for example: one little girl of 7 complained that her father and girl friend squirted tea in a syringe up 'her front'; one little boy of 4 spoke of an iron bar being pushed up his bottom; one boy said he had a toilet roll pushed up as a punishment. In several instances children who were later found to have been abused at home engaged in sexualised behaviour towards each other or with other children at school.

Pressure to Keep the Secret
17. Many children who have been subject to sexual abuse are put under pressure from the perpetrator not to tell; there may be threats of violence to the child or that the perpetrator will commit suicide, of being taken away from home and put into care, threats that someone they love will be angry with them, or that no-one would believe them. Children may elect not to talk because of a genuine affection for the perpetrator and an awareness of the consequences to the perpetrator, to the partner, to the family unit, or for an older child an understanding of the economic considerations in the break-up of the family and the loss of the wage earner. The secretive element persists. Professor Sir Martin Roth in evidence said: — 'There is a powerful disincentive to disclosing the fact that one has been subject to sexual abuse. The person who discloses this has fears that he may be regarded as having permitted himself, as having collaborated in it, as having been lastingly damaged in a sexual way. He is likely to fear ridicule, humiliation, obloquy and so on'.
18. This pressure upon the child not to tell and the desire of all to keep the secret is also apparent in the pressure brought upon children to retract once they have made a complaint. The pressure comes from the family, mother, siblings and the extended family as well as the abuser. The withdrawal of the complaint is a common situation with child complainants and presents particular difficulties for the police.
19. In Cleveland we heard of examples of pressure on children. A girl of 12 told the Official Solicitor that her step-father said no-one would believe her. A girl of 8 expressed relief at the death of her father who committed suicide after she revealed the abuse. One little girl of 5 told the police that her father had sexually abused her. According to a letter from her mother she explained why she had not told before: — 'It was because my daddy told me I would lose my voice if I told anyone'. The mother wrote: — 'These are the things she has told me: — she was told, somebody will come and take her away, people would hit her for telling lies, Mammy will cry if you tell her'.

The Children may become 'Double Victims'
20. Those who fear a child has been sexually abused naturally wish to protect the child from further assaults; to stop the abuser having the opportunity to abuse again. The ideal would be to protect the child within his or her home and neighbourhood, preferably after identifying and excluding the abuser. However, if, as is often the case, the perpetrator is unknown, or is suspected but denies the abuse, how can the child be protected? In practice, it is the child who is taken away from home, friends and school and it is the child who is placed in hospital, in a childrens' home or in a foster home, in strange surroundings and among strangers.
21. The plight of the 'double victim' is well illustrated by what happened to one of the children in Cleveland. The girl told the police that she had been sexually abused by her father. She said that the threat from the perpetrator was that she would be taken away from home and placed in care if she told anyone what was going on. As it happened the effect of the complaint was a place of safety order and she was removed from home, and suffered twice over. That child retracted her story.

Relationships within the Family
28. The mother, we are told, is by no means certain to be the protector of the child. Some may have themselves been abused as children. Some may be afraid of the man, inadequate personalities ill-equipped to give the child protection, or even prefer him to pay attention to the child rather than to themselves. Some mothers can not or will not believe it to be possible. There is a very acute dilemma for a mother in the conflict between her man and her child, in which the relationship with the man, the economic and other support which she received from him may disincline her to accept the truth of the allegation. Some mothers choose sexual offenders as partners more than once.
   Again quoting Professor Sir Martin Roth: – 'In many cases mothers play a role in the genesis of the sexual abuse of their daughters. They may be too physically ill or inadequate in personality to provide proper care and protection for their children. In other cases mothers elect the eldest or one of the oldest daughters to the role of 'child mother'. The girl in her early teens or even earlier is expected to take the responsibility for the caring of younger children whose mothering role is allowed to slide into a sexual relationship with the father. This is tolerated with little or no protest. I refer to lack of protest on the part of the mother for a variety of reasons and the mother may in such cases deny what is happening. She conceals the truth from herself as well as others; the relationship continues and when the situation is brought to light it may be insisted by the mother that it had been unknown to her'.
29. In the evidence presented to the Inquiry several children who described abuse indicated that their mothers either were present or knew what was going on.

The Lasting Effects of Sexual Abuse in Childhood
30. We have been provided with a considerable amount of written material on various aspects of the long term effects on the abused child. . . .
33. Professor Sir Martin Roth told us in evidence of the serious harm sexual abuse had done to some of his patients. He warned that 'Those who have been intimidated by threats into incestuous relationships in childhood proved to be at high risk of abusing their own children thus transmitting the effects of deprivation. The ill effects are not confined to feelings of guilt, self-reproach and humiliation aroused after incest has begun or when its character has come to be appreciated. Emotional development may be seriously deranged or arrested and ability to form normal personal and sexual relationships to be fulfilled and happy in marriage and to prove emotionally equal to the responsibility of rearing children suffer lasting impairment. Although it is the more intrusive and more aggressive forms of abuse that cause the most grave damage, forms of incestuous relationship that leave no sign may inflict a lasting wound.'

Question

There were some 18 reports of child abuse inquiries between 1973 and 1980 (see DHSS, 1982), beginning with Maria Colwell (1973) and including Susan Auckland (p. 372, above) and Wayne Brewer (1977). Between 1980 and 1989 there were at least 19 more (see DH, 1991). Apart from Cleveland (p. 375, above), the most influential were Jasmine Beckford (1985), Heidi Koseda (1986), Tyra Henry (1987) and Kimberley Carlile (1987). All but Cleveland concerned the authorities' failure to protect children from physical abuse or neglect either at home or in care. In Cleveland the concern was that the authorities might have been too anxious to protect the children. What difference does the nature of the alleged abuse make?

2 The search for explanations

Some impression of the huge research literature is given by Jenny Clifton in her account of *Factors Predisposing Family Members to Violence*, in the Scottish Social Work Services Group's collection of papers on *Violence in the Family* (1982):

The main perspectives from which researchers have attempted to explain the violence of family members are: the childhood experiences of violent individuals, pathological conditions, social stress and family interaction. These will be explored here, together with a brief mention of the victim's role as perceived by researchers. Each perspective will be explored in the context first of child abuse and then of wife battering.

Childhood experience
A number of researchers have found that the parent who abuses his or her child is likely to have been mistreated as a child. On this evidence it has been argued that a cycle of violence can occur whereby violent treatment of children is passed on from generation to generation (Ounsted and Lynch 1976; Court 1974). What this research fails to clarify is whether the important factor is violence to a child or neglect or rejection with which violence may be closely associated.

Two important studies which bear on this issue are those by Steele and Pollock (1968) and the NSPCC (1975), both of which emphasise the importance of early emotional experience. The mother's role as the attacker in both studies was attributed to her greater contact with the child and in Steele and Pollock's work the early emotional deprivation of both parents was felt to be of significance. The latter study describes parents who had experienced a lack of 'basic mothering', harsh discipline, conditional affection and high expectations of consistently good behaviour. The NSPCC study confirms the picture of poor emotional experience, actual physical abuse being less in evidence in the backgrounds of their mothers than severe disruptions and changes in caretaker. This study suggests that such emotional experiences seemed to be replicated in the following generation, the links being inadequate parental role models and the importance of a nurturing mother child relationship in the development of a healthy personality. The NSPCC study, however, admits to this being only a partial explanation and points out the unanswered questions. Why was the parental deprivation manifested in child abuse rather than some other form of disturbed behaviour? Why do not other parents with impoverished early lives batter their children? The study concludes that there remains 'little conception of the necessary or sufficient causes of child abuse' and that an emotionally deprived childhood is but one, albeit an important one. . . .

The interpretation of research into the impact of childhood experience of violence in the context of wife beating is complicated by lack of clarity about what counts as crucial violent history: whether it be the experience of violence or its observation and whether it is the wife's or the husband's experience which is more significant. The oft-quoted studies which investigate this are those of Gayford (1975) and Gelles (1972). The former was based on interviews with women at Chiswick Women's Aid refuge and has been severely criticised on methodological grounds (Wilson 1976). The findings clearly do need more careful testing. In a study likely to include the more extreme cases of battering, just 40% of wives said that their husbands had either been subjected to or had witnessed violence in childhood. Among the women themselves, 20% reported such experiences. Questions remain about the violent behaviour or victim status of the remainder. Gelles' study also leaves these unanswered questions. He concludes that those spouses who, whether as victims or witnesses, had experienced violence in childhood were more likely to be violent to their own spouse. Yet just as 50% of those in his sample who had witnessed violence engaged in it as adults, so the other half of that group did not become violent. Among those who had never experienced violence at the hands of their parents, 40% became violent to their spouse. As Marsden (1978) has said: 'It is not clear how much violence or what intensity, needs to be experienced as victim or witness in the family or via the media for it to be significantly associated with the later development of violent behaviour'. The value of Gelles' work to an understanding of this complex issue is his evidence on the widespread use of force in childhood socialisation which represents a general approval of violence. . . .

Pathology
Many attempts have been made to define the disturbed individual who is likely to batter his or her child. A wide range of psychiatric illnesses have been found to exist among battering parents, but there is no clear association between any of them and the phenomenon of child abuse. Frequently the only evidence claimed for the existence of a disturbed personality which is then said to be cause of violence, is the violence itself — a tautological argument at best. . . .

Some writers have attempted to delineate a particular personality type, independent of specific personality disorders and psychiatric illness, who might be violence-prone. Thus Steele and Pollock (1968) depict a type of person who has a very high expectation of the child's performance and a corresponding disregard for his needs and helplessness. Such a parent, feeling insecure and unloved, looks to the child for reassurance. Bad behaviour is interpreted as lack of such reassurance and violence can erupt. Steele and Pollock offer reasons for assaults on a particular child, such as sex or position in the family, and jealousy and compulsive behaviour figure in the pathology they propose. They quote a case:

'Kathy made this poignant statement: "I have never felt really loved all my life. When the baby was born, I thought he would love me, but when he cried all the time, it meant he didn't love me, so I hit him". Kenny, aged three weeks, was hospitalised with bilateral subdural haematomas.'

It is clear, however, that many of the families in the studies which attempt to describe a particular personality type face a range of stresses which might equally be used to explain their resort to violence.

As with parental abuse of children, it appears that some men who batter their wives are suffering from mental illness and that this plays the largest part in bringing about their violence. Studies such as those of Faulk (1974) and quoted by Scott (1974) indicate a high incidence of disturbance among battering men. However, much of this research has been based on highly selected, often criminal, populations. Erin Pizzey (1974) has spoken of battering men as psychopaths and cases of pathological jealousy are evidenced in the literature. Gelles (1972) quotes an example where a woman described her husband's harassment for her supposed infidelity:

'He would just keep it up until out of desperation I would admit anything in the world to get him to shut up. He would keep it up for five hours and not let me sleep. I would say, "Yes, I did, are you glad?" and then he would beat me.'

The instances quoted by Pizzey (1974) and by Dobash and colleagues (1978) of frequent attacks when a wife is pregnant, may indicate pathological jealousy of the impending baby. . . .

There is not always a clear association between violence to a wife and violence to outsiders. While sub-culture theories and the idea that a man with a violent lifestyle or job will carry this behaviour into his family life and acquire an immunity to the effects of violence have been explored (Wolfgang and Ferracuti 1967; Westley 1970), it has not yet been substantiated that such men form the majority of battering husbands. Indeed it has been proposed that a more common situation may be that of the 'Jekyll and Hyde' marriage where the husband, while violent to his wife, is a perfectly respectable and pleasant person to everyone else (Marsden and Owens 1975). . . .

Some men, then, who beat their wives have personalities which lead them to be consistently violent and some are suffering from a range of psychiatric illnesses. The violence of some of these men will be exhibited more broadly than within marriage. However, it is unknown how many battering men fall into such categories and unclear how many 'ordinary' men engage in violence only to their wives and perhaps then only spasmodically. It is difficult too to reach any firm conclusions when the whole issue involves the contentious boundaries between pathology and normality.

Social stress
A number of writers on child abuse have noted the existence of a combination of stresses impinging on battering parents and often rely for their explanation of the violence on a stress-induced model. Writers have found poor housing, financial difficulties, social isolation, unemployment and illness among these parents. Gil (1973) argues that poverty is likely to be associated with abuse both because it weakens the parents' self-control and because there are distinct subcultural patterns of child rearing among poorer groups. The increased likelihood of the use of physical discipline may, it is suggested, spill over into violence of a more severe nature among poor working-class families where there are overcrowded living conditions and greater

anxiety about adequate means of support. Steinmetz and Straus (1974) support this contention of the likelihood that violence will occur in association with stress factors, but argue against any simple assumption that child abuse is a working class phenomenon. They suggest that stress factors will press harder on poor families and increase the tendency for abuse to occur, so that stress rather than class is the important factor. The evidence is limited and it must be said that the apparent link between social stress and child abuse may well be due to the social class bias of the samples used in many studies. Most writers conclude that abused children come from all strata of society but that social deprivation and poor health are interacting factors which together increase the risk of violence. Whether the cause can be located in stress factors is perhaps less crucial to establish than the recognition that social deprivation enhances the likelihood of other problems or disorders associated with child abuse.

Stress as a factor in wife battering has been examined in a variety of ways. Some writers have suggested that such stress-inducing experiences as unemployment are associated with violence and have referred to the increased recorded incidence of violence in times of severe unemployment. In the present author's study of women who had used a refuge (Clifton 1980) several women attributed the violence they had experienced to pressures and anxieties about money, the impact of which were sometimes increased when the husband had a drinking problem. Gelles (1972) argues that attacks by husbands on their wives can be seen as rational in the context of a response to stress which is translated into violence by means of a number of triggering factors such as alcohol. He maintains that alcohol is only indirectly related to violence through the release of inhibitions and that the use of alcohol may in itself be a response to stress. He feels that the link between violence and excessive drinking has been misrepresented and that drink may provide a rationalisation for violence. . . .

Family interaction
The quality of the marital relationship between the parents of the abused child has been considered by a number of authors but no single pattern of interaction is represented in the studies. Some have found considerable marital disharmony (Smith 1975) and others an extremely close and claustrophobic type of relationship (Ounsted and Lynch 1976). Problems of lack of support for a young mother and unwanted pregnancies have been found to be common among abusing mothers and in a number of studies there is a high proportion of single parents (Smith 1975; Gil 1973). The NSPCC studies (1975) have reflected upon the frequency of collusion in families of injured children. It may also be important to consider the impact of a father's lack of support in caring for the family when mother is under strain or is ill, as well as the pressures upon one partner not to seek advice although aware of his or her spouse's violence towards the child. In some instances both parents are emotionally vulnerable and there may be a complex chain of interaction whereby stress on one member may be felt by another whose response to the pressure is a violent one (Skinner and Castle 1969).

Another kind of stress has been posited as significant by those who seek for explanations in the arena of husband-wife interaction. O'Brien (1971) argues that status inconsistency in marriage may lead to violence. This may occur when a husband feels threatened by his wife's superior achievement or ascribed status, or where he is an under-achiever in the work setting. The likelihood of a particular individual perceiving this status inconsistency as a threat requires further explanation but it has been suggested by Pagelow (1977) that socialisation into and acceptance of the dominant role will vary in extent and that a man who has come to view male superiority as essential will be more likely to find such inconsistency stressful.

The role of the victim
There are indications in the research on child abuse that certain characteristics of the child may enhance the potential for abuse. Gelles (1972) has said that it is the very young child who is most at risk and that this ties in with unrealistic demands and expectations on the part of the parents. The premature baby is frequently over-represented in research samples (Skinner and Castle 1969; Lynch 1975). This has been explained in terms of the association of premature birth with lack of intimate contact between mother and child in the early weeks and the consequent prevention of bonding. Stress and ill-health in the mother and child may be common after premature birth, connecting prematurity and abuse in a different manner. A child who is particularly unresponsive or who cries excessively from birth may create unbearable stress for a parent and several studies have found innate variations between infants on a number of such behavioural factors (Schaffer and Emerson 1964; Birns et al 1969). Illegitimacy, the child's position in the family and his or her resemblance to another family member are all factors which have been considered significant (Allan 1978).

The consideration of the wife's role in cases of wife abuse has tended to focus less on passive factors and more on the question of provocation. Nagging, verbal aggression, even over-submission are all used in explanation and even justification in the literature (Storr 1974; Jobling 1974). It is hard, upon examining some of the case histories of battered women, to credit arguments that provoking words or actions could justify the type of torture and excessive beating inflicted upon them. Given the common acceptance of a husband's assumption of authority as head of the household, there is a wide range of behaviour which could be construed as challenging such dominance and which might lead to violence against the wife. In studying the evidence from their research the Dobashes (1980) concluded: 'The only pattern discernible in these lists (of provocative behaviour) is that the behaviour whatever it might be, represents some form of failure or refusal on the part of the woman to comply with or support her husband's wishes and authority'.

Questions

(i) Bromley in his textbook on *Family Law* (5th edn, 1976), however, used to argue that 'no spouse ought to be allowed to rely on the other's past conduct as a justification for living apart' where there is no probability of recurrence: (a) do you agree? (b) What if a wife could put an end to the beating by obeying her husband's unreasonable orders? (c) What if she could do so by obeying his *reasonable* orders? (d) Can you think of some orders so reasonable that disobedience would merit a beating? (e) If you can, would the wife be unable to get a divorce under s. 1(2)(b) of the Matrimonial Causes Act 1973 (see p. 199 above)?

(ii) Dobash and Dobash (1980) call the idea of provocation in these cases 'naive and insidious', naive 'because it represents a failure to see the marital relationship within which the wife must negotiate with her husband in order to conduct her daily life' and 'insidious because what is being said is that the woman has no real right to negotiate with her husband about how their money is spent . . .': is community of property (see p. 155, above) or dual employment the solution?

This points to an important argument which concentration on the personalities and motivations of individuals obscures. As Jenny Clifton herself points out:

While it is possible to examine the research into child abuse and wife battering within the same categories, there are several reasons for discussing the two forms of violence separately. Researchers have approached the two topics from different implicit theoretical standpoints and have asked different questions, making comparison difficult. The extent of overlap between different forms of violence in the same family is unclear but a link is not inevitable, and greater understanding may be gained from a focus on the differences in context between parent-child relationships and marital ones (Dobash and Dobash 1980). If the specific context of marital violence is fully considered, it proves possible to make sense of the direction of such violence — overwhelmingly from husband to wife (Lystad 1975) — by exploring attitudes to women rather than simply to violence.

Borkowski, Murch and Walker (1983) report that in a survey of recently divorced men and women, 40% reported some violence in their previous marriage. As Elizabeth Wilson (1976) comments, the scale of the problem may be some indication of causes:

If you are one of only 500 women in a population of 50 million then you have certainly been more than unlucky and there may perhaps be something very peculiar about your husband, or unusual about your circumstances, or about you; on the other hand, if you are one of 500,000 women then that suggests something very different — that there is something wrong not with a few individual men, or women, or marriages, but with the *situation* in which *many* women and children regularly get assaulted — that situation being the home and the family.

Lorna Smith expands upon this in *Domestic Violence: an Overview of the Literature* (1989):

Feminist explanations

At the core of feminist explanations is the view that all violence is a reflection of unequal power relationships: domestic violence reflects the unequal power of men and women in society and also, therefore, within their personal relationships. It is a view propounded by sociologists (for example, Dobash and Dobash, 1980; Edwards, 1985), psychologists (for example, Walker, 1984), lawyers (for example, Freeman, 1979; 1984) and practitioners in the criminal justice system (for example, Pence, 1985) alike.

Dobash and Dobash (1980, 1984) employ the notion of patriarchy to explain women's subordinate status. Patriarchy comprises two elements: the structural — that is those societal institutions which define and maintain women's subordinate position and thus prevent them from influencing or changing the social order — and the ideological — that is the socialisation process which ensures acceptance of that order. Both the Dobashes (1981) historical analysis of legal sources and their empirical 'context specific' study (1979, 1984) demonstrate how husbands have sought and still seek to control their wives by violence.

Pahl (1985) has explicitly pointed out that the 'taken-for-granted assumptions' about marriage and the role of the family shape the ways in which the roles of women are defined, the ways in which domestic violence is perceived and thus also agencies' response to domestic violence. The ideology of the family and the privacy accorded the family in our society mean that women are, and are seen to be, subordinate to the men they live with. Men are expected to assume their 'natural' role as the dominant adult within the family. Indeed, Wilson (1983) has argued that domestic violence can be better understood if it is seen as an extreme form of normality — an exaggeration of how society expects men to behave as the authority figure in the family — and both Freeman (1980) and Edwards (1985) argue that the legal system both reflects and sustains this male supremacy. The pathology is, therefore, moved from that of the individual or even of the individual family to the family structure itself and its unequal power structure. Moreover, the family is seen as a microcosm of an unequal society. Domestic violence thus becomes a symptom of the more general demonstration of male violence, a demonstration of the male ethos and the male domination of women.

A number of writers have drawn attention to the economic dependency of women (see, for example, Chapman and Gates, 1978; Homer *et al.*, 1985; Kalmuss and Straus, 1981; Kaufman Kantor and Straus, 1987; Martin, 1976; 1978). Pahl's empirical study (1985) attests to the importance of the allocation of the control of money within the household. Although Pahl, herself, did not see this as important when she began her study, the women in her sample drew such consistent attention to it that she systematically investigated it: more than three quarters of the women named money a problem area. Husbands seemed to use the control of money as part of a more general attempt to control and subordinate wives. It appeared to be the key element in a marital relationship in which the husband assumed he would be the dominant partner. This finding is consistent with other studies. The Dobashes (1980) found that the majority of arguments preceding violence focusses on husband's jealousy, differing expectations regarding the wife's domestic duties and the allocation of money. Roy (1977), in her American study, found that the four factors most often leading to violence were, in order of importance, arguments over money, jealousy, sexual problems and alcohol. Evason (1982), too, paid particular attention to financial arrangements within marriage. Her sample compared groups of women who had been victims of domestic violence with those who had not: those who had experienced violence were more likely to have had husbands who kept control over finances and who gave their wives money as and when they thought fit. Non-violent husbands were more likely to have opted for joint management of money. Assumptions and expectations about wives' appropriate behaviour were also identified as important by Evason (1982) and Klein (1982). Evason, for example, found that although there were no differences between her violent and non-violent groups in terms of education, social class, age at marriage or length of courtship prior to marriage, wives who had been abused were particularly likely to have had husbands who favoured a traditional model of marriage in which the husband was 'master in his own home'. Any attempt by wives to assert themselves or question that authority was interpreted as wives 'getting above themselves' and, therefore, they had to be 'put back in their place'.

Morash (1986) has pointed out that socio-structural cultural explanations and feminist explanations are not necessarily antithetical despite their use of different paradigms for theory building. . . .Straus (1977), for example, agrees with feminists that:

'The most fundamental set of factors bringing about wife beating are those connected with the sexist structure of the family and society . . . The cultural norms and values permitting and sometimes encouraging husband-to-wife violence reflect the hierarchical and male-dominant type of society which characterises the Western world.'

Moreover, some feminists (for example, Dobash and Dobash, 1980) would not reject the relevance of family history, social stresses, use of alcohol, sexual problems and so on, but argue rather that their explanatory power is not sufficient. Emphasising such factors leaves the question unanswered: why are women most frequently the victim?

Questions

(i) Why, then, do most men *not* beat their wives?

(ii) Do you think, as the magistrates (but not the Family Division) did in *Bergin v Bergin* [1983] 1 WLR 279, that a wife who accepted three black eyes 'as part of married life' can reasonably be expected to go on living with her husband when he next turns violent?

3 But is it not a crime?

According to Erin Pizzey, in the book which first alerted the public to the modern realities of wife-beating, *Scream Quietly or the Neighbours will Hear* (1974):

The police attitude to wife-battering reveals an understandable but unacceptable schizophrenia in their approach to violence. Imagine that Constable Upright is on his beat one night and finds Mr Batter mugging a woman in the street. Mr Batter has already inflicted heavy bruises to the woman's face and is just putting the boot in when Constable Upright comes on the scene. The constable knows his duty and does it. He arrests Mr Batter, who is charged with causing grievous bodily harm and goes to prison for ten years.

Ten years later Constable Upright is on his beat when he is sent to investigate screaming which neighbours have reported coming from the home of the newly released Mr Batter. Mr Batter is mugging his wife. He's thrown boiling water at her, broken her nose, and now he's trying for her toes with a claw hammer. When Constable Upright arrives what does he do? Does he make an arrest? Of course not.

He knocks on the door and Mr Batter tells him to 'sod off'. He tells Mr Batter that the neighbours are complaining and he wishes to see his wife. Mr Batter says they have been having a minor row and he gets his wife who is looking bruised round the face and crying. The policeman will not arrest. In one case the husband even assaulted his wife in front of a policeman but still there was no arrest. All that he did was to advise her to go to the local magistrates' court the next morning and take out a summons against her husband, but he knew that she was unlikely to do this because she would have to live in the same house as her husband while she was taking him to court.

Much confirmation for what she said came from the evidence of various police bodies to the House of Commons Select Committee on *Violence in Marriage* (1975). Thus the Association of Chief Police Officers:

. . . Whilst such problems take up considerable Police time . . . in the majority of cases the role of the Police is a negative one. We are, after all dealing with persons 'bound in marriage', and it is important, for a host of reasons, to maintain the unity of the spouses. Precipitate action by the Police could aggravate the position to such an extent as to create a worse situation than the one they were summoned to deal with. . . .

Questions

(i) This is borne out by Jan Pahl's research (1982), which indicated that the police were far more likely to take action themselves if (*a*) the woman had already left for a refuge, or (*b*) although still under the same roof, the woman was not married to the man: can you list the 'host of reasons' why this might be?

(ii) How many of the reasons which might disincline a policeman to intervene appear to you to be valid?

(iii) What powers does Constable Upright have, if told to 'sod off' by a man who is apparently beating his wife inside the matrimonial home? (Consult *R v Thornley* (1980) 72 Cr App Rep 302.)

There may well be a difference between perceptions of seriousness in violence between husband and wife and those, for example, in violence between parent and child. But even if there were not, Mildred Dow puts her finger on one difficulty in *Police Involvement*, her contribution to *Violence in the Family* (edited by Marie Borland in 1976):

It has, however, been recognised in law for many centuries that the sanctity of marriage is something special. Until recent times a wife was seen as a chattel of her husband and had no real rights. In recent years it has become obvious to the writer, through years of police experience as a practical officer, that however often one says to a wife, 'Your rights are . . .' she will invariably be re-influenced by her husband and refuse to give the necessary evidence. Whether this is basically due to personal fear or to an essentially sexual attraction and influence, or to fear for the children of the union, it is difficult to determine. I only know how frustrating it is for a police officer who has taken much care and trouble in the preparation of the presentation of the case at court to be let down because his principal witness has had 'second thoughts'. If positive action is desirable when injury has been caused, quite often severe injury, we must overcome the problem of the wife who is unwilling to give evidence. Often her decision not to do so is made at the last minute, either as a result of reconciliation or perhaps through fear of retribution. From a practical viewpoint it would appear better to charge the husband and keep him in custody, rather than to follow the practice in some few police areas where the husband is reported for summons, thus giving him time to influence his wife. If some aggressive husbands are, by these means, kept away from the matrimonial home, more wives may be prepared to give the relevant evidence.

Question

A young constable is called to a 'domestic' dispute, in which (it turns out) the wife has suffered three cracked ribs and a dislocated collar bone in addition to numerous cuts and bruises. He arrests her husband, who is convicted of causing her grievous bodily harm and imprisoned. The constable later gives evidence in support of the wife's petition for divorce, which is granted. Three months after the husband is released from prison, the couple marry one another again. Has all his work been wasted?

In any event, both Dobash and Dobash (1980) and Wasoff (1982) in Scotland found that claims about wives dropping charges were 'greatly exaggerated', as did Tony Faragher, discussing *The Police Response to Violence against Women in the Home* (1985):

The degree of police concern over possible withdrawal of the complaint is not matched, however, by the frequency with which this occurs in practice. Only one in ten women in a local study were found to have withdrawn their complaint (Dawson and Faragher, 1977, 142). The only way in which this low level of withdrawal can be accounted for is that the police are extremely selective about who they sponsor to take legal action. This is borne out by observation at the scene of 'domestics' — women are time and again asked whether they really want to take legal action. Alternatively women are given time to 'think it over' in the belief that an 'unemotional' decision made the next day will be more realistic. In this sense the police abrogate their protective role, for their judgment is heavily influenced by prognoses of the woman's reliability as a witness in court proceedings.

Before the Police and Criminal Evidence Act 1984, the House of Lords held in *Hoskyn v Metropolitan Police Comr* [1979] AC 474, [1978] 2 All ER 136, HL that a wife could not be compelled to give evidence against her husband in these cases. Lord Edmund Davies, who dissented, summed up the opposing viewpoints thus:

The noble and learned Lord, Viscount Dilhorne, has spoken of the repugnance created by a wife being compelled '. . . to testify against her husband on a charge involving violence, no matter how trivial and no matter the consequences to her and to her family'. For my part I regard as extremely unlikely any prosecution based on trivial violence being persisted in where the injured spouse was known to be a reluctant witness. Much more to the point, as I think, are cases such as the present . . ., arising from serious physical maltreatment by one spouse of the other.

Such cases are too grave to depend simply on whether the injured spouse is, or is not, willing to testify against the attacker. Reluctance may spring from a variety of reasons and does not by any means necessarily denote that domestic harmony has been restored. A wife who has once been subjected to a 'carve up' may well have more reasons than one for being an unwilling witness against her husband. In such circumstances, it may well prove a positive boon [for] her to be directed by the court that she has no alternative but to testify. But, be that as it may, such incidents ought not to be regarded as having no importance extending beyond the domestic hearth. Their investigation and, where sufficiently weighty, their prosecution is a duty which the agencies of law enforcement cannot dutifully neglect.

Questions

(i) How many reasons can you think of why a victim of violence within the family might not wish to give evidence?
(ii) What should the judge do if she refuses (see *R v Renshaw* [1989] Crim LR 811; Edwards, 1989; Brownlee, 1990)?

The arguments for and against 'diverting' cases out of the criminal justice system are put by Susan Maidment in *The Relevance of the Criminal Law to Domestic Violence* (1980):

In this country police diversion occurs for all the wrong reasons. Police reluctance to prosecute arises from the fact that the wife often becomes subsequently a reluctant victim or witness, unwilling to give evidence against her husband; from a belief in victim precipitation; from a misplaced emphasis on a successful conviction rate as a measure of police efficiency; from an unwillingness to spend what is considered to be an exorbitant amount of time on relatively minor family disputes; from the dangers in the United States to the police if they get caught in the crossfire between husband and wife; and in general from what is considered to be a time-consuming distraction to the overall police effort, leading to job demoralisation, because it is incompatible with the obligations of a law-enforcement agency.

The reasons for police diversion may be considered to be wrong, but the fact of police diversion is further evidence of a general belief in society, as seen also in Parliament's provision of more and better civil remedies, that domestic violence should not be dealt with as a matter for the criminal law. As yet however police diversion has not been institutionalised, as it has for example in respect of juveniles in the juvenile liaison bureaux. . . .

Strong arguments can be put forward why the criminal law should be used in all cases of domestic violence. It would be a clear affirmation of social values, of condemnation by society, and a clear statement of the personal responsibility and accountability of the offender. We know that the criminal law can provide an effective and prompt protection for the victim. The criminal law can at least attempt to prevent an escalation of violence either through incarceration, or by making at the outset the strongest statement that society can make denouncing the act. The police are in any case often involved in emergency calls, and they may be the only agency with the authority and ability to cope with such volatile situations.

On the other side there are arguments against the use of the criminal law. It is a blunt tool. It misplaces emphasis on the offender, not the victim. There is no facility for treatment within the system, for example, for understanding and attempting to control aggression, except probation, but then the husband is still at large. No attempt is made to improve the marital relationship, to develop mutual respect between husband and wife. On a more technical level, there are problems of proof in criminal law, as compared with the easier standard of proof for an injunction. This may lead to some acquittals purely on technical grounds. For the wife however this means a lack of protection.

In more general terms a criminal conviction and sentence for the husband may be counter-productive for the wife in many ways. There may be financial disadvantage to the wife, emotional loss to the children. It may only escalate the problem because of the husband's anger and grudge against her; imprisonment is only a temporary respite (though this argument could equally apply to injunctions). It may not be what the wife really wants — she would like to have him treated. She may feel guilty and responsible for him being punished or locked away. Indeed her initial call to the police may not be a cry for criminal action at all; it is simply the only place she knows to turn to in an emergency.

Indeed the present operation of the criminal law, when it is invoked in these cases, makes a mockery of the criminal process, because of the derisory sentences that are passed, even for example where the charge is actual bodily harm (House of Commons, 1975; Pizzey, 1974). The basic problem to which the use of the criminal law gives rise has been well expressed in the following statement:

> 'Of all the areas in which an alternative to criminal treatment seems justified, the area of marital disputes is the most obvious. This is not to say that violence, theft or neglect between spouses should be ignored, but it does appear that these cases deserve different treatment than they are now given. Whether prosecution is decided upon or not, it would seem that beyond the point of immediate police response to danger, the criminal process is largely irrelevant in these cases. If anything, its very invocation may exacerbate poverty-related and/or psychological problems. The summary, rather shallow treatment given these complainants does not answer the need that they have expressed for help.' (Subin, 1966)

Nevertheless there are some cases where the criminal law has to be used. These cases should be restricted to those occasions when there is a need present for coercive prevention of violence in view of serious physical or emotional danger to the wife. It is all the other cases, where there is a choice between the civil and criminal remedy, which give rise to problems of decision-making. At present the choice of remedy is, as already described, haphazard. It depends partly on the wife's choice as to whether she goes to a solicitor or to the police, and on the police as to whether they are willing to prosecute. In practice the choice will effectively be made by the police since they will usually be involved in the very initial stages. But the fact is that the choice of remedy can and ought to be a professional principled decision. There are some clear issues to be considered, and serious arguments for and against the use of the criminal law as already described. A professional decision needs to be arrived at after full consideration of the alternative remedies available.

Questions

(i) Which professionals might those be? Why should they be better qualified to decide than the police or the woman herself?

(ii) Do we need to distinguish between what Constable Upright does when called to the house in the middle of the night and what Inspector Morse or the Crown Prosecution Service do the next day?

A new wind has certainly begun to blow, as evidenced by the recent Home Office Circular (60/1990) on *Domestic Violence*:

Nature and extent of problem
2. Chief officers will be aware of the wide range of abuse which is covered by the term 'domestic violence'. It encompasses all aspects of physical, sexual and emotional abuse, ranging from threatening behaviour and minor assaults which lead to cuts and bruises to serious injury, and sometimes even death. (In about 44% of homicide cases where the victim is a female the suspect is or was married to or lived with her.) Research has shown that, although the severity of the abuse varies, incidents of domestic violence have several common characteristics. They are rarely isolated occurrences. They tend to be repeated over a period of time, often increasing in their severity, and are particularly common during the woman's pregnancy. They often extend beyond the woman to children living within the home. The offender is likely to come from a family in which violence was used against women, but he may be in any stratum of society; domestic violence occurs across the whole social spectrum.
. . .
4. Domestic violence is not simply a challenge for the criminal justice system. Victims will often need assistance which is beyond the capacity of the police to provide, requiring close co-operation with medical, social work and housing authorities and with victim support groups. Domestic violence is, however, a crime and it is important that the police should play an active and positive role in protecting the victim and that their response to calls for help is speedy and effective.
. . .

Force policy statements
11. The Home Secretary recommends that chief officers should consider issuing a force policy statement about their response to domestic violence . . . Central features of the force policy statement should be: —
    — the overriding duty to protect victims, and children, from further attack;
    — the need to treat domestic violence as seriously as other forms of violence;
    — the use and value of powers of arrest;
    — the dangers of seeking conciliation between assailant and victim;
    — the importance of comprehensive record-keeping to allow the chief officer to monitor the effectiveness of the policy in practice.

Initial police response to incidents
(a) *Distinguish violent/non-violent incidents*
12. The first contact between a victim and the police is likely to be by telephone when a victim seeks police intervention or protection. The first priority for police officers answering such calls is to find out whether immediate police help is required, or whether there is no imminent danger of an assault. Even if immediate help is not sought, the call must be recorded and there should always be some sort of positive action to investigate the case — for instance, an interview with the victim to establish in more detail what prompted her call and whether it was part of a history of violence.

(b) *Check previous history of relationship*
13. All complaints of domestic violence by victims or witnesses should be properly recorded in the same way as similar incidents involving strangers. The seriousness of an incident should not be downgraded because it takes place in a domestic context and no incident should be 'no-crimed' unless the police conclude, after investigation, that the report was inaccurate or false.
. . .

(c) *Action at the scene of the incident: the victim*
14. In the past, police officers arriving at the scene of domestic violence have often tried to smooth over the dispute and reconcile the partners. Research suggests that this is not necessarily the best course of action and that what victims want is the enforcement of the law. Police officers should rarely attempt conciliation if the victim has been, or claims to have been, violently assaulted (bruises may not develop for some time after the incident so the absence of obvious injury may not be significant). Wherever possible, it is desirable for a woman police officer to be available to attend the incident so that the victim may be given a choice about the sex of the officer who assists her. If the victim is interviewed on the spot, the interview should

not take place in the presence of her alleged assailant so that she does not feel pressurised into relating the incident in front of him. However, if she *chooses* to repeat the allegation in his presence and hearing, it may be given in evidence by the police at any subsequent court hearing. The victim should never be asked in the alleged assailant's presence whether she will be prepared to give evidence against him. In some cases, however, the immediate priority will simply be to remove her (and any children) to a place of safety.
. . .

(d) *Action at the scene of the incident: the assailant*
16. Police officers should be aware of their powers in respect to domestic violence . . . Experience in other countries suggests that the arrest of an alleged assailant may act as a powerful deterrent against his re-offending — at least for some time — and it is an important means of showing the victim that she is entitled to, and will receive, society's protection and support. The arrest and detention of an alleged assailant should therefore always be considered, even though the final judgement may be that this is inappropriate in the particular case.

(e) *Action at the scene: witnesses*
17. In view of the difficulties in bringing a prosecution in cases of domestic violence, there is a particular need to establish whether there are witnesses such as other members of the family or neighbours who can give evidence.

Action after the incident
(a) *Charging the suspect*
18. In considering whether or not to initiate criminal proceedings, police officers will wish to take into account the same factors as those which are relevant in the case of attacks by strangers. The fact that some women, having made a complaint, subsequently decide that they are not prepared to give evidence at court should not affect a police officer's decision to charge in a case in which the evidence justifies that course of action. Many women will be in a state of shock when the police first arrive, and unable to contemplate the prospect of a court case. With proper support, however, they may gain in confidence and, following discussion of all the aspects of their case, they may well come to recognise that prosecution is in their own interest. When there is sufficient evidence to justify a prosecution the police should charge the suspect and refer the case to the Crown Prosecution Service.
. . .

(c) *Reports to the Crown Prosecution Service*
21. Just as police officers will find it essential to have background information about the nature and history of the relationship readily to hand in order to deal with an incident, so Crown Prosecutors need the same information in order to prosecute the case effectively and ensure the protection of the victim and any children by the imposition of bail conditions or a remand in custody. In particular, Crown Prosecutors need to be kept informed if circumstances change. The information which is required by the Crown Prosecutor includes
   (i)   the composition of the family;
   (ii) the nature of the relationship — marital status of the parties, history of the relationship including previous attacks if known, likelihood of recurrence if not self-evident;
   (iii) domestic arrangements (relevant to bail);
   (iv) the future of the relationship — whether complainant has ended/intends to end relationship, whether a reconciliation is in progress or seems likely, whether or not she seeks/intends to seek non-molestation order in civil courts. (This information may best be obtained in the presence of a third person eg relative or social worker or, at this early stage, the victim may not be able to discuss rationally the future of the relationship.)
. . .

Withdrawal of victim's complaint
24. In the past, the likelihood of the victim's withdrawing her complaint has often been used to justify not taking criminal proceedings against the alleged assailant. Recent research has established, however, that withdrawal of complaint is less common than has been supposed. The victim's refusal to testify against her partner may considerably lessen the prospect of a conviction, however. The CPS has power, under section 97 of the Magistrates' Courts Act 1980 or Section 80 of the Police and Criminal Evidence Act 1984 to seek to compel a spouse or partner to attend court for the purpose of giving evidence. The power is used infrequently and a decision to use it can only be taken in the light of the circumstances of the case, including the reasons

why the complainant does not wish to give evidence and the views of the officer in the case. This underlines the need to give close support to the victim during the pre-trial period, so that she will feel sufficiently self-confident to give evidence.

Questions

(i) There is, of course, a public interest in the prevention and prosecution of crime: is there also a public interest in the reconciliation and preservation of viable family units? What is viable for this purpose?

(ii) Is prosecution more likely to be favoured (*a*) by a person who subscribes to the individual pathology theory of causation, or (*b*) by a person who subscribes to the family theory?

(iii) How many of the arguments for and against prosecution apply with equal force to the prosecution of parents who neglect or abuse their children?

Michael Freeman takes a pragmatic view of prosecution for child abuse in *Violence in the Home* (1979):

The criminal law as a mechanism to protect children from abuse is ineffective. It is often extremely difficult to obtain a conviction: there are problems of evidence and proof. An acquittal may be seen by the parent as a vindication of the legitimacy of his behaviour and this in turn makes therapeutic intervention impossible. Successful prosecutions, on the other hand, which are few and far between do not act as deterrents but tend instead to confirm the parent in his 'negative self-image'. There is also the danger that a parent who knows he may be prosecuted may neglect or delay to seek medical treatment for his injured child because of fear of the consequences. Furthermore, prosecutions may divide families. There is no doubt, though, that in really serious cases prosecutions must and do take place.

Questions

(i) Do you have any qualms about confirming the negative self-image of a parent who neglects or abuses his child? Or her child?

(ii) What about a step-parent? (Note that in all the child deaths reviewed by the DH, 1991, where a step-father was present in the household, he was convicted.)

(iii) Farmer and Parker (1985) found that long delays and numerous interim care orders in care proceedings were associated with prosecuting the parents, yet the High Court has held that care proceedings need not be adjourned pending the outcome (*R v Inner London Juvenile Court, ex p G* [1988] FCR 316, [1988] 2 FLR 58; *R v Exeter Juvenile Court ex p DLH; R v Waltham Forest Juvenile Court, ex p KB* [1988] FCR 474, [1988] 2 FLR 214): which is more prejudicial (*a*) to the parents, or (*b*) to the child?

(iv) Section 97 of the Children Act 1989 removes the privilege against self-incrimination for any person called to give evidence in an application for a care, supervision, emergency protection or child assessment order, although the answers are not then admissible in any criminal proceedings against the person (or his spouse) except for perjury: is this the right balance between punishing the abuser and protecting the child?

4 The search for alternative protection for the battered woman

Jenny Clifton's review of the literature (1982) points to some of the difficulties which women face in taking action:

It is important to view the battered wife in the context of a family network which may tacitly or explicitly support the husband's position. The problems of the wife who does not think she will be believed if she tells how her apparently normal husband is a batterer . . . represent a crucial component of the explanation for women remaining in a violent relationship. Women's own hopes and expectations of marriage and family life, added to the pressures from others to keep the family together, the very real hardships of life alone and the social disadvantages of divorced status offer plenty of scope for the explanation of women's apparent tolerance of a violent relationship without recourse to suppositions that women must need the violence in a pathological way (Holman 1970; Marsden 1978; Barker and Allen 1976; Hart 1976). This is not to say that conflict which may occasionally spill into violence does not sometimes become an integral part of a marital relationship (Cade 1978) but the consistent picture from research studies is that women who are beaten do not come to need or enjoy their victimisation (Dobash and Dobash 1980). Neither are conflict-ridden marriages and relationships which occasionally involve physical combat quite the same as marriages in which the wife is frequently and brutally subjected to physical force.

Dobash and Dobash (1980) point to other difficulties too:

The pattern of staying, leaving, and returning is not related just to personal concerns, say, the children's happiness, but also to structural or material factors such as financial support, accommodation, and child care. In order for a woman to get out of the house even if it is only to escape the violence temporarily, she must have some money and a place to stay. In order for her to leave permanently, she must have sufficient funds to support herself and her children and be able to find suitable accommodation. Involved in this are a whole host of material problems which are sometimes insurmountable and over which the woman may have little or no control.

Despite the fact that a substantial proportion of women are now the sole wage earners in their families and an even larger proportion of couples jointly support their families, many women are either completely or substantially dependent upon their husbands for financial support. The concept of the dependent wife does, of course, continue to permeate most of our social institutions and results in many arrangements that limit the battered woman's opportunities to become financially independent and thus able to establish a reasonable life, or any life at all, apart from her violent husband.

As John Stuart Mill pointed out in 1869, 'it is contrary to reason and experience to suppose that there can be any real check to brutality, consistent with leaving the victim still in the power of the executioner'. The first step had therefore to be to improve and extend the procedures for releasing wives from their lifelong promise and legal duty to live with their husbands. But it is one thing to be told that you need no longer live with your husband, and another thing to pluck up the courage to live through the interim before the divorce and to find somewhere to live both then and thereafter.

The remedies developed in family law are explained by the Law Commission in their Working Paper on *Domestic Violence and Occupation of the Family Home* (1989):

Injunctions issued ancillary to matrimonial proceedings
2.2 The principles relating to the grant of injunctions against molestation or excluding a spouse from the matrimonial home were first evolved by the courts in considering applications made ancillary to proceedings for divorce, judicial separation or nullity [e.g. in *Silverstone v Silverstone* [1953] P 174, [1953] 1 All ER 556]. While matrimonial proceedings are pending a spouse has the right to pursue remedies in the courts free from threats, intimidation or coercion.

If such interference were found, the courts would assist by ensuring that the victimised spouse was not prevented from pursuing the action. Initially the intervention of the court included the grant of an injunction to exclude the husband from the matrimonial home, provided that the husband's conduct complained of made it 'impossible' for her to live in the house while he was living there too. It was therefore in this context that the advantages of ouster injunctions as an effective protection against domestic violence first became apparent [Maidment, 1977].

Later case law placed less emphasis on blame and concentrated more on the issue of what in the circumstances was fair, just and reasonable. Frequently on the facts of those cases the children's interests were found to be the deciding factor [e.g. *Stewart v Stewart* [1973] Fam 21, [1973] 1 All ER 31; *Phillips v Phillips* [1973] 2 All ER 423, [1973] 1 WLR 615; *Bassett v Bassett* [1975] Fam 76, [1975] 1 All ER 513; *Walker v Walker* [1978] 3 All ER 141, [1978] 1 WLR 533].

2.3 In accordance with the general rule that an injunction will only be granted to support a legal right, the majority of matrimonial injunctions were obtained ancillary to proceedings for divorce. Although it was clear that if proceedings for divorce were pending there was a sufficient nexus between the petition and the protection sought, it was not clear what other proceedings must be pending before the court had jurisdiction to grant injunctive relief. In particular, it might be necessary to distinguish between injunctions against violence and other forms of molestation, which might be justified either by the need to protect litigants or by the general law of tort, and injunctions excluding one party from the home, which might depend upon their respective claims to occupy it [cf. *Winstone v Winstone* [1960] P 28, [1959] 3 All ER 580; *McGibbon v McGibbon* [1973] Fam 170, [1973] 2 All ER 836].

Rights of occupation
2.4 At common law the contract of marriage imposes a mutual obligation on spouses to live together. Flowing from this is the right of each spouse to share in the occupation of the matrimonial home irrespective of ownership. . . .
2.5 Since 1967 the non-entitled spouse has also enjoyed statutory rights of occupation under the Matrimonial Homes Act. The 1967 Act was principally passed to reverse the House of Lords' decision in *National Provincial Bank Ltd v Ainsworth* [1965] AC 1175, [1965] 2 All ER 472. Its main purpose was therefore to turn the personal right of occupation enjoyed by the non-owning spouse into a land charge which could be protected by registration against dispositions to third parties by the owning spouse. . . .
2.6 Of equal importance in the long run, however, have been the powers given by the Matrimonial Homes Act to regulate and adjust the respective rights of occupation between the spouses themselves. Originally, the courts had power to uphold or to end the occupation rights of a non-owing spouse but it was held in *Tarr v Tarr* [1973] AC 254, [1972] 2 All ER 295 that the 1967 Act gave no power to exclude the legal owner altogether. This again was remedied by the Domestic Violence and Matrimonial Proceedings Act 1976, which also introduced a new power to adjust the occupation rights of spouses who were joint owners or tenants. Since then, the legislation [ss. 1(2), 9(1) of the Matrimonial Homes Act 1983] has provided that either of the spouses may apply to the court for an order: —
 — declaring, enforcing, restricting or terminating the rights of occupation of a non-owning spouse;
 — prohibiting, suspending or restricting the exercise by either spouse of the right to occupy the dwelling house; or
 — requiring either spouse to permit the exercise by the other of that right.
2.7 The Matrimonial Homes Act has taken on new significance since the decision of the House of Lords in *Richards v Richards* [1984] AC 174, [1983] 2 All ER 807 (p. 394, below). Before *Richards v Richards* the Matrimonial Homes Act was not extensively used at all. It was not passed to provide a remedy for a wife threatened with violence but to ensure that any deserving spouse had a roof over her head. Until 1976, it did not provide for an owning spouse to be excluded. Nor is there any express power to protect against molestation before or after the hearing. The provisions of the Matrimonial Homes Act could never be said to have been designed for those women, popularly named 'battered wives', on whose plight public concern was focusing in the early 1970s.

Actions in tort
. . .
2.9 As between spouses, there was little need to resort to tort law, because matrimonial remedies were available. As between cohabitants and other family members however, an action in tort might be the only way to proceed. This is not wholly appropriate in the context of domestic violence because the main object of the tort system is financial compensation and in

most cases this will either not be available or will reduce the resources otherwise used to maintain the family. Injunctions can nonetheless be effective remedies for the torts of assault, battery, nuisance or trespass. In the High Court, such injunctions might be the only relief claimed, whereas in county courts they have generally to be ancillary to a claim for damages or some other cause or matter within the court's jurisdiction.

The Domestic Violence and Matrimonial Proceedings Act 1976
2.10 In February 1975 a Select Committee was appointed to consider the extent, nature and causes of problems of families where there is violence between the partners or where children suffer non-accidental injury. The committee concentrated on the 'battered wife' aspect of its terms of reference, women, that is:
   '[who] are often with inadequate means and with dependent children, and in need of shelter
   or help or advice for themselves and their families.'
While admitting that no laws, however well enforced, could prevent marital assaults, the Select Committee made a number of recommendations for new powers to be applied in all courts. Jo Richardson M.P. introduced a private Member's Bill which became the Domestic Violence and Matrimonial Proceedings Act 1976. It was said, by Lord Salmon in *Davis v Johnson* [1979] AC 264, 340, to have been:
   'hurried through Parliament to provide urgently needed first aid for "battered wives" '.
2.11. The new provisions overcame the lack of jurisdiction that had previously prevented a county court from granting an injunction unless it could be shown to be incidental to other proceedings. Section 1(1) of the 1976 Act gave jurisdiction to all county courts to grant the following types of injunction whether or not there were other proceedings before the court: —
   — restraining the other party to the marriage from molesting the applicant;
   — restraining the other party from molesting a child living with the applicant;
   — excluding the other party from the matrimonial home or a part of the matrimonial home
   or from a specified area in which the matrimonial home is included;
   — requiring the other party to permit the applicant to enter and remain in the matrimonial
   home or a part of the matrimonial home.
These powers were to apply both between parties to a marriage and between 'a man and woman who are living with each other in the same household as husband and wife' [s. 1(2)].
2.12 Initially it was thought that section 1 of the 1976 Act was only a procedural provision overcoming the previous limitations on the county courts' powers. It was not thought to have altered the substantive law so as to enable the court to override common law property rights. However, in *Davis v Johnson* [1979] AC 264, [1978] 1 All ER 1132 the House of Lords held, by a majority of 4 to 1, that section 1 of the Act did give a county court jurisdiction to exclude both a spouse and, as in this case, a cohabitant from the matrimonial home irrespective of any right of property vested in the person excluded whether he be the sole or joint owner or tenant. Section 1, however, can only give temporary relief and its purpose is not to affect existing property rights but to override or interfere with the enjoyment of such rights. As Lord Scarman explained,
   'the purpose of the section is not to create rights but to strengthen remedies.'
2.13 Taking note of the heartfelt complaints made by many women that, because of the slow enforcement procedures, civil injunctions were not worth the paper they were written on, the Select Committee had also recommended that the courts have power to attach a police power of arrest to injunctions. This recommendation was implemented by section 2 of the Domestic Violence and Matrimonial Proceedings Act 1976. This applies to all injunctions restraining violence or excluding one party from the home, whatever the proceedings in which they were granted, but as with section 1, only between spouses or people living together as such.

Jurisdiction of the magistrates' courts
2.14 The matrimonial jurisdiction of the magistrates' courts evolved in response to a particular concern about the position of working class women who suffered repeated physical assaults from their husbands. In 1878 the Matrimonial Causes Act gave magistrates' courts the power to grant a separation order, with maintenance and custody of children under ten, to a wife whose husband had been convicted of an aggravated assault on her, 'if satisfied that the future safety of the wife (was) in peril'. The separation order had the force and effect of a decree of judicial separation on the ground of cruelty. Except in so far as the award of maintenance provided wives with a limited financial means of escape, the award of a separation order did little else to ensure personal safety.
2.15 The 1978 Act abolished the separation order and provided new remedies specifically designed to protect a spouse, usually the wife, or child from a violent and dangerous husband within the matrimonial home. . . . Two new remedies were created:

'the personal protection order which will merely prohibit him (the husband) from behaving in a way which is dangerous to this wife and children (and) the exclusion order . . . which will have the positive and drastic result of preventing the husband from living in his own home'. [Law Commission, 1976, para. 3.18]

These powers are quite independent of any other claim, for example to financial relief, and either party may apply. The court may also attach a power of arrest to an order. These powers are essentially emergency measures and were not intended to resolve long term occupation rights between spouses.

Question

The grounds for personal protection and exclusion orders are set out in the *Domestic Proceedings and Magistrates' Courts Act 1978*:

16. – (2) Where on an application for an order under this section the court is satisfied that the respondent has used, or threatened to use, violence against the person of the applicant or a child of the family and that it is necessary for the protection of the applicant or a child of the family that an order should be made under this subsection, the court may make one or both of the following orders, that is to say –
  (a) an order that the respondent shall not use, or threaten to use, violence against the person of the applicant;
  (b) an order that the respondent shall not use, or threaten to use, violence against the person of a child of the family.
  (3) Where on an application for an order under this section the court is satisfied –
  (a) that the respondent has used violence against the person of the applicant or a child of the family, or
  (b) that the respondent has threatened to use violence against the person of the applicant or a child of the family and has used violence against some other person, or
  (c) that the respondent has in contravention of an order made under subsection (2) above threatened to use violence against the person of the applicant or a child of the family,
and that the applicant or a child of the family is in danger of being physically injured by the respondent (or would be in such danger if the applicant or child were to enter the matrimonial home) the court may make one or both of the following orders, this is to say –
  (i) an order requiring the respondent to leave the matrimonial home;
  (ii) an order prohibiting the respondent from entering the matrimonial home.

If one of the declared objects of the legislation was to avoid unnecessary anomalies between the magistrates' and higher courts (Law Commission, 1976), why were the magistrates' powers limited (*a*) to cases involving the use or threat of violence, and (*b*) to husband and wife?

Some of the reasons why women found that non-molestation orders were 'not worth the paper they were written on' are illustrated by Erin Pizzey (1974):

Joan took her husband before the High Court eleven times before she finally got him put in prison with a one-year sentence. The first time he broke in the police refused to come as they said there was nothing they could do on a High Court injunction. He beat her up and she came to Women's Aid. After that the poor woman yo-yoed back and forth with her three children using us as a refuge when her husband was around. Eventually she went back and tried to live in the home that the court said was hers when the divorce had been granted. He broke in, beat her up, punctured her ear-drum and raped her at the point of a knife. When she got him back into the High Court, the judge did not appear to have read the previous judges' notes and accepted the husband's story that he dropped in for some urgent papers at 3 a.m. and his wife had refused to let him have them. The judge gave him seven days and told him in effect that he was a naughty boy.

Part of Joan's problem was that whenever she took her husband to court they appeared in front of a different judge, and none of the judges bothered to read the file of her husband's atrocities, which was steadily getting thicker and thicker.

She gave up trying to live in 'her' home and moved in with us. Her husband broke our windows, screamed and raged outside the house, pestered the school and tried to snatch the children. We took him back to court and this time saw the same judge twice. He did read the case and was appalled enough to put him inside for a year. It was too late for Joan to claim her council house, though — the rent arrears had mounted up and the council had taken it back.

Not surprisingly, women consider an ouster injunction more effective. Getting one, however, is more difficult. The principles were settled by the House of Lords in a case which did not involve violence but has affected the courts' approach in all types of case.

Richards v Richards
[1984] AC 174, [1983] 2 All ER 807, [1983] 3 WLR 173, [1984] FLR 11, 13 Fam Law 256, House of Lords

The wife petitioned for divorce, relying upon allegations of behaviour, but remained in the matrimonial home for nearly three months performing 'wifely duties' but not sleeping with her husband. She then left taking the children, a girl of six and a boy of four, to a friend's cottage. She sought and obtained an order, inter alia, for the husband to leave the home. She then returned with the children; the parties had since arranged that she lived with them there during the week and the father lived with them there at weekends. The husband's appeal to the Court of Appeal was dismissed and he appealed to the House of Lords.

Lord Brandon of Oakbrook: . . . My Lords, Judge Pennant, when he came to give judgment on the wife's application, expressed himself as being in a legal dilemma. He had been referred by counsel for the husband to the decision of one division of the Court of Appeal in *Myers v Myers* [1982] 1 All ER 776, [1982] 1 WLR 247, in which it was held that the judge below had erred in principle in failing to consider whether on the facts before him the wife's conclusion that she was unwilling to return to the matrimonial home while the husband was still there was a reasonable conclusion having regard to the personalities of both the husband and the wife. The judge had also been referred by counsel for the wife to the decision of another division of the Court of Appeal in *Samson v Samson* [1982] 1 All ER 780, [1982] 1 WLR 252, in which it was held that, where there were young children, the first consideration was their welfare, and that the court should not consider whether the wife was justified in leaving and refusing to return to the matrimonial home while the husband was still there or not. The judge, correctly in my view, regarded these two decisions of different divisions of the Court of Appeal as incompatible with each other, and asked himself the difficult question which of them he should follow. . . .

My Lords, so far as the facts of the case are concerned the judge made the following findings: (1) that the practical probability was that the children would continue to live with the wife; (2) that the allegations in the wife's petition relating to the behaviour of the husband were 'rubbishy' and 'very flimsy indeed'; (3) that the elder child, Melanie, did not want her parents to separate; (4) that the wife was living in overcrowded accommodation not fit as a home for the children; (5) that the wife had no reasonable grounds for refusing to return to live in the same house as the husband; and (6) that the wife's assertion that she could not bear to live in the same house as the husband was untrue, the reality being that she was a strong-willed woman who simply did not wish to do so. On these facts he said that he thought that it was thoroughly unjust to turn the husband out, but justice no longer seemed to play any part in this branch of the law. The matrimonial home was a house provided by the public as a home for the four persons concerned, and, that being so, the public interest was best met by installing the children in that home, which meant in practice installing the wife there also. He went on to say that it was by no means certain that there would be a divorce on the existing grounds, and he had come to the conclusion that, although it was unjust to the husband, it seemed right to grant the ouster order sought in the interests of the children. It will be apparent that, in reaching that conclusion, he decided to apply *Samson v Samson* rather than *Myers v Myers*. . .

. . .

Before 1967 the only power which the High Court had to make an ouster order was the general power to grant injunctions conferred on it by s. 45(1) of the Supreme Court of Judicature (Consolidation) Act 1925. That subsection provided, so far as material:

'The High Court may grant . . . an injunction . . . by an interlocutory order in all cases in which it appears to the court to be just and convenient.'

The subsection replaced in substantially the same terms s. 25(8) of the Supreme Court of Judicature Act 1873, in respect of which it had been long held that, despite the apparently wide words of the subsection, the High Court only had jurisdiction to grant injunctions for the purpose of protecting legal or equitable rights: see *North London Ry Co v Great Northern Ry Co* (1883) 11 QBD 30 at 40 per Cotton LJ. It follows that s. 45(1) of the 1925 Act, and s. 37(1) of the Supreme Court Act 1981, by which it has now been replaced in substantially the same terms, must be interpreted as subject to the like limitation in their scope.

My Lords, until the radical social changes which have occurred in this country during the last two or three decades, the usual situation with regard to the ownership of a matrimonial home was that the whole estate in it, both legal and equitable, was vested in the husband. It followed from this that most wives could not apply for an ouster order under s. 45(1) of the 1925 Act on the ground that they had any legal or equitable interest in the matrimonial home which such an order could protect. However, a wife against whom no disqualifying matrimonial offence had been proved had a common law right to be provided by her husband with a home in which to live, and the High Court regarded itself as having jurisdiction under s. 45(1) of the 1925 Act to make an ouster order against a husband in order to protect that right pending suit: see *Silverstone v Silverstone* [1953] 1 All ER 556, [1953] P 174; *Gurasz v Gurasz* [1969] 3 All ER 822, [1970] P 11.

Parliament, however, did not regard this limited right of protection under s. 45(1) of the 1925 Act as adequate, as a result of which it passed the Matrimonial Homes Act 1967.

His Lordship then sets out the relevant provisions of the 1967 Act and later amendments, since consolidated in the Matrimonial Homes Act 1983 (p. 49, above), and of the 1976 Act and continues:

I conclude that it was the intention of the legislature, in passing and later amending and extending the scope of the 1967 Act, and in passing the 1976 Act, that the power of the High Court to make, during the subsistence of a marriage, orders relating to the occupation of a matrimonial home, including in particular an ouster order, which had previously been derived from s. 45(1) of the 1925 Act, should for the future be derived from, and exercised in accordance with, s. 1 of the 1967 Act. In this connection it is to be observed that, in s. 1(1) of the 1967 Act as originally enacted, it was expressly provided that, where one of the spouses was entitled to occupy the matrimonial home by virtue of any estate, interest or contract, and the other spouse was not so entitled, the latter should have rights of occupation, including a right 'not to be evicted or excluded . . . *except with the leave of the court given by an order under this section*' (my emphasis). If spouse A can only oust spouse B pursuant to an order made under s. 1 of the 1967 Act, it must surely follow that spouse B can only oust spouse A pursuant to a like order.

I reach a similar conclusion with regard to ouster orders made in a county court, namely that it was the intention of the legislature that the power of a county court to make ouster orders, which had been previously derived from the very general provisions of s. 74 of the County Courts Act 1959, should for the future be derived from, and exercised in accordance with, the provisions of the 1967 Act, county courts were given an additional power to make ouster orders by s. 1 of the 1976 Act, but it seems to me to be a necessary inference that the legislature intended such additional power to be exercised in accordance with the principles laid down in the 1967 Act.

. . . Those principles are contained in s. 1(3), the essential parts of which I set out earlier. That subsection requires the court to make such order as it thinks just and reasonable having regard to a number of specified matters. The matters so specified are these: (1) the conduct of the spouses to each other and otherwise; (2) the respective needs and financial resources of the spouses; (3) the needs of any children; and (4) all the circumstances of the case. With regard to these matters it is, in my opinion, of the utmost importance to appreciate that none of them is made, by the wording of s. 1(3), necessarily of more weight than any of the others, let alone made paramount over them. All the four matters specified are to be regarded, and the weight to be given to any particular one of them must depend on the facts of each case.

My Lords, I do not go so far as to say that the conduct of an applicant wife in the particular respect under discussion is necessarily and in all cases decisive, in a manner adverse to her, of the question whether the order for which she has applied should be made or not. It is, however, an important factor to be weighed in the scales, along with the other matters specified in s. 1(3) of the 1967 Act; and in a substantial number of cases at any rate it will be a factor of such weight as to lead a court to think that it would not be just or reasonable to allow her application. . . .

The approach adopted in *Samson v Samson* [1982] 1 All ER 780, [1982] 1 WLR 252 comes very near to treating the needs of any relevant children, not just as one of a number of matters to which s. 1(3) of the 1967 Act requires the court to have regard, but as a paramount matter overriding all others. That approach would certainly be justified in a case to which s. 1 of the Guardianship of Minors Act 1971 applied, including in particular a case in which the custody or upbringing of a child was in question. In my opinion, however, s. 1 of the 1971 Act, which re-enacted in like terms s. 1 of the Guardianship of Infants Act 1925, only applies where the custody or upbringing of a child is directly in question, and does not apply to a case where such matters are not directly in question but only arise incidentally in relation to other matters which are directly in question. In this connection it is to be observed that s. 1 of the Guardianship of Infants Act 1925 was in force when s. 1, including in particular sub-s. (3) of that section, was enacted, and the only inference which can, in my view, be drawn is that, in relation to ouster orders, s. 1(3) of the 1967 Act, making the needs of any children only one of a number of factors to be considered, was intended to exclude the paramount status which such needs would have had if s. 1 of the 1925 Act were treated as applicable.

Lord Scarman, however, disagreed on the law but not on the merits:

. . . It is clear that, as a matter of strict literal construction, the section imposes the principle of paramountcy only where the legal custody (or the property of the child) is in issue and has to be decided. But, unless it can be shown to have been excluded by express enactment or by necessary implication, the principle must guide the exercise of a court's discretion in every case in which the court is required to consider the welfare and upbringing of minor children. It would be contrary to the will of Parliament for a court to make an order directly affecting the rights, duties and responsibilities of parents in respect of the personal life of their children without ensuring that its order did not obstruct, or offend against the principle which must govern judicial decision as to legal custody. On this broad ground I would hold that, unless expressly or by necessary implication excluded by statute, the principle of s. 1 of the Guardianship Act applies wherever there are children whose interests must be considered before an order is made excluding one parent from the family home.

. . . When an ouster order is sought in pending divorce proceedings, the court is being invited to intervene at a most critical period in the lives of the children, the relationship between their parents having broken down (possibly irretrievably). The court is seized with the question of their welfare and upbringing. If ever there was a time to apply the principle of paramountcy of their needs and interest, it is in pending divorce proceedings. . . . In other proceedings also for an ouster order, where there are children but custody is not directly in issue, the courts should apply the principle of paramountcy for the reason I have earlier given, namely that the question whether or not to make the order cannot be considered without having regard to the issue of custody. . . .
Appeal allowed.

Questions

(i) Until the 1976 amendments, the 1967 Act did not allow the court to exclude a spouse who was either sole or joint tenant in law; how could it have laid down principles for doing so?

(ii) John Eekelaar (1986) asks 'Why then did the House of Lords re-write history and distort the flow of the development of the jurisprudence on matrimonial injunctions into the straitjacket of the 1967 (now 1983) Act? The answer, it seems, lies in the political climate regarding the effects of divorce on the interests of divorced men at the time the case arose.' To what is he referring?

(iii) Consider the following extract from *Myers v Myers* [1982] 1 All ER 776, [1982] 1 WLR 247, CA:

Arnold P: . . . The judge excluded the husband from the house, subject to giving him permission to return thereto during weekday evenings, when the wife was doing her part-time job, to look after the child of the marriage, a little girl called Naomi who is 2 years old. The foundation of the judge's order was substantially that these two young people could not live together in the same premises, at any rate for the time being, because the wife had come to a conclusion that she would not do so, the court drawing the conclusion, as the judge said, that she really did mean that and it was not merely a passing whim. The wife said that she had reached that conclusion because she was scared.

When one looks at the history of the marriage, which had in fact endured for about two years although there had been a similar period of cohabitation previously, one finds that the basis of her fear was not very large, looking at it in the terms of her own evidence. She said that he had a tendency to violent outbursts (which I take to be verbal abuse) even prior to the marriage; over the last few months matters have deteriorated; she says he is continuing to drink very heavily and to take drugs (he says that is cannabis); that he goes out drinking twice a week, mainly at weekends, and when he returns home after his drinking sessions he very easily loses his temper and then becomes violent; except in so far as it is later particularised, there are no details about that. Then she says that he constantly abuses her, and indeed in a measure that is agreed by the husband. She says he is jealous and makes accusations of infidelity against her and related threats and that this is distressing to her and the marriage.

Then there are three specific allegations of violence. The first one which took place a fortnight before they were married was something which arose in the course of an argument in the street. The judge, rightly in my view, discounts that because it is so very shortly before the marriage.

Then there was an occasion a few months later, sometime in 1979 apparently, when the husband tipped the wife out of bed but no-one seems to have attached very much importance to that.

Then there was a substantial and most unhappy occasion of physical violence on 16 October 1981. There had been some disagreement between the parties at a dance to which they had gone, the husband resenting what he regarded as 'flighty behaviour' on the part of his wife, and in particular in one instance an impermissible approach by some man with whom she was dancing towards her. But the immediate occasion of the violence was that, when they got home, both of them being sensible of the desire for a reconciliation after the upsets of the evening, they went to bed and started to make love. At this time she was having some difficulty in this context of her marriage and at some late stage, so it is said by the husband, in the course of that contact she wished to terminate it and did so, much to the annoyance and frustration of the husband who gave her a 'thumping', as it is called. That the judge, in the face of a disputed piece of evidence, believed. The wife maintained before the judge, and here he did not believe her, that the marriage was all over. To quote the judge: 'She said consistently in the witness box that the marriage was at an end and that she cannot go back. I am not satisfied that is what in fact the future does hold.' Later on he says: 'I hope a reconciliation may still be possible', and then he said he thought 'it is more likely to occur if the parties are apart than if the wife is kept away or if they live under the same roof'.

Even given the law as stated in *Richards v Richards* would you have allowed the husband's appeal?

The Law Commission outline the criticisms of *Richards* in their *Working Paper* (1989):

3.19 The reasoning of the House of Lords in *Richards v Richards* has attracted serious criticism [e.g. Eekelaar, 1986]. More importantly, for our purposes, the position which has since developed could be thought unsatisfactory for a number of reasons. First, the application of the Matrimonial Homes Act criteria to all cases fails to distinguish between the very different situations in which exclusion may be sought: (i) there may be an immediate need for protection against violence or other forms of abuse; (ii) there may be an immediate need to regulate a couple's short term accommodation needs in a period of disharmony, possibly leading up to divorce; (iii) where the couple have mutual rights of occupation in the home, there may be a need for a longer term adjustment of those rights.

3.20 Secondly, the criteria were first enacted in 1967 before many of the most significant developments in this field: before the awakening of public concern in the problems of violence and abuse within the family; before the replacement of the doctrine of the matrimonial offence with the concept of irretrievable breakdown of the marriage as the sole ground for divorce; before the introduction of powers of property adjustment on divorce; and before any serious consideration had been given to the problems of cohabiting couples and their children. As the 1967 Act was principally designed to give protection against dispositions to third parties, the original purpose was to identify those non-owning spouses who were sufficiently deserving of long term accommodation in the family home to entitle them to resist such dispositions.

3.21 Hence the criteria could be said to give inadequate protection against violence, by requiring conduct to be balanced against other factors, and not acknowledging that in such cases personal protection for the victims should be given priority over the hardship to respondent. Although the remedy is discretionary in magistrates' courts, there is no indication in the 1978 Act that the court should be investigating any mitigating factors in the violence or that it must be serious if it is to justify the victim in her desire to live apart for a while. The success rate for applications for injunctions under the 1976 Act is high, but there is considerable variation over the country. Magistrates, on the other hand, refuse very few applications [Smith, 1989, pp. 90–91].

3.22 A further criticism, relating to cases in which an ouster injunction is sought during marital breakdown and where divorce proceedings have already begun or are being considered by one or both parties, is of the necessity for holding a trial of the parties' conduct at this interlocutory stage. Allegations of violence or of other types of unacceptable behaviour constituting conduct relevant to the granting of ouster injunctions may also be cited in an existing or subsequent divorce petition based on the respondent's 'behaviour' under section 1(2)(d) of the Matrimonial Causes Act 1973. The court is then placed in the difficult position of having to make findings of fact for one purpose in advance of the trial of the same issue for another purpose. A further result of pre-divorce litigation involving issues of conduct is that it is likely, on the one hand, to cause delay in just those cases where a leaving should take place quickly, and on the other hand, to impede reconciliation, where that is appropriate, by protracted battles between the parties as to allegations of not only past, but continuing conduct. This is contrary to the general trend of divorce law in reducing the need for recrimination and fault-finding, with all the bitterness and conflict which this can entail. It is a particular cause for concern that the need to provide a period of calm during which the parties may perhaps become reconciled has been held to be irrelevant [*Summers v Summers* [1986] 1 FLR 343].

3.23 Above all, criticism has been made of the risk that the children's welfare will be given insufficient weight in the balancing exercise [Eekelaar, 1986; Edwards and Halpern, 1988]. In *Richards* itself, there was no evidence at all that the children's welfare was suffering from the presence of both parties in the home: quite the reverse, as the couple had made arrangements to share their care between them. In *Summers v Summers* [1986] 1 FLR 343, however, the judge found that it was not in the children's interests to witness continuing bitter quarrels between the parties in which (it appears) furniture was broken and objects smashed. He also thought that it would be beneficial for all to have a break for some time. It was held that he appeared to have given too much weight to the interests of the children as against the draconian nature of the order, where the couple were equally to blame for the situation which had developed. This is inconsistent with the general trend of the law to give increased, if not predominating weight to the interests of children, even in relation to matters of finance and property. . . .

3.24 The courts have often referred to the draconian nature of an ouster order, and indeed its effects will often be severe, particularly if it is granted at short notice without giving much time to arrange alternative accommodation. This in itself can produce circular arguments, where the remedy is thought so severe that it is only appropriate where the risk of harm is such that it must be granted in terms which increase its severity [e.g. *Burke v Burke* [1987] 2 FLR 71]. Yet there are obviously cases in which one of the parties can arrange alternative accommodation, with family or friends or commercially, at least for a short time and without suffering severe or even appreciable hardship. There are equally obviously cases where the hardship caused to one party if the other is allowed to remain will be much more severe than the effects of ouster. Thus although it will often be a severe remedy, the assumption that it is so in all cases can obscure the considerable differences between the circumstances of the parties and in which the remedy is sought. Even where it is severe, it may be the only proper solution to the problem.

3.25 Finally, the 1967 criteria are not easily applicable to cases between unmarried couples [see Chapter 8, above]. There is, for example, no indication of the relevance, if any, of their respective property rights. As between married couples, the Matrimonial Homes Act 1983 provides mutual rights of occupation and procedures specifically designed to enforce or adjust these irrespective of whether the couple intend to divorce. On divorce or judicial separation, the Matrimonial Causes Act 1973 gives power to adjust the property rights themselves. Neither statute applies to unmarried couples, who will normally have to resort to actions under the ordinary law unless they can obtain relief under section 1 of the 1976 Act.

Question

Is it possible to provide *both* effective protection against family violence *and* a sensible method of resolving accommodation problems when a relationship is breaking down?

The *Family and Civil Committees of the Council of Her Majesty's Circuit Judges* (1990), in their response to the Law Commission's Working Paper, make some radical proposals:

POLICY OBJECTIVES: THE CONTEXT

In 1976, when Parliament enacted the Domestic Violence and Matrimonial Proceedings Act, the perceived problem needing to be addressed was the need for immediate intervention of the law to protect battered women and children. In 1989, with the development of the concepts and practice of conciliation or mediation, we believe that domestic violence needs to be considered in a broader context than short-term protection. In some cases which reach the courts a long-term chronic history of violence presents. Even in these cases our anecdotal experience shows that women quite often resume cohabitation after having obtained an injunction.

In other cases, there is no chronic history of violence, but violence has happened in the context of the rupture of the family, for example when one partner discovers that the other has formed a relationship with a third party. In such cases the violence is the symptom, not the cause, of the problem and a knee-jerk response of an application for or the grant of an order under the Domestic Violence and Matrimonial Proceedings Act 1976 alone may exacerbate the problem rather than help the partners move into constructive resolution of their family crisis. Thus, we argue, injunctions for personal protection need to be considered in the context of the future relationships of the family as a whole.

CHILDREN AND ANTI-MOLESTATION ORDERS

Although some courts refuse to grant an injunction without seeking to address problems relating to contact between children and the respondent, quite often orders are granted without effective inquiry into such contact. The effect on children of having their father ordered to leave the home may be beneficial where the children or their mother have endured violence, but in many cases the sudden enforced departure of their father may be extremely disturbing and damaging to children.

. . .

PROPOSALS FOR DECLARATION OF POLICY

1. In relation to friction associated with the breakdown of families and to molestation, violence and other damaging behaviour, an object of the law and of legal process while any legal proceedings are pending is to contrive a truce between the parties and to direct them towards constructive resolution of their problems and away from destructive recrimination. While adjudication should remain available for deciding issues that cannot be resolved by agreement, constructive readjustment by agreement should manifestly be encouraged by legal process.

2. Legal process should enable the parties to proceedings related to the breakdown of a family to arrive at a truce and to work towards constructive resolution of their problems wherever practicable without having to make an application to the court based on allegations of misconduct.

3. A truce available through legal process should be available wherever practicable without the emotional and financial cost of an application based on allegations of misconduct.

4. An injunction should not be granted to one party to a marriage or a cohabitation directing the conduct of the other party unless the court is of the opinion that:
   (i) an automatic truce binding on both parties is insufficient to protect a party or a child of the family; and
   (ii) no child of the family would unreasonably be affected by the proposed injunction.

PROPOSALS FOR REFORM
1. Automatic Injunctive Direction to Both Parties to Family Proceedings
We consider that the most effective way to give effect to the policy advocated above might well be to provide that upon either party to a marriage or a cohabitation making any application to a court in relation to the breakdown of the family (divorce, separation, residence of or contact with children, occupation or ownership of the matrimonial home, financial relief, possession or ownership of property, etc.), there should automatically and at once be applied an injunctive direction to both parties. The direction should forbid each of the parties:
- (i) to use any violence against or otherwise to molest the other party or any child of either party;
- (ii) to destroy, dispose of or dissipate any family property or assets;
- (iii) to use any force, intimidation or molestation to gain care of or contact with any child of either party;
- (iv) to use any force, intimidation or molestation to remove the other party from the matrimonial home.

The automatic direction should remain in force while the proceedings are pending unless superseded by an order of the court or by mutual undertakings given to the court.

2. Exclusion and Ouster from the Matrimonial Home and Powers of Arrest
We propose that these remedies should be available only upon the court being of the opinion that the evidence shows that:
- (i) an automatic direction as set out above is insufficient to protect the applicant or any child of either party; and
- (ii) no child of the family would unreasonably be affected by such an order.

3. Mutual Undertaking
We propose that, whether or not proposals 1 and 2 above are adopted, upon an inter partes application being heard by the court, if both parties attend they should be invited to resolve, as far as possible, their differences by mutual undertakings.

4. Distinguishing Short-Term Protection Orders from Long-Term Readjustment Orders
Although the working paper refers to the difference between short-term protection and longer-term orders, in our opinion the working paper does not carry this to its logical conclusion. We propose that there should be two separate and distinct types of order:
- (a) short-term protection orders (STP)
- (b) long-term readjustment orders (LTR)

Both types of orders should be able to deal with: (1) the home and personal property; (2) residence of and contact with children.

The judges were influenced by what they had been told of the practice in California. However, not everyone in America is convinced of the merits of an automatic truce, as the following account of the *Report of the New York Task Force on Domestic Violence* (1987) shows:

Mutual orders of protection direct each party not to harass, menace, recklessly endanger, attempt to assault or assault the other party. The Task Force found that many family court judges routinely enter mutual orders of protection in family-offense proceedings upon the mere oral request of respondents or *sua sponte* without prior notice to petitioners and without an opportunity for rebuttal testimony by petitioners. Nearly two-thirds of male (sixty-five percent) and female (sixty-six percent) survey respondents reported that judges 'often' or 'sometimes' issue mutual orders even though respondents have not filed petitions.

Mutual orders of protection issued in this manner create the appearance that both parties have been found to be violent, not withstanding the absence of proof of the petitioner's conduct. As Judge Richard Huttner testified:

'[T]he woman who came to court for help, is now herself a subject of the order of protection, having had no notice of the allegations made by the respondent, totally unprepared to meet them, not having had the opportunity to consult with an attorney beforehand, the man had usually six weeks to seek counsel and to prepare his case, and the lady six seconds. This is not due process, and it is unfair.'

In subsequent family court proceedings, the petitioner will be seen as aggressive, provocative or violent — equally responsible for the violence or abuse. As a result, the court may be reluctant to grant a more restrictive order of protection directing the respondent to stay away from the marital home or to hold the respondent in contempt if there is another violent incident. The domestic-violence victim with a mutual order of protection is in a worse position than if she had no order.

'The issuance of such orders reinforce[s] the historical fallacy that battered women are responsible for partners' behavior and are equal and active participants in the violence. . . . A woman who experiences difficulty in [en]forcing a mutual order of protection is left with little protection and her partner is given the message that his behavior is excusable and he will not be held accountable for his violence, thus perpetuating the cycle of battering.'

A mutual order gives police ambiguous direction regarding its enforcement. Officers are put in the position of doing nothing or of arresting both parties because of a violation of the order.

'The police don't know what to do with [mutual orders]. They go into a domestic violence situation and are very confused, getting conflicting reports of what happened. And I've talked with them, and when there is a mutual order of protection, they throw up their hands. They have no guidance. They don't know what to do, and, in general, arrests are not made.'

The victim may withdraw the request for police assistance because the arrest of both parents requires placement of the children with child protective services. She may be unaware of the true import of a mutual order and call the police, to her ultimate regret.

One rationale proffered for issuing mutual orders of protection is that women sometimes request orders of protection as 'tactics' in matrimonial actions. Orders of protection are, therefore, made mutual to 'neutralize' perceived tactical advantages.

The Task Force believes this view to be ill-founded. Women often seek an order of protection after starting a matrimonial action because this is when violence is most likely to occur.

'[P]ost service of matrimonial summons is an extremely dangerous point in the violent relationship. The service of a matrimonial summons is a statement of assertiveness. The woman is standing up for herself. She is asserting her right to control her own life. The one thing the wife-beater does not allow is his wife to assert herself.'

Moreover, there exist profound disincentives to a petitioner's requesting an order of protection as a mere litigation tactic. If the family court petition and divorce complaint have the same allegations, a dismissal of the petition could be given collateral estoppel effect in the matrimonial action. The family court hearing gives the respondent discovery of the petitioner's cause of action for divorce to which the respondent would not be entitled in the matrimonial action. Finally, the petitioner is required to try her case twice, creating a record that can be used against her on cross-examination in a subsequent proceeding. These factors make it unlikely that petitioners will misuse family-offense proceedings as tactics in matrimonial actions.

Questions

(i) In *The Mail on Sunday*, 5 May 1991, Julie Burchill began:

A woman was this week found stabbed to death inside a London police station. She had been left with her husband to discuss 'their' problems in a sinisterly titled 'domestic violence unit'. Far from being the tragic freak accident it has been painted, this took the modern craze for non-specific 'conciliation' to its logical conclusion. . . . It's just another way of the State washing its hands of the problems of the weak and oppressed, and pressurising them to simply rub along with those who seek to make their lives a misery.

Do you agree?

(ii) Mary Hayes (1990) suggests we build on the Domestic Proceedings and Magistrates' Courts Act 1978 and provide almost automatic personal protection and ouster orders in cases of violence; but what should we do about cases like *Wiseman v Simpson* [1988] 1 All ER 245, [1988] 1 FLR 490, where 'the judge found that the parties were two young people who had simply ceased to be in love with each other, that, as they had agreed, there was no prospect that they could live together under the same roof and that the tension between them was retarding the development of the child'? (The judge granted the order, but the Court of Appeal ordered a new trial.)

(iii) What, too, should be done about forms of molestation falling short of violence? As the Law Commission point out in their *Working Paper* (1989):

3.27 . . . Molestation includes, but is wider than, violence.
'Violence is a form of molestation but molestation may take place without the threat or use of violence and still be serious and inimical to mental and physical health.' [*Davis v Johnson* [1979] AC 264, 334]
'Pester' has been suggested as a synonym, [*Vaughan v Vaughan* [1973] 3 All ER 449, [1973] 1 WLR 1159] and it has also been said that molestation applies to any conduct which can properly be regarded as such a degree of harassment as to call for the intervention of the court. [*Horner v Horner* [1982] Fam 90, [1982] 2 All ER 495]. Hence the relief available under the 1976 Act or in matrimonial causes covers a wide range of behaviour which can cause particular problems when a family relationship is breaking down but which does not necessarily involve the commission of a tort. However, it has recently been held that there is no tort of harassment in English law, and hence no protection for those who do not fall within the ambit of the Act [*Patel v Patel* [1988] 2 FLR 179].

(iv) Should non-molestation orders be available (*a*) to former spouses, (*b*) to former cohabitants, (*c*) to other people sharing a household, including gay and lesbian couples, or (*d*) to other members of the family? What makes households or families more deserving of such a remedy than other victims of harassment or molestation?

(v) If the police begin to implement the new policy (p. 387, above), would it benefit the victims to give the police power to apply for civil remedies on their behalf?

(vi) Under the Domestic Violence and Matrimonial Proceedings Act 1976, powers of arrest can only be attached as follows:

2. – (1) Where, on an application by a party to a marriage, a judge grants an injunction containing a provision (in whatever terms) –
    (*a*) restraining the other party to the marriage from using violence against the applicant, or
    (*b*) restraining the other party from using violence against a child living with the applicant, or
    (*c*) excluding the other party from the matrimonial home or from a specified area in which the matrimonial home is included,
the judge may, if he is satisfied that the other party has caused actual bodily harm to the applicant or, as the case may be, to the child concerned and considers that he is likely to do so again, attach a power of arrest to the injunction.

Bearing in mind the problems of enforcement (p. 393, above), should powers of arrest be attached automatically in all cases of violence? Or should they be abandoned as an anomaly in civil proceedings and no longer necessary in the light of the new police policy?

Another problem is graphically illustrated by Erin Pizzey (1974):

Going to court is quite an ordeal. The High Court in the Strand is as awe-inspiring as it sounds. It is a massive crenellated building with white towers and spires outside and a huge arched hall inside. The place is honeycombed with narrow corridors that run off the central hall to the small courtrooms. Everywhere ant-like uniformed figures bustle around. Barristers stride along in their black flapping gowns and wrinkled white wigs, best-suited solicitors scurry in their wake, blue-suited ushers look officious. The people waiting in little knots look shabby and out of place in this impersonal palace of justice.
If the case is to be heard in the morning we have to be there by 10. Waiting to meet the solicitor is always an anxious time because if the husband has been told to attend the court too, it will be the first time that his wife has had to face him since she ran away.
If you manage to avoid meeting him before, you usually find him crouched on the hard little benches that line the ill-lit, crowded corridor outside the courtroom. There, knee to knee and face to face, the couple must wait, sometimes for hours, before they are called into court.
My first time was with Lesley. Pat had come along to hold her other hand and together we

had to hold Lesley upright because she was in such a state of fear at the prospect of seeing her husband. He had a terrible reputation, and on the night she had left him, he'd gone to see her friends with a gang and broken into the house. The gang beat up the old couple upstairs and their two sons. It took ten policemen to get them out, and though he was charged he was released on bail. Now we were in court to ask for an injunction to give her custody of the three children, maintenance while her divorce petition went through and a non-molestation order to keep him from carrying out his threat to kill her.

Waiting to go into the courtroom, we were all frightened. The solicitor and the barrister were quite unperturbed, and the barrister gave the impression that Lesley was making an unnecessary fuss. We were due in court mid-morning, so we settled down on the little benches to wait, morosely contemplating the other silent people waiting, and gazing at the stained walls.

The tedium and the peace were disturbed by the arrival of Lesley's husband and his henchmen. Then began a cat-and-mouse shuffle as we moved round the narrow corridors trying to prevent him upsetting Lesley even more. By the time it was our turn Lesley was speechless with fright and we half carried her between us into the court.

PRACTICE NOTE

FAMILY DIVISION

The President is greatly concerned by the increasing number of applications being made ex parte in the Royal Courts of Justice for injunctions, which could and should have been made (if at all) on two clear days' notice to the other side, as required by the rules.

An ex parte application should not be made, or granted, unless there is real immediate danger of serious injury or irreparable damage. A recent examination of ex parte applications shows that nearly 50% were unmeritorious, being made days, or even weeks, after the last incident of which complaint was made. This wastes time, causes needless expense, usually to the Legal Aid Fund, and is unjust to respondents.

Where notice of an application for an injunction is to be given and an early hearing date is sought, practitioners are reminded of the special arrangements which exist at the Royal Courts of Justice whereby the applicant's solicitor is able to select for the hearing any day on which the court is sitting. . . .

RL BAYNE-POWELL
Senior Registrar

26 June 1978

Questions

(i) If the relevant question is 'real immediate danger', is it obviously unmeritorious to apply 'days, or even weeks', after the last incident?
(ii) Which is the more unjust: making an alleged batterer leave the home for a short while before he has an opportunity of defending himself against the allegations, or making the alleged victim leave for a short while before she has an opportunity of putting her case before a court?
(iii) Would you favour (*a*) adopting the higher standard of proof applicable in criminal cases, or (*b*) abandoning the hearsay rule entirely, or (*c*) both, in ex parte applications?

PRACTICE NOTE

FAMILY DIVISION

To secure uniformity of practice, the President has issued the following note with the concurrence of the Lord Chancellor.
1. Section 1(1)(*c*) of the Domestic Violence and Matrimonial Proceedings Act 1976 empowers a county court to include in an injunction provisions excluding a party from the matrimonial home or a part of the matrimonial home or from a specified area in which the matrimonial home is included. Where a power of arrest under s. 2 of the 1976 Act is attached to any injunction containing such provisions, the respondent is liable to be arrested if he enters the matrimonial home or part thereof or specified area at any time while the injunction remains in force.

2. It is within the discretion of the court to decide whether an injunction should be granted and, if so, for how long it should operate. But whenever an injunction is granted excluding one of the parties from the matrimonial home (or a part thereof or specified area), consideration should be given to imposing a time limit on the operation of the injunction. In most cases a period of up to three months is likely to suffice, at least in the first instance. It will be open to the respondent in any event to apply for the discharge of the injunction before the expiry of the period fixed, for instance on the ground of reconciliation, and to the applicant to apply for an extension.

RL BAYNE-POWELL
21 July 1978   Senior Registrar

Questions

What would you advise a battered wife to do once the three months are up if she is still very frightened of her husband, but does not want a divorce because of the various legal and other advantages to her of remaining married? Does the Matrimonial Homes Act 1983 any longer provide her with a remedy? What can an unmarried woman do? (See Chapter 8, above.)

PRACTICE NOTE

FAMILY DIVISION

The police are holding some thousands of orders containing a power of arrest made under s. 1(1)(c) of the Domestic Violence and Matrimonial Proceedings Act 1976. Experience has shown that the police are rarely called on to take action on an injunction which is more than three months old, and the requirement that they should retain indefinitly the orders containing a power of arrest imposes an unnecessary burden upon them. . . .

To assist in easing the burdens of the police and in enabling them to concentrate on the cases where action may be required, judges should consider, at the time a power of arrest is attached to an injunction, for what period of time this sanction is likely to be required. Unless a judge is satisfied that a longer period is necessary in a particular case, the period should not exceed three months. In those few cases where danger to the applicant is still reasonably apprehended towards the expiry of three months, application may be made to the court to extend the duration of the injunction.

RL BAYNE-POWELL
22 December 1980   Senior Registrar

Questions

(i) Would a criminal court regard three months as an appropriate period for the suspension of a sentence of imprisonment for occasioning (a) actual or (b) grievous bodily harm?
(ii) Do these practice notes help us to understand why the WAFE study of women in refuges (Binney, Harkell and Nixon, 1981) found (a) that a power of arrest had little effect upon police willingness to arrest and prosecute; (b) that only 8% of the women left the refuges to return to live alone in their homes and only 4% were still there a year after the original interview; and (c) that the women had found refuges and self-help organisations more helpful than the official agencies?

In *Violence Against Women* (1985), a Working Group of the Women's National Commission commented:

108. The Working Group received evidence that these apparently helpful legislative measures have, in practice, achieved much less than was anticipated. . . . Many battered women are wholly ignorant of the law and are deterred from consulting solicitors because too afraid or believing it would be too costly. The Courts have proved suspicious of the wide powers which can be taken against the allegedly violent partner including removing him from his own property, and if they agree to grant injunctions they may limit the period these remain in force. Practical difficulties for complainants and their solicitors have proved to be great: the procedures are cumbersome and time consuming; it is virtually impossible for the police to assist in enforcing an injunction with no powers of arrest attached, and, probably through lack of specific training and lack of serious concern with domestic matters, police have often proved ill-informed about what to do, and sluggish to act, even where powers of arrest exist. . . .

111. Parker (1985) refers to the fact that in 1980, out of 6,400 injunctions granted under Section 1 of the DVA, only 24% had powers of arrest attached to them (in the North East only 10%). Other authorities discuss in greater detail the practical difficulties solicitors for battered women and the women themselves may encounter in obtaining injunctions. Violent husbands can be clever and elusive. They may return during the night to the home from which they are excluded by injunction to attack their wife. Wives may have difficulty in establishing that a breach of the injunction has occurred. Injuries may need to be grave and obvious to convince sceptical authorities. If a power of arrest is attached, police may nevertheless be very reluctant to act and have to be convinced that a breach has occurred. Where there is no power of arrest, the battered wife has to apply to the Court for her husband to *be charged with contempt of court*, first ensuring notice is served on him. . . . The period of any legal delays can be most dangerous for wives as violent men are often inflamed by wives taking legal steps. . .

113. The Working Group accepts that there are intrinsic difficulties for the Courts in establishing when violent partners should be subject to injunctions, especially when this makes a man homeless. If injunctions were granted to women without enquiry, judges would be criticised with some justification for failing to give a fair hearing to husbands to whom the asset of their home and the stability this represents for them will normally be very important. However, the Working Group urge judges to consider the frequently desperate situation of battered wives, who are obliged to seek safety and redress for acts of what may be extreme violence through an inadequate mechanism. They would like to see powers of arrest attached to all injunctions made under the DVA, unless the judge is satisfied that there is no danger of physical attack. It would be desirable if legislation could be amended to incorporate this principle.

They go on to discuss alternative solutions:

115. . . . An alternative to restraining the man is to remove the woman to a place of safety where she can begin a new separate existence if she wishes. . . . Women's Aid refuges serve a number of purposes admirably, and are an exceedingly welcome development which needs supporting. But women often return to violent husbands because of concern about the quality of their own and their children's lives in refuges, which are often overcrowded. This underlines the importance of the Housing (Homeless Persons) Act 1977, which defines women victims of domestic violence as in 'priority need' and obliges a local authority to find permanent accommodation for them. Women's Aid groups normally find that the existence of the Act now enables them to negotiate some permanent local authority accommodation for women living in their refuges. But local authorities tend to strictly ration what is available. The assumption sometimes made that a very high proportion of women in refuges return permanently to their violent partners is not true. One research study undertaken by Jan Pahl (1985) found that:

> 'Out of the 42 women, 20 (48%) never lived with their husbands again after leaving the refuge, while only two lived with their husbands continuously from the time they left the refuge until the time of the second interview (about two years later). The remaining 20 of the women (48%) made between one and nine attempts at reconciliation. . . . Of these only nine couples were still together at the second interview. . . .'

Lack of a housing offer amongst other factors has forced large numbers of women to try again with their husbands and to suffer further violence. The Working Group therefore urge Housing Authorities to accept their responsibilities in relation to battered wives. It has been suggested that if Housing Authorities had a policy of seeking to find some accommodation (temporary or permanent) for violent husbands they would enable battered wives and children to remain in the family home in family sized accommodation which would be under-utilised by the man himself. To effect this kind of sensible solution probably requires multi-agency working groups to be set up on which police, personal social services, housing authority, and women's organisations representatives could serve.

Questions

(i) Knowing that a woman with children who is not intentionally homeless has a priority need under (now) Part III of the Housing Act 1985, would you be more or less inclined to grant an order ousting her husband from the matrimonial council house?

(ii) If you do, will (*a*) the local authority, or (*b*) the court be able to transfer the tenancy into her name (see p. 51, above)?

(iii) What if they are not married to one another (see *Ainsbury v Millington* [1986] 1 All ER 73)?

(iv) As the House of Commons Select Committee on *Violence in Marriage* (1975) asked during its proceedings, why do we not create hostels to receive the battering men?

(v) Imagine that when Barbara Auckland left her husband (p. 373, above), she had pushed Susan's pram, not to an aunt who contacted the local social services department, but (*a*) to the local police station, or (*b*) to a women's refuge in Barnsley. What might each have advised in 1974? Or in 1983? Or in 1990?

Before concluding that either might have saved Susan's life, consider what the social workers *might* have done, then or now. We shall turn to the specific remedies available to them in Chapter 13, but first we must consider generally the legal relationship between parents, their children and the state.

CHAPTER 10

Parental responsibility

ARTICLE 8

(1) Everyone has the right to respect for his private and family life, his home and his correspondence.
(2) There shall be no interference by a public authority with the exercise of this right except such as is in accordance with the law and is necessary in a democratic society in the interests of national security, public safety or the economic well-being of the country, for the prevention of disorder or crime, for the protection of health or morals, or for the protection of the rights and freedoms of others.

ARTICLE 9

(1) Everyone has the right to freedom of thought, conscience and religion; this right includes freedom to change his religion or belief and freedom, either alone or in community with others and in public or private, to manifest his religion or belief, in worship, teaching, practice and observance.
(2) Freedom to manifest one's religion or beliefs shall be subject only to such limitations as are prescribed by law and are necessary in a democratic society in the interests of public safety, for the protection of public order, health or morals, or for the protection of the rights and freedoms of others.

PROTOCOL NO. 1, ARTICLE 2

No person shall be denied the right to education. In the exercise of any functions which it assumes in relation to education and to teaching, the State shall respect the right of parents to ensure such education and teaching in conformity with their own religious and philosophical convictions.

Thus the *European Convention of Human Rights* seeks to achieve a free and plural society through, among other things, a proper balance between family privacy and the right to learn. Relying on parents to bring up their children is seen as an essential feature of Western democratic society. But is this for the parents', the children's or society's sake? When should a child's interests or wishes prevail over his parents'? How much help should the parents be given to perform their task? These are large issues which can only be touched on here, but they serve as an introduction to the new philosophy of the Children Act 1989, with its transition from rights to responsibility for parents.

1 Parental rights and children's welfare

The concept of parental 'rights' achieved its greatest legal prominence in the nineteenth century. An example of eighteenth century thinking is provided by Sir William Blackstone in the first volume of his *Commentaries on the Laws of England* (1765):

1. And, first, the duties of parents to legitimate children: which principally consist in three particulars; their maintenance, their protection, and their education.

The duty of parents to provide for the *maintenance* of their children is a principle of natural law; an obligation, says Puffendorf, laid on them not only by nature herself, but by their own proper act, in bringing them into the world: for they would be in the highest manner injurious to their issue, if they only gave the children life, that they might afterwards see them perish. By begetting them therefore they have entered into a voluntary obligation, to endeavour, as far as in them lies, that the life which they have bestowed shall be supported and preserved. And thus the children will have a perfect *right* of receiving maintenance from their parents. And the president Montesquieu has a very just observation upon this head: that the establishment of marriage in all civilized states is built on this natural obligation of the father to provide for his children; for that ascertains and makes known the person who is bound to fulfil this obligation: whereas, in promiscuous and illicit conjunctions, the father is unknown; and the mother finds a thousand obstacles in her way; — shame, remorse, the constraint of her sex, and the rigor of laws; — that stifle her inclinations to perform this duty: and besides, she generally wants ability.

After discussing the relevant provisions of English law, including its deficiencies in the matter of education, he continues:

2. The *power* of parents over their children is derived from the former consideration, their duty; this authority being given them, partly to enable the parent more effectually to perform his duty, and partly as a recompence for his care and trouble in the faithful discharge of it. And upon this score the municipal laws of some nations have given a much larger authority to the parents, than others. The ancient Roman laws gave the father a power of life and death over his children; upon this principle, that he who gave had also the power of taking away. . . .

The power of a parent by our English laws is much more moderate; but still sufficient to keep the child in order and obedience. He may lawfully correct his child, being under age, in a reasonable manner; for this is for the benefit of his education. The consent or concurrence of the parent to the marriage of his child under age, was also *directed* by our ancient law to be obtained: but now it is absolutely *necessary*; for without it the contract is void. And this also is another means, which the law has put into the parent's hands, in order the better to discharge his duty; first, of protecting his children from the snares of artful and designing persons; and, next of settling them properly in life, by preventing the ill consequences of too early and precipitate marriages. A father has no other power over his son's *estate*, than as his trustee or guardian; for, though he may receive the profits during the child's minority, yet he must account for them when he comes of age. He may indeed have the benefit of his children's labour while they live with him, and are maintained by him: but this is no more than he is entitled to from his apprentices or servants. The legal power of a father (for a mother, as such, is entitled to no power, but only to reverence and respect) the power of a father, I say, over the persons of his children ceases at the age of twenty one: for they are then enfranchised by arriving at years of discretion, or that point which the law has established (as some must necessarily be established) when the empire of the father, or other guardian, gives place to the empire of reason. Yet, till that age arrives, this empire of the father continues even after his death; for he may by his will appoint a guardian to his children. . . .

3. The *duties* of children to their parents arise from a principle of natural justice and retribution. For to those, who gave us existence, we naturally owe subjection and obedience during our minority, and honour and reverence ever after; they, who protected the weakness of our infancy, are entitled to our protection in the infirmity of their age; they who by sustenance and education have enabled their offspring to prosper, ought in return to be supported by that offspring, in case they stand in need of assistance. Upon this principle proceed all the duties of children to their parents, which are enjoined by positive laws.

Questions

(i) How much of this represents the modern law?
(ii) Do you think that Blackstone's account of the rationale underlying parental power is equally applicable today?

If parents have rights, there might be two ways of enforcing them: either by an action in tort against anyone who interfered or by an action to recover the child and impose the parental will upon him. There was a common law action in tort, but only if the third party, either by enticement, seduction or harbouring, or by a wrongful act against the child, caused a loss of services actually being rendered by the child to the father. These actions were abolished in 1970 and 1982 respectively. Hence in *F v Wirral Metropolitan Borough Council* [1991] 2 All ER 648, [1991] 2 WLR 1132, Stuart-Smith LJ announced that 'In my judgment [counsel's] submission that this court could now declare that a parent had an action for damages for interference with his or her right as a parent was wholly misconceived.' However, various remedies were available to recover a child and enforce the father's wishes as to his upbringing (see Pettitt, 1957). These reached their peak in a case which Lord Upjohn in *J v C* [1970] AC 668, [1969] 1 All ER 788, p. 411, below, could 'only describe as dreadful'.

Re Agar-Ellis, Agar-Ellis v Lascelles
(1883) 24 Ch D 317, 53 LJ Ch 10, 50 LT 161, 32 WR 1, Court of Appeal

A Protestant father agreed at his marriage that any children would be brought up Roman Catholics, but at the birth of the first child he changed his mind. The mother, however, taught the children Roman Catholicism and eventually they refused to go to a Protestant church. The father made them wards of court and the court (see (1878) 10 Ch D 49, 48 LJ Ch 1) restrained the mother from taking them to confession or to a Roman Catholic church and left the father to do what he thought fit for their spiritual welfare. He therefore took the children from their mother and placed them with other people, allowing her to visit only once a month and censoring her letters. In 1883, the second daughter, then aged 16, wrote to the judge begging to be allowed the free exercise of her religion and to live with her mother. The father agreed to the former but not the latter. Accordingly, she and her mother petitioned the court to allow them a two-month holiday together and freedom of correspondence and access. The father opposed this because he feared that the mother would alienate his child's affections. Pearson J dismissed the petition on the ground that the court had no jurisdiction to interfere with the father's legal right to control the custody and education of his children, in the absence of any fault on his part. The petitioners appealed.

Brett MR: . . . But the law of *England* has recognised the natural rights of a father, not as guardian of his children but as the father, because he is the father . . . The law recognises the rights of the father because it recognises the natural duties of the father. Now the natural duties of a father are to treat his child with the utmost affection and with infinite tenderness, to forgive his child without stint and under all circumstances. None of those duties are expected of a testamentary guardian, but they are the natural duties of a father, which, if he breaks, he breaks from all that nature calls upon him to do; and if he breaks from these duties, the law may not be able to insist upon their full performance. The law cannot inquire in every case how fathers have fulfilled their duties. The law does not interfere because of the great trust and faith it has in the natural affection of the father to perform his duties, and therefore gives him corresponding rights. . . .

But there are limits to the forbearance and patience of the law in particular cases, . . . If, for instance, a father by his immoral conduct has become a person who really is unfit in the eyes of everybody to perform his duties to his child, and, therefore, to claim the rights of a father towards his child, the Court then will interfere. That is, if the child be a ward of Court; for unless the child be a ward of Court, the Court has no greater jurisdiction as between the father and child than it has between any other persons. But if the child be a ward of Court, and if the father has been guilty of that amount of immorality which convinces the Court that he is not fit to claim his rights as a father, the Court will, at the instance of the ward, interfere. And so, if the father has allowed certain things to be done, and then, out of mere caprice, has counter-ordered them, so as, in the eyes of everybody, to cause an injury to the child, then the Court will not allow the capricious change of mind, although if the thing had been done originally the Court could not have interfered. I am not prepared to say that the patience of the Court, in the case of its ward, might not be exhausted by other conduct of the father — by cruelty to a great extent, or pitiless spitefulness to a great extent. . . .

The rights of a father are sacred rights because his duties are sacred duties. . . .

Bowen LJ: . . . This is a case in which, if we were not in a Court of Law, but in a court of critics capable of being moved by feelings of favour or disfavour, we might be tempted to comment, with more or less severity, upon the way in which, so far as we have heard the story, the father has exercised his parental right. But it seems to me the Court must not allow itself to drift out of the proper course; the Court must not be tempted to interfere with the natural order and course of family life, the very basis of which is the authority of the father, except it be in those special cases in which the state is called upon, for reasons of urgency, to set aside the parental authority and to intervene for itself. . . .

. . . Judicial machinery is quite inadequate to the task of educating children in this country. It can correct abuses and it can interfere to redress the parental caprice, and it does interfere when the natural guardian of the child ceases to be the natural guardian, and shews by his conduct that he has become an unnatural guardian, but to interfere further would be to ignore the one principle which is the most fundamental of all in the history of mankind, and owing to the full play of which man has become what he is. . . . If that were not so we might be interfering all day and with every family. I have no doubt that there are very few families in the country in which fathers do not, at some time or other, make mistakes, and there are very few families in which a wiser person than the father might not do something better for that child than is being done by the father, who however has an authority which never ought to be slighted. *Appeal dismissed.*

Questions

(i) Take out the sex discrimination and apply these arguments to a couple's decision: (*a*) that their child shall not go on the school trip to France; (*b*) that their child shall go to Sunday school every week; (*c*) that their child shall not be vaccinated against whooping cough; or (*d*) that their child should not receive sex education or attend 'peace studies' in school. Should the law interfere?

(ii) How relevant to your view of the *Agar-Ellis* decision was it (*a*) that mother and father disagreed with one another, and (*b*) that the child was, by the hearing, aged 17?

The position, at least between mother and father, was radically altered on or before the *Guardianship of Infants Act 1925* (later superseded by the Guardianship of Minors Act 1971):

Whereas Parliament by the Sex Disqualification (Removal) Act, 1919, and various other enactments, has sought to establish equality in law between the sexes, and it is expedient that this

principle should obtain with respect to the guardianship of infants and the rights and responsibilities conferred thereby:

Be it therefore enacted, etc.

1. Where in any proceeding before any court (whether or not a court within the meaning of
the Guardianship of Infants Act, 1886) the custody or upbringing of an infant, or the administration of any property belonging to or held on trust for an infant, or the application of the
income thereof, is in question, the court, in deciding that question, shall regard the welfare of
the infant as the first and paramount consideration, and shall not take into consideration
whether from any other point of view the claim of the father, or any right at common law
possessed by the father, in respect of such custody, upbringing, administration or application
is superior to that of the mother, or the claim of the mother to that of the father.

This principle was then applied to disputes between parents and non-parents
in what became the leading case:

J v C
[1970] AC 668, [1969] 1 All ER 788, [1969] 2 WLR 540, 113 Sol Jo 164,
House of Lords

It is almost impossible to summarise the facts dispassionately, but Lord
Guest perhaps comes closest to doing so:

The story began in the autumn of 1957 when the infant's parents came to Britain from Madrid
for the purpose of bettering their financial position by entering domestic service. The father
was at that time a very lowly-paid worker living in poor housing conditions in Madrid. They
are both of the Roman Catholic faith. They left behind a daughter then aged 4 who lived with
the maternal grandmother. The mother became pregnant shortly after their arrival in Britain
and the infant was born in hospital on 8 May 1958. As the mother was found to be suffering
from tuberculosis and had to remain in hospital for some considerable time a home was found
for the infant through the kind offices of a married couple who have been called the 'foster
parents'. The infant was taken care of, from the age of four days, by them in their house in
Northamptonshire while the mother remained in hospital. The foster parents had been both
previously married and between them have four children by their previous marriages and now
have two by their own marriage. The infant continued to remain with the foster parents until
the mother was discharged from hospital in April 1959. The infant's father remained in
employment near the foster parents' house and visited the infant from time to time. The infant
thereafter rejoined his parents who had obtained employment in Surrey. The foster parents had
also moved to Surrey. The infant remained with his parents at C for about ten months: the
foster mother assisted the mother in looking after the infant and the parents kept in touch with
the foster parents' family. In February 1960, the mother again became pregnant. As she was
afraid of having another baby in this country she and her husband went back to Madrid taking
the infant with them.

During the infant's stay in Madrid in the summer of 1960 his parents lived in what has been
described as little better than a 'hovel'. The father was still a lowly-paid worker and the family
lived in what were virtually slum conditions. In the summer heat of Madrid the infant's health
rapidly deteriorated due to malnutrition and the local conditions which did not suit him. He
only remained in Madrid with his parents for 17 months. In July 1961, he returned to Britain
to stay with the foster parents. This move was made at the specific request of the parents who,
through the intermediary of a Spanish maid of the foster parents, M, conveyed their request
to the foster parents. This request was made on the ground of the infant's health. On his return
to this country the infant's health rapidly improved and he has continued thereafter to enjoy
good health. He has not lived with his parents since July 1961, and has continued to live with
the foster parents ever since.

The parents were content at this time to leave the infant with the foster parents. There was
some suggestion that the parents should return to England to take up domestic service, so
that the infant could be with them, and the foster parents in fact made some arrangements to
this end. But these arrangements came to nothing. In the winter of 1961 the parents went to
Hamburg with the idea of further bettering their financial position in order to be able to obtain
a house of their own in Madrid in more salubrious surroundings. They had left their elder

daughter with the maternal grandmother in Madrid and they remained in Hamburg until the early part of 1963. In February 1963, the grandmother died and this necessitated the parents' return to Madrid, first the mother and latterly the father.

Up to this point of time the parents had evinced no wish to the foster parents to have the infant back with them in Madrid apart from a suggestion for a holiday. But in July 1963, the foster mother wrote to the mother what has been described as a tactless and most unfortunate letter. In this letter she described how the infant had become integrated with their family; he had gone to an English school and he had grown up an English boy with English habits, and that it would be most disturbing for him to have to return to live with his parents in Madrid. She also made critical remarks about the infant's father. This letter produced the not unexpected reaction from the mother who, after some previous correspondence, wrote on 25 September 1963, to the Surrey County Council, in whose official care the infant was, asking for the infant's return. The local authority did not act with conspicuous consistency or good sense. After appearing to agree to the mother's request they subsequently, after receipt of a letter from the foster parents expressing their point of view, resolved, on the advice of counsel, to apply to the Chancery Division to have the infant made a ward of court, which was done on 16 December 1963.

The proceedings took some considerable time to reach the judge and the parents were unfortunately led to believe by a letter from the Surrey County Council that they would be represented by counsel at the hearing who would state their case for them. For this reason the parents only lodged written representations which had been prepared for them by a Spanish lawyer. These, however, did express their wish for the infant's return. Affidavits were lodged by various other parties. After a hearing on 22 July 1965, Ungoed-Thomas J ordered that the infant remain a ward of court, that the care and control be committed to the foster parents, that the infant be brought up in the Roman Catholic faith and in the knowledge and recognition of his parents and in knowledge of the Spanish language.

Two years were to elapse before the final stage of the proceedings took place before the same judge. This stage had been initiated by the parents' summons – asking that they should have the care and control of the infant. This was made on 10 May 1967. An application was also made by the foster parents in January 1967, that the infant be brought up in the Protestant faith. This request for a change in the boy's religious upbringing was prompted by a desire on the foster parents' part that he should enter a choir school so as to avoid expense. The most convenient school was a Protestant school. The official solicitor also entered the proceedings, having been appointed next friend. On this occasion the judge heard evidence from all the parties and his judgment was given on 31 July 1967. No order was made on either application and his order was dated 20 September 1967. Owing to various delays, for which none of the parties is responsible, the Court of Appeal hearing did not take place until 5 July 1968, and the order of the Court of Appeal refusing leave to appeal was made on 30 July 1968.

In retrospect it is unfortunate that at the first hearing in 1963 before the judge the full facts were not before him. It is apparent that at that stage he was uncertain of the ability of the mother on the ground of her health, to look after the child and he was not sure in his own mind that the parents genuinely desired the infant's return. It may be that if more expedition had been exercised by the parties in bringing the case to trial and the full facts had been known at the time, the judge's decision might well have been different in 1963. In 1963 when the parents first asked for the infant's return he was only 5 years old and he had only been parted from his parents for a matter of two years. Even in 1965 he was only 7 years old, but at the time of the second hearing he was 9½ and he is now 10½ years old. He has been at school in England since January 1963. He has not seen his parents since 1961 when he was 3, and apart from a matter of 27 months he has been living continually in the home of the foster parents with their family. There is no doubt, as the learned judge found, that the infant lives in happy surroundings in a united and well-integrated family. The mixed families have made it particularly easy for him to become integrated. He speaks English and only pidgin Spanish. He is especially friendly with P the child of the marriage of the foster parents who is only a little younger than him.

It is right at this stage to say that the house in which the parents now live in Madrid is entirely suitable for the reception of the infant. It contains three bedrooms and is in a modern block of flats in quite different surroundings from the previous home. The father is in good steady employment at a weekly wage of about £18 and the mother's health has been completely restored.

The reason which has impelled the judge to take the unusual step of taking the care and control from the parents and giving it to strangers is that, in his view, the risk of plunging this boy of 10½ years into a Spanish family, where he has not seen his parents since he was aged 3 and into a foreign country, would be too great to take and that the adjustment necessary might well permanently injure the infant's health at the impressionable age at which he has arrived. The judge has regarded the infant's welfare as the paramount consideration and he has decided that this demands that he should remain with his foster parents.

The account of the law which has been most frequently quoted in subsequent decisions is that of Lord MacDermott:

All parties were agreed that the courts had jurisdiction and a duty to interfere with the natural right of parents to have the care, control and custody of their child if the welfare of the child required and the law permitted that course to be taken. But there agreement ended. For the parents it was submitted that the courts were in law bound to presume that the welfare of the child was best served by allowing him to live with his parents unless it was shown that it was not for his welfare to do so because of their conduct, character or station in life. Counsel for the infant and counsel for the foster parents submitted, on the other hand, that there was no such presumption of law, that the paramount and governing consideration was the welfare of the child and that the claim of natural parents, although often of great weight and cogency and often conclusive, had to be regarded in conjunction with all other relevant factors, and had to yield if, in the end, the welfare of the child so required.

The question of law under discussion is therefore whether there now is such a presumption as that contended for by the parents, or whether the correct process of adjudication is, instead, to consider all material aspects of the case, including the claims of the parent, and then to decide in the exercise of a judicial discretion what is best for the welfare of the child. I have already mentioned counsel for the parents' concession as to the position if his argument does not prevail. I may add here that if it does prevail the appeal, in my opinion, is bound to succeed since: (*a*) the evidence shows no defects of character or conduct on the part of the parents sufficient to disentitle them to custody; and (*b*) their position in life has so improved as to be no longer capable in itself of constituting an answer to their claim.

His lordship then reviews the developments in case law and statute before 1925 and continues:

I have referred to these Acts because, as in the case of the authorities, they record an increasing qualification of common law rights and the growing acceptance of the welfare of the infant as a criterion. In this way, and like the trend of the cases, they serve to introduce the enactment which has been so closely canvassed on the issue of law under discussion. It is s. 1 of the Guardianship of Infants Act 1925 [see above, p. 410].

The part of this section referring to 'the first and paramount consideration' has been spoken of as declaratory of the existing law. See *Re Thain, Thain v Taylor* [1926] Ch 676, 95 LJ Ch 292 per Lord Hanworth MR (p. 689) and Sargant LJ (p. 691); and *McKee v McKee* [1951] AC 352 at 366 per Lord Simonds. There have been different views about this, but whether the proposition is wholly accurate or not, the true construction of the section itself has to be considered as a matter of prime importance.

Two questions arise here. First, is the section to be read as referring only to disputes between the parents of the child? In *Re Carroll (No 2)* [1931] 1 KB 317, 100 LJKB 113, Slesser LJ appears to have approved such an interpretation for he said (p. 355):

'This statute, however, in my view, has confined itself to questions between the rights of father and mother which I have already outlined — factors which cannot arise in the case of an illegitimate child . . .'

Now, the latter part of the section is directed to equalising the legal rights or claims of the parents, and the preamble speaks only of achieving an equality between the sexes in relation to the guardianship of infants. But these considerations, do not, in my opinion, suffice to constrict the natural meaning of the first part of the section. The latter part beginning with the words 'shall not take into consideration . . .' does not call for or imply any such constriction for it does not necessarily apply to all the possible disputes which the earlier part is capable of embracing; and as for the preamble, it could only be used to restrict the applicability of the earlier part of the section if that part were ambiguous. See *A-G v HRH Prince Ernest Augustus of Hanover* [1957] AC 436 at 463 per Viscount Simonds. Having read the whole Act, I cannot find this important earlier part to be other than clear and unambiguous. On the contrary, its wording seems to be deliberately wide and general. It relates to *any* proceedings before *any* court, and as Eve J said in *Clarke-Jervoise v Scutt* [1920] 1 Ch 382 at 388: '"Any" is a word with a very wide meaning, and prima facie the use of it excludes limitation.'

Thus read the section would apply to cases, such as the present, between parents and strangers. This construction finds further support in the following considerations. In the first place, since (as the Act and authorities already mentioned by way of background show) welfare was being regarded increasingly as a general criterion which was not limited to custody disputes between parents, it would be more than strange if the earlier part of s. 1 were meant to apply only to that single type of dispute. Secondly, the questions for decision which are expressly mentioned — custody, upbringing, administration of property belonging to or held in trust for the infant, and the application of the income thereof — are of a kind to suggest the involvement not only of parents but of others such as guardians or trustees. And thirdly, there is nothing in the rest of the Act to require a limited construction of s. 1. Section 6, indeed, would seem to point the other way for it provides for the settlement by the court of differences between joint guardians affecting the welfare of an infant and there is no apparent reason for confining this relief to differences between parents or taking proceedings therefore out of the ambit of s. 1. For these reasons I would hold that the present proceedings are proceedings within that section.

The second question of construction is as to the scope and meaning of the words '. . . shall regard the welfare of the infant as the first and paramount consideration.' Reading these words in their ordinary significance, and relating them to the various classes of proceedings which the section has already mentioned, it seems to me that they must mean more than that the child's welfare is to be treated as the top item in a list of items relevant to the matter in question. I think they connote a process whereby, when all the relevant facts, relationships, claims and wishes of parents, risks, choices and other circumstances are taken into account and weighed, the course to be followed will be that which is most in the interests of the child's welfare as that term has now to be understood. That is the first consideration because it is of first importance and the paramount consideration because it rules on or determines the course to be followed. It remains to see how this 'first view', as I may call it, stands in the light of authority.

After a review of the authorities, he concludes:

. . . I conclude that my first view construction of s. 1 should stand, and that the parents' proposition of law is ill-founded and must fail. The consequences of this present little difficulty, but before coming to them I would add in summary form certain views and comments on the ground surveyed in the hope that they may serve to restrict misunderstanding in this difficult field. These may be enumerated as follows:

1. Section 1 of the Act of 1925 applies to disputes not only between parents, but between parents and strangers and strangers and strangers.

2. In applying s. 1, the rights and wishes of parents, whether unimpeachable or otherwise, must be assessed and weighed in their bearing on the welfare of the child in conjunction with all other factors relevant to that issue.

3. While there is now no rule of law that the rights and wishes of unimpeachable parents must prevail over other considerations, such rights and wishes, recognised as they are by nature and society, can be capable of ministering to the total welfare of the child in a special way, and must therefore preponderate in many cases. The parental rights, however, remain qualified and not absolute for the purposes of the investigation, the broad nature of which is still as described in the fourth of the principles enunciated by FitzGibbon LJ in *Re O'Hara* [1900] 2 IR 232 at 240. [I.e. the court should act cautiously, and in opposition to the parent only when judicially satisfied that the welfare of the child requires it.]

4. Some of the authorities convey the impression that the upset caused to a child by a change of custody is transient and a matter of small importance. For all I know that may have been true in the cases containing dicta to that effect. But I think a growing experience has shown that it is not always so and that serious harm even to young children may, on occasion, be caused by such a change. I do not suggest that the difficulties of this subject can be resolved by purely theoretical considerations, or that they need to be left entirely to expert opinion. But a child's future happiness and sense of security are always important factors and the effects of a change of custody will often be worthy of the close and anxious attention which they undoubtedly received in this case.

The conclusions I have reached on the parents' proposition of law make it unnecessary to enter on a review of the facts and circumstances which are material here. When the evidence and the judgments are examined the result is only to confirm the propriety of counsel for the parents' concession. The learned judge applied the appropriate principles of law and I can find no ground for interfering with the manner in which he exercised his discretion. On these grounds I am of opinion that the appeal fails and should be dismissed.

Their lordships all concurred in dismissing the appeal but on two points they are not quite unanimous. Lords Upjohn and Donovan state quite clearly that s. 1 of the 1925 Act changed the law. Lord MacDermott, as we have seen, expresses no definite view on the previous law, while Lord Guest concludes his review of the earlier authorities thus:

It is clear to me that even prior to the Act of 1925 the paramount consideration in regard to the custody of infants was the infant's welfare. The father's wishes were to be considered but only as one of the factors bearing on the child's welfare. The father had no 'right' as such to the care and control of his infant children. The comparative absence of authority in the intervening years between 1900 and 1925 may have been due to the fact that the change in the climate of social conditions was taking place gradually and its influence on the courts was almost inperceptible and was taking place in the chambers of the Chancery Courts. But whatever may have been the state of the law prior to the Act of 1925, s. 1 of that Act set any doubts at rest and made it perfectly clear that the first and paramount consideration was the welfare of the infant. I do not agree with the parents' construction of s. 1. It is, in my view, of universal application and is not limited in its application to questions as between parents.

Lord Upjohn, however, has this to say:

My Lords Eve J [in *Re Thain* [1926] Ch 676] said that among other considerations the wishes of an unimpeachable parent undoubtedly stand first, and I believe, as I have said, that represents the law. . . . The natural parents have a strong claim to have their wishes considered; first and principally, no doubt, because normally it is part of the paramount consideration of the welfare of the infant that he should be with them but also because as the natural parents they have themselves a strong claim to have their wishes considered as normally the proper persons to have the upbringing of the child they have brought into the world. It is not, however, a question of the onus being on anyone to displace the wishes of the parents; it is a matter for the judge. . .

Lord Donovan's short, sharp speech contains the following:

I think the section means just what it says — no more and no less; and although the claim of natural parents to the custody and upbringing of their own children is obviously a most weighty factor to be taken into consideration in deciding what is in the best interests of the infant, yet the legislature recognised that this might not always be the determining factor, whether the parents were unimpeachable or not.

Lord Pearson agrees with Lord MacDermott.

The Law Commission discuss the point of principle in their Working Paper on *Custody* (1986):

6.20 There may still be doubts whether the child's 'best interests' should determine the issue between parents and non-parents. Respect for family life is guaranteed under the European Convention on Human Rights [p. 407, above] and parents may require protection from unwarranted interference. Local authorities are not permitted compulsorily to intervene in the care of children simply because they could provide something better, but only where specific shortcomings in the home or the parents can be proved. In adoption, parental agreement is required, unless it can be dispensed with on defined grounds, and the child's welfare is only the 'first' rather than the 'paramount' consideration. In relation to custody and upbringing, however, the House of Lords decided in *J v C* that there is no presumption in favour of even the 'unimpeachable' natural parents of the child, although their relationship with the child will often carry great weight as they 'can be capable of ministering to the total welfare of the child in a special way'.
6.21 Although we recognise that this is a difficult question, several arguments persuade us that the present position in English law should be maintained. First, the child may have a much closer relationship with someone other than his 'natural' parent. The emotional and psychological bonds which develop between a child (especially a very young child) and those who are

bringing him up are just as 'natural' as are his genetic ties. To give preference over such a 'psychological' parent to one whose interest may be based solely on a blood tie could on occasion be highly detrimental to the child. Secondly, the analogy with intervention by local authorities is not exact. By definition, the authority cannot be or become such a 'psychological' parent. Whereas a non-parent applicant will usually be seeking to secure the child's existing home and an established relationship, the local authority will usually be seeking to remove him from such a home in favour of an unspecified alternative. Unlike a case between private individuals, the court is not faced with a choice between two (or more) identifiable homes. There are also strong objections in principle to the authority of the State being used to impose standards upon families unless it can be shown that the children are suffering, or are likely to suffer, unacceptable harm.

6.22 We conclude, therefore, that the welfare of each child in the family should continue to be the paramount consideration whenever their custody or upbringing is in question between private individuals.

Questions

(i) Do you agree?

(ii) It is one thing to decide between competing sets of parents, one 'natural' and the other 'social': but what about interfering in a particular upbringing decision made by otherwise 'unimpeachable' parents?

Of course, some decisions are more important than others:

Re D (a minor) (warship: sterilisation)
[1976] Fam 185, [1976] 1 All ER 326, [1976] 2 WLR 279, 119 Sol Jo 696, High Court, Family Division

D, now aged 11, was born with 'Sotos syndrome', the symptoms of which included epilepsy, clumsiness, an usual facial appearance, behavioural problems, and some impairment of intelligence. Her mother was convinced that she was seriously mentally handicapped and would be unable to care either for herself or a child of her own. The paediatrician who had taken an interest in her case from an early stage took a similar view. When she reached puberty, therefore, mother and paediatrician arranged with a gynaecologist that she should be sterilised immediately, because they were afraid that she might be seduced and bear an abnormal child. The people responsible for her education, however, thought that it would be wrong to perform an irreversible and permanent operation upon her; her behaviour and social skills were improving steadily; she was of dull normal intelligence and it was common ground that she had sufficient intellectual capacity to marry in due course. The educational psychologist therefore made her a ward of court and applied for an order continuing the wardship in order to delay or prevent the proposed operation. It was not proposed that D should be removed from the care and control of her widowed mother, who had looked after her 'splendidly.'

Heilbron J: . . .

Is wardship appropriate?
I have first of all to decide whether this is an appropriate case in which to exercise the court's wardship jurisdiction. Wardship is a very special and ancient jurisdiction. Its origin was the sovereign's feudal obligation as parens patriae to protect the person and property of his

subjects, and particularly those unable to look after themselves, including infants. This obligation, delegated to the chancellor, passed to the Chancery Court, and in 1970 to this division of the High Court.

The jurisdiction in wardship is very wide, but there are limitations. It is not in every case that it is appropriate to make a child a ward, and counsel for Mrs B has argued with his usual skill and powers of persuasion that, as this case raises a matter of principle of wide public importance, and is a matter which affects many people, continuation of wardship would be inappropriate.

In his powerful argument, counsel for the Official Solicitor, on the other hand, submitted that the court in wardship had a wide jurisdiction which should be extended to encompass this novel situation, because it is just the type of problem which this court is best suited to determine when exercising its protective functions in regard to minors. As Lord Eldon LC said many years ago in *Wellesley v Duke of Beaufort* (1827) 2 Russ 1, 5 LJOS 85:

'This jurisdiction is founded on the obvious necessity that the law should place somewhere the care of individuals who cannot take care of themselves, particularly in cases where it is clear that some care should be thrown around them.'

It is apparent from the recent decision of the Court of Appeal in *Re X (A Minor)* [1975] Fam 47, [1975] 1 All ER 697 that the jurisdiction to do what is considered necessary for the protection of an infant is to be exercised carefully and within limits, but the court has, from time to time over the years, extended the sphere in the exercise of this jurisdiction.

The type of operation proposed is one which involves the deprivation of a basic human right, namely the right of a woman to reproduce, and therefore it would, if performed on a woman for non-therapeutic reasons and without her consent, be a violation of such right. . . . As the evidence showed, and I accept it, D could not possibly have given an informed consent. What the evidence did, however, make clear was that she would almost certainly understand the implications of such an operation by the time she reached 18.

This operation could, if necessary, be delayed or prevented if the child were to remain a ward of court, and as Lord Eldon LC, so vividly expressed it in *Wellesley's* case: 'It has always been the principle of this Court, not to risk the incurring of damage to children which it cannot repair, but rather to prevent the damage being done.'

I think that is the very type of case where this court should 'throw some care around this child', and I propose to continue her wardship which, in my judgment, is appropriate in this case.

The operation — should it be performed?
In considering this vital matter, I want to make it quite clear that I have well in mind the natural feelings of a parent's heart, and though in wardship proceedings parents' rights can be superseded, the court will not do so lightly, and only in pursuance of well-known principles laid down over the years. The exercise of the court's jurisdiction is paternal, and it must be exercised judicially, and the judge must act, as far as humanly possible, on the evidence, as a wise parent would act. As Lord Upjohn pointed out in *J v C* [1970] AC 668, [1969] 1 All ER 788 the law and practice in relation to infants —

'have developed, are developing and must, and no doubt will, continue to develop by reflecting and adopting the changing views, as the years go by, of reasonable men and women, the parents of children, on the proper treatment and methods of bringing up children; for after all that is the model which the judge must emulate for . . . he must act as the judicial reasonable parent.'

It is of course beyond dispute that the welfare of this child is the paramount consideration, and the court must act in her best interests.

The judge then reviews some of the evidence and arguments, including the facts that D had as yet shown no interest in the opposite sex, and had virtually no opportunities for promiscuity; that other methods of contraception or even abortion would be available should the need arise; and that there was no therapeutic reason for performing the operation now. She continues:

Dr Gordon, however, maintained that, provided the parent or parents consented, the decision was one made pursuant to the exercise of his clinical judgment, and that no interference could be tolerated in his clinical freedom.

The other consultants did not agree. Their opinion was that a decision to sterilise a child was not entirely within a doctor's clinical judgment, save only when sterilisation was the treatment of choice for some disease, as, for instance, when in order to treat a child and to ensure her direct physical well-being, it might be necessary to perform a hysterectomy to remove a malignant uterus. Whilst the side effect of such an operation would be to sterilise, the operation would be performed solely for therapeutic purposes. I entirely accept their opinions. I cannot believe, and the evidence does not warrant the view, that a decision to carry out an operation of this nature performed for non-therapeutic purposes on a minor, can be held to be within the doctor's sole clinical judgment.

It is quite clear that once a child is a ward of court, no important step in the life of that child can be taken without the consent of the court, and I cannot conceive of a more important step than that which was proposed in this case.

A review of the whole of the evidence leads me to the conclusion that in a case of a child of 11 years of age, where the evidence shows that her mental and physical condition and attainments have already improved, and where her future prospects are as yet unpredictable, where the evidence also shows that she is unable as yet to understand and appreciate the implications of this operation and could not give a valid or informed consent, but the likelihood is that in later years she will be able to make her own choice, where, I believe, the frustration and resentment of realising (as she would one day) what had happened could be devastating, an operation of this nature is, in my view, contra-indicated.

For these, and for the other reasons to which I have adverted, I have come to the conclusion that this operation is neither medically indicated nor necessary, and that it would not be in D's best interests for it to be performed.

Questions

(i) If the proceedings had not been brought and the operation had gone ahead as planned, would the gynaecologist have committed a battery upon D (see *Re B (a minor) (wardship: sterilisation)* [1988] AC 199, [1987] 2 All ER 206)?

(ii) What difference, if any, would it have made: (*a*) to question (i) above, or (*b*) to the result of the wardship case, if D had been 15 and able to understand the consequences of the operation (see *Re R (a minor) (wardship: medical treatment)* (1991) Times, 31 July)?

(iii) What difference, if any, would it have made if the operation, although controversial, had been therapeutically indicated: for example, an abortion (see *Re P (a minor)* [1986] 1 FLR 272)?

(iv) What difference would it have made if the operation had been necessary to save D's life?

The courts have had to grapple with the problem of life-saving treatment for severely handicapped children in three reported cases, of which the following is the most recent:

Re J (a minor) (wardship: medical treatment)
[1990] 3 All ER 930, [1991] 2 WLR 140, Court of Appeal

J was a ward of court who had been born very prematurely. He suffered very severe and permanent brain damage at the time of his birth, the brain tissue then lost being irreplaceable. He was epileptic and the medical evidence was that he was likely to develop serious spastic quadriplegia, would be blind and deaf and was unlikely ever to be able to speak or to develop even limited intellectual abilities, but it was likely that he would feel pain to the same extent as a normal baby. His life expectancy was uncertain but he was expected to die before late adolescence, although he could survive for a few years. He had been ventilated twice for long periods when his breathing stopped, that treatment being both painful and hazardous. The medical prognosis was that any further collapse which required ventilation would be fatal. However he was neither on the point of death nor dying. The question arose whether if he suffered a further collapse the medical staff at the hospital where he was being cared for should reventilate him in the event of his breathing stopping. The judge, exercising the court's parens patriae jurisdiction, made an order that J should be treated with antibiotics if he developed a chest infection but should not be reventilated if his breathing stopped unless the doctors caring for him deemed it appropriate given the prevailing clinical situation. The Official Solicitor appealed . . .

Lord Donaldson MR: . . . Before considering these submissions, it is sensible to define the relationship between the court, the doctors, the child and its parents.

The doctors owe the child a duty to care for it in accordance with good medical practice recognised as appropriate by a competent body of professional opinion (see *Bolam v Friern Hospital Management Committee* [1957] 2 All ER 118, [1957] 1 WLR 582). This duty is, however, subject to the qualification that, if time permits, they must obtain the consent of the parents before undertaking serious invasive treatment.

The parents owe the child a duty to give or to withhold consent in the best interests of the child and without regard to their own interests.

The court when exercising the parens patriae jurisdiction takes over the rights and duties of the parents, although this is not to say that the parents will be excluded from the decision-making process. Nevertheless in the end the responsibility for the decision whether to give or to withhold consent is that of the court alone.

It follows from this that a child who is a ward of court should be treated medically in exactly the same way as one who is not, the only difference being that the doctors will be looking to the court rather than to the parents for any necessary consents.

No one can *dictate* the treatment to be given to the child, neither court, parents nor doctors. There are checks and balances. The doctors can recommend treatment A in preference to treatment B. They can also refuse to adopt treatment C on the grounds that it is medically contra-indicated or for some other reason is a treatment which they could not conscientiously administer. The court or parents for their part can refuse to consent to treatment A or B or both, but cannot insist on treatment C. The inevitable and desirable result is that choice of treatment is in some measure a joint decision of the doctors and the court or parents. . . .

Taylor LJ: The plight of baby J is appalling and the problem facing the court in the exercise of its wardship jurisdiction is of the greatest difficulty. When should the court rule against the giving of treatment aimed at prolonging life?

Three preliminary principles are not in dispute. First, it is settled law that the court's prime and paramount consideration must be the best interests of the child. That is easily said but not easily applied. What it does involve is that the views of the parents, although they should be heeded and weighed, cannot prevail over the court's view of the ward's best interests. In the present case the parents, finding themselves in a hideous dilemma, have not taken a strong view so that no conflict arises.

Second, the court's high respect for the sanctity of human life imposes a strong presumption in favour of taking all steps capable of preserving it, save in exceptional circumstances. The problem is to define those circumstances.

Third, and as a corollary to the second principle, it cannot be too strongly emphasised that the court never sanctions steps to terminate life. That would be unlawful. There is no question of approving, even in a case of the most horrendous disability, a course aimed at terminating life or accelerating death. The court is concerned only with the circumstances in which steps should not be taken to prolong life.

Two decisions of this court have dealt with cases at the extremes of the spectrum of affliction. *Re C (a minor) (wardship: medical treatment)* [1990] Fam 26, [1989] 2 All ER 782 was a case in which a child had severe irreversible brain damage such that she was hopelessly and terminally ill. This court held that the best interests of the child required approval of recommendations designed to ease her suffering and permit her life to come to an end peacefully with dignity rather than seek to prolong her life.

By contrast, in the earlier case of *Re B (a minor) (wardship: medical treatment)* (1981) [1990] 3 All ER 927, [1981] 1 WLR 1421, the court was concerned with a child suffering from Down's syndrome, who quite separately was born with an intestinal obstruction. Without an operation this intestinal condition would quickly have been fatal. On the other hand, the operation had a good chance of successfully removing the obstruction, once and for all, thereby affording the child a life expectation of some 20 to 30 years as a mongol. The parents genuinely believed it was in the child's interests to refrain from operating and allow her to die. The court took a different view. Templeman LJ said that the court had to decide—

'whether the life of this child is demonstrably going to be so awful that in effect the child must be condemned to die, or whether the life of this child is still so imponderable that it would be wrong for her to be condemned to die. There may be cases, I know not, of severe proved damage where the future is so certain and where the life of the child is so bound to be full of pain and suffering that the court might be driven to a different conclusion, but in the present case the choice which lies before the court is this: whether to allow an operation to take place which may result in the child living for 20 or 30 years as a mongoloid or whether (and I think this must be brutally the result) to terminate the life of a mongoloid child because she also has an intestinal complaint. Faced with that choice I have no doubt that it is the duty of this court to decide that the child must live . . . The evidence in this case only goes to show that if the operation takes place and is successful then the child may live the normal span of a mongoloid child with the handicaps and defects and life of a mongol child, and it is not for this court to say that life of that description ought to be extinguished.'

(See [1990] 3 All ER 927 at 929, [1981] 1 WLR 1421 at 1424.)

Dunn LJ said ([1990] 3 All ER 927 at 930, [1981] 1 WLR 1421 at 1424–1425):

'. . . there is no evidence that this child's short life is likely to be an intolerable one. There is no evidence at all as to the quality of life which the child may expect. As counsel for the Official Solicitor said, the child should be put into the same position as any other mongol child and must be given the chance to live an existence. I accept that way of putting it.'

Those two cases thus decide that where the child is terminally ill the court will not require treatment to prolong life; but where, at the other extreme, the child is severely handicapped although not intolerably so and treatment for a discrete condition can enable life to continue for an appreciable period, albeit subject to that severe handicap, the treatment should be given.

I should say that, in my view, the phrase 'condemned to die' which occurs twice in the passage cited from the judgment of Templeman LJ is more emotive than accurate. As already indicated the court in these cases has to decide, not whether to end life, but whether to prolong it by treatment without which death would ensue from natural causes.

It is to be noted that Templeman LJ did not say, even obiter, that where the child's life would be bound to be full of pain and suffering there would come a point at which the court should rule against prolonging life by treatment. He went no further than to say there may be cases where the court might take that view.

This leads to the arguments presented by counsel for the Official Solicitor. His first submission propounded an absolute test, that, except where the ward is terminally ill, the court's approach should always be to prolong life by treatment if this is possible, regardless of the quality of life being preserved and regardless of any added suffering caused by the treatment itself. I cannot accept this test which in my view is so hard as to be inconsistent at its extreme with the best interests of the child. Counsel for the Official Solicitor submits that the court cannot play God and decide whether the quality of life which the treatment would give the child is better or worse than death. He referred to dicta in *McKay v Essex Area Health Authority* [1982] QB 1166, [1982] 2 All ER 771. That case involved a quite different situation since a claim was being made for damages for negligence against doctors for allowing a gravely damaged infant plaintiff to be borne at all after his mother had contracted German measles. The exercise of weighing the disability against the alternative of not being born at all was, therefore, in a damages context. But Stephenson LJ said ([1982] 2 All ER 771 at 781, [1982] QB 1166 at 1180):

'Like this court when it had to consider the interests of a child born with Down's syndrome in *Re B (a minor) (wardship: medical treatment)* ([1990] 3 All ER 927, [1981] 1 WLR 1421), I would not answer until it is necessary to do so the question whether the life of a child could be so certainly "awful" and "intolerable" that it would be in its best interests to end it and it might be considered that it had a right to be put to death.'

Again there is reference in that passage to the possibility of a child being 'put to death'. I repeat, because of its importance, the debate here is not about terminating life but solely whether to withold treatment designed to prevent death from natural causes.

Ackner LJ said ([1982] 2 All ER 771 at 787, [1982] QB 1166 at 1189):

'But how can a court begin to evaluate non-existence, "The undiscovered country from whose bourn no traveller returns?" No comparison is possible and therefore no damage can be established which a court could recognise.'

Despite the court's inability to compare a life afflicted by the most severe disability with death, the unknown, I am of the view that there must be extreme cases in which the court is entitled to say: 'The life which this treatment would prolong would be so cruel as to be intolerable.' If, for example, a child was so damaged as to have negligible use of its faculties and the only way of preserving its life was by the continuous administration of extremely painful treatment such that the child either would be in continuous agony or would have to be so sedated continuously as to have no conscious life at all, I cannot think counsel's absolute test should apply to require the treatment to be given. In those circumstances, without there being any question of deliberately ending the life or shortening it, I consider the court is entitled in the best interests of the child to say that deliberate steps should not be taken artificially to prolong its miserable life span.

Once the absolute test is rejected, the proper criteria must be a matter of degree. At what point in the scale of disability and suffering ought the court to hold that the best interests of the child do not require further endurance to be imposed by positive treatment to prolong its life? Clearly, to justify withholding treatment, the circumstances would have to be extreme. Counsel for the Official Solicitor submitted that if the court rejected his absolute test, then at least it would have 'to be certain that the life of the child, were the treatment to be given, would be intolerably awful'.

I consider that the correct approach is for the court to judge the quality of life the child would have to endure if given the treatment and decide whether in all the circumstances such a life would be so afflicted as to be intolerable to that child. I say 'to that child' because the test should not be whether the life would be tolerable to the decider. The test must be whether the child in question, if capable of exercising sound judgment, would consider the life tolerable. This is the approach adopted by McKenzie J in *Re Superintendent of Family and Child Service and Dawson* (1983) 145 DLR (3d) 610 at 620–621 in the passage cited with approval by Lord Donaldson MR. It takes account of the strong instinct to preserve one's life even in circumstances which an outsider, not himself at risk of death, might consider unacceptable. The circumstances to be considered would, in appropriate cases, include the degree of existing disability and any additional suffering or aggravation of the disability which the treatment itself would superimpose. In an accident case, as opposed to one involving disablement from birth, the child's pre-accident quality of life and its perception of what has been lost may also be factors relevant to whether the residual life would be intolerable to that child.

Counsel for the Official Solicitor argued that, before deciding against treatment, the court would have to be *certain* that the circumstances of the child's future would comply with the extreme requirements to justify that decision. Certainty as to the future is beyond human judgment. The courts have not, even in the trial of capital offences, required certainty of proof. But, clearly, the court must be satisfied to a high degree of probability.

In the present case, the doctors were unanimous that in his present condition, J should not be put back on to a mechanical ventilator. That condition is very grave indeed. I do not repeat the description of it given by Lord Donaldson MR. In reaching his conclusion, the judge no doubt had three factors in mind. First, the severe lack of capacity of the child in all his faculties which even without any further complication would make his existence barely sentient. Second, that, if further mechanical ventilation were to be required, that very fact would involve the risk of a deterioration in B's condition, because of further brain damage flowing from the interruption of breathing. Third, all the doctors drew attention to the invasive nature of mechanical ventilation and the intensive care required to accompany it. They stressed the unpleasant and distressing nature of that treatment. To add such distress and the risk of further deterioration to an already appalling catalogue of disabilities was clearly capable in my judgment of producing a quality of life which justified the stance of the doctors and the judge's conclusion. I therefore agree that, subject to the minor variations to the judge's order proposed by Lord Donaldson MR, this appeal should be dismissed.

Appeal dismissed. No order for costs.

Questions

(i) Is it indeed a question to be governed by the 'best interests of the child' when the choice is between life and death?

(ii) Ian Kennedy, in *The Karen Quinlan Case: Problems and Proposals* (1976) supports the view of a *doctor's* obligations to his patient put forward in 1957 by Pope Pius XII:

Doctors, he said, were obliged to continue with 'ordinary' measures but were not obliged to carry out 'extraordinary' measures. The latter he defined not in terms of what a doctor would regard as extraordinary or non-standard procedures, a definition which would change as developments occurred, but rather as whatever 'cannot be obtained or secured without excessive expense, pain or other inconvenience for the patient or for others, or which, if used, would not offer a reasonable hope of benefit to the patient'.

Does this also strike you as a reasonable definition of the limits of a parent's duty (under s. 1(2)(*a*) of the Children and Young Persons Act 1933) to secure adequate medical aid for his child?

(iii) Do you agree that the test of 'best interests' in matters of life and death should be what the disabled child himself would have wanted? Or should the court adopt the 'same attitude as a responsible parent . . . in the case of his or her own child' (per Balcombe LJ in *Re J*)? What difference would it make?

(iv) How would you judge the child's 'best interests' when deciding whether he (*a*) should have complicated and risky surgery to alleviate a gross deformity of the face, or (*b*) should have relatively simple surgery to correct a cleft palate and hare-lip?

(v) In *Gillick v West Norfolk and Wisbech Area Health Authority* [1986] AC 112, [1985] 3 All ER 402, HL (p. 428, below), Lord Scarman described the rule that the child's welfare is paramount as 'a warning that parental right must be exercised in accordance with the welfare principle and can be challenged, even overriden, if it be not'. Can this be the case in choosing (*a*) where the family should go on holiday, or (*b*) where each of several children should go to school?

(vi) Might you answer to the last question be affected by the following information, from *Social Trends 21* (1991)?

Table 3.11: **Pupils in independent schools as a proportion of all pupils[1]: by sex and age[2]**
Great Britain   Percentages

	1976	1981	1986[3]	1988	1989
Boys aged:					
Under 11	4	4	5	5	5
11–15	7	6	7	8	8
16 and over	16	17	19	19	19
All ages	6	6	6	7	7
Girls aged:					
Under 11	4	4	5	5	5
11–15	6	6	6	7	7
16 and over	13	12	14	15	15
All ages	5	5	6	6	6
All pupils	5	5	6	7	7

1 At January.
2 Ages are as at December of the previous year for 1976 and 1981. Thereafter ages are as at previous August for England and Wales and December for Scotland.
3 Includes estimates for Scotland.
Source: Department of Education and Science

In 1989, 7 per cent of all pupils in Great Britain attended independent schools compared to 5 per cent in 1976 (Table 3.11). Pupils aged 16 and over formed the highest percentage of children attending independent schools in all years shown. The gap between the proportion of boys and the proportion of girls attending independent schools widened with age in each of the years shown in the table.

Re D and *Re J* concerned a single, albeit vital, question about the child's upbringing. There was no dispute about where the child should live or who should bring him up. But when the state wishes to challenge the parents' claim to bring the child up at all, should it be enough to prove that the state will probably be able to provide the child with a better life than they can? There were some (e.g. Eekelaar, Dingwall and Murray, 1982) who thought that the wardship jurisdiction had almost developed that far, at least in theory. The *Review of Child Care Law* (1985), however, signalled a halt:

2.12 . . . We have had to consider whether a simple welfare or 'best interests' test should now be adopted where the state, in the shape of local authority, is in conflict with the parents.
2.13 We are firmly of the opinion that it should not and that in cases where compulsory committal to local authority care is in issue the present balance between the welfare of the child and the claims of his parents should be maintained. Taken to its logical conclusion, a simple 'best interests' test would permit the state to intervene whenever it could show that the alternative arrangements proposed would serve the children's welfare better than those proposed by their parents. But 'the child is not the child of the state' and it is important in a free society to maintain the rich diversity of lifestyles which is secured by permitting families a large measure of autonomy in the way in which they bring up their children. This is so even, or perhaps particularly, in those families who through force of circumstances are in need of help from social services or other agencies. Only where their children are put at unacceptable risk should it be possible compulsorily to intervene. Once such a risk of harm to the child has been shown, however, his interests must clearly predominate. [Later on:]
15.11 We have considered whether it would be sufficient to qualify a broad welfare test by a requirement that, as in family cases, the responsible body should first be satisfied that there are exceptional circumstances making it impracticable or undesirable that the child should be entrusted to his parents or to some other person. In our view that criterion would add very little to the broad welfare ground, given that only in exceptional circumstances would a court or local authority even consider compulsory intervention and given the readiness of the courts in applying section 1 of the 1971 Act to assume that generally a child's welfare is best served by his being brought up by his parents [see *J v C* [1970] AC 668]. The judges of the Family Division in proposing the criterion agreed that it might leave too much to subjective interpretation by the courts. We did consider whether adding guidelines to the criterion might overcome its apparent drawbacks, as has been suggested to us. However we doubt that these would be sufficient to direct the court's mind to the principles underlying restrictions on state intervention.

Questions

(i) We shall come to the new 'threshold conditions' for state intervention in Chapter 13, but how would you define the cases where a child is 'put at unacceptable risk'?
(ii) The threshold conditions apply before a child can be placed in care or under supervision, but not where a social worker, educational psychologist, doctor or other representative of the caring agencies of the state seeks a 'specific issue order' dealing with a particular aspect of how the child should be brought up, such as having an operation: can this distinction be justified?
(iii) Do you think that any of this will make much difference to what courts actually do?

2 Arguments for parental autonomy

In *Beyond the Best Interests of the Child* (1973), Goldstein, Freud and Solnit produced a powerful argument for legal standards which would secure the continuity and stability of relationships between a child and his psychological parents, even if this conflicted with the claims of his family of birth. In a second book, *Before the Best Interests of the Child* (1980), the same authors employ the same concepts of a child's development to support their argument for severe limitations upon the state's power to intervene between parent and child:

. . . Constantly ongoing interactions between parents and children become for each child the starting point for an all-important line of development that leads toward adult functioning. What begins as the experience of physical contentment or pleasure that accompanies bodily care develops into a primary attachment to the person who provides it. This again changes into the wish for a parent's constant presence irrespective of physical wants. Helplessness requires total care and over time is transformed into the need or wish for approval and love. It fosters the desire to please by compliance with a parent's wishes. It provides a developmental base upon which the child's responsiveness to educational efforts rests. Love for the parents leads to identification with them, a fact without which impulse control and socialization would be deficient. Finally, after the years of childhood comes the prolonged and in many ways painful adolescent struggle to attain a separate identity with physical, emotional, and moral self-reliance.

These complex and vital developments require the privacy of family life under guardianship by parents who are autonomous. The younger the child, the greater is his need for them. When family integrity is broken or weakened by state intrusion, his needs are thwarted and his belief that his parents are omniscient and all-powerful is shaken prematurely. The effect on the child's developmental progress is invariably detrimental.[1] The child's need for safety within the confines of the family must be met by law through its recognition of family privacy as the barrier to state intrusion upon parental autonomy in child rearing. These rights — parental autonomy, a child's entitlement to autonomous parents, and privacy — are essential ingredients of 'family integrity.' 'And the integrity of that life is something so fundamental that it has been found to draw to its protection the principles of more than one explicitly granted Constitutional right.'

Two purposes underlie the parents' right to be free of state intrusion. The first is to provide parents with an uninterrupted *opportunity* to meet the developing physical and emotional needs of their child so as to establish the familial bonds critical to every child's healthy growth and development. The second purpose, and the one on which the parental right must ultimately rest, is to safeguard the *continuing maintenance* of these family ties — of psychological parent-child relationships — once they have been established. . . .

Put somewhat differently, two stages in the parent-child relationship generally define the right of family integrity that deserves recognition and protection from interruption by the state. The first is the stage at which the *opportunity* for the development of psychological ties between parent and child exists; the right usually comes about through a child's being placed with natural parents at birth, or through legally sanctioned adoption. These opportunities merit protection from state intrusion because it is only through continuous nurture of the child within the privacy of the family that the second stage can be reached. At that stage, primary psychological ties between parent and child have been established and require for their *maintenance* continuous nurture free of state intrusion. The liberty interest in these familial bonds, including bonds established between children and longtime fostering adults who are not their parents, has not yet been clearly perceived or firmly established in law. It is as deserving of recognition and protection as is the first stage, normally associated with biological reproduction or with adoption.

---

1. The authors' footnote here refers to Rutter (1972; now 1981), Clarke and Clarke (1976), Tizard (1977), Kearsley, Zelazo, Kagan and Hartmann (1975) and Kagan, Kearsley and Zelazo (1978), but suggests that these authors' 'reliance on the resilience of cognitive function as evidence of the child's well-being is simplistic,' whereas their own 'psychoanalytic theory, along with Piaget's work on cognitive development, recognizes that maturational capacities and social environmental experiences are dynamically involved in the child's developmental capabilities and progression.' (Eg Piaget, 1937; Freud and Burlingham, 1944; Bowlby, 1965.)

Beyond these biological and psychological justifications for protecting parent-child relationships and promoting each child's entitlement to a permanent place in a family of his own, there is a further justification for a policy of minimum state intervention. It is that the law does not have the capacity to supervise the fragile, complex interpersonal bonds between child and parent. As *parens patriae* the state is too crude an instrument to become an adequate substitute for flesh and blood parents. The legal system has neither the resources nor the sensitivity to respond to a growing child's ever-changing needs and demands. It does not have the capacity to deal on an individual basis with the consequences of its decisions, or to act with the deliberate speed that is required by a child's sense of time. Similarly, the child lacks the capacity to respond to the rulings of an impersonal court or social service agencies as he responds to the demands of personal parental figures. Parental expectations, implicit and explicit, become the child's own. However, the process by which a child converts external expectations, guidance, commands, and prohibitions into the capacity for self-regulation and self-direction does not function adequately in the absence of emotional ties to his caretakers.

A policy of minimum coercive intervention by the state thus accords not only with our firm belief as citizens in individual freedom and human dignity, but also with our professional understanding of the intricate developmental processes of childhood.

The authors therefore distinguish between two forms of legislation which curtail parental autonomy:

The first has been to set relatively precise limits on parental judgment concerning matters about which there is a clear societal consensus. For example, parents are not free to send their children into the labor market or to refuse to let them attend school or be immunized against certain contagious diseases. Legislative enactments like those concerned with child labor, compulsory education, and immunization are infringements upon parental autonomy which give parents fair warning of what constitutes a breach of their child care responsibilities and provide advance notice of the extent of the state's power to intervene. In thus defining the authority to intrude in precise terms, legislatures also restrict the power of administrative agencies and courts to breach the state's general commitment to family privacy and parental autonomy. . . .

This second form of legislation, unlike the first form, invests judges and state agency personnel as *parens patriae* with almost limitless discretion in areas generally under the exclusive control of parents. Such legislation is used to justify the *ad hoc* creation of standards of intervention in case-by-case determinations to investigate, supervise, and supervene parental judgments. It invites the exploitation of parents and children by state officials. Acting in accord with their own personal child-rearing preferences, officials have been led to discriminate against poor, minority, and other disfavored families.

Questions

(i) Is there a 'clear societal consensus' in this country in favour of vaccination against whooping cough?
(ii) Would it trouble you if a child's belief that his parents are omniscient and all powerful is broken prematurely?

There is also the question of the role of the state where parent and child are at odds with one another. This issue has arisen in the United States in connection with the right of parents to 'volunteer' their children for treatment in a psychiatric hospital. The following anonymous discussion of the *Mental Hospitalisation of Children and the Limits of Parental Authority* (1978) provides a summary of the arguments:

Five justifications are most often advanced to support parental authority. They may for convenience be termed *social pluralism, social order, parental privilege, family autonomy* and *child's welfare*. Once each of these proffered justifications has been considered, the constitutional limits on a parent's power to admit his child to a mental hospital will emerge.

A. Social pluralism

It is a 'fixed star in our constitutional constellation,' especially with respect to the education of children, that the state shall not impose an orthodoxy 'in politics, nationalism, religion, or other matters of opinion.' And, especially in matters that relate to families and childrearing, the Constitution also disfavors state practices that threaten to impose on all a single conception of a worthwhile way of life. The institution of parental authority, by fragmenting decisions about the goals and methods of childrearing, serves to militate against such an orthodoxy. This, historically, has been part of its rationale and is today one reason for treating parental authority, when asserted against the state, as a constitutional right. It is therefore not surprising that the Supreme Court has acted more readily to protect parental authority against state intrusion when the threat to social pluralism has been acute.[2]

. . . Yet where, as here, the conflict under consideration is between parents and their children, the social pluralism rationale offers little direct guidance. Although a rule favoring parents over the state will always be a bulwark against a state-imposed orthodoxy of social values, a rule favoring parents over their children may or may not have that effect. The goal of social pluralism might just as well be advanced by allowing children to decide for themselves. . . .

B. Social order

Historically, the law recognized society's interest in having children reared so that as adults they would be economically self-sufficient and would conform their conduct to society's norms. Parents, according to one court, were ordinarily entrusted with this task 'because it [could] seldom be put into better hands,' but they were subject to state supersession if they failed. Parents are still, to some extent, viewed as child-socialization agents of the state. . . .

To the extent that parents actually do admit their children to mental hospitals as a method of social control, they are acting in their role of child-socialization agents of the state and are, therefore, subject to the same constitutional constraints as would apply if the state had acted directly. . . .

C. Parental privilege

It is not uncommon for parents to seek to express their own personalities through their children. This interest of parents may serve as the basis for the claim they advance to have 'the power to dictate their [children's] training, prescribe their education and form their religious opinions.' To the extent that the law protects this claim of parents, it creates a *parental privilege* − that is, a prerogative of a parent to rear his child to be a person whose conduct, character, and belief conform to standards of the parent's choosing. There can be no doubt that this interest of parents, when asserted against the state, is within the scope of liberty protected by the Constitution. But in situations in which a parent's choice conflicts not with the state but with the preferences of his own child, parental privilege as a justification for parental authority is less deserving of support. . . .

It is regarded by many as unjust for one adult to impose his conception of the good life on another and as demeaning to another's dignity not to respect his choice of his own life plan. Psychological studies show that at adolescence, children of normal intellect are in this respect substantially like adults: they have the basic cognitive capacities to choose intelligently among competing values and to formulate their own life plans. So, as applied to adolescents, parental privilege − the prerogative of parents to impose on their children values and styles of life that best express the *parents'* personalities − is especially hard to justify on moral grounds. These

---

2. The author's footnote reads: Compare *Wisconsin v Yoder* 406 US 205 (1972) (invalidating state compulsory education law as applied to Amish children) and *Pierce v Society of Sisters* 268 US 510 (1925) (invalidating state law requiring parents to send their children only to public schools) with *Prince v Massachusetts* 321 US 158 (1944) (upholding statute prohibiting street solicitation by children as applied to Jehovah's Witness distributing religious literature). The Court in *Yoder* noted especially that the statute as applied 'substantially interfer[ed] with the religious development of the Amish child and his integration into the way of life of the Amish faith community' and 'carrie[d] with it a very real threat of undermining the Amish community and religious practice.' 406 US at 218. Enforcement of the statute in *Prince*, however, posed no such threat to the Jehovah's Witnesses' way of life; the Court in *Prince* took pains to note that its holding left parents free to accomplish the religious training and indoctrination of their children by all means 'except the public proclaiming of religion [by their children] in the streets.' 321 US at 171. More importantly, in *Yoder* and *Pierce* but not in *Prince* the effect of a holding in favour of the state would have been to compel children to confront daily a set of religious and social values antagonistic to those that their parents sought to foster.

moral considerations derive implicit legal sanction from those court decisions that permit an adolescent to act on his own values over the objection of his parent. . . .

D. Family autonomy
The state's interest in preserving the family unit is often cited to justify state sanction of parental authority. But protecting the family from outside interference is quite distinct from fortifying the family's power over one of its members. . . .

When a parent, in his role of family governor, exercises authority over the child, his action has a moral basis that the exercise of bare parental privilege lacks. But there are other criteria for the moral assessment of social institutions — whether an institution that makes claims against some provides some reciprocal benefit for each of those whose liberty it restricts, or whether it makes an equal relative contribution to the good life of each of its participants. Although family life may often require that some good of one individual be foregone for the well-being of the family as a whole, a family that excessively derogates the interests of one for the sake of the others undermines its own moral basis.

These moral considerations suggest a legal norm. The state need not intervene in every family dispute, but if it does, it must treat each family member affected as having a distinguishable interest, which is equally entitled to the protection of the state. And, in particular, where parents solicit or simply avail themselves of the sanction of law to augment their controls over family life, the child's own individual interest must be taken into account. Therefore, if it is based on the family autonomy rationale, the legitimacy of state sanction of parental authority with respect to a certain class of decisions depends on the consequences of those decisions for family well-being, on what the child is being asked to sacrifice for the sake of his family, and on what he ultimately stands to gain.

E. Child's welfare
The last of the proffered justifications of parental authority is that it serves the child's welfare. It has been suggested that allowing parents to be the supreme arbiters of their child's fate is justified because it is conducive to the child's long term psychological health. More commonly, parental authority is defended on the ground that someone must choose for children since they lack the capacity to choose for themselves; parents are assigned this role because they are presumed to be better able to perform the task than anyone else.

The legitimacy of parental authority based on the child's welfare rationale depends primarily on the child's capacity to choose for himself. This capacity will vary with age. Parental authority over preadolescents is justified because the assumption that children are not competent to make their own choices is, as applied to them, generally correct. Since, however, parents under this rationale are presumed to act as guardians of the child's interests, parental authority would lose its underlying legitimacy if exercised for purposes unrelated to the child's welfare or in ways that create for the child a substantial risk of harm. . . .

For the adolescent, the situation is more complex. Psychologists agree that about the time of adolescence a major transformation occurs in the quality of a child's thought. As a consequence of a shift to what is called formal operational thought, the youngster is capable of abstract, logical, and scientific thinking, which enables him to see the practical possibilities of real-life situations and to anticipate and evaluate the consequences of his own conduct. Simultaneously, or perhaps as a consequence of the same underlying process, the individual acquires an appreciation for the social ramifications of individual conduct, and a capacity to formulate his own personal and social ideals.

When a person makes choices after having identified the likely consequences for himself and others and having evaluated those alternatives in light of an overall life plan, he has chosen intelligently, even if unwisely from someone else's point of view. By this criterion, the psychological evidence shows that the typical adolescent will have acquired a basic capacity for intelligent choice by about fourteen years old.

Question

It is easy to conclude how the author would approach the question of a 15-year-old boy 'volunteered' against his will for psychiatric treatment, or a 15-year-old girl whose parents refused to consent to the abortion she desired, but to what extent would the same arguments apply to the case of D on p. 416, or of B, referred to on p. 418, above?

3 Children's rights

That last point makes it clear that we are here considering a tri-partite relationship: between parents and the state (or other third parties) and between parents and children, but also between children and parents and children and the state.

Gillick v West Norfolk and Wisbech Area Health Authority
[1986] AC 112, [1985] 3 All ER 402, [1985] 3 WLR 830, [1986] 1 FLR 224, House of Lords

The plaintiff, mother of five daughters under the age of 16, sought a declaration that the guidance issued by the DHSS, to the effect that in exceptional circumstances a doctor might give contraceptive advice and treatment to a girl under 16 without her parent's consent, was unlawful. She failed at first instance, but succeeded in the Court of Appeal. On appeal to the House of Lords:

Lord Fraser of Tullybelton: . . . Three strands of argument are raised by the appeal. These are: (1) whether a girl under the age of 16 has the legal capacity to give valid consent to contraceptive advice and treatment including medical examination; (2) whether giving such advice and treatment to a girl under 16 without her parents' consent infringes the parents' rights; and (3) whether a doctor who gives such advice or treatment to a girl under 16 without her parents' consent incurs criminal liability. I shall consider these strands in order.

1. *The legal capacity of a girl under 16 to consent to contraceptive advice, examination and treatment*
    There are some indications in statutory provisions to which we were referred that a girl under 16 years of age in England and Wales does not have the capacity to give valid consent to contraceptive advice and treatment. If she does not have the capacity, then any physical examination or touching of her body without her parents' consent would be an assault by the examiner. One of those provisions is s. 8 of the Family Law Reform Act 1969, which is in the following terms:
    '(1) The consent of a minor who has attained the age of sixteen years to any surgical, medical or dental treatment which, in the absence of consent, would constitute a trespass to his person, shall be as effective as it would be if he were of full age; and where a minor has by virtue of this section given an effective consent to any treatment it shall not be necessary to obtain any consent for it from his parent or guardian. . .
    (3) Nothing in this section shall be construed as making ineffective any consent which would have been effective if this section had not been enacted.'
    The contention on behalf of Mrs Gillick was that sub-s (1) of s. 8 shows that, apart from the subsection, the consent of a minor to such treatment would not be effective. But I do not accept that contention because sub-s (3) leaves open the question whether consent by a minor under the age of 16 would have been effective if the section had not been enacted. That question is not answered by the section, and sub-s (1) is, in my opinion, merely for the avoidance of doubt. . . .
    The statutory provisions to which I have referred do not differentiate so far as the capacity of a minor under 16 is concerned between contraceptive advice and treatment and other forms of medical advice and treatment. It would, therefore, appear that, if the inference which Mrs Gillick's advisers seek to draw from the provisions is justified, a minor under the age of 16 has no capacity to authorise any kind of medical advice or treatment or examination of his own body. That seems to me so surprising that I cannot accept it in the absence of clear provisions to that effect. It seems to me verging on the absurd to suggest that a girl or a boy aged 15 could not effectively consent, for example, to have a medical examination of some trivial injury to his body or even to have a broken arm set. Of course the consent of the parents should normally be asked, but they may not be immediately available. Provided the patient, whether a boy or a girl, is capable of understanding what is proposed, and of expressing his or her own wishes, I see no good reason for holding that he or she lacks the capacity to express them validly and

effectively and to authorise the medical man to make the examination or give the treatment which he advises. After all, a minor under the age of 16 can, within certain limits, enter into a contract. He or she can also sue and be sued, and can give evidence on oath. Moreover, a girl under 16 can give sufficiently effective consent to sexual intercourse to lead to the legal result that the man involved does not commit the crime of rape: see *R v Howard* [1965] 3 All ER 684 at 685, [1966] 1 WLR 13 at 15, . . .

Accordingly, I am not disposed to hold now, for the first time, that a girl aged less than 16 lacks the power to give valid consent to contraceptive advice or treatment, merely on account of her age.

2. *The parents' rights and duties in respect of medical treatment of their child*
. . . It was, I think, accepted both by Mrs Gillick and by the DHSS, and in any event I hold, that parental rights to control a child do not exist for the benefit of the parent. They exist for the benefit of the child and they are justified only in so far as they enable the parent to perform his duties towards the child, and towards other children in the family. If necessary, this proposition can be supported by reference to *Blackstone's Commentaries* (1 Bl Com (17th edn, 1830) 452), where he wrote: 'The power of parents over their children is derived from . . . their duty.' The proposition is also consistent with the provisions of the Guardianship of Minors Act 1971, s. 1, as amended, as follows:

'Where in any proceedings before any court . . . (*a*) the legal custody or upbringing of a minor . . . is in question, the court, in deciding that question, shall regard the welfare of the minor as the first and paramount consideration, and shall not take into consideration whether from any other point of view the claim of the father in respect of such legal custody, upbringing, administration or application is superior to that of the mother, or the claim of the mother is superior to that of the father.'

From the parents' right and duty of custody flows their right and duty of control of the child, but the fact that custody is its origin throws but little light on the question of the legal extent of control at any particular age. . . .

It is my view, contrary to the ordinary experience of mankind, at least in Western Europe in the present century, to say that a child or a young person remains in fact under the complete control of his parents until he attains the definite age of majority, now 18 in the United Kingdom, and that on attaining that age he suddenly acquires independence. In practice most wise parents relax their control gradually as the child develops and encourage him or her to become increasingly independent. Moreover, the degree of parental control actually exercised over a particular child does in practice vary considerably according to his understanding and intelligence and it would, in my opinion, be unrealistic for the courts not to recognise these facts. Social customs change, and the law ought to, and does in fact, have regard to such changes when they are of major importance. An example of such recognition is to be found in the view recently expressed in your Lordships' House by Lord Brandon, with which the other noble and learned Lords who were present agreed, in *R v D* [1984] AC 778 at 806, [1984] 2 All ER 449 at 457. Dealing with the question of whether the consent of a child to being taken away by a stranger would be a good defence to a charge of kidnapping, Lord Brandon said:

'In the case of a very young child, it would not have the understanding or the intelligence to give its consent, so that absence of consent would be a necessary inference from its age. In the case of an older child, however, it must, I think be a question of fact for a jury whether the child concerned has sufficient understanding and intelligence to give its consent; if, but only if, the jury considers that a child has these qualities, it must then go on to consider whether it has been proved that the child did not give its consent. While the matter will always be for the jury alone to decide, I should not expect a jury to find at all frequently that a child under 14 had sufficient understanding and intelligence to give its consent.'

Once the rule of the parents' absolute authority over minor children is abandoned, the solution to the problem in this appeal can no longer be found by referring to rigid parental rights at any particular age. The solution depends on a judgment of what is best for the welfare of the particular child. Nobody doubts, certainly I do not doubt, that in the overwhelming majority of cases the best judges of a child's welfare are his or her parents. Nor do I doubt that any important medical treatment of a child under 16 would normally only be carried out with the parents' approval. That is why it would and should be 'most unusual' for a doctor to advise a child without the knowledge and consent of the parents on contraceptive matters. But, as I have already pointed out, Mrs Gillick has to go further if she is to obtain the first declaration that she seeks. She has to justify the absolute right of veto in a parent. But there may be circumstances in which a doctor is a better judge of the medical advice and treatment which will conduce to a girl's welfare than her parents. . . .

The only practicable course is, in my opinion, to entrust the doctor with a discretion to act in accordance with his view of what is best in the interests of the girl who is his patient.

He should, of course, always seek to persuade her to tell her parents that she is seeking contraceptive advice, and the nature of the advice that she receives. At least he should seek to persuade her to agree to the doctor's informing the parents. But there may well be cases, and I think there will be some cases, where the girl refuses either to tell the parents herself or to permit the doctor to do so and in such cases the doctor will, in my opinion, be justified in proceeding without the parents' consent or even knowledge provided he is satisfied on the following matters: (1) that the girl (although under 16 years of age) will understand his advice; (2) that he cannot persuade her to inform her parents or to allow him to inform the parents that she is seeking contraceptive advice; (3) that she is very likely to begin or to continue having sexual intercourse with or without contraceptive treatment; (4) that unless she receives contraceptive advice or treatment her physical or mental health or both are likely to suffer; (5) that her best interests require him to give her contraceptive advice, treatment or both without the parental consent. . . .

Lord Scarman: . . . It is, of course, a judicial commonplace to proclaim the adaptability and flexibility of the judge-made common law. But this is more frequently proclaimed than acted on. The mark of the great judge from Coke through Mansfield to our day has been the capacity and the will to search out principle, to discard the detail appropriate (perhaps) to earlier times and to apply principle in such a way as to satisfy the needs of his own time. If judge-made law is to survive as a living and relevant body of law, we must make the effort, however inadequately, to follow the lead of the great masters of the judicial art. . . . Approaching the earlier law in this way, one finds plenty of indications as to the principles governing the law's approach to parental right and the child's right to make his or her own decision. Parental rights clearly do exist, and they do not wholly disappear until the age of majority. Parental rights relate to both the person and the property of the child: custody, care and control of the person and guardianship of the property of the child. But the common law has never treated such rights as sovereign or beyond review and control. Nor has our law ever treated the child as other than a person with capacities and rights recognised by law. The principle of the law, as I shall endeavour to show, is that parental rights are derived from parental duty and exist only so long as they are needed for the protection of the person and property of the child. The principle has been subjected to certain age limits set by statute for certain purposes; and in some cases the courts have declared an age of discretion at which a child acquires before the age of majority the right to make his (or her) own decision. But these limitations in no way undermine the principle of the law, and should not be allowed to obscure it. . . .

. . . The underlying principle of the law was exposed by Blackstone and can be seen to have been acknowledged in the case law. It is that parental right yields to the child's right to make his own decisions when he reaches a sufficient understanding and intelligence to be capable of making up his own mind on the matter requiring decision. Lord Denning MR captured the spirit and principle of the law when he said in *Hewer v Bryant* [1970] 1 QB 357 at 369, [1969] 3 All ER 578 at 582:

'I would get rid of the rule in *Re Agar-Ellis* (1883) 24 Ch D 317 and of the suggested exceptions to it. That case was decided in the year 1883. It reflects the attitude of a Victorian parent towards his children. He expected unquestioning obedience to his commands. If a son disobeyed, his father would cut him off with 1s. If a daughter had an illegitimate child, he would turn her out of the house. His power only ceased when the child became 21. I decline to accept a view so much out of date. The common law can, and should, keep pace with the times. It should declare, in conformity with the recent report on the Age of Majority that the legal right of a parent to the custody of a child ends at the eighteenth birthday; and even up till then, it is a dwindling right which the courts will hesitate to enforce against the wishes of the child, the older he is. It starts with a right of control and ends with little more than advice.'

But his is by no means a solitary voice. It is consistent with the opinion expressed by the House in *J v C* [1970] AC 668, [1969] 1 All ER 788, where their Lordships clearly recognised as out of place the assertion in the *Agar-Ellis* cases (1878) 10 Ch D 49; (1883) 24 Ch D 318 of a father's power bordering on 'patria potestas'. It is consistent with the view of Lord Parker CJ in *R v Howard* [1965] 3 All ER 684 at 685, [1966] 1 WLR 13 at 15, where he ruled that in the case of a prosecution charging rape of a girl under 16 the Crown must *prove* either lack of her consent or that she was not in a position to decide whether to consent or resist and added the comment that 'there are many girls who know full well what it is all about and can properly consent'. And it is consistent with the views of the House in the recent criminal case where a father was accused of kidnapping his own child, *R v D* [1984] AC 778, [1984] 2 All ER 449, a case to which I shall return. . . .

In the light of the foregoing I would hold that as a matter of law the parental right to determine whether or not their minor child below the age of 16 will have medical treatment terminates if and when the child achieves a sufficient understanding and intelligence to enable him or her to understand fully what is proposed. It will be a question of fact whether a child seeking advice has sufficient understanding of what is involved to give a consent valid in law. Until the child achieves the capacity to consent, the parental right to make the decision continues save only in exceptional circumstances. Emergency, parental neglect, abandonment of the child or inability to find the parent are examples of exceptional situations justifying the doctor proceeding to treat the child without parental knowledge and consent; but there will arise, no doubt, other exceptional situations in which it will be reasonable for the doctor to proceed without the parent's consent.

Lord Bridge agreed with them both. For him, however, the main ground for decision was that the DHSS guidance could only be challenged through judicial review, whereas Lord Scarman had held that private rights were involved. Lord Brandon of Oakbridge did not discuss the rights of parents or children because he concluded from the provisions of the Sexual Offences Act 1956 relating to unlawful sexual intercourse that the provision of contraceptive facilities was unlawful in any event.

Lord Templeman: . . . A parent is the natural and legal guardian of an infant under the age of 18 and is responsible for the upbringing of an infant who is in the custody of that parent. The practical exercise of parental powers varies from control and supervision to guidance and advice depending on the discipline enforced by the parent and the age and temperament of the infant. Parental power must be exercised in the best interests of the infant and the court may intervene in the interests of the infant at the behest of the parent or at the behest of a third party. The court may enforce parental right, control the misuse of parental power or uphold independent views asserted by the infant. The court will be guided by the principle that the welfare of the infant is paramount. But, subject to the discretion of the court to differ from the views of the parent, the court will, in my opinion, uphold the right of the parent having custody of the infant to decide on behalf of the infant all matters which the infant is not competent to decide. The prudent parent will pay attention to the wishes of the infant and will normally accept them as the infant approaches adulthood. The parent is not bound by the infant's wishes, but an infant approaching adulthood may be able to flout the wishes of the parent with ease. . . .

I accept also that a doctor may lawfully carry out some forms of treatment with the consent of an infant patient and against the opposition of a parent based on religious or any other grounds. The effect of the consent of the infant depends on the nature of the treatment and the age and understanding of the infant. For example, a doctor with the consent of an intelligent boy or girl of 15 could in my opinion safely remove tonsils or a troublesome appendix. But any decision on the part of a girl to practise sex and contraception requires not only knowledge of the facts of life and of the dangers of pregnancy and disease but also an understanding of the emotional and and other consequences to her family, her male partner and to herself. I doubt whether a girl under the age of 16 is capable of a balanced judgment to embark on frequent, regular or casual sexual intercourse fortified by the illusion that medical science can protect her in mind and body and ignoring the danger of leaping from childhood to adulthood without the difficult formative transitional experiences of adolescence. There are many things which a girl under 16 needs to practise but sex is not one of them. Parliament could declare this view to be out of date. But in my opinion the statutory provisons discussed in the speech of my noble and learned friend Lord Fraser and the provisions of s. 6 of the Sexual Offences Act 1956 indicate that as the law now stands an unmarried girl under 16 is not competent to decide to practise sex and contraception. . . .

. . . In my opinion a doctor may not lawfully provide a girl under 16 with contraceptive facilities without the approval of the parent responsible for the girl save pursuant to a court order, or in the case of emergency or in exceptional cases where the parent has abandoned or forfeited by abuse the right to be consulted. Parental rights cannot be insisted on by a parent who is not responsible for the custody and upbringing of an infant or where the parent has abandoned or abused parental rights. And a doctor is not obliged to give effect to parental rights in an emergency.

Appeal allowed.

Questions

(i) Are all four of their Lordships saying the same thing? Does parental right yield to the child's autonomy? Can a parent override the dissent of an autonomous child (see *Re R (a minor) (wardship: medical treatment)* (1991) Times 31 July)? Or does the child's autonomy allow a third party to take over the decision of what will be best?

(ii) Following *Gillick*, the GMC advised doctors that the decision does not guarantee confidentiality for children who are found by the doctor to be insufficiently mature to give consent: is this advice correct in law (see Grubb and Pearl (1986, at p. 240) and Montgomery (1987))?

(iii) Is there anything in these speeches which might have led counsel in *F v Wirral Metropolitan Borough Council* [1991] 2 All ER 648, [1991] 2 WLR 1132, p. 409, above, to put forward the argument described by Stuart-Smith LJ as 'wholly misconceived'?

In *The Emergence of Children's Rights* (1986) John Eekelaar discusses the concept of children's rights, and distinguishes three different kinds of interest they may have:

We may accept that the *social perception* that an individual or class of individuals has certain interests is a precondition to the conceptualization of rights. But these interests must be capable of isolation from the interests of others. I might believe that it is in my infant daughter's interests that I (and not she) take decisions concerning her medical welfare. This may even be supportable by objective evidence. But my interest, or right, to take such decisions is not identical with her interests. I might make stupid or even malicious decisions. Her interest is that I should make the best decisions for her. I am no more than the agent for fulfilling her interests. Hence we should be careful to understand that when we talk about rights as protecting interests, we conceive as interests only those benefits which the subject himself or herself might plausibly claim in themselves. This point is of great importance in the context of modern assertions of the right to parental autonomy. This has been advanced as a fuller enhancement of children's rights. Goldstein, Freud and Solnit [see p. 424, above] construct the concept of 'family integrity' which is a combination of 'the three liberty interests of direct concern to children, parental autonomy, the right to autonomous parents and privacy'. But can we say the children might plausibly claim any of these things in themselves? If they are claimed (which they may be) it will be because they are believed to advance other desirable ends (perhaps material and emotional stability) which are the true objects of the claims. Observe that the formulation refers to claims children might plausibly make. Not, be it noted, what they actually claim. We here meet the problem that children often lack the information or ability to appreciate what will serve them best. It is necessary therefore to make some kind of imaginative leap and guess what a child might retrospectively have wanted once it reaches a position of maturity. In doing this, values of the adult world and of individual adults will inevitably enter. This is not to be deplored, but openly accepted. It encourages debate about these values. There are, however, some broad propositions which might reasonably be advanced as forming the foundation of any child's (retrospective) claims. General physical, emotional and intellectual care within the social capabilities of his or her immediate caregivers would seem a minimal expectation. We may call this the 'basic' interest. What a child should expect from the wider community must be stated more tentatively. I have elsewhere [Eekelaar, 1984] suggested the formulation that, within certain overriding constraints, created by the economic and social structure of society (whose extent must be open to debate), all children should have an equal opportunity to maximize the resources available to them during their childhood (including their own inherent abilities) so as to minimize the degree to which they enter adult life affected by avoidable prejudices incurred during childhood. In short, their capacities are to be developed to their best advantage. We may call this the 'developmental' interest. The concept requires some elaboration.

It seems plausible that a child may expect society at large, no less than his parents, to ensure that he is no worse off than most other children in his opportunities to realize his life-chances. Could a child also plausibly claim that he should be given a *better* chance than other children, for example, by exploitation of his superior talents or a favoured social position? As an expectation addressed to the child's parents, such a claim might have some weight. A child of rich parents might retrospectively feel aggrieved if those resources were not used to provide him with a better chance in life than other children. On the other hand, such an expectation is less plausibly addressed to society at large, except perhaps with respect to the cultivation of singular talents. But from the point of view of a theory of rights, it does not much matter whether we decide that a privileged child has an interest in inequality favourable to himself. For, if the interest is to become a right, it must be acknowledged in the public domain as demanding protection for its own sake. As far as the 'developmental' interest is concerned, therefore, societies may choose to actualize it in harmony with their overall social goals, which may (but not necessarily) involve creating equality of opportunity and reducing socially determined inequalities, but encouraging diversity of achievement related to individual talent.

There is a third type of interest which children may, retrospectively, claim. A child may argue for the freedom to choose his own lifestyle and to enter social relations according to his own inclinations uncontrolled by the authority of the adult world, whether parents or institutions. Claims of this kind have been put forward on behalf of children by Holt (1975) and by Farson (1978). We may call them the 'autonomy' interest. Freeman (1983) has argued that such interests might be abridged insofar as children also have a right to be protected against their own inclinations if their satisfaction would rob them of the opportunity 'to mature to a rationally autonomous adulthood . . . capable of deciding on [their] own system of ends as free and rational beings'. This may be no more than a version of the developmental interest defined earlier. The problem is that a child's autonomy interest may conflict with the developmental interest and even the basic interest. While it is possible that some adults retrospectively approve that they were, when children, allowed the exercise of their autonomy at the price of putting them at a disadvantage as against other children in realizing their life-chances in adulthood, it seems improbable that this would be a common view. We may therefore rank the autonomy interests subordinate to the basic and the developmental interests. However, where they may be exercised without threatening these two interests, the claim for their satisfaction must be high.

'Basic' interests are served by care proceedings, at that time under s. 1 of the Children and Young Persons Act 1969 (now under s. 31 of the Children Act 1989, p. 607, below):

. . . the statute does not confer rights to be free of deprivations suffered by parents which are reflected on the children. But it does, as applied in practice, seem to give children rights to be removed from the adverse consequences of care by parents who suffer social or personal inadequacy. The imposition of these duties is primarily perceived by the enforcement agencies as directed at advancing the interests of the rightholders, and represents a total reversal of earlier characterizations of the child-parent relationship. This reflects not only the social recognition of the basic interests of the rightholders as ends in themselves, but also a societal decision of the priority to be applied where those interests conflict with the interests of others, in this case, the parents.

'Developmental' interests present more problems:

When we turn to the developmental interests, there is more difficulty. The requirement to allocate resources so that an individual child does not suffer such deprivations during childhood that he is disadvantaged disproportionately, when compared to children generally, in the outset of his or her adult life, can for a large part be met only by the community at large. The cost appears in such areas as children's medical services and education. The duties lie primarily in the political domain and therefore become enmeshed in still broader considerations of public policy. Their legal articulation is at a very broad level of generality. . . .

While children are resident with their parents, the law imposes no duty on the parents to fulfil the developmental interests, apart from ensuring their education. This is the legacy of the vacuum left by the common law which has been referred to earlier. We can, perhaps, safely assume that while the family remains intact, family resources will be used as far as possible to satisfy them, and that compromises will be fairly arrived at. Or, if we are unhappy about making such an assumption, we may believe that legal intrusion over the disposition of the resources of the intact family is inappropriate, at least if the basic interests are not threatened. However we may justify it, the developmental interest for the vast majority of children is not protected as a right, but owes its satisfaction to the natural workings of the economies of families which are themselves dependent on the wider social and economic mechanisms of the community. Where, however, the family is split apart, the regulation of the distribution of resources between the families is thrown into the public domain. Failure to ensure some such distribution carries the risk of visible impoverishment of the mother and child, with attendant threats to social stability and community welfare funds. The developmental interests of children are also threatened in these circumstances, so it is of interest to discover how far the legal regulation of income distribution after family separation can be characterized as the protection of that interest. The interests of parents are in strong contention here: their interests in releasing themselves from a disliked marriage and in entering a new one (with sufficient resources); their interests in using their resources, capital and income, as they think fit; their interests in freedom of movement; their interests in pursuing new relationships free from the influences of the past; their interests in salvaging a relationship with their children. It is important to realize that separation and divorce do give rise to serious conflicts between the interests of parents and children. Martin Richards [1986] has suggested that failure to recognize such conflicts is the source of much of the guilt which surrounds divorce. But it is not enough simply to recognize the conflicts. They need resolution. The children's interests cannot be characterized as rights if they are equated with, or subservient to, those of the adults. Nor can they be so treated if the resolution of such conflicts is abandoned to the uncontrolled discretion of adjudicators.

After analysing the deficiencies of *Richards v Richards* [1984] AC 174, [1983] 2 All ER 807, HL (p. 394, above) in this respect, he comments:

The set-back to children's rights represented in *Richards* may be thought to be curious in the light of its apparent success in the 'first' consideration clause in the 1984 Act. In fact, it may be more significant as showing the fragility of the statutory principle when faced with strongly opposed adult interests. In the divorce context, contemporary society has still to determine the full extent of what the interests of children are and the degree to which, by restraining the fulfilment of conflicting interests of adults, the children's interests should be promoted to the status of rights.

Finally, he discusses the autonomy interest in the light of *Gillick*:

. . . Of the nine judges who gave a decision in this litigation, five were in favour of the plaintiff. This perhaps illustrates the ambiguity in current perceptions of the proper scope of children's autonomy interests. But the majority decision of the House of Lords has implications which extend beyond the parent-child relationship and into the scope of state power over the lives of children themselves.

Both Lord Scarman and Lord Fraser adopted the major premise that once a child had attained sufficient understanding and maturity, he had full capacity to enter legal relationships without the consent of his parents. The consistency of this position with authority and principle has already been demonstrated. Lord Scarman then concluded that as soon as a child reached this position, any parental right within the relevant area, terminated. The parental right 'yielded' to the child's right. Lord Fraser, however, was less clear about this. In the medical context, he seemed to say that a doctor would only be 'justified' in treating a child without parental consent if this was in the child's best interests, and, as far as contraceptive treatment was concerned, this would normally entail involvement of the parents, although this could be avoided if the child refused to permit it, and the protection of (her) physical and mental health required such treatment despite lack of parental knowledge and consent. This might mean that, in certain situations, the parental right survives the minor child's acquisition of capacity and with judicial support, could prevent such a child from acting according to her wishes if her interests demanded such restriction. But an alternative interpretation of the speech is possible. This would permit anyone to deal lawfully with a minor child who had acquired capacity, and restrict the requirement to consult parents (outside exceptional situations) to a rule of good practice applicable only in medical matters and enforceable only through professional discipline. No help is obtained from Lord Bridge, who simply agreed with both Lord Scarman and Lord Fraser. Lord Templeman, who dissented on the issue as far as it related to *contraceptive* treatment, seemed to express a view close to that of Lord Scarman as far as other medical matters were concerned.

The significance of Lord Scarman's opinion with respect to children's autonomy interests cannot be over-rated. It follows from his reasoning that, where a child has reached capacity, there is no room for a parent to impose a contrary view, *even if this is more in accord with the child's best interests*. For its legal superiority to the child's decision can rest only on its status as a parental right. But this is extinguished when the child reaches full capacity. More importantly, the argument catches the court itself. Should the child be warded, custody of the child vests in the court. The inherent jurisdiction of the High Court to intervene in the lives of children rests on the doctrine of the Crown's role as *parens patriae*. But on what principle can the Crown retain the parental jurisdiction when the parent himself has lost it, not through deprivation, but due to the superior right of the child? The primary question in wardship cases involving older children can no longer be: what is in the best interest of the child? It must be, has the child capacity to make his own decisions?

This recognition of the autonomy interests of children can be reconciled with their basic and developmental interests only through the empirical application of the concept of the acquisition of full capacity. This, as Lord Scarman made clear, may be no simple matter. The child must not only understand the nature of the transaction, but be able to evaluate its implications. Intellectual understanding must be supplemented by emotional maturity. It is easy to see how adults can conclude that a child's decision which seems, to the adult, to be contrary to his interests, is lacking in sufficient maturity. In this respect, the provision of the simple test of age to provide an upper limit to the scope of a supervisory, paternalistic power has advantages. We cannot know for certain whether, retrospectively, a person may not regret that some control was not exercised over his immature judgment by persons with greater experience. But could we not say that it is on balance better to subject all persons to this potential inhibition up to a defined age, in case the failure to exercise the restraint unduly prejudices a person's basic or developmental interests? It avoids judgments in which questions of fact and value will be impenetrably mixed. But the decision, it seems, has been taken. Children will now have, in wider measure than ever before, that most dangerous but most precious of rights: the right to make their own mistakes.

Questions

(i) Would you give priority to an older child's interests or to his wishes?

(ii) Might not recognising the child's 'autonomy interest' itself be a means of recognising his 'basic' and 'developmental' interests (see, for example, Adler and Dearling, 1986)?

(iii) To what extent would you give priority to any of these interests, if they conflicted with those of adults?

(iv) Eekelaar acknowledges the political implications of society recognising the developmental interests of children: how far is it possible to go in a democracy?

(v) 'Is it not almost a self-evident axiom that the State should require and compel the education, up to a certain standard, of every human being who is born its citizen?' (Mill, 1859)

In fact, although the authors of *Before the Best Interests of the Child* (1980) appear to regard compulsory education as unproblematic, this can be a most difficult area in which to reconcile the rights of the child with the values of a free and plural society. In *Wisconsin v Yoder* 406 US 205 (1972), the United States Supreme Court invalidated a state compulsory education law insofar as it compelled Amish children to stay at school beyond the age (14) at which their parents believed it might prejudice their upbringing in the Amish way of life. The European Convention of Human Rights deals with the matter in article 2 of Protocol No. 1 (p. 407, above), the interpretation of which was discussed in the following case:

Campbell and Cosans
(1982) 4 EHRR 293 European Court of Human Rights, Strasbourg

Mrs Campbell's son, Gordon, attended a primary school in Scotland at which corporal punishment was used for disciplinary purposes, although in fact Gordon was never so punished while he was at that school. Mrs Cosans' son, Jeffrey, attended a secondary school where corporal punishment was also used. On his father's advice, Jeffrey refused to accept corporal punishment for trying to take a prohibited short cut on his way home from school. As a result, he was suspended from school until such time as he was willing to accept the punishment. He remained suspended from September to the following May, when he ceased to be of compulsory school age. Each mother claimed a violation of the second sentence of Article 2, Protocol No. 1, and Mrs Cosans claimed that Jeffrey's suspension violated his right to education under the first sentence of that Article. (They also claimed breach of the prohibition of 'torture' or 'inhuman or degrading treatment or punishment' in Article 3 of the Convention, but the Court found that no such treatment had taken place.)

Judgment of the court: . . . in the submission of the Government, the obligation to respect philosophical convictions arises only in relation to the content of, and mode of conveying, information and knowledge and not in relation to all aspects of school administration.
   As the Government pointed out, the *Kjeldsen, Busk Madsen and Pedersen* judgment states:
   'The second sentence of Article 2 implies . . . that the State, in fulfilling the functions assumed by it in regard to education and teaching, must take care that information or knowledge included in the curriculum is conveyed in an objective, critical and pluralistic manner. The State is forbidden to pursue an aim of indoctrination that might be considered as not respecting parents' religious and philosophical convictions. That is the limit that must not be exceeded.'
   However, that case concerned the content of instruction, whereas the second sentence of Article 2 has a broader scope, as is shown by the generality of its wording. This was confirmed by the Court in the same judgment when it held that the said sentence is binding upon the Contracting States in the exercise, inter alia, of the function 'consisting of the organisation and financing of public education'. . . .
   The Government also contested the conclusion of the majority of the [European Commission of Human Rights] that the applicants' views on the use of corporal punishment amounted to 'philosophical convictions', arguing, inter alia, that the expression did not extend to opinions on internal school administration, such as discipline, and that, if the majority were correct, there was no reason why objections to other methods of discipline, or simply to discipline in general, should not also amount to 'philosophical convictions'. . . .
   Having regard to the Convention as a whole . . . the expression 'philosophical convictions' in the present context denotes, in the Court's opinion, such convictions as are worthy of respect in a 'democratic society' . . . and are not incompatible with human dignity; in addition, they must not conflict with the fundamental right of the child to education, the whole of Article 2 being dominated by its first sentence. . . .
   The applicants' views relate to a weighty and substantial aspect of human life and behaviour, namely the integrity of the person, the propriety or otherwise of the infliction of corporal punishment and the exclusion of the distress which the risk of such punishment entails. They are views which satisfy the various criteria listed above; it is this that distinguishes them from opinions that might be held on other methods of discipline or on discipline in general. . . .
   Mrs Campbell and Mrs Cosans have accordingly been victims of a violation of the second sentence of Article 2 of Protocol No. 1. . . .
   The right to education guaranteed by the first sentence of Article 2 by its very nature calls for regulation by the State, but such regulation must never injure the substance of the right nor conflict with other rights enshrined in the Convention or its Protocols. . . .
   The suspension of Jeffrey Cosans — which remained in force for nearly a whole school year — was motivated by his and his parents' refusal to accept that he receive or be liable to corporal punishment. . . . His return to school could have been secured only if his parents had acted contrary to their convictions, convictions which the United Kingdom is obliged to

respect under the second sentence of Article 2. . . . A condition of access to an educational establishment that conflicts in this way with another right enshrined in Protocol No. 1 cannot be described as reasonable and in any event falls outside the State's power of regulation under Article 2.

There has accordingly also been, as regards Jeffrey Cosans, breach of the first sentence of that Article.

Questions

(i) In the *Kejeldsen, Busk Madsen and Pedersen* case (7 December 1976, Series A, No. 23) the court held that compulsory sex education in state schools was *not* a contravention of the duty to respect the parents' religious and philosophical convictions: can you explain why?

(ii) What would have been the position if Jeffrey Cosans had wanted to exercise his right to education, but his parents had prevented him?

(iii) In the event, the Government found it impossible to legislate to allow parents to choose and the Education (No. 2) Act 1986 bans corporal punishment for all state-educated pupils: is this a victory for parents' or children's rights?

4 Parental responsibility

The *Children Act 1989* uses the basic concept of 'parental responsibility', defined as follows:

3. — (1) In this Act 'parental responsibility' means all the rights, duties, powers, responsibilities and authority which by law a parent of a child has in relation to the child and his property.

(2) It also includes the rights, powers and duties which a guardian of the child's estate (appointed, before the commencement of section 5, to act generally) would have had in relation to the child and his property.

(3) The rights referred to in subsection (2) include, in particular, the right of the guardian to receive or recover in his own name, for the benefit of the child, property of whatever description and wherever situated which the child is entitled to receive or recover.

(4) The fact that a person has, or does not have, parental responsibility for a child shall not affect —

  (a) any obligation which he may have in relation to the child (such as a statutory duty to maintain the child); or

  (b) any rights which, in the event of the child's death, he (or any other person) may have in relation to the child's property.

. . .

The reasons for what might be thought a purely cosmetic change appear in the Law Commission's Report on *Guardianship and Custody* (1988):

Parental responsibility

2.4 Scattered through the statute book at present are such terms as 'parental rights and duties' or the 'powers and duties', or the 'rights and authority' of a parent. However, in our first Report on Illegitimacy we expressed the view that 'to talk of parental "rights" is not only inaccurate as a matter of juristic analysis but also a misleading use of ordinary language.' The House of Lords, in *Gillick v West Norfolk and Wisbech Area Health Authority* [[1986] AC 112, [1985] 3 All ER 402, HL (p. 428, above)] has held that the powers which parents have to control or make decisions for their children are simply the necessary concomitant of their parental duties. To refer to the concept of 'right' in the relationship between parent and child is therefore likely to produce confusion, as that case itself demonstrated. As against third parties, parents clearly have a prior claim to look after or have contact with their child but, as the House of Lords has recently pointed out in *Re KD (A Minor) (Ward: Termination of Access)* [1988] AC 806, [1988] 1 All ER 577, HL, that claim will always be displaced if the interests of the child indicate to the contrary. The parental claim can be recognised in the rules governing the allocation of parental responsibilities, but the content of their status would be more accurately reflected if a new concept of 'parental responsibility' were to replace the ambiguous and confusing terms used at present. Such a change would make little difference in substance but it would reflect the everyday reality of being a parent and emphasise the responsibilites of all who are in that position. . . .

2.5 One further advantage is that the same concept could then be employed to define the status of local authorities when children have been compulsorily committed to their care. The reports of the inquiries into the deaths of Jasmine Beckford and Tyra Henry indicate how helpful this would be in emphasising the continuing parental responsibility of the local authority even if the child has been allowed to live at home.

(a) The scope of parental responsibility

2.6 The concept of 'parental responsibility' can be defined by reference to all the incidents, whether rights, claims, duties, powers, responsibilities or authority, which statute and common law for the time being confer upon parents. It would be superficially attractive to provide a list of these but those who responded to our Working Paper on Guardianship recognised the practical impossibility of doing so. The list must change from time to time to meet differing needs and circumstances. As the *Gillick* case itself demonstrated, it must also vary with the age and maturity of the child and the circumstances of each individual case.

2.7 Three points should, however, be made clear. First, the incidents of parenthood with which we are concerned are those which relate to the care and upbringing of a child until he grows up. This does include some power to administer the child's property on his behalf but it does not include the right to succeed to the child's property on his death (which will almost always be without leaving a will because children under 18 can only make wills in very exceptional circumstances). The right to succeed is a feature of being related to the deceased in a particular way and operates irrespective of who has responsibility for bringing him up. . . .

2.8 Secondly, it might also be helpful to clarify the nature and extent of a parent's powers to administer or deal with a child's property, for the law on this is most obscure . . . a particular uncertainty is whether the parents have the same powers as do guardians, for example to receive a legacy on the child's behalf. Our provisional proposal that parents should be in no worse position than guardians in this respect was approved on consultation and we so recommend.

2.9 Thirdly, the fact that a person does, or does not, have parental responsibility for the care and upbringing of a child does not affect the rights of the child, in particular to be maintained or to succeed to a person's estate. The principle that children should have the same rights whatever the marital status of their parents was an essential feature of our recommendations on illegitimacy [see pp. 469 et seq, below] which have recently been implemented by the Family Law Reform Act 1987. . . .

Question

What do you think the Commission meant when they argued that the concept of parental 'responsibility' would 'reflect the everyday reality of being a parent'?

John Eekelaar, in *Parental Responsibility: State of Nature or Nature of the State?* (1991), has pointed out that the concept of parental responsibility can be used in two rather different senses:

It was . . . in the context of appreciation that parental 'rights' needed to be exercised for the benefit of the child that the Law Commission (1982) first suggested that it might be more appropriate to talk about parental responsibilities than parental rights. Similarly, the Commission's confirmation in paragraph 1.11 of its 1985 Working Paper on Guardianship of its preference for speaking of 'powers and responsibilities' rather than 'rights and duties' follows the observation that a parent 'will not . . . be permitted to insist upon action which is contrary to (the welfare of the child) or to resist action which will promote it' (Law Commission, 1985). The shift in terminology reflects a similar change made in West Germany as long ago as 1970, when 'parental power' (*elterliche Gewalt*) was replaced by 'parental care' (*elterliche Sorge*) (Frank, 1990) and the conception of 'parental responsibilities' recommended by the Committee of Ministers of the Council of Europe in 1984 (Recommendation No. R(84)4, February 28, 1984), which states that 'parental responsibilities are a collection of duties and powers which aim at ensuring the moral and material welfare of the child, in particular by taking care of the person of the child, by maintaining personal relationships with him and by providing for his education, maintenance, his legal representation and the administration of his property.' I shall refer to this sense of 'responsibility' as *responsibility (1)*.

However, also in paragraph 1.11 of its 1985 Working Paper, the Commission introduced a different concept of responsibility. 'Further,' they wrote, 'to the extent that the law enables parents to decide how to bring up their children without interference from others or from the state, it does so principally because this is a necessary part of the parents' responsibility for that upbringing and in order thus to promote the welfare of their children'. 'Responsibility' does not here refer to the way in which a parent behaves *towards* his child (as is reflected in the references to duties and supervision over parental conduct made earlier) but rather to a role which is to be exercised by the parent rather than some other entity. Of course, the assumption of responsibility for a child in this sense is not necessarily inconsistent with the presence of duties towards the child (as we shall see, it is sometimes thought that it encourages their performance). But the focus is not upon those duties but rather upon the distance between the parent and others in making provision for the child; indeed, on the degree of *freedom* given to parents in bringing up their children. And the more scope that is given to parental autonomy, the less room there is for external supervision over the way duties (under *responsibility (1)*) towards children are discharged. This will be referred to as *responsibility (2)*.

Question

As various provisions of the Children Act 1989 appear, try to identify whether they owe more to responsibility (1) or responsibility (2).

The *Children Act 1989* also deals with some important features of parental responsibility:

2.—. . .(5) More than one person may have parental responsibility for the same child at the same time.

(6) A person who has parental responsibility for a child at any time shall not cease to have that responsibility solely because some other person subsequently acquires parental responsibility for the child.

(7) Where more than one person has parental responsibility for a child, each of them may act alone and without the other (or others) in meeting that responsibility; but nothing in this Part shall be taken to affect the operation of any enactment which requires the consent of more than one person in a matter affecting the child.

(8) The fact that a person has parental responsibility for a child shall not entitle him to act in any way which would be incompatible with any order made with respect to the child under this Act.

(9) A person who has parental responsibility for a child may not surrender or transfer any part of that responsibility to another but may arrange for some or all of it to be met by one or more persons acting on his behalf.

(10) The person with whom any such arrangement is made may himself be a person who already has parental responsibility for the child concerned.

(11) The making of any such arrangement shall not affect any liability of the person making it which may arise from any failure to meet any part of his parental responsibility for the child concerned.

3. — . . .(5) A person who —

(a) does not have parental responsibility for a particular child; but

(b) has care of the child.

may (subject to the provisions of this Act) do what is reasonable in all the circumstances of the case for the purpose of safeguarding or promoting the child's welfare.

Once again, these are explained in the Law Commission's *Report* (1988):

(b) *The power to act independently*
2.10 . . . We believe it important to preserve the equal status of parents and their power to act independently of one another unless and until a court orders otherwise. This should be seen as part of the general aim of encouraging both parents to feel concerned and responsible for the welfare of their children. A few respondents suggested that they should have a legal duty to consult one another on major matters in their children's lives, arguing that this would increase parental co-operation and involvement after separation or divorce. This is an objective which we all share. However, whether or not the parents are living together, a legal duty of consultation seems both unworkable and undesirable. The person looking after the child has to be able to take decisions in the child's best interests as and when they arise. Some may have to be taken very quickly. In reality . . . it is that person who will have to put those decisions into effect and that person who has the degree of practical control over the child to be able to do so. The child may well suffer if that parent is prevented by the other's disapproval and thus has to go to court to resolve the matter, still more if the parent is inhibited by the fear that the other may disapprove or by the difficulties of contacting him or of deciding whether what is proposed is or is not a major matter requiring consultation. In practice, where the parents disagree about a matter of upbringing the burden should be on the one seeking to prevent a step which the other is proposing, or to impose a course of action which only the other can put into effect, to take the matter to court. Otherwise the courts might be inundated with cases, disputes might escalate well beyond their true importance, and in the meantime the children would suffer. We recommend, therefore, that the equal and independent status of parents be preserved and, indeed, applied to others (principally guardians) who may share parental responsibility in future. This will not, of course, affect any statutory provision which requires the consent of each parent, for example to the adoption of the child.

(c) *The effect of court orders*
2.11 Allied to this is the principle that parents should not lose their parental responsibility even though its exercise may have to be modified or curtailed in certain respects, for example if it is necessary to determine where a child will live after his parents separate. Obviously, a court order to that effect will put many matters outside the control of the parent who does not have the child with him. However, parents should not be regarded as losing their position, and their ability to take decisions about their children, simply because they are separated or in dispute with one another about a particular matter. Hence they should only be prevented from acting in ways which would be incompatible with an order made about the child's upbringing. If, for example, the child has to live with one parent and go to a school near home, it would be incompatible with that order for the other parent to arrange for him to have his hair done in a way which will exclude him from the school. It would not, however, be incompatible for that parent to take him to a particular sporting occasion over the weekend, no matter how much the parent with whom the child lived might disapprove. These principles form part of our general aim of 'lowering the stakes' in cases of parental separation and divorce, and emphasising the continued responsibility of both parents, to which we shall return [see p. 543, below]. However, they are equally important where children are committed to local authority care. The crucial effect of a care order is to confer parental responsibilities upon the authority and there will be detailed regulations about how these are to be exercised. But the parents remain the parents and 'it will continue to be important in many cases to involve the parents in the child's care'. Clearly, the order will leave little scope for them to carry out their responsibilities, save to a limited extent while the child is with them, because the local authority will be in control of so much of the child's life [see p. 612, below]. But the parents should not be deprived of their very parenthood unless and until the child is adopted or freed for adoption.

(d) *Arrangements and agreements with parents and others*
2.12 . . .
2.13 It is clearly important to maintain the principle that parental rights or responsibility cannot be legally surrendered or transferred without a court order and we so recommend. Equally, it is always possible, and a common practice, for parents to delegate the exercise of some or all of their parental responsibilities either between themselves or to other people or agencies, such as schools, holiday camps, foster parents or local authorities. It would be helpful for the law to recognise this expressly, for two reasons. First, parents are now encouraged to agree between themselves the arrangements which they believe best for their children, whether or not they are separated. It is important, therefore, that they should feel free to do so. Secondly

. . . it is helpful if, for example, a school can feel confident in accepting the decision of a person nominated by the parents as a temporary 'guardian' for the child while they are away. . . .

2.14 We do not recommend, however, that such arrangements should be legally binding so that the parents cannot revoke or change them. . . . It would scarcely be in the best interests of children for parents to be bound by such arrangements should they wish to change them. No court would uphold them if they were contrary to the child's interests but the burden of taking the case to court should not lie with the parents. This is particularly important in the context of arrangements made with or through local authorities. Both the Review of Child Care Law and the Government's response to it have emphasised that these should always be voluntary and that court proceedings should be required before any compulsory interference with the parents' responsibilities.

2.15. . . As between those who share parental responsibility, . . . a provision for legally binding agreements might inhibit them from making whatever arrangements seem best at the time for fear that it might later be difficult to change them. Any disagreement will eventually have to be resolved by a court and in practice the burden will still lie on the one wishing to change the agreed arrangements. The court, in deciding what is best for the child, will no doubt take account of the arrangements agreed, the reasons for them, and the risks of changing them. But if they have already been changed in fact it would be wrong for there still to be a bias in favour of the previous agreement. . . .

(e) *The position of those without parental responsibility*

2.16 However, it would be helpful to clarify the position of those who have actual care of a child without having parental responsibility for him in law. . . . There is criminal liability for, *inter alia*, ill-treatment, neglect and failure to educate, whether or not a person has legal custody. . . . But there may be confusion about the power of such people to take certain decisions about the child. We therefore recommend that it be made quite clear that anyone with actual care of a child may do what is reasonable in all the circumstances of the case for the purpose of safeguarding or promoting the child's welfare. The obvious example is medical treatment. If the child is left with friends while the parents go on holiday, it would obviously not be reasonable to arrange major elective surgery, but it would be reasonable to arrange whatever was advised in the event of an accident to the child. . . .

The Department of Health's *Introduction to the Children Act 1989* (1989) sums it all up like this:

1.4 The Act uses the phrase '*parental responsibility*' to sum up the collection of duties, rights and authority which a parent has in respect of his child. That choice of words emphasises that the duty to care for the child and to raise him to moral, physical and emotional health is the fundamental task of parenthood and the only justification for the authority it confers.

1.5 The importance of parental responsibility is emphasised in the Act by the fact that not only is it unaffected by the separation of parents but even when courts make orders in private proceedings such as divorce, that responsibility continues and is limited only to the extent that any order settles certain concrete issues between the parties. That arrangement aims to emphasise that interventions by the courts where there is family breakdown should not be regarded as lessening the duty on both parents to continue to play a full part in the child's upbringing.

Questions

(i) Do you really believe that parents are for children rather than children for parents?

(ii) If you do, would you introduce any controls over who is allowed to have children (see also p. 495, below)?

The *United Nations Convention on the Rights of the Child* (1989) includes the following:

WELFARE PRINCIPLE
Article 3
1 In all actions concerning children, whether undertaken by public or private social welfare institutions, courts of law, administrative authorities or legislative bodies, the best interests of the child shall be a primary consideration.

FAMILY LIFE
Article 9
1 States Parties shall ensure that a child shall not be separated from his or her parents against their will, except when competent authorities subject to judicial review determine, in accordance with applicable law and procedures, that such separation is necessary for the best interests of the child.
   Such determination may be necessary in a particular case such as one involving abuse or neglect of the child by the parents, or one where the parents are living separately and a decision must be made as to the child's place of residence.

CHILD'S WISHES
Article 12
1 States Parties shall assure to the child who is capable of forming his or her own views the right to express those views freely in all matters affecting the child, the view of the child being given due weight in accordance with the age and maturity of the child.
2 For this purpose, the child shall in particular be provided the opportunity to be heard in any judicial and administrative proceedings affecting the child, either directly, or through a representative or an appropriate body, in a manner consistent with the procedural rules of national law.

FREEDOM OF EXPRESSION
Article 13
1 The child shall have the right to freedom of expression; this right shall include freedom to seek, receive and impart information and ideas of all kinds, regardless of frontiers, either orally, in writing or in print, in the form of art, or through any other media of the child's choice.

PARENTAL SUPPORT
Article 18
1 States Parties shall use their best efforts to ensure recognition of the principle that both parents have common responsibilities for the upbringing and development of the child. Parents or, as the case may be, legal guardians, have the primary responsibility for the upbringing and development of the child. The best interests of the child will be their basic concern.

MINORITY RIGHTS
Article 30
In those States, in which ethnic, religious or linguistic minorities or persons of indigenous origin exist, a child belonging to such a minority or who is indigenous shall not be denied the right, in community with other members of his or her group, to enjoy his or her own culture, to profess and practice his or her own religion, or to use his or her language.

Questions

(i) Why is the Convention not called the Convention on the Responsibilities of Parents and Others for Children?

(ii) We have moved from parental rights to parental responsibilities. Should we also move from children's rights to children's responsibilities?

CHAPTER 11

Who is a parent?

Once upon a time, it was the *child* of unmarried parents who was thought to be the problem. Now the law tries to treat the child himself just like any other but still distinguishes between different sorts of parent.

The *Family Law Reform Act 1987* provides:

GENERAL PRINCIPLE

1.—(1) In this Act and enactments passed and instruments made after the coming into force of this section, references (however expressed) to any relationship between two persons shall, unless the contrary intention appears, be construed without regard to whether or not the father and mother of either of them, or the father and mother of any person through whom the relationship is deduced, have or had been married to each other at any time.

(2) In this Act and enactments passed after the coming into force of this section, unless the contrary intention appears—

    (*a*) references to a person whose father and mother were married to each other at the time of his birth include; and

    (*b*) references to a person whose father and mother were not married to each other at the time of his birth do not include.

references to any person to whom subsection (3) below applies, and cognate references shall be construed accordingly.

(3) This subsection applies to any person who—

    (*a*) is treated as legitimate by virtue of section 1 of the Legitimacy Act 1976;

    (*b*) is a legitimated person within the meaning of section 10 of that Act;

    (*c*) is an adopted child within the meaning of Part IV of the Adoption Act 1976; or

    (*d*) is otherwise treated in law as legitimate.

(4) For the purpose of construing references falling within subsection (2) above, the time of a person's birth shall be taken to include any time during the period beginning with—

    (*a*) the insemination resulting in his birth; or

    (*b*) where there was no such insemination, his conception.

and (in either case) ending with his birth.

The *Children Act 1989*, however, provides:

2.—(1) Where a child's father and mother were married to each other at the time of his birth, they shall each have parental responsibility for the child.

(2) Where a child's father and mother were not married to each other at the time of his birth—

    (*a*) the mother shall have parental responsibility for the child;

    (*b*) the father shall not have parental responsibility for the child, unless he acquires it in accordance with the provisions of this Act.

(3) References in this Act to a child whose father and mother were, or (as the case may be) were not, married to each other at the time of his birth must be read with section 1 of the Family Law Reform Act 1987 (which extends their meaning).

(4) The rule of law that a father is the natural guardian of his legitimate child is abolished.

To appreciate the magnitude of the legal revolution involved, we must look first at the old law of legitimacy and illegitimacy, then at developing patterns of child-bearing and family formation, before considering the new law, which is still controversial. More controversial still is the law's approach to the parenthood of children born as a result of sperm or egg donation, embryo transfer, or surrogacy arrangements. These raise in the most fundamental way the question 'who is a parent?'

1 The old law

The bastard, like the prostitute, thief, and beggar, belongs to that motley crowd of disreputable social types which society has generally resented, always endured. He is a living symbol of social irregularity, and undeniable evidence of contramoral forces; in short, a problem — a problem as old and unsolved as human existence itself.

These are the opening words of Davis' seminal article on *Illegitimacy and the Social Structure* (1939), in which the sociologist identified two approaches to the problem of illegitimacy — the 'social welfare' and the 'sociological'. The social welfare approach seeks to discover why individual women become unmarried mothers (or even why individual men become unmarried fathers) and then to cure their deviant tendencies. It was as much a development from the earlier deterrent attempts of church and state as is the same approach to the prevention of crime. Deterrence began in the medieval ecclesiastical courts, but the secular authorities took a hand once it appeared that failures in spiritual control were likely to cost the community money. The following example, and an explanation, are offered by Peter Laslett in *The World We Have Lost* (1971):

Anyone who committed or tried to commit a sexual act with anyone not his spouse, whether or not conception took place, ran the risk of a summons to the archdeacon's court — the lowest in the hierarchy of spiritual courts — a fine, and then penance in church at service time, or in the market place. If a person about whom a *fame of incontinency* had got abroad (that is a suspicion of a sexual escapade) ignored the summons or refused the punishment, then excommunication followed. This meant exile from the most important of all social activities, isolation within the community.

The lay courts and lay authority could be invoked for the more serious offences, and this often happened for the begetting of bastards. . . .

If the records of the church courts are filled with notices of sexual incontinence, those of the magistrates courts are studded with measures taken in punishment of unmarried mothers, and sometimes of unmarried fathers too, with provision for the upkeep of the child:

'Jane Sotworth of Wrightington, spinster, swears that Richard Garstange of Fazarkerley, husbandman, is the father of Alice, her bastard daughter. She is to have charge of the child for two years, provided she does not beg, and Richard is then to take charge until it is twelve years old. He shall give Jane a cow and 6s. in money. Both he and she shall this day be whipped in Ormeskirke.'

So ordered the Lancashire justices at the Ormskirk Sessions on Monday, 27 April 1601, though the language they used was Latin and lengthier. At Manchester, in 1604, they went so far as to require that Thomas Byrom, gentleman, should maintain a bastard he had begotten on a widow, and be whipped too. On 10 October 1604, he was whipped in Manchester market place. . . .

The institutions of the old world must be looked upon in this way, as expedients to provide permanence in an environment which was all too impermanent and insecure. The respect due to the old and experienced, the reverence for the Church and its immense, impersonal antiquity, the spontaneous feeling that it was the family which gave a meaning to life because the family could and must endure, all these things helped to reconcile our ancestors with relentless, remorseless mortality and mischance. But they must not deceive the historian into supposing that the fixed and the ancient were the only reality: an unchanging, unchangeable social structure may well be essential to a swiftly changing population.

The legal warrant for Thomas Byrom's punishment is explained by Elisofon in *A Historical and Comparative Study of Bastardy* (1973):

The year 1576 was especially important in relation to rights of the bastard child; for this was the first time in English history that a duty of support was imposed upon the parents of an illegitimate child. The statute passed by Parliament read, in part:

'Concerning bastards begotten and born out of lawful matrimony (an offence against God's law and man's law), the said bastard being now left to be at the charge of the parish where they be born, to the great burden of the same parish, and in defrauding of the relief of the impotent and aged true poor of the same parish, and to the evil example and encouragement of lewd life; it is ordained and enacted that two justices of the peace, upon examination of the cause and circumstances, shall and may by their discretion take order as well for the *punishment of the mother and reputed father* of such bastard child, as also for the better relief of every such parish in part or in all, and shall make likewise by like discretion, take order for the keeping of every such bastard child, *by charging such mother or reputed father with payment of money weekly or other substentation for the relief of such child* and such ways as they think covenant. And if. . . the reputed mother and father shall not observe and perform the order, then the party making the default in not performing the order, be committed to the common gayle.' (emphasis added) . . .

Question

Which do you suppose was the more serious — the offence against God's law or burden of the parish?

The deterrent approach was thus carried on through the poor law. Its more recent history is taken up by Sir Morris Finer and Professor O.R. McGregor, in *A History of the Obligation to Maintain*, printed as an appendix to the Report of the Committee on One-Parent Families (1974). They begin with the report of the royal commissioners on the poor laws which led to the 'new' poor law of 1834:

56. In the case of such a mother, the report did not recommend any change in the methods of relief, but it urged the repeal of all legislation which punished or charged the putative father of a bastard who should become, the Commissioners said:

'what Providence appears to have ordained that it should be, a burden on its mother, and, where she cannot maintain it, on her parents. The shame of the offence will not be destroyed by its being the means of income and marriage, and we trust that as soon as it has become both burthensome and disgraceful, it will become as rare as it is among those classes in this country who are above parish relief. . . . If we are right in believing the penalties inflicted by nature to be sufficient, it is needless to urge further objections to any legal punishment. . . . In affirming the inefficiency of human legislation to enforce the restraints placed on licentiousness by Providence, we have implied our belief that all punishment of the supposed father is useless.'

Behind this extreme statement of the providential foundations of the double standard of sexual morality lay the experience of abuses under the old bastardy laws. Under these, if a single woman declared herself pregnant and charged a man with being responsible, the overseers of the poor or any substantial householder could apply to any justice of the peace for a committal warrant. This would issue unless the accused man could give security to indemnify the parish or to enter into a recognisance to appear at Quarter Sessions and to perform any order which might there be made. The Commissioners thought that poor men were at the mercy of blackmail and perjury by unscrupulous women, and that the bastardy laws promoted social demoralisation.

57. The bastardy clauses of the Act of 1834 were in line with the opinions of the Poor Law Commissioners. . . .

However, not all sections of society took the same view of the problem:

59. With the dislike of Tories for the centralising tendency of Benthamite administrative reforms, went also a different view of sexual morality and obligation. The urban Victorians inherited a strict moral code. They got it from evangelical religious teachers who imposed it on the new middle class, the executive agents of the expanding industrial economy; and they planted it, as far as they could, on their lower orders. Their bookshelves carried the weight of such typical products of the evangelical outlook as Thomas Bowdler's *The Family Shakespeare, In which nothing is added to the Text; but those Words and Expressions are omitted which cannot with Propriety be read aloud in a Family*. These ten volumes reached a sixth edition in 1831, six years before the adolescent Victoria came under the influence of her first prime minister, a cultivated Whig who had been heard to respond to an evangelical sermon with the observation that 'things are coming to a pretty pass when religion is allowed to interfere with private life'. 'Thad d – d morality' which disturbed Lord Melbourne did not result from religious enthusiasm only. Differing provisions for the inheritance of family property were an important factor, too. The sexual waywardness of the territorial aristocracy did not endanger the integrity or succession of estates which were regulated by primogeniture and entail. Countless children of the mist played happily in Whig and Tory nurseries where they presented no threat to the property or interest of heirs. But middle class families handled their accumulating industrial wealth within a system of partible inheritance which demanded a more severe morality imposing higher standards upon women than upon men. An adulterous wife might be the means of planting a fraudulent claimant upon its property in the heart of her family; to avoid this ultimate catastrophe, middle class women were required to observe an inviolable rule of chastity. Just as the new poor law of 1834 represented a political triumph for philosophic radicalism by establishing an effective means of policing poverty, so it imposed middle class morality upon pauper women by seeking to police their sexual virtue.

60. Despite protests, the Poor Law Commissioners remained stout, for a time, in their insistence that to afford the mother of an illegitimate child a direct claim against the putative father for its maintenance would, by extending the rewards of matrimony to the unqualified and undeserving, tend to the destruction of the institution. In their sixth annual report in 1840, they printed with approval a report on the law of bastardy submitted to them by Sir Edmund Head, an Assistant Commissioner. We reproduce an extract which illustrates our earlier contention that the poor law contained within itself a special system of family law which applied exclusively to paupers and shows, also, the basis of the urban middle class fear of illegitimacy:

'. . . it is most characteristic of our legislation that questions of such moment as the *status* of illegitimate children, and rights and duties of their parents, should hardly be discussed at all, except in connection with Poor Laws. That the whole subject is one of extreme importance there can be no doubt. The framework of society in modern Europe rests on the institution of marriage. The church has dignified that rite with all its attributes of sanctity, and the state has endowed it with the most valuable civil privileges. In no country is respect for marriage more generally professed and more readily entertained than in England. . . . The recognition of a civil contract as the groundwork of matrimony in the Registration Bill was a great scandal to many persons. . . . We were told by many eminent members of the legislature that, to afford a woman who had once broken the marriage tie an opportunity of even seeing her children for a few minutes was an encroachment on the privileges of wives who had remained faithful, and in this way a direct encouragement to immorality. If this be so, what shall we say to the infringement of the exclusive privileges of the married state implied by conferring on the mother of a bastard that claim for its support from a definite father, which it is one great object of matrimony to secure? Does not the principle that anything short of marriage is sufficient to fix the paternity of the child involve in itself a direct attack on that institution?'

Against such arguments were set the findings of the Commissioners of Inquiry for South Wales who were appointed to investigate the Rebecca Riots. They reported in 1844 that the bastardy laws had:

'altogether failed of the effect which sanguine persons calculated they might produce on the caution or moral feelings of the weaker sex. (There was little prostitution in South Wales but) subsequent marriage – and that not a forced one – . . . almost invariably wiped out the light reproach which public opinion attached to a previous breach of chastity. (Now subsequent marriage was becoming rarer and women were exposed to) all the temptations of a life of vice (while) the man evades or defies the law, with a confidence and effrontery which has outraged the moral feeling of the people to a degree that can hardly be described.'

61. In the end, the Poor Law Commissioners gave ground and recommended in their tenth annual report that a mother should be given a civil action for maintenance against the putative father of her child. The Poor Law Amendment Act 1844 made a complete change by taking bastardy proceedings out of the hands of the poor law authorities and turning them into a civil matter between the parents. . . .

62. The Poor Law Amendment Act 1868 restored to the parish the power to recover from the putative father the cost of maintenance of a bastard child by providing that, where a woman who had obtained an order against the father of her child herself became a charge of the parish, the justices might order the payments to be made to the relieving officer. . . .

64. If the history of the legal rules which determine responsibility for the maintenance of bastards and their mothers is complicated, their treatment under the poor law was entirely straightforward. The mother was regarded as an able-bodied woman of demonstrated immorality, and relief was accordingly provided on a strictly deterrent basis in the workhouse. Mothers and babies were separated after the confinement and initial period of nursing. Most unmarried mothers could only use the workhouse as an immediate refuge during childbirth, after which they abandoned their children within it. Such unfortunates shared the fate of orphans and other deserted children who suffered deprivation as pauper children. But girls suffered worse than boys, because the workhouse served as a manufactory of prostitutes. Frances Power Cobbe's observation in 1865 remained true throughout the nineteenth century:

'The case of the girls is far worse than of the boys, as all the conditions of workhouse management fall with peculiar evil on their natures. . . . Among all the endless paradoxes of female treatment, one of the worst and most absurd is that which, while eternally proclaiming "home" to be the only sphere of a woman, systematically educates all female children of the State, without attempting to give them even an idea of what a home might be. . . .'

Workhouse children gained in the later decades of the nineteenth century from such advances in institutional care as cottage homes, sheltered homes and boarding out. But the need for change was only just beginning to be recognised in the early years of this century. . . .

. . .

74. One significant expression of the 'children's century' was the foundation in 1918 of the National Council for the Unmarried Mother and her Child. Lettice Fisher, the Council's first chairman, records that 'child welfare work went with a swing' in the immediate post-war search for a better life and that the council was not at first exclusively concerned with the unmarried mother and her child:

'The new Council was expected to work out schemes which could, if necessary, include not only unmarried mothers, but deserted or widowed mothers, and should aim at the provision of homes for expectant mothers, and small homes or foster-parents for such babies as could not be kept with their mothers.'

But the difficulty of raising money soon led to the abandonment of the original intention to care for all one-parent families, and the council had to restrict its work to the 'reform of the existing Bastardy and Affiliation Acts' and to securing 'the provision of adequate accommodation to meet the varying needs of mothers and babies throughout the country, with the special aim of keeping mother and child together'. The council stood for the public denial of the Victorian belief that the inferior status of bastardy, with its stigma for admittedly blameless children, was an essential buttress for the institution of monogamous marriage. Early successes were the Adoption and Legitimacy Acts 1926. . . .

75. The Adoption of Children Act 1926 made a momentous break with the law's age-long insistence upon a parent's inalienable rights over his child by enabling adopters to step into the shoes of the natural parents. Similarly, the Legitimacy Act 1926 brought into English law the *legitimatio per subsequens matrimonium* of Roman Law which the canon lawyers had unsuccessfully proposed when the Statute of Merton was debated in 1236. All that was achieved in 1926 was the concession of legitimation to the progeny of single persons who subsequently married. The Act did not apply to a child born of an adulterous union, that is, where either parent was married to someone else at the time of the birth. This limitation was imposed because, as the Home Office explained in an official memorandum:

'to allow children born in adultery to have the benefit . . . may remove a deterrent to adulterous intercourse, and may therefore be prejudicial to family life (which) in the interest of children generally is more important than the interest of a comparatively few illegitimate children.'

Children born of an adulterous union were not brought within the scope of legitimation until 1959. A decade later, the Family Law Reform Act 1969, enacting the main recommendations of the Committee on the Law of Succession in Relation to Illegitimate Persons, established near-equality of inheritance for all children. With this measure, English society has not completed but has come within the sight of completing a legal process achieved in countries which have altogether abolished the status of illegitimacy.

Questions

(i) Does the difference in patterns of inheritance between the landed aristocracy and the commercial bourgeoisie strike you as a plausible explanation for the difference in their attitudes to illegitimacy?

(ii) Why, then, did English law establish 'near-equality of inheritance' for all children before tackling many of their other disabilities?

Davis' second, or 'sociological' approach to the problem of illegitimacy may help us to answer the second question. Davis explains the approach thus:

Its central thesis is epigrammatically stated in Brinton's words (1936):
'Bastardy and marriage in this world are quite supplementary — you cannot have one without the other. In another world, you may indeed separate the two institutions and eliminate one of them, either by having marriage so perfect — in various senses — that no one will ever commit fornication or adultery, or by having fornication so perfect that no one will ever commit marriage. But these are definitely other worlds.'
. . . The gist of the theory is that the function of reproduction can be carried out in a socially useful manner only if it is performed in conformity with institutional patterns, because only by means of an institutional system can individuals be organized and taught to co-operate in the performance of this long-range function, and the function be integrated with other social functions. The reproductive or familial institutions constitute the social machinery in terms of which the creation of new members of society is supposed to take place. The birth of children in ways that do not fit into this machinery must necessarily receive the disapproval of society, else the institutional system itself, which depends upon favorable attitudes in individuals, would not be approved or sustained. . . .
People are not supposed to have illegitimate children, but when they do an emergency machinery is set into operation to give the child a status (though an inferior one) and to define the positions of the parents. In this way society continues. No one ever completely transcends the institutional boundaries. If he did, he would not be human. On the other hand, no one ever remains completely within the narrowest institutional boundaries. If he did, he would not be human. The fundamental explanation of nonconformity to the marital institutions is the same as the explanation of institutional nonconformity in general. . . .
The question as to why the child is punished for the sins of its parents is wrongly put. It assumes an explanation of what has yet to be explained. It should read: What is the status of the illegitimate child, and why is he given this status? Perhaps his status is partly explicable in terms of punishment, but not primarily. . . . punishment for parental sin is not the sole motive for the treatment of illegitimate children and does not deserve the primacy generally given it. The inquiry must be pushed to a deeper level which will explain both the legal disabilities (concerning descent, inheritance, support, and domicile) and the social disabilities (concerning public opinion, folkways, and mores).

In other words, in order to understand the treatment meted out by society and the law towards those born outside marriage, we have to understand what marriage itself is designed to achieve. Lucy Mair, an anthropologist, discusses this in the first chapter of her book, *Marriage* (1971), intriguingly entitled, 'What is a husband for?' She first outlines Robin Fox's theory that in primitive societies, marriage is a mechanism for persuading father to stay at home in order to protect and support his children and their mother. She then examines some cultures in which, even though 'it is an ideal in all known societies that the begetting of children should be formally licensed in some way', illegitimacy is common. She concludes:

If it were essential for the protection — in modern times rather for the economic support — of a woman with young children that the father of her children should be legally tied to her, these populations would not be able to survive. But they do. So we come back to the question, what is a husband for?

Husbands, considered as recognized fathers, are most important where they are the source of their children's social status and claims to inheritance. . . .

In the greater part of the world children take their status from the father; and even where the line of descent is traced through the mother it is usually no disadvantage to have a father of high status. There are societies. . . . that are divided into *patrilineal* or *agnatic lineages*, groups recruited by descent through males and recognizing common descent as far back as the members can trace their ancestry. A lineage has its patrimony, in land, cattle or capital, and as long as commercial activity is not much developed men depend on inheritance more than on acquisition; where there is commercial activity there is still nothing like inheritance to give you a good start in life. Men are always informally ranked by wealth, and where there is a formal ranking system it is legitimate descent that assigns places in it. Public office is often hereditary; so is the ability to approach nonhuman beings in ritual to secure their benevolence towards the society or some section of it. Because of the rules that define whom one may or may not marry, status by descent is significant when one is seeking a spouse.

The implications of this aspect of husbandhood and fatherhood are much wider than practical matters of economic support. . . .

A man is anxious to be the head of a numerous household when this provides him with a large working team; to be a member of a numerous lineage when this may be necessary for defence. He looks to his sons for support when he is old or sick. In societies organized in agnatic lineages religion is commonly focused on the cult of ancestors, and every man wishes to have descendants to make offerings to his spirit so that he will be commemorated in whatever is considered the appropriate way. In China up to the Communist revolution it was the first duty of a son to marry and produce a son to carry on the ancestor cult. The ancient Romans had very similar ideas. In lineage-based societies, and indeed in many others, marriage is an important way of forming alliances; this is one reason why men wish to become husbands as distinct from fathers.

In societies so organized, then, men wish to marry and women have no choice. Women do not have difficulty in inducing their consorts to marry them; but they are often penalized for entering into unlegalized unions, at any rate if these produce offspring.

Question

Engels (1884) described the development of such societies as the 'world historical defeat of the female sex . . . In order to make certain of the wife's fidelity and therefore of the paternity of her children, she is delivered over unconditionally into the power of her husband . . . [This type of marriage] is based on the supremacy of the man, the express purpose being to produce children of undisputed paternity; such paternity is demanded because these children are later to come into their father's property as his natural heirs'. In modern times, the reason given for the strength of the common law presumption that a child born to a married woman is her husband's child was that both woman and child would otherwise suffer the disabilities attached to adultery and illegitimacy. Is it at least possible that those disabilities were the *result*, not the cause, of that presumption?

The primacy of succession is reflected in the view of Sir William Blackstone, in his *Commentaries on the Laws of England* (1765):

The incapacity of a bastard consists principally in this, that he cannot be heir to any one, neither can he have heirs, but of his own body; for, being *nullius filius*, he is therefore of kin to nobody, and has no ancestor from whom any inheritable blood can be derived. A bastard was also, in strictness, incapable of holy orders; and, though that were dispensed with, yet he was utterly disqualified from holding any dignity in the church: but this doctrine seems now obsolete; and in all other respects, there is no distinction between a bastard and another man. And really any other distinction, but that of not inheriting, which civil policy renders necessary, would, with regard to the innocent offspring of his parents' crimes, be odious, unjust, and cruel to the last degree.

Thus, if inheritance has been the principal explanation for our laws of both marriage and legitimacy, it has little importance in the modern world. The expectations which a child may have of his parents were spelled out by the Court of Appeal when allowing the appeal of a millionaire father against an order that, on divorce, he should settle £25,000 on each of his children:

Lord Lilford v Glyn
[1979] 1 All ER 441, [1978] 1 WLR 78, Court of Appeal

Orr LJ: . . . One finds in s. 25(2) of the 1973 [Matrimonial Causes] Act, which lays down the duty of the court in deciding whether to exercise its powers under (inter alia) s. 24(1)(*b*), that the court is so to exercise the power to order a settlement, like the other powers there referred to, as to place the child '. . . in the financial position in which the child would have been if the marriage had not broken down and each of the parties to the marriage had properly discharged his or her financial obligations and responsibilities towards him'. Whatever the precise meaning of that phrase a father, even the richest father, ought not to be regarded as under 'financial obligations or responsibilities' to provide funds for the purposes of such settlement as are envisaged in this case on children who are under no disability and whose maintenance and education are secure. . . .

There is not in this context, one rule for millionaires and another for less wealthy fathers, and in our judgment there was no means of judging whether the father, if the marriage had continued, would or would not have made a settlement in favour of the daughters. He might or he might not, and there was no reason to suppose that the first course was more likely than the other in view of the fact that he had already made a substantial settlement for the daughters in the form of the trust deed.

Similarly, under the Inheritance (Provision for Family and Dependants) Act 1975 (p. 176, above) children of the deceased can only upset the provisions of his will or the rules of intestacy if these fail to make 'such financial provision as it would be reasonable in all the circumstances of the case for the applicant to receive for his maintenance' (s. 1(2) (*b*)). The leading case is *Re Coventry* [1980] Ch 461 (doubting *Re Christie* [1979] Ch 168 and applied in *Re Dennis* [1981] 2 All ER 140). The Court of Appeal upheld the decision of Oliver J that a 46 year old son was not entitled to a share in his father's estate, even though they had shared a house for 19 years, which the son would now have to leave, while the deceased and his widow (who was entitled to the whole estate under the rules of intestacy) had lived apart. Buckley LJ said this:

His approach was that where an applicant is an adult male in employment, and so capable of earning his own living, some special circumstance is required to make a failure on the part of the deceased to make some financial provision for the applicant unreasonable.

The judge said:

> 'An application in such circumstances [he is referring to the character of the applicant in the present case] would not have been possible at all before 1st April 1976 but the 1975 Act now enables a child of the deceased to apply for provision even though that child is male, of full age, and suffering from no disability. Nevertheless, applications under the 1975 Act for maintenance by able-bodied and comparatively young men in employment and able to maintain themselves must be relatively rare and need, I should have thought, to be approached with a degree of circumspection.'

Later on he said:

> 'It seems to me, however, that in regarding the circumstances and in applying the guidelines set out in s 3, it always has to be borne in mind that the 1975 Act, so far as it relates to applicants other than spouses, is an Act whose purpose is limited to the provision of reasonable maintenance. It is not the purpose of the Act to provide legacies or rewards for meritorious conduct. Subject to the court's powers under the 1975 Act and to fiscal demands, an Englishman still remains at liberty at his death to dispose of his own property in whatever way he pleases or, if he chooses to do so, to leave that disposition to be regulated by the laws of intestate succession. In order to enable the court to interfere with and reform those dispositions it must, in my judgment, be shown, not that the deceased acted unreasonably, but that, looked at objectively, his disposition or lack of disposition produces an unreasonable result in that it does not make any or any greater provision for the applicant and that means, in the case of an applicant other than a spouse, for that applicant's maintenance.'

In my judgment the judge there correctly states the problem, and I think he states the appropriate test to be applied.

The view that children are entitled to be maintained but not necessarily to inherit may help to explain why the *Report of the Committee on the Law of Succession in relation to Illegitimate Persons* (the Russell Report, 1966) took a simple line on intestate succession to both mother and father:

> 19. At the root of any suggestion for the improvement of the lot of bastards in relation to the laws of succession to property is, of course, the fact that in one sense they start level with legitimate children, in that no child is created of its own volition. Whatever may be said of the parents, the bastard is innocent of any wrongdoing. To allot to him an inferior, or indeed unrecognised, status in succession is to punish him for a wrong of which he was not guilty.

All children do not start level, however, if they have not had what the modern world thinks is due to every child — proper attention to their physical, emotional and intellectual needs throughout childhood. Modern society sees marriage as the framework within which mother and father co-operate to provide this. Increasingly, as we have already seen, they are choosing to do so outside marriage and the law is seeking to ensure that the child is not disadvantaged as a result.

2 The factual background

The first graph overleaf, from *Social Trends 21* (1991), shows how the percentage of births outside marriage has changed during this century. There is a marked difference between the age groups, not only in their tendency to have children, but also in their tendency to do so outside marriage, as the second graph, also from *Social Trends 21*, (1991) shows.

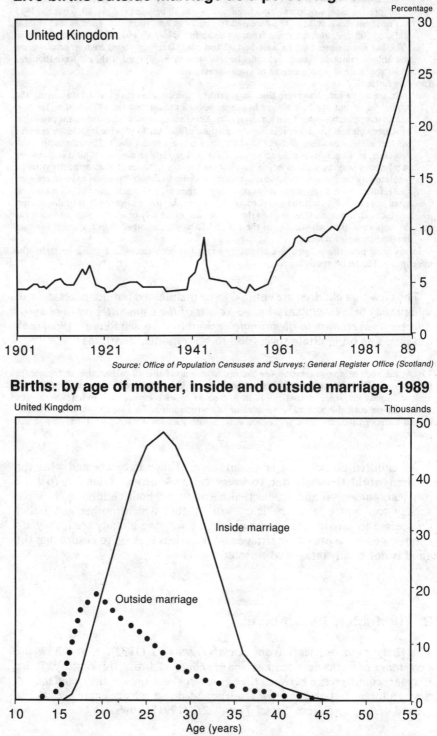

Live births outside marriage as a percentage of all births

Percentage

United Kingdom

Source: Office of Population Censuses and Surveys: General Register Office (Scotland)

Births: by age of mother, inside and outside marriage, 1989

United Kingdom

Thousands

Inside marriage

Outside marriage

Age (years)

Source: Office of Population Censuses and Surveys: General Register Office (Scotland):
General Register Office (Northern Ireland)

Questions

(i) Does this suggest anything to you about *why* people have children outside marriage?

(ii) In particular, can you account for the fact that during the 1970s the *proportion* of births outside marriage rose, although *numbers* fell?

(iii) Why, do you think, has the birth rate been rising again in recent years?

The underlying causes are no doubt complicated, but some light may be cast by looking at how the outcome of all conceptions, in or out of marriage, has altered over the past 20 years. Once again, the table overleaf comes from *Social Trends 21* (1991).

Questions

(i) Why do you think that 'shot-gun' marriages are so clearly on the decline?

(ii) As such marriages have traditionally been twice as likely to break down (see Rowntree, 1964; Gibson, 1974; Haskey, 1983), is this a good thing or a bad thing?

(iii) Does the dramatic rise in births as well as abortions outside marriage indicate (*a*) that more women (or girls) are not being left 'holding the baby', or (*b*) that more women (or girls) are quite happy to bear a child outside marriage?

(iv) Does the rising proportion of joint registrations of births outside marriage indicate (*a*) that more are the product of stable cohabitations, or (*b*) that more men are prepared to take some responsibility for their children, or (*c*) that more women are prepared to recognise their child's right to know his origins or (*d*) anything else?

Apart from undoubted improvements both in societal attitudes towards and in the economic circumstances of single mothers which have taken place in the last two decades, it is generally accepted that a large but variable proportion of these children are born into what used to be called 'stable illicit unions'. The National Child Development Study followed the careers of *all* children born in this country in a single week in 1958. In *Children in Changing Families* (1980), Lydia Lambert and Jane Streather studied the data from the follow-up at the age of 11 (for an earlier follow-up at age 7, see Crellin, Kellmer Pringle and West, 1971). They wished to compare the development of children born outside marriage who had stayed with their mothers, children who had been adopted by strangers, and children who had been born to married parents. These are their findings on the children's 'family situation' (percentages within each birth status):

Legitimacy status	Natural parents	Step-parents	Adoptive parents	Mother alone	Father alone	Other situations
Illegitimate	41%	24%	0	20%	1%	14%
Adopted	0	0	93%	0	0	7%
Legitimate	91%	3%	*	4%	1%	1%

* Three legitimate children were adopted between 7 and 11, but another 15 were excluded from the study because they had been adopted before the follow-up at the age of 7.

. . . As expected, the majority (74%) of the 409 illegitimately born children were living in a two-parent family at age eleven. This number includes the children who had subsequently been adopted, but when they are excluded, the pattern is still clear. Out of the 294 illegitimate

2.26 Conceptions: by age of woman, marital status and outcome
England & Wales

Percentages and thousands

	1971	1976	1981	1986	1987	1988
Conceptions to women aged under 20						
Inside marriage						
Maternities	33.2	29.8	23.2	13.1	11.7	10.5
Legal abortions[1]	0.6	1.1	0.9	0.6	0.6	0.5
Outside marriage						
Maternities inside marriage	30.0	20.0	15.4	9.5	8.2	7.2
Maternities outside marriage[2]						
− joint registration	5.8	8.7	14.8	26.6	28.5	29.9
− sole registration	13.5	13.4	14.8	17.4	17.0	16.7
Legal abortions[1]	16.9	27.0	31.0	32.8	34.0	35.3
All conceptions (= 100%) (thousands)	133.1	105.7	115.2	118.8	123.2	120.7
All conceptions						
Inside marriage						
Maternities	72.6	707.7	65.9	58.1	55.8	54.1
Legal abortions[1]	5.2	6.1	5.6	4.7	4.6	4.5
Outside marriage						
Maternities inside marriage	8.1	5.8	5.5	5.1	4.9	4.7
Maternities outside marriage[2]						
− joint registration	3.5	4.2	6.8	12.6	14.1	15.2
− sole registration	4.1	3.8	4.8	6.1	6.3	6.3
Legal abortions[1]	6.7	9.4	11.4	13.4	14.4	15.2
All conceptions (= 100%) (thousands)	835.5	671.6	752.3	818.9	850.4	849.5

1 Legal terminations under the 1967 Abortion Act
2 Births outside marriage can be registered by the mother only (sole registrations) or by both parents (joint registrations)
Source: Office of Population Censuses and Surveys

children who had not been adopted, 195 were living in two-parent families (65%). The proportion of illegitimate children living with both their natural parents at 11 (41%) was very similar to that at 7.

It is not possible to know whether this pattern is typical of the family situations of illegitimate children of this age in the general population. However, a study of 2511 children aged 9 to 14 years in Aberdeen found that at the time of interview 73% of the illegitimately born children were living in a two-parent situation of some kind and of these 34 per cent (25% overall) were living with their natural parents (Gill, 1977), figures which are very similar to our own.

In a later chapter, the authors comment:

When current theories about the family . . . have been matched against the reality of demographic facts, the discrepancy between the ideal of the conventional nuclear family and the actual diversity of family life has been obvious. While it is true that the majority of children continue to live with both their own parents, the rates of separation and divorce are such that increasing proportions of families are broken, for a time at least, and many are then reconstituted following remarriage. Gill (1977) has pointed out that the pathways of care for legitimate children are towards fatherlessness while those for illegitimate children are away from it. This pattern, and the resulting diversity of family life, is apparent when the parental-care situations at the age of 11 of the children in the present study are examined.

A more precise study of the fate of those born outside marriage was carried out by Richard Leete, in *Adoption Trends and Illegitimate Births 1951–1977* (1979). He calculated the numbers of these children in a given year who had subsequently been adopted by a parent, adopted by strangers, legitimated or had died. The following brief extracts summarise his results:

The figures show that between 7 and 8% of the generations born in the 1950s and 1960s were, or can be expected to be adopted by age 16 by couples of whom one at least is a parent. . . .

The level of adoption of illegitimate children by non-parents is very much higher than that by parents. . . . some 20% of children born illegitimate between 1951 and 1968 were, or can be expected to be, adopted by non-parents by the time they become adults; . . . Since 1968 the rate of adoption in the first years of life has fallen greatly. Thus, just 9 per cent of children born illegitimate in 1974 had been adopted by age two, just half the proportion found for generations born during the early and mid 1960s. . . .

Among generations born in the mid and late 1960s it is likely that some 20% of illegitimate children will have been legitimated by age 16. For generations born during the 1970s there has been a sharp fall in the level of legitimation . . .

Percentage of selected generations of illegitimate children alive and still illegitimate by given age, England and Wales

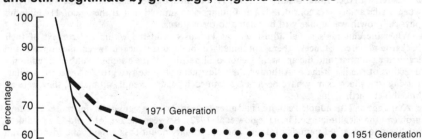
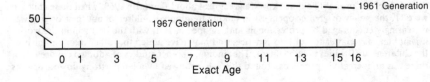

The main causes of attrition from illegitimacy have been non-parental adoptions and legitimations. Other things being equal, it follows that when the rate at which these events occur falls, as it has done since the late 1960s, increasing proportions of children born illegitimate can be expected to continue as such.

Questions

(i) Why do *you* think there has been a fall in *both* adoptions by strangers *and* legitimation?

(ii) Might it not have been expected that legitimation would increase following the Divorce Reform Act 1969?

(iii) Do these figures suggest anything to you about what the law should be?

Lambert and Streather set out to answer the question 'does birth status matter?' The raw data showed that the children who remained with their mothers were generally less likely to be living in favourable circumstances: 16% had been in local authority care at some time in their lives, compared with 3% of the marital children; only 12% were in non-manual ('middle class') homes, compared with 34% of the marital and 60% of the adopted; many more of their mothers had 'come down in the world' from their social class of origin; 35% were receiving supplementary benefit or free school meals, compared with 13% of the legitimate and 4% of the adopted; they were also more likely to be over-crowded, less likely to have sole use of basic amenities, and less likely to be owner-occupiers, even when both parents were together. But when the authors studied the children's physical development and school attainment after making allowances for their family situation and environmental circumstances, a different picture emerged:

When no allowance was made for background circumstances, adopted children were, for example, reading better at 11, on average, than either legitimate children or illegitimate children. This achievement deserves to be commended, but when we looked at the reading scores of children who came from homes with similar environmental characteristics, illegitimate as well as legitimate children were reading just as well as the adopted. Conversely, where the home circumstances were less favourable, illegitimate children were not reading any worse than other children in such circumstances. The fact that illegitimate children were more likely than other children to be living in disadvantaged situations, rather than their birth status, was associated with their lower reading scores at 11. For most of the children the same was also true when maths ability was considered. The findings also showed that at the age of 11 children's physical growth was unlikely to be related to birth status.

When the children's social adjustment at 11 was considered within the context of their background circumstances, there continued to be a difference between illegitimate and legitimate children, and the apparently equivocal position of the adopted children tilted in the direction of the illegitimate. Although the adjustment of these two groups appeared similar, varying stress factors may have been at work in each group, even if, ultimately, they were all linked with birth status.

At the age of 7 the adopted children had already been showing signs of having more behaviour problems than legitimate children (Seglow et al, 1972). Between the ages of 7 and 11 all children are likely to have had periods of doubt and uncertainty about their origins and identity, and all but a handful of the adopted children knew for a fact that they were born to a different parents [sic] but probably did not know a great deal about them. By 1969, when these children were 11, the policy of greater openness in talking to adopted children about their origins was increasingly encouraged by professionals and the media. But, with the best will in the world, it is not an easy matter to put into practice, and may have added to, rather than diminished, the children's difficulties in adjustment. The finding, in other studies of adopted children, that there was an increase in problems around this age, followed by a later settling down, suggests that it may be a healthy sign that the adopted children in the NCDS were more troublesome in mid-childhood. It will be extremely interesting to study their adjustment at 16 to see what was happening during adolescence. Obviously teachers and parents would be right to show concern for difficulties in social adjustment at any age, but it may be the case that these are only an indication of possible maladjustment if they persist.

Illegitimate children who were not adopted were also more likely than legitimate children to have experienced difficulties in resolving uncertainties about their origins. Their mothers may have been more reluctant than adoptive parents to discuss the subject, and while some of the children were living with their own fathers, others may have been told even less about them than adopted children. However, the illegitimate children had been less well adjusted than legitimate children at the age of 7, which suggests that unless uncertainty about their origins was the contributory reason at both ages, other factors, such as the greater amount of change in their environmental circumstances, were also associated with their relatively poorer social adjustment at 11.

In conclusion
The general lack of association between children's physical development or their school attainment at the age of 11 and their birth status is a salutory reminder of the powerful influence of the environment for good or ill. Some children were fortunate and lived in an exceptionally favourable environment, and many of the adopted children were among this group. For other children, living in families with poor housing and low income, and experiencing the difficulties mainly associated with low social status were far more pressing and ever-present problems than whether their parents had been married when they were born.

Even if they were legitimately born, diversity in family life was becoming the experience of an increasing proportion of children, as their parents' marriages were broken or remade. The importance of birth status fades before a recognition of the practical needs of families for such things as adequate incomes and adequate housing if children are to grow up without disadvantage.

Questions

(i) Does not the association between birth outside marriage and poorer environmental circumstances at least suggest something *to* the child's mother?
(ii) Could the greater tendency of these children to show signs of stress, both at seven and at eleven, have anything to do with their birth status as such?
(iii) Do you think that the findings of a similar study of children born during 1991 would be the same?
(iv) If not, why not?

3 Proving paternity

Proving paternity has always been thought to be a problem. Somehow it is easier to remember the first part of Lancelot's speech to Old Gobbo — 'It's a wise father, that knows his own child' — than the second — 'Truth will come to light; murder cannot be hid long, a man's son may; but in the end, truth will out'. Hence there is a presumption that any child born to a married woman is her husband's child. This used to be extremely difficult to rebut. There was also a procedure for conclusively determining a person's legitimacy. Both are amply illustrated by the following case:

The Ampthill Peerage Case
[1977] AC 547, [1976] 2 All ER 411, [1976] 2 WLR 777, 120 Sol Jo 367,
House of Lords' Committee of Privileges

In 1921, Christobel, wife of the man who was later to become third baron
Ampthill, gave birth to Geoffrey, who had been conceived by external
fertilisation while his mother was still a virgin. Her husband petitioned for
divorce, alleging that this was the result of Christobel's adultery. At the trial,
the husband gave evidence that he had had no sexual intimacy of any kind
with his wife at the probable date of conception and was granted a decree.
On appeal, the House of Lords decided that evidence of non-access by a
husband or a wife was inadmissible both in legitimacy proceedings and in
divorce proceedings (*Russell v Russell* [1924] AC 687, 93 LJP 97: the rule
was subsequently reversed in the Law Reform (Miscellaneous Provisions)
Act 1949, s 7(1)). The divorce decree was rescinded. In 1925, the High Court
made a declaration that Geoffrey was the legitimate child of Christobel and
her husband. Under the Legitimacy Declaration Act 1858, such declarations
were binding on all the world, but could not prejudice anyone who had not
been given notice or made a party (or did not claim through such a person)
or if obtained by fraud or collusion. The marriage was eventually dissolved
in 1937. In 1950, a son John was born of the third baron's third marriage.
The third baron died in 1973 and both Geoffrey and John claimed to succeed
him. Geoffrey relied upon the declaration, but John alleged that this was not
binding, inter alia, because it had been procured by fraud. Blood samples
were available from Christobel and the third baron, but not from Geoffrey.

Lord Wilberforce: . . . There can hardly be anything of greater concern to a person than his
status as the legitimate child of his parents; denial of it, or doubts as to it, may affect his
reputation, his standing in the world, his admission into a vocation, or a profession, or into
social organisations, his succession to property, his succession to a title. It is vitally necessary
that the law should provide a means for any doubts which may be raised to be resolved, and
resolved at a time when witnesses and records are available. It is vitally necessary that any such
doubts once disposed of should be resolved once for all. . . .

Lord Simon of Glaisdale: . . . There is one status for which Parliament, in the wisdom of
experience, has made special provision. This is the status of legitimacy. Status means the
condition of belonging to a class in society to which the law ascribes peculiar rights and duties,
capacities and incapacities. Such, for example, is the status of a married person or minor.
Legitimacy is a status: it is the condition of belonging to a class in society the members of which
are regarded as having been begotten in lawful matrimony by the men whom the law regards
as their fathers. Motherhood, although also a legal relationship, is based on a fact, being proved
demonstrably by parturition. Fatherhood, by contrast, is a presumption. A woman can have
sexual intercourse with a number of men any of whom may be the father of her child; though
it is true that modern serology can sometimes enable the presumption to be rebutted as regards
some of these men. The status of legitimacy gives the child certain rights both against the man
whom the law regards as his father and generally in society. Among the peculiar rights which
a child is entitled to enjoy by virtue of the status of legitimacy is the right to succeed to a
hereditary title of honour. If the hereditary title of honour is a peerage of the United Kingdom,
the oldest legitimate son when of full age is entitled to be called to your Lordships' House on
the death of the man whom the law regards as his father.

It was probably for two reasons that Parliament made special provision for judgment
as to the status of legitimacy. First, no doubt, because, since fatherhood is not factually
demonstrable by parturition, it is questionable; and it is generally in the interest of society that
open questions should be finally closed. Second, no doubt, because since the legitimate child, by
virtue of his legal relationship with the man whom the law regards as his father, is entitled to
certain rights both as against the father and generally in society, it is desirable that the legal
relationship between father and child should be decisively concluded.

His lordship then reviews the law and the evidence and concludes that the decree was not obtained by fraud or collusion, not least because, as the law stood in 1925, Geoffrey was entitled to the benefit of the presumption *even if* his mother had confessed to committing adultery at the relevant time. Finally:

. . . The law, in response to society's needs, enjoins that civil strife should be concluded by the final judgment of a court of law. To this there are well-recognised exceptions demanded by considerations of justice: where the judgment has been obtained by fraud, by collusion or by such a procedural irregularity as is liable to cause a failure of justice. John is seeking to add two further, unauthorised and undesirable, exceptions: first, where technological developments have furnished new modes of proof; and, secondly, where there has been a change in the law of evidence. Such further exceptions are undesirable, because if admitted there is no reason why there should be any end to litigation. The bitter waters would never ebb. . . .
Their lordships advised that Geoffrey had made out his claim to the barony.

Questions

(i) How many of the concerns suggested by Lord Wilberforce seem relevant to ordinary people today?
(ii) This case demonstrates the strength of the courts' traditional reluctance to bastardise a child, but we repeat an earlier question: were the disabilities attached to adultery and bastardy the *result*, rather than the cause, of the need to presume that the husband was father to his wife's children?
(iii) Now that most of the legal distinctions between birth in and outside marriage have been removed, is there any longer a need for this presumption?
(iv) Is it so obvious these days who is a child's mother (see p. 490 below)?

However, the position has changed. First, the *Family Law Reform Act 1969* now provides:

26. – Any presumption of law as to the legitimacy or illegitimacy of any person may in any civil proceedings be rebutted by evidence which shows that it is more probable than not that that person is illegitimate or legitimate, as the case may be, and it shall not be necessary to prove that fact beyond reasonable doubt in order to rebut the presumption.

The leading case on the meaning of this was decided shortly afterwards:

S v S; W v Official Solicitor
[1972] AC 24, [1970] 3 All ER 107, [1970] 3 WLR 366, 114 Sol Jo 635, House of Lords

Both were divorce cases in which the husband denied paternity of a child to whom the presumption of legitimacy applied. They arose before the Family Law Reform Act 1969 gave the courts power to direct that blood samples be taken from mother, child and any party alleged to be the child's father, in the course of any civil proceedings in which paternity is in issue. They were thus mainly concerned with whether the court had power to order that the child's blood be tested, but the speeches remain of interest upon the question of whether a court *should* now direct that blood tests be used.

Lord Reid: . . . The law as to the onus of proof is now set out in s 26 of the Family Law Reform Act 1969, . . .

That means that the presumption of legitimacy now merely determines the onus of proof. Once evidence has been led it must be weighed without using the presumption as a make-weight in the scale for legitimacy. So even weak evidence against legitimacy must prevail if there is not other evidence to counterbalance it. The presumption will only come in at that stage in the very rare case of the evidence being so evenly balanced that the court is unable to reach a decision on it. I cannot recollect ever having seen or heard of a case of any kind where the court could not reach a decision on the evidence before it. . . .

. . .

I think that it was implicit in the argument of the Official Solicitor that to take a blood test is to imperil the child's status of legitimacy. But that must be on an assumption that if the case was decided without the blood test it would be held that the child is legitimate. Now that this depends simply on balance of probabilities it is very often impossible to forecast how the case will go. If one knew or suspected that on the other evidence the child would be held to be illegitimate then it would be in the child's interest to have a blood test because that would afford some chance that the decision would go the other way.

But that is only one reason why it is so difficult to assess the child's interest. On the one hand, it is said that with rare exceptions it is always in the child's interest to have a decision that it is legitimate. On the other hand, it is said that the value to a child of a finding of legitimacy is now much less than it used to be, and that it is generally better for the child that the truth should out than that the child should go through life with a lurking doubt as to the validity of a decision when evidence, which would very likely have disclosed the truth, has been suppressed.

. . . I accept the view that on average it is still a considerable disadvantage to be illegitimate. But I doubt whether, again on average this disadvantage would be greatly diminished by a decision in favour of legitimacy seen to have been based on inadequate evidence after refusal to allow a blood test. I think that the final abolition of the old strong presumption of legitimacy by s 26 of the 1969 Act shows that in the view of Parliament public policy no longer requires that special protection should be given by the law to the status of legitimacy. . . .

Lord Hodson: . . . In paternity cases such as those under consideration by your Lordships the court is not truly exercising the custodial jurisdiction in which the interests of the child are paramount but the duty of arbitrament between parties in which their interests are relevant and must be considered as well as the interests of the infant whose body it is sought to examine. Were it otherwise I think that the task of the court in deciding whether or not to order a blood test in the case of a child would in many, perhaps in most, cases be exceedingly difficult. Who is to say what is in the interests of the child and whether knowledge of true paternity would or would not favour his or her future prospects in life? How are these interests to be assessed? I find these questions especially difficult to answer in view of the fact that it must surely be in the best interests of the child in most cases that paternity doubts should be resolved on the best evidence, and, as in adoption, the child should be told the truth as soon as possible.

Compare Lord Reid's remarks upon the standard of proof required for a married man to establish that he is *not* the father of his wife's child with those of Ormrod LJ in *Re JS* [1981] Fam 22, [1980] 1 All ER 1061, CA as to the standard of proof required to establish that a particular man *is* the father:

. . . The burden might be formulated on analogous lines, 'the plaintiff (or the party on whom the burden rests) must satisfy the court that it is reasonably safe in all the circumstances of the case to act on the evidence before the court, bearing in mind the consequences which will follow'.

The learned judge, rightly in our opinion, adopted this test. In the course of her judgment she said: 'The degree of probability in an issue of paternity should, in my opinion, be commensurate with the transcending importance of that decision to the child.'

Questions

(i) *Re JS* was applied in *W v K (proof of paternity)* [1988] 1 FLR 86. Mr and Mrs B and Mr and Mrs W agreed to swap partners. Mrs B became pregnant and only Mr B or Mr W could be father. Earlier sperm tests indicated that Mr B was likely to be infertile. Blood tests on Mr W indicated as follows:

(1) A combination of tests used in this investigation would be expected to exclude at least 95% of wrongly accused men.

(2) It is not the primary purpose of blood tests to attempt to prove paternity. Nevertheless, by comparing the chances that those genes, for which blood tests have been carried out, which the child must have inherited from its true father, have come from a putative father rather than a random man, a paternity index can be calculated. In this case the paternity index for Mr W and the baby is 97.4%

(a) Would you have found that the presumption of legitimacy had been rebutted? (b) Would you have found that Mr W was the father? (c) Would you have found that Mr W was the father if the paternity index had been lower? (d) Would you have found that Mr W was the father if there had been *no* blood test evidence at all?
(ii) If your answer to (a) is 'yes', should the law allow you to answer 'no' to (b), (c), or (d)?
(iii) Do you think that the standard of proof of paternity should be the same (a) if the mother is applying for financial provision or a property settlement for her child, or (b) if the father is applying for a contact, residence or parental responsibility order, or (c) if the child is applying for a binding declaration of parentage?

There used to be further obstacle to proving paternity for the purpose of establishing the father's financial liability, in that any evidence given against him by the mother had to be corroborated. In 1968 the Law Commission agreed that there was a 'danger of a perjured claim in this sort of case' but in their Working Paper on *Illegitimacy* (1979) they argued:

9.47 . . . There are three reasons why we do not at present favour a formal requirement of corroboration. First, such a requirement can easily lead to a waste of time and money. Under the affiliation procedure, if the mother fails for lack of corroboration in the first instance, she is entitled to try again with better evidence: the first hearing is treated as having ended by her being non-suited, and the res judicata rule accordingly does not apply. Secondly, we do not think that a formal requirement is necessary in order to avoid injustice. A court will be aware of the risks attached to the acceptance of uncorroborated evidence, and this will affect the weight of evidence which is in practice required to discharge the burden of proof. Although civil cases are proved by preponderance of probability, the degree of probability depends on the subject matter, and we would expect courts to require paternity to be convincingly established. Thirdly, the formal requirement of corroboration may well have been justified in former times when it might have been difficult for the respondent to produce positive evidence to the contrary; but blood testing has changed the position. We therefore conclude that corroboration should be a relevant factor in evaluating the evidence to which it relates, but not a formal prerequisite. . . .

Questions

(i) Why exactly was perjury thought likely in these cases? Was it (a) because a lot of money might be involved; or (b) because the fact that a woman has sexual intercourse outside marriage makes her unreliable and untruthful as a witness; or (c) because complainants are invariably women and defendants invariably men; or (d) for any other reason?
(ii) If the answer to question (i) is (a), why is corroboration not required in any other civil litigation?

(iii) If the answer to question (i) is (*b*), why did the Report of the Advisory Group on the Law of Rape (Heilbron, 1975) feel able to reject the idea as an 'anachronism', whereas the Law Commission apparently did not?

Under the Family Law Reform Act 1987, both affiliation proceedings and the formal requirement of corroboration have disappeared. Moreover, provisions in the draft Bill attached to the Commission's original Report on *Illegitimacy* (1982), requiring paternity to be proved 'to the satisfaction of the court' were dropped from the revised version attached to the Commission's *Second Report* (1986), for these reasons:

3.18 It is not entirely clear what the effect of such a provision will be upon the standard of proof, but if there is an invariable and significant difference between the usual standard of proof upon the balance of probabilities and proof to the satisfaction of the court, the results could be unacceptable. Since 1969 the standard of proof used in rebutting the presumption of legitimacy is the balance of probabilities. It cannot be right that, as a matter of law, the standard of proof required to show that a particular man is not the father is necessarily less than the standard of proof required to show that he is. As a matter of evidence, it may be easier to show the one than the other, although with the advent of modern blood testing it is often possible to prove a likelihood of paternity to a degree of probability far higher than is possible for many other facts which may be in issue in litigation. The courts will also bear in mind, in appropriate cases, the general principle that the degree of proof should be commensurate with the gravity of the subject matter in dispute.

3.19 We therefore think that it would be unsatisfactory if some special standard of proof were automatically to prevent a child being granted access to or financial support from a man who, after fully fought proceedings, was shown on a balance of probabilities to be the father. Such a special provision might be seen as unnecessarily marking out the issue of paternity amongst the many issues faced by the courts in civil proceedings and as such contrary to the general principle of eliminating unnecessary discrimination in the law. Accordingly, except in relation to declarations, the new Bill does not include express requirements that paternity should be established to the court's satisfaction.

Questions

(i) To what would you attribute the Commission's change of heart?
(ii) Do you think that dropping the formal requirement will lead to a judicial change of heart?

The whole debate has now been overtaken by a scientific development, known as 'DNA profiling' or 'fingerprinting', and explained by Cellmark Diagnostics, who have patented the process, in their *DNA Fingerprinting Information and Procedures Guide*:

WHAT IS DNA FINGERPRINTING?
The technique known as DNA fingerprinting, or genetic fingerprinting, was developed by Professor Alec Jeffreys FRS, who is a Lister Institute Research Fellow at Leicester University. It has the ability to positively demonstrate relationships between individuals and is the subject of various patent applications by the Lister Institute of Preventive Medicine [UK Patent No. 2166445]. DNA is the genetic material contained in all living cells which makes every individual different (except for genetically identical twins) and can be extracted from blood, semen, hair roots or other body tissues that contain DNA. A blood sample taken under medical supervision is usually the simplest form of material that is used for testing. A pattern of chemical signals has been discovered within the DNA molecule which is as unique and individual to each person as their actual fingerprint, hence the colloquial term 'DNA finger-printing'. This pattern is visualised by the laboratory process shown below as a series of bands on an X-Ray film, rather like the bar codes now found on a wide variety of retail goods.

THE DNA FINGERPRINTING PROCESS

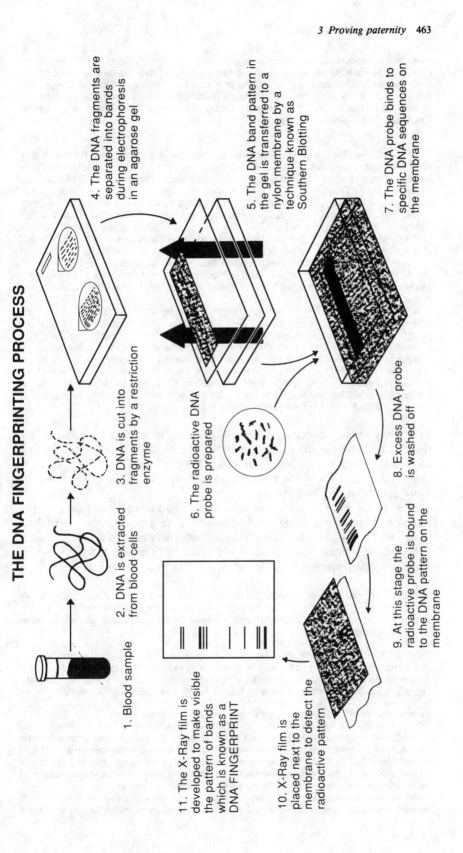

1. Blood sample

2. DNA is extracted from blood cells

3. DNA is cut into fragments by a restriction enzyme

4. The DNA fragments are separated into bands during electrophoresis in an agarose gel

5. The DNA band pattern in the gel is transferred to a nylon membrane by a technique known as Southern Blotting

6. The radioactive DNA probe is prepared

7. The DNA probe binds to specific DNA sequences on the membrane

8. Excess DNA probe is washed off

9. At this stage the radioactive probe is bound to the DNA pattern on the membrane

10. X-Ray film is placed next to the membrane to detect the radioactive pattern

11. The X-Ray film is developed to make visible the pattern of bands which is known as a DNA FINGERPRINT

WHAT WILL IT RESOLVE?
Conventional methods previously used to resolve paternity/maternity may be lengthy and involve up to 17 different blood tests. They may only show whether an individual *is not* the father or mother of a child. DNA fingerprinting, in one single test, can show with certainty that an individual either *is* or *is not* the father or mother of a child, or whether a child is related to a particular individual.

HOW DOES THE TEST WORK?
As previously described, a genetic fingerprint is producted as a series of bands on an X-Ray film. Just as all of us inherit out basic physical characteristics from our parents, then so do we inherit the DNA bands in our DNA fingerprint. Approximately half a person's DNA bands are inherited from the father and half from the mother. Positive proof of paternity is established by firstly identifying a child's maternally-inherited DNA bands by comparison of the DNA fingerprints from the mother and child. Any bands in the child's DNA fingerprint which do not match with the mother can only have been inherited from the true biological father. Analysis of the alleged father's DNA fingerprint will show that he has bands present in his DNA fingerprint which match the paternal bands in the child if he is indeed the true father. The statistical chance that a randomly-selected unrelated individual could possess all the same bands as the true father has been calculated to be as small as 30000 million to 1. In other words, if the father's bands and the child's paternal bands match, paternity is confirmed. [This is illustrated by the diagrams on the opposite page.]

In order to provide *positive* proof of a relationship, a blood sample is required from the alleged father, the child *and* the mother. Testing *can* be carried out in cases where one of the parents may be deceased or simply unavailable for testing, but the method of analysis used is then based upon looking for the statistically expected band-sharing that is normally seen between related individuals. With just two individuals, the test will clearly indicate whether or not they are related but the nature of that relationship, i.e. mother to child, or aunt to nephew, can only be assessed upon the relative degree of band-sharing found. Therefore in this instance, the Test Report will indicate whether or not the DNA fingerprint analysis is *consistent* with that claimed relationship, rather than providing positive proof of it.

There may be some concerns over quality control in the forensic context, but there is no doubt as to the reliability of the technique in the family law context, where good quality samples are readily available (either by court order under Part III of the Family Law Reform Act 1969, as amended, or more commonly by agreement).

Thus far we have been looking at standards and methods of proof for the purpose of legal proceedings, but of course there are other people (such as social workers or personal representatives) who may have to decide the facts. What other sources of information are available? One is birth registration. The Law Commission's *Working Paper* (1979) had this to say:

9.18 For birth registration purposes the registrar should be entitled to accept a paternity statement from either parent without the explicit consent of the other parent —
   (i) where the registration reflects the application of the presumption of paternity based on marriage; or
   (ii) where paternity has been established by a court order.
This would constitute a change in the law only to the extent that it would allow a father to insist on his fatherhood appearing on the register (if necessary, by re-registration), where he has either obtained a declaration of parentage under the procedure dealt with below, or where an order giving him custody or access, or ordering him to pay maintenance, has been made. . . .

Formal methods of acknowledging paternity other than by court order
9.23 A considerable number of other jurisdictions, including New Zealand, most of the Australian states, Ontario, parts of the United States, and many civil law countries, have provided for acknowledgement of paternity otherwise than through the register of births. In New Zealand, for instance, an instrument of acknowledgment executed by the father and mother either as a deed or in the presence of a solicitor constitutes prima facie evidence of paternity. Such an instrument may be filed with the Registrar General.
9.24 We entirely agree that voluntary acceptance of paternal responsibilities is to be encouraged, but we suggest that the formal adoption of any such procedures here, by legislation,

Analysis of DNA Fingerprints in Paternity Testing

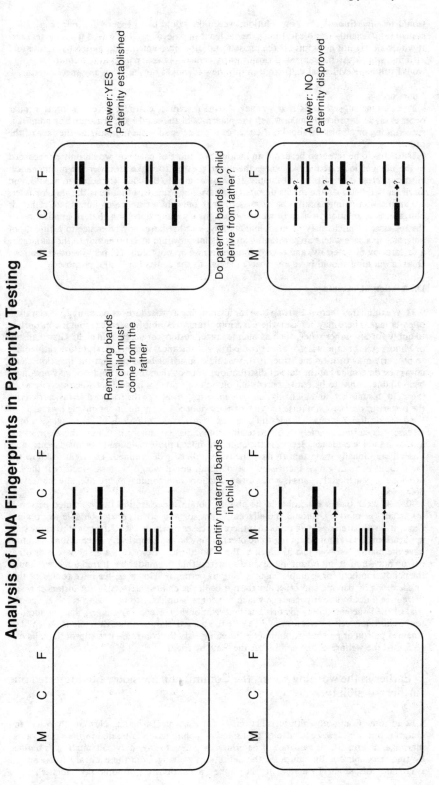

Identify maternal bands in child

Remaining bands in child must come from the father

Do paternal bands in child derive from father?

Answer: YES
Paternity established

Answer: NO
Paternity disproved

M   C   F

M   C   F

M   C   F

M   C   F

M   C   F

M   C   F

would be superfluous. The best solution, we think, would be to ensure that our registration system is sufficiently flexible to enable the evidence of paternity to be derived from the register. It would clearly not be helpful if the register and other instruments recognised by statute told different stories. An instrument recording an agreement between parties as to a child's paternity would still have evidential value; but in our view it should not be given any special status.

Court orders

9.27 . . . Our suggestion is that whenever a maintenance, custody, access or other similar order is made in proceedings in which the paternity of the child has been found or admitted, such finding or admission should, if either of the parties so wishes, appear on the face of the order. . . .

9.28 It should be repeated here that an incidental finding of paternity would only be recorded in the manner indicated above where the court goes on to make an order for maintenance, custody, access or the like. For example, if a man applies to the court for access to a child, and an order is refused on the merits despite the court being satisfied that he is the child's father, his application should simply be dismissed. It is only the existence of immediate rights or obligations in relation to a child which would justify the proposition that an application to the registrar of births may be made unilaterally. Furthermore, any reference to a finding of paternity in a case where no substantive order is made would be tantamount to the making of a declaration of paternity, and (as we argue later) we do not think that persons other than the child in question should have unrestricted access to the courts for such a purpose. . . .

Declaration of parentage
. . .

9.33 We think that there is a strong case for introducing a procedure for obtaining a declaration of parentage. There may be cases where it is important to establish parentage, but inappropriate to apply for any other relief, such as maintenance, custody or access under the Guardianship of Minors Acts or otherwise. We have two particular instances in mind. First, future entitlement to property may turn on the issue. It is, we think, insufficient to say that the question could always be determined at the date of distribution, since by then the best evidence may no longer be available. It has to be remembered that blood test evidence is most satisfactory only when the child, his mother, and all likely fathers can be tested. Hence the sooner a test is carried out the better, in order to minimise the risk of the evidence becoming unobtainable by reason of the death or disappearance of relevant persons. In any event, questions of parentage cannot in all cases be determined solely by blood testing, and it may be important to have those concerned available to give evidence. Secondly the child, or indeed those claiming to be his parents, may think it emotionally important to have the issue judicially determined. The right to know the facts about one's origins is increasingly recognised, and it would be unsatisfactory if the law provided only artificial means (such as an application for a nominal award of maintenance) for doing so. . . .

9.40 It is clear that a child should be able to obtain a declaration that a named person is his father (or mother). Should the alleged parent, or any other person, be able to obtain a declaration of parentage? We think that there are cases in which it would be right to allow such applications. First, those claiming to be parents may have a proprietary or emotional claim to have the matter resolved just as much as the child himself. Secondly, a grandparent or other person may think it important in the child's interest that the matter be cleared up, even though the child's mother, for example, is unwilling to permit it. However, we have to accept that applications by parents and others might not be in the child's interests — for instance, where there is real doubt about parentage which the court is unlikely to be able to resolve, and the trial of the issue could only disturb a settled relationship. Hence we suggest that, in addition to the child, any other person should be able to seek a declaration that the child is the child of a named person or persons if, but only if, he can satisfy the court that it is appropriate, having regard to the welfare of the child, that the issue be tried.

Earlier in the working paper, the Commission considered but rejected one further possibility:

9.12 In some Commonwealth jurisdictions — for example Tasmania, New South Wales and Ontario, but not New Zealand or Queensland — cohabitation is treated in the same way as marriage, as prima facie evidence of paternity. Needless to say, only cohabitation as defined by statute counts for this purpose, the definitions ranging from the arbitrary (for example twelve months, as in Tasmania) to the vague ('a relationship of some permanence', as in

Ontario). We incline to the view that this complication should not be introduced into the law. The value of a 'prima facie evidence rule' lies in its general applicability without further evidence. . . . But cohabitation (or rather, cohabitation 'as husband and wife', for only such cohabitation can be relevant) is by no means self-proving, especially if there are further statutory definitions going to the durability of the relationship.

Questions

(i) Was your stereotype of the unmarried father a man who was anxious to avoid his responsibilities or a man who was anxious to assert his relationship in the face of the mother's determination to have nothing more to do with him? Should the law on establishing paternity be the same in each case?

(ii) How easy is it to judge what will be in the child's best interests? Suppose, for example, that Miss B has been brutally raped by Mr X, who is a very rich man, and a child Y results. Will it be in the best interests of Y to declare or register Mr X as his father at the time when X sought and was denied an order to have contact with baby Y, if 20 years later X is killed in a road accident having left no will?

(iii) Do you agree with the National Council for One-Parent Families (1980) that the proposal only to record 'incidental' findings of paternity was a 'deliberate restriction on the child's right to know the identity of his or her father' and, presumably, regrettable?

(iv) If so, do you think that the matter should be obliged to name the father (*a*) for the purpose of claiming benefits (so that steps can be taken to recover a contribution from him), or (*b*) in all cases?

Given the current enthusiasm, in the Child Support Act 1991 (see *Children Come First* (1990), para. 5.33 and p. 129, above), for obliging mothers to name their children's fathers, the Law Commission's doubts about extending the formal machinery for recognising paternity seem somewhat out of date. Their Working Paper's proposals about birth registration were enacted in s. 10 of the Family Law Reform Act 1987. Their proposals for declarations of paternity had a more chequered history. In their first Report on *Illegitimacy* (1982), the Commission no longer thought that there was such a 'strong case' for these:

10.6 It is now necessary to record the anxiety which we have felt about the consequences of introducing a declaration procedure. First, there is the potential which proceedings for a declaration of parentage might have for disruption, not least by putting at risk the established relationships of the child whose parentage is at issue. Secondly, there is a problem relating to proof of parentage in particular where entitlement to British citizenship may be a consequence. . . .
10.7 . . . The arguments which we put forward in the Working Paper . . . do not, it may be said, take account of the potential use of such proceedings by the deluded or obsessed, or even for blackmailing or vindictive purposes. The distress and harm caused by the proceedings — perhaps merely the institution of proceedings — could greatly exceed any good which could be achieved for the claimant even if he succeeded. . . .
10.8 . . . Not infrequently, where no dispute arises [during childhood], a secure and contented childhood is provided for non-marital children by some family arrangement which ignores or conceals the true parentage. A claim to a declaration, pursued by a child when adult, could be intrusive or disturbing to the alleged parents and to their separate families. . . .
10.10 . . . There must . . . be some concern lest the court should regard itself as bound to grant a declaration merely because *some* evidence tending to establish paternity had been led and not contradicted. . . .

10.11 The problem of finding a satisfactory standard of proof in declaration proceedings is exacerbated by the fact that . . . the English court normally determines issues by adversarial means, that is on the basis of evidence which the parties choose to put before it. In a paternity dispute where, for example, financial provision is sought for the child, the applicant's assertion as to paternity is likely to be challenged by the respondent if the assertion is false. There is in such a case a 'proper contradictor', to test the applicant's evidence. There would often be no such contradictor in proceedings for a declaration of parentage.

10.12 . . . The risk of a false case being put forward and not contradicted is likely to be greater in cases where the successful applicant will gain a considerable advantage, at no cost to any other individual. . . . The risk is probably likely to be greatest in claims to British citizenship. . . .

Hence the Commission concluded that only the child himself should be able to apply, and only where he was born in England or Wales. He should be required to state the effect of a declaration upon his citizenship and the declaration should only bind the Crown if the Attorney General was a party to the proceedings. The court should have power to call for blood tests from *any* party of its own motion and to dismiss the application if these are not forthcoming. The court should make a declaration only if parentage was proved to its satisfaction.

After this Report, however, the Commission's later Report on *Declarations in Family Matters* (1984), which among other things updated the procedure for declarations of legitimacy, was implemented by the Family Law Act 1986. In their *Second Report* (1986), therefore, the Commission argued:

3.14 . . . Should our Report on Illegitimacy also be implemented, such need as there is for separate declarations of legitimacy and legitimation will be yet further reduced. In most cases, a declaration of parentage coupled with a declaration (where necessary) that those parents were married to one another at a relevant time, will be sufficient. However, it may be necessary to retain these special declarations to meet some very exceptional cases [see *Re MacDonald* (1964) 44 DLR (2d) 208]. If such declarations are to remain, we think that all should be subject to the same rules, for example as to jurisdiction and effect. Furthermore, it would not be right that those children of unmarried parents who had been obliged to seek a declaration of parentage should be subject to a more limited or onerous regime than those who are able to apply for declarations of legitimacy or legitimation when the essential issue is the same. Hence we recommend that declarations of parentage be assimilated to and integrated with the scheme for declarations of legitimacy and legitimation.

Section 22 of the 1987 Act provides a new s. 56 to the *Family Law Act 1986* accordingly:

56. – (1) Any person may apply to the court for a declaration –
   (a) that a person named in the application is or was his parent; or
   (b) that he is the legitimate child of his parents.
   (2) Any person may apply to the court for one (or for one or, in the alternative, the other) of the following declarations, that is to say –
   (a) a declaration that he has become a legitimated person;
   (b) a declaration that he has not become a legitimated person.
   (3) A court shall have jurisdiction to entertain an application under this section if, and only if, the applicant –
   (a) is domiciled in England and Wales on the date of the application; or
   (b) has been habitually resident in England and Wales throughout the period of one year ending with that date.
   (4) Where a declaration is made on an application under subsection (1) above, the prescribed officer of the court shall notify the Registrar General, in such a manner and within such period as may be prescribed, of the making of that declaration.
   (5) In this section 'legitimated person' means a person legitimated or recognised as legitimated –

(*a*) under section 2 or 3 of the Legitimacy Act 1976;
(*b*) under section 1 or 8 of the Legitimacy Act 1926; or
(*c*) by a legitimation (whether or not by virtue of the subsequent marriage of his parents) recognised by the law of England and Wales and effected under the law of another country.

Questions

(i) How relevant is it that the Family Law Reform Act 1987 contains no provisions about nationality? Can you think of any reason other than a desire for British citizenship which would lead a person to seek a declaration knowing that the evidence was false or very weak?
(ii) Do you support the limitation of declaration proceedings to the child himself? What about a grandchild?
(iii) Looking back at the *Ampthill Peerage* case (p. 458), do you see any reason for retaining separate declarations of legitimacy and legitimation, now that anyone can obtain a declaration of parentage in the same way and with the same effect? In what circumstances could the *status* achieved by being born to particular parents still be a problem?

4 The child's position

The differences at that time between legitimacy and illegitimacy were summarised thus in the Law Commission's Working Paper on *Illegitimacy* (1979):

Discrimination directly affecting the illegitimate child
2.10 It may be that the biggest discrimination suffered by a person born out of wedlock is the legal characterisation of him as 'illegitimate': we deal with the perpetuation of this label in Part III of this paper. The main practical areas in which there is legal discrimination are:
   (i) the maintenance of an illegitimate child is subject to the restrictions affecting the jurisdiction of the magistrates' courts: no lump sum exceeding £500 can be awarded and financial provision cannot be secured;
   (ii) although an illegitimate child can now inherit on the intestacy of either of his parents, he cannot take on the death intestate of any remoter ascendant or any collateral relation. In effect, therefore, he is treated as having no grandparents, brothers or sisters;
   (iii) despite recent reforms, an illegitimate child cannot succeed as heir to an entailed interest or succeed to a title of honour; and
   (iv) an illegitimate child if born outside the United Kingdom is not entitled as of right to United Kingdom citizenship even if both his parents are United Kingdom citizens.[1]

Discrimination affecting the father of an illegitimate child
2.11 From a strictly legal point of view, the father of an illegitimate child is today probably at a greater disadvantage than the child himself; and while many fathers may take little or no interest in their children born out of wedlock, other fathers who have lived with the mothers for perhaps many years are clearly affected by the discrimination. This discrimination takes a number of different forms:
   (i) the father has no automatic rights of guardianship, custody or access, even where an affiliation order has been made against him. Any such rights are obtainable by him only by court order or, if the mother has died, under the mother's will. The basic principle is set out in section 85(7) of the Children Act 1975: 'Except as otherwise provided by

---

1. Under the British Nationality Act 1981, s. 50(9), an illegitimate child may claim citizenship through his mother but not through his father.

or under any enactment, while the mother of an illegitimate child is living she has the parental rights and duties exclusively'.
(ii) Even if the father is awarded custody, he (unlike the father of a legitimate child) cannot obtain maintenance for the child from the mother, whatever her means.
(iii) The father's agreement to the child's adoption is not required unless he has already been granted custody or has become the child's guardian by court order or by appointment under the mother's will. His position is therefore different from that of the mother, and of both parents of a legitimate child, whose agreement is required.
(iv) The father's consent to a change of the child's name is not required unless he has become the legal guardian of the child by court order or under the mother's will.
(v) The father's consent to the marriage of the child during the child's minority is not required unless he has been granted custody of the child or has become the child's guardian under the mother's will.
(vi) There is no legal procedure by which the father can establish his paternity without the consent of the child's mother.

Procedural discrimination
2.12 There are, in addition, a number of procedural matters which point to the illegitimate child as 'different':
(i) Maintenance for an illegitimate child involves the institution by the mother of a special form of proceedings (affiliation proceedings) which many people regard as involving a stigma.
(ii) The mother cannot obtain maintenance for the child unless she is a 'single woman' at the date of the application for maintenance, or was so at the date of the child's birth. The phrase 'single woman' includes not only an unmarried woman (spinster, widow or divorcee) but also a married woman who is living apart from her husband and who has lost the right at common law to be maintained by him.
(iii) Only the magistrates' court has jurisdiction in affiliation proceedings, whereas the High Court, the county court and the magistrates' court all have jurisdiction in cases where maintenance is sought for legitimate children.
(iv) Subject to certain exceptions, an application for maintenance by way of affiliation proceedings must be made within three years of the child's birth. There is no such time limit as respects legitimate children.
(v) There is a special rule of evidence applicable to affiliation proceedings: if the mother gives evidence, her evidence must be corroborated.
(vi) There is a special form of appeal from a magistrates' court in affiliation proceedings.

Questions

(i) Why, do you suppose, did the Law Commission choose the word 'discrimination' instead of, for example, 'distinction'?
(ii) Should the lack of an automatic relationship with the father be classified as 'discrimination affecting the father' or 'discrimination affecting the child' or both?
(iii) Why are the matters described in paragraph 2.12 not labelled discrimination against the mother?

The Law Commission went on to survey the basic question of discrimination in this way:

3.2 . . . It is not now easy to put convincing arguments in favour of discrimination, because such arguments would logically justify a return to the strict common law position, and it is difficult to believe that there would be any substantial support for turning the clock back in this way. Nevertheless, arguments in favour of preserving the principle of discrimination may still be used by those who are prepared reluctantly to accept, as an accomplished fact, the changes which have already been made towards improving the legal status of the illegitimate child, but think that no further reform should be made. We therefore briefly summarise the arguments in favour of discrimination. They are three in number though they are perhaps not altogether distinct.

3.3 First, it is said that the legal distinction between 'legitimacy' and 'illegitimacy' reflects social realities. This was certainly true at one time. The birth of an illegitimate child was regarded as bringing disgrace not only on the mother but also on her immediate family. The child could no more expect to be recognised as a member of the family and be received into the family home than he could expect to inherit family property. He was not a real member of the family group. However, although there may still be cases where the illegitimate child is in this position, the evidence suggests that a significant and increasing proportion of all illegitimate children born each year are recognised by both their parents, at least if the parents have a relationship of some stability. . . .

3.4 Secondly, it is said that the distinction serves to uphold moral standards and also to support the institution of marriage. In relation to the preservation of moral standards, it is difficult to say how far the fear of producing illegitimate children influenced sexual behaviour in the past; since the risk of an unwanted pregnancy can now usually be avoided by contraceptive measures it seems improbable that such fears still influence sexual behaviour to any substantial extent. Support for the institution of marriage is of course of great importance, especially in the present context, because a married relationship between parents should in principle be more stable than an unmarried one, so creating a better environment for the child's upbringing. However, many marriages are not stable, and statistically it seems that marriages entered into primarily for the purpose of ensuring that an expected child is not born illegitimate are especially at risk. In a large proportion of marriages where the girl is under 20 she is also pregnant; and the failure rate of marriages where the girl married young is statistically high. We therefore find it difficult to accept that the institution of marriage is truly supported by a state of the law in which the conception of a child may encourage young couples to enter precipitately into marriages which may have little chance of success.

3.5 The third argument in favour of preserving discriminatory treatment asserts that the legal relationship between the child's parents should be relevant in determining the child's legal status: that as the legal relationship of marriage results in legitimate status for the child, so a relationship which does not accord with the norm should not result in normal status for the child. On this view it is regarded as significant not only that a legitimate child is the issue of a legally recognised union, the incidents of which are fixed by law and which can only be dissolved by formal proceedings but also that marriage, at least in its inception, is intended to be permanent. The relationship of an illegitimate child's parents, on the other hand, is not in general legally recognised and may never have been intended to be more than transient. However this argument is based on the premise that a child's status ought to be affected by that of his parents. This is the proposition which we do not accept; it is, after all, the child's status, and the nature of the relationship between his parents need not and should not affect this.

3.6 In general, where a child is involved, the law is that his welfare is the first and paramount consideration, transcending even the consideration of doing justice between his parents or between his parents and outsiders. We do not think that the arguments mentioned above in favour of discrimination are sufficiently strong to justify a refusal, as a matter of law, to apply the same welfare principle to children simply on the ground that they have been born out of wedlock. In particular, we see no justification for preserving the status quo. . . .

Two further reasons for reform were put forward in the Scottish Law Commission's Consultative Memorandum on *Illegitimacy* (1982):

1.15 Reform would be in line with this country's treaty obligations. The United Kingdom has ratified the *European Convention on the Legal Status of Children born out of Wedlock*. The preamble to this Convention notes that in a great number of member States of the Council of Europe efforts have been, or are being, made to improve the legal status of children born out of wedlock by reducing the differences between their legal status and that of children born in wedlock which are to their legal or social disadvantage. It records that the signatory States believe that the situation of children born out of wedlock should be improved and that the formulation of certain common rules concerning their legal status would assist this objective. The Convention then binds each Contracting Party to ensure the conformity of its law with the provisions of the Convention. A State is, however, allowed to make not more than three reservations. The present law of Scotland [and England] does not conform to two provisions of the Convention and the United Kingdom accordingly reserved the right not to apply, or not to apply fully, those provisions in relation to Scotland.[2] The policy of the Convention

---

2. The provisions in question are: — Art. 6(2) 'Where a legal obligation to maintain a child born in wedlock falls on certain members of the family of the father or mother, this obligation

is to allow 'progressive stages for those States which consider themselves unable to adopt immediately' all of its rules and reservations are valid for only five years at a time. It is clear that the general policy of the Convention is the reduction of legal discrimination against illegitimate children and that the United Kingdom's position would be more in accord with that policy if the reservations were unnecessary.

1.16 The United Kingdom is also a party to the *European Convention on Human Rights*. [See article 8, p. 407, above.] It has been held in the case of *Marckx v Kingdom of Belgium* that the provisions of Belgian law prohibiting an illegitimate child from inheriting from his close maternal relatives on their intestacy contravened Article 8 and that these different inheritance rights of legitimate and illegitimate children lacked objective and reasonable justification. In Scots law, as in Belgian law, an illegitimate child has no such inheritance rights, so that changes are necessary to prevent the continuing breach of Article 8 by the United Kingdom.

Having concluded that there was no justification for retaining the status quo, the English Law Commission (1979) went on to discuss two possible models for reform:

(b) First model for reform: abolition of adverse legal consequences of illegitimacy
3.8 In this model the concepts of legitimacy and illegitimacy are preserved, but further steps are taken to remove by statute certain of the practical and procedural consequences of illegitimacy: in particular, all consequences which are adverse to the child. Thus, affiliation proceedings would be abolished and the illegitimate child would be given a legal right, under the Guardianship of Minors Acts 1971 and 1973, to support from both his parents; he would be capable of succeeding on the intestacy of ascendant and collateral relatives as if he had been born legitimate, and so on.

3.9 The particular reforms for inclusion within such a scheme could be selective; and the model has what some may regard as the advantage of not necessarily involving the automatic removal of all discrimination against the father of an illegitimate child. . . .

(c) Second model for reform: abolition of the status of illegitimacy
3.14 This model involves the total disappearance of the concept of 'legitimacy' as well as of 'illegitimacy', for the one cannot exist without the other. It goes beyond the mere assimilation of the legal positions of children born in and out of wedlock, since that solution, which has been considered above, would still preserve the caste labels which help artificially to preserve the social stigma now attached to illegitimacy.

3.15 The case for abolishing illegitimacy as a status is in our view supported by the fact that such a change in the law would help to improve the position of children born out of wedlock in a way in which the mere removal of the remaining legal disabilities attaching to illegitimacy would not. No change in the law relating to legitimacy would help to improve the economic position of a child born out of wedlock in so far as he suffers from being the child of a 'one-parent family'; but an illegitimate child suffers a special disadvantage which does not affect the child of a widow or divorcee. He has a different *status*, even if the incidents of that status do not differ greatly from those attached to the status of a legitimate child; attention is thus focussed on the irrelevant fact of the parents' marital status. We believe that the law can help to lessen social prejudices by setting an example clearly based upon the principle that the parents' marital relationship is irrelevant to the child's legal position. Changes in the law cannot give the illegitimate child the benefits of a secure, caring, family background. They cannot even ensure the he does not suffer financially, since his father may not be in a position to support him. But they can at least remove the *additional* hardship of attaching on opprobrious description to him. . . .

3.16. If the law were changed so that there was no longer a legal distinction between the illegitimate child, it would also follow that in principle there would be no distinction between parents: both parents would have equal rights and duties unless and until a court otherwise ordered. . . . We have tentatively concluded that the advantages of removing the status of illegitimacy altogether from the law outweigh the disadvantages of giving all fathers parental rights.

---

shall also apply for the benefit of a child born out of wedlock.'
Art. 9 'A child born out of wedlock shall have the same right of succession in the estate of its father and its mother and of a member of its father's or mother's family, as if it had been born in wedlock.'

The response of the National Council for One-Parent Families, *An Accident Birth* (1980), supported the end but not the means:

In discussing the abolition of illegitimacy, we believe that it is necessary to draw a clear distinction between the rights of the child and the rights of the parents. We do not believe that the two models — that of abolishing the status of illegitimacy and that of preserving some distinction between the parental rights and duties of married and unmarried parents — are necessarily mutually exclusive. We believe that by giving all children equal rights, irrespective of the marital status of their parents, the status of illegitimacy is abolished. Any remaining difference in the custodial relationship of parents is a consequence of the status of marriage, of which we are not proposing the abolition. We recognise the need for reform in the area of parental rights, and would certainly support an increase in father's rights to encourage unmarried fathers to play a greater role in the upbringing of their children. However, we feel that there are strong arguments against giving all fathers *automatic* equal parental rights. . . .

    (*a*) In our experience, the majority of illegitimate children during early childhood are living with and being cared for by their mothers alone, and either have no contact, or very erratic contact, with their natural fathers. We believe that giving fathers automatic rights will remove the existing protection and security an unmarried mother has in bringing up her child alone, and will lead to increased pressure and distress, caused not only in the event of intervention by an estranged father, but also by the uncertainty of never knowing whether or not the father will exercise his rights, unless the issue is decided by the court.

    (*b*) If an unmarried father is to be given automatic parental rights, the question of establishing paternity takes on increased significance. We believe that many mothers will be deterred from entering the father's details on the birth certificate or will deny the identity of the father if automatic parental rights flow from paternity being established. This will act against the child's right to know the facts about his or her origins and will undermine the Law Commission's recommendation on this subject.

[However:] . . . There is a need to provide a procedure available to all unmarried parents, whether cohabiting or not, to make a *mutual declaration* of parentage and joint custody, and to register it with the court. Simple forms could be available at the Municipal Offices where births are registered, where such a declaration could be formalised. This would give full custody rights to unmarried fathers where the mother consents. Although we believe that such a consensual arrangement is the only one having a reasonable chance of success, it could be viewed as giving an unjustifiable veto to the mother. We therefore recommend that a further amendment should be made to the Guardianship of Minors Act 1971, to allow unmarried fathers to apply to the court for joint custody if the mother should not agree to a mutual declaration. In reaching its decision, the court would have to apply the cardinal principle of family law in regarding the welfare of the child as paramount.

[Finally:] We deplore the Law Commission's statement that 'One-parent families remain a major social problem'. The one-parent family is not problematic per se and it is not a deviation from the two-parent family. Despite the fact that one-parent families suffer both economic and social discrimination we believe that a one-parent family is a normal and viable family form in its own right and is able to carry out required family functions such as parenting. Given such negative attitudes it is not surprising that laws developed to suit a two-parent family fit so awkwardly on a one-parent family.

Residual social stigma affects the confidence of single women in their undoubted ability to provide a satisfactory upbringing for their children. Attitudes towards illegitimacy are part of wider social and moral codes affecting sexual behaviour and particularly attitudes towards women. The sense of shame, of feeling different and inferior, which has been the experience of so many illegitimate children in the past, is the result of society's punishing attitude towards the mother for contravening the moral code. In our concern to give equality to all children, we should not overlook that in the early childhood years, the fate of many children will be in the hands of one custodian only, usually the mother. The law must strike a balance which protects and respects her as custodian whilst at the same time keeping open the channels of access to the father.

Somewhat similar criticisms were voiced by Mary Hayes in her comment on the Working Paper (1980):

One weakness of their paper is that only superficial attention is given to the practical implications of giving rights to fathers, while the emotional dimensions of implementing such a change are virtually ignored. Furthermore the effect of giving rights to fathers is not tested against the welfare principle; this means that the Law Commission fail to ask themselves some fundamental questions before they conclude, at an early stage, that abolishing illegitimacy promotes the welfare of the child.

The Commission's Report on *Illegitimacy* (1982) therefore paid much greater heed to the arguments against according automatic rights to fathers:

4.26 . . .

(*a*) It was said that automatically to confer 'parental rights' on fathers could well result in a significant growth in the number of mothers who would refuse to identify the father of their child. Mothers would be tempted to conceal the father's identity in order to ensure that in practice he could not exercise any parental rights. If this were to happen, it would detract from the desirable objective of establishing, recognising and fostering genuine familial links.

(*b*) It was said that to confer rights on the father might well be productive of particular distress and disturbance where the mother had subsequently married a third party, who had put himself *in loco parentis* to the child. The possibility — however unlikely in reality — of interference by the child's father could well engender a damaging sense of insecurity in the family; matters would be all the worse if the father did intervene. Some commentators argued that the result in such a case might be that the mother and her new partner would seek, for instance by an application for custody or adoption, to forestall any possible intervention by the natural father with the result that the child would be prematurely denied the possibility of establishing a genuine link with him.

(*c*) It was said that automatically to confer 'rights' on the father of a child born outside marriage could put him in a position where he might be tempted to harass or possibly even to blackmail the mother at a time when she might well be exceptionally vulnerable to pressure. In this context a number of commentators made what seems to us to be the valid point that what is in issue is not so much how the law is perceived by the professional lawyer or the experienced social worker, but how it might be perceived by a fearful and perhaps ill-informed mother. Sometimes what the law is thought to be may be almost as important as what it in fact is. Thus the partners of a child might well attach more significance to the fact that the law had given the father 'rights' than would a lawyer who is accustomed to the forensic process and able dispassionately to consider the likelihood of a court in fact permitting a father to exercise those rights, given its overriding concern to promote the child's welfare.

(*d*) It was also suggested that the experience of countries which have sought to abolish the discrimination affecting those born outside marriage is generally against automatically conferring 'parental rights' on the father of an illegitimate child. In most of those countries the father does not have the full range of parental rights unless he has obtained a court order or he falls within a delimited category of fathers in whom the law automatically recognises parental rights.

(*e*) Finally it was suggested that if all fathers automatically possessed parental authority over their illegitimate children, practical difficulties would be encountered where the child was in the care of a local authority under section 2 of the Child Care Act 1980. These would arise because a local authority is not entitled to keep a child in its care if a person having parental rights expresses a desire to take over the child's care. The result might therefore be either that the father would, contrary to its best interests, take the child out of care, or alternatively that long-term planning for the child's future would be delayed until the father's rights had been terminated. In such cases the child might well suffer.

Questions

(i) Is it possible to abolish the status of illegitimacy (and for that matter legitimacy) without giving automatic parental responsibility to all fathers? (ii) Which of the following do you think would be the best for most children: (*a*) abolishing the status and giving *all* fathers automatic parental responsibility: (*b*) abolishing the child's exclusion from his father's lineage, giving him the same claims to financial provision and property adjustment as any other child, but not giving the father automatic parental responsibility; or (*c*) abolishing the status and giving *no* fathers automatic parental responsibility?

In their First Report on *Illegitimacy* (1982), the Law Commission answered the first question in the negative, but opted for a package of reforms corresponding to model (*b*):

4.44 . . . Some commentators expressed the view . . . that it would be perfectly possible to abolish the status of illegitimacy whilst preserving the existing rules whereby parental rights vest automatically only in married parents. We do not accept this view. The argument for 'abolishing illegitimacy' (rather than merely removing such legal consequences of that status as are adverse to the child) is essentially that the abolition of any legal distinction based on the parents' marital status would itself have an influence on opinion. The marital status of the child's parents would cease to be *legally* relevant, and thus the need to refer to the child's distinctive legal status would (in this view) disappear. This consequence could not follow if a distinction − albeit relating only to entitlement to parental rights − were to be preserved between children which would be based solely on their parent's status. There would remain two classes of children: first, those whose parents were married and thereby enjoyed parental rights; secondly, those whose parents were unmarried and whose fathers did not enjoy such rights. . . .
4.45 We believe, therefore, that it is impossible to avoid the stark choice between abolition of the status of illegitimacy and its retention (albeit coupled with a removal of the legal disadvantages of illegitimacy so far as they adversely affect the child).
4.49 In the result, we have come to the conclusion that the advantages of abolishing the status of illegitimacy are not sufficient to compensate for the possible dangers involved in an automatic extension of parental rights to fathers of non-marital children. . . .
4.50 Accordingly, . . . we can no longer adhere to the provisional proposal made in the Working Paper, that the status of illegitimacy be abolished. We are in no doubt that the law should be reformed so as to remove all the legal disadvantages of illegitimacy so far as they discriminate against the illegitimate child, but we do not think that parental rights should vest in the fathers of non-marital children without prior scrutiny of the child's interests by the courts. . . .
4.51 For almost all purposes the effect of the changes which we recommend will be that all children − irrespective of their parents' marital status − will be treated alike by the law. However, in a few areas (the most important of which is obviously the question of entitlement to parental rights) there will continue to be a difference between those children whose parents have married and those whose parents have not. To this extent it will be necessary to preserve the concepts of 'legitimacy', 'illegitimacy' and 'legitimation'. On the question of terminology, however, we would at this stage make one small, but we think important, recommendation: namely, that whenever possible the terms 'legitimate' and 'illegitimate' should cease to be used as legal terms of art. The expressions that we favour in their stead, and that we use generally in this Report and in the draft legislation attached hereto, are 'marital' and 'non-marital', which avoid the connotations of unlawfulness and illegality which are implicit in the term 'illegitimate'.

The Scottish Law Commission, in their Report on *Illegitimacy* (1984), reached the same conclusions about what the law should be, but approached the questions of terminology and status in this way:

9.2 . . . We would endorse the view of the Law Commission for England and Wales that the terms 'legitimate' and 'illegitimate' should, wherever possible, cease to be used as legal terms of art. We do not agree with the Law Commission, however, that it would be desirable to replace these terms with 'marital' and 'non-marital'. This is just another way of labelling children, and experience in other areas, such as mental illness, suggests that new labels can rapidly take on old connotations. In our view it should so rarely be necessary to discriminate between children on the basis of whether their father was married to their mother that no special legal label is required for this purpose. There are already children, for example, whose fathers, although married or formerly married to the mother, have been deprived of custody and other parental rights. It has not been found necessary to invent a special legal label for them. In short, we would not wish to see a discriminatory concept of 'non-maritality' gradually replace a discriminatory concept of 'illegitimacy'. We would rather see future legislation distinguish, where distinctions based on marriage are necessary, between fathers rather than between children. Where it is thought necessary to distinguish between people on the basis of whether or not their parents were married to each other at any relevant time − and we hope this will be a very rare exception − we would suggest that this should be done expressly in those terms. . . .
9.3 *The legal status of illegitimacy.* Implementation of our recommendations would remove most remaining legal differences between children which depend on whether or not their parents

are, or have been, married to each other. It would not, however, remove all and, as we have seen, the words 'legitimate' and 'illegitimate' would not be entirely removed from the statute law. In these circumstances, it would be a matter for argument whether it was any longer justifiable to refer to a legal status or illegitimacy in Scots law. This, in our view, is not a matter on which it would be appropriate to legislate. Legislation is concerned with rules. Whether minor differences in the rules applying to different classes of persons justify the ascription of a distinct status is a matter for commentators rather than legislators.

Questions

(i) On terminology, the Law Commission in their Second Report (1986) agreed with the Scots (see s. 1 of the Family Law Reform Act 1987, p. 443, above): do you?
(ii) On status, could they have gone further and purged the statute book of the concepts of legitimacy and legitimation altogether?

The Family Law Reform Act 1987 did remove virtually all the law's discrimination against the child. The new general rule of construction (p. 443, above) applies to the rules of intestacy and to other dispositions. The child is only now excluded from his father's lineage for the purposes of nationality and titles of honour. Affiliation proceedings were replaced with a general power to make financial provision and property adjustment orders for the benefit of *any* child, equivalent to those available on divorce (now contained in Sch. 1 to the Children Act 1989). The offending label 'illegitimate' was removed from most of the child law statutes (now in any event replaced by the Children Act 1989) and the Lord Chancellor given power to remove it from other legislation by statutory instrument.

Questions

(i) In practice, however, how much is likely to change?
(ii) Consider the cases of *Tanner v Tanner* [1975] 3 All ER 776, [1975] 1 WLR 1346 (p. 348, above) and *Lord Lilford v Glyn* [1979] 1 All ER 441, [1979] 1 WLR 78 (p. 450, above): now that the courts have power to make capital settlements for all children will they use it?

5　A new status for fathers

Because of the new general rule of construction, 'parent' now always includes the child's mother and father. Both are financially liable to maintain their child in public and private law. But the Family Law Reform Act 1987 and, now, the Children Act 1989 (p. 443, above) preserve the rule that only the mother has parental responsibility for bringing the child up from the moment of birth. The *Children Act 1989*, however, provides for several ways in which the father may come to share it with her:

4.–(1) Where a child's father and mother were not married to each other at the time of his birth—
    (*a*) the court may, on the application of the father, order that he shall have parental responsibility for the child; or
    (*b*) the father and mother may by agreement ('a parental responsibility agreement') provide for the father to have parental responsibility for the child.

(2) No parental responsibility agreement shall have effect for the purposes of this Act unless—
    (*a*) it is made in the form prescribed by regulations made by the Lord Chancellor; and
    (*b*) where regulations are made by the Lord Chancellor prescribing the manner in which such agreements must be recorded, it is recorded in the prescribed manner.
(3) Subject to section 12(4), an order under subsection (1)(*a*), or a parental responsibility agreement, may only be brought to an end by an order of the court made on the application—
    (*a*) of any person who has parental responsibility for the child; or
    (*b*) with leave of the court, of the child himself.
(4) The court may only grant leave under subsection (3)(*b*) if it is satisfied that the child has sufficient understanding to make the proposed application.
12.—(1) Where the court makes a residence order in favour of the father of a child it shall, if the father would not otherwise have parental responsibility for the child, also make an order under section 4 giving him that responsibility.
(4) Where subsection (1) requires the court to make an order under section 4 in respect of the father of a child, the court shall not bring that order to an end at any time while the residence order concerned remains in force.

Section 4(1)(*a*) replaces s. 4 of the Family Law Reform Act 1987. The purpose and effect of this were explained by the Law Commission in their *Second Report* (1986) like this:

3.1 At present, an unmarried father may be granted legal custody of his child, but he cannot share that custody with the mother. The Report Bill provided that a court could grant him the full legal status of parenthood, that is all the parental rights and duties, usually sharing these with the mother in the same way that married parents do. It was thought that such an order would normally be sought where the mother and father were living together and both wanted it, or where the mother had died without appointing the father testamentary guardian (although in that case he may at present apply to be made guardian), or where the parents had separated and he wanted full parental status rather than simply legal custody. However, in providing that the father should share that status with the mother 'unless otherwise directed,' the Report Bill incidentally gave the court the unprecedented power to remove all the mother's parental authority. We think that this result was unintentional and could be undesirable. . . .
3.2 The new clause 4 [permits] the court to order that the father shall have all parental authority, sharing it with the mother. Such an order will place him in essentially the same position as a married father. Once the father has acquired full parental status in this way, disputes between the parents will usually be dealt with in the same way as disputes between married parents, . . .
3.3 There is one respect in which the position of a father who has been granted all the parental rights and duties by means of an order under clause 4 of the draft Bill will differ from that of a married father, in that the court will have power to revoke the order. This was provided for in our earlier Report and, in the present state of the law relating to family responsibilities, we consider that it should be retained. We recognise that, owing to the widely varying extent to which unmarried fathers in fact assume responsibility towards their children (and indeed towards the mothers who bring those children up), it would not be in the best interests of the children if fathers were automatically to enjoy full parental status. Where the parents are in fact living together and co-operating in bringing up their children, we hope that such orders will frequently be applied for and granted. However, unless the courts are able to remove parental powers where it subsequently proves not to be in the child's best interests for the father to have them, the courts may be reluctant to make such orders at all. A court will necessarily have to have regard to the extent to which it will be able to protect the child's interests should the need arise in the future and under the present law the powers of the divorce courts in relation to married couples are somewhat more extensive than those under the Guardianship of Minors Acts. The time may come when the general framework of the law relating to the responsibilities of parents, not only towards their children but also towards one another, is such that this can be reconsidered. . . .

Questions

(i) Do you think that it should be reconsidered straightaway?

(ii) Do you think that the mother's consent should be required to an application for full parental status, unless it could be dispensed with in the same way as in adoption?

D v Hereford and Worcester County Council
[1991] 2 All ER 177, [1991] 2 WLR 753, Family Division

The child's father and mother lived together for the first few months of his life and the father played an active part in looking after him. There was regular contact after the parents separated. Then the mother began a relationship with a man who had committed a sexual offence against another child and all her children were taken into care. At first, the father was allowed contact with his child, but this was ended by the local authority, and at that time he had no legal remedy to challenge this. As soon as s. 4 of the Family Law Reform Act 1987 came into force, he applied for an order. The magistrates granted it and the local authority appealed, arguing that parental 'rights and duties' (as they then were) included an enforceable right to access and custody, and that accordingly a s. 4 order was incompatible with the local authority's responsibilities under the care order.

Ward J: . . . As the law stood at the time of the father's application and the justices' adjudication thereon, this father had no other legal remedy available to him to seek the determination of his right to respect for his family life. I phrase it thus in order, for the moment, to adopt the language of the European Convention for the Protection of Human Rights and Fundamental Freedoms. The father could not have applied in wardship because the court would not exercise its jurisdiction: *A v Liverpool City Council* [1982] AC 363. The father could not have applied under the Guardianship of Minors Act 1971 for legal custody or access for the same reason: *Re M and H (Minors)* [1990] 1 AC 686. The father could not have applied for access under Part 1A of the Child Care Act 1980 because the rights there conferred are given only to, 'parent, guardian or custodian' and, being unmarried, he would not have qualified: see s. 87(1) of the Child Care Act 1980. That lacuna had not been cured by the Family Law Reform Act 1987 and it needed para. 35 of sch. 12 to the Children Act 1989, enacted on November 16, 1989, to give the unmarried father that remedy. Only if this application succeeded was the door to the court left open.

   . . .

   In my judgment, the father's case is preferable for these reasons.

   (1) The Family Law Reform Act 1987 is, to quote the preamble

   'An Act to reform the law relating to the consequences of birth outside marriage: to make further provision with respect to the rights and duties of parents and the determination of parentage and for connected purposes.'

That reform was the culmination of long deliberation and consultation. The Law Commission published its first Working Paper on Illegitimacy in 1979. The logic of sweeping away the legal distinction between the illegitimate child and the legitimate child was that in principle there should be no distinction between the parents and each should have equal parental rights and duties. As the Law Commission's Report, No. 118 of 1982, made clear, that sweeping approach did not find favour and the Report recommended instead that the law should provide machinery giving legal recognition to the familial links between a non-marital child and his father whenever it would be in the child's interests to do so. In 1986 the Scots Law was amended. So, the Law Commission in its second report, No. 157 in 1986, stated that the policy emerging was that to the greatest extent possible the legal position of the child born to unmarried parents should be the same as that of one born to married parents, but as between the parents themselves, the mother alone should have the parental rights and duties, although the father should be able to acquire these by legal process. The Law Commission accordingly recommended in para. 3.2: [see p. 477, above.] The effect of the s. 4 order is, in the appropriate case, to give the father rights he did not have before that order was made. The result of his being given those rights is that he is then in the same position *vis-à-vis* the child as is the mother, and in the same position *vis-à-vis* the mother as is the married father. . . .

(3) To introduce, as [counsel for the local authority] does, this element of enforceable right is to introduce at once the element of confrontation. That would be furthest from the minds of the mother and father who cohabit happily together and wish to use s. 4 constructively to place themselves and their child to all intents and purposes in the position that would obtain were they married. As [counsel for the father] submits, the s. 4 order gives the unmarried father some status and standing.

. . .

(6) In my judgment, there is no logic in nor justification for the . . . proposition upon which the whole of the local authority's case depends. . . . I am strengthened in my conclusion by the persuasive but *obiter* view expressed by Balcombe, L.J. in *Re H (Minors) (Putative Fathers' Rights)* [1989] 2 All ER 353 at 357, [1989] 1 WLR 551 at 557, which I gratefully adopt:

'. . . that submission [that the effect of *Re M and H* still applied] was mistaken because a parental rights order under s. 4 of the Family Law Reform Act 1987 will not interfere with the local authority's exercise of their statutory rights over the children, but will merely give the father a *locus standi* and place him in the same position as the parent of a legitimate child to make the necessary applications to the court. That, it seems to me, is the difference between a parental rights order (giving *locus standi*) and a custody order (under the Guardianship of Minors Act 1971) which would, if given effect to, interfere with the local authority's rights in relation to children in their care.'

. . . The essence of the question for the justices is, 'Can this respondent show that he is a father to the child', not in the biological sense but in the sense that he has established or is likely to establish such a real family tie with the boy that he should now be accorded the corresponding legal tie. It would be easier to ask under the Children Act 1989, but the essence is the same: 'Has he behaved, or will be behave, with parental responsibility for the child?' These real links are not established simply upon proof of, or acknowledgement of, paternity. That option was ruled out by the Law Commission, which also recommended against the automatic conferring of rights on the father, leaving it to the mother to apply to displace them. There is, therefore, a burden of proof on the father. No one factor can ever be conclusive, but some will obviously weigh more heavily than others. Each case will inevitably depend upon its own facts, but some guidance may be helpful to the justices in this and other cases.

There may be obvious reasons for rejecting the application. By way of statistically unlikely example, the claim of the rapist. A more common event may be such implacable hostility from mother to the intervention of father into her life, perhaps after the most casual relationship, that no benefit would ensue to the child. If the father has nothing to offer the child it would be right to refuse his application.

There may also be clear reasons for admitting the claim, for example, if it has the full consent of the mother, free from any improper pressure from the father. The fact of mother and father having cohabited together, perhaps not only at birth (the criterion of New Zealand) but also in circumstances which establish a substantial familial connexion, is also a powerful factor. Such a positive participation in the child's upbringing may well constitute such a contribution to his welfare that the reality of the paternal link should be cemented by granting personal rights and imposing parental duties. Past participation may have forged that link strongly enough for it to endure even though the parents separate. Separation may then affect the position in two ways. It may have such devastating consequences upon the relationship of the father and mother and/or father and child that the application is rejected, or an existing order discharged. If, however, the parents thereafter disagree only about the way in which a particular element of parental rights is exercised, then they may seek directions under the Guardianship of Minors Act 1971 or the Guardianship Act 1973.

As for the child in care, the making of a care order and the consequential long-term plans for the child to the exclusion of the father may affect the parental rights application in different ways. At one extreme, one may have a violent father living with a terrified mother, unable to protect her child who then suffers serious non-accidental injury at the father's hands. His participation in the past will have been so negative, and his exclusion from the future so final, that his application would have little merit. At the other extreme, a couple devoted to each other and to the child over a number of years may suffer misfortune leading to their inability to provide a home for the child in the immediate future. The care order does not deprive the mother of her parental rights, though her right to the actual custody is suspended and her right of access controlled. In such circumstances, the father should be entitled to be placed in the same position as the mother, in resisting the termination of access and in objecting to the proposed adoption.

. . . The matter will have to be remitted to the justices so that they may hear all the evidence and then exercise their discretion afresh with such help as I have been able to give them. To that extent the appeal must be allowed.

Appeal allowed.

Questions

(i) Under s. 34(1) of the Children Act 1989 (p. 613, below), the local authority has a duty to allow reasonable contact between the child and his father, and the father can go to court if there is any dispute: will it be necessary or desirable to make a s. 4 order in such cases?

(ii) This decision was effectively approved by the Court of Appeal in *Re H (minors) (local authority: parental rights)*, [1991] 2 All ER 185, [1991] 2 WLR 763: the court held that a s. 4 order ought to have been made so as to enable the father to oppose an application to free the child for adoption, even though they then decided that the father's agreement to the adoption should be dispensed with on the ground that it was unreasonably withheld: is it for the benefit either of the child or of his father to do this? (Can it be reconciled with the views of the Law Commission on whether a right of access should entitle the father to withhold his agreement to an adoption, see p. 483, below?)

(iii) The court must make a s. 4 order if it makes a residence order in the father's favour (p. 477, above): do these decisions suggest that it should also do so if it makes a contact order? Do you think it should?

(iv) What do you think that mothers will think of this?

We have already mentioned One-Parent Families' proposal for a voluntary sharing procedure (p. 473, above). The Law Commission's response in their first Report on *Illegitimacy* (1982) was this:

4.39 It may, however, be argued that the father should be entitled to parental rights in cases where *both* parents of the child agree that he should. After all (it might be argued) the law already accords parental rights to all married parents without any prior scrutiny of what is in the child's best interests. Why should it not equally accord such rights to unmarried parents who are in agreement? We see force in this argument, but have nevertheless rejected it. The most powerful factor influencing our decision was the strong body of evidence from those best acquainted with the problems of the single parent family about the vulnerable position of the unmarried mother in many cases. Such mothers may well be exposed to pressure, and even harassment, on the part of the natural father; and it would, in our view, give unscrupulous natural fathers undesirable bargaining power if they were to be placed in a position where they might more easily extort from the mother a joint 'voluntary' acknowledgement, having the effect of vesting parental rights in the father, perhaps as the price of an agreement to provide for the mother or her child, or even as the price of continuing a relationship with the mother. For this reason, we think it appropriate for the court to investigate and sanction even a joint request that parental rights vest in the father. In reaching this conclusion we have, as we have said, been particularly impressed by the need to protect single mothers from the risk of pressure. But we should make it plain that we do not, in any event, accept the argument that since a couple can acquire parental rights over their child by marriage they should be able to do so by some other formal act. Apart from the consideration (to which some will attach considerable importance) that to do so would debase the institution of marriage, it must be borne in mind that marriage is still, in principle, a permanent relationship. In contrast, there is no such unifying factor in the case of unmarried relationships, which are infinitely variable in their nature and in the intentions of the partners to them. This diversity suggests to us that scrutiny by a court is a not unreasonable protection for the interests of the child of unmarried parents.

Questions

(i) Is not the threat of legal proceedings just as much harassment for the mother, at least if her consent is not required for an order?

(ii) Does not the new order debase the institution of marriage just as much as a voluntary agreement might do?

(iii) Why should a parent be able to appoint a guardian to share parental status with the other parent after her death, but not to share her own status while she is alive?

The Commission were able to return to this question in the course of their review of the whole of the private law relating to the upbringing of children. In their Report on *Guardianship and Custody* (1988) they concluded:

2.18 ... In our Working Paper on Guardianship, we pointed out that such judicial proceedings may be unduly elaborate, expensive and unnecessary unless the child's mother objects to the order. We suggested, therefore, that the mother might be permitted to appoint the father guardian to share responsibility while she was alive. A large majority of those who responded, including the leading organisations representing single parents and children's interests, supported this suggestion. It was pointed out, however, that it would be more consistent with the primary concept of parenthood if the father were to acquire the same status by such an appointment as he would by a court order. We therefore recommend that mother and father should be able to make an agreement that the father shall share parental responsibility with the mother. This will have the same effect as a court order. Both, for example, will confer upon him the power to give or withhold agreement to the child's adoption or to appoint a guardian. More importantly perhaps, both an agreement and an order may only be brought to an end by a court order made on the application of either parent (or a guardian). The child should also be able to make such applications, but only if the court is satisfied that he has sufficient understanding to do so.

2.19 For this reason, we also recommend that the agreement be made in a prescribed form. . . . The object is to ensure that, as far as possible, both parents understand the importance and effects of their agreement. Overall, this should provide a simple and straightforward means for unmarried parents to acknowledge their shared responsibility, not only for the support, but also for the upbringing of their child.

2.20 This procedure will serve to distinguish the private appointment of the father to share parental responsibility during the mother's life-time from the private appointment of a guardian to take a parent's place after his death. The effect upon the person appointed is the same, in that he acquires full parental responsibility, but the effect upon the appointer is quite different, in that she loses sole control over certain decisions. Given the serious concern about the pressures to which mothers may be subject, which was expressed at the time of our first Report on Illegitimacy, it is appropriate for the machinery for such sharing appointments to be different from, and more formal and deliberate than, the machinery for appointment of a guardian. However, although it is hoped that more and more unmarried parents will agree to share parental responsibility, there may still be cases in which they would prefer the mother to have sole responsibility during her life-time but for the father to assume it in the event of her death. It should therefore remain possible for the mother to appoint him guardian. . . .

If the parents have not agreed or been ordered to share parental responsibility, the question is still what view the courts will take of the best interests of the child when the father applies for contact, residence or to oppose an adoption. Where the dispute is between a mother and father who have lived together with their child, the reported cases suggest that the court should not distinguish between married and unmarried parents (see, e.g., *B v T (custody)* [1990] FCR 31, [1989] 2 FLR 31; *Re K (a minor) (custody)* [1990] 3 All ER 795, [1990] 2 FLR 64, see also p. 630, below). We have no means of knowing how representative this is of actual practice. Where mother and father have not lived together, however, the issues are rather more complex.

S v O (illegitimate child: access)
(1977) 3 FLR 15, 8 Fam Law 11, High Court, Family Division

The mother and father, then both in their teens, had an association which lasted some time. Their son was born in January 1976. Before and up to the birth, the mother was in a home, and after the birth the child was fostered for a short while. The father had only seen his son three times, and explained this by the rows which had accompanied his break-up with the mother. In March 1977, he applied to a magistrates' court for access and this was granted. The mother appealed.

Baker P: . . . It is not unusual for illegitimate mothers, when they have had a row, or rows, with the father and the association has broken up, to try to keep the father out of the child's life. The matter was not debated in the course of the case but it is worth remembering that so often in these cases, if there is no access, either because of an order or because the [father] has not, for some reason or other, availed himself of the possibility of seeing the child, and after a year or two the mother marries or forms a permanent association, questions of adoption arise. If she does marry, and an adoption application is made, the natural biological father is in a hopeless position because the mother is able to say: 'Well, he has not seen the child for so many years, and has not done anything about trying to develop, or even keep, a relationship.' It may be that this mother has not thought as far ahead, but the fact is that this is a little boy who has no father-figure at the present time and the question that the magistrates I think had to ask themselves — and did ask themselves — was: 'Is it for the boy's welfare, is it in his interests, that the natural biological father should be seeing the child?' — in other words that he should have a father or father-figure, there being no other.

The way the magistrates dealt with this in their reasons is as follows, and I shall quote various passages.

'The father' [they said] 'desired to bring a father's influence into the child's life; the mother, to close an unhappy chapter and to make a new life for the child. Had the child been legitimate then there could have been little dispute as to the father's rights. Because he was not so, the father's rights were virtually non-existent. Such rights as he had were to be looked at in the light of the child's welfare. Basing our decision on that approach we concluded that access was in the child's interest and we granted the order.'

They could, of course, have expanded the law on this matter, but basically I think they were absolutely right to look at the question in the light of the child's welfare. They found, in particular, that the father wished to get to know his son and to do all that he could for him. Their conclusion was that it was in the child's interest to know his father. . . .

As has been said many times in this court, and in a decision by a full Divisional Court of this Division, *M v M (child: access)* [1973] 2 All ER 81 [see p. 523, below], access is a right of the child. In that case it was held that no court should deprive a child of access [to] either parent unless it was wholly satisfied that it was in the interests of the child that access should cease, and that was a conclusion at which the court should be extremely slow to arrive.

I, for my part, take the view that that applies equally to illegitimate parents. Children, whether born in wedlock or not, need fathers. If there is a father then he should have the opportunity of developing the relationship. Nothing that has been said in this case and nothing in the evidence satisfies me that there would be any detrimental effect upon this child, either at present or necessarily in future if access is given.

The magistrates went on to say, having dealt with the concepts which have changed:

'When there is a father who is willing and able to act as such within the limits of an illegitimate relationship, and at the same time that father gives evidence of being responsible and conscientious within the moral code that governs both parents, then we do not think the child should be robbed of that influence. Accordingly, being each of us agreed on this decision, we granted a right of reasonable access.'

In the end, of course, this was a decision in the discretion of the magistrates. Have they wrongfully exercised this discretion? Did they act contrary to the law in coming to the conclusion that they did? I think the exercise of their discretion cannot possibly be faulted. . . .

This does not of course mean that every application will succeed: see *M v J (illegitimate child: access)* (1977) 3 FLR 19 and *B v A (illegitimate children: access)* (1981) 3 FLR 27.

Questions

(i) Would your decision in this case have been different, (a) on the facts as they were, or (b) if the mother had married another man during 1976?

(ii) Suppose that the father sees his child for three or four years and then the mother marries: what do you think should happen then?

(iii) Do you think that, if the father has been granted a contact order, his agreement to the child's adoption should be necessary unless it can be dispensed with?

In their original Report on *Illegitimacy* (1982), the Law Commission thought that it should; but in their *Second Report* (1986), they argued thus:

3.4 The Report Bill provided that the father's agreement to the child's adoption or freeing for adoption would be required, not only where he had full parental status or, as at present, custody by court order but also where he had a right of access only. Furthermore, before freeing the child for adoption, a court would have to be satisfied that the father did not intend to apply for any of these orders or that if he did so apply the application would be likely to be refused. Our earlier Report recognised that the arguments for and against including a mere right of access were finely balanced. On the one hand, 'such an order clearly suggests that the court believed that a link between father and child should be recognised and fostered'. On the other hand, a father with access can be heard on the merits of the adoption order in any event. A court which considers that it is in the best interests of the child for the father to continue to have the right of access can always refuse the order, whereas if his agreement is required that agreement may only be dispensed with in defined and limited circumstances in which the interests of the child are not the first and paramount consideration. We now consider that a right to access, which may be very limited and may or may not be being exercised, is too flimsy a basis on which to give the father rights which may not be in the best interests of the child. This argument applies with even more force where the court is contemplating freeing the child for adoption before the father has made any application to the court at all.

This last comment refers to the requirement (see Adoption Act 1976, s. 18(7)) that before freeing a child for adoption, the court must be satisfied that the father does not intend to apply for parental responsibility, or that if he did so, he would be likely to fail. But if a father without custody or full parental status objects to the child's adoption, how likely is he to succeed? Once upon a time, his chances were slim:

Re E (P) (an infant)
[1969] 1 All ER 323, [1968] 1 WLR 1913, 133 JP 137, 112 Sol Jo 821, Court of Appeal

A boy was born to unmarried parents in October 1965. In February 1966 the justices awarded the father access for two hours a week and made an affiliation order. The mother refused to marry the father and married another man in August 1967. In 1968 she and her husband applied to adopt. The father applied for custody in order to oppose the adoption and retain access. The adoption was granted and the father appealed.

Harman LJ: . . . The objection is a curious one. It is not because of the unsuitability of the adoption in itself; it is because the father wishes to maintain his connection with the child. He says that it is better for the child that it should remain under the stigma of bastardy because there will be compensations in the fact that he will keep in touch and will, as he says, later on send the boy to a grammar school if he is bright enough. The mother not unnaturally objects.

She says — or it is said on her behalf; she is still an infant[3] and represented by her husband — that this child is being brought up in the house as one of the family and his position ought to be regularised as soon as possible, and that the best thing for him is to make a clean cut; and the judge has so found.

I for my part do not feel any hesitation in saying that I think that the judge was right. It is quite true that the father has shown himself a devoted father — so far as he can; two hours a week — and wishes to maintain himself in the picture. But I cannot think that in so doing he is considering the real advantages of the child. What he is doing is to forward his own pleasure. He has the pleasure at present of paternity without the trouble of bringing the child up. Two hours a week on Sunday morning is an agreeable interlude in his life, and that he wishes should continue. It does not seem to him to matter that the child will remain a bastard. The effect of the Adoption Act 1958, is to remove that stigma, so far as it can be removed, and to give children in that unfortunate position a fresh start in life without the slur attaching to their origin. I cannot help thinking that so solid an advantage certainly ought not to be thrown away in order that the father may have the pleasure of seeing the child and dandling him on his knee two hours a week on Sunday morning before he goes off to play football.

It is said that the judge paid insufficient attention to the evidence of a psychiatrist. I wish to say as little as I can about that. The psychiatrist, as usual, only saw one side; he never saw the mother or her husband, and he, as he says, 'acted on his brief'. I cannot think that his opinions, under those circumstances, ought to have weighed very heavily with the judge — indeed, I think they did not — and I for one endorse that point of view. This is a question of fact — what is the best for the child? It is best for the child that he should be adopted and become so far as possible a respectable member of society, and I would, therefore, dismiss both appeals, for if the adoption is made, the question of custody or access for the father must fail with it because he will necessarily lose any standing in the matter whatever and the child will, as in all adoption cases, be deprived of his real father. Counsel for the father says that that is very shocking; but it is the inevitable result of all adoptions. I for one think that the advantages much outweigh any disadvantages that there may be, and I would, therefore, dismiss these appeals.

Questions

(i) Has the 'stigma of bastardy' now been removed?
(ii) In Chapter 12, we shall look at the arguments for and against adoption by step-parents after divorce: are they any different in a case such as this?
(iii) In Chapter 14, we shall look at the differences between adoption and residence orders: would residence or a modified form of adoption be better for the child in a case such as this?

Re J (a minor) (adoption order: conditions)
[1973] Fam 106, [1973] 2 All ER 410, [1973] 2 WLR 782, 117 Sol Jo 372, High Court, Family Division

An adoption application by the mother and step-father of a boy of six was countered by a wardship application by his natural father, who sought reasonable access. The case was eventually compromised on the following terms:

'It is in pursuance of the said Act ordered that the applicant be authorised to adopt the said minor upon the conditions set out in the Second Schedule hereto.'
Schedule 2 reads as follows:
'1. The Official Solicitor may at his sole and absolute discretion (a) arrange visits from time to time to be made by a member of his staff or other suitable person to the home

---

3. She was about 20: this was before the age of majority was reduced from 21 to 18 by the Family Law Reform Act 1969.

or school of the minor; (*b*) give such information as he thinks fit concerning the health, education and welfare of the minor to his natural father; (*c*) supervise any future access by the minor to his natural father.

'2. The adopters and the survivor of them shall consult and pay due regard to the advice of the Official Solicitor as to (*a*) the future education of the minor; (*b*) the nature and extent of any communication between the minor and his natural father; (*c*) the resumption and continuance of access by the natural father to the minor.'

In approving this settlement, Rees J rehearsed the arguments on each side:

The case on behalf of the father was . . . [that] because of his racial characteristics which J shares he has a special contribution to make in the future upbringing of J. The father puts himself forward as a devoted and loving parent who has established a lasting relationship with J during the three years before the separation and the contact with him since. Some evidence of his interest in the boy is that the father had made J a devisee by his will of a large house and land in the country and a beneficiary under a substantial discretionary trust. In all these respects J has been treated on a basis of equality with the father's legitimate children. . . . Several witnesses deposed to the father's devotion to J and to his suitability to maintain contact with him.

The case for the adopters is that continued contact between J and his father is not in the best interests of J for two main reasons. The first is that the father's mode of life and moral character render him wholly unfit to have contact with, and to exercise influence over, J. . . . It is also alleged against the father that he is a ruthless and dominating person and that these characteristics tell against contact with a very young child. The second reason advanced on behalf of the adopters is that the evidence in their possession establishes that J was seriously and adversely affected by the access to his father . . . This evidence asserts that J showed a number of signs of stress immediately following each period of access followed by more or less lasting symptoms of insecurity and tension. . . .

As I have indicated, no criticism of any kind has been made of the adopters in relation to their capacity as parents or of their affection or ability to provide an excellent home, education and guidance for J. There can be no doubt but that the mother's husband is willing and able to provide for all the needs of J, financially and otherwise, as if he were his natural son. . . .

In summary form, . . . the Official Solicitor . . . was of opinion that an adoption order would be in the best interests of J. In reaching that conclusion he took full account of the difficulties involved in an adoption order in the present case where the child has a firm recollection of his natural father which will never be erased from his mind, especially where there has been regular contact between the child and the natural father until the child was almost five years of age. He was also of opinion that some suitable arrangements should be made so that contact can be re-established between J and his natural father when J has developed a sufficient degree of maturity to make that course desirable in his best interests. The Official Solicitor relies on the opinion of the consultant physician appointed by the court that this stage might be reached in about five or six years from now when J becomes 11 or 12 years of age. The Official Solicitor recognises the manifold difficulties which arise in a case wherein it is contemplated, notwithstanding that an adoption order is made, that at some time in the future it may be in the best interests of the child that contact with his known natural father should be resumed.

After reviewing the adoption legislation and the authorities, including *Re B (MF) (an infant)* [1972] 1 All ER 898, [1972] 1 WLR 102 (p. 652, below), the judge concluded:

The conclusion which I draw from the terms of the 1958 Act and from the authority cited above is that the general rule which forbids contact between an adopted child and his natural parents may be disregarded in an exceptional case where a court is satisfied that by so doing the welfare of the child may be best promoted. I have no doubt that the instant case is an exceptional one and also that there are very strong grounds existing at present to support the view that at the right time and in the right manner contact between J and his father is likely to be for J's real and lasting benefit.

Questions

(i) Which circumstances do you think exceptional (*a*) that the father was very rich; (*b*) that the father was Jewish and wanted to ensure that his son was provided with a barmitzvah ceremony when he was 13; or (*c*) that the father had established a relationship which he was genuinely anxious to maintain in some way?

(ii) Would the decision have been the same if the child had been a girl?

(iii) If this case suggests an acceptable compromise between the child's 'right to know' his origins and the advantages of adoption, is there any reason to reserve it for 'exceptional' cases?

(iv) How many of the arguments in favour of continued contact in this case would have applied with equal force had the child been placed for adoption with strangers?

Although the court has power to make continued contact a condition of an adoption order (or to make a contact order after an adoption), only in exceptional cases will this be done if the adoptive parents disagree (see *Re C (a minor) (adoption: conditions)* [1989] AC 1, [1988] 1 All ER 705, HL, p. 653, below). But what if the mother wants the child adopted and the father wants to offer him a home? The case below caused a great stir at the time.

Re C (MA) (an infant)
[1966] 1 All ER 838, [1966] 1 WLR 646, 130 JP 217, 110 Sol Jo 309, 64 LGR 280, Court of Appeal

A son was born in July 1964 to a 23-year-old mother and a 47-year-old father. While pregnant the mother decided not to marry the father. When the child was two months old, he was placed with prospective adopters, where he remained. The father became reconciled with his wife and they wished to bring up the boy together. The mother, however, denied the father all contact with the child. Adoption proceedings were begun in a county court. The father applied to the High Court for custody. The county court proceedings were then stayed and the adopters applied to the High Court. Both applications came before Ungoed-Thomas J in December 1965, when the child was 17 months old. The judge awarded custody to the father and the adopters appealed.

Russell LJ: . . . It is, I think, plain that in weighing up the pro's and contra's the judge did attach a great deal of weight to the personality and character of the father's wife, and to the importance of the natural link with the father in the circumstances of this case. I say this because numerically there are several other matters weighing the scales in favour of leaving the boy where he is. I instance the risk point; the relative ages of the proposed adopters and of the father and his wife; the probability of a youthful brother or sister for the boy (by adoption if not by natural birth) if he stays where he is; the stability prognosis of the two marriages, as to which I will say something later; the mother's wish that the boy should be brought up in the Roman Catholic faith; the possibility, if adopted, that the boy will never realise his illegitimacy, and the certainty that with the father he must do so at some time. I am not, however, persuaded that, regarding the welfare of the infant as the paramount consideration, the judge has in weighing all these matters decided wrongly. I myself do attach great weight to the blood tie. If a father (as distinct from a stranger in blood) can bring up his own son as his own son, so much the better for both of them, whether or not by the accident of events the legitimate relationship exists. (Here indeed there was an accident of events, for the child was conceived with the intention of marriage with the mother, and only the mother's change of heart or conscience prevented the link being legitimate.) As to knowledge of his illegitimacy, the circumstances which reveal that will reveal also the determination of his father to be his father; the determination that he should not be a boy with an unknown and perhaps abandoning father, which is a factor which can have bad effects on an adopted child, though usually only if the adoption has not been a success. In this connexion it was also argued that he would find out that his mother was prepared to abandon him to strangers; but this may be softened by telling him the reasons which she herself gives, that she thought it better for him that he should be brought up by two people than by one.

On the question of the prognosis of the stability of the two marriages, that of the proposed adopters is undoubtedly very good, for reasons which I need not set out. It is said that the prognosis for the stability of the father's marriage is not good having regard to his matrimonial history, and that a risk of breakdown, with ill-effects to the child, exists. In making that prognosis, however, it is of the first importance to consider the circumstances in which the father's marriage has been reconstituted. When I consider the single-mindedness with which the father has pursued the aim of securing to himself (with the aid of his wife) the upbringing of his son, and the impact made on the judge by the personality of the wife, the conclusion that I reach is that if the child is given to the custody of the father, that will act as a cement to the marriage which at least over-sets a prognosis founded on the father's matrimonial history. The situation is wholly different from that which those who are experienced in adoptions view with misgiving, namely, when two spouses hope by adoption of a stranger child to patch up a crumbling marriage. I would weigh this point of relative stability of marriage very lightly in the scales.

Harman LJ took it for granted that a natural father and step-mother, even if illegitimate, were preferable to adoptive parents (compare his views in *Re E (P) (An Infant)* [1969] 1 All ER 323, [1968] 1 WLR 1913, p. 483, above), although he did express some doubt about the passage of time. Willmer LJ, however, dissented, partly because of the age of the father and his wife and of his doubts about the stability of their marriage, but mainly because his interpretation of the medical evidence was that the risks of uprooting the child from the prospective adopters were far greater than the 'rather shadowy and conjectural advantages possibly to be derived from being brought up by his natural father and his exceedingly competent wife.' The medical evidence on the comparative value of the 'blood tie' as against the risks of disturbing the status quo was thus of vital importance. The fullest account of that evidence appears in the judgment of Russell LJ:

The written statement of Dr Soddy I divide into seven aspects. (i) The established relationship with the adopting mother is good, and the parental care excellent. (ii) The boy is perfectly normal. (iii) As a general proposition a change of mother after the age of six months is attended by a risk of lasting adverse effects, even if the substituted or second mother's care is adequate; this risk progressively increases when the change happens after six months, with a high level between twelve and thirty months, when the risk level begins to decline. (iv) (I read this as an aspect of adverse effect) Change between nine and eighteen months is attended with a particularly serious risk of long or even permanent impairment of the child's capacity to form relationships. (v) There is the additional danger that the disturbance in any particular case caused by the change may lead to demonstrations of rejection of the second mother, and the latter, unless unusually patient and loving may react to such demonstrations, leading to a vicious circle. (vi) The proposed second mother (the father's wife) may be to some extent not best situated to cope with the situation and to offset the risk, owing to her age, to the many years since she mothered a small child, and to the fact that, not being the natural mother, she can have no instinctual pull towards the child. (vii) A change would be to take an unjustifiable risk with the child's future.

Dr Soddy's oral evidence is at some points confusing, partly I think because of technical misunderstandings in question and answer. There was much discussion about instinctual ties, and it was submitted for the appellants that Dr Soddy did not give any evidence that the fact that a man is the biological or natural parent is to be expected to contribute something to the welfare and personality of a child brought up by him as his child which is not to be expected of a man who is not the biological or natural parent. I cannot agree. It is quite clear that the instinctual tie, to which reference was so freely made, is the pull which draws the actual parent to the child because it is known by him to be the child of the parent's body, and if it was irrelevant to the welfare of the child brought up by the natural parent I cannot imagine why it was ever brought in. At one point Dr Soddy's evidence was this:

'Q. – Do you attach any importance to the instinctual relationship, to the relationship between the child and the biological father? A. – Yes, indeed. Q. – And that, of course, is a crucial matter in this case? A. – Yes.'

He then said that the instinctual relationship between biological father and child became 'distinctly important' (which must mean to the child) at about eighteen months. Later on there is confusion between question and answer, to which my lord has already referred, which I think is cleared up shortly afterwards. The confusion is caused by a failure to appreciate that an infant has no instinctual tie or pull towards his parent; that tie or pull derives from communication. At this point appears the following statement by Dr Soddy:

'Unless there is communication between the two (i.e. the natural mother and child) the mother's instinctive factor can have no effect on the child.'

This indicates that the special instinctive factor of a natural mother *has* an effect on the child, if there is communication. This is made clear in the succeeding questions and answers:

'Q. – But assuming access in the case of the non-biological mother and the biological mother, would the instinctive one-way working of the biological relationship from the mother to the child (but not, as you said, vice versa), affect the upbringing or development of the child? Is that an important factor in the development of the child? A. – It is an important factor provided it is there at certain key periods. Q. – Which are they? A. – This is the nub of the whole issue. As far as the mother is concerned it is the period before six months which is vital, which is important in terms of instinct. As far as the father is concerned it does not seem to be. We might put it up a year. Q. – From a year? A. – To about eighteen months. We might raise the age to around eighteen months. Q. – From a year to eighteen months? A. – From eighteen months, around eighteen months. Q. – To when, in the case of a boy? A. – To two and a half or three.'

In the light of that expert evidence I think that it must be said that the boy in this case will lose an important factor in the development of his personality if he is not brought up by his natural father.

I turn next to the ultimate scope of Dr Soddy's evidence on the risk to the child's personality of a change from the proposed adopters to the father and his wife. He perfectly correctly agreed that for the full assessment of this risk in the particular case his data were incomplete, since he had no knowledge, on which he could place reliance, of the father and the wife; though, as indicated above, he attached importance to the instinctual tie of the natural father to the child. The quantitive degree of risk cannot be estimated by psychiatrists, because there are no means of telling how many cases there are in which a child has survived a crucial change of mothering without lasting adverse effects; such cases would naturally not come to the notice of the experts, and there is no occasion to study their case histories; their number is wholly unknown. He agreed that in cases of disturbed personality (I hope that that is not a misused technical phrase) a change of mother, if it has occurred, may be only one of the contributing factors. This I take to mean that in observed cases of disturbed personality the change of mother might not have had any lasting adverse effect but for its combination with other predisposing factors. Here Dr Soddy's evidence is that there does not appear to be any other observable predisposing factor, for he says that the boy is a perfectly normal child. In relation to the assessment of the risk, Dr Soddy accepted that the temperament and character of the transferee mother (here the father's wife) were 'crucial', were 'extremely relevant to the decision to be made about this child', and that in assessing the likely effect of a change of mothering to the father's wife her temperament and character were a 'highly relevant factor'. As stated, Dr Soddy had indicated what he considered to be certain prima facie possible disadvantages in the position of the father's wife; and on reading part of her evidence he speculated whether she had not an underlying motive in her desire to mother her husband's bastard, I think that of gratitude to him for the past and anxiety to reconstitute the marriage; but he said that he did not care to base any judgment on that foundation. Finally under this head Dr Soddy was asked, in connexion with the character of the father's wife and her situation:

'Q. – Would they reduce the effect of the risk of which you have spoken? A. – Under certain circumstances, yes. Q. – Would you expect them to be capable of completely nullifying effects? A. – It is a speculative question. I should doubt it, but I can only answer speculatively.'

And generally speaking on the question of risk, Dr Soddy said:

'There is an element of risk that depends on the combination of the particular circumstances in the case.'

Questions

(i) Is the risk one which you would have taken in this case?

(ii) Does this case strike you as: (*a*) an undesirable resurrection of old-fashioned ideas about the ties of blood; (*b*) a pioneering recognition of the claims of unmarried fathers; or (*c*) a straightforward application of the principle that the welfare of the child is the first and paramount consideration in any proceedings in which his upbringing is in issue?

6 What is a parent?

As a result of their provisional recommendation that illegitimacy be abolished and automatic parental status be conferred upon all fathers, the Law Commission in their Working Paper (1979) were obliged to consider the position of children born as a result of artificial insemination using sperm from a donor other than the mother's husband:

10.8 On one view, there is no need to make any special provision to deal with A.I.D. conceptions: the fact that an anonymous and untraceable donor would, in consequence of the proposed change in the law, have 'rights' which he would never be able to enforce does not (it may be said) justify interfering with the law, since this gives rise to no difficulty in practice. However, we do not find this argument convincing. Couples should not be put into a position, as they now are, where they are strongly tempted (and perhaps even advised) to make a false declaration on registering the birth; it brings the law into disrepute if it is believed that it can safely be defied. . . .

10.9 The policy of the legislation, we are at present inclined to think, should therefore be that where a married woman has received A.I.D. treatment with her husband's consent, the husband rather than the donor should, for all legal purposes, be regarded as the father of a child conceived as the result. . . .

10.11 The simplest way of implementing the policy which we have suggested would be a statutory provision deeming the husband to be the father of an A.I.D. child born to his wife; the only ground on which the husband could challenge the operation of this deeming provision would be that he had not consented to his wife receiving A.I.D. treatment. This approach seems to us to have the merit not only of simplicity, but also of giving effect to the likely feelings and wishes of the wife and husband. We note that statutory provision of the type we envisage has been made in several States of the USA. . . .

10.17 Although there are many advantages to such a statutory deeming provision, there are two main objections to it. The first involves a major point of policy: it could be said that the proposal involves a deliberate falsification of the birth register. The second objection is more theoretical: that the proposal would involve a transfer of legal rights from the donor to the husband, and that the law should accurately mirror that transfer.

A comment upon the first objection may be taken from a Ciba Foundation Symposium on the *Law and Ethics of A.I.D. and Embryo Transfer* (1973):

McLaren [geneticist]: Even though the genetic register which Canon Dunstan proposed might not be very useful, through being erroneous (owing to the possibility that occasionally the supposedly infertile husband fertilizes the egg), our present registry system is itself erroneous in all those cases where the husband is not actually the father of the child. Are there any statistics on how common this is? This is probably more frequent than the cases where a supposedly infertile husband was really the father of an A.I.D. child.

Philipp [consultant obstetrician and gynaecologist]: We blood-tested some patients in a town in south-east England, and found that 30% of the husbands could not have been the fathers of their children . . .

JH Edwards [geneticist]: . . . Analysis of some blood group data, making allowance for the fact that one could not detect all the illegitimacies, showed that in the 1950s in the West Isleworth area about 50% of premarital conceptions were not fathered by the apparent father. As the apparent fathers were questioned while visiting their wives immediately after the birth, most of them obviously thought they were the father. I think the group Mr Philipp referred to is also highly biased. In spite of much talk about artificial insemination by donor and all the difficulties with genetics and so on, natural insemination by donor is practised on quite a substantial scale on an amateur basis.

The Commission therefore recommended that the mother's husband be treated for all purposes as if he were the child's father, unless it was proved that he had not consented to the insemination. This was implemented by s. 27 of the Family Law Reform Act 1987. Meanwhile, however, the Government had set up the Warnock Committee of Inquiry into Human Fertilisation and Embryology. This dealt with other techniques for counteracting infertility, which are usefully summarised in the DHSS Consultation Paper on *Legislation on Human Infertility Services and Embryo Research* (1986):

In vitro fertilisation
8. This technique is used mainly where a woman has no fallopian tubes or they are blocked. Currently about 1,000 births in the UK are thought to have involved IVF. It has also been used in dealing with some types of male infertility and where the cause of infertility is unknown. A ripe egg is taken from the woman's ovary shortly before it would have been released naturally. It is then mixed with sperm in a dish (in vitro) so that fertilisation can occur. Once the fertilised egg has started to develop it is transferred back to the woman's womb. If a pregnancy is to be established the embryo must then implant in the womb.
9. IVF although simple in concept is not an easy technique in practice. To increase the chances of success (currently the success rate is thought to be of the order of 15 per cent) it is usual to create and transfer to a woman more than one embryo. Several eggs are thus required. To obtain these eggs the woman is given superovulatory drugs which ensure that a number of eggs is produced in one menstrual cycle and these are available for fertilisation.
10. Fertilisation of these eggs may result in more embryos than it is appropriate to transfer to the woman's womb. These embryos can then be preserved by freezing for later transfer to the womb or scientific use or they may be left to perish. At present it is not possible for embryos to grow outside a woman's body for longer than 9–10 days.

Egg donation
11. The IVF technique allows a pregnancy to be achieved where the woman cannot produce an egg. An egg by another woman is fertilised with the husband's sperm in vitro and the resulting embryo is then transferred to the infertile woman. One case involving sisters was reported in this country in 1985.

Embryo donation
12. In this case donated eggs and sperm would be used to create an embryo for transfer to the infertile woman. The technique could apply where both partners are infertile. Embryo donation is thought not yet to have been used in the UK.

Surrogacy
13. This practice involves one woman carrying a child for another with the intention that the child be handed over after birth. Surrogacy can make it possible for a woman to obtain a child in cases where she cannot carry the pregnancy at all, or for long enough for the fetus to be capable of being born alive. Artificial insemination of the surrogate mother by sperm of the commissioning mother's husband makes it possible for that child to be conceived without the need for sexual intercourse. However, by means of IVF it may be possible in some instances for the commissioning mother's eggs to be used.

As the Warnock Committee pointed out in their *Report* (1984):

6.8. Egg donation produces for the first time circumstances in which the genetic mother (the woman who donates the egg), is a different person from the woman who gives birth to the child, the carrying mother. The law has never, till now, had to face this problem. There are inevitably going to be instances where the stark issue arises of who is the mother. In order to achieve some certainty in this situation it is our view that where a woman donates an egg for transfer to another the donation should be treated as absolute and that, like a male donor she should have no rights or duties with regard to any resulting child.

The policy in s. 27 of the 1987 Act has therefore been taken several stages further in the *Human Fertilisation and Embryology Act 1990*:

27.—(1) The woman who is carrying or has carried a child as a result of the placing in her of an embryo or of sperm and eggs, and no other woman, is to be treated as the mother of the child.

. . .

28.—(1) This section applies in the case of a child who is being or has been carried by a woman as a result of the placing in her of an embryo or of sperm and eggs or her artificial insemination.

(2) If—

(a) at the time of the placing in her of the embryo or the sperm and eggs or of her insemination, the woman was a party to a marriage, and

(b) the creation of the embryo carried by her was not brought about with the sperm of the other party to the marriage,

then, subject to subsection (5) below, the other party to the marriage shall be treated as the father of the child unless it is shown that he did not consent to the placing in her of the embryo or the sperm and eggs or to her insemination (as the case may be).

(3) If no man is treated, by virtue of subsection (2) above, as the father of the child but—

(a) the embryo or the sperm and eggs were placed in the woman, or she was artificially inseminated, in the course of treatment services provided for her and a man together by a person to whom a licence applies, and

(b) the creation of the embryo carried by her was not brought about with the sperm of that man,

then, subject to subsection (5) below, that man shall be treated as the father of the child.

(4) Where a person is treated as the father of the child by virtue of subsection (2) or (3) above, no other person is to be treated as the father of the child.

(5) Subsections (2) and (3) above do not apply—

(a) in relation to England and Wales and Northern Ireland, to any child who, by virtue of the rules of common law, is treated as the legitimate child of the parties to a marriage,

. . .

(6) Where—

(a) the sperm of a man who had given such consent as is required by paragraph 5 of Schedule 3 of this Act was used for a purpose for which such consent was required, or

(b) the sperm of a man, or any embryo the creation of which was brought about with his sperm, was used after his death,

he is not to be treated as the father of the child.

(7) The references in subsection (2) above to the parties to a marriage at the time there referred to—

(a) are to the parties to a marriage subsisting at that time, unless a judicial separation was then in force, but

(b) include the parties to a void marriage if either or both of them reasonably believed at that time that the marriage was valid; and for the purposes of this subsection it shall be presumed, unless the contrary is shown, that one of them reasonably believed at that time that the marriage was valid.

. . .

29.—(1) Where by virtue of section 27 or 28 of this Act a person is to be treated as the mother or father of a child, that person is to be treated in law as the mother or, as the case may be, father of the child for all purposes.

(2) Where by virtue of section 27 or 28 of this Act a person is not to be treated as the mother or father of the child, that person is to be treated in law as not being the mother or, as the case may be, father of the child for any purpose.

(3) Where subsection (1) or (2) above has effect, references to any relationship between two people in any enactment, deed or other instrument or document (whenever passed or made) are to be read accordingly.

(4) In relation to England and Wales and Northern Ireland, nothing in the provisions of section 27(1) or 28(2) to (4), read with this section, affects —

(a) the succession to any dignity or title of honour or renders any person capable of succeeding to or transmitting a right to succeed to any such dignity or title, or

(b) the devolution of any property limited (expressly or not) to devolve (as nearly as the law permits) along with any dignity or title of honour.

Questions

(i) How many arguments can you think of for making (a) the carrying mother, or (b) the genetic mother the mother in law?

(ii) Are the arguments for recognising 'social' rather than 'genetic' fatherhood stronger or weaker?

(iii) Does the widespread availability of donor insemination, whether by artificial or more conventional methods, on a 'do-it-yourself' basis, affect matters?

(iv) Why should not the same provisions apply when a husband accepts his wife's naturally born child by another man?

(v) Is it right to extend 'social' fatherhood beyond marital relationships?

(vi) What if the husband or partner consented to *in vitro* fertilisation of the woman's egg by a donor's sperm and the resulting embryo was frozen for some years before implantation? Should he be able to change his mind?

(vii) As donors can never be fathers, what do you think of the re-introduction of a class of children who are inevitably 'fatherless by law'?

(viii) Do you think that all this is, or is not, in the best interests of the children?

The Law Commission (1982) also considered a further problem raised by their basic approach:

10.25 A problem which would arise whichever method were used for dealing with A.I.D. is whether or not legal provision should be made so that the child would be entitled to ascertain the facts about his parentage. Under the present law and practice the truth about the child's genetic identity may well be concealed from him if he has been registered as the legitimate child of the mother and her husband; in any event it is up to his mother and her husband to decide whether or not to disclose the fact that he is an A.I.D. child. Even if they do decide to tell him what they know, they will not usually be able to tell him who the donor was.

10.26 The argument in favour of a procedure giving the child the right to know the facts about his conception is essentially that a person has the right to know the truth about his origins. This principle is now accepted in adoption law, and an adopted child is entitled to discover the recorded facts about his natural parentage on attaining his majority. It therefore seems logical that an A.I.D. child should have the same right. On the other hand, if the only fact which the child is able to discover is that he is not genetically the offspring of his mother's husband, but of a donor wholly unknown not only to him but to his mother and her husband, it is difficult to see that this would be of any real advantage to him. To go further, by giving the child the right to know the identity of the donor would involve a major, and probably unacceptable, change of policy and practice.

The Warnock Committee's *Report* (1984) took much the same view:

4.19 It is the practice of some clinics in the USA to provide detailed descriptions of donors, and to permit couples to exercise choice as to the donor they would prefer. In the evidence there was some support for the use of such descriptions. It is argued that they would provide information and reassurance for the parents and, at a later date, for the child. They might also be of benefit to the donor, as an indication that he is valued for his own sake. A detailed description also offers some choice to the woman who is to have the child, and lack of such choice can be said to diminish the importance of the woman's right to choose the father of her child.

4.20 The contrary view, also expressed in the evidence, is that detailed donor profiles would introduce the donor as a person in his own right. It is also argued that the use of profiles devalues the child who may seem to be wanted only if certain specifications are met, and this may become a source of disappointment to the parents if their expectations are unfulfilled.

4.21 As a matter of principle we do not wish to encourage the possibility of prospective parents seeking donors with specific characteristics by the use of whose semen they hope to give birth to a particular type of child. We do not therefore want detailed descriptions of donors to be used as a basis for choice, but we believe that the couple should be given sufficient relevant information for their reassurance. This should include some basic facts about the donor, such as his ethnic group and his genetic birth. A small minority of the Inquiry, while supporting the principle set out above, and without compromising the principle of anonymity, consider that a gradual move towards making more detailed descriptions of the donor available to prospective parents, if requested, could be beneficial to the practice of AID, provided this was accompanied by appropriate counselling. **We recommend that on reaching the age of eighteen the child should have access to the basic information about the donor's ethnic origin and genetic health and that legislation be enacted to provide the right of access to this.** This legislation should not be retrospective.

4.22 We were agreed that there is a need to maintain the absolute anonymity of the donor, though we recognise that in privately arranged donation, for example between brothers, a different situation would of course apply; such domestic arrangements, however, fall outside any general regulation. Anonymity would give legal protection to the donor but it would also have the effect of minimising the invasion of the third party into the family. Without anonymity, men would, it is argued, be less likely to become donors . . . We recognise that one consequence of this provision would be that AID children, even if informed about the circumstances of their conception would never be entitled to know the identity of their genetic fathers.

The contrary point of view is succinctly put by Eric Blyth in his article, *Assisted reproduction: what's in it for the children?* (1990):

However, available evidence serves to undermine justification of both donor anonymity and secrecy. Research conducted in Sweden (Sverne, 1986), Australia (Daniels, 1989) and New Zealand (Daniels, 1987) indicates that sperm donors would be prepared to continue to donate in the absence of anonymity. A report prepared for the European Commission (Glover, 1989) recommends the removal, for an evaluated trial period, of donor anonymity.

Empirical evidence concerning AR families is restricted to those brought about following DI, but this clearly reveals both the disadvantages of maintaining secrecy and the benefits of openness. Secrecy, it appears, can only be sustained at high psychological cost to the parent(s). It deprives them of social support, whilst inadvertent disclosure remains a potentially lifelong fear. Children who found out about their genetic origins by less than direct means often expressed bitterness about their experiences (Snowden and Snowden, 1984).

Conversely, children whose parents had been open with them valued their parents' honesty, experienced few emotional consequences of being told, and fears about the specific effect of openness on the father-child relationship were not substantiated. Parents who were open felt that they no longer had to carry the burden and guilt of secrecy and were able to obtain support from others (Snowden and Snowden, 1984). The task of telling children at an early age about the nature of their conception could be considerably lightened by the development of story books similar to those currently available for adopted children.

The positive experiences of 'open' AR families are supported by the experience of both traditional adoption (McWhinnie, 1984) and more recent practices of 'open adoption' where contact between the child and birth-parent(s) is maintained (Fratter, 1989).

Nigel Bruce takes the argument a stage further in a later article, on *The importance of genetic knowledge* (1990):

Adopted young people now have the legal right in Britain, on reaching maturity, to see their original birth certificates. Those conceived by means of DI do not as yet enjoy this legal right. The main purpose of this article is to argue that, at least in the contemporary culture of Western Europe, such young people have strong moral claims to know their genetic identities; and that these moral claims should now be converted to legal rights.

In any civilised moral code, the truth is preferable to deception; without respect for truth, social institutions could not operate. Truth-telling is a basic legal, as well as moral, principle; the courts oblige us to swear or affirm to tell the truth, and they can punish us if we resort to deception.

In any civilised moral code, trustworthiness is more meritorious than unreliability. Sociologists say that society depends upon honesty and trustworthiness if it is to function properly. Psychologists say that trust is a basic component in the social development of the child.

In any civilised moral code, individual members of of society have a *prima facie* right to personal autonomy. They must not be enslaved or imprisoned without trial; they must not be bought or sold; and they have legal rights not to be discriminated against or unjustly treated. In contemporary Western law, this personal autonomy also includes the right to personal information about themselves which may be held on official commercial or welfare files. John Harris (1985, p. 209) discussed personal autonomy in relation to medical ethics in *The Value of Life* and reached the conclusion that 'if one clear principle emerges from this discussion of autonomy, it is that there is an obligation to tell all to those who wish to be told'.

Linked with this claim to autonomy is the need which we all have to possess and develop a personal identity. There are two aspects of the term 'identity': the objective identity perceived by authority, which we possess; and the subjective identity which we develop within our 'selves' and which is the way we perceive and come to terms with our 'selves'.

The United Nations Declaration of the Rights of the Child (1959) referred only to the objective aspect of identity when it declared in Principle 3: 'The child shall be entitled from his birth to a name and a nationality'. The new United Nations Convention on the Rights of the Child (1989) contains a broader concept of identity in Articles 7 and 8. Article 7 requires that:

'. . . the child shall be registered immediately after birth and shall have the right to a name, the right to acquire a nationality, and as far as possible the right to know and be cared for by his or her parents.'

Article 8 requires the States Parties:

'. . . to respect the right of the child to preserve his or her identity, including nationality, name and family relations as recognised by law, without unlawful interference.'

The Convention also contains an Article 13 on freedom of expression and of information, which must surely include the right to obtain medical information about one's conception and birth. Even if the release of such information may be seen as an infringement of the privacy of the adults involved, it is now well established in the law of most developed countries that when there is a conflict between the interests of children and adults, the interests of the children should be paramount. Principle 2 of the UN Declaration of the Rights of the Child states that 'in the enactment of laws for this purpose, the best interests of the child shall be the paramount consideration'. Article 3 of the UN Convention contains the less definitive statement that:

'. . . in all actions concerning children, whether undertaken by public or private social welfare institutions, courts of law, administrative authorities or legislative bodies, the best interests of the child shall be the primary consideration.'

Thus the claim that children should be legally as well as morally entitled to know the facts of their conception and birth rests equally on the argument that it is in their best interests to be treated with honesty and respect and on the relevance of the legal provisions prohibiting traffic in children, protecting their mental health and guaranteeing free access to information.

Questions

(i) Section 31 of the Human Fertilisation and Embryology Act 1990 leaves it to regulations to specify what information about the donor should be given to people born as a result of licensed treatment services (i.e. egg or sperm donation or *in vitro* fertilisation) when they grow up, but insists that information identifying the donor cannot be released unless regulations provided for this at the time of the donation: should such regulations be made now or should they wait until public opinion has developed further? (ii) If they should be made now, should they provide (*a*) for identifying information to be released if the donor consents, or (*b*) for such information to be released even if he or she does not consent, and (c) what other information about the donor should be provided to his or her offspring?

The concern here is with the long-term welfare and interests of a person who has been born as a result of licensed treatment. But what about the welfare of children who *may be* born if treatment is given? Section 13(1) of the 1990 Act provides that it shall be a condition of every licence to provide treatment service under the Act that:

13. — (5) A woman shall not be provided with treatment services unless account has been taken of the welfare of any child who may be born as a result of the treatment (including the need of that child for a father), and of any other child who may be affected by the birth.

The Lord Chancellor explained what this meant to the House of Lords (*Hansard* (H.L.), vol. 516, c.1097) thus:

I think everyone would agree that it is important that children are born into a stable and loving environment and that the family is a concept whose health is fundamental to the health of society in general. A fundamental principle to our law about children, including the legislation which this House considered in such detail last Session and which became the Children Act 1989, is that the welfare of children is of paramount consideration. I think that it is, for these general reasons, entirely right that the Bill should be amended to add that concept. It could be argued that the concept of the welfare of the child is very broad and indeed all-embracing. That I think is inevitable given the very wide range of factors which need to be taken into account when considering the future lives of children who may be born as a result of techniques to be licensed under the Bill. My attention has been drawn to a New Zealand case where Mr. Justice Hardie Boyce dealt with this concept in *Walker v Harrison* [1981] New Zealand Recent Law vol. 257. I think his remarks, which were cited by the Law Commission in a recent working paper on family law, indicate very well the wide range of circumstances and meanings which the concept of welfare involves.
     He said:
     ' "Welfare" is an all-encompassing word. It includes material welfare, both in the sense of an adequacy of resources to provide a pleasant home and a comfortable standard of living and in the sense of an adequacy of care to ensure that good health and due personal pride are maintained. However, while material considerations have their place, they are secondary matters. More important are the stability and the security, the loving and understanding care and guidance, the warm and compassionate relationships, that are essential for the full development of the child's own character, personality and talents'.
The amendment will place on clinicians in statutory form a responsibility which I believe most, if not all, of them already perform. I accept that that is an important responsibility and it may in particular cases be far from easy to discharge.
     Among the factors which clinicians should take into account will be the material circumstances in which the child is likely to be brought up and also the stability and love which he or she is likely to enjoy. Such stability is clearly linked to the marital position of the woman and in particular whether a husband or long-term partner can play a full part in providing the child with a permanent family setting in the fullest sense of that term, including financial provision.
     The House does not need to be reminded of the plight of childless people and the very strong and deeply felt emotions which those in that position experience. We may on the one hand pay the tribute which is due to the importance of ensuring that children are born into the family environment by specifically excluding from treatment women who are not married or have no stable partner to be involved in the decision about treatment and in counselling beforehand, but I wonder what will happen if we do that. Surely there is a risk that such women, driven by the very strong desire for a child, may turn elsewhere for treatment. I am advised that it is a relatively easy matter for AID to be carried out in clinically unsupervised conditions. It may be that the result of the amendment would be to encourage those few single woman who are infertile to seek unsuitable donors if we were to introduce such a restriction. Any children who may be born as a result of uncontrolled treatment are at risk of serious disease, including HIV infection.
     On the other hand, if the law recognises that in a very small number of cases single women will come forward for treatment, it may be better to encourage them to seek clinical advice.

With the child and welfare amendments we have just discussed there is a likelihood that through counselling and discussion with those responsible for licensed treatment they may be dissuaded from having children once they have fully considered the implications of the environment into which their child would be born or its future welfare.

Questions

(i) Blyth (1990) points out that 'the extent to which welfare principles might apply to children in the field of AR is questionable . . . Firstly, it is hardly valid to claim that anyone would have been better off not having been born in the first place. Secondly, the implication that alternatives exist from which a choice may be made does not hold'. Do you agree?

(ii) In *R v Ethical Committee of St Mary's Hospital (Manchester), ex p H* [1988] 1 FLR 512, the hospital's policy of refusing treatment to those who did not satisfy the general criteria of suitability for adoption was not challenged: but might it be a breach of the 'right to marry and found a family', guaranteed by article 12 of the European Convention of Human Rights to deny (*a*) a married, or (*b*) an unmarried couple treatment, using (*a*) their own, or (*b*) donated gametes, on the ground that they might not be able to bring the child up properly?

(iii) Would the same apply to a single, virgin or lesbian woman?

(iv) Does the greater threat of a 'brave new world' come from artificial or assisted reproduction or controlling parenthood?

(v) The Human Fertilisation and Embryology Authority is required to give guidance about the account to be taken of the welfare of children who may be born or affected by treatment in its Code of Practice (s 25(2) of the Human Fertilisation and Embryology Act 1990): try to draft it.

Blyth (1990) also has some interesting observations about controlling access to assisted reproduction which might be applied in a wider context:

. . . the Warnock Committee itself recognised the problems of restricting access to AR services on social grounds and that it would not be possible to 'draw up comprehensive (social) criteria that would be sensitive to the circumstances of every case' (1984). Such reservations are justified given the discriminatory criteria currently employed by some AR practitioners (Snowden and Mitchell, 1981). That intentions to be more open about receipt of AR should be perceived as a potential contra-indication for treatment is an extreme but iniquitous example (Braidwood, 1989: Saunders, 1980).

Although the use of a screening process has been justified by reference to the potential psychopathology of infertile people, recent studies indicate a lack of support for the existence of a psychogenic basis to infertility. Similarly, the extent to which infertility inevitably represents a 'psychic trauma' can be challenged (e.g. Edelmann and Connolly, 1986).

Conventional assumptions about the 'ideal' environment for child-rearing, based on theological doctrine and the stereotype of the contemporary, white, westernised middle class nuclear family, result in the denial of parental aspirations to those who do not conform to the norm. Specifically, the claims to AR services by single women and lesbians are rejected as a 'threat to normal family life' by failing to provide children with a 'nurturing father-figure' (Council for Science and Society, 1984). Similarly the Warnock Committee believed that it would be 'morally wrong' for the state to deliberately seek to create single parent families.

Golombok *et al.* (1983), who have provided empirical evidence about both single parent and lesbian families, complain that the debate has been characterised by 'dogma rather than argument'. Their own research failed to substantiate generally held stereotypes about lesbian families, at the same time concluding that the deprivations children in both single parent and lesbian households did experience were essentially the result of societal prejudice.

In a recent literature review evaluating the impact of a variety of family forms on children's psychological development, Schaffer (1988, p. 95) concluded there was:

'. . . no indication that departures from the conventional norm of family structures are necessarily harmful to children; psychologically healthy personalities can develop in the context of a great variety of social groupings.'

Evidence to support the validity of selection criteria is scarce. There has been little follow-up of children born following AR or their families or of those who have been rejected for treatment (Snowden and Snowden, 1984). Outcomes of adoption might be seen to offer some guidance, although these are not without their difficulties. . . .

Criteria for successful child care placements are also somewhat elusive, although some studies have identified certain factors contributing to successful adoption placements: parental attitudes and the adopted child's perception of being fully accepted and integrated into family life, although the mechanics of telling and talking about adoption appear not to be significantly associated with outcome (Smith, 1984). Tresiliotis' recent review of studies of foster placements (1989) identifies certain factors associated with *unsuccessful* outcomes which appear to be of relevance to AR:

(i) the child's ignorance about her or his origins;

(ii) the carer's ambivalence/hostility towards genetic parents.

There is considerable evidence of the limitations on the ability to successfully predict 'good parents' and indeed define with any degree of confidence what characteristics one should even be looking for, let alone try and find. Smith (1984) catalogues the specific problems associated with the implementation of selection criteria in adoption practice:

(i)   restrictions on the time available for this process limit the depth of investigation;

(ii) applicants have a lot at stake and are out to impress;

(iii) social workers' skills in assessment are not particularly sophisticated;

(iv) there are few generally accepted assessment techniques for determining who will make a good or bad parent, or clear cut predictors of potential for successful parenthood.

Some adoption workers have explicitly abandoned conventional practices of 'matching' and 'assessment' on the grounds that:

'. . . there is no evidence to indicate that social workers have any proven expertise in the prediction of which adoptive parents are likely to provide a continuing, stable relationship and a secure family environment for an adopted child (Howell and Ryburn, 1987, p. 38)'

In their place they have developed practice which focuses on *preparation and education* designed to help applicants decide if adoption is for them and provide the necessary information and support. Similar practices could well be developed in AR.

Finally, there is surrogacy, which may involve either sperm donation alone, or egg and sperm donation. The Warnock Committee's *Report* (1984) summarised the arguments like this:

Arguments against surrogacy

8.10 There are strongly held objections to the concept of surrogacy, and it seems from the evidence submitted to us that the weight of public opinion is against the practice. The objections turn essentially on the view that to introduce a third party into the process of procreation which should be confined to the loving partnership between two people, is an attack on the value of the marital relationship. Further, the intrusion is worse than in the case of AID, since the contribution of the carrying mother is greater, more intimate and personal, than the contribution of a semen donor. It is also argued that it is inconsistent with human dignity that a woman should use her uterus for financial profit and treat it as an incubator for someone else's child. The objection is not diminished, indeed it is strengthened, where the woman entered an agreement to conceive a child, with the sole purpose of handing the child over to the commissioning couple after birth.

8.11 Again, it is argued that the relationship between mother and child is itself distorted by surrogacy. For in such an arrangement a woman deliberately allows herself to become pregnant with the intention of giving up the child to which she will give birth, and this is the wrong way to approach pregnancy. It is also potentially damaging to the child, whose bonds with the carrying mother, regardless of genetic connections, are held to be strong, and whose welfare must be considered to be of paramount importance. Further it is felt that a surrogacy agreement is degrading to the child who is to be the outcome of it, since, for all practical purposes, the child will have been bought for money.

8.12 It is also argued that since there are some risks attached to pregnancy, no woman ought to be asked to undertake pregnancy for another, in order to earn money. Nor, it is argued should a woman be forced by legal sanctions to part with a child, to which she has recently given birth, against her will.

Arguments for surrogacy

8.13 If infertility is a condition which should, where possible, be remedied it is argued that surrogacy must not be ruled out, since it offers to some couples their only chance of having a child genetically related to one or both of them. In particular, it may well be the only way that the husband of an infertile woman can have a child. Moreover, the bearing of a child for another can be seen, not as an undertaking that trivialises or commercialises pregnancy, but, on the contrary, as a deliberate and thoughtful act of generosity on the part of one woman to another. If there are risks attached to pregnancy, then the generosity is all the greater.

8.14 There is no reason, it is argued, to suppose that carrying mothers will enter into agreements lightly, and they have a perfect right to enter into such agreements if they so wish, just as they have a right to use their own bodies in other ways, according to their own decision. Where arguments are genuinely voluntary, there can be no question of exploitation, nor does the fact that surrogates will be paid for their pregnancy of itself entail exploitation of either party to the agreement.

8.15 As for intrusion into the marriage relationship, it is argued that those who feel strongly about this need not seek such treatment, but they should not seek to prevent others from having access to it.

8.16 On the question of bonding, it is argued that as very little is actually known about the extent to which bonding occurs when the child is *in utero*, no great claims should be made in this respect. In any case the breaking of such bonds, even if less than ideal, is not held to be an overriding argument against placing a child for adoption, where the mother wants this.

The Committee were divided between those who wanted an almost complete ban on the practice and those who wanted only profit-making agencies banned. The Surrogacy Arrangements Act 1985 banned commercial agencies and advertising of and for surrogacy services. The *Human Fertilisation and Embryology Act* inserted a further provision making all surrogacy arrangements unenforceable (and see *A v C* (1978) [1985] FLR 445). However, it also provided a convenient method of avoiding its own rules about parentage and allowing the commissioning parents to take over:

30. – (1) The court may make an order providing for a child to be treated in law as the child of the parties to a marriage (referred to in this section as 'the husband' and 'the wife') if –
  (*a*) the child has been carried by a woman other than the wife as the result of the placing in her of an embryo or sperm and eggs or her artificial insemination,
  (*b*) the gametes of the husband or the wife, or both, were used to bring about the creation of the embryo, and
  (*c*) the conditions in subsections (2) to (7) below are satisfied.

(2) The husband and the wife must apply for the order within six months of the birth of the child or, in the case of a child born before the coming into force of this Act, within six months of such coming into force.

(3) At the time of the application and of the making of the order –
  (*a*) the child's home must be with the husband and wife, and
  (*b*) the husband or the wife, of both of them, must be domiciled in a part of the United Kingdom or in the Channel Islands or the Isle of Man.

(4) At the time of the making of the order both the husband and the wife must have attained the age of eighteen.

(5) The court must be satisfied that both the father of the child (including a person who is the father by virtue of section 28 of this Act), where he is not the husband, and the woman who carried the child have freely, and with full understanding of what is involved, agreed unconditionally to the making of the order.

(6) Subsection (5) above does not require the agreement of a person who cannot be found or is incapable of giving agreement and the agreement of the woman who carried the child is ineffective for the purposes of that subsection if given by her less than six weeks after the child's birth.

(7) The court must be satisfied that no money or other benefit (other than for expenses reasonably incurred) has been given or received by the husband or the wife for or in consideration of –
  (*a*) the making of the order,
  (*b*) any agreement required by subsection (5) above,
  (*c*) the handing over of the child to the husband or the wife, or

(*d*) the making of any arrangements with a view to the making of the order,
unless authorised by the court.

. . .

(9) Regulations may provide —
  (*a*) for any provision of the enactments about adoption to have effect, with such
    modifications (if any) as may be specified in the regulations, in relation to orders under
    this section, and applications for such orders, as it has effect in relation to adoption,
    and applications for adoption orders, and
  (*b*) for references in any enactment to adoption, an adopted child or an adoptive
    relationship to be read (respectively) as references to the effect of an order under
    this section, a child to whom such an order applies and a relationship arising by virtue
    of the enactments about adoption, as applied by the regulations, and for similar
    expressions in connection with adoption to be read accordingly.
and the regulations may include such incidental or supplemental provision as appears to the
Secretary of State necessary or desirable in consequence of any provision made by virtue of
paragraph (*a*) or (*b*) above.

Questions

(i) In *A v C* (1978) [1985] FLR 445, Ormrod LJ referred to a surrogacy
arrangement (from which the mother had repented) as a 'quite bizarre and
unnatural arrangement' and Cumming-Bruce J called it a 'kind of baby-
farming operation of a wholly distasteful and lamentable kind': do you
agree?
(ii) How much of the law relating to adoption (see Chapter 14, below) would
you apply to the procedure under s. 30?
(iii) (*a*) In 1987, Mrs Pat Anthony gave birth to triplets. Doctors in South
Africa had implanted into her eggs from her daughter Karen which had been
fertilised by Karen's husband's sperm. Mrs Anthony therefore became the
world's first surrogate grandmother (see Reid, 1988). Should treatment be
provided in such a case? (*b*) In 1989, an English husband, infertile as a
result of mumps, was told that it was 'ethically impossible' for his wife to be
artificially inseminated with his brother's sperm. Can you think what the
ethical objection might be? (*c*) How relevant are the Houghton Committee's
doubts (p. 650, below) about adoption by relatives?
(iv) What, if anything, should the Human Fertilisation and Embryology
Authority say about surrogacy in its Code of Practice?
(v) Why do we not feel able to allow the carrying mother to decide what she
finds 'inconsistent with [her] human dignity'?

CHAPTER 12

When parents part

Doreen: I feel very angry sometimes, that a man can literally decide that he wants to be free, free of responsibilities that *somebody* must take. Somebody needs to when children are involved. But men can just walk off. I think because they know that the woman is going to be the strong one, that *she* will not . . . walk away.

Michael: The effects on my career have hurt. . . . The company begins to assess you a bit lower perhaps because your mind has family welfare as a higher priority than it should be. . . . I took Anne down to junior church as I always have done . . . but I'd never brushed her hair before or tied ribbons, and this was actually impossible to me.

These two lone parents, and others, talked about their lives to Catherine Itzin for her book on *Splitting Up* (1980). This chapter is concerned with how it is decided what should happen to the children when their parents part. We shall look first at what is known of the practice of the courts under the law as it was before the Children Act 1989, including some illustrative cases, then at what some of the 'experts' think that they should be doing, before turning to the new law and the reasons for it.

1 What courts do

We cannot tell how many couples with children separate each year, because the fact is not always officially recorded. The first graph opposite, from *Social Trends 19* (1989) shows the numbers of children under 16 whose parents divorce. The next two graphs, from *Social Trends 21* (1991), show the rise in one parent families of all types and the increasing proportion which result from separation or divorce.

Children of divorcing couples: by age

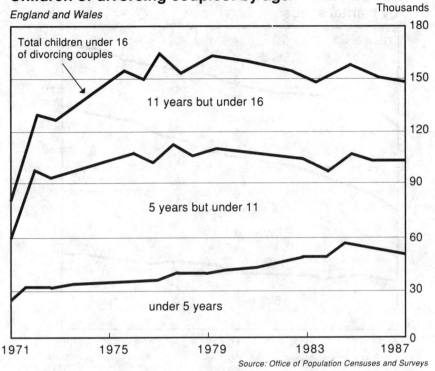

England and Wales

Total children under 16
of divorcing couples

11 years but under 16

5 years but under 11

under 5 years

Thousands

Source: Office of Population Censuses and Surveys

Proportions[1] of all families with dependent children headed by lone mothers and lone fathers

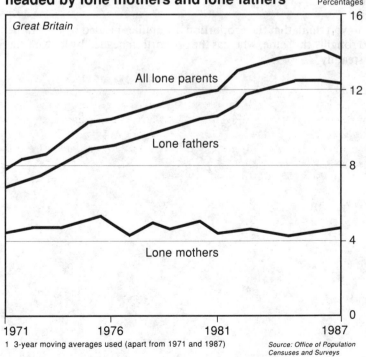

Great Britain

Percentages

All lone parents

Lone fathers

Lone mothers

1 3-year moving averages used (apart from 1971 and 1987)

Source: Office of Population Censuses and Surveys

Lone mothers with dependent children: by marital status

Percentages[1]

1 3-year moving averages used (apart from 1971 and 1987).

Source: Office of Population Censuses and Surveys

Question

Why do you think that the proportion of families headed by lone fathers has stayed roughly the same, whereas the proportion headed by lone mothers has risen steadily?

The most recent study of *Custody Orders in Practice in Divorce and Domestic Courts* (1986), by Jacqueline Priest and Jonathan Whybrow, was published as a supplement to the Law Commission's Working Paper on Custody. The following table collects statistics from various sources to show how the usual outcome on divorce has changed in recent years:

Table 6: Custody orders in divorce proceedings (Percentages)

Study	Year of Data	Custody of Wife	Custody of Husband	Joint Custody	Others	Total Number[7]
Maidment[1]	1973	77.6	19.0	3.4	0	58
Wolfson[2]	1974	81.4	13.2	5.2	.2	428
Bristol[3]	1979–80	81.4	11.6	7.0	0	1,290
National[4]	1985	77.4	9.2	12.9	.7	82,059
Bristol(2)[5]	1985	73.0	9.6	16.9	.5	4,676
Wolfson(2)[6]	1985	72.2	9.2	18.1	.5	12,771

Notes to Table 6
1. A random sample of 95 undefended divorce petitions involving children, which had been filed in a North Midlands county court in 1973: Maidment, 'A Study in Child Custody' (1976) 6 Fam Law 195 and 236, p. 198.
2. A study of 625 divorces involving children in 1974, from a sample of 10 courts selected to reflect a cross-section of the divorcing population: Eekelaar and Clive with Clarke and Raikes, *Custody After Divorce*, Family Law Studies No. 1, Centre for Socio-Legal Studies, Wolfson College, Oxford, Table 33.
3. Research into 1,550 children's appointments between May 1979 and June 1980 in five courts in the Western Circuit and two courts on the Wales and Chester Circuit: Davis, MacLeod and Murch, 'Undefended Divorce: Should Section 41 of the Matrimonial Causes Act 1973 be Repealed?' (1983) 46 M.L.R. 121, 132.
4. The figures collected from the returns of 174 divorce registries in 1985.
5. The courts used by the Bristol study, updated using the figures noted in 4.
6. The courts used by the Wolfson study, updated using the figures noted in 4. These are the county courts at Birmingham, Bournemouth, Carmarthen, Guildford, Lincoln, Newcastle-upon-Tyne, Nottingham, Sheffield and Shrewsbury, and P.R.F.D. The latter's returns have been extrapolated from our own survey's results (see para. 5.30).
7. The total number of custody orders made by the divorce court, that is excluding care committals and previous courts' orders. In rows 1, 2 and 3 orders splitting the children between husband and wife have been counted as orders in favour of *each* of them.

At first sight, it would appear that the increase in joint custody has been largely at the expense of husbands who would otherwise have sole custody. A more complex picture emerges, however, from detailed returns from ten divorce courts. These were deliberately chosen to provide a range of high and low proportions of joint custody. However high the rate of joint custody, the children's residence was remarkably consistent, as shown opposite. There was also a wide geographical variation in joint custody orders, as shown by the map on p. 506.

The authors summarise the possible explanations, gleaned from interviews with judges, thus:

5.6 Why is there regional variation in joint custody orders? *Some* joint custody orders are made in every divorce court. Our inquiries suggest that disparity in orders reflects differences both in the courts' approaches and in the proposals put forward by spouses across the country. The regional pattern masks a consensus amongst the judges interviewed that, where possible, both parents should continue to be involved in their children's upbringing after divorce. However, from the interviews, three different approaches to joint custody were apparent: promotion of the joint option; a non-interventionist or laissez-faire attitude towards the parties' proposals as to custody; and scepticism about or discouragement of joint custody. Indeed, several of the judges commented that they felt they were working in isolation: they were not aware of the practice in other courts and, prior to their appointment, usually working as barristers, they had gained little or no experience of children's cases.

Question

What explanation would you give for the regional differences?

Returns from the ten courts, which were not necessarily representative, did provide a little more detail about who went where:

Table 7: Children subject to custody orders by age and sex (percentages) n. = 2927

Proportion of children in each category subject to wife, husband and joint orders.

Custody Orders	Boys	Girls	0–5	Age of Children 6–10	11–15	16+
Wife Orders	71	73	80	72	67	61
Husband Orders	8	6	3	6	12	22
Joint Custody	21	21	16	23	21	16
Total Number (= 100%)	1497	1430	760	778	778	173

4.24 From Table 7 several propositions may be made:—
1) At all age groups mothers were more likely to be granted sole custody than fathers (on average at a ratio of 10: 1).
2) Mothers were marginally less likely to receive sole custody of boys than girls.
3) Fathers were relatively more likely to receive the sole custody of boys than girls.
4) The older the child the more likely the father was to be granted sole custody.

The proportion of orders in ten courts under which child's residence with wife

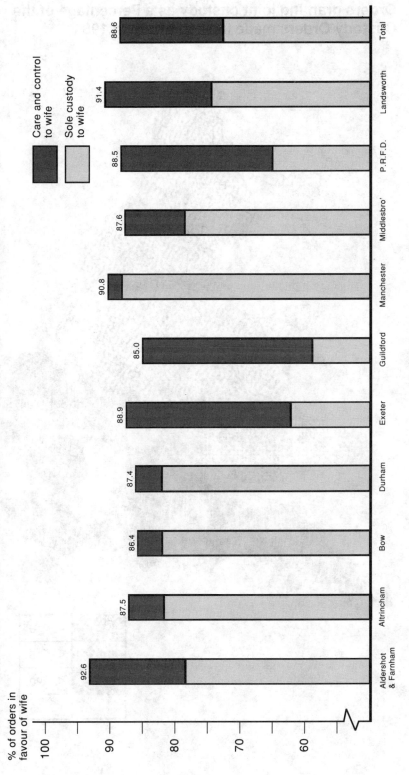

Orders granting joint custody as a Percentage of the Custody Orders made in each group in 1985

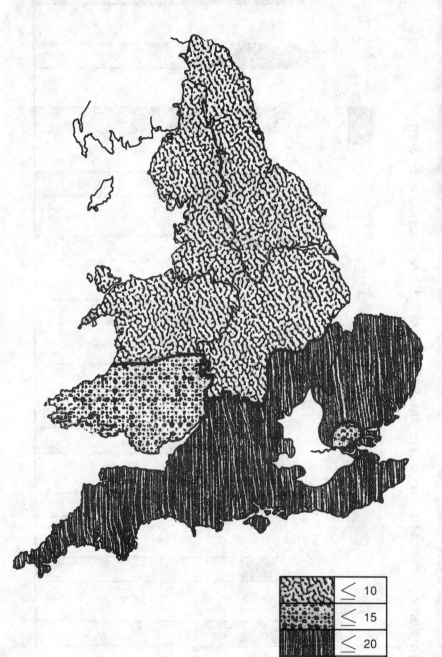

▨	≤ 10
▦	≤ 15
▥	≤ 20
☐	≤ 25

This study did not examine the court records in detail, as the Wolfson study, *Custody after Divorce* (1977) by John Eekelaar and Eric Clive, with Karen Clarke and Susan Raikes, had done. This revealed more about the parties' behaviour:

13.7 Proposals of the parties
The vast majority of petitioners/pursuers simply sought the court's approval for the continuation of the existing state of affairs. In England and Wales only 4.8% of petitioners and in Scotland only 2.5% of pursuers proposed any substantial change in the child's residence, and those cases generally contained some abnormal feature (e.g. the children were in care or with third parties). . . . Since children generally lived with their mother, this meant that petitioners/pursuers generally wished this to continue. Indeed, it was relatively rare for a husband to challenge the continued care for his children by the mother. In England and Wales husbands expressed an initial intention to apply for custody of children currently in their wife's care only in 10.3% of such cases, whereas in 34.3% of cases where the children were living with the husband, the wife expressed an initial intention to seek custody herself. However, in only a few of these cases was the challenge pressed to a contest in the court. . . . In Scotland . . . as well as England and Wales . . . the evidence showed a very strong tendency on the part of mothers to claim custody of children in contrast to the fathers.

Earlier, the authors comment:

3.6 . . . Wives are more tenacious than husbands in their attempts to obtain possession of the children. In most cases the husbands are content to leave to the wife the task of bringing up the children. If they seek to do so themselves, they are far more likely to be challenged by the wife than is a wife who keeps the children. That the wife is seen as prima facie the proper person to have care of the children therefore appears as a factor of community opinion which is shared by the parties themselves. However, the very low success rate of wives where they did challenge their husbands' possession of the children shows that the courts do not necessarily share that assumption, or, if they do, they have regard to other factors in making their decisions.

This last point becomes clearer when the outcome of the small proportion of cases in which custody was contested is discussed:

6.1 Thirty-nine cases (6.0% of the sample) were classified as being contested on the custody issue at hearing and 6 more contested on access only. However, it is possible that a further 9 were contested on the custody issue and a further 3 on access alone. But only the clearly contested cases are analyzed in this chapter.
6.3 Well over half the contested cases were adjourned on decree nisi. . . . In nearly half of those adjourned, a welfare report was ordered, but in just over a third no steps are recorded in the documents, probably because further negotiations took place between the parties. . . . In all, welfare reports were available in 53% of contested cases. Because the total numbers are so small it is not easy to deduce any factor especially associated with the ordering of welfare reports in these cases, other than, perhaps, that a report is more likely to be ordered if the child is resident with the husband . . ., and if it is proposed the child should move. . . . Perhaps this indicates that the courts will look more seriously at proposals that a child should move from the husband than that it should move from the wife.
6.4 Of the 39 custody contests, custody was awarded to the husband in 4 cases, to the wife in 17, to the parties jointly in 5, and the children were divided in 4 cases. In one, custody was awarded to the husband's sister and in 7 others no order was made. In 3 of the 5 joint awards, care and control was given to the wife and in the other two to the husband. But in only 5 cases did the child's residential status quo change. Since this happened in only 13 instances in the whole sample, it is clear that, where a child's residence is to change, it is likely to be in the context of a custody dispute. . . .
6.5 In only two of the five cases . . . did the court order itself bring about a change of residential status quo, and, although they were both in favour of the wife, one of them also re-united separated siblings. Although, therefore, our study provided evidence of a certain judicial caution

about allowing husbands to look after children, apart from these two cases, the principle in favour of the status quo prevailed even when contested by the wife. There were seven such cases, involving, in all, 1 boy and 1 girl under 4, 3 boys aged 5–11, and 4 girls in the same age bracket, and 2 boys and a girl between 12 and 15. In 6 of them, however, the court acted on the advice of a welfare officer's report. Furthermore, in all 4 cases where the children were divided between the parents, the court was maintaining the residential status quo. . . . Yet it is notable that, in the only two cases where the status quo was changed, in one the judge ignored the recommendation of the welfare report and in the other there was no report. . . . A similar observation was made in the context of uncontested cases.

The authors conclude:

13.29 Another striking finding emerged in the examination of the contested cases. This is that the courts did not favour either sex as the more suitable custodian (although they displayed more caution when the husband was the custodian), nor did they appear to operate in accordance with presumptions relating to the age or sex of the children. Instead, they followed the principle advocated by Goldstein, Freud and Solnit . . . of minimum disruption to the child's existing emotional ties.

These findings are highly comparable with those in Maidment's study (1976). Eekelaar's later study (1982) confirmed the finding that mothers are more likely than fathers to dispute the other's custody, but he also found that at least one child was moved in no less than seven out of the 31 cases in which custody was disputed. Three were moved from mother to father and four from father to mother. The welfare officer was in favour of this in three cases, against it in two, and undecided in two. However, 'although when the father's sole custody was challenged by the mother he was less likely to retain them than when he challenged the mother's sole custody, a father is nevertheless more likely to retain custody than to lose it. If he loses custody this will usually have the approval of the welfare officer.' Fathers who want their children and are prepared to fight, therefore, would appear, statistically at least, to have a reasonable chance of success. The reasons why fathers do not fight, however, are likely to vary. Some are suggested by Martin Richards in his discussion of *Post Divorce Arrangements for Children: A Psychological Perspective* (1982):

Mother or father?
Though the law itself does not favour mothers or fathers as potential custodial parents, if all else is equal and, especially if the children are young ('of tender years'), the mother is more likely to be granted custody in a dispute. Not all would concur with this point, but I think the weight of the evidence from reported cases and the surveys support a principle of a presumption that custody should be vested in the mother. Of course, I am not suggesting that the courts are entirely responsible for the fact that only in a small percentage of cases does a father have custody of his children after a divorce. In most cases the father has not sought custody and does not challenge his wife's claim. The main reason for this situation is that the general assumptions that are held about the sexual division of labour within marriage are extended to the post-divorce situation. Within most marriages, the prime responsibility for childcare falls on women and so it is after the marriage ends. A small and probably increasing proportion of men would like to have the custody and care and control of their children. In many of these cases it seems that they are so certain that this will not be granted to them that they do not bother to raise the issue with their solicitors. One man I interviewed recently thought that it was 'against the law' for men to have custody 'especially if they had daughters.' (He, incidentally, was looking after his children on his own and had consulted a solicitor. Later, after he received some counselling, he asked for and got the custody and care and control of his children.) In turn, solicitors are unlikely to suggest to their male clients that they might seek custody (or joint custody). If the client does bring it up the common advice seems to be that it is not worthwhile to proceed unless their partners will agree to the proposal. So [in] almost all cases where a man does get custody, it is because the spouses have agreed to this, or because the wife has left the matrimonial home and has not maintained contact with the children.

Question

But might there be another reason not to fight? As the *New English Bible* relates:

So they went on arguing in the king's presence. . . . Then he said, 'Fetch me a sword.' They brought in a sword and the king gave the order: 'Cut the living child in two and give half to one and half to the other.' At this the woman who was the mother of the living child, moved with love for her child, said to the king, 'Oh! sir, let her have the baby; whatever you do, do not kill it.' The other said, 'Let neither of us have it; cut it in two.' Thereupon the king gave judgement: 'Give the living baby to the first woman; do not kill it. She is its mother.

Can you think of less drastic ways in which a legal system might try to achieve the same?

For most children, therefore, the vital question is not where, or with whom, they will live but how their parents will resolve what Murch (1980) has called the 'fundamental dilemma facing divorcing parents. This is how to disengage from the broken marriage while preserving a sense of being a parent with a part to play in the children's future.' The evidence about how many 'absent' parents do in fact lose touch with their children is limited and contradictory. The Wolfson study of *Custody After Divorce* (Eekelaar and Clive, 1977) found a marked falling off in contact over time:

England and Wales	Access by time from separation						
Whether access exercised	Time from separation in years						
	0-½	½-1	1-2	2-3	3-5	5-10	over 10
Access exercised %	66.6	59.0	50.6	49.6	48.6	33.3	18.1
Access not exercised %	28.3	33.7	37.7	37.6	38.9	56.1	54.5
Access infrequent[1] %	5.1	7.4	11.7	12.8	12.5	10.5	27.3
Total number of cases[2]	99	95	77	125	72	57	11

1 Once or twice in previous year or since separation
2 Excluding cases where exercise of access unknown

Murch (1980), however, found that only one in four of the parents he interviewed was dissatisfied with the arrangements for access (some had none). Ann Mitchell's study of *Children in the Middle* (1985) also presents a more encouraging picture:

According to the parents, 40 per cent of the children had seen their other parent at least once a week after separation, 20 per cent once a month, 15 per cent rarely and 25 per cent never. Fathers were far more likely than mothers to say that their children had, initially, kept in touch with the other parent.

But not all the parents' accounts were accurate:

Elaine and her mother gave quite different accounts of what had happened after the father had left home. Both told me that he used to bring maintenance payments to the mother regularly. There, the similarity ended between the stories. The mother was one of the few whose husbands, they said, had brought money to the house without asking to see the children. Four years after separation, she told me, he began to bring birthday and Christmas presents for the children, who then occasionally visited him. Elaine told me that, when her father brought money, he quite often arranged to take the children out, 'to buy clothes, to the zoo quite a few times, to a safari park, places like that'. She had also 'kept in touch' with her father by going to see him in his new home, alone and by bus. She had not told her mother who, she knew, would have disapproved. If asked where she'd been, she said she'd been to see a friend. Unfortunately, someone happened to tell the mother that she had seen Elaine on a bus. 'I got in trouble with my Mum and my Mum stopped him from seeing us for about a year.' Elaine had defied the ban once or twice, but her mother had found out and belted her. She then had to stop seeing her father, apart from a few minutes each week when he brought maintenance money to her mother. About a year later, Elaine 'told my mother to grow up' and allow her children to see their father again. Thereafter, Elaine had been free to see her father whenever she wanted. . . .

For the children, the pattern of access immediately after separation clearly set the pattern for the future, as Wallerstein and Kelly (1980) had also found. The sooner and the more frequently that children had access, the more likely were they to continue to keep in touch with the absent parent. Those who had no access in the beginning found difficulties first in restoring broken relationships and then in maintaining them.

Martin Richards (1982) also addresses the question 'why do non-custodial parents disappear?'

Almost all the evidence we have is about absent fathers so I will discuss this. However, there is no reason to think that male non-custodial parents disappear any more or less often than female ones, although the reasons may differ somewhat in the two cases. I will list some of the reasons that have been uncovered in the research studies.

(*a*) Some men believe that it is in their children's interests for them to disappear. They may feel that their visits will upset the children or that their continued presence makes it less likely that their ex-spouses will settle down with a new partner. Often, and especially in the early days after separation, a child's upset at what has happened is most likely to be apparent before and after a visit from the father. This may lead either parent to try to reduce or stop the visiting. It is hardly surprising that the child's feelings are most likely to be expressed at these times as they will be the most vivid reminders of what has happened. Indeed, it would be odd if any child accepted such a radical change in their lives without upset and in the long term it is probably much better that these feelings are expressed at the time. The real issue here is the capacity of the parents to accept the expression of such feelings at a time when they are likely to be feeling very vulnerable and upset themselves.

(*b*) It is often said, not least by mothers with custody that some fathers are uninterested in their children. Doubtless this is sometimes true but I suspect that this reason is often used to cover others.

(*c*) Some men believe, incorrectly of course, that if they do not see their children they will not be required to pay maintenance. More realistically, others assume that if they have no contact with their old families it will be hard for them to be traced and forced to pay maintenance. Others connect maintenance and access in another way so that they see the money they pay as an entitlement to visit. If they can only afford a little, they see themselves as having little entitlement to visit.

(*d*) Some men are prevented from seeing their children by their ex-spouse. Preventing contact with children is the most obvious weapon available to a custodial parent and some use it. After a long journey the father arrives to find the house empty. Or perhaps a child may always turn out to be 'ill' on access days. More bluntly, a father may simply be told at the doorstep that he cannot see his children. As I have mentioned above, the sanctions are few in such cases and without persistence and the ability to find the right kind of help the situation may seem hopeless.

(*e*) Some men feel that after a separation they want to move away and start again. Particularly if their spouse has a new partner, they may not want to live nearby. Distance may then create too many problems for the visiting arrangements to survive.

(*f*) A new partner may be very resentful of the contact with the children of the first marriage and bring pressure to try to end it. Not infrequently the custodial parent will attempt to argue for access orders which try to prevent the children having contact with a new partner. Although it is not hard to understand the feelings that give rise to such attempts, these are unrealistic and unreasonable from the point of view of both the adults and children and, in general, courts have not sanctioned them. But pressures from both the new and old spouse may effectively reduce access.

(*g*) Access visits may be so painful and upsetting that a father cannot bear to continue with them. This may be because the visits involve meeting the ex-spouse or because the father finds it very difficult to readjust to a new kind of relationship with his children. The latter is particularly likely if access visits are brief. Sometimes the conditions in an access order are such that it seems impossible that any parent could conform, e.g. two hours a month in the old matrimonial home in the presence of the ex-spouse (and often her new partner). If access is brief and the father's home is far away there is the problem of where to take the children. There is also the 'father Christmas syndrome' — where the father seems only able to relate to his children by giving gifts and treats. Anything more realistic and normal may seem threatening to his relationship with the children. As one might expect the problems of access are most acute at the beginning and they usually resolve over time provided, of course, that access continues.

(*h*) Last among the reasons I shall mention, but certainly not least, is the point made to me by many men I have interviewed — that all too often continued contact is not supported or encouraged by anyone. Indeed, I have been told of men being advised by a whole variety of professional people that access was a kind of selfish private indulgence they should give up as soon as possible. Very few had received any sensible advice or help — if they had it was usually from a court welfare officer, one of the few solicitors who specialise in family law or from another parent who had experienced a divorce. . . .

On the basis of current evidence it would be very difficult to give any indication of the frequency of the various reasons I have described. However, a recent study by Eekelaar (1982) does give some clues. This study concerns cases where there were disputes concerning children and relies on information provided by court welfare officers. Where access was infrequent or never occurred the officers gave the following explanations:

Reason	No. of cases
Lack of interest by absent parent	14
Consideration for the children	6
Consideration for other parent	2
'Legal advice'	1
Injunction against absent parent	5
Hostile attitude of other parent	5
Opposition by children	5
Practical difficulties	22
Unknown	3

Question

Eekelaar also found that children living with their fathers were less likely to retain a good relationship with their mothers than vice versa: why might that be?

Reported decisions are of limited relevance in children cases, and even less so now that the law has been changed, but a selection is given below to indicate the position which the courts had reached before the Children Act 1989 and the reports which led to it. The general principles are well illustrated by the first:

Re K (Minors) (Wardship: Care and Control)
[1977] Fam 179, [1979] 1 All ER 647, [1977] 2 WLR 33, 121 Sol Jo 84, Court of Appeal

The parents married in 1969. They had a son in 1971, who was now aged 5, and a daughter in 1974, who was now two and a half. The father was a Church of England clergyman. Through church activities, the mother met a young man named Martin in 1973. By March 1975, their friendship had become adulterous. The father wished the mother to give up her relationship with Martin and be reconciled. The mother wished to leave the father and set up home in a house to be bought jointly with Martin, but she was unwilling to go without the children. Accordingly, in May 1976 she applied to the local magistrates' court for their custody. The father halted those proceedings by applying to make the children wards of court. Reeve J granted care and control to the mother and the father appealed.

Stamp LJ: Before turning to the facts of the case, I would make some introductory observations. In the first place the law which is to be applied is not in doubt. It is that the welfare of the children is, in the words of the statute, the first and paramount consideration. It was stated with clarity and precision by Lord MacDermott in *J v C* [1970] AC 668, [1969] 1 All ER 788 [p.411, above] in a passage in his speech which should be in the mind of every judge who tries an infant case, . . .

> 'The second question of construction is as to the scope and meaning of the words ". . . shall regard the welfare of the infant as the first and paramount consideration". Reading these words in their ordinary significance, and relating them to the various classes which the section has already mentioned, it seems to me that they must mean more than that the child's welfare is to be treated as the top item in a list of items relevant to the matter in question. I think they connote a process whereby, when all the relevant facts, relationships, claims and wishes of parents, risks, choices and other circumstances are taken into account and weighed, the course to be followed will be that which is most in the interests of the child's welfare as that term has now to be understood. That is the first consideration because it is of first importance and the paramount consideration because it rules on or determines the course to be followed.'

Applying the law so stated, this court in *S (BD) v S (DJ)* (*infants: care and consent*) [1977] Fam 109, [1977] 1 All ER 656 held that the earlier case of *Re L* (*infants*) [1962] 3 All ER 1, [1962] 1 WLR 886, where this court appears to have balanced the welfare of the child against the wishes of an unimpeachable parent or the justice of the case as between the parties, was no longer to be regarded as good law. . . .

The second thing I would say at the outset is, . . . that although one may of course be assisted by the wisdom of remarks made in earlier cases, the circumstances in infant cases and the personalities of the parties concerned being infinitely variable, the conclusions of the court as to the course which should be followed in one case are of little assistance in guiding one to the course which ought to be followed in another case.

Thirdly I would emphasise that where a judge has seen the parties concerned, has had the assistance of a good welfare officer's report and has correctly applied the law, an appellate court ought not to disturb his decision unless it appears that he has failed to take into account something which he ought to have taken into account or has taken into account something which he ought not to have taken into account, or the appellate court is satisfied that his decision was wrong; it is not enough that a judge of the appellate court should think, on reading the papers, that he himself would on the whole have come to a different conclusion. . . .

It is clear that, from the point of view of the children, nothing could be much worse than a continuation of the situation which the judge described, to which must be added the fact that the mother is, as I have indicated, continuing her intimate association with M and that one of them at least knows that something is wrong, and that both the children are, so it appears, fond of M, with whom they have become very well acquainted. As I have indicated, the father, because of his beliefs, will not divorce his wife, or consent to a divorce, so that the couple face for a period of five years during which they cannot marry, a situation which cannot I think continue from the point of view of any of the three adults concerned, or which could be tolerable for any lengthy period. To the extent that it does endure, the strains will become intolerable and the damage to the children incalculable.

The mother appears to have been somewhat ambivalent on the question whether if care and control were denied to her, she would stay in the home to look after the children, maintaining her liaison with M, or whether she would go and live with him. The judge thought that she could not contemplate the possibility of giving up either her children or M, but he considered that if care and control were given to the father, the greatest possibility was that she would go and live with M alone, but of course what she wants to do is to set up home with M and the children.

The arrangements which the father would make if he were to have care and control and the mother in fact went to live with M were summarised by the judge thus:

> 'Moreover, I bear this matter in mind. That the arrangements which the father can make — I refer to the roster which is exhibited to one of his affidavits — is on the face of it satisfactory in that these children will be cared for by worthy persons at all hours of the day, nevertheless it is not a satisfactory way, through no fault of the father's, in having children cared for. As has been pointed out, during the course of one week there may be five different persons who may be responsible for looking after these children. There will

be some continuity in the care that the father can lavish on them. Nevertheless there would be a succession of other persons who would be assisting in that regard. That, as I say, is not the fault of the father, he is making the best arrangements that he can.'

...

I agree with the learned judge that the arrangements are far from satisfactory and that if the matter rested there it could hardly be doubted that it would be for the benefit of these children that effect should be given to the dictates of nature which make the mother the natural guardian, protector and comforter of the very young. But, as the judge pointed out in a judgment which shows the greatest possible sympathy with the father — a sympathy which I would emphasise that I share — in considering the welfare of the children one has to look also to their moral and spiritual welfare.

The father, who naturally holds his beliefs very strongly, not only wants to live according to his faith, but wants his children to be brought up in that faith, to hold the same beliefs as he does and to live their lives as he intends to live his life. I cannot do better than quote the words in which the learned judge put it; he said this:

'And he takes the view that if the care and control is committed to the mother this may do considerable harm, and he would put it a little higher perhaps, very considerable harm, to the children in that it would be hurtful to them spiritually. He does not attach so much importance to the difficulty which might exist in explaining to these children what it entails if their mother is living in sin, if one can use that old fashioned Victorian expression, with M. He does not attach any great importance to the difficulty that there no doubt will be in due course if the children are committed to the care and control of their mother of explaining to them how professed Christians can ignore one of the commandments, or any of them. But what he feels will do very considerable harm to these children is that they should be brought up in a home where their mother and another man are living together in blatant defiance of church doctrine and all that the father believes in. And as appears very clearly from their demeanour in the witness box where those two persons with whom the children would be living in those circumstances show no repentance.'

The judge remarked that there was considerable force in that argument.

But unfortunately, as the judge pointed out, if one yielded to that submission and committed the care of these children to the father, it would not in great measure protect them from the moral and spiritual harm which the father fears. The plain fact is that the children's mother intends to live with a young man who is not her husband. No one suggests that she should be denied access to the children and the judge thought, and I share that view, that it would have to be liberal access, including staying access. How could the children then fail to be aware, and constantly aware, that their mother was living with M in, to quote the judge's words 'blatant defiance of church doctrine and all that [the father] believes in'? And, if, as appears to be the case, the children are children who love their mother and are fond of M, to deprive them of her would, in my judgment, be as likely as not to cause a revolt against the very teaching that the father would have them imbibe and a revolt, so I would have thought, which in due course would be a revolt against the father himself. ....

One cannot be sure that the relationship between the mother and M will remain a stable one; the judge said that that was possibly one of the most difficult aspects of the case on which to express a view with any degree of certainty. He said of it:

'That is possibly one of the most difficult aspects of this case on which to express a view with any degree of certainty. I know that they met in January 1975 [that was a slip for 1973], that their adulterous association has continued for about a year now and that at the moment there can be no question that they feel they are going to stay with each other and that the union between them, whether they are married or not, is going to be a permanent one. Moreover M has purchased a house which would be the "matrimonial home". I appreciate that there must be some question that this association between them may be no more than a temporary infatuation which will burn itself out when the glamour of what I suppose one could call their courtship over the last few months has gone. I face that danger. It is also submitted that if I took the children away from the home which the boy has known for over three years, and that is really the whole of his life which he can remember (and this is the only home that the girl has known) that that would cause a great upheaval in their lives. I attach no importance to that. These children would settle down perfectly well in any other environment if they are with their mother.'

...

I turn now to how the learned judge described the mother; at one point in his judgment he said this:

'But again I can appreciate the situation in which she now is. She is a desperately unhappy person. She cannot control her own emotions. She has the laudible and natural maternal instincts for her children. For that she can only be praised. But unfortunately — and the fact I criticise her for this is neither here nor there — she has equally strong emotions for M and those two emotions are so strong that she can write the notes to which I have referred but not in detail and are so strong that she cannot really see the wickedness of the step that she is taking in disrupting this family. And also she cannot see the very real goodness that there is in her husband both as a husband and as a father.'

The judge also says this of her earlier in his judgment:

'So far as their material welfare is concerned no sort of criticism has been made against the mother. As a mother she has been quite excellent. And there is no reason to suppose that in that regard she will change. These children will need for nothing if they are being fed, clothed and brought up in all those material particulars by their mother; they could not expect to have a better mother'

and it was at that point that the judge went on to point out that he also had to consider the children's spiritual and moral welfare. I would add this, that it is not suggested that the mother is in any degree lacking in the warmth which such very young children so much need.

The judge made it abundantly clear that if he were deciding the case by trying to do justice between the father and the mother, there could be only one way in which he could possibly decide it, and that was in favour of the father; but he correctly applied what was laid down in *J v C* and refused to set that consideration against the welfare of the children. The judgment, of which I have only quoted parts, is if I may say so, full, careful and thoughtful.

. . .

He expressed himself towards the conclusion of his judgment in these terms:

'I propose to commit the care and control of these children to the mother. That has been obvious for some period during my judgment. Having thus stated my conclusion the mother is already feeling much happier. She will be able to act more naturally. She will be able to see the goodness in her husband that she has not been able to until this moment when she has heard my decision. I take the view that she is really a very nice person. It is a tragedy that her emotions have been such that she is blind to all advice and she really cannot control herself. But she is really a very nice person. Now that she has got what she wants, her children and her lover, I feel that she will be able to see that there is a lot of good in her husband, not only as a husband (though that is of no importance now because this marriage has irretrievably broken down whatever the father may think) but may also be able to see his goodness as a father. I have no fear in committing the care and control of these children to her that she will try and build up M as the father of these children. That last consideration is not the reason why I commit the care and control of these children to the mother. The real reason is this. Nothing that I have heard would induce me to take away a little girl who is not yet 2½ from a really good mother, and nobody has suggested that these children should be separated. It might cause untold harm to the little girl if she were taken away from her mother now.'

I can only say that I am quite unable to conclude that the judge came to a wrong conclusion; I agree with it and would dismiss this appeal.

Ormrod LJ: . . . For my part, I do not think that justice between parents in these cases is ever simple. On the contrary, it is a highly complex question which can very rarely be answered satisfactorily, and then only after exhaustive investigation. In the present case this aspect of it was, quite rightly, not pursued in any detail, because I do not think the welfare of the children required any such enquiry. So I prefer to keep an open mind as to where the justice of the case, as between the father and the mother, lies. It seems to me that all experience shows that, particularly serious-minded people such as the mother in this case, do not break up their marriages unless their relationship with their spouses has deteriorated very severely indeed. So I hesitate to make moral judgments in this class of case; I do not find it particularly helpful. . . . *Appeal dismissed.*

Questions

(i) Do you consider that this decision was 'unfair' to the father?

(ii) If you do think it unfair, is that because: (*a*) the law requires the court to determine the case on the basis of the children's welfare and not upon the rights and wrongs of the marital dispute, or (*b*) the court gave effect to the 'dictates of nature which make the mother the natural guardian, protector and comforter of the very young'?

(iii) Following this case, is it ever relevant that one of the parents is determined to break up the home whereas the other is anxious to hold it together?

(iv) What do you think was best for these two children?

On the third point made by Lord Justice Stamp, the House of Lords has affirmed the role of appellate courts in children cases:

G v G (Minors) (Custody: Appeal)
[1985] 2 All ER 225, [1985] 1 WLR 647, [1985] FLR 894, [1985] Fam Law 321, House of Lords

Lord Fraser of Tullybelton: . . . We were told by counsel that practitioners are finding difficulty in ascertaining the correct principles to apply because of the various ways in which judges have expressed themselves in these cases. I do not think it would be useful for me to go through the cases and to analyse the various expressions used by different judges and attempt to reconcile them exactly. Certainly it would not be useful to inquire whether different shades of meaning are intended to be conveyed by words such as 'blatant error' used by the President in the present case, and words such as 'clearly wrong', 'plainly wrong', or simply 'wrong' used by other judges in other cases. All these various expressions were used in order to emphasize the point that the appellate court should only interfere when they consider that the judge of first instance has not merely preferred an imperfect solution which is different from an alternative imperfect solution which the Court of Appeal might or would have adopted, but has exceeded the generous ambit within which a reasonable disagreement is possible. The principle was stated in this House by my noble and learned friend Lord Scarman in *B v W (wardship: appeal)* [1979] 3 All ER 83, [1979] 1 WLR 1041: . . .

'But at the end of the day the court may not intervene unless it is satisfied either that the judge exercised his discretion upon a wrong principle or that, the judge's decision being so plainly wrong, he must have exercised his discretion wrongly.'

The same principle was expressed in other words, and at slightly greater length, in the Court of Appeal (Stamp, Browne and Bridge LJJ) in *Re F (a minor) (wardship: appeal)* [1976] Fam 238, [1976] 1 All ER 417, CA . . . Browne LJ said:

'Apart from the effect of seeing and hearing witnesses, I cannot see why the general principle applicable to the exercise of the discretion in respect of infants should be any different from the general principle applicable to any other form of discretion.'

. . . The decision in *Re F* is also important because the majority rejected, rightly in my view, the dissenting opinion of Stamp LJ, who would have limited the right of the Court of Appeal to interfere with the judge's decision in custody cases to cases 'where it concludes that the course followed by the judge is one that no reasonable judge having taken into account all the relevant circumstances could have adopted'. That is the test which the court applies in deciding whether it is entitled to exercise judicial control over the decision of an administrative body, see the well-known case of *Associated Provincial Picture Houses Ltd v Wednesbury Corpn* [1948] 1 KB 223. It is not the appropriate test for deciding whether the Court of Appeal is entitled to interfere with the decision made by a judge in the exercise of his discretion.

Questions

(i) 'But to say that the judge below is deemed to have "exceeded the generous ambit within which a reasonable disagreement is possible" is surely to say no more, nor less, than that his decision was one which no reasonable judge could make' (Eekelaar, 1985)?

(ii) How much importance should be attached to 'the effect of seeing and hearing witnesses' in children cases?

(iii) Do you think appeals should be encouraged or discouraged? Why?

One reason could be that the appeal court will usually have to send the case back to be heard again. A recent rare exception was the following:

Re A (a minor)
(1991) Times, 24 April, Court of Appeal

Butler Sloss LJ: said that K's parents, both caring people, separated in 1989 after 20 years together. K, the youngest of their six children, described as a bright, happy and independent child, had continued living in the former matrimonial home with her father and three brothers together with a housekeeper who had cared for her and her brother aged nine since their births.

The judge had ordered [that] K's sister aged 11 be in the mother's custody: an inevitable order in the circumstances. He had then considered K, stating that there was an acute balance of arguments. He concluded by rejecting the *status quo* argument and accepting the mother's case that it was natural for a mother to have the care of her daughter aged six.

In so concluding, the judge had misunderstood the decision of the Court of Appeal in *Re H (a Minor)* (*The Times* June 20, 1990) where it was said that although it was natural for young children to be with their mothers, where there was a dispute, it was but one consideration, not a presumption.

If a child had remained throughout with the mother and was young, the unbroken relationship of the mother and child was one which it would be very difficult to displace, unless the mother was unsuitable to care for the child.

But where the mother and child had been separated and the mother sought the return of the child, other considerations applied and there was no starting point that the mother should be preferred to the father.

Here the mother and K had been separated at the time of the hearing for 12 months and at the age of six she was not in the category of very young children.

The judge had applied the wrong test. Moreover, he had relied on factors which he should not have relied on in the exercise of his discretion. His decision was fatally flawed and could not stand.

Two courses could be taken: either to remit the case for a rehearing or for the court to exercise its discretion on the facts available to it, both those available to the judge and fresh evidence which the court had allowed the parties to adduce.

Decisions as to children ought not to be delayed. This little girl had been the centre of dispute ever since her mother left home in October 1989. It was important that she should know where she was going to make her home and should not, alone of the children, remain in limbo for a further period. It was urgent that a decision be made. There was enough material on which to make one.

The points in favour of K not being uprooted were strong. She was settled where she was.

Without criticising the mother or her ability to care for K, it would plainly be wrong to move her at this stage. The appeal should be allowed and an order that the father have custody substituted.

Question

Is it at all relevant *why* the status quo has lasted for so long since the parents separated? Or the circumstances in which they did so?

This case is a good illustration of the conflict between the two factors which traditionally loom largest in the reported cases, the so-called 'maternal preference' and a reluctance to disturb the 'status quo':

Re W (a minor)
(1982) 4 FLR 492, 13 Fam Law 47, Court of Appeal

A little girl was born in May 1980 and cared for by her mother for nine months, until the mother left the matrimonial home in February 1981. She wished to take the baby, but the father would not agree. From February to

July 1981, the baby was cared for by the father, with help from his family while he was at work. The father did everything for her while at home and formed a much closer relationship with her than 'most young fathers'. Since July 1981, the baby had largely been cared for by Mrs C, who became the father's cohabitant. Custody proceedings between the parents were first heard by magistrates in May 1981, when interim custody was awarded to the father, with daily access to the mother. In July, this was reduced to reasonable access, later fixed as weekly, with every other weekend spent at the mother's home. The case was transferred to the High Court, but not heard until July 1982, when Ewbank J awarded custody to the mother. The father appealed.

Cumming-Bruce LJ: . . . [Counsel for the father] submits that . . . the judge was weighing the scales too heavily against the father . . . [the judge] put it in this way:
'. . . the courts consider that a child of this age and a child considerably older than this too ought to be with the mother if other things are equal unless there is some strong ground for saying that the child's best interests will be away from her mother'.
I would not myself think it wise to make such a generalisation about the view of the courts. I would prefer to say that, as a matter of general experience, culled from the evidence that has been given in court, including the evidence of paediatricians, sociologists, social scientists, social workers and many varieties of educational people, is to this effect. First, the individual circumstances of every case vary so much that any generalisation has to be qualified in the light of a sensitive grasp of the realities of all the relationships between the child and the various grown-ups concerned. Secondly, the capacity of the grown-ups, who are put forward as claimants for care and control, is of immense importance in proving their capacity for forming affectionate, loving relationships with the child or children concerned.
Thirdly, if all such factors are nicely balanced, then probably it is right for a child of tender years to be brought up by his or her natural mother.
Fourthly, when, as a result of separation of the parents, the natural mother has been cut off for a significant period of continuous care for a small child, and the father and/or the father and another lady have stepped into the breach so that for months or years the child has been learning to place its security upon the father and/or the father's other lady, it becomes in each case a very delicate weighing exercise to decide whether it is now right, in the interests of the child, to take the risk of uprooting him or her in order that it may continue to be brought up by the natural mother. . . .
I would think it safer if one is trying to formulate the test, to substitute for the words 'unless there is some strong ground for saying that the child's best interests would be away from the mother', the words 'unless there is some ground for saying that the child's best interests would be away from the mother', though speaking for myself, the appreciation of the relevant factors varies so immensely in every single case that an attempt by a lawyer to grasp such a formulation is likely to be unhelpful. But in practical affairs, of course, particularly in the Law Courts, we have to try to formulate our criteria.
. . . When it came to the weighing exercise which the judge had to do, I am satisfied that he reached his conclusion because he was confident that the reality of the situation was that the child had in early life been in the care of her mother, who was ready and willing to go on bringing up her daughter and with whom throughout she had preserved a relationship; that although the roots of the child were in her father and his home, the discontinuity of contact with the mother had not been such as to make it sensible to prevent the mother resuming the full time upbringing of her daughter. . . .
Appeal dismissed.

Question

Counsel for the husband complained that the trial judge had not explained *why* it was in the child's long term interests to be brought up by her mother: do you think that the Court of Appeal provided a satisfactory answer?

In the following very similar case, however, the status quo prevailed:

B v B (Custody of Child)
[1985] FLR 462, [1985] Fam Law 29, Court of Appeal

The parties were married in April 1979. They had one child, PM, a boy born in November 1980, who was just three at the time of the Court of Appeal hearing. In October 1981, the mother left the father and went to live with a Mr K. In December 1981, a consent order was made by magistrates giving custody to the father. The mother had gone through an unsettled time when the parties separated, but now had a suitable home with Mr K. In 1983, the parties were divorced and the mother applied for custody. The judge dismissed her application and she appealed.

Heilbron J: . . . There is no doubt that both parties love this child and that he not only likes but is attached to his mother and likes Mr K. The quality of his attachment to his father, however, is very strong, and it is to be expected that it should be so, because from a bare recital of the dates and facts to which I have referred it is quite obvious that this child has really had no one else to bring him up except his father, he has known no other home than the former matrimonial home, and there is no doubt, on the evidence — and the judge so found — that the father was a very responsible and caring young man. Although the father had had a job which took him away from the house all day (except on Fridays and, of course, Sundays), he made very careful arrangements to see that his son did not suffer in any way from his absence at work. In the first place he arranged for his mother and sister, Mrs U, to look after the child, but when his mother unfortunately died his sister continued to look after PM when the father was unable so to do. He took his son the 3 or 4 miles to Mrs U's house. She is a very competent and caring mother with three young children of her own, and no one could find fault with her care of PM. Not only that, but she apparently used her good offices to assuage the bitterness that so often occurs in cases of this kind so that, as we are now told, access is working very well and the bitterness has, to a large extent, subsided between former husband and wife.

That the father had to use the services of Mrs U was a matter of some concern to the welfare officer as well as to the judge, because it meant that the child had to be taken to her early in the day and brought home by his father on his return from work. Nevertheless, even at that period this child went home to his own bed 7 nights a week, was put to bed by his father, bathed, fed, looked after and cared for in a way which has not been criticized by anyone.

The judge, on those facts, found that the father was a responsible and satisfactory parent. The situation was not ideal (it never is ideal when a marriage breaks up in these circumstances), but he had no doubt that Mr and Mrs U were eminently suitable people to look after PM while his father was at work, that PM fitted in well with the family; and that, even in those circumstances, he was receiving better attention and more love than he would have been if his father were to put him in a day nursery while he was at work. The situation at that stage was such that the judge came to the conclusion that although the mother would be a competent mother there was no tangible evidence to that effect, . . .

Miss Renton [Counsel for the mother], in a most persuasive address, has urged upon the court that the judge was wrong even in the then circumstances. She says that since the decision of the judge, access has taken place, it has been successful; but, Miss Renton says, in addition to that the child has a good relationship with his mother and one has always to predicate the possibility of some risk when there is a change. She submitted further that although, admittedly, the mother did go through an irresponsible period, she has now matured and would be a responsible mother. She said that the judge took too greatly into account his view (indeed, she submits, it was an overwhelming feature of his judgment) that the child would suffer, or would be likely to suffer, some risk as a result of a transfer.

Miss Renton, in my opinion quite rightly, did not submit that in every case a child of this age should be with its mother. Indeed, this case is a good illustration of the sort of situation where a young child may be well looked after, its welfare may be well served and it may be as well cared for by a loving and responsible father. . . .

Since the appellant's application for custody was dismissed the husband points out, in his up-to-date affidavit, his own situation has altered and this has affected the arrangements for looking after PM. Briefly, what has happened is that this is not the case of a father who has deliberately given up work in order to go on social security: circumstances have forced him to give up work because the firm asked him — indeed, required him — to go on shift work and this was obviously incompatible with continuing to look after PM in the way that he would wish to do, so that he reluctantly had to refuse that offer. There were other qualifications which now no longer exist and the fact is that he is now unemployed and is likely to be for some little time. He hopes that when PM goes to school — and there does not seem to be any reason why this hope should not be fulfilled — he will be able to undertake part-time work, which I understand is what the mother is now doing.

So far as the case is concerned today — although this was not before the judge — the position has, if anything, improved from the point of view of the father: no longer does he have to take his son the 3-miles journey 3 days a week.

On the other hand, Miss Renton counters that by saying: 'Well, here is a man living on social security, that is a disadvantage and is not a good thing'. I do not think there is anything in that point in this case; the facts are vastly different from the sort of case where a father deliberately gives up work in order to go on social security so as to keep or obtain custody of a child. This is a continuing situation. Through no fault of his own, the father is now unemployed. It so happens that it puts him in a position whereby he can devote even more time to looking after this child, who will benefit thereby.

Appeal dismissed.

Questions

(i) What factors can you find to distinguish this case from *Re W*? In which direction do they point?

(ii) Would it make any difference in cases like these if (*a*) the father deliberately refused to let the mother take the child with her, and (*b*) refused to let her have any access after she had gone, and (*c*) delayed the hearing of her applications for custody and access as long as possible? Should it?

(iii) What do you think of the distinction drawn by the judge between different classes of unemployed fathers? Or between unemployed fathers and unemployed mothers?

(iv) Go back to what the Warnock Report (p.497, above) had to say about motherhood: do you think that the fact that the mother has carried and given birth to the child is relevant at all?

There are, of course, other considerations apart from 'maternal preference' and 'status quo', as illustrated by the following cases:

C v C (a minor) (custody: appeal)
[1991] FCR 254, [1991] 1 FLR 223, Court of Appeal

The parties married and had a daughter (now nearly seven) in 1983. They separated in 1984 and divorced in 1988. The mother had care and control, with reasonable access to the father. The mother became a prison officer, fell in love with a woman prisoner, and on the woman's release went to live with her, with the child. The father remarried. In October 1989, while the child was staying with her father and step-mother at half-term, the mother and partner were evicted from their home and the mother asked the father to keep the child for a little while. The father decided that she would be better off with him and applied for custody. At the hearing in June 1990, the judge awarded care and control to the mother, for the following reasons:

It's not an easy case and I have come to my conclusion not without hesitation, but in the end as it seems to me the question of the lesbian relationship is one which is there anyway, and the child is going to have to cope with anyway. I don't think there can be much difference in the speed with which that problem will come to the child's consciousness, whichever decision I make. It seems to be being accepted that it would come to the child's consciousness sooner if she's living with mother. I wonder about that. Secondly, I can't see that there is going to be a great deal of difference between the way in which she will be assisted in tackling that, because if she is living with father she will spend the bulk of her time in a household where lesbian relationship is not seen favourably and therefore there's a balance of easing her task in accepting the problem in living with mother, but I don't think that's a great feature to put into the balance. If I were being asked here to choose between a child being brought up wholly ignorant of lesbian relationships and untouched on the one hand, and on the other hand in heterosexual relationships, it seems to me there might be an appreciable balance one way in favour of what, unlike the welfare officer, I do see as 'the normal', but in the end I have come to the conclusion that the most important factor in this case, and one which is not outweighed by the advantages the other way, is the strong bond, and the one which until October 1989 was almost untampered with, between the child and her mother. On balance, I come to the conclusion that she is better living with her mother, and I award care and control to her with reasonable access which I have every confidence will be sorted out by the parties in the co-operative way they have been able to work hitherto.

The father appealed.

Glidewell LJ: . . . it is my clear view . . . that, with all respect to the judge, the conclusion at which he arrived in relation to the effect on C of her mother's lesbian relationship was plainly wrong. I have reached this conclusion for the following reasons.

Despite the vast change over the past 30 years or so in the attitudes of our society generally to the institution of marriage, to sexual morality, and to homosexual relationships, I regard it as axiomatic that the ideal environment for the upbringing of a child is the home of loving, caring and sensible parents, her father and her mother. When the marriage between father and mother is at an end, that ideal cannot be attained. When the court is called upon to decide which of two possible alternatives is then preferable for the child's welfare, its task is to choose the alternative which comes closest to that ideal.

Even taking account of the changes of attitude to which I have referred, a lesbian relationship between two adult women is an unusual background in which to bring up a child. I think that the mother herself recognises this, because the judge recorded her as saying that she was sensitive to the problems that could arise, and did not flaunt the sexual nature of her relationship.

The judge had no evidence, and thus we have none, about the effect on a young child of learning the nature of a lesbian relationship and of her friends learning about it. Nevertheless, it seems that the judge accepted, and it is certainly my view, that it is undesirable that this child should learn or understand at an early age the nature of her mother's relationship. The judge seems to have thought that she was just as likely to acquire this knowledge and understanding if living with her father and stepmother and staying from time to time with her mother, as she would if she lived permanently with her mother. In this respect, I think the judge was plainly wrong.

Moreover, he seems to have disregarded the effect on C of her school friends learning of the relationship. If or when they do, she is bound to be asked questions which may well cause her distress or embarrassment. If she is at school in Shrewsbury, living in a heterosexual household, it is much less likely that she will be exposed to this.

These are factors to which, as I have said, the judge gave no weight. He struck the balance as if there were no lesbian relationship. If there had not been, his decision could not be faulted. But his disregard of these factors was in my judgment a plain error.

I make it clear that I am not saying that the fact that a mother is living in a lesbian relationship is conclusive, or that it disqualifies her from ever having the care and control of her child. A court may well decide that a sensitive, loving lesbian relationship is a more satisfactory environment for a child than a less sensitive or loving alternative. But that the nature of the relationship is an important factor to be put into the balance seems to me to be clear.

For this reason I would allow the appeal and set aside the judge's order. There remains the question what order this court should make. Although I am very conscious that it is desirable that a final decision in this matter should be made as soon as possible, I nevertheless consider

that the proper course is for us to order a rehearing, at which the judge can decide afresh the proper weight to give to all the factors, including those to which I have referred.
. . . .

Balcombe LJ: . . . One thing is however clear: in making a decision on welfare the judge should not be influenced by subjective considerations. To take an example: the issue may be whether the child is to be brought up in the faith of religion A or in that of religion B. The judge may be a member of religion A, and a firm believer in its tenets: nevertheless, he must try to ensure that his personal beliefs do not affect his judicial function in deciding where the child's welfare lies.

Nevertheless, although the judge may not allow his subjective views to affect his decision on what the child's welfare requires, he cannot abdicate responsibility merely because the issue is a sensitive one on which differing views are held. What standards then should he apply if he is not to apply his own subjective views?

In my judgment, he should start on the basis that the moral standards which are generally accepted in the society in which the child lives are more likely than not to promote his or her welfare. As society is now less homogeneous than it was 100 or even 50 years ago, those standards may differ between different communities, and the judge may in appropriate cases be invited to receive evidence as to the standards accepted in a particular community, but in default of such evidence and where, as here, the child does not come from a particular ethnic minority, the judge is entitled, and indeed bound, to apply his or her own experience in determining what are the accepted standards.

. . . Of course, the fact that the mother has a lesbian partner is not of itself a reason for denying the mother the care and control of her daughter; the question is: in conducting the balancing exercise what weight should the judge give to the fact that, if care and control is given to the mother, the child's home will be the mother's home, with all that that involves? I agree with Glidewell LJ that in those circumstances the judge can only start with the approach that in our society it is still the norm that children are brought up in a home with a father, mother and siblings (if any) and, other things being equal, such an upbringing is most likely to be conducive to their welfare. If, because the parents are divorced, such an upbringing is no longer possible, then a very material factor in considering where the child's welfare lies is which of the competing parents can offer the nearest approach to that norm. In the present case it is clearly the father.

If the judge had adopted that approach and had then come to the conclusion that the advantages of the child being with the mother outweighed all other relevant factors, this court could not have interfered with his decision: see *G v G (Minors) (Custody Appeal)* [1985] FLR 894. . . .

Appeal allowed. Case remitted for rehearing.

Questions

(i) Whose reasoning do you prefer?

(ii) Do you regard it as axiomatic that the ideal environment for the upbringing of a child is the home of loving, caring and sensible parents?

(iii) If so, should the court be looking for something as close as possible to that ideal? Is this what Goldstein, Freud and Solnit (p.532, below) mean by the 'least detrimental alternative'?

(iv) Do you think that the judge can avoid letting his subjective views affect his decision?

May v May
[1986] 1 FLR 325, [1986] Fam Law 105, Court of Appeal

The parties were married in 1978. They had two sons, one born in 1977 before their marriage, and the other born in 1979. In 1983, the mother left the father, taking both children with her, and went to live with a Mr Mitchell, with whom she was still living. In 1985, the judge granted the parents joint custody, with care and control to the father. The mother appealed.

Ackner LJ: . . . The judge commented, as I would wish to, on the extremely helpful and balanced reports of the welfare officer, . . . upon whom he clearly relied in regard to her views about the children, the parents and Mr Mitchell. The welfare officer, in a telling phrase, said that the conflict was not as to the competence of either of the parents. It was a conflict of different values. In her conclusions, . . . she said:

'Here one has an invidious role in trying to assist in the choice between two parents who in any other circumstances would never be under scrutiny and who by all standards have done a marvellous job together in bringing up these little boys so far.'

In her report she commended the mother for the affection and care which she had lavished on the children. The judge in terms accepted that. In regard to the father, she said this:

'Mr May has always taken a full share in the care of his sons, the more so because his wife had been employed in the evenings and at weekends, so he had a substantial part in the children's day-to-day care — feeding, bathing and putting to bed. It is quite evident when seeing the children with their father that they are well used to being in his sole care and that he has a constructive, stimulating and loving relationship with them. He and his older son are, I think, especially close; nevertheless, the responses of both children are so natural as to indicate his longstanding share in their upbringing.'

. . . In her conclusion she said that she was confident that the boys would be well cared for by either party.

'Not only have they a concerned and capable mother, they have a concerned and capable father who is just as well versed in their practical needs as his wife and who has made sensible arrangements to enable him to assume their care.'

Those arrangements involve his agreeing with his employer, the local authority, by whom he is employed as a cost accountant, to work very restricted hours, from 9 a.m. to 4 p.m., thereby enabling him to take the children to school and to be available to collect them or be at home when they come home. He has extensive holidays, and any need to increase the time spent with the children in case there was some illness could be made up so far as his employers were concerned by his working at home.

'There is a conflict of values between the parents — differences in which the parties could have complemented each other if the marriage had continued. Mr May does, I think, place greater emphasis on fostering academic achievement. He would also inculcate different values — for example he chose to put some of Russell's birthday money in a building society account; Mrs May felt he should be allowed to spend it all. Mrs May says that her husband has said things to distress the children, but perhaps underestimates the distress which her own decision has caused both the children and her husband. Mr Mitchell says he does indeed have different attitudes from Mr May.'

I intervene here to say that, without criticizing him, he has a much freer and easier approach to life, and his approach to the discipline of the children, (the time they should spend working, the time they should spend watching television and the like) and the emphasis on academic achievements would be significantly different from that of Mr May. The welfare officer says:

'. . . my discussions with Mr May have shown him sensitive to and concerned for his sons in all aspects of their life, and in his dealings with them he is warm and demonstrative. Both Mr May and Mr Mitchell are keen sportsmen and can foster athletic development. Mrs May, because of her quiet nature, will need the support of her partner as the boys grow to test parental discipline.'

In her penultimate paragraph . . .

'The frequent access visits to the matrimonial home have helped to maintain the anchor for the children and there would be little trauma for them in returning there.' [She concluded by saying:] 'Both parents love these little boys; one of them is going to be dreadfully hurt by the decision of the court with regard to care and control and whatever that decision this is clearly a case where joint custody should be granted.'

It is quite clear from her report that the welfare officer did not think it appropriate to make any criticism of either of the two alternatives offered to the judge that the children should stay with the mother and Mr Mitchell (whom she intends to marry) where the children have been for some 18 months, or go to the father, subject to course to generous access to the mother. The judge said in terms that in this sort of case

'. . . neither party can win. There are losers on both sides. The real losers are the children, whose parents have split up.'

. . . The judge accepted that there was this conflict as to values, a conflict as to standards. He accepted that the question of discipline was one very much in the mind of the father, the discipline meaning learning to discipline and organize one's own life. It is not a question of acceding to demands as a result of being shouted at. He accepted that the access which was available to the father was not sufficient to enable him to take a full part in developing the boys' character in the way that he would wish to do. He accepted that the father believed that with the assistance of his parents, who run a hotel nearby and who are young grandparents, he would be able to bring up the children in a more disciplined way than the mother. The judge commented: 'He may be right in that. Time will tell.' However, he concluded that it was in the children's best interests that they should be in the care and control of the father, and that was obviously designed to enable the father to bring up the children in the way that the father thought was appropriate and which was designed to stimulate them from the educational point of view and to develop their character in a manner which he thought was appropriate. To my mind it is perfectly clear that the judge accepted that it was in the best interests of the children to have the values of the father upon which to base their upbringing rather than those in the mother's house, which were different.
[Having rehearsed the grounds of appeal, he could find nothing sufficient to disturb the exercise of the judge's discretion.]
Appeal dismissed.

Questions

(i) Would you have moved children after 18 months because of a 'conflict of values' of this nature?
(ii) Do you think that it made any difference that they were both boys?
(iii) In Lord Justice Ackner's view, 'the judge did not base his decision upon the circumstances in which the wife left her husband, but he was perfectly entitled to point out that [these] in no way reflected upon the character or conduct of the father. On the contrary, if it reflected at all it reflected upon the mother.' He went on to say that this was relevant to the future permanence of the relationship between the mother and Mr Mitchell. Do you think that there may be a conflict of values between Lord Justice Ackner and Lord Justice Ormrod (at p. 514, above)?

If the courts have found some difficulty in balancing the status quo against the claims of the parent whom they feel most suitable to meet the child's needs, they have found far less difficulty in insisting upon the child's need to maintain contact with both parents. Eekelaar (1973) was inclined to describe access as one of the few remaining 'rights' of parenthood. Since then, the courts have turned the terminology, but not the practice, on its head:

M v M (child: access)
[1973] 2 All ER 81, High Court, Family Division

The parents married in 1956 and adopted the child, a boy now aged seven, in 1966. The mother was not able to give him 'full maternal care' and in 1969 a supervision order was made. In 1970, the mother left both father and boy. Her matrimonial complaint to the local magistrates' court was unsuccessful and custody was awarded to the father, with reasonable access to the mother. Access did not run smoothly, because of the parties' extreme hostility to one another. Each began to commit adultery, but once the mother became pregnant, the father refused to allow her to see the boy. She applied for access to be defined; the father applied for it to be revoked. By the time of the hearing she had not seen the boy for a year. There was evidence that access had an extremely disturbing effect upon the boy and the justices revoked it. The mother appealed.

Wrangham J: . . . it seems to me . . . that the companionship of a parent is in any ordinary circumstances of such immense value to the child that there is a basic right in him to such companionship. I for my part would prefer to call it a basic right in the child rather than a basic right in the parent. That only means this, that no court should deprive a child of access to either parent unless it is wholly satisfied that it is in the interests of that child that access should cease, and that is a conclusion at which a court should be extremely slow to arrive. It is not without significance that Edmund Davies LJ in *B v B* [1971] 3 All ER 682, [1971] 1 WLR 1486, CA said:

'For a court to deprive a good parent completely of access to his child is to make a dreadful order. That is what has been done here, and the impact on both parent and child must have lifelong consequences. Very seldom can the court bring itself to make so Draconian an order, and rarely is it necessary.'

I should add that in that case the boy was in his teens, so that there was little prospect of making a change in the access arrangements later. The order cutting off access could only in the circumstances of that case be regarded as effectively final, whereas of course in many cases, and this is one, there would be no reason for supposing that the cessation of access need be final.

I think before parting with *B v B* one should also note that the members of the Court of Appeal criticised very strongly the mother who had had the care and control of this boy during the years in which he grew up and had used it to alienate him from his father. I cite the words of Edmund Davies LJ, who quoted the report of the Official Solicitor, who said he did not suggest that the mother had wilfully attempted to turn the boy against his father, but, because she honestly believed it was not in the interests of the boy for there to be access, she had done nothing towards creating an atmosphere in which the boy would willingly go to the father for access. Edmund Davies LJ's comment was this:

'In general, one parent who takes that attitude in relation to the other parent is undertaking a tremendous responsibility and discharging it thoroughly badly. Again speaking generally, it is the duty of parents, whatever their personal differences may be, to seek to inculcate in the child a proper attitude of respect for the other parent.'

For these reasons I do not think it can be said that the justices, in reaching the conclusion which they did, were acting contrary to the law as laid down by the Court of Appeal. Quite clearly they placed before themselves the rule that the welfare of the child is the paramount consideration; they say so in terms; and they came to their conclusion on the ground that the welfare of the child would not be promoted by the continuance of access and would be promoted by the cessation of access. . . .

Latey J: . . . Where one finds, as one does for example in *S v S and P* [1962] 2 All ER 1, [1962] 1 WLR 4452, a reference to the basic right of a parent to access to the child, I do not accept that the meaning conveyed is that a parent should have access to the child although such access is contrary to the child's interests, and when one reads *S v S and P* in conjunction with the more recent decisions of the Court of Appeal, to which Wrangham J has referred, I agree entirely, and as emphatically as I can, that what is meant is this: where the parents have separated and one has the care of the child, access by the other often results in some upset in the child. Those upsets are usually minor and superficial. They are heavily outweighed by the long term advantages to the child of keeping in touch with the parent concerned so that they do not become strangers, so that the child later in life does not resent the deprivation and turn against the parent who the child thinks, rightly or wrongly, has deprived him, and so that the deprived parent loses interest in the child and therefore does not make the material and emotional contribution to the child's development which that parent by its companionship and otherwise would make.

Appeal dismissed.

Questions

(i) How does one distinguish between upset to a child which is 'minor and superficial' and upset which is seriously damaging to the child?

(ii) Is the damage any less serious to the child even if the upset is caused by the attitude of the custodial parent (cf. *Re E (a minor: access)* [1987] 1 FLR 368, [1987] Fam Law 90, CA)?

The problems of the law in attempting to enforce this 'right' against the wishes of the parent with whom the child lives are demonstrated in the following case:

V-P v V-P (access to child)
(1978) 1 FLR 336, 10 Fam Law 20, Court of Appeal

The parents married in 1971. The father came from Mauritius and was at that time working as a clerical officer in the civil service. The mother came from a Welsh farming family and was working in London as an assistant architect. They had one daughter, now aged six, but the father had an older son by an earlier relationship. They divorced in 1977 and custody of the daughter was awarded to the mother, but the mother strongly opposed access from the outset. In February 1978, the judge ordered that the father should have reasonable access, and made a supervision order. This order was unsuccessful and in May the judge ordered specified access. The mother permitted the first visit, but thereafter totally refused access and refused to co-operate with the welfare officer. The judge appointed the Official Solicitor to represent the child, but when the matter came before him in November, the mother was still opposed to access. The judge made no order as to access and the father appealed.

Ormrod LJ: [After reciting the facts:] That is the situation which led the learned judge to make the order which he did and far be it from me to criticize him for doing so. But the situation as it presents itself to my mind is this: the mother has put forward no real grounds at all for refusing access to the father. The evidence of the upset to this child is minimal. It is totally uncorroborated in any way and it is in direct conflict with the impression that Mr Dunning, the supervising officer, obtained. He thought that the child was delighted to see her father and enjoyed it. Indeed the school mistress thought also that the child had benefited very much by seeing her father: she had come alive, as it were. So far as all the independent evidence is concerned, it is absolutely clear that there is nothing to suggest that F herself suffers in any way from seeing her father; in fact the suggestion is to the contrary.

That being so, a serious situation obviously arises. It is a difficult situation and one with which the court is not unfamiliar. An implacable opposition by one parent about access always means, of course, that it is nothing whatever to do with the child, but it is everything to do with the parents. What the background of the relationship between the father and mother is none of us knows. All we do know is that the mother seems to have been a very clever girl who got to London, got into higher education and started training as an architect. She has reached the stage of being an architectural assistant and is obviously, therefore, a person of great intelligence, who has retreated back into a very rural community, where it is reasonably obvious that her marriage to her husband is a matter of acute embarrassment to her and no doubt equally an acute embarrassment to her mother, because she has in fact, since her father's death, left her husband and gone back to her mother. . . .

Where this passionate opposition to access is coming from, whether it is really coming from the mother, who wants to put this mistaken marriage completely behind her, or whether it is coming from her mother, who totally disapproves of it, one does not know. But that the child is suffering as a consequence of this attitude of her mother and grandmother is abundantly plain and that she will certainly suffer in the future is even clearer. . . .

It is difficult to know whether the mother appreciates what she is doing. I suppose that probably she does not see the full implications. No-one wants to make threats or to adopt a hostile, compulsive attitude in this kind of situation, but the court cannot possibly accept a situation like this unless the evidence leading to it is really conclusive. I have already said the evidence as to the upset of this child in respect of one period of access on May 23 is really much too slight to act upon. On the other hand, I fully appreciate the Official Solicitor's representative's view that head-on confrontations at this stage with mother and grandmother are not likely to be productive. But the court is dealing today with a woman who is highly educated, even if still perhaps rather unsophisticated. She must be a woman who has a sufficient moral sense to understand her duty to this child. She may be unable to deal with her own mother — I do not know whether that is so or not — but the responsibility that is resting upon her at this moment in refusing access to the father is very very great indeed. I hope that she at least will understand that, as a responsible member of society and a responsible mother, she has a duty to comply with orders made by courts in this regard. It should not be necessary when dealing with intelligent people for the court to be thinking in terms of sanctions. One only uses sanctions to compel the stupid to do things, or the obstinate. But if the court, having seriously considered the welfare of this child, comes to the conclusion that there should be access, the court is entitled to expect that the mother will seriously consider what this court says and will do her best to co-operate with it.

I have said that I do not want to issue threats, but the mother should, I think, realize this: the father has a home with the half brother in it, he is unemployed, he is available to look after both these children full time. The mother is fully occupied, so that the grandmother is playing a very important part in this child's life. The child is in a totally feminine environment at the present moment and one does not want a repetition of the situation where the mother has grown up under the domination of her mother. I would imagine the mother does not want to produce a situation in which, when this child is 12 or 13, she revolts against this feminine environment and goes to her father, which is a possibility.

That being so, it would be a mistake on the part of the mother, in my judgment, to assume that the order for custody in her favour is inevitable; it is not and if the situation goes on as it is at present then it may be necessary to reconsider the question of custody. I say no more, because no-one would willingly take this child away from her mother unless there were strong reasons for doing so, but there are what look to me like potentially strong reasons for taking that course if we are going to be confronted with a total non-cooperation on the part of the mother. I do not hold out any hopes for the father, it would be quite wrong that he should build any hopes on this, but in my view the right way to deal with this case is to make an order which demonstrates clearly to the mother and to her mother the view of the court.

Appeal allowed. Order varied to provide that there shall be access at the discretion of the supervising officer. . . . Custody to be reviewed within 12 months. . . .

Questions

(i) If you were faced with a child's mother such as this, would you be inclined to do what one of the judges in Dodds' (1981) survey suggested: 'Persuade. Threaten. Give Up.'?

(ii) Have you noticed how many of the cases in which the judiciary have emphasised the importance of retaining ties with both parents concern cross-cultural relationships? What effect, if any, do you think this factor may have had upon the court?

(iii) The law reports cannot reveal the other side of the coin, which may be a more common problem: if continued contact is the 'right of the child,' how can the law enforce the corresponding duty of the non-custodial parent?

In *Divorce and the Reluctant Father* (1980), Anne Heath-Jones gives a vivid account of the problem and her solution to it:

When my husband and I separated 12 years ago, we had two children who were then one and three years of age with long years of childhood ahead of them. . . .

James was never a doting father, which had been one of the problems of the marriage. In effect I had always been a single parent. The boys were very young and their awareness of, and attachment to, their remote father was slight. James was all set to vanish from our lives completely.

But somehow in all the mess, in all my own grief and loneliness, and in spite of all the bitterness I harboured against him, I knew that if I had strength to fight for anything it should be to maintain contact between the children and their father. . . .

In those early years the fact that he saw them at all was due to every imaginable ploy. Persuasion, appeal, anger and tears. I met him more than half-way on any arrangement that he was prepared to concede. I would deliver them to his flat and collect them. If he refused to have them to stay overnight then I settled for one day — or half a day. I felt anything was better than that they should lose touch and become strangers.

Meanwhile, I kept James informed of progress at nursery and later primary school. I made sure the boys remembered his birthday; I showed him school reports. I begged him (swallowing large hunks of indigestible pride) to attend school open days, birthday parties and Guy Fawkes parties. Most important of all I kept his image intact for his children. They never heard from me any criticism of his character, or knew of my deep hurt and resentment that their father needed so much coercion to see them or be involved in their lives.

For many years all the initiative for contact came from us. He never 'phoned or wrote or asked to see them. Then slowly, very slowly, the years of effort began to pay off. The boys and I moved from London into the country. James came down occasionally for the weekend and I would clear off and leave the cottage to them. After he re-married a more or less regular arrangement was worked out for the school holidays.

We were lucky in his choice of a new wife. She was friendly and accepted her two stepsons, and in time they formed an easy relationship with her. Christmases were now peopled with a whole new branch of extended family. Instead of moping alone with me (and some Christmases were very mopey) they had a welcome at their father's and his relations and even at the big family gatherings of his new wife. . . .

Now, 1967 seems a long time ago and their childhood is nearly over. The relationship with their father now is mutually warm, positive and spontaneous. At times the price to pay for nurturing that relationship has been high. If you idealise the absent parent you must be prepared for the consequences.

When life got tough for us, when the boys were unhappy with school or friends, or when they sobbed for the father whose contact I had so carefully preserved, the cry was 'I want to live with Dad.' It hurt of course because I had provided the years of love and security, it hurt because I knew their father wouldn't want them and it hurt because that was the last thing in the world that I could explain to the crying child.

In spite of the upheavals of those early years we have all survived. They now have a father they can respect and admire, a man they can talk to and learn from, and a model to emulate when they become husbands and fathers themselves.

The differences between disputes about children and other types of litigation, and the inherent difficulties involved in knowing what the best solution will be, are spelled out by Robert H. Mnookin in *Child Custody Adjudication: Judicial Functions in the Face of Indeterminacy* (1975):

At the core of adjudication is the notion that government exercises authority through a process in which the persons affected can participate. Each party has an 'institutionally guaranteed . . . opportunity to present proofs and arguments for a decision in his favour.' A neutral judge resolves the dispute by ascertaining past events and evaluating those past events against articulated and described legal standards that are generally applicable. As part of this process, the judge is obliged to reconcile the rules used to evaluate these past events with those announced and applied in earlier disputes of the same sort. The parties then usually may ask some higher court to review the decision to determine whether the appropriate rules were applied and, to a limited extent, whether the past events were accurately ascertained. Child-custody disputes resolved under the broad best-interests-of-the-child principle differ from this model of adjudication in several closely interrelated ways.

1. 'Person-oriented' not 'act-oriented' determinations
The first and most striking difference relates to a distinction suggested by Lon Fuller: custody disputes under the best-interests principle require 'person-oriented,' not 'act-oriented,' determinations. Most legal rules require determination of some event and are thus 'act-oriented' (1971). A 'person-oriented' rule, on the other hand, requires an evaluation of the 'whole person viewed as a social being.' Several of the other important ways in which child-custody disputes differ from the paradigm of adjudication follow from this feature of person- rather than act-orientation. . . .

In deciding [ordinary] litigation, it will not be remotely relevant which disputant has more money, is more humane, works harder, gives more to charity, follows better religious practices, or takes better care of his house. The resolution will only be person-oriented to the extent that the judge must evaluate each as a social being in order to determine whether one should be considered more credible than the other.

Resolution of a custody dispute by the best-interests-of-the-child principle stands in sharp contrast to the foregoing. In a divorce custody fight, a court *must* evaluate the attitudes, dispositions, capacities, and shortcomings of each parent to apply the best-interest standard. Indeed, the inquiry centers on what kind of person each parent is, and what the child is like. That there is, however, nothing inherent in custody disputes requiring resolution by a person-oriented rule is shown by the nineteenth century examples of act-oriented rules for custody disputes between a child's parents.

2. Predictions not determinations of past acts
Adjudication usually requires the determination of *past* acts and facts, not a prediction of *future* events. Applying the best-interests standard requires an individualized prediction: with whom will this child be better off in the years to come? Proof of what happened in the past is relevant only insofar as it enables the court to decide what is likely to happen in the future. . . .

3. Interdependence of outcome-affecting factors
Because custody disputes involve *relationships* between people, a decision affecting any one of the parties will often necessarily have an effect on the others. The resolution of a custody dispute may permanently affect—or even end—the parties' legal relationship; but the social and psychological relationships will usually continue. The best-interests principle requires a prediction of what will happen in the future, which, of course, depends in part on the future behavior of the parties. Because these parties will often interact in the future, this probable interaction must be taken into account in deciding what the outcome is to be. For example, awarding custody to the mother may affect the father's behavior, which, in turn, can affect the mother's behavior and the child. The possibility of such feedback must be considered in applying the best-interests standard. Most disputes resolved by adjudication do not require predictions involving appraisals of future relationships where the 'loser's' future behavior can be an important ingredient.

4. Findings, precedent, and appellate review
A determination that is person-oriented and requires predictions necessarily involves an evaluation of the parties who have appeared in court. This has important consequences for the roles of both precedent and appellate review in custody cases. The result of an earlier case involving different people has limited relevance to a subsequent case requiring individualized evaluations of a particular child and the litigants. Prior reported cases now provide little basis for controlling or predicting the outcome of a particular case. Moreover, the trial court in custody disputes is often not required to make specific findings of fact, much less write an opinion about the case or reconcile what has been done in this case with what has happened before.

All of this makes the scope of appellate review extremely limited. Because the trial court's decision involves an assessment of the personality, character and relationship of people the judge has seen in court, appellate courts are extremely loath to upset the trial court's determination on the basis of a transcript. In the words of an English judge, 'So much may turn, consciously or unconsciously, on estimates of character which cannot be made by those who have not seen or heard the parties.' As Professor Fuller has written, 'It would be hard [for an appellate court to pass an intelligent judgment on the trial court's decision] unless it were prepared to summon the husband, wife and child before it and try the case over again.'

5. Participation by all affected parties
Normally, parties most obviously affected by a dispute have a right to participate in the adjudicatory process. *The* issue in a child-custody dispute is what will become of the child, but ordinarily the child is not a true participant in the process. While the best-interests principle requires that the primary focus be on the interests of the child, the child ordinarily does not define those interests himself, nor does he have representation in the ordinary sense. Even in states that allow for independent representation for the child in the dispute, the role of the child's advocate is different from that in normal adjudication. A lawyer usually looks to his client for instructions about the goals to be pursued. Except in the case of older children, a child's representative in a custody dispute must himself normally define the child's interests.

Having concluded that child custody adjudication cannot fit the usual model of litigation, Mnookin goes on to consider whether it can fit a managerial model of rational decision-making:

Decision theorists have laid out the logic of rational choice with clarity and mathematical rigor for prototype decision problems. The decision-maker specifies alternative outcomes associated with different courses of action and then chooses that alternative that 'maximizes' his values, subject to whatever constraints the decision-maker faces. This involves two critical assumptions: first, that the decision-maker can specify alternative outcomes for each course of action; the second, that the decision-maker can assign to each outcome a 'utility' measure that integrates his values and allows comparisons among alternative outcomes. . . .

From the perspective of rational choice, the judge would wish to compare the expected utility for the child of living with his mother with that of living with his father. The judge would need considerable information and predictive ability to do this. The judge would also need some source for the values to measure utility for the child. All three are problematic.

a. The need for information: specifying possible outcomes
One can question how often, if ever, any judge will have the necessary information. In many instances, a judge lacks adequate information about even the most rudimentary aspects of a child's life with his parents and has still less information available about what either parent plans in the future. . . .

b. Predictions assessing the probability of alternative outcomes
Obviously, more than one outcome is possible for each course of judicial action, so the judge must assess the probability of various outcomes and evaluate the seriousness of possible benefits and harms associated with each. But even where a judge has substantial information about the child's past home life and the present alternatives, present-day knowledge about human behaviour provides no basis for the kind of individualized predictions required by the best-interests standard. There are numerous competing theories of human behavior, based on radically different conceptions of the nature of man, and no consensus exists that any one is correct. No theory at all is considered widely capable of generating reliable predictions about the psychological and behavioral consequences of alternative dispositions for a particular child.

While psychiatrists and psychoanalysts have at times been enthusiastic in claiming for themselves the largest possible role in custody proceedings, many have conceded that their theories provide no reliable guide for predictions about what is likely to happen to a particular child. Anna Freud, who has devoted her life to the study of the child and who plainly believes that theory can be a useful guide to treatment, has warned: 'In spite of . . . advances there remain factors which make clinical foresight, i.e. prediction, difficult and hazardous,' not the least of which is that 'environmental happenings in a child's life will always remain unpredictable since they are not governed by any known laws. . . .' (1958) . . .

c. Values to inform choice: assigning utilities to various outcomes
Even if the various outcomes could be specified and their probability estimated, a fundamental problem would remain unsolved. What set of values should a judge use to determine what is in a child's best interests? If a decision-maker must assign some measure of utility to each possible outcome, how is utility to be determined? . . .

Moreover, whether or not the judge looks to the child for some guidance, there remains the question whether best interests should be viewed from a long-term or a short-term perspective. The conditions that make a person happy at age 7 to 10 may have adverse consequences at age 30. Should the judge ask himself what decision will make the child happiest in the next year? Or at 30? Or at 70? Should the judge decide by thinking about what decision the child as an adult looking back would have wanted made? In this case, the preference problem is formidable, for how is the judge to compare 'happiness' at one age with 'happiness' at another age?

Deciding what is best for a child poses a question no less ultimate than the purposes and values of life itself. Should the judge be primarily concerned with the child's happiness? Or with the child's spiritual and religious training? Should the judge be concerned with the economic 'productivity' of the child when he grows up? Are the primary values of life in warm, interpersonal relationships, or in discipline and self-sacrifice? Is stability and security for a child more desirable than intellectual stimulation? These questions could be elaborated endlessly. And yet, where is the judge to look for the set of values that should inform the choice of what is best for the child? Normally, the custody statutes do not themselves give content or relative weights to the pertinent values. And if the judge looks to society at large, he finds neither a clear consensus as to the best child rearing strategies nor an appropriate hierarchy of ultimate values.

Question

Do the cases selected earlier support his analysis?

2 What do the 'experts' think?

Judges profess to be sceptical of the evidence which 'experts' may give in children cases. As Lord Upjohn said in *J v C* [1970] AC 668, [1969] 1 All ER 788, HL, p. 411, above:

In the case of a happy and normal infant in no need of medical care and attention for any malady or condition who is sent to a psychiatrist or other medical practitioner for the sole purpose of calling the practitioner to give quite general evidence on the dangers of taking this, that or the other course . . . such evidence may be valuable if accepted but it can only be as an element to support the general knowledge and experience of the judge in infancy matters. . . .

Indeed, judges have frequently said that children must not be taken by one parent to see such practitioners without the consent of the other parent or the leave of the court (*Re S (an infant)* [1967] 1 All ER 202, [1967] 1 WLR 396). Nevertheless, Michael King in *Childhood, Welfare and Justice* (1981) argues that it is not surprising that judges faced with difficult and emotionally charged decisions about children

. . . should search around for help both in making those decisions and in justifying them after they have been made. No more is it surprising that they should seek to give their decisions an aura of scientific respectability by making it appear that those whose advice they have accepted are indeed experts, and that the quality of their expertise is equated with that of a doctor over physical health or a scientist who makes discoveries and so advances our knowledge about the physical world.

Furthermore, judges seek to put into effect the values which they believe acceptable in society:

Not so long ago, the judiciary perceived these social values as being based upon Christian morality. Today, however, given the decline of the Church and the growth of pluralism, the only universally accepted truths . . . appear to be those manufactured by scientists.

It is therefore worth taking a brief look at some of the theories about child development which have both informed public opinion and formed the basis of much of the 'medical evidence' such as that given in *Re C (MA) (An Infant)* [1966] 1 All ER 838, [1966] 1 WLR 646, which is extensively quoted on pp. 487–488, above. Prime amongst these was the work of John Bowlby, whose popular book *Child Care and the Growth of Love* was first published in 1953. The gist of his theory is stated at the outset:

. . . What is believed to be essential for mental health is that an infant and young child should experience a warm, intimate, and continuous relationship with his mother (or permanent mother-substitute — one person who steadily 'mothers' him) in which both find satisfaction and enjoyment. It is this complex, rich and rewarding relationship with the mother in the early years, varied in countless ways by relations with the father and with the brothers and sisters, that child psychiatrists and many others now believe to underlie the development of character and of mental health.

A state of affairs in which a child does not have this relationship is termed 'maternal deprivation'. This is a general term covering a number of different situations. Thus, a child is deprived even though living at home if his mother (or permanent mother-substitute) is unable to give him the loving care small children need. Again a child is deprived if for any reason he is removed from his mother's care. . . .

The ill-effects of deprivation vary with its degree. Partial deprivation brings in its train anxiety, excessive need for love, powerful feelings of revenge, and, arising from these last, guilt and depression. A young child, still immature in mind and body, cannot cope with all these emotions and drives. The ways in which he responds to those disturbances of his inner life may in the end bring about nervous disorders and instability of character. . . .

Bowlby goes on to explain why the discussion in the book concentrates upon the mother and does not deal in detail with the father:

The reason for this is that almost all the evidence concerns the child's relation to his mother, which is without doubt in ordinary circumstances by far his most important relationship during these years. It is she who feeds and cleans him, keeps him warm and comforts him. It is to his mother that he turns when in distress. In the young child's eyes father plays second fiddle and his value increases only as the child becomes more able to stand alone. Nevertheless, as the illegitimate child knows, fathers have their uses even in infancy. Not only do they provide for their wives to enable them to devote themselves unrestrictedly to the care of the infant and toddler, but, by providing love and companionship, they support the mother emotionally and help her maintain that harmonious contented mood in the atmosphere of which her infant thrives.

Question

It is noticeable that this paragraph is phrased, not in terms of how things necessarily *should* be, but of how they in fact are: do you think that his estimate of the respective roles of mother and father in caring for very young children generally holds good today?

It is scarcely surprising that those who do not accept the roles described should have attacked Bowlby's theories, although it is more surprising that his empirical base should have proved so vulnerable (Morgan, 1975). In *Maternal Deprivation Reassessed* (1981), Michael Rutter examined the components of the theory and concluded that various modifications are required. In particular:

A further point of departure from Bowlby's views concerns the supposedly special importance of the mother. He has argued that the child is innately monotropic and that the bond with the mother (or mother-surrogate) is different in kind from the bonds developed with others. The evidence on that point is unsatisfactory but what there is seems not to support that view. Two issues are involved. The first is whether or not the main bond differs from all others. It is suggested here that it does not. The chief bond is especially important because of its greater strength, but most children develop bonds with several people and it appears likely that these bonds are basically similar. The second concerns the assumption that the 'mother' or 'mother-surrogate' is the person to whom the child is necessarily most attached. Of course in most families the mother has most to do with the young child and as a consequence she is usually the person with whom the strongest bond is formed. But it should be appreciated that the chief bond need not be with the chief caretaker and it need not be with a female.

Furthermore, it seems to be incorrect to regard the person with whom there is the main bond as necessarily and generally the most important person in the child's life. That person will be most important for some things but not for others. For some aspects of development the same-sexed parent seems to have a special role, for some the person who plays and talks most with the child and for others the person who feeds the child. The father, the mother, brothers and sisters, friends, school-teachers and others all have an impact on development, but their influence and importance differs for different aspects of development. A less exclusive focus on the mother is required. Children also have fathers!

It is not, and could not be, our purpose to evaluate these competing views, but rather to demonstrate the effect which they have had upon the development and practice of the law. In their influential book *Beyond the Best Interests of the Child* (1973), Joseph Goldstein, Anna Freud and Albert J. Solnit, respectively a lawyer, a psychoanalyst and a psychiatrist collaborate in an attempt to use 'psychoanalytic theory to develop generally applicable guidelines to child placement.' That theory 'establishes, for example, as do developmental studies by students of other orientations, the need of every child for unbroken continuity of affectionate and stimulating experiences with an adult.' The authors develop three basic concepts. The first is that of the relationship between a 'psychological parent' and a 'wanted child' whom they later define as follows:

A wanted child is one who receives affection and nourishment on a continuing basis from at least one adult and who feels that he or she is and continues to be valued by those who take care of him or her.

A psychological parent is one who, on a continuing, day-to-day basis, through interaction, companionship, interplay, and mutuality, fulfills the child's psychological needs for a parent, as well as the child's physical needs. The psychological parent may be a biological . . ., adoptive, foster, or common law . . . parent, or any other person. There is no presumption in favor of any of these after the initial assignment at birth. . . .

Secondly, they stress the need for continuity in this relationship:

Continuity of relationships, surroundings, and environmental influence are essential for a child's normal development. Since they do not play the same role in later life, their importance is often underrated by the adult world.

Physical, emotional, intellectual, social, and moral growth does not happen without causing the child inevitable internal difficulties. The instability of all mental processes during the period of development needs to be offset by stability and uninterrupted support from external sources. Smooth growth is arrested or disrupted when upheavals and changes in the external world are added to the internal ones.

Disruptions of continuity have different consequences for different ages:

In *infancy*, from birth to approximately 18 months, any change in routine leads to food refusals, digestive upsets, sleeping difficulties, and crying. Such reactions occur even if the infant's care is divided merely between mother and baby-sitter. They are all the more massive where the infant's day is divided between home and day care center; or where infants are displaced from the mother to an institution; from institutional to foster care; or from fostering to adoption. Every step of this kind inevitably brings with it changes in the ways the infant is handled, fed, put to bed, and comforted. Such moves from the familiar to the unfamiliar cause discomfort, distress, and delays in the infant's orientation and adaptation within his surroundings.

Change of the caretaking person for *infants and toddlers* further affects the course of their emotional development. Their attachments, at these ages, are as thoroughly upset by separations as they are effectively promoted by the constant, uninterrupted presence and attention of a familiar adult. When infants and young children find themselves abandoned by the parent, they not only suffer separation distress and anxiety but also setbacks in the quality of their next attachments, which will be less trustful. Where continuity of such relationships is interrupted more than once, as happens due to multiple placements in the early years, the children's emotional attachments become increasingly shallow and indiscriminate. They tend to grow up as persons who lack warmth in their contacts with fellow beings.

For *young children* under the age of 5 years, every disruption of continuity also affects those achievements which are rooted and develop in the intimate interchange with a stable parent figure, who is in the process of becoming the psychological parent. The more recently the achievement has been acquired, the easier it is for the child to lose it. Examples of this are cleanliness and speech. After separation from the familiar mother, young children are known to have breakdowns in toilet training and to lose or lessen their ability to communicate verbally.

For *school-age children*, the breaks in their relationships with their psychological parents affect above all those achievements which are based on identification with the parents' demands, prohibitions, and social ideals. Such identifications develop only where attachments are stable and tend to be abandoned by the child if he feels abandoned by the adults in question. Thus, where children are made to wander from one environment to another, they may cease to identify with any set of substitute parents. Resentment toward the adults who have disappointed them in the past makes them adopt the attitude of not caring for anybody; or of making the new parent the scapegoat for the shortcomings of the former one. In any case, multiple placement at these ages puts many children beyond the reach of educational influence, and becomes the direct cause of behavior which the schools experience as disrupting and the courts label as dissocial, delinquent, or even criminal.

With *adolescents*, the superficial observation of their behavior may convey the idea that what they desire is discontinuation of parental relationships rather than their preservation and stability. Nevertheless, this impression is misleading in this simple form. It is true that their revolt against any parental authority is normal developmentally since it is the adolescent's way toward establishing his own independent adult identity. But for a successful outcome it is important that the breaks and disruptions of attachment should come exclusively from his side and not be imposed on him by any form of abandonment or rejection on the psychological parents' part.

Adults who as children suffered from disruptions of continuity may themselves, in 'identifying' with their many 'parents,' treat their children as they themselves were treated — continuing a cycle costly for both a new generation of children as well as for society itself.

Thus, continuity is a guideline because emotional attachments are tenuous and vulnerable in early life and need stability of external arrangements for their development.

Thirdly, they discuss the child's sense of time:

A child's sense of time, as an integral part of the continuity concept, requires independent consideration. That interval of separation between parent and child which would constitute a break in continuity for an infant, for example, would be of no or little significance to a school-age youngster. The time it takes to break an old or to form a new attachment will depend upon the different meanings time has for children at each stage of their development.

Unlike adults, who have learned to anticipate the future and thus to manage delay, children have a built-in time sense based on the urgency of their instinctual and emotional needs. As an infant's memory begins to incorporate the way in which parents satisfy wishes and needs, as well as the experience of the reappearance of parents after their disappearance, a child gradually develops the capacity to delay gratification and to anticipate and plan for the future.

Emotionally and intellectually an infant and toddler cannot stretch his waiting more than a few days without feeling overwhelmed by the absence of parents. He cannot take care of himself physically, and his emotional and intellectual memory is not sufficiently matured to enable him to use thinking to hold on to the parent he has lost. During such an absence for the child under two years of age, the new adult who cares for the child's physical needs is latched onto 'quickly' as the potential psychological parent. The replacement, however ideal, may not be able to heal completely, without emotional scarring, the injury sustained by the loss.

For most children under the age of five years, an absence of parents for more than two months is equally beyond comprehension. For the younger school-age child, an absence of six months or more may be similarly experienced. More than one year of being without parents and without evidence that there are parental concerns and expectations is not likely to be understood by the older school-aged child and will carry with it the detrimental implications of the breaches in continuity we have already described. After adolescence is fully launched an individual's sense of time closely approaches that of most adults.

Finally, they point to the limits of the law's ability to supervise personal relationships and of knowledge to predict long-range outcomes:

While the law may claim to establish relationships, it can in fact do little more than give them recognition and provide an opportunity for them to develop. The law, so far as specific individual relationships are concerned, is a relatively crude instrument. It may be able to destroy human relationships; but it does not have the power to compel them to develop. It neither has the sensitivity nor the resources to maintain or supervise the ongoing day-to-day happenings between parent and child – and these are essential to meeting ever-changing demands and needs. Nor does it have the capacity to predict future events and needs, . . . [However] placement decisions can be based on certain generally applicable and useful predictions. We can, for example, identify who, among *presently available adults*, is or has the capacity to become a psychological parent and thus will enable a child to feel wanted. We can predict that the adult most likely suited for this role is the one, if there be one, with whom the child has already had and continues to have an affectionate bond rather than one of otherwise equal potential who is not yet in a primary relationship with the child. Further, we can predict that the younger the child and the more extended the period of uncertainty or separation, the more detrimental it will be to the child's well-being and the more urgent it becomes even without perfect knowledge to place the child permanently.

Beyond these, our capacity to predict is limited.

These concepts lead the authors to propose the following guidelines for all child placement decisions:

As an overall guideline for child placement we propose, instead of the 'in-the-best-interests-of-the-child' standard, 'the least detrimental available alternative for safeguarding the child's growth and development.' The new standard has as its major components the three guidelines which we have already described. The least detrimental alternative, then, is that specific placement and procedure for placement which maximizes, in accord with the child's sense of time and on the basis of short-term predictions given the limitations of knowledge, his or her opportunity for being wanted and for maintaining on a continuous basis a relationship with at least one adult who is or will become his psychological parent.

However, the reasoning behind this proposal also reveals how unhelpful it is in the normal custody dispute between parents:

To use 'detrimental' rather than 'best interest' should enable legislatures, courts, and child care agencies to acknowledge and respond to the inherent detriments in any procedure for child placement as well as in each child placement decision itself. It should serve to remind decision-makers that their task is to salvage as much as possible out of an unsatisfactory situation. It should reduce the likelihood of their becoming enmeshed in the hope and magic associated with 'best,' which often mistakenly leads them into believing that they have greater power for doing 'good' than 'bad'.

The concept of 'available alternatives' should press into focus how limited is the capacity of decisionmakers to make valid predictions and how limited are the choices generally open to them for helping a child in trouble. If the choice, as it may often be in separation and divorce proceedings, is between two psychological parents and if each parent is equally suitable in terms of the child's most immediate predictable developmental needs, the least detrimental standard would dictate a quick, final, and unconditional disposition to either of the competing parents.

It is difficult not to sympathise with the comment of Mnookin (1975):

I believe that psychologists and psychiatrists can rather consistently differentiate between a situation where an adult and a child have a substantial relationship of the sort we characterize as parent-child and that where there is no such relationship at all. But I do not think that existing psychological theories provide the basis to choose generally between two adults where the child has some relationship and psychological attachment to each. . . .

Often each parent will have a different sort of relationship with the child, with the child attached to each. One may be warm, easy-going, but incapable of discipline. The other may be fair, able to set limits, but unable to express affection. By what criteria is an expert to decide which is less detrimental? Moreover, even the proponents of psychological standards have acknowledged how problematic it is to evaluate relationships from a psychological perspective unless a highly trained person spends a considerable amount of time observing the parent and child interact or talking to the child. Superficial examinations by those without substantial training may be worse than nothing. And yet, that is surely a high risk. . . .

While the psychologists and psychiatrists have made substantial therapeutic contributions, they are not soothsayers capable of predicting with any degree of confidence how a child is likely to benefit from alternative placements. When the expert does express a preference, it too often is based on an unexpressed value preference. What is psychologically least detrimental will usually be no more determinate for expert and nonexpert alike than what is in a child's best interests; and to reframe the question in a way that invites predictions based on the use of labels and terminology developed for treatment is both demeaning to the expert and corrupting for the judicial process.

Questions

(i) Dingwall and Eekelaar (1986) would go further: 'Psychology is used selectively to legitimate an ideal of social organisation so that moral or political choices are made to appear matters of natural law.' How would you describe the moral and political choices of Goldstein, Freud and Solnit?

(ii) Goldstein, Freud and Solnit's footnote to the last passage quoted from their book suggests that 'a judicially supervised drawing of lots between two equally acceptable psychological parents might be the most rational and least offensive process for resolving the hard choice.' Do you agree?

(iii) Might your view on question (ii) be affected by the clear evidence from empirical studies that contested custody cases take much longer to reach final settlement?

Goldstein, Freud and Solnit's arguments, however, did lead to some firm and controversial conclusions on post-separation contact:

Children have difficulty in relating positively to, profiting from, and maintaining the contact with two psychological parents who are not in positive contact with each other. Loyalty conflicts are common and normal under such conditions and may have devastating consequences by destroying the child's positive relationships to both parents. A 'visiting' or 'visited' parent has little chance to serve as a true object for love, trust, and identification, since this role is based on his being available on an uninterrupted day-to-day basis.

Once it is determined who will be the custodial parent, it is that parent, not the court, who must decide under what conditions he or she wishes to raise the child. Thus, the noncustodial parent should have no legally enforceable right to visit the child, and the custodial parent should have the right to decide whether it is desirable for the child to have such visits. What we have said is designed to protect the security of an ongoing relationship — that between the child and the custodial parent. At the same time the state neither makes nor breaks the psychological relationship between the child and the noncustodial parent, which the adults involved may have jeopardized. It leaves to them what only they can ultimately resolve.

There is certainly ample evidence, particularly from studies of the 1950s and 1960s, of the problems that contact can cause. These are recounted by Susan Maidment in *Access Conditions in Custody Orders* (1975):

The most noticeable fact in the writings of sociologists and psychiatrists on the subject of marriage breakdown is that access is always mentioned as a potential source of difficulty both for the parents and the child. It might be argued that their accounts are unrepresentative, that they focus on the abnormal, rather than the normal situation which, because it works, does not get mentioned. Yet it is believed here that access is a greater problem than is generally realised. Even where relations between the parents are good:

'(a)ccess, even at best, is unsettling. A child may appear to be coping with the emotional strain, but there are still the practical problems of too little time and of opportunities having to be missed. This is one of the hard facts about divorce. Parents can help by accepting it and showing restraint in the demands they make.' (Sanctuary and Whitehead, 1970)

However, access also provides the perfect opportunity for continuing the battle and bitterness between the couple. Thus Goode (1956) suggests that sometimes the children are actually used by the parents for their own ends:

'Whatever the custodial arrangements, these marriages usually continued after the divorce, through the lives of the children. . . . This relationship is often the only channel through which the other spouse can make legitimate demands upon the other: (a) the wife by support demands; (b) the husband by visitation demands. It may also offer the most convenient means for learning about the activities of the other spouse.

Further, this relationship contains the most important weapons in the conflict of wills between ex-spouses, both during the divorce conflict and afterwards. This exploitation of the parent-child relationship may, of course, be unconscious, since few parents can admit that they use their children as punitive instruments.'

The two main techniques for using the children are:

(a) threatening to withhold visits, or making them difficult; and (b) persuading the children to dislike or be suspicious of the other parent.

But even where the parents are not consciously or unconsciously using the children in this way, there is also the problem that the visits themselves will cause stress. Marsden (1969), writing about the problem of poverty as it affects the fatherless family, observed that:

'(t)ensions were most pronounced in the minority of families where the father had continued to visit frequently after separation or divorce. If the mother still had a lingering affection for him she fostered the children's loyalties and memories and supported his visits. But where, as usually happened, resentment built up between the parents, all too easily the father's visits or contacts with the children became a battle for their affections. Young children soon forgot even violence and neglect and were puzzled and distressed that the father could not stay. Happy visits when he was able to indulge their wants contrasted with the pinching and scraping and bad temper which were too often the result of the mother's financial position.'

Similar observations were made by Goode:

'The relationship between the usually absent parent and the child at such visits is nagged by the fact that the parent and child will separate once again; that the advice and corrections of the absent parent will be overruled; while the assurances of love must carry their own proof during his absence. Since it is a rare young child who sees any reason for his parents to divorce, the haunting suspicion of abandonment gnaws at the enjoyment of the visits.'

The net result of these problems associated with access seems to be that visits become less frequent and regular. Thus Marsden says:

'In the light of these difficulties it was easy to understand why only one of the fathers who now visited had been coming for as long as five years. The usual story appeared to be that visits which began well tailed off. . . . Repeated contacts with the father only served to dramatise and exacerbate the conflict of affection, and by active discouragement — or by an equally eloquent display of 'neutrality' when the child appealed to her for a decision about writing to or seeing the father — the mother worked to bring the relationship to an end.'

George and Wilding (1972) in a study of motherless families, reported similar findings:

'Our impression from the fathers' answers is that there is a tendency for visits to diminish in frequency and regularity with the passage of time. . . . (M)others, fathers, and children find that visits make demands on them all which generate stresses and conflicts that eventually tend to reduce the frequency of visits.'

In *Post-Divorce Arrangements for Children: A Psychological Perspective* (1982), however, Richards argues that continued contact is so much in the interests of the child that the system should try harder to encourage it. In discussing the needs of children, he first points to the lack of good direct evidence either way, and continues:

There are a couple of findings in the psychological studies which have turned up several times and are at least consistent with my hypothesis. The first is that some of the long-term disruptive effects on children whose parents divorce are most marked if the separation comes earlier (say before the age of five) rather than later (eg Douglas, 1970). Several explanations are possible but one of these is that the likelihood of losing contact with the non-custodial parent will increase over time and so is most likely to be lost after an earlier separation. A similar explanation can be given of the evidence that divorce is more upsetting for children who remain with their mothers if those mothers remarry (Douglas, 1970), as the presence of a step-father almost always reduces contact with the father (Furstenberg, 1981).

The nearest we get to a direct study of the question of continuing contact is an American one where groups of children spending varying amounts of time with each of their divorced or separated parents were compared (Keshet and Rosenthal, 1978). Here the children (and parents) who spent at least 25% of their time with each of their parents seem to adjust best. However, in this study we cannot be certain that factors other than the post-separation arrangements determined the outcome. For instance, it could be that parents who decide to share their time with their children after separation are also parents who prepare their children for the separation and support them before it occurs. However, this evidence is in the same direction as the hints which can be found in all the recent studies of children of divorced parents that continuing relations with both parents are desirable from the point of view of the children's adjustment (Weiss 1975, 1979; Wallerstein and Kelly, 1980). . . .

A continued relationship with the non-custodial parent would appear to offer many psychological advantages for children. One of the most obvious is that it offers a wider variety of experience; the experience of a relationship with a second parent. A child is not denied a close and continuing relationship with a parent of each gender. This may be of special value in the development of his or her own gender identity (which has been shown to be disturbed in some studies of children of divorce) (Hetherington, 1972). With two parents a child is given the opportunity of learning how to move from one relationship to another. Often this is seen in a rather negative sense as something a child must learn to cope with. But I think we should see it much more positively as a very necessary skill for adult life that allows us to live within a whole network of relationships of differing kinds and qualities. It might be argued that these aspects of development should be satisfied equally by any two (or more) adults, not just a child's parents. To some extent this may be true, but there are many indications that parental relations are usually very special and cannot be replaced by other adults in any easy way. To say this is not to evoke any concept of a blood tie but one of a psychological parent. The potency of a psychological parent lies in the continuity of the relationship with their child and their symbolic position as a parent. A separation that does not involve the loss of one parent is likely to be much less disturbing of a child's social connections outside the immediate family. Friends and relatives of the non-custodial parent are not lost to the child. The child has a much better chance of maintaining links with both sets of grandparents.

At a separation, it is usual that among the many feelings a child is likely to experience is anger (Wallerstein and Kelly 1980). This anger is associated with the wish or fantasy that the parents will come back together again and it is generally expressed towards the parent who spends most time looking after the child regardless of their role in the separation. If a child is able to maintain a relationship with both parents this anger gradually dissipates as the child begins to feel confident in the new kind of relationship that develops with both parents. The separation of the parents gradually ceases to be the total threat to the child's life it once had seemed. In a case where the child does not have contact with the non-custodial parent the resolution of the anger at the parents' separation may be much more complex and prolonged. The absent parent, just because he or she is absent, may be built up into a totally idealised figure while the custodial parent's role is seen as that of the person who has driven out the 'ideal' parent. Everything that goes wrong or frustrates the child may be laid at the door of the custodial parent. Under this emotional pressure even the strongest of parents begins to react so that the child may feel signs of rejection or anger in return. This in turn increases the child's anger and insecurity. Of course, not all children of divorce react in this way, but those who do are probably those who have lost contact with one parent.

It has been suggested that a continued relationship with both parents makes the acceptance of a step-parent much more difficult for a child. There is no evidence to support this idea, which is improbable in view of our understanding of a child's parental relations. The unlikely assumption here is that a child has the capacity for two parental relations and if both spaces are filled there will be no space for anybody else. In fact there is great variation in number and kind of relations that a child can maintain (Shaffer and Emerson, 1964). It seems much more likely that if children feel confident that they are going to lose neither of their parents despite the marital separation, that they will accept a new adult more easily. Certainly, we need to move beyond the simplistic notion of very fixed parental roles which can be occupied by anybody that a parent or a court chooses to place in that position.

At the social level there are several very powerful arguments that can be given for the maintenance of ties with both parents.

For many, if not most children, a marital separation is followed by a permanent or temporary period in a single-parent family. We have abundant evidence that these families suffer from many disadvantages (Ferri, 1976). Among these are the effects of a single person providing for all the children's needs day in and day out and the low incomes typical of such families. Both of these are likely to be reduced by continuing [contact] with the non-custodial parent. Such a parent not only provides the child with an alternative home but is also a relief for the custodial parent. These breaks allow the custodial parent to recharge emotional batteries and indulge in some adult life uninterrupted by the demands of childcare.

In principle, there is no connection between access and the payment of maintenance by non-custodial parents. However, this is not the way it is always seen by those involved. Parents who have regular contact with their children and maintain a close relationship are much more likely to want to pay maintenance and feel that it is fair and reasonable to do so. If the contact is maintained the needs of the children including financial ones will be more obvious and are likely to be more freely met.

One can also see the non-custodial parent as a kind of insurance policy for children. Lives of custodial parents cannot be predicted with certainty; changes may occur which make it very difficult or impossible for them to cope with children. If there is a disaster a second parent who is in close touch can often take the children and so avoid another major upheaval.

But what of the negative side — what arguments are there against the continuing involvement of both parents? There is a general belief, which is borne out by the research studies, that many difficulties are associated with access visits. However, the extent of these should not be exaggerated. Murch's study (1980), for instance, found a majority who are satisfied with their access arrangements and he also noted that initial difficulties often resolved in time. That difficulties occur around access visits is hardly surprising as this will often be the one point of contact between spouses (Eekelaar, 1982). The remedy of cutting off the contact may be superficially attractive, but in the long term is unlikely to help the adults to resolve their difficulties, apart from its likely effects on the children.

Part of our ambivalence about access is expressed in the common attitude that, though access is desirable, it can easily be overdone and so it is necessary to limit visits in terms of both their duration and frequency. Over-long or frequent visits are held to lead to confusions of loyalty for the children and to undermine their security in their main home. Clearly, if two parents are determined to continue their battles via their children, heavy pressures can be brought to bear which, if long-lasting, could make life a misery for children. However, such battles are usually relatively short-lived. As the separated parents begin to rebuild their lives and acquire new concerns and interests the old battles begin to lose their fire. Also children are surprisingly resourceful in avoiding situations which cause them pain.

One of the feelings that most concerns children at a parental separation is the fear of loss of both parents. If one parent has chosen to leave home and live elsewhere, why should not the other one make the same decision at a future date? The only way in which these fears can be countered is by a demonstration that there is continuity in the new arrangements. But it is not always understood that a child's fears are best countered if continuity is demonstrated in *both* parental relationships. Part of the mistaken fear that access visits are disturbing rests on the assumption that they may unsettle the relationship with the custodial parent. However, unless the child has a reasonable amount of time with the non-custodial parent there is no chance to regain confidence in that relationship.

Perhaps the most common cause of difficulties in access is that visits are too brief. We are well-used to descriptions of the Sunday afternoon access visit spent in the park and cafe. Only a moment's reflection is required to see how difficult or impossible it would be to recreate a normal parental relationship on that kind of basis. What children and adults need is the chance to share some of the very ordinary and routine aspects of life. Access visits must be long enough to remove the sense that they are a special occasion. Excessive gifts and the provision of 'treats' are sure signs that an ordinary relationship has not been recreated. The matter was summed up very clearly by a man I interviewed who told me that it was only after he had first got angry with his children during a visit that he began to feel that they were getting back to a reasonable relationship.

Given the many factors that will influence a particular situation and the practical constraints in making visiting arrangements I feel it would be unwise to try to lay down norms for the length of visits. However, I think it is fairly obvious that difficulties will be more common if overnight stays are not possible.

Sometimes it is felt important that things like rules about bedtimes should be as similar as possible in the two homes. Children often make comparisons and talk about any differences they have noted. In general, I would take the ability to talk openly about such differences as evidence that they were coming to terms with the separateness of their parents. Children will, of course, also try to exploit differences between the homes, supposed and real, to get what they want from a parent. But it is simple enough to make it clear to them that rules between the homes may differ and the fact that they are allowed to do X in the other house is no reason why they should do it here. Far from seeing differences in rules and routines in the two homes as confusing for children, I think there are good reasons for viewing them as advantages. They are ways of seeing something of variety in life and learning that there is not always a single answer to a problem. If different activities are possible in the two homes, just as the two relationships with the two parents will each have its own characteristics, so much the better for the children.

Richards makes several suggestions about how we might encourage continued contact but primarily he says this:

> The awarding of custody to a single parent at divorce is a public acknowledgment and notice that the role of the non-custodial parent is expected to be reduced. My first suggestion is that we cease to give such notice in the majority of cases. Much more appropriate would be a public reaffirmation that, in spite of the adults' separation, parental duties persist. The most obvious way in which this could be done is by making joint custody the norm — courts could either automatically make such an order unless strong and specific arguments against it were brought forward or they could make no order as to custody in this situation so that the position existing before divorce could persist. There are many indications that more parents are pressing for joint custody and this trend needs every encouragement. Those who continue to believe that such orders always lead to trouble must be prepared to back their beliefs with some hard evidence.

We have already seen (pp. 503 et seq., above) that there was a considerable, if geographically patchy, rise in joint custody orders before the Children Act 1989. In their Working Paper on *Custody* (1986) the Law Commission discuss the reasons:

Joint custody

4.35 A number of factors have contributed to the rise in popularity of joint custody orders in this country and elsewhere. First, there has been an increasing recognition that the task of bringing up children is not the exclusive responsibility of one parent but a shared responsibility of them both. [Rapoport, Rapoport and Strelitz, 1977] . . .

4.36 Secondly, . . . it is widely thought that continued contact with both parents is the best way of promoting the children's welfare. If so, joint custody may encourage the parent with whom the children are no longer living to play a greater role. It avoids the 'public acknowledgement and notice that the role of the non-custodial parent is expected to be reduced' [Richards, 1982, above]. At the very least, it should improve his position during access and perhaps his willingness to exercise access at all. It avoids the hurtful 'winner takes all' impression which a sole custody order may give [Luepnitz, 1982; Patrician, 1984].

4.37 Thirdly, the increase in divorce, its relative acceptability and the wider range of circumstances in which it may be granted have perhaps increased the number of cases in which there is the possibility of close cooperation between the parents following their divorce. These facts may also have contributed to the view that the 'once and for all' disposition which was appropriate when divorce was a rare (and perhaps a shameful) event is no longer appropriate when it is the experience of so many children. They should be able to feel that their lives have been disrupted as little as possible by their parents' separation.

4.38 This may have been further encouraged by the reduction in the relevance of matrimonial fault, both in the ground for divorce and in the allocation of custody in disputed cases. There is an understandable desire to treat each parent equitably, and in some cases perhaps to award joint custody as a 'consolation prize' to the parent, usually the father, with whom the children will no longer be living. In one study [Eekelaar and Clive, 1977] it appeared that joint custody was more commonly awarded where custody had originally been contested. Although this is probably less so today, it may be a tempting means of achieving a settlement, which in itself can be in the best interests of children who would otherwise suffer from the delay, uncertainty and bitterness engendered by a contest. . . .

On the other hand:

4.40 Although these orders have gained in popularity in some parts of the country (largely in the south), in others (largely in the north) they are still quite rare [Priest and Whybrow, 1986]. The attitudes and expectations of courts, legal practitioners and the parties themselves must play some part in this. In any event, these orders clearly have disadvantages. The main benefit appears to be purely symbolic, in recognising the continued parental status of the other parent. But this is not a genuine sharing of parental responsibility, for all the major burdens of looking after and bringing up the child are still carried by the parent with whom the children are living. To the extent that it may encourage the other parent to interfere in day-to-day matters it is obviously undesirable [Shulman and Pitt, 1982; Weitzman, 1985]. Lack of clarity about the division between 'strategic' and 'day-to-day' matters can only make this worse.

4.41 Furthermore, it is in many cases almost impossible to separate strategic decisions from the day-to-day responsibilities of care and control. If the parent with whom the children are no longer living is able to play an equal part in deciding where they shall go to school or to church, it is the parent with whom they live who will usually have to put this decision into practice, by taking the children there or insisting that they go. Even 'strategic' responsibilities cannot in practice be exercised without also having care and control of the child. There is thus a considerable danger that joint custody will become either 'power without responsibility' or, what may be worse, responsibility without power.

4.42 Research indicates that the majority of joint custody orders result in the mother taking care and control where otherwise she would have obtained sole custody [Priest and Whybrow, 1986]. The traditional division of responsibility, in which the mother carries the day-to-day burden but the father is able to exercise some control over how this is done, may thus be perpetuated. Yet the more popular such orders become, the more difficult the mother may find it to resist one even when it is not so appropriate in her case.

4.43 Finally, there are still cases in which the needs of the child and the custodial parent to feel secure and free from even the unlikely threat of interference must be put before the symbolic advantages of joint custody, even if this also increases the risk of the child and the non-custodial parent losing touch with one another.

Shared custody

4.44 The objections to joint custody according to the model in England and Wales might not apply so strongly were care and control itself to be shared or more evenly divided. In the United States of America, the reaction against divisive custody dispositions which give the non-custodial parent 'little chance to serve as a true object for love, trust and identification since this role is based on being available on an uninterrupted day to day basis' [Goldstein, Freud and Solnit, 1973], has been answered by a movement towards joint physical custody. There has been much research, albeit of limited general applicability, which points to the success of joint custody after divorce in providing for emotional continuity and a network of support for children [Ahrons, 1981; Luepnitz, 1982]. Some States have therefore enacted a presumption in favour of joint custody, which includes joint physical custody, which can on occasions be applied irrespective of the wishes of the parents.

4.45 We see the force of the arguments in favour of joint custody in the sense of sharing the benefits and burdens of being a parent. However, although on occasion it may be difficult to distinguish from sole custody with liberal staying access, it seems that shared care and control is most exceptional on this side of the Atlantic. There are strong doubts as to whether joint physical custody in the American sense is generally practicable. It particularly relies on the feasibility of joint child care to which society is not generally geared. Also the imposition of joint custody in cases where one parent is reluctant may cause much stress and practical difficulty for the child and parents [Steinman, 1981; Luepnitz, 1982; Goldzband, 1982]. For some children the dividing of time between two homes may be against their best interests, particularly if it involves switching between schools and friends. A child who moves between two families may not regard himself, or be regarded, as a full member of either. For his parents, running two homes may duplicate expenditure and add to their financial problems. It has thus been argued that it could lead to decreased maintenance for the mother, whose fixed costs nevertheless remain as high as if she had sole custody [Weitzman, 1985]. Finally, if the sharing does not turn out to be equal the order may be little different from joint custody in the English sense.

3 The law

(a) THE ORDERS AVAILABLE

The *Children Act 1989* replaces the old orders for custody, joint custody, care and control, access, and the resolution of disputes about the exercise of parental rights, as follows:

8.—(1) In this Act—
'a contact order' means an order requiring the person with whom a child lives, or is to live, to allow the child to visit or stay with the person named in the order, or for that person and the child otherwise to have contact with each other;
'a prohibited steps order' means an order that no step which could be taken by a parent in meeting his parental responsibility for a child, and which is of a kind specified in the order, shall be taken by any person without the consent of the court;
'a residence order' means an order settling the arrangements to be made as to the person with whom a child is to live; and
'a specific issue order' means an order giving directions for the purpose of determining a specific question which has arisen, or which may arise, in connection with any aspect of parental responsibility for a child.
(2) In this Act 'a section 8 order' means any of the orders mentioned in subsection (1) and any order varying or discharging such an order.
(3) For the purposes of this Act 'family proceedings' means any proceedings—
  (*a*) under the inherent jurisdiction of the High Court in relation to children; and
  (*b*) under the enactments mentioned in subsection (4).
but does not include proceedings on an application for leave under section 100(3) [see p. 609, below].
(4) The enactments are—
  (*a*) Parts I, II and IV of this Act;
  (*b*) the Matrimonial Causes Act 1973;
  (*c*) the Domestic Violence and Matrimonial Proceedings Act 1976;
  (*d*) the Adoption Act 1976;
  (*e*) the Domestic Proceedings and Magistrates' Court Act 1978;
  (*f*) sections 1 and 9 of the Matrimonial Homes Act 1983;
  (*g*) Part III of the Matrimonial and Family Proceedings Act 1984.

As between parents (married or unmarried) these may be made in the following circumstances:

10.—(1) In any family proceedings in which a question arises with respect to the welfare of any child, the court may make a section 8 order with respect to the child if—
  (*a*) an application for the order has been made by a person who—
    (i) is entitled to apply for a section 8 order with respect to the child; or
    (ii) has obtained the leave of the court to make the application; or
  (*b*) the court considers that the order should be made even though no such application has been made.
(2) The court may also make a section 8 order with respect to any child on the application of a person who—
  (*a*) is entitled to apply for a section 8 with respect to the child; or
  (*b*) has obtained the leave of the court to make the application.
. . .
(4) The following persons are entitled to apply to the court for any section 8 order with respect to a child—
  (*a*) any parent or guardian of the child;
  (*b*) any person in whose favour a residence order is in force with respect to the child.

There are also various supplementary provisions:

11.—(3) Where a court has power to make a section 8 order, it may do so at any time during the course of the proceedings in question even though it is not in a position to dispose finally of those proceedings.

(4) Where a residence order is made in favour of two or more persons who do not themselves all live together, the order may specify the periods during which the child is to live in the different households concerned.

(5) Where—
    (*a*) a residence order has been made with respect to a child; and
    (*b*) as a result of the order the child lives, or is to live, with one of two parents who each have parental responsiblity for him,
the residence order shall cease to have effect if the parents live together for a continuous period of more than six months.

(6) A contact order which requires the parent with whom a child lives to allow the child to visit, or otherwise have contact with, the other parent shall cease to have effect if the parents live together for a continuous period of more than six months.

(7) A section 8 order may—
    (*a*) contain directions about how it is to be carried into effect:
    (*b*) impose conditions which must be complied with by any person—
        (i)   in whose favour the order is made;
        (ii) who is a parent of the child concerned;
        (iii) who is not a parent of his but who has parental responsibility for him; or
        (iv) with whom the child is living,
        and to whom the conditions are expressed to apply;
    (*c*) be made to have effect for a specified period, or contain provisions which are to have effect for a specified period;
    (*d*) make such incidental, supplemental or consequential provision as the court thinks fit.

. . .

13.—(1) Where a residence order is in force with respect to a child, no person may—
    (*a*) cause the child to be known by a new surname; or
    (*b*) remove him from the United Kingdom;
without either the written consent of every person who has parental responsibility for the child or the leave of the court.

(2) Subsection (1)(*b*) does not prevent the removal of a child, for a period of less than one month, by the person in whose favour the residence order is made.

(3) In making a residence order with respect to a child the court may grant the leave required by subsection (1)(*b*), either generally or for specified purposes.

These provisions are explained in the Law Commission's Report on *Guardianship and Custody* (1988):

Orders between parents

4.2 There are three main difficulties with the present law. First,. . . the orders available differ according to the proceedings brought. Divorce courts may allocate 'custody', 'care and control' and 'access' in any way they see fit. . . . Domestic courts hearing applications for financial relief under the Domestic Proceedings and Magistrates' Court Act 1978 and all courts hearing applications for custody or access under the Guardianship of Minors Act 1971 can only make orders for 'legal custody' and 'access'. They cannot make orders for joint legal custody as such although they can give the same power of veto over specified or even all decisions apart from actual custody. It is doubtful whether they can make orders relating to actual custody alone, for example that it be shared. . . .

4.3 The second difficulty is that the effect of these orders is no longer clear or well-understood. Parents not unnaturally think that a sole custody order puts the custodial parent in sole control, but the Court of Appeal appeared to say otherwise in *Dipper v Dipper* [1981] Fam 31, [1980] 2 All ER 722. Parents who are reluctant to concede sole custody are advised that joint custody is 'an important ratification of their continued parental role' [Priest and Whybrow, 1986, para. 8.4]. Parents with care and control who see joint custody as a threatening interference are told that it is simply 'a matter of words'. In most cases, this is obviously right, because the strategic matters over which a power of veto might be exercised very rarely arise. The fact that a joint custody order technically gives a power of veto may not be generally appreciated. Certainly, both judges and solicitors have reported difficulty in explaining the effect of orders to clients [Ibid., para. 5.25].

4.4 The third difficulty is that the views and practices of courts differ very considerably, largely because of differences of opinion amongst judges, legal practitioners and clients about the merits of joint custody orders. While some see them as an important means of encouraging the 'non-custodial' parent to remain involved, others see them as a purely symbolic exercise which is unnecessary if the couple will co-operate in any event and a recipe for continual conflict if they cannot. The result is that the place at which the parents divorce is likely to have a considerable effect upon the orders made, even though the practical outcome, in terms of where the child lives, is much the same. . . .

4.5 In framing a scheme of orders to replace the present law, we have had in mind throughout the clear evidence that the children who fare best after their parents separate or divorce are those who are able to maintain a good relationship with them both [e.g. Wallerstein and Kelly, 1980; Lund, 1987; Richards and Dyson, 1982; Maidment, 1984]. The law may not be able to achieve this — indeed we are only too well aware of the limits of the law in altering human relationships — but at least it should not stand in their way. Our respondents were generally agreed on three points. Where the parents are already able to co-operate in bringing up their children, the law should interfere as little as possible. Where they may be having difficulty, it should try to 'lower the stakes' so that the issue is not one in which 'winner takes all' or more importantly 'loser loses all'. In either case, the orders made should reduce rather than increase the opportunities for conflict and litigation in the future.

4.6 The scheme which we provisionally proposed in the Working Paper had three basic elements. The first, as we have already explained, [see p. 440, above] is that the parents should retain their equal parental responsibility and with it their power to act independently unless this is incompatible with the court's order. A parent who does not have the child with him should still be regarded in law as a parent. He should be treated as such by schools and others, so that he can be given information and an opportunity to take part in the child's education. He should not be able to exercise a power of veto over the other, but should be able to refer any dispute to the court if necessary. A parent who does have the child with him should be able to exercise his responsibilities to the full during that time.

. . .

4.8 The second element in our proposals was designed to reflect the practical reality that parental status is largely a matter of everyday responsibility rather than rights. It is 'a mistake to see custody, care and control and access as differently-sized bundles of powers and responsibilities in a descending hierarchy of importance'. Most parental responsibilities can only be exercised while the parent has the child, for only then can the parent put into effect the decisions taken. Equally, however, it is then that the parent must be in a position to meet his responsibilities as the circumstances and needs of the child dictate. Parental responsibilities, therefore, largely 'run with the child'. Clearly, in most cases, one parent carries a much heavier burden of that responsibility than does the other. The present system of orders, by concentrating on the allocation of 'rights', appears more concerned with whether one parent can control what the other parent does while the child is with the other, than with ensuring that each parent properly meets his responsibilities while the child is with him. The practical question in most cases is where the child is to live and how much he is to see of the other parent. Hence we provisionally proposed that custody and access orders should be replaced by a single order, possibly termed 'care and control', allocating the child's time between the parents.

. . .

4.10 However, several respondents who approved of the general thrust of our provisional proposals suggested different terminology from 'care and control' which still carries some of the proprietorial connotations of 'custody'. There is also a practical disadvantage in having only a single order which divides the child's time between his parents. Most children will live with one parent for most of the time and spend variable amounts of time with the other. The usual order at present is for 'reasonable' access. Our respondents did not think it desirable for orders to spell this out in any more detail unless and until disputes arose. Parents are usually able to agree upon their own arrangements, which have to be flexible enough to meet changing needs and circumstances. Rather than being required to specify the periods of time intended, therefore, the court should normally deal with where (or, more accurately, with whom) the child is to live, whom he should see, and any other specific matters which have to be resolved.

. . .

(a) *Residence orders*
4.12 Apart from the effect upon the other parent, . . . the main difference between a residence order and a custody order is that the new order should be flexible enough to accommodate a much wider range of situations. In some cases, the child may live with both parents even though they do not share the same household. It was never our intention to suggest that children should share their time more or less equally between their parents. Such arrangements will rarely be practicable, let alone for the children's benefit. However, the evidence from the United States is that where they are practicable they can work well and we see no reason why they should be actively discouraged. None of our respondents shared the view expressed in a recent case [*Riley*

v Riley [1986] 2 FLR 429] that such an arrangement, which had been working well for some years, should never have been made., More commonly, however, the child will live with both parents but spend more time with one than the other. Examples might be where he spends term time with one and holidays with the other, or two out of three holidays from boarding school with one and the third with the other. It is a far more realistic description of the responsibilities involved in that sort of arrangement to make a residence order covering both parents rather than a residence order for one and a contact order for the other. . . .

4.14 The effect of a residence order is simply to settle where the child is to live. If any other conditions are needed they must usually be specified. However, the Matrimonial Causes Rules 1977 at present specify two conditions which must be included in divorce court custody orders unless the court otherwise directs. First, the parent with custody must not change the child's surname without the written consent of the other parent or the leave of a judge. The child's surname is an important symbol of his identity and his relationship with his parents. While it may well be in his interests for it to be changed, it is clearly not a matter on which the parent with whom he lives should be able to take unilateral action. . . .

4.15 Secondly, a divorce court order for custody or care and control must provide for the child not to be removed from England and Wales without leave of the court except on such terms as the court may specify in the order. This means that, unless the court makes an exception at the outset, the child cannot be taken on holiday abroad (or even to Scotland), even if the other parent agrees, without the trouble and expense of an application for leave. This is clearly quite unrealistic these days and we suspect that the requirement is often ignored. Otherwise, an order for legal custody does not permit a person to arrange the child's emigration unless he is a parent or guardian but the order contains no more stringent requirement unless the court specifically prohibits removals and we understand that it rarely does so. The matter could be dealt with entirely by the criminal law [s. 1, Child Abduction Act 1984]. However, taking the child abroad indefinitely can obviously have a serious effect upon his relationship with the other parent and it may be important to remind the residential parent of this, and of the steps to be taken if she wishes to do so. A simple, clear general rule seems most likely to be remembered and observed.

. . .

(b) *Contact orders*

4.17 Where the child is to spend much more time with one parent than the other, the more realistic order will probably be for him to live with one parent and to visit the other. There are important differences between this and the present form of access order. It will not provide for the 'non-custodial' parent to have access to the child. It will provide for the child to visit and in many cases stay with the parent. While the child is with that parent, the parent may exercise all his parental responsibilities. He must not do something which is incompatible with the order about where the child is to live. The court may also attach other conditions if there are particular anxieties or bones of contention but these should rarely be required. If visiting is not practicable, the court may nevertheless order some other form of contact with the child, including letters or telephone calls or visits to the child. We would expect, however, that the normal order would be for reasonable contact, which would encompass all types. . . .

(c) *Specific issue orders*

4.18 Specific issue orders may be made in conjunction with residence or contact orders or on their own. . . . As with conditions attached to other orders, the object is not to give one parent or the other the 'right' to determine a particular point. Rather, it is to enable either parent to submit a particular dispute to the court for resolution in accordance with what is best for the child. A court can determine in the light of the evidence what decision will be best for the child at the time. It may equally be content for decisions to be taken by each parent as they arise in the course of everyday life in the future. It may even attach a condition to a residence or contact order that certain decisions may not be taken without informing the other or giving the other an opportunity to object. But to give one parent in advance the right to take a decision which the other parent will have to put into effect is contrary to the whole tenor of the modern law [e.g. the disapproval of the old form of 'split' orders, giving custody to one and care and control to the other, *Williamson v Williamson* [1986] 2 FLR 146]. A court can scarcely be expected to know in advance that the first parent's decision will be the best for the child.

4.19 However, a specific issue order is not intended as a substitute for a residence or contact order. There is obviously a slight risk that they might be used, particularly in uncontested cases, to achieve much the same practical results but without the same legal effects. We recommend, therefore, that it should be made clear that a specific issue order cannot be made with a view to achieving a result which could be achieved by a residence or contact order.

(d) *Prohibited steps orders*

4.20 Prohibited steps orders are also modelled on the wardship jurisdiction. The automatic effect of making a child a ward of court is that no important step may be taken without the court's leave. An important aim of our recommendations is to incorporate the most valuable features of wardship into the statutory jurisdictions. It is on occasions necessary for the court to play a continuing parental role in relation to the child, although we would not expect those occasions to be common. If this is in the best interests of the child, it should be made clear exactly what the limitations on the exercise of parental responsibility are. Hence, instead of the vague requirement in wardship, that no 'important step' may be taken, the court should spell out these matters which will have to be referred back to the court. We would expect such orders to be few and far between, as in practice the wardship jurisdiction is more often invoked to achieve a particular result at the time than to produce the continuing over-sight of the court. One example, however, might be to ensure that the child is not removed from the United Kingdom, especially in a case where there is no residence order and so the automatic prohibition cannot apply. As with specific issue orders, however, we recommend that these orders should not be capable of being made with a view to achieving a result which could be achieved by a residence or contact order.

(e) *Supplemental provisions*

4.21 The courts have interpreted their powers under section 42 of the Matrimonial Causes Act 1973 so flexibly as to enable them to make interim orders, delay implementation or attach other special conditions. The other legislation contains specific provisions for similar purposes. The object of our recommendation is to preserve the present flexibility of the divorce courts' powers within the new scheme of orders. We would not expect these supplemental powers to be used at all frequently, as most cases will not require them and all are subject to the general rule that orders should only be made where they are the most effective means of safeguarding or promoting the child's welfare.

Questions

(i) The new scheme of orders has to be read in conjunction with the provisions on shared parental responsibility, discussed on pp. 437–441 earlier. Assuming that the object is to recognise and encourage both parents' continued involvement in their children's upbringing, do you prefer (*a*) joint legal custody under the previous law; (*b*) time-divided shared care as recommended by the Working Paper; or (*c*) the Children Act scheme? Can you tell the difference?

(ii) Feminists, on the whole, did not like joint legal custody: can you explain why? Would they like shared care any better?

(iii) Or do you think that Goldstein, Freud and Solnit were right after all?

(b) THE WELFARE PRINCIPLE

The *Children Act 1989* restates the welfare principle (first enacted in s. 1 of the Guardianship of Infants Act 1925, p. 410, above) with additions:

1.—(1) When a court determines any question with respect to—

(*a*) the upbringing of a child; or

(*b*) the administration of a child's property or the application of any income arising from it, the child's welfare shall be the court's paramount consideration.

. . .

(3) In the circumstances mentioned in subsection (4), a court shall have regard in particular to—

(*a*) the ascertainable wishes and feelings of the child concerned (considered in the light of his age and understanding);

(*b*) his physical, emotional and educational needs;

(c)   the likely effect on him of any change in his circumstances;
(d)   his age, sex, background and any characteristics of his which the court considers relevant;
(e)   any harm which he has suffered or is at risk of suffering;
(f)   how capable each of his parents, and any other person in relation to whom the court considers the question to be relevant, is of meeting his needs;
(g)   the range of powers available to the court under this Act in the proceedings in question.
(4) The circumstances are that—
(a)   the court is considering whether to make, vary or discharge a section 8 order, and the making, variation or discharge of the order is opposed by any party to the proceedings; or
(b)   the court is considering whether to make, vary or discharge an order under Part IV [see p. 607, below].

Section 1(1), however, differs in two respects from the recommendations of the Law Commission:

3.13 We suggested, however, two modifications in the present formulation of the paramountcy rule. First, the interests of the child whose future happens to be in issue in the proceedings before the court should not in principle prevail over those of other children likely to be affected by the decision. Hence their welfare should also be taken into consideration. Secondly, the world 'first' had caused confusion in that it had in the past led some courts to balance other considerations *against* the child's welfare rather than to consider what light they shed upon it [e.g. *Re L (infant)* [1962] 3 All ER 1, [1962] 1 WLR 886]. Since *J v C* [1970] AC 668 [p. 411, above], that view has been decisively rejected in the courts [*Re K (a minor) (children: care and control)* [1977] Fam 179, [1977] 1 All ER 647, p. 511, above] and a modern formulation should reflect this. These proposals were approved by all those who commented upon them.

3.14 It could be said that, given its recent interpretation in the courts, retaining the present formula does no harm. However, merely to drop 'first', as a piece of 'draftsman's duplicity (now obsolete)' [Bennion, 1976], does nothing to resolve the earlier confusion. Litigants might still be tempted to introduce evidence and arguments which had no relevance to the child's welfare, in the hope of persuading the court to balance one against the other. The whole aim of these proposals is to state the modern law simply and clearly. We recommend, therefore, that in reaching any decision about the child's care, upbringing or maintenance, the welfare of any child likely to be affected by the decision should be the court's only concern. . . .

Questions

(i) Is there a difference between a 'paramount' and a 'sole' consideration?
(ii) If other considerations can be taken into account, should they include, for example, (a) the 'justice' of the matrimonial dispute, (b) the need to minimise public expenditure, or (c) the wishes and feelings of any of the adults involved?
(iii) What would an economist or utilitarian think of a law which, in theory, required that a small gain to the child's welfare, in living with the marginally more suitable parent, should outweigh a much greater detriment to the welfare of a parent who would be devastated by the loss of his or her child?

The Law Commission went on to explain the 'checklist' in s. 1(3) like this:

3.18 The 'checklist' received a large majority of support from those who considered the matter. It was perceived as a means of providing a greater consistency and clarity in the law and was welcomed as a major step towards a more systematic approach to decisions concerning children. Respondents pointed out that it would help to ensure that the same basic factors were being used to implement the welfare criterion by the wide range of professionals involved, including judges, magistrates, registrars, welfare officers, and legal advisers. One respondent, for example, who is a magistrates' clerk, thought that the list would be particularly useful when advising magistrates in making decisions in contested custody cases and in formulating reasons in the event of an appeal. It would also provide a practical tool for those lacking experience and confidence in this area. Perhaps most important of all, we were told that such a list could assist both parents and children in endeavouring to understand how judicial decisions are made. At present, there is a tendency for advisers and their clients (and possibly even courts) to rely on 'rules of thumb' as to what the court is likely to think best in any given circumstances. A checklist would make it clear to all what, as a minimum, would be considered by the court. At the very least, it would enable the parties to prepare and give relevant evidence at the outset, thereby avoiding the delay and expense of prolonged hearings or adjournments for further information. Moreover, we were informed that solicitors find the checklist applicable to financial matters most useful in focussing their clients' minds on the real issues and therefore in promoting settlements. Anything which is likely to promote the settlement of disputes about children is even more to be welcomed. We recommend, therefore, that a statutory checklist similar to that provided for financial matters be provided for decisions relating to children.

3.19 We recognise, however, that a statutory checklist contains certain dangers against which the legislation must be careful to guard. It should not appear to increase the burden upon courts in uncontested cases and thus encourage them to intervene unnecessarily in the course of considering the arrangements proposed for the children. There is no evidence at all that the checklist for financial matters has had this effect. The courts would only apply it where an issue had arisen. Secondly, while the checklist may provide a clear statement of what society considers the most important factors in the welfare of children, it must not be applied too rigidly or be so formulated as to prevent the court from taking into account everything which is relevant in the particular case. Thirdly, a statutory checklist is only practicable if it is confined to the major points, leaving others to be formulated elsewhere. If a detailed checklist is provided, it cannot be appropriate to all types of decision and thus separate lists would be needed to deal with each issue. This would lead to unnecessary complexity, not only in the statute, but also in legal proceedings, where issues of custody and access (or residence and contact) often go side-by-side. The more detailed the list, the greater the risk of an appeal if the court were to fail to cover every single point in the course of explaining its decision. Finally, if a detailed list is prescribed by statute, it can only be changed by statute, yet knowledge and understanding of children and their needs is developing all the time and the courts must be able to keep pace with this.

Questions

(i) The list deliberately steers clear of statements like 'young children need their mothers', or 'boys need a masculine influence', or 'brothers and sisters need to stay together': is this a good thing?

(ii) Turn to the cases on pp. 511–526, above: would any of them have been decided — or expressed — differently if the checklist had been in force?

(iii) Factor (g) was added later: why?

(c) THE NON-INTERVENTION PRINCIPLE

Section 1 of the *Children Act 1989* contains another, important, but novel principle:

1.–(5) Where a court is considering whether or not to make one or more orders under this Act with respect to a child, it shall not make the order or any of the orders unless it considers that doing so would be better for the child than making no order at all.

The Law Commission's explanation was this:

3.2 A tendency seems to have developed to assume that some order about the children should always be made whenever divorce or separation cases come to court. This may have been necessary in the days when mothers required a court order if they were to acquire any parental powers at all, but that is no longer the case. Studies of both divorce and magistrates' courts have shown that the proportion of contested cases is very small so that orders are not usually necessary in order to settle disputes. Rather, they may be seen by solicitors as 'part of the package' for their matrimonial clients and by courts as part of their task of approving the arrangements made in divorce cases [Priest and Whybrow 1986, para. 8.2]. No doubt in many, possibly most, uncontested cases an order is needed in the children's own interest, so as to confirm and give stability to the existing arrangements, to clarify the respective roles of the parents, to reassure the parent with whom the children will be living, and even to reassure the public authorities responsible for housing and income support that such arrangements have in fact been made. However, it is always open to parents to separate without going to court at all, in which case there will be no order. If they go to court for some other remedy, they may not always want an order about the children. The proportion of relatively amicable divorces is likely to have increased in recent years and parents may well be able to make responsible arrangements for themselves without a court order. Where a child has a good relationship with both parents the law should seek to disturb this as little as possible. There is always a risk that orders allocating custody and access (or even deciding upon residence and contact) will have the effect of polarising the parents' roles and perhaps alienating the child from one or other of them.

3.3 For these reasons, the Working Paper proposed a more flexible approach, in which it was not always assumed that an order should be made, but the court would be prepared to make one even in uncontested cases if this would promote the children's interests. Most of those who responded agreed with this approach. Such a change would be consistent with the view that anything which can be done to help parents to keep separate the issues of being a spouse and being a parent will ultimately give the children the best chance of retaining them both. [Clulow and Vincent, 1987]. On the other hand, the impression should not be given that an application or an order is a hostile step between them. We therefore recommend that the court should only make an order where this is the most effective way of safeguarding or promoting the child's welfare.

This is closely linked to the role of the court in all divorce cases where there are relevant children of the family, whether or not the parents are agreed:

3.5 . . . one possible reason why orders are almost always made at present is the divorce court's present duty under section 41 of the Matrimonial Causes Act 1973 to declare itself satisfied as to the arrangements made for the children of the family before making absolute a decree of nullity or divorce or making a decree of judicial separation. Magistrates' domestic courts have a similar duty [s. 8(1) of the Domestic Proceedings Magistrates' Courts Act 1978] not to dismiss or to make a final order on an application for financial relief without deciding what order, if any, to make about the children.

3.6 The original main aims [Royal Commission on Marriage and Divorce 1951–1955, 1956, paras. 366 et seq.] of section 41 procedure were to ensure that divorcing parents made the best possible arrangements for their children and to identify cases of particular concern where protective measures might be needed. In our Working Paper on Custody we concluded that the procedure had not been successful in achieving either of these aims. The information currently available to the court is too limited, being based on a brief statement from the petitioner alone; the arrangements are usually discussed in a short interview with the judge, which cannot be other than perfunctory in many cases; and, most importantly, the practical power of the court to produce different outcomes is very limited, nor can it ensure that the approved arrangements are subsequently observed. Although there are undoubtedly exceptional cases in which protective measures of supervision or even care may be needed, the present process is not principally designed to discover these.

3.7 Hence the Working Paper provisionally proposed replacing the divorce court's present duty to declare that the arrangements are 'satisfactory' or 'the best that can be devised in the circumstances' with the domestic court's more modest duty to consider what order, if any, to make. To help the court to decide this question, procedural improvements along the lines recommended by the Booth Committee [1985, paras. 4.3–4.37] might be made. These included an expanded statement of arrangements, allowing or requiring the respondent to join with the petitioner's statement or to file his own, and considering these at an earlier stage in the proceedings than at present.

3.8 There was a large measure of support for these proposals . . . But it was thought by some of our respondents that a duty invariably to have decided what order to make before granting the decree absolute went too far. We accept that this requirement would be too strong if it meant that no divorce could be granted while a custody dispute existed. This would create a serious risk of children becoming pawns in their parents' own battles. A parent opposed to the divorce might drag out the dispute indefinitely if divorce were thereby unobtainable. Such a bar would in fact be more onerous than the present law, as declarations may be granted even where the resolution of a custody dispute is still outstanding [*A v A* [1979] 2 All ER 493, [1979] 1 WLR 533]. Moreover, satisfactory arrangements are often most difficult to devise where the family circumstances are particularly desperate, so that to deny the relief associated with divorce may make matters even worse.

3.9 We recommend, therefore, that once divorce, nullity or judicial separation proceedings have been initiated, the court should have a duty to consider the arrangements proposed for the children in order to decide whether to exercise any of its powers under this legislation. Where this is so, but only in exceptional circumstances, the court should also have power to direct that the decree absolute (or a decree of judicial separation) cannot be made until the court allows it.

The Children Act accordingly substitutes a new s. 41 in the Matrimonial Causes Act 1973.

Questions

(i) Would you prefer to have your proposals labelled 'satisfactory' or 'the best that can be devised in the circumstances'?
(ii) In what circumstances do you think that it would be 'better' for the child to make an order when his parents part?
(iii) Did you think it was the law that there *had* to be an order of some sort in a divorce case?
(iv) Are we in danger of throwing the baby out with the bath water?

(d) THE CHILD'S SENSE OF TIME

There is one value judgment in the *Children Act 1989* about what is good for children:

1.—(2) In any proceedings in which any question with respect to the upbringing of a child arises, the court shall have regard to the general principle that any delay in determining the question is likely to prejudice the welfare of the child.

The Law Commission are to blame:

4.55 . . . Prolonged litigation about their future is deeply damaging to children, not only because of the uncertainty it brings for them, but also because of the harm it does to the relationship between the parents and their capacity to co-operate with one another in the future. Moreover, a frequent consequence is that the case of the parent who is not living with the child is severely prejudiced by the time of the hearing. Regrettably, it is almost always to the advantage of one of the parties to delay the proceedings as long as possible and, what may be worse, to make difficulties over contact in the meantime. At present, particularly in divorce courts, the responsibility for the progress of the proceedings lies principally with the adult parties, although a considerable source of delay is the time taken to prepare welfare officers' reports and sometimes to attempt conciliation between the parties.

4.56 . . . there is serious concern, particularly among the judiciary, about the present delays and . . . action is required to remedy the situation. There may be problems in preparing welfare reports, given the other constraints within which welfare officers have to work, and in some cases time may be beneficial in enabling an agreed solution to emerge, perhaps with the help of conciliation. Nevertheless, the 'child's sense of time' is quite different from the adults' and it is the child's interests which should prevail.

4.57 The most effective practical action which can be taken to remedy matters is to place a clear obligation upon the court to oversee the progress of the case and to ensure that the court regards all delay as prejudicial to the child's interests unless the contrary is shown. (An example might be where the benefit to the child from a thorough report outweighed the detriment of having to wait for it, but the Court of Appeal has said that if one has to wait as long as nine months it is better to do without one [*Re C (a minor) (custody of child)* (1980) 2 FLR 163].) This approach is something of a novelty within our legal system, which is generally content to leave such matters to the parties themselves.

(e) THE VIEWS OF THE CHILD

Item (*a*) in the checklist, p. 545, above, covers the 'wishes and feelings' of the child himself, as recommended by the Law Commission:

3.22 The Working Paper on Custody provisionally that, at least in contested cases, the court should have to ascertain the 'wishes and feelings' of the child and give due consideration to them in the light of his age and understanding. Such a requirement already exists in adoption cases [s. 6 of the Adoption Act 1976]. Views were invited upon whether the requirement should be expressed independently or as part of a 'checklist' and on whether it should extend to uncontested cases. The two questions are related for, as we have already seen, the effect of including the requirement in a checklist is in practice to limit it to contested cases.

3.23 The opinion of our respondents was almost unanimously in favour of the proposal to give statutory recognition to the child's views. Obviously there are dangers in giving them too much recognition. Children's views have to be discovered in such a way as to avoid embroiling them in their parents' disputes, forcing them to 'choose' between their parents, or making them feel responsible for the eventual decision. This is usually best done through the medium of a welfare officer's report, although most agreed that courts should retain their present powers to see children in private. Similarly, for a variety of reasons the child's views may not be reliable, so that the court should only have to take due account of them in the light of his age and understanding. Nevertheless, experience has shown that it is pointless to ignore the clearly expressed wishes of older children [*M v M* (transfer of custody: appeal) [1987] 1 WLR 404, [1987] 2 FLR 146]. Finally, however, if the parents have agreed on where the child will live and made their arrangements accordingly, it is no more practicable to try to alter these to accord with the child's views than it is to impose the views of the court. After all, united parents will no doubt take account of the views of their children in deciding upon moves of house or employment but the children cannot expect their wishes to prevail [King, 1987, p. 190].

3.24 These considerations all point towards including the child's views as part of a statutory checklist, which in practice will be limited to contested cases, rather than as a separate consideration in their own right. This solution was generally favoured by our respondents and we so recommend. Were there not to be a statutory checklist, however, the increasing recognition given both in practice and in law to the child's status as a human being in his own right [*Gillick v West Norfolk and Wisbech Area Health Authority* [1986] AC 112], rather than the object of the rights of others, would clearly require an independent duty in the court to take account of his views to the same extent as that in adoption cases.

3.25 . . . The courts' present powers to make custody and access orders endure until the child reaches 18, although the court will rarely, if ever, make a custody order which is contrary to the wishes of a child who has reached 16 [*Hall v Hall* (1945) 175 LT 355]. Any other approach is scarcely practicable, given that this is the age at which children may leave school and seek full-time employment and become entitled to certain benefits or allowances in their own right. However, the matter goes beyond the question of what is practicable. There are powers of direct enforcement of custody orders which operate upon the child rather than the adults involved [e.g. s. 34 of the Family Law Act 1986]. The older the child becomes, the less just it is even to attempt to enforce against him an order to which he has never been party. As we explain below, it is usually thought unnecessary to accord party status to children in family disputes and in general we would not disagree. We recommend, therefore, that orders relating to the child's residence, contact or other specific matters of upbringing should not be made in respect of a child who has reached 16 unless there are exceptional circumstances and that orders made before that age should expire then unless in exceptional circumstances the court orders otherwise.

Questions

(i) Does this go far enough? Do you think that children should be separately represented in all proceedings about their future? If so, should this be done by a lawyer or a social worker or both?

(ii) The child himself may apply for a s. 8 order, with the court's leave, if he has 'sufficient understanding' (s. 10(8)): can you think of any orders which the court might make in such a case?

(iii) Would you agree with the following recommendation of the Justice Report on *Parental Rights and Duties and Custody Suits* (1975)?

89. . . .
  (*h*) The family court would include among its staff a new officer, having training in both law and applied social sciences. Among other things, his duty would be to act as overseer of children's interests in custody suits. We have referred to him already in our report as the 'Children's Ombudsman.'. . .

91. The role we envisage for the Children's Ombudsman includes that of a clearing agency, one branch at each family court. Everyone would know of his existence and would be expected to report to him. All relevant information would end up under one hand. He would have the power to request a welfare report whenever he thought it necessary. On behalf of a child the subject of a custody suit, he would act as the child's spokesman and would have the duty of instructing solicitors and counsel to represent the child's interests so that the interests of the child might be separately represented to the court independently of the adults and local or other authorities concerned. (He would have the power to do so in other legal proceedings as well.) As the child's spokesman, it would be his particular duty to ensure that the views of any child able to express them, verbally or otherwise, were ascertained in the absence of the parents or other adult 'custodian' and then made known to the tribunal. He would be responsible to the Lord Chancellor (the traditional delegate of the Crown as *parens patriae*).

4 Court welfare officers

The court welfare officers so frequently referred to above are usually probation officers and do not, in fact, provide welfare services for children or families. Their principal function is to investigate and make reports to the court; this is usually regarded as the appropriate way in which to ascertain the child's own views and put them before the court. Welfare officers may also be involved in providing formal or informal help with a particular problem, for example over visiting arrangements. This used to be known as 'supervision', but under s. 16 of the Children Act 1989, orders of this type will become family assistance orders (supervision orders, to protect the child from a risk of significant harm, are dealt with in Chapter 13). Welfare officers may also offer conciliation to help the parents resolve their disputes without the need for the court's decision, but this should be kept quite separate from their reporting function (*Re H (conciliation: welfare reports)* [1986] 1 FLR 476) (conciliation is discussed in Chapter 15).

The Wolfson study of *Custody after Divorce* (Eekelaar and Clive, 1977) found that there were welfare officers' reports in 53% of contested and 8.2% of uncontested cases, but it was difficult to know how many cases remained contested to the bitter end. Later enquiries (Priest and Whybrow, 1986) suggest that, although practice may vary, it is rare for a report not to be available if there is a full-blown contest about where the child should live. The Wolfson study also showed that in 45% of cases it took more than six months from the adjournment for a report before the case got back to court. Sometimes, therefore, the court may have to choose between the damage done by deciding the case without a report and the damage done by waiting for one (see *Re C (a minor) (custody of child)* (1980) 2 FLR 163). The court is entitled to come to a different conclusion from the welfare officer (*S v S (custody of children)* (1978) 1 FLR 143) but should not depart from a clear recommendation without making its reasons plain (*Re T (a minor) (welfare report recommendation)* (1977) 1 FLR 59). It is therefore important to see what these reports are trying to do. The following is an (updated) example which has been used by welfare officers themselves for training purposes. The characters are, of course, fictitious.

SPECIMEN WELFARE REPORT

BLANKSHIRE PROBATION & AFTER-CARE SERVICE

WOOD & WOOD

Applicant:	Mrs Jean WOOD	— 22 years
Respondent:	Mr John WOOD	— 35 years
Child concerned:	Richard WOOD	— 5.5.87–3 years
Child:	Amanda FORBES	— 6 years
Respondent's co-habitee:	Janet SMITH	— 32 years
Children:	Mary SMITH	— 6 years
	Brian SMITH	— 5 years

1. ENQUIRIES:

I have read the Court file concerning this matter
I have had discussions with:
— the Applicant with Richard
— the Respondent and Co-habitee with Richard
— Richard by himself
I have had a telephone conversation with the Housing Department
I have had a telephone conversation with Dr Jones, the Respondent's Physician

2. BACKGROUND RELATING TO THE CHILD

I understand from both parties that initially their relationship was good though the Applicant claims the Respondent spent too much time with his mother. In March 1990 Mr Wood's father died and he invited his mother to live with him and his wife. The Applicant and her mother-in-law had never enjoyed a good relationship and there were immediate problems. Mrs Wood senior it is claimed assumed control of the family, gradually taking over responsibility for the housework and the care of both the Respondent and the child—Richard. There were constant quarrels and in November 1990 following a violent disagreement, the Applicant left the matrimonial home on an impulse and stayed for a short period with a relative. Being without accommodation she did not feel it fair to Richard to take him with her at that time. Within three weeks she had found accommodation in a very small bedsitting room sharing a kitchen and bathroom with a family of five people; again a situation she felt unsuitable for Richard.

3. APPLICANT MOTHER

Mrs Jean WOOD — Mrs Wood, a full time housewife, impressed as a bright, outgoing young woman who is obviously deeply attached to her son. She told me she had found the situation in the former matrimonial home quite intolerable from the time her mother-in-law moved in. She claimed Mrs Wood senior had undermined her discipline of Richard and had tried to cause difficulties between her and the Respondent. She said that her reason for staying had been the fear that she might lose Richard and that she left only when she felt she could no longer cope with the situation. I understand that Richard's behaviour was untypically bad from the time she left home causing the Respondent to contact the family doctor. I am told the child's behaviour returned to normal once contact with his mother was re-established in December 1990. Mrs Wood visits Richard twice weekly at the former matrimonial home. The Respondent has been quite adamant that he will not allow her to take the child away from the home. Until very recently, there were no difficulties with contact. The Applicant feels, however, that the atmosphere has become tense since the Respondent's co-habitee moved into the home in January 1991 whereupon the grandmother left.

4. Of her own relationship with her co-habitee, Mr Forbes, the Applicant tells me she had known him some years ago and met him again soon after leaving her husband. She has lived with Mr Forbes since the beginning of January 1991 and has already formed an excellent relationship with his daughter, Amanda, who lives with them. The Applicant and Mr Forbes plan to marry as soon as both are free to do so.

5. The Applicant Mother feels very strongly that she is the appropriate person to have the day to day care of Richard. She feels he has already been subjected to too many changes and that she can now offer him the stability he needs. She has made tentative enquiries concerning a playschool for Richard, but if he comes to live with her would delay any decision until he was completely settled in his new home. Mrs Wood appears to fully appreciate the importance of the child having regular contact with the Father and would have no objection to reasonable contact which she suggests could be staying on alternate weekends.

6. APPLICANT'S CO-HABITEE

Mr Michael FORBES — Mr Forbes presented as a pleasant, mature personality. He told me he had married very young, that his wife had had difficulty in managing on a low income and the resulting debts had caused difficulties between them. He told me that his wife left him 2 years ago and he has not heard from her since. He has made enquiries concerning her whereabouts as he is anxious now to petition for divorce. Mr Forbes has had the care of his daughter since his wife left and has coped admirably with the help of a neighbour. He is employed as a clerk. He tells me that because of the demands made on him in caring for his daughter, he has not been able to take advantage of promotion. However, now that the Applicant is caring for his daughter Amanda, he feels his employment prospects are excellent. Because the Respondent has refused to allow Richard to leave the home with his mother, Mr Forbes has not met the child. He is realistic about the possible difficulties should Richard come to live with them but feels his experience with his own child will help.

7. APPLICANT'S HOME

The home is a 2-bedroomed flat which is adequately furnished and well kept. Mr Forbes expects to move to a 3-bedroomed maisonette in the near future having negotiated an exchange with another family. I have contacted the Housing Department who confirm that there are no objections to this transfer.

8. RESPONDENT

Mr John WOOD — Mr Wood is a quiet, introspective man. He tells me he was the youngest son in a large family. He has always enjoyed a very close relationship with his mother who did not approve of his relationship with the Applicant. Mr Wood tells me that his wife coped well with the home and the child until his mother moved in with them. He claims that the Applicant then became lazy and lost interest in the home, leaving everything to the grandmother. The Respondent is employed as a Sales Manager. In the course of his work he travels extensively, often away overnight and sometimes travels abroad. His co-habitee—Mrs Smith—has lived with him since mid January 1991 and although he has not known her for very long, the relationship appears to be sound and based on mutual interests. The Respondent told me that Richard has caused him some anxiety since Mrs Smith arrived and the grandmother left the home. He has again consulted the family doctor but feels that if a firm line is taken with Richard, he will quickly adapt to the new situation. The Respondent tells me that he is asking Richard to stay with him as he does not wish to have another man involved in bringing up his son. He also feels he is in a better position to care for Richard's material needs than is the Applicant. He would have no objection to the present arrangement for contact being continued but would oppose staying visits.

9. RESPONDENT'S CO-HABITEE

Mrs Janet SMITH — Mrs Smith is a quiet, intelligent woman who is studying for a degree with the Open University and would like a teaching career. She talked frankly about her own children saying that she was not very maternal and although she very much enjoys her children's monthly visits, she does not wish to see them more often. She expressed some reservations about bringing up Richard, especially with the Respondent being often away from home. She told me, however, that she is fond of Richard and is anxious to do whatever Mr Wood wishes.

10. RESPONDENT'S HOME

The home is a spacious, 4-bedroomed house where material standards are high. The property is owned by Mr Wood subject to a mortgage.

11. CHILD CONCERNED

Richard WOOD — Richard is a bright and lively child, obviously well cared for. I have seen him with the Applicant and also separately with the Respondent. When I saw Richard with the Respondent and Mrs Smith, he appeared to be anxious to do and say the right thing and was quieter and more subdued than when I interviewed him with the Applicant. With the Applicant, Richard was talkative and lively and very upset when the time came for her to leave. Although Richard is hardly 4, it appears that given the choice, he would wish to spend most of his time with his mother.

12. CONCLUSION

From my enquiries, it would appear that both parents care about Richard's welfare and either could offer him a good home. The Respondent is in a position to offer material advantages and wishes Richard to be privately educated. The Applicant Mother's means are more modest but the bond between mother and child is particularly close and the separation was of such short duration that it appears to have done no damage to the relationship. It has not been possible to see the Applicant's co-habitee with the child. On the other hand the child's relationship with the Respondent's co-habitee is not yet a close one. In fact, the child appears to be having some difficulty in relating to a third mother figure.

13. In view of the very close relationship between mother and child, it would appear to be in Richard's long-term best interests if he were to live with his Mother.

14. Should this course of action be followed the Court may feel, in view of the Respondent's particular interest in Richard's education, that the parties should share responsibility for any major decision concerning Richard's education. It is clear that whatever the decision Richard will experience problems in adjusting to the new step-parent. The Court may consider, therefore, that a short period of assistance would be of benefit to Richard in making this adjustment. During the enquiries a good working relationship has been established between the Welfare Officer, the parties, and more particularly Richard, which indicates that such an Order may be more appropriately made to the Probation Service to allow continuity.

February 1991   *Court Welfare Officer*

Questions

(i) If you were counsel for the mother in this case, what features of the report would you emphasise to the court?

(ii) If you were counsel for the father, would you advise him to settle the dispute along the lines suggested by the welfare officer? How does the new law differ from the old?

(iii) If the father wished to fight the case, which features would you as counsel emphasise to the court?

(iv) As counsel for the father, how would you go about challenging the suggestion in para. 11 of the report that 'although Richard is hardly four, it appears that given the choice, he would wish to spend most of his time with his mother'?

(v) In *Re W* (1982) 4 FLR 492 above, the Court of Appeal was highly critical of a welfare officer who had not made it her business to observe the child and her relationships within each of the competing households: why are the welfare officer's observations of those relationships apparently as significant as the evidence given at the trial?

(vi) Is this a case in which it will be better for the child to make an order?

5 Step-families

As every child knows, there have always been step-parents, but their stereotype is the wicked step-mother who invades the family after their real mother is dead. Nowadays, however, the more appropriate stereotype would be the divorced father who has gradually faded out of his own children's lives, and has now married a woman who has children from a previous marriage or relationship. As Jacqueline Burgoyne and David Clark point out in *Reconstituted Families* (1982):

There is considerable evidence that the obligations and responsibilities of fatherhood are very diffusely defined in our own society; mothers are felt to be mainly responsible for the welfare and public behaviour of children (eg Newson, 1972); fatherless families are expected to manage on their own, albeit in reduced circumstances, although we do not have similar expectations of motherless families (see George and Wilding, 1972); fathers continue to play little or no part in the care of babies or toddlers in many families (eg Oakley, 1979). The obligations of fatherhood are most clearly articulated in terms of being a good provider, ensuring economic security for the mother who takes direct responsibility for the care of his children. . . . Therefore, even if divorced parents consciously desire to exercise a shared responsibility for the care of their children there are important informal pressures tending to undermine this intention especially where one or both of them has remarried.

Although there is insufficient data to draw very definite conclusions, it does seem from the limited evidence available that many non-custodial fathers lose contact with their children from their first marriage and may eventually become step-fathers to some-one else's children.

As to the scale of step-parenthood, John Haskey draws some conclusions on the family circumstances of *Children of Families Broken by Divorce* (1990):

The General Household Survey (GHS), includes questions on each respondent's marital history and on women's past child-bearing. Two recent studies [Clarke, 1989; Clarke and Eldridge, 1989] have extracted some useful information from this source to give the family circumstances of children of women aged from 18 to 49 living in Great Britain in 1985. Using the sample numbers from which these results were obtained, very approximate estimates can be made that, of all children who were *not* living with both their natural parents in 1985, about one half were living with a non-cohabiting lone mother; about one third were living their natural mother who had remarried — that is, in a step-father family — and about one in 12 were living with their natural mother who was cohabiting — that is, in a 'de facto step-father family'. In addition, about one in 11 children were living either with their father, or with neither parent.

These proportions refer to *all* children who were not living with both their natural parents in 1985; of more interest in the present context is the sub-set of all these children who were not living with both their natural parents *because of divorce*. Using results from other studies on one-parent families [Haskey, 1989] and on cohabitation [Haskey and Kiernan, 1989] and assuming that all remarried women with children had remarried after divorce, estimates of the required proportions can be derived from those given above. The resulting rough estimates are that, of all children not living with both their natural parents because of divorce, just over one third live with their non-cohabiting lone divorced mother; about one half live with their remarried mother and stepfather; and about one in 15 live with their lone divorced mother, who is cohabiting. A very small proportion — about one in 30 — live with their father, and a similar proportion live with neither parent.

Question

It also appears that women with young children are more likely to remarry than those without; can you think why (see also p. 108, above)?

The complexities of the step-relationship are explored from the point of view of a step-mother by Brenda Maddox in her book, *Step-parenting* (1980):

If families in which there is a step-parent differ from adoptive families, they differ far more from ordinary families. The reason is that the basic rules that govern family life are disturbed in families where the children are not the biological offspring of both the husband and wife in the household. These rules concern sex and money: who may have sexual relations with whom, who must support whom and who may inherit from whom. Father sleeps with a woman who is not his son's mother, and is therefore not explicitly forbidden to the son by the recognised incest taboo. The child sits at the table of the breadwinner of the household, but the child is actually supported by a father living somewhere else. Often children who ordinarily would expect to inherit from their father and mother find their parent's new spouse will take away some or all of what might have been their portion. Or, if there are children of the new marriage as well as of a former marriage, there often exists an uncomfortable situation in which there are two sets of children who live under the same roof, or who spend vacations together, but who have quite different financial expectations. One might be, say, the daughter of the late Aly Khan and the other of Orson Welles. . . .

Still, there is no model for how a step-parent should behave. The parent's obligations, by contrast, are clear. The anthropologist Bronislaw Malinowski has pointed out that 'the mother, besides feeling inclined to do all she does for her child, is none the less obliged to do it'. Step-parents often do not feel inclined to do anything for their step-children, yet they feel strong pressure from the community, and from their spouse, to do something. But what? For natural parents, not only the obligations but the ideals are clear. . . .

The social questions posed by the remarriage of parents have hardly been faced by a society that ostensibly accepts divorce as the right solution to an unhappy marriage. We have been told that the marriage bond is the structural keystone in our kinship system and that our identity depends entirely on the marriage unit (unless we come from old-established lineage like the Devonshires or the Rothschilds). Who we are depends entirely on two families — our family of origin and our family of procreation; we are the children of our parents and the parents of our children. But we are not told how to preserve our sense of identity if we have a mother in one family, a father in another, a son in a third, and a daughter in a fourth.

Burgoyne and Clark (1982) draw upon their research with step-families in Sheffield to reach the following conclusions:

We have tried to suggest that it is still often the case that step-families are reconstituted according to a normative blueprint which is based on the unbroken nuclear family. Those who marry again are, therefore, heavily reliant on criteria of success, failure and adequacy which are drawn from 'normal' family life. Consequently evaluations of stepfamily life are typically made according to criteria of 'ordinariness'. However it is clear that stepfamilies differ in the extent to which they consciously attempt to 'pass' as an unbroken nuclear family by, for example, taking a new job and moving to a new area. Naturally this may seem to be the most obvious strategy; it brings about the normalisation of family life and, in the case of young adults with small children where divorce and custody are uncontested, this may well prove to be both practical and expedient. However, this may be impossible for other families. Where legal aspects of custody, access and maintenance arrangements are disputed and where older children and non-custodial parents are in regular contact, then the stepfamily is less likely to succeed in attempts at normalisation. For these families two possible strategies are available. Some may, out of a sense of guilt, propriety or confusion, choose to fly in the face of the structural factors which make their existence as a stepfamily both visible and incontrovertible. The pursuit of the goal of normal family life is inevitably frustrated, as subjective ideals clash continually with external and material constraints. Others, to the extent that they recognise the nature of these problems, may reject, either explicitly or implicitly, such a course. Members of these families, sensitised by media coverage of trends in divorce and remarriage, see themselves as pioneers of an alternative life. Having accepted their situation, they formulate an ideology and practice to match it. In marked contrast to some of the literature which emphasised the negative aspects of step-relationships, they are clear that their way of life may also represent a source of potential rewards and satisfactions of a type absent from more conventional nuclear families. Typically, these step-families emphasise the material and social benefits which stepsiblings derive from one another's presence in the family, the value and importance of additional parental figures, and the fulfillment which results from reconstituting a single family from its disparate elements.

In *Making a Go of It* (1984), they construct the following typology to reflect these variations:

Table 6.1: A typology of stepfamilies

1 *'Not really a stepfamily'*
The stepchildren of the family were young at the time of divorce and remarriage; within a short time they were able to think of themselves as an 'ordinary' family.
Children of new marriage confirm this.

2 *'Looking forward to the departure of the children'*
Older couples with teenage children await departure of dependent children so that they can enjoy their new partnership more fully.
Too old for children in new marriage.

3 *The 'progressive' stepfamily*
Prototype 'new' stepfamily in which conflicts with ex-partners have been resolved. They stress the advantages of their circumstances.
Few barriers to additional children of new marriage.

4 *The successful conscious pursuit of an 'ordinary' family life together*
Stepparent becomes full 'social' parent transferring allegiance to stepchildren. Their initial problems are solved or successfully ignored. Children of new marriage symbolise 'normality' of their family life.

5 *The conscious pursuit of 'ordinary' family life frustrated*
The legacy of their past marriage(s) frustrates their attempts to build an ordinary family life together.
Children of new marriage are unlikely because of continuing problems.

Until the mid-seventies, the common solution to the contradictions of the step-parent role was to adopt the children, but this practice came under increasing attack from, in particular, social workers who acted as guardian ad litem for the child in the proceedings. In 1970, a Departmental Committee on the Adoption of Children (then under the chairmanship of Sir William Houghton) published a *Working Paper* which made the following radical suggestion:

92. About half the adoptions by a natural parent and a step-parent are of legitimate children, the application being made jointly by one of the child's parents and a new spouse following divorce or death of the child's other parent. Adoptions of legitimate children by a parent on remarriage after divorce could well increase if there is an increase in the divorce rate. Family circumstances in these cases may be very varied. Although the consent of the first partner is required unless dispensed with by the court and although the consent of a minor child to his adoption is required in Scotland and the wishes of the infant are taken into consideration in England and Wales, such adoptions hold the serious implication of effectively cutting children off from one of their natural legitimate parents with whom they may have lived for a considerable time; these are the adoptions most likely to involve older children. The child may not wish to lose contact with the other parent, for whom he may well have deep feelings and a sense of loyalty. He may not want to have his name changed. He may suffer from severance of contact not only with one parent, but with siblings (e.g. if the divorce court divided custody of the children between the two parents) and other relatives. He may lose rights of inheritance. Circumstances may indeed later arise in which his return to the other parent would be desirable, e.g. on the breakdown of the second marriage of the parent having his custody. Some, though not all, of these considerations apply on remarriage after death of the first spouse as well as after divorce.

93. Just as openness about adoption and illegitimacy is desirable, so is it desirable to recognise openly the fact and the consequences of divorce and of death. One of the consequences of divorce is that many children are living with a parent and a step-parent and retain contact with, or even live for part of the time with, their other parent, who may also have remarried. Such a situation may well be disturbing to the child, but it is not appropriate to use adoption in an attempt to ease the pain or to cover up these consequences of divorce. The legal extinguishment of a legitimate child's links with one half of his own family, which adoption entails in such circumstances, is inappropriate and may well be damaging. We consider therefore that adoption of a legitimate child by a natural parent and step-parent should no longer be possible.

94. We recognise that we are drawing a distinction between legitimate and illegitimate children in that a step-parent will be able to adopt his step-child only if the child is illegitimate. This distinction might be regarded as invidious, and it may be thought that adoption by a step-parent should be available in both cases or in neither. On the other hand the two situations are not truly analogous. An illegitimate child, by adoption, obtains a legal status and a family which he did not have before. A legitimate child does not gain a more favourable legal status; he exchanges one set of family relationships for another, and almost inevitably severs existing family links. . . . What is required is a legal procedure which recognises the position and the responsibility of the step-parent with whom such a child is living, enabling the step-parent to act as guardian of the child jointly with his spouse. The extension of guardianship law to permit step-parents to apply to be appointed guardians would provide the requisite procedure, enabling questions of custody and access to be decided by the court from time to time in accordance with the welfare of the child.

The final *Report* of the Committee (1972) stated that:

108. The evidence we received was overwhelmingly opposed to our suggestion. Some witnesses pointed to the positive advantages of adoption to a legitimate child whose other parent is dead or where contact with that parent and his family is negligible or non-existent. Others were strongly opposed to the distinction between legitimate and illegitimate children, pointing out that a parent may have a legitimate and an illegitimate child and on the remarriage of the parent the illegitimate child could be adopted by the step-parent but not the legitimate child.

This Children Act 1975 accordingly introduced statutory discouragement of all types of step-parent adoption, although at first only the provisions relating to divorce were implemented. These required the court to refuse a step-parent adoption if the matter could be 'better dealt with' by some form of custody order in the divorce proceedings. The courts have always been reluctant to dispense with the agreement of an estranged father who does not want his children adopted, but they had difficulty in working out when they ought to refuse an adoption which everyone wanted.

Re D (minors) (adoption by step-parent)
(1980) 2 FLR 102, 10 Fam Law 246, Court of Appeal

The parents of two girls, now aged 13 and 10½, were divorced in 1973. In 1976 the mother married her present husband, who was also divorced and had the custody of the two children of his first marriage. The girls' name was changed to his by deed poll with the consent of their father. There was contact between the father and the eldest child until the end of 1977 and between him and the younger child until September 1978. In 1980 the mother and step-father applied to adopt the girls and the father consented. Both girls indicated to the guardian ad litem that they wished to be adopted. The family planned to emigrate to Australia. The guardian ad litem, after a thorough examination of the advantages and disadvantages, concluded that on balance the adoption order should not be made. The judge reached the same conclusion and the applicants appealed.

Ormrod LJ: . . . It is a very difficult decision to make because it is extremely difficult to know what criteria should be used in reaching the decision. The various financial provisions of the Matrimonial Causes Act 1973 and the Family Law Reform Act 1969 as well have now extended to the point when it is almost impossible to show any financial benefit from an adoption order. . . . So the court has to consider very difficult psychological issues in coming to the conclusion that the matter can be better dealt with in one way or the other.

. . . Obviously an important factor in the matter, although by no means conclusive, is the fact that, under [s 6 of the Adoption Act 1976], the court, in considering making an adoption order, is required by statute to ascertain, so far as practicable

'the wishes and feelings of the child regarding the decision and give due consideration to them . . .'

That, to my mind, must be an important consideration when dealing with children of the age of these children. They are fully old enough to understand, as I have said before, the broad implications of adoption and, if they actively wish to be adopted, even if they cannot give a very coherent reason for that wish, to refuse an adoption order in the face of that wish does require, as Brandon LJ said in the course of argument, some fairly clear reason. . . .

I have mentioned other matters in this case which distinguish it from the run of these cases; and I think those can be summarized in a sentence by saying that the natural father of these children has dropped out of their lives both physically and psychologically to an extent which is much greater than one usually meets in this type of post-divorce situation. It is reasonable to infer that the children see themselves as members of the D family to a much, much greater extent than children of divorced parents normally do. There is no question of regarding Mr D as 'Uncle Tom' or whatever his name is. They clearly regard him as 'Dad'.

So it is a case in which, to my mind, all the indications are in favour of making an adoption order, more particularly as the family is about to emigrate to Australia. I can well understand the adults feeling that it would put their position in their new country much more clearly and explicitly if they go there with these two children as the adopted children of the family.

The points which troubled [the guardian ad litem] mainly seem to me to be, first, the fact that the children in this case had a full recollection of their natural father, and so it was not one of those cases such as *Re S* (1974) 5 Fam Law 88 where the children themselves have no recollection of their natural father and where the making of an adoption order gives legal effect to a situation which already exists in fact. But, to my mind, this is not a crucial distinction. The fact that they remember their natural father cannot be, in itself, a reason for not making an adoption order if the other indications suggest that it would be desirable. Of course these children remember their father.

Then it is said that the effect of an adoption order is to cut them off entirely from their father's family — to which, to my mind, the answer is that it may or may not do so. There is no magic in an adoption order. The fact that the child becomes a child of the new family does not, in itself, automatically cut off the children from the natural family. Of course it may do. An adoption order has that effect when the child is very young. I am always impressed by the differences in the considerations to be taken into account where one is concerned with the adoption of a small child, say up to two years, and an older child. The effect of adoption of a child up to two is to effect a complete severance with the natural family and, hopefully, a complete integration into the new family; but, once the child is older than that and has experience of a natural parent, adoption can never have that effect in fact. It may have in law that effect, but there is no reason why, if everyone is agreeable, children like these should not see their [paternal] grandparents should it be desirable. In fact, in this case we are told they are completely out of touch with the whole of the father's family, not only with the father himself. So that, with respect to [the guardian] and recognizing his extreme care in this case, I personally do not attach great significance to the fact that the children are fully aware of the existence of their natural father.

He was also troubled by what he thought would be the disturbing effect of the adoption order on the existing family unit. That I find hard to understand, because there seems to be no indication that an adoption order will materially alter anything in this new family except, if anything, to increase its cohesion and not diminish it. The judge was worried that, possibly, after an adoption order had been made, one of the children might turn on the adoptive father and challenge him as not being their own father. But, with respect, that point must apply with even more force to a situation where Mr D's position is simply that of a joint custodian under the Matrimonial Causes Act.

He also took the point — and one sees the force of it again — that there was a distinction here between the two children that we are dealing with and the two children of the husband because there was no suggestion of an application by the step-mother, Mrs D, for an adoption order in respect of them. We are told that the reason for that is that their mother, that is the first Mrs D, has so completely disappeared out of the children's lives that the proposed adopters in this case regarded proceedings for an adoption order in respect of those children as being quite superfluous and unnecessary. If that is right — and it seems to me, on the face of it, reasonable to suppose that it is — then there does not seem to be any serious objection from that point of view. . . .

Appeal allowed.

Question

Why do you think the couple were so much more anxious that the step-father should adopt his wife's children than that the step-mother should adopt her husband's? Does it bear out what Burgoyne and Clark (pp. 555, above) suggest about fatherhood?

The local courts hearing adoption applications also had divergent views, as Judith Masson, Daphne Norbury and Sandra Chatterton found in their study of step-parent adoptions in three court areas, *Mine, Yours or Ours? A Study of Step-parent Adoption* (1984):

There was little variation in outcome between the three areas in 1975, but by 1978 the differences were enormous. In area 1 *post-divorce* step-parents continued to get adoption orders just as they had before this Act. In area 2 judges held strong views on step-parent adoption. By 1978, adoption had become virtually unattainable for *post-divorce* step-parents in this area. The percentage of full orders granted changed from 91% in 1975 to 9% in 1978. In area 3 where there were several circuits, the picture was less clear cut. *Post-divorce* applications were scrutinised and often unsuccessful but orders continued to be made. However, here too they fell from 87% of applications in 1975 to 64% in 1978.

Under the Children Act 1989, an adoption application is 'family proceedings', so that the court may make any s. 8 order instead of an adoption order whenever it wishes, although it has no duty to consider doing so. Step-parent adoptions are no longer expressly discouraged. If the child is treated as a 'child of the family' (see p. 5, above) of the new marriage, the step-parent is always entitled to apply for a residence or contact order (s. 10(5)(a)). He may be ordered to make financial provision for the child, although he will not be automatically liable under the new child support scheme (see Chapter 4). The child may also apply for family provision from his estate (see p. 176, above). So what does an adoption order do that a residence order in favour of parent and step-parent does not? Most of the cases concern emigration and change of surname, which are prohibited under both the old and the new law, unless the other parent consents or the court gives leave (see p. 542, above).

Barnes v Tyrrell
(1981) 3 FLR 240, Court of Appeal

The mother had custody of the two children of her former marriage, a boy now 12 and a girl now 11. Since the divorce in 1977, the father had had liberal access. The mother was now married to an Australian and wished to return with him to Australia. Her first application to take the children was refused, because of the welfare officer's evidence that the boy might be upset at losing regular contact with his father. After a successful holiday in Australia, however, the boy changed his mind and both children now wished to go, although also to keep contact with their father. The judge granted leave to take the children permanently, with an annual holiday in this country. The father appealed.

Dunn LJ: . . . In these cases one always has a great deal of sympathy for the parent who is, in effect, left behind. What is said in this appeal on behalf of the father is that the judge gave insufficient weight to the fact that these children had had very regular contact with the father, notwithstanding the breakdown of the marriage. It was not a case such as *P (LM)) (otherwise E) v P (GE)* [1970] 3 All ER 659, where there was a very young child who hardly knew his father, but in this case the children obviously have a good relationship with their father and have been cared for by him for a period after the mother left.

Then it was said that these children of 11 and 12 would be uprooted from their schools, they would be sent to an entirely new system of education in Australia, and they would be taken away from what is nowadays called their 'extended' family, namely their grandparents, uncles and aunts and cousins, and would go to a strange country where they would only have their mother as a blood relation.

Speaking for myself it seems to me that all these matters were taken into account by the judge before he made the order. The principle which is followed by the court in these cases was stated by Sachs LJ in *P (LM)) (otherwise E) v P (GE)* [1970] 3 All ER 659 at 662, where he said:

'When a marriage breaks up, a situation normally arises when the child of that marriage, instead of being in the joint custody of both parents, must of necessity become one who is in the custody of a single parent. Once that position has arisen and the custody is working well, this court should not lightly interfere with such reasonable way of life as is selected by that parent to whom custody has been rightly given. Any such interference may . . . produce considerable strains which would not only be unfair to the parent whose way of life is interfered with but also to any new marriage of that parent. In that way it might well in due course reflect on the welfare of the child. The way in which the parent who properly has custody of a child may choose in a reasonable manner to order his or her way of life is one of those things which the parent who has not been given custody may well have to bear, even though one has every sympathy with the latter on some of the results.'

The judge plainly had that passage in mind because he dealt at length with the arrangements for these children in Australia. He had the evidence not only of the mother and Mr B, but also of Mr B's father as to what the circumstances were in Australia. It appears from the evidence, which the judge accepted, that Mr B's financial prospects are better in Australia than they are in this country. He would be likely to command a better salary there than he does here. There is apparently a suitable house in a suburb of Sydney, where his parents live, and the judge had evidence from Mr B's father as to the schools available in Australia. The judge summed it up in this way:

> 'The prospect of the family, accordingly, is one of prosperity in Australia, or a very much more uncertain prospect in England. Mr B is very anxious to go back to his home. The baby is an Australian, and he would wish to bring her up in Australia.'

The judge came to the conclusion, accordingly, that the mother's wish to take the children to Australia was an entirely reasonable one and upon that basis he made the order.

Appeal dismissed.

Questions

(i) What difference might it have made if the mother had not remarried but was herself an Australian and wished to return with the children (see *Tyler v Tyler* [1990] FLR 22, [1989] 2 FLR 158)?

(ii) Or are the courts likely to see things differently after the Children Act in any event?

Fathers who are anxious to maintain links with their children may be just as anxious to avoid a change of surname as they are to oppose an adoption. The courts have expressed differing views:

R (BM) v R (DN)
[1978] 2 All ER 33, [1977] 1 WLR 1256, 121 Sol Jo 758, Court of Appeal

The case was a custody dispute about whether the youngest of four children, a boy now aged 6½, should continue to live with his father and new partner or should join the other children, who lived with their mother and her new partner, in army quarters at the rural camp where he was stationed. The trial judge gave custody to the mother and Stamp LJ described the father's appeal as 'hopeless'. One element in the father's objections to the transfer was the fact that the three older children were using the surname of their mother's new partner, Sergeant W:

Ormrod LJ: . . . I remember that [the original rule] was directed to preventing parents with custody or care and control orders changing children's names by deed poll or by some other formal means, but, unfortunately, it now seems to be causing a great deal of trouble and difficulty to school authorities and to children and the very last thing that any rule of this court is intended to do is to embarrass children. It should not be beyond our capacity as adults to cope with the problem of dealing with children who naturally do not want to be picked out and distinguished by their friends and known by a surname other than their mother's, if they are thinking about it at all. It is very embarrassing for school authorities and indeed to the court if efforts have to be made to stop a little girl signing her name 'W' when it really is 'R'. We are in danger of losing our sense of proportion. All one can say in this particular case is that one can understand the situation, which is not at all unusual, and I just hope that no one is going to make a point about this name business, in other words, to treat it as a symbol of something which it is not. There is nothing in this case that suggests that the mother or Sergeant W want to make a takeover bid for this family from the father and turn these children into their own children, nothing at all. Therefore, I hope that it can be treated as counsel in his exchanges with the learned judge below observed, 'This is a peripheral matter.' I would endorse that strongly.

W v A (child: surname)
[1981] Fam 14, [1981] 1 All ER 100, [1981] 2 WLR 124, 124 Sol Jo 726, 11
Fam Law 22, Court of Appeal

The parents separated in 1971 when their children were aged 3 and 1½. They
were granted joint custody, with care and control to the mother and
reasonable access, which was exercised, to the father. After divorce, both
remarried; the mother married an Australian who wished to return with her
and the children to his home country. The father agreed, provided that the
mother undertook not to change the children's surname. The mother and
both children, now aged 12 and 10, wished to use the step-father's name. The
trial judge refused leave to change and the mother appealed.

Dunn LJ: . . . When the question of the change of name came before the judge, he was faced
with the dilemma that there are two apparently conflicting lines of authority in this court on
the question of changing children's surnames. The first is that the change of a child's surname
is an important matter, not to be undertaken lightly. The second is that the change of a child's
surname is a comparatively unimportant matter. The judge, faced with the choice between those
two lines of authority, opted for the first.
   . . . As in all cases concerning the future of children whether they be custody, access,
education or, as in this case, the change of a child's name, s. 1 of the Guardianship of Minors
Act 1971 requires that the court shall regard 'the welfare of the [child] as the first and paramount
consideration'. It is a matter for the discretion of the individual judge hearing the case, seeing
the witnesses, seeing the parents, possibly seeing the children, to decide whether or not it is in
the interests of the child in the particular circumstances of the case that his surname should or
should not be changed; and the judge will take into account all the circumstances of the case,
including no doubt where appropriate any embarrassment which may be caused to the child
by not changing his name and, on the other hand, the long-term interests of the child, the
importance of maintaining the child's links with his paternal family, and the stability or
otherwise of the mother's remarriage. I only mention those as typical examples of the kinds of
considerations which arise in these cases, but the judge will take into account all the relevant
circumstances in the particular case before him. . . .
   Speaking for myself, I think the judge was entirely right not to attach decisive importance
to the views of two young children of 12 and 10 who were about to embark on the excitement
of going to Australia with their mother and their new stepfather.
   Other criticisms were made of the judge. It was said that there were positive advantages to
these children in changing their surname. They were about to make a fresh start in a new country
and it would be an advantage to them to go out as a united family. A change of name, it was
said, would not make much difference to the father because the children would be at the other
end of the world and he has two sons by his second marriage, so the name of A will survive
in Gloucestershire. It is also said that, when they get older, if the children wished to change their
name back to A they could always do so.
   I have no doubt that the judge had all these matters in mind and there is nothing in his
reasons, in his short judgment, which leads me to suppose that he did not. On the contrary,
it seems to me that the judge approached this matter entirely rightly.
Appeal dismissed.

Questions

(i) Do you think that children of this age are any less entitled to a view on
this point than they are on adoption?
(ii) Do you think that *either* of the opposing camps in the Court of Appeal
is indeed putting the children's interests before those of the adults?
(iii) There are many cases in which a child's surname might be changed
without resort to litigation — for example, if any of these fathers had
consented, or if they were dead, or if the children had used their names

although the parents were unmarried — are the arguments against allowing this any less strong in such cases?

The empirical evidence in support of a child's 'right to know' has been collected in studies of children fostered or adopted by strangers (see Chapter 14). Wallerstein and Kelly's study of children and their parents in 60 divorced families in California gives further indications of the children's needs. In *Surviving the Break-up* (1980) they discuss 'fathers versus step-fathers':

The child's relationship with stepfather and father, and the various ways in which this issue was resolved by the child and adults or continued as a source of open conflict, was of central importance in the psychological development and adjustment of the child within the remarried family. The extent to which the child was able to share in the benefits of the marriage depended in large measure on the satisfactory resolution of this conflict by the adults and the children.

Many children were able to maintain and enjoy both relationships. The father and the step-father did not occupy the same slot in the child's feelings and the child did not confuse the relationship with the two men. Mostly, children enlarged their view of the family and made room for three major figures, all of whom were potentially and actually of major importance in shaping the child's psychological, social, and moral development and ultimately important life choices. . . .

The expectation of many people that the children would necessarily experience conflict as they turned from father to stepfather during their growing-up years was not borne out by our observations. Nor was the expectation that in the happily remarried family the biological father was likely to fade out of the children's lives. . . .

The stepfather's influence, in turn, was not undone by the child's continued visiting with the father. Neither divorce nor remarriage appeared to change substantially the importance or the emotional centrality of both biological parents for the growing child. At the same time, the stepfather's influence was enormous. He, clearly, could greatly enhance the child's development — broadening his or her intellectual horizons, strengthening moral development, and exercising a far-reaching, beneficial effect on every aspect of the child's character structure which was still in the process of formulation. Conversely, the stepfather could constrict the child's emotional life, narrow his or her vision of the world, increase unhappiness, or decrease self-esteem. But even with this major potential influence, the stepfather did not replace the departed father. Only when the child *voluntarily* rejected the father, or counter-rejected the father and voluntarily disidentified with the father and placed the stepfather in the father's role, did replacement occur. . . .

Masson, Norbury and Chatterton (1983) found, as others have done, that step-parents are not very interested in an alternative to adoption. They discuss a new way of giving them some status:

Perhaps the strongest arguments against returning to the old law relate to the needs step-families have and the reasons they give for adoption. Applicants we interviewed had little or no idea of the legal implications of adoption. They wanted to make the family like a 'proper family' but did not intend that the child be considered as 'adopted' rather than as 'their own'. Mothers did not want to become adoptive mothers and some were disturbed that the birth certificate had to be replaced with an adoption certificate. What they appeared to want was recognition for the step-parent, permission to change the child's name and something to reassure them that their family was secure. Adoption went far beyond this and legally made fundamental changes in the family structure. The belief that adoption is essential if members of the step-family are to be treated as belonging to a complete family unit or the step-parent is to enjoy legal rights arises largely from ignorance. . . .

There is need for recognition of the step-parent during the life of his spouse: a need currently met, albeit inadequately for a minority, by adoption. The criticisms of the present and former laws suggest that whether or not there is a thorough investigation of the family, it has simply not been possible to assess families for a different status because there are no accepted criteria. If this is true, it follows that any new status should be available to all step-parents on demand. If there were no assessment and no selection then there would be no place for either a guardian *ad litem* or a judge. An administrative process could be used, just as adoption applicants themselves had expected in the past.

If a status is to be available without investigation to all who seek it, it should involve neither the exclusion of the other natural parent nor the creation of extra rights in the step-family. This could be achieved by a change in legislation enabling the step-parent to *share those parental rights which his spouse has*. There would be no need for the law to allocate these rights between the parent and the step-parent; this would be a matter for the parties, as it is in families of first marriage. Both parent and step-parent, and the other natural parent, would be able to challenge a decision or refer a dispute to the court, as can parents and guardians at present. Disputes would be settled applying the welfare principle. . . . It would avoid the necessity of the natural parent naming the step-parent as guardian by will or deed if she wished him to act in the event of her death. The status which a step-parent can be given on the death of his spouse would exist *during* the marriage, thus problems would not arise as they do now merely because the natural parent dies intestate. . . . This new status would not automatically provide for inheritance between the child and step-parent on intestacy; this would, perhaps, be too fundamental a change in English law. Nor would it permit the *post-divorce* parent and step-parent to change the child's name without the permission of either the other natural parent or the court. In fact, the status provided would be similar to the guardianship which the step-parent (or any other person) may obtain on the parent's death.

The Inter-departmental Review of the Adoption Law, in its Discussion Paper on *The Nature and Effect of Adoption* (1990), wonders whether the Houghton Committee's objections to step-parent adoptions still have some force and considers some alternative suggestions:

131. It would be possible to provide that on remarriage the step-parent acquired the same parental responsibility as the parent simply by application with proof of marriage or that this status might be acquired automatically on marriage. Masson, Norbury and Chatterton suggested that a certificate could be given to document the new status and that it might also be possible to mark the occasion with a short ceremony in which the child could participate.
132. It would also be possible to provide for the acquisition of parental responsibility by agreement subject to judicial confirmation. This could mean agreement of parent and step-parent, and/or of the child once a certain age has been reached. Agreement of the other birth parent would not be required as his status would not be affected. A judicial hearing could ensure that proper consideration was given to the interests of the child, perhaps by the compulsory appointment of a guardian ad litem in such cases. However, once judicial confirmation is required it becomes difficult to distinguish this approach from an application for a residence order.
133. The vexed question of name change remains a problem. Presumably the right to change the child's name would not be an integral part of acquisition of parental responsibility by a step-parent but would remain a matter for the agreement of the other birth parent or the leave of the court.
134. Under the Children Act [s. 2(5)] any number of people may have parental responsibility for a child and so its acquisition in one of the ways outlined above would not cut out the birth father of his relatives. The idea of transferring parental responsibility by administrative means was canvassed by the Law Commission in its Working Paper on Guardianship [1985] but provoked a mixed reaction, particularly for post-divorce cases. While it may be appropriate in some situations, in others it might provoke hostility and problems between the children and their step-parent. Creating more than two parents could also be confusing for children. Accordingly, the idea was not pursued in the Commission's Report on Guardianship and Custody [1988]. On the other hand the high number of second marriages means that step-families and therefore step-parents are far more common than they used to be and there is recognition that children's affections are capable of embracing the new parent and sibling and yet distinguishing between the existing and the new relatives. It seems appropriate to raise this option again in the context of adoption where it may receive a wider airing. If an administrative solution were thought preferable, should this entail the abolition of adoption for step-parents?

Questions

(i) In *Re M (minors)* [1990] FCR 993, CA, the father had reluctantly agreed
to an adoption, but wanted it set aside because the mother died shortly afterwards and the step-father could not cope: is this a problem any more
common to step-parent adoptions than to others? What is the solution?
(ii) Go back to the typology of step-families on p. 557: do the 'sharing' solutions work equally well for all of them?

CHAPTER 13

Social services for children and families

Local authority social services departments provide for three broad types of children, dubbed by Packman (1986, p. 578, below) the 'victims', the 'villains', and the 'volunteered'. The legal and factual categories do not always coincide, but an indication of both is given in the latest figures (see Hansard (H.C.), vol. 190, 1991, WA, col 364) for children in care in England on 31 March 1989:

Reason for entering care	1989
Received into care under section 2 of the Child Care Act 1980	
Short-term illness of parent or guardian	1,668
Long-term illness or incapacity of parent	1,122
Confinement of mother	199
Family homeless	304
Parents are dead/no guardian	317
Abandoned or lost	1,122
Death of parent	895
Deserted by parent	3,134
Parent or guardian in prison or custody	414
Unsatisfactory home conditions	5,460
Other reasons	9,072
Sub-total	23,707
(Percentage of total)	(38%)
Committed into care by order of the courts	
On remand or committed for trial	615
Subject to interim care order	2,101
Sub-total	2,716
Committed by care orders made under the Children and Young Persons Act 1969:	
S. 1(2)(*a*) neglect, ill treatment	14,990
S. 1(2)(*b*) neglect, ill treatment of another child in household	1,699
S. 1(2)(*bb*) member of household convicted of an offence against children	296
S. 1(2)(*c*) moral danger	957
S. 1(2)(*d*) beyond parental control	1,911
S. 1(2)(*e*) not receiving full time education	1,070
Ss. 1(2)(*f*)/7(7) guilty of an offence	2,122
S. 15(1) in place of a supervision order	790
Ss. 25(1)/26(2) transfer of a care order	29
Sub-total	23,864
Committed by care orders made under other Acts	
Section 43(1) of the MCA 1973	3,627
Section 10(1) DPMCA 1978	160
Section 7(2) of the FLRA 1969	6,409

Section 2(2)(*b*) of the GA 1973   1,180
Section 17(1)(*b*) of the CA 1975   16
Others   469
Total number of children in care   62,148

We shall look briefly at how this came about, before turning to the comprehensive new code in the Children Act 1989. A recurring theme has been the risk of confusion, both in law and in practice, between *providing a service* for children in need and *compulsory intervention* to protect either the child from his family or society from the child. The 1989 Act aims to draw a clear distinction.

1 Out of the Poor Law

Jean Heywood explains the beginnings of the public service for the deprived child in her classic history of *Children in Care* (now 1978):

In pre-Reformation England the orphaned or illegitimate child had a place in a feudal and employed community, though opportunities were open and found for human nature to exploit him. His safeguard, if it existed, lay in the communal nature of the society and its ethical canons, expressed — though not always observed — in the teaching against usury, on the duty of almsgiving, on the efficacy of the corporal works of mercy. In the fact that life was centred round the community rather than the family there lay the possibility of opportunity and protection for the unwanted child. In the community obligations of medieval society a way could be found to provide for him and the family setting was less vital to him than it is to us today. The medieval Church had exalted not the private family but rather the greater one, Christian society, endowing chastity, asceticism and celibacy with greater virtue than the sacrament of marriage. It was at the Reformation period when economic as well as religious changes were taking place, that men turned from the Church's teaching on celibacy, and as they found the social order crumbling away they discovered that in family life there could also be an opportunity to witness to the glory of God.

The ideal of the small home and personal family life could hardly be achieved until a middle class came into existence. The sixteenth century Tudor households of yeomen farmers, of small merchants and tradesmen provided the setting in which real family life became possible, and in a growing urban society, which was neither stable economically, nor ruled any longer by a philosophy on the good of a united community, the family became of major significance. Without it the individual was unsupported in society and became without identity.

The spread of destitution which followed the social and economic changes of the sixteenth century was the cause of the increasing legislation dealing with poor relief in the Tudor era. Vagrancy increased with unemployment, and everywhere the old order was breaking down and a new and as yet unstable society being formed.

The discharging of servants and apprentices increased the numbers of deprived children while the growth of poverty, vagrancy and unemployment made it more difficult for them to find a home or to be fitted in to the pattern of village life. Collections made for the poor in the parish churches were unable to meet the demand for alms. The dissolved houses of the monks and nuns were no longer able to provide out-relief, and the hospitals were falling into decay. In consequence laws were passed to make each parish responsible for providing a place where the sick, the old and the 'succourless poor child' could receive shelter and care. At this time, too, the right of destitute children to beg was recognised and they were given a licence.

. . . In 1530, authority was first given for the compulsory apprenticing of vagrant children between the ages of five and fourteen, though sixteen years afterwards further legislation had to reduce the severity of apprenticeship regulations and give justices power to liberate children badly treated by master and mistress.

The crowds of vagrants and unemployed at this time (which included the child 'unapt to learning') were seen not only as a chronic nuisance but a serious danger to society, as social failures for whom the community was now legally and financially responsible. . . .

So many of the composite hospitals which were established at this time, at first by persuasive and finally by compulsory taxation, for the relief of the poor became also houses of correction and punishment for the idle, as well as technical schools for the young. The deprived child, in need of training, and old and sick people in need of care were accommodated together with vagrants sent for punishment. The degradation of the pauper had begun.

It was the Elizabethan statute, the Poor Relief Act of 1601, which set the pattern for our system of relief to the poor until 1948. Those responsible for the care of deprived children, the churchwardens and the parish overseers, were to take such measures as were necessary for setting them to work or binding them as apprentices. These bald embodiments of a constructive principle of care remained unaltered in our legislation for three hundred and forty-seven years, until the shadow of a grim farm-house fell across them, and darkened them for ever.

However, Heywood also notes that the Report of the Committee on Parish Apprentices (1815) stated that in London poor relief was 'seldom bestowed without the parish claiming the exclusive right of disposing, at their pleasure, of all the children of the person claiming relief'. The parental right of custody emerged as a powerful factor in upper class litigation during the nineteenth century (p. 409, above) and began to pose a challenge both for the poor law authorities and for the philanthropists seeking to rescue children from their supposedly corrupting environment:

In all the planning of the various systems of care for the deprived child, the natural family, where it existed, remained a problem which, if it was not being treated, was certainly to be reckoned with. Separating the child and the unfit parent or relative of bad influence was a definite attempt to prevent pauperism reproducing itself in the next generation, but the policy was often difficult to effect even if it was considered ethically sound. The constructive work which the poor law attempted by providing a better environment for the child was frequently brought to nothing by what was described as the 'pernicious influence of the child's relations' particularly when the children passed out of the guardians' care at 16. Two solutions were found for coping with this problem:. . .

Boards of Guardians were empowered under the Poor Law Amendment Act of 1850 to emigrate orphan or deserted children under the age of 16 years, provided the child gave his consent. There were real opportunities, particularly in Canada where there was a shortage of labour and where food was cheap, and the guardians made use of these opportunities, though not to any great extent. In general voluntary organisations, such as Dr Barnardo's Homes or the Roman Catholic Emigration Agency, were used as agents, the fittest and most promising of the eligible pauper children being chosen for this new life.

The more difficult problem of the child and the unfit parent was grappled with by Acts of 1889 and 1899. These gave the boards of guardians in England and Wales authority to assume complete rights and responsibilities of a parent over a child in care until he reached the age of 18. Such rights could be assumed only in respect of deserted children at first, but in 1899 their application was widened to include orphans and children of parents who were disabled or in prison, or unfit to have the care of them. This power to assume parental rights by the state was an expression of the public interest in the welfare of children and was intended to lay down a definite standard of parental care. . . .

However, the standard of care provided by the local authorities which became responsible for administering the poor law left a great deal to be desired. The 'grim farmhouse' to which Heywood refers was where Dennis O'Neill died in 1945, as recounted by Sir Walter Monckton in his *Report* (1945):

2. . . . Dennis and Terence O'Neill were born respectively on the 2 March 1932, and the 13 December 1934, and were the children of Thomas John O'Neill, a labourer, of Newport, Monmouthshire, and Mabel Blonwyn O'Neill, his wife. On the 30 May 1940, Dennis and Terence were committed by the Newport Juvenile Court to the care or protection of the Newport County Borough Council, as a 'fit person' within the meaning of Sections 76 and 96 of the Children and Young Persons Act 1933, hereinafter referred to as the 1933 Act. Dennis was boarded out at Bank Farm, Minsterley, Shropshire, on the 28 June 1944. The foster-parents were Reginald Gough and Esther Gough, his wife, Terence joined Dennis at Bank Farm on the 5 July 1944. Dennis died there on the 9 January 1945. Terence was removed from Bank Farm to a place of safety on the 10 January 1945.

3. An inquest was held on the boy Dennis. The coroner's jury returned a verdict that his death was due to acute cardiac failure following violence applied to the front of the chest and back while in a state of under-nourishment due to neglect and added a rider that there had been a serious lack of supervision by the local authority. Reginald and Esther Gough were charged with manslaughter. At Stafford Assizes on the 19 March 1945, Reginald Gough was found guilty of manslaughter and was sentenced to six years' penal servitude. Esther Gough was found not guilty of manslaughter but guilty of neglect and was sentenced to six months' imprisonment.

The children had been boarded out with the Goughs in an emergency, but thereafter there had been no adequate inquiry into their suitability, no medical examination, and no proper supervision. Sir Walter concluded, however, that little change in the law was needed:

54. . . . What is required is rather that the administrative machinery should be improved and informed by a more anxious and responsible spirit. . . . The personal relation in which the local authority, which has undertaken care and protection stands to the child should be more clearly recognized. . . . It may well be that, in order to ensure that those who supervise are competent for the purpose, some training or instruction should be required; but this is a question which would need fuller consideration. The duty to be sure in the care of children must not be put aside, however great may be the pressure of other burdens.

By that time, however, plans were already afoot to abolish the Poor Law and a different approach was being urged to the care of children:

WHOSE CHILDREN?
WARDS OF STATE OR CHARITY

To the Editor of *The Times*

Sir,

Thoughtful consideration is being given to many fundamental problems, but in reconstruction plans one section of the community has, so far, been entirely forgotten.

I write of those children who, because of their family misfortune, find themselves under the guardianship of a Government Department or one of the many charitable organisations. The public are, for the most part, unaware that many thousands of these children are being brought up under repressive conditions that are generations out of date and are unworthy of our traditional care for children. Many who are orphaned, destitute, or neglected, still live under the chilly stigma of 'charity'; too often they form groups isolated from the main stream of life and education, and few of them know the comfort and security of individual affection. A letter does not allow space for detailed evidence.

In many 'Homes', both charitable and public, the willing staff are, for the most part, over-worked, underpaid, and untrained; indeed, there is no recognised system of training. Inspection, for which the Ministry of Health, the Homes Office, or the Board of Education may be nominally responsible, is totally inadequate, and few standards are established or expected. Because no one Government Department is fully responsible, the problem is the more difficult to tackle.

A public inquiry, with full Government support, is urgently needed to explore this largely uncivilised territory. Its mandate should be to ascertain whether the public and charitable organisations are, in fact, enabling these children to lead full and happy lives, and to make recommendations how the community can compensate them for the family life they have lost. In particular, the inquiry should investigate what arrangements can be made (by regional reception centres or in other ways) for the careful consideration of the individual children before they are finally placed with foster-parents or otherwise provided for; how the use of large residential homes can be avoided; how staff can be appropriately trained and ensured adequate salaries and suitable conditions of work, and how central administrative responsibility can best be secured so that standards can be set and can be maintained by adequate inspection.

The social upheaval caused by the war has not only increased this army of unhappy children, but presents the opportunity for transforming their conditions. The Education Bill and the White paper on the Health Services have alike ignored the problem and the opportunity.

Yours sincerely,

Marjory Allen of Hurtwood.
Hurtwood House, Albury, Guildford.

15 July 1944.

The public inquiry was conducted by the Care of Children Committee, chaired by Miss Myra Curtis, 'into the existing methods of providing for children who from loss of parents or from any cause whatever are deprived of a normal home life with their own parents or relatives'. This covered almost 125,000 children, some 57,000 of whom were cared for under the poor law. The *Curtis Report* (1946) paints a gloomy picture:

138. . . . . It was clear that in some areas the workhouse served as a dumping ground for children who could not readily be disposed of elsewhere, and that in some districts where children's Homes provided insufficient accommodation, or boarding out had not been well developed, older children, for whom there had never been any properly planned accommodation, were looked after in the workhouse for a considerable length of time.
. . .
140. An example of this kind of motley collection was found in one century-old Poor Law institution providing accommodation for 170 adults, including ordinary workhouse accommodation, an infirmary for senile old people and a few men and women certified as either mentally defective or mentally disordered. In this institution there were twenty-seven children, aged 6 months to 15 years. Twelve infants up to the age of 18 months were the children of women in the institution, about half of them still being nursed by their mothers. In the same room in which these children were being cared for was a Mongol idiot, aged 4, of gross appearance, for whom there was apparently no accommodation elsewhere. A family of five normal children, aged about 6 to 15, who had been admitted on a relieving officer's order, had been in the institution for ten weeks. This family, including a boy of 10 and a girl of 15, were sleeping in the same room as a 3 year old hydrocephalic idiot, of very unsightly type, whose bed was screened off in the corner. The 15 year old girl had been employed in the day-time dusting the women's infirmary ward. These children had been admitted in the middle of the night when their mother had left them under a hedge after eviction from their house. No plan appeared to have been made for them.
. . .
144. One nursery which was structurally linked to the Public Assistance Institution had sunk to the lowest level of child care which has come under our notice. . . . The healthy children were housed in the ground floor corrugated hutment which had been once the old union casual ward. The day room was large and bare and empty of all toys. The children fed, played and used their pots in this room. They ate from cracked enamel plates, using the same mug for milk and soup. They slept in another corrugated hutment in old broken black iron cots some of which had their sides tied up with cord. The mattresses were fouled and stained. On enquiry there did not appear to be any available stocks of clothes to draw on . . . The children wore ankle length calico or flanelette frocks and petticoats and had no knickers. Their clothes were not clean. Most of them had lost their shoes; . . . Their faces were clean; their bodies in some cases were unwashed and stained.

This nursery was an exception, and some were very good, but even for the children who found their way into children's homes, conditions might not be much better:

171. . . . In another Single Home with accommodation for 18 boys there were 24 present at the time of our visit. They had only one small sitting room for meals, reading and play. The dormitories were tightly packed and there was no room for any provision in the way of lockers or other receptacles for the boys' own possessions, though they were said to be on order. Outside was a small asphalt yard.

It was attitudes, as much as organisation and resources, which were to blame:

154. . . . We do not mean to suggest that we found evidence of harshness for which the staff was responsible. Except in the one instance of the nursery unit described in paragraph 144 the ill-usage was of a negative rather than a positive kind and elsewhere sprang directly from unsuitability of buildings, lack of training and of appreciation of children's needs. Officials of local authorities suggested that the children suffered from the attitude of the public to children maintained under the poor law. This attitude had affected some members of the Public Assistance Committees, some of whom had survived as Committee members from the days of

the old Boards of Guardians and still held old-fashioned views about what was suitable for a destitute child.

This spilled over into other aspects of the children's lives:

193. . . . We gained the impression that many of the children in the Homes were educationally retarded. This may, of course, have been due to their unfortunate history rather than to the conditions of their lives, but it was surprising to find in some Homes that few of the children could tell the time, and that many of them did not know the date of their birthdays. The contact between the Home and the school was often unsatisfactory. There seemed to be a lack of cooperation. Some of us were concerned to notice a certain prejudice against 'Home' children in the schools. It was difficult to tell whether the fact that the majority of Homes had sent no children to Secondary or Technical Schools for a number of years was due to the poor quality of intelligence of children in the Homes or to the fact that their interest in school work or in future opportunities was not sufficiently encouraged; or to any other disadvantages which attached to their living in a Public Assistance Home. . . . [This] reflects in a serious way a failure to compensate the child deprived of a normal home life; not only because they are not getting the opportunities open to normal children, but because the lack of individual attention and of special teaching and stimulus in the infant and toddler stages may have directly contributed to their failure to reach the necessary standard.

The Committee also visited some of the 27,800 children who were boarded out:

370. . . . 'The contrast between the children in Homes and the boarded out children was most marked. The boarded out children suffered less from segregation, starvation for affection and lack of independence. They bore a different stamp of developing personality, and despite occasional misfits were manifestly more independent. For example, they were much more indifferent to visitors, were much better satisfied by their environment (by which we mean the special features of security and love). There was, we thought, much greater happiness for the child integrated by boarding out into a family of normal size in a normal home.'

Question

Why was the fact that the children 'were much more indifferent to visitors' regarded as a good sign?

When it came to recommending solutions, the Committee assumed that most of the children would remain in public care for a long time. It was clear about what their substitute home *should* provide:

427. . . . If the substitute home is to give the child what he gets from a good normal home it must supply —
   (i)   Affection and personal interest; understanding of his defects; care for his future; respect for his personality and regard for his self esteem.
   (ii) Stability; the feeling that he can expect to remain with those who will continue to care for him till he goes out into the world on his own feet.
   (iii) Opportunity of making the best of his ability and aptitudes, whatever they may be, as such opportunity is made available to the child in the normal home.
   (iv) A share in the common life of a small group of people in a homely environment.
Some at least of these needs are supplied by the child's own home even if it is not in all respects a good one; it is a very serious responsibility to make provision for him to be brought up elsewhere without assurance that they can be supplied by the environment to which he is removed.

Hence:

447. . . . Every effort should be made to keep the child in its home, or with its mother if it is illegitimate, provided that the home is or can be made reasonably satisfactory. The aim of the authority must be to find something better − indeed much better − if it takes the responsibility of providing a substitute home. The methods which should be available may be treated under three main heads of adoption, boarding out and residence in communities. We have placed these in the order in which, subject to the safeguards we propose and to consideration of the needs of the individual, they seem to us to secure the welfare and happiness of the child.

Question

Do you agree with this order to priorities?

The Committee's main solution was for new local authority Children's Departments to take responsibility for all kinds of children's homes, including approved (reform) schools, boarding out, and adoption, and for children found in need of care and protection by a court. At its head would be a universal mother:

441. . . . We desire . . . to see the responsibility for the welfare of the deprived children definitely laid on a Children's Officer. This may indeed be said to be our solution of the problem referred to us. Throughout our investigation we have been increasingly impressed by the need for the personal element in the care of children, which Sir Walter Monckton emphasised in his report on the O'Neill case. No office staff dealing with them as case papers can do the work we want done − work which is in part administrative, but also in large part field work, involving many personal contacts and the solution of problems by direct methods. . . .
443. . . . She (we use the feminine pronoun not with any aim of excluding men from these posts but because we think it may be found that the majority of persons suitable for the work are women) will of course work under the orders of her committee or board but she will be a specialist in child care as the Medical Officer of Health is a specialist in his own province and the Director of Education is in his; and she will have no other duties to distract her interests. She would represent the council in its parental functions. The committal of the child to the care of a council which takes over parental rights and duties is not without incongruity. To be properly exercised the responsibility must be delegated to an individual, and that individual one whose training has fitted her for child care and whose whole attention is given to it. . . .

Hence the Children Act 1948 set up the new departments and gave them, among other things, the duty to care for orphaned, abandoned or deprived children, the power to assume parental rights over children in their care who had no parents or parents who were in some way incapable or unfit to look after them, and the duty to act as a fit parent for children compulsorily removed from home by a court.

However, children compulsorily removed from home fell into three different categories, which were eventually brought together in s. 1 of the Children and Young Persons Act 1969. John Eekelaar, Robert Dingwall and Topsy Murray in *Victims or Threats? Children in Care Proceedings* (1982) explain how this came about:

. . . A significant report published in 1816 by an unofficial Committee of the Society for Investigating the Causes of the Alarming Increase of Juvenile Delinquency in the Metropolis, attempted a radical assessment of the problem. Although it is sometimes thought that the significance of the home and community environment among the causative factors of delinquency is a modern realisation, this is not so. The 1816 Report numbered 'the improper conduct of parents, the want of education and the want of suitable employment' as the first of the five most significant causes of delinquency. Here is a recognition of human nature as being a product of environment, of behaviour being socially caused. The work of the reformatory movement was inspired by the same idea and it received statutory recognition in the Youthful Offenders Act 1854. But the scope of reform schools in combating juvenile delinquency was restricted by the major limitation that children were committed there only after having been convicted of an offence. . . .

[Nineteenth century reformers] maintained a distinction in classification between children who had committed offences and those who had not. They were to be kept in separate establishments. The industrial schools, which catered for the latter category, were a development of the 'ragged schools' of the eighteenth century which, as the Departmental Committee on Young Offenders of 1927 noted 'were an attempt to deal more radically with the problem of child welfare by providing education and industrial training for the class of children from whom delinquents were mainly drawn.'. . .

Yet it is clear that the children in industrial schools were there at least as much because they were thought of as being a *risk* to society as being *at risk* themselves and already by 1870 the Inspector of Industrial Schools reported that those schools had been assimilated to reformatories 'in their necessary arrangements and regulations and the main features of their management.' The children were sent there by warrant of a magistrate. The schools had become 'houses of detention for the young vagabond and petty misdemeanant.' . . .

The third source which makes up the composition of section 1(2) of the 1969 Act had its origin in the Prevention of Cruelty to and Protection of Children Act 1889. The most significant provision of this Act created an offence if anyone over 16 who had custody, control or charge of a boy under 14 or a girl under 16 wilfully ill-treated, neglected or abandoned the child in a manner likely to cause unnecessary suffering or injury to health. On conviction of a parent for this offence, the court could commit the child to the charge of a relative or anyone else willing to have the care of the child who would have 'like control over the child as if he were its parent and shall be responsible for its maintenance, and the child shall continue under the control of such person, notwithstanding that it is claimed by its parents.'

The necessity of conviction of the parent is significant, for it reflects the basis of the justification for state intervention on which this provision rests. This is that the *parent's conduct* offends against the moral conception of society held by the Act's proponents. The purpose for the intervention was, indeed, to protect children, but the method by which this was sought was morally to reform the parents. . . .

But in 1933 this category of children was included in the category of children formerly covered by the industrial schools legislation as being 'in need of care and protection.' This was a highly significant move for, as we have seen, children found to be in need of care and protection could be committed to approved schools as young offenders could be. It seems odd to find children who, even more clearly than the 'neglected' category, were in need of protection *from* adults, being dealt with under the very same statutory provisions, and indeed, court procedure, as children from whom the community sought to protect itself. It is revealing therefore to discover how this happened. The 1927 Committee was required 'to inquire into the treatment of young offenders and young people who, owing to bad associations or surroundings require protection and training.' They considered that their inquiry was concerned not only with the 'young offender' but also with 'the neglected boy or girl who has not yet committed offences but who, owing to want of parental control, bad associations or other reasons needs protection and training.' . . . However, the Committee went on to say: 'There are also young people who are the victims of cruelty or other offences committed by adults and whose natural guardianship having proved insufficient or unworthy of trust must be replaced.' We may note here what has been characteristic of all these investigations into the condition of children, that the concern has primarily been with the problem of troublesome children, and the question of child protection has been tagged on very much as a subsidiary and secondary question. . . .

There is no doubt that the result was to strengthen the provisions for protecting such children because local education authorities were now placed under a duty to inquire into such cases and bring them before a court and the courts were empowered to commit them into the care of local authorities. But these children had now become irredeemably intertwined with a group of children with entirely different problems and who were regarded by society as virtually inseparable from delinquent children.

In the meantime another significant development had been occurring in attitudes towards neglected and abused children. The evangelical movement had declined, but the growth of community health services provided an alternative model for intervention in family life. . . . The immediate impetus arose from the prosecution by the NSPCC of a blind couple for neglecting their children, and in 1952 the Children and Young Persons (Amendment) Act removed the requirement of prosecution of parents as a condition precedent for finding a child to be in need of care and protection within the 1933 Act. Hence forward it would be enough if the child had no parent or guardian or if his parent or guardian was 'unfit to exercise care or guardianship or (was) not exercising proper care and guardianship' and 'he was being ill-treated or neglected in a manner likely to cause him unnecessary suffering or injury to health.' Failure (for whatever cause) in the parenting function leading to a specified condition in the child became a ground for intervention. Although the approach is now overtly welfarist, the requirement that the child's condition should arise from parental failure still serves to maintain a distinction between this class of children and those from whom society sought to protect itself. The distinction was not to last for long.

The Ingleby Committee (1960) and the 1969 Act
. . . In dealing with the general issue of the circumstances in which the state may properly intervene in proceedings against parents for child neglect, the Committee states that 'difficulty has not arisen for several years over the reasonable requirements for nutrition, housing, clothing and schooling' although there had been some cases where parents had refused to give their children proper medical attention. No mention is made at all by the Committee of child abuse cases and the Committee proceeds, throughout the rest of the chapter, to consider the issue solely in terms of delinquency cases. By 1960, then, our society had become blind to potential conflicts between family autonomy and child protection. Apart from a few troublesome cases involving unconventional religious sects, the resolution of welfarist child protection and family autonomy was considered simple and unproblematic. In fact, it had been obscured by the overwhelming pre-occupation with delinquency. . . .

The two Government White Papers, *The Child, the Family and the Young Offender* and *Children in Trouble* (Home Office, 1965 and 1968) were, as their titles indicate, wholly concerned with the problem of juvenile delinquents. They set the basis for the policy of the 1969 Act. One cornerstone of that policy was that children should progressively cease to be prosecuted for offences and should, instead, be made subject to care proceedings under the Act. Accordingly, the grounds for bringing care proceedings were to be extended to include a ground that the child had committed an offence (excluding homicide). Child offenders were now to be treated under (almost) exactly the same process as troublesome children who were not offenders. And, as we have seen, child *victims* had by now been assimilated into this category. The logic of this assimilation compelled the abandonment, *for all categories of these children*, of any reference to parental inadequacy among the conditions precedent to bringing care proceedings. For, as the Home Office observed in its official guide to the Act, such a provision 'meant that proceedings inevitably appeared to cast blame for the child's situation or behaviour directly into his parents or those looking after him' a fact which was quite irrelevant for the delinquent child (though, as will be argued below, crucially relevant in the case of the child victim). The Act, therefore, took the line originally proposed by the Ingleby Report and simply required that it be shown that the child was in need of 'care of control' which he would not receive if an order was not made.

Implementation of the 1969 Act, which tried to cater for the villains and the victims by the same process, coincided with the Local Authority Social Services Act 1970, which amalgamated the children's services with those provided for the old, the mentally disordered or handicapped, and the abled, into new all-purpose social services departments. As Jean Packman explains in *The Child's Generation* (1981):

Developments in prevention and work with delinquency not only strained, modified and redefined the original aims and methods of the child care service; they also contributed to its eventual demise. The pursuit of both policies increased the children's departments' involvement with and dependence upon other agencies and threw into relief their relationship with one another and the illogical and wasteful effects of the fragmented pattern of personal social services. As the two policies drew closer together, with prevention of neglect being seen more and more as a key means of forestalling delinquency, the pressure to change that pattern and to provide an integrated 'family service' in its place mounted.

However, not everyone was delighted:

Oxfordshire's Children's Committee, in preparing its own evidence to Seebohm, said 'it would in our opinion, for instance, be damaging to the highly personal type of work done by the child care service to place it in such a large and general group of functions that the old pattern of the former Public Assistance Service might recur, with the disadvantages that would entail'. The spectre of the Poor Law still haunted the local councillors.

Question

If local councillors are to be haunted, should Dennis O'Neill (p. 569, above), Susan Auckland (p. 372, above) or Jasmine Beckford (p. 618, below) be the most potent spectre?

2 Children's services today

The key provisions of the *Children Act 1989* are these:

17. — (1) It shall be the general duty of every local authority (in addition to the other duties imposed on them by this Part) —
   (a) to safeguard and promote the welfare of children within their area who are in need; and
   (b) so far as is consistent with that duty, to promote the upbringing of such children by their families,
by providing a range and level of services appropriate to those children's needs.
   (2) For the purpose principally of facilitating the discharge of their general duty under this section, every local authority shall have the specific duties and powers set out in Part 1 of Schedule 2.
   (3) Any service provided by an authority in the exercise of functions conferred on them by this section may be provided for the family of a particular child in need or for any member of his family, if it is provided with a view to safeguarding or promoting the child's welfare.
   . . .
   (10) For the purposes of this Part a child shall be taken to be in need if —
   (a) he is unlikely to achieve or maintain, or to have the opportunity of achieving or maintaining, a reasonable standard of health or development without the provision for him of services by a local authority under this Part;
   (b) his health or development is likely to be significantly impaired, or further impaired, without the provision for him of such services; or
   (c) he is disabled,
and 'family', in relation to such a child, includes any person who has parental responsibility for the child and any other person with whom he has been living.
   (11) For the purposes of this Part, a child is disabled if he is blind, deaf or dumb or suffers from mental disorder of any kind or is substantially and permanently handicapped by illness, injury or congenital deformity or such other disability as may be prescribed; and in this Part —
   'development' means physical, intellectual, emotional, social or behavioural development; and
   'health' means physical or mental health.

Part I of Sch. 2 lists a great many specific services for children living at home or elsewhere. Day care is dealt with in ss. 18 and 19. Section 20 deals with the provision of accommodation:

20. — (1) Every local authority shall provide accommodation for any child in need within their area who appears to them to require accommodation as a result of —
   (a) there being no person who has parental responsibility for him;
   (b) his being lost or having been abandoned; or
   (c) the person who has been caring for him being prevented (whether or not permanently, and for whatever reason) from providing him with suitable accommodation or care.
   (2) Where a local authority provide accommodation under subsection (1) for a child who is ordinarily resident in the area of another local authority, that other local authority may take over the provision of accommodation for the child within—

(*a*) three months of being notified in writing that the child is being provided with accommodation; or

(*b*) such other longer period as may be prescribed.

(3) Every local authority shall provide accommodation for any child in need within their area who has reached the age of sixteen and whose welfare the authority consider is likely to be seriously prejudiced if they do not provide him with accommodation.

(4) A local authority may provide accommodation for any child within their area (even though a person who has parental responsibility for him is able to provide him with accommodation) if they consider that to do so would safeguard or promote the child's welfare.

(5) A local authority may provide accommodation for any person who has reached the age of sixteen but is under twenty-one in any community home which takes children who have reached the age of sixteen if they consider that to do so would safeguard or promote his welfare.

(6) Before providing accommodation under this section, a local authority shall, so far as is reasonably practicable and consistent with the child's welfare—

(*a*) ascertain the child's wishes regarding the provision of accommodation; and

(*b*) give due consideration (having regard to his age and understanding) to such wishes of the child as they have been able to ascertain.

(7) A local authority may not provide accommodation under this section for any child if any person who—

(*a*) has parental responsibility for him; and

(*b*) is willing and able to—

(i) provide accommodation for him; or

(ii) arrange for accommodation to be provided for him,

objects.

(8) Any person who has parental responsibility for a child may at any time remove the child from accommodation provided by or on behalf of the local authority under this section.

(9) Subsections (7) and (8) do not apply while any person—

(*a*) in whose favour a residence order is in force with respect to the child; or

(*b*) who has care of the child by virtue of an order made in the exercise of the High Court's inherent jurisdiction with respect to children,

agrees to the child being looked after in accommodation provided by or on behalf of the local authority.

(10) Where there is more than one such person as is mentioned in subsection (9), all of them must agree.

(11) Subsections (7) and (8) do not apply where a child who has reached the age of sixteen agrees to being provided with accommodation under this section.

The 'continuum' of services provided under the Act can be traced back to the ideas in the Curtis Report (p. 571, above). Jean Packman, in *The Child's Generation* (1981), explains the development, after the 1948 Act, of the concept of 'prevention':

Research studies of the period [principally Bowlby (1953), see p. 530, above) stressed the importance of the mother-child relationship and the damaging effects on a child's mental, emotional and even physical development, if the relationship were inadequate, disturbed or broken. Most studies examined the latter — deprivation by separation — the phenomenon in its most readily observable form. The emphasis therefore tended to rest on the temporary, or even irreversible damage caused to children by removing them from home. To these studies were added the observations of the child care workers themselves. Seeing, at first hand, the unhappiness and distress of many children in care, they were naturally spurred to seek ways of avoiding admissions. Depressingly, too, they saw that many deprived children themselves grew up to be inadequate parents whose children were, in turn, deprived. A 'cycle of deprivation' was acknowledged long before it became a political catchphrase.

To this central concern to avoid separating children from their parents, was added the complicating factor that some families were clearly incapable of providing even a minimum of physical or emotional care and stability for their children. Social workers were therefore faced with decisions about whether or not the deprivations suffered by a child within his family were worse and more hazardous than those he would suffer by removal from home. Such decisions were also affected by estimates of their own skills and the resources available to them, to intervene and *improve* the family situation, to the child's benefit; and by the standards of substitute care that might offset and compensate the child for the effects of separation.

Prevention thus came to be a two-pronged concept; prevention of admission to care; and prevention of neglect and cruelty in the family. A variety of methods of working towards each of these ends can be seen emerging, in response to the differing circumstances of the families concerned. With some families the work was clearly directed to their weaknesses, whether these were problems of poor home management and low standards of hygiene, or of disturbed and volatile relationships. . . .

In other situations more stress was laid on family and community strengths. Child care workers were aware that many children came into care at a time of family crisis, for lack of any alternative. It was their task to explore and encourage links with kin or with neighbours who could offer care for the children in a familiar environment. . . .

A third dimension to preventive work grew from the knowledge that some families collapsed through external pressures which were beyond their control, yet were within the power of children's departments to influence. A prime example lies in the field of housing. As early as 1951 concern was expressed at the effects on children, separated from their parents because of homelessness. . . .

Packman also quotes John Stroud's more cynical view from *The Shorn Lamb* (1960):

'When I first came galloping out of the University, in shining armour and with all pennants flying, it was to the Rescue of the Deprived Child. Light and air were going to be flooded into the dark places, all those miserable public waifs were going to have a new square deal. And indeed over the years this had happened, we had brought a measure of increased happiness to the children in care. What we hadn't stopped to consider was how they managed to get there in the first place. . . . But we'd only taken a few cautious steps in this direction when Whitehall seized upon the development with glee: here was an even better and even *cheaper* way of caring for children, so cheap it didn't cost anything! Don't care for them at all!'

The variety of purposes which admission to care, whether voluntary or compulsory, could serve is discussed by Jean Packman, John Randall and Nicola Jacques, in their study of decisions taken in two similar places, 'Clayport' and 'Shiptown', in *Who Needs Care?* (1986):

. . . Admission to care is not a unitary concept: it clearly has several purposes, and is a response to a wide range of different problems and situations, as this study has underlined. At its simplest, there are at least three distinct sorts of public child care on offer. One is for families who are beset by difficulties or handicaps which interrupt or interfere with their capacity to look after their children. Their problems may be acute or chronic, one-dimensional or, more usually, multifaceted and interconnected, and they are likely to be short on supportive networks of relatives or friends to help out, and without the means to pay for child-care services outside these networks. For such families the local authority can provide — and, indeed, is legally obliged to provide (under the old 1948 Act and its 1980 successor) — a child-care service. Provided that it is judged to be in the interests of the child's welfare, no limits are set on the circumstances in which an admission can take place, nor (apart from an upper age limit) to the time the child may spend in care. Parents can and do request such admissions (more properly, 'receptions' into care), though they can also be effected in their absence. In the words of one commentator, it 'does not imply any criticism of parents who may seek care for their child as a solution to a crisis. It can be a very constructive move by the parents.' [Holden, 1980] It is therefore a type of admission that responds to parents as unfortunate rather than blameworthy, and casts the local authority in the role of the child's caretaker, acting on the parents' behalf. As such, it can be seen to be at one end of a continuum of services which includes domiciliary help and day care for children. It therefore forms, in our view, part of a range of child-care services for *families* and not, as the narrower interpretations of 'care' and 'prevention' would imply, a stark alternative to such services. Given the severity of poverty and disruption in most of the families with whom social-services departments come into contact, and the undoubted increase in their number through rising rates of unemployment and divorce, it is disturbing that the provision of such a service seems to be shrinking, relative to other forms of public child care.

A second type of admission provides a protection and rescue service for children who are thought to be in danger, whether it be physical, sexual, moral, emotional or developmental. Here the emphasis is on parental faults and failings and on the child as a victim of inadequate or inappropriate parenting. The local authority intervenes on the child's behalf, and, more often than not, if an admission is arranged (and even if it is requested by the parents) the local authority itself takes over parental rights as well as duties. In essence, the child-care service offered is protection for very vulnerable *children*.

The third type of admission relates to the child whose own behaviour is causing problems. Children whose behaviour troubles no one but their own families, or who behave in ways which adults too easily overlook — depressed and withdrawn children, for example — are unlikely candidates for care. But children whose disruptive and antisocial behaviour spreads beyond the family, and is visible to schools, police, neighbours and strangers, may well be so. For them, admission to care has a more ambiguous meaning. The intentions of the 1969 Children and Young Persons Act were to cast admitted 'villains' in the role of 'victims' of another sort — vulnerable youngsters from difficult backgrounds who had succumbed to family, neighbourhood and societal pressures, and were in need of care or control not otherwise available to them. In practice, familiar elements of punishment, containment and deterrence are also in the minds of decision-makers and, it must be said, the parents themselves. In the event, the child-care service offered to this group is as much a retributive and protective service for the *public* as it is a 'care' service for the young people themselves.

Earlier, they pointed out that:

. . . The public child-care system is permeable. Its boundaries are not a Rubicon that is crossed in only one direction. The majority of children (three out of five in the study) return from care within a short time — some of them within days or weeks. On the other hand, children whose admission is prevented at one point in time may well come in later — one in five of our original group of non-admitteds had done so by follow-up. Some children even cross and recross the boundaries several times (a third of our admitteds had already been in care at least once before). So sharp distinctions between 'admitted' and 'not-admitted' status are false, and turn a situation that is actually grey and fluid into a misleadingly static picture in black and white.

Failure to realise this, and to appreciate the variety of situations to which care is a response could have unfortunate consequences:

Statements that assert that 'admission to care should be a last resort' or that 'it is to be prevented at all costs', and policies which equate low admission rates with good child care, for example, seem to us to be singularly unhelpful — yet they were much in evidence in departmental documents and in discussions with staff at many levels. . . . There is also a sense in which a defensive 'last resort' stance — much the most common reaction, in our experience, though it is based in part on obvious faults in the child-care system itself — actually contrives to *reinforce* these failings, ensuring that public care is indeed something to be avoided. Some of the precipitate entrances into care, with their distressing lack of preparation, hastily arranged placements, and all the attendant risks of breakdown and further disruptions to follow, seemed to be directly attributable to such negative attitudes. A 'rule of pessimism' [cf. p. 620, below] operated about the care system, which meant that admission was sometimes almost unthinkable, until it became too late to think at all. 'Last resorts' are, after all, seldom desirable or constructive places to be.

Another important finding was a considerable discrepancy between the two authorities in the legal route chosen, as shown by the table. The consequences and conclusions to be drawn from this are also important:

. . . For the children concerned, being *compelled* into care carries a high risk that the admission itself will be hasty, ill prepared and even traumatic. Place of Safety Orders ['POSOs'; see p. 600, below] are the extreme case, where entry is so managed that children rarely have the comfort of familiar adults around them, or any foreknowledge of where they are to go, as they make the transition from home to 'care'. Indeed, for some it will mean literally being carried off, protesting, and for a few it can apparently involve a dramatic entrance to a 'safe place' in handcuffs! And though POSOs *are* the extreme case, they are also so much a part of normal child-care practice that they formed over a *third* of all admissions and 60 per cent of all compulsory admissions in the monitoring year. For most children, compulsion is also likely to

Table 4.2: Summary of decisions made

	Clayport (No.)	(%)	Shiptown (No.)	(%)
Admitted at first decision	61	37	100	51
Not admitted at first decision	105	63	95	49
Legal route of admissions				
Voluntary (Child Care Act 1980, section 2)	36	59	35	35
POSO — social-service department initiated	11	18	20	20
POSO — police initiated	5	8	18	18
Remand	4	6	15	15
Children and Young Persons Act 1969, care orders and interim care orders	4	6	6	6
Matrimonial care orders (and others)	1	2	6	6
All compulsory admissions	25	41	65	65

mean placement in *residential* care (as distinct from fostering) and the imposition of restrictions on contact with family members. It also increases the chances that the children will remain in care for a long time. (Half with compulsory admissions were still in care at follow-up, compared with less than a third of the voluntary group).

For parents, compulsory removal has other implications. The majority will experience loss of control over decisions which affect their children's lives — not only at the point of entry, but throughout the time their children remain in care. They may be 'told' rather than consulted about plans for their children's future, or may even be kept in ignorance of what such plans are, or whether they exist at all. Many are likely to feel angry, frustrated and resentful at this perceived takeover, and to interpret events as a betrayal. . . .

By comparison, voluntary reception into care is generally better managed and much more acceptable to parents. For some, (though by no means all) there is planning and preparation. Children are more likely to be introduced to placements in advance and to be accompanied to them by familiar adults, and they are more likely to go into foster homes. Most will return home fairly swiftly. Parents are much more likely to be consulted, to feel involved and to have a sense of sharing in plans and decisions for their child. Social workers are similarly happier with these admissions and more often judge them to be appropriate and beneficial.

There seems every reason, therefore, to think very carefully before the legal means of entry is chosen; for there is certainly a choice to be made. Despite the evident differences in emphasis in the child and family problems with which alternative routes into care have become associated — the *behavioural* focus of many compulsory removals and the large number of teenagers amongst their ranks, compared with the *situational* stress to which much voluntary care is a response, and the younger age group that is usually involved — there is much overlap. 'Victims' and 'volunteered' share very similar deprivations and disadvantages, and official concern over standards of parental care is manifest for both. Even the older 'villains', for all the *relative* stability and comfort of their home base, have been, and usually remain, subject to stressful family relationships. Children who enter care therefore form another continuum — of age and family circumstances — and where they are placed on that continuum, and what is therefore considered to be the best means of effecting their admission, is a matter of interpretation and emphasis.

The Review of Child Care Law (1985) and the Government's White Paper on *The Law on Child Care and Family Services* (1987), which led to the 1989 Act, were heavily influenced by these views:

18. It is proposed to give local authorities a broad 'umbrella' *power* to provide services to promote the care and upbringing of children, and to help prevent the breakdown of family relationships which might eventually lead to a court order committing the child to the local authority's care. Within this power the local authority will be able to provide services to a child *at home*, for example a family aide to assist within the home; at a *day centre*, for example a day nursery for pre-school children, an after school scheme for school age children or placement with a childminder; or *residential facilities* allowing a child to stay for short or long periods

away from home, say with a foster family or in a children's home. The local authority will also be able to offer financial assistance in exceptional circumstances. . . .

20. Local authorities have a duty under current legislation to receive children into their care in special circumstances, generally where there is a need to care for the child away from home because of the absence or incapacity of parents. This duty will be maintained broadly as at present. So will the duty to return the child to his family where this is consistent with his welfare.

21. The Government wish to emphasise, however, that the provision of a service by the local authority to enable a child who is not under a care order to be cared for away from home should be seen in a wider context and as part of the range of services a local authority can offer to parents and families in need of help with the care of their children. Such a service should, in appropriate circumstances, be seen as a positive response to the needs of families and not as a mark of failure either on the part of the family or those professionals and others working to support them. An essential characteristic of this service should be its voluntary character, that is it should be based clearly on continuing parental agreement and operate as far as possible on a basis of partnership and co-operation between the local authority and parents.

Hence the abolition of the power to assume parental rights by resolution and the insistence (in s. 20(8), (9) and (10)) that any person who is entitled to have the child living with him may remove the child from local authority accommodation at any time. One reason for this emphasis on the voluntary provision of services was the recommendation of the Review of Child Care Law (1985) that child care legislation should be combined with the health and welfare legislation, under which services are provided for mentally handicapped and disabled children, to embody the best features of both. The White Paper agreed:

16. The health and welfare legislation generally makes no provision for the supervision of the welfare of individual children provided with services. Thus, for example, under this legislation a child may remain away from home for long periods without any legal requirement for the caring agency to review his case, or to give first consideration to his welfare or to consult him where practicable in taking any decisions about him all of which are requirements under child care law. Nor are there any provisions about local authority responsibilities to children when they leave facilities provided under this legislation. This again contrasts with child care law. There are also inconsistencies between health and welfare legislation and child care law over such matters as charging for services.

17. The Government therefore propose the unification of these two sets of legislation as recommended by the Review. In reaching this decision the Government considered carefully the reservations expressed by some that this would cause concern to those parents of handicapped and disabled children who provide expert and devoted care but from time to time need respite care provided by the local authority. This concern it was said flowed from the perception that reception into care by local authorities under the present legislation was frequently associated with parental shortcomings. . . . The intention of the Government is to ensure that in all cases the children concerned receive the standard of care and protection and professional review appropriate to their needs and that those ends are achieved where possible in a partnership with parents.

A clear distinction should therefore be drawn between children 'in care', who are the subject of care orders (see p. 607, below), and other children who are simply provided with accommodation by the authority. A sharp eye, however, is needed to recognise the differences in the sections of the 1989 Act dealing with all children being 'looked after':

22. – (1) In this Act, any reference to a child who is looked after by a local authority is a reference to a child who is –
   (*a*) in their care; or
   (*b*) provided with accommodation by the authority in the exercise of any functions (in particular those under this Act) which stand referred to their social services committee under the Local Authority Social Services Act 1970.

(2) In subsection (1) 'accommodation' means accommodation which is provided for a continuous period of more than 24 hours.

(3) It shall be the duty of a local authority looking after any child —

(a) to safeguard and promote his welfare; and

(b) to make such use of services available for children cared for by their own parents as appears to the authority reasonable in his case.

(4) Before making any decision with respect to a child whom they are looking after, or proposing to look after, a local authority shall, so far as is reasonably practicable, ascertain the wishes and feelings of —

(a) the child;

(b) his parents;

(c) any person who is not a parent of his but who has parental responsibility for him; and

(d) any other person whose wishes and feelings the authority consider to be relevant,

regarding the matter to be decided.

(5) In making any such decisions a local authority shall give due consideration —

(a) having regarded to his age and understanding, to such wishes and feelings of the child as they have been able to ascertain;

(b) to such wishes and feelings of any person mentioned in subsection (4)(b) to (d) as they have been able to ascertain; and

(c) to the child's religious persuasion, racial origin and cultural and linguistic background.

(6) If it appears to a local authority that it is necessary, for the purpose of protecting members of the public from serious injury, to exercise their powers with respect to a child whom they are looking after in a manner which may not be consistent with their duties under this section, they may do so.

(7) If the Secretary of State considers it necessary, for the purpose of protecting members of the public from serious injury, to give directions to a local authority with respect to the exercise of their powers with respect to a child whom they are looking after, he may give such directions to the authority.

(8) Where any such directions are given to an authority they shall comply with them even though doing so is inconsistent with their duties under this section.

Question

(i) Subsections (6) to (8) of s. 22 stem from the Children and Young Persons Act 1969, when local authorities were given responsibility for most juvenile offenders: now that committal to local authority accommodation is no longer available as a disposal in criminal cases (except on remand or as a short residential condition in a supervision order) can they still be justified? (ii) Why are they not limited to 'children in care'?

23. — (1) It shall be the duty of any local authority looking after a child —

(a) when he is in their care, to provide accommodation for him; and

(b) to maintain him in other respects apart from providing accommodation for him.

(2) A local authority shall provide accommodation and maintenance for any child whom they are looking after by —

(a) placing him (subject to subsection (5) and any regulations made by the Secretary of State) with —

(i) a family;

(ii) a relative of his; or

(iii) any other suitable person,

on such terms as to payment by the authority and otherwise as the authority may determine;

(b) maintaining him in a community home;

(c) maintaining him in a voluntary home;

(d) maintaining him in a registered children's home;

(e) maintaining him in a home provided by the Secretary of State under section 82(5) on such terms as the Secretary of State may from time to time determine; or

(f) making such other arrangements as —

(i) seem appropriate to them; and

(ii) comply with any regulations made by the Secretary of State.

(3) Any person with whom a child has been placed under subsection (2)(*a*) is referred to in this Act as a local authority foster parent unless he falls within subsection (4).

(4) A person falls within this subsection if he is —
  (*a*) a parent of the child;
  (*b*) a person who is not a parent of the child but who has parental responsibility for him; or
  (*c*) where the child is in care and there was a residence order in force with respect to him immediately before the care order was made, a person in whose favour the residence order was made.

(5) Where a child is in the care of a local authority, the authority may only allow him to live with a person who falls within subsection (4) in accordance with regulations made by the Secretary of State.

(6) Subject to any regulations made by the Secretary of State for the purposes of this subsection, any local authority looking after a child shall make arrangements to enable him to live with —
  (*a*) a person falling within subsection (4); or
  (*b*) a relative, friend or other person connected with him,
  unless that would not be reasonably practicable or consistent with his welfare.

(7) Where a local authority provide accommodation for a child whom they are looking after, they shall, subject to the provisions of this Part and so far as is reasonably practicable and consistent with his welfare, secure that —
  (*a*) the accommodation is near his home; and
  (*b*) where the authority are also providing accommodation for a sibling of his, they are accommodated together.

(8) Where a local authority provide accommodation for a child whom they are looking after who is disabled, they shall, so far as is reasonably practicable, secure that the accommodation is not unsuitable to his particular needs.

(9) Part II of Schedule 2 shall have effect for the purposes of making further provision as to children looked after by local authorities and in particular as to the regulations that may be made under subsections (2)(*a*) and (*f*) and (5).

One of the key paragraphs of Part II of Sch. 2 deals with keeping in touch:

15. — (1) Where a child is being looked after by a local authority, the authority shall, unless it is not reasonably practicable or consistent with his welfare, endeavour to promote contact between the child and —
  (*a*) his parents;
  (*b*) any person who is not a parent of his but who has parental responsibility for him; and
  (*c*) any relative, friend or other person connected with him.

(2) Where a child is being looked after by a local authority —
  (*a*) the authority shall take such steps as are reasonably practicable to secure that —
    (i) his parents; and
    (ii) any person who is not a parent of his but who has parental responsibility for him, are kept informed of where he is being accommodated; and
  (*b*) every such person shall secure that the authority are kept informed of his or her address.

. . .

The *Arrangements for Placement of Children (General) Regulations 1991* require:

3. — (4) In any other case [i.e. except when child is 16 and agrees to be accommodated under s. 20(11), above] in which a child is looked after or accommodated but is not in care the arrangements shall so far as reasonably practicable be agreed by the responsible authority with —
  (*a*) a person with parental responsibility for the child, or
  (*b*) if there is no such person the person who is caring for the child
before a placement is made and if that is not practicable as soon as reasonably practicable thereafter.

By reg. 4(2), these must if practicable include the matters listed in Sch. 4:

MATTERS TO BE INCLUDED IN ARRANGEMENTS TO ACCOMMODATE
CHILDREN WHO ARE NOT IN CARE

1. The type of accommodation to be provided and its address together with the name of any person who will be responsible for the child at that accommodation on behalf of the responsible authority.
2. The details of any services to be provided for the child.
3. The respective responsibilities of the responsible authority and —
   (a) the child;
   (b) any parent of his; and
   (c) any person who is not a parent of his but who has parental responsibility for him.
4. What delegation there has been by the persons referred to in paragraph 3(b) and (c) of this Schedule to the responsible authority of parental responsibility for the child's day to day care.
5. The arrangements for involving those persons and the child in decision making with respect to the child having regard —
   (a) to the local authority's duty under sections 20(6) (involvement of children before provisions of accommodation) and 22(3) to (5) of the Act (general duties of the local authority in relation to children looked after by them);
   (b) the duty of the voluntary organisation under section 61(1) and (2) of the Act (duties of voluntary organisations); and
   (c) the duty of the person carrying on a registered children's home under section 64(1) and (2) of the Act (welfare of children in registered children's homes).
6. The arrangements for contact between the child and —
   (a) his parents;
   (b) any person who is not a parent of his but who has parent responsibility for him; and
   (c) any relative, friend or other person connected with him,
and if appropriate, the reasons why contact with any such person would not be reasonably practicable or would be inconsistent with the child's welfare.
7. The arrangements for notifying changes in arrangements for contact to any of the persons referred to in paragraph 6.
8. In the case of a child aged 16 over whether section 20(11) (accommodation of a child of 16 or over despite parental opposition) applies.
9. The expected duration of arrangements and the steps which should apply to bring the arrangements to an end, including arrangements for rehabilitation of the child with the person with whom he was living before the voluntary arrangements were made or some other suitable person, having regard in particular, in the case of a local authority looking after a child, to section 23(6) of the Act (duty to place children where practicable with parents etc.) and paragraph 15 of Schedule 2 to the Act (maintenance of contact between child and family).

Questions

(i) The Review of Child Care Law (1985, para. 7.16) recommended against 'allowing legal powers over a child to be settled by informal agreement in individual cases. Great care would need to be taken to ensure that the parent was fully aware of the consequences of such an agreement and was in no way overawed or pressurised (however unwittingly) by the person obtaining consent.' What is the legal effect of the agreed arrangements under these regulations?

(ii) What is the position of a parent who wishes herself to meet one of the parental responsibilities delegated in the agreement (see p. 441, above)?

(iii) What is a parent to do if (a) the agreed arrangements for contact are not kept, or (b) she wishes to make some different arrangements?

(iv) Do you think that the parent will see herself as being in partnership with the local authority (or voluntary organisation) to look after her child?

(v) What is meant by an 'other person connected with him' (in Sch. 2, para. 15(1)(c) of the Children Act 1989, and para. 6(c) above)? What if a 13 year old girl in local authority accommodation has a boyfriend (*a*) to whom the local authority objects but the parents do not, or (*b*) to whom the parents object but the local authority does not?

One problem with the idea of partnership is the length of time that many children stay in care. The mismatch between the ideals of prevention and rehabilitation and the reality was first exposed by Jane Rowe and Lydia Lambert in *Children Who Wait* (1973):

The growth of the illusion
Following the Children Act 1948 with its stress on the need to return children to their parents and the Children and Young Persons Act 1963 with its stress on prevention, the idea of bringing up children in care went very much out of fashion. Many social workers had become acutely aware of the problems of children who had been cut off from their families. They strove to emphasise plans for maintaining family ties and returning children home. There was therefore comparatively little interest in providing permanence or continuity or in the way an agency should carry out its parental role in relation to the children in its care. . . .

The findings of the study
The stark reality disclosed by this study is that if a pre-school or primary school age child has been in care for as long as six months, his chances of returning to his parents are slim. On the most liberal interpretation of the study figures little more than one child in four was expected to return to his family before he reached school leaving age. . . .

The national picture
Over the country as a whole, there are probably at least 6,000 children of pre-school or primary school age who are in the care of social agencies and who need a substitute family. This estimate is based on the study finding that *626 children, or 22% of the total number surveyed, were thought by their social workers to need placement in a foster or adoptive home.*

The findings of more recent research into what happens to children looked after by local authorities are depressingly summarised by the DHSS in *Social Work Decisions in Child Care* (1985):

1) *Far less attention is given to what is to happen after admission than to whether or not to admit and if children stay long in care, social work attention fades.*
'The system itself is geared towards placing an emphasis on the justification for intervention rather than what intervention would achieve.' (Hilgendorf, 1981)
'This study has highlighted with considerable precision a situation that has long been known — that unless a child leaves care quickly, that is within six weeks — he or she has a very strong chance of being in care in two years time. Yet, the administrative arrangements within social services and social work practice often do not reflect this acutely short time scale. We find a time perspective entertained by social workers which is greatly at variance with the urgency experienced by the child and family or which, this study demonstrates, is in their best interests.' (Dartington, 1986)
2) *Children in care are likely to experience many changes of placement.*
The instability of 'in care' placements is hammered home to the reader of these research studies by the depressing similarity of their findings.
'Four out of five admitted children had moved at least twice and a quarter at least four times, in the space of a few months.' (Packman, 1986)
'In relation to their most recent admissions, 33% of children had two or three placement changes and 17% four or more.' (Marsh & Fisher, 1986)
Over a two year period '56% of the children will have had three or more placements and 14% of them will have had more than four.' (Dartington, 1986)
The Dartington study reveals that of 170 children still in care after two years, 63 were thought by their social workers to be unsuitably placed.
They report: —
'Transfer and breakdown of children in placements selected by social workers are common. . . .
This propensity to breakdown is only slightly less common among young children than adolescents and is as likely to occur in foster as in residential care . . . Seven out of the fifteen

infants admitted to care before the age of two have suffered a placement breakdown, three of them under crisis conditions.' (Dartington, 1986)

3) *Discharge or remaining in care is not usually the result of social work planning.*

'Remaining in care is not always the outcome of a decision, but may be the outcome of not taking a decision . . . It was rarely possible to pin-point when, or how, the decision that they would not return home had been taken . . . Many children remained in care or in a particular placement, not as the result of an explicit decision that this would be the best course of action . . . but by default.' (National Children's Bureau, 1986)

'A good number of discharge processes (according to both families and social workers) occurred without the active involvement of the social worker . . . (In general), the process of leaving care was not accorded much attention by most social workers.' (Marsh & Fisher, 1986)

4) *Family links are seldom given much consideration. As a result, circumstantial barriers to access may go unrecognised and little practical help is offered to encourage parents' visits. When links wither, chances of the child's return home are diminished.*

'Parent-child contact was not a feature relayed by social workers as of importance in relation to placement . . . Although in the majority of cases parental contact was not being discouraged, the stance was being adopted of waiting and seeing what the parents did . . . Social workers invariably commented that they left this (visiting arrangements) to be worked out between the foster parents and the parent.' (National Children's Bureau, 1986)

'Only two sets of parents said their social workers had actually helped them over visiting.' (Packman, 1986)

'The propensity of many placements to frustrate links . . . often passes quite unrecognised by social workers.' (Dartington, 1986)

In the Dartington cohort, only 36% of families had *specific* restrictions imposed on their access, but 66% experienced *non-specific* barriers of distance, travel problems, rules about visits, unwelcoming attitudes etc. At the two year stage, 41 of the 170 children still in care had a mother who did not know their address.

'Even after controlling for other variables, we find that a weakening of parental links is strongly associated with declining chances for the child of returning home. Naturally parental links are not a sufficient condition to ensure exit from care . . . (but they are) a necessary condition for exit.' (Dartington, 1986)

'We were frequently dismayed and sometimes angered by the way in which social workers so often failed to provide the necessary support and encouragement to maintain visiting. Sometimes they actually seemed to set up 'no win' situations for natural parents, first discouraging visits 'to let the children settle' and later saying that after such a long gap renewed visiting would be upsetting. But this way is by no means the whole story. We found that ambivalence towards visiting seemed to be a prevalent attitude in natural parents and foster children as well as in social workers and foster parents. Everyone seemed to draw back from the pain and potential conflict involved.' (Rowe, 1984)

5) *Difficulties in maintaining links are exacerbated for both children and social workers by the rapidity with which the families of children in care change and re-constitute themselves.*

'Many of these family structures underwent radical changes during the child's absence, even though the stay in care was short . . . By six months, nearly half of the children will have had a major change in their family structure . . . These oscillations are most noticeable among the families of younger children, a factor which not only prevents their return home and affects their wider relationships but also greatly hinders contact between parents and children.' (Dartington, 1986)

6) *Parents of children in care may feel pushed aside and disillusioned.*

'At present many parents seem to feel totally devalued. 'They just don't care about us' was an all too frequent comment . . . It was clear from many records that natural parents had been allowed — almost encouraged — to lose contact with the department as well as with their children . . . During the 12 months preceding the study social workers had been in touch with only one-third of the children's "primary" parents.' (Rowe, 1984)

'Eventually, parents' sense of violation and powerlessness encourages passivity and assumed indifference. However skilled the social worker may be, this is an extremely difficult situation in which to assess parents' long-term viability to care . . . Parents feel unwanted and that they have nothing more to contribute to the well-being of their children. This feeling increases after time. As contact with the social worker declines, the children settle down and inertia steals over the child care scene, parents feel abandoned and angry.' (Dartington, 1986)

7) *Tension and misunderstandings are often caused by differing values and attitudes to child rearing held by parents, social workers and residential staff.*

'The evaluations of parents focussed on the extent to which the care their child was receiving corresponded to a pre-existing framework about appropriate ways of dealing with children

. . . Social work intervention was apt to miss the importance of discipline in the eyes of the parents . . . These discrepancies (in perception of the purpose of care and of the parents' continued sense of responsibility), were rooted in different concepts of appropriate parenting and were to have long-term consequences for the children's experiences of care and for the parents' acceptance of care as an appropriate solution to their difficulties.' (Marsh & Fisher, 1986)

The 1989 Act tries to address some of these concerns, not only by the provisions quoted above on consultation and contact, but also in s. 26, which requires regular reviews of why and how children are being looked after and a formal complaints mechanism:

26. – (3) Every local authority shall establish a procedure for considering any representations (including any complaint) made to them by –
(a) any child who is being looked after by them or who is not being looked after by them but is in need;
(b) a parent of his;
(c) any person who is not a parent of his but who has parental responsibility for him;
(d) any local authority foster parent;
(e) such other person as the authority consider has a sufficient interest in the child's welfare to warrant his representations being considered by them,
about the discharge by the authority of any of their functions under this Part in relation to the child.
(4) The procedure shall ensure that at least one person who is not a member or officer of the authority takes part in –
(a) the considerations; and
(b) any discussions which are held by the authority about the action (if any) to be taken in relation to the child in the light of the consideration.
. . .
(7) Where any representation has been considered under the procedure established by a local authority under this section, the authority shall –
(a) have due regard to the findings of those considering the representation; and
(b) take such steps as are reasonably practicable to notify (in writing) –
(i) the person making the representation;
(ii) the child (if the authority consider that he has sufficient understanding); and
(iii) such other persons (if any) as appear to the authority to be likely to be affected, of the authority's decision in the matter and their reasons for taking that decision and of any action which they have taken, or propose to take.
(8) Every local authority shall give such publicity to their procedure for considering representations under this section as they consider appropriate.

Questions

(i) You are a child aged 15 being looked after by Blankshire County Council in a small residential home. You like this because it is near to your school and friends. Visits to or from your family are easy. Blankshire then decides to privatise its provision of residential care and to close the home. You are likely to be sent to a similar home 50 miles away. What can you do?
(ii) Your mother is a disabled widow who found it impossible to look after you as well as your two sisters because your mild mental handicap has made your adolescence difficult for both of you. The relationship between you is still very close. What can she do?
(iii) Your mother's sister would have you to live with her, provided that she can have some financial and social work support. You have mixed feelings about this, but would prefer it to moving away. What can she do (see also p. 635, below)?

(iv) Your 16 year old sister thinks you have a lovely life in the home and would like to join you. What can she do?

(v) Your 21 year old boy friend would like to visit you in the home, but the home's rules prohibit such visits. What can he do?

(vi) Blankshire thinks that returning you to your family at this crucial stage in your education and development will not be for the best. If your mother decides that the only solution is to take you away from them, what can they do?

This last question involves the use of compulsion against parents, which is dealt with below (p. 605). Remember, however, that compulsion is also used against the children themselves: this is Susan's story from *The Pindown Experience and the Protection of Children: The Report of the Staffordshire Child Care Inquiry 1990* (1991):

11.17 Susan, who was born in 1976, was put into Pindown when she was 9 years old.

11.18 At the beginning of 1986 Susan, her half-sister aged 13, and her mother were living with the maternal grandfather. Her half-sister is the child of her mother's former marriage. Susan's father was one of her mother's subsequent boyfriends.

11.19 Over a period of about a month, in early 1986, the mother contacted Staffordshire social services on a number of occasions requesting help with coping with Susan's behaviour. Susan was said to be mixing with older girls and smoking, stealing and upsetting her grandfather who did not want her to remain in his home.

11.20 Susan was then received into care and placed at 245 Hartshill Road.

11.21 She went straight into Pindown. The first entry in the log book was as follows: '(Susan) admitted – *very basic programme be very nasty to her*' (emphasis added).

11.22 Susan was required to wear pyjamas and kept in a sparsely furnished room. She was not allowed contact with other children or non-Pindown staff and was not permitted to attend school. She was required to knock on the door before going to the toilet. She remained in Pindown for a week and then returned home. Subsequently five 'family reviews' were held at The Birches at about weekly intervals before social services contact with the family ceased and the case was closed.

11.23 Immediately after Susan's admission to Pindown an entry in the log book at 245 Hartshill Road recorded a residential worker's conversation with her headmaster: he was concerned that she was in care because she was no trouble at all in school being a good attender, well-behaved, and a hard worker. She was also in his view very bright.

11.24 Further entries in the log book during her week in Pindown included:
   - 'wants to go to the toilet a lot, soon put a stop to that. Had harsh words twice. Once for calling through the bedroom wall (to another child in Pindown).'
   - 'will try anything to get out of her room, after several telling offs (sic) she stopped trying.'
   - 'she thinks I'm room service, hasn't anyone told her its not an hotel.'
   - 'the little knocker has not knocked so much tonight, when I go in I usually look for a tip as I feel like a waiter.'

11.25 On the evening of Susan's third day in Pindown a 'review' was held. Neither the log book nor the social services file on Susan records who was present. 'Susan's problems' were 'highlighted'. It was noted that the grandfather would not allow her back and her mother was prepared to move out of his home. It was 'agreed that (Susan) remain in care'. It was recorded in the log book that 'mother saw her 2 mins. Cried a little. Then later cried wanting to go home. Was her mother still here. Explained review system. Spoke to her about contract and may well come back if she breaks the rules. Bath, bed. Toilet a lot still. First sign of hope for her, maybe!!!'

11.26 Susan is twice recorded in the log book as 'working hard'. What she was doing in the Pindown room is not specified.

11.27 A further 'review' was held after Susan had been in Pindown for 7 days. It was agreed that she should 'return home' on various conditions, one of which was that she should write a letter of apology to her grandfather.

11.28 Susan returned to the home of her grandfather. Soon afterwards she and her mother and half-sister were re-housed.

11.29 Just over a year later, the mother again brought Susan, then aged 10, to the social services office. She said that she had been having problems with Susan's behaviour for some considerable time. She would not do what she was told, called her mother unpleasant names and embarrassed her in public. The mother said that she had eventually lost her temper and attempted 'to strangle' Susan. She could not look at Susan without wanting to attack her and Susan was unrepentant about her behaviour. There were also problems with the mother's boyfriend who was living in their home and about whom Susan complained.

11.30 Susan was again received into care and placed into Pindown. The entry in the log book at 245 Hartshill Road records that '(Susan) admitted to pindown after family meeting . . . she is an extremely naughty and manipulative little girl: so much so that she has driven her mother to the point of violence. *Basic Pindown—plenty of schoolwork.*' Later on the day of admission to Pindown it is recorded that 'if she knocked on the door once, she knocked ten thousand times. Other than that *no* problems, she did *not* eat much tea, had a bath at 6-30 tucked up in bed 7 p.m.'

11.31 Three days later the following entry was made in the log book: '(Susan) reviewed this afternoon. She fully expected to go home. When she realised that this wasn't going to happen she became very upset. Cried off and on until 8-30—at times becoming hysterical. She will go to school on Monday; she understands that this is a privilege and is the only she will be given for some time to come.'

11.32 After ten days of Pindown it was noted by the child's social worker in the social services file that 'there are no complaints about (Susan's) behaviour at Hartshill Road but she is in no position to misbehave as she is restricted'.

11.33 Subsequently the mother recognised that 'problems can only be resolved at home' and Susan spent some of her time at home and some in Pindown at 245 Hartshill Road. It would seem that she actually spend some 20 days in Pindown before being transferred to The Birches.

11.34 After spending about 3 months at The Birches during which time she spent regular weekends at home, Susan was moved to another children's home. She eventually went home at the beginning of 1988, some six months after being received into care for the second time. More recently further problems occurred and Susan was placed in a foster home.

11.35 Susan at 9 years of age was one of the youngest children placed in Pindown. During her two spells in care in 1986 and 1987 she spent at least 27 days in the unit.

Questions

(i) Why should it be regarded as a privilege to be allowed to go to school?
(ii) Under s. 36 of the Education Act 1944, 'It shall be the duty of the parent of every child of compulsory school age to cause him to receive efficient full-time education suitable to his age, ability and aptitude and to any special educational needs he may have, either by regular attendance at school or otherwise'; under s. 114(1) (as amended by the Children Act 1989), 'parent' includes 'any person (*a*) who is not a parent of his but has parental responsibility for him, or (*b*) who has care of him' but for this purpose only includes such a person if he is an individual: should local authorities be under the same legal obligation as others to educate the children they are looking after properly?

There are limits on the circumstances in which children may be placed in 'secure accommodation', now contained in the *Children Act 1989*:

25.—(1) Subject to the following provisions of this section, a child who is being looked after by a local authority may not be placed, and, if placed, may not be kept, in accommodation provided for the purpose of restricting liberty ('secure accommodation') unless it appears—
  (*a*) that—
    (i) he has a history of absconding and is likely to abscond from any other description of accommodation; and
    (ii) if he absconds, he is likely to suffer significant harm; or

(b) that if he is kept in any other description of accommodation he is likely to injure himself or other persons.

(2) The Secretary of State may by regulations —
  (a) specify a maximum period —
    (i) beyond which a child may not be kept in secure accommodation without the authority of the court; and
    (ii) for which the court may authorise a child to be kept in secure accommodation;
  (b) empower the court from time to time to authorise a child to be kept in secure accommodation for such further period as the regulations may specify; and
  (c) provide that applications to the court under this section shall be made only by local authorities.

Questions

(i) Why is this not restricted to 'children in care'?
(ii) What legal action (if any) might be available to Susan and others like her?
(iii) Section 51 of the Act allows the Secretary of State to exempt from criminal liability for harbouring or assisting runaways specified voluntary organisations and others who provide refuges for children 'at risk': is this a better solution?
(iv) Why should we tolerate a public care system from which children want to run away?

3 Investigating child abuse

One of the startling things about the death of Susan Auckland (p. 372, above), as in almost all the other cases on which there have been official inquiries (see DHSS, 1982; DH, 1991), is that the family was well known to the social services and other agencies, 'to such an extent that the family can almost be seen as a demonstration of how the welfare state operates'. Co-operation between health, education and social services, and the police, is seen as the key to effective protection by the DH in *Working Together — A guide to arrangements for inter-agency co-operation for the protection of children from abuse* (1991 draft). It defines child abuse thus:

6.14 The following categories of registration of abuse are not necessarily exhaustive nor are they mutually exclusive. The term 'child abuse' in this guide is intended to cover all these categories. . . .
  Neglect: The persistent or severe neglect of a child (for example, by exposure to any kind of danger, including cold and starvation) which results in serious impairment of the child's health or development, including non-organic failure to thrive.
  Physical abuse: Physical injury to a child, including deliberate poisoning, where there is definite knowledge, or a reasonable suspicion, that the injury was inflicted or knowingly not prevented.
  Sexual abuse: The involvement of dependent, developmentally immature children and adolescents in sexual activities they do not truly comprehend, to which they are unable to give informed consent, or that violate the social taboos of family roles.
  Emotional abuse: The severe adverse effect on the behaviour and emotional development of a child caused by persistent or severe emotional ill-treatment or rejection. All abuse involves some emotional ill-treatment; — this category should be used where it is the main or sole form of abuse.
  Grave concern: This category should not be used lightly and should be needed only in exceptional circumstances for children whose situations do not currently fit the above

categories. This may be where there is an explicit and serious concern that the child is not developing as would be expected (and all medical causes have been eliminated) or there is a sudden, unexplained change in that child's normal behaviour pattern. If the cause of the child's condition is later established as fitting one of the above categories, a case conference should amend the cause of registration.

The process starts with referral:

5.9 The starting point of the child protection system in England and Wales is that any person who has knowledge or a suspicion that a child is being abused or is at risk of abuse should refer their concern to one or more of the agencies with statutory duties and/or powers to investigate and intervene. These are the 'investigating agencies', ie the social services department, the NSPCC and the police.

For health professionals, this overrides the normal rules of confidentiality:

5.4 Ethical and statutory codes concerned with confidentiality and data protection are not intended to prevent the exchange of information between different professional staff who have a responsibility for ensuring the protection of children. The Annual Report 1987 of the General Medical Council gives unequivocal advice on this matter in cases of child abuse, including child sexual abuse:
> 'The Council's published guidance on professional confidence states that doctors may disclose confidential information to the police who are investigating a grave or very serious crime, provided always that they are prepared to justify their actions if called upon to do so. However, a specialist in child psychiatry recently drew to the Council's attention that its guidance does not specifically address the question of whether a doctor may properly initiate action in a case of this kind, as opposed to responding to a request. Both the British Medical Association and the medical defence societies have expressed the view that in such circumstances the interests of the child are paramount and that those interests may well override the general rule of professional confidence. On the recommendation of the Standards Committee, the Council in November 1987 expressed the view that, if a doctor has reason for believing that a child is being physically or sexually abused, not only is it permissible for the doctor to disclose information to a third party but it is a duty of the doctor to do so.'

This is still the stance of the General Medical Council.

Question

Despite what the guide says, health professionals are under no legally enforceable duty to report suspicions of child abuse: should they be? What about other people?

D v National Society for Prevention of Cruelty to Children
[1978] AC 171, [1977] 1 All ER 589, [1977] 2 WLR 201, 121 Sol Jo 119, 76 LGR 5, House of Lords

Lord Diplock: . . . The uncontradicted evidence of the director of the NSPCC is that the work of the society is dependent upon its receiving prompt information of suspected child abuse and that, as might be expected, the principal sources of such information are neighbours of the child's family or doctors, school-teachers, health visitors and the like who will continue to be neighbours or to maintain the same relationship with the suspected person after the matter has been investigated and dealt with by the NSPCC. The evidence of the director is that without an effective promise of confidentiality neighbours and others would be very hesitant to pass on to the society information about suspected child abuse. There is an understandable reluctance to 'get involved' in something that is likely to arouse the resentment of the person whose suspected neglect or ill-treatment of a child has been reported. . . .

The fact that information has been communicated by one person to another in confidence, however, is not of itself a sufficient ground from protecting from disclosure in a court of law the nature of the information or the identity of the informant if either of these matters would assist the court to ascertain facts which are relevant to an issue on which it is adjudicating. . . . The private promise of confidentiality must yield to the general public interest that in the administration of justice truth will out, unless by reason of the character of the information or the relationship of the recipient . . . to the informant, a more important public interest is served by protecting the information or the identity of the informant from disclosure in a court of law. The public interest which the NSPCC relies on as obliging it to withhold from the respondent and from the court itself material that could disclose the identity of the society's informant is analagous to the public interest that is protected by the well-established rule of law that the identity of police informers may not be disclosed in a civil action, whether by the process of discovery or by oral evidence at the trial (*Marks v Beyfus* (1890) 25 QBD 494; 59 LJQB 479) . . . in *Rogers v Home Secretary* [1973] AC 388, [1972] 2 All ER 1057 this House did not hesitate to extend to persons from whom the Gaming Board received information for the purposes of the exercise of their statutory functions, under the Gaming Act 1968, immunity from disclosure of their identity analogous to that which the law had previously accorded to police informers. Your Lordships' sense of values might well be open to reproach if this House were to treat the confidentiality of information given to those who are authorised by statute to institute proceedings for the protection of neglected or ill-treated children as entitled to less favourable treatment in a court of law than information given to the Gaming Board so that gaming may be kept clean. . . .

Question

The identity of informants is still protected under the Access to Personal Files Act 1987 and Access to Personal Files (Social Services) Regulations 1989, reg. 9(3): should busy-bodies be encouraged or discouraged?

Part of the investigation should include a case conference:

6.1 A case conference is a multi-disciplinary meeting called to formulate advice on a specific issue. Case conferences are an essential feature of inter-agency co-operation and the need for holding a conference should always be identified at an early stage. Case conferences should have a clear purpose, they are not an end in themselves. If they are too large, wrongly timed, have no clear purpose, involve the wrong people or are poorly conducted they may not only fail to facilitate good practice but may also bring inter-agency working into disrepute and undermine good practice.

6.2 Case conferences provide a forum for the exchange of information between professionals involved with the child and family and allow for inter-agency, multi-disciplinary discussion of allegations or suspicions of abuse; the outcome of investigation, assessments for planning; an action plan for protecting the child and helping the family and reviews of the plan. The Chairman of the conference must be able to call upon the attendance of a lawyer from the local authority's legal section to assist in making recommendations for court applications. The result of the discussions are recommendations to individual agencies for action. While the decision to implement the recommendations must rest with the individual agency concerned, any deviation from them should not be made, except in an emergency, without informing other agencies through the key worker.

6.3 For reasons of both efficiency and confidentiality the number of people involved in a case conference should be limited to those with a need to know or those who have a contribution to make to the task involved. A case conference may be larger in the early stages of work, when a number of agencies may be contributing to an investigation or to an assessment for planning. Once a long-term plan has been formulated, however, a small group including the key worker, should be identified as the core group who agree to work together to implement and review the plan.

. . .

6.6 A case conference is an inter-professional meeting but on occasion it may wish to invite a non-professional who is working with the child or family, for example, foster parents or

volunteer workers. In this event, the key worker or professional most closely involved with the non-professional should undertake to brief him or her beforehand about the purpose of the conference, the duty of confidentiality and the primacy of the child's interests over that of the parents' interests if a conflict of interest arise.
6.7 Case conferences should be convened by the social services department or the NSPCC on its behalf but other agencies should be able to request one in the expectations that the request will not be refused without good reason.

Involvement of children and parents
6.8 It is important that parents and/or carers be informed about the basis of an investigation or intervention and are consulted and informed at all stages thereafter. Openness and honesty are an important basis on which to build a foundation of understanding and respect between parents and professionals which will often be essential for a satisfactory outcome for the child. Parents' views should be sought on the issues to be raised prior to a case conference to afford them the opportunity to seek advice and prepare their point of view. They should be invited to case conferences unless in the view of the Chairman of the conference their presence will preclude a full and proper consideration of the child's interests. Where this is the case, or the parents decline to attend, this should be recorded with the reason given, it should be arranged for their point of view to be presented to the case conference, and they should be informed of the outcome as soon as is practicable. . . .
6.9 A local authority has a specific duty to promote the welfare of the child it is looking after. In relation to any decisions taken, the authority has a duty to ascertain as far as is practicable his or her wishes and feelings and give due consideration to them, having regard to his or her age and understanding. Whenever children are old enough to express their wishes and feelings and to participate in the process of assessment, planning and review, arrangements should be made which allows them to attend the case conference. . . . If they do not wish to attend, or their age and/or understanding make this inappropriate, the case conference should be provided with a clear and up to date account of their views by the professionals who are working with them. The case conference should, therefore expect the key worker to be able to inform them about the views of a child who is not attending the meeting. Equally the child should be kept informed of the progress of the inter-agency work by the professional working with him or her.
6.10 When an agreement has been reached in a case conference to place the child's name on the child protection register and to formalise inter-agency co-operation, the parents or carers and where it is appropriate, the child should be informed formally of this agreement and its purpose, even if they attended the case conference. The function of case conferences and the child protection register in facilitating the inter-agency work should be explained at the same time. Parents should be advised of the procedure for removal of the child's name and when registration might end and that they will be informed if and when this happens. They should also be informed about how they will be involved in planning for the child.

Apart from the services to be provided and the possibility of legal proceedings, case conferences discuss whether children should be placed on the child protection register:

6.13 In each area covered by a social services department a central register must be maintained which lists all the children in the area *who are considered to be suffering from or likely to suffer, significant harm and for whom there is a child protection plan.* This is *not* a register of children who have been abused but of children for whom there are currently unresolved child protection issues and for whom there is an inter-agency protection plan. The register should include children who are recognised to be at risk and who are placed in the local authority's area by other local authorities or agencies.
. . .
6.15 The entry of a child's name on the register should normally only occur following discussion at a case conference when abuse or potential abuse is confirmed and an inter-agency agreement is made to work co-operatively to protect the child. The exception is that when a registered child moves the child should be registered at once pending the first case conference in the new area.
6.16 A child's name will normally only be removed from the register when it is agreed in a case conference or by exchange of minutes that formal inter-agency working is no longer necessary

to protect the child. Once a child's situation is identified as fitting one of the above categories the child's name and details should be entered on the register with a record of the plan for the child and the services to be provided. A child, if of sufficient understanding, and his parents should be informed of the entry and the parents should be told of the possibility of challenging the details or making representations about the entry.

6.17 The purpose of the register is to provide a record of all children in the area who are currently the subject of an inter-agency protection plan and to ensure that the plans are formally reconsidered at least every six months. The register will provide a central point of speedy inquiry for professional staff who are worried about a child and want to know whether the child is the subject of an inter-agency protection plan; and will provide information for managers and the [area child protection committee].

Some parents find all this rather unfair and heavy-handed. As 'Mrs Jones', the mother who burned her child (p. 371, above), says:

'You know, once you get the authorities in you never get them out. They look at everything you do. Never a week goes past without there's somebody in our flat checking up. They think you'll think it's just a social visit — but it's not, you know what they're looking for. Once you're on their books! They keep having case conferences about our family, I think it's appalling: *it's wrong*! They call them without you knowing, they hold them behind your back and so many outsiders go to them. People you've never met before know you. You go in and there's a new doctor, and when you give your name they say, Oh, *hello* Mrs Jones! — just like that — and you know they know all about you. I mind it, I really do mind it. All sorts of people who've got no reason to know about me get told all the details — they sit in on conferences about me, that I know nothing about, and *I'm* not told about them. I don't think it's right. I feel I've no privacy left at all'.

R v Harrow London Borough, ex p D
[1990] Fam 133, [1990] 3 All ER 12, [1989] 3 WLR 1239, [1989] FCR 729, [1990] 1 FLR 70, Court of Appeal

Following divorce proceedings, the mother was granted custody of three children, with fortnightly access to the father and a supervision order to the local authority. Access to the two elder children had been a cause of continuing litigation between the parents and there was a dispute over the paternity of the youngest child. In May 1986, following the father's allegations that the children were victims of physical abuse by the mother, the eldest child was examined by a paediatrician who found serious bruising and formed the view that the injuries were non-accidental. The child accused the mother of inflicting the injuries. A place of safety order was obtained and the two elder children were detained overnight in hospital and were examined by a consultant paediatrician the following day. The youngest child was never removed from home. The paediatrician found injuries to the eldest child which were incompatible with the mother's account. In June 1986 a case conference was convened, attended by the two paediatricians and the headmistress of the children's school. The mother's request to attend was refused but she was allowed to and did make written representations. As a result of the conference, the names of the children and the mother were placed on the 'at risk' register. The two children were then returned home. The mother applied for judicial review of the local authority's decision, on the basis that the conclusion of the case conference and the subsequent placing of the mother's and children's names on the register were unfair and unreasonable and contrary to natural justice. The judge dismissed the application and the mother appealed. The local authority contended, *inter alia*, that judicial review did not lie in respect of a decision to place a name on the register.

Butler-Sloss LJ: . . . Before the judge it was argued that the mother should have been permitted to attend the case conference and to have been heard. That suggestion is not pursued before this court. Rather, it is urged upon us that the lowest degree of fairness to the mother, the opportunity to know about and to be allowed to meet the material allegations made against her, was not afforded to her. It is said that the decision was unfair, and the decision-making process was defective on *Wednesbury* principles.

Mr Scrivener, for the appellant mother, made a number of points. The effect of entry on the register, even if the names of the children are subsequently removed, is to leave a stigma on the character of the mother. He asserts that the inclusion of the name of the mother in the register was the equivalent of a 'finding of guilt', that she had physically abused J. The record of J reads:

'3. Nature of injury and by whom inflicted, whether child abuse has been substantiated: bruise on back and forehead, graze on side of nose, near eye (black eye), inflicted by mother. Child abuse substantiated.'

That finding had to be on the basis of suitable evidence which she was entitled to know about and to have an opportunity to answer. He accepts that not all the minutiae require to be disclosed, but asserts that relevant and important matters were taken into account without prior disclosure.

The case conference was given background information about the family, which included the information that the child J had previously been on the register shortly after birth in 1979 for about 2 years. The mother says that she was unaware of that fact, and the accuracy of that statement was not explored. There were other matters relating to why J did not attend swimming lessons, why the children did not drink milk at school, the failure of the mother to take the youngest for medical check-ups, the explanation for an earlier accident to D and the failure of the social workers to ask the mother for an explanation of the injuries to J.

In the context of these facts, the earlier registration was of peripheral relevance.

What was critical was whether the mother was responsible for J's injuries. What the mother required was an opportunity of giving her account as to how these injuries could have occurred, and this was given to her by the consultant paediatrician. She took advantage of the opportunity to give her account, both orally and in written representations.

The child J was clearly on the register as a result of the findings and conclusions of the consultant paediatrician, together with the allegations of the child J and the unsatisfactory explanations of the mother. The failure of a social worker to elicit an explanation from the mother was not only understandable but, in my view, probably wise. In allegations of physical injury, the most appropriate person to be given the account of the parent is likely to be the paediatrician who is often specially qualified to assess its probability in the light of the type, place, severity and other aspects of the injuries which have occurred.

Although the mother's request to attend, be represented and speak at the case conference was refused, Mr Scrivener does not submit that the case conference erred in that respect. She was permitted to make written representations, both from herself and a friend. The representations were placed before the case conference. The decision to place the name of J on the register cannot, in my view, be faulted. Mr Scrivener accepts that if J's name was properly there, the inclusion of the other children was reasonable since they would be at risk.

I am satisfied that the procedure and the result did not in any way offend the *Wednesbury* principles. The conclusion of the judge was that the appellant failed '. . . to show that the decision was in any way unfair, unreasonable, or contrary to natural justice' (see [1989] 2 FLR 51, at p. 55F).

I agree with him.

That would be sufficient to dispose of this matter, but it has been contended by the respondent council that judicial review does not lie in respect of a decision to place a name upon the child abuse register. Mr McCarthy also submits that the decision of Waite J to grant judicial review of such a decision in *R v Norfolk County Council, ex p X* [1989] 2 FLR 120 was wrong. The facts in the *Norfolk* case were very different, of a plumber working in a house where a teenage girl made allegations of sexual abuse by him. She had twice previously been the victim of sexual abuse, and a few days later made similar allegations against another man. The plumber's name was entered in the child abuse register as an abuser, after a case conference. His employers were informed and suspended him, pending an internal inquiry. The first knowledge the plumber had of the allegations was the letter informing him of the decision to place his name on the register. He was not told that his employers had been informed.

Although the contents of the register are confidential, a significant number of people inevitably have to aware of the information contained in it. As the *Norfolk* case demonstrates, the effect upon outsiders may be dramatic. If the decision to register can be shown to be utterly unreasonable, in principle I cannot see why an application to review the decision cannot lie. In coming to its decision, the local authority is exercising a most important public function which can have serious consequences for the child and the alleged abuser. I respectfully agree with the decision of Waite J.

It would also seem that recourse to judicial review is likely to be, and undoubtedly ought to be, rare. Local authorities have laid on them by Parliament the specific duty of protection of children in their area. The case conference has a duty to make an assessment as to abuse and the abuser, if sufficient information is available. Of its nature, the mechanism of the case conference leading to the decision to place names on the register, and the decision-making process, is unstructured and informal.

It is accepted by Mr Scrivener that it is not a judicial process. It is part of a protection package for a child believed to have been the victim of abuse.

In balancing adequate protection to the child and fairness to an adult, the interest of an adult may have to be placed second to the needs of the child. All concerned in this difficult and delicate area should be allowed to perform their task without looking over their shoulder all the time for the possible intervention of the court.

Appeal dismissed.

Questions

(i) Do you agree that it was 'probably wise' of the social worker not to 'elicit an explanation' from the mother?

(ii) What are the objections to parental attendance at case conferences? What are the advantages?

(iii) What are the objections to a more structured and formal procedure at case conferences? What are the advantages (*a*) to the child, (*b*) to the parents or carers, or (*c*) to third parties (e.g. plumbers)?

Section 47 of the Children Act 1989 imposes extensive obligations upon local authorities to investigate and take action where necessary and upon other agencies to assist them. The reasons appear in the White Paper, *The Law on Child Care and Family Services* (1987):

42. Under existing legislation the local authority have a duty to investigate cases where information is received which suggests that there are grounds for care proceedings. The Review proposed that this should be replaced by a more active duty to investigate in any case where it is suspected that the child is suffering harm or is likely to do so. The Government endorse that proposal and accept that the enquiries made should be such as are necessary to enable the local authority to decide what action, if any, to take.

43. The Jasmine Beckford Report declared that there were powerful reasons why the duty on local authorities or health authorities to co-operate under section 22 of the NHS Act 1977 should in the context of child abuse be made more specific, to include the duty to consult and the duty to assist by advice and the supply of information so as to help in the management of such cases. Such a duty would, it was argued, operate as a positive and practical step to promote multidisciplinary working in this area, which is important not only at the stage of identification of abuse but also in subsequent follow-up action. The Government accept this view, and therefore intend to make legal provision for co-operation between statutory and voluntary agencies in the investigation of harm and protection of children at risk.

Question

In *The Protection of Children* (1983), Robert Dingwall, John Eekelaar and Topsy Murray suggest that the fragmentation of responsibility between different agencies is a useful means in a liberal democracy of reducing the power of the state to police families: would you rather rely upon organisational inadequacies or legal rights for that purpose?

An increasingly important part of the investigation, particularly when sexual abuse is suspected, is to 'interview' the child. Any interview which does not follow the guidance given in the *Report of the Inquiry into Child Abuse in Cleveland 1987* (1988) will certainly attract judicial criticism and will probably lose the case (see *Re E* [1990] FCR 793):

Introduction
12.1 An essential part of the investigation of an allegation or a complaint of sexual abuse will be an interview with the child if he or she is old enough to say what did nor did not happen to them. The child telling of abuse was often referred to as 'in disclosure' and assisting the child to talk of it as 'disclosure work'. The use and potential abuse of 'disclosure work' was the subject of a considerable amount of evidence to the Inquiry. Dr David Jones defined 'disclosure' as:
— 'a clinically useful concept to describe the process by which a child who has been sexually abused within the family gradually comes to inform the outside world of his/her plight'. He defined 'disclosure work' as: — the 'process by which professionals attempt to encourage or hasten the natural process of disclosure by a sexually abused child'.

When the child speaks of abuse
12.2 The young child may speak innocently of behaviour which an adult recognises as abuse; an older child may wish to unburden and tell of abuse to anyone they may trust and that may occur informally to, for instance, a parent, school teacher, paediatrician on a medical examination or foster mother. Dr Zeitlin told us that: — 'There is evidence that material produced spontaneously without prompting is undoubtedly the most reliable form of statements that children make, and often these have been made before disclosure interviews to various people.' However as a step in the inter-disciplinary investigation of sexual abuse there needs to be the formal process of interviewing the child.
12.3 During the Inquiry the question as to whether any child involved was or was not telling the truth was not an issue. The problems related to the interpretation by professionals of the comments of children who were not making clear allegations against their parents. Nevertheless, the question of whether or not to believe the child where there is concern about sexual abuse is important and evidence was given to the Inquiry about it.
12.4 What should an adult do when a child speaks of abuse? According to Dr Bentovim, until a few years ago, it was the practice for professionals to disbelieve the child. He said: — 'If a child described a sexual experience, you first of all disbelieved and it had to be proven to you, rather than you first of all taking it seriously and saying he is entitled to belief and then obviously investigating it properly and thoroughly.'
12.5 In the [draft] DHSS paper 'Child Abuse — Working Together' (April 1986) it is stated:
— 'A child's statement that he or she is being abused should be accepted as true until proved otherwise. Children seldom lie about sexual abuse.' . . .
  Professor Kolvin said that the Royal College of Psychiatrists was not happy with the statement of the DHSS document: — 'They felt that a statement by the child that sexual abuse has occurred should be taken seriously, but you are pre-judging the issue if you say that you believe it; in other words that you believe the child entirely.' He went on to say: — 'Always listen to the child and always take what they say seriously.' . . .

The interview with the child
12.10 When the possibility of sexual abuse is raised the formal interview with a child of sufficient age and understanding is a necessary step in the investigation. Different types of interview must be distinguished and the purposes for which the interview is being held must be clear.
12.11 In Cleveland there was confusion as to whether some interviews were being conducted to ascertain the facts or for therapeutic purposes or a mixture of both. It must also be clear

whether it is intended to 'facilitate' or assist the child to speak and if so in what way and using which aids.

. . .

Disclosure work

12.18 The problem arises when there is reason to believe there may be abuse and the child may need help to tell, or where the assessment to that date is inconclusive and then a somewhat different type of interview may take place. This is a second or so-called facilitative stage which needs further consideration. The interviewer at this time may be trying a more indirect approach, with the use of hypothetical or leading questions, or taking cue from the child's play or drawings. According to Dr Bentovim, it should be used sparingly by experts, who may include suitably trained social workers. . . . .

12.19 There is a danger, which should be recognised and avoided from the experience in Cleveland, that this facilitative second stage may be seen as a routine part of the general interview, instead of a useful tool to be used sparingly by experts in special cases. In the first stage the child tells the interviewer. The second stage is a process whereby the professional attempts to encourage the child who may be reluctant to tell the story.

. . .

Disagreement between the professionals

12.27 The main area of disagreement between the child psychiatrists from whom the Inquiry received contributions, is as to the desirability of and limits upon the facilitative second stage.

12.28 On the one hand, in Dr Bentovim's opinion the use of leading, alternative, hypothetical questions should be available 'but it is very important that whoever uses such techniques should be very aware of what the consequences are in terms of the fact that the interviewer immediately has problems in terms of its probability, in terms of evidential value and there is always a balance between those factors. . . . My reading of the research is that a free statement, a spontaneous statement made by a child is going to be the most acute.'

12.29 The experience of his team was that children were usually highly relieved by the interview.

On the other hand, Professor Kolvin said: — 'I am uneasy with the concept of disclosure, which really goes hell-bent for trying to get some idea of 'yes' or 'no' on the basis of almost a coercive interview with the child and also does not take into consideration the possibility that perhaps nothing has happened or that perhaps we will not know.'

. . .

Agreement of the professionals

12.34 All those who provided evidence to the Inquiry were agreed on the following points to be observed in conducting all interviews. We endorse their views:

1. The undesirability of calling them 'disclosure' interviews, which precluded the notion that sexual abuse might not have occurred.
2. All interviews should be undertaken only by those with some training, experience and aptitude for talking with children.
3. The need to approach each interview with an open mind.
4. The style of the interview should be open-ended questions to support and encourage the child in free recall.
5. There should be where possible only one and not more than two interviews for the purpose of evaluation, and the interview should not be too long.
6. The interview should go at the pace of the child and not of the adult.
7. The setting for the interview must be suitable and sympathetic.
8. It must be accepted that at the end of the interview the child may have given no information to support the suspicion of sexual abuse and position will remain unclear.
9. There must be careful recording of the interview and what the child says, whether or not there is a video recording.
10. It must be recognised that the use of facilitative techniques may create difficulties in subsequent court proceedings.
11. The great importance of adequate training for all those engaged in this work.
12. In certain circumstances it may be appropriate to use the special skills of a 'facilitated' interview. That type of interview should be treated as a second stage. The interviewer must be conscious of the limitations and strengths of the techniques employed. In such cases the interview should only be conducted by those with special skills and specific training.

Parents at interviews

12.35 The professionals who gave evidence to the Inquiry were unanimous about the unsuitability of having a parent present at an interview held because of the suspicion of sexual abuse. Dr Bentovim said the presence of parents made the interview very difficult, but the presence of a person familiar to the child, such as teacher or social worker, may be helpful to the child. However he/she must not take part in the interview.

. . .

Disclosure work in Cleveland

12.40 In Cleveland before 1987 sexual abuse had been identified by complaint from the child or from an adult. The need to interview children believed to be sexually but reluctant to disclose such abuse was not widely recognised and there was a lack of expertise in the Cleveland area (and almost certainly in many other areas) in this specialised field. A number of social workers had attended conferences and work shops on the subject, some of them at Great Ormond Street.

12.41 During 1987 there appears to have been an immediate response to a suspicion of child sexual abuse that somebody should do disclosure work with the child. It is not clear whether this was intended to listen to the child's account or to use specialised techniques learnt at workshops attended by some professionals.

12.42 There can however be no doubt that there were interviews carried out in Cleveland during 1987 which fall into the type of interviews criticised in the Family Law Reports. It was apparent that various feelings came together at the time of interviewing some at least of these children—anxiety, the need for a solution, beliefs about 'denial' and the therapeutic benefits for children of talking about abuse, the perceived need to believe the child and some learnt information about techniques of interviewing. These included matching the pressure on the child not to tell with pressure by the interviewer on the child at the interview. There was in many instances a presumption that abuse had occurred and the child was either not disclosing or denying that abuse. There was insufficient expertise, over-enthusiasm, and those conducting the interviews seemed unaware of the extent of pressure, even coercion, in their approach. There were dangers, which became apparent in some cases, of misinterpretation of the content of the interview. Some interviews we saw would not be likely to be acceptable in any court as evidence of sexual abuse. The Official Solicitor refers to an aspect of this—the dangers with such interviews of costly and protracted litigation. There is also a danger with a great deal of written material available on how to conduct an interview, of the inexperienced interviewer going through each of a number of stages with each child interviewed, rather than considering the best way to interview a particular child.

Anatomically correct or complete dolls

12.54 These dolls were according to Dr Bentovim, imported by his team at Great Ormond Street during 1982/1983 from the United States. They have found the dolls to be extremely helpful to enable children to speak of their experiences, particularly for young children or older children with difficulties in communication. He said: — 'Inevitably as accurate diagnosis is the first step in treatment we began to use the dolls increasingly during the diagnostic assessment phase of our work.'

12.55 Over the years the Great Ormond Street team have developed a particular expertise in interviewing the children generally and in the use of these dolls. The Inquiry does not in any way wish to criticise the use of these dolls in the hands of such experts.

12.56 The problem from the evidence to the Inquiry appears to arise when well-meaning professionals, some of whom have attended Great Ormond Street workshops, or who have read of their work or the work in the United States on the techniques of interviewing children and the use of dolls as an initial part of such interviewing techniques, take to using these dolls as part of the standard interviewing process. There are dangers in their use at too early a stage in the evaluation, in the hands of the inexperienced operator.

12.57 We were concerned to learn of the provision of such dolls as basic equipment for police, social workers or clinical psychologists in Cleveland during the crisis without perhaps sufficient expertise in their use.

. . .

12.60 Dr Cameron in his paper to the Inquiry said of the dolls: — 'These are often sadly misused as the first line of approach to a possibly sexually abused child. These dolls are very potent cues, and it must be borne in mind that the more helpful the cue, the greater the possibility of a false positive result.

'It is now accepted that the majority of sexually abused children are likely to make the dolls behave in a sexually explicit manner; in contrast to the majority of non-abused children who use the dolls for non-sexual play (enacting tea parties and other family gatherings). However it must be borne in mind that some non-sexually abused children will make these dolls pretend to pass urine, and possibly even pretend to have intercourse. This serves to highly the fact that a 'positive' response to the dolls is only an indicator that the child may have been sexually abused, and is *not* an absolute diagnostic test.'

Questions

(i) This chapter of the Report ends by quoting the Children's Legal Centre:

'We are very concerned that the desire for "inter-agency co-operation" and "multi-disciplinary team approaches" to child abuse can conflict with childrens' desire, need and right to speak in confidence to others about things that concern them. . . . The Childrens' Legal Centre believes that childrens' right to and need for confidential advice and counselling has been ignored by many if not all the agencies involved in investigating and seeking to prevent child abuse.'

Can you see an answer which reconciles the child's right to privacy (article 16 of the United Nations Convention on the Rights of the Child) with his right to protection from neglect and abuse (articles 3, 9, 34 and 39)?
(ii) *Working Together* (1991 draft) now says this about the child's 'testimony':

5.25 . . . A child's statement about an allegation of abuse, whether in confirmation or denial, should always be taken seriously. A child's testimony should not be viewed as inherently less reliable than that of an adult. However, professionals need to be aware that allegations may be a sign of a disturbed family environment and an indication that the child may need help. . . .

Do you think this is an improvement on the draft referred to above?
(iii) If a child's statement is needed to prove the case, what is the best way of presenting it to the court: (*a*) by the child giving sworn or unsworn evidence in court (see s. 96(1) and (2) of the Children Act 1989), (*b*) by a professional witness giving evidence about what the child has said (s. 96(3) to (7)), (*c*) by a lay witness, such as a foster parent, giving evidence about what the child has said (ibid), (*d*) by a party, such as a parent, giving evidence about what the child has said, (*e*) by a video recording of the child being interviewed (what sort of evidence is this?), (*f*) by a welfare officer, guardian ad litem or the Official Solicitor reporting what the child has said (see *H v H (minor)* [1990] Fam 86, sub nom *H v H and C (child abuse: evidence)* [1989] 3 All ER 740), or (*f*) by the judge or magistrates seeing the child privately?

4 Assessment and protection orders

As we have seen (p. 580, above) Packman found that a high proportion of compulsory admissions began with a 'place of safety' order, which could be obtained ex parte and last for up to 28 days with no right of appeal. The proportion found by Dartington (1986) was even higher. The House of Commons Social Services Committee Report on *Children in Care* (1984) voiced a general concern:

123. Place of safety orders are primarily intended to ensure that children at risk of abuse or neglect or beyond control can be removed from immediate danger until a decision is made as to their longer-term future. They are thus likely to be the first formal step towards care for children who have suffered abuse or neglect, or who are in moral or other danger — for example, through solvent abuse. There is growing disquiet at the way in which place of safety orders are in fact being used. Dr Jean Packman of the University of Exeter submitted a cogent memorandum based on her recent research which suggested that some practice represented an abuse or misinterpretation of the powers given by statute. Representatives of the Magistrates' Association had found that orders were being used increasingly as a means of commencing care proceedings rather than as an emergency measure; one magistrate from Wales referred to that being so in 90 per cent of the cases, another to 50 per cent. . . .

124. There is insufficient evidence to be able to determine whether or not place of safety procedures are in fact being abused; but what evidence is to hand on, for example, the high proportion of teenagers subject to such orders, and research evidence showing the proportion of children returned home at the expiry of an order without even being made subject to a supervision order, does suggest that there are good grounds for anxiety. Various propositions were made to the Committee for altering the statutory basis of such orders, generally involving a strict limitation of the time for which orders could run and the introduction of a court hearing at as early a stage as possible.

Evidence of something remarkably like abuse, however, was found in the *Cleveland Report* (1988):

Place of safety orders
10.6 The initial route to the Juvenile Court was by way of place of safety orders. Between 1st January and 31st July 1987, 276 place of safety orders were applied for by social workers under the powers granted in s. 28 of the Children and Young Persons Act 1969. . . . All but one application appears to have been made ex parte, that is to say without the parent present, and none appears to have been refused. . . .
10.7 The Social Services Department operated a highly interventionist policy in the use of place safety orders. The effect of their general approach to the use of these orders was accentuated by the memorandum of the 29th May issued by Mr Bishop, directing social workers to apply for them on receiving a diagnosis of child sexual abuse from a paediatrician. Further a trend away from applications for the maximum 28 days to periods not exceeding 7 days as advocated in their manual was not maintained in 1987 and was specifically reversed in early June . . .
10.8 Before the crisis period of May/June and before the 29th May memorandum a number of place of safety orders in cases of diagnosis of sexual abuse were applied for and granted for 28 days. The reason for the longer order was not so much the need to protect the child as the need perceived by social workers to have sufficient time to engage in 'disclosure work' with the child.
10.9 Of the 276 orders were applied for out of hours by the Emergency Duty Team. The majority of the orders were likely to have been granted during the day. We learnt however that of those 227, 174 were heard by a single magistrate at home, during the hours of court sittings, despite a clear understanding between the Clerk to the Justices and the Social Services Department that social workers would make these applications in the first instance to the full court. . . .

Interim care orders
10.10 During early June the numbers of interim care orders applied for dramatically increased. On Monday 8th June there were 45 applications for interim care orders waiting to be heard. This increase in the workload led the Clerk to the Justices, Mr Cooke, to talk to one of the Court Liaison Officers, Mr Morris to discuss the implications for resources and to ask for a meeting with the Director of Social Services. In the evidence to the Inquiry there was some difference of recollection as to what was said between Mr Cooke and Mr Morris. Mr Morris went away with the impression that Mr Cooke was suggesting that Social Services should apply for 28 day orders to ease the strain on the courts, and he then advised the Emergency Duty Team to apply for 28 day orders.

Level of concern
10.13 Mr Davies said that there were three matters of special concern to magistrates receiving the applications.

1. The effect on the courts of applications which were increasing in volume and complexity. There was great concern about the backlog of cases and the delay to the regular work of the courts.
2. Prior to 1987 it was not the practice of the Social Services Department to refuse access to parents on the obtaining of a place of safety order and this approach was known to the Bench. Mr Morris told us that in the past access was almost invariably granted and denial was a marked change of policy. The requirement of separation of child from parents during 'disclosure work', which might take weeks or months was a new development. Mr Davies said that the denial of access on a place of safety order or on an interim care order was recognised by the magistrates as a most serious deprivation for parents and children and knowledge that it was now a common practice was a matter of deep concern. The reason for denying access in particular circumstances was known to the magistrates but there was unease that access might be denied too readily.
3. The conflict of medical evidence was also of great concern. Mr Davies told us that: — 'It was the first time in my experience that Teesside magistrates had been invited to assess the quality of conflicting medical evidence provided by experts in child abuse.' Mr Cooke said that his magistrates were not used to dealing with that sort of thing. . . .

Questions

(i) Look back at the account of child sexual abuse on pp. 375: what level of concern do you think might justify removing a child and keeping him away from his parents for weeks in order to undertake disclosure work?

(ii) Look back to the discussion of ex parte orders in domestic violence cases on p. 403: why do you think that well-meaning social workers prefer to remove the child before telling the parents that they are bringing proceedings?

Working Together (1991 draft) encourages a different approach to removing children from home:

5.15 Except in an emergency the arrangements and timing for the removal of children from their homes should be agreed following consultation with all appropriate professionals (which may include paediatricians and psychiatrists) and should take account of the likely effect on the child and other members of the family. It may be possible on occasions when it is necessary to remove both adults and children (for example, in order to prevent intimidation) for the children to be moved to safe accommodation by the social services separately from any arrest of adults by police. Any decision to move the child should balance the potential effect this would have in itself on the child and his family with the need to obtain as much information as possible to assess the scale and characteristics of any abuse.

As for the law, the Cleveland Report supported the proposals, made in the Review of Child Care Law (1985) and the White Paper (1987), to replace place of safety orders with a new Emergency Protection Order. The changes are explained by the DH in *Court Orders* (1991), volume 1 of their Guidance and Regulations on the Children Act 1989:

4.28 Emergency protection orders replace the much-criticised place of safety orders which could be obtained under a number of provisions in previous legislation. The purpose of the new order, as its name suggests, is to enable the child in a genuine emergency to be removed from where he is or be kept where he is, if and only if this is what is necessary to provide immediate short-term protection. Nearly every aspect of the new provisions, including the grounds for the order, its effect, opportunities for challenging it and duration, are different.
4.29 The essential features of the new provisions are:
   (*a*) the court has to be satisfied that the child is likely to suffer significant harm or cannot be seen in circumstances where the child might be suffering significant harm;
   (*b*) duration is limited to eight days with a possible extension of seven days;

(c)   certain persons may apply to discharge the order (to be heard after 72 hours);

(d)   the person obtaining the order has limited parental responsibility;

(e)   the court may make directions as to contact with the child and/or medical or psychiatric examination or assessment;

(f)   there is provision for a single justice to make an emergency protection order;

(g)   applications may be made in the absence of any other interested parties (ie *ex-parte*), and may, with the leave of the clerk of the court, be made orally;

(h)   the application must name the child, and where it does not, must describe him as clearly as possible.

4.30 These key provisions have been limited to what is necessary to protect the child, but it remains an extremely serious step. It must not be regarded — as sometimes was the case with place of safety orders — as a routine response to allegations of child abuse or as a routine first step to initiating care proceedings. The new grounds require some evidence that the situation is sufficiently serious to justify such severe powers of intervention being made available.

Nevertheless decisive action to protect the child is essential once it appears that the circumstances fall within one of the grounds in section 44(1). Under section 47(6) the authority must apply for an emergency protection order or another of the orders specified if they are refused access to the child or denied information about his whereabouts while carrying out enquiries, unless they are satisfied that the child's welfare can be satisfactorily safeguarded without their taking such action. . . .

The grounds for an order are these:

44. — (1) Where any person ('the applicant') applies to the court for an order to be made under this section with respect to a child, the court may make the order if, but only if it is satisfied that —

(a)   there is reasonable cause to believe that the child is likely to suffer significant harm if —

(i)   he is not removed to accommodation provided by or on behalf of the applicant; or

(ii)   he does not remain in the place in which he is then being accommodated;

(b)   in the case of an application made by a local authority —

(i)   the enquiries are being made with respect to the child under section 47(1)(b); and

(ii)   those enquiries are being frustrated by access to the child being unreasonably refused to a person authorised to seek access and that the applicant has a reasonable cause to believe that access to the child is required as a matter of urgency; or

(c)   in the case of an application made by an authorised person —

(i)   the applicant has reasonable cause to suspect that a child is suffering, or is likely to suffer, significant harm;

(ii)   the applicant is making enquiries with respect to the child's welfare; and

(iii)   those enquiries are being frustrated by access to the child being unreasonably refused to a person authorised to seek access and the applicant has reasonable cause to believe that access to the child is required as a matter of urgency.

As the DH Guidance observes:

4.44 As with all orders under the Act, even where the above conditions apply the court will not automatically make an emergency protection order. It must still consider the welfare principle and the presumption of no order [see pp. 545 and 547, above]. In most cases it is unlikely that the parents will be present at the hearing. With only one side of the case before it the court will want to examine very carefully the information it is given, especially where the basis of the application is likelihood of future harm or inability to see the child. It may be that the initial order will be made for a very short time such as the next available hearing date so that an extension to the order will be on notice to parents and others.

Section 44(1)(b) (local authorities) and (c) (authorised persons, see p. 608, below) seek to provide for children like Kimberley Carlile (see Greenwich, 1987), where the social worker was refused access but did not feel that he had sufficient cause to seek a place of safety order under s. 28 of the Children and Young Persons Act 1969 or a warrant under s. 40 of the Children and Young Persons Act 1933 (also repealed). The Review of Child Care Law

(1985), White Paper (1987), and Cleveland Report (1988) did not adopt the idea of a 'lesser' order requiring the parents to co-operate with a multi-disciplinary assessment of the child, but this found its way into the Children Act 1989 during its passage through Parliament. Its purpose is explained in the DH Guidance as follows:

4.6 The child assessment order, established by section 43, had no parallel in previous legislation. It deals with the single issue of enabling an assessment of the child to be made where significant harm is suspected but the child is not thought to be at immediate risk (requiring his removal, or keeping him in hospital), the local authority or authorised person considers that an assessment is required, and the parents or other persons responsible for him have refused to co-operate. Its purpose is to allow the local authority or authorised person to ascertain enough about the state of the child's health or development or the way in which he has been treated to decide what further action, if any, is required. It is less interventionist than the emergency protection order, interim care order and interim supervision order and should not be used where the circumstances of the case suggest that one of these orders would be more appropriate.
. . .
4.9 A child assessment order will usually be most appropriate where the harm to the child is long-term and cumulative rather than sudden and severe. The circumstances may be nagging concern about a child who appears to be failing to thrive; or the parents are ignorant of or unwilling to face up to possible harm to their child because of the state of his health or development; or it appears that the child may be subject to wilful neglect or abuse but not to such an extent as to place him at serious immediate risk. Sexual abuse, which covers a wide range of behaviour, can fall in this category: The harm to the child can be long-term rather than immediate and it does not necessarily require emergency action. However, emergency action should not be avoided where disclosure of the abuse is itself likely to put the child at immediate risk of significant harm and/or where there is an urgent need to gather particular forensic evidence which would not otherwise be forthcoming in relation to the likelihood of significant harm.
. . .
4.12 The court can allow up to 7 days for the assessment. The order must specify the date which the assessment is to begin. The applicant should make the necessary arrangements in advance of the application, so that it would usually be possible to complete within such a period an initial multi-disciplinary assessment of the child's medical, intellectual, emotional, social and behavioural needs.
. . .
4.15 Section 43(9) provides for keeping the child away from home for the purposes of the assessment. This is intended to be a reserve provision, and if used the number of overnight stays should be kept as low as possible. The assessment should be conducted with as little trauma for the child and parents as possible. It is important that the child assessment order is not regarded as a variant of the emergency protection order with its removal power: The purposes of the two orders are quite different. The child may only be kept away from home in the circumstances specified, namely:

    (*a*) the court is satisfied that it is necessary for the purposes of the assessment;
    (*b*) it is done in accordance with directions specified in the order; and it is limited to such period or periods (which need not be the full period of the order) specified in the order.

Questions

(i) Are you convinced by these arguments of the need for a child assessment order?
(ii) Why is it thought less drastic than an emergency protection order?
(iii) The DH Guidance talks about removing the alleged abuser rather than the child:

4.31 Where the need for emergency action centres on alleged abuse of the child the local authority will always want to explore the possibility of providing services to and/or accommodation for the alleged abuser as an alternative to the removal of the child. This could be on a voluntary basis backed up by the provisions of schedule 2 paragraph 5 which gives authorities the discretion to provide assistance with finding alternative housing or cash assistance to the person who leaves the family home. Such practical assistance may be crucial in persuading the alleged abuser to co-operate in this way. Existing legislation makes no public law provision empowering a court to order an alleged abuser out of the family home. However, in certain circumstances private law remedies may be used to achieve the same effect, and the local authority should explore these where it is in the child's best interest to do so. The non-abusing parent may agree to apply to the county court for a short-term ouster injunction under section 1 of the Domestic Violence and Matrimonial Proceedings Act 1976 or to the magistrates' court for an exclusion order under section 16 of the Domestic Proceedings and Magistrates' Court Act 1978, forcing the alleged abuser out of the home. This may be particularly appropriate in sexual abuse cases where the non-abusing parent has no wish to protect or shield the alleged abuser and where immediate removal of the child is not always in the child's best interests.

The Law Commission, in their Working Paper on *Domestic Violence and Occupation of the Family Home* (1989) suggest that the court might have power, during or instead of an emergency protection or interim care order, to order a suspected abuser to leave the home. What are the arguments for and against this?

(iv) Under s. 46, where a police officer has reasonable cause to believe that a child would otherwise be likely to suffer significant harm, he may take the child into police protection for up to 72 hours: why should such a power be thought necessary?

5 Care proceedings

Care proceedings no longer cover both the villains and victims: they are designed solely for cases where the parental shortcomings are such that the local authority should assume parental responsibility for the child. In reality, as Robert Dingwall, John Eekelaar and Topsy Murray observed in *Care or Control?* (1981), the summary of their study of child protection work, this was what usually happened:

We then describe what we hold to be the central issues in care proceedings: that is, the matters which tend to be primarily in contention before the court. The first is the condition of the child. However, we observe that allegations concerning a child's physical condition are not often contested in court: medical evidence on this matter is rarely challenged. This evidence is seen as being of a factual nature. However, medical evidence often extended to surmises of the causes of the child's condition and, although the parents might dispute this in abuse cases, it seems rare for this to be done by the production of opposing evidence, perhaps due to the difficulty of persuading one doctor to testify against another in matters of this kind. In neglect cases it seems unlikely that medical evidence on causation will be strongly challenged at all. We suggest that written medical evidence of this nature should be admissible if all parties agree. We were also struck by the lack of resort to expert testimony when the emotional condition of the child was in question. The reason may lie in lawyers' distrust of psychiatric evidence, but is more likely to be found, in our view, in the readiness of lay people to resort to their common sense notions of normality in making these assessments. This attitude is taken further when attempts are made to assess the effects on a child of its environment. Fieldworkers and courts are prepared to use such concepts in determining the degree of deviance in parental behaviour (and, accordingly, the child's upbringing) and to impute from that consequences for the child. . . .

This leads us to consider the central issue in care proceedings as being assessment of parental competence. We build our discussion of this around a particular case (Leonard). . . . The main point in dispute was whether a burn had been deliberately inflicted on the child. Nevertheless, as we show, the character of the child's parents was examined from a multitude of facets and the picture revealed was crucial to the outcome of the case. We also show how significant, in this and in other cases, is the issue of the preparedness of the parent to co-operate with social services and to accept the legitimacy of their concern. All these matters are as crucial in court as they are in the earlier stages of the process: they amount, in effect, to the construction of a case against the parent, which the parent is obliged to 'answer'.

We argue next that a third major issue in care proceedings relates to the plans regarding the child and the family held by the authority should they establish their case. However, the technical division of care proceedings into two stages (based on the criminal model), if strictly applied, would relegate this matter to consideration after the finding had been made that a ground for making an order had been established. Insistence on the two-stage procedure seemed to vary and to depend heavily on the view of its appropriateness held by the local authority lawyers in the area. Our data suggested that the division was, in practice, difficult, if not impossible, to maintain, and indeed its observation might be inconsistent with the 'care or control' test. However, we saw no attempts to distinguish evidence presented to establish one of the 'grounds', and evidence directed at the 'care or control' test.

. . . We revert to our contention that the purpose of seeking care proceedings may frequently have as its prime object the acquisition of greater control over family functioning, and that care orders are frequently used for this purpose. We consider the propriety of using care orders in this way and conclude by referring to the very limited opportunities, in the available methods of disposition, for making orders which specify with any degree of refinement or precision, the measures that may be taken concerning the child.

The idea that the criteria for care and supervision orders should focus upon the condition of the child, the shortcomings of the home and the comparative advantages of local authority intervention can also be found in the recommendations of the *Review of Child Care Law* (1985):

15.12 In our view the primary justification for the state to initiate proceedings seeking compulsory powers is actual or likely harm to the child. . . .

. . .

15.14 We consider that newly drafted grounds should make it clear that 'harm' consists of a deficit in or detriment to the standard of health, development and well-being which can reasonably be expected for the particular child. By 'development' we mean not only his physical progress but also his intellectual, emotional and social or behavioural development, so that it is clear that a child who is failing to learn to control his anti-social behaviour as others do is included. We refer to the standard expected for the particular child because some children have characteristics or handicaps which mean that they cannot be expected to be as healthy or well-developed as others, but equally it must be clear that if the child needs special care or attention (perhaps, for example, because he is unusually difficult to control) then this is to be expected for him. However, the standard should only be that which is reasonable to expect, rather than the best that could possibly be achieved, for each particular child. To apply the 'best' standard would be to introduce by other means the risk that a child could be removed from home simply because some other arrangements could cater better for his needs than care by his parents.

15.15 We consider that, having set an acceptable standard of upbringing for the child, it should be necessary to show some *substantial* deficit in that standard. Minor short-comings in the health care provided or minor deficits in physical, psychological or social development should not give rise to compulsory intervention unless they are having, or are likely to have, serious and lasting effects upon the child. The courts are used to assessing degrees of harm, for example in the context of prosecution for assaults, and we consider that they could also do so here.

15.16 The inclusion of 'well-being' in the standard to be expected is intended to cover those deficits which cannot necessarily be described in terms of health or development but which may equally amount to 'harm' to a child. Principal amongst these is ill-treatment. A child who has suffered non-accidental injury may not have suffered any lasting impairment in his health and the resulting emotional damage may be difficult to prove. The same may be said of older children who suffer sexual abuse. We consider that the concept of substantial detriment to their well-being will cover such cases and adequately distinguish between cases of real harm to the child and cases of acceptable variation in parenting standards.

. . .

15.18 In our view, a requirement that the harm be 'likely' will place a burden of proof upon local authorities which will be sufficiently difficult for them to discharge, especially in relation to mental or emotional harm, and this will prevent unwarranted intervention. A substantial or serious likelihood would be much more difficult to assess than substantial or serious harm and is not recommended. We have also considered whether anticipatory harm should be restricted by reference to specific circumstances from which risk could be inferred. . . . However, a list would inevitably leave gaps unless the categories of risk were themselves very broadly expressed. Such broad expression would defeat the purpose of having express reasons for apprehended harm. In any event, it would perpetuate the arbitrariness and unfairness complained of by the Select Committee, would be complex and unwieldy, and would amount to a consolidation of the existing conditions rather than a genuine simplification in the law. . . .

15.20 As regards more specific free-standing conditions, . . . we do not consider them desirable. Their operation can be arbitrary or unfair and we doubt the traditional claim that specific preconditions of that sort operate to protect parents and children against unwarranted interference by the state. Rather we consider that such specific preconditions in practice may have the opposite effect and operate as magnets for drawing children within the sphere of compulsory care. . . . Overall, there is a danger that very specific preconditions lead to a generalised view that once the conditions are satisfied an order follows unless there is some special reason for refusing one. What is more, the section 3 grounds, by focusing on parental unfitness, may have a stigmatising effect which may itself provoke unnecessary conflict and be detrimental to all concerned by unnecessarily prolonging proceedings and adding to their traumatic effects. We therefore, recommend that the sole primary ground should be actual or likely harm.

15.23 In our view the ground should also require that the source of the harm is the absence of a reasonable degree of parental care. Put another way, the court should be expressly required to find that the care available to the child is not merely wanting, but falls below an objectively acceptable level or that he is beyond parental control so that he cannot benefit from the care on offer. At present, the use of words such as 'prevented or neglected' or 'avoidably impaired', together with the care or control test in section 1(2), carry with them the flavour of lack of parental care. They fail, however, to express it clearly and more importantly give no indication of how great that failure must be. . . .

15.24 We also consider that the grounds should in future make a clear reference to the likely effectiveness of an order. At present in section 1(2) there is the requirement that the child's need for care or control is unlikely to be met unless the court makes an order. Our impression is that the test is often satisfied by proof that his needs will not be met outside care, rather than by positive proof that a care order or supervision order will result in his needs being met or at least better catered for, and further that intervention will not do more overall harm than good. In our view the matter should be put beyond doubt. We consider that this might be achieved best by linking the idea of effectiveness with the child's best interests, that being the ultimate purpose of an order and in our view itself a matter which needs to be drawn expressly to the court's attention. Accordingly, we think there is a strong case in future for requiring the court to be satisfied before it makes an order that it is the most effective means available to it (including refusing an order) of safeguarding and promoting the child's welfare.

The *Children Act 1989* provides as follows:

31. – (1) On the application of any local authority or authorised person, the court may make an order –

(a) placing the child with respect to whom the application is made in the care of a designated local authority; or

(b) putting him under the supervision of a designated local authority or of a probation officer.

(2) A court may only make a care order or supervision order if it is satisfied –

(a) that the child concerned is suffering, or is likely to suffer, significant harm; and

(b) that the harm, or likelihood of harm, is attributable to –

(i) the care given to the child, or likely to be given to him if the order were not made, not being what it would be reasonable to expect a parent to give to him; or

(ii) the child's being beyond parental control.

(3) No care order or supervision order may be made with respect to a child who has reached the age of seventeen (or sixteen, in the case of a child who is married).

(4) An application under this section may be made on its own or in any other family proceedings.

(5) The court may –

(a) on an application for a care order, make a supervision order;

(b) on an application for a supervision order, make a care order.

(6) Where an authorised person proposes to make an application under this section he shall –

(*a*) if it is reasonably practicable to do so; and

(*b*) before making the application,

consult the local authority appearing to him to be the authority in whose area the child concerned is ordinarily resident.

(7) An application made by an authorised person shall not be entertained by the court if, at the time when it is made, the child concerned is —

(*a*) the subject of an earlier application for a care order, or supervision order, which has not been disposed of; or

(*b*) subject to —

(i) a care order or supervision order;

(ii) an order under section 7(7)(*b*) of the Children and Young Persons Act 1969; or

(iii) a supervision requirement within the meaning of the Social Work (Scotland) Act 1968.

(8) The local authority designated in a care order must be —

(*a*) the authority within whose area the child is ordinarily resident; or

(*b*) where the child does not reside in the area of a local authority, the authority within whose area any circumstances arose in consequence of which the order is being made.

(9) In this section —

'authorised person' means —

(*a*) the National Society for the Prevention of Cruelty to Children and any of its officers; and

(*b*) any person authorised by order by the Secretary of State to bring proceedings under this section and any officer of a body which is so authorised;

'harm' means ill-treatment or the impairment of health or development;

'development' means physical, intellectual, emotional, social or behavioural development;

'health' means physical or mental health; and

'ill-treatment' includes sexual abuse and forms of ill-treatment which are not physical.

(10) Where the question of whether harm suffered by the child is significant turns on the child's health or development, his health or development shall be compared with that which could reasonably be expected of a similar child.

(11) In this Act —

'a care order' means (subject to section 105(1)) an order under subsection (1)(*a*) and (except where express provision to the contrary is made) includes an interim care order made under section 38; and

'a supervision order' means an order under subsection (1)(*b*) and (except where express provision to the contrary is made) includes an interim supervision order made under section 38.

Questions

(i) How many of the following might be covered by the threshold criteria in s. 31(2): (*a*) a ten year old girl whose mother had recently begun cohabiting with a man previously convicted of sexual offences (cf. s. 1(2)(*bb*) of the Children and Young Persons Act 1969; (*b*) an 18 month old boy accommodated by the local authority since birth, whose mother had then been homeless and immature but had kept in touch as much as she could and now had a decent home to offer (cf. *W v Sunderland Borough Council* [1980] 2 All ER 514, [1980] 1 WLR 1101; (*c*) an unborn child expected by a mentally disturbed mother with a history of drug abuse (cf. *Re F (in utero) (wardship)* [1988] Fam 122, [1988] 2 FLR 307); (*d*) a three year old boy who has been in and out of care because his mother recognised that, from time to time, because of her own problems, the local authority could care for him better than she could (cf. *O'D v South Glamorgan County Council* (1980) 78 LGR 522); (*e*) an eight year old girl boarded to foster parents as a baby when her parents came to this country to pursue their education, who has remained with the same foster parents almost since birth, but whose parents now wish to take her home with them (cf. *J v C* [1970] AC 668, [1969] 1 All ER 788);

(*f*) a six year old boy whose father has shown little interest since arranging for him to be accommodated by the local authority after his mother died when he was four; or (*g*) a mentally handicapped girl of 14 who has been abandoned by her parents since entering residential care when she was two?

(ii) The Review (1985) and White Paper (1987) proposed that the local authority might be able to apply to become guardian in cases such as (*f*) and (*g*): why in the end was this not thought necessary?

(iii) Does the idea of a 'similar' child in s. 31(10) mean a child (*a*) with similar physical or psychological characteristics, or (*c*) of a similar racial, ethnic or religious background?

(iv) If (*b*) and (*c*) are included, can this be reconciled with the philosophy of the Review of Child Care Law (1985) (p. 423, above)?

(v) As well as the threshold criteria, the court must also apply the welfare test in the light of the 'checklist' (p. 545, above) and the 'non-intervention principle' (p. 547, above): do these amount to the same thing as the 'effectiveness test'?

(vi) The checklist requires the court to consider alternatives: care and supervision orders can only be made on application, but the court may make s. 8 orders (see p. 541, above) of its own motion instead: can you think of the sort of s. 8 orders which might be made (not only in cases like *Re L (a minor) (care proceedings: wardship)* [1990] FCR 509, [1991] 1 FLR 14 and *Re L (a minor) (care proceedings: wardship) (No 2)* [1991] 1 FLR 29, p. 616, below)?

(vii) These criteria have to cater for every case in which a child requires compulsory care or supervision (cf. ss. 9(2) and 100(2) of the Children Act 1989): can they do so?

(viii) Local authorities can only invoke the inherent (wardship) jurisdiction of the High Court in order to achieve a result which cannot be achieved by an order under the Act and only then if there is reasonable cause to believe that the child is otherwise likely to suffer significant harm (s. 100(3) to (5)): can you think of an example?

Section 100 is one of the most controversial provisions of the Act:

Restrictions on use of wardship jurisdiction
100. — (1) Section 7 of the Family Law Reform Act 1969 (which gives the High Court power to place a ward of court in the care, or under the supervision, of a local authority) shall cease to have effect.

    (2) No court shall exercise the High Court's inherent jurisdiction with respect to children —
      (*a*) so as to require a child to be placed in the care, or put under the supervision, of a local authority;
      (*b*) so as to require a child to be accommodated by or on behalf of a local authority;
      (*c*) so as to make a child who is the subject of a care order a ward of court; or
      (*d*) for the purpose of conferring on any local authority power to determine any question which has arisen, or which may arise, in connection with any aspect of parental responsibility for a child.

    (3) No application for any exercise of the court's inherent jurisdiction with respect to children may be made by a local authority unless the authority have obtained the leave of the court.

    (4) The court may only grant leave if it is satisfied that —
      (*a*) the result which the authority wish to achieve could not be achieved through the making of any order of a kind to which subsection (5) applies; and
      (*b*) there is reasonable cause to believe that if the court's inherent jurisdiction is not exercised with respect to the child he is likely to suffer significant harm.

    (5) This subsection applies to any order —
      (*a*) made otherwise than in the exercise of the court's inherent jurisdiction; and

(*b*) which the local authority is entitled to apply for (assuming, in the case of any application which may only be made with leave, that leave is granted).

These restrictions on local authority use of wardship were indirectly the result of the following case:

A v Liverpool City Council
[1982] AC 363, [1981] 2 All ER 385, [1981] 2 WLR 948, 145 JP 318, 125 Sol Jo 396, 79 LGR 621, House of Lords

This was a 'leap-frog' appeal direct from the High Court to the House of Lords against the decision of Balcombe J that he was bound by authority to dismiss a mother's application to have her child made a ward of court without investigating the merits of her case.

Lord Roskill: . . . The relevant facts can be shortly stated. On 10 March 1980 the local authority obtained a care order pursuant to s. 1(2)(*a*) and (3) of the Children and Young Persons Act 1969 in respect of K. He was then placed with foster parents but the mother was allowed weekly access. That access continued until 16 June 1980 when the mother was told that henceforth only monthly supervised access would be allowed. That access was to take place at a day nursery and was to be limited to one hour. The local authority's stated reason was that 'rehabilitation' of the mother and K was not in K's best interest. Accordingly there was no point in maintaining regular access when no such 'rehabilitation' was still planned.

The local authority refused to reconsider its decision and it was with the intention of challenging that decision as 'wholly unreasonable' and 'arbitrary' that the present wardship proceedings were begun. The summons issued by the mother not only sought from the court an order for defined access but also care and control of K. The learned judge, rightly in my view, declined to express any view on the facts, being of the opinion as already stated that he was bound by authority to discharge the wardship proceedings. . . .

My Lords, I do not think it necessary to review the authorities on the interrelationship between prerogative and statutory powers. The basic principles were authoritatively determined by your Lordships' House in *A-G v De Keyser's Royal Hotel Ltd* [1920] AC 508: see especially the speech of Lord Summer ([1920] AC 508 at 561). My Lords, I do not doubt that the wardship jurisdiction of the court is not extinguished by the existence of the legislation regarding the care and control of deprived children, a phrase I use to include children whose parents have for some reason failed to discharge their parental duties towards them. I am not aware of any decision which suggests otherwise. It is helpful to examine the unsuccessful submissions in *Re A B* [1954] 2 QB 385 at 389–390 of J E Simon QC for the foster parents and the successful submission of R J Parker for the local authority. Mr Parker argued that 'the court's powers as parens patriae are limited by the Children Act 1948 by which Parliament has committed, in certain cases, the task and the right of the supervision of the welfare of children to local authorities'. It was this argument which Lord Goddard CJ was accepting (see [1954] 2 QB 385 at 398, [1954] 2 All ER 287 at 291). Indeed, Donovan J concurring on this point said ([1954] 2 QB 385 at 401, [1954] 2 All ER 287 at 293):

'Thus far, at any rate, Parliament has entrusted the welfare of the child to the local authority, and to that extent the prerogative right to secure the welfare of the child is, in my view, by necessary implication, restricted. Accordingly . . . the court cannot intervene simply because it differs from the local authority as to what is best for the child.'

It was this view which found favour with the Court of Appeal in *Re M*. Lord Evershed MR, with whom Upjohn and Pearson LJJ expressly concurred, stated his first two conclusions thus ([1961] Ch 328 at 345, [1961] 1 All ER 788 at 795):

'(i) The prerogative right of the Queen as parens patriae in relation to infants within the realm is not for all purposes ousted or abrogated as the result of the exercise of the duties and powers by local authorities under the Children Act, 1948: in particular the power to make an infant a ward of court by invocation of s. 9 of the Act of 1949 is unaffected.

(ii) But even where a child is made a ward of court by virtue of the Act of 1949, the judge in whom the prerogative power is vested will, acting on familiar principles, not exercise control in relation to duties or discretions clearly vested by statute in the local authority, and may, therefore, and in a case such as the present normally will, order that the child cease to be a ward of court.'

The statutory codes which existed in 1954 and in 1961 have been elaborated and extended and amended several times since these decisions as the social needs of our society have changed and, unhappily, the number of deprived children in the care of local authorities has tragically increased. It cannot possibly be said that the massive volume of legislation since 1961 culminating in the Child Care Act 1980, a consolidating Act which, though repealing the whole of the 1948 Act, left intact the early part of the 1969 Act has lessened the responsibilities of local authorities. This hardly suggests an intention by Parliament to restrict the scope of the statutory control by local authorities of child welfare in favour of the use by the courts of the prerogative wardship jurisdiction. On the contrary, the plain intention of this legislation is to secure the continued expansion of that statutory control.

I do not think that the language of s. 1 of the Guardianship of Infants Act 1925 and of its statutory successor in any way points in a contrary direction. The former statute, as its preamble shows, was largely designed to secure equality of rights as between father and mother in relation to their children and making the welfare of those children paramount in relation to those two henceforth equal interests. Nor do I think that the emphasis laid on that section in your Lordships' House in *J v C* [1970] AC 668, [1969] 1 All ER 788 [p. 411, above] casts any doubt on the correctness of the several earlier decisions to which I have already referred.

I am of the clear opinion that, while prerogative jurisdiction of the court in wardship cases remains, the exercise of that jurisdiction has been and must continue to be treated as circumscribed by the existence of the far-ranging statutory code which entrusts the care and control of deprived children to local authorities. It follows that the undoubted wardship jurisdiction must not be exercised so as to interfere with the day-to-day administration by local authorities of that statutory control.

My Lords, to say that is not to suggest that local authorities are immune from judicial control: in an appropiate case, as Lord Evershed MR himself said in *Re M*, the *Wednesbury* principle is available. The remedy of judicial review under RSC Ord 53 is also available in an appropriate case.

Appeal dismissed.

Questions

(i) Is this reasoning on the inter-relationship of prerogative and statutory powers convincing?

(ii) Does it apply equally to the inter-relationship between the statutory powers of local authorities and the *statutory* powers of the courts (e.g. under the Guardianship of Minors Act 1971)?

(iii) If the *Wednesbury* principle applies, should not the remedy always be judicial review (see *Re DM* [1986] 2 FLR 122)? Do you agree with the Law Commission (1987) that there must be 'concern that nothing can be done for the child's welfare even where a local authority have acted in breach or disregard of their statutory responsibilities'?

The problem is that, while parents, children, relatives and foster parents could not use wardship to challenge what the local authority was doing, the local authority was in a very different position, as the Law Commission point out in their Working Paper on *Wards of Court* (1987):

3.30 The increased use of wardship by local authorities has been the outstanding feature of its development over the past 15 years. In 1985, local authorities were involved in approximately 40% of the wardship cases initiated, in some 36% as plaintiff. In recent years, they have often been encouraged to make use of wardship if it is felt that their statutory powers are insufficient to enable them to protect the interests of children.

Questions

(i) The Law Commission canvassed several general solutions. In the local authority context, these would mean: (*a*) retain wardship and allow anyone to invoke it, even in care cases against a local authority; (*b*) retain wardship and allow it to be invoked in care cases against a local authority only if *Wednesbury* principles applied; (*c*) retain it as a residuary jurisdiction to make good the deficiencies in the statutory code; or (*d*) abolish it altogether and incorporate its best features into the statutory code. What are the advantages and disadvantages of each?

(ii) In relation to (*c*), do you agree with the Law Commission that 'It may be possible to recognise the difference between a hole in a blanket, which needs to be patched, and a hole in Swiss cheese, which is part of the fabric and virtue of the cheese itself, but it is difficult to describe it in legislative language'?

(iii) Which solution does s. 100 most resemble?

The *Children Act* also clarifies the relationship between care orders and other orders under the Act:

9. – (1) No court shall make any section 8 order, other than a residence order, with respect to a child who is in the care of a local authority.

(2) No application may be made by a local authority for a residence order or contact order and no court shall make such an order in favour of a local authority.

. . .

91. – (1) The making of a residence order with respect to a child who is the subject of a care order discharges the care order.

(2) The making of a care order with respect to a child who is the subject of any section 8 order discharges that order.

(3) The making of a care order with respect to a child who is the subject of a supervision order discharges that other order.

(4) The making of a care order with respect to a child who is a ward of court brings that wardship to an end.

(5) The making of a care order with respect to a child who is the subject of a school attendance order made under section 37 of the Education Act 1944 discharges the school attendance order.

(6) Where an emergency protection order is made with respect to a child who is in care, the care order shall have effect subject to the emergency protection order.

. . .

The effect of a care order is the same as the effect of a residence order in favour of a non-parent (p. 636, below), except for the following:

33. – (3) While a care order is in force with respect to a child, the local authority designated by the order shall –

(*a*) have parental responsibility for the child; and

(*b*) have the power (subject to the following provisions of this section) to determine the extent to which a parent or guardian of the child may meet his parental responsibility for him.

(4) The authority may not exercise the power in subsection (3)(*b*) unless they are satisfied that it is necessary to do so in order to safeguard or promote the child's welfare.

(5) Nothing in subsection (3)(*b*) shall prevent a parent or guardian of the child who has care of him from doing what is reasonable in all the circumstances of the case for the purpose of safeguarding or promoting his welfare.

. . .

(9) The power in subsection (3)(*b*) is subject (in addition to being subject to the provisions of this section) to any right, duty, power, responsibility or authority which a parent or guardian of the child has in relation to the child and his property by virtue of any other enactment.

34. – (1) Where a child is in the care of a local authority, the authority shall (subject to the provisions of this section) allow the child reasonable contact with –

    (*a*) his parents;

    (*b*) any guardian of his;

    (*c*) where there was a residence order in force with respect to the child immediately before the care order was made, the person in whose favour the order was made; and

    (*d*) where, immediately before the care order was made, a person had care of the child by virtue of an order made in the exercise of the High Court's inherent jurisdiction with respect to children, that person.

(2) On an application made by the authority or the child, the court may make such order as it considers appropriate with respect to the contact which is to be allowed between the child and any named person.

(3) On an application made by –

    (*a*) any person mentioned in paragraphs (*a*) to (*d*) of subsection (1); or

    (*b*) any person who has obtained the leave of the court to make the application;

the court may make such order as it considers appropriate with respect to the contact which is to be allowed between the child and that person.

(4) On an application made by the authority or the child, the court may make an order authorising the authority to refuse to allow contact between the child and any person who is mentioned in paragraphs (*a*) to (*d*) of subsection (1) and named in the order.

(5) When making a care order with respect to a child, or in any family proceedings in connection with a child who is in the care of a local authority, the court may make an order under this section, even though no application for such an order has been made with respect to the child, if it considers that the order should be made.

(6) An authority may refuse to allow the contact that would otherwise be required by virtue of subsection (1) or an order under this section if –

    (*a*) they are satisfied that it is necessary to do so in order to safeguard or promote the child's welfare; and

    (*b*) the refusal –

        (i) is decided upon as a matter of urgency; and

        (ii) does not last for more than seven days.

(7) An order under this section may impose such conditions as the court considers appropriate.

(8) The Secretary of State may by regulations make provision as to –

    (*a*) the steps to be taken by a local authority who have exercised their powers under subsection (6);

    (*b*) the circumstances in which, and conditions subject to which, the terms of any order under this section may be departed from by agreement between the local authority and the person in relation to whom the order is made;

    (*c*) notification by a local authority of any variation or suspension of arrangements made (otherwise than under an order under this section) with a view to affording any person contact with a child to whom this section applies.

(9) The court may vary or discharge any order made under this section on the application of the authority, the child concerned or the person named in the order.

(10) An order under this section may be made either at the same time as the care order itself or later.

(11) Before making a care order with respect to any child the court shall –

    (*a*) consider the arrangements which the authority have made, or propose to make, for affording any person contact with a child to whom this section applies; and

    (*b*) invite the parties to the proceedings to comment on those arrangements.

On contact, the DH Guidance says this:

3.77 The presumption that contact is allowed for certain named people, and the pro-active role given to the court reflect the importance of this subject. Regular contact with parents, relatives and friends will usually be an important part of the child's upbringing in his new environment and is essential to successful rehabilitation. Lack of contact can, over a period, have vital consequences for the rights of parents and children; it can be a major factor in deciding whether to discharge a care order or to dispense with parental agreement to adoption. This is too important to be regarded as simply a matter of management within the sole control of the local authority. The new scheme is intended to provide a basis for good practice and remove the perceived unfairness in previous arrangements. It is separate from the contact provisions in

Part II of the Act; a section 8 contact order cannot be made when a child is in local authority care (section 9(1)), and an existing order is automatically discharged on the making of a care order (section 91(2)).

Questions

(i) The principle behind s. 34 seems much the same as that behind s. 8 contact orders (see p. 541, above): can you think why a different technique was used for care order children?

(ii) Why should the court have so much control over contact between the child and his family and so little over how he is actually looked after while in care?

The explanation may be traced to the *Review of Child Care Law* (1985):

Courts and local authorities

2.20 One of our guiding principles has been that the court should be able to determine major issues such as the transfer of parental rights and duties where there is or may be a dispute between parents and local authorities, while the management of the case should be the responsibility of the local authority. This followed the Select Committee's general principle that 'the courts should make long-term decisions impinging directly on the rights and duties of children or their parents, and that the local authority or other welfare agency should make decisions on matters which, although they may be of equal or greater importance, are not susceptible to clear and unambiguous resolution' [1984].

2.21 While there is room for debate as to which decisions ought to fall into which category we believe this gives a valuable working rule. Decisions on such matters as the adoption or change of name of a child are made by the court whereas decisions such as the best placement for a child are made by the professional staff of the local authority. Access arrangements have features of both types of decision because they can affect later decisions on the transfer of rights (eg through applications to discharge the child or to free the child for adoption); . . .

2.22 It is a separate question whether local authority decisions and actions should be open to greater challenge by parents and children in the courts. This is usually argued to give parents and children greater voices in the various decisions taken by local authorities as well as to discourage drift and lack of positive planning for the children involved. A variety of proposals have been put forward for achieving these aims, including care orders for a limited period; automatic periodic reviews by the courts or a review on the application of a parent; prior approval for certain strategic decisions with potentially long term effects, such as that to abandon rehabilitative efforts or to change from residential to foster care or from one type of fostering to another; or the notification of such decisions with a right to challenge them in the courts. These proposals do not always distinguish between two different functions, the regular review of the circumstances and future of each individual child in care, and the resolution of disputes relating to particular decisions which have been or are to be taken about him.

2.23 The expertise of a court lies in its ability to hear all sides of the case, to determine issues of fact and to make a firm decision on a particular issue at a particular time, in accordance with the applicable law. It cannot initiate action to provide for the child, nor can it deliver the services which may best serve the child's needs. It is arguable that only if it were given the power to choose the precise placement of the child and the resources to ensure that a sufficient range of placements was made available, could a court realistically be given the function of undertaking regular reviews of the future of each child in care.

2.24 It is not only important that the reviewing body should itself have the power to deliver the care which it considers best for the child: it is also necessary that the body with day to day responsibility for the child should have a positive duty to 'take a grip on' the case and make firm and early decisions without the temptation to pass responsibility to another body. The encouragement of positive attitudes and practices, as well as subjecting them to informed scrutiny, is more important than what could only ever be a limited form of judicial review. We therefore support the emphasis currently placed by the Government on improving the working of the system of reviews by local authorities of all children in their care at fixed intervals under the existing legislation.

2.25 The particular strength of the courts or any other independent body lies in the resolution of disputes. We have no doubt that some machinery for the resolution of disagreements relating to children in care should be provided. The views expressed to us suggest that not all local authorities yet have a satisfactory system for dealing with disputes and complaints. Yet in deciding the exact machinery most appropriate for any particular dispute it is necessary to bear in mind some of the disadvantages of the court process. First, courts must maintain a certain formality in their procedures and there are some disputes which may be better resolved by more informal means. A dispute process which is inaccessible and intimidating to the people concerned will be of little value to them. Secondly, even a well managed court with resources to hear cases speedily will take time to resolve disputes, because of the need for the parties to prepare their case and for the court to conduct any independent investigations. Such delays can be highly detrimental to all concerned, especially to the younger child for whom time can be of crucial importance. Thirdly, a speedier and more informal means of resolving disagreement could be applied to a much wider range of decisions than could realistically be subject to referral to a court.

Questions

(i) Do you find this the slightest bit convincing?
(ii) Turn back to the questions on pp. 587–588: what different does it make if you are subject to a care order?

Of course, a care order is not the only solution available. One alternative is a supervision order which is apparently not widely used in child abuse cases, according to the *Review of Child Care Law* (1985):

18.5 The Select Committee were concerned about the small number of cases in which supervision orders were made (in 1983 there were about 1,400 supervision orders made in care proceedings as compared with about 3,000 care orders). They suggested that the reason was the perceived ineffectiveness of supervision orders and that these might be used more widely if the supervisor were given greater powers not only over the child but over the parents as well. In particular supervision might be used instead of a care order where the local authority intended to place the child at home on trial if a care order was obtained.

Imposing requirements on parents
18.6 One way forward would be to enable the court to impose conditions on the parent or whoever has the actual custody of the child provided that the actual custodian has had an opportunity to be heard. . . .
18.7 Whether the requirements under a supervision order are met may depend on the parent rather than the child, especially where the child is young. At present orders may be frustrated, for example simply by the parent refusing the supervisor access to the child. Refusal to allow a supervised child to be visited or medically examined is now automatically reasonable cause for suspicion so that a warrant to search for and remove the child may be obtained. Nevertheless, where the object of the supervision is in fact to impose requirements on the parents for the protection of the child we consider that the court should have express power to do so. . . .
18.9 As to what requirements precisely the court should be able to impose on adults the follow-ing list has occurred to us:
 a. to keep the supervisor informed of his address and that of the child;
 b. to allow the supervisor access to the child in the home and to assess the child's welfare, needs and condition;
 c. to allow the child to be medically examined;
 d. to comply with the supervisor's direction to attend with the child at a specified place (such as a clinic or day centre) for the purpose of medical examination, medical or psychiatric treatment, or participation in specified activities;
 e. to permit the child to receive medical or psychiatric treatment; and
 f. to comply with the supervisor's directions on matters relating to the child's education.
18.15 The power to require the child to live with a named individual will in our view be largely overtaken by our recommendation that the court in care proceedings should have power to

grant legal custody to another person for example a relative or friend and should therefore be abolished. This will have the advantage of clarifying the legal status of the other person and enabling him to combine both the powers and responsibilities of a parent. The order could be coupled with a supervision order if required.

Question

The Children Act 1989 implements these recommendations in s. 15 and Sch. 2, Parts I and II: are social workers reluctant to use supervision orders for much the same reason that they were ready to use place of safety orders (see p. 601, above)?

Another alternative, introduced by the Children Act 1989, is to make s. 8 orders (see p. 541), in any permitted combination, and either initially or on discharging a care order. Some judges were ahead of this:

Re L (a minor) (care proceedings: wardship) (No 2)
[1991] 1 FLR 29, Crown Court and High Court

The child was made the subject of a care order in care proceedings following certain unexplained injuries sustained by her. Both the parents and the grandparents had had access to the child. The local authority decided not to rehabilitate the child with her parents. There was no discussion at the case conference about the child going to either the maternal or paternal grand-parents. Arrangements were made for her long-term fostering with a view to adoption. Access to the relatives were terminated. The parents applied to the juvenile court for the discharge of the care order and for an access order to the child. The maternal grandparents requested the local authority to consider them as long-term alternative carers for the child. That request was rejected. They then obtained leave to appear on the application to discharge the care order. The juvenile court dismissed both applications for discharge of the care order and for an access order. In this sequel, the parents appealed to the Crown Court against the refusal to discharge the care order, and, at the same hearing in the Crown Court, arrangements were made for the judge hearing the appeal to sit as a High Court judge in wardship.

Willis J: . . . On 21st February 1989 the case conference decided not to rehabilitate K with her parents. It is now accept by all parties that that decision was correct. The only other course of action discussed was that of adoption and we understand there was no discussion about K going to either the maternal or paternal grandparents. A decision was made to terminate access. The last access visit took place on 2 March 1989, followed by a meeting between the mother, the maternal grandmother and a friend, with Mr C, the assistant director of social services, to explain the situation to them.
. . .
  The whole crux of this case depends on how much weight should be given to the various 'pros' and 'cons' for the two alternative courses for this child, namely, going to the grandparents or being adopted. We received the impression from the guardian, as we did from the local authority witness also, that they are far too keen on adoption and consider it the panacea for all problems. They all expressed a number of concerns or problems which might arise in the maternal grandparents' extended family if K is there. None of them envisaged any real problem in adoption in a child of this age. The impression they tried to give was that, as in every good fairy story, after placement, 'everyone lives happily ever after'. We pressed Mrs G particularly on this matter. We asked her for the 'pros' and 'cons' of adoption and she could only find

matters in favour. She said there were very few problems in adoption and placement. She gave no consideration at all to any possible psychological problems which adoptive children can have as to their roots and the fact of adoption. She said that when K reaches 18 she can have a life story book and find her natural family if she wants to, as if this would then provide the child with its natural family as well as her adoptive family. It is, of course, then far too late. The guardian ad litem admitted that in the past there had been terrible psychological problems caused to adoptive children, but suggested those were due to old adoptive practices which are now perfected. She had to admit, however, that it is impossible to research these new techniques for some years to come.

Mrs G and the local authority witnesses expressed a number of concerns should K be placed with her grandparents. These were very ably and concisely put by Mr T for the local authority in his closing address:

(1) That it would be extremely difficult for the grandparents to regulate the parents' contact with K in the long term. We do not accept this. For several months yet the mother will be at [an establishment] coping with her new baby, and thereafter we consider the maternal grandmother has a sufficiently strong character to be able to regulate the position and control her daughter.

(2) That the mother will be deprived of assistance from her mother when she most needs it. It has also been argued that the maternal grandmother was too over-protective with her daughter so as to delay her maturity. This could be the making of the mother by getting her to stand on her own two feet. She is not entirely without help and support because she has two sisters and a husband and other members of the extended family – all of whom are very close.

(3) There will be difficult emotional aspects between grandparents and parents. It is suggested that the parents might want the child to go to them and that the grandparents might wish that also. This was suggested because there was a time earlier when the maternal grandparents naturally advocated that K should go to her parents first of all, and only if that failed come to them. We believe they have moved on considerably from that point and they now realise, especially having heard the evidence in these proceedings, and earlier proceedings, that permanency is a necessity for K's well-being. Given time, and if hopefully they make a success of their new baby, I think the parents will adjust to their first child being cared for by grandparents.

(4) There is a high potential for the family situation to develop into a stressful one. As Dr C put it, every family has problems and they have the ability to sort them out as they arise. We believe this will happen here.

(5) There is a real risk of ambiguity that the child may grow up with divided loyalties, particularly if it sees a parallel happy family at the parents' house, and this will create problems. This could be overcome with careful handling.

(6) Siblings in the parallel happy family could cause problems.

(7) Another move in one or two years' time which cannot be ruled out would be disruptive. This we believe the parents and grandparents accept, so it should not occur.

(8) To return the child at that stage, to a vulnerable couple in one or two years' time, could be an additional risk. This is not really contemplated within this application.

(9) Grandparents and parents are too closely involved so that a two home problem could develop with the child being torn between both. Careful handling will obviate this.

(10) The question of co-operation by the maternal grandparents with the social services. The establishment to which the parents are going is a privately run organisation, not part of the local authority's social services department. We believe any advice from them will be fully acceptable. Further, once K is with them their anger and frustration, which earlier was fully justified, is not likely to reappear, providing they are dealt with in a sensible and sensitive way.

(11) Ability to deal with K's questions about why she is not with her parents: this problem also sometimes arises in adoption. We do not believe that in the wider family context this will prove a problem at all. Children will accept most situations providing they are happy.

(12) The [establishment to which the parents are going]: if it fails will this trigger further family stress? It might well do, but we do not think it will affect K when she is firmly bonded with her grandparents.

(13) There is the question of the mother's personality or immaturity. Who produced this? It may well have been over-protectiveness by the maternal grandmother. There is no reason to suppose that this will be repeated with K. Although we do not know the reason for it, it could be that the mother was over-protected because she was the youngest, and possibly not so bright as her two elder sisters.

The local authority's case is that there are far too many problems if K goes back to the family, i.e. to grandparents, and that a fresh start with adoption is a less risky course. K will be 'grafted' into a new family with the absence of access problems. This argument, however, fails to address the considerable problems which are more likely to arise in adoption, namely the psychological worry of who and what her family are, why she is not with them and why she was adopted. We heard evidence about this from Mrs Y who takes the oppositive view to the local authority. She is very highly qualified in this field as a guardian ad litem and social worker and she did considerable investigation into this particular case. We prefer and accept her evidence that any confusion by being brought up by grandparents can be overcome and that it is not insoluble. The great advantage in staying with the wider family is that the child maintains her roots. We consider this a very important aspect which has been totally ignored by the local authority and also by the guardian ad litem. Mrs Y considers that K can only benefit from hers being an unusually closely knit family. With that we also agree. Adoption is a trial and error situation about which too little is known. Many adopted people start looking for their roots, particularly in adolescence. Dr C, a most eminent psychiatrist and child specialist of more than 30 years, supports the grandparents' case. He said that it is always better to be brought up in your own family. He was particularly impressed with the breadth of the extended family who are all in touch with each other. K would be part of a very supportive family structure. We fully agree with Mrs Y's evidence that adoption should only be the last resort when no one in the wider family is available and suitable to look after a child. parentage is not always perfect, but parentage in the family is preferable to the unknown risk of adoption, even though we accept that adoption assessments these days are very carefully carried out. We consider that every child has a right, whenever it is possible, to be brought up in its own genetic family. That right should not be taken away from it except in the last resort when there are strong, cogent and positive reasons for so doing. All the local authority's arguments are based on concerns which may or may not happen. Even if they did, the risk to K, we feel, would be less than the risks inherent in adoption.

For the above reasons, we have no hesitation in deciding that it is appropriate, and in K's best interest, to discharge the care order. Her welfare and the transition to the care of the maternal grandparents will be safeguarded by wardship proceedings.

We have set out above some of the long category of failures by the local authority in giving proper consideration to their duties. So that these mistakes do not happen again it is very important that they look very carefully at their procedures and their attitudes so far as fostering and caring in the immediate family are concerned. They should reconsider their facile approach to adoption, which they appear to see as a neat and clean solution to any problems.

Questions

(i) Would you have done the same?
(ii) Return to this question after you have read Chapter 14: does it change your mind?

Nevertheless, the choice generally lies between finding a permanent substitute home with strangers and reuniting the child with his family. We shall discuss the former in the next chapter, but what should be the criterion for the latter? Once a child has been removed from home, should his future be governed by what is in his best interests or should the parents be entitled to have him back once the conditions which led to the care order no longer exist? Robert Dingwall's commentary on *The Jasmine Beckford Affair* (1986) gives some indication of the complexities:

Jasmine Beckford became the subject of a care order to the London Borough of Brent in September 1981 following a non-accidental injury for which her father, Morris Beckford, was subsequently convicted. At the care proceedings, Willesden magistrates added a rider, hoping that the child would be rehabilitated. Brent Social Services initially arranged for Jasmine to be fostered but subsequently returned her home under their close supervision in April 1982. The department was satisfied with the progress of the family and Jasmine was removed from the at-risk register in November 1982. Revocation of the care order was refused by the magistrates in June 1983 but Brent Social Services scaled down their work on the case and were considering renewing their attempt to revoke the order when Jasmine was killed in July 1984. Post-mortem examination showed that the child had suffered repeated severe beatings over the period since her return home and that there was also clear evidence of failure to thrive.

The panel [see Brent Council, 1985] allocated equal responsibilities to the social worker *and* the health visitor involved. Neither of them had been callous or indifferent but neither was adequately trained, experienced or supervised. The blame was shared, therefore, with their immediate superiors who had assigned them to this work and failed to give appropriate support or guidance. Criticism is also addressed to the magistrates for overstepping their powers by adding the rider to their Care Order and to the Social Services courts officer for failing to take this up and to advise the department to disregard it. More specifically, the front-line workers and their supervisors are variously censured for their poor liaison with Jasmine's school, for their failure to diagnose her injuries, for their misconceptions of the meaning of a Care Order, for their emphasis on the parents rather than the child as their primary client, for their reluctance to exercise authority and for unsatisfactory relationships of professional accountability. The report concludes

'We think in fact we have identified and isolated one fundamental aspect of professional response to child abuse that has been overlooked or discarded by modern social work training and practice. It is that the making of a Care Order invests Social Services with pervasive parental powers. By such a judicial act society expects that a child at risk from abuse by its parents will be protected by Social Services personnel exercising parental powers effectively and authoritatively on behalf of society. Such a child is a child in trust.'

The full radicalism of such a proposal is obscured in the report. Nevertheless it is clear here and elsewhere that the effective aspiration of the panel is to reverse the dominant decision-rule in child care, that parents should receive the benefit of any genuine doubt or uncertainty.

It will, however, be argued that it is possible, in principle, to show that most of the 'failings' documented by the report result from this decision-rule and that its operation derives from the essential nature of child protection in a liberal democracy. . . .

The report is highly critical of the social workers' apparent focus on Morris Beckford and Beverly Lorrington rather than on their children, who were the subject of care orders. Indeed, this becomes a central justification for the inquiry's recommendation for the dismantling of generic social service departments in favour of a more child-centred agency. But that focus is understandable in work of this kind. After all, when you have parents who have abused their children, it is generally their behaviour that you will want to change. The predominant theory of child abuse in Britain sees it as a product of an interaction between vulnerable individuals and a stressful environment. If you are operating on the principle that parents should not be avoidably deprived of their children, you will focus your work on relieving the stresses, which are generally fairly obvious, poor housing, lack of money, etc., even if the agency's resources are limited, or on strengthening the individuals by encouraging the development of self-control or supportive relationships.

On the evidence in the report, Brent social workers were quite successful at this. Joan Court's independent social work report to the 1981 care proceedings encouraged the view that more adequate housing would enable the family to be safely reunited. The family were re-housed. Morris Beckford held down a stable, well-paid job. The relationship between himself and Beverly Lorrington appeared secure and reasonably harmonious by the standards of a deprived inner-city community.

From the time Jasmine was returned from foster care to the time of her death, then, she was seen to be living in a material and social environment that was better than that of many other children in Brent. As has been shown previously, under such circumstances allegations of abuse are consistently difficult to make [Dingwall, Eekelaar, and Murray, 1983]. Child protection workers throughout the country would tend to resolve ambiguities in the parent's favour. So when Gun Wahlstrom failed to interpret Jasmine's disordered gait in March 1984 as evidence of a fractured femur rather than as the uncertain steps of a developmentally delayed child in a deprived community, this cannot justifiably be read as 'negligence' but is the predictable outcome of the decision-rules used to reduce the proportion of the child population investigated as potential victims to a manageable size.

. . . The final example is another recurrent criticism of the social workers, namely their apparent failure to exercise 'authority'. The panel simply cannot comprehend the social workers' reluctance to use the extensive powers conferred by the Care Orders on Jasmine and Louise Beckford. This failure provokes a sweeping attack on the whole occupation for its 'negation of any authoritarian role in the enforcement of Care Orders'. . .

The report assumes a traditional picture of local authorities and their officers as 'creatures of statute', existing only in and through a framework of law.

The reality is more complex. As we have previously observed,

'Doctors, health visitors and social workers are not law-enforcement officers, permanently and selectively attuned to discovering breaches of statute. They are better characterized as problem-solving agents for whom the law exists as one possible resource for dealing with social troubles.'

. . . On this sort of reading, it is possible to identify local pressures which compound what has elsewhere been called 'the rule of optimism.' [Dingwall, Eekelaar, and Murray, 1983] In a complex information-processing situation, a social worker in Brent has to recognise that the literal enforcement of a care order will produce both organisational trouble, in a demand for overstretched resources and possibly community trouble, in the sensitive relations between metropolitan social services departments and minority ethnic communities, and professional trouble, in raising issues about the permissible extent of intrusion into family privacy. All of these are more immediate contingencies to influence the use of discretion under a care order than the letter of legalism. . . .

The bulk of child protection work involves uninvited surveillance or private behaviour. The apparent weakness of agencies engaged in this task is a mark of a liberal state: indeed the contrary is often regarded as a key symbol of authoritarian societies. The rule of optimism is the product of a fundamental conflict of values about the relationship between the families and the state which receives, at best, a nodding acknowledgement in the Beckford Report.

Question

Is Dingwall applying the same 'rule of optimism' to social workers as they apply to parents? And for the same reasons?

6 How far have we come?

The ideals of the public care system have been set out by an advisory group convened by the DH in *The Care of Children — Principles and Practice in Regulations and Guidance* (1990):

1) Children and young people and their parents should all be considered as individuals with particular needs and potentialities.
2) Although some basic needs are universal, there can be a variety of ways of meeting them.
3) Children are entitled to protection from neglect, abuse and exploitation.
4) A child's age, sex, health, personality, race, culture and life experiences are all relevant to any consideration of needs and vulnerability and have to be taken into account when planning or providing help.
5) There are unique advantages for children in experiencing normal family life in their own birth family and every effort should be made to preserve the child's home and family links.
6) Parents are individuals with needs of their own.
7) The development of a working partnership with parents is usually the most effective route to providing supplementary or substitute care for their children.
8) Admission to public care by virtue of a compulsory order is itself a risk to be balanced against others. So also is the accommodation of a child by a local authority.
9) If young people cannot remain at home, placement with relatives or friends should be explored before other forms of placement are considered.
10) If young people have to live apart from their family of origin, both they and their parents should be helped to consider alternatives and contribute to the making of an informed choice about the most appropriate form of care.
11) When out-of-home care is necessary, active steps should be taken to ensure speedy return home.
12) Parents should be expected and enabled to retain their responsibilities and to remain as closely involved as is consistent with their child's welfare, even if that child cannot live at home either temporarily or permanently.
13) Siblings should not be separated when in care or when being looked after under voluntary arrangements unless this is part of a well thought out plan based on each child's needs.

14) Family links should be actively maintained through visits and other forms of contact. Both parents are important even if one of them is no longer in the family home and fathers should not be overlooked or marginalised.
15) Wider families matter as well as parents—especially siblings and grandparents.
16) Continuity of relationships is important, and attachments should be respected, sustained and developed.
17) Change of home, caregiver, social worker or school almost always carries some risk to a child's development and welfare.
18) Time is a crucial element in child care and should be reckoned in days and months rather than years.
19) Every young person needs to develop a secure sense of personal identity and all those with parental or caring responsibilities have a duty to offer encouragement and support in this task.
20) All children need to develop self confidence and a sense of self worth, so alongside the development of identity, and equally important is self esteem.
21) Since discrimination of all kinds is an everyday reality in many children's lives, every effort must be made to ensure that agency services and practices do not reflect or reinforce it.
22) Corporate parenting is not 'good enough' on its own.
23) Young people should not be disadvantaged or stigmatised by action taken on their behalf, e.g. as a result of admission to care or to special residential provision.
24) Children's long-term welfare must be protected by prompt, positive and pro-active attention to the health and education of those in both short and long-term care.
25) Young people's wishes must be elicited and taken seriously.
26) As young people grow up, preparation for independence is a necessary and important part of the parental role which child care agencies carry for young people in long-term care.

Question

Looking back at this chapter and on to the next, can you trace where these ideas stem from? Are they a pious hope or a realistic aspiration?

CHAPTER 14

The tug of love: parents by birth, fostering and adoption

Former foster child A: It was only recently I was told that my natural parents could have removed me at any time if they wanted to. Even now when I think of it I shudder. . . . For me they would have been total strangers. Why remove me when I was so happy? I have met my natural mother recently and I see her from time to time. There is no bond between us. My 'mum' is my foster mum and my 'dad' is my foster dad. If I call my natural mother 'mum' when I meet her it is just for saving face. . . .

Former foster child D: I must have been 7 when I went to live with my foster parents. They were the second family I went to. The first family went abroad after promising to take me with them. They didn't and it broke my heart at the time. . . . The [foster parents] had two of their own and another foster child. Somehow I never felt I belonged there. We foster children did not fit in very well. I cannot say that I developed much attachment to them. My foster mother often threatened to send me back to the Corporation. Sometimes she would ring them but they would make her change her mind. I suppose I was difficult too, and I would hark back or argue. She would then smack me and send me to bed . . . I could be nasty and so could my foster mother . . . I left at 17 when our quarrels became worse, and I went to live in a hostel.

These two extracts from John Triseliotis' study, *Growing Up in Foster Care and After* (1980), tell us a great deal about the problems of providing substitute family care for children separated from their families of birth. The findings of Rowe and Lambert (p. 585, above), along with others, led not only to an increasing emphasis on positive planning for children in care but also to much more strenuous attempts to find substitute families, often on a more permanent basis than before. At the same time the supply of babies whose natural parents wish them to be adopted by another family has been diminishing (see pp. 639–640, below). These developments have contributed to a significant and highly controversial reappraisal of the relative legal claims of natural parents, substitute parents and the children themselves, which it is the task of this chapter to examine. However, one of the difficulties for lawyers is that their involvement begins with the 'tug of love' where one family disputes with another the future of a hapless child. The considerations applicable, and the judgments appropriate, at that stage may be quite different from those applicable at the point where the social worker begins, with a child who has just been or is about to be separated from his natural family.

1 The dilemmas of fostering

The view taken following the Children Act 1948 is summed up by Jean Packman in *The Child's Generation* (1981):

Originally, fostering had frequently been seen as an *alternative* to parental care, when the latter had proved inadequate. Before children's departments existed many children who were fostered lost all contact with their natural families and the fostering became a 'de facto' adoption . . . The Children Act, moving away from this position, stipulated that children must be rehabilitated with their own families, when this was consistent with their welfare, and . . . the concept was increasingly applied. Though fostering was the favoured method of care, promising as it did a 'natural' upbringing and the warmth and intimate relationships that children need, it was now more often a short-term or impermanent arrangement, incorporating a far greater degree of sharing. If children were to be rehabilitated, they must be kept in close touch with their natural parents. . . . What was expected of foster parents became at once more subtle and more difficult. They must confer on the child all the benefits of loving family care, but should not seek to replace the parents in his affections. Their compassion and acceptance must be extended from the child himself, to his parents as well — even where the latter seemed 'to blame' for some of his past deprivations. They should act toward him as a good parent, yet give him up when the department judged the time to be ripe.

That expectation to some extent reflects the concept of 'inclusive' fostering described by Robert Holman (who refers to his own work as 'Holman') in his seminal article on *The Place of Fostering in Social Work* (1975):

Inclusive fostering
. . . The inclusive concept is based on a readiness to draw the various components into the fostering situation. The foster parents can offer love without having to regard themselves as the real parents. Their attitude is that of the 36% identified by Holman (1973) who said 'I know he's not mine but I treat him the same'. A significant number did not wish to adopt, but this did not mean they lacked affection. The willingness to include others is further seen in the 31% of Holman's sample and 54% in Adamson's (1973) who considered that natural parents should see their children. Natural parents are regarded more positively, with a greater willingness that the children should possess full knowledge about them. The social workers are also included. Adamson records that over 50% of the foster mothers looked forward to visits from the social workers, and would immediately contact them if difficulties rose. Such foster parents, George (1970) pointed out, defined the social workers as official colleagues rather than informal friends. They were also more likely to regard themselves as possessing special skills which merited payment.
   Within the inclusive concept, emphasis is placed on the children's need to obtain a true sense of their present identity and past history within a framework of affection. It accords with Ruddock's (1972) model of a role tree in which realistic grasp of personal identity is necessary so that the person can integrate various parts into a coherent pattern which will both satisfy him internally and allow him to find satisfactory external roles. Moreover, it accepts that the inclusion of all the fostering participants — foster parents, children, natural parents and social workers — are needed in order to facilitate rehabilitation of the children if that is possible.

This he contrasts with a quite different type of fostering, the 'exclusive,' which he describes thus:

Exclusive fostering
Exclusive fostering may be so termed in that it attempts to contain the foster child within the foster family while excluding other connections. Thus Holman's study revealed that 63% of local authority foster parents regarded the children 'as their own' and would like to have adopted. Similarly, Adamson found that over half did not think of themselves as foster mothers. George records that 62.1% considered 'own parent' as the best description of their position. Seeing themselves as the parents, such foster parents want to exclude the natural parents. George established that 56% did not think the real parents had even a conditional right to visit. Of Holman's local authority foster mothers 35% thought natural parents should not be encouraged to visit while, in addition, a slightly smaller proportion thought it conditional upon suitable attitudes and intentions. Adamson confirmed that 46% thought it best if foster children did not see their own families. This negative attitude, Holman shows, is encapsulated in hostile opinions of the natural parents (such as 'She's disgusting', 'She doesn't deserve to have children') and is revealed in an unwillingness to accept or talk to the foster children about their background. It follows that if the children are regarded as natural ones then the social workers

too cannot be fully accepted as having an official interest in them. Accordingly, George discovered that 48.6% of foster parents described their social workers only as 'friends', while 64.6% would not think it necessary to inform the social workers even if the foster children stole. Adamson also noted that a considerable number of foster parents felt unease about social workers' visits, while 34% would not have initiated contact with them even concerning a serious problem.

The exclusive fostering concept appears to stem from a two-fold premise. Foster children need to be sheltered from the influence of, even knowledge about, natural parents. Further, the foster children and foster parents' greatest need is freedom from any fear that the fostering will be disturbed or even that the fact of fostering will be brought to their attention. In many ways, it is strikingly similar to the 'fresh start' which dominated much boarding out under the nineteenth century Poor Law.

He then quotes the following studies of foster children which suggest that they benefit from parental contact:

1. Weinstein (1960) established that regular natural parent contact was associated with the foster children achieving high scores on present and future 'well-being' scales.
2. Jenkins (1969) found that 57% of foster children aged over 1½ years at placement with no parental contact were 'disturbed' as against only 35% with regular contact. Similar findings were reported for those under 1½ years.
3. Holman (1973) observed that in general the less the contact the higher the incidence of certain emotional and physical symptoms such as soiling and ill-health.
4. Thorpe's (1974) recent work revealed a trend suggesting a relationship between satisfactory adjustment and contact (although it was not statistically significant except for 11- to 13-year-olds).

From these he concludes that:

In general, fostering success bears a closer relationship with the inclusive than with the exclusive type of fostering. The explanation, Holman suggests, is that foster parents of the exclusive kind in regarding themselves as natural parents create situations of role conflict or confusion. For at times their conception must be challenged by the reality of social workers' visits, natural parent contact, or questions from the children. The resultant anxiety and confusion can be conveyed to the whole family.

Nevertheless:

The association between fostering success and inclusive fosterings would be less noteworthy if they constituted the typical foster home. But a further implication [of the research studies quoted] is that a substantial number of long-term foster homes operate on the exclusive concept.

Furthermore:

The intensity of foster parent feeling has meant that social workers are also drawn into the fostering dilemma. The research suggests that most social workers hold the inclusive concept of fostering. They frequently work with foster parents who possess the opposite view, at a time of foster parent shortage. The social workers thus find themselves believing that foster children should be encouraged to know or know about their natural parents yet aware that to do so would endanger the fostering. . . . George's work suggests that generally the social workers collude with the foster parents. He found that only 3.8% of natural parents were encouraged to see their children . . . [he] concludes his study . . . by saying that social workers and foster parents 'by their active hostility or passive inaction towards natural parents have forced or have merely allowed natural parents to alienate themselves from their children. This alienation has in turn been used as evidence for the natural parents' lack of interest in their children and for their inability to care for them adequately.' . . . The studies concur in finding some workers so caught by the need not to disturb foster homes that they find themselves reinforcing the very concept of fostering with which they disagree.

Holman's call is for greater efforts among social workers to find foster parents who *can* accept the inclusive model and to make it work. However, there are certain assumptions underlying his whole argument which require closer examination. As Jane Rowe points out in her account of *Fostering in the 1970s* (1977):

Much of the social work writing about fostering has stressed the foster parents' difficulties in understanding their role, and their tendency to think of themselves as substitute parents when the agency wishes them to assume the role of caretaker or therapist. In reality a foster parent's role — like that of a residential worker — is always a combination of caretaker, therapist, compensatory parent and substitute parent, though the mix will vary according to the type of placement and age of the child, and may change from time to time during the child's stay in the foster home. . . .

Social workers are often more confused than foster parents about the appropriate division of role within the triangular fostering situation in which natural parents, foster parents and agency all carry some responsibility for the child. A foster parent's role must always depend upon which aspects of the parental role are still being exercised by the natural parents and which are being undertaken by the agency. The foster parent's difficult task is to fill in the gaps. . . .

The purpose of placement and the likely length of stay are crucial to role definition. . . . Divisions of responsibility which are satisfactory in the short term may become intolerable in the long term and, with young children in particular, caretakers quickly slip into a substitute parenting role unless natural parents remain closely involved.

On the likely length of stay, she observes:

In social work literature, there is a generally held assumption that most foster homes nowadays are of the indefinite/medium length type and discussions about the foster parents' role are based on the expectation that the child will be going back to his family of origin. The fact is, however, that except for the fostering of teenagers, there are comparatively few medium-length fostering placements. *Children Who Wait* (Rowe and Lambert, 1973) and subsequent studies have shown that if children do not return home within a few months, they are likely to remain in care for a very long time and it is now only too clear that rehabilitation to parents is frequently difficult to achieve. Major findings from *Children Who Wait* were that 72% of the children needing foster home placements were thought to need a 'permanent home' and only half of those for whom a foster home for an indeterminate period was being sought were actually thought likely to return to their parents.

A detailed study of the foster children in one local authority by Shaw and Lebens (1976) showed that 88% were expected to remain in care until their eighteenth birthday, 54% of the children had already been in their foster homes for more than five years and a further 22% for between two to five years.

The discrepancy between social work theory and the fostering realities which these figures demonstrate is a serious threat to good practice. It goes a long way towards explaining the gap between social work emphasis on the need for foster parents to avoid possessiveness, and not become too emotionally involved with the child, and foster parents' persistence in considering themselves as substitute parents. It is clearly very difficult for foster parents to maintain a somewhat detached professional role for an extended period, but social workers often continue to apply expectations and policies that are out of keeping with the facts and with the psychological realities.

Jane Rowe, Hilary Cain, Marion Hindleby and Anne Keane studied 200 foster placements which had lasted for at least three years, 55 with relatives and 145 with non-relatives, reported in *Long-Term Foster Care* (1984):

. . . The children did not just live with their foster families, they became part of them. The importance that the youngsters themselves placed on being in a family can scarcely be over-emphasized and not one of those we interviewed would have preferred to be in residental care. They spoke of their foster parents with genuine affection and almost all were well accepted by foster grandparents and other relatives. They were growing up as normal members of their neighbourhoods and communities and after leaving care had a home base from which to start adult life.

. . . Nevertheless, questions still remain about whether fostering provides a 'good enough' experience of family life in the sense of promoting the child's overall welfare. From the welfare perspective, our findings are not clear-cut but give grounds for some concern. Behaviour problems were much in evidence among the study children. Enuresis, destructiveness, tantrums and stealing were all more frequent than in the general population. The disproportionate number of study children who were not reaching their potential at school was a pointer to emotional blocks in the development of some children, and more than half of those whom we interviewed had feelings of discomfort over their status.

. . . There were a handful of truly 'inclusive' placements where children retained close links with natural parents and where rehabilitation, though not foreseen, could have been achieved without undue difficulty if the natural parents' circumstances changed. There were some other placements where there was genuine 'shared care' between foster parents and agency and where the social worker played a very positive part, but these were rare. It was our very strong impression that, although many of the placements we studied were working well, they were doing so in spite of the system rather than because of it.

The placements we studied would almost all be designated as 'exclusive' in that neither natural parents nor social workers played a significant role in the child's life. . . .

. . . However, the children did not necessarily feel secure and the number of changes that occurred while the study was in progress, plus the fact that nearly half the placements had been in some sort of jeopardy at some stage showed that their fears were not without foundation.

Being a foster child is not easy. The study children have revealed something of the stresses of having to answer questions, of feeling different and of anxieties and unanswered questions about the past and the future. . . . Our findings confirm those of Triseliotis (1983) and of Fanshel and Shinn (1978). Summing up the differences between young adults who had been adopted as older children and young adults who had been fostered, Triseliotis concluded:

> 'Compared to those who grew up in long-term fostering, adoptees in general appeared more confident and secure with fewer doubts about themselves and about their capacity to cope with life . . . In spite of the strong psychological bonds between those fostered and their foster parents, the ambiguous nature of the arrangement seemed to have a qualitative impact on the former's sense of identity.'

A very similar conclusion is drawn by Fanshel and Shinn (1978) though they, too, are tentative. At the end of their massive five-year longitudinal study of 624 children, these authors support the view that children should be afforded permanency in their living arrangements if at all possible, though they hasten to add that they do not take this position on the basis of their data but because:

> 'We are not completely sure that continued tenure in foster care over extended periods is not in itself harmful to children . . . We fear that in the inner recesses of his heart, a child who is not living with his own family or who is not adopted may come to think of himself as being less than first-rate, as an unwanted human being.'

. . . The inescapable conclusion of our findings is that many long-term foster children would be better off if they were adopted by their foster parents, not because being fostered is so bad but because it is not quite good enough. However, one must hasten to add that it would be a serious mistake to assume that *all* long-term foster children could or should be adopted. . . .

Distinguishing which children should be adopted is not easy and cannot be done by any general rule about length of stay or even on the basis of parental contact, though both may be useful guides. In our study we had examples of children who were in touch with parents but who nevertheless wanted very much to be adopted. There were a few children who had no parental contact who, nevertheless felt a strong sense of natural family identity. For them, adoption would have seemed like an intrusion. . . . there are also foster parents who do not want to adopt even though they have a strong bond to the child and are committed to providing a permanent home. A crucial issue is whether or not the child *feels* secure.

Of course, contact with, knowledge of, and returning to one's family are three quite separate things. Rosamund Thorpe, in *The Experience of Children and Parents Living Apart* (1980) studied (in 1971) the psychological adjustment of all children aged five to 17 in the care of one local authority who had been in their current foster home with non-relatives for at least one year. She too found a higher rate of disturbance than among the general population, indeed higher than that in Rowe's study. She goes on to discuss the children's needs:

The foster child's perception and experience of placement: the need for security
. . . 87% of the children were expected by their social workers to remain in the foster home until and beyond their discharge from local authority care at the age of 18 years; and 75% of the children identified with their foster parents and wanted to remain living with them. Despite the extent of expected permanence, concern with their security of tenure in the foster home nevertheless coloured the interview responses of several of the children. . . .

Thus the first and major conclusion must be that children in care need to know what is going to happen to them, whatever it is. Whilst, clearly, those children who have already spent a high proportion of their life in a foster home may need to be assured that they can remain there, for other children it may be necessary to plan and work more positively than hitherto for rehabilitation or a more appropriate placement. And for yet other children there will be a need for them to be aware when their future is uncertain. For knowledge of uncertainty is shared and thus bearable, whereas uncertainty of knowledge can be frightening, even disturbing, since in the absence of facts, fantasies and fears will run wild.

The need for a sense of identity
. . . Almost all of the children were concerned to know much more about their natural parents, and many were keen to retain or re-establish contact with them. For example, *Jane* (12 years), recently re-introduced to her natural mother, explained:

'I saw Mum last week — the first time for five years. I was ever so pleased. She's nice; she talks nice and looks nice and dresses nice — but I don't know really because I don't live with her. She's not really as I imagined her. I thought she'd be all fussy sort of thing, but she weren't — only a little. It's a bit confusing. I'm very pleased to have seen her and if I don't see her it bothers me a bit in bed at night sometimes. I think it's best to see her once or twice. I don't really know why. I just think so. I want to see her again; I'd like to see her. I like staying here but I'd like to see my mum occasionally.

My dad, he's gone back to India. I've never seen him in my life. I would like to have seen him just once because I'd like to see my own dad instead of thinking someone else is my dad when they're not. It didn't bother me before when I was little, but I'd like to find out now that I'm bigger.'

What Jane had to say highlights not only the need foster children have for a sense of genealogical roots in fixing the boundaries to a sense of self-identity, but also the way that, in the absence of facts, children will develop fantasies. Such fantasy pictures of natural parents may become extreme or bizarre, and this can lead to insecurity; this is further compounded by the fact that fantasies consume a great deal of emotional energy which cannot then be channelled into learning or making relationships. This in turn leads to the not unfamiliar picture of the child in care who is either under-achieving in school, or having difficulty in making relationships, or both. And this would account for the relationship between self-knowledge and emotional adjustment in foster children. . . .

The need for contact between foster child and natural parent
. . . There is a popular belief that children in foster homes experience a conflict of loyalties between their natural and their foster parents and feel 'different' because of this. However, this was not substantiated by my research. When the adults — natural and foster parents — accepted each other, the foster children appeared to experience no conflict of loyalties and accepted the foster situation with equanimity, understanding the reasons why it had to be this way for them. By contrast, when children could not identify with their natural parents, through a lack of knowledge or contact, they seemed to experience a sense of stigma in being fostered. *Robert* (15 years) is perhaps a good example:

'It is probably slightly harder being fostered just because you've got to fight this conscious fact of being fostered and not having parents of your own. For example, if you have the micky taken out of you at school — or fear they might find out and take the micky. It's just your fact and you have to put up with it. It's really just mostly a joke — they don't mean to hurt, they only think it's a game — but others may not.'

This experience of stigma in being 'different' links in with the theoretical view that children often experience the separation from natural parents entailed in coming into care as rejection, and that their feelings of rejection may undermine their sense of personal worth. This was apparent in my research, in that those children who were in contact with their natural parents seemed reassured that they were loved, rather than rejected. They understood that the reasons for their being in care were not because they were bad, unlovable or 'no-good'; as a result they could tolerate the 'difference' implicit in being a foster child.

Questions

(i) Do these findings give us some explanation for the apparently surprising finding (Rowe *et al.*, 1984) that children fostered by relatives seemed to be doing better in virtually all respects than those fostered by non-relatives? Why do you think that was?

(ii) For those who are not in touch with their natural families, do you think that the law can provide some answer to the 'stigma in being "different" '?

In *Foster care outcomes: a review of key research findings* (1989), John Triseliotis surveys the factors associated with successful outcomes. Among those related to the child were:

- The child's understanding of the circumstances of his or her in-care situation, fostering placement, origins and genealogical circumstances and background contribute to placement stability and to a sense of well-being in the child (Weinstein, 1960; Thorpe, 1974; Aldgate, 1980; Fanshel & Shinn, 1978; Triseliotis, 1980; Berridge & Cleaver, 1987). Rowe et al (1984) also add that the disturbed children in their studies were more confused about their status than were those who were better adjusted.
- The majority view among researchers is that children who experience consistent parental contact are more stable and settled in their foster care placements (Weinstein, 1960; Thorpe, 1974; Berridge & Cleaver, 1987). Berridge & Cleaver, when referring to both short-term and intermediate fostering, claimed that placements in which there was no contact between child and parents were much more likely to prove unsuccessful. In the case of short-term placements the likelihood of disruption was three times greater. On the other hand, erratic visits or the appearance of parental figures after a long absence or a reduction in contact may unsettle and upset the child.
- A mixed picture emerges with regard to children placed with siblings, with most studies suggesting that such placements lead to few disruptions or that the children are better adjusted (Trasler, 1960; Triseliotis, 1980; Berridge & Cleaver, 1987; Hill et al, 1989). Other studies, though, have found that the outcome of placements was not affected by the presence of siblings and in fact George (1970) and Napier (1972) found that foster children not placed with siblings were more successful. In addition, Rowe et al (1984) comment that the foster child's adjustment was unrelated to the presence or absence of siblings. The answer to this mixed picture may lie in the kind of relationships the children had before separation. It seems safer to start with the principle of keeping siblings together unless there are compelling reasons not to.

Among those related to the foster parents were:

- Where foster carers are inclusive of the family of origin there is also evidence of success (Weinstein, 1960; Thorpe, 1974; Triseliotis, 1980; Berridge & Cleaver, 1987). Yet Rowe et al (1984) observed that most long-term foster care remains essentially traditional and 'exclusive' and the social workers' as well as the natural family's involvement remains problematic. Most conflicts about parental contact and visits usually arise over what are meant to be intermediate type placements. According to Rowe et al (1984) social workers took a passive role towards visiting, whilst foster carers generally expected visits but were glad when they did not happen. Wilkinson (1988) also observed that as the placement period grew 'foster parents tended to be openly critical and often hostile to the child's family'.
- Foster placements with relatives are generally more successful than the rest (Rowe et al, 1984; Millham et al, 1986; Berridge & Cleaver, 1987). Rowe et al's (1989) latest study though was not so optimistic, possibly because the results, as they suggest, were depressed through the presence of more long-term placements with relatives compared to others.

Among those associated with the parents were:

• There is considerable agreement among a number of studies that consistent parental visiting to children either in residential or foster care results in the quicker return of the child home (Jenkins & Norman, 1973; Aldgate, 1977; Millham et al, 1986). The evidence also suggests that as length of placement increases parents tend to visit less and less. Rowe et al (1984) confirmed that the younger the child at admission the less sustained was the visiting. This was especially true of children admitted when less than six months old. With children aged five or more at admission to care, 'parental interest may well remain high even if visiting ceases'. Overall though, only 21 per cent of the children had 'even casual contact with a parent in the previous year'.
• The factors that impede or encourage parental visiting to children in foster care appear to be connected with the parents' belief in their own importance to their children's lives; the social worker's encouragement, or lack of it; the attitude of the foster family to visiting; and the circumstances of the natural family. Aldgate's (1977) study of 244 Scottish families with children in voluntary care showed that there was significantly greater contact between parents and children in residential care than between parents and children in foster care. The interviews conducted with the parents suggested very strongly that foster homes presented more difficulties for them to visit than children's homes, a point confirmed also by Colton (1988).
• Reference has already been made to Wilkinson's (1988) small-scale, but in-depth, study which showed that with the passage of time foster carers tended to become increasingly critical of and hostile to the child's family. Both Wilkinson and Berridge & Cleaver (1987) found less antagonism towards birth parents by specialist foster carers compared to traditional ones. The Strathclyde study (1988) reported that when foster families were asked about their likes and dislikes about fostering, 'dislike of contact with natural parents was frequently mentioned'. Millham et al (1986) also noted that with increasing time, the involvement with the birth family became less and less. This may be acceptable in long-term fostering where the children are well settled and there is no likelihood of them returning home, but not in those situations where rehabilitation is still a possibility.
• The studies seem to suggest that there is a gap between hectic activity at the start of the placement becoming increasingly episodic or reactive until it ceases in most long-term cases. Our study in freeing children for adoption (Lambert, Buist, Triseliotis & Hill, 1989) suggests that the scrutiny exercised by courts when considering freeing applications has contributed to increased social work efforts in rehabilitative work.

Questions

(i) The last point reminds us that the court's scrutiny of the child's future often comes at the end of a long and complex history of placement and contact decisions taken by others: what function can the court then have?
(ii) What do you think the views of the various researchers are on the relative merits of (*a*) reuniting the child with his birth family, (*b*) continued local authority care, (*c*) permanent fostering, and (*d*) adoption?

2 Foster parents — how the law has changed

We have already seen how, in *J v C* [1970] AC 668, [1969] 1 All ER 788 (p. 411, above), the House of Lords decided that there was no presumption in favour of the child's parents: the child's welfare is paramount in disputes between parents and foster parents just as it is in disputes between parents. However, we have also seen (p. 610, above) that the courts will not normally allow the wardship jurisdiction to be invoked to challenge decisions taken by local authorities about children in their care. Even if the child is not in care, the foster parents may have difficulty in keeping the child if the local authority favours rehabilitation:

Re K (a minor) (wardship: adoption)
[1991] FCR 142, [1991] 1 FLR 57, Court of Appeal

The parents had two older children and, despite some social services involvement with the family, there was no question of removing them. The marriage
was a stormy one, the father was addicted to gambling and had a criminal
record, and the mother was receiving treatment for heroin addiction. The
mother became unexpectedly pregnant with this child, N, during a particularly difficult time. A private arrangement was made to hand the child over
to foster parents, as they thought permanently. This was done when the child
was six weeks old but less than three months later the mother wanted her
back. The foster parents made the child a ward of court and obtained interim
care and control. When the child was seven and a half months old, the judge
gave them care and control with a view to adoption and terminated the
mother's access. Mother, father and local authority all appealed.

Butler-Sloss LJ: . . . This is a very sad case in which the little girl was handed over by the
mother at a time of great stress and financial difficulty within 6 weeks of the birth of the child
to a much older couple who are childless and have for some years hoped to care for a child on
a long-term basis. The mother and the father have repented of their decision to hand over N
and wish to reintroduce her into the family with her elder brother and sister. She has, however,
settled into a warm and loving family who are currently caring for her admirably and wish to
continue to do so. If she moves there will be inevitable upheaval and upset for the child. If she
goes back to her natural family there are question marks as to their suitability. There are also
question marks as to the long-term suitability of the family with whom she is at present. It is
a sad example of the unwisdom of private arrangements made in the absence of intervention
and assistance by the agencies, principally the social services. It presents a very anxious and
difficult problem for the decision of the court. . . .

The judge was faced with three possible orders: to place the child back with the parents, to
approve of the child remaining with the plaintiffs, or to place the child in care with a view to
being placed with another long-term family. The third option was not seriously canvassed either
before the judge or before us.

The core of counsel's submissions on behalf of the mother was that the judge correctly stated
the law but did not apply it. The judge referred to . . . the decision in *Re K (A Minor) (Custody)*
[1990] 2 FLR 64. 67F in which Fox LJ stated:

'I come now to the law. In *Re KD (A Minor) (Access Principles)*, Lord Templemen said:
"The best person to bring up a child is the natural parent. It matters not whether the
parent is wise or foolish, rich or poor, educated or illiterate, provided the child's moral
and physical health are not endangered."
Lord Oliver of Aylmerton, at [1988] 2 FLR 139, 156B-C, cited the observations of Fitz-
Gibbon LJ in *Re O'Hara* [1900] 2 IR 232 at page 240 [see also p. 414, above]:
"In exercising the jurisdiction to control or to ignore the parental right the court
must act cautiously, not as if it were a private person acting with regard to his own
child, and acting in opposition to the parent only when judicially satisfied that the
welfare of the child requires that the parental right should be suspended or
superseded."
The judge properly directed himself as to the existence of that principle, but in my view
he did not apply it. What he did was to apply a quite different test. In effect, he asked
himself the question: who would provide a better home for R, the father or Mr and Mrs
E? Thus, the judge sought to balance the consideration of normal family life in an exceptionally good home (which he concluded would be provided by Mr and Mrs E) against the
fostering of the natural relationship which existed between a father and son . . . That, in
my view, was the wrong approach. The question was not where would R get the better
home? The question was: was it demonstrated that the welfare of the child positively
demanded the displacement of the parental right? The word "right" is not really accurate
insofar as it might connote something in the nature of a property right (which it is not) but
it will serve for present purposes. The "right", if there is one, is perhaps more than of the
child.'

Waite J, (in *Re K*) at [1990] 2 FLR 64, 70C, said:

'The principle is that the court in wardship will not act in opposition to a natural parent unless judicially satisfied that the child's welfare requires that the parental rights should be suspended or superseded.'

. . .

The difficulty in this case is that if the child had not been placed in such an unorthodox fashion with the plaintiffs and had been put into short-term care to help the mother it is most unlikely that efforts would not have been made to reintroduce the child back to her mother and brother and sister, unless there were exceptional circumstances which do not, in my view, arise in this case.

The mother must be shown to be entirely unsuitable before another family can be considered, otherwise we are in grave danger of slipping into social engineering. The question is not: would the child be better off with the plaintiffs? but: is the natural family so unsuitable that, as Fox LJ said, 'the welfare of the child positively demanded the displacement of the parental right'? I agree with Fox LJ that it is the right of the child rather than the parent and, borrowing from the philosophy of the Children Act 1989, I would rephrase it as the displacement of the parental responsibility. Once the judge found that this mother genuinely wanted her child back and was a mother who cared properly for the other two children, not to give her at least an opportunity to try to rehabilitate the family was to deprive the child of any chance of her own family. I recognise that the placement of the child back with the natural family poses considerable risks and requires careful consideration from the local authority concerned. But, backed as it is by all the professionals who gave evidence, it cannot be said to be wholly unreasonable. One attempt at rehabilitation with a young baby and a mother capable of loving her children would have been likely to have been attempted if this private arrangement had not been entered into and, instead, N had been placed by social workers with foster-parents where the mother had originally said she wanted to place her for adoption and had then changed her mind, not an unusual occurrence. . . .

There is a second matter raised in the arguments of the local authorities. . . . the position of the plaintiffs as permanent caretakers presents its own problems and would have done so even if the natural family had been entirely unsuitable.

The plaintiff husband is now 55 and the wife is 47. They are childless, having had the misfortune not to be able to have children and their efforts to adopt a baby have been unsuccessful. They were born and brought up in Cyprus and are Greek Cypriot in origin but are now British subjects. They married in England in 1965 and have ever since been settled here. The husband runs a Greek restaurant and they live in a pleasant house which they own. The husband speaks fluent English with a strong Greek accent. The wife understands and speaks English but her command of the language is imperfect and much less than her husband's. They are Greek Orthodox in religion. . . . They are quite simply outside the age group which would ordinarily be considered suitable as adopters of a baby. The question of age was considered to be an important factor by both Mr T and Mrs P [social workers]. It is not only a question of physical fitness but also the generation gap. Mrs P was concerned that the plaintiffs would make N the whole, the centre of their life and would find it very difficult to let go as she got older. In addition, there are problems of matching the child to a suitable family. This child is Irish. Although chosen by the natural family, the plaintiffs are in every way different from N's background, in origins, language and religion. In certain cases such difference should not be allowed to predominate over the needs of the child. But, I agree with counsel for the local authority that this is not such a case. The evidence of Mr T on attachment was that a child of a few months or, indeed, under 2, can move relatively easily, whereas an older child would be more adversely affected and, therefore, the exceptional factors so attractively urged upon us by counsel for the plaintiffs do not, in my view, arise and N would not be likely to suffer long-term harm by being moved from her present home. The third and, in a contested matter such as this, important aspect is the knowledge of the natural parents as to where the child would be living. The plaintiffs want no further contact with the natural parents and this knowledge of the address is, to say the least, most unsatisfactory for the child's future welfare. . . .

I am also concerned at the course that the arrangements for this child have taken and that the order of the judge terminating access and placing the child for adoption has circumvented the normal slow, careful, sometimes protracted process preparatory to an adoption application.

Appeal allowed.

Questions

(i) Do you agree with the actual result in this case?

(ii) Can the approach taken by Fox LJ in *Re K (a minor) (custody)* [1990] 2 FLR 64 and by Butler-Sloss LJ in this case be reconciled, either with *J v C* [1970] AC 668 (p. 411, above), or with s. 1(1) of the Children Act 1989 (p. 545, above)?

(iii) By the time the Court of Appeal decided the case, the child was a year old: what might Mr T's evidence about bonding have been then?

(iv) Why is age such an important disqualification for foster parents who want to adopt but not, apparently, for grandparents (see p. 650, below)?

As long ago as 1972, the *Report of the Departmental Committee on the Adoption of Children* (the Houghton Report) had expressed concern at the all or nothing choice facing most foster parents and relatives:

116. There are many children who are not being brought up by their natural parents but are in the long-term care of foster parents or relatives. These people normally have no legal status in relation to the child, and the law provides no means by which they can obtain it without cutting his links with his natural family by adoption. They are faced with the choice of doing without the legal security, which may be damaging to the child, or applying for an adoption order. This is one reason why . . . adoption is frequently applied for in inappropriate circumstances, particularly by relatives.

. . .

120. We suggested in our working paper that the right to apply for custody under guardianship legislation should be made available to relatives and foster parents already caring for a child, subject to certain limitations. The evidence we received strongly supported this, particularly in the case of relatives.

121. There were more reservations about guardianship for foster parents, but we think there are some circumstances where guardianship by foster parents would be appropriate. We have in mind situations where the parents are out of the picture, and the foster parents and the child wish to legalise and secure their relationship and be independent of the local authority or child care agency, but the child is old enough to have a sense of identity and wishes to keep this and retain his own name. There are also a few cases where the parents are actively in touch with the child and the foster parents, and where this bond is secure, but the parents recognise that they will never be able to provide a home for the child. There are other cases in which for financial reasons the foster parents may feel unable to seek adoption but guardianship with financial assistance may be appropriate [but see p. 657, below].

122. There must be some restriction on the circumstances in which foster parents can apply for guardianship. While courts would not be likely to accede to an application by foster parents who had cared for a child for a short period, the natural parents ought not to be caused the anxiety of being involved in such proceedings. We therefore recommend that, as in the case of adoption [see now Adoption Act 1976 s. 13(2)] foster parents should not be allowed to apply for guardianship unless they have cared for the child for 12 months.

. . .

125. Since a guardianship order can be reviewed by the court at any time, we do not propose any formal provisions for the giving of parental consent. The parents of the child should be notified of the application, as well as the local authority and any other interested person or body (including a local authority or voluntary society having care of the child), and they should all be parties to the application, with a right to attend and be heard.

126. We envisage that most guardianship orders would be made with the agreement of the natural parent, and that a natural parent who was unwilling to consent to the final severance of legal ties by an adoption order would sometimes be willing to consent to guardianship. . . .

127. In deciding whether to make a guardianship order the court would be required to follow the principle in the existing guardianship law and regard the welfare of the child as the first and paramount consideration. In deciding whether an order would be for the child's welfare, the court would be able to consider all the relevant factors, including the wishes of the child, where he was old enough to form a view; the wishes of his parents; and the suitability of the applicants.

. . .

144. We suggested in our working paper that where foster parents had cared for a child for five years they should be able to apply to the court for adoption and the position should be frozen pending the court hearing even if the mother had not consented. . . .

. . .

146. . . . There was a strong body of opinion, particularly from those experienced in the child care field, that the effect of our proposals would be to increase the number of 'tugs-of-war' between natural parents and foster parents in the courts; that the result would be a reduction in the number of children fostered and an increase in the number accommodated in children's homes, or kept by their mothers even if their situation was such that it was in the children's interest to be fostered; and thus changes in the law designed to further the welfare of some children might be harmful to the welfare of many others. It was argued that the number of cases in which children were reclaimed against their interests did not justify putting at risk the whole fostering system. . . .

The Children Act 1975 gave relatives and foster parents the right to apply for 'custodianship' but only if they had looked after the child for a minimum period which varied according to whether or not they were related to the child and whether or not they had the consent of a parent. The provisions were only brought into force on 1 December 1985 but appear to have been relatively little used. Emma Bullard and Ellen Malos summarise the results of their study of *Custodianship* (1990) thus:

9.31 The largest group of applicants were the grandparents applying for young children who had been living with them for all or most of their lives. The mothers themselves were likely either to have been in their teens at the time of their child's birth or to be in their early twenties and to be described as 'immature' either by their parents and the social workers or, among those we interviewed, to have that perception of themselves.

9.32 In the majority of such cases the reason for the application was the desire of the grandparents to safeguard the children's place with them, to be given a clear legal right to make the normal day-to-day decisions about their upbringing and to symbolise the child's place in the family.

9.33 In the cases involving relatives it appeared that the need for such an order arose most often in situations where there had been a substantial degree of agreement by the parents to the placement but also an element of uncertainty about its stability or about the formal powers of the carers to make day-to-day decisions about the children's care. In some cases the uncertainty was not a result of any sense of potential conflict with parents but because of a discovery that only a formal endorsement of the placement could convey such powers; the most frequently mentioned being that of consenting to medical treatment.

9.34 In some cases there had been a background of concern about the children's well-being while they were living with their parents and in a smaller number of cases the children had come into the grandparents' care from that of a local authority social services department following physical or sexual abuse.

9.35 There were also other circumstances in which relatives applied for custodianship but these were more common in the wider family than among grandparents. These included bereavement and marital breakdown and the most unusual case was one where custodianship was granted in adoption proceedings to an aunt who had taken over the care of the daughter of her brother and sister-in-law who were living in the same multi-generation family household.

9.37 The circumstances in which the children came into the care of the unrelated foster carers had features in common with those where relatives were caring for children following bereavement or marital breakdown or where the children had suffered or had been at risk of neglect or abuse. There were a small number of cases where children who had been in care before the application were suffering from severe health problems or disabilities.

9.38 There was also a blurring of the distinction between foster carers and relative applicants because in some cases the children had been boarded-out with the relatives while in the care of the local authority prior to the custodianship application.

They also looked into the reasons for *not* applying for custodianship:

9.39 . . . Most of the responses received were from unrelated foster carers. 14% of the respondents had not heard of custodianship until receiving our letter and questionnaire. The great majority (90%) of non-users described it as an advantage that, under a custodianship order,

the child in their care could not be moved to another placement by a social worker. Nevertheless they had not wanted to apply for custodianship, and gave a variety of reasons for their decision.
9.40 Apart from the people who had not heard of custodianship, there was a group who had heard of it but had found the available information confusing and inadequate. Some carers had decided that adoption was preferable, while others said simply that they could see no advantages to be gained by applying for custodianship. Financial considerations were mentioned by some carers who were caring for a child with special needs or who were dependent on state benefits. A number of respondents felt that they needed continued social work support for a variety of reasons such as making access arrangements, the child's special needs, or behaviour problems in adolescence.

Although numbers were small, and in the case of private carers represented the 'tip of the iceberg', the researchers concluded that 'there was and will continue to be a need for some such provisions as custodianship'. Quite what these might be is discussed by the Law Commission in their Working Paper on *Custody* (1986):

Custodians
5.15 Custodianship was devised to meet two distinct needs. The Houghton Committee on the Adoption of Children was mainly concerned to provide an alternative to adoption by step-parents (which had by then become very common, especially after divorce) [see p. 558, above] or by relatives such as grandparents. Both will sever the child's legal relationship with one side of his family, which may be detrimental in emotional and financial terms. Both also carry the risk of confusion and distress to the child, through the distortion of his relationship, not only with the adopters but also with his parents. Grandparent adoption, which makes the grandparent a parent and the parent a sibling, is a vivid example of this. The risk of damage caused by later discovery of the truth might also be greater than in more conventional adoptions.
. . .
5.17 Secondly, the Committee had in mind the need to provide security and status for some foster parents, in particular where 'the parents are out of the picture, and the foster parents and the child wish to legalise and secure their relationship and be independent of the local authority or child care agency, but the child is old enough to have a sense of identity and wishes to keep this and retain his own name'. There might also be cases where the parents were still in touch but recognised that they would never be able to provide a home for the child. Finally, some foster parents might not be able to afford to adopt, but could become guardians if financial assistance were available.
5.19 In the event, while the Committee's recommendations for adoption were implemented without significant change, further qualifications were imposed for 'custodianship.' It might have been argued that no special qualifications were needed, as the courts would be able to take all the relevant factors into account when deciding what would best promote the child's welfare. However, that would have increased the courts' powers to review the placement decisions made by local authorities. Such an 'open door' might also have added to the concern that parents would lose their confidence in the child care service [see Holman, 1975], and that foster parents (and others) would be encouraged to exclude rather than work with the natural parents, to the detriment of the child's relationships and sense of identity. Further, it could have been and subsequently has been argued that if a permanent substitute home is required nothing short of adoption can provide the necessary security and commitment on both sides [see Adcock, 1984].
. . .
5.23 . . . It would appear that the qualifications for custodianship do not entirely meet any of their declared objectives. They are not consistently less stringent than those for adoption. They cannot invariably spare parents the pain of unwarranted applications. . . .

Later, they make proposals for reform:

5.37 The simplest way of removing the arbitrariness, gaps and inconsistencies in the present law is to allow non-parents the same rights to apply for custody as have parents. They already have the right to apply for care and control in wardship proceedings, so that no new principle is involved in extending the statutory procedures to them. Given the large numbers of children who have experienced divorce, after which in theory any person can intervene to seek custody (or indeed access), it might not be such a radical step in practice as it at first sight appears.

. . .

5.39 It may therefore be that a requirement of leave, which currently applies to most interventions in divorce suits, would be a sufficient deterrent against unwarranted applications and would allow the court to judge whether the applicant stood a reasonable prospect of success in the light of all the circumstances of the case.

Special consideration is needed, however, for children in care:

5.41 As already seen, children in care are treated differently from others in both the matrimonial and wardship jurisdictions and the restrictions in custodianship have been devised partly with their special circumstances in mind. Most children are received into care under section 2 of the Child Care Act 1980 without any compulsory measures against them or their parents. . . . Under the Review's recommendations, local authorities would only compulsorily acquire parental rights if they could show, not only that they could do better than the parents, but also that the child was suffering or was likely to suffer harm as a result of shortcomings in his home. It would therefore be surprising if local authority foster parents could acquire the parental right of custody more readily than could the authority.

5.42 The unqualified right in foster parents to apply for custody could also be seen as an unprecedented interference in the child care responsibilities of the local authority. As has recently been emphasised, both by the Review of Child Care Law and by the report of the inquiry team in the Jasmine Beckford case, it is important to strengthen rather than to undermine the responsibility of local authorities to make the best possible provision for each child in their care. If foster parents were able to challenge their placement decisions in the courts, there would clearly be even greater pressure to allow parents to do so.

5.46 . . . The security and stability which might be gained from a custodianship order must be set against the difficulties which premature applications might cause in the making and realisation of the local authority's plans, particularly for children who have been compulsorily removed from inadequate homes. Current child care practice places great emphasis upon planning a secure and permanent home for children who might otherwise have to grow up in care. This may be achieved either through making strenuous efforts to solve the family's problems and reach a position where parents and child may be reunited or through finding an alternative family which can provide the sort of care which is best suited to the child's needs. Such plans may obviously take some time to formulate and put into effect.

The end result, in the *Children Act 1989*, is a modified 'open door'. We have already seen (p. 541, above) how s. 10(1) and (2) provide for the court to make any s. 8 order, either in any family proceedings or on free-standing application, and that applications can be made either by people entitled to do so or by anyone with the court's leave. The section continues:

10. — (5) The following persons are entitled to apply for a residence or contact order with respect to a child —
  (*a*) any party to a marriage (whether or not subsisting) in relation to whom the child is a child of the family;
  (*b*) any person with whom the child has lived for a period of at least three years;
  (*c*) any person who —
    (i) in any case where a residence order is in force with respect to the child, has the consent of each of the persons in whose favour the order was made;
    (ii) in any case where the child is in the care of a local authority, has the consent of that authority; or
    (iii) in any other case, has the consent of each of those (if any) who have parental responsibility for the child.
  (6) A person who would not otherwise be entitled (under the previous provisions of this section) to apply for the variation or discharge of a section 8 order shall be entitled to do so if —
  (*a*) the order was made on his application; or
  (*b*) in the case of a contact order, he is named in the order.
  (7) Any person who falls within a category of person prescribed by rules of court is entitled to apply for any such section 8 order as may be prescribed in relation to that category of person.
  (8) Where the person applying for leave to make an application for a section 8 order is the child concerned, the court may only grant leave if it is satisfied that he has sufficient understanding to make the proposed application for the section 8 order.

636   Chapter 14   The tug of love: parents by birth, fostering and adoption

(9) Where the person applying for leave to make an application for a section 8 order is not the child concerned, the court shall, in deciding whether or not to grant leave, have particular regard to—
  (a) the nature of the proposed application for the section 8 order;
  (b) the applicant's connection with the child;
  (c) any risk there might be of that proposed application disrupting the child's life to such an extent that he would be harmed by it; and
  (d) where the child is being looked after by a local authority—
    (i) the authority's plans for the child's future; and
    (ii) the wishes and feelings of the child's parents.
(10) The period of three years mentioned in subsection (5)(b) need not be continuous but must not have begun more than five years before, or ended more than three months before, the making of the application.

However, those local authority foster parents who require leave have an additional hurdle to surmount:

9.—(3) A person who is, or was at any time within the last six months, a local authority foster parent of a child may not apply for leave to apply for a section 8 order with respect to the child unless—
  (a) he has the consent of the authority;
  (b) he is a relative of the child; or
  (c) the child has lived with him for at least three years preceding the application.
(4) The period of three years mentioned in subsection (3)(c) need not be continuous but must have begun not more than five years before the making of the application.

The consequences of obtaining a residence order are spelled out later (and see p. 439, above, for the consequences for the parents):

12.—(2) Where the court makes a residence order in favour of any person who is not the parent or guardian of the child concerned that person shall have parental responsibility for the child while the residence order remains in force.
(3) Where a person has parental responsibility for a child as a result of subsection (2), he shall not have the right—
  (a) to consent, or refuse to consent, to the making of an application with respect to the child under section 18 of the Adoption Act 1976;
  (b) to agree, or refuse to agree, to the making of an adoption order, or an order under section 55 of the Act of 1976, with respect to the child; or
  (c) to appoint a guardian for the child.

Questions

(i) Do you approve either of the 'open door' or of the restrictions on local authority foster parents?
(ii) Notice that the 'checklist' (pp. 545-6, above) does not include the 'wishes and feelings' of the child's parents: should it?
(iii) The long-term foster parents studied by Rowe et al. (1984) were 'certainly not enthusiastic' about the possibility of custodianship and Bullard and Malos (p. 633, above) indicate that it has been more popular with relatives: will the same apply to residence orders?
(iv) How many reasons can you think of for preferring a residence order to adoption for (a) the applicants, (b) the birth parents, (c) the child, and (d) everyone else?

3 Adoption past

Adoption means a great many different things. For a summary of the extra-ordinary diversity of the institution, we may turn to *Adoption: A Second Chance* (1977), Barbara Tizard's account of her study comparing the adop-tion or rehabilitation of children in care:

The essence of adoption is that a child not born to you is incorporated into your family as though he were your own. This practice can be found in some form in most cultures — one of the best-known early adoptions was that of Moses. But just as the family, although a constant feature of all societies, has assumed many different forms and functions, so the characteristics of adoption have varied enormously during history. Today most people think of adoption as a process in which a young child, usually an infant, is permanently incorporated into a family into which he was not born. Typically, the adoptive parents and the biological parents are strangers, and the adoption is arranged through an agency or other third party. Great stress is laid on keeping the two sets of parents from meeting or even knowing each others' identity. All links between the adopted child and his natural parents are severed, and the adopted child has all the rights, and is treated in the same way, as a natural child of his new family. The primary purpose of the adoption is seen to be the satisfaction of the desire of a married couple to rear a child; at the same time, a home is provided for a child whose natural parents are unable to rear it. . . .

Perhaps the greatest contrast is with the custom of child exchange, or kinship fostering, formerly prevalent in Polynesia and parts of Africa. In these societies children were often not reared by their biological parents but sent to be raised by relatives, sometimes after wean-ing, sometimes from the age of 6 or 7. The exchange of children was arranged by the parents, who continued to maintain some contact with their biological child. It was believed that aunts, uncles and grandparents would bring children up and train them more effectively than their parents. This custom of child exchange seems to have been part of a system of mutual kinship obligations.

Adoption played a very different role in such ancient civilisations as the Babylonian, Chinese and Roman. There, its function was primarily to ensure the continuity of wealthy families by providing for the inheritance of property and the performance of ancestral worship. Roman law, for example, permitted adoption only in order to provide an heir to the childless, and laid down that the adopters must be past child-bearing age and the adoptee must be an adult. Until recently, the adoption laws of many European countries were influenced by Roman law; often adoptive parents had to be childless and over the age of 50.

Hindu law also recognised adoption as a method of securing an heir, both for religious purposes and for the inheritance of property. It specified, however, that the adopted child should be if possible a blood relative, and that the transaction must take place directly between the two sets of parents. For this reason, orphans could not be adopted. In most ancient civil-isations adoption was only one among several possible ways of providing an heir, and often not the preferred one. In Islam, for example, divorce and remarriage, polygamy, and the legitimisation of children by maidservants were common practices, while adoption was not permitted.

In all these societies adoption was essentially concerned with preserving the property and the religious observances of the families of the ruling class. It was very much a service for the rich, and for men; it was men who wanted heirs, and for this purpose they wanted boys. The emotional needs of childless wives were not recognised; indeed if they did not produce an heir they were likely to be divorced or otherwise replaced. Nor was it a service for homeless children; the adoptees were often adult, or, if children, they were given to the adoptive parents by their biological parents in order to better their social status.

Question

It may be easy to see why the modern idea of providing a home for an illegi-timate and often pauper child found little favour in medieval England, but how do you account for the fact that the great English families did not wish to do as the Romans had done — so that, even now, an adopted child cannot succeed to a peerage or other hereditary title?

Tizard resumes her account thus:

It is only relatively recently that adoption has become a recognised practice in Western society. Before this time bastards were sometimes legitimised by the rich, but the orphans and illegitimate children of the poor were sent to the workhouse and contracted out as soon as possible to private employers for domestic service, or work in factories, mills or mines. Often, of course, the orphans of both rich and poor were cared for by relatives, but they were rarely accorded the same status as the biological children of the family. The position of illegitimate children was worse, because of the social and moral stigma attached to illegitimacy, coupled with a strong belief in the inheritance of moral qualities. Not only the unmarried mother but also her child were regarded as morally inferior. There was also a general belief that to care for the illegitimate child would condone or even encourage the immorality of his mother. People were reluctant even to admit illegitimate children into a household; it was thought that 'bad blood will out', and the sins of the mother would be visited on the child.

It was in the United States, where more egalitarian ideas prevailed, heredity was at a discount, and human labour was in short supply, that the modern practice of adoption began to evolve. The first modern adoption law was enacted in Massachusetts in 1851. But long before that time American homesteaders took homeless children and reared them, benefiting in exchange from their help on the farm. Often, these children were treated very much as second-class citizens. Indeed, for half a century after adoption was legitimised in the U.S.A. it continued to be seen as a charitable act, and the adopted child was expected to work harder than a natural child and repay his debt of gratitude. . . .

Adoption at this stage, then, was a way of giving a homeless child a more humane upbringing than he would have received in an institution, with the expectation of receiving services from the child in return. It was only gradually that adoption began to be seen as a way of giving infertile couples all the emotional satisfaction that they would have had from a biological child.

The English were still deeply suspicious. In 1921, the Hopkinson Committee reported in favour of providing for legal adoption, but its recommendations proved so controversial that a second Committee was appointed, under the chairmanship of Mr Justice Tomlin. The *Report of the Child Adoption Committee* in 1925 is far from enthusiastic:

4. . . . There have no doubt always been some people who desire to bring up as their own the children of others but we have been unable to satisfy ourselves as to the extent of the effective demand for a legal system of adoption by persons who themselves have adopted children or who desire to do so. It may be doubted whether any such persons have been or would be deterred from adopting children by the absence of any recognition by the law of the status of adoption. The war led to an increase in the number of de facto adoptions but that increase has not been wholly maintained. The people wishing to get rid of children are far more numerous than those wishing to receive them and partly on this account the activities in recent years of societies arranging systematically for the adoption of children would appear to have given to adoption a prominence which is somewhat artificial and may not be in all respects wholesome. The problem of the unwanted child is a serious one; it may well be a question whether a legal system of adoption will do much to assist the solution of it.

. . .

9. [Nevertheless] . . . we think that there is a measure of genuine apprehension on the part of those who have in fact adopted other people's children, based on the possibility of interference at some future time by the natural parent. It may be that this apprehension has but a slight basis in fact notwithstanding the incapacity of the legal parent to divest himself of his parental rights and duties. The Courts have long recognised that any application by the natural parent to recover the custody of his child will be determined by reference to the child's welfare and by that consideration alone. The apprehension, therefore, in most cases has a theoretical rather than a practical basis. There is also a sentiment which deserves sympathy and respect, that the relation between adopter and adopted should be given some recognition by the community. We think, therefore, that a case is made out for an alteration in the law. . . .

Having reluctantly reached that conclusion, the Committee went on to consider how adoption should take place, and to what effect. Some of their arguments cast an interesting light upon more recent debates:

11. . . . some form of judicial sanction should be required. . . . The transaction is one which may affect the status of the child and have far-reaching consequences and from its nature is not one which, without judicial investigation, there is likely to be any competent independent consideration of the matter from the point of view of the welfare of the child.

Inasmuch as many cases of adoption in fact have their origin in the social or economic pressure exercised by circumstances upon the mother of an illegitimate child, it is desirable that there should be some safeguard against the use of a legal system of adoption as an instrument by which advantage may be taken of the mother's situation to compel her to make a surrender of her child final in character though she may herself, if a free agent, desire nothing more than a temporary provision for it. Further, there are many who hold that a system of adoption so far as it tends to encourage or increase the separation of mother and child may of itself be an evil and should be therefore, if introduced, operated with caution. . . .

. . .

15. . . . Whichever be the tribunal selected it is important that the judicial sanction, which will necessarily carry great weight, should be a real adjudication and should not become a mere method of registering the will of the parties respectively seeking to part with and take over the child. To avoid this result we think that in every case there should be appointed . . . some body or person to act as guardian ad litem of the child with the duty of protecting the interests of the child before the tribunal.

. . .

18. . . . No system of adoption, seeking as it does to reproduce artificially a natural relation, can hope to produce precisely the same result or to be otherwise than in many respects illogical, and this is made apparent in the diversity of provisions in relation to succession and marriage which appear in the adoption laws of other countries.

19. We think that in introducing into English law a new system it would be well to proceed with a measure of caution and at any rate in the first instance not to interfere with the law of succession . . . it does not require any profound knowledge of the law of succession to bring home to an enquirer (1) the impracticability of putting an adopted child in precisely the same position as a natural child in regard to succession, and (2) the grave difficulties which would arise if any alteration were to be made in the law of succession for the purpose of giving an adopted child more limited rights . . . but . . . the tribunal which sanctions the adoption should have power if it thinks fit, to require that some provision be made by the adopting parent for the child.

Question

What, if anything, was so different about the system of succession in classical Roman law that the complete absorption of the adopted child into his new family presented none of the difficulties apparently so obvious to English lawyers in 1925?

If these passages in the report betray (although they do not confess to) deep-seated attitudes about 'natural' and 'artificial' relationships, there is one point upon which the Committee's views have a decidedly modern ring:

28. . . . Certain of the Adoption Societies make this feature an essential part of their policy. They deliberately seek to fix a gulf between the child's past and future. This notion of secrecy has its origin partly in a fear (which a legalised system of adoption should go far to dispel) that the natural parents will seek to interfere with the adopter and partly in the belief that if the eyes can be closed to facts the facts themselves will cease to exist so that it will be an advantage to an illegitimate child who has been adopted if in fact his origin cannot be traced. Apart from the question whether it is desirable or even admissible deliberately to eliminate or obscure the traces of a child's origin . . . we think that this system of secrecy would be wholly unnecessary and objectionable in connection with a legalised system of adoption.

The first cautious steps were taken in the Adoption of Children Act 1926. In 1927, just under 3,000 adoption orders were made in England and Wales (mainly by juvenile courts) and numbers rose steadily year by year. During and after the second world war, they rose more sharply, reaching a peak of over 21,000 in 1946. There was then a decline to 12,700 in 1950 followed by a gradual recovery to an all-time peak of 24,800 in 1968, since when there has been a considerable fall. The following chart, from *Social Trends 21* (1991), tells us something about the changing number and character of adoptions, but we are woefully short of more detailed information:

Adoptions: by age of child

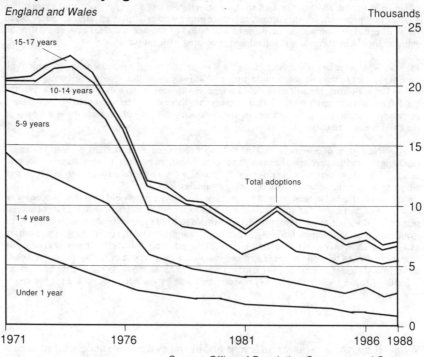

England and Wales   Thousands

Source: Office of Population Censuses and Surveys

Questions

(i) When did the adoption of children under the age of one begin to decline? Can you think why?

(ii) To what would you attribute the dramatic decline, particularly in the adoption of older children, in the mid-1970s?

(iii) Would you expect adoption to decrease, increase, or stay much the same in the future?

4   Today's 'traffic in children'

As Jean Heywood reports in *Children in Care* (1978):

The very popularity of adoption since it became legal in 1926 had led to an increase in the number of adoption societies and an extension of their activities, as well as an increase in the numbers of private individuals who arranged the placement of babies. Adoption work was entirely unsupervised and uncontrolled and the standard was naturally extremely variable and sometimes haphazard. . . . A committee of inquiry was set up in January 1936 under the chairmanship of Miss Florence Horsbrugh, MP whose recommendations were embodied in the Adoption of Children (Regulation) Act 1939. This legislation empowered the Secretary of State to make regulations about the way in which adoption societies conducted their work, and also laid certain duties with regard to them on the local authorities. Adoption societies must be registered as approved by the local authorities before they could place children for adoption; and the local authority was required to be notified seven days in advance of all children placed by private persons acting as third parties for adoption, and to supervise these placings until the adoption came to the court.

Question

Who do *you* think would be more suitable to bring up a little girl of two, recently released for adoption by her mother, who had found it impossible to cater for either her physical or her psychological needs: (*a*) a childless couple in their 30s, who have turned to adoption in desperation after unsuccessful attempts to cure the wife's infertility, or (*b*) a couple in their 40s whose own three children are now aged 18, 15 and 10 and who have been acting as short-term foster parents but would prefer a permanent placement?

The increasing professionalism of adoption societies led to an increasing concern about the private placement of children for adoption, discussed in the *Report of the Departmental Committee on the Adoption of Children* (the Houghton Report) in 1972:

83. The Hurst Committee estimated that in 1954 more than one-third of non-relative adoptions resulted from placements by third parties or by the natural parents. The 1966 survey figures [Grey, 1971] . . . show that the proportion was then very much less. Nevertheless there were some 1,500 children a year placed in this way. There are a number of reasons why people make independent arrangements without using agency services. One is the inaccessibility of agencies in some areas, which our recommendations [on p. 643, below] are designed to remedy. Others are people's dislike of the idea of enquiries by an agency, a desire to keep control of the situation themselves, or their trust in a person known to them, such as their family doctor. Some would-be adopters have been turned down by agencies, and others may seek independent placements because they realise that no adoption agency would consider them suitable.

84. Much concern has been expressed about these placements. The decision to place a child with a particular couple is the most important stage in the adoption process. Adoption law must give assurance of adequate safeguards for the welfare of the child at this stage, otherwise it is ineffective. This assurance rests mainly upon the skilled work of the adoption services, which includes preparation for adoptive parenthood. An independent adoption is one in which this assurance is lacking. We therefore suggested in our working paper that independent placements with non-relatives should no longer be allowed.

85. The evidence we received was divided. The main arguments against our proposal were that it was an interference with individual liberty, particularly in the case of direct placements by the mother; that there was no research evidence to prove that independent placements were any worse than agency placements, and that they should not be banned until agency work had improved; and that the investigation by the guardian ad litem and a court hearing were sufficient safeguards against adoption orders being made in respect of unsuitable placements.

86. Virtually no recent research has been done to compare the outcome of independent placements with that of agency placements, but there is no lack of evidence of unsatisfactory independent placements. Information received from the Church of England Board for Social Responsibility, which has contact with agencies working with unmarried mothers, revealed that in the course of a year a considerable number of highly unsatisfactory independent placements came to the notice of the social workers. Local authorities with experience of acting as guardians ad litem or carrying out welfare supervision of children placed for adoption have come across unsatisfactory independent placements which would not have been made by a reputable adoption agency. This is confirmed by the written and oral evidence we have received and by the personal experience of some of our members.

87. . . . The greater imbalance between the numbers of couples wishing to adopt and the number of babies needing adoption could lead to an increase in third party activity in future. We have received no direct evidence of financial transactions in third party placements, but it is within the knowledge of some of our members that couples have alleged that they have paid an inflated fee for the investigation of infertility on the understanding that a child would be found for them to adopt, and that mothers have alleged that services, such as nursing home facilities, have been provided on the understanding that the child would be available for adoption.

88. Adoption is a matter of such vital importance to a child (who is usually too young to have any say in the matter) that society has a duty to ensure that the most satisfactory placements are made. Society manifestly does not do so while it is open to anybody to place a child for adoption. While the court hearing is intended as a final safeguard, safeguards are needed much earlier. Moreover courts are in difficulty about refusing to make an adoption order because there is no agency to which the child can be returned. Adoption agencies are increasingly staffed by social workers whose professional skills and knowledge are increasing. Agency practice has built-in safeguards through the Adoption Agencies Regulations and through general accountability to the public. We therefore adhere to the view expressed in our working paper that independent placements should not be allowed once the new registration system for adoption agencies is in force, when these safeguards will be even greater. We include in this proposal direct placements by the parents, although, if they wished a particular placement to be made, the agency arranging the adoption should give this sympathetic consideration.

Questions

(i) What is so wrong about paying an unmarried mother to let you have her baby?

(ii) Can it be distinguished from paying a doctor to inseminate you with the semen of an unknown donor?

(iii) Or paying a woman to bear your child? (see p. 497, above).

(iv) Wait a moment — is not that what husbands do?

In *Growing Up Adopted* (1972), Jean Seglow, Mia Kellmer Pringle and Peter Wedge report upon a follow-up study of all the children born in a single week in 1958 who were adopted by non-parents: they were studied at birth, then again at seven, and further enquiries were made of their adoptive parents in 1967 and 1971. (For a comparison of their lives with those of children who were not adopted, see extracts from Lambert and Streather. *Children in Changing Families*, p. 453, above). As Jane Rowe says in her foreword:

The outstanding fact to emerge from this careful study is the power of the environment to affect children's development for good or ill. The adopted children are shown to have enjoyed a more favourable environment than the much larger group of illegitimate children who remained with their natural mothers. The illegitimate children were found to be vulnerable at birth. By the age of 7 years, the care, affection and material advantages provided by their new parents had enabled the adopted children to overcome their earlier handicaps and to compare very favourably with their peers in the general population. . . .

[Nevertheless] no-one reading this book carefully could spring to the conclusion that adoption is an easy solution to the problems of illegitimacy or childlessness. Not all the placements were happy and successful. Some of the agencies' work was evidently poor. Adoption is shown to have its own built in stresses. Many of the cherished theories of agency policy are once more challenged by the findings that factors such as age, health, social class and family composition are rather unimportant, while the authors demonstrate over and over again the importance of such intangible factors as attitudes, feelings and expectations.

One of the greatest advantages of agency placement might be thought by lay people to be the enhanced opportunities it provides for suiting the child to the particular adopters, but Mia Kellmer Pringle has this to say:

'Matching' for similarities in physical appearance, temperament, intelligence, etc., is yet another myth which needs to be abandoned for a number of reasons. Being led to expect similarities between their adopted children and themselves, adoptive parents will feel cheated and justifiably resentful if their expectations are subsequently not fulfilled. Also, the younger the baby the more impractical it is to ensure any measure of success. Moreover, it increases the risk of playing into the hands of those adoptive parents who want to deny the reality of adoption.

But perhaps most important of all 'none of the evidence showed matching to be a favourable factor. The only associations, in fact, were in the opposite direction. Families in the "very high" match group on physical resemblance and ethnic background had more children in the problem groups at follow-up, and those in the "very low" match group had fewer children showing problems' (Ripple, 1968). In matching for intelligence it has been shown that children with a very unpromising background who are placed into adoptive homes of a much superior level tend to develop intellectual abilities more closely in keeping with those of their adoptive parents.

Perhaps, therefore, it is not surprising that in discussing the overall results of the study, Peter Wedge reports:

Privately placed children accounted for some 21% of our sample. The remainder were placed by recognized adoption agencies. The former group of children did not differ significantly from children placed by an agency when their overall assessment of success in adoption was considered. The importance of this is not only that private placements seemed to be no less successful than agency placements, but that agency placements were no more successful than private placements. One would have expected that, where children were placed by agencies (presumably using specialist staff), then those children would have a more successful outcome than children placed privately, and so relatively haphazardly. If the practice of private placements justifies the criticism that has been frequently levelled at it, then now how necessary is it that the whole standard of adoption work among agencies should be raised above the level implied by this finding? Rather than banning independent arrangements, the first step must surely be to improve the alternative. . . .

Nevertheless, most private placement is now a criminal offence (s. 11 of Adoption Act 1976). Sections 1 and 2 of the 1976 Act, which are designed to provide a comprehensive agency service, result from the following recommendations of the *Houghton Report*:

33. . . . Over Great Britain as a whole, local authorities have made no systematic attempt to assess the needs of their areas and to develop services accordingly, and we have been told of areas which are ill-served. Moreover, where local authorities do provide a service, not all have integrated their adoption work with their other services for children and families.

34. These factors influence considerably the kinds of people, whether children, natural parents or prospective adopters, to whom a service is available and the quality of the service which is offered. What is needed is a service which is comprehensive in scope and available throughout the country.

The objectives and organisation of a comprehensive service

35. The service must meet the needs of children, persons wishing to adopt and natural parents. Local authority social services departments and voluntary organisations with a range of services for children should be able to offer a better and more comprehensive service for children than purely placement agencies, since they have a wider range of resources. This is particularly important where children with special needs are concerned . . . where more time is needed to find suitable homes, as well as good assessment facilities and highly developed casework skills.

36. If adoption is a child-centred service, aimed at providing homes for children, the service which an agency will offer to couples wishing to adopt will be ancillary to this central aim. . . .

...
38. What then should a comprehensive service cover? We consider that it should comprise a social work service to natural parents, whether married or unmarried, seeking placement for a child (which would include channels of communication with related community resources); skills and facilities for the assessment of the parents' emotional resources, and their personal and social situation; short-term accommodation for unsupported mothers; general child care resources, including short-term placement facilities for children pending adoption placement; assessment facilities; adoption placement services; after-care for natural parents who need it; counselling for adoptive families. In addition, it should have access to a range of specialised services, such as medical services (including genetic, psychiatric and psychological assessment services, arrangements for the examination of children and adoptive applicants, and a medical adviser) and legal advisory services.

Improved standards in agencies would permit the relationship of the other social work functions in the adoption process (ss. 13, 22, 23 and 65):

Welfare supervision
237. We are in no doubt about the need for a settling-in period, and a period of supervision and help. This was introduced in 1949 and its value is well established. The Guide to Adoption Practice describes the aim of welfare supervision as being 'to offer a supporting service to adopters, help them to focus on the essential task of integrating the child into their family life, and look forward confidently to the future. The welfare supervisor . . . should concentrate on the particular needs of this period: the adoptive parents' pre-occupation with the physical care of the child, their adaptation to new family roles and changed relationships'. We are convinced that this kind of help can best be offered by the agency responsible for choosing the adoptive home and placing the child. The agency is in the best position to help the couple to adapt to their new role and to deal with any problems they may have. . . .

Information to the court
244. . . . We consider that the law ought to recognise the decisive part played by the agency in arranging the adoption by making the agency accountable to the court. The court will have to make judgments on assessments and decisions made by the agency. It ought to have a first hand account of them and the opportunity to question the agency about them. The agency should therefore make a comprehensive report to the court and should have the opportunity of explaining to the court the reasons for that particular placement.

The guardian ad litem
252. . . . The appointment of the guardian should be at the discretion of the court. Courts might regard some types of adoption application as requiring the automatic appointment of a guardian, for instance, where there is an application to dispense with consent. Agencies may often be able to advise the court about cases which might warrant the appointment of a guardian, thus reducing the risk of delay.
253. Where the court decides to appoint a guardian, it would be helpful if it would indicate the aspects of the case which give rise to concern or uncertainty and in respect of which it particularly needs help. We think it should be a matter of good practice for the guardian to make his enquiries of the agency or local authority in the first instance, so as to avoid unnecessary duplication of enquiries and to acquire an understanding of the background of the case.

Question

The Tomlin Committee thought a guardian ad litem essential so that there should be a real adjudication (see p. 639, above): yet as judges almost always follow the guardian's advice, does it matter whether the court is advised by the agency or an independent person?

Behind these changes in policy and practice, however, lies a much more fundamental change in attitudes towards adoption, explained thus by Tizard in *Adoption: A Second Chance* (1977):

The fall in 'non-parent' adoptions since 1968 no doubt reflects the decline in the number of illegitimate births that took place during the period following the passing of the Abortion Act of 1967 – while the illegitimacy rate remained constant, the absolute number of illegitimate births fell by 10,000 between 1968 and 1973. It may also reflect the increased financial assistance available for single parents, and the widespread change of social attitudes, so that it is not only financially but also socially easier for the unmarried mother to bring up her child.

The present 'famine' of babies must also represent an increase in the number of couples wanting to adopt. Unfortunately this figure is not anywhere available, but since the number of babies adopted by persons other than a parent was actually higher in 1973 than in 1958 it is clear that there is no shortage of babies by pre-1960s standards. . . . A much larger sector of society began to see adoption as an acceptable solution to infertility, or as an acceptable way of adding to their family. . . . For the first time, would be adoptive couples are faced with the choice of either waiting for years, often without success, for a healthy white infant, or adopting an infant with a physical or mental disability, whose mother feels unable to accept it, or a child well past infancy, often of a different race.

This situation is leading to a changing conception of adoption in our society. Since the twenties adoption had been seen primarily as a service for childless couples – a way of providing them with a substitute child to satisfy their emotional needs and cement their marriage.

The essence of the new view of adoption is that it is a form of child care, one among several possible ways of rearing children whose parents can't, or won't, look after them. At first sight this change in emphasis may seem to be only a verbal distinction, since adoption must necessarily provide a service to both adoptive parent and homeless child. The implications of the two viewpoints are, however, very different – different couples and different children are considered suitable for adoption, depending on whether adoption is seen primarily as a cure for infertility or as a form of care. According to the first viewpoint, which until recently prevailed, only infertile couples would be offered a child. Prolonged investigations into infertility were the rule, because it was assumed that if the couple subsequently had a child of their own they would reject the adopted child. The health, racial origins and family history of the infant were closely examined, because it would not be 'fair' to place with the couple a child dissimilar to the healthy infant who under optimal circumstances might have been born to them. Only healthy infants with a 'good' family history were offered.

Much social work went into 'matching' the physical characteristics and family background of the child and adoptive couple, with the object of ensuring that the adopted child could be assimilated into his new family as completely as possible. . . .

For the same reason only infants were offered for adoption, so as to approximate as closely as possible to the normal way of acquiring children. Because of the emphasis on meeting the needs of the parents, children with any visible imperfections or whose family history contained evidence of any abnormality were not considered suitable for adoption.

If, however, adoption is seen primarily as a way of providing care for a child outside his natural family, then any child in need can be considered for adoption, whatever his colour, family history, state of health or age. Adoptive parents for these children are selected not for their infertility but because of evidence (often from the rearing of their own children, or from the kind of work they have done) that they are likely to provide a loving, stable home for a child in need.

Question

What do you think makes it possible for one person to love and care for another person's child as if he were her own? Are you in any way surprised that it is possible? Why do you think that English policy-makers have found it so surprising until so very recently?

This 'child-centred' view of adoption is enshrined in the following section of the *Adoption Act 1976*:

Duty to promote welfare of child
6. – In reaching any decision relating to the adoption of a child a court or adoption agency shall have regard to all the circumstances, first consideration being given to the need to safeguard and promote the welfare of the child throughout his childhood; and shall so far as practicable

ascertain the wishes and feelings of the child regarding the decision and give due consideration to them, having regard to his age and understanding.

5 A legal transplant?

The next step after the first cautious moves in 1926 is described by Heywood in *Children in Care* (1978) thus:

> The policy reflected in legislation for adoption . . . has moved on from providing legal *status*, for those who lacked this, to providing a legal *relationship* between adopted child and adopters as similar as possible to that which exists between a child and his natural parents. This principle was expressed in the Adoption of Children Act 1949, introduced as a private members' bill by Sir Basil Nield. The Act took great care to see, particularly by the safeguarding of consents, that the divestment of the natural family, and particularly the mother, should not be lightly undertaken, but that, where it was, the integration of the child with his new family should be complete and natural.

The process was still not complete, as the *Houghton Report* (1972) explains:

Interpretation of wills and other instruments

326. The present law provides that for the purposes of inheritance (in Scotland, succession) and of the interpretation of dispositions made after an adoption order, an adopted person shall be treated as if he is a child born to the adopter in lawful wedlock and not the child of any other person. This means that an adopted child has the same rights on an intestacy occurring after the adoption order as a child born to the adopter in wedlock. In England and Wales an adopted person does not, however, benefit under a general gift to, say, grandchildren of the testator, where the disposition was made before the date of the adoption order unless it can be construed to include adopted children as such. . . .

327. If adoption means the complete severance of the legal relationship between the child and his natural parents and the establishment of a new and irrevocable relationship, designed to make the child a full member of another family, it follows that that child should have exactly the same rights under wills and other instruments as a natural child of the adoptive family. We proposed that this should be the case and none of the evidence dissented from our proposition. It was pointed out to us that the passing of the Family Law Reform Act 1969 had placed illegitimate children in England and Wales in a better position than adopted children by providing, in section 15, that an illegitimate child may take under any disposition made after the Act came into force whether he was born before or after the disposition.

These recommendations were implemented in 1975, so that there are now only three important exceptions to the principle that an adopted child is the same as a child born to married parents: he cannot succeed to peerages and similar dignities; the rules prohibiting marriages with certain relatives in his birth family remain and he is only debarred from marriage with his adoptive parent in the new family; and if he is adopted abroad he will not gain the same rights under nationality and immigration laws as would a child born abroad to United Kingdom parents or adopted here.

Nevertheless, a total legal transplant does not mean a total physical or psychological transplant, as shown by these quotations from adopted adults who had sought their original birth certificates, as then permitted by Scottish but not English law, in John Triseliotis' study *In Search of Origins* (1973):

> 'You look at yourself in the mirror and you can't compare it with anybody. You're a stranger because you don't know what your real mother looks like or what your father looks like. . . .'

'All through my life I had the feeling of unreality about myself; a feeling of not being real, something like an imitation antique . . . I have been told that I was born in the Poor House and that my birth mother was a bad lot. This has been haunting me. I tried desperately to avoid being like her but then who am I like? I feel I have nothing to pass on to my children. . . .'

'My parents were kind people but very isolated. We had few relatives calling and we had no habit of calling on others. My parents' relatives meant nothing to me and I must have meant nothing to them. . . . When I was 15 or 16 I was very curious to know "who I was" and especially to know about my natural parents and their families. With your adoptive family you can only go as far back as they are and not beyond. But with your natural ones you feel you want to go further back. . . .'

The adopted person's needs are discussed by Christine Walby and Barbara Symons in *Who am I?* (1990):

The need to know

A major task faced by adopted people is the development of a sense of separate identity out of what Sants in 1967 called 'genealogical bewilderment'. Triseliotis in 1974 posed the question of 'how far adopted people face similar or different developmental tasks from those who have not been adopted'. These 'growing-up' tasks may be seen as achieving a mature independence and a clear sense of identity, and being able to give and receive love. They are inextricably linked with knowledge and feelings about heritage and about how other people see us and behave towards us.

Thus while the growing-up tasks may be common to all, the adopted person's development may be hampered by lack of knowledge. Margaret Kornitzer described the situation graphically in 1971 when writing of the effect upon the adopted person's natural development of a sense of identity when there has been a failure to provide information about 'blood and bones':

'Background knowledge of one's family is like baby food — it is literally fed to a person as part of the normal nourishment that builds up his [or her] mental and emotional structure and helps the person to become acquainted with what he [or she] is so that he can seize his inheritance of himself.'

She goes on to discuss the importance of knowing what our (biological) parents were like in understanding much about ourselves, and of the reality being 'healthier' than the fantasy. The point is made that simply being honest with adopted children is not enough: 'Even those adopted children whose adopters have been quite honest with them do feel left out on a limb at a certain point in their development because they can have no visual or mental picture of the couple who gave them their physical continuity in the chain of life': a fact denied by many practitioners and adopters.

At a more mundane level, as McWhinnie [1970] reports, the simplest tasks of adult life, such as completing medical data on forms, can become an ordeal because of the adopted person's lack of very basic information about biological background which others possess as a matter of course.

An adopted person has, in Triseliotis' view, to base his or her identity on 'the concept of two sets of parents'. Rowe [1970], Kirk [1964], Triseliotis [1974] and Rosner [1961] agree that adopters need to feel and experience the child as their own, and have confidence in the validity of their family. Jan de Hartog, a novelist and adopter, goes as far as to say that the adoptive mother should totally exclude the birth mother for a time in order to make the child her own.

The crucial issue, says Rowe, is that adopters should not pretend that being an adoptive parent is the same as being a biological parent, but should have a 'sturdy belief that their form of parenthood really is parenthood'. They also need to be able to feel 'some sense of kinship with the people who gave their child birth', and truly absorb the child's background into their family traditions.

Attitudes in the outside world

Unfortunately, as Triseliotis illustrated, the problems encountered by adopted persons in the maturation process are not limited to the resolution of attitudes, roles and relationships within the family. The community too has a subtle but profound effect: 'However successful adoptive parents are in their parental task, they cannot protect the child from the nuances of the outside world'. He also refers to 'covert negative messages', which are best illustrated by some of his examples from discussion with adopted people:

'When I told my fiance I was adopted his reply was "I do not know what my father and mother will feel . . ."

When my boy was born and my mother-in-law visited me in hospital she exclaimed: "Thank God that he has taken from our side of the family." I know what she was getting at and it hurt.

Somehow I felt that my parents were ashamed to talk about it and they gave me the feeling that adoption was unnatural . . .'

Thus the concept of access to birth records must be considered against a shifting foundation of confusion about the real nature of adoption. On the one hand we have absolute legal precision about the status of adoption and on the other, highly complex cultural and emotional uncertainty. It is in this context, and that of the complicated development of maturity and independence, that adopted people seek information on, and sometimes direct contact with, their origins.

The arguments for and against access to birth records were summarised in the *Houghton Report* (1972):

301. . . . It seems that where an adopted person has been told of his adoption at an early age and his relationship with his adopters is good he is less likely to seek access to his original birth record. Two-thirds of those in [Triseliotis'] sample who sought this information came to know about their adoption when they were 11 or more years old, half of them being 16 or over and one as old as 40. Only two-fifths of those who applied had been told of their adoption by their adoptive parents, the others finding out by discovering documents or letters or from chance remarks by people outside the family, mainly other children. For many of them the late disclosure of their adoption came as a shock, and they had difficulty in coming to terms with it. It was also noticeable that two out of every five who sought this information had lost one or both adoptive parents by death, separation or divorce before they reached the age of 16, and in one-third of all the applications it was the death of an adoptive parent that triggered off the search for information about the natural parents. Two-thirds of those who sought this information had the immediate reaction that it was helpful or of some help to them, while one-third felt very upset by the information they had obtained. Some were unhappy to discover that they were illegitimate, while the few who were legitimate were equally sad to think that their parents, although married, had 'given them away'. When seen four months later, however, nine out of ten had no regrets about having taken steps to find out this information.

302. The other evidence we received was divided. . . . Some witnesses urged that the right of an adult adopted person to know the names of his natural parents was a basic human right. Others were concerned about the distress which might be caused as a result of widespread attempts by adopted children to seek out their original parents. The Scottish research showed that although 42 adopted persons, or 60% of the sample, sought to trace their natural parents, only four succeeded in doing so, although seven others were able to contact blood relations. The Deputy Registrar General for Scotland said that he could not recall any complaint made by natural relatives who had been traced through the Registrar General's records. The fear of being traced may therefore have been unduly magnified, particularly as all the indications are that the climate of opinion is changing and mothers are becoming less concerned to conceal the fact that they have had an illegitimate child. Research into the views of a sample of adoptive parents revealed that 63% considered that their adoptive children should be allowed free access to their original records.

303. The weight of the evidence as a whole was in favour of freer access to background information, and this accords with our wish to encourage greater openness about adoption. . . . We therefore recommend that all adopted adults in England and Wales, whenever adopted, should in future be permitted to obtain a copy of their original birth entry.

This probably provoked more public debate and controversy than all the other recommendations in the report. For example, on 10 October 1976, the *News of the World* declared:

Thousands of women are facing the fear that a secret shadow from the past may soon knock at their door and wreck their marriages. They are the mothers who have never told their husbands and their families that they had an illegitimate baby whom they gave for adoption.

As a compromise, all those adopted before 12 November 1975, when the Children Act 1975 was passed, were obliged to accept counselling before gaining access to their original birth certificate. John Triseliotis looked at the debate and at the various studies of how the provisions had operated, in *Obtaining Birth Certificates* (1984) and concluded:

Only a minority of adopted people seek access to their birth records . . . The calamities anticipated by sections of the media, politicians, and some organizations have not materialized. The various studies carried out so far suggest that the vast majority of adoptees act thoughtfully and with great consideration for the feelings of both their birth and adoptive parents. The value of access facility is not now in dispute. . . . The vast majority of adoptees had no intention of setting out on a quest. Their main explanation was that they had parents, their adoptive ones, they were leading a 'happy' life and they were not interested in quests or in meetings with an original parent. . . .

It is difficult to escape my earlier conclusions that though there is a curiosity and deep psychological need in every adoptee to know about his background and personal history, the need for access to records, for meetings or reunions with birth parents is frequently a characteristic of those who were not given reasonable explanations and information about their origins, of those who have recently gone through some major event or crisis in their lives, or of those who may have experienced unsatisfactory growing-up experiences. Contrary to some assumptions identity confusion does not necessarily go with adoption. Studies have shown that the vast majority of adopted people have a firm and secure sense of self.

Walby and Symons, however, were able to explore the feelings of their small sample in some depth:

One of the most interesting facts to emerge from this data is that those respondents who were voluntarily told of their adoption by their parents did not necessarily feel better about their situation than those who were not told. The crucial elements appear to be the amount and the accuracy of the information available, the ability of the adoptive parents to recognise and share in the feelings of the adopted child about the adoption, and particularly their appreciation of the child's need to explore the question 'Who am I?'. The experiences and feelings of respondents in both groups were markedly similar.

No respondents had received any meaningful information about their origins; many spoke of extreme tensions and even taboo preventing any discussion of adoption; all had feelings ranging from discomfort in their difference from others, and anger about not having information to which they felt entitled, to guilt about causing distress to their adoptive parents. The majority felt stigmatised by their adoptive state. In terms of Goffman's [1963] description of the three main types of stigma, this feeling would derive from 'abominations of the body' and 'blemishes of individual character', the first a subtle product of common attitudes towards childlessness (traditionally the main motivation to adoption), the second a more obvious, and for the respondents more potent, reaction to illegitimacy.

Questions

(i) Is this a question of psychological welfare or human rights? In *R v Registrar General, ex p Smith* [1990] 2 QB 253, the Divisional Court held that, on public policy grounds, the Registrar General could refuse to disclose the original birth certificate to an adopted man who had committed a brutal and sadistic murder and while in prison had killed another prisoner whom he thought was his adoptive mother: was this right?

(ii) If the 1975 provision established the child's right to know his origins, why should it not apply equally to a child born of AID, egg donation or embryo transfer (see pp. 492 et seq., above)?

In *Adoption, Identity and Social Policy* (1985), Erica Haimes and Noel Timms point to some further difficulties which the changing character of adoption may bring:

In terms of adoption practice in general, there is a risk with these developments that two styles of adoption will develop: that for the placing of young babies and that for the placing of the older child, especially with the continuance of institutional secrecy over the birth certificate. Whilst older children will remember their previous name and will, therefore, require explanations for the change, the baby will undergo the change unknowingly and will remain dependent on the adoptive parents for any information. For any adult enquiring . . . in the future (and if placed after November 1975) routes to detailed information will be more difficult without a counsellor as a guide. Conversely, the difficulties for the social worker holding the adoption files will begin when the adoptee has found the route, for then the judgement of how much information to give, difficult enough now, will be crucial. . . . Up to now the nature of the difficulty has been to tell someone they were illegitimate. . . . However, many adoptees had already worked this out and for others it was not very important anyway, given their other interests and perhaps the social climate. Does this mean though that children currently being placed will be able to work out along similar lines that they had perhaps been neglected or physically abused by their natural parent(s)? Or that they had been the subject of a contested adoption? Social workers will have to confront those facts themselves first and decide how much and in what way they will be able to tell a person face-to-face.

Question

If the child has the right to know his identity, should the natural parent (particularly if she did not consent to the adoption) have the right to know the identity of her child?

This leads us to an issue about which the Houghton Committee's views may seem contradictory. On the one hand, they gave considerable encouragement to adoptions of older hard-to-place children or by long term foster parents. On the other hand, the more the 'total transplant' view took hold, the more disquiet was felt about adoptions, especially those by relatives or step-parents, where this could not be achieved (see p. 632, above). Once custodianship was brought into force, the Children Act 1975 obliged the court to consider it as an alternative to adoptions sought by relatives or step-parents. One court did so even before then:

Re O (a minor) (adoption by grandparents)
[1985] FLR 546, [1985] Fam Law 305

Applicants for adoption appealed against the justices' decision to make an interim order, giving the applicants legal custody for one year, in the hope that the custodianship provisions would be implemented before it expired.

Hollis J: . . . The facts, very shortly, are these. The child concerned is a little girl who is now just over 5 years old. She is the illegitimate daughter of the appellants' adopted son and apparently in May 1980 the mother of the child left her with the father who immediately handed her over to his parents. She has lived with her grandparents ever since then with some contact with the father but none with the mother; the mother now being abroad. The father is apparently a registered drug addict. Both the parents consented to an adoption order being made in this case and the fact of adoption was supported also by the guardian ad litem, who of course made various inquiries as to the case. In the justices' reasons for their decision they said this:

'5. [The grandmother] (aged 54) impressed us as a motherly figure who might well make a suitable adopter. We felt far less sure about [the grandfather]. Although he is 66, not 67 as stated in the report, he appeared to us to be an oldish 66 and, looking ahead, his age could be a considerable problem in future. Moreover, there is no young person in the household although the father does make visits. We felt anxious about the plan, if there was no adoption, for the applicants to appoint their son as testamentary guardian and, on their own admission, he is, at present at least, an irresponsible drug addict. In addition, we could not altogether overlook the fact that their adopted son's upbringing had not been a success, although the extent of their own responsibility for this is quite unclear.

6. In the forefront of our minds is the need to give first consideration to the need to safeguard and promote the welfare of the child throughout its childhood . . . this led us to the conclusion that in the present circumstances adoption is inappropriate. On the other hand, we accepted the grandparent's desire for some security in the relationship with [the child] is legitimate and, had Part II of the Children Act 1975 been in force, we might well have made a custodianship order.'

. . .

The question is: Do those factors, so far as they are legitimately found by the magistrates, support their conclusion that in the present circumstances adoption is inappropriate? I find that a difficult question to answer, and I bear this in mind, that their answer to that was really to postpone the decision. I ask myself what assistance could postponement of the year give? First the grandfather would be a year older, as indeed would everybody else, but it seems highly unlikely that any decision could have been taken by then as to a testamentary guardian. Furthermore, I would have thought that it was not appropriate to weigh in the scales the factor of the grandparents' upbringing of their own son. We simply do not know enough about it and nor did the justices.

I have come to the conclusion, therefore, that in para. 6 of the reasons, when they reach the conclusion that adoption is inappropriate, the magistrates have fallen into error.
Appeal allowed.

Re S (a minor) (adoption or custodianship)
[1987] Fam 98, [1987] 2 All ER 99, [1987] 2 WLR 977, Court of Appeal

The applicants were the mother's father and his second wife, who had taken full responsibility for the child (now 4) since he was 6 months old. The mother had consented to adoption, but the local authority favoured custodianship, because adoption would not enhance the quality of the relationship between the applicants and the child and could confuse existing relationships. The judge made a custodianship order and the applicants appealed.

Sir Roualeyn Cumming-Bruce: . . . It seems to me that the paramount factor affecting his future welfare is to make an order that will secure him in his de facto relationships in such a way as to minimise the risk of the natural mother, or anyone else, seeking to disrupt them. This an adoption order can achieve with a greater prospect of success than a custodianship order. The legal relationships will then coincide with the actual relationships on which T is, by now, totally reliant. It seems to me that an adoption order will promote the welfare of T in another way. When he is tactfully introduced to the true facts about his parentage, the adoption order will have already conferred upon him the legal status of child of the applicants. This is likely to reduce, not increase, the risk of emotional confusion, or the onset of insecurity.

Glidewell LJ: . . . In this case, however, whether T is adopted or not, he will be brought up by the applicants, and the decision when and how to tell him will be made by them. The female applicant said in her evidence in the county court: "T will grow up understanding; we've spoken to him already about adoption." She also then said, and counsel repeated before us, that she and her husband would seek the help and advice of the county council social workers. That being so, whatever the prospects are of T being in a state of some confusion when he not only knows but is old enough to appreciate and understand the true relationships in his family, I cannot see how that confusion will be greater, or its effect made worse, if he is adopted than if the applicants are his custodians.
Appeal allowed.

Questions

(i) Do you find the reasons given for preferring adoption in either of these cases convincing?

(ii) Would they have been more or less convincing if the mother had refused to agree to adoption?

There is another group where similar problems might arise, and where the courts might also take a different view from that taken by social workers:

Re B (MF) (an infant) Re D (SL) (an infant)
[1972] 1 All ER 898, [1972] 1 WLR 102, Court of Appeal

Two brothers, then aged four and one, were removed from their parents as being in need of care. They were fostered with the appellants, with whom they 'made great strides' and were 'undoubtedly happy and extremely well cared for.' Their natural parents' home was 'nothing like as satisfactory,' they had three other young children and were in 'constant financial difficulties,' partly because of the father's psychiatric difficulties. After three years, the foster parents applied to adopt the boys and the natural parents both consented, but the county court judge refused to make the order. The foster parents appealed.

Salmon LJ: . . . Apparently the view which the county council take is that it would be better for the status quo to be preserved, that is to say for the children to remain as foster children with the appellants. It would have the advantage, so the county council think, of keeping the position fluid. There is no doubt that the position would remain fluid, but I am by no means persuaded that that fluidity could conceivably be in the interests of the children. Once an adoption order is made, then the children's position vis-à-vis the appellants is assured. The appellants would have the same legal obligation to the children as if they were their own natural children. I am not suggesting for a moment that they would not in any event continue to treat the children with the same affection and take the same interest in them and accept the same responsibility for them as they do now; and, of course, I know that the county council has no present intention of taking the children away from them. But the appellants feel — and indeed they feel rightly — that just as the children would have no legal rights against them unless an adoption order is made, so they would have no legal right to keep the children should the county council, in their wisdom, decide to remove the children in the future. I would have thought the insecurity which they not unnaturally feel would be just as unsatisfactory from the point of view of their relations with the children as it would be unsatisfactory for the children to have no security and no legal rights as against their adopters.

The only other point that I should deal with is the fact that the appellants take the view that Mr and Mrs D, for whom they have much sympathy, should from time to time visit the children, and particularly that these two boys should be kept in touch with their sister Pauline. It is quite true that in law Pauline will cease to be their sister after the adoption order is made, but Pauline will remain their natural sister and no order of any court can alter that fact.

As a rule, it is highly undesirable that after an adoption order is made there should be any contact between the child or children and their natural parents. This is the view which has been taken, and rightly taken, by adoption societies and local authorities as it has been by the courts in dealing with questions of adoption. There is, however, no hard and fast rule that if there is an adoption it can only be on the terms that there should be a complete divorce of the children from their natural parents. . . . Although the courts will pay great attention to the general principle to which I have referred, namely, that it is desirable in normal circumstances for there to be a complete break, each case has to be considered on its own particular facts.

The facts of this case are exceptional. Although it may be — I know not — that it would be a good plan if there were a complete break here between Mr and Mrs D and the two boys, the appellants (who I suspect know a good deal more about the situation than I do) consider that the occasional encounters between Mr and Mrs D and the boys and Pauline [are] for their good.

It is suggested that in the future the fact that the boys know the appellants as 'Mummy' and 'Daddy' and their parents as 'Daddy D' and 'Mummy D' may lead to stresses and strains. Mr and Mrs D are not prepared to have these children back. It is all they can do to cope with the three young ones they have at home now, and without any disrespect to Mr and Mrs D, through circumstances over which they have no control, it is obvious that it would be very much more in the interests of the two boys to stay where they have been so well cared for during the last three years.

Appeal allowed.

Re C (a minor) (adoption: conditions)
[1989] AC 1, [1988] 1 All ER 705, [1988] 2 WLR 474, House of Lords

C was taken into care, together with her two older brothers, at a very early age. C became very attached to her brother M during the next seven years, spent mainly in children's homes, and remained in touch with him after her placement with the prospective adopters. C wanted to be adopted, but her mother withheld agreement in case adoption might weaken her relationship with M. The judge thought this should be preserved at all costs. Both the judge and the Court of Appeal refused to dispense with the mother's agreement, being doubtful of the power to make continued contact a condition of the adoption order. The prospective adopters appealed.

Lord Ackner: . . . It seems to me essential that, in order to safeguard and promote the welfare of the child throughout his childhood, the court should retain the maximum flexibility given to it by the Act and that unnecessary fetters should not be placed on the exercise of the discretion entrusted to it by Parliament. The cases to which I have referred illustrate circumstances in which it was clearly in the best interests of the child to allow access to a member of the child's natural family. The cases rightly stress that in normal circumstances it is desirable that there should be a complete break, but that each case has to be considered on its own particular facts. No doubt the court will not, except in the most exceptional case, impose terms or conditions as to access to members of the child's natural family to which the adopting parents do not agree. To do so would be to create a potentially frictional situation which would be hardly likely to safeguard or promote the welfare of the child. Where no agreement is forthcoming the court will, with very rare exceptions, have to choose between making an adoption order without terms or conditions as to access, or to refuse to make such an order and seek to safeguard access through some other machinery, such as wardship. To do otherwise would be merely inviting future and almost immediate litigation.

The cases in the Court of Appeal have essentially been concerned with the question of whether provision can properly be made in an adoption order for access to a natural parent or parents. Although it is one of degree, a distinction can properly be drawn between access to natural parents on the one hand and other natural relatives on the other. Other relatives and, in particular, brothers and sisters have no parental rights which by the adoption order are being extinguished and then vested in the adopters. The Court of Appeal was, in my judgment, correct in paying no regard to the suggestions made by the judge that if C were told that M was no longer her brother, she would be bitterly and desperately hurt. Fresh evidence put before the Court of Appeal established that C, when interviewed a little over a year ago, had made it clear that she wanted to be adopted, that to her adoption meant that 'she would then know that no one could ever take her away from her mum and dad' (the appellants). She said she could not see how it would affect her relationship with M or how she felt for him and he for her. Even without this additional evidence, it seems to me that the judge's evaluation of C's reaction to learning that technically M was no longer her *legal* brother was quite unreal.

. . .

The order which the judge made sacrificed the benefits of adoption in order to provide for an event which might never eventuate, namely the failure of the adopters properly to co-operate in maintaining access between C and M. The fresh evidence put before the Court of Appeal established that there continued to be no obstacles put by the appellants in the way of such access and none were anticipated by M. Indeed, your Lordships have been informed, without objection, that the appellants took C to London twice last year so that she could visit M, and had invited M to come to see his sister in Norfolk. Contact had continued by phone and letter. Moreover, the judge failed to appreciate that, were it to become necessary to enforce access between C and M, to do so through the machinery of wardship was no easier and, indeed, might be more complex, than by seeking to enforce a term or condition of the adoption order. *Appeal allowed*.

Questions

(i) But what if the local authority had been unable to find prospective adopters who could recognise and respect the child's relationship with her brother?

(ii) Does the distinction drawn between birth parents and other relatives make sense?

Despite the misgivings of some courts and local authorities and of the Houghton Committee, a more 'open' view of adoption has been developing, particularly for older children who need a secure placement but retain a knowledge of their origins. Open adoption has been pioneered in New Zealand, and the results appear in the *Report of the Adoption Practices Review Committee* (1990):

WHAT IS OPEN ADOPTION?
Open adoption can mean different things to different people and can take different forms. Social work practices differ throughout the country. At one end of the spectrum, it involves nothing more than an exchange of letters and photographs, sometimes through the mediation of the Department. At the other end of the spectrum, it can mean a degree of co-parenting between the birth and adoptive parents. In between, there is a wide range of different styles of contact, co-operation and mutual care. Open adoption may involve not just the parents, but also the families, and we have heard of moving experiences as families get to know each other and share their lives a little.

Whatever the nature of open adoption for particular individuals, it is important to emphasise that everyone should enter upon the process with the right attitude — an attitude of openness, respect and willingness to explore the options in the interests of the child.

POPULARITY OF OPEN ADOPTION
The evidence we have received strongly supports open adoption. This support comes from all quarters — adopted persons, birth parents, adoptive parents, families, social workers, and experts in the field. Although we cannot be sure what effect open adoption will have long-term on adoptive people, given that it is only recently that the practice has begun, we are confident that it provides a more satisfactory basis for the vast majority of permanent placements of children. . . .

Open adoption appears to be in the best interests of the child for several reasons:

   (i) To develop socially, emotionally, physically and intellectually, the child should have a sense of personal identity. Knowledge of genetic inheritance, whakapapa and roots is a component of identity formation. Open adoption is one of several ways of preserving to varying degrees the child's cultural background.
   (ii) For a child to be accepted fully in the adoptive family, there is a need for the child's origins to be known and accepted by the whole family . . .
   (iii) There is research and inherited wisdom that children can maintain more than one relationship simultaneously and indeed may benefit from so doing, provided that there is no threat to the permanency of placement with the principal family.

ONGOING SUPPORT
While the endorsement of open adoption is overwhelming, there are points of concern. Open adoption is sometimes presented as if it were the ideal answer and simple to carry through. The reality is that, even in the best of open adoption arrangements, there can be problems, unforeseen issues, tensions, changes of circumstances and changes of heart. These are all perfectly

natural, given that we are dealing with human nature. Sometimes they may stem from the different socio-economic backgrounds of the birth and adoptive parents.

It must be recognised that open adoption needs working at, that the parties sometimes need assistance to make it work, and that each relationship is different. Under 'the new adoption', adoption is a process and not an event. It is important therefore that practice does not suddenly end. It is equally as important that the preparation of the parties be realistic, point out the pitfalls as well as the joys, and get people to think long-term about the arrangement that they come to. Sometimes, for example, a birth mother may want minimal contact for the first few years but feel more confident about herself and the relationship with her child later on. The adopted person may not place much store beside contact with birth parents in the first few years of life but feel quite the opposite as the teenage years are lived. It must be remembered that the welfare of the child is the deciding factor, and security and permanency of placement is a principle which we accept.

The idea has been taken up by the Inter-Departmental Review of Adoption Law here. In its discussion paper on *The Nature and Effect of Adoption* (1990), Option A is to retain the existing concepts of adoption and residence orders, but with possible modifications to the former:

97. One of the great benefits of adoption and its essential feature in contrast to other orders is the permanent status it confers on both child and adoptive parents as members of the new family, the security this gives to them all, and the commitment it demands of the adoptive parents. Given the importance with which permanence has been regarded in social work philosophy in recent years, it is not surprising that the irrevocability of adoption has made it attractive to those involved in finding substitute care for children. Furthermore, this new relationship continues into adulthood and throughout the lives of all involved. . . .

Suggested modifications: openness
98 Given these advantages, would it be better to modify adoption within its existing legal framework, rather than to create new alternatives? One option would be to facilitate greater openness in the form of pre- or post-adoption contact, while leaving the legal effects of adoption essentially unchanged. . . .

Pre-adoption contact
100. One form of openness would allow greater involvement of the birth parents, usually the mother, in the selection of adopters. Birth parent involvement might range from actual selection, for example from a number of prospective adopters approved by the agency, to exchange of photographs. It is difficult to say to what extent this is happening already; the legislation itself gives no guidance on the issue and is predicated on the assumption that no such involvement takes place. Legally however there is nothing to stop pre-adoption involvement of birth parents and one option would be to leave this to developments in agency practice. The extent of such links would obviously be related to the post-adoption position, as were there to be contact after adoption, pre-adoption meetings would be a natural corollary.

Openness and the legal process
102. A further corollary of increased openness before and after adoption is to move towards less secrecy at the time of the proceedings. Anecdotal evidence suggests that in many cases serial numbers are applied for as a matter of course without necessarily any regard to the particular circumstances of the child. One option would be to reduce the use of the serial number procedure by making it available only with leave of the court.

Post-adoption contact
103. If the existing approach is retained and adoption continues to effect a transfer should it necessarily sever all of the links with the child's birth family after adoption? Increased openness might make adoption the favoured solution for some children for whom long-term foster care had seemed the only possibility, even though rehabilitation with the birth family was out of the question. This could include children whose parents do not agree to adoption and children needing contact with relatives.
104. Although the Adoption Act 1976 allows conditions to be included in adoption orders the courts have been reluctant to attach access provisions [see p. 653, above]. However, evidence from one research sample of 'special needs' adoptions showed that contact with parents

and siblings continued in a small percentage of cases. Thus, while few adoption orders actually include an access clause, access may continue as a result of informal agreement.

105. The Children Act 1989 will allow a contact order to be added to an adoption order and the court to prescribe the type and extent of contact. This might range from staying access at one end to the exchange of cards on birthdays and special occasions at the other. The act will also allow a contact order to be attached to a freeing order and so for the first time a child could be freed with a condition of access. Adopters would know that in these circumstances there would be less risk of the parents withdrawing their agreement and their acceptance of the access could be explored at an early stage. This would be a major development for the courts which at present regard access as exceptional and are extremely unlikely to grant it without the adopters' agreement. It would also be a major development for agencies.

106. Again, should developments in post-adoption contact be left to practice or is there a need for legislation? Statutory encouragement of the use of contact orders, perhaps in the form of a duty on the court to consider them in every case where an adoption order is made, is one way in which additional flexibility could be achieved whilst retaining the basic status quo. Or should the use of orders to regulate post-adoption contact be restricted, for example to those cases where the parties themselves have reached agreement? What other restrictions, if any, might there be on the use of post-adoption contact orders? The court could of course refuse to make the order, where it was of the view that this would not be in the child's best interests.

108. It would also be possible to make provision for the court to direct the adoption agency to continue to pass on information to birth parents after adoption. The cooperation of the adoptive parents would obviously be necessary for this to work in practice. Another possibility would be to increase the opportunity for birth parents and relatives to obtain information about the adopted person once he or she had grown up.

Suggested modifications: encouraging the use of alternative orders (the 'menu' approach)
110. Under the Children Act 1989 the court will have a power of its own motion to make section 8 orders, either as an alternative or in addition to adoption orders [see p. 541, above]. . . . At present there is no statutory duty on the court to consider making section 8 orders in adoption applications, comparable to that in section 1(3)(g) of the 1989 Act [p. 546, above], although it has the power to select from the 'menu' thereby placed at its disposal. Should the court be under a duty when hearing adoption applications to consider the available alternatives? This could easily be fitted into the legislation. If so, should there be guidelines for the court to follow and what factors should the court take into account when making the choice? There is also the question as to whether the court's duty under the Children Act section 1(5) should apply generally in adoption proceedings (namely the duty on the court, when considering making an order under the Act, not to make any order unless it considers it would be preferable to no order at all).

Residence orders as alternatives
111. The advantage of residence orders is that they confer parental responsibility without interfering with the child's identity and family relationships. They can be combined with contact orders if appropriate. They can, however, be revoked. This may be seen as a weakness from the perspective of those caring for a child who value the permanence of adoption. In practice a residence order *will* generally provide the necessary permanence for the family concerned, as once a child is settled the courts are reluctant to disturb the status quo and are most unlikely to discharge it in favour of another party. It appears from the research that some foster parents and children are more worried that the local authority might remove the children than that the parents will do so. Former local authority foster parents with a residence order will be in the same position in relation to the local authority as other parents, in that a care order will be necessary for the authority to take back responsibility for a child against their will. The local authority will still have power to pay an allowance if appropriate. Thoburn [1990] writes that a majority of research studies into long-term foster care and adoption found that children find foster care status acceptable when it is *seen* as permanent.
. . .

113. Under the Children Act 1989 the court can, when dealing with any application for a Children Act order, prohibit any named person from applying for an order under the Act without the court's leave [s. 91(14)]. This power could be used to increase the permanent element of a residence order, for example to prevent birth parents applying for residence or contact where foster parents have obtained a residence order, or, in a step-parent case, to prevent the birth parent who is undesirable or long out of the picture from making upsetting or unexpected applications. Further, although the absent parent technically retains 'parental responsibility', the court could also make a 'prohibited steps' order restraining the parent from exercising any authority without its permission.

Suggested modifications: revocability

114. At present, the law provides expressly for revocation in limited circumstances only . . . Other mistakes are put right, if at all, by the somewhat artificial route of giving leave to appeal out of time [see *Re M (minors)* [1990] FCR 993, CA; *Re F(R)* [1970] 1 QB 385, [1969] 3 All ER 1101, CA]. Legislation in some of the Australian jurisdictions, at least on its face, gives greater scope to discharge an adoption order. In several jurisdictions an adoption order may be discharged in circumstances along the following lines:

(a) where the adoption order or agreement was obtained by fraud or duress or other improper means; or

(b) some other exceptional reason exists why, subject to the welfare and interests of the child, the adoption order should be discharged.

Questions

(i) Option B was to have two different types of irrevocable order, one transferring the child from one family to another, the other transferring only parental responsibility for bringing the child up (which might be called 'simple' rather than 'full' adoption, or guardianship, or permanent residence, depending on precisely what was involved): is this really necessary?

(ii) The Children's Legal Centre (1991) would prefer there to be three different types of residence order ('basic', 'midway', and 'permanent'); they argue that 'the concept of adoption reinforces the notion of children as property *par excellence*'. Do you agree?

One last aspect of the blurring of distinctions between fostering and adoption is the implementation in 1982 of the following recommendation of the *Houghton Report* (1972):

Should adoption be subsidised?

93. We suggested in our working paper that consideration should be given to the possibility of guardians and adopters being paid regular subsidies in appropriate cases, and we said that we would welcome views on this. While there was considerable support for allowances for guardians . . ., many witnesses saw a clear distinction between adoption and guardianship and opposed the idea of any payments to adopters. Some took the view that payment would conflict with the principle that adoption should put the child in precisely the same position as a child born to the adopters. While some agreed with our suggestion that, if allowances were payable, more homes might be found for children with special needs, others said that it would be unfair to the parents of handicapped children if the adopters of these children could get an allowance which was not available to their natural parents. Some said that the law should not forbid agency payments to adopters but that there should be no national system of allowances.

94. We recognise the objection to singling out handicapped adopted children for special payments, and we do not advocate payments for adopters generally. However, we still think that there is a case for allowances in some circumstances, for example, where suitable adopters are available for a family of children who need to be kept together but, for financial reasons, adoption is not possible if an allowance cannot be paid. Although most witnesses were opposed to our suggestion, we should like to see a period of experiment during which evidence could be gathered. But at present even experiment is not possible, because it would contravene the law, and we recommend that the law should be amended so as to enable payments to be made by a few charitable bodies specially authorised by the Secretary of State for this purpose. There may be a number of difficulties, and we suggest pilot schemes which could be reviewed after, say, seven years, although the subsidy would have to be continued to those who had adopted on that basis for as long as they needed it.

Question

How many views about the 'deservingness' of foster parents are coloured by the fact that they receive an allowance, however inadequate, for their pains?

6 The parents' wishes and the child's best interests

At the heart of most of the dilemmas discussed in this chapter lies the weight to be given to the parents' wishes. As we have seen (p. 638, above), the Tomlin Committee treated adoption as a 'transaction' between natural and adoptive parents, in which the court's task was to ensure that the private agreement did not prejudice the welfare of the child. Later developments placed more and more emphasis on the need for expert intermediaries who must now arrange and supervise the placement. Parents who want their child to be adopted can no longer choose who should have him; they cannot complain if they do not know his new parents' name; the only preference which agencies have any duty to respect is as to their religion (s. 7 of the Adoption Act 1976). The agreement of each parent or guardian, is, however, required to the particular adoption order, unless it can be dispensed with on defined grounds or the child has already been freed for adoption (s. 16(1) of the 1976 Act). The Tomlin Committee assumed that parental consent would be required unless the parent had 'disappeared, abandoned the child, or become incapacitated from giving such consent.' Over the years, the circumstances in which the court has been empowered to dispense with the parent's consent have increased. The present list is in s. 16 of the *Adoption Act 1976*:

16 (2) . . . that the parent or guardian—
   (*a*) cannot be found or is incapable of giving agreement;
   (*b*) is withholding his agreement unreasonably;
   (*c*) has persistently failed without reasonable cause to discharge the parental duties in rela-
          tion to the child;
   (*d*) has abandoned or neglected the child;
   (*e*) has persistently ill-treated the child;
   (*f*) has seriously ill-treated the child (subject to subsection (5)).
. . .
   (5) Subsection (2)(*f*) does not apply unless (because of the ill-treatment or for other reasons) the rehabilitation of the child within the household of the parent or guardian is unlikely.

Question

Compare these grounds with those for making a care order under s. 31 of the Children Act 1989 (see p. 607, above). Do these grounds appear to you to be wider or narrower? Do the differences seem, at least at first sight, to be justified by the different circumstances in which the procedures are used?

In practice, dispensing with parental agreement to an adoption order arises in two quite different contexts: first, the parent who places her child for adoption and later changes her mind, and second, the parent who has never agreed to adoption.

(a) THE PARENT WHO CHANGES HER MIND

Re W (An Infant)
[1971] AC 682, [1971] 2 All ER 49, [1971] 2 WLR 1011, 115 Sol Jo 286,
House of Lords

The mother was unmarried, in her early 20s. She was living in one room with her two little girls by an earlier relationship, now broken, when she found herself unintentionally pregnant again. She was a good mother to the girls but was doubtful of her ability to cope with a third child in that accommodation. Accordingly she made arrangements before the birth for the child to be adopted. She was offered better accommodation just before the birth, but still had doubts and so did not alter the arrangement. The child went to the applicants as temporary foster parents when he was 8 days old and had been there ever since. They began adoption proceedings when he was 10 months old, and the mother signed the consent form a few days later. She withdrew that consent the day before the hearing was first due to take place. She was now well settled with her two daughters and a cousin in her new flat, but she had had no contact at all with the child, who was 16 months old when the county court judge came to decide the case. He decided that she was withholding her consent unreasonably and made the order. Her appeal to the Court of Appeal was upheld, on the ground that her conduct had not been 'culpable' or 'blameworthy' ([1970] 2 QB 589, [1970] 3 All ER 990, CA) but a differently constituted Court of Appeal refused to follow this test in *Re B (CHO) (an infant)* [1971] 1 QB 437, [1970] 3 All ER 1008, CA and the applicants in this case appealed to the House of Lords.

Lord Hailsham of St Marylebone LC: . . . [Section 16(2)(*b*)] lays down a test of reasonableness. It does not lay down a test of culpability or of callous or self-indulgent indifference or of failure or probable failure of parental duty. . . . It is not for the courts to embellish, alter, subtract from, or add to words which, for once at least, Parliament has employed without any ambiguity at all. I must add that if the test had involved me in a criticism of the respondent involving culpability or callous or self-indulgent indifference, I might well have come to the same conclusion on the facts as did Sachs and Cross LJJ. But since the test imposed on me by the Act is reasonableness and not culpability I have come to the opposite conclusion.
   The question then remains as to how to apply the correct test. The test is whether at the time of the hearing the consent is being withheld unreasonably. As Lord Denning MR said in *Re L (an infant)* (1962) 106 Sol Jo 611:
   'In considering the matter I quite agree that: (1) the question whether she is unreasonably withholding her consent is to be judged at the date of the hearing; and (2) the welfare of the child is not the sole consideration; and (3) the one question is whether she is unreasonably withholding her consent. But I must say that in considering whether she is reasonable or unreasonable we must take into account the welfare of the child. A reasonable mother surely gives great weight to what is better for the child. Her anguish of mind is quite understandable; but still it may be unreasonable for her to withhold consent. We must look and see whether it is reasonable or unreasonable according to what a reasonable woman in her place would do in all the circumstances of the case.'
This passage was quoted with approval by Davies LJ in *Re B (CHO) (an infant)* by Lord Sorn in *A B and C B v X's Curator,* by Pearson LJ in *Re C* [1971] 1 QB 437, [1970] 3 All ER 1008, *Re C (L)* [1965] 2 QB 449, [1964] 3 All ER 483 and by Winn LJ in *Re B (CHO)*. In my view, it may now be considered authoritative. . . .
   From this it is clear that the test is reasonableness and not anything else. It is not culpability. It is not indifference. It is not failure to discharge parental duties. It is reasonableness, and reasonableness in the context of the totality of the circumstances. But, although welfare per se is not the test, the fact that a reasonable parent does pay regard to the welfare of his child must enter into the question of reasonableness as a relevant factor. It is relevant in all cases if and

to the extent that a reasonable parent would take it into account. It is decisive in those cases where a reasonable parent must so regard it. . . .

I only feel it necessary to add on this part of the case that I entirely agree with Russell LJ when he said in effect ([1970] 2 QB 589, [1970] 3 All ER 990) that it does not follow from the fact that the test is reasonableness that any court is entitled simply to substitute its own view for that of the parent. In my opinion, it should be extremely careful to guard against this error. Two reasonable parents can perfectly reasonably come to opposite conclusions on the same set of facts without forfeiting their title to be regarded as reasonable. The question in any given case is whether a parental veto comes within the band of possible reasonable decisions and not whether it is right or mistaken. Not every reasonable exercise of judgment is right, and not every mistaken exercise of judgment is unreasonable. There is a band of decisions within which no court should seek to replace the individual's judgment with his own.
Appeal allowed.

Question

How many points of difference can you find between this case and *Re K (a minor) (wardship: adoption)* [1991] FCR 142, [1991] 1 FLR 57 (p. 631, above)? Are they enough to account for the difference in result?

Re H (infants) (adoption: parental consent)
[1977] 2 All ER 339, [1977] 1 WLR 471, 121 Sol Jo 303, Court of Appeal

An unmarried mother of about 20 gave birth to twins in January. They were fostered until April when she signed a provisional form of consent to adoption and the children were placed with the applicants. In May she signed the formal consent forms but still had doubts. In July she indicated that she opposed the adoption. The hearing took place in December. The trial judge found that the children had formed a special attachment to the adoptive mother which it might be harmful to break and that the mother was immature and vacillating. He dispensed with her agreement and the mother appealed.

Ormrod LJ, delivering the first judgment at the invitation of Stamp LJ, stated the facts and said that it was impossible for the court to come to any other conclusion than that the judge's judgment must be upheld. His Lordship continued: The attitude of the court to the question of dispensing with consent, or holding that the consent is unreasonably withheld, has changed over the years, since adoption became possible in 1926. It has changed markedly since Lord Denning MR's judgment in *Re L (an infant)* and perhaps even more markedly since the House of Lords' decision in *Re W (an infant)* and probably it will change even more in consequence of the Children Act 1975, although, at the moment, this court has said that s. 6 of the Adoption Act 1976 does not apply to this particular issue *Re P (an infant) (adoption: parental consent)* [1977] Fam 25, [1977] 1 All ER 182). However, it is safe to say this: the relative importance of the welfare of the children is increasing rather than diminishing in relation to dispensing with consent. That being so, it ought to be recognised by all concerned with adoption cases that once the formal consent has been given or perhaps once the child has been placed with the adopters, time begins to run against the mother and, as time goes on, it gets progressively more and more difficult for her to show that the withdrawal of her consent is reasonable.
Appeal dismissed.

Question

Do you think that, on its proper construction, s. 6 of the Adopton Act 1976 (p. 645, above), should apply to the court's decision about whether the parent's decision to withhold agreement is unreasonable?

(b) THE PARENT WHO HAS NEVER AGREED

Cases where the parent has never consented usually arise after a child has been taken into care, either under a care order or in wardship, and the local authority plans a permanent substitute home rather than rehabilitation. The court's approach is first to decide 'where does the child's future lie?'; if it lies in a substitute home, the court must then decide whether a hypothetical reasonable parent would object. The law is the same whether it is an application to adopt or to free the child for adoption.

Re D (a minor) (adoption: freeing order)
[1990] FCR 615, [1991] 1 FLR 48, Court of Appeal

The child was 4½ years old. The father played no part in her life, the mother's relationship with him having ended before the child's birth. Following unexplained injuries and evidence of emotional deprivation, a care order was made. The child was placed with short-term foster-parents and access visits with the mother were arranged. At about the same time the mother gave birth to a second child by another man. The relationship between the mother and that other man was unstable. The child returned home to the mother on trial with intense social work involvement. However, rehabilitation was unsuccessful. The child had a continuing loss of weight and suffered unexplained injuries. There was hostility by the mother towards the child. Subsequently, the child was again placed with foster-parents. The local authority decided not to try further rehabilitation but to consider adoption. The mother was at first in favour of adoption but later changed her mind. By this time the mother was living with a different man. The mother's access to the child continued, albeit infrequently, after she was placed with prospective adopters. The local authority applied to free the child for adoption. The judge dismissed that application and the local authority appealed.

Butler-Sloss LJ: . . . Mr Wall for the local authority has criticised the judge's approach to both tests of welfare and consent. The first ground is that the judge confused the two tests and did not apply them in two stages. The judge said:
'I have been referred to a large number of authorities and there are two questions:
(1) Is adoption in the best interests of the child?
(2) Is the natural mother unreasonable in withholding her consent?
Whether these two matters should be dealt with separately or together is arguable, there being conflicting authorities, but the end result in this case in my opinion is the same.'
In our judgment, the judge, having correctly identified the questions to be asked, fell into a fundamental error in considering it made no difference whether they were dealt with separately or together. Our understanding is that there are not now any conflicting authorities on the matter and none was cited to us. Moreover, . . . the test under s. 6 is not the same as the test under s. 16(2), to which we shall refer later. This fundamental misapprehension has fatally flawed the course of the judge's reasoning and he has throughout his judgment confused the two tests.
The second criticism relates to the first test, whether it is in the child's best interests that she should be adopted. Having set out very briefly some of the relevant facts and considered access to the mother and her present position in somewhat more detail the judge said:
'What I have to decide is not whether it is in K's interests in the near or foreseeable future or perhaps the long-term future that she should remain with the prospective adopters, but whether it is in K's interests, at this time and at this age, that her right of contact with her mother and with her half-sister should be terminated. Notwithstanding the present careful reports to the contrary, I find it difficult to hold that it is in her best interests

that contact should cease. Access is taking place, she enjoys it and it is causing no ill-effects.'

Mr Wall has argued with considerable cogency that the judge never addressed the underlying question of the welfare of the child, nor did he analyse objectively the value of access to the child. That value in turn depended upon the quality of the relationship between the mother and the child. How strong was the bond between them? Mr Wall showed us all the relevant passages in the evidence about the strength of that relationship. There was no evidence of any real bond between the mother and child, not surprisingly with the history of interrupted care throughout her short life, and some evidence of rejection by the mother during each of the two periods when K was returned to the mother's care. She had a period of one year between October 1985 and October 1986 with her mother, followed by a gap of 9 months away from her. She returned in July 1987 for 7 months and thereafter, in the subsequent 16 months had seen her mother, at most, five or six times. The evidence of the social worker was that she was indifferent to access. It was a time for her to play with toys. She was happy there and happy to say goodbye. The social worker also said that she did not believe that there was a meaningful relationship between the mother and the child and that she would not suffer from the cessation of access by her mother. None of that evidence was referred to by the judge. Further, although he referred to the reports, he did not refer specifically to the report of the child's guardian ad litem, who found a lack of sustained commitment by the mother to access over the year up to the hearing and gave careful reasons on behalf of the child why he recommended adoption.

The judge also failed to make a finding as to whether the child was likely to return to the mother in the foreseeable future. This was a matter of importance in applying both the first and second tests. The undisputed evidence before him was that the child would remain with the prospective adopters whatever the outcome of the application, even if they had to be redesignated long-term foster-parents. The local authority had a full care order and unless the mother succeeded in revoking it, an application for which was not in prospect, the child would not be likely to return home. The purpose of access, therefore, had to be considered: was it to create a greater bond between them which might lead to a change of heart by the local authority; or was it to be contact access for a few times a year to keep alive the child's knowledge of her mother? The amount of access was entirely within the control of the local authority and unless they terminated it, upon which the mother could apply to juvenile court, she had no redress as to the number of times they might allow access to take place. Reasons for continuing the second type of access were given to the judge by junior counsel then appearing for the mother, as he informed us. But it is unclear which sort of access the judge had in mind and whether he believed that a return to the mother was feasible. If rehabilitation was not feasible, the realities of the situation of access as the child grew older and became more settled with long-term foster-parents did not appear to have been considered by the judge.

For all these reasons we are satisfied that the judge failed to look beneath the surface and did not look at all the circumstances. He gave what he thought was the desirability of access continuing at this time predominant weight over all other factors. He did not give sufficient consideration to the child's long-term welfare throughout her childhood and did not correctly apply the test under s. 6. In our judgment he erred in law in his approach to the first stage.

We now turn to the second stage. The test under s. 16(2) as to whether a parent is withholding his or her agreement unreasonably is entirely different from that under s. 6. . . .

From *Re W (An Infant)* [p. 659, above] and subsequent speeches in the House of Lords and judgments of this court it is clear that reasonableness is to be judged by an objective and not a subjective test. Would a reasonable parent have refused consent? (per Lord Reid in *O'Connor v A and B* [1971] 1 WLR 1227, 1229). This involves considerations of how a parent in the actual circumstances of this mother, but (hypothetically) endowed with a mind and temperament capable of making reasonable decisions, would approach a complex question involving a judgment as to the present and the future and the probable impact upon the child (per Lord Reid in *Re D* [1977] AC 602, 625). There has become a greater emphasis upon the welfare of the child as one of the factors (but not the overriding one), and the chances of a successful reintroduction to or continuance of contact with the natural parent is a critical factor in assessing the reaction of that hypothetical reasonable parent (per Purchas LJ in *Re H: Re W (Adoption: Parental Agreement)* (1983) 4 FLR 614, 625). This test is to be applied at the time of the hearing and the court is not entitled simply to substitute its own view for that of the parent (*Re W (An Infant)* (above) at p. 659).

In his judgment, the judge said:

> 'Miss D looks forward to the eventual reunification of K and S with her and Mr B. Although Miss D has not really explained all of the past, on the evidence I have heard from her I do not consider her aspiration eventually to have K back to be an unreasonable one. She has not said precisely how she expects this to come about. She is after

all in the hands of the local authority, but I do not regard her aspiration as being
unreasonable.'

Since the judge in considering the first test had never decided whether such an aspiration was
objectively reasonable, the criticism of Mr Wall that this was a subjective approach of the judge
is, in our judgment, well-founded. The judge went on to say:

'Apart from eventual reunification there is access continuing and I do not see how I can
say that she is being unreasonable to want it to continue as she thinks it is for the benefit
of K and S. Especially when it is going on with no ill-effect to K.'

Again, since there was, as we have already set out under the first test, no finding as to
the purpose or long-term benefit of access to K, Mr Wall's criticism applies equally to this
passage. . . .

The question then arises as to whether this court should substitute its own discretion upon
the facts before us or remit the application to the county court for a rehearsing and reassessment
of the two tests. . . . We are satisfied that in this case this court has sufficient information to
enable it to consider the test of welfare and the objective assessment as to whether a hypothetical
reasonable parent in the circumstances of this mother ought to have given her consent. On the
first test we are entirely satisfied that there is no prospect whatever of this child returning to
live with her mother. There is no evidence of a real relationship between the mother and the
child. . . . Further, the contact of K with her half-sister, S, has been infrequent and at their
respective ages and in the circumstances it was not suggested by any one that any relationship
at all has developed. We are satisfied that there is ample evidence upon which to answer the
first test under s. 6: the adoption would safeguard and promote the welfare of K throughout
her childhood.

The second test of consent is more difficult and we keep well in mind the importance of 'the
band of decisions within which no court should seek to replace the individual's judgment with
its own'.

Looking at the hypothetical reasonable parent in the circumstances of this mother, we see that
the factors in her favour are: she is the mother and the child lived with her for two main periods
totalling about 18 months: she now has a settled home with a potential step-father and S has
returned to live with her and is being cared for satisfactorily — if she were not, no doubt the
local authority would have intervened; she desires to reunite the family; she is continuing to
have access and the child on one level enjoys it and is having no ill-effects from it.

The contrary factors are: the efforts at rehabilitation have failed in the past, not only because
the child was not well cared for and there was suspected non-accidental injury which may have
been attributable to the then co-habitee, but also a failure of bonding, and hostility and rejection by the mother; K has not lived with her mother since 19 February 1988; there is no present
evidence of any close or warm or effective relationship between them nor any foundation upon
which to recreate it; there is no evidence of any relationship between the half-sisters; there is
no real possibility of rehabilitation not only in the foreseeable future, but since children cannot
wait for ever and will settle where they are, at any time thereafter — consequently the entirely
natural aspirations of the mother to have K back and reunite the family are unrealistic; in the
absence of eventual rehabilitation and without an adequate existing relationship, the continuance of access in the long term is not likely to be beneficial to the child in any real sense; contact a few times a year without any firm basis of a relationship between the mother and child
for a child of 4½ years old would at best be entirely superficial and more for the adult than
the child, and at worst, as the child settled with the present family and grew older, might be
unsettling and upsetting. . . .

In our judgment, a reasonable parent in the position of the mother would recognise the overwhelming force of the negative points and the unreasonableness of refusing to agree to the freeing for adoption. We, therefore, hold that the mother has unreasonably withheld her agreement
under s. 16(2). We allow the appeal and accede to the application of the local authority to free
K for adoption.

Appeal allowed.

Question

In a somewhat similar case, *Re L (a minor) (adoption: statutory criteria)*
[1990] 1 FLR 305, Balcombe LJ stated: '[counsel for the mother] submitted
that there was a presumption in the case of all children that access by the
natural parent was desirable, and the onus ought to be on those who sought

to stop access to prove it. It seems to me that that submission is . . . misconceived'. But if this presumption applies between separated parents, why should it not apply between birth parents and prospective adopters?

Re B (a minor) (adoption: parental agreement)
[1990] FCR 841, [1990] 2 FLR 383; Court of Appeal

After a history of neglect and inadequate parenting by the mother, care orders were made in respect of two children, N and S. The children were placed with foster-parents. Access was granted to the mother. N settled well into the foster-family but S was unhappy and disruptive. The local authority decided to terminate access for a trial period to see how the children would respond. The mother applied to a magistrates' court for an access order. The guardian ad litem did not support a termination of access. A compromise was reached between the local authority and the mother whereby access would be restored and the mother's application adjourned. When access was reintroduced, there was a marked difference in the attitude between the two children: S wanted access to continue but N was diffident. S was subsequently returned to the mother and the care order in respect of her was revoked. N continued to see his mother but not as often as under the terms of the compromise. He was relieved with the departure of S and regarded access as an intrusion. The foster-parents decided to apply to adopt N. Access was terminated but N was encouraged by the foster-parents to have some residual contact with S and his mother. At the adoption hearing in the county court, the judge found that adoption would be in the best interests of N, but decided that he could not say that the mother's refusal to agree fell outside the band of reasonable parental decisions. Accordingly, he refused to dispense with the mother's agreement. The foster-parents appealed.

Butler-Sloss LJ: . . . In the careful judgment of the judge, he was satisfied under [s. 6 of the Adoption Act 1976] (1) that the welfare of the child during his childhood would be met by the adoption; and (2) that the boy himself wanted to be adopted. The boy was angry that the adoption proceedings were adjourned and, according to the judge, would be 'devastated if it did not take place,' and he was a very vulnerable child. He saw his sister as a threat in the home and was relieved when she left. He was not close to his sister. He regarded access as an intrusion and his attitude to it was ambivalent. He did not want to see his mother now, although he might wish to see her in the future. The judge was satisfied on the basis of welfare that the balance was in favour of adoption, although not overwhelming; and, from the wishes of the child to be adopted, he was satisfied that adoption was in the best interests of the boy. The only issue was the refusal of the mother to agree.
    . . . The judge correctly set out the objective test that was to be applied. In my judgment, however, he did not go on to consider the effect upon a reasonable mother faced with this situation, a boy of 11, whose view was strongly held, who had lived with the foster family for 7 years at the time of the hearing before the judge and was entirely integrated within that family; a very vulnerable child who would be devastated by the result if the adoption did not take place. . . .
    The continuing contact between the mother and the son is undoubtedly an important factor, as indeed Purchas LJ said in Re H; W (Adoption: Parental Agreement) (1983) 4 FLR 614, at p. 625A:
    'The chances of a successful reintroduction to, or continuance of contact with, the natural parent is a critical factor in assessing the reaction of a hypothetical, reasonable parent as was recognised in Re F.'
    This, however, is an unusual case with unusually understanding foster-parents said by the judge to be 'quite wonderful and selfless'. They have not sought in the past to prevent contact

between the boy and his mother and sister, and there is nothing to indicate that they would do so in the future. . . . The judge would not have granted access at this time, if asked, but he took the view that estrangement was not complete; he found it difficult to contemplate that the dialogue would not continue and attached considerable importance to it. The dialogue at that time was telephone calls and cards.

In refusing the adoption the judge referred to the possible effect of a Pyrrhic victory and the possibility that it might bring about the cessation of the very contact that the mother was wishing to have. He does not, however, appear to have considered that aspect of the problem within the situation of the mother and her refusal to consent. At the age of this child, his view of being in touch with his mother with or without an adoption order would carry a great deal of weight with these appellants and with any court who might in future consider whether access should be granted. The mother's position for herself and for her daughter in respect of contact with N is more likely to be secure with adoption than in a situation where the adoption was refused.

The judge was also, in my view, over-influenced by the position of S, which was undoubtedly different from that of the boy, N. She was isolated and alone, whereas he had his foster-brother and foster-sister. The position appeared to be very different to that in *Re C (A Minor) (Adoption: Conditions)* [1989] AC1, [1988] 1 All ER 705 [1987] 2 FLR 383 [p. 653, above], where there was a real danger that the girl would lose contact with her brother after adoption and that was seen to be of substantial importance to her. In this case, the contact with his sister is not of great importance to N. The effect upon the sister, which is understandably in the mind of the mother, should not, in my judgment, in the circumstances of this case have assumed great importance in the assessment by a reasonable mother.

The other matter of which the judge took some account is that of the grievance of the mother. In my judgment, he misdirected himself in putting that into the balance, particularly since he found that the grievance was not justified since October 1984. There can, in my view, only be rare instances when a sense of grievance can justifiably have an important effect upon a reasonable parent with a decision to refuse consent, and I find it difficult to envisage when that could occur.

This was a difficult and worrying case in which the judge wanted to make an adoption order, but refused to do so on grounds which, in my judgment, were untenable. This was one of those cases in which the welfare of the child was decisive and a reasonable parent should have come to the conclusion that adoption was in the best long-term interests of this boy. I too would allow this appeal.

Appeal allowed.

Questions

(i) Was this a case for an access condition or contact order? If not, why not?

(ii) If the court first concludes that adoption is in the best interests of the child, how can it then conclude that the mother is reasonable in objecting?

(iii) How might a mother's *justifiable* sense of grievance be taken into account (see *Re E (minors) (adoption: parental agreement)* [1990] 2 FLR 397)?

(iv) Why were these cases argued under 'unreasonable withholding' rather than one of the other grounds for dispensing with parental agreement?

(v) Would a different type of order have been appropriate in either of them?

(c) 'FREEING FOR ADOPTION'

The *Houghton Report* (1972) recommended a new procedure which might help in solving both types of consent problem:

168. . . . There is considerable dissatisfaction with the timing and nature of the present consent procedure. Parental rights and obligations are not terminated at the time the parent signs the consent document. They continue until an adoption order is made some weeks or months later.

The argument in favour of this system is that there is never a period when the child is not the legal responsibility of either natural or adoptive parents. But there is evidence that this procedure imposes unnecessary strain and confusion on the mother. Moreover, it may encourage indecisiveness on her part; and by maintaining her legal responsibility for the child until the adoption order is made, it may prevent her from facing the reality of her decision and planning her own future. This period of uncertainty can be considerably prolonged if there is a delay in the adoption arrangements.

169. The disadvantages for the adoptive parents are obvious. The welfare of the child is at risk while his future remains in doubt and there is a possibility that he may be moved. Even though this happens only in a small minority of cases, the knowledge that it is possible may give rise to anxiety on the part of all prospective adopters, who may hesitate to give total commitment to a child whom they may not be allowed to keep.

170. We suggested in our working paper that in agency cases it should be possible for consent to become final before an adoption order was made. We outlined a system similar to that followed in some overseas countries, notably many states in the United States of America, which enables parents to take an irrevocable decision to give up their child for adoption, and to relinquish parental rights and obligations, before the child is placed. These rights and obligations are transferred by the court to an adoption agency, and in due course are transferred by the agency to the adopters when an adoption order is made. This enables the mother to give up parental rights and obligations before an adoption order is made, while providing for their exercise by the agency in the meantime . . .

. . .

221. There is known to exist a sizeable number of children in the care of local authorities and voluntary societies for whom no permanent future can be arranged for a variety of reasons, for example, because the parents cannot bring themselves to make a plan, or do not want their child adopted but are unable to look after him themselves. Some of these children may have no contact with their parents and would benefit from adoption, but the parents will not agree to it. In other cases a parent may have her child received into care shortly after birth and then vacillate for months or even years over the question of adoption, thus depriving her child of the security of a settled family home life.

. . .

223. In some of these cases a court might well consider that there were statutory grounds for dispensing with the parents' consent because they had persistently failed to discharge the obligations of a parent, or were withholding consent unreasonably. Under the present law there is no way of testing this without first placing the child with prospective adopters and awaiting a court decision after at least three months care and possession by them. If the court then decides that there are insufficient grounds for dispensing with the parents' consent the child must be returned to the agency. Moreover, unless the child is in the care of a local authority which has parental rights, or a care order has been made, the parents can frustrate the proceedings by removing the child before the court hearing. Agencies are therefore understandably reluctant to place these children for adoption.

224. We accept the principle that the natural family should be preserved wherever reasonably possible. But where a child is in care with no satisfactory long-term plan in mind, and lacking the possibility of long-term stable relationships, we think that it should be open to a local authority or a registered adoption agency to apply to a court for the parents' consent to be dispensed with on one of the statutory grounds, for parental rights to be transferred to the agency and the child thus freed for placement for adoption. The parents should not be permitted to remove the child from the agency's care without the leave of the court while the application is pending. This procedure would enable a decision to be taken without a child first being placed for adoption. The hearing would be in the nature of a relinquishment hearing but with the application made by the local authority or agency. Such an application would be made only where there was every prospect of a satisfactory placement for the child, and if it were granted the agency would have parental rights and obligations until an adoption order was made.

The resulting recommendations are contained in ss. 18 to 20 of the *Adoption Act 1976*:

Freeing child for adoption
18. – (1) Where, on an application by an adoption agency, an authorised court is satisfied in the case of each parent or guardian of the child that
　　(a) he freely, and with full understanding of what is involved, agrees generally and unconditionally to the making of an adoption order, or

    (*b*) his agreement to the making of an adoption order should be dispensed with on a ground specified in section 16(2),

the court shall make an order declaring the child free for adoption.

(2) No application shall be made under subsection (1) unless —

    (*a*) it is made with the consent of a parent or guardian of a child, or

    (*b*) the adoption agency is applying for dispensation under subsection (1)(*b*) of the agreement of each parent or guardian of the child, and the child is in the care of the adoption agency.

    (3) No agreement required under subsection (1)(*a*) shall be dispensed with under subsection (1)(*b*) unless the child is already placed for adoption or the court is satisfied that it is likely that the child will be placed for adoption.

. . . .

These provisions have not yet quite lived up to expectations, as Nigel Lowe reports in *Freeing for Adoption — the Experience of the 1980s* (1990):

. . . What emerged from our survey was that the practice differed greatly from one agency to another, often with neighbouring agencies having quite opposite policies.

What are the different policies?

(a) *The Use of Freeing in Uncontested Cases.*   With regard to the use of freeing in uncontested cases we found (through various interviews with practitioners) that, as envisaged both by Houghton and the Local Authority Circular, some agencies felt that, where young babies are involved, the freeing procedure is helpful when the mother agrees to the adoption and wants to put the issue behind her as quickly as possible. It was suggested that in these cases, the freeing procedure helps to confirm the baby's future if there is any doubt about the mother's intentions and motivation.

The procedure was also felt to be useful by the same agencies in cases where the natural parents have consented but for whatever reason the child cannot be placed immediately. In cases where placement can be expected to take more time, perhaps because the child is handicapped or older or where there are two or more siblings, the birth parents, by agreeing to freeing, are able to relinquish their responsibilities and involvement sooner.

(b) *The Use of Freeing in Contested Cases.*   We found that, unforeseen by the Houghton Committee though contemplated by the Local Authority Circular, the freeing procedure is frequently used in cases that are likely to be contested. Agencies feel that the advantage of freeing in such cases is that it protects the prospective adopters by alleviating some of their anxiety because it is the adoption agency which takes on the contest with the natural parents. The freeing procedure means that the adopters should avoid the ordeal of appearing in court (although in some freeing cases prospective adopters have apparently been asked to appear in court). Any adjournments in the case directly affect just the agency thus further insulating the adopters from extra stress. Furthermore, prospective adopters have the worry of legal costs removed if the freeing procedure is used because the local authority foots the bill whereas in contested adoption cases the prospective adopters may have to pay some legal costs. Several authorities have more legal experience and will present the case better than solicitors in private practice who may be less experienced in the field of child care law. Furthermore by keeping it 'in house,' local authorities can see the process through.

As far as benefits to the child are concerned, some agencies suggested that freeing lessens disruption to the child both directly and indirectly. The court can give leave for the child not to be present at the hearing. For children who are older it is helpful to know as soon as possible that the legal uncertainties are over and that they can attach themselves unreservedly to their new family.

The freeing procedure is also seen as a useful way of testing a borderline case (as envisaged by the Circular) where parental agreement is withheld before going ahead with a permanent placement for the child.

(c) *Why Freeing is not being used*

    (i) *Delays in the procedure.*   Time and again agencies mentioned delays. One agency expressly decided not to use freeing where there was no parental consent but to opt instead for contested adoption because of the delays in processing freeing cases. . . .

The interaction between freeing and adoption proceedings and termination of access
It became apparent in our investigations that there are varying policies and practices regarding the use of freeing and the termination of access.

One adoption worker explained that where the care plan for the child was adoption they would try to deal with termination of access in parallel with freeing thereby allowing the whole issue to be decided by the county court in one hearing. They would do so only where there was very clear and overwhelming evidence to support the view that the grounds for termination. . . .

He went on to explain that when the freeing provisions were first implemented his agency had instituted care proceedings at birth. They then dealt with termination of access and after that was resolved, with the freeing. The result was that it had taken up to two years to obtain a freeing order and the child was in a state of limbo often with highly attached foster parents. It was because they wished to reduce the traumas that this process caused that they then applied for freeing in parallel with termination of access.

Another adoption worker commented that his agency would not use freeing primarily as a method of terminating access because it is almost impossible to find prospective adopters who could tolerate access until such time as a freeing order was made. On the other hand, we have been also told of instances where freeing orders have been granted with access in fact continuing. . . .

Conclusions
Although, as has been said, practice varies over the use of freeing, overall it seems fair to say that the process has not lived up to expectations. As one respondent put it to the Bristol research team:
> 'I think freeing should work in theory. It should be helpful. I think that the practical reality is that it does not work. It delays the process for whatever reason so I do not think that it has fulfilled its promise.'

Whether the process can be reformed so as to make it work is an interesting question, but perhaps before that is tackled it ought to be asked if the process in its current form, at any rate, should be retained at all. Even before its implementation not everyone was enthusiastic about the process. Having to have two sets of legal proceedings was certainly not everyone's ideal solution. One commentator [Eekelaar, 1978] suggested, before its implementation, that freeing should be an administrative process, as in Australia, so that once a parent has agreed to the child's adoption that agreement should automatically become irrevocable after a set period. The Australian experience of that type of provision certainly merits investigation but while it may offer a solution in uncontested cases it leaves the contested cases unresolved.

Following their research in Scotland, Lambert, Buist, Triseliotis and Hill [1989] concluded that the freeing process should be retained, but improved. They considered the process to be a useful option in child care planning. At any rate, as they put it, it deserves a second chance to prove itself. A similar conclusion may be take with regard to the position in England and Wales. Freeing does have a useful role to play particularly in contested cases where it is both important for the child and fair to the parents that the local authority's adoption plan is tested early on. The usefulness of that role, however, is dependent upon proceedings being heard quickly.

Questions

(i) Freeing transfers parental responsibility for the child's upbringing to the agency (until he is adopted or the freeing order revoked): but is he still related to his birth parents and relatives? Can he succeed to their property?

(ii) In *Re E (a minor: adoption)* [1989] FCR 118, [1989] 1 FLR 126, Balcombe LJ commented: 'So the hypothetical reasonable mother could also take into account — although I doubt whether she could properly place much weight on this factor — that the choice lay between the family unit, with all its known deficiencies, with which [the children] have never lost contact, and a new and untried (though carefully vetted) placement with adopters': why should she not give this great weight, especially if adopters who can handle the child's continuing relationship with his birth family are hard to find?

7 A wider dimension

The following story is told by Barbara Tizard in *Adoption: A Second Chance* (1977):

The fifth set of foster parents, a comfortably-off middle-class couple in their 50s, had fostered children, mainly babies, for many years. Mrs E thought of 'David' as one of her own children. He had taken her name, and addressed her as 'Mummy'. There was, however, no possibility of adoption because his mother would not allow it.

She had placed David in care at the age of two months hoping to reclaim him in two years when she had finished her nursing training. Before this time however, she married, had another child and stopped visiting David. Since her husband didn't want to accept David, she planned to send him to her parents in Jamaica. The grandparents, however, had a large family of their own, and were reluctant to take him till he was 7. It was decided to keep him in the children's home, and hope that he would eventually be united with his family. His mother didn't visit him for two years, but when he was 4 she reappeared, and talked of taking him and leaving her husband. Since she did not do so, David was eventually fostered with Mrs E at the age of 5. From this time, his only contact with his mother was via occasional telephone calls.

Foster mother 'He can't go back to her or even visit her, because the man she's married to just won't have him in the house. And she's got four children by this man. But she won't give David up — she feels that he's still her son, and she thinks that he might return to her when he's older, and stick up for her. But the thing is, he won't know her, he'll have no genuine feeling for her. He'll know that she's his mother, because she's black, but that's about all.'

Mrs E not only acted as a mother to David, but kept in close touch with his mother and gave her a lot of support.

Foster mother 'I'm the shoulder that she cries on. If things get on top of her, or she finds she's pregnant again she rings me up. My husband and I slip over occasionally, if I know that she's a bit down, and take some toys or clothes for her children. She usually sends David a pound at Xmas, and sometimes she writes to him but she doesn't see him.'

Mrs E tried to help David understand his position.

Foster mother 'I tell him that his Mummy just can't have him, because her husband doesn't want him living there. So he has to stay with us. He wanted to know who his Daddy was, and what he was like — how tall he was — how black he was — where he came from — things like that. So I contacted his Mummy, and then I told him the basics. I've skimmed over the bad side of his father and given him a fair picture of him. One day, when I feel the time is right, I'll tell him his father left his mother in the lurch. I try to keep to the nicer side about his mother too, and make his family background sound as nice as possible. She rings me up and tells me about her parents and grandparents, and I pass it on to David. I think it's important he should have some background of his own.'

Partly because David is very black — both parents were West Indian — Mrs E tried to foster a pride in his colour in him.

Foster mother 'Although he's been brought up white, I think he should never forget he's coloured, that he's got something to be proud of. He'll need this in a white community — He gets "Sambo" and "Nig-nog" at school already — if he's proud of himself it will be easier for him in the long run.'

Although Mrs E was 'only' a foster mother, she seemed to have the same deep commitment to David as if he were her own child.

Foster mother 'When he came to me he was a chronic asthma sufferer. He never ran — if he walked up the stairs he'd have to stop and get his breath back. Now he never sits still — he's out on a bike all day. He had his last attack 16 months ago — it was a very bad one. I never went to bed for three nights. The doctor wanted him to go to hospital, but I said I'd rather nurse him at home — if he were to get worse, then I'd go with him into hospital, I wouldn't leave him.'

. . . .

The issue of adoption did not arise, because Mrs E knew that David's mother would not consider it. Nevertheless, she felt quite secure in her relationship with David because she knew that there was no possibility of his developing a relationship with his mother. In this situation she was able to support his mother, whilst treating David as her own child.

Foster mother 'I think every mother if she's honest, has individual feelings for every child she's got. You feel differently about each of your children. I won't say I feel the same about David as the others — I feel differently about them all — but he's just like my own.'

. . . None of the foster parents saw this situation, however, as ideal — they would have pre-ferred adoption.

> *Foster mother* 'I'm a firm believer that the mother is the person to have a child. But as far as David is concerned, there could never be a very good relationship, because the man she's married to won't have him — and she's got the other children to look after. That sort of mother is no good to the child, is she?'

Compare that with the following legal case:

Re N (a minor) (adoption)
[1990] 1 FLR 58, Family Division

The child, N, was born in 1984 of Nigerian parents who were not married. The mother placed her with white foster parents, the Ps, two weeks after birth and went to the USA. The father lived there but they did not live together. The father took an interest in the child and sought consistently to have care for her, but there were visa difficulties. In 1987, the foster parents applied to adopt and then dispense with the mother's agreement. The father, with the mother's support, applied for care and control. He proposed a gradual transition, through a relative or bridging placement.

Bush J: . . . The most important question to decide is where does N's future lie. We are all of us parents or potential parents and it is very difficult and sad for us to say that a child should be brought up by someone other than the natural parents. It should of course always be borne in mind that in English law N is a person in her own right and not just an appendage of her parents. . . .

Not only does the court in this case have to cope with practical difficulties involved in a transfer of N from the Ps to the father in a foreign land where the father will have to work long hours, and Miss F too has to work long hours, but I have also been bombarded by a host of theories and opinions by experts who derive their being from the political approach to race rela-tions in America in the 1960s and 1970s. The British Agencies for Fostering and Adoption forcefully expressed the view that black children should never be placed with white foster-parents. That that part of the approach was politically inspired seems clear from reading the summary to a practice note, the date of which is not clear. Nevertheless, it is an approach which due to the zeal of its authors has persuaded most local authorities not to place black children with white foster-parents. The summary note reads as follows:

> 'Over and above all these basic needs, children need to develop a positive identity, including a positive racial identity. This is of fundamental importance since ethnicity is a significant component of identity. Ideally such needs are met within the setting of the child's birth family. Historically black people have been victims of racism for centuries. This has manifested and continues to manifest itself in many forms. Racism permeates all areas of British society and is perpetuated through a range of interests and influences, including the media, education and social service policies and practices. Negative and stereotypical images and actions can have a major impact on black children through the internalisation of these images, resulting in self-hate and identity confusion. Black children therefore require the survival skills necessary to develop a positive racial identity. This will enable them to deal with the racism within our predominantly white society.'

As Dr B, an eminent and experienced child psychiatrist . . . pointed out . . . there seems little real evidence, save anecdotal, to suggest that black-white fosterings are harmful. Indeed, Dr B says that her experience . . . indicates to the contrary namely, that the placement of black children with white foster-parents works just as well as black foster-children with black foster-parents, and the real problem, of course, is that black foster-parents are in short supply in this country.

In my view — and I have no wish to enter into what is clearly a political field — the emphasis on colour rather than cultural upbringing can be mischievous and highly dangerous when you are dealing in practical terms with the welfare of children. Also, the fact remains that this child has been placed with white foster-parents and they have been the only real family she has ever known. I do not for one moment think that the father subscribes to this dogma. He does not have to be condescended to because he is black; he has made his way and his children will make their own way in the world because of intelligence and flair. To suggest that he and his children need special help because they are black is, in human terms an insult to them and their abilities. Yet it is to this principle that a whole social work philosophy has been dedicated. I do not need persuading that if at all possible the parents being suitable, a child should be brought up by its natural parents. Nor do I need persuading that experience tells us that particularly during teenage years there is a desire in children who have not been brought up by their natural parents, or who have not been having a regular access to them, to seek them out and that, if the whole of their placement has not been handled responsibly and delicately throughout their childhood, and sometimes even then, there may be psychological problems. There are of course serious psychological problems likely to arise when an effort is made to part a 4½-year-old child from the only carers she has ever known. . . .

There is, of course, a very important question which relates not so much to colour as to national origins. The father and mother are Nigerian. The father is under some pressure from his father, who will be disgraced if it appears that even an illegitimate child has been abandoned. The father is a Roman Catholic, and I accept that he has a genuine desire to bring up his own child. An older illegitimate child of his, a boy, lives with a different mother in Nigeria and visits his father at regular intervals.

The evidence of Mrs B, a consultant social worker, as to Nigerian practice is of use. . . . She said there is no concept of adoption in Nigerian society. It is the normal cultural pattern for children to be brought up by others, often for most of their minority, and to be aware of their birth parents. Adoption rather than fostering of a West African child has particular difficulties. Adoption is to transfer a child from one family into another permanently and although the adoptive parents strive to inform the child about its origins in adoption it is clear the child is as if it were born to the adopters. In fostering, even long-term carers and the child are aware this is another and different family from a true family. If the child is moved from a white foster home to Nigerian culture, with his foster-parents not wanting the child to go, this can be devastating. Growing up with a set of values, a way of looking at family life, is constant in the same culture. However, to move from a British family with a closeness, autonomy and freedom to express what you want and to do what you want to a place where you cannot can be very distressing long-term. The damage of losing the people you trust at the same time as the trauma can be life-long.

. . . I am satisfied, as are the local authority and the guardian ad litem that N could be moved without immense harm to her psychological development and her psychiatric health, both now and in the future. The later harm that may arise in her teens when she wished to seek out her cultural roots can best be dealt with by sympathetic understanding and education, upon which the Ps have already embarked, and it can also hopefully be met by the father continuing his interest and having access to N. It can only be helped if the father accepts the situation and enjoys access not on the basis of an expected rehabilitation but on the basis of a contact access designed to keep N in touch with her origins. If the father cannot accept this, then it may be that for N's security access would have to cease.

The Ps want adoption with an access order. The local authority and the guardian ad litem oppose adoption on the ground: (i) that the father has a useful and important part to play in the child's life in the future, particularly when she is nearing adulthood; (ii) that access to which the Ps are to some extent agreeable might very well be imperilled, the fact being that an adoption would result in the father and the whole of his family losing face. The father told me, and I have no reason to disbelieve, in the course of his argument that in his culture adoption is viewed as a restoration of slavery, which would be a deep and hurtful blow to him and his family. The question one has to ask oneself is whether the security that adoption would give to both the Ps and to N is offset by the fact that it clearly would not be in N's interests for her father to feel the shame and distress that in his culture an adoption order would bring. . . .
. . . .

I know all the arguments, I have heard them many times, about the security that an adoption could give and in the main I accept the arguments and have in the past acted upon them, but in the particular circumstances of this case I would not think it right to make an adoption order. Circumstances of course may change in the future. The guardian ad litem is most concerned, as we all are, that what has really become open warfare between the Ps and the father should cease. It is in the interests of that it should so cease. I accept that the father is bitterly hurt and distressed and feels utterly betrayed by the Ps, and no doubt my decision has distressed him even more. However, the future of N throughout her childhood lies with the Ps and the father is intelligent enough and dedicated enough to his daughter to appreciate that changes of attitude on his part must come about. . . .

Accordingly, the order that I make is that the wardship shall continue, that there be care and control to Mr and Mrs P, that there be reasonable access to the father to be agreed. In default of agreement it should be access once a year over a period of one week to begin with and that access to take place in England.

Questions

(i) Rowe (1984) found that 'the 29 black children who were interviewed mostly shrugged off colour differences as being unimportant but a few of the older teenagers were now facing problems because they had grown up in a white world'. Should white families be allowed to foster or adopt black children? What is black for this purpose?

(ii) Do you consider David's case (a) a perfect example of 'inclusive' fostering working to the benefit of all; or (b) a case in which the additional security of adoption would have benefited both child and foster parents?

(iii) Re N was not (a), but was it (b)?

Issues of race and ethnic origin arise even more acutely when prospective adopters seek to adopt a child from another country. The Department of Health's approach is explained in a Circular on Adoption of Children from Overseas (1990, CI(90)17):

1. The Department's approach to intercountry adoption is influenced by the provisions of the 1986 United Nations Declaration on Social and Legal Principles relating to the Protection and Welfare of Children, with special reference to Foster Placement and Adoption Nationally and Internationally. This provides that:
   (a) intercountry adoption may be considered as an alternative means of providing a family for a child who cannot be cared for in any suitable manner in his own country;
   (b) in all matters relating to the placement of a child outside the care of the child's own parents, the best interests of the child should be the paramount consideration;
   (c) safeguards and standards equivalent to those which apply in national adoption are to be applied in intercountry adoption to protect the welfare of the children concerned.
2. Social Services Departments have a vital role to play in safeguarding the welfare of children who came from overseas for adoption. This includes:
   (a) advising and counselling those who are considering adopting a child from overseas;
   (b) assessing the suitability of prospective adopters;
   (c) supervising placements and making reports and recommendations to the courts when children arrive from overseas for adoption.
. . .
6. It is for the Home Office to decide whether a child will be admitted to the UK. If the Home Office are satisfied that there are no immigration reasons for refusal and that the proposed adoption involves a genuine transfer of parental responsibility on the grounds of the parents' inability to care for the child, they will look to this Department for advice on welfare aspects of the proposed adoption.
7. In giving advice the Department's central concern is to give first consideration to the welfare of the child. This is the test in section 6 of the Adoption Act 1976 which requires a court hearing a subsequent adoption application to give first consideration to the welfare of the child. The Department needs to be satisfied on the following matters:
   (a) the reasons for the proposed adoption; evidence of the child's identity and as much information about his circumstances, history and background as can be discovered, including a health report on the BAAF Intercountry Medical Form;
   (b) evidence that the child is legally available for adoption and that the appropriate authorities support the adoption plans and have authorised the child's departure from the country of origin for the purposes of adoption;
   (c) there is either a valid parental consent, in a form which is acceptable to a UK court, given freely and with full understanding of the effects of a UK adoption order, or official certification that the child has been genuinely abandoned and the parents cannot be found;
   (d) the prospective adopters are recommended by their Social Services Department as suitable adopters for the child.

8. The Department relies on reports from the authorities in the child's country of origin, supplemented where necessary by enquiries made by the Entry Clearance Officer in that country, and on information provided by prospective adopters, in order to be satisfied about (*a*), (*b*) and (*c*), above. The Department relies on the prospective adopters' SSD for a report and recommendation on their suitability (or otherwise) as adopters.

This all looks splendid until tested by a couple who went strictly 'by the book':

R v Secretary of State for Health, ex p Luff
(1991) Guardian, 29 March, High Court

The facts
Mr and Mrs Luff who are aged 53 and 37 wish to adopt two Romanian orphans — a boy born in October 1987 and a girl born in May 1988. The Luffs applied to the Home Office for entry clearance in respect of the two children who are presently living in appalling conditions in Romanian orphanages. The London Borough of Bexley's adoption panel approved the Luffs as prospective adopters. However, the Health Department had medical reports on Mr Luff who had had coronary artery bypass graft surgery. The first report had said Mr Luff was suitable as a prospective adopter but the medical officer changed her mind after seeing the opinion of consultant cardiologists. She then advised that because of Mr Luff's limited life expectancy, it was not recommended that he be allowed to adopt young children. The Health Secretary advised the Home Office that 'Mr and Mrs Luff are unable to offer the long-term security throughout childhood and adolescence that is considered necessary in adoption.' The Home Office rejected the application for entry clearance. The Luffs applied for judicial review of the Health Secretary's advice.

The decision
Mr Justice Waite said that the only function of the Health Secretary in the case of foreign adoptions was to advise the Home Secretary who had the ultimate decision. It was conceded that the Health Secretary's advice was susceptible of judicial review, but the court was reminded that in reviewing advice as opposed to decisions, a judge is acting at the extremity of his powers and should confine himself to deciding whether the proposition of law is erroneous and avoid expressing opinions in areas of controversy.

Favourable recommendations had been given in 150 out of 160 foreign adoption applications. It was not realistic nor fair to foist upon the Health Secretary, in the absence of any evidence to support it, an automatic assumption that the only alternative to adoption by the Luffs for these children would be internment until majority in their present orphanages.

It was also said that the Health Secretary had displayed an obsessive preoccupation with speculative medical evidence about Mr Luff's life expectancy so as to exclude other considerations altogether or alternatively to give it undue importance. However, it appeared that the Health Secretary asked himself what the appropriate advice to give was on these facts. That included the ages of the parties and the circumstances in which the medical advice was given. It was wholly a matter for the Health Secretary to decide what weight to give any one factor over another and the weighing process was not one with which the court could interfere.

It was then claimed that the Health Secretary had brushed aside the advice of the Bexley Adoption Panel, notwithstanding that the panel was the 'lynchpin' of the adoption system. His Lordship could not accept the assertion that the Health Secretary, although not bound by the panel, was disabled from rejecting the panel's advice unless it was so demonstrably absurd as to be overturned on judicial review. The panel's advice was an opinion which the Health Secretary was invited to and did take into account.

The principal ground of attack was the irrationality of the Health Secretary's advice. His Lordship said no one disputed that many people, perhaps a majority of concerned, sympathetic and understanding people, would take the view that these two children had pressing needs. The Luffs were admirably suited to undertaking the special care these children required.

There was however another view. It might only appeal to a minority because it proceeded in the cold light of caution rather than the warm glow of hope. But the people to whom it might appeal are people with the same qualities of concern, sympathy and understanding. That view would say of these children that they had already endured physical and emotional suffering which threatened to scar them psychologically for life. Their most pressing need therefore was stability. The risks of future trauma could never be eliminated but they could be reduced to the lowest level that human endeavour could achieve. They should therefore be adopted by people whose health held out at least a reasonable prospect that they would be spared the pain of family bereavement in their teenage years.

Both those views were tenable. Both were supported on grounds of humanity. Both could claim to have the children's best interests at heart. It followed therefore that the advice tendered by the Health Secretary was cogent and rational advice, incapable of being struck down by the process of judicial review.

Questions

(i) If you had been advising the Secretary of State in this case, what would your advice have been?

(ii) Is it consistent with the view you took on the case of *Re K (a minor) (wardship: adoption)* [1991] 1 FLR 57 (p. 630, above)?

(iii) Left to yourself, would you (*a*) ban inter-country adoption altogether, (*b*) set up an agency to arrange placements properly, or (*c*) recognise all foreign adoption orders?

CHAPTER 15

Adjudication and conciliation

Americans preach that the procedure of the family court must be therapeutic. This means no more (but no less) than that, just as the juvenile court seeks to do what is best for the child, so the family court should approach its wider jurisdiction inspired by a similar philosophy. In every case it would seek to diagnose and cure the underlying cause of the family disorder. Thus, in divorce it would think first of marriage-mending before marriage-ending. For this remedial function it would need to be buttressed with adequate expert assistance, whether within the court or in the local community. Where, however, cure proved impossible, the family court would perform its legal operation (such as divorce) with the least traumatic effect on the personalities involved.

This extract from Neville Brown's discussion of *The Legal Background to the Family Court* (1966) would be highly controversial today. The object of this chapter is to look at the role of the courts and other agencies in the resolution of conflict in the family.

1 The family courts debate

The first comprehensive official discussion of family courts came in the *Report of the Committee on One-Parent Families* (the Finer Report) in 1974. The Report deals first with general principles:

CRITERIA

4.282 Our approach owes little to American experience or writings, or to any preconceived attachment to the notions of a 'family court'. We have been guided pragmatically by specific considerations emerging from our study of the matrimonial law and courts in this country, which has established for us the need for and the character of the institution we have in mind. We have, in the first place, traced the personal and social mischiefs to which the dual system of matrimonial jurisdiction gives rise. We have also shown how this system offers financial provision to wives, mothers and their children by means of orders which in many cases are not honoured by those whose obligation to maintain their dependants has been affirmed by the courts. To ensure that these women and children survive, the social security authorities provide the subsistence which the law promises. The contribution of the private obligation to maintain is interstitial; that of social security is fundamental. We therefore conclude that only an institution which is shaped by the recognition of these facts can adequately serve the needs of broken families. The second major point is that members of families which have collapsed come to court at a stage when critical decisions will have to be taken about issues, other than those directly affecting matrimonial relief or finance, around which conflicts are likely to develop. There may be disputes over the custody of the children, or the ownership or occupation of the matrimonial home. Such practical matters have to be settled or determined at some time, and the presence of the parties in court provides the best opportunity that may ever occur for discussion and decision. Thus, we have come to think of the family court as an institution which will improve on our inherited system by eliminating the overlap, the contradictions and the other

weaknesses and defects of the legal jurisdictions we have exposed earlier in this Part of the Report, and which at the same time will also improve the machinery and services which are available to deal realistically with the practical problems resulting from marriage breakdown.
4.283 In the light of the foregoing considerations, we set out the six major criteria which a family court must in principle satisfy:

(1) the family court must be an impartial judicial institution, regulating the rights of citizens and settling their disputes according to law:

(2) the family court will be a unified institution in a system of family law which applies a uniform set of legal rules, derived from a single moral standard and applicable to all citizens;

(3) the family court will organise its work in such a way as to provide the best possible facilities for conciliation between parties in matrimonial disputes;

(4) the family court will have professionally trained staff to assist both the court and the parties appearing before it in all matters requiring social work services and advice;

(5) the family court will work in close relationship with the social security authorities in the assessment both of need and of liability in cases involving financial provision;

(6) the family court will organise its procedure, sittings and administrative services and arrangements with a view to gaining the confidence and maximising the convenience of the citizens who appear before it.

Criterion (1) is elaborated thus:

THE FAMILY COURT AS A JUDICIAL INSTITUTION

4.285 The fundamental principle which must govern the family court is that it shall be a judicial institution which, in dealing with family matters, does justice according to law. This may seem to be so obvious a point as hardly to be worth mentioning; but the need to emphasise it arises from the nature of a jurisdiction which aims to do good as well as to do right. To promote welfare is an unusual function for a court of law. To some extent, the courts which deal with matrimonial disputes and with children are already familiar with that function through references in the statutes to reconciliation in husband and wife disputes, and through the statutory obligation in many forms of proceedings which involve children to have first and paramount regard, in any decision the court may reach, to their welfare. But the deliberate attempt to expand and systematise the welfare function, which is an essential part of the family court concept, carries risks, as well as potential advantages, which can be eliminated only by clear thinking and firm practice regarding boundaries and priorities. The court must remain, and must be seen to remain, impartial. This is of particular importance now that local authorities and governmental agencies of various kinds have powers and duties imposed on them which bring them into the proceedings, either as interested parties or as advisers to the court. The object of achieving welfare must not be permitted to weaken or short cut the normal safeguards of the judicial process — the dispassionate examination of evidence properly adduced to the court, regular procedures which promote an orderly and fair hearing, and the allowance of legal representation. The court must not see the men, women and children with whom it is concerned as 'clients', and still less as 'patients' for whom the court process is one form of, or a preliminary to, 'treatment'. Professional staff serving the court, including any who are responsible for assisting the court to reach sound conclusions on welfare issues, must be answerable to the court for what they do and how they do it. The aim must be to make adjudication and welfare march hand in hand, but there should be no blurring of the edges, either in principle or in administration. Through the family court it should be possible to make a new and highly beneficial synthesis between law and social welfare, and the respective skills, experience and efforts of lawyers and social workers; but the individual in the family court must in the last resort remain the subject of rights, not the object of assistance.

Question

To what extent have criteria (2) and (5) been overtaken by later developments?

The Finer Committee were heavily influenced by the differences between the higher courts, the magistrates' courts, and the social security authorities in their approach to financial relief (see Chapters 3 and 4, above). The plethora of jurisdictions relating to children was, however, even more confusing, as the following imaginary history (taken from Hoggett, 1986) illustrates:

Johnny's parents were divorced when he was ten years old. Custody was granted to his mother, partly because his father worked abroad as an engineer for long periods. The divorce was granted by the county court in Muncaster, where Johnny's mother was living at the time, although it could have been granted in any divorce county court.

Shortly afterwards, his mother moved to Loamshire, where she had a nervous breakdown and Johnny was received into the care of the Loamshire County Council. No enquiries were made of Johnny's father, because he did not have custody and the mother insisted that he was not interested. Her illness turned out to be severe, and Loamshire passed a resolution assuming her parental rights and duties over Johnny. She challenged this in the Loamshire juvenile court, for jurisdiction lies with the juvenile court for the local authority's area. She lost before the juvenile court and on appeal to the Family Division of the High Court.

Meanwhile, Johnny was boarded out with foster parents in the metropolitan borough of Bigborough. They were only interested in a permanent arrangement and found it increasingly hard to cope with visits and other contacts from Johnny's mother. Because of his mother's mental state, Johnny also found them distressing. After a few months, Loamshire decided that it would be impossible to reunite Johnny and his mother. They therefore served notice upon the mother, terminating her access to him. She challenged this in the Loamshire juvenile court, for this jurisdiction also lies with the court for the local authority's area. At the same time, however, she applied for the resolution to be determined, on the ground that she had now recovered and established a new home in a special housing association development in County Fairacre. This application had to be made to the juvenile court for the area where she was living, in Fairacre.

However, with the support of the Loamshire County Council, the foster parents then applied to adopt Johnny. Such applications may be made to the High Court or the county court or domestic court for the area where the child is, and they chose the Bigborough county court.

As the adoption proceedings were pending, the local authority persuaded the Loamshire juvenile court to adjourn the mother's application for access and the Fairacre juvenile court to adjourn her application to end the resolution. She therefore appealed to the High Court, to compel each juvenile court to continue to hear her application. She succeeded in the case of the access application, but not in the other. Her application was eventually heard and failed.

In the adoption proceedings, the foster parents had applied for the mother's agreement to be dispensed with because it was being unreasonably withheld, and the father's because he could not be found. However, in the course of further enquiries ordered by the court, he was found working on a pipeline in the Philippines. Immediately he returned to this country, not only to oppose the adoption, but also to apply to the Muncaster county court for a custody order in his favour.

Loamshire County Council, realising that it might be difficult to proceed with the adoption, decided that Johnny must leave the foster parents and go to a children's home in Loamshire, so that he could start spending weekends with his father and the woman his father plans to marry. Johnny was very upset by this, as he had not seen his father for a long time, did not like his proposed step-mother, and wanted to stay with the foster parents. He started running away from the home and sleeping rough. Eventually, the local authority decided that they would have to put him in secure accommodation and applied to the Loamshire juvenile court for authority to do so. This was granted, but Johnny's appeal to the Crown Court was successful.

For the time being, he is back with the foster parents, who were waiting for the custodianship provisions of the Children Act 1975 to come into force, but have also applied to the Muncaster county court for leave to intervene in the divorce suit so that they may apply for custody in those proceedings.

The criticisms of this state of affairs are set out by the Law Reform Commission of Canada in their Working Paper on *The Family Court* (1974):

Despair, confusion and frustration
The most distressing effect of the present state of affairs is the despair, confusion and frustration it causes to the participants. It should not be necessary nor even feasible to apply to one

court for maintenance upon desertion, another for custody, a third for wardship or adoption, and yet another for divorce. As far as the general public is concerned there appears to be no reason why all legal matters arising from a matrimonial or family dispute should not be dealt with by a single court. Public expectations of a family court may far exceed the realistic potential of any court of law since there is no legal process which can solve all of the problems arising from marriage or family breakdown, but to circumvent the existing maze of jurisdictions seems a step in the right direction.

Overlapping jurisdiction
. . . 'Forum-shopping' can also develop from the existing situation. Certain parties may prefer a court bound by formal rules and procedures to an informal, conciliatory chamber. This may affect the outcome of hearings and lead to results that are not in the best interests of all parties. There have been instances where actions commenced in a family court have been barred by the opposing party taking the same issue to a higher court.

Cost
Present systems cause duplication of effort by judges, lawyers, witnesses, court administrators and the parties themselves and this naturally leads to increased costs. Consolidation of family law jurisdiction in a single court would reduce the cost of legal services to the individuals, although an effective system of family courts with access to support services would not necessarily reduce the financial cost to the state.

Inability of courts to deal with the total problem
By forcing parties to go to different courts in relation to different facets of a single problem, the process denies any one court the opportunity to view the problem as a whole. As a result no one person sees all the evidence, and remedies may be granted which are not the best.
   We consider that family conflicts require special procedures, designed to help individuals to reconcile or settle their differences and where necessary to obtain assistance. Therefore, the resolution of family conflicts, particularly those involving children, require some modification of the traditional adversary process. To leave reconciliation and settlement of issues exclusively in the hands of the lawyers is inadequate.

Lack of respect for the courts and the law
A system of law that prevents parties from finding simple, dignified means of solving their problems within a reasonable time, often while they are under very great emotional strain, encourages distrust of the legal process as a means of solving family problems.

Reform of the substantive law can, however, lead to changes in the courts. Thus the Department of Health in *An Introduction to the Children Act 1989* (1989) explain the main features of the new code of remedies:

3.4 The Children Act creates a single code for court orders about the welfare of children. The main features of this code are that for the first time:
   (*a*) each court which is considering a matter affecting a child's future will be able to make orders in the interests of the child's welfare;
   (*b*) any person will be able to apply to court for an order concerning a child's upbringing (either with or without the court's leave);
   (*c*) the range of orders available in each court and the criteria applied by the courts will be the same;
   (*d*) the effect of court orders is clarified, including the effect of one order on another;
   (*e*) where aspects of a case affecting the same child come before more than one court, the proceedings can be brought together in one venue.

Their guidance on *Court Orders* (1991) explains the new concurrent jurisdiction thus:

1.13. The Children Act creates a concurrent system of jurisdiction for a wide range of family proceedings in new magistrates' family proceedings courts, county courts and the High Court. Rules governing the allocation and transfer of cases either vertically between the various tiers, or horizontally within tiers, will ensure that cases are directed to the most appropriate court.

1.14. In practice the majority of public law cases will be heard entirely in the magistrates' family proceedings court as usually this will be the most appropriate court. Different considerations apply to private law cases where for the time being it will continue to be possible to exercise free choice about which court is used.

1.15. Most public law applications will start in the magistrates' family proceedings court but in certain circumstances can be transferred to a higher court. Subject to the overriding principle that delay is likely to prejudice the welfare of the child the criteria for transfer are:

    (*a*) exceptional complexity, importance or gravity;
    (*b*) the need to consolidate with other proceedings;
    (*c*) urgency.

Questions

(i) Think back to the issues discussed in Chapters 9, 10 and 13: do you think that magistrates' family proceedings courts will usually be the 'most appropriate court' to handle public law cases?

(ii) Why should the applicant local authority not be allowed to choose where to bring the case?

(iii) Could we not achieve a family court by the simple expedient of abolishing the family jurisdiction of magistrates' courts?

(iv) What are the objections to doing that?

It was the inefficiency of overlapping jurisdictions and inconsistent remedies which most concerned the Interdepartmental Review of Family and Domestic Jurisdictions (Consultation Paper, 1986) and which has now been addressed to some extent in the Children Act 1989. Others have been more concerned that the nature of family disputes, and hence the functions of the courts in relation to them, demand a rather different sort of court. This appears from the report of a working party set up by British Agencies for Adoption and Fostering and the Association of Directors of Social Services on *Family Justice* (1986):

29 We identified three essential functions for a family court:
— to resolve disputes whether arising from family breakdown or from the state's intervention in family life on behalf of children
— to assert a state interest in agreements between parties where, had agreement not been reached, resolution would require a decision by the court. This would be necessary, for example, to record a change of status, protect an economically weaker party or safeguard the interests of children.
— to provide a means of enforcing orders, including those made by consent
30 We then identified certain fundamental characteristics shared by family matters which indicate the way in which the court's functions should be carried out:
a) Any incident which results in recourse to a court administering family law occurs in the context of historical developments, present disruption and significant changes in personal status and relationships which are likely to result from a resolution of the case. In order to reach a decision the court should take account of past events but must also appreciate the future consequences of any resolution which may be reached. This point bears on the attitude, approach and breadth of understanding which the court is required to bring to a case.
b) The practical arrangements and social dynamics which characterise family life are complicated and interrelated. Any reorganisation of these matters may involve the court in dealing with a range of problems which cannot be treated in isolation. Matrimonial proceedings may require attention to disputes concerning financial support, occupation of the family home, ownership of assets, custody of children, access. The resolution of child care issues occurring, for example, in care or access proceedings should be considered in relation to future consequences and options for safeguarding the long-term welfare of children.
c) Decisions in family matters have far-reaching consequences for the adults and children concerned. Those who have to dispense justice require not only a thorough knowledge of complex

areas of law and a consistent response to difficult aspects of interpretation but also an understanding of the social and emotional factors which influence the well-being of individuals.
d) Those adults and children who come into contact with the courts through civil proceedings
are likely to be experiencing considerable stress and to be angry with or alienated from each
other. At the same time they may have to cope with readjustments in personal, social, economic
and other practical areas of their lives. Personal satisfaction and the ability to deal constructively with the legal resolution of disputes will be affected by the degree of privacy, respect,
sensitivity and efficiency which is reflected in all aspects of the court's operation. . . .
g) Delays in the resolution of family disputes can have extremely detrimental effects, particularly if they involve subjecting children to prolonged uncertainty about their future. Delay
may in some circumstances actually become the principal factor dictating the outcome of a
dispute.
31 We concluded that the characteristics outlined point to the need for a court whose judiciary
and staff develop special skills to enable them to deal with these difficult areas of emotional
conflict, and whose atmosphere is as conducive as possible to achieving conciliated outcomes.

Questions

(i) Do you think that some or all family cases should be heard in private?
If so, which? What are the advantages and disadvantages of privacy for (*a*)
adult parties, (*b*) children, or (*c*) courts?
(ii) Cases heard in private cannot be reported in the media unless the court
allows this. What, if any, restrictions should there be on the reporting of
family cases?
(iii) Do you think that 'special skills' are needed by the judiciary in family
cases? If so, what are they?

A recurring theme of discussions about family courts has been the need
for greater informality and for inquisitorial rather than adversarial procedures. The *Finer Report* (1974) had this to say:

4.404 We are impressed by the unanimity of the commentators in favour of greater informality
in family matters. But we are impressed, too, by the lack of studies of the effect of legal ritual
upon citizens who use the courts. We do not know how representative a figure is the trade union
leader who observed of the Industrial Relations Court that, if his members are to be sent to
prison for contempt of court, he desires it to be done by a judge properly robed in scarlet and
ermine. On these aspects of court procedure, we think that decisions should be delayed until
they can be based on knowledge of what will best satisfy the citizen user's desire for fairness
and dignity in the determination of matrimonial cases.
4.405 Another much canvassed procedural question is how far the hearings in the family court
should be inquisitorial rather than adversary in nature. In the accusatorial or adversary form
of procedure, as it characterises our civil litigation, the parties not only choose the issues which
form the subject matter of the dispute, but also determine what evidence shall be brought before
the court. The court has no right and no means to act as its own fact-gatherer. In the inquisitorial form of procedure, the court is not confined to acting as a referee, but may, so far as
it has the means, take steps of its own to inform itself of the facts and circumstances it considers
it ought to know in order to make a just determination. But the two forms of procedure are
not, in truth, mutually exclusive. In the divorce jurisdiction, the court has always been charged
with the duty of being 'satisfied' that it can grant relief, which must involve, in appropriate
cases, a duty to enquire into matters as to which the parties themselves may not be in dispute.
So again, in matters affecting custody of and access to children the court has to have regard
to the child's paramount interests, which is a matter which the views of the parties, even to the
extent that they coincide, do not determine. The proper balance of the two forms of procedure
in the family court should, in our view, be determined by the following considerations. It is
desirable that the court itself should not come into the arena. To the extent that the court
requires assistance by way of investigation or expert assessment of circumstances which it considers material, this function should be discharged by ancillary services which are attached to
or can be called upon by the court, but whose personnel are not themselves members of the

court. The bench of the family court is to consist only of judges, professional or lay, and experts or assessors should not be constituents. On the other hand, the bench as so constituted should, in every aspect of its jurisdiction, be able to call upon the aid of a competent person to make social and welfare enquiries and reports.

Similar caution is voiced by Elizabeth Szwed, in *The Family Court*, her contribution to Michael Freeman's collection on *The State, the Law and the Family: Critical Perspectives* (1984):

I believe that there is a real possibility that enthusiasm for the therapeutic and conciliatory, or the reassuring and accessible, atomosphere could produce unfair and adverse consequences. Unbridled abrogation of the customary rules of court proceedings is probably more likely to result in sloppiness and disrespect rather than reassurance. But, more importantly, as the history of the American juvenile courts illustrates, over-hasty abandonment of the essential features of the judicial process could seriously jeopardize those legal safeguards that ensure, and as I have already argued, justify, the existence of a court rather than a panel.

Questions

Should a judge dress up in purple dressing gown and curly wig (*a*) to grant an adoption order to which the birth parents have agreed, or (*b*) to try a hotly contested parental dispute about where the children are to live, or (*c*) to decide whether or not a ten-year-old girl has been sexually abused, or (*d*) to grant or enforce an ouster injunction against a violent man, or (*e*) to decide whether a child should be called by a new surname?

Behind all these questions lies the essential role of the court in family cases: is it there to regulate and supervise family life, to help solve family problems, to resolve disputes by adjudication or by other means, or all of these things? We shall look at each of them in turn.

2 Public regulation or private ordering?

Robert Mnookin's celebrated article *Bargaining in the Shadow of the Law — The Case of Divorce* (1979) begins:

I wish to suggest a new way of thinking about the role of law at the time of divorce. It is concerned primarily with the impact of the legal system on negotiations and bargaining that occurs *outside* of court. Rather than regard order as imposed from above, I see the primary function of contemporary divorce law as providing a framework for divorcing couples themselves to determine their respective rights and responsibilities after dissolution. This process, by which parties to a marriage are empowered to create their own legally enforceable commitments, I shall call '*private ordering*'.

In *Divorce Bargaining: The Limits on Private Ordering* (1984), he explains both the advantages and the disadvantages which have to be countered:

THE ADVANTAGES OF PRIVATE ORDERING
Let me begin with the arguments supporting the presumption in favour of private ordering. The core reason is rooted in notions of *human liberty*. Private ordering is supported by the liberal ideal that individuals have rights, and should largely be left free to make of their lives what they wish. In Charles Fried's words, a regime of law that 'respects the dispositions

individuals make of their rights, carries to its logical conclusion the liberal premise that individuals have rights'.

Private ordering can also be justified on grounds of *efficiency*. Ordinarily, the parties themselves are in the best position to evaluate the comparative advantages of alternative arrangements. Each spouse, in the words of John Stuart Mill, 'is the person most interested in his own well-being: . . . with respect to his own feelings and circumstances, the most ordinary man or woman has means of knowledge immeasurably surpassing those that can be possessed by anyone else.' Through negotiations, there are opportunities for making *both* parents better off than either would be if a court or some third party simply imposed a result. A consensual solution is, by definition, more likely to be consistent with the preferences of each spouse than would a result imposed by a court. Parental preferences often vary with regard to money and child-rearing responsibilities. Through negotiations, it is possible that the divorcing spouses can divide money and child-rearing responsibilities to reflect their own individual preferences.

Finally, there are obvious and substantial *savings* when a couple can resolve the distributional consequences of divorce without resort to formal adjudication. The financial cost of litigation, both private and public, is minimized. The pain of the formal adversarial proceedings is avoided. A negotiated settlement allows the parties to avoid the risks and uncertainties of litigation, which may involve all-or-nothing consequences. Given the substantial delays that often characterize contested judicial proceedings, agreement can often save time and allow each spouse to proceed with his or her life. In short, against a backdrop of fair standards in the shadow of which a couple bargains, divorcing couples should have very broad powers to make their own arrangements. Significant limitations are inconsistent with the premises of no-fault divorce. Parties should be encouraged to settle the distributional consequences of divorce for themselves, and the state should provide an efficient and fair mechanism for enforcing such agreements and for settling disputes when the parties are unable to agree.

CAPACITY

On an abstract level, I find the general defense of private ordering both appealing and persuasive. But it is premised on the notion that divorce bargaining involves rational, self-interested individuals — that the average adult has the intelligence and experience to make a well-informed judgment concerning the desirability of entering into a particular divorce settlement. Given the tasks facing an individual at the time of divorce, and the characteristics of the relationship between divorcing spouses, there are reasons to fear that this may not always be the case.

Informed bargaining requires a divorcing spouse to assess his or her own preferences concerning alternative arrangements. Radical changes in life circumstances complicate such assessments. Within a short period of time, separation and divorce often subject spouses to the stresses of many changes: '[S]pouses need to adjust to new living arrangements, new jobs, financial burdens, new patterns of parenting, and new conditions of social and sexual life.' It may be particularly difficult for a parent to assess custodial alternatives. The past will be a very incomplete guide to the future. Preferences may be based on past experiences in which child-rearing tasks were performed in an ongoing two-parent family, and dissolution or divorce inevitably alters this division of responsibilities.

. . .

Separation often brings in its wake psychological turmoil and substantial emotional distress that can make deliberative and well-informed judgments unlikely. It can arouse 'feelings about the former spouse, such as love, hate, bitterness, guilt, anger, envy, concern, and attachment; feelings about the marriage, such as regret, disappointment, bitterness, sadness, and failure; and more general feelings such as failure, depression, euphoria, relief, guilt, lowered self-esteem, and lowered self-confidence.' Isolini Ricci has suggested that for many individuals 'the emotions of ending a marriage' characteristically go through five stages during a two or three year period. . . . The third stage, which follows the separation, arouses strong emotions that are 'both natural and nasty'. 'Emotional roller-coasters are common at this stage, causing many people to feel permanent emotional instability.' According to Ricci, 'this is the worst possible time to make any permanent decisions — especially legal ones. Thinking and believing the worst about each other is one of the chief hazards of this stage, and such thoughts, exaggerated and extended, can lead to serious complications.' . . .

Some might think that the stresses and emotional turmoil of separation and divorce undermine the essential premise of private ordering — the idea that individuals are capable of deliberate judgments. I disagree. After all, for most persons the emotional upheaval is transitory, and the stresses are an inevitable consequence of having to make a new life. Temporary incapacity does not justify state paternalism for an extended period of time. Nonetheless, safeguards are necessary, and the wooden application of the traditional contract defense of 'incompetence' may not provide sufficient protection. . . .

Professor Eisenberg recently suggested a concept of 'transactional incapacity' to capture the notion that 'an individual may be of average intelligence and yet may lack the aptitude, experience, or judgmental ability to make a deliberative and well-informed judgment concerning the desirability of entering into a given complex transaction.'. . .

An analogous concept could be applied to divorce bargaining within a system that encourages private ordering at the time of divorce. When one spouse knows or has reason to know of the diminished capacity, and exploits this incapacity, a court should reopen the agreement. Proof of exploitation is essential, however. For this I would require a showing that the terms of the agreement considered as a whole fall outside the range of what would have been acceptable to a competent person at the time of the settlement. By providing a remedy only if a party exploited the other side's incapacity by securing an unusually one sided bargain, this test will not create uncertainty in most cases.

A second prophylactic to guard against transitory diminished capacity would involve a 'cooling-off' period, during which either party would be free to rescind a settlement agreement. In a commerical context, this period is often very short — typically three days. In the divorce context, I would make it considerably longer — perhaps sixty or ninety days. Like any safeguard, this one has costs. Some agreements may come apart even though they involve no exploitation whatsoever, simply because of ambivalence or a change of heart. Moreover, this cooling-off period might be used strategically by a party — a tentative agreement may be reached, only to be later rescinded, in order to wear an opponent down.

. . .

UNEQUAL BARGAINING POWER

Let me now turn to a second possible justification for imposing limits on private ordering — the basic idea is simple; in negotiations between two competent adults, if there are great disparities in bargaining power, some bargains may be reached that are unconscionably one-sided.

The notion of bargaining power has intuitive appeal, but turns out to be very difficult to define. Without a complete theory of negotiations, it is hard to give precise substantive content to the notion of bargaining power, much less define precisely the idea of 'relative bargaining power'. Nonetheless, by briefly analyzing the five elements of the bargaining model I described in an earlier article, it is possible to suggest why some divorcing spouses may be seen as having unequal bargaining power.

First, there are *the legal endowments*. The legal rules governing marital property, alimony, child support, and custody give each spouse certain claims based on what each would get if the case goes to trial. In other words, the outcome the law will impose if no agreement is reached gives each parent certain bargaining chips — an endowment of sorts.

. . .

Second, a party's bargaining power is very much influenced by his or her *preferences* — i.e., how that party subjectively evaluates alternative outcomes. These preferences are not simply matters of taste — they can depend upon a party's economic resources and life circumstances. The parties' relative bargaining power depends on how they both subjectively evaluate the outcome a court would impose.

A third element that effects bargaining power has to do with uncertainty, and the parties' attitudes towards risk. Often the outcome in court is far from certain, and the parties are negotiating against a back-drop clouded by substantial uncertainty. Because the parties may have different risk preferences, this uncertainty can differentially affect the bargaining power of the two spouses. If there is substantial variance among the possible court-imposed outcomes, the relatively more risk averse party is comparatively disadvantaged.

A fourth element that can create differences in bargaining power relates to the differential ability to withstand the transaction costs — both emotional and economic — involved in negotiations. A party who is in no hurry, enjoys negotiations, and has plenty of resources to pay a lawyer, has an obvious advantage over an opponent who is impatient, hates negotiations, and cannot afford to wait.

A fifth element concerns the bargaining process itself, and strategic behaviour. In divorce bargaining, the spouses may not know each other's true preferences. Negotiations often involve the attempts by each side to discern the other side's true preferences, while making credible claims about their own, and what they intend to do if a particular proposal is not accepted. 'Bargainers bluff, argue for their positions, attempt to deceive or manipulate each other, and make power plays to gain an advantage.' Some people are more skilled negotiators than others. They are better at manipulating information and managing impressions. They have a more refined sense of tactical action. These differences can create inequalities in negotiations.

EXTERNALITIES – THIRD PARTY EFFECTS

Third party effects provide the last set of reasons that justify limiting private ordering. . . .

A divorce settlement may affect any number of interests not taken into account in the spouses' negotiations. The state's fiscal interests can be affected, for example. The economic terms of the bargain between the two spouses may substantially affect the odds that a custodial parent will later require public transfer payments. The most important third party effects concern the children, although there can be externalities with respect to other family members as well. At a conceptual level, it is easy to see how a negotiated settlement may reflect parental preferences but not the child's desires or needs. . . .

Concerns about the effects of the divorce on the children underlie many of the formal limitations on private ordering – e.g., the requirement of court review of private agreements relating to custody and child support; the legal rules prohibiting parents from making nonmodifiable and binding agreements concerning these elements. . . .

I believe divorcing parents should be given considerable freedom to decide custody matters – subject only to the same minimum standards for protecting the child from neglect and abuse that the state imposes on *all* families. The actual determination of what is in fact in a child's best interests is ordinarily quite indeterminate. It requires predictions beyond the capacity of the behavioural sciences and involves imposition of values about which there is little consensus in our society. It is for this reason that I conclude that the basic question is who gets to decide on behalf of the child.

A negotiated resolution is desirable from the child's perspective for several reasons. First, a child's social and psychological relationships with both parents ordinarily continue after the divorce. A process that leads to agreement between the parents is preferable to one that necessarily has a winner and a loser. A child's future relationship with each of his parents is better ensured and his existing relationship less damaged by a negotiated settlement than by one imposed by a court after an adversary proceeding. Notions of child protection hardly justify general judicial suspicion of parental agreements; the state's interest in the child's well-being in fact implies a concomitant interest in facilitating parental agreement.

Second, the parents will know more about the child than will the judge, since they have better access to information about the child's circumstances and desires. Indeed, a custody decision privately negotiated by those who will be responsible for care after the divorce seems much more likely than a judicial decision to match the parents' capacities and desires with the child's needs.

Because primary responsibility for child-rearing after divorce does and *should* remain with parents there should be a strong presumption in favor of the parental agreement and limits on the use of coercive state power by judges or other professionals to force parents to do what the professional thinks is best. On the other hand, I think the state has an important interest in encouraging parents to understand that the responsibility for their children extends beyond the divorce, that children are in many ways at risk during the divorcing process, and that in deciding about the child-rearing arrangements, the parents have an important obligation to meet their children's needs. Moreover, there is reason to think that by facilitating parental agreement, and helping the parents transform their old relationship into one in which they can now do business together with respect to the children's future needs, the interests of the children are being served.

Questions

(i) Why are significant limitations on private ordering 'inconsistent with the premises of no-fault divorce'?

(ii) How far does English law now reflect Mnookin's model?

(iii) How far would it do so if the Law Commission's recommendations on the ground for divorce (see p. 236, above) were to be enacted?

(iv) Do the arguments in favour of allowing people to make their own arrangements when they separate or divorce apply equally to allowing them to make pre-marital or pre-cohabitation contracts (see p. 344, above)?

(v) What if the parties find it difficult to make their own arrangements? What help should they be given?

(vi) How far, if at all, does the concept of private ordering help us to decide what sort of court would be best suited to adjudicating upon those issues which the parties cannot decide for themselves?

One suggestion is put forward by Mervyn Murch in *Justice and Welfare in Divorce* (1980):

(i) Primary task
The participant model defines the primary task of legal and welfare processes in a new way. It starts from the assumption that there is a common objective about which all parties could reach agreement, even though they may differ as to the means of reaching that objective. This common objective is that of arriving at a fair and reasonable basis upon which the family can reconstitute itself following divorce, paying due regard to the interests of the children. In other words, the primary task of divorce machinery is to find a way of providing for the interests and welfare of family members after divorce. I doubt very much whether more than a small minority of divorcing parents would not subscribe to this objective, likewise few lawyers or welfare officers would dissent fundamentally.

(ii) Membership of the conflict-resolving system
Once it is accepted that there is a common objective, all the actors within the machinery of justice — judges, members of the Bar, solicitors, welfare officers and the family members themselves, who have temporarily become part of the system — can be perceived as being bound together in a common pursuit of an agreed objective. This becomes the task, and each actor within the system has a responsibility to work towards the common goal. To a large extent therefore the task of working towards the common goal becomes itself an authority from which the actors derive their responsibility and by which their roles are defined and differentiated.

Question

Michael Freeman (1981) asks 'But is there a "common objective" and, if so, who defines it?'

Freeman is afraid that Murch's model of 'participant justice' would 'become a cloak to enable yet another group of professionals to take over'. This brings us to whether the court's role is to help solve family problems or simply to resolve their disputes.

3 Marriage mending or marriage ending?

Explicit in Neville Brown's conception of a family court was a commitment to 'marriage mending' — a court-based attempt to solve the family's problems and reunite the parties. The *Finer Report* (1974) recounts the English experience:

Reconciliation in the divorce jurisdiction
4.290 In 1946, the Lord Chancellor, Viscount Jowitt, appointed a committee under the chairmanship of Lord Denning (then Mr Justice Denning):
'to examine the present system governing the administration of the law of divorce and nullity of marriage in England and Wales; and, on the assumption that the grounds upon which marriages may now be dissolved remain unchanged, to consider and report upon which procedural reforms ought to be introduced . . . in particular whether any (and if so, what) machinery should be made available for the purpose of attempting a reconciliation between the parties, either before or after proceedings have been commenced.'
The report laid great stress on the importance of preserving the marriage tie and attempting reconciliation in every case where there was a prospect of success. It examined the role of the

Service Departments during the then recently ended war in effecting reconciliation between serving men and their wives, and the part played by voluntary organisations such as the Marriage Guidance Council. The principal conclusion in this area was:

'There should be a Marriage Welfare Service to afford help and guidance both in preparation for marriage and also in difficulties after marriage. It should be sponsored by the State but should not be a State institution. It should evolve gradually from the existing services and societies just as the probation system evolved from the Court Missionaries and the Child Guidance Service from the children's clinics. It should not be combined with the judicial procedure for divorce but should function quite separately from it.'

It was also recommended that welfare officers should be appointed to give guidance to parties who resorted to the divorce court or contemplated doing so, and that where there were dependent children the court should at any time after the petition had been filed be entitled to refer the case to the court welfare officer for enquiry and report. The recommendation for a marriage welfare service fell by the wayside. . . .

The English experience of reconciliation through the courts

4.298 It may, indeed, be said to be the virtually unanimous opinion of those who have the relevant experience that there is little room for optimism when the court to which the parties have presented themselves to formalise or regulate the breakdown of the marriage seeks to use that occasion for mending it. The Denning Report [1947] concluded on the evidence it received:

'The prospects of reconciliation are much more favourable in the early stages of marital disharmony than in the later stages. At that stage both parties are likely to be willing to co-operate in an effort to save the marriage; but if the conflict has become so chronic that one or both of the parties has lost the power or desire to co-operate further, the prospects sharply diminish. By the time the conflict reaches a hearing in the divorce court, the prospects are as a rule very small. It is important therefore that the general public should be brought to realise the importance of seeking competent advice, without delay, when tensions occur in marriage.'

4.299 The Morton Royal Commission on Marriage and Divorce [1956] which took a good deal of evidence on this subject, recorded:

'If matters are allowed to develop into a condition of chronic disharmony one or perhaps both of the spouses will probably have lost the ability or desire to make any attempt to restore the marriage, and by the time steps have been taken to institute divorce proceedings the prospects of bringing husband and wife together again are greatly reduced. This view won a wide measure of support from our witnesses.'

4.300 The Law Commission [1966] considered that reconciliation procedures started after the filing of the petition achieve little success and 'have tended to become pointless and troublesome formalities'.

The Law Society took a similar view in *A Better Way Out* (1979):

178. . . . It is generally accepted that, by the time either spouse reaches the stage of consulting a solicitor about divorce proceedings, the breakdown of the marriage has reached the point of no return and it is too late for there to be any real prospect of reconciliation. If the spouses wanted help in saving the marriage, they will have sought it before then from family, friends or marriage guidance counsellors.

Gwynn Davis and Mervyn Murch, however, in *Grounds for Divorce* (1988) report that:

The results of our 'consumer' interviews indicate beyond doubt that this assessment is seriously wide of the mark. In particular, it fails to take account of the fact that the whole divorce process has speeded up, with many petitions being filed whilst the parties are still living together.

Earlier, they point to the evidence suggesting that, nowadays, the possibility of reconciliation may exist in a great many cases:

In support of this, the evidence of the judicial statistics points to a very significant 'fall-off' in numbers from petition to decree nisi and then from decree nisi to decree absolute. This is not a consequence of delay in the award of the decree, or of fluctuations in the divorce rate: the fall-off in numbers occurs *every* year. For example, from 1980 to 1983, the difference between the numbers of decrees nisi and decrees absolute varied from just under 3,000 per annum to over 5,000 per annum. This represents a 'fall-off' rate of around 2 per cent. We do not know in what proportion of these cases the parties resumed cohabitation, but the figures certainly suggest a higher reconciliation rate than is generally assumed.

The 'fall-off' at an earlier stage — from petition to decree nisi — is even more pronounced. From 1980 to 1983 there were, each year, some 20,000 fewer decrees nisi than petitions filed — a shortfall of between 12 and 15 per cent. It is likely that 'double petitioning' (in which one set of proceedings is abandoned, only for another to take its place) accounts for the majority of these. Nevertheless we are left with an interesting question concerning the number of reconciliations which may have contributed to this gulf between the two sets of figures.

Our own research also suggests that there is a potential for reconciliation in a significant number of divorce cases. Even in the course of the Special Procedure survey (from which initially defended cases were excluded) 39 per cent of respondents and 23 per cent of petitioners claimed that they would have preferred to remain married to their former partner. In at least 50 per cent of these cases it appeared that the marriage breakdown reflected the will of only one party. Given that our interviews usually took place some months after the award of the decree nisi — and in some cases, several years after the initial separation — it is likely that the number wishing to continue with their marriage had, at the outset of proceedings, been even greater.

Amongst our later Conciliation in Divorce sample, which included initially defended suits, 40 per cent said they would have preferred to remain married: 51 per cent of men and 29 per cent of women. Of the 71 cases in which we interviewed both parties to the divorce, there were only 21 (29.5 per cent) in which the marriage breakdown had been accepted on each side. We should acknowledge that there is a risk that some of those interviewed may have interpreted our question hypothetically — rather than as pertaining to the actual circumstances of their marriage. However, in the Special Procedure survey we were on slightly firmer ground because we also asked respondents whether they believed that their own marriage had 'irretrievably broken down'. Fifteen per cent denied that it had done so, with a further 10 per cent saying that they were 'uncertain'. Few, if any, of those interviewed in the course of this research had attempted to defend the divorce petition.

This evidence of *doubt* or *regret* should not be taken as an indication that a great many of these marriages could have been 'saved'. . . .

The findings of the Law Commission's *Court Record Study* (1990) also lend support to the view that there is more scope for reconciliation during divorce proceedings than had previously been acknowledged:

13. The original 477 files resulted in one nullity decree, five judicial separation decrees, 433 decrees nisi of divorce and 418 decrees absolute. One decree nisi was later rescinded. Thus 53 cases (11.1% of the total) fell by the wayside at some stage, 28 without any decree at all, and 15 between decree nisi and decree absolute. These included one case (mentioned earlier) where the fact was not recorded. Otherwise, Table 6 shows the facts relied on in the unsuccessful petitions:

Table 6 Facts relied on in unsuccessful petitions

	No.	(%)	% of petitions on that fact
Adultery	13	(24.5%)	9.3%
Behaviour	30	(56.6%)	16.2%
Desertion	0	(0%)	0%
Two years	6	(11.3%)	5.4%
Five years	4	(7.5%)	11.1%
Total:	53	(99.9%)	

14. The behaviour cases did tend to run into more difficulty than the others, but it is significant that more than a quarter of these couples were still living at the same address at the date of the petition. This in itself was associated with a higher rate of failure to proceed.

15. It was not always possible to deduce the reason why a case had failed to reach decree or decree absolute. It was rarely associated with, let alone attributable to, the intervention of the court. The most common reason appeared to be reconciliation; there were also some who had obtained non-molestation or ouster injunctions but apparently gone no further, some where the proceedings on the file had been superseded by a new petition in that or another court, and some which proceeded no further than notification of an intention to defend.

Questions

Davis and Murch nonetheless conclude 'It would be absurdly facile to assume, just because some couples decide, in the end, to remain together, that *courts* have much (if any) role in the marriage mending business. Perhaps the most we can ask of courts and legal procedure is that they do not make life *even more difficult* for couples facing these decisions.' (*a*) Do you agree? (*b*) In what respects might the present law make life even more difficult?

The law gives some encouragement to reconciliation: s. 6(2) of the Matrimonial Causes Act 1973 allows the court to adjourn divorce proceedings for an attempt to reconcile the parties if at any stage it appears that there is a reasonable possibility of success; s. 26 of the Domestic Proceedings and Magistrates' Courts Act 1978 gives similar powers in relation to applications for financial provision (but not protection from domestic violence). Another provision is explained in the Law Commission's *Court Record Study* (1990):

Reconciliation certificates
21. A solicitor acting for a petitioner is obliged, under section 6(1) of the 1973 Act, to file with the petition a certificate stating whether or not he has discussed reconciliation with the client or given the client the names and addresses of persons qualified to assist. There were at least five cases in which certificates were filed apparently unnecessarily because the solicitor was not acting for the purposes of the petition; and four cases where there was no certificate but there should have been. Hence there were certificates in 121 of the 125 cases in which solicitors were acting.
22. Generally, therefore, solicitors were fulfilling their duty to file certificates. More interestingly, perhaps, they gave positive responses in what might be thought a surprisingly high proportion of cases. Thus 85 out of the 125 certificates reported that the solicitor *had* discussed reconciliation with his client, and 29 reported that they had referred the client to other agencies.

Solicitors now rarely act for the purposes of the petition itself, because of the special procedure (see p. 215, above). The perhaps surprisingly high proportion (also found by Davis and Murch) who had nevertheless discussed 'reconciliation' or made referrals may have done so because of a practice direction (see p. 693, below) that 'reconciliation' can also include 'conciliation'. The *Finer Report* drew the following distinction:

4.288 In the discussion which follows we shall be using the terms 'reconciliation' and 'conciliation' to denote two different concepts. By 'reconciliation' we mean the reuniting of the spouses. By 'conciliation' we mean assisting the parties to deal with the consequences of the established breakdown of their marriage, whether resulting in a divorce or a separation, by reaching agreements or giving consents or reducing the area of conflict upon custody, support, access to and education of the children, financial provision, the disposition of the matrimonial home, lawyers' fees, and every other matter arising from the breakdown which calls for a decision on future arrangements.

4.289 The distinction between reconciliation and conciliation, and the influence which the family court may bring to bear in promoting either of them, is of cardinal importance in the consideration of any proposal for a family court.

To some extent, this distinction may have reflected a change in emphasis and approach in the world of marital counselling, as described in *Marriage Matters* (1979), a consultative document issued by a working party on marriage guidance set up by the Home Office in consultation with the DHSS:

1.12 The pioneers of the marriage councils were as clear in their avowed aims as they were prudent, able and persuasive in the pursuit of them, and in their first selection and training of counsellors. They were out to save marriages — to 'mend' them, not to 'end' them. The aim appealed to intelligent and compassionate people everywhere, particularly among those with an educated understanding of the problem, and sufficient leisure to offer their services for its remedy. It appealed to the churches because it was wholly consistent with their theological understanding of marriage as a lifelong and exclusive relationship. It appealed to the growing profession of social work, particularly those branches of it concerned with children whose welfare was jeopardized by broken homes. It appealed to the State, because the aiding of divorce litigation was expensive, as was the social and material care of children and others disadvantaged by divorce. People unhappy in their marriages were to be helped, then, towards reconciliation, to live again within the institution of marriage. . . .

A gradual change of objective
1.15 The avowed objective of 'marriage guidance' work, to mend marriages, changed under the influence of a number of factors. There were changes in the public attitude towards marriage and divorce, and in the divorce law itself. Legal aid, social and economic factors, including a wider liberty for women to support themselves by working outside the home, contributed to a growing resort to divorce — though not necessarily to a growing incidence of marital breakdown. These and other changes reduced the pressure to 'keep couples together'. The practice of marital counselling itself was a powerful contributor to change. The training of counsellors, specialist and lay, disseminated to a wider public some of the insights into the dynamics of human behaviour, including marital behaviour, derived from psycho-analysis. Methods of 'case-work' were developed: for a generation they were the staple of practice and training in social work. They were designed to enable the client to understand more of himself and his problems, and, in understanding, to help himself. Out of this grew 'marital counselling' rather than 'marriage guidance' — a change of name denoting a sensitive shift of method and intent.
1.16 . . . in a long-established moral and pastoral tradition, the 'counsel' has denoted some fairly clearly directed course of action, stronger than 'advice', which the recipient was told to pursue for his good. Early social work, and perhaps early marriage guidance work, stood in, or in the penumbra of, this tradition. Some persons may still need it and profit from it; and some ready helpers are willing to give it. But the giver seldom knows the meaning of the advice to the receiver or how he will distort it; and the very giving of advice may entrench the giver in an unhelpful relationship. So it is only the most skilled and sensitive counsellor who may safely offer it. By and large, 'counselling' is now by another way: the counsellor offers the client a relationship in which he may discover himself and find resources within himself — and within his marriage — by which to help himself and find his own way; in short, to enlarge his area of freedom and to move within it. The outcome may be a marriage mended — renewed ability and will to continue and improve the matrimonial life; or it may be a marriage ended, though with less hurt, perhaps less insult to the emotions and spiritual relationship, than otherwise there might have been.

After discussing the Finer Report's distinction between reconciliation and conciliation, they offer their own model for a 'court conciliation service':

7.10 The conciliation service we envisage would be on lines similar to that proposed in the Finer Report and would exist side by side with the legal structure. Whereas the function of the courts is judicial, the main purpose of the conciliation service would be to help individuals and couples to sort out their views, attitudes and feelings, make decisions which are most beneficial to the mental and emotional health of themselves, their spouses and their children, and begin to adapt themselves to the implications of those decisions. The court assumes that people are clear what they want and adjudicates when there is a clash of interest between spouses. However, many people experiencing marital breakdown who go through legal process for divorce or separation have conflicting feelings at various stages or indeed throughout. Sometimes this ambivalence may be apparent at the point of their first consulting a solicitor; sometimes it may surface as legal action is taking place and uncertainty about the future model of life highlights the forgotten positive aspects of the relationship that is being terminated; sometimes the permission to divorce, perhaps at the granting of the decree nisi, provides such a shift in the marital relationship that the old marriage can be resumed on a new basis.

7.11 The divorce process is thus often accompanied by feelings of uncertainty, sadness, panic, bitterness or regret or even reluctance; individuals or couples can benefit from talking these through with a counsellor or welfare officer experienced in conciliation. In particular it is important for time to be available for each parent to talk about his or her feelings about the children, and about the future plans for the children's welfare, including arrangements for continuing the relationship with the parent who will then be absent from them. The continuing role of parent, after both parents are no longer cohabiting is fraught with difficulty. Often some supervision of the children will be necessary for some time, either to help with any bitterness transmitted into the post-divorce relationships with children or to safeguard access arrangements. These are all matters of fundamental importance with which the law as a judicial agent is not well placed to help. It is not a question of either legal process or a conciliation service. Many couples have need of both, and both have a complementary role to fulfill. From our viewpoint, an undue share of time, skill and finance goes into the execution of the law, and we think more resources of all sorts should be diverted to the process of conciliation in the wide sense we have used it here.

This definition still sounds more like counselling them conciliation even in the Finer sense. Lisa Parkinson, in *Conciliation in Separation and Divorce* (1986) also has some criticisms of Finer:

This definition continues to be widely quoted as the most authoritative and comprehensive definition of conciliation in separation or divorce, but it is unsatisfactory for several reasons. In many cases, the breakdown of the marriage is not 'established' in any formal sense, since statements made by one partner may be strenuously denied by the other. Disagreement about the divorce itself is very common and conciliation may be needed on this primary issue. Secondly, the Finer Committee's definition could apply to conciliatory advice from solicitors or other professionals, rather than to a formal process of conciliation undertaken by a neutrally placed conciliator. Some lawyers define 'conciliation' as 'a settlement of cases without recourse to contentious litigation, as an essential function of the lawyer practising in these matters' (Jackson, 1983). Many registrars and judges use a conciliatory approach not only at initial hearings or section 41 appointments but also in the context of contested proceedings in which judicial authority may be used to persuade the parties to accept a consent order. Some court welfare officers consider that in their statutory work for the court 'the two processes of investigation and conciliation are . . . inextricably interwoven and very largely interdependent' (Wilkinson, 1981). Partly as a result of the ambiguity in the Finer Committee's definition, 'conciliation' had become a fashionable portmanteau word carrying whatever bundle of meanings and values its user chooses to pack into it. Many professionals see it as an intrinsic part of their work which can be combined with our tasks. Wilkinson (1981) stated that 'the task of conciliation is implicit in all that the welfare officer undertakes' and he used the term synonymously with counselling by suggesting that the term 'personal conciliation' could be applied to 'the work undertaken with the person who is so depressed and debilitated by divorce that he is not only unable to cope with the separate demands of separate living, but is equally incapable of contemplating his single future as anything other than arid and meaningless.'

She offers her own definition thus:

Conciliation may be defined as a structured process in which both parties to a dispute meet voluntarily with one or more impartial third parties (conciliators) who help them to explore possibilities of reaching agreement, without having the power to impose a settlement on them or the responsibility to advise either party individually.

Question

Is the real distinction that 'reconciliation' is an outcome, whereas 'counselling' and 'conciliation' are processes?

There is obviously still considerable potential for confusion between the differing objectives and processes involved. In their Report on *The Ground for Divorce* (1990), the Law Commission try to sum up the different kinds of help which might be wanted or needed:

Counselling, conciliation and mediation

5.29 . . . The umbrella term 'counselling' is used in Australia and New Zealand to encompass a variety of different types of help. All share the characteristic of keeping an open mind about the eventual outcome, while helping the couple or individuals involved to gain a greater understanding of their situation and to reach their own decisions about the future. The focus and method, however, can differ sharply, as can the organisational context in which the service is offered.

5.30 Broadly speaking, there are three different types of activity which may be involved:

(i) Marital counselling is offered, either to a couple or to an individual spouse, with a view to helping the couple to strengthen or maintain their marital relationship. If they are estranged or separated, the aim is to reconcile or reunite them. Historically, attempts at reconciliation were part of the role of 'police court missionaries' who became the probation and divorce court welfare service of today. Generally speaking, however, such services are offered by voluntary organisations, principally Relate Marriage Guidance. Relate counsellors are carefully selected and trained, but do not hold any particular professional qualification and offer their services voluntarily;

(ii) Divorce counselling and other forms of therapy aim to assist individuals, couples, and their children, to come to terms with the fact that their relationship is breaking down, to reduce the sense of personal failure, anger and grief, to disengage from and negotiate a new relationship with the former spouse and with the children, and eventually to move on to new relationships with confidence, avoiding the mistakes of the past. In other words, it seeks to minimise the harm done to either partner and to their children by the breakdown of their marriage. Once again, this is generally offered by voluntary organisations such as Relate, although some probation services offer divorce experience courses, and specialist therapy may be available privately or in some parts of the health service;

(iii) Conciliation or mediation is a way of resolving disputes without resort to traditional adjudication. The aim is to help the couple to reach their own agreements about the future, to improve communication between them, and to help them to co-operate in bringing up their children. Conciliation in this country developed first in the context of resolving disputes about children, often through the efforts of registrars and divorce court welfare officers at the court where a custody or access dispute was to be tried, but also through independent conciliation services, most of which are now affiliated to the National Family Conciliation Council. Conciliators generally hold professional qualifications in social work, undergo specialist training in family conciliation, and are paid for their services. The costs and benefits of various conciliation services have recently been the subject of a major research study conducted by the University of Newcastle. This has revealed that conciliation is indeed effective, both in reducing the areas of conflict and in increasing the parents' well-being and satisfaction with the arrangements made. In general, these benefits are greater when the service is provided away from the courts. The problems with conciliation conducted by or at the court, valuable and effective though it can often be, include the inevitable pressure to reach a settlement quickly, the inevitable authority of the registrar or court welfare officer conducting it, which may unconsciously or consciously dictate the outcome, and the risks of confusing the welfare officer's different roles of reporting to the court and assisting the couple to reach agreement. However, this is a fast-moving field in which developments are taking place all the time. For example, the independent sector is beginning to develop methods of comprehensive mediation, covering property and finance as well as child-related issues.

As had the Finer Report, but for rather different reasons, they concluded that reconciliation attempts should *not* be a mandatory part of the divorce process:

5.33 Some of our respondents argued that counselling aimed at saving the marriage should be a compulsory part of the divorce process, but most were opposed to this. The matter has been considered on many previous occasions, most notably by the Denning Committee on Procedure in Matrimonial Causes in 1947, by the Royal Commission on Marriage and Divorce in 1956, by the Law Commission in The Field of Choice in 1966, and by the Finer Committee on One-Parent Families in 1974. They all concluded that mandatory reconciliation attempts within the court process were unlikely to succeed. We do not take the view that no reconciliation is possible once a person has taken the momentous step of consulting a solicitor and making a statement of marital breakdown: the evidence suggests that, even under the present law, couples become reconciled between petition and decree, and even between decree nisi and decree absolute. Removing the need to separate or to make hostile allegations against one another should increase the prospect of reconciling those who can be reconciled; but we do not believe that the courts should require them, on pain of punitive sanctions, to make the attempt. There are several reasons for this. First, there are the views of the organisations at present involved in providing these services. They would of course like there to be a properly funded network of services readily available to all who wish to use them. But such counselling is a two-way process which can only be offered to volunteers, not conscripts. The hostility and bitterness induced by conscription is unlikely to lead to a real and lasting resolution. Secondly, and perhaps more importantly, there are some marriages which it would be wrong in principle to attempt to save. A wife who is regularly subjected to violence or abuse from her husband needs rescuing from her marriage, not pressure to return to it. A system of mandatory reconciliation could not be justified without some attempt to distinguish between marriages, which would only reintroduce the very inquiry into past misbehaviour which it is the object of these proposals to avoid. Thirdly, it would be impossible to justify the enormous public expenditure which would be involved in requiring such attempts in every case, without a better prospect of success than can be demonstrated at present. Finally, it was felt by some respondents that *conciliation* might, paradoxically, be more likely to result in reconciling some couples, by encouraging them to find a way through their difficulties relating to future arrangements while they were still amenable to discussion.

Questions

(i) Do you agree that 'there are some marriages which it would be wrong in principle to attempt to save'?
(ii) Can you think of other ways in which encouragement to seek whatever help might be needed by either party could be built into the divorce process?
(iii) Do you think that it is the role of the state to provide such help?
(iv) If you do, how might it be funded? Would a levy on banns, licences, and certificates to marry be appropriate? It not, why not?

Conciliation and mediation are more obviously connected with the role of the courts in resolving disputes: we must therefore examine them in rather more detail before deciding how the law might provide for them.

4   Conciliation and mediation

A history of the development of family conciliation in this country is given in the University of Newcastle's Conciliation Project Unit's Report to the Lord Chancellor on the *Costs and Effectiveness of Conciliation in England and Wales* (1989):

Industrial Conciliation

2.20 Conciliation, as a means of informally resolving disputes, has, of course, deep roots in the area of industrial relations and dates from the very beginnings of collective bargaining. A Royal Commission, reporting in 1891, recommended that the government should play an active role in urging the parties to major industrial disputes to resort to boards of conciliation which had been set up in various industries and this was implemented by the Conciliation Act of 1896. The major development of the twentieth century was the creation of a national service, financed by the Exchequer and known initially as the Industrial Relations Service. In 1974, this became independent both of government and of statutory control, and assumed its present form of the Advisory Conciliation and Arbitration Service (ACAS (1979)).

Early Forms of Family Conciliation

2.21 Conciliation in the area of family disputes has been a relatively recent development in England and Wales. It is difficult to trace its precise source simply because the further one delves into the past the greater the confusion between 'conciliation' and 'reconciliation' (Eekelaar and Dingwall (1988)). 'Conciliation' is reported to have been widely practised in the magistrates' courts before the Second World War — and not only by the probation service — but the context makes it clear that the primary aim was to preserve the marriage relationship and, in particular, to persuade wives not to pursue legal claims against their husbands (Manchester and Whetton (1974)).

2.23 The notion that divorce procedures should enable parties to resolve their differences with the minimum of bitterness and conflict, once the breakdown of the marriage was irretrievable, can be discerned in the change of attitude to collusion which, in 1969, became a discretionary, rather than an absolute bar to divorce (see the remarks of Lord Scarman in *Minton v Minton* [1979] AC 593, 608). The first official, explicit recognition of the distinction between 'conciliation' and 'reconciliation' would appear to be the Practice Direction of the President of the Family Division, issued on 27 January 1971 (*Practice Note (Divorce: Conciliation)* [1971] 1 WLR 223), and which coincided with the coming into force of the Divorce Reform Act 1969:

> 'Where the Court considers that there is a reasonable possibility of reconciliation *or that there are ancillary proceedings in which conciliation might serve a useful purpose*, the Court may refer the case, or any particular matter or matters in dispute therein, to the Court Welfare Officer.'

The Court Welfare Officer would then, if he decided that conciliation 'might assist the parties to resolve their dispute', refer the case on to a probation officer, a marriage guidance counsellor or 'some other appropriate person or body indicated by the special circumstances . . . of the case'.

The Finer Report and its Aftermath

2.24 The impact of the 1971 Practice Direction on the divorce courts is unclear, but when the Finer Committee investigated the question it found that the court welfare services had concentrated almost exclusively on reconciliation rather than conciliation (Finer (1974)). . . .

2.25 Having reviewed conciliation and reconciliation practices both in Britain and in some foreign jurisdictions, the committee concluded that, whereas reconciliation procedures undertaken at the time when parties seek to formalise their marriage breakdown have small success, 'conciliation procedures conducted through the court at this same stage have substantial success in civilising the consequences of the breakdown'. In its view, the policy of the law should be that:

> 'dead marriages should be decently buried. Decency in this connection involves diagnosing the practical needs of the family at the time when the court assumes control over the relationship between its members and their affairs, invoking the help of other appropriate agencies to minister to those needs, and encouraging the victims of the family breakdown to wind up their failure with the least possible recrimination, and to make the most rational and efficient arrangements possible for their own and their children's future'.

The Committee envisaged that the 'agencies' referred to would comprise not only the court welfare service but also other bodies, including the social services and specialised organisations offering marriage guidance.

2.26 These suggestions for conciliation were made in the context of the Finer proposals for a family court and this may help to explain why they elicited no centralised response. Instead, initiatives were taken at a local level by different groups with different aims. Indeed, the very breadth of the Finer definition of conciliation encouraged a multitude of approaches. . . . Parkinson [1986] lists six concerns which, in her view, fuelled the rapid growth of conciliation in Britain from 1975:

> (i) to provide an alternative to the adversarial system in the divorce courts;

     (ii) to protect children involved in their parents' divorce;
    (iii) to give people more control over their own affairs and reduce their reliance on formal institutions;
    (iv) to achieve greater administrative efficiency by processing contested cases more quickly;
    (v) to reduce public expenditure, particularly on legal aid;
    (vi) to stem the rising tide of divorce. (Parkinson (1986)).

The Development of In-Court Conciliation
2.27 The first attempt to institute a formal conciliation service within the court process took place at the Bristol County Court. The Avon Probation Service, as a response to the Finer proposals, had organised a specialist civil work team and, following discussions with the judiciary, a system of preliminary appointments in defended divorced cases was set up in 1976. In 1978, the service was extended to cases of disputes over custody or access, the term 'mediation' being used to describe appointments in cases of this kind (Parmiter (1981)).
2.28 The focus by researchers and others on the Bristol experiment (Davis and Bader (1983a); Davis and Bader (1983b); Davis and Bader (1985); Fraser (1980)) has had the unfortunate consequence that schemes in other courts of no less importance, and sometimes adopting different approaches, have not received the same attention; no systematic account of their development exists. What is clear is that growth has been very rapid, particularly in areas where the enthusiasm of the probation service was matched by that of local judges or registrars. . . .
2.29 Legally, it is clear that parties cannot be compelled to attend conciliation appointments (*Clarkson v Winkley* [1987] FCR 33) but there is evidence that they perceive the process to be compulsory (Davis and Bader (1985)). As will be revealed elsewhere in this Report, both the style of the conciliation appointment and the procedure of referral vary considerably. In some courts, once the existence of a dispute has been located, the parties are invited to an appointment with a court welfare officer. In others, the process is initiated by a registrar who seeks to identify the area of disagreement and then encourages the parties to meet with the conciliator in a separate room, with the possibility of a further appointment should this be necessary.
2.30 It was this approach to conciliation which the Booth Committee, reporting in July 1985, found to be so appealing, for it squared with its own view that much of the difficulty and cost associated with matrimonial litigation could be reduced by earlier institutional interventions, primarily through an 'initial hearing' which would take place as soon as practicable after the filing of the petition (Booth (1985)). . . .
2.31 The Booth Committee also had to grapple with what has become, perhaps, the most contentious issue concerning court-based conciliation: its relationship to the more traditional function undertaken by the probation service in preparing welfare reports. The Committee considered that there was a clear difference between the goals of the two forms of intervention:

    'whilst conciliation is directed towards achieving an agreed solution, the object of the welfare report is to assist the court in deciding a contested matter . . . It is for the reporting officer but not for the conciliator to assess the situation and propose his own solution' (ibid: para 4.62).

Judges have expressed the same view, holding in particular that the same officer should not both conciliate and prepare a report in a given case (*Re H* [1986] 1 FLR 476; *Scott v Scott* [1986] 2 FLR 320; *Clarkson v Winkley* [1987] FCR 33; *Merriman v Hardy*, ibid. See also the letter of the President of the Family Division, Sir John Arnold, addressed to the probation service (ACOP Information Bulletin No 87, March 1986) and the Practice Direction of the Senior Registrar of the Principal Registry of the Family Division, 28 July 1986). The distinction drawn by the Committee and the judges has been sharply criticised by some members of the service (see especially Pugsley et al (1986)). They argue that there is no such thing as 'pure' conciliation or 'pure' reporting; rather, in preparing a report, an officer will appreciate the value of exploring the issues *with* the parties and attempt to promote acceptance by them of the report to which they contribute and conciliation involves an inquiry by the conciliator and an attempt to move the parties to agreement.

The Development of Independent Conciliation Services
2.34 It has been argued by some that conciliation is most effective when undertaken independently of the judicial process (Davis and Bader (1985)). As recognised by the Booth Committee (para 3.12), this is, in part, based on a belief that the earlier the intervention the better, and court services can, of course, only be used when proceedings have begun. But other advantages are also regarded as important (Parkinson (1986): p 76), such as quick accessibility in crisis situations and availability to unmarried as well as married couples and to those who wish to avoid court proceedings. It has also been argued (Roberts (1983) and (1987)) that the essence

of conciliation being to enable the parties themselves to make joint decisions on disputed matters, the process may be seriously inhibited by its location within the institutional framework of the courthouse or any connection with it.

2.35 Arguments such as these were deployed by those, including lawyers, who helped to launch the independent conciliation services. As with court schemes, Bristol took the lead with the establishment of the Bristol Courts Family Conciliation Service in 1979 (the word 'Courts' was abandoned in 1987 to avoid confusion with the court-based service). Perhaps the other most important pioneering service was the South-East London Family Conciliation Bureau, established also in 1979 at Bromley. . . .

2.37 While finance remains the main concern of the independent services, their character as predominantly autonomous institutions, introducing a novel service to the community, has given rise to other problems. Many services have a disappointingly low number of referrals even after sustained publicity. Much depends on relationships with, and attitudes of, local practitioners, registrars and judges. A most significant development in this respect may have been the Practice Direction of the Senior Registrar of the Principal Registry, issued on 28 July 1986 with the approval of the President of the Family Division and the concurrence of the Lord Chancellor:

> 'A Judge or Registrar, before ordering an enquiry and report by a Court Welfare Officer, should, *where local conciliation facilities exist*, consider whether the case is a suitable one for attempts to be made to settle any of the issues by the conciliation process, and if so, a direction to this effect should be included in the order.'

2.38 A second important issue concerns the qualifications and experience of those acting as conciliators. Unlike those practising in court-based schemes, conciliators in independent services come from diverse backgrounds. The NFCC requires, as a condition of affiliation, that conciliators have undergone social work or marriage guidance training and it has also formulated a code of practice. But it still remains an open question whether professional regulation in the conventional sense is appropriate.

Thus the big debate, apart from whether conciliation is appropriate at all, is about whether it should be provided as part of the court's own processes. An Inter-departmental Committee in 1983 had favoured 'in court' conciliation, whereas the *Report of the Matrimonial Causes Procedure Committee* (the Booth Report) was in favour of conciliation both in and out of court:

3.11 . . . There are three main factors which lead us to the conclusion that conciliation should be available to parties to matrimonial litigation. The first is that conciliation places responsibility squarely on the parties to seek agreement. This is consistent with our fundamental approach to matrimonial litigation, that contested proceedings are generally only appropriate where parties have been unable to reach agreement after being given every assistance and encouragement to do so. Secondly, conciliation, by its very nature, emphasises that parties are jointly responsible for dealing with the consequences of marriage breakdown and that it is not a matter just to be left to lawyers. This is particularly important in relation to children, for if both parents are to remain involved in the children's care and upbringing it is necessary that they should co-operate in making the necessary arrangements. Thirdly, we believe that if conciliation were generally available early in the proceedings it would encourage parties to face up to difficulties which might otherwise be suppressed, only to emerge at a later date as contested issues. *However, we do not think that conciliation should be concerned with the deep-seated and complex and emotional problems which stem from marriage breakdown: counselling for those problems should be available elsewhere.* The object of conciliation is to marshal such reasonableness and objectivity as exist and to direct the parties towards solving the essentially practical problems which arise.

3.12 Under our proposals the obvious place for conciliation is at the initial hearing. However, we have been greatly impressed by the view that in many cases conciliation is likely to be most effective before court proceedings have been started. *We also see much force in the argument that the distinction between out-of-court and in-court conciliation is somewhat arbitrary and is not necessarily relevant to the central question as to what form of conciliation service is likely to be most effective. We remain convinced that early intervention can be a major factor in developing a positive and conciliatory approach. Equally, we think that conciliation has a crucial role to play in helping parties to resolve issues which arise, or emerge, only when proceedings have started.*

The Newcastle unit were asked to investigate the comparative costs and effectiveness of various types of conciliation service. As Jan Walker, one of the unit's directors, points out in *Conciliation Research*, her contribution to *Family Conciliation within the United Kindgom* (1990), large claims have been made for them:

The claims have fallen into two main categories:
  (1) Quality-of-life benefits – those which suggest that conciliation reduces bitterness between separating couples, encourages parents to take responsibility for decision-making, and promotes consensual agreements.
  (2) Cost-reduction benefits – those which argue that conciliation reduces the financial costs associated with legal battles, thus reducing both state legal aid expenditure and referrals for divorce welfare reports.
Not surprisingly, the practitioners most closely involved with the development and provision of conciliation have been motivated by the 'quality of life' benefits, viewing the 'cost-reduction' benefits as important spin-offs, providing a forceful argument to be used in campaigning for funds. The constant threat of inadequate or non-existent funding has been a major difficulty for independent services placing considerable public emphasis on the cost reduction benefits in order to impress government and other potential funding bodies. To some extent this has been unfortunate since it is by those criteria that conciliation has then been expected to prove its worth, despite the fact that cost-saving has never been one of its principal or high-priority aims. Indeed, conciliators would probably argue that conciliation is so much better for families, and therefore for society, that it is morally right to fund it even if it does not save money (Walker, 1987).

Nevertheless, it was the task of the *Newcastle Report* to evaluate those claims. For the purpose of analysis, services were classified into four types:

Category A: court-based conciliation with high judicial control – Birmingham, Bristol, Mid-Glamorgan, Principal Registry;
Category B: court-based conciliation with low judicial control – Lancashire, Stoke;
Category C: independent conciliation with probation control – Ipswich, South-East London;
Category D: independent conciliation with no probation control – Birmingham, Bristol, Cleveland, Sheffield;

There were also two control areas, Derby and Lincoln, without a conciliation service.
On costs, the Report concluded as follows:

20.5 In summary, the results of our statistical analysis of costs indicate that conciliation, whether court-based or independent, involves a significant net addition to the overall resource cost of settling disputes. More specifically, having compared conciliated and non-conciliated disputes, all of which were associated with cases passing through the county courts, it would appear that the net impact of court-based conciliation is to add, on average, about £150.00 to the cost of settling a dispute, of which only about £25.00 to £30.00 represents costs borne by the parties themselves – the balance of the cost falling upon the public sector. Our conclusions on independent services must be more tentative since there was no evidence of judicial proceedings in the majority of cases in our sample and conciliation in some of these may have obviated the need for litigation. But subject to this, and setting aside Category C for which the sample size was inadequate, we estimate that the net impact of conciliation is to add approximately £250.000 to the overall cost of settling a disputed child issue associated with a case passing through the county court, of which some £40.000 is borne by the parties themselves.

Questions

(i) As they could only look properly at the comparative costs of conciliated and non-conciliated cases going through the courts, are their data sufficient

for us to evaluate the claim that conciliation saves public money?
(ii) Can it reasonably be expected that a new service, introduced in the
course of legal proceedings, will result in a transfer of funds away from the
legal profession?
(iii) Should it be?

However, even if conciliation could not be shown to save money, it could
be effective:

Effectiveness Analysis
20.6 . . . evaluating the effectiveness of conciliation has not been a simple task. Our research
has confirmed that the families referred to conciliation services were a heterogeneous population in terms both of social and personal circumstances and of the issues in dispute. The conciliation intervention was itself variable with important differences in emphasis, ranging from
settlement-seeking to improving the relationships between parties, in the length of the process
and in the conciliators' practice styles. In addition, there was the problem of attribution, as it
was not always possible to know whether a particular process created an observed change or
whether other factors external to the process, such as improvements in personal circumstances
or the mere passage of time, were responsible. We sought to overcome these difficulties by using
a variety of quantitative and qualitative methods of analysis. . . .
20.7 In terms of dispute-resolution, our primary findings on effectiveness were as follows
   (a) *Reduction of Disputed Issues*. The largest reduction in the number of issues over which
       parties disagreed was reported by parties who had attended conciliation of Catego-
       ries B and C, though similar levels of reduction occurred among the area comparator
       groups.
   (b) *Agreed Arrangements*. In general terms, users of conciliation reported agreements on
       some issues in 71 per cent of cases and 74 per cent of these described themselves as
       satisfied with the agreements reached. In relation to the reaching of agreements, there
       was, however, a tendency for Category A conciliation to do less well than the other three
       categories.
   (c) *Satisfaction with Arrangements*. At the end of the study period, users of Category A
       conciliation were significantly less likely to be satisfied with arrangements for access
       than those in other conciliated and non-conciliated categories. No significant differ-
       ences, as regards satisfaction with access arrangements, emerged between the latter
       categories and there were no significant differences between any of the categories
       regarding custody arrangements.
20.8 In terms of therapeutic and analogous goals, the effectiveness study yielded the following
findings.
   (a) *Relationships*. There was an improvement in the quality of relationships among parties
       who attended conciliation in Categories A, B and D, but there were no significant differ-
       ences between conciliated and non-conciliated cases. Thus, there was no evidence that
       conciliation had an impact on relationships.
   (b) *Well-Being*. Users of independent conciliation (Categories C and D) experienced signif-
       icant improvements in psychological well-being during the study period, suggesting that
       this form of intervention resulted in making parties *feel* better.
   (c) *Satisfaction with Conciliation*. Only a small percentage of parties (15 per cent) were
       dissatisfied with the process of conciliation and three-quarters of the users said they
       would recommend it to others. Satisfaction was less apparent in relation to Category
       A conciliation than to the other categories.
   (d) *Aims of Conciliation*. Category D conciliation was generally regarded as the most suc-
       cessful in achieving the various aims of conciliation; this was especially the case regard-
       ing counselling and dealing with personal feelings.
   (e) *Helpfulness of Conciliators*. Most people who used conciliation thought that conci-
       liators were helpful in enabling them to reach agreements with their partners. Con-
       ciliators in independent schemes were regarded as the most helpful.
20.9 These findings lead us to the general conclusion that court-based services in Category A
were less successful than conciliation in other categories. While there were few significant differences in the effectiveness of services between Categories B, C and D, independent schemes
in Category D seem to have been the most successful.
20.10 On some measures of effectiveness we failed to find significant differences between conciliated and non-conciliated cases. It would, however, be misguided to draw the inference from

this that traditional legal procedures are as effective in relation to disputed child issues as conciliation. In the first place, in many of the non-conciliated cases the disputes were less difficult to settle than those which arose in conciliated cases. This was particularly true in the two comparator areas, Lincoln and Derby: compared with cases from other areas, the reported degree of the *severity* of the disputes which went to these two courts was significantly lower, even though the *number* of disputed issues in individual cases was approximately the same. Secondly, in those two courts, the probation service in the exercise of its statutory duties adopted a style of welfare investigation which in many ways was similar to conciliation and which we have referred to as 'conciliatory'. These findings suggest that it may be possible to achieve some of the aims of conciliation without drawing clear boundaries between that process and the welfare-reporting function. . . .

20.18 Our research suggests that there are five factors in particular which critically contribute to the effectiveness of conciliation and thus serve to explain the results reported in 20.6 to 20.9.

(a) *Difficulty of Case.* The population receiving conciliation varied markedly between the court-based and independent services. The cases referred to court-based services, particularly those in Category A, were more difficult to resolve and the disputes were more likely to be entrenched. Many of these cases had a long history of disputes so that for some of them any success, however small, was to be applauded; but it may be that conciliation was not the most appropriate intervention to deal with many of them. Significantly, the area comparator cases in Derby and Lincoln appeared to be less difficult to resolve than conciliated cases in Category A; they also contained a smaller proportion of what we have referred to as 'formal disputes' (where the existence of the dispute is manifest on the face of the court papers).

(b) *Issues.* The range of issues dealt with in conciliation also varied between services. Court-based services tended to restrict their remit to dealing *only* with custody and access, while independent services (with the exception of . . .) South-East London . . . dealt with a wider range and combination of issues (for example, with the breakdown of marriage and with defended divorces) and in so doing were more likely to adopt a practice style which incorporated an element of counselling. Our study shows that it was unusual for couples to be in dispute about a single issue: those who could not agree about the custody of, and/or access to, children were likely to be in dispute about other matters. As one dispute was apparently 'settled', other disagreements might emerge, thus undermining the effectiveness of the settlement of the single issue. The lastingness of agreements in services which focused on settling one dispute was problematic. This was especially marked in relation to . . . South-East London . . . which had a deliberately narrow focus on access disputes. Agreements reached in other independent services were, however, more likely to be complied with than those reached in court-based services. It seems clear that couples in dispute about future arrangements for children are typically not able to segregate those disputes from others.

(c) *Content and Location of Conciliation.* We found no evidence to suggest that the amount of time spent in conciliation was itself a significant factor in accounting for effectiveness; the *content* of the process seemed to be more relevant. In independent services, more time was usually allocated to exploring the issues in dispute, recognising the emotional state of each party and reaching settlements according to the pace set by the parties. In contrast, in the court-based services, not only was the time allocated for each case comparatively brief but also the interviews were (except in Lancashire) usually conducted on court premises, signifying the pressure of 'authority' to reach speedy settlements. For probation officers conciliating in the court, there appeared to be a tension between their statutory duties as agents of the court and their desire to offer a client-focused service. Two further findings add support to this interpretation of the effectiveness data. The first was that, on the whole, men were more satisfied with court-based services and women more satisfied with independent services. Since the disputed issue was very often access and mothers were likely to be the custodial parent, they felt considerable pressure to agree to access in the court environment, without being able to explain fully their objections and anxieties. The more in-depth exploration of issues by independent services gave mothers the opportunity to do this, not always to the advantage of fathers (though men were equally as likely as women to view the process in the independent services and its outcome positively). Secondly, the conciliation provided by the Lancashire Probation Service appeared to be better received by clients than that of other court-based services. Under the Lancashire scheme it will be recalled that the invitation to attend conciliation came from the service, rather than the courts, and that officers specialising in conciliation undertook the process wherever possible in premises used only for that purpose. The clients' perception of the service with its complete separation from the courts and legal process was thus somewhat akin to that of an independent service.

(*d*) *Terminology*. Our findings confirmed that separating and divorcing couples do not easily understand the nature of conciliation. There would seem to be a number of factors which inhibit such understanding.

    (i)   The term 'conciliation' is itself problematic since it is frequently confused with 'reconciliation' (which one partner may be hoping for anyway). Although some services used the term 'mediation' this was no less obscure; and where both terms were used to describe different processes within the same service greater confusion was apparent.

    (ii)   Couples were rarely adequately prepared for conciliation before attending the service. Although independent schemes usually sent leaflets about the service, these did not always explain clearly the nature of the conciliation process, nor its relationship to other legal processes encountered in separation and divorce. Court-based services typically gave much less information, some none at all. Unless clients were given an explanation by their solicitors, most had little idea about the purpose of conciliation, its structure and place within the legal context.

    (iii) The lack of helpful information was compounded for couples attending court-based services by the fact that conciliation there was but one intervention in a series of legal and welfare processes. . . .

(*e*) *Overlapping Processes*. The overlapping of legal, judicial, welfare and conciliation processes was most apparent for clients who attended court-based services and, of course, where such overlap occurred, the clients' confusion was not merely as to terminology. They found it difficult to understand the difference between the processes and not easy to 'switch gear' between them. It seemed to be unrealistic to expect couples to be 'reasonable' and 'conciliatory' on the issues relating to children while some other issues were being dealt with by means of solicitor negotiation or adjudication. Many couples attending independent services were not so obviously faced with this contradiction since the referral to conciliation often took place prior to the commencement, or after the completion, of legal proceedings.

The National Family Conciliation Council provides the following leaflet, *Are you separating or divorcing? Perhaps we can help*:

In the process of Separation or Divorce?

Is it hard to talk with your former partner about matters which you should be discussing together?
Are your children brought into your conflicts?
Are you uncertain or confused about the legal steps to take?
Are you worried about short-term and long-term arrangements?
Although it may be difficult, would a meeting with your former partner be useful?

NFCC could offer you just the help you need

What is the NFCC?

The National Family Conciliation Council, and the fifty local Family Conciliation Services affiliated to it, offer help to couples, married or unmarried, who are in the process of separation or divorce. Conciliators (sometimes called Mediators) help couples to settle some of their disputes by making joint decisions, particularly about arrangements for their children. This can reduce bitterness, and can save unnecessary solicitors' costs.

What can NFCC Services offer you?

    ■ A 'neutral' place where you and your former partner can meet, with an impartial Conciliator, to work out solutions to some of your difficulties.
    ■ A special interest in making things go well for your children.
    ■ Information, if required, about counselling, divorce experience courses, and other facilities.
    ■ Confidentiality.

What local service is there in your area?

> Telephone or write to our National Office to find the Service closest to you or ask solicitors or Advice Centres in your area.

Question

How useful do you think this is in helping people to understand the nature of conciliation?

The *Newcastle Report* draws the following broad policy conclusions:

> 20.19 Our identification of the factors which, as regards existing services, seem to hinder the effectiveness of conciliation leads us to the view that conciliation:
>   (*a*) should not be mandatory for all couples;
>   (*b*) should not focus exclusively on child issues;
>   (*c*) should not be surrounded by ambiguous terminology; and
>   (*d*) should not overlap with other legal and welfare processes.
> More positively, for effectiveness to be maximised, we believe that:
>   (*e*) conciliation should be recognised as an alternative mechanism to legal, adjudicatory procedures for the resolution of disputes and be identifiable as a discrete, unambiguous process;
>   (*f*) its distinguishing feature should be to enable couples to retain control of the decision-making process consequent on separation and divorce, encouraging them to reach their own agreements; and
>   (*g*) the arena in which it takes place should be conducive to civilised discussion with an appropriate degree of informality.

The Law Commission in their Report on *The Ground for Divorce* (1990) were heavily influenced by these conclusions in making their recommendations on conciliation and the legal process:

> 5.34 A more difficult question, therefore, is whether conciliation or mediation should be mandatory, if not in all cases at least in those which the court identifies as suitable for it. Once again, however, the majority of our respondents thought it should not. The professionals practising in the field said that mandatory conciliation or mediation was unlikely to be successful and indeed might be counter-productive. The Newcastle research indicated that the greatest benefits came from independent conciliation which was clearly distinguished from the coercive setting of the court. It is also clear that, whatever its benefits in some cases, there are many issues or relationships in which it is quite unsuitable. If so, the aim must be to ensure that adequate services are available to those who wish to use them, and to secure efficient information and referral machinery, rather than coercive sanctions to achieve this. There are also dangers in relying too heavily upon conciliation or mediation instead of more traditional methods of negotiation and adjudication. These include exploitation of the weaker partner by the stronger, which requires considerable skill and professionalism for the conciliator to counteract while remaining true to the neutral role required; considerable potential for delay, which is damaging both to the children and often to the interests of one of the adults involved; and the temptation for the court to postpone deciding some very difficult and painful cases which ought to be decided quickly. It is important that, whatever encouragement is given by the system to alternative methods of dispute resolution, the courts are not deterred from performing their function of determining issues which require to be determined. Where time permits, alternative methods can be explored so as to enable the parties to try and reach their own agreements away from the pressures of the court door. Where, however, an immediate decision is needed in the interests of either party or of their children, the courts should be prepared to give it.
> 5.35 We therefore *recommend* that undertaking either relationship counselling whether reconciliation or divorce motivated, or conciliation or mediation should be purely voluntary.
> 5.36 We further *recommend* that opportunities and encouragement to resolve matters amicably should be built into the system where appropriate. The first opportunity will be when the statement of marital breakdown is made; the second will be at the preliminary and subsequent assessments by the court; and the third will be whenever any contested issue arises for decision.

Throughout, it can be encouraged by placing obligations upon the parties' legal advisers as to the provision of information and discussing the possibilities of both reconciliation and conciliation.

5.37 Furthermore, although participation in conciliation or mediation should be voluntary, we *recommend* that the court should have two additional powers to encourage it. Neither of these powers should be seen as placing any pressure on the parties to participate. They are designed to ensure that the parties are better-informed and to facilitate participation if they wish. They are also designed to some extent to regulate what happens informally at present. . . .

Referral for an explanation of conciliation or mediation

5.38 It is likely that in a number of cases one spouse, or perhaps both spouses, will not appreciate the nature and effectiveness of conciliation or mediation, or even if aware have a totally closed mind on the subject. Many people are confused about the distinctions between counselling, reconciliation and conciliation and are instinctively resistant to reconciliation. We therefore *recommend* that the court should have power, whether on application or of its own motion, to give a direction that the spouses meet a specified conciliator or mediator, in order to discuss the nature and potential benefits of conciliation or mediation in their case. . . . The object of such a meeting would be to enable the parties to reach a better informed decision as to whether or not they wished to embark upon conciliation or mediation and to offer them an opportunity of participating should they agree to do so. We also *recommend* that the conciliator or mediator specified should be under a duty to report back to the court within a given time limit on whether or not the parties have kept the appointment and whether or not they have agreed to take up an offer of conciliation and mediation. We understand that this is how the new referral procedure in Scotland operates and that the first indications are that it is working well.

Adjournment for participation

5.39 We further *recommend* that, where the parties are in dispute about any issue arising in the context of divorce or separation, the court should have power, whether on application or of its own motion, to adjourn the hearing of that issue, for the purpose of enabling them to participate in conciliation or mediation, or generally with a view to the amicable resolution of the dispute. In deciding to do this, the court should take the interests of any children into account (whether, for example, they will be more helped by the amicable resolution or harmed by the delay). It should, of course, be open to the parties not to participate and if either of them feels unable to do so this should not affect the handling of the case thereafter. It is also important to avoid this being used as a method of procrastination and manipulation. We therefore recommend that any such adjournment should be for a fixed period, and that one or both parties should be required to report back to the court on the outcome. . . .

This is all very encouraging to the conciliation movement. Nevertheless, there are serious doubts and dangers which have to be addressed. These are spelled out from a feminist perspective by Anne Bottomley, in *Resolving family disputes: a critical view*, her contribution to Michael Freeman's collection on *The State, the Law and the Family: Critical Perspectives* (1984):

The idea of conciliation has an older pedigree than is often assumed. It is one of the basic models of dispute resolution identified in anthropological literature where it is more usually and more correctly named as 'mediation' (Roberts 1979, 1983). Other forms of dispute resolution share the objective of agreement rather than judgement; however in conciliation it is the parties who are deemed to be in control. The presence of a third party is simply to further face-to-face negotiations by 'assisting in' helping communication (the language here slips often into a quasi-therapeutic discourse) and, when necessary, to give technical assistance with the symbols of social recognition of an agreement having been reached, whether by eating and drinking or by the drafting of a document. The anthropological literature has long alerted us to the need to look behind the presentation of such a form of dispute resolution and ask two questions. First, is there equality of power in the relationship between the parties, and between the parties and the mediator? Such an 'open' process is open to manipulation. To be persuaded may be an invidious form of judgement and control. Second, despite the presentation of the mediator in terms of neutrality and objectivity the mediator may be the purveyor of a particular pattern of beliefs that would tend to favour a particular 'resolution' to which the parties give their formal agreement.

I have stressed the need to examine the model of conciliation for two reasons. First, there is too often a blur between 'conciliation' and what is essentially a process of arbitration, or indeed informal adjudication; in both cases the essential factor is the power of the 'conciliator' over the parties rather than the party control which is deemed the essence of conciliation. Second, it is to highlight a fundamental ambiguity in the role of the conciliator. In the literature the hall-marks of a conciliator are those of neutrality, objectivity, and 'assistance' rather than control. Whether such a role is actually achievable in the majority of case, or indeed whether in some cases it is actually desirable, are moot points.

. . . Apart from the possible covert use of conciliation to 'provide a cover for value-laden tampering with family life' (Roberts 1983: 139) or simply a slippage back into old ways in which guidance and support mean in reality direction and control by experts, too often there is also a conflation of dispute resolution with therapy. Parkinson increasingly alludes in her work to therapeutic techniques and in a recent article on conciliation refers to 'conflict resolution' rather than 'dispute resolution' (Parkinson 1983b). This is consistent with a welfare-orientated approach which would reject as false the abstraction of legal from emotional problems. Davis (1983a: 139) quotes the Finer Report as positing the legal system as one which 'treats people . . . in the last resort as the subject of rights, not as . . . patients for whom the legal process is just another kind of treatment'. However for two professional groups involved in the field of family law the emphasis would be on the latter and conciliation a further opportunity for penetration into the formal system of rights and due process.

Why is this a problem? First, because it attacks the credibility of the very idea of conciliation itself; the parties are transformed into clients. Second, because the conciliator is clearly not neutral but the purveyor of certain ideologies and practices. Psychology, therapy, or social policy are not neutral bodies of knowledge. . . . Social workers and probation officers tend to share a common belief in the functionalism of the family, and a particular familial ideology in which roles are cast and those who do not fit are deemed not to be fit. They also share a concern with the increase in divorce and the need somehow to 'normalize' divorce so that it becomes less challenging to the images of stability and continuity that remain at the core of the family image. Much emphasis is placed on the fact that parents never divorce, only spouses: 'The court is asked in a divorce petition to dissolve the legal bonds of marriage, not the bonds of parenthood' (Parkinson 1983a: 24). Normalization is best achieved through images of continuity and consensus. Davis (1983a: 134–35) warns of the problems of a 'fabricated consensus'.

> 'An understandable human reaction to conflict is to pretend it does not exist, or at least, that it is not too serious or may be overcome. There are two reasons for this. First, conflict is painful. . . . Secondly, to pretend that conflict does not exist may be useful in getting one's own way.'

There are actually three forms of conflict that need to be addressed. First, there is the form I think is usually meant by many conciliators, that of general conflict between the parties. Second, there is the lawyers' perception of a conflict of interests; this is, I believe, far more specific and addressed to particular legal issues. The concern of lawyers to recognize conflicts of interest gives rise to the one-dimensional caricature of their approach as 'entirely adversarial'. It may be true that some lawyers exacerbate general conflict but there is much evidence to suggest that family law practitioners spend time 'cooling out' clients. Nor should we forget that the reality of practice is that bilateral bargaining results in the vast majority of cases being settled out of court. The third aspect of conflict, one rarely recognized, is, that of a more structural character; it is the conflict between the interests and needs of men and women. To ignore such structural conflict is merely to reproduce an existing power relationship and not in any way to mitigate or challenge it. Women's needs, the consequence of their continuing position of disadvantage in society, their lack of bargaining power *vis-à-vis* individual men, and the conflation of their rights with their role as mothers, make them particularly vulnerable in conciliation procedures. Those of us who see the family as the site of women's oppression must necessarily be highly critical of any social policy that holds as its core familial ideology and uses the 'welfare' of children as its major access point (Wilson 1977). . . .

Having explored some of the problems of what is actually meant by 'assisting' the parties, we must now necessarily question the nature of an 'agreement'. Have the parties been persuaded as to what is best rather than having decided for themselves? . . .

What we are experiencing at the moment is a pincer movement. On the one hand family law is being squeezed out of the formal legal system on arguments of cost and on the other hand it is being enticed out with promises of more fruitful pastures elsewhere. This shift towards de-legalization (Glendon 1977) must not be simply accepted but must be more closely examined. We need to recognize that the process of de-legalization is not one of de-regularization but is a shift from one form of social discipline to another. While the articulate middle classes will continue to buy the services of professional groups, others will become more and more the subjects of control by 'welfarism' (Donzelot 1980). Those who are most vulnerable will be caught between the unequal power relations of private ordering and a familial ideology rendered benign by welfarism in informal dispute resolution.

Questions

(i) Is conciliation simply a form of alternative dispute resolution in family cases or is it yet another cloak for yet another type of professional to take over?

(ii) How far might these concerns be dismissed as lawyers' special pleading?

(iii) How far do the Law Commission's proposals meet them?

(iv) If conciliation fails or is inappropriate, should the court procedure seek to promote a non-adversarial approach in more conventional dispute resolution?

(v) What is a non-adversarial approach? Is it the same thing as an informal approach? Or an inquisitorial approach?

(vi) We are, of course, civilised people: go back for a moment to the case of Barbara Auckland (p. 372, above) — what sort of family court would have catered best for her family's needs?

(vii) Can the same system be made to work *both* for matrimonial and for child care cases?

Index